The Victorians

B

BLACKWELL ANTHOLOGIES

TheVictorian
An Anthology of Poetry & Poetics

Edited by Valentine Cunningham

Editorial Advisers

Rosemary Ashton, University of London; Gillian Beer, University of Cambridge; Gordon Campbell, University of Leicester; Terry Castle, Stanford University; Margaret Ann Doody, Vanderbilt University; Richard Gray, University of Essex; Joseph Harris, Harvard University; Karen L. Kilcup, University of North Carolina, Greensboro; Jerome J. McGann, University of Virginia; David Norbrook, University of Oxford; Tom Paulin, University of Oxford; Michael Payne, Bucknell University; Elaine Showalter, Princeton University; John Sutherland, University of London; Jonathan Wordsworth, University of Oxford.

Blackwell Anthologies are a series of extensive and comprehensive volumes designed to address the numerous issues raised by recent debates regarding the literary canon, value, text, context, gender, genre and period. While providing the reader with key canonical writings in their entirety, the series is also ambitious in its coverage of hitherto marginalized texts, and flexible in the overall variety of its approaches to periods and movements. Each volume has been thoroughly researched to meet the current needs of teachers and students.

THE VICTORIANS

AN ANTHOLOGY OF POETRY & POETICS

EDITED BY **VALENTINE CUNNINGHAM**

BLACKWELL
Publishers

Copyright © Blackwell Publishers Ltd 2000
Editorial introduction, selection and arrangement copyright
© Valentine Cunningham 2000

First published 2000
2 4 6 8 10 9 7 5 3 1

Blackwell Publishers Ltd
108 Cowley Road
Oxford OX4 1JF
UK

Blackwell Publishers Inc.
350 Main Street
Malden, Massachusetts 02148
USA

British Library Cataloguing in Publication Data
A CIP catalogue record for this book is available from the British Library.

Library of Congress Cataloging-in-Publication Data
The Victorians: an anthology of poetry and poetics/edited by
Valentine Cunningham.
p.   cm.—(Blackwell anthologies)
Includes bibliographical references and index.
ISBN 0–631–19915–2 (hardbound: alk. paper). — ISBN 0–631–19916–0 (pbk.: alk. paper)
1. English poetry—19th century.   2. English poetry—19th century—History and criticism.
I. Cunningham, Valentine.   II. Series.
PR1223.V54   1999   821'.808—dc21   99–34412   CIP

Typeset in Garamond on 9.5/11 pt by
Kolam Information Services Pvt Ltd, Pondicherry, India
Printed in Great Britain by T.J. International, Padstow, Cornwall
This book is printed on acid-free paper

Contents

List of Authors

Acknowledgements

Brontë, Branwell, 'Why dost thou sorrow for the happy dead?' from (ed. Tom Winnifrith) *The Poems of Patrick Branwell Brontë* (Shakespeare Head Press, 1983).

Brontë, Branwell, 'Thorp Green' from (ed. Tom Winnifrith) *The Poems of Patrick Branwell Brontë* (Shakespeare Head Press, 1983).

Brontë, Branwell, 'When all our cheerful hours seem gone for ever' from (ed. Tom Winnifrith) *The Poems of Patrick Branwell Brontë* (Shakespeare Head Press, 1983).

Brontë, Emily, 'What winter floods, what showers of spring' from (ed. Janet Gezari) *Emily Jane Brontë, The Complete Poems* (Penguin, Harmondsworth, 1992).

Brontë, Emily, 'Long neglect has worn away' from (ed. Janet Gezari) *Emily Jane Brontë, The Complete Poems* (Penguin, Harmondsworth, 1992).

Brontë, Emily, 'The night is darkening round me' from (ed. Janet Gezari) *Emily Jane Brontë, The Complete Poems* (Penguin, Harmondsworth, 1992).

Brontë, Emily, 'All hushed and still within the house' from (ed. Janet Gezari) *Emily Jane Brontë, The Complete Poems* (Penguin, Harmondsworth, 1992).

Brontë, Emily, 'O Dream, where art thou now?' from (ed. Janet Gezari) *Emily Jane Brontë, The Complete Poems* (Penguin, Harmondsworth, 1992).

Brontë, Emily, 'How still, how happy! those are words' from (ed. Janet Gezari) *Emily Jane Brontë, The Complete Poems* (Penguin, Harmondsworth, 1992).

Brontë, Emily, 'Mild the mist upon the hill' from (ed. Janet Gezari) *Emily Jane Brontë, The Complete Poems* (Penguin, Harmondsworth, 1992).

Brontë, Emily, 'No coward soul is mine' from (ed. Janet Gezari) *Emily Jane Brontë, The Complete Poems* (Penguin, Harmondsworth, 1992).

Clare, John, 'I wish I was were I would be' from (ed. Eric Robinson and David Powell) *The Later Poems of John Clare 1837–1864* (Clarendon Press, Oxford, 1984, reproduced with permission of Curtis Brown Ltd, London, on behalf of Eric Robinson. Copyright Eric Robinson, 1984).

Clare, John, 'Here is the scenes the rural poet made' from (ed. Eric Robinson and David Powell) *The Later Poems of John Clare 1837–1864* (Clarendon Press, Oxford, 1984, reproduced with permission of Curtis Brown Ltd, London, on behalf of Eric Robinson. Copyright Eric Robinson, 1984).

Clare, John, 'I've had many an aching pain' from (ed. Eric Robinson and David Powell) *The Later Poems of John Clare 1837–1864* (Clarendon Press, Oxford, 1984, reproduced with permission of Curtis Brown Ltd, London, on behalf of Eric Robinson. Copyright Eric Robinson, 1984).

Clare, John, 'Sonnet: The Nightingale' from (ed. Eric Robinson and David Powell) *The Later Poems of John Clare 1837–1864* (Clarendon Press, Oxford, 1984, reproduced with permission of Curtis Brown Ltd, London, on behalf of Eric Robinson. Copyright Eric Robinson, 1984).

Clare, John, 'Sonnet: I am' from (ed. Eric Robinson and David Powell) *The Later Poems of John Clare 1837–1864* (Clarendon Press, Oxford, 1984, reproduced with permission of Curtis Brown Ltd, London, on behalf of Eric Robinson. Copyright Eric Robinson, 1984).

Clare, John, 'The Round Oak' from (ed. Eric Robinson and David Powell) *The Later Poems of John Clare 1837–1864* (Clarendon Press, Oxford, 1984, reproduced with permission of Curtis Brown Ltd, London, on behalf of Eric Robinson. Copyright Eric Robinson, 1984).

Clare, John, 'Sonnet: The Crow' from (ed. Eric Robinson and David Powell) *The Later Poems of John Clare 1837–1864* (Clarendon Press, Oxford, 1984, reproduced with permission of Curtis Brown Ltd, London, on behalf of Eric Robinson. Copyright Eric Robinson, 1984).

Clare, John, 'Pleasant Sounds' from (ed. Eric Robinson and David Powell) *The Later Poems of John Clare 1837–1864* (Clarendon Press, Oxford, 1984, reproduced with permission of Curtis Brown Ltd, London, on behalf of Eric Robinson. Copyright Eric Robinson, 1984).

Clare, John, 'To Miss Mary Ann C.' from (ed. Eric Robinson and David Powell) *The Later Poems of John Clare 1837–1864* (Clarendon Press, Oxford, 1984, reproduced with permission of Curtis Brown Ltd, London, on behalf of Eric Robinson. Copyright Eric Robinson, 1984).

Clare, John, 'The Bean Field' from (ed. Eric Robinson and David Powell) *The Later Poems of John Clare 1837–1864* (Clarendon Press, Oxford, 1984, reproduced with permission of Curtis Brown Ltd, London, on behalf of Eric Robinson. Copyright Eric Robinson, 1984).

Clare, John, 'Song' from (ed. Eric Robinson and David Powell) *The Later Poems of John Clare 1837–1864* (Clarendon Press, Oxford, 1984, reproduced with permission of Curtis Brown Ltd, London, on behalf of Eric Robinson. Copyright Eric Robinson, 1984).

Clare, John, 'There is a charm in Solitude that cheers' from (ed. Eric Robinson and David Powell) *The Later Poems of John Clare 1837–1864* (Clarendon Press, Oxford, 1984, reproduced with permission of Curtis Brown Ltd, London, on behalf of Eric Robinson. Copyright Eric Robinson, 1984).

Clare, John, 'There's music in the songs of birds' from (ed. Eric Robinson and David Powell) *The Later Poems of John Clare 1837–1864* (Clarendon Press, Oxford, 1984, reproduced with permission of Curtis Brown Ltd, London, on behalf of Eric Robinson. Copyright Eric Robinson, 1984).

Clare, John, 'Song: The hurly burly wind' from (ed. Eric Robinson and David Powell) *The Later Poems of John Clare 1837–1864* (Clarendon Press, Oxford, 1984, reproduced with permission of Curtis Brown Ltd, London, on behalf of Eric Robinson. Copyright Eric Robinson, 1984).

Clare, John, 'The Dark Days of Autumn' from (ed. Eric Robinson and David Powell) *The Later Poems of John Clare 1837–1864* (Clarendon Press, Oxford, 1984, reproduced with permission of Curtis Brown Ltd, London, on behalf of Eric Robinson. Copyright Eric Robinson, 1984).

Clare, John, 'Song: O sweet is the song o'the Thrush' from (ed. Eric Robinson and David Powell) *The Later Poems of John Clare 1837–1864* (Clarendon Press, Oxford, 1984, reproduced with permission of Curtis Brown Ltd, London, on behalf of Eric Robinson. Copyright Eric Robinson, 1984).

Clare, John, 'The Nursery Garden' from (ed. Eric Robinson and David Powell) *The Later Poems of John Clare 1837–1864* (Clarendon Press, Oxford, 1984, reproduced with permission of Curtis Brown Ltd, London, on behalf of Eric Robinson. Copyright Eric Robinson, 1984).

Clare, John, 'Fragment' from (ed. Eric Robinson and David Powell) *The Later Poems of John Clare 1837–1864* (Clarendon Press, Oxford, 1984, reproduced with permission of Curtis Brown Ltd, London, on behalf of Eric Robinson. Copyright Eric Robinson, 1984).

Clare, John, 'The Rawk o'the Autumn' from (ed. Eric Robinson and David Powell) *The Later Poems of John Clare 1837–1864* (Clarendon Press, Oxford, 1984, reproduced with permission of Curtis Brown Ltd, London, on behalf of Eric Robinson. Copyright Eric Robinson, 1984).

Eliot, George, 'In a London Drawingroom' from Bernard J. Paris, 'George Eliot's Unpublished Poetry', *Studies in Philology* 56.3 (July 1959) 539, reproduced by courtesy of Jonathan G. Ouvry.

Eliot, George, 'Notes on Form in Art' from unpublished manuscript, written in 1868, now in Yale University Library, Beinecke Rare Book and Manuscript Collection, reproduced by courtesy of Jonathan G. Ouvry.

Gray, John, 'April' from (ed. Ian Fletcher) *The Poems of John Gray* (ELT Press, Department of English, University of North Carolina, 1988, reproduced by courtesy of Father Bede Bailey, The Archives of the English Province of the Order of Preachers, Edinburgh).

Housman, A. E., 'Oh who is that young sinner' from Laurence Housman, *A.E.H.: Some Poems, Some Letters and a Personal Memoir by His Brother* (Jonathan Cape, 1937, The Society of Authors as the literary representative of the Estate of A. E. Housman).

Housman, A. E., 'Diffugere Nives' from *More Poems* (Alfred A. Knopf, New York, 1936, The Society of Authors as the literary representative of the Estate of A. E. Housman).

Housman, A. E., 'A.J.J.' from *More Poems* (Alfred A. Knopf, New York, 1936, The Society of Authors as the literary representative of the Estate of A. E. Housman).

Housman, A. E., 'R.L.S.' from *Collected Poems* (Jonathan Cape, 1939, The Society of Authors as the literary representative of the Estate of A. E. Housman).

Housman, Laurence, 'Dark was the night' ('Love Importunate') from *The Collected Poems of Laurence Housman* (Sidgwick & Jackson, 1937, courtesy of Random House UK Ltd).

McGonagall, William, 'The Tay Bridge Disaster' from *Poetic Gems: Selected from the Works of William McGonagall, Poet and Tragedian* (David Winter and Son, Dundee, 1947).

McGonagall, William, 'Death and Burial of Lord Tennyson' from *The Last Poetic Gems: Selected from the Works of William McGonagall, Poet and Tragedian* (David Winter and Son, Dundee, 1968).

Siddal, Elizabeth, 'A Silent Wood' from (ed. Roger C. Lewis and Mark S. Lasner) *Poems and Drawings* (The Wombat Press, Wolfville, Nova Scotia, 1978).

Siddal, Elizabeth, 'Lord May I Come?' from (ed. Roger C. Lewis and Mark S. Lasner) *Poems and Drawings* (The Wombat Press, Wolfville, Nova Scotia, 1978).

Siddal, Elizabeth, 'Dead Love' from (ed. Roger C. Lewis and Mark S. Lasner) *Poems and Drawings* (The Wombat Press, Wolfville, Nova Scotia, 1978).

Siddal, Elizabeth, 'Worn Out' from (ed. Roger C. Lewis and Mark S. Lasner) *Poems and Drawings* (The Wombat Press, Wolfville, Nova Scotia, 1978).

Introduction

The keynote of Victorian culture and society is numerosity – bigness, density, multiplicity, mass-ness. This was 'the age of great cities', of massive agglomerations of people, huge productivity of things, vast fortunes, and gigantic outputs of printed words – newspapers, books, novels, poems. There were more writers making their mark than ever before in Britain. When Tennyson was made Poet Laureate in 1850 he began to receive, he said, 'such shoals of poems' through the post that he was 'almost crazed with them, the two hundred million poets of Great Britain deluge me daily with poems'. Two hundred million was rather an exaggeration, but the size of the writerly crowd was indeed big and growing all the time, in step with an expanding literary market in Britain, America and the colonies – an insatiable demand for the written word. 'The number of readers grows daily', complained Walter Bagehot; 'young men and tired men are thrown among a mass of books.' And so readers become, he claimed, 'hasty readers', in their effort to keep up with the newest 'excite-ment, which in turn stimulates for an instant, and then is past by for ever'; literature thus becomes 'dressy' and 'exaggerated' in order to catch the eye of these hasty readers, all faced with just too much material, especially (Bagehot thought) the woman reader. It all meant a bad time for what in his lengthy grumble of 1864, 'Wordsworth, Tennyson, and Browning; or Pure, Ornate, and Gro-tesque Art in English Poetry', he called Pure writing.

But one of the great attractions of Victorian poetry is precisely its impurity, the way it is so open to the new and the newly felt multitudinousness of the Victorian experience. The vessel of Victor-ian verse delights precisely for its extreme porosity. So much leaks in; this body of writing is noth-ing if not pervious. There was so much for the imagination to comprehend in a writing, to cope with, and copiousness became literature's responsive and responsible way. 'There's copiousness!' exclaimed Tennyson of one of Browning's poems. He meant its great length: 'His new poem has 15,000 lines: there's copiousness!' But whatever the length of poems might be – and they come, of course, in every kind of size – Victorian verse is noteworthy for its reach and variety, its sheer scope, the extraordinary amplitude of its subjects, its modes, its moods. Such omnivorous-ness, a national compendium of poetic kinds and contents on this scale, had been seen nowhere before.

When, in the important Preface to the first edition of his *Poems* (1853), Matthew Arnold declared (following Aristotle) that 'the eternal objects of poetry' were 'actions; human actions', everybody could see not only how limiting that formula was in general, but also how unapt it was in particular to contemporary poetic production. 'We have poems to the Lesser Celandine, to a Mouse, to the Skylark...which...are purely descriptive of natural objects', and not at all about human action, objected W. C. Roscoe. And Arnold conceded the rebuke, in his Preface to the second edition of his *Poems* (1854). He was wise to give in, for Victorian poetry could name, could say, any number of things. It embraced an exuberant variousness and variety this Anthology tries very hard to reflect.

So here are poems about cod-liver oil, railway lines and railway trains, chairs, soup, soap, paint-ings, omnibuses, going to the dentist, Grimm's Law, weather in the suburbs, dead dogs, cricket players, a cabbage leaf, Missing Links, tobacco, booze, snow, sado-masochism, Psychical Research, leeks, onions, genitalia, war, New Women, fairies, love, death, God, pain, poverty, poems, faith, doubt, science, poets, poetry. 'Cakes abundant be and buns;/Cakes of mace and marzipan;/Saffron cake and cakes of bran;/Gingerbreads and sallylunns': thus John Gray at the end of the century (1896), his Browningesque list of desired eating stuffs an allegory of the Victorian poem's huge appetite for ingestion. 'The crumping of cat-ice and snow down wood rides, narrow lanes and every street causeways. Rustling through a wood, or rather rushing while the wind hallows in the oak tops like thunder. The rustles of birds wings startled from their nests, or flying unseen into the bushes./The whizzing of larger birds over head in a wood, such as crows, puddocks, buzzards &c': thus John Clare, around the beginning of Victoria's reign, listing 'Pleasant Sounds', his post-Romantic haul of natural phenomena an allegory of the very many noises Victorian poets have us listening to. And there's always an Etcetera.

Just so, the mood of Victorian poetry oscillates hugely – from grave to gay, indeed all the way from the most serious to the very lightest. The comic poets, the nonsense mongers, the mockers and *pasticheurs* (too neglected in many visions of the period) – Charles Neaves, R. E. Egerton Warburton, H. S. Leigh, Locker-Lampson, C. S. Calverley, J. K. Stephen, Mortimer Collins, W. H. Mallock, H. Cholmondeley Pennell, G. R. Sims, as well as the better known W. S. Gilbert, Edward Lear and Lewis Carroll – are strongly represented here because they're so dominant a period presence. And so too are the hopeful, the cheering, the consolers, and the whistlers in the dark – the kind of poet Robert Browning was commonly misrepresented as being (as in Robert Buchanan's satirical 'Doctor B.'). But of course even the Christians found simple contentment hard. 'Believe not those who say/The upward path is smooth', wrote Anne Brontë. And she and Christina Rossetti, that most devoted of devout Anglo-Catholic believers, join the large roster of quite infidel endurers such as the uncowardly souled Emily Brontë or the Latinate pagan stoic A. E. Housman – the steely bearers-up against the known bad odds, the refusers of consolation, the deliberate residents in that *penultimate*, Beckettian place of Tennyson's character Ulysses, morbidly minded, alert to impending death and annihilation, but still determined not to throw in the towel and to do something more 'ere the end'. The spleenful abound too, and spleen can be a great enlivener of poetry, as angry Alfred Tennyson, for one, amply shows. But so also, and even more so, do the utterly discomfited abound, the sad, the dispirited, those from Tennyson to Amy Levy, from John Clare to John Davidson, from James Thomson to Thomas Hardy, poets driven, by grief or poverty or a sense of failure or the awfulness of the city or the loss of faith or inherited black blood, into dark nights of the soul, depression, neurasthenia, madness and suicidal thoughts. Melancholic moods are prevalent all over the period. 'No funeral gloom, my dears, when I am gone', urged William Allingham; it was a rare sentiment. Albrecht Dürer's engraving of *Melencolia* (1514) haunts the poetry (James Thomson said Dürer's mournful female figure was the ghostly urban spirit of his *The City of Dreadful Night*). Autumnal feelings keep invading the Victorian garden, keep dominating the period's numerous pastorals. Being on 'Dover Beach' with Matthew Arnold listening to the 'melancholy, long, withdrawing roar' of a receding faith is (in the words of a twentieth-century parody of Arnold's poem) a bitch the period is extremely familiar with. 'And some grow mad', as Wilde's *The Ballad of Reading Gaol* has it. Indeed they did. It's most striking that in his attack on 'The Pathetic Fallacy', John Ruskin should claim that *prosopopoeia*, the extremely basic poetic trope that he's objecting to, the trope of personification without which scarcely any poetry exists, is itself a kind of madness.

Assorted moods. And they enjoy assorted modes of poetic transport. There are poems made eloquent, not to say grandiloquent, by the emotional extremes they register, and poems reduced to quietness, to silence even, by the very same affects (Alice Meynell is not the only poet of the time writing in what keeps proving a necessary 'Silent Time'). And as degrees of eloquence vary so do poetic kinds. The variety of Victorian poetic modes is simply astonishing by its abundance. There are elegies, the poetry of mourning and melancholia, elegies simply everywhere (and everywhere taking their cue, as it were, from that great central Tennysonian text of mourning, *In Memoriam*). And there are love poems, outdoing even elegies in number, for this is one of the great ages of poetic love, and it is, of course, a poetry of love expressing enormous varieties and variations of desire – desire heterosexual, homosexual, religious; desire reciprocated, thwarted, twisted into hatred; perverse desire, banally ordinary desire; love triumphant, love downcast, love enduring every sort of ruin ('Love Among the Ruins' indeed); married love, domestic bliss, married horror. And there are sonnets, and pastoral poems, hymns, songs, odes, *ballades*, street ballads, and protest poems (so many of these, all across the period, not just in and around the protesting forties, what Charles Kingsley called 'Poems of 1848'): poems siding with the victims of despots and slavery, war, prejudiced law-makers, capital punishment and capitalism, and with the destitute and prostitutes, the 'Low' of all sorts, the ill-paid worker sweating at home, in a factory, or down a mine. And there are dramatic monologues, and epics (only shadows and traces of those here, of course: length is a perennial problem for anthologies), and imitations, parodies, poems in novels, versified stories, poems for children, realist poems, surrealist ones, Nonsense verses ('Nonsense' being one of the great Victorian innovations), Christian poems (for this is an age of great faith), anti-Christian ones (for this is an age of great doubt), dialect poems, Spasmodic poems, Impressionist poems, Decadent poems, Gothic poems, Symbolist ones.

And the poets, the producers of this great variety of material, comprise for their part an utterly motley band, their class, and selfhood, their voices, all as various as their subjects and their modes. They are English (the majority), but also Scottish, Irish, Anglo-Irish (one keeps being reminded of the close nineteenth-century ties between England and Ireland), and (a few) Welsh. They are men and women (with the numbers of women poets increasing mightily as the period goes on); and writers in standard English, but also subtle and unmisgiving departers from standard (Hardy the greatest case of this), writers in regional dialect, Scots, of course, but also other dialects (William Barnes, the Dorset poet, being the most notable advocate of an English regional ideolect); poets from the north of Britain and from the south; poets from cities, London dominantly, but also Edinburgh, Nottingham, Manchester, Glasgow, Birmingham, and poets from the countryside; poets utterly home-grown and home-bound, and poets with strong overseas, especially imperial, connexions – poets actually born in the colonies, like Kipling and Thackeray who were both born in India, children of empire, sons and daughters of colonial administrators, traders, soldiers, teachers and missionaries, and poets whose money came from family involvement in Caribbean plantations formerly worked by slaves. And there are poets born poor (like Thomas Hardy, or Gerald Massey, born in a hut on the canal near Tring to utterly illiterate parents, or the Midlands peasant John Clare, or Edward Lear, born poor in London's Holborn), and poets from the middle classes, and poets born into extremely rich families, like Swinburne or William Morris, R. E. Egerton-Warburton and Walter Savage Landor; and poets making great sums from their sales (the later Tennyson, Kipling, Macaulay, Martin Tupper) and poets making nothing at all from their verse (like the Brontës) or making scarcely enough, as John Davidson put it, to keep them in tobacco; poets armed with a classical education (like the huge roster of men from Oxford and Cambridge colleges – men because women were mainly excluded from the kind of classical education which dominated the men-only Public, i.e. private, Schools and the all-male, until late on in the period, Oxford and Cambridge), and poets who got up their knowledge autodidactically from books more or less by themselves (women, of course, in some number, though women from well-off families were often rather well educated by parents and tutors and schools for girls, but above all the many men who were too poor to go to school for long or to university at all); and poets who were Christians (a majority, but a mixed breed, from all the possible Victorian varieties of sect and creed and practice, a great restless crowd, much in motion, agitated often in their faith, to-ing and fro-ing, especially the ones who 'nightly pitched their moving tent/A day's march nearer Rome' (as one hymn parody had it), members of the Church of England becoming Anglo-Catholics, Anglo-Catholics becoming Roman Catholics), and on the other hand poets who were losing their traditional faith (Matthew Arnold-like), or who had lost it altogether, like Clough and Swinburne and Hardy and many another (*Loss and Gain*, the title of John Henry Newman's novel of 1848, summed up much of this religious scene).

And if the poets and their poems were so extraordinarily various, so was the implied reader of poetry – man, woman, straight, gay, believer, atheist, agnostic, politically conservative, politically radical, imperialist, anti-imperialist, proletarian, comfortably off, adult, child, Bible reader, up in the classics, interested in poeticity, interested, by contrast, though not necessarily by contrast, rather in Nature and in things.

The absoluteness of all this wondrous variety should not, however, be exaggerated. Variety did not please all Victorians. There were strong and illiberal efforts afoot to direct and to constrain utterance. Everything was more or less speakable, and somewhere or other was actually spoken. But publicly allowed speech came patchily. Even canonical poets, like Shakespeare and Chaucer, were made to appear in bowdlerized versions. The ruder Classical authors – Juvenal, Catullus, and so on – were regularly censored in school and university editions. Robert Buchanan's barbed assaults on 'The Fleshly School' of Rossetti and Swinburne were characteristic of a widespread censorious attitude, a resistance to plain speaking or enthusiasm in sexual and bodily matters. Francis Palgrave, editor of the most famous Victorian anthology, *The Golden Treasury of the Best Songs and Lyrical Poems in the English Language* (1861), left out poems he thought 'too high-kilted' for the ordinary poetry reader, that is ones with their skirts hitched up, too erotically or bodily explicit, such as Edmund Spencer's 'Epithalamium'. That poem was, as he put it, ' "Pueris" rather than "Virginibus" ' – for the boys rather than for virgins. And poets were mindful of embargoed areas. The homosexual verse of William (Johnson) Cory, for instance, remained coy and hintful rather than explicit, at least in its public versions. And unmindful, or risk-taking, poets were soon reminded of public resistances. Swinburne's publisher suppressed the first edition of *Poems and Ballads* (1866); Henry Vizetelly, publisher of Zola's novels in translation, was sent to jail for his temerity. Pater worried enough over his Conclusion to *The Renaissance* to suppress it for a while. A. E. Housman thought it more prudent not to publish his poem about the imprisonment of Oscar Wilde, 'Oh who is that young sinner with the handcuffs on his wrists', in his own lifetime. Some 'tears', in the words W. H. Auden used of Housman, were best kept 'like dirty postcards in a drawer'.

And if not all subjects were easily available to all readers, not every kind of poet was equally on hand for public consumption. While it is true that all sorts and conditions of men and women did indeed produce verse and get published there was still a good deal of socially lopsided homogeneity about the person of the published poet. Children of the bourgeoisie simply predominated. A Gerald Massey, a Thomas Hardy, a Clare, were the rarity, and, as the headnotes in this anthology reveal with daunting clarity, the majority of Victorian poets came from the professional classes, were children of the middle and upper-middle classes. The poor come almost nowhere, statistically speaking. Very few shopkeepers, either, had poetic offspring. The large number of poetic men from Oxford and Cambridge colleges, especially rich ones like Trinity College, Cambridge, tells this social story loudly; the numbers of poets who were called to the Bar but did not practise (because they did not need the money) puts the matter even more clamantly. One of the best ways of ensuring that you would turn out a poet in Victorian times was to make sure you were born into a clergyman's family. The darlings of the Victorian canon started off very often as the little darlings of some dotingly literatured bourgeois family (as the Brontës, for example, did).

And if the heterogeneity of the poets is not a simple matter, nor is that engaging heterogeneity of Victorian subject-matter. At least, the fetchingly alert engagement of the poetry with the great variety of Victorian phenomena is never just a matter of innocent report or uncomplicated reflection. The Victorian real comes inflected by a particular Victorian-ness, indeed by a particular set of Victorian-nesses, by what Matthew Arnold recognized as the peculiar *modernity* of the times. 'Modern problems have presented themselves', to the poet and to poetry, is the way he put this in his 1853 Preface. The problems he went on to indicate are, naturally enough, old problems of world and self, but they have assumed distinctly modern shape: what to make of the world now, what the present times have made and are making of the world; and what the self, the individual, the subject, especially the reflecting, story-making, speaking subject – the poetic self – makes, can make, might make, of itself and of its speaking, its art, in the world in which it presently finds itself, the world which it finds itself obliged now to make out and to make up – in other words, to invent, in every sense, for now.

The Victorian version of such perennial questions of epistemology and hermeneutics – that is, questions of knowing and of interpreting – were especially focused in the fierce realism debate and in the nearly neurotic concern with the nature, the being, the soul, as the Victorians put it, of the poet. The *real* had become in many ways overwhelmingly confusing, chaotic, bad. The commonest posture to the world among writers was counter, aggressive, satirical, appalled. William Morris talked, quite representatively, of 'all the fifth of civilisation'. The city, increasingly regarded as typical modern, industrialized, mass existence, is a place of horror, distress, oppression, loneliness – to be angrily registered in all the poems about the urban poor, mental darkness in the city, loneliness in London, jumpers off Thames bridges, 'Chrismassing à la Mode de Slumopolis' (as the poem by G. R. Sims has it). Escapism, naturally, attracts – hence, not least, the large swathe of wistful, desirous, pastoral poems – literal pastoral celebrations from Arnold's 'Thyrsis' and 'Scholar-Gipsy' to

Tennyson's 'Come into the garden, Maud' and T. E. Brown's 'A garden is a lovesome thing, God wot', pastorals multiplying in number as the dire urbanizing century advanced (from the likes of Mathilde Blind, G. A. Simcox, Edward Dowden, Augusta Webster, W. E. Henley, Margaret Veley), and also metaphorical pastorals (the domestic pastoral of, say, Coventry Patmore's celebrations of Christian marriage, *The Angel in the House*, or Gerard Manley Hopkins's outdoor world of 'God's Grandeur', or Francis Thompson's rapturous snowflake in 'To a Snow-flake', and all that). But, equally characteristically, the pastorals are also notably frail and tending to dissolution. Maud's garden proves no hedge against modern dementias; the lovely garden of Katharine Tynan's 'Sheep and Lambs' – 'All in the April evening' – is where the Lamb of God is crucified on 'a Cross of shame'; and God will not send rain even upon Gerard Hopkins's 'dry roots'; and autumn comes, and harsh snows, the typically awful weather of the Victorian outdoors poem; and Housman's lovely 'blue remembered hills' are 'the land of lost content', 'Where I went/And cannot come again'.

The real proves, in fact, difficult to envisage as not in some way or another grotesque – much too grotesque, certainly, for some readers. 'Grotesque realism', a 'taste for ugly reality', is what appals Walter Bagehot about Robert Browning's poetry. There's no relish in Bagehot's aesthetic for what the dyspeptic, suicidal John Davidson celebrated as 'Pre-Shakespearianism', namely a poetic receptivity to 'the offal of the world'. And Victorian aesthetics split along these lines. You could, according to George Henry Lewes's essay of 1865, have too much of a certain 'detailism'. Portrait-painters should concentrate on the philosopher's face, not his waistcoat or the upholstery of the chair he sits in. 'Realism' has become 'unhealthy'. 'There are other truths besides coats and waistcoats, pots and pans, drawing-rooms and suburban villas.' It's hard not to read Lewes's polemic as a particular swipe at his life-partner George Eliot, the novelist who theorized the importance of pots and pans and the poet who wrote about a London Drawingroom, as well as its being a general gibe at whole swathes of Victorian novels and poems whose grasp of the real rested upon just such knowable materialisms. In effect Lewes was at one with Dickens in his role as self-elected art critic, when the latter objected in 1850 to the representation of ugly bodies in the Pre-Raphaelite John Everett Millais's painting *Christ in the Carpenter's Shop*. Instead of 'tender, awful, sorrowful, ennobling, sacred, graceful, or beautiful associations', Millais gave you 'the lowest depths of what is mean, odious, repulsive, and revolting': 'Wherever it is possible to express ugliness of feature, limb, or attitude, you have it expressed. Such men as the carpenters might be undressed in any hospital where dirty drunkards, in a high state of varicose veins, are received. Their very toes have walked out of St Giles's.' St Giles was a notorious London slum parish. An anonymous carpenter was Millais's model for St Joseph, Jesus's father. The saint patently has dirt in his fingernails. And Dickens was, evidently, on the side of the clergy in Browning's 'Fra Lippo Lippi' who want the artist to 'Paint the soul, never mind the legs and arms'. Which is only a step away from objecting, with Robert Buchanan's notorious flyting attack on 'The Fleshly School' – on the sons of Browning, in fact – to any fleshliness at all.

But the body, and the eroticized body not least, would not go away. Its celebration, once begun, as it were, by Browning and his poetic offspring, would spread across the frank pages in particular of decadent, and perverse, and gay poets – from Swinburne's exuberant S-M celebrations of the bloodied and pained body, through Edward Carpenter's Whitmanesque hymnings of the admired male body ('Beautiful is the figure of the lusty full-grown groom on his superb horse'), to Arthur Symons's feasting on 'the white fragrant apple of a breast' ('Hallucination I': it's his Bianca's body which 'satisfies my soul'), or John Gray's sly allusions to Jules Laforgue's diaphanous geraniums (metaphor for female genitalia) in 'The Barber'. And so it would go on, on into the pages of the modernist and Laforgue-obsessed T. S. Eliot. (John Gray's dream of being a barber is characteristic. The decadents really go to town on that Victorian body-part so persistently fetishized all across the period, the hair. The fragrance of hair was especially enticing. 'Is it perfume from a dress/That makes me so digress?' T. S. Eliot's Prufrock would ask himself. For the Victorians it was the scentedness of hair that was particularly arousing. 'Even now the fragrant darkness of her hair/Had brushed my cheek' (Ernest Dowson, 'Terre Promise'). The arousing scentedness of hair was utterly central to the current bodily erotics. Arthur Symons prefaced the second edition of his

Silhouettes (1896) with 'A word on Behalf of Patchouli'. The devoutest of Christians, such as Isa Craig Knox and Richard Le Gallienne, are specially drawn to the Gospel tradition of Mary Magdalene's anointing Christ's feet with a boxfull of spikenard and then wiping them with her hair: the odour of poetic sanctity is the odour of perfume on a fallen woman's hair.)

What the resort to bodiliness signals, of course, is the quest for some ground of certainty in a confused world. For the body, even at its pained worst, was reassuring because – as Aldous Huxley would put it later (in his novel *Eyeless in Gaza* in 1936) as part of his explanation for the body's increasing importance in the modern imagination – the body was 'indubitably there'. The materiality, and especially the bodily materiality, of Victorian writing is, clearly, so much there in the writing, because it is so knowably there in the world. Matthew Arnold talked rather plaintively of the need to find touchstones for critical judgement in a world of faltering critical standards; what Buchanan and Dickens and the rest thought of as gross materialism becomes a sort of guarantee of something fixed in a time when so much is in danger of becoming unglued. The material becomes a touchstone of certainty, in effect, for an era when the Grand Narratives of the Christian tradition, the biblical myths of origins and ends, the old cosmic certainties of the Creation story, the old reliable narratives of God's Big Book and of all other people's books of wisdom, were under vivid threat.

The poetry – Tennyson's and Arnold's, Clough's and Hardy's poetry, of course, but also the poetry of others, Alfred Domett it might be, or W. E. Henley ('A Desolate Shore'), or A. M. F. Robinson (her 'Men and Monkeys'), or L. S. Bevington's 'Egoisme à Deux' – earnestly registers the post-Christian loosening and loss of cosmic grip in the wake of Darwin and the geologists and the biblical critics. Naturally the Christians try to fight back with some assertiveness, as in Buchanan's 'Nietzsche' and Edward Dowden's 'Seeking God' and in Charles (Tennyson) Turner's sonnets such as '*Leben Jesu* and *Vie de Jésus*' and 'The "Higher Criticism"'. But the wrestle for certainties and confidence remains a real struggle. Which side convinces the more, for example, in the crucial battle for the truth of Christmas it would be hard to say. The huge number of poems sited about the December celebrations of the birth of Jesus witness the importance of Christmas's meanings for the claims of the old creed. What was at stake at Christmas was that it was either a living witness to the historical origins of the Christian faith and to its continuing theological value and meaning or a hollow ritual, historically void, a sign of Christianity's discontinued value. It's no accident that one of the very finest Christian poems in the whole period should be Christina Rossetti's 'A Christmas Carol' – 'In the bleak mid-winter' – but no accident either that *In Memoriam*, that great poem of religious hesitation and question, that long journal of repeatedly staggered faith, should be built around three Christmas-tides.

And meanwhile the scepticism stakes were being raised as Browning's eloquently unreliable narrators signalled the sort of untrustworthiness of all perceivers and tellers which became a main plank of modernism; and impressionism (fetchingly lovely, of course, in a painterly imagistic poem by a William Renton, a Wilde, or a Symons) was just impressionism, the poeticity of a frail subjectivity; and transcendence found itself dumbed down (in the hands of Matthew Arnold and Pater and Housman) into the merely aesthetic. No wonder the thisness, the thereness, the materiality, of the body, or of the upholstery – even if the upholstery was grotesquely torn and the body grimly sick (Henley's '*vers libres* on his scrofula', as Wilde sneeringly put it) – possessed such appeal. Even – perhaps especially – for Christians. 'All things counter, original, spare, strange: whatever is fickle, freckled (who knows how)', to quote Hopkins's 'Pied Beauty': they were, as the man said, indubitably there.

But all the same, even for Hopkins, the orthodox Catholic priest asserting the eternal and divine origin of the lovely thinginess that so attracts his aestheticizing gaze ('He fathers-forth whose beauty is past change: Praise him') there's the persistence of the worrying doubting parenthesis: 'who knows how'. And if the identity and nature of things, *out there*, was questionable even for the believing Christian, the question of the poet's own identity, the nature of things as it were *in here*, was all the more pressing. For Arnold, modern problems presented themselves first and foremost as 'the dialogue of the mind with itself'. Victorian modernity engendered self-debate; the question of the self was now uppermost. Even for the Luther-admiring Protestant poet Robert

Browning, the old 'here stand I' of Carlyle's Luther, the self armed with a sturdily reliant Protestant self-conscience, had fractured into the dramatic monologue's multitude of dubious, errant, misled and miseleading personae. Strikingly, the most militant of possible British self-identifications, that of Christian soldier, the righteous male heroic self (the guardian of the borders and bridges against encroachments of otherness, as in Macaulay's parable of soldierly faithfulness, *Horatius*), tapers off, despite all assertions from Henry Newbolt and Conan Doyle and even Tennyson, to the contrary, into the tremors of Tennyson's ageing Ulysses, Crimean War recriminations, and Kipling's imperialist forebodings. For his part, Swinburne is attracted to the dualities of hermaphroditism. Gender positives were becoming unstuck. The old ecclesiastically affirmed gender fences were beginning to stagger under the push of so many homosexual apologiae. A poet called Michael Field proves to be a pair of lesbians. And self-naming becomes a kind of mere shadow-boxing with identity. What, where, precisely is the centre of being for the narrator of *Maud*? What exactly does he feel? His *I* becomes a very kaleidoscope of possibilities and parts. Now his *I* hates, now scorns, now is one with his kind. 'So dark a mind within me dwells'; no wonder any certainty about himself does not last long. '*If* I be dear...', he says. If. This Hamlet is indeed a thing of shreds and patches. The same goes for Yeats's poetic self. Who actually speaks his late-century poems? The names, the self-labellings, keep being switched and swapped. The nineties blurring caps the period's long process of lapsing, loose, losing, self-identification attempts. 'I know not what I am. – Oh dreadful thought' (J. A. Symonds, 'Personality'). 'Like smoke I vanish' (W. H. Mallock, 'Human Life'). 'On ne saurait dire à quel point un homme, seul dans son lit et malade, devient personnel' (that's Henley's epigraph to his *In Hospital* sequence): when, indeed, does a sick man become a person? 'I tell my secret?' No, Christina Rossetti's Hamlet won't tell; perhaps because she cannot.

And these identity problems *within* poems are closely related with the identity problems *of* poems. For a most striking feature of Victorian poetry is just how much of it is preoccupied with poetry itself. The poems themselves are busy to an extraordinary degree with constructing a poetics. There's a great Babel of voices talking about poetry – claiming poetic status ('We are the music-makers'); wondering what poetry is, what taste, who the poet, whether poets are born rather than made, what hope there is for modern rhyme, and what the progress of poetry has been; seeking to define art, and prose, and rhyme, and the ministry of song, and writing, and the sonnet; fawning on fellow practitioners (Tennyson accumulates a large poetic fan club; women poets queue to admire Felicia Hemans, and L.E.L., and Elizabeth Barrett Browning; Arnold celebrates his dead poetic friend Clough, and the Brontës; and so on), but also jeering at aesthetical persons and 'aesthetic adjectives', mocking and pastiching, especially knocking modern hits like Adelaide Procter's 'The Lost Chord', and putting acknowledged modern masters like Tennyson and Browning in their place.

This incessant conversation about poetry is, of course, like all post-classical, all modern, literary discourses, afflicted by the anxiety of belatedness, the late arrival's fear there is nothing left to say or sing, no real role for the poetic newcomer. 'Have not all songs been sung – all loves been told?/ What shall I say when nought is left unsaid?' (Margaret Veley, 'Sonnet'). The greatness of past poems makes the newcomer's efforts seem very small. 'I will not sing my little puny songs', declares Digby Mackworth Dolben, at least not 'After Reading Aeschylus'. The Gospel parable about what the latecomers to the vineyard should be paid grips the poetic imagination (see the poems titled 'Unto this Last' by Isa Craig Knox and by Francis Thompson). But all the anxiety over the value of the belated one's contribution never really abates the desire to join in the chorus of valued old voices, to become part of the – or a – admired tradition. 'O may I join the choir invisible/Of those immortal dead who live again/In minds made better by their presence' (George Eliot). The strong question is whether the tradition might live on in the new individual talent. But it does still remain a heartfelt question whether the literary dead ever really live again. Is immortality possible for anyone? Can, in fact, the admired poetic Lazarus be raised from the dead, come forth from the tomb of the past, to live on in the person of his, or her, successor? It is much to the point that Victorian elegy – suffused as is all elegy with the provoking desire to recall the dead to life in some form, to have them live again and speak still – is very frequently a dead poets', not just a dead persons', society: it grieves over Cowper and Keats, Clough, 'Poor Hood', Arthur Hallam,

Felicia Hemans, L.E.L., Tennyson himself. They are the voices the poets would above all like to have speaking again, and, it's hoped, through them.

Claiming affinities, seeking active commerce with the dead is, of course, what tradition-making – and canon-building – are all about. By such means living poets seek to prove their own legitimacy, their non-bastardy, their rights to some aesthetic inheritance – and so they name their ancestors, call on their fathers and mothers in the poetic line, claiming and identifying their own poetic place and character by declaring their nurturing predecessors. Sometimes this claiming is made by filial acts of translation (Carlyle, it might be, translates Luther; J. M. Neale translates medieval hymn writers); sometimes by discipular remouthings of admired old words (as Newman recycles the Mass in *The Dream of Gerontius*, and scores of poems recycle biblical texts), or by retellings of old stories (as Tennyson rewrites Homer's and Dante's Ulysses, and Browning reanimates a line from *King Lear*, 'Childe Roland to the Dark Tower Came'), or by assuming past artistic personae (Browning's painters and musicians; Yeats's Irish mages); or by meditations on valued old aesthetic products such as paintings (that repeated practice of L.E.L., and Dante Gabriel Rossetti, and Michael Field).

The affiliation process is not all joy; there are losses as well as gains to be made in these jostlings for poetic kin, lost leaders as well as leaders (as in Browning's negative celebration of Wordsworth in 'The Lost Leader'), painful examples as well as benedictory ones. William Cowper is a superb if downcast ruralist predecessor for John Clare, but for Anne Brontë and Elizabeth Barrett Browning a melancholy Calvinist suffering moods a Christian poet need not share: 'O poets! From a maniac's tongue, was poured the deathless singing!' Just so, Sappho was a great inspiriter of Victorian women who wanted to sing their own sex, but her suicide (the story was she threw herself off a cliff) was also the stuff rather of melancholic meditation and self-pitying reminders, which easily attached to the suicide of Amy Levy if not actually to the mysterious death of L.E.L. And Victorian women poets were not shy at utilizing the large gallery of negative history and myth for their self-modellings, even though the implications were evidently gloomy and the task a kind of masochism. L.E.L. watches the ocean with Calypso, who was abandoned by Ulysses; Michael Field contemplates a drawing of Leda raped by the swan. And, to be sure, the mythic women who haunt the poems of men as well as women tend to be fearful models of the female rather than otherwise – even if, in the prevailing and repeated cases of Circe and Persephone and Salomé and Mary Magdalene, there's much dark sexual pleasure to compensate the male poet, a Swinburne, a Rossetti, say, for the terrors he's carefully troubling himself with. 'Could you hurt me, sweet lips?' – as Swinburne puts it to 'Our Lady of Pain' in his 'Dolores (Notre Dame des Sept Douleurs)'. (It's been left out of this anthology only because Swinburne's quota of painful somaticism had been used up.)

These attempted discipleships and willed associations are, of course, an important and necessary, if often rather extreme, part of the Victorians' urgent attempts to find 'the words to say it'. The words: getting them right is always the poet's chief problem. And Victorian poetry is well recognized to have, taken as a whole, a difficulty over the words. Its diction can so often be so slack, so breezily casual and cliché-ed, seemingly so uncared-for. Auden's thought – it's one of his best critical-historical speculations (in his Introduction to his lovely anthology *Nineteenth Century Minor Poets*, 1967) – was to blame bourgeois male education in the Public School system, where the first practice a boy had in versifying was in a foreign language – imitating Latin and Greek verses as part of his lessons. Long habituation in this, lessons dinned in by the cane, resulted, Auden suggests, in the evident facility and confidence about metre which is all over the Victorian scene (Victorian poets can turn their hand now to this metre, now to that; their expertise is manifest), but also in a kind of ingrained heedlessness about diction (for in translating, as the classroom tyro in Latin and Greek verse was constantly doing, you get used to settling for less than the *mot juste* and to not quite saying what you might or should). This theory would not by itself explain women writers' practice, since they weren't put through the male classical mill. But it is a radical thought; certainly one to set alongside the counter-fact that Victorian poets and the Victorian readership prove everywhere to be extremely preoccupied with the exact state of poetic words.

The vicious early criticism of Tennyson, the wide hostility to Browning, are rooted in critics not being prepared to condone what they read as Tennyson's sloppiness and Browning's harshness of vocabulary. No sign there of a readiness to let just anything go. And the poets themselves are to be observed pushing the words hard all over the poetic scene – there's Hopkins, it might be, experimenting in language as well as in metre, and William Barnes carefully investing in Dorset dialect, and Hardy consciously disproportioning his words, and Browning and his gruff school effortfully working their guttural, plosive, consonantal magic, and vowel-minded Tennyson (the poet with the proverbially good ear, one of the very few English poets to make one really believe in onomatopoeia), rightly admiring his own vowel-skill in 'The moan of doves' lines in 'Come down, O maid' in *The Princess*, and so on and on. Careless about words the most arresting of the poets certainly are not. And in fact so urgent is the quest for the words which will tell best, that Victorian poets go to extremes which anticipate and even rival the extremes of modernist verbal experiment. I mean so-called Nonsense writing and its close neighbours, the various kinds of what we might call Victorian glossolalia, language on the compelling edge of gibberish. Victorian poetic rhetoric quite often gives itself over to a very risky kind of raw, uncooked linguisticity, close to the primitivity of onomatopoeia, and goes in rather often also for the parallel risks of a helter-skelter rhyming in which the signifiers accumulate more for the vertiginous excitements of the mere noise they make than for any rational senses they might carry.

Theo Marzials's 'A Tragedy' (happily brought to my attention by that most wide-ranging contemporary period guide, *Victorian Poets* (1852), by the American critic Edmund Clarence Stedman, which I stumbled on in a seaside book-bin) will stand nicely for the practice of the uncooked, with its watery 'Flop, plop, Plop, plop, drip, drop, Plop' sequences; and Henry Bellyse Baildon's 'A Bluebottle' for helter-skelter rhyming ('Buzzes, bustles,/Fumes and fustles'; 'Still abusing, random cruising,/Still unflagging, zig-a-zagging'). The tone of such moments as these is light, comic, or near-comic (W. S. Gilbert's comic rhymes come to mind). The word-music being made here is also primitive, the jingling stuff of popular song (the 'Rink-a-tink, rink-a-tink, rink-a-tink-a-tink' of Mary Howitt's 'Barley-Mower's Song', it might be), and of nursery rhyme and playground chant, the archaic aurality of the young and the small. And it's no accident that 'Nonsense' should have been directed at children or the child-like, that its proponents, such as Edward Lear, should have taken such delight in the childish pleasures of onomatopoetic imitation (his way with train noises has become appropriately famous), nor, indeed, that such plays of archaic poeticity should occur in the vicinity of dinkified characters and subject-matter. '[H]obbling,/Flying, running, leaping,/Puffing and bowing,/Chuckling, clapping, crowing,/Clucking and gobbling,/Mopping and mowing': that's Christina Rossetti's little men in her 'Goblin Market'. The immense Victorian investment in fairy fellers, little people, childishness, nursery joys, nursery songs, puppets, toys, dolls, doll-like little girls, water-babies, Wee Willie Winkie, Letty and her globe, all the shrunken, the midget, the minute things and persons of William Allingham, Charles (Tennyson) Turner and William Miller, of Robert Louis Stevenson, William Brighty Rands, Coventry Patmore, George MacDonald, Andrew Lang, Lear, Carroll and the rest is part and parcel of, as it helps to sustain and fire, the often frenzied plunge into raw signifying.

This is language on edge, close up to un-meaning, to mere babble and *néant*, to the incantatory mystagogic babbling of modernist texts. And if babble excites (the great modernist linguist Ferdinand de Saussure takes seriously the glossolalia of the Geneva medium Mme Smith, and inaugurates an era in which the idea of signifiers floating free of significds will scducc litcrary thcorists), it also frightens the rational (the jabbering of Africa in Conrad's end-of-century *Heart of Darkness* is an essence of estrangement and otherness). And the association of the uncooked Victorian linguisticity with the world of the tiny tot only affirms such worriedness. Tininess unsettles the fully grown. The art of the minute wears its neuroses openly. The neurotically tiny fairy paintings of Richard Dadd (notably *Contradiction: Oberon and Titania* and *The Fairy Feller's Master Stroke*) are not only typical of the fairy genre of Victorian painting, but their freaky miniaturized controllings, their desire to dominate by a miniaturizing excess, seem not at all unconnected with the murderous intentions – Dadd killed his father – that got their painter into the Bethlem mad-house and the Broadmoor Hospital for the criminally insane, where he did his paintings. The minute handwriting of the young Brontës in their midget hand-made notebooks seems as much a sign of obsession and neurosis (like a carving of the Lord's Prayer on a grain of rice) as of laudable nursery creativity.

Christina Rossetti's goblins are full of extremest menace. So are the tiny objects in Wilde's *The Ballad of Reading Gaol* – the Chaplain's 'little tract', the hangman's 'little bag', the 'little ticks' of the doctor's time-piece – not to mention the doomed innocence of the condemned man's boyish cricket cap. Tiny prosopopoeias can be far more uncanny than full-size ones (it's the lesson of the little shops of repro-Victorian nightmares in Hollywood Gothic or the toyshop horrors of Angela Carter's stories, as it is of shrunken Alice in her Wonderland). In James Thomson's poem 'In the Room' pieces of furniture come alive and discuss the horrors they've witnessed, and in particular the body of a suicide lying on the bed. A mirror recalls a little cousin being used to check whether a dead man was breathing; a little phial of poison tells how the dead suicide on the bed drank from it. And it's the littleness of these personifications which deepens the uncanniness.

Disconcertingly animated furniture. Thomson's bedroom nightmare is not unreminiscent of Rhoda's in Virginia Woolf's *The Waves* when her bedroom walls and furniture wave and wobble about her, modernistically endorsing some kind of dissolution of the self. So once again Victorian imaginings seem oddly proleptic of modernist ones. And this two-faced doubleness, the realist tendency jostling the anti-realist, is, of course, a ground of the greatest tension within the Victorian age and its writing – namely, the way the period's great confidences and certainties about persons and texts, politics and morality, its assertive realisms, its buoyant materialisms, the hard-edgedness of its ideologies, are attended by constant doubts, waverings and hesitations of all sorts, by conflictedness of the self and gender, of theology and politics, by epistemological doubts and narrative uncertainties, by shakings of the foundations and rattlings of linguistic order. In other words, the Victorian is never far from the modernism to come. It's a paradoxical blend, a whole set of contraries, nicely emblematized by this anthology's cover painting, J. M. W. Turner's *The Fighting Temeraire tugged to her last berth to be broken up, 1838.*

Here, in a painting first exhibited at the Royal Academy, May 1839, is a pictorial paean to maritime might, a memorial to England's great naval power, to her sheer imperialist force, the far-flung battle-line that Kipling would write about (the *Temeraire* was one of the old sailing ships of the line, designed for a main place in the naval line of battle). Named after a famous French ship, *Le Téméraire*, captured in 1758, it was in the forefront of what was for the Victorians the greatest sea victory ever, the defeat of Napoleon's navy at the Battle of Trafalgar in 1805 – a victory led by Admiral Horatio Nelson in his flagship *Victory*, a vessel commanded by Captain Thomas Masterman Hardy, Thomas Hardy's renowned naval ancestor. The painting was a celebration in many ways appropriate to the beginning of the new queen's reign (Victoria was crowned 28 June 1838), highly appropriate to the feelings Victorians expressed, and would go on expressing in, so to say, old-order poems – imperialistic, male, championing power, appealing to force. Words adapted from a poem by Thomas Campbell, the renowned pre-Victorian poet of empire, 'Ye Mariners of England: A Naval Ode', were attached to the picture (Turner had already done water-colour illustrations for *The Poetical Works of Thomas Campbell*, 1837, including the Nelson-eulogizing poem, 'The Battle of the Baltic'). Turner's *Temeraire* was, Thackeray thought, in his role of journalistic art critic, 'a magnificent national ode'. And the painting did indeed inspire verse – an imperialist song by J. Duff (1857), imperialist poems by Richard Monckton Milnes, by Gerald Massey ('The Fighting Temeraire Tugged to Her Last Berth', in *Havelock's Last March and Other Poems*, 1851), and by Henry Newbolt ('The Fighting Téméraire', in *Admirals All*, 1897):

> Oh! To see the linstock lighting
> And to hear the round shot biting
> For we're all in love with fighting
> On the fighting Téméraire.

But of course that old imperial, naval order was changing even as it was being celebrated. The great sailing ship's fabled career was over, and it was being towed to the breaker's berth, tugged along with great modern-age indignity by what Thackeray described as a 'little, spiteful, diabolical steamer'. The celebratory painting was also a feast of regret, an essay in nostalgia, an elegy for the sort of uncluttered imperialist gloryings that would become less and less simple as Victoria's reign proceeded (the appearance of the Massey poem in his volume featuring the mixed glories of the Indian Mutiny indicates the kind of unbucklings the old sentiments would more and more endure). The sun in the painting is setting, setting in splendour, but still setting. In his book *Turner* (1891), the poet Cosmo Monkhouse said the picture 'was penetrated with a sentiment which finds an echo in every heart' – and that sentiment was highly elegiac, to do with 'the fate of all created things'. A passing was being recorded, which included, we might conclude, poetic as well as military certitudes. The 'brave old ship' had 'death, as it were, written on her', Thackeray wrote; and the sense of mortality was about art as much as about politics and history. 'The flag which braved the battle and the breeze,/No longer owns her' was the little poem Turner wrote and attached to his picture. It was cobbled together out of words from Campbell. 'Whose flag has braved, a thousand years,/The battle and the breeze', Campbell wrote. 'No longer owns her' was Turner's own addition – a dyspeptic supplement signifying the Admiralty's abandonment of the old national favourite, but also in effect a revision of Campbell's versified imperialism, an amendment of a poeticized politics and a politicized poetics. 'But in England's song for ever/She's the Fighting Téméraire', Newbolt would assert – and right at the end of the century too. But even Newbolt has to remind himself that the ship 'was fading down the river'. And so, evidently, certainly by 1897, was any consensus about 'England's song'. By 1897 many other, newer songs than confidently male, heroic, nationalist and imperialist ones had been and were being sung. And what's most striking is that these newer, more complex, rhetorics were being announced, implicitly, but still clearly, by the stylistics of Turner's painting. Already in 1838, right at the beginning of Victoria's reign, here is this ur-modernist production – hazy, impressionistic, hesitant about seeing and knowing, a painting about the unreliable narrativity of painting, a declaration of painting's fictionality, a lesson to viewers in the necessity of non-realism, and the realistic nature of the invented, the made-up. It's an example of the 'mad, late-Turner rendering' which Hardy praised in 1887, the year of Victoria's Golden Jubilee – Hardy, himself on the cusp of the post-Victorian, recognizing in Turner, Turner the early Victorian, the presented 'secret' of an utterly modern and modernist art, that is, 'how to produce by a false thing the effect of a true'. The ending-up, backwards-looking poetics of Turner's version of the *Temeraire*'s last days was also inseparably linked, in penetrating ways, with the art of the future. The paradoxically mixed nature of Victorian art – and poetry – could scarcely be more suggestively broached.[1]

All anthologies are funny about their predecessors. They're greedily parasitical upon them, but at the same time like to feel they are different from them, even uniquely so. This one is no exception. It has been greatly helped, inspirited even, by several earlier collections: by William Davenport Adams's *The Comic Poets of the Nineteenth Century: Poems of Wit and Humour by Living Writers* (1876) – a lucky find in the depths of the Oxford English Faculty Library; by W. H. Auden's *Nineteenth Century Minor Poets* (1967), another lucky *trouvaille*, this time in the stacks of the Konstanz Universität library; by Derek Stanford's *Pre-Raphaelite Writing* (1973); Kingsley Amis's *New Oxford Book of Light Verse* (1978); Brian Maidment's *The Poorhouse Fugitives: Self-Taught Poets and Poetry in Victorian Britain* (1987); Jennifer Breen's *Victorian Women Poets 1830–1901* (1994); by the truly pioneering *Victorian Women Poets*, edited by Angela Leighton and Margaret Reynolds (1995); the even larger *Nineteenth-Century Women Poets*, edited by Isobel Armstrong, Joseph Bristow and Cath Sharrock (1996); by R. K. R. Thornton's *Poetry of the 1890s* (1970; revised with Marion Thain, 1997); and Daniel Karlin's capacious *Penguin Book of Victorian Verse* (1997), which came out not quite too late for me, but nearly so. Most pointers and, yes, inspiration, came from Christopher Ricks's magnificent *New Oxford Book of Victorian Verse* (1990) – which broke so much overgrown and neglected ground and splendidly redrew the maps of Victorian poetry for all his successors. But – and here comes the claim of special difference – all these collections, like all anthologies, have their peculiar interests, devotions, intentions, ideologies, and so drawbacks, which, naturally, this anthology seeks to

I'm grateful to the *Temeraire* researches of Judy Egerton, *Making and Meaning: Turner, The Fighting Temeraire* (National Gallery Publications, Yale University Press, 1995).

counter. *Comic, Light Verse, Minor, Self-Taught, Women*: those titles and bits of titles spell out special leanings. But the grandly bland *Victorian* professes some sort of consensus about what the 'Victorian' is, about what the good or interesting or important Victorian poets and poems are, about who or what is in or out, effectively about what the Victorian canon is, a consensualism which is however denied on many pages the title presides over. And inevitably so. There will never be absolute agreement. Specialism, even special pleading, are the order of the day, the nature of the case. Editors must choose, and in choosing they can't help define a partial Victorianism which will be partly or even greatly their own. All anthologies have their preferences, their ideology, which are not admitted in their titles, even in specialized titles. Leighton and Reynolds, for instance, play up the role of unmarried women poets and are especially keen on lesbians. Christopher Ricks is noticeably drawn to quirkiness and oddity of subject, as well as to stoical doubt and unbelief rather than to poems of faith, and he likes poems about the fickleness of women (he can also, by the way – though this enormous critical power is actually not at all by the way but right in the centre of the track – tell a good poem when he sees one, many a time singling out the one poem that passes the Housman tingle-factor test from a whole volume of the otherwise dire and drossy). For his part, Daniel Karlin has gone hunting for the minor and the provincial authors that others have too commonly left shelved. No one's space allows for more than glimpses of the long poem. And so on.

This anthology's claim is to be bigger, more comprehensive, more liberally inclusive of varieties of author, subjects and kinds, than anyone else's. Its great size tells. There are 158 named poets here, as against Ricks's 112 and Karlin's 145. This greater range – which includes giving, in most cases, more than just a single poem, certainly more than just a single short poem, from each represented author – is, it's hoped, more than ever before answerable to the great scope and variety of Victorian verse. This anthology also strives to use its bulk to reflect the presence and the force of long poems and sequences (all of Macaulay's *Horatius*, of *In Memoriam* and *Maud*, of Henley's *In Hospital* sequence, George Eliot's *Brother and Sister* group, Wilde's *The Ballad of Reading Gaol*, Fitz-Gerald's *Rubáiyát of Omar Khayyám*, Hopkins's *The Wreck of the Deutschland*, Newman's *The Dream of Gerontius*, Clough's *Amours de Voyage*, Carroll's *The Hunting of the Snark*, Aytoun's spoof review of *Firmilian*, and so on). Other anthologies have some of these things; nobody else has all of them. The usual space problems, even in an anthology this big, mean, alas, only parts of Elizabeth Barrett Browning's *Sonnets from the Portuguese*, Meredith's *Modern Love*, Thomson's *The City of Dreadful Night*, and nothing much from Tennyson's *The Princess* and *Idylls of the King*, and nothing at all from the period's most extraordinary and very important long poem, Robert Browning's *The Ring and the Book*.

If there is a desire here to do more than keep a liberal open house and to try and respect the great variety of Victorian poetry, it is the wish to register in particular the variety, strength and importance, poetically, culturally, historically, on the one hand of poetry about poetry, the great poetics debate and conversation conducted within and through poetry itself, and on the other hand of Christian and Christianity-concerned verse – and not least devotional writing, especially the still too neglected work of women hymn-writers. A secularized time such as ours should not lose sight of the centrality of the religious in the poetry of its immediate past. An unhappy peculiarity of recent Victorian anthology-making is that the extremely welcomable rise and rise of the Anglo-Catholic Christina Rossetti is being accompanied by the puzzling diminishment of the Roman Catholic Gerard Hopkins. In this volume they both assume – or resume – their most significant place in the immensely important band of Victorian Christian, Christianized, and Christianity-obsessed poetic pilgrims.

Nothing is more contentious among anthologies than the boundaries of the 'Victorian'. Everyone accepts that the main criterion for inclusion should be publication within the dates of Victoria's reign by poets living and writing during that time, but nobody disputes that the mere dates of that reign – 20 June 1837 to 22 January 1901 – will not do just by themselves as demarcators, and that 'Victorian' is more than just an accident of the timing of publication, or even of writing. Many poets everybody would accept as utterly Victorian also write and publish either before or after Victoria. The major Victorian Gerard Hopkins was completely unknown to the Victorian public, because almost nothing of his was published until the reign of George V. There are several important poems by other main Victorians – Emily Brontë, A. E. Housman, Robert Louis Stevenson, William Allingham – which did not see the light of public day until after Victoria died. There's a great deal of early work by poets who became Victorian by virtue of surviving into the new queen's reign, but which was written and published beforehand. It would be absurd to exclude from a Victorian collection Tennyson's 'The Lady of Shalott' because it was first published in 1832, or Robert Browning's 'Porphyria's Lover' because it came out in January 1836, or, for that matter, Tennyson's 'Ulysses' because, though published in 1842, it was written in 1833. Equally absurd, of course, to think of Wordsworth's *The Prelude* as a Victorian poem because it was published in 1850, or of Shelley's 'Defence of Poetry' as a piece of Victorian poetics because it was published in 1840. Mere chronological criteria will not always do. Publication dates, like the careers of authors, simply refuse to comply snugly with the chronology of monarchs' reigns. There is some case, I'd suggest, for believing that 'Victorian' poetry begins with Tennyson's *Poems* of 1832, or with the death of Arthur Hallam in 1833. (The deaths of Walter Scott and George Crabbe in 1832, and Coleridge in 1834, signal some kind of poetic era's end; but these are more or less purely accidental; and where does mere chronology leave someone like Leigh Hunt, born, as Arthur Symons points out in his Introduction to *Essays by Leigh Hunt*, in the year of Dr Johnson's death and dying only two years earlier than Elizabeth Barrett Browning?) This anthology unapologetically includes poems by Hallam, because of his crucial relationship with Tennyson – as it includes poems of John Keble from *The Christian Year* of 1827, and Newman's 'Lead Kindly Light' (published 1836) because of their main and emblematic role for the Victorian Christian imagination and in particular for the Anglo-Catholic movement. At the same time Felicia Hemans is excluded – even though she was a best-selling poet in Victorian times, and a vivid part of the consciousness of many women Victorian poets – with the excuse that she died in 1836. (Like Charlotte Mew, whose first volume was not until 1916, Felicia Hemans is a huge presence in the Leighton–Reynolds collection: but they do, I think, push the boundaries of 'Victorian' much too far.)

Such discrepancies, these tendentious inclusions and exclusions, are the inevitable stuff of editorial life. However, a feature of this anthology is that every version of every poem comes tagged with a clear identification of what it is and where it comes from. Readers will thus know at every point where they stand in relation to the identity of the text in front of them: its author, its title, the timing of its publication, and often of its writing, and where this particular version of the poem was, and is, to be found. This is most important for this body of poetry because of the awkward tendency of Victorian poets to fiddle with their texts, to rejig the titles both of poems and also of the volumes in which poems occur, as well as to travel under various personal names – the ones they acquired at birth, pseudonyms, official and private changes of name, and, in the case of women, married (and re-marriage) names. Other anthologies can be vexingly vague about such details, so that in them a given text may well have a wrong title, be said to come from a wrong volume, and carry an authorial name it did not bear at the time of alleged publication. Sorting out these data is tricky (and some errors may well remain). Much of this working through the labyrinth has been done with the unsurpassable aid of the Bodleian Library's great holdings, and the quirkier but still indispensable resources of the London Library, as well as, of course, with the necessary help of the toiling army of editors of modern editions of main, and other, authors, to whom massive tribute must be paid. Venturing into the maze of Victorian poetry publication is daunting – and not helped, I'm afraid, by some modern editorial practices, such as making synoptic, synthetic texts out of what seem to editors the best bits of various published versions, and, especially, the misguided practice of the otherwise wonderful Longman's Annotated Poets series of modernizing the poets' English.

Unless there is some pressing reason why not, the texts offered here are those of first-volume publication, with all the spelling oddities and anomalies of those first appearances – the variations of practice, for example, as to the accentuation of final -*ed* forms or the capitalizing of the deity's pronouns, *He, Him, His.* The most prominent exception to the first-volume rule is that Tennyson's 1832 poems appear in their 1842 versions – because he carefully revised his first published efforts with notable poetic effect. (The idea that the revisions of a poet, above all his last words, should in general be taken as definitive does not bear much critical scrutiny.) Poets appear in sequence by date of birth, and poems usually by date of volume publication and by their order within their original volumes. Where the order of composition is known for all or much of a poet's work, that is followed. Authors appear with the name they are, or were, usually known by, but all of their known given names and their variations of nomenclature appear at the head of their headnotes. The headnotes are unashamedly full of biographical and contextual material: no text ever appeared without an author somewhere behind it; all texts have contexts. The headnotes would have been impossible without the aid of dozens of people's researches, but in particular not without the assistance of the glorious *Dictionary of National Biography*, and *The Feminist Companion to Literature in English: Women Writers from the Middle Ages to the Present*, ed. Virginia Blain, Patricia Clements and Isobel Grundy (1990), and S. Austin Allibone's truly invaluable three-volume *Critical Dictionary of English Literature and British and American Authors, Living and Deceased, From the Earliest Accounts, to the Latter Half of the Nineteenth Century* (J. B. Lippincott, Philadelphia, 1877) – which I found tucked away in the Corpus Christi College Library. Annotations are kept to a bare minimum: foreign words are translated, biblical and Classical allusions are identified, some now less familiar names and items clarified (with the occasional name or quotation utterly defeating me). I am deeply indebted to colleagues who have been liberal with help on the annotation front – John Kelly, Helen Moore, Nicholas Shrimpton, and in particular Corpus Christi College's team of Classicists: Ewen Bowie, Stephen Harrison, Robin Osborne and John Elsner, without whom even these minimalia would have been impossible. Annotation is minimal, of course, because the pleasure of reading, the pleasures of the text, come, surely, from readers being left to do most, if not absolutely all, of the work of reading for themselves, and certainly not from being constantly told how some interfering editor thinks the poem should be read.

Pleasures of the text. It is the prime hope of this compiler and editor that, everything else notwithstanding, this anthology's contents will give pleasure. The words with which Francis Palgrave ended the Preface of his *Golden Treasury* (1861) are still in this regard worth the savouring.

> Throughout this vast and pathetic array of Singers now silent [he was talking of his Anthology's exclusions], few have been honoured with the name Poet, and have not possessed a skill in words, a sympathy with beauty, a tenderness of feeling, or seriousness in reflection, which render their works … better worth reading than much of what fills the hours that most men spare for self-improvement, or for pleasure in any of its more elevated and permanent forms. – And if this be true of even mediocre poetry, for how much more are we indebted to the best! … Poetry gives treasures 'more golden than gold' … But she speaks best for herself. Her true accents, if the plan has been executed with success, may be heard throughout the following pages: – wherever the Poets of England are honoured, wherever the dominant language of the world is spoken, it is hoped that they will find fit audience.

CCC, Oxon.
May 1999

To My Father
Valentine Cunningham
Man of Donegal and the Bible
A grand reciter of Anglo-Irish Verse

Anon. Street Ballads

People sing – everywhere. Songs are a key kind of poetry. The street ballads of Victorian England were thus a poetry of the populace. They were hawked on single sheets of paper, known in printers' jargon as *broadsheets*, on the streets of cities, towns and villages, wherever anybody might be persuaded to part with a halfpenny or penny for a song. Hawkers often sang their wares, as they had done for hundreds of years, as an inducement to sales. Many ballads were reprints of popular songs, traditional folk-songs, recitations, poems. But any subject of the moment could be balladized, from a coronation to a murder, a battle to a lock-out, a boxing-match to a tax law. Every British town had printers who would run off topical broadsheets (in prose as well as verse) at the drop of a hat. Ballads were not there merely for the pleasure of singers but acted, along with the prose broadsheets, as the people's newspapers – with all the zest for sensation, melodrama and gore of the modern tabloid press. Printers kept local poets in business at a shilling a ballad. But anybody, striker, preacher, salesman, malcontent, local Tory, was free to put his versified story to the public. Hundreds of thousands of ballads were printed in nineteenth-century Britain. The London printing firm of Catnach is said to have sold millions of copies of just two broadsheets featuring murders in the later 1840s. John Clare reported that whilst the common people might know the name of Shakespeare, 'the ballad-monger who supplys hawkers with their ware is poets with them & they imagine one as great as the other'. When the time comes for Dickens's Mr Boffin in *Our Mutual Friend* to seek literary instruction he naturally turns to Silas Wegg the ballad-seller for it. The simple, singable rhymes, rhythms and stanza forms of the ballad are – like those of the hymn – never far away from the formal repertoire of even the most sophisticated of Victorian poets. The street ballad invites critical dismissal by no means inevitably.

ALBERT'S FASHIONS, AND DESCRIPTION OF ENGLAND

Tune – 'Unhappy Jeremiah'

We daily meet with something,
We never need be undone,
Now search old England through & through
And all the streets in London.
Victoria's name is going by,
That once caus'd such a bother,
And now, it's Albert every thing,
From one end to the other.

Chorus
From John-o-Groats to the Land's-end,
From thence right up to Dover,   10
You will meet with Albert everything,
The country all over.

There's Albert pokers, Albert tongs,
Prince Albert's chairs and tables,
Albert fenders, Albert songs,
And Albert's german cradles,
Albert's peas, and Albert's sprats,
And Albert's summer cabbages,
Prince Albert's four and ninepenny hats,
And Albert's german sausages.   20

Albert's coats, and Albert's shoes,
Albert's Congreve matches,
Albert's matchless ginger pop,

And Albert's buckskin breeches.
Albert's Yarmouth bloaters fine,
Albert's pickles and capers.
Albert's blacking and hot pea-soup,
And Albert's baked potatoes.

Prince Albert's oranges, Albert's mice,
And Albert's dancing monkeys,   30
Albert's cakes, penny a slice,
And Albert's pigs and donkeys.
Albert's crabs, and perry-winks,
Albert's clocks, and muscles,
Albert's tags, and Albert's boots,
And Albert's dandy bustles.

Albert's shipping, Albert's carts,
And Albert's prigs and tailors.
Albert's soldier's ladies' joy,
And Albert's flashing sailors.   40
Albert's horses, Albert's cakes,
Albert's dustmen, wives and cronies,
Albert's coffee, Albert's tea
And Albert's little polonies.

Albert's mustard, Albert's salt,
Albert's mackintosh and mantles,
Albert's codfish, Albert's trout,
And Albert's half-penny candles.
Albert's doors and frying-pans,
And thousands at the least then,   50
Of Albert's wooden rolling-pins,
And Albert's gay policemen.

There is Albert's greens, & Albert's pork,
And if I am not mistaken,
There is Albert's geese and bullocks heads
And Albert's Wiltshire bacon.
There is Albert's snuff, and Albert's gin,
Prince Albert's rum and brandy,
There is Albert's wine in Petticoal,
And Albert's sugar candy.   60

There is Albert's stockings, Albert's boots,
And Albert's floors to plank it,
Albert's sheets, and bugs and fleas,
And Albert's Witney blankets.
Albert's soap and Albert's starch,
Albert Jews and Quakers,
Albert Costermongers arch,
And Albert undertakers.

Albert snobs and Albert snips,
And Albert sausage-makers,   70
Albert dishes, smoking hot.
Albert dusty bakers.
Some Albert things are very nice,
They are, depend upon it,
Albert husbands the ladies want,
And Albert dandy bonnets.

We have got a Albert parliament,
Who will soon keep John Bull still,
If they don't send across the seas,
The cursed Albert corn bill.   80
From John-o-Groats to the Lands-end,
From thence right up to Dover,
You will meet with Albert every thing,
The country all over.

Printed by T. BIRT, Printer, 39, Great St. Andrew Street, Seven Dials.
Printing of every description done Cheap.

Bodleian Library: John Johnson Collection, Street Ballads 73.

ARRIVED AT LAST: AN HEIR TO THE THRONE OF ENGLAND

Tune – 'The Roast Beef of Old England'

Hark! Hark! How the bells do merrily ring,
And the lads and the lasses do merrily sing,
We are sure of a queen, if we don't have a king,
For in England there is safely landed,
A blooming young heir to the throne.

To Buckingham Palace some thousands did flock,
Last Saturday evening about three o'clock
At the doors of the palace they loudly did knock
Singing, God Save the Queen of old England,
Who has brought us an heir to the throne.   10

Let us drink her a health in a bumper of purl,
And the banner of freedom Great Britain unfurl,
Here's a health to the Queen and her sweet little girl,
She has brought us a fine little daughter,
And we hope she will soon have a son.

Look out for halfpence the heiress to keep,
The news shall fly speedily over the deep,
And poor uncle Ernest in sorrow will weep,
When he hears that in England's arrived,
A sweet little heir to the throne,   20

Won't Prince Albert be proud when she sits in his lap,
He will put on her napkins and tie up her cap,
When he sits by the fire to feed it with pap,
Singing, oh! what a dear little creature,
A sweet little heir to the throne.

He will send to his father and mother you'll see,
Who lives in the mountains of High Germany,
Fader you now must a grandfader be
To the sweet little rose of Old England,
My wife's got an heir to the throne.   30

All the towns throughout Germany will be in bloom,
Uncle Cobug, and Humbug, and Aunt buy-a-broom,
Will sail for old England you'll see very soon,

With presents for Prince Albert's daughter,
Hurrah for the heir to the throne.

Grandfather and grandmother will soon be here,
To look at the face of the sweet little dear,
And bring a ship load of bergami pears,
For the Queen of Old England's daughter,
The sweet little heir to the throne.   40

The people of Britain long time will remember,
Eighteen hundred and forty the twenty-first of November,
When the Queen brought Old England so charming and tender,
A fine little beautiful daughter,
A sweet little heir to the throne.

Printed by T. BIRT, Printer, 39, Great St. Andrew Street, Seven Dials.
Printing of every description done Cheap.

Bodleian Library: John Johnson Collection, Street Ballads 74.

HAVE YOU BEEN TO THE CHRYSTAL PALACE

In great Hyde Park, like lots of larks,
They work with expedition,
Like swarms of bees, among the trees,
At the great Exhibition.
Talk of Mount Vesuvivus,
Or the Tower of Babylonia,
It is nothing to it, or Noah's Ark,
Or the whale that swallowed Jonah.

I went to see on Sunday last.
With every rank and station,   10
The Palace where is to be the Ex-
hibition of all Nations.

There I beheld some panes of glass,
So beautifully stained sirs,
As thick as Nelson's Monument,
And as long as Salisbury Plain, sirs;
I saw a man with seven heads,
With a face as black as tinder,
And five and twenty wooden legs
A peeping through the window.   20

I saw the tail of a woman's smock,
Which made folks pull wry faces,
Would cover the West India Docks,
And reach to Epsom Races.
I saw a lady's bustle too;
The females to adorn there,
Nine times as thick as Old St. Paul's,
And as wide as Hyde Park Corner.

I saw a prize from Germany,
A sausage made of strength, sirs,   30
Three hundred and twenty inches thick,

And fifteen miles in length, sirs.
I saw a handsome silver watch,
Made by a man called Jenkin,
Nearly twenty times as big
As the great Tom of Lincoln.

I saw a rat, and two tom cats,
Among the people mingling,
Bigger my friends than any bulls
You ever saw in England.   40
I saw ten thousand men at work,
And numbers more were flocking,
They were so far apart they couldn't
Hear each other knocking.

The prettiest thing I did behold,
My friends depend upon it,
Was a little woman without a head,
Who did not wear a bonnet.
Her husband led a quiet life,
Happy was his position,   50
He thinks to surely gain a prize
At the National Exhibition

I saw a pig on thirteen legs,
Around the Palace did run,
I saw a teapot seven times
As big as the Tower of London.
I saw a mouse brought from Canton,
As big as a Russian monkey;
And I saw a mite in a Glo'ster cheese,
Five times as big as a donkey.   60

The prizes all are coming in,
As plainly may be seen, sirs,
And all the towns of England
Are coming up by steam, sirs.
Some bring their bedding on their backs,
Because they will be right slap;
And all who come to town to stop,
Will have to bring their night caps.

I saw a lass, none can surpass,
They call her Madame Chambert,   70
She had eleven kids in seven months,
As big as old Daniel Lambert.
I saw a pie, it is no lie,
With the crust together knocked hard,
Made of shrimps and sloes, and pigeon's toes,
As big as Woolwich Dock Yard.

I saw a pair of babies shoes,
Believe me what I say now,
I'll take an oath they were as big
As any brewer's dray now.   80
I saw a handsome frying pan,
The size of half a farden;
And I saw a stunning halfpenny roll,
As big as Covent Garden.

I saw a jew's harp made of gold,
And a silver copper fiddle;
I saw a lady's thing em bob,
All hairy down the middle.
I saw a dandy victorine,
With a yellow, blue, and green coat;   90
And a pair of lady's ear-rings
Seven times as big as a steam boat.

I have not told you half I saw
The Palace going over,
It would take a sheet of paper that
Would reach from here to Dover.
I saw a man who had twenty wives,
And fed them all on Mondays,
He had one for every day in the week,
And fourteen left for Sundays.   100

Have you been to see, as well as me,
The wonders in each station,
In great Hyde Park among the trees,
The Exhibition of all Nations.

BIRT, Printer, 39, Great St. Andrew Street, Seven Dials, London

Bodleian Library: John Johnson Collection, Street Ballads 91.

A CHAPTER OF CHEATS, OR THE ROGUERY OF EVERY TRADE

Attend you blades of London and listen unto me,
While I sing to you a ditty of the tradesmen's roguery;
And when you hear my ditty through you cannot fail to laugh.
For you lately have been bothered with a little bit of chaff.

Chorus
And they're all a-cheating, cheat, cheat, cheating,
In country and in town, in country and in town.

Now the first it is a lawyer, to bother and to jaw,
He knows well how to cheat you with a little bit of law;
And the next it is a doctor, to handle you he's rough,
He will charge you half-a-crown for six pennyworth of stuff.   10

The pawnbroker comes next with a ticket in his hand,
To cheat you like the devil for the interest is his plan;
The grocer sands his sugar and he sells sloe leaves for tea,
And then there's the dusty miller, where's a bigger rogue than he?

The next it is the butcher, all with his greasy hat,
And underneath his scale is stuck a dirty lump of fat;
Well, then there comes the baker with his alum bread and starch,
In the dishes hot potatoes he will not forget to search.

The cobbler mends your boots and shoes, in cold and rainy weather;
He will mend the sole and upper too, and all with rotten leather;   20

Now the tailor as you all do know is always full of sloth:
He will think no sin to cabbage up[1] a yard and more of cloth.

Now the barber when he shaves you will cut you in the chin;
The chandler's shop will cheat you and will think it not a sin;
And rotten wood the wheelwright he will put into a wheel;
The blacksmith he will sell you iron and swear that it is steel.

The hatter sells his hats and he calls them waterproof;
They are plastered up with horse-dung, it is nothing but the truth;
The carpenter will hammer in your table broken nails;
And I know the police will very quickly pop you into jail.   30

The linen draper will mark up things – he knows it makes you grin,
And he is sure enough to cheat you when his shop you enter in;
The cheesemonger will cut his cheese, his butter and his lard,
And cheat you with his bacon – oh, the times are very hard.

The costermonger's next, with his measures but half full;
The tater merchant washes his potatoes in a pool;
The tallow chandler cheats you until he makes you grin;
The porkman he does stuff his sausages with skin.

And there's the hackney coachman will cheat you like the devil,
And a pretty girl will drain your money, and all the time be civil;   40
Old iron shops buy stolen goods, it's true I do declare;
If a chimney sweep comes to your house he'll steal away your ware.

Bricklayers, weavers, maltsters, will cheat you in a bother;
If a glazier mends one pane of glass he's sure to break another;
The undertaker'll cheat you, believe me it is so;
If the body-snatchers get you, to the doctor's off you go.

Stay-stitchers, bonnet-makers, they look so very shy,
The bill-stickers sell their paper and swear it is a lie;
The coal merchants in a sack of coals will use you very rough;
The tobacconist will sell you fine sand instead of snuff.   50

The next is the gin-shop, how they will take you in.
There's such a load of vitriol in a half a pint of gin;
The landlord for rent, too often he will call,
And he that gathers taxes is the greatest rogue of all.

Printed by Ford, Chesterfield (Derby Public Library).

THE COTTON LORDS OF PRESTON

Have you not heard the news of late
About some mighty men so great?
I mean the swells of Fishergate,
The Cotton Lords of Preston.
They are a set of stingy blades,
They've locked up all their mills and shades,

A CHAPTER OF CHEATS

1   to take remnants of cloth (leftovers) as his own.

So now we've nothing else to do
But come a-singing songs to you.
So with our ballads we've come out
To tramp the country round about,   10
And try if we cannot live without
The Cotton Lords of Preston.

Chorus
Everybody's crying shame
On these gentlemen by name.
Don't you think they're much to blame,
The Cotton Lords of Preston?

The working people such as we
Pass their time in misery,
While they live in luxury,
The Cotton Lords of Preston.   20
They're making money every way
And building factories every day,
Yet when we ask them for more pay,
They had the impudence to say:
'To your demands we'll not consent;
You get enough, so be content' –
But we will have the ten per cent
From the Cotton Lords of Preston.

Our masters say they're very sure
That a strike we can't endure;   30
They all assert we're very poor,
The Cotton Lords of Preston.
But we've determined every one
With them we will not be done,
And we will not be content
Until we get the ten per cent.
The Cotton Lords are sure to fall,
Both ugly, handsome, short and tall;
For we intend to conquer all
The Cotton Lords of Preston.   40

So men and women, all of you,
Come and buy a song or two,
And assist us to subdue
The Cotton Lords of Preston.
We'll conquer them and no mistake,
Whatever laws they seem to make,
And when we get the ten per cent
Then we'll live happy and content.
Oh then we'll dance and sing with glee
And thank you all right heartily,   50
When we gain the victory
And beat the Lords of Preston.

Printed by Harkness, Preston. The great Preston cotton-mills
strike/lock-out of 1853 was the trigger for Dickens' Hard Times *(1854).*
(Cambridge University Library: Madden Collection)

Eliza Lynn Linton (1822–98)

Eliza Lynn Linton was born at Keswick, 10 February 1822, daughter of a vicar and granddaughter of a bishop (James Lynn, her father, was vicar of Crosthwaite, Cumberland; her mother Charlotte was daughter of Samuel Goodenough, bishop of Carlisle). She fell out with her family and moved to London in 1845 to make her way as a novelist and journalist. She soon joined the staff of the *Morning Chronicle* – the first woman newspaper writer in Britain to get a fixed wage. Brought up on books in her father's library she rather naturally went in for rehashing old scholarship in novels about the ancient world before tackling more modern themes in *Realities* (1851). This being lampooned for great unreality she lost heart in novel writing and went off to work as a journalist in Paris until 1854. She was an admirer of Mary Wollstonecraft, in favour of women's property rights (she inherited the house Gad's Hill which she sold to Dickens) and of divorce (her marriage in 1858 to a widower, the engraver William James Linton, didn't work and the two soon separated), but still she was clamantly hostile to many of the moves and positions of Victorian feminism. Prolific and successful as an acerbic London journalist she was notorious not least for her *Saturday Review* article (14 March 1868) 'The Girl of the Period', lampooning the 'Shrieking Sisterhood' of the day (it was collected in *The Girl of the Period and Other Essays*, 2 vols, 1883). When she took up the novel again she achieved popularity. Among her twenty-five or so novels her Gospel-story update *Joshua Davidson* (1872) and *The Autobiography of Christopher Kirkland* (1885), her own story as it were masculinized, were especially well known. Her waspishness never mellowed, though, and she couldn't resist, even as an old lady, satirizing the latest crusading females and latest feminist developments – as witness *The One Too Many* (1894), cruel about 'The Girton Girl' (neurasthenic, freaky, sexless), and *In Haste and At Leisure* (1895), harsh about the mannishness of the women's clubs movement (smoking, short-haired, *Angst-voll*). She was no less unkind to George Eliot in her volume on that novelist (1897) in the Women Novelists of Queen Victoria's Reign series. She was recruited for *Household Words* and *All the Year Round* through Dickens's co-editor W. H. Wills, whom she met in Paris – from where her first *HW* contributions came. Dickens relied on her as an all-round contributor: 'Good for anything, and thoroughly reliable.' Sometimes he thought her too 'bawdy' for his papers. 'I don't know how it is that she gets so near the sexual side of things as to be a little dangerous to us at times.' She retired to Malvern about three years before her death, but died at Queen Anne's Mansions, London, 14 July 1898, aged 76.

William Henry (Harry) Wills (1810–80)

Born in Lynmouth, 13 January 1810, son of a wealthy shipping magnate whose fortunes later crashed, Harry Wills was a journalist who became Charles Dickens's close friend and colleague and essential right-hand man at both *Household Words* and *All the Year Round*. Wills was one of the founders of *Punch* (first number, 17 July 1841) and its regular drama critic. His contacts with Dickens began with articles submitted to *Bentleys' Miscellany* when Dickens was its editor. Wills became Dickens's secretary in the run-up to the founding of the *Daily News*, where he worked under the editorship of Dickens and then of John Forster. He went briefly north to edit *Chambers's Journal* (and married Janet Chambers, sister of the publishing Chambers brothers), but was soon invited back to London, at Forster's suggestion, to become co-editor and a proprietor of *HW*. At *HW*, as later at *AYR*, Wills managed the paper, kept the accounts and records, inviting contributions, editing, sub-editing, cutting, revising, reading proofs. He wrote numerous pieces of his own, significantly rewrote many pieces, collaborated intensely on others. Dickens didn't think much of Wills's writing talents – 'decidedly of the Nutmeg-Grater, or Fancy-Bread-Rasper School' – but couldn't have managed his papers without him. As all the London literary world knew. 'If only there were another Wills, my fortune would be made', said Thackeray when he took on the editorship of the *Cornhill*. (The best indication of his work is to be found in *Household Words: A Weekly Journal 1850–1859, Conducted by Charles Dickens . . . based on the Household Words Office Book*, ed. Anne Lohrli, University of Toronto Press, 1973.) Wills sometimes went with Dickens on investigative journalistic trips. He was on Dickens's 1851 theatrical tour for the benefit of the Guild of Literature and Art and became the Guild's Secretary. Through Dickens he became confidant, secretary and financial adviser to the philanthropist Angela Burdett-Coutts in her considerable charitable endeavours. When he was blacklisted for membership of the Garrick Club Dickens and Wilkie Collins both resigned. He edited anthologies of *Spectator* articles, comic poems, and *HW* pieces (*Old Leaves: Gathered from*

Household Words, 1860). He left *AYR* after a riding accident whilst out hunting, retired to Welwyn, Hertfordshire, and became a magistrate and chairman of the Board of Poor Law Guardians (who ran the local workhouse: a not un-ironic fate for a friend of Dickens whose fiction so lampooned workhouses). He died at Welwyn, 1 September 1880.

Street Minstrelsy

The harp, fiddle, and cornet which ply their trade at my window, although they annoy me while I am writing, are disseminating among the populace, the politest strains of the Opera. Whenever they commence, we know who inspired their open-air music – whether it be Donizetti, Verdi, Mercandanti, or Bellini. Nothing is too high for them; and if, like the jolly guest at the Three Pigeons in She Stoops to Conquer, they had bears to dance, they would dance them to the genteelest of tunes – much more genteel ones than Water Parted from the Sea or the minuet in Ariadne. They convey fashionable melodies to the ears of the cook as she ends her gossip with the grocer's man at the area steps: Mario and the glorious Royal Italian Opera band float the same notes more thrillingly and exquisitely, it is true, under the bandeaux of the beauties in the grand tier; but they *are* the same. We will not enter into the question of comparative merit of execution, for perhaps even that street orchestra is beyond cook's musical education, and the superiority of Mario and the Royal Italian Opera band would be simply lost upon her. There is a point in every education beyond which degrees of excellence are blurred and blotted into one, like distant forms to the short-sighted.

Although the best composers are known and popular, the strains of the classical and fashionable poets never permeate down among the masses. These have an Anthology and Parnassus of their own. When you see a few hundreds of penny ballads stuck against a hoarding, and a few more hundreds boiling over the edges of a huge basket in some half-finished street, you wonder who the authors are. Do they live in garrets, after the fashion of the good old Grub Street days, and spin their brains into rhymes for the milkwoman's score and the dinner bill? Who write the people's ballads? What manner of men? of what status in society? and of what, or how much, sympathy with their audience? We might almost prove the Grub Street theory from some of the songs in that osier cauldron; songs with evident power and education in them, but slipshod and hurried, as if written while the dun stood threatening at the door, or the sheriff's officer was pacing before it. In the days (which have passed away for all except the retained of advertising tailors) when the Puff Poets were in fashion, and every razor-strop vendor, lottery-office keeper, and blacking maker kept a lyrist on his premises, the emoluments of the profession could not have been very high. Indeed, only recently a printer and publisher of halfpenny ballads complained to a friend of mine that his principal poet – on whom he depended for the versification of battles, murders, and sudden deaths reported in the newspapers – 'wouldn't put pen to paper under five shillings.'

It is, however, good to know that, at this day, the songs and ballads which take firmest hold of the people's heart and voice are written by the most refined masters of their art. Barry Cornwall, whose verses charm the most critical taste and delight the finest ear, is one of the worshipped of the million for his song of The Sea. Such men, having the strongest sympathy for the people, are enabled to understand their needs and to elevate their tastes. They are the real reformers of street songs, and have driven the coarse ballad into the obscure corner: they have staked it out into nooks and angles. This is no small gain, when we consider that once, almost all street ballads were morally objectionable, and that now there is a rich collection of pure and singularly beautiful songs written for, and enjoyed by, the people. When we compare even the least unworthy of the former favourites with the poems of Barry Cornwall, Charles Mackay, William Allingham, Gerald Massey, W. C. Bennett, and others, we cannot fail to be struck by the difference lying between the two classes.

On a queer-looking sheet before me, with dull woodcut headings, and type and paper so very bad that they are only just within the pale of legibility, are pasted some two dozen popular ballads. Most of them are Irish; some with the Irish grace scattered here and there, like dewdrops on the grass; very few with any real Irish fun, and one or two simply barbarous jangles on passing stories or events. For instance, we have a –

LAMENTATION

ON THE BARBAROUS AND INHUMAN

MURDER OF MRS. KIRWAN,

WHO WAS BRUTALLY MURDERED BY HER OWN

HUSBAND

– a doggerel narrative of a recent cause célèbre, with paper, printing, style, and spelling all of a piece, and headed by a tremendous representation of Blue Beard and Fatima, flanked by two side-way vignettes, pourtraying black, smeared, and therefore incomprehensible tragedies.

On the same sheet is a new song in praise of Bishop M'Hale; which sounds very strange to Anglo-Saxon and Protestant ears. He is designated 'A pious prelate of wit sublime,' and a brilliant star in his church. He is the great M'Hale from the rock of Naifin; the bright star of Erin; and the pride of Mayo. Dr. Cahill also comes in for his laudation, in an appeal to all true Romans to unite in combination against England, and a vile heretic tribe, and clear heresy out of the land. O'Connell, typified as Erin's Green Linnet (not so very green, we should have thought) is not forgotten. 'I hope that the Lord for his pains will reward him, for seeking the rights of old Erin-go-bragh,' says the songster, piously, after praising the Linnet's lovely green wings with which he hovered so brisk and airy. Brave, bluff, obese, old Daniel O'Connell, green, brisk, and airy!

Side by side with these are pasted some really attractive street music; dulcet, simple, as belongs to true ballad poetry; love songs, with the delicate shadings and tender tones, characteristic of love poetry; telling the old, sad story of desertion and heart-break, or the brighter tale of successful, if marauding love; songs that would do no one any harm to hear: which cannot be said of the eroticisms that flowed from the tavern poets of the old time. Nanny's Sailor Lad, the Abbey of Assaroe, Among the Heather, and the Girl's Lamentation, have seldom been exceeded for pathos and simplicity, especially the last. The Winding Banks of Erne is an established street favourite in the Ballyshannon district; especially among departing emigrants. All these songs, sung constantly in the highways and byeways of Ireland, are, it appears, written by an Irish poet whose muse has long been recognised by critics of the highest rank, for tenderness, grace, and polish – Mr. William Allingham.

Here is a natural bit of peasant portraiture representing Lovely Mary Donnelly:

> Her eyes like mountain water that's flowing on a rock,
> How clear they are, how dark they are! and they give me many a shock.
> Red rowans warm in sunshine and wetted with a shower,
> Could ne'er express the charming lip that has me in its power.
>
> Her nose is straight and handsome, her eyebrows lifted up,
> Her chin is very neat and pert, and smooth like a china cup;
> Her hair's the brag of Ireland, so weighty and so fine;
> It's rolling down upon her neck, and gather'd in a twine.
>
> The dance of Whitsun Monday exceeded all before,
> No pretty girl for miles about was missing from the floor;
> But Mary kept the belt o' love, and O but she was gay!
> She danced a jig, she sung a song, that took my heart away.
>
> When she stood up for dancing, her steps were so complete,
> The music nearly kill'd itself to listen to her feet;
> The fiddler moan'd his blindness, he heard her so much praised,
> But bless'd himself he wasn't deaf when once her voice she raised.

The quaint inconsistency of all street ballad illustrations is not absent from the halfpenny print in which Mr. Allingham's popular works are inscribed. Our sentiments for the milkmaid who is wooed and won by a young squireen, are stimulated by the figure of an elephant, at the head, and by a cut of a goat nibbling chopped sticks on the edge of a precipice, at the foot.

On this side of the Irish Channel, no one has ever touched the people more deeply than our own thoroughly British (for he is half Scotch) Charles Mackay. His are really the people's songs; and he has made himself heard and appreciated throughout the length and breadth not only of this land, but of every other land over which Englishmen are spread. 'There's a Good Time Coming, Boys,' took the very nation by storm. It shared in the honours given to such confessed master-pieces as Dibdin's sailor songs: which, however, had the additional chance of gaining popular favour by having been written for a purpose, and of expressing a deep national sentiment which they neither created nor directed. The man who can originate the thought or feeling to which he addresses himself, is a more profound master of his art, than one who merely takes advantage of a general enthusiasm. There's a Good Time Coming is the epitome of political forbearance and manly patience. Less passionate than the Marseillaise, it is yet as heart-searching, and in the trial would, perhaps, be found as powerful to restrain, as the other has been to excite. It is not a song of action; but it is one full of quiet heroism and the patient hope, which is not supineness, but rather an act of distinct mental energy. For is there not an energy that represses, as well as one that incites, the passions of men? 'Cheer Boys, Cheer' – one of the emigrant series – is another most popular song by Doctor Mackay. It is *the* song of the emigrants. Several of the later writers on our colonies, detailing their voyages, and the incidents of ship-board and coast-life, mention the thrilling effect of this song, as it bursts with passionate force from the crowded decks of the out-ward bound; or rises, almost like a prayer, as the new comers rush forward to the new land. It is a great gift, that of stirring, and swaying, the hearts of the masses; and Charles Mackay has had this gift lavishly dealt out to him. 'The Souls of the Children,' again, is a poem which met with great success. It was reprinted in a separate form by desire of certain friends of popular education, and above fifty thousand copies of it were sold, or distributed, among the people.

Charles Mackay is the poet of common sense; the idealiser of those homely, every-day truths which go so near to be essential wisdom. He amplifies with ballads the same wise, good axioms that other people condense into proverbs. He is not in the least degree sentimental, though with abundance of healthy sentiment; but the words have different meanings, and most of my readers can understand the difference. The tone of all his poetry is manly; his grasp is like the grasp of a man with muscles hardened by honourable work. His John Brown is the type of the ideal working Englishman. He impersonates the brave, frank, loving, but insensitive and anti-sentimental Anglo Saxon. We cannot do better than read him once again:

A PLAIN MAN'S PHILOSOPHY

I

I've a guinea I can spend,
I've a wife and I've a friend,
And a troop of little children at my knee, John Brown;
I've a cottage of my own,
With the ivy overgrown,
And a garden with a view of the sea, John Brown;
I can sit at my door,
By my shady sycamore,
Large of heart, though of very small estate, John Brown;
So come and drain a glass
In my arbour as you pass,
And I'll tell you what I love and what I hate, John Brown.

II

I love the song of birds,
And the children's early words,
And a loving woman's soul, low and sweet, John Brown;
And I hate a false pretence,
And the want of common sense,

And arrogance, and fawning, and deceit, John Brown;
    I love the meadow flowers,
    And the brier in the bowers,
And I love an open face without guile, John Brown;
    And I hate a selfish knave,
    And a proud, contented slave,
And a lout who'd rather borrow than he'd toil, John Brown.

III

    I love a simple song
    That awakes emotions strong,
And the word of hope that raises him who faints, John Brown;
    And I hate the constant whine
    Of the foolish who repine,
And turn their good to evil by complaints, John Brown;
    But even when I hate,
    If I seek my garden gate,
And survey the world around me and above, John Brown,
    The hatred flies my mind,
    And I sigh for human-kind,
And excuse the faults of those I cannot love, John Brown.

IV

    So if you like my ways,
    And the comfort of my days,
I will tell you how I live so unvex'd, John Brown:
    I never scorn my health,
    Nor sell my soul for wealth,
Nor destroy one day the pleasures of the next, John Brown.
    I've parted with my pride,
    And I take the sunny side,
For I've found it worse than folly to be sad, John Brown;
    I keep a conscience clear,
    I've a hundred pounds a-year,
And I manage to exist and to be glad, John Brown.

Is not this a better song for our working-men than the unseemly parodies, and something worse, which are not yet wholly exorcised from the repertory of street songs? Doctor Mackay has done his part towards raising the taste of the humbler public, and elevating and purifying the thoughts which find expression in song; and so have many other poets who rank high in the courtliest drawing-rooms. But it has been given to Charles Mackay and to Barry Cornwall (who cannot be too often mentioned in this connection), to strike deeper down into the hearts of the people than others have done.

Turning back to street-music – properly so called – what a run the Ethiopian Serenaders had! But the 'darkies,' like everything else, have had their day: there is a night for every noon, a nadir for every zenith. I confess to never having shared in the horror which it was thought drawing-room good taste to affect against those poor soot-begrimed artists, with their striped cottons and huge linen collars, knocking their tambourines on their heads, and worn out elbows, and rattling their bones with fifty-horse power. The soot I shall not enlarge upon; but the melodies themselves, and the genuine songs, are very taking and spirited. Lucy Neil and Mary Blane may stand side by side with any love laments in the language; and Old Uncle Ned, too, who went where the good niggers go, was by no means a disreputable old 'chattel.' The livelier songs were nothing worse than simply comic, and not half so vulgar as the ditties which divided the favour of the town some years ago. The Ohio Boatman, who dances all night, and goes home with the pretty girls in the morning, is a right good fellow, only with less sentiment and vastly more fun in him than his Canadian brother, who used to sing nightly to our fathers of how the rapids were won and the danger was passed. The Buffalo Girls who are incited to come out to-night, are no whit worse than Moore's lady who desired to take advantage of the young May Moon which is beaming love, or than Lilian, who is awakened at untimely hours, and bidden to be lovingly cognisant of the fact. What a marked peculiarity about lovers in books and poems it is, that they have the most extra-ordinary ideas of time, and never trouble themselves with proprieties in hours, or the natural divisions of the day and night! It is always full-moon with them, and a perpetual summer, rendering night walks in muslin dresses practicable to a degree unheard of in the bills of health. The Buffalo Girls are of this kind: but then the summers of Ole Virginny have nights of which we know nothing.

The negro melodies are childish, certainly: they belong to a childish race, and naturally follow the national bent; if, indeed, we may say that a race of slaves has anything national at all about it! But, although they show very little intellectual culture, they are never coarse nor indelicate, and have a natural and unaffected tone, which I presume contains the secret of their success. The world is so overlaid with cant in various forms, that anything genuine stands out with double force and lustre.

Household Words, *vol. 19, no. 478 (21 May 1859), 577–80.*

William Wordsworth (1770–1850)

William Wordsworth, Poet Laureate in succession to Robert Southey for seven years from April 1843, was born at Cockermouth, 7 April 1770, the son of a Cockermouth lawyer John Wordsworth (yet one more fatherly John) and his wife Anne, a mercer's daughter from Penrith. Wordsworth remained as much the rough northerner as Tennyson did the unsmooth Lincolnshire man. His father and mother were both dead by the time he was thirteen. His guardians managed, though, to scrape together the funds to send him (and his brother Christopher) to Cambridge. He graduated from St John's College in January 1791 without Honours, more impressed by the French Revolution he'd encountered the previous summer on a continental walking tour than by his books ('Bliss was it in that dawn to be alive'). He returned to revolutionary France at the end of 1791 and had an affair with Annette Vallon. They had a daughter, born in December 1792, when he returned to London a convinced republican and sympathizer with the proletariat. He walked a lot, turned to poetry as occupation rather than the Law his people would have preferred, and became friends with Coleridge, producing the poetically and politically revolutionary *Lyrical Ballads* (1798) with his friend. It became the poetic guidebook of the British Romantic Movement. Prefaces to subsequent editions (1801, 1802) made clear the preferred mode of composition (the emotional experience of nature relived later as trigger for poems) and the rejection of specifically 'poetic' diction in favour of the language really used by ordinary people. On the strength of a large legacy Wordsworth married a childhood friend, Mary Hutchinson (they had five children), but he remained extremely close to his only sister and muse Dorothy. He soon lost faith with the French Revolution and Napoleon, fell out and in again with Coleridge, but never lost faith in a beneficent Nature and a morally necessary sympathy with the rural poor. He worked continually to the end of his life at his great, posthumously published autobiographical poem *The Prelude* – now thought of as three distinct poems in the versions of 1799, 1805 and 1850. It is generally held that, in common with other Romantics, Wordsworth revised only to dilute and spoil and this charge parallels the view that the later, ageing patriotic, more conservative Wordsworth (he strongly feared the results of the 1832 Reform Bill) was less and less good as a poet. But though he did perhaps, like Charles (Tennyson) Turner, write too many sonnets, the verses he was still producing into Victoria's reign – let alone the last version of *The Prelude* – can be strong, even extremely strong. Though canonical in his own lifetime, never no capable of transforming lives, and almost the contemporary representative of the poetic *per se* (John Stuart Mill, converted from arid Benthamism to culture by reading Wordsworth, offers this poet in his *Autobiography* (1873) as, so to say, the spiritual and the aesthetic as such), Wordsworth's poetic reputation was also heavily criticized – not least by Coleridge in Chapter 14 of his *Biographia Literaria* (1817). As for the Wordsworthian religion of Nature and Romantic pantheism – these were, the novelist Mark Rutherford (William Hale White) objected plaintively in his autobiographical novel *Mark Rutherford's Deliverance* (1885), all very well for those with ready access to the countryside, but misleading and useless for 'the millions of sensitive persons' locked up in the great towns such as London. Wordsworth died on 23 April 1850 and was buried in Grasmere churchyard beside his two dead children Catharine and Thomas.

A POET! – He hath put his heart to school,
Nor dares to move unpropped upon the staff
Which Art hath lodged within his hand – must laugh
By precept only, and shed tears by rule.
Thy Art be Nature; the live current quaff,
And let the groveller sip his stagnant pool,
In fear that else, when Critics grave and cool
Have killed him, Scorn should write his epitaph.
How does the Meadow-flower its bloom unfold?
Because the lovely little flower is free   10
Down to its root, and, in that freedom, bold;
And so the grandeur of the Forest-tree
Comes not by casting in a formal mould,
But from its *own* divine vitality.

Written, probably, 1842. Poems Chiefly of Early and Late Years *(Edward Moxon, 1842).*
(Added as vol. 7 to Poetical Works, *6 vols, Edward Moxon, 1840.) Text,* Poetical Works,
7 vols (Edward Moxon, 1849) ('A New and Revised Edition'), VI.

The most alluring clouds that mount the sky
Owe to a troubled element their forms,
Their hues to sunset. If with raptured eye
We watch their splendour, shall we covet storms,
And wish the Lord of day his slow decline
Would hasten, that such pomp may float on high?
Behold, already they forget to shine,
Dissolve – and leave to him who gazed a sigh.
Not loth to thank each moment for its boon
Of pure delight, come whencesoe'er it may,   10
Peace let us seek, – to stedfast things attune
Calm expectations, leaving to the gay
And volatile their love of transient bowers,
The house that cannot pass away be ours.

Written, probably, 1842. Poems Chiefly of Early and Late Years *(1842).*
Text, Poetical Works *(1849), VI.*

ON THE PROJECTED KENDAL AND WINDERMERE RAILWAY

Is then no nook of English ground secure
From rash assault?[1] Schemes of retirement sown
In youth, and mid the busy world kept pure
As when their earliest flowers of hope were blown,
Must perish; – how can they this blight endure?
And must he too the ruthless change bemoan
Who scorns a false utilitarian lure
Mid his paternal fields at random thrown?
Baffle the threat, bright Scene, from Orrest-head
Given to the pausing traveller's rapturous glance: 10
Plead for thy peace, thou beautiful romance

ON THE PROJECTED KENDAL AND WINDERMERE RAILWAY

1 The degree and kind of attachment which many of the yeomanry feel to their small inheritance can scarcely be over-rated. Near the house of one of them stands a magnificent tree, which a neighbour of the owner advised him to fell for profit's sake. 'Fell it!' exclaimed the yeoman, 'I had rather fall on my knees and worship it.' It happens, I believe, that the intended railway would pass through this little property, and I hope that an apology for the answer will not be thought necessary by one who enters into the strength of the feeling. [Author's note]

Of nature; and, if human hearts be dead,
Speak, passing winds; ye torrents, with your strong
And constant voice, protest against the wrong.

12 October 1844. First published, Morning Post*, 16 October 1844.*
Poems: A New Edition *(Edward Moxon, 1845). Text,* Poetical Works *(1849), VI.*

Forth from a jutting ridge, around whose base
Winds our deep Vale, two heath-clad Rocks ascend
In fellowship, the loftiest of the pair
Rising to no ambitious height; yet both,
O'er lake and stream, mountain and flowery mead,
Unfolding prospects fair as human eyes
Ever beheld. Up-led with mutual help,
To one or other brow of those twin Peaks
Were two adventurous Sisters wont to climb,
And took no note of the hour while thence they gazed,   10
The blooming heath their couch, gazed, side by side,
In speechless admiration. I, a witness
And frequent sharer of their calm delight
With thankful heart, to either Eminence
Gave the baptismal name each Sister bore.
Now are they parted, far as Death's cold hand
Hath power to part the Spirits of those who love
As they did love. Ye kindred Pinnacles –
That, while the generations of mankind
Follow each other to their hiding-place   20
In time's abyss, are privileged to endure
Beautiful in yourselves, and richly graced
With like command of beauty – grant your aid
For MARY's humble, SARAH's silent, claim,
That their pure joy in nature may survive
From age to age in blended memory.

1845

Poetical Works *(1849), II.*

ILLUSTRATED BOOKS AND NEWSPAPERS

Discourse was deemed Man's noblest attribute,
And written words the glory of his hand;
Then followed Printing with enlarged command
For thought – dominion vast and absolute
For spreading truth, and making love expand.
Now prose and verse sunk into disrepute
Must lacquey a dumb Art that best can suit
The taste of this once-intellectual Land.
A backward movement surely have we here,
From manhood – back to childhood; for the age –   10
Back towards caverned life's first rude career.
Avaunt this vile abuse of pictured page!
Must eyes be all in all, the tongue and ear
Nothing? Heaven keep us from a lower stage!

1846

Poetical Works *(1849), VI.*

Walter Savage Landor (1775–1864)

Walter Savage Landor, born 30 January 1775 at Rugeley in Staffordshire, was an irascible dilettante of letters whose generous and aesthetically inclined life, much of it passed in Italy, was funded by rents from considerable estates purchased on the sale and redistribution of the family lands in Staffordshire and Warwickshire. He was never not at odds with someone. He insulted his headmaster at Rugby School and was withdrawn so as to avoid the stigma of expulsion. Behaving like a 'mad Jacobin' at Trinity College, Oxford (writing an Ode to Washington, going about with unpowdered hair), he was rusticated in 1794 (i.e. sent away from the university for a period) for firing a pistol at the windows of a Tory student he disliked, and never returned. He was later (1818) expelled from Como in Italy for insulting the authorities in a Latin poem. He would be expelled from Florence a bit later. His marriage to Julia Thuillier, a Swiss, broke up in the mid-1830s, owing to his terrible temper. In 1857, in rather great old age, he had to flee from England because of embroilment in a libel suit. His lifelong brand of aristocratic republicanism did not extend to sympathy with Napoleon. In 1808 he went voluntarily to fight with the Spaniards against the French at Coruña and became an honorary Spanish Colonel (though, par for the course, he handed his commission back when Spain afterwards restored the Jesuits). His classicizing tendencies kept him from real sympathy with the Romantics – he'd sooner write a Latin poem than any other kind – but his acquaintance was always on the fringes of Romantic circles. He denounced the Convention of Cintra with Wordsworth and Southey and was on good terms with Hazlitt and Leigh Hunt. Southey and Coleridge enthused over his epic *Gebir* (1798). De Quincey claimed that he and Southey were the poem's two sole purchasers. Shelley raved about it when he was an undergraduate at Oxford (1811). Fox recruited Landor as an anti-government journalist. He contributed to many papers, including *Leigh Hunt's Journal*. Dying in 1843, Southey is said to have babbled of Landor. Landor's friendship with Dickens lasted from 1840 until the end of Landor's life (he had one poem in *Household Words*, 19 June 1858). Dickens's friend and biographer John Forster helped Landor assemble his Collected Works in two great volumes (1846) and wrote a Life (1869). Dickens put Landor cruelly into *Bleak House* (1852–3) as John Jarndyce's exaggerating friend Boythorne who has a standing land-rights feud with his neighbour Sir Leicester Dedlock. From the 1820s on Landor put much creative energy into his series of prose *Imaginary Conversations* between notable literary and political figures (first series, 1824). Once greatly admired for their style, they now fall pawkily between the stools of the Platonic dialogues they're clearly inspired by and the intellectual drama they are vainly trying to be (and, to be sure, Landor did write three plays in the late thirties). Rather ruined financially in his late-fifties libel case, a sort of refugee in his favourite Florence (only 'eighteenpence in his pocket'), he was greatly helped out by Robert Browning. He died in Florence in the Via Nunziata, 17 September 1864. Swinburne had been one of his recent visitors – and dedicated 'Atalanta in Calydon' to him.

Twenty years hence my eyes may grow
If not quite dim, yet rather so,
Still yours from others they shall know
   Twenty years hence.
Twenty years hence tho' it may hap
That I be call'd to take a nap
In a cool cell where thunder-clap
   Was never heard.
There breathe but o'er my arch of grass
A not too sadly sigh'd *Alas*,
And I shall catch, ere you can pass,
   That winged word.

    10

Works, 2 vols (Edward Moxon, 1846), II, 625.

Yes; I write verses now and then,
But blunt and flaccid is my pen,
No longer talkt of by young men
  As rather clever:

In the last quarter are my eyes,
You see it by their form and size;
Is it not time then to be wise?
    Or now or never.

Fairest that ever sprang from Eve!
While Time allows the short reprieve,   10
Just look at me! would you believe
    'Twas once a lover?

I can not clear the five-bar gate,
But, trying first its timber state,
Climb stiffly up, take breath, and wait
    To trundle over.

Thro' gallopade I can not swing
The entangling blooms of Beauty's spring:
I can not say the tender thing,
    Be't true or false,   20

And am beginning to opine
Those girls are only half-divine
Whose waists yon wicked boys entwine
    In giddy waltz.

I fear that arm above that shoulder,
I wish them wiser, graver, older,
Sedater, and no harm if colder
    And panting less.

Ah! people were not half so wild
In former days, when, starchly mild,   30
Upon her high-heel'd Essex smiled
    The brave Queen Bess.

Sent to John Forster, c. November 1844. Works (1846), II, 651. Acquired title 'Sedater Pleasures,' subsequently.

To Robert Browning

There is delight in singing, tho' none hear
Beside the singer: and there is delight
In praising, tho' the praiser sit alone
And see the prais'd far off him, far above.
Shakespeare is not our poet, but the world's,
Therefore on him no speech! and brief for thee,
Browning! Since Chaucer was alive and hale,
No man hath walkt along our roads with step
So active, so inquiring eye, or tongue
So varied in discourse. But warmer climes   10
Give brighter plumage, stronger wing: the breeze
Of Alpine highths thou playest with, borne on
Beyond Sorrento and Amalfi, where
The Siren waits thee, singing song for song.

The Morning Chronicle (22 November 1845), 5. Reprinted as leaflet by Robert Browning's father (only extant copy: pasted into copy of Browning's Bells and Pomegranates given to Alfred ('Waring') Domett and signed: 'Sent out to New Zealand to me in 1845 by R. Browning'). Works (1846), II, 673. Text, 1846.

Ebenezer Elliott (1781–1849)

Ebenezer Elliott, the Yorkshire Corn-Law Rhymer, was born 17 March 1781 at Masborough, near Rotherham, the son of a radical nonconformist Calvinist iron-worker. There were eleven children; schooling was minimal; Ebenezer was regarded as a dunce. But from about the age of fourteen he read widely in books bequeathed his father by a poor cleric, including the poems of Young and Shenstone. He wandered much around the countryside, becoming expert in plants and flowers. Aged seventeen, he wrote his *Vernal Walk* in imitation of Thomson's *Seasons* and dedicated it to Jane Austen. From the age of sixteen to twenty-three he worked for his father for little more than pocket money. After he married, he put his wife's little money into his father's business – which went bankrupt. At the age of forty, however, he managed to set up for himself as an iron-founder in Sheffield and prospered greatly. He was active as a Chartist (he was a Sheffield delegate to the great Chartist Rally at Westminster in 1838), but left the movement when it stopped agitation for repeal of the Corn Laws. Elliott attributed all his father's and his own financial difficulties, as well as those of the whole country, to these laws which kept bread prices artificially high. His politics turned his writing away from its early rural and gothic preoccupations to direct campaigning in his *Corn-Law Rhymes* (1831) against a regime that made 'Bread dear and labour cheap'. In his long article on Elliott in the *Edinburgh Review* (July 1832), Carlyle warmed to this Sheffield worker in brass and iron, who describes himself as "one of the lower, little removed above the lowest class"'. 'It used to be said that lions do not paint, that poor men do not write; but the case is altering now.

Here is a voice coming from the deep Cyclopean forges, where Labour, in real soot and sweat, beats with his thousand hammers "the red son of the furnace"; doing personal battle with necessity, and her dark brute powers, to make them reasonable and serviceable; an intelligible voice from the hitherto Mute and Irrational, to tell us at first hand how it is with him.... To which voice ... let good ear be given.' Elliott, says Carlyle, is woefully short of humour, and he can be too imitative of certain available styles – Crabbe's (which is understandable given his subject), Byron's (which is irrelevant) and Mrs Hemans's, which is disconcerting ('but what if there were a slight bravura dash of the fair tuneful Hemans?') – but he's always *genuine*. And while deploring the 'corrosive' spirit of Elliott's radicalism, Carlyle grants the inevitable and compelling nature of his alliance between poetry and politics. This alliance ran all through Elliott's doings. There was a bust of Shakespeare in his counting-house and casts of Achilles, Ajax and Napoleon in his workshop. He gave lectures to northern working men – talking, for instance, on poetry and on poets such as Cowper, Burns and Milton at Mechanics' Institutes in Sheffield and Hull. He was a great and rightly renowned spokesman for the working poor. He and his wife had thirteen children. When he retired from business in 1841 he made his home at Great Houghton, near Barnsley. Happily, he lived to see the hated 'Bread Tax' repealed in 1846. After his death, 1 December 1849, the workmen of Sheffield subscribed the immense sum of £600 for a bronze statue in his honour (erected in the city's market-place in 1854). Walter Savage Landor composed an Ode for the occasion.

SONNET

In these days, every mother's son or daughter,
Writes verse, which no one reads except the writer,
Although, unink'd, the paper would be whiter,
And worth, per ream, a hare, when you have caught her.
Hundreds of unstaunch'd Shelleys daily water
Unanswering dust; a thousand Wordsworths scribble;
And twice a thousand Cornlaw Rhymers dribble
Rhym'd prose, unread. Hymners of fraud and slaughter,
By cant call'd other names, alone find buyers –
Who buy, but read not. 'What a loss in paper,'
Groans each immortal of the host of sighers!
'What profanation of the midnight taper
In expirations vile! But I write well,
And wisely print. Why don't my poems sell?'

10

More Verse and Prose by the Cornlaw Rhymer, *2 vols (Charles Fox, 1850), I.*

WOMAN

1

What highest prize hath woman won
   In science, or in art?
What mightiest work, by woman done,
   Boasts city, field, or mart?
'She hath no Raphael!' Painting saith;
   'No Newton!' Learning cries;
'Show us her Steam-ship! her Macbeth!
   Her thought-won victories.'

2

Wait, boastful Man! Though worthy are
   Thy deeds, when thou art true,   10
Things worthier still, and holier far,
   Our sister yet will do;
For this the worth of woman shows,
   On every peopled shore,
That still as man in wisdom grows,
   He honours her the more.

3

Oh, not for wealth, or fame, or power,
   Hath man's meek angel striven,
But, silent as the growing flower,
   To make of earth a heav'n!   20
And in her garden of the sun
   Heaven's brightest rose shall bloom;
For woman's best is unbegun!
   Her advent yet to come![1]

More Verse and Prose by the Cornlaw Rhymer *(1850)*, I.

EPIGRAM

What is a communist? One who hath yearnings
For equal division of unequal earnings:
Idler, or bungler, or both, he is willing
To fork out his penny, and pocket your shilling.[1]

More Verse and Prose by the Cornlaw Rhymer *(1850)*, I.

SONG

1

Donought would have everything;
Eat the lark, and use its wing;
Sip the sweet, and be the sting:
Donought is the only King.

WOMAN

1 Educated woman, through her self-denying, self-aggrandising refu-
sal to marry, without first securing a certain standard of comfort, is des-
tined to save mankind, and in the language of St. Paul, 'Lift us up!'
[Author's note]

EPIGRAM

1 And he has two names, Legion and Danger. [Author's note]

2

Donought is an alchemist;
Hencock is a communist;
Idle head is heavy fist;
Will's a right line – with a twist.

3

Hark! the throstle! what sings he?   10
'Worm, my Beauty, come to me!'
Yet all lovely things are free:
'Chain'd and happy, cannot be.'

4

'See the daisies, how they grow!'
When they list, the breezes blow:
Why can't weary man do so?
All enjoy, and nothing owe?

5

'Mouth, keep open! Eyes, be shut!'
Take no care for back or gut:
Best of women is the slut:
Hey, for cattle cook'd and cut!   20

More Verse and Prose by the Cornlaw Rhymer *(1850), I.*

(James Henry) Leigh Hunt (1784–1859)

Leigh Hunt, critic, essayist and second-wave Romantic poet, was born in Southgate, Middlesex, 19 October 1784. His parents were both of English descent, but his father, the Revd Isaac Hunt, was born in Barbados into a creolized planter family, and his mother, Mary Shewell, was from a Quaker family in Philadelphia, USA, and niece of the wife of the American painter Benjamin West. Isaac attended college in Philadelphia, followed his father into the Anglican ministry, wrote against Tom Paine and American Republicanism, turned Unitarian (was preacher at Bentinck Chapel, Paddington), and ended up a Universalist. Leigh Hunt, fifth son of the family, delicate, swarthy (looking every bit a Creole), went to Christ's Hospital School, then in Newgate Street, London (Coleridge and Charles Lamb were recent Old Boys). He wrote much schoolboy verse in imitation of Gray, Collins, Thomson. His family prevented him from going on to university on the grounds of delicacy and a stutter (his mother pampered him greatly). His adoring papa sponsored his first volume, *Juvenilia* (1801), fed him books, and encouraged him into writing for the *Traveller* as 'Mr Town, Junior, Critic and Censor-general'. His precocious theatre reviews were collected as *Critical Essays on the Performers of the London Theatres, including General Remarks on the Practice and Genius of the Stage* (1807), and Hunt's career as one of the most renowned reviewers, essayists and book-makers of his time was under way. After brief work in the law firm of one of his brothers, and a short spell in the War Office (his father knew the Prime Minister), he and his brother John set up the humanitarian, liberal, satirical *Examiner* (1809), in which Hunt wrote for thirteen years. He married Marianne Kent (1809), though he would remain all his life a notorious flirt and womanizer. He and his brother were jailed for two years and fined hugely in February 1812 for lampooning the Prince Regent – though Hunt's cell in Horsemonger Lane Gaol became a bower of editorial bliss, underwritten by Shelley's money, with a piano, venetian blinds, flowered wallpaper and painted blue-sky on the ceiling, in which the hero of radical journalism held court to all the radicals and liberal-aesthetic giants of the day – James Mill, Jeremy Bentham, Benjamin Haydon, Hazlitt, Lamb, Byron; kept the *Examiner* coming out; and wrote most of *The Story of Rimini*, his long poem (1816) on the Paolo and Francesca story. After prison Hunt settled in the Vale of Health, Hampstead, relied heavily on Shelley for cash, became close to Keats, promoted the genius of Keats and Shelley in the *Examiner*, and defended Shelley's morality. *Foliage; or Poems, Original and Translated* appeared in 1818. Hunt was a prime target of the scurrilous Tory-critical attacks on the so-called Cockney School of poetry in *Blackwood's Magazine* and the *Quarterly Review* – though the sneers at the baroque tendencies of his vocabulary did have a certain point. He joined Shelley and Byron in Italy in 1822 to edit the short-lived *Liberal*, was present when the body of the drowned Shelley was burned (July 1822), and wrote the epitaph for Shelley's tomb in Rome. He quarrelled with Byron, was destitute in Florence (he would be in financial straits all his life), and wrote furiously to survive (as he would have to for the rest of his life). The *Examiner* had been run in parallel with the *Reflector* and, eventually, the *Indicator* (which nearly killed him, Hunt said). But he couldn't resist the journalistic bug. He founded the *Literary Examiner*, the *Companion*, the *Chat of the Week*, the *Tatler*, *Leigh Hunt's London Journal*, *Leigh Hunt's Journal*, wrote for the *New Monthly Magazine*, the *Atlas*, *Ainsworth's Magazine*, *Fraser's Magazine*, the *Spectator*, and edited the *Monthly Repository*. The first collected edition of his poems appeared in 1832, financed by public subscription. In the same year his *Christianism* appeared, financed by John Forster: it led to Hunt's lifelong friendship with Carlyle (whom Hunt lived next door to in Cheyne Row, Chelsea, 1833–40). He is said to have dined frugally, often just on bread and water, by choice; but he relied heavily on Forster's charity, Dickens's benefit dramatic performances, royal grants, money from the Shelley estates, and eventually a Civil List pension of £200 a year from 1847 – though his fictionalized portrait as the sweet scrounger Harold Skimpole in Dickens's *Bleak House* makes him appear carelessly spendthrift as

well as needy. His mind was as miscellaneous as his pleasantly capacious, garrulous fireside essays (he'd be 'interested', he said, from moment to moment during the day 'in things great or small, in a print, in a plaster-cast, in a hand-organ...in the flower on my table, in the fly on my paper while I write'. He wrote endlessly – poems, translations, drama, fictions, adaptations, treatments, rewrites, paraphrases and summaries, prefaces, introductions; edited numerous anthologies of other authors' works in prose and verse; and of course continually recycled his own vast journalistic output in book form. The death of his son Vincent in 1852 is the subject of one of his finest poems. His wife died in 1857 – the year a two-volume edition of his *Poetical Works* appeared in the USA. He continued writing to the end and died, simply worn out, 28 August 1859. He was buried in Kensal Green Cemetery. Ten years later a bust was unveiled over his grave with a motto from his best-known poem, the genial 'Abou Ben Adhem': 'Write me as one that loves his fellow-men'. His son Thornton edited the 'final' *Poetical Works* (1860) and the *Correspondence* (2 vols, 1862). Arthur Symons brought out a selection of the *Essays* (1887) with a superior Introduction.

ABOU BEN ADHEM

Abou Ben Adhem (may his tribe increase!)
Awoke one night from a deep dream of peace,
And saw, within the moonlight in his room,
Making it rich, and like a lily in bloom,
An angel writing in a book of gold: –
Exceeding peace had made Ben Adhem bold,
And to the presence in the room he said,
'What writest thou?' – The vision rais'd its head,
And with a look made of all sweet accord,
Answer'd, 'The names of those who love the Lord.'   10
'And is mine one?' said Abou. 'Nay, not so,'
Replied the angel. Abou spoke more low,
But cheerly still; and said, 'I pray thee then,
Write me as one that loves his fellow-men.'

The angel wrote, and vanish'd. The next night
It came again with a great wakening light,
And showed the names whom love of God had bless'd,
And lo! Ben Adhem's name led all the rest.

First published in S. C. Hall, Book of Gems, III (1838). Poetical Works,
Now Finally Collected, Revised by Himself, and Edited by His Son,
Thornton Hunt (Routledge, Warne, and Routledge, 1860).

RONDEAU

Jenny kiss'd me when we met,
  Jumping from the chair she sat in;
Time, you thief, who love to get

Sweets into your list, put that in:
Say I'm weary, say I'm sad,
    Say that health and wealth have miss'd me,
Say I'm growing old, but add,
    Jenny kiss'd me.

First published in The Monthly Chronicle *(November 1838), with* Nelly *for*
Jenny, *and* jaundiced *for* weary. Poetical Works *(1860).*

ON THE DEATH OF HIS SON VINCENT

Waking at morn, with the accustomed sigh
For what no morn could ever bring me more,
And again sighing, while collecting strength
To meet the pangs that waited me, like one
Whose sleep the rack hath watched: I tried to feel
How good for me had been strange griefs of old,
That for long days, months, years, inured my wits
To bear the dreadful burden of one thought.
One thought with woful need turned many ways,
Which, shunned at first, and scaring me, as wounds   10
Thrusting in wound, became, oh! almost clasped
And blest, as saviours from the one dire pang
That mocked the will to move it.

First published in The Correspondence of Leigh Hunt, *ed. by his eldest son*
[*Thornton Hunt*], 2 vols (Smith, Elder & Co., 1862), II, 146–7. Poetical Works,
ed. Humphrey Milford (Oxford, 1923).

Charlotte Elliott (1789–1871)

One of the most renowned of Victorian hymn-writers, Charlotte Elliott was born, 17 March 1789, into the heart of Anglican Evangelicalism, or Church Methodism – the so-called Clapham Sect. Her mother Eling Venn was daughter of the famous Revd Henry Venn; her brothers were the Revd Henry Venn Elliott and Edward Bishop Elliott. The Clapham Sect, a clan or cousinhood of well-off, high-bourgeois Christians, personally devout and pietistic, but also devoted to human welfare, spearheaded much of the period's philanthropic and reformist work. Early on inclined to witty versifying, Charlotte abandoned worldliness after the severe illness in 1821 which made her a permanent invalid. After that she mainly read the Bible and wrote the 150 or so hymns that reached a very wide audience. *Hymns for a Week* (1839) sold over 40,000 copies. *Hours of Sorrow Cheered and Comforted; or, Thoughts in Verse Chiefly Adapted to Seasons of Sickness* (1836) went into numer-ous editions. 'Just As I Am', which first appeared in *The Invalid's Hymn Book* (1836), was extraordinarily popular, travelling the globe in large numbers of translations. Henry Venn Elliott, in whose *Psalms and Hymns for Public, Private, and Social Worship* (1835–48) many of her hymns appeared, signed C. E., said of this hymn: 'In the course of a long ministry, I hope I have been permitted to see some fruits of my labours; but I feel that far more has been done by a single hymn of my sister's.' Many of Miss Elliott's hymns appeared in *The Christian Remembrancer Pocket Book*, which she edited 1834–59. Unmarried, she lived with her father Charles Elliott in Clapham (where she passed most of the first thirty-two years of her life) and at Brighton. After a spell in Torquay (1845–57) she returned to Brighton where she died, 22 September 1871, aged 82.

JUST AS I AM

'Him that cometh to Me I will in no wise cast out.'
John vi. 37

Just as I am – without one plea
  But that Thy blood was shed for me,
  And that Thou bid'st me come to Thee –
    O Lamb of God, I come!

Just as I am – and waiting not
  To rid my soul of one dark blot,
  To Thee, whose blood can cleanse each spot –
    O Lamb of God, I come!

Just as I am – though toss'd about,
  With many a conflict, many a doubt,   10
  Fighting and fears within, without –
    O Lamb of God, I come!

Just as I am – poor, wretched, blind;
  Sight, riches, healing of the mind,
  Yea, all I need, in Thee to find –
    O Lamb of God, I come!

Just as I am – Thou wilt receive,
  Wilt welcome, pardon, cleanse, relieve,
  Because Thy promise I believe –
    O Lamb of God, I come!   20

Just as I am – Thy love unknown
  Has broken every barrier down;
  Now to be Thine, yea, Thine alone –
    O Lamb of God, I come!

Just as I am – of that free love,
  The breadth, length, depth, and height to prove,
  Here, for a season, then above –
    O Lamb of God, I come!

Text, Selections from the Poems of Charlotte Elliott, With a Memoir by
Her Sister, E.B. *[Mrs E. Babington] (Religious Tract Society, 1874). (Frontispiece
item; clearly the star attraction.)*

THY WILL BE DONE

My God and Father! while I stray
  Far from my home, in life's rough way,
  Oh! teach me from my heart to say,
    'Thy will be done!'

Though dark my path and sad my lot,
  Let me 'be still' and murmur not;
  Or breathe the prayer divinely taught,
    'Thy will be done!'

What though in lonely grief I sigh
For friends belov'd, no longer nigh,   10
Submissive still would I reply,
    'Thy will be done!'

Though Thou hast call'd me to resign
What most I priz'd, it ne'er was mine:
I have but yielded what was thine: –
    'Thy will be done!'

Should grief or sickness waste away
My life in premature decay;
My Father! still I strive to say,   20
    'Thy will be done!'

Let but my fainting heart be blest,
With thy sweet Spirit for its guest;
My God! to thee I leave the rest:
    'Thy will be done!'

Renew my will from day to day!
Blend it with thine; and take away
All that now makes it hard to say,
    'Thy will be done!'

*Hours of Sorrow: or, Thoughts in Verse, Chiefly Adapted to Seasons
of Sickness, Depression, and Bereavement (James Nisbet & Co., 1836).*

John Keble (1792–1866)

John Keble, founding father of the Oxford Movement, the Anglo-Catholic party in the Church of England, was born at Fairford, Gloucestershire, 25 April 1872, into a dynasty of Anglican clergy. His father was vicar of Colm St Aldwins; his mother was the daughter of a vicar. Keble had three sisters and a younger brother. The brothers were educated at home and both became scholars at their father's old college, Corpus Christi, Oxford. John's career was hugely successful, laden with prizes and First Classes in examinations. In 1812 he became a Fellow of Oriel, an association he maintained until 1823, when he left Oxford upon the death of his mother. He was ordained an Anglican priest in 1816. He worked in his father's parish from 1826 (one sister having died, another being a permanent invalid), turning down many offers of other posts until his father's death in 1835 and his marriage to Charlotte Clarke in the same year induced him to accept the living of Hursley, near Winchester, in 1836. There he stayed for the rest of his life, combining the ordinary activities of parish priest with an intensely engaged career as a chief polemicist for his ecclesiastical party. The anonymous publication in 1827 of his sequence of verses for use alongside the Church of England's Book of Common Prayer, *The Christian Year: Thoughts in Verse for the Sundays and Holydays Throughout the Year*, made his name as a main Christian poet of his time. Stanzas from 'Bless'd are the pure in heart', for instance, would eventually be in every Christian denomination's repertoire. Wordsworth offered to help Keble polish up the roughnesses of some of his rhymes, but even without his help the volume sold in hundreds of thousands. The follow-up volume, *Lyra Innocentium: Thoughts in Verse on Christian Children, their Ways, and their Privileges* (1846), became almost as well known as *The Christian Year*, for all its rarified obsession with the purity of the baptismally regenerated child. In 1831 Keble was elected Professor of Poetry at Oxford (and served until 1841, when his lectures, originally delivered in Latin, were published). His Oxford Assize Sermon of 1833 on 'National Apostacy' was rightly considered by John Henry Newman to have started the Oxford Movement, and Keble remained an extremely key player in the campaign to restore and build up the pre-Reformation features of the Church of England: in *The Library of the Fathers* scheme with Newman and Pusey (1838 onward); in the highly controversial *Tracts for the Times* sequence (Keble wrote seven of them – numbers 4, 13, 52, 54, 57, 60, 89); in the *Library of Anglo-Catholic Theology* project (begun in 1846). Keble published sermons, wrote poems and articles for the *British Magazine*, and intervened steadily in the main doctrinal debates rocking the Church of England. After his death many more sermons, poems and doctrinal materials were published, sealing his reputation as the doyen of Anglo-Catholicism. For though many Anglo-Catholics had followed the logic of Keble's polemics and gone over to the Roman Catholic Church, including to Keble's immense sorrow his friend and ally Newman, he himself stayed loyally within the National Church in order to inspire and steady the movement he had helped found. Drained by the death of his remaining sister in 1860 and the illness of his wife, he suffered a stroke in 1864, and he died, 29 March 1866, at Bournemouth, where he and his wife were wintering for the sake of his health. She died six weeks later. In 1869 Keble College was opened in his memory at Oxford, built by adoring subscribers to provide affordable education for Anglo-Catholic men – and especially to provide recruits for the Anglo-Catholic ministry.

MORNING

His compassions fail not; they are new every morning.
Lament. iii. 22, 23

Hues of the rich unfolding morn,
That, ere the glorious sun be born,
By some soft touch invisible
Around his path are taught to dwell; –

Thou rustling breeze so fresh and gay,
That dancest forth at opening day,
And brushing by with joyous wing,
Wakenest each little leaf to sing; –

Ye fragrant clouds of dewy steam,
By which deep grove and tangled stream   10
Pay, for soft rains in season given,
Their tribute to the genial heaven; –

Why waste your treasures of delight
Upon our thankless, joyless sight;
Who day by day to sin awake,
Seldom of heaven and you partake?

Oh! timely happy, timely wise,
Hearts that with rising morn arise!
Eyes that the beam celestial view,
Which evermore makes all things new![1]   20

New every morning is the love
Our wakening and uprising prove;
Through sleep and darkness safely brought,
Restored to life, and power, and thought.

New mercies, each returning day,
Hover around us while we pray;
New perils past, new sins forgiven,
New thoughts of God, new hopes of heaven.

If on our daily course our mind
Be set to hallow all we find,   30
New treasures still, of countless price,
God will provide for sacrifice.

Old friends, old scenes, will lovelier be,
As more of heaven in each we see:
Some softening gleam of love and prayer
Shall dawn on every cross and care.

As for some dear familiar strain
Untir'd we ask, and ask again,
Ever, in its melodious store,
Finding a spell unheard before;   40

Such is the bliss of souls serene,
When they have sworn, and stedfast mean,
Counting the cost, in all to' espy
Their God, in all themselves deny.

O could we learn that sacrifice,
What lights would all around us rise!
How would our hearts with wisdom talk
Along Life's dullest dreariest walk!

We need not bid, for cloister'd cell,
Our neighbour and our work farewell,   50
Nor strive to wind ourselves too high
For sinful man beneath the sky:

The trivial round, the common task,
Would furnish all we ought to ask;
Room to deny ourselves; a road
To bring us, daily, nearer God.

MORNING
1   Revelations xxi. 5. [Author's note]

Seek we no more; content with these,
Let present Rapture, Comfort, Ease,
As Heaven shall bid them, come and go: –
The secret this of Rest below.   60

Only, O Lord, in thy dear love
Fit us for perfect Rest above;
And help us, this and every day,
To live more nearly as we pray.

The Christian Year: Thoughts in Verse for the Sundays and Holydays Throughout the year, 2 vols (J. Parker, Oxford; C. & J. Rivington, London, 1827), I. (First poem in the collection; containing the verses which formed the famous hymn, 'New every morning is the love'.)

SEPTUAGESIMA SUNDAY

The invisible things of Him from the creation of the world are clearly seen, being understood by the things that are made.

Romans 1.20

There is a book, who runs may read,
    Which heavenly truth imparts,
And all the lore its scholars need,
    Pure eyes and Christian hearts.

The works of God above, below,
    Within us and around,
Are pages in that book, to show
    How God himself is found.

The glorious sky embracing all
    Is like the Maker's love,   10
Wherewith encompass'd, great and small
    In peace and order move.

The Moon above, the Church below,
    A wondrous race they run,
But all their radiance, all their glow
    Each borrows of its Sun.

The Saviour lends the light and heat
    That crowns his holy hill;
The saints, like stars, around his seat,
    Perform their courses still.[1]   20

The saints above are stars in Heaven –
    What are the saints on earth?
Like trees they stand whom God has given,[2]
    Our Eden's happy birth.

Faith is their fix'd unswerving root,
    Hope their unfading flower,
Fair deeds of charity their fruit,
    The glory of their bower.

The dew of Heaven is like thy grace,[3]
    It steals in silence down;   30
But where it lights, the favour'd place
    By richest fruits is known.

One Name above all glorious names
    With its ten thousand tongues
The everlasting sea proclaims,
    Echoing angelic songs.

The raging Fire,[4] the roaring Wind,
    Thy boundless power display:
But in the gentler breeze we find
    Thy Spirit's viewless way.[5]   40

Two worlds are ours: 'tis only Sin
    Forbids us to descry
The mystic heaven and earth within,
    Plain as the sea and sky.

Thou, who hast given me eyes to see
    And love this sight so fair,
Give me a heart to find out thee,
    And read thee every where.

The Christian Year (1827), I.

SEPTUAGESIMA SUNDAY
1 Daniel 12.3.
2 Isaiah 60.21.
3 Psalm 68.9.
4 Hebrews 12.29.
5 St John 3.8.

THE PURIFICATION

Blessed are the pure in heart: for they shall see God.
St Matthew v. 8

Bless'd are the pure in heart,
   For they shall see our God,
The secret of the Lord is theirs,
   Their soul is Christ's abode.

Might mortal thought presume
   To guess an angel's lay,
Such are the notes that echo through
   The courts of Heaven to-day.

Such the triumphal hymns
   On Sion's Prince that wait,   10
In high procession passing on
   Towards His temple-gate.

Give ear, ye kings – bow down,
   Ye rulers of the earth –
This, this is He; your Priest by grace,
   Your God and King by birth.

No pomp of earthly guards
   Attends with sword and spear,
And all-defying, dauntless look,
   Their monarch's way to clear;   20

Yet are there more with him
   Than all that are with you –
The armies of the highest Heaven,
   All righteous, good, and true.

Spotless their robes and pure,
   Dipp'd in the sea of light,
That hides the unapproached shrine
   From men's and angels' sight.

His throne, thy bosom blest,
   O Mother undefil'd[1] –   30
That throne, if aught beneath the skies,
   Beseems the sinless child.

Lost in high thoughts, 'whose son
   'The wondrous Babe might prove,'

Her guileless husband walks beside,
   Bearing the hallow'd dove;

Meet emblem of His vow,
   Who, on this happy day,
His dove-like soul – best sacrifice –
   Did on God's altar lay.   40

But who is he, by years
   Bow'd, but erect in heart,
Whose prayers are struggling with his tears?[2]
   'Lord, let me now depart.

'Now hath thy servant seen
   'Thy saving health, O Lord;
''Tis time that I depart in peace,
   'According to thy word.'

Yet swells the pomp: one more
   Comes forth to bless her God: 50
Full fourscore years, meek widow, she
   Her heaven-ward way hath trod.[3]

She who to earthly joys
   So long had given farewell,
Now sees, unlook'd for, Heaven on earth,
   Christ in His Israel.

Wide open from that hour
   The temple-gates are set,
And still the saints rejoicing there
   The holy Child have met.   60

Now count his train to-day,
   And who may meet him, learn:
Him child-like sires, meek maidens find,
   Where pride can nought discern.

Still to the lowly soul
   He doth himself impart,
And for His cradle and His throne
   Chooseth the pure in heart.

The Christian Year *(1827), II.*

THE PURIFICATION
1 the Virgin Mary.

2 Simeon: Luke 2.25ff.
3 Anna: Luke 2.36ff.

HOLY MATRIMONY

(To be sung at the Commencement of the Service)

A threefold cord is not quickly broken.
Eccles. iv. 12

The voice that breathed o'er Eden,
    That earliest wedding-day,
The primal marriage blessing,
    It hath not passed away.

Still in the pure espousal
    Of Christian man and maid,
The holy Three are with us,
    The threefold grace is said.

For dower of blessèd children,
    For love and faith's sweet sake,   10
For high mysterious union,
    Which nought on earth may break.

Be present, awful Father,
    To give away this bride,
As Eve Thou gav'st to Adam
    Out of his own pierced side:

Be present, Son of Mary,
    To join their loving hands,
As Thou didst bind two natures
    In Thine eternal bands: 20

Be present, Holiest Spirit,
    To bless them as they kneel,
As Thou for Christ, the Bridegroom,
    The heavenly Spouse dost seal.

O spread Thy pure wing o'er them,
    Let no ill power find place,
When onward to Thine altar
    The hallowed path they trace,

To cast their crowns before Thee
    In perfect sacrifice,   30
Till to the home of gladness
    With Christ's own Bride they rise. Amen.

July 12, 1857

Miscellaneous Poems of the Rev. J. Keble, MA., Vicar of Hursley
(Oxford and London, 1869).

John Clare (1793–1864)

John Clare was born, 13 July 1793, in Helston, Northamptonshire, on the edge of the Peterborough Fen, between Stamford and Peterborough, eldest child of an illegitimate thresher (or whopstraw) and village wrestling champion called Parker Clare. His mother was completely illiterate. His father, who could only read a bit in the Bible and such-like texts, did, though, have scores of ballads at his command. Minding sheep and geese, threshing corn from an early age to help ease the family's dire poverty, Clare was still sent, on and off, to school. He read eagerly in the Bible, the Prayer Book, chapbooks, *The Pilgrim's Progress*, a *Robinson Crusoe* which came his way. A battered Thomson's *Seasons*, lent him by some Methodist friends – who favoured Charles Wesley's hymns more – caused his heart to 'twitter' with joy. He raised the shilling necessary to purchase his own copy in Stamford. He took intensively to reading and 'scribbling' and to 'muttering' his verse as he went about. His mother mistakenly plundered his hoard of early work, hidden in some hole in the wall – using his scribbled-on bits of old wrapping paper and overwritten copybook pages as 'kettle holders and firelighters'. Clare worked at several casual and seasonal rural jobs

– horse-boy, plough-boy, gardener, lime-burner. He joined the local militia (1812). He fell easily in love – with Mary Joyce, farmer's daughter, who rejected him and would haunt him all his life; with Martha Turner (Patty), whom he reluctantly married, on 16 March 1820, when she was eight months pregnant (they had eight children in all). After certain unsuccessful to-ings and fro-ings he eventually found a firm of publishers who would issue his poems – John Taylor, in fact, publisher of Keats – and *Poems Descriptive of Rural Life and Society* appeared on 21 January 1821. This book was a hit, and Clare was taken up by literary London, meeting Hood, William Hone, James Montgomery and Cary the Dante translator. The well-disposed Taylor touched patrons and put together a £40 annuity – scarcely enough for the huge Clare family, but a help. But success was short-lived, *The Village Minstrel* (1821) and *The Shepherd's Calendar* (1827) selling few, and *The Rural Muse* (1835) scarcely any. In 1832 the Clare family moved three miles from Helston to Northborough – an utterly estranging distance for the poet ('How every tree is strange to me', as his pained poem 'The Flitting' has it). His vision darkened; violence and cruelty featured more in his writing. A tiny man (5′ 2″), and a lifelong weakling, he was given to depression and subject to epileptic-type fits. In the mid-thirties he was suffering loss of memory and delusions. In 1837, on Taylor's advice, he entered Matthew Allen's leniently run asylum in Epping Forest in Essex. In July 1841, improved in body though not in mind, he escaped, tramping the 80 miles home to Northborough in search of 'Mary'. Utterly penniless, he was driven to eat grass on the way (it tasted, he said, 'something like bread'). Around this time he was working on his long poems in homage to Byron, *Don Juan* and *Child Harold*. In December 1841 he was certified insane and put in the new St Andrew's County Lunatic Asylum in Northampton, and there he stayed until his death, 20 May 1864. He was allowed to wander around, mooch in the church porch and write. The house-steward of the Asylum, W. F. Knight, transcribed many of the vast number of poems Clare composed. These were shown to lots of people, and a few were published in provincial newspapers. One oddity of the Knight relationship is that the manuscript originals of all his transcriptions have disappeared, leaving us only with versions greatly tidied up as to spelling and punctuation (and with some evident mis-transcriptions). Deeply troubled, Clare had serious delusions of being Byron, Shakespeare, Horatio Nelson, Wellington with his head shot off at Waterloo. He imagined Mary to be his first wife, Patty only his second. He remembered and celebrated a vast confused cast of women (his 'fancys') in his verses – Ruth, Liza, Isabel, Hellen, Eleanor, Betsy, Arabella, Peggy, Ellen, Mary, Kate, Mary Ann, Bessy, Rachael, Nancy, Susannah, and so on. (He is one of the period's best love poets.) A depressed weed, he kept thinking he was a famous pugilist – 'they're feeding me up for a fight but they can get nobody able to strip to me'. The exquisite poems arising from an extraordinarily close attention to nature (he 'kicked' verses 'out of the clods', he said; or, less harshly put, 'I hunted curious flowers in rapture and muttered thoughts in their praise') now merged into the numerous simple 'Halfpenny Ballads' he poured out, and his haunted, introspective, visionary, even Blakean poems. Most of the later writing, including *The Mid-Summer Cushion*, the collection of poems he was preparing through the thirties, remained unpublished until long after his death. Whatever his mood or his mode, Clare is a major poet – and all the more remarkable for being so close to England's unlettered underclass and for crossing so frequently over the borders of sanity.

SONG

I wish I was where I would be
Alone with beauty & the free
I wish I was where I have been
A lover on the village green
Where old pits swell'd & mosses grew
Along with one who loved so true
Hath time made no changes then love is the same
Through calm & through danger dishonour & fame
What e'er I encounter what e'er I pursue
Human love may be frail – but mans honour is true   10

Canst thou feel what I breathed on thy bosom that eve
If thy love was a womans thoult ne'er disbelieve
But walk in thy fancys through meadow & glen
Aye walk & be happy & think it agen
There's the hills in thy fancy the Park in thy eye
& in midnight so guiltless that beautiful sky
& the stars looked upon us so lovely & warm
& thy own native star shed its beauty so calm
That said in bright colours love never should part
When I lay on thy bosom the man of thy heart   20

The prude may rail on love & falsehood declaim
Mock love is their liscence & falshood their fame
In abscence they scandalize wrong & decieve
& laugh at their fondness when women believe
But man never wronged them & Eden I see
Where man ever loved & a woman is free
Then leave me still free with thy love to be blest
On the bosom of woman my wishes are blest

Oer the hills & the hollows on that happy Eve
True love was the welcome that cannot decieve   30

Dated, early 1845. Text, The Later Poems of John Clare 1837–1864,
*ed. Eric Robinson, David Powell and Margaret Grainger, 2 vols
(Clarendon Press, Oxford, 1984), I. Northampton Asylum MS.*

Here is the scenes the rural poet made
So famous in his songs – the very scenes
He painted in his words that warm & shade
In winters wild waste & springs young vivid greens
Alcove & shrubbery – & the tree that leans
With its oerweight of Ivy – Yardley oak
The peasants nest & fields of blossomed beans
The bridge & avenue of thick set oak
The wilde[r]ness – here Cowpers spirit spoke

Dated, early 1845. Text, The Later Poems of John Clare, *I. Northampton Asylum MS.*

I'VE HAD MANY & ^{CR1}

1
I've had many an aching pain,
A for sake o' somebody:
I have talked, but o' in vain,
When I thought o' somebody.

2
Nought could please me any where,
I could heed nor smile, nor tear;
And yet I sighed, for half a year!
And that for sake o' somebody.

3
She was like the lily fair,
The rose it blushed, for somebody;   10
Her neck was white, her cheek was rare,
I wot it smiled on somebody; –

4
Here's good luck to somebody;
And best o' health for somebody;
The dearest thought I keep mysell,
I keep for sake o' somebody.

Dated, 17 July 1844. Text, The Later Poems of John Clare, *I.
Transcript made by W. F. Knight, house-steward at Northampton Asylum.*

I'VE HAD MANY & ^{CR}
1   etcetera.

SONNET

The Nightingale

This is the month, the Nightingale, clod-brown,
  Is heard among the woodland shady boughs;
This is the time when, in the vale, grass-grown
  The maiden hears at eve, her lovers vows.
  What time the blue mist, round her patient cows,
Dim rises from the grass, and half conceals
  Their dappled hides, – I hear the Nightingale,
That from the little blackthorn spinny steals,
  To the old hazel hedge that skirts the vale,
And still unseen, sings sweet: – the ploughman feels   10
  The thrilling music, as he goes along,
And imitates and listens, – while the fields
  Lose all their paths in dusk, to lead him wrong
Still sings the Nightingale her sweet melodious song.

Dated, 12 June 1844. Published, Worcester Journal *(29 August 1844). Text,*
The Later Poems of John Clare, *I. W. F. Knight transcript.*

SONNET

'I Am'

I feel I am; – I only know I am,
And plod upon the earth, as dull and void:
Earth's prison chilled my body with its dram
Of dullness, and my soaring thoughts destroyed,
I fled to solitudes from passions dream,
But strife persued – I only know, I am,
I was a being created in the race
Of men disdaining bounds of place and time: –
A spirit that could travel o'er the space
Of earth and heaven, – like a thought sublime,   10
Tracing creation, like my maker, free, –
A soul unshackled – like eternity,
Spurning earth's vain and soul debasing thrall
But now I only know I am, – that's all.

Text, The Later Poems of John Clare, *I. W. F. Knight transcript.*

THE ROUND OAK

1

The Apple top't oak in the old narrow lane
And the hedge row of bramble and thorn
Will ne'er throw their green on my visions again
As they did on that sweet dewy morn
When I went for spring pooteys and birds nests to look
Down the border of bushes ayont the fair spring
I gathered the palm grass close to the brook
And heard the sweet birds in thorn bushes sing

2

I gathered flat gravel stones up in the shallows
To make ducks and drakes when I got to a pond   10

The reed sparrows nest it was close to the sallows
And the wrens in a thorn bush a little beyond
And there did the stickleback shoot through the pebbles
As the bow shoots the arrow quick darting unseen
Till it came to the shallows where the water scarce drebbles
Then back dart again to the spring head of green

3

The nest of the magpie in the low bush of white thorn
And the carrion crows nest on the tree o'er the spring
I saw it in march on many a cold morn
When the arum it bloomed like a beautiful thing   20
And the apple top't oak aye as round as a table
That grew just above on the bank by the spring
Where every saturday noon I was able
To spend half a day and hear the birds sing

4

But now there's no holidays left to my choice
That can bring time to sit in thy pleasures again
Thy limpid brook flows and thy waters rejoice
And I long for that tree – but my wishes are vain
All that's left to me now I find in my dreams
For fate in my fortune's left nothing the same   30
Sweet Apple top't oak that grew by the stream
I loved thy shade once – now I love but thy name

Dated, 19 June 1846. Text, The Later Poems of John Clare, I. W. F. Knight transcript.

SONNET

The Crow

How peaceable it seems for lonely men
To see a crow fly in the thin blue sky
Over the woods and fealds, o'er level fen
It speaks of villages, or cottage nigh
Behind the neighbouring woods – when march winds high
Tear off the branches of the hugh old oak
I love to see these chimney sweeps sail by
And hear them o'er the knarled forest croak
Then sosh askew from the hid woodmans stroke
That in the woods their daily labours ply   10
I love the sooty crow nor would provoke
Its march day exercises of croaking joy
I love to see it sailing to and fro
While feelds, and woods and waters spread below

Text, The Later Poems of John Clare, I. W. F. Knight transcript.

PLEASANT SOUNDS

The rustling of leaves under the feet in woods and under hedges. The crumping of cat-ice and snow down wood rides, narrow lanes and every street causeways. Rustling through a wood, or rather rushing while the wind hallows in the oak tops like thunder. The rustles of birds wings startled from their nests, or flying unseen into the bushes.

The whizzing of larger birds over head in a wood, such as crows, puddocks, buzzards, & ͨ ͵͵
The trample of roburst wood larks on the brown leaves, and the patter of Squirrels on the green moss. The fall of an acorn on the ground, the pattering of nuts on the hazel branches, ere they fall from ripeness. The flirt of the ground-larks wing from the stubbles, how sweet such pictures on dewy mornings when the dew flashes from its brown feathers.

Text, The Later Poems of John Clare, *I. W. F. Knight transcript.*

TO MISS MARY ANN C.[1]

There is a land of endless life
Where lovers pass away
And leave these coarser scenes of strife
And unrefined clay
A land of love and pure delight
In never fading flowers
There Mary's love shall take its flight
From this cold world of ours

2

Thy beaming eyes shall brighter be
Thy cheeks pure roses glow   10
Thy person with the clime agree
More white than driven snow
That bosom in itself a soul
Shall be immortal soon
Where each one hides a happy mole
Like burs around the moon

3

Thyself shall be the angel there
Mid scenes for ever green
In flowers for ever bright and fair
Shall Mary live serene   20
I'll kiss the mole on either breast
Where mortals ne'er reprove
And share in my eternal rest
Her everlasting love

Text, The Later Poems of John Clare, *I. W. F. Knight transcript.*
A parody of Isaac Watts's hymn 'There is a land of pure delight'.

THE BEAN FIELD

A Bean field full in blossom smells as sweet
As Araby or Groves of orange flowers
Black eyed and white and feathered to ones feet
How sweet they smell in mornings dewy hours
When seething night is left upon the flowers
And when morns bright sun shines oer the field
The pea bloom glitters in the gems o' showers
And sweet the fragrance which the union yields
To battered footpaths crossing o'er the fields.

Text, The Later Poems of John Clare, *I. W. F. Knight transcript.*

TO MISS MARY ANN C.
1 Possibly Mary Ann Collingwood.

SONG

Sweet is the violet scented pea
Haunted by red legged sable bee
But sweeter far than all to me
Is her I love so dearly
Than perfumed pea or sable bee
The face I love so dearly

2

Sweet as the hedge row violet blue
Than apple blossoms streaky hue
The black eyed bean flower bleb'd with dew
Is her I love so dearly   10
Than apple flowers or violets blue
The cheeks I love so dearly

3

Than woodbines upon branches thin
The clover flower all sweets within
Which pensive bees do gather in
Three times as sweet or nearly
Is the cheek the lip the eye the chin
Of her I love so dearly

Text, The Later Poems of John Clare, *I. W. F. Knight transcript.*

There is a charm in Solitude that cheers
A feeling that the world knows nothing of
A green delight the wounded mind endears
After the hustling world is broken off
Whose whole delight was crime at good to scoff
Green solitude his prison pleasure yields
The bitch fox heeds him not – birds seem to laugh
He lives the Crusoe of his lonely fields
Which dark green oaks his noontide leisure shields

Text, The Later Poems of John Clare, *I. W. F. Knight transcript.*

1

There's music in the songs of birds
There's music in the bee
There's music in a womans voice
When sitting on your knee
While walking in the mossy vales
Beneath the spreading beech
Song lives in singing nightingales
And in a womans speech

2

To hear her wisper in the dark
'Tis heavens melody   10
Her calm reply her wise remark
Is more than song to me
The harp can touch no sweeter chord
In music's thrilling choice
Nor music breath[e] a sweeter word
Than comes from womans voice

3

There's music in the singing lark
That carols to the sky
To hear her wisper in the dark
'Tis heavens melody   20
There's music in a womans voice
While sitting on your knee
And Emma is my own heart's choice
When e'er she chooses me

Text, The Later Poems of John Clare, *I. W. F. Knight transcript.*

SONG

1

The hurly burly wind
And it whirls the wheat about
While its comeing in the ear
And the barley's on the sprout
It whirls the wheat about me
In its suit of sunny green
And my lassie need not doubt me
She's the sweetest ever seen

2

Her hair is of the auburn
And her cheek is of the rose   10
And my bonny Sarah Ann is
The sweetest flower that grows
Her lips are like the cherry
And her skin is lilly white
Her tongue is ever merry
Her smiles are all delight

3

The hurly-burly wind
And it whirls the wheat about
The billows swab behind
And the headaches scrail without   20
The bluecaps in the green
Eddie like Butterflies
And nothing still is seen
Where e'er we turn our eyes

4

My love is like the wild scene
Her gown is floating free
And I have like a child been
To seek her company
And I must like a child be
In fancy's to delight   30
So I walk to see the wild bee
And butterfly till night

Text, The Later Poems of John Clare, *I. W. F. Knight transcript.*

THE DARK DAYS OF AUTUMN

The dark days of Autumn grows cloudy and rainy
The sun pales like sulphur the shadows grow long
To me the dull season the sweetest of any
I love to see yellow leaves fall in my song
The rush covered green and thistle capped mountain
The dead leaves a falling and winds singing round
The willow and ash leaves they choak up the fountain
There's health i' the strife o't and joy i' the sound

I love there to loiter wi' winds blowing round me
Till the strong eddies past and the rain gust is over   10
Wild pigeons fly over the instance looks downy
With <stunt> willow rows [and] pieces of clover
Brown pieces o' stubbles ground o' turnips bright green
The crows flying over the lakes silver light
Scarce a wild blossom left to enliven the scene
Rauk and mist are for ever in sight

     Text, The Later Poems of John Clare, *II. W. F. Knight transcript.*

SONG

O sweet is the song o' the Thrush i' the spring mornings
And sweet is the Chaffinch that sings o' the Thorn
And lovely and pleasant are natures adornings
To walk out wi Rachael in loves dewey morn
When the hare licks her coat i' the dewey mist clover
And the rabbit pit patters upon the Molehill
And the Wren i' the furze bush wi flowers golden over
Builds her green mossy nest by the side o' the hill

Ill ramble the wood side and down the green lane go
And court my young Rachael while milking the Kye   10
The Blackbird sings loud as a Lady's piano
With a yellow gold ring round his violet eye
O Rachael is fair as the dew pearls o' morning
And Rachael is sweet as the buds o sweet brere
Her dark jetty curls oer her eye lashes dawning
The moss on the Rose is'nt nothing so dear

O Rachael looks sweet in her new Sunday gown
And her bonny lace cap makes her neck look so fair
Shes the prettiest Girl in all the whole Town
Through her cap you may see the fine comb in her hair   20
Her breasts underneath her green gown bosom lye
Like a pair o' white Doves in a lilly white nest
O red was her ripe lips & bright was her eye
I courted her long & I loved her the best

     Text, The Later Poems of John Clare, *II. W. F. Knight transcript.*

THE NURSERY GARDEN

There is an hidden history, in the trees,
The various shades of green, and shapes of leaves,
The nursery grounds, all stirred with the mild breeze,
My mind from lonesome weariness relieves,
Leaf shedding some, midst evergreen young firs,
Whisper, and talk to every wind which stirs.

2

I love the nursery calm – or stirr'd by winds,
Sweet chesnut, beech, and broad leaf'd sycamore,
Fruit trees, and shrubs, and trees of various kinds,
While o'er the varied scene the wind waves o'er;   10
The poplar, broom, and oak that trees excel,
The nursery – Oh! I love the nursery well!

3

I love the nursery, with its trees and bushes,
Where gold beak'd blackbirds build their nests & fly,
To hear neath pine clumps shade, the singing thrushes,
Hiding her Heaven tint eggs, from every eye,
I love the nursery with its shades of green,
At early morn, or in calm eve serene.

4

The nuts, and filberts with their soft broad leaves,
Throw shadows on the path of russet brown,   20
The willows grey, a summer chaplet weaves,
For nights dull visions, when the sun goes down,
I love the nursery, with its paths and trees,
Its songs of birds, and summer panting bees.

5

I love the nursery, 'tis a pleasant place,
To spend ones leisure hours, on summer's day,
To mark the various tree's, throughout the space,
Noting dark clumps, where leaves exclude bright day,
I love the nursery, where the breezes leave,
A whispering song of melody at eve.   30

Text, The Later Poems of John Clare, *II. W. F. Knight transcript.*

FRAGMENT

Vetches; both yellow, and blue,
Grew thick in the meadow lane,
Isabellas shawl kept off the dew,
As thickly upon her it came,
A thorn bush caught her umbrella,
As though it would bid her to stay,
But the loving, and loved Isabella,
Went laughing, and walking away.

Text, The Later Poems of John Clare, *II. W. F. Knight transcript.*

THE RAWK[1] O' THE AUTUMN

The rawk o' the Autumn hangs over the woodlands
Like smoke from a City dismember'd and pale
The sun without beams burns dim o'er the floodlands
Where white Cawdymaws[2] slow swiver and sail
The flood froths away like a fathomless ocean
The wind winnows chill like a breeze from the sea
And thoughts of my Susan give the heart an emotion
To think does she e'er waste a thought upon me

Full oft I think so on the banks of the meadows
While the pale Cawdymawdy flies swooping all day   10
I think of our true love where grass & flowers hid us
As by the dyke side o' the meadows we lay
The seasons have chang'd since I sat wi my true love
Now the flood roars & raves o'er the bed where we lay
There the bees kiss'd the flowers – Has she got a new love
I feel like a wreck of the flood cast away

The rawk of the Autumn hangs over the woodland
Like smoke from a City sulphurously grey
The Heronshaw lonely hangs over the floodland
And cranks its lone story throughout the dull day   20
There's no green on the hedges no leaves on the darkwood
No cows on the pasture or sheep on the lea
The Linnets cheep still & how happy the lark would
Sing songs to sweet Susan to remind her of me

Text, The Later Poems of John Clare, *II. W. F. Knight transcript.*

Henry Francis Lyte (1793–1847)

Henry Francis Lyte, the hymn-writer, was born at Ednam, near Kelso, in Scotland, 1 June 1793, second son of Captain Thomas Lyte. The father moved his family to Ireland, then separated from his wife, who left for London in 1801 or 1802 and never saw her children again. Shortly after, the father was posted to Jersey and saw his sons only occasionally – and later posed, in fact, as their uncle, with his second wife merely as their aunt. Henry Francis was educated at Portora Royal School, Enniskillen, and later at Trinity College, Dublin – where he was a Scholar and won the English Poem prize three times. His original intention was to become a physician but he altered course for theology. He graduated in 1814 and was ordained in the Established Church in 1815. Greatly vexed by ill health, he would all his life travel much abroad looking for cures and respite. In 1817 he became minister in Marazion, Cornwall, where he married Anne Maxwell, heiress of the Revd Dr W. Maxwell of County Monaghan in Ireland (who wrote

Chapter 24 of Boswell's *Life of Johnson*). In 1819, greatly moved by the illness and death of a fellow-clergyman, he went through a life-altering evangelical transformation. Shortly afterwards, he moved to Lymington, where he wrote *Tales in Verse* (published 1826). In 1823 he became Perpetual Curate at the sea-port of Lower Brixham in Devon, his post for the last twenty-five years of his life. His volumes of Christian verse are *Poems Chiefly Religious* (1833; enlarged 1845) and *The Spirit of the Psalms* (1834) – rather heavy versions of the biblical Psalms originally done for his Lower Brixham congregation. *Miscellaneous Poems* (posthumously published, 1868) reprints the 1833 volume. Arthur Sullivan set Lyte's secular poem 'On a Naval Officer' to music. Lyte collected the *Sacred Poems* of Henry Vaughan (1846) and wrote the biographical preface. He became extremely well known in English-speaking Christendom as the author of the hymns 'God of mercy, God of Grace', 'Pleasant are Thy courts above', 'Praise,

2 gulls.

my soul, the King of Heaven', but above all for 'Abide with me', based on the moment in the Gospel story of Jesus being revealed to two disconsolate disciples at Emmaus when they ask him to stay at the end of the day (Luke 24.29): 'Abide with us, for it is toward evening, and the day is far spent.' Themes of separation, the desire for union with mother and father, especially with the divine father, celebrations of God's fatherliness ('Father-like he tends and spares us;/Well our feeble frame he knows;/In his hands he gently bears us,/Rescues us from all our foes':

'Praise, my soul, the King of Heaven') are dominant notes in the verses of this once abandoned child. 'Abide with me' was written not long before his death, after one of his last sermons in Devon, given against family advice because of his severely lapsing health, on 4 September 1847. He died at Nice in the South of France on 20 November of the same year. His daughter Anna Maria Maxwell Hogg tells the story of 'Abide with me' and other writing in her prefatory Memoir to Lyte's *Remains* (1850).

ABIDE WITH ME

'Abide with us: for it is towards evening, and the day is far spent.'
St Luke xxiv. 29

Abide with me! Fast falls the eventide;
The darkness deepens: Lord, with me abide!
When other helpers fail, and comforts flee,
Help of the helpless, O abide with me!

Swift to its close ebbs out life's little day;
Earth's joys grow dim; its glories pass away:
Change and decay in all around I see;
O Thou, who changest not, abide with me!

Not a brief glance I beg, a passing word,
But as Thou dwell'st with Thy disciples, Lord,   10
Familiar, condescending, patient, free,
Come, not to sojourn, but abide, with me!

Come not in terrors, as the King of kings;
But kind and good, with healing in Thy wings:
Tears for all woes, a heart for every plea.
Come, Friend of sinners, and thus bide with me!

Thou on my head in early youth didst smile,
And, though rebellious and perverse meanwhile,
Thou hast not left me, oft as I left Thee.
On to the close, O Lord, abide with me!   20

I need Thy presence every passing hour.
What but Thy grace can foil the Tempter's power?
Who like Thyself my guide and stay can be?
Through cloud and sunshine, O abide with me!

I fear no foe with Thee at hand to bless:
Ills have no weight, and tears no bitterness.
Where is death's sting? where, grave, thy victory?
I triumph still, if Thou abide with me.

Hold then Thy cross before my closing eyes;
Shine through the gloom, and point me to the skies: 30

Heaven's morning breaks, and earth's vain shadows flee.
In life and death, O Lord, abide with me!

Berryhead, September, 1847

Originally published in pamphlet form, 1847. Text: Remains of the Late
Rev. Henry Francis Lyte, MA., with a prefatory Memoir by the Editor,
A.M.M.H. [*Anna Maria Maxwell Hogg*] *(Francis & John Rivington, 1850).*
Hymn-books usually omit stanzas 3–5.

Janet (Thompson) Hamilton (1795–1873)

Janet Hamilton, self-educated, and blind for many years, became one of the Victorian era's most celebrated working-class authors. She was born Janet Thompson in Shotts, Lanarkshire, 12 October 1795, into a poor family. Her father was intermittently a cobbler and farm-labourer. She did spinning and weaving, married at the age of fourteen or so a cobbler who worked for her father, had ten children, but also found time to read the Bible, Shakespeare, Milton, Burns, standard histories, biographies and essays. A good Scottish Calvinist, she wrote religious verses when she was young, in a pseudo-oriental handwriting she concocted for herself. But being a hard-pressed housewife and mother unsurprisingly distracted her from writing until, in her mid-fifties, she returned to composition – for Cassell's *Working Man's Friend.* Her writing in verse and prose – forthright, indignant, canny about Scot-

tishness, the plight of the poor, worldwide oppression, war, slavery, drunkenness, Sabbath-breaking – was collected in several volumes in the sixties and seventies. Blind for her last eighteen years, she relied on her husband John Hamilton and daughter Marion to read to her and on her son James to act as amanuensis (she taught all her children their reading and writing). She became rather celebrated and received distinguished visitors, including Garibaldi's son (Italian liberation was one of her causes). A petition to Prime Minister Disraeli brought her a £50 grant from the Royal Bounty. She was said never to have travelled more than twenty miles from her married home in Langloan, Lanarkshire, in all her sixty years there. She died on 27 October 1873, at the good old age of seventy-eight.

WOMAN

There is an element of power
That suits the needs of every hour –
All wants to which our state gives birth –
The life, the mind, the home, the hearth.

'Tis Woman. From the mother's breast
The babe draws life and strength and rest;
She soothes its pains, its wants supplies,
With yearning love in heart and eyes.

A prudent, gentle, loving wife,
The boon most precious to the life   10
Of him to whom her all is given,
Save love of God, and hope of heaven.

And who shall teach the infant mind
The way of truth and peace to find?
Who teach in wisdom's paths to tread,
But she who gives his daily bread?

A guiding star to shed and shine
Soft radiance on the household shrine,

And from her sphere – a span of earth –
Pour light and love on home and hearth.   20

And such should Woman ever prove –
The pole-star of domestic love,
To which the youthful circle tend,
As mother, guardian, teacher, friend.

There is an element of ill –
Of power to soil, deface, and kill
The buds, the flowers, the fruits of life –
The careless mother, worthless wife.

O careless mother, why neglect
The early buds of vice to check   30
In your untutored boys and girls,
Ere cast on life – its sins and perils?

Your children's blood you would not shed;
Yet, cruel mother, on your head
The blood of souls uncared-for lies –
That blood to Heaven for ever cries.

Oh, woe for him who finds on earth
No spot so dreary as the hearth
Where sits the partner of his life,
A shrewish, wasteful, worthless wife!   40

O Woman, much to thee is given –
Thy mission comes direct from Heaven;
The priceless gems of human life –
A careful mother, virtuous wife.

Poems, Essays, and Sketches *(James Maclehose, Glasgow, 1870).*

The Horrors of War

Verses Suggested by the War in the Crimea, 1854

Flapping fierce her gory pinions,
    Whetting sharp her crimson beak,
Vulture War her barbarous minions,
    Calls their ghastly prey to seek.

Now her hideous form comes swooping
    From the thundering ramparts' height,
O'er the carnaged valley stooping,
    Gorged with slaughter – horrid sight!

Shot and shell, the dark air rending –
    Sulphurous flash, and bayonets' gleam –   10
Shouts and shrieks, and groans wild blending,
    With her loud discordant scream.

High the purple tide is swelling,
    O'er the dark ensanguined plain,
From a thousand bosoms welling,
    Mangled limbs and shattered brain!

Oh! for angel eye and station,
    Far above the battle-cloud,
Whence I'd view the dread migration
    Of the unbodied spirit-crowd!   20

Through eternity's dark portals
    To the abodes of weal or woe,
Swiftly rush the new immortals –
    Lord, how long shall it be so?

Summerland – Oh! beauteous region,
    Rich in foliage, flowers, and fruit,
Shall the foe, whose name is Legion,
    Keep and tread thee under foot?

Round thy leagured port and city
    Volleying thunders ceaseless roar,   30
Earth affords not aid or pity –
    They shall fall to rise no more!

Poems, Essays, and Sketches *(1870).*

Our Local Scenery

Smoorin' wi' reek an' blacken'd wi' soot
Lowin' like Etna an' Hecla to boot,
Ought o' our malleables want ye to learn? –
There's chappin' an' clippin' an' sawin' o' airn;
Burnin' an' sotterin' reengin' an' knockin';
Scores o' puir mortals roastin' an' chokin'.
Gizzen'd an' dry ilka thrapple an' mouth,
Like cracks in the yird in a het simmer drouth;
They're prayin', puir chiels, for what dae ye think?
It's no daily bread, it's drink, 'Gi'e us drink!'   10
'Callan,' quo' I, 'ye maun rin like a hatter,
Bring up twa pails fou o' clear caller water;
Be aff, noo, ye imp! come back at a canter,
Keep oot o' the store, or I'll fell ye *instanter*!'
Wae on the store an' the publican's bar,
It's no a haet better – sometimes it's waur;
Men, whan they're het, hoo they sweat an' they swear
Coup up the whisky an' toom doun the beer.

While droonin' their brains an' tooming their purses
The verra air rings wi' oaths an' wi' curses.   20
It's no just a pay or an orra bit fuddle –
Aft in a day they guzzle an' muddle.

The puir wifie says there's little comes till her,
It's the drink, it's the drink that licks up the siller.
Licks up the siller! wha is't that can count,
Reckon an' add up the fearfu' amount
Wasted on drink at ilk airn-makin' station –
Drink, ever drink, the curse o' our nation?
An' O siccan Sabbaths! O siccan weans!
Rantin' an' playin' an' castin' o' stanes.   30
Hearken, thae toddlin' wee things hoo they swear;
Had I wings like a doo I wadna be here –
I wad flee far awa' an' seek oot a rest
Whaur drinkin' an' swearin' nae mair wad molest.

Poems, Essays, and Sketches *(1870).*

COMPARATIVE SLAVERY

Tell me not of negro slavery,
　Of its shackles, stripes, and woes –
Shackles stronger, stripes more cruel,
　Deeper woe the drunkard knows.

Ah! what fetters adamantine
　Bind and hold him in their thrall,
Oft the scorpion scourge of horror
　On his shrinking soul will fall.

Tell me not of buying, selling,
　Like the beasts in field or fold,　　　　10
Human beings – lo! the drunkard –
　Body, soul, and heart hath sold.

Sold! is it to plant the cotton,
　Hoe the soil, and pick the pod?
No; to drink the demon tyrant,
　Foe to man, accursed of God.

Tell me not the negro mother
　Rears her children for the mart,
To be torn, when master wills it,
　From her clinging arms and heart.　　　20

We have thousand British mothers
　Who, in want, neglect, and cold,
See their infant victims pining
　To the fiend intemperance sold.

Do we loathe the beastly orgies
　Of the negro breeding pens?
Look within our thousand brothels,
　Viler far then negro dens.

Why do we descern so clearly
　Beams that dim our brother's eye,　　　30
While the motes, that mar our vision,
　We so seldom can descry?

Heritage of British freeman
　Never can a drunkard claim;
Slave of drink, and thrall of misery,
　His the heritage of shame.

Men of temperance, men of action,
　Ye who work, and think, and feel,
For the cause heaven smiles upon you,
　Labouring for your country's weal.　　　40

On the battle-field of temperance,
　Are no garments rolled in blood!
Nor the sound of shouting warrior
　Wading in the purple flood.

Patriotic zeal and pity,
　Effort born of brother love,
These your arms go on and conquer,
　Success waits you from above.

Poems, Essays, and Sketches *(1870)*.

Thomas Carlyle (1795–1881)

Thomas Carlyle, Victorian England's most important social critic, prophet and historian – Germanizing, Shandeyesque, post-Christian – was born 4 December 1795, at Ecclefechan, in Annandale, Scotland, into a devout working-class Calvinist family, members of the so-called Burghers faction of the eighteenth-century Kirk Secessionist church. First child of his builder father James Carlyle and his second wife Janet Aitken, Carlyle had three brothers and five sisters. A violently bad-tempered but bright lad, he progressed from his mother's reading lessons, to the village school, to Annan Grammar School, to Edinburgh University (November 1809: he walked the hundred miles to get there). Loss of orthodox Christian faith caused his abandonment of plans for ordination as a Christian minister after graduation. He later gave up studying for the Scottish bar. While schoolmastering temporarily at Kirkcaldy Carlyle began his great friendship with Edward Irving, who would lead the charismatic-prophetic movement which resulted in the Irvingites, or Catholic Apostolic Church. Irving, at one time London's most fashionable

preacher, became for Carlyle a model of both the power and also the dangers of charismatic rhetoric. In October 1826 Carlyle married Jane Baillie Welsh, a feistily independent and clever woman, a descendant of John Knox the founding father of Scottish Calvinism (she had been a tutee of Irving, who dearly wanted to marry her). The Carlyles' marriage was stormy; he was often neglectful (devoted to his studies) as well as violent and (probably) sexually inadequate. His lifelong dyspeptic stomach problems can't have helped. In the middle of 1821 he wrestled sleeplessly with the ghosts of his Christianity (a struggle greatly inspirited by his reading of Goethe), moving into a classically privatized form of Victorian humanism – 'Scottish Calvinism without the dogma', it's been called. He worked as a tutor, shuttled between Scotland and London, improved his German, and slowly wormed his way into literary journalism as a writer, in particular, on German literary topics. His early career was greatly helped by sponsorship from Francis Jeffrey, founder and editor of the *Edinburgh Review*. Carlyle's translation of *Wilhelm Meister* brought him into a long-standing friendship with Goethe. He spent several years reading and writing keenly, very short of money, in the Scottish isolation of Craigenputtock (not good for Jane), before settling in June 1834 at No. 5 Cheyne Row in Chelsea, in 'the din of this monstrous city of London'. His first great work, *Sartor Resartus* – wryly metatextual, lovely Shandeyesque meditations on the scope of meaning and the force of text in a post-Christian world – struggled for recognition; but his radical tracts on the dire condition of capitalist England, *Chartism* (1839) and *Past and Present* (1843), made his name as the nation's foremost social observer and critic. It's no surprise that Dickens should have dedicated his novel *Hard Times* (1854) to Carlyle (Carlyle's vision widely inflects Dickens's). Worry, though, over the perils of the individual in modern mass society led to increasing strain in Carlyle's writing. Terror of revolutionary terror infects his great history *The French Revolution* (1837: its first volume had to be rewritten after J. S. Mill's maid-servant allegedly mistook the heap of MSS for rubbish and lit fires with it). Carlyle became more and more devoted to a salvationist vision of the Strong Man as necessary Leader: a line of thought running through his *Heroes and Hero-Worship* (1841), *Oliver Cromwell's Letters and Speeches* (1845), the four-volume *Cromwell* (1850), *Latter-Day Pamphlets* (1850) and the monstrously protracted *History of Frederick the Great* (1858–65). Carlyle's late article 'Shooting Niagara: And After?' (*Macmillan's Magazine*, 1866), inspired by the Second Reform Bill agitations, is truly hectic and disturbingly inflammatory in its panics over democracy. Carlyle was foremost among supporters of the Liberals' *bête noire*, Governor Edward Eyre of Jamaica, vicious repressor of the revolt of Jamaican blacks in 1865. Mussolini was a great admirer of Carlyle's; so was Bismarck. Carlyle hated much – cant; the ballot-box; poetry. He was always advising poets to try prose instead (Tennyson, he said, was 'a life-guardsman spoilt by making poetry': such views did not spoil their great mutual affection). The death of his wife on 21 April 1866 did not contribute to any sweetening of Carlyle's later mood (she was severely hurt when a cab knocked her down in a London street in August 1863 and never fully recovered). In the seventies, Carlyle drifted gradually towards death, cantankerously leonine, bitingly reminisciential (at work on the wonderfully revealing *Reminiscences*), intensely renowned, greatly bent with age, accepting honours from Prussia but not from Tory Prime Minister Disraeli. He died on 4 February 1881, and was buried in Ecclefechan Kirk-yard (his known opposition to the Anglican Funeral Service precluded the offered interment in Westminster Abbey). Carlyle is the truest, most honest, crankiest polemicist of his times, as well as its most annoyingly circumlocutionary but also most torrentially exciting stylist. Robert Browning's impromptu 'Terse Verse, being a contribution to Scottish Anthology', rightly casts him as a Bunyanesque hero – 'He, ordained to close with and cross-buttock/Cant, the giant' (it's in Hallam Tennyson's *Memoir* of Tennyson, ii. 230). Cross-buttock to rhyme, of course, with Craigenputtock.

LUTHER'S PSALM

Among Luther's Spiritual Songs, of which various collections have appeared of late years,[1] the one entitled *Eine feste Burg ist unser Gott* is universally regarded as the best; and indeed still retains its place and devotional use in the Psalmodies of Protestant Germany. Of the Tune, which also is by Luther, we have no copy, and only a secondhand knowledge: to the original Words, probably never before printed in England, we subjoin the following Translation; which, if it possess the only merit it can pretend to, that of literal adherence to the sense, will not prove unacceptable to our readers. Luther's music is heard daily in our churches, several of our finest Psalm-tunes being of his composition. Luther's sentiments also are, or should be, present in many an English heart; the more interesting to us is any the smallest articulate expression of these.

The great Reformer's love of music, of poetry, it has often been remarked, is one of the most significant features in his character. But indeed, if every great man, Napoleon himself, is intrinsically a poet, an idealist, with more or less completeness of utterance, which of all our great men, in these modern ages, had such an endowment in that kind as Luther? He it was, emphatically, who stood based on the Spiritual World of man, and only by the footing and miraculous power he had obtained there, could work such changes in the Material World. As a participant and dispenser of divine influences, he shows himself among human affairs; a true connecting medium and visible Messenger between Heaven and Earth; a man, therefore, not only permitted to

LUTHER'S PSALM
1   For example: *Luthers Geistliche Lieder, nebst dessen Gedanken über die Musica* (Berlin, 1817); *Die Lieder Luthers gesammelt von Kosegarten und Rambach, & c.* [Author's note]

enter the sphere of Poetry, but to dwell in the purest centre thereof: perhaps the most inspired of all Teachers since the first Apostles of his faith; and thus not a Poet only, but a Prophet and god-ordained Priest, which is the highest form of that dignity, and of all dignity.

Unhappily, or happily, Luther's poetic feeling did not so much learn to express itself in fit Words that take captive every ear, as in fit Actions, wherein truly, under still more impressive manifestation, the spirit of spheral melody resides, and still audibly addresses us. In his written Poems we find little, save that strength of one 'whose words,' it has been said, 'were half battles;' little of that still harmony and blending softness of union, which is the last perfection of strength; less of it than even his conduct often manifested. With Words he had not learned to make pure music; it was by Deeds of love or heroic valour that he spoke freely; in tones, only through his Flute, amid tears, could the sigh of that strong soul find utterance.

Nevertheless, though in imperfect articulation, the same voice, if we will listen well, is to be heard also in his writings, in his Poems. The following, for example, jars upon our ears: yet there is something in it like the sound of Alpine avalanches, or the first murmur of earthquakes; in the very vastness of which dissonance a higher unison is revealed to us. Luther wrote this Song in a time of blackest threatenings, which however could in nowise become a time of despair. In those tones, rugged, broken as they are, do we not recognise the accent of that summoned man (summoned not by Charles the Fifth, but by God Almighty also), who answered his friends' warning not to enter Worms, in this wise: 'Were there as many devils in Worms as there are roof-tiles, I would on;' – of him who, alone in that assemblage, before all emperors and principalities and powers, spoke forth these final and forever memorable words: 'It is neither safe nor prudent to do aught against conscience. Here stand I, I cannot otherwise. God assist me. Amen!'[2] It is evident enough that to this man all Pope's Conclaves, and Imperial Diets, and hosts, and nations, were but weak; weak as the forest, with all its strong *trees*, may be to the smallest spark of electric *fire*.

Eine feste Burg ist unser Gott

Eine feste Burg ist unser Gott,
Ein gutes Wehr und Waffen;
Er hilft uns frey aus aller Noth,
Die uns jetzt hat betroffen.
Der alte böse Feind
Mit Ernst ers jetzt meint;
Gross Macht und viel List
Sein grausam' Rüstzeuch ist,
Auf Erd'n ist nicht seins Gleichen.

Mit unsrer Macht ist Nichts gethan,   10
Wir sind gar bald verloren:
Es streit't für uns der rechte Mann,
Den Gott selbst hat erkoren.
Fragst du wer er ist?
Er heisst Jesus Christ,
Der Herre Zebaoth,
Und ist kein ander Gott,
Das Feld muss er behalten.

Und wenn die Welt voll Teufel wär,
Und wollt'n uns gar verschlingen,   20
So fürchten wir uns nicht so sehr,
Es soll uns doch gelingen.

---

2 'Till such time as, either by proofs from Holy Scripture, or by fair reason or argument, I have been confuted and convicted, I cannot and will not recant, *weil weder sicher noch gerathen ist, etwas wider Gewissen su thun. Hier stehe ich, kann nicht anders. Gott helfe mir. Amen!* [Author's note]

Der Fürste dieser Welt,
Wie sauer er sich stellt,
Thut er uns doch Nichts;
Das macht er ist gerichtt,
Ein Wörtlein kann ihn fällen.

Das Wort sie sollen lassen stahn,
Und keinen Dank dazu haben;
Er ist bey uns wohl auf dem Plan   30
Mit seinem Geist und Gaben.
Nehmen sie uns den Leib,
Gut', Ehr', Kind und Weib,
Lass fahren dahin.
Sie haben's kein Gewinn,
Das Reich Gottes muss uns bleiben.

A safe stronghold our God is still,
A trusty shield and weapon;
He'll help us clear from all the ill
That hath us now o'ertaken.
The ancient Prince of Hell
Hath risen with purpose fell;
Strong mail of Craft and Power
He weareth in this hour,
On Earth is not his fellow.

With force of arms we nothing can,   10
Full soon were we down-ridden;
But for us fights the proper Man,
Whom God himself hath bidden.
Ask ye, Who is this same?
Christ Jesus is his name,
The Lord Zebaoth's Son,
He and no other one
Shall conquer in the battle.

And were this world all Devils o'er,
And watching to devour us,   20
We lay it not to heart so sore,
Not they can overpower us.
And let the Prince of Ill
Look grim as e'er he will,
He harms us not a whit:
For why? His doom is writ,
A word shall quickly slay him.

God's Word, for all their craft and force,
One moment will not linger,
But spite of Hell, shall have its course,   30
'Tis written by his finger.
And though they take our life,
Goods, honour, children, wife,
Yet is their profit small;
These things shall vanish all,
The City of God remaineth.

Fraser's Magazine, no. 12 (1831). Essays, Critical and Miscellaneous, 7 vols.
Collected and Republished (1839–69), vol. III (Chapman & Hall, 1872), 61–4.

CLOTHES FOR THOUGHTS & THOUGHTS ON CLOTHES

Prospective

The Philosophy of Clothes is now to all readers, as we predicted it would do, unfolding itself into new boundless expansions, of a cloudcapt, almost chimerical aspect, yet not without azure loomings in the far distance, and streaks as of an Elysian brightness; the highly questionable purport and promise of which it is becoming more and more important for us to ascertain. Is that a real Elysian brightness, cries many a timid wayfarer, or the reflex of Pandemonian lava? Is it of a truth leading us into beatific Asphodel meadows, or the yellow-burning marl of a Hell-on-Earth?

Our Professor, like other Mystics, whether delirious or inspired, gives an Editor enough to do. Ever higher and dizzier are the heights he leads us to; more piercing, all-comprehending, all-confounding are his views and glances. For example, this of Nature being not an Aggregate but a Whole:

'Well sang the Hebrew Psalmist: "If I take the wings of the morning and dwell in the uttermost parts of the universe, God is there."[1] Thou too, O cultivated reader, who too probably art no Psalmist, but a Prosaist, knowing GOD only by tradition, knowest thou any corner of the world where at least FORCE is not? The drop which thou shakest from thy wet hand, rests not where it falls, but to-morrow thou findest it swept away; already, on the wings of the Northwind, it is nearing the Tropic of Cancer. How came it to evaporate, and not lie motionless? Thinkest thou there is aught motionless; without Force, and utterly dead?

'As I rode through the Schwarzwald, I said to myself; That little fire which glows star-like across the dark-growing (*nachtende*) moor, where the sooty smith bends over his anvil, and thou hopest to replace thy lost horse-shoe, – is it a detached, separated speck, cut off from the whole universe; or indissolubly joined to the whole? Thou fool, that smithy-fire was (primarily) kindled at the Sun; is fed by air that circulates from before Noah's Deluge, from beyond the Dogstar; therein, with Iron Force, and Coal Force, and the far stronger Force of Man, are cunning affinities and battles and victories of Force brought about: it is a little ganglion, or nervous centre, in the great vital system of Immensity. Call it, if thou wilt, an unconscious Altar, kindled on the bosom of the All; whose iron sacrifice, whose iron smoke and influence reach quite through the All; whose Dingy Priest, not by word, yet by brain and sinew, preaches forth the mystery of Force; nay preaches forth (exoterically enough) one little textlet from the Gospel of Freedom, the Gospel of Man's Force, commanding, and one day to be all-commanding.

'Detached, separated! I say there is no such separation: nothing hitherto was ever stranded, cast aside; but all, were it only a withered leaf, works together with all; is borne forward on the bottomless, shoreless flood of Action, and lives through perpetual metamorphoses. The withered leaf is not dead and lost, there are Forces in it and around it, though working in inverse order; else how could it *rot*? Despise not the rag from which man makes Paper, or the litter from which the Earth makes Corn. Rightly viewed no meanest object is insignificant; all objects are as windows, through which the philosophic eye looks into Infinitude itself.'

Again, leaving that wondrous Schwarzwald Smithy-Altar, what vacant, high-sailing air-ships are these, and whither will they sail with us?

'All visible things are Emblems; what thou seest is not there on its own account; strictly taken, is not there at all: Matter exists only spiritually, and to represent some Idea, and *body* it forth. Hence Clothes, as despicable as we think them, are so unspeakably significant. Clothes, from the King's-mantle downwards, are Emblematic, not of want only, but of a manifold cunning Victory over Want. On the other hand, all Emblematic things are properly Clothes, thought-woven or hand-woven: must not the Imagination weave Garments, visible Bodies, wherein the else invisible creations and inspirations of our Reason are, like Spirits, revealed, and first become all-powerful; – the rather if, as we often see, the Hand too aid her, and (by wool Clothes or otherwise) reveal such even to the outward eye?

'Men are properly said to be clothed with Authority, clothed with Beauty, with Curses, and the like. Nay, if you consider it, what is Man himself, and his whole terrestrial Life, but an Emblem; a Clothing or visible Garment for that divine ME of his, cast hither, like a light-particle, down from Heaven? Thus is he said also to be clothed with a Body.

'Language is called the Garment of Thought: however, it should rather be, Language is the Flesh-Garment, the Body, of Thought. I said that Imagination wove this Flesh-Garment; and does she not? Metaphors are her stuff: examine Language; what, if you except some few primitive elements (of natural sound), what is it all but Metaphors, recognised as such, or no longer recognised; still fluid and florid, or now solid-grown and colourless? If those same primitive elements are the osseous fixtures in the Flesh-garment, Language, – then are Metaphors its muscles and tissues and living integuments. An unmetaphorical style you shall in vain seek for: is not your very *Attention* a *Stretching-to?*[2] The difference lies here: some styles are lean, adust, wiry, the muscle itself seems osseous; some are even quite pallid, hunger-bitten, and dead-looking; while others again glow in the flush of health and vigorous self-growth, sometimes (as in my own case) not without an apoplectic tendency. Moreover, there are sham Metaphors, which overhanging that same Thought's-Body (best naked), and deceptively bedizening, or bolstering it out, may be called its false stuffings, superfluous show-cloaks (*Putz-Mäntel*), and tawdry woollen rags: whereof he that runs and reads may gather whole hampers, – and burn them.'

Than which paragraph on Metaphors did the reader ever chance to see a more surprisingly metaphorical? However, that is not our chief grievance; the Professor continues:

'Why multiply instances? It is written the Heavens and the Earth shall fade away like a Vesture; which indeed they are: the Time-vesture of the Eternal. Whatsoever sensibly exists, whatsoever represents Spirit to Spirit, is properly a Clothing, a suit of Raiment, put on for a season, and to be laid off. Thus in this one pregnant subject of CLOTHES, rightly understood, is included all that men have thought, dreamed, done, and been: the whole external Universe and what it holds is but Clothing; and the essence of all Science lies in the PHILOSOPHY OF CLOTHES.'

Towards these dim infinitely-expanded regions, close-bordering on the impalpable Inane, it is not without apprehension, and perpetual difficulties, that the Editor sees himself journeying and struggling. Till lately a cheerful daystar of hope hung before him, in the expected Aid of Hofrath Heuschrecke; which daystar, however, melts now, not into the red of morning, but into a vague, gray, half-light, uncertain whether dawn of day or dusk of utter darkness. For the last week, these so-called Biographical Documents are in his hand. By the kindness of a Scottish Hamburgh Merchant, whose name, known to the whole mercantile world, he must not mention; but whose honourable courtesy, now and often before spontaneously manifested to him, a mere literary stranger, he cannot soon forget, – the bulky Weissnichtwo Packet, with all its Customhouse seals, foreign hieroglyphs, and miscellaneous tokens of Travel, arrived here in perfect safety, and free of cost. The reader shall now fancy with what hot haste it was broken up, with what breathless expectation glanced over; and, alas, with what unquiet disappointment it has, since then, been often thrown down, and again taken up.

Hofrath Heuschrecke, in a too long-winded Letter, full of compliments, Weissnichtwo politics, dinners, dining repartees, and other ephemeral trivialities, proceeds to remind us of what we knew well already: that however it may be with Metaphysics, and other abstract Science originating in the Head (*Verstand*) alone, no Life-Philosophy (*Lebensphilosophie*), such as this of Clothes pretends to be, which originates equally in the Character (*Gemüth*), and equally speaks thereto, can attain its significance till the Character itself is known and seen; 'till the Author's View of the World (*Weltansicht*), and how he actively and passively came by such view, are clear: in short, till a Biography of him has been philosophico-poetically written, and philosophico-poetically read.' 'Nay,' adds he, 'were the speculative scientific Truth even known, you still, in this inquiring age, ask yourself, Whence

---

2   *Attention* from Latin *attendere*, to stretch towards.

came it, and Why, and How? – and rest not, till, if no better may be, Fancy have shaped out an answer; and, either in the authentic lineaments of Fact, or the forged ones of Fiction, a complete picture and Genetical History of the Man and his spiritual Endeavour lies before you. But why,' says the Hofrath, and indeed say we, 'do I dilate on the uses of our Teufelsdröckh's Biography? The great Herr Minister von Goethe has penetratingly remarked that "Man is properly the *only* object that interests man:"[3] thus I too have noted, that in Weissnichtwo our whole conversation is little or nothing else but Biography or Autobiography; ever humano-anecdotical (*menschlich-anek-dotisch*). Biography is by nature the most universally profitable, universally pleasant of all things: especially Biography of distinguished individuals.

'By this time, *mein Verehrtester* (my Most Esteemed),' continues he, with an eloquence which, unless the words be purloined from Teufelsdröckh, or some trick of his, as we suspect, is well-nigh unaccountable, 'by this time, you are fairly plunged (*vertieft*) in that mighty forest of Clothes-Philosophy; and looking round, as all readers do, with astonishment enough. Such portions and passages as you have already mastered, and brought to paper, could not but awaken a strange curiosity touching the mind they issued from; the perhaps unparalleled psychical mechanism, which manufactured such matter, and emitted it to the light of day. Had Teufelsdröckh also a father and mother; did he, at one time, wear drivel-bibs, and live on spoon-meat? Did he ever, in rapture and tears, clasp a friend's bosom to his; looks he also wistfully into the long burial-aisle of the Past, where only winds, and their low harsh moan, give inarticulate answer? Has he fought duels; – good Heaven! how did he comport himself when in Love? By what singular stair-steps, in short, and subterranean passages, and sloughs of Despair, and steep Pisgah hills, has he reached this wonderful prophetic Hebron (a true Old-Clothes Jewry)[4] where he now dwells?

'To all these natural questions the voice of public History is as yet silent. Certain only that he has been, and is, a Pilgrim, and Traveller from a far Country; more or less footsore and travel-soiled; has parted with road-companions; fallen among thieves, been poisoned by bad cookery, blistered with bugbites; nevertheless, at every stage (for they have let him pass), has had the Bill to discharge. But the whole particulars of his Route, his Weather-observations, the picturesque Sketches he took, though all regularly jotted down (in indelible sympathetic-ink[5] by an invisible interior Penman), are these nowhere forthcoming? Perhaps quite lost: one other leaf of that mighty Volume (of human Memory) left to fly abroad, unprinted, unpublished, unbound up, as waste paper; and rot, the sport of rainy winds?

'No, *verehrtester Herr Herausgeber*,[6] in no wise! I here, by the unexampled favour you stand in with our Sage, send not a Biography only, but an Autobiography: at least the materials for such; wherefrom, if I misreckon not, your perspicacity will draw fullest insight; and so the whole Philosophy and Philosopher of Clothes stand clear to the wondering eyes of England; nay thence, through America, through Hindostan, and the antipodal New Holland, finally conquer (*einnehmen*) great part of this terrestrial Planet!'

And now let the sympathising reader judge of our feeling when, in place of this same Autobiography with 'fullest insight,' we find – Six considerable PAPER-BAGS, carefully sealed, and marked successively, in gilt China-ink, with the symbols of the Six southern Zodiacal Signs, beginning at Libra; in the inside of which sealed Bags, lie miscellaneous masses of Sheets, and oftener Shreds and Snips, written in Professor Teufelsdröckh's scarce-legible *cursiv-schrift*,[7] and treating of all imaginable things under the Zodiac and above it, but of his own personal history only at rare intervals, and then in the most enigmatic manner!

Whole fascicles there are, wherein the Professor, or, as he here speaking in the third person calls himself, 'the Wanderer,' is not once named. Then again amidst what seems to be a Metaphysico-theological Disquisition, 'Detached Thoughts on the Steam-engine,' or 'The continued Possibility

---

3 In *Wilhelm Meister* (1795–6), II. iv.

4 Slough of Despond (in Bunyan's *The Pilgrim's Progress*); Pisgah (mountain from which Moses viewed Promised Land he could not enter); Hebron (where, for instance, David was king); Old Jewry (London street, once a ghetto).

5 invisible ink (becomes visible when paper is warmed).

6 'most honoured Mr Editor.'

7 joined-up handwriting.

of Prophecy,' we shall meet with some quite private, not unimportant Biographical fact. On certain sheets stand Dreams, authentic or not, while the circumjacent waking Actions are omitted. Anecdotes, oftenest without date of place or time, fly loosely on separate slips, like Sibylline leaves.[8] Interspersed also are long purely Autobiographical delineations, yet without connexion, without recognisable coherence; so unimportant, so superfluously minute, they almost remind us of 'P. P. Clerk of this Parish.'[9] Thus does famine of intelligence alternate with waste. Selection, order appears to be unknown to the Professor. In all Bags the same imbroglio; only perhaps in the Bag *Capricorn*, and those near it, the confusion a little worse confounded. Close by a rather eloquent Oration 'On receiving the Doctor's-Hat,' lie washbills marked *bezahlt* (settled). His Travels are indicated by the Street-Advertisements of the various cities he has visited; of which Street-Advertisements, in most living tongues, here is perhaps the completest collection extant.

So that if the Clothes Volume itself was too like a Chaos, we have now instead of the solar Luminary that should still it, the airy Limbo which by intermixture will farther volatilise and discompose it! As we shall perhaps see it our duty ultimately to deposit these Six Paper Bags in the British Museum, farther description, and all vituperation of them, may be spared. Biography or Autobiography of Teufelsdröckh there is, clearly enough, none to be gleaned here: at most some sketchy, shadowy, fugitive likeness of him may, by unheard-of efforts, partly of intellect partly of imagination, on the side of Editor and of Reader, rise up between them. Only as a gaseous-chaotic Appendix to that aqueous-chaotic Volume can the contents of the Six Bags hover round us, and portions thereof be incorporated with our delineation of it.

Daily and nightly does the Editor sit (with green spectacles) deciphering these unimaginable Documents from their perplexed *cursiv-schrift*; collating them with the almost equally unimaginable Volume, which stands in legible print. Over such a universal medley of high and low, of hot, cold, moist and dry, is he here struggling (by union of like with like, which is Method) to build a firm Bridge for British travellers. Never perhaps since our first Bridge-builders, Sin and Death, built that stupendous Arch from Hell-gate to the Earth, did any Pontifex, or Pontiff, undertake such a task as the present Editor. For in this Arch too, leading as we humbly presume, far otherwards than that grand primeval one, the materials are to be fished up from the weltering deep, and down from the simmering air, here one mass, there another, and cunningly cemented, while the elements boil beneath: nor is there any supernatural force to do it with; but simply the Diligence and feeble thinking Faculty of an English Editor, endeavouring to evolve printed Creation out of a German printed and written Chaos, wherein, as he shoots to and fro in it, gathering clutching, piecing the Why to the far-distant Wherefore, his whole Faculty and Self are like to be swallowed up.

Patiently, under these incessant toils and agitations, does the Editor, dismissing all anger, see his otherwise robust health declining; some fraction of his allotted natural sleep nightly leaving him, and little but an inflamed nervous-system to be looked for. What is the use of Health, or of Life, if not to do some work therewith? And what work nobler than transplanting foreign Thought into the barren domestic soil; except indeed planting Thought of your own, which the fewest are privileged to do? Wild as it looks, this Philosophy of Clothes, can we ever reach its real meaning, promises to reveal new-coming Eras, the first dim rudiments and already-budding germs of a nobler Era, in Universal History. Is not such a prize worth some striving? Forward with us, courageous reader; be it towards failure, or towards success! The latter thou sharest with us, the former also is not all our own.

Old Clothes

As mentioned above, Teufelsdröckh, though a Sansculottist,[10] is in practice probably the politest man extant: his whole heart and life are penetrated and informed with the spirit of Politeness; a

---

8   In Virgil's *Aeneid*, the Sibyl of Cumae reads off prophecies from leaves blown about by inspiriting wind.

9   Parodic memoir by Alexander Pope and John Gay, *Memoirs of P. P. Clerk of this Parish* (1728).

10   (French) revolutionary.

noble natural Courtesy shines through him, beautifying his vagaries; like sun-light, making a rosy-fingered, rainbow-dyed Aurora out of mere aqueous clouds; nay, brightening London smoke itself into gold vapour, as from the crucible of an alchemist. Hear in what earnest though fantastic wise he expresses himself on this head:

'Shall Courtesy be done only to the rich, and only by the rich? In Good-breeding, which differs, if at all, from High-breeding, only as it gracefully remembers the rights of others, rather than gracefully insists on its own rights, I discern no special connexion with wealth or birth: but rather that it lies in human nature itself, and is due from all men towards all men. Of a truth, were your School-master at his post, and worth any thing when there, this, with so much else, would be reformed. Nay, each man were then also his neighbour's schoolmaster; till at length a rude-visaged, unmannered Peasant, could no more be met with than a Peasant unacquainted with botanical Physiology, or who felt not that the clod he broke was created in Heaven.

'For whether thou bear a sceptre or a sledge-hammer, art thou not ALIVE is not this thy brother ALIVE? "There is but one Temple in the world," says Novalis, "and that Temple is the Body of Man. Nothing is holier than this high Form. Bending before men is a reverence done to this Revelation in the Flesh. We touch Heaven, when we lay our hands on a human Body."

'On which ground, I would fain carry it farther than most do; and whereas the English Johnson only bowed to every Clergyman, or man with a shovel-hat, I would bow to every Man with any sort of hat, or with no hat whatever. Is he not a Temple, then; the visible Manifestation and Impersonation of the Divinity? And yet, alas, such indiscriminate bowing serves not. For there is a Devil dwells in man, as well as a Divinity; and too often the bow is but pocketed by the *former*. It would go to the pocket of Vanity (which is your clearest phasis of the Devil, in these times); therefore must we withhold it.

'The gladder am I, on the other hand, to do reverence to those Shells and outer Husks of the Body, wherein no devilish passion any longer lodges, but only the pure emblem and effigies of Man: I mean, to Empty, or even to Cast Clothes. Nay, is it not to Clothes that most men do reverence; to the fine frogged broad-cloth, nowise to the "straddling animal with bandy legs" which it holds, and makes a Dignitary of? Who ever saw any Lord my-lorded in tattered blanket, fastened with wooden skewer? Nevertheless, I say, there is in such worship a shade of hypocrisy, a practical deception: for how often does the Body appropriate what was meant for the Cloth only! Whoso would avoid Falsehood, which is the essence of all Sin, will perhaps see good to take a different course. That reverence which cannot act without obstruction and perversion when the Clothes are full, may have free course when they are empty. Even as, for Hindoo Worshippers, the Pagoda is not less sacred than the God; so do I too worship the hollow cloth Garment with equal fervour, as when it contained the Man: nay, with more, for I now fear no deception, of myself or of others.

'Did not King *Toomtabard*, or, in other words, John Balliol, reign long over Scotland; the man John Balliol being quite gone, and only the "Toom Tabard" (Empty Gown) remaining? What still dignity dwells in a suit of Cast Clothes! How meekly it bears its honours! No haughty looks, no scornful gesture; silent and serene, it fronts the world; neither demanding worship, nor afraid to miss it. The Hat still carries the physiognomy of its Head: but the vanity and the stupidity, and goose-speech which was the sign of these two, are gone. The Coat-arm is stretched out, but not to strike; the Breeches, in modest simplicity, depend at ease, and now at last have a graceful flow; the Waistcoat hides no evil passion, no riotous desire; hunger or thirst now dwells not in it. Thus all is purged from the grossness of Sense, from the carking Cares and foul Vices of the World; and rides there, on its Clothes-horse; as, on a Pegasus, might some skyey Messenger, or purified Apparition, visiting our low Earth.

'Often, while I sojourned in that monstrous Tuberosity of Civilised Life, the Capital of England; and meditated, and questioned Destiny, under that ink-sea of vapour, black, thick, and multifarious as Spartan broth;[11] and was one lone Soul amid those grinding millions; – often have I turned into their Old-Clothes Market to worship. With awe-struck heart I walk through that Monmouth Street, with its empty Suits, as through a Sanhedrim of stainless Ghosts. Silent are they, but expressive in their silence: the past witnesses and instruments of Woe and Joy, of Passions, Virtues, Crimes, and all the fathomless tumult of Good and Evil in "the Prison called Life." Friends! trust not the heart of that man for whom Old Clothes are not venerable. Watch too, with reverence, that bearded Jewish Highpriest, who with hoarse voice, like some Angel of Doom, summons them from the four winds! On his head, like the Pope, he has three Hats, – a real triple tiara; on either hand, are the similitude of Wings, whereon the summoned Garments come to alight; and ever, as he slowly cleaves the air, sounds forth his deep fateful note, as if through a trumpet he were proclaiming: "Ghosts of Life, come to Judgment!" Reck not, ye fluttering Ghosts: he will purify you in his Purgatory, with fire and with water; and, one day, new-created ye shall reappear. Oh! let him in whom the flame of Devotion is ready to go out, who has never worshipped, and knows not what to worship, pace and repace, with austerest thought, the pavement of Monmouth Street,[12] and say whether his heart and his eyes still continue dry. If Field Lane,[13] with its long fluttering rows of yellow handkerchiefs, be a Dionysius' Ear,[14] where, in stifled jarring hubbub, we hear the Indictment which Poverty and Vice bring against lazy Wealth, that it has left them there cast out and trodden under foot of Want, Darkness, and the Devil, – then is Monmouth Street a Mirza's Hill,[15] where, in motley vision, the whole Pageant of Existence passes awfully before us; with its wail and jubilee, mad loves and mad hatreds, church-bells and gallows-ropes, farce-tragedy, beast-godhood, – the Bedlam of Creation!'

To most men, as it does to ourselves, all this will seem overcharged. We too have walked through Monmouth Street; but with little feeling of 'Devotion:' probably in part because the contemplative process is so fatally broken in upon by the brood of money-changers, who nestle in that Church, and importune the worshipper with merely secular proposals. Whereas Teufelsdröckh might be in that happy middle-state, which leaves to the Clothes-broker no hope either of sale or of purchase, and so be allowed to linger there without molestation. – Something we would have given to see the little philosophical Figure, with its steeple-hat and loose-flowing skirts, and eyes in a fine frenzy, 'pacing and repacing in austerest thought' that foolish Street; which to him was a true Delphic avenue, and supernatural Whispering-gallery,[16] where the 'Ghosts of Life' rounded strange secrets in his ear. O thou philosophic Teufelsdröckh, that listenest while others only gabble, and with thy quick tympanum hearest the grass grow!

At the same time, is it not strange that, in Paperbag Documents, destined for an English Work, there exists nothing like an authentic diary of this his sojourn in London; and of his Meditations among the Clothes-shops only the obscurest emblematic shadows? Neither, in conversation (for, indeed, he was not a man to pester you with his Travels), have we heard him more than allude to the subject.

For the rest, however, it cannot be uninteresting that we here find how early the significance of Clothes had dawned on the now so distinguished Clothes-Professor. Might we but fancy it to have been even in Monmouth Street, at the bottom of our own English 'ink-sea,' that this remarkable Volume first took being, and shot forth its salient point in his soul, – as in Chaos did the Egg of Eros, one day to be hatched into a Universe!

Sartor Resartus, *Book I, ch. II; Book III, ch. 6* (Fraser's Magazine, *Nov. 1833–August 1834*) (US editions, 1836, 1837; first British edition, 1838). Fraser's Magazine *text.*

12   old clothes centre of London (featured by Dickens in *The Uncommercial Traveller*).

13   'the emporium of petty larceny' (*Oliver Twist*, ch. 26), where Fagin and his boys dispose of their stolen 'wipes'.

14   echo-chamber device by which tyrant of Syracuse overheard what was said in his prison.

15   in Addison's famous 'Vision of Mirza', *Spectator*, 1 Sept. 1711.

16   gallery up in the echoing dome of St Paul's Cathedral.

Mary (Wright) Sewell (1797–1884)

Mary Sewell was born 6 April 1797, the daughter of Quaker parents, John and Anne Wright, in Sutton, Suffolk. Educated mostly at home, though with one year away at school in Tottenham, she had become an avid reader by the age of fifteen, when regular education ceased. For a time she worked as a governess. In 1819 she married Isaac Sewell, a leading Yarmouth Quaker who ended up as a banker in Brighton. Mary Sewell's first writings were for her two children. In 1835 she became an Anglican. She was deeply involved in religious philanthropic work, not least as a member of the Anti-Slavery Association. At the late age of sixty she started seriously to write long sentimental ballads promoting the moral virtues she held dear. Immense success with the public ensued. *Homely Ballads for the Working Man's Fireside* (1858) sold in the scores of thousands. *Mother's Last Words* (1860), about two lads kept on the moral rails by adhering to their dying mother's advice, sold over a million copies. *Our Father's Care* (1861) sold three-quarters of a million. Her crippled daughter Anna Sewell (1820–78) evidently inherited her mother's touch for tear-jerking Christian moralism – she was the author of the phenomenally successful equine autobiography *Black Beauty* (1877), written to protest against the harsh treatment of horses and a kind of foundational text for the work of the characteristically Victorian RSPCA (the Royal Society for the Prevention of Cruelty to Animals). Much of Mary Sewell's writing was done at Wick (between Bristol and Bath). She moved to Old Cotton in Norfolk in 1867, where her husband and daughter predeceased her (both in 1878). She died on 10 June 1884, aged 87, and is buried in the Quaker burial ground at Lama, Norfolk.

The London Attic (Another Story)

Fast fades the year, and Christmas time
    Has travelled round again;
The naked trees are shivering
    Upon the barren plain.

The birds are mute, the bees are still,
    Their pleasant mirth is done;
There's not a fly, to hum or buzz
    Beneath December's sun.

But men and boys are shouting there,
    And beat the bushes round,   10
And huntsmen in their scarlet coats
    Are riding o'er the ground.

And they will ride, and laugh, and shout,
    As long as they can see;
Then hasten home to blazing fires,
    And jovial company.

But we will leave the Christmas sports,
    And all the Christmas fare,
To watch a lady, in a court
    Of London town, so fair.   20

Take care! take care! the place is dark,
    That narrow stair is steep –
And broken, too, and dangerous –
    She'll scarce her footing keep.

But up she goes – she's at the door,
    And trembles now with fear;

She'd better far go back again –
    The dwelling looks so queer.

One cannot tell what people dwell
    In such abodes as these;   30
The worst of thieves, or murderers,
    Might shelter here with ease.

But there she stops – she fears to knock,
    Yet will not go away;
For she has heard the folks will starve
    If left another day.

She stands, and listens for a while –
    The door is just ajar –
And dimly now she can observe
    A boy and woman there.   40

The woman's voice is sweet and low,
    Her face is very pale;
But there's a calm upon her brow,
    That tells a thoughtful tale.

What have they in that dismal place?
    The room looks very bare;
There's something like a wretched bed,
    And children sleeping there.

And what beside? there is no fire;
    And this is Christmas eve!   50
And not a sign of any food.
    That she can yet perceive.

The woman's light is burning low;
  She lays her work aside;
And still keeps talking to the boy,
  Who listens at her side.

'I do not yet despair, my child,
  We've been as low before,
And God has not forgot His way
  Unto the widow's door.   60

'We have no food nor work to do,
  We've neither light nor fire;
But still, my heart says God is true,
  Though man may be a liar.

'I've proved Him oft, through year and year,
  That He will not forsake –
Will not forsake me utterly,
  Though sore my heart may ache.

'He feeds the ravens when they call;
  He clothes the lilies fine;   70
And He has numbered every hair
  Upon your head and mine.

'I say it, James, with sense of sin,
  And yet with humble trust,
That we have tried to do His will,
  And sought His kingdom first.

'I do not claim, as our desert,
  That God should give us bread;
But He has promised that He will,
  And there my faith is stayed.   80

'Your father on the day he died,
  In deep and earnest prayer
Gave up his helpless family
  To God's Almighty care.

'He knew the world was rough and wild,
  And all its ways uneven;
He knew we should have weary feet
  Before we got to heaven.

'His prayer was heard, and heeded too,
  And registered on high: 90
I've always felt that he was heard,
  Through all our poverty.

'What but the grace of God has kept
  Our hands and hearts from sin,
When day and night we've wanted bread,
  And nothing coming in?

'Oh, Jemmy, lad! it was the Lord
  Who kept you in the street
From joining in with wicked boys,
  Or stealing food to eat.   100

'Oh! many a time, and many, child,
  My heart has trembled through,
Lest hunger, and temptation sore,
  Should be too strong for you.

'But you are my sweet comfort, James,
  My good, my honest son!
And we will trust our Father still,
  And say, "Thy will be done."

'I once had hoped on Christmas-day
  That you might have a treat,   110
But now, I fear, the little ones
  Will cry for bread to eat.

'The Lord can send it, if He will;
  We cannot beg or steal;
He knows we've tried in vain for work,
  And now have not a meal.

''Twas on this evening, Jemmy dear!
  Our Saviour came to earth;
A lowly manger was His bed,
  And poor men hailed His birth.   120

'And now He'll not forget the poor,
  In poverty's dark hour;
He died to save us from our sins,
  And lives to give us power.

''Tis hard, I know, 'tis very hard,
  To bear these things in mind,
When all the world, and every thing,
  Looks hopeless and unkind.

'But 'tis in worst extremity,
  The Saviour draweth nigh;   130
We'll tell Him, once again, my child,
  Of all our poverty.'

She knelt beside the flickering light,
  Upon that naked floor,
And lifted up her voice to God,
  His mercy to implore.

And angels bowed their heads to hear –
  It was a solemn sight
To see those lonely pleaders there,
  In that dark attic height, –   140

Speaking to Him who guides the stars,
  Who makes the welkin ring,
And 'taketh up the islands
  As a very little thing;'

Pleading with Him as children plead
  Who know their parent's heart –
Not with a wordy eloquence,
  Nor speeches framed with art;

But in a language clear and full,
    And simple and sincere,   150
As if they knew that every word
    Would reach their Father's ear.

And thankful praise ascended, too,
    For mercies even then;
And Jemmy, with his youthful voice,
    Responded his 'Amen.'

And when they both had risen up
    From off that hallowed floor,

The lady, with a swelling heart,
    Tapped gently at the door.   160

We need not tell what then befel,
    But this can truly say,
That theirs was not an empty board
    Upon that Christmas day;

Because the God of Providence
    Is watching everywhere,
And sending forth His ministers
    To answer faithful prayer.

Poems and Ballads, 2 vols (Jarrold & Sons, 1886), II.

James Henry (1798–1876)

James Henry, eminent Virgil scholar, medical doctor, wonderfully cranky, witty, scathing versifier, was born into the Protestant Ascendancy in Dublin, 13 September 1798, eldest son of a woollen-draper, Robert Henry, and his wife Kathleen Olivia Elder. His religious scepticism was fuelled early on by Unitarian schoolmasters. He fell in love with Virgil as a child, and from the age of eleven formed the habit of carrying a copy of the *Aeneid* in his left breast-pocket (over the heart, of course). At Trinity College, Dublin, he was a Classical scholar, and graduated in 1819 with the Gold Medal for Classics (Oscar Wilde was a later winner). He turned to medicine, at which he was a great success too. He completed an MD thesis on malaria fever (1832), and became Vice-President of the Royal College of Physicians in Ireland. A satirical bent – his satirical pamphlets, modelled on Swift's, lampooning everything from temperance campaigns to medical practice – combined attractively with a kind of eccentric humanity (he refused to charge the standard one-guinea fee – no doctor being worth more than five shillings, he said). In 1826 he married Anne Jane Patton from an Evangelical Donegal family, and they had three daughters – only the last one, Katharine Olivia, born 20 November 1830, surviving infancy. Henry's Virgilian studies began in earnest with the discovery of serious textual and hermeneutical problems when he set out to translate the *Aeneid*. He came into an inheritance around 1845, and gave up his medical practice for his lifelong career of eccentrically criss-crossing Europe on foot, with his womenfolk in tow, visiting Virgilian sites and collating manuscripts of the *Aeneid* in university libraries. He was drawn again and again to Dresden – with its great classical library – and many of his books were published there, including his *Notes of a Twelve Years' Voyage of Discovery in the First Six Books of the Eneis* (1853), his main volumes of verses, *A Half Year's Poems* (1854) and *Poems Chiefly Philosophical* (1856), *Thalia Petasata: a Foot Journey from Carlsruhe to Bassano* (1859), as well as the *Menippea* – satires which include rewrites of Genesis – and *Poematia* (both 1866). Most of his writings were privately printed. Early in 1849 Henry's wife died unexpectedly in the Austrian Tirol, but he and his daughter Katharine carried on their immense scholarly – and pedestrian – labours. This included crossing the Alps on foot about seventeen times. Katharine became a considerable Virgil expert in her own right, her father's indispensable right-hand assistant, as he kept acknowledging. She died, of what sounds like stomach cancer, 11 December 1872. Deeply cast down, her father did not long survive her. He died in Dublin, 14 July 1876. The first volume of the great *Aeneidea* father and daughter had laboured on so long was published in London in 1873; the three subsequent parts appeared posthumously in Dublin, 1877–9.

'Album mutor in alitem.' [1]

The Roman Lyrist's soul, 'tis said,
Oút of his body when it fled,
Entered the body of a swan,
And thére continued to sing ón.

'THE ROMAN LYRIST'S SOUL, 'TIS SAID'

1   'I am changed into a white bird', Horace, *Odes*, II. xx. 10.

But whén the bard of Ambleside,[2]
Fóllowing the example, died,
Hís spirit – never of much use –
Éntered the body of a goose,
And, faithful to its ancient knack,
Kept gabbling ever, gak gak gak.   10

Composed during the night in bed, Trompeter-Schlösschen, Dresden, Febr. 18–19, 1854

A Half Year's Poems *(C. C. Meinhold & Sons, Dresden, 1854).*

Odds bóbs, brother Tom, do you knów, by the Pówers,
It's a míghty fine wórld this, this fine world of ours,
With its rolicking, frolicking, eating and drinking;
The ónly one bád thing I knów in it's thinking.

He's a jolly old fellow, that round red-faced Sun,
That so knowingly loóks down all day on our fun.
As cantering, cápering, on we go hopping
From one spreé to another without ever stopping;

And though Mistress Moon's whéy-faced and modest and shy,
Yet she's wélcome for áll that, when nobody's by,   10
To peép through the branches where under a tree
My árm's round my doxy and hér arm's round me.

Yet fine as this wórld is, and we áll know it's fine,
'Twere a poór drimly drúmly world, sure, without wine;
So to pále water-drinkers let's leáve cares and pains,
And with lífe's true elixir replenish our veins.

We'll drink eách to the other and health to his lass;
Tom, sénd round the bottle and fill up your glass;
Let Jóve keep his Nectar, so we have the vine –
Anóther dozen, fellow – it's cápital wine.   20

God bléss Queen, lords, commons, and country, and town;
God keép our friends úp and our enemies down;
And may Brítons live happy and mighty and free,
As lóng as Great Britain's shore's wáshed by the sea.

Trompeter-Schlösschen, Dresden, March 28, 1854

A Half Year's Poems *(Dresden, 1854).*

I am a versemaker by trade
And vérses of all kinds have made,
Bád ones to win me fame and pelf,
And goód ones to amuse myself.
Of várious humor grave and gay
I póetise the livelong day
And sómetimes sit up half the night
Some flúent nonsense to indite
Aboút an élephant or a fly,
Or Ánnabel's bewitching eye,   10
Aboút past, present, or to come,
Aboút America, Carthage, Rome,

Aboút high, lów, or great, or small,
Or máybe ábout nóthing at all.
I wish you saw me when I write
Vérses for mine own delight;
I cán't sit still, I jump about
Úp and dówn stairs, in and out;
My cheéks grow red, my eyes grow bright,
You'd sweár I'd lost my senses quite.   20
But when I'm set a verse to spin
That shall be sure applause to win,
Lórd, but it is an altered case!
I woúldn't my foé see in my place;

2 Wordsworth.

n vaín my locks I twirl and pull,
And bíte my nails, and thúmp my skull,
My spírit's ebbed, my wit's at null;
Gods, but it's hárd work to write dull!
Thrice-gifted Wordsworth – happy bard
To whóm that task was never hard! –   30
Teách me the árt intó my Muse
Not 'géntle pity' to infuse,
Or feár or hópe or jealousy,
Or sweét love or philosophy
And reáson strong and manly sense,
But páltry cunning, sleek pretence,
And hów to give no vice offence,
That sits installed in station high
And míxes with good company;
In áll, sufficient skill to cook   40
Some fiddle faddle, pious book
On dráwing-room table fit to lie
And cátch the idle visitor's eye

And hélp the aúthor ón to fame
And pénsion and a poet's name.
Don't ásk me can I nothing find
More fitting to employ my mind
And whíle away my idle time
Than 'strínging blethers up in rhyme'
For yoú and other fools to sing,   50
For I'm as happy as a king:
My tróchees are my diamond crown,
My ánapests my purple gown,
My pén's my sceptre, my inkstánd
Sérves me for révenues and land,
And as for súbjects – every thing
In heáven and eárth owns mé for king;
So mány háve I that I choose,
And táke the good, the bad refuse;
In the whole wórld, I'd like to know,
Where's th' óther king that can do so?

Walking from Beuern to Weingarten (Baden), Octob. 14–15, 1854

Poems Chiefly Philosophical *(C. C. Meinhold & Sons, Dresden, 1856)*.

'Two hundred men and eighteen killed
   For want of a second door!
Ay, for with two doors, each ton coal
   Had cost one penny more.

And what is it else makes England great,
   At home, by land, by sea,
But her cheap coal, and eye's tail turned
   Toward strict economy?

But if a slate falls off the roof
   And kills a passer-by,   10
Or if a doctor's dose too strong
   Makes some half-dead man die,

We have coroners and deodands[2]
   And inquests, to no end,
And every honest Englishman's
   The hapless sufferer's friend,

And householder's or doctor's foe,
   For he has nought to lose,
And fain will, if he can, keep out
   Of that poor dead man's shoes.   20

But if of twice a hundred men,
   And eighteen more, the breath
Is stopped at once in a coal pit,
   It's quite a natural death;

For, God be praised! the chance is small
   That either you or I
Should come, for want of a second door,
   In a coal pit to die.

Besides, 'twould cost a thousand times
   As much, or something more,   30
To make to every pit of coal
   A second, or safety door,

As all the shrouds and coffins cost
   For those who perish now
For want of a second door, and that's
   No trifle, you'll allow;

And trade must live, though now and then
   A man or two may die;
So merry sing 'God bless the Queen,'
   And long live you and I;   40

'TWO HUNDRED MEN AND EIGHTEEN KILLED'
1 At ten o'clock on the morning of Thursday, January 16, 1862, the great iron beam of the steam-engine which worked the pumps of the Hester coal pit near Hartley in Northumberland, snapped across, and a portion of the beam, 40 tons in weight, fell into the shaft, tearing away the boarded lining so that the earthy sides collapsed and fell in, filling up the shaft in such a manner as not only to cut off all communication between the interior of the pit and the outer world, but entirely to obstruct all passage of pure air into, and of foul air out of, the pit. All the persons who were at work below at the time, two hundred and eighteen in number, were of course suffocated, nor was it until the seventh day after the accident that access could be had to the interior of the pit, or anything, beyond the mere fact of their entombment, ascertained concerning the helpless and unfortunate victims of that 'auri sacra fames' which so generally, so heartlessly, so pertinaciously refuses the poor workers in the coal mines of England, even the sad resource of a second staple or air shaft. See the Illustrated London News of Jan. 25, and Febr. 1, 1862. [Author's note]
2 forfeits to the Crown, on grounds of having caused death.

And, Jenny, let each widow have
   A cup of congo[3] strong,
And every orphan half a cup,
   And so I end my song,

With prayer to God to keep coal cheap,
   Both cheap and plenty too,
And if the pit's a whole mile deep,
   What is it to me or you?

For though we're mortal too, no doubt,
   And Death for us his sithe   50
Has ready still, the chance is small
   We ever die of stithe.[4]

And if we do, our gracious Queen
   Will, sure, a telegram send,
To say how sore she grieves for us
   And our untimely end;

And out of her own privy purse
   A sovereign down will pay,
To have us decently interred   6c
   And put out of the way;

And burial service shall for us
   In the churchyard be read,
And more bells rung and more hymns sung
   Than if we had died in bed:

For such an accident as this
   May never occur again,
And till it does, one door's enough
   For pumps, air, coal, and men;

And should it occur – which God forbid! –
   And stifle every soul,   7c
Remember well, good Christians all,
   Not one whit worse the coal.

Casa Cartoni ai Cavalleggieri, Leghorn, 25 February, 1862

Poematia (C. C. Meinhold & Sons, Dresden, 1866).

---

*'Huic monstro Volcanus erat pater; illius atros
Ore vomens ignis, magna se mole ferebat.*

. . . .

*Ille autem. . . . .
Faucibus ingentem fumum, mirabile dictu,
Evomit, involvitque domum caligine caeca,
Prospectum eripiens oculis, glomeratque sub antro
Fumiferam noctem commixtis igne tenebris.
Non tulit Alcides animis."*

I am the pink of courtesy
   As I smoke my cigar,
And whiff and puff, and spit about,
   And near, am smelt, and far.

Yet come not near, sweet ladies dear,
   If you'd not burn your clothes;
See how the sparks fly from the quid
   Sticks out below my nose.

I vow and swear I take all care
   To save your crinolines,   10
But sparks will fly, and fire will burn,
   Were ye all sceptered queens.

The smell is not of violets,
   I never will deny,

And delicate olfactories
   Will dó well to fight shy,

And keep full six yards off from me
   Here in wide open street,
And quick let both the sashes down,
   In steamcoach when we meet.   20

There's not a morning comes, but I
   Take pains to brush away
From coat, necktie and gloves, the stale
   Odour of yesterday;

In spite of all my pains, I own,
   Some hangs about me still,
But, well I know, so good your hearts,
   Ye will not take it ill.

You're bound in love, in duty bound,
   So much from us to bear,   30
The smell of a cigar will not
   Weigh in the scale one hair.

But that we should the same from you
   Take patiently in turn,
And only love you all the more,
   The more our clothes ye burn,

---

3   congo: black China tea.
4   ? suffocation.
'I am the pink of courtesy'
1   *Aeneid* viii, 198ff. 'The father of this monster [Hercules] was Vulcan,
and it was his father's black fire he vomited from his mouth as he
moved his massive bulk...[ ] There was no escape for him [Cacus]
now, but he [Hercules] vomited thick smoke from his monstrous
throat and rolled clouds of it all round his den to blot it from sight.
Deep in his cave he churned out fumes as black as night and the dark-
ness was shot through with fire. Hercules was past all patience.' David
West translation (Penguin, 1991).

The more of yesterday's cigar
   Your silks are redolent,
The more reichsthaler, every year,
   Are in the luxus spent,   40

The more your lips are red and swelled,
   The less your breath is sweet –
That is a creed I never held,
   Since first I strode the street.

A schoolboy rule is tit for tat,
   Not fit for ladies' use,
And that good sauce for gander is
   What góod sauce is for goose.

For though your woman's stomach's made
   Of the same stuff as ours,   50
And thirsts and hungers, every day,
   At the same stated hours,

Yet kindly Nature has on you,
   So much the weaker sex,
Bestowed immunity from qualms
   Which mightiest heroes vex;

And you can keep your spirits up,
   And healthy appetite sound,
Without one whiff of a cigar
   The whole, long twelvemonth round.   60

Favored of heaven, ye know not what
   He bears, the wretched man,
Who, with bare five cigars a day,
   Must put up as he can;

Who has not his Havana fresh,
   To keep him in right tune,
Before and after every meal,
   Morning, and night, and noon;

One to enable him his eyes
   To open to the light,   70
And, when that's done, another one,
   And so on until night;

And one while for the bed he strips,
   And one, when he gets in;
And, if he's restless in the night,
   A little one's no sin,

And with another little one
   Eked out, will keep away

Qualms, which without his nicotine
   Beset him, night and day.   80

How blest your lot, ye little wot,
   Who, if such qualms ye feel,
Have resolution from all eyes
   Your sufferings to conceal.

Angels ye are who not alone
   So well your own griefs bear,
But even for griefs imposed by us
   Some patience have to spare.

We need it all, and count on you –
   Let us not count in vain;   90
Some twelve cigars per day allow,
   And we will not complain;

But, in all due acknowledgment,
   As often as we meet,
Whether on hórseback or on foot,
   In park or open street,

Out of our mouths will take cigar
   Till you have clear passed by,
Showing, alike, respect for you,
   And magnanimity;   100

And he who can't so long abstain,
   Or will not, if he can,
It's not enough to call him rude,
   He is not even a man.

But I, who can and will – I am
   Of courtesy the star,
And, to each lady passing by,
   I lower my cigar,

In sign how much I honor her,
   How little for self care,   110
What sore privation for her sake
   I'm ready still to bear.

Deservedly is Bacchus praised,
   Well earned Gambrinus' fame,
But I revere and honor more
   Jean Nicot's glorious name.[2]

Hurrah, then, for Havana mild!
   For Nicot loud hurrah! –
Sir, might I have a little fire?
   I thank you, sir – hurrah!   120

Struvestrasse, Dresden, March 3, 1866

Poematia *(Dresden, 1866).*

2   1530–1600. Introduced tobacco plant into France: named Nicoti-
ana after him.

Mary (Botham) Howitt (1799–1888)

Mary Howitt was born at Coleford, Gloucestershire, 12 March 1799, the daughter of well-off Staffordshire Quakers, Samuel and Anne Botham. Her mother, Anne Wood, was a descendant of the notorious Andrew Wood, the man with the licence to produce Wood's Irish pence, lampooned by Jonathan Swift in *The Drapier's Letters* (1724). Mary was educated at Quaker schools in Croydon, Uttoxeter and Sheffield. Her writing career was intimately bound up with that of her Quaker husband William Howitt, who for a long time ran a chemist's shop in Nottingham. Known jokingly as William and Mary after the onetime King and Queen of England, they (and their periodical *Howitt's Journal*) were at the forefront of progressive causes – against the Corn Laws, enclosures of common land, slavery, vivisection, factory abuses, and in favour of extension of the suffrage and Catholic Emancipation. Mary Howitt contributed poems widely to journals and annuals, edited the *Drawing-Room Scrap Book*, wrote novels, *A Popular History of the United States* (1859), most of *The Literature and Romance of Northern Europe* (1852), was a successful writer of children's books and an important translator from Swedish and Danish (among other things, Hans Christian Andersen's stories and Fredrika Bremer's novels). Elizabeth Barrett Browning praised the 'simplicity and sweetness' of her *Ballads and Other Poems* (1847) in which 'The Barley-Mower's Song' appeared. As a woman of letters, living by her pen, she frequented literary company and was friends with many of the period's writers – Felicia Hemans, Mary Russell Mitford, L.E.L., Leigh Hunt, Tennyson, the Rossettis, as well as Barbara Leigh Smith (later Madame Bodichon) and Bessie Rayner Parkes of the 'Langham Place' group to which Mary Howitt's daughter Anne Mary belonged. She had five children, and several miscarriages, the usual losses and gains of Victorian motherhood – none of which, though, must be let interfere too much with the pressures of earning a living ('Poor dear Claude!...How often did he beg and pray of me to put aside my translation just for that one day, that I might sit by him and talk or read to him? I never thinking how near his end was – said "Oh, no! I must go on yet a page or two"'). Religiously, Mary Howitt drifted from the Quakers to Unitarianism and then in the 1850s went in heavily for Spiritualists, including Daniel Dundas Hume, the religious crook satirized by Robert Browning in 'Mr Sludge, "The Medium"' (1864). In April 1879, upon the death of her husband, she received a Civil List Pension of £100 per annum and moved to the Tirol. In her early eighties, still on the religious move, she converted to Roman Catholicism. She died in Rome, 30 January 1888, but was buried by special dispensation in the Protestant Cemetery there.

THE BARLEY-MOWERS' SONG

Barley-mowers here we stand,
One, two, three, a steady band;
True of heart and strong of limb,
Ready in our harvest-trim;
All arow, with spirits blithe,
Now we whet the bended scythe.
   Rink-a-tink, rink-a-tink, rink-a-tink-a-tink!

Side by side now, bending low,
Down the swaths of barley go;
Stroke by stroke, as true as chime
Of the bells we keep in time:
Then we whet the ringing scythe,
Standing 'mid the barley lithe.
   Rink-a-tink, rink-a-tink, rink-a-tink-a-tink!

After labour cometh ease;
Sitting now beneath the trees,
Round we send the barley-wine,
Life-infusing, clear and fine;

Then refreshed, alert and blithe,
Rise we all, and whet the scythe.   20
   Rink-a-tink, rink-a-tink, rink-a-tink-a-tink!

Barley-mowers must be true,
Keeping still the end in view;
One with all, and all with one,
Working on till set of sun;
Bending all with spirits blithe,
Whetting all at once the scythe.
   Rink-a-tink, rink-a-tink, rink-a-tink-a-tink!

Day and night, and night and day,
Time, the mower, will not stay: 30
We may hear him in our path
By the falling barley-swath;
While we sing with spirits blithe,
We may hear his ringing scythe.
   Rink-a-tink, rink-a-tink, rink-a-tink-a-tink!

Time the mower cuts down all,
High and low, and great and small:
Fear him not, for we will grow
Ready like the field we mow;
Like the bending barley lithe,   40
Ready for Time's whetted scythe.
   Rink-a-tink, rink-a-tink, rink-a-tink-a-tink!

Ballads and Other Poems *(Longman, Brown, Green, 1847).*

Thomas Hood (1799–1845)

Thomas Hood, journalist, humorist and poetic crusader for the poor, was born 23 May 1799 in the Poultry, in the City of London. His father was a bookseller, his mother the sister of an engraver. His health was poor from an early age – causing him to leave the counting-house he entered at the age of thirteen, to abandon an engraving apprenticeship, and to spend many years living abroad, in Coblenz and Ostend, as a convalescent. He turned to journalism in 1821, working as a sub-editor on the *London Magazine* (where he got to know De Quincey, Hazlitt and Charles Lamb), going on variously to edit *The Gem* annual from 1829 (which published early Tennyson among others), the *Comic Annual* (from 1830), the *New Monthly Magazine* (from August 1841) and *Hood's Magazine* (founded in 1844). Hood had poor financial luck, leading to loss of all his assets in 1834, and worse health. A long-time consumptive, he broke down completely just before Christmas 1844, leaving him and his wife pretty destitute. Prime Minister Robert Peel came up with a Civil List Pension of £100, assigned to Mrs Hood because Thomas was not expected to live long. He died, 3 May 1845, in the Finchley Road. Throughout his short life he produced a stream of writing – novelettes, a three-decker novel *Tylney Hall* (1834), and much verse: *Whims and Oddities* on the one hand, as one volume of his prose and verse had it; much more serious writing on the other, including some of the period's most famous and pathos-full poems, in particular 'The Bridge of Sighs' and, of course, 'The Song of the Shirt' (published anonymously in the Christmas number of *Punch*, 1843: it 'wrung many compassionate but ineffectual tears from the daughters of the bourgeoisie', whinged Engels in *The Condition of the Working Class in England in 1844*); and verses playing the serious and the comic notes simultaneously – like the long parodic epic *Miss Kilmansegg and Her Precious Leg*. His *Complete Works* (1882–4) came to eleven volumes. He married Jane Reynolds in 1824. The death of their first child is the subject of Charles Lamb's poem 'On an Infant Dying as soon as Born'. In 1854, as a direct consequence of Eliza Cook's lamenting in her 'Poor Hood' that there was no public monument, one was erected to him by public subscription in Kensal Green Cemetery, with bas-reliefs depicting scenes from his works, including 'The Bridge of Sighs', and inscribed 'He sang the Song of the Shirt'.

A DROP OF GIN

Gin! Gin! a drop of Gin!
What magnified monsters circle therein!
   Ragged, and stained with filth and mud,
   Some plague-spotted, and some with blood!
Shapes of misery, shame, and sin!
   Figures that make us loathe and tremble,
   Creatures scarce human that more resemble
Broods of diabolical kin,
Ghost and vampyre, demon and Jin![1]

Gin! Gin! a drop of Gin!   10
The dram of Satan! the liquor of sin! –
   Distilled from the fell
   Alembics of hell,
By Guilt and Death, – his own brother and twin! –
   That man might fall
   Still lower than all
The meanest creatures with scale and fin.
But, hold; – we are neither Barebones nor Prynne,[2]
   Who lashed with such rage   20
   The sins of the age;
Then, instead of making too much of a din,
   Let Anger be mute,
   And sweet Mercy dilute,
With a drop of pity, the drop of Gin!

Gin! Gin! a drop of Gin! –
When, darkly, Adversity's day's set in,
   And the friends and peers
   Of earlier years
Prove warm without, but cold within,   30
   And cannot retrace
   A familiar face
That's steeped in poverty up to the chin;
But snub, neglect, cold-shoulder, and cut
The ragged pauper, misfortune's butt;
Hardly acknowledged by kith and kin,
   Because, poor rat!
   He has no cravat,
A seedy coat, and a hole in that! –
No sole to his shoe, and no brim to his hat;
Nor a change of linen – except his skin;   40
   No gloves, no vest,
   Either second or best;
And, what is worse than all the rest,
No light heart, though his trousers are thin –
   While time elopes
   With all golden hopes,
And even with those of pewter and tin;
   The brightest dreams,
   And the best of schemes,

A DROP OF GIN
1 djinn: genies, often evil; in bottles or other magic containers, waiting to be released.

2 Praise-God Barebones, who gave name to Cromwell's Barebones Parliament, 1643; William Prynne, 17th-century Puritan scourge, especially of the theatre.

All knocked down, like a wicket by Mynn,[3] –   50
   Each castle in air
   Seized by giant Despair,
No prospect in life worth a minnikin pin;[4]
   No credit, no cash,
   No cold mutton to hash,
   No bread – not even potatoes to mash;
No coal in the cellar, no wine in the binn –
   Smashed, broken to bits,
   With judgments and writs,
Bonds, bills, and cognovits distracting the wits,   60
In the webs that the spiders of Chancery spin –
   Till, weary of life, its worry and strife,
   Black visions are rife of a razor, a knife;
Of poison – a rope – 'louping over a linn.'

Gin! Gin! a drop of Gin!
Oh! then its tremendous temptations begin,
   To take, alas!
   To the fatal glass; –
And happy the wretch that it does not win
   To change the black hue   70
   Of his ruin to 'blue' –
While angels sorrow, and demons grin –
   And lose the rheumatic
   Chill of his attic
By plunging into the Palace of Gin!

First published Punch, *November 1843. Text,* The Works of Thomas Hood.
Comic and serious, in Prose and Verse, *Ed., with Notes by His Son*
*[Thomas Hood], 7 vols (Edward Moxon & Co., 1862), VI. (*it *supplied in line*
69 – as in other versions.)

The Song of the Shirt

With fingers weary and worn,
   With eyelids heavy and red,
A woman sat, in unwomanly rags,
   Plying her needle and thread –
     Stitch! stitch! stitch!
In poverty, hunger, and dirt,
   And still with a voice of dolorous pitch
She sang the 'Song of the Shirt.'

'Work! work! work!
While the cock is crowing aloof!   10
   And work – work – work,
Till the stars shine through the roof!
It's O! to be a slave
   Along with the barbarous Turk,
Where woman has never a soul to save,
   If this is Christian work!

---

3 cricketer Alfred Mynn (1807–61), 'the Lion of Kent': right-handed   4 very small pin.
batsman and right-arm bowler.

'Work – work – work
Till the brain begins to swim;
    Work – work – work
Till the eyes are heavy and dim!
Seam, and gusset, and band,
    Band, and gusset, and seam,
Till over the buttons I fall asleep,
    And sew them on in a dream!   20

'O! Men, with Sisters dear!
    O! Men, with Mothers and Wives!
It is not linen you're wearing out,
    But human creatures' lives!
        Stitch – stitch – stitch,
    In poverty, hunger, and dirt,   30
Sewing at once, with a double thread,
    A Shroud as well as a Shirt.

'But why do I talk of Death?
    That Phantom of grisly bone,
I hardly fear his terrible shape,
    It seems so like my own –
    It seems so like my own,
    Because of the fasts I keep,
Oh, God! that bread should be so dear,
    And flesh and blood so cheap!   40

'Work – work – work!
    My labour never flags;
And what are its wages? A bed of straw,
    A crust of bread – and rags.
That shatter'd roof – and this naked floor –
    A table – a broken chair –
And a wall so blank, my shadow I thank
    For sometimes falling there!

'Work – work – work!
From weary chime to chime,
    Work – work – work –   50
As prisoners work for crime!
    Band, and gusset, and seam,
    Seam, and gusset, and band,
Till the heart is sick, and the brain benumb'd,
    As well as the weary hand.

'Work – work – work,
In the dull December light,
    And work – work – work,
When the weather is warm and bright –   60
While underneath the eaves
    The brooding swallows cling
As if to show me their sunny backs
    And twit me with the spring.

'Oh! but to breathe the breath
Of the cowslip and primrose sweet –
    With the sky above my head,
And the grass beneath my feet,

For only one short hour
　　To feel as I used to feel,   70
Before I knew the woes of want
　　And the walk that costs a meal!

'Oh but for one short hour!
　　A respite however brief!
No blessed leisure for Love or Hope,
　　But only time for Grief!
A little weeping would ease my heart,
　　But in their briny bed
My tears must stop, for every drop
　　Hinders needle and thread!'   80

With fingers weary and worn,
　　With eyelids heavy and red,
A woman sate in unwomanly rags,
　　Plying her needle and thread –
　　　Stitch! stitch! stitch!
　　In poverty, hunger, and dirt,
And still with a voice of dolorous pitch,
Would that its tone could reach the Rich!
She sang this 'Song of the Shirt!'

First published Punch, *Christmas Number, 1843*. Poems of Thomas Hood, *2 vols*
(Edward Moxon, 1846), I.

THE BRIDGE OF SIGHS

'Drown'd! drown'd!'
Hamlet[1]

One more Unfortunate,
Weary of breath,
Rashly importunate,
Gone to her death!

Take her up tenderly,
Lift her with care;
Fashion'd so slenderly,
Young, and so fair!

Look at her garments
Clinging like cerements;   10
Whilst the wave constantly
Drips from her clothing;
Take her up instantly,
Loving, not loathing. –

Touch her not scornfully;
Think of her mournfully,

Gently and humanly;
Not of the stains of her,
All that remains of her
Now is pure womanly.   20

Make no deep scrutiny
Into her mutiny
Rash and undutiful:
Past all dishonour,
Death has left on her
Only the beautiful.

Still, for all slips of hers,
One of Eve's family –
Wipe those poor lips of hers
Oozing so clammily.   30

Loop up her tresses
Escaped from the comb,

THE BRIDGE OF SIGHS

1   words of the Queen upon hearing of Ophelia's death, *Hamlet* IV.
vii. 183.

Her fair auburn tresses;
Whilst wonderment guesses
Where was her home?

Who was her father?
Who was her mother?
Had she a sister?
Had she a brother?
Or was there a dearer one   40
Still, and a nearer one
Yet, than all other?

Alas! for the rarity
Of Christian charity
Under the sun!
Oh! it was pitiful!
Near a whole city full,
Home she had none.

Sisterly, brotherly,
Fatherly, motherly   50
Feelings had changed:
Love, by harsh evidence,
Thrown from its eminence;
Even God's providence
Seeming estranged.

Where the lamps quiver
So far in the river,
With many a light
From window and casement,
From garret to basement,   60
She stood, with amazement,
Houseless by night.

The bleak wind of March
Made her tremble and shiver;
But not the dark arch,
Or the black flowing river:
Mad from life's history,
Glad to death's mystery,
Swift to be hurl'd –

Any where, any where   70
Out of the world!

In she plunged boldly,
No matter how coldly
The rough river ran, –
Over the brink of it,
Picture it – think of it,
Dissolute Man!
Lave in it, drink of it,
Then, if you can!

Take her up tenderly,   80
Lift her with care;
Fashion'd so slenderly,
Young, and so fair!

Ere her limbs frigidly
Stiffen too rigidly,
Decently, – kindly, –
Smooth, and compose them;
And her eyes, close them,
Staring so blindly!

Dreadfully staring   90
Thro' muddy impurity,
As when with the daring
Last look of despairing
Fix'd on futurity.

Perishing gloomily,
Spurr'd by contumely,
Cold inhumanity,
Burning insanity,
Into her rest. –
Cross her hands humbly,   100
As if praying dumbly,
Over her breast!

Owning her weakness,
Her evil behaviour,
And leaving, with meekness,
Her sins to her Saviour!

First published Hood's Magazine, *May 1844.* Poems *(1846), I.*

I REMEMBER, I REMEMBER[1]

I
I remember, I remember,
The house where I was born,
The little window where the sun
Came peeping in at morn;
He never came a wink too soon,
Nor brought too long a day,

But now, I often wish the night
Had borne my breath away!

II
I remember, I remember,
The roses, red and white,   10
The vi'lets, and the lily-cups,

I REMEMBER, I REMEMBER
1   a title re-used by Philip Larkin, *The Less Deceived* (1955).

Those flowers made of light!
The lilacs where the robin built,
And where my brother set
The laburnum on his birth-day, –
The tree is living yet!

III

I remember, I remember
Where I was used to swing,
And thought the air must rush as fresh
To swallows on the wing;   20
My spirit flew in feathers then,
That is so heavy now,

And summer pools could hardly cool
The fever on my brow!

IV

I remember, I remember
The fir trees dark and high;
I used to think their slender tops
Were close against the sky:
It was a childish ignorance,
But now 'tis little joy   30
To know I'm farther off from heav'n
Than when I was a boy.

Poems *(1846), II.*

Charles (Lord) Neaves (1800–76)

Charles Neaves, eminent Scottish lawyer, man of letters, philologist and satirist, was born in Edinburgh, 14 October 1800. His father was a lawyer; so was his wife's father. He attended Edinburgh High School and Edinburgh University, and progressed far in the Law, becoming a judge and a Lord of Justitiary. He was Solicitor-General for Scotland in Lord Derby's administration (until Derby's resignation in January 1853). A great 'case lawyer' with a formidable memory for the legal cases with precedent power, Neaves was also a regular contributor to *Blackwood's Edinburgh Magazine* and a key literary figure in his home city – there at the banquet in 1827 when Scott divulged his authorship of the Waverley Novels, at the banquet to honour Dickens in 1841, and the one for Thackeray in 1857. He was, on the side, a renowned stu-

dent of philology, on which he published articles, a book (*A Glance at Some of the Principles of Comparative Philology*, 1870) and poems (including 'Grimm's Law'). He was also a classicist of some merit (his book on *The Greek Anthology* appeared in Blackwood's Ancient Classics series, 1870). As a satirist he combined sting nicely with a punchy grace. His best comic and satirical verses were gathered in *Songs and Verses, Social and Scientific* (Edinburgh, 1868; second edition, 1872). Among his other books is *On Fiction as a Means of Popular Teaching* (1869). He was awarded the degree of LL.D by Edinburgh University (1860) and elected Lord Rector of St Andrew's University in 1872. He died 23 December 1876, leaving a widow and several daughters – one of whom was, of course, married to a judge.

GRIMM'S LAW[1]

A New Song

Air: Old Homer, – but with him what have we to do?

Etymology once was a wild kind of thing,
Which from any one word any other could bring:
Of the consonants then the effect was thought small,
And the vowels – the vowels were nothing at all.
Down a down, down, &c.

GRIMM'S LAW

1 [*In a late Number of the 'Anthropological Review' Grimm's law is explained in what is at least an ingenious manner. After describing an Aryan, or 'articulate-speaking man,' setting out to teach language to some rude owners of the 'kitchen-middens' of the primeval age, who are supposed to be speechless, a distinguished Anthropologist thus reports the result of the attempt: 'But now assume the 200 [kitchen-middeners] to be mutes, and follow the leader of the Aryans in his first lesson to the crowd around him. Naturally he would get the crowd to pronounce after him some short syllables, such as* pa, ta, ka, *to illustrate the use of lips, palate, and throat, and very naturally the four or five men (or women more likely) just in* front of him would pronounce them rightly; but not one man in fifty can tell the real effect of his work on a crowd. On their returning to their wigwams, much would be the emotion of risibility and imitativeness displayed that night among the natives; and next morning the chances are that the majority who stood some distance from the speaker would have fixed for ever upon the whole nation the wrong utterance of ba, da, ga. The main point of my whole argument is, that such a result would most naturally follow among mutes, but would never happen among speaking men.' – Extract from Paper read before the Anthropological Society by the Rev. D. I. Heath, M.A. – 'Anthropological Review,' April 1867.] [Author's note]

But that state of matters completely is changed,
And the old school of scholars now feels quite estranged:
For 'tis clear that whenever we open our jaw,
Every sound that we utter comes under some Law.

Now one of these laws has been named after Grimm,
For the Germans declare it was found out by him: 10
But their rivals the Danes take the Germans to task,
And proclaim as its finder the great Rasmus Rask.

Be this as it may, few have sought to explain
How it came that this law could its influence gain:
Max Müller has tried, and, perhaps, pretty well;
But I don't understand him, and therefore can't tell.

Anthropologists say, after Man had his birth,
There were two human races possessing the earth;
One gifted and graced with articulate speech,
And another that only could gabble and screech.   20

The Aryans could speak, and could build, and could plough,
And knew most of the arts we are practising now;
But the Dumbies that dwelt at those vile Kitchen-Middens
Weren't fit but to do their Superiors' biddings.

So an Aryan went forth to enlighten these others,
And to raise them by speech to the level of brothers;
On the Mutes of the Middens he burst with eclàt,
And attempted to teach them the syllable PA.

This PA was intended to set things a-going
For a lot of Good Words very well worth the knowing;   30
Such as Pater, and πολις,² and Panis, and Pasco;
But the Midden performers made rather a *fiasco*.

Scarce one of them all would say PA for a wonder,
But each blundered away with a different blunder:
Some feebly cried A, and some, crow-like, said KA,
While the nearest they came to was FA or was BA.

Then the Aryan propounded the syllable TA,
Which his pupils corrupted to THA and to DA:
Even KA, when they tried it, they never came nearer
Than to HA or to GA, or to something still queerer.   40

So slow were their senses to seize what was said,
That they never could hit the right nail on the head;
And the game of cross purposes lasted so long,
That it soon was a rule they should always go wrong.

Thus the Dumbies for ever said Father for Pater,
And Bearing and Brother for Ferens and Frater:
The Aryan cried Pecu, the Midden-man Fee,
In which Doctors and Lawyers to this day agree.

2   *polis*, city (Greek).

Jove's Tonitru sank into Old Saxon Thunner,
Which the High-German dunderheads changed into Donner;   50
From Domo came Tame, and from Domus came Timmer,
While the hissing Helvetians said Zämen and Zimmer.

From θυρα[3] came Door, and from θυγατηρ[4] Dochter,
Which dwindled away into Türe and Tochter;
From Hortus and Hostis came Garden and Guest,
And from χολη[5] came Gall, which so bothers the best.

The Old Aryan GAU was the Kitchener's Koo
(Though some tribes were contented to call the beast Boo):
If your wife in her καρδια[6] would give you a Cornu,
The Midden-man said, 'In her Heart she would Horn you.'   60

Such a roundabout race I can only compare
To the whirligig engines we mount at a fair;
Where each rides as in fear lest his steed be forsaken,
But he ne'er overtakes, and is ne'er overtaken.

A theory seldom is free from a flaw,
But the story I've told may account for Grimm's law:
Though some others suggest, if the Bible's no fable,
That Grimm's law was what caused the confusion at Babel.
                    Down a down, down, &c.

                              December 1867

Songs and Verses, Social and Scientific, By An Old Contributor to 'Maga'
(4th edn, Enlarged, Blackwood, Edinburgh and London, 1875).

O WHY SHOULD A WOMAN NOT GET A DEGREE?

On Female Graduation and Ladies' Lectures

Air: Argyll is my name.

Ye fusty old fogies, Professors by name,
A deed you've been doing of sorrow and shame:
Though placed in your Chairs to spread knowledge abroad,
Against half of mankind you would shut up the road:
College honours and lore from the Fair you withdraw,
By enforcing against them a strict Salic law:
Is it fear? is it envy? or what can it be?
And why should a woman not get a degree?

How ungrateful of You, whose best efforts depend
On the aid certain Ladies in secret may send: 10
CLIO[1] *here* writes a lecture, URANIA[2] *there*,

---

3 *thura*, door (Gr.).
4 *thugater*, daughter (Gr.).
5 *chole*, gall, bile (Gr.).
6 *kardia*, heart (Gr.).

O WHY SHOULD A WOMAN NOT GET A DEGREE?
1 Clio: Muse of history.
2 Urania: Muse of astronomy.

And more Muses than one prompt the Musical Chair.
CALLIOPE[3] sheds o'er the Classics delight,
And the lawyers have meetings with THEMIS[4] by night;
Yet, if VENUS de' Medici[5] came, even She
Could among her own Medici get no degree.

In Logic a woman may seldom excel;
But in Rhetoric always she bears off the bell.
Fair PORTIA will show woman's talent for law,
When in old Shylock's bond she could prove such a flaw.[6]   20
She would blunder in Physic no worse than the rest,
She could leave things to Nature as well as the best;
She could feel at your wrist, she could finger your fee;
Then why should a woman not get a degree?

Your Lectures for Ladies some fruit may produce;
For a Course of good lectures is always of use.
On a married Professor your choice should alight,
Who may lecture by day – as he's lectured at night.
And allow me to ask, what would Husbands become,
If they weren't well lectured by women at home?   30
When from faults and from follies men thus are kept free,
There surely the woman deserves a degree.

Yet without a degree see how well the Sex knows
How to bind up our wounds and to lighten our woes!
They need *no* Doctor's gown their fair limbs to enwrap,
They need ne'er hide their locks in a Graduate's cap.
So I wonder a woman, the Mistress of Hearts,
Would descend to aspire to be Master of Arts:
A Ministering Angel in Woman we see,
And an Angel need covet no other Degree.   40

Songs and Verses, Social and Scientific *(4th edn, 1875).*

LET US ALL BE UNHAPPY ON SUNDAY

A Lyric for Saturday Night

Air: We bipeds made up of frail clay.

We zealots, made up of stiff clay,
    The sour-looking children of sorrow,
While not over-jolly to-day,
    Resolve to be wretched to-morrow.
We can't for a certainty tell
    What mirth may molest us on Monday;
But, at least, to begin the week well,
    Let us all be unhappy on Sunday.

That day, the calm season of rest,
    Shall come to us freezing and frigid;   10

<hr>

3 Calliope: chief of Muses.
4 personification of divine justice and legality on earth, worshipped widely in ancient Greece.

5 famous Roman statue of 'Venus', owned by the Medici of Rome (patrons of arts); since 1680 in Uffizi Gallery, Florence.
6 in Shakespeare's *The Merchant of Venice.*

A gloom all our thoughts shall invest,
    Such as Calvin would call over-rigid.
With sermons from morning till night,
    We'll strive to be decent and dreary:
To preachers a praise and delight,
    Who ne'er think that sermons can weary.

All tradesmen cry up their own wares;
    In this they agree well together:
The Mason by stone and lime swears;
    The Tanner is always for leather.   20
The Smith still for iron would go;
    The Schoolmaster stands up for teaching;
And the Parson would have you to know,
    There's nothing on earth like his preaching.

The face of kind Nature is fair;
    But our system obscures its effulgence:
How sweet is a breath of fresh air!
    But our rules don't allow the indulgence.
These gardens, their walks and green bowers,
    Might be free to the poor man for one day;   30
But no, the glad plants and gay flowers
    Mustn't bloom or smell sweetly on Sunday,

What though a good precept we strain
    Till hateful and hurtful we make it!
What though, in thus pulling the rein,
    We may draw it so tight as to break it!
Abroad we forbid folks to roam,
    For fear they get social or frisky;
But of course they can sit still at home,
    And get dismally drunk upon whisky.   40

Then, though we can't certainly tell
    How mirth may molest us on Monday;
At least, to begin the week well,
    Let us all be unhappy on Sunday.

            Songs and Verses, Social and Scientific *(4th edn, 1875)*.

Thomas Babington (First Baron) Macaulay (1800–59)

Thomas Babington Macaulay was born 25 October 1800, eldest child of Zachary Macaulay, the great Evangelical Christian crusader for African liberation and anti-slavery campaigner, and his wife, Selina Mills, daughter of a Quaker bookseller from Bristol. Macaulay grew up in the family home in High Street, Clapham, at the heart of the Evangelical 'Clapham Sect' of wealthy, high-minded moralists and reformers – Wilberforces, Buxtons, Thorntons, Venns. He was the pet of Hannah More, the crusading Evangelical novelist, and an indulged child prodigy – able to recite long poems by heart, composing hymns, beginning a universal history at the age of seven, writing at the age of eight a treatise for the conversion of the natives of Malabar to Christianity. His prodigious memory never failed him and he would claim to be able to reproduce all of *Paradise Lost* and *The Pilgrim's Progress* by heart. After attending a private Evangelical school run by a Revd Mr Preston he went up to Trinity College, Cambridge (October 1818), where he lodged with Henry Sykes Thornton (eldest son of Henry Thornton, leader of the Clapham Sect); was a friend of Winthrop Mackworth Praed; starred at the Union; won prizes for Latin declamation and the English Poem (*Pompeii*, 1819; *Evening*, 1821). After Cambridge he studied for the Bar, involved himself with the Anti-Slavery Society, started his renowned career as a writer in the *Edinburgh Review* with an essay on Milton (August

1825). He entered Parliament in April 1830 and remained one of the most exciting orators the House of Commons had ever known. He was as persuasively pugnacious and acrimonious in the debating Chamber of the House as he was in his *Edinburgh* reviewing. In 1834 he left for India to become a member of the East India Company's supreme council at a £10,000 annual salary – he needed the money, his father's huge fortune having been diminished by the bad business dealings of trusted people, though Macaulay, a confirmed bachelor, was extremely reluctant to move away from his sisters (Hannah, in fact, accompanied him to India, and he would continue living with her even after her marriage to Sir Charles Trevelyan). In India he worked hard to reform the criminal law, and at other reformist measures in keeping with his professed Whiggish principles, though his momentous Minute on Indian Education, 2 February 1835, was also responsible for establishing English rather than oriental studies as the basis of the colonists' education system (he had not found one Orientalist 'who could deny that a single shelf of a good European library was worth the whole native literature of India and Arabia'). Back in London at the end of the thirties, now a rich man, Macaulay became again an MP (for Edinburgh), pursued his career as an essayist, started his great project of *The History of England*, and became Secretary of War and a member of the Cabinet. He assembled his *Collected Essays* in 1843 (they'd started appearing in pirated collections in the USA) and they went on selling in thousands for the rest of his life. His *Lays of Ancient Rome* appeared in October 1842 – they were stimulated by his Italian travels of autumn 1838 –

and were an immediate best-seller (18,000 copies sold in ten years; 100,000 by 1875). On the political side he worked at copyright law, was Paymaster General in Lord Russell's administration, but lost his Edinburgh seat in 1847. The authorized edition of his *Speeches* appeared in 1854. Meanwhile, the *History* – robust, partial, full of purple patches, the work of a novelist *manqué* – took up more and more of his time. The first two volumes (November 1848) had a novel's success – 13,000 copies sold in just four months. Volumes three and four (December 1855) blitzed the market even more successfully – 26,500 copies sold in ten weeks, a cheque from Longmans for £20,000 four months after publication, sales rivalling the Bible in the USA. In 1857 he became Baron Macaulay of Rothley under Palmerston's premiership, but his health had been failing for some years and he died 28 December 1859, whilst reading the first number of the *Cornhill Magazine*, his *History* unfinished and a career in the House of Lords unassayed. He thought he had significantly contributed to the moulding of the form of the English essay. Remarkably, given the admiration for deftness with soldierly implements evinced in his 'Horatius' he was a physically clumsy man, unable to do up his own neck-cloth or shave himself properly. The male heroic of the poem, and its imperialistic feel for resisting the barbarian at the gate, come as less of a surprise, given – not least – his defence of English education in India. He was buried in Westminster Abbey, 9 January 1860, in Poets' Corner at the foot of Joseph Addison's statue – a pair of renowned essayists together.

HORATIUS

A Lay Made About the Year of the City CCCLX[1]

XI
Lars Porsena of Clusium
  By the Nine Gods he swore
That the great house of Tarquin
  Should suffer wrong no more.
By the Nine Gods he swore it,
  And named a trysting day,
And bade his messengers ride forth,
East and west and south and north,
  To summon his array.

II
East and west and south and north   10
  The messengers ride fast,
And tower and town and cottage

Have heard the trumpet's blast.
Shame on the false Etruscan
  Who lingers in his home
When Porsena of Clusium
  Is on his march for Rome.

III
The horsemen and the footmen
  Are pouring in amain,
From many a stately market-place;   20
  From many a fruitful plain;
From many a lonely hamlet,
  Which, hid by beech and pine,
Like an eagle's nest, hangs on the crest
  Of purple Apennine;

HORATIUS
1 the City of Rome; dates were counted from the year of its founding.

IV

From lordly Volaterræ,
  Where scowls the far-famed hold
Piled by the hands of giants
  For godlike kings of old;
From seagirt Populonia,   30
  Whose sentinels descry
Sardinia's snowy mountain tops
  Fringing the southern sky;

V

From the proud mart of Pisæ,
  Queen of the western waves.
Where ride Massilia's triremes
  Heavy with fair-haired slaves;
From where sweet Clanis wanders
  Through corn and vines and flowers;
From where Cortona lifts to heaven   40
  Her diadem of towers.

VI

Tall are the oaks whose acorns
  Drop in dark Auser's rill;
Fat are the stags that champ the boughs
  Of the Ciminian hill;
Beyond all streams Clitumnus
  Is to the herdsman dear;
Best of all pools the fowler loves
  The great Volsinian mere.

VII

But now no stroke of woodman   50
  Is heard by Auser's rill;
No hunter tracks the stag's green path
  Up the Ciminian hill;
Unwatched along Clitumnus
  Grazes the milk-white steer;
Unharmed the water fowl may dip
  In the Volsinian mere.

VIII

The harvests of Arretium,
  This year, old men shall reap;
This year, young boys in Umbro   60
  Shall plunge the struggling sheep;
And in the vats of Luna,
  This year, the must shall foam
Round the white feet of laughing girls
  Whose sires have marched to Rome.

IX

There be thirty chosen prophets,
  The wisest of the land,
Who always by Lars Porsena
  Both morn and evening stand:
Evening and morn the Thirty   70
  Have turned the verses o'er,
Traced from the right on linen white
  By mighty seers of yore.

X

And with one voice the Thirty
  Have their glad answer given:
'Go forth, go forth, Lars Porsena;
  Go forth, beloved of Heaven;
Go, and return in glory
  To Clusium's royal dome;
And hang round Nurscia's altars   80
  The golden shields of Rome.'

XI

And now hath every city
  Sent up her tale of men;
The foot are fourscore thousand,
  The horse are thousands ten.
Before the gates of Sutrium
  Is met the great array.
A proud man was Lars Porsena
  Upon the trysting day.

XII

For all the Etruscan armies   90
  Were ranged beneath his eye,
And many a banished Roman,
  And many a stout ally;
And with a mighty following
  To join the muster came
The Tusculan Mamilius,
  Prince of the Latian name.

XIII

But by the yellow Tiber
  Was tumult and affright:
From all the spacious champaign   100
  To Rome men took their flight.
A mile around the city,
  The throng stopped up the ways;
A fearful sight it was to see
  Through two long nights and days.

XIV

For aged folks on crutches,
  And women great with child,
And mothers sobbing over babes
  That clung to them and smiled.
And sick men borne in litters   110
  High on the necks of slaves,
And troops of sun-burned husbandmen
  With reaping-hooks and staves

XV

And droves of mules and asses
  Laden with skins of wine,
And endless flocks of goats and sheep,
  And endless herds of kine,
And endless trains of wagons
  That creaked beneath the weight
Of corn-sacks and of household goods,   120
  Choked every roaring gate.

XVI

Now, from the rock Tarpeian,
  Could the wan burghers spy
The line of blazing villages
  Red in the midnight sky.
The Fathers of the City,
    They sat all night and day,
For every hour some horseman came
  With tidings of dismay.

XVII

To eastward and to westward   130
  Have spread the Tuscan bands;
Nor house, nor fence, nor dovecot
  In Crustumerium stands.
Verbenna down to Ostia
  Hath wasted all the plain;
Astur hath stormed Janiculum,
  And the stout guards are slain.

XVIII

I wis, in all the Senate,
  There was no heart so bold,
But sore it ached, and fast it beat,   140
  When that ill news was told.
Forthwith up rose the Consul,
  Up rose the Fathers all;
In haste they girded up their gowns,
  And hied them to the wall.

XIX

They held a council standing
  Before the River-Gate;
Short time was there, ye well may guess,
  For musing or debate.
Out spake the Consul roundly: 150
  'The bridge must straight go down;
For, since Janiculum is lost,
  Nought else can save the town.'

XX

Just then a scout came flying,
  All wild with haste and fear:
'To arms! to arms! Sir Consul:
  Lars Porsena is here.'
On the low hills to westward
  The Consul fixed his eye,
And saw the swarthy storm of dust   160
  Rise fast along the sky.

XXI

And nearer fast and nearer
  Doth the red whirlwind come;
And louder still and still more loud,
From underneath that rolling cloud,
Is heard the trumpet's war-note proud,
  The trampling and the hum.
And plainly and more plainly

Now through the gloom appears,
Far to left and far to right,   170
In broken gleams of dark-blue light,
The long array of helmets bright,
  The long array of spears.

XXII

And plainly and more plainly,
  Above that glimmering line,
Now might ye see the banners
  Of twelve fair cities shine;
But the banner of proud Clusium
  Was highest of them all,
The terror of the Umbrian,   180
  The terror of the Gaul.

XXIII

And plainly and more plainly
  Now might the burghers know,
By port and vest, by horse and crest,
  Each warlike Lucumo.
There Cilnius of Arretium
  On his fleet roan was seen;
And Astur of the fourfold shield,
Girt with the brand none else may wield,
Tolumnius with the belt of gold,   190
And dark Verbenna from the hold
  By reedy Thrasymene.

XXIV

Fast by the royal standard,
  O'erlooking all the war,
Lars Porsena of Clusium
  Sat in his ivory car.
By the right wheel rode Mamilius,
  Prince of the Latian name;
And by the left false Sextus,
  That wrought the deed of shame.   200

XXV

But when the face of Sextus
  Was seen among the foes,
A yell that rent the firmament
  From all the town arose.
On the house-tops was no woman
  But spat towards him and hissed,
No child but screamed out curses,
  And shook its little fist.

XXVI

But the Consul's brow was sad,
  And the Consul's speech was low,   210
And darkly looked he at the wall,
  And darkly at the foe.
'Their van will be upon us
  Before the bridge goes down;
And if they once may win the bridge,
  What hope to save the town?'

XXVII

Then out spake brave Horatius,
    The Captain of the Gate:
To every man upon this earth
    Death cometh soon or late,   220
And how can man die better
    Than facing fearful odds,
For the ashes of his fathers,
    And the temples of his Gods,

XXVIII

'And for the tender mother
    Who dandled him to rest,
And for the wife who nurses
    His baby at her breast,
And for the holy maidens
    Who feed the eternal flame,   230
To save them from false Sextus
    That wrought the deed of shame?

XXIX

'Hew down the bridge, Sir Consul,
    With all the speed ye may;
I, with two more to help me,
    Will hold the foe in play.
In yon strait path a thousand
    May well be stopped by three.
Now who will stand on either hand,
    And keep the bridge with me?'   240

XXX

Then out spake Spurius Lartius;
    A Ramnian proud was he:
'Lo, I will stand at thy right hand,
    And keep the bridge with thee.'
And out spake strong Herminius;
    Of Titian blood was he:
'I will abide on thy left side,
    And keep the bridge with thee.'

XXXI

'Horatius,' quoth the Consul,
    'As thou sayest, so let it be.'   250
And straight against that great array
    Forth went the dauntless Three.
For Romans in Rome's quarrel
    Spared neither land nor gold,
Nor son nor wife, nor limb nor life,
    In the brave days of old.

XXXII

Then none was for a party;
    Then all were for the state;
Then the great man helped the poor,
    And the poor man loved the great;   260
Then lands were fairly portioned;
    Then spoils were fairly sold;
The Romans were like brothers
    In the brave days of old.

XXXIII

Now Roman is to Roman
    More hateful than a foe,
And the Tribunes beard the high,
    And the Fathers grind the low.
As we wax hot in faction,
    In battle we wax cold;   270
Wherefore men fight not as they fought
    In the brave days of old.

XXXIV

Now while the Three were tightening
    Their harness on their backs,
The Consul was the foremost man
    To take in hand an axe;
And Fathers mixed with Commons,
    Seized hatchet, bar, and crow,
And smote upon the planks above,
    And loosed the props below.   280

XXXV

Meanwhile the Tuscan army,
    Right glorious to behold,
Came flashing back the noonday light,
    Rank behind rank, like surges bright
        Of a broad sea of gold.
Four hundred trumpets sounded
    A peal of warlike glee,
As that great host, with measured tread,
And spears advanced, and ensigns spread,
Rolled slowly towards the bridge's head,   290
    Where stood the dauntless Three.

XXXVI

The Three stood calm and silent,
    And looked upon the foes,
And a great shout of laughter
    From all the vanguard rose:
And forth three chiefs came spurring
    Before that deep array;
To earth they sprang, their swords they drew
And lifted high their shields, and flew
    To win the narrow way;   300

XXXVII

Aunus from green Tifernum,
    Lord of the Hill of Vines;
And Seius, whose eight hundred slaves
    Sicken in Ilva's mines;
And Picus, long to Clusium
    Vassal in peace and war,
Who led to fight his Umbrian powers
From that gray crag where, girt with towers,
The fortress of Nequinum lowers
    O'er the pale waves of Nar.   310

XXXVIII

Stout Lartius hurled down Aunus
    Into the stream beneath:

Herminius struck at Seius,
　　And clove him to the teeth:
At Picus brave Horatius
　　Darted one fiery thrust;
And the proud Umbrian's gilded arms
　　Clashed in the bloody dust.

XXXIX
Then Ocnus of Falerii
　　Rushed on the Roman Three;　　　　　　320
And Lausulus of Urgo,
　　The Rover of the sea;
And Aruns of Volsinium.
　　Who slew the great wild boar,
The great wild boar that had his den
Amidst the reeds of Cosa's fen,
And wasted fields, and slaughtered men,
　　Along Albinia's shore.

XL
Herminius smote down Aruns:
　　Lartius laid Ocnus low:　　　　　　330
Right to the heart of Lausulus
　　Horatius sent a blow.
'Lie there,' he cried, 'fell pirate!
　　No more, aghast and pale,
From Ostia's walls the crowd shall mark
The track of thy destroying bark.
No more Campania's hinds shall fly
To woods and caverns when they spy
　　Thy thrice accursed sail.'

XLI
But now no sound of laughter　　　　　　340
　　Was heard among the foes.
A wild and wrathful clamor
　　From all the vanguard rose.
Six spears' length from the entrance
　　Halted that deep array,
And for a space no man came forth
　　To win the narrow way.

XLII
But hark! the cry is Astur:
　　And lo! the ranks divide;
And the great Lord of Luna　　　　　　350
　　Comes with his stately stride.
Upon his ample shoulders
　　Clangs loud the fourfold shield,
And in his hand he shakes the brand
　　Which none but he can wield.

XLIII
He smiled on those bold Romans
　　A smile serene and high;
He eyed the flinching Tuscans,
　　And scorn was in his eye.
Quoth he: 'The she-wolf's litter　　　　　　360

Stand savagely at bay;
But will ye dare to follow,
　　If Astur clears the way?'

XLIV
Then, whirling up his broadsword
　　With both hands to the height,
He rushed against Horatius,
　　And smote with all his might.
With shield and blade Horatius
　　Right deftly turned the blow.
The blow, though turned, came yet too nigh;　　370
It missed his helm, but gashed his thigh:
　　The Tuscans raised a joyful cry
　　To see the red blood flow.

XLV
He reeled, and on Herminius
　　He leaned one breathing-space;
Then, like a wild cat mad with wounds,
　　Sprang right at Astur's face.
Through teeth, and skull, and helmet
　　So fierce a thrust he sped,
The good sword stood a hand-breadth out　　380
　　Behind the Tuscan's head.

XLVI
And the great Lord of Luna
　　Fell at that deadly stroke
As falls on Mount Alvernus
　　A thunder-smitten oak.
Far o'er the crashing forest
　　The giant arms lie spread;
And the pale augurs, muttering low,
　　Gaze on the blasted head.

XLVII
On Astur's throat Horatius　　　　　　390
　　Right firmly pressed his heel,
And thrice and four times tugged amain
　　Ere he wrenched out the steel.
'And see,' he cried, 'the welcome,
　　Fair guests, that waits you here!
What noble Lucumo comes next
　　To taste our Roman cheer?'

XLVIII
But at this haughty challenge
　　A sullen murmur ran,
Mingled of wrath, and shame, and dread,　　400
　　Along that glittering van.
There lacked not men of prowess,
　　Nor men of lordly race;
For all Etruria's noblest
　　Were round the fatal place.

XLIX
But all Etruria's noblest
　　Felt their hearts sink to see

On the earth the bloody corpses,
　In the path the dauntless Three:
And, from the ghastly entrance　　　　410
　Where those bold Romans stood,
All shrank, like boys who unaware,
Ranging the woods to start a hare,
Come to the mouth of the dark lair
Where, growling low, a fierce old bear
　Lies amidst bones and blood.

L

Was none who would be foremost
　To lead such dire attack:
But those behind cried 'Forward!'
　And those before cried 'Back!'　　　　420
And backward now and forward
　Wavers the deep array;
And on the tossing sea of steel,
To and fro the standards reel;
And the victorious trumpet-peal
　Dies fitfully away.

LI

Yet one man for one moment
　Stood out before the crowd;
Well known was he to all the Three,
　And they gave him greeting loud:　　　430
'Now welcome, welcome Sextus!
　Now welcome to thy home!
Why dost thou stay, and turn away?
　Here lies the road to Rome.'

LII

Thrice looked he at the city;
　Thrice looked he at the dead;
And thrice came on in fury,
　And thrice turned back in dread:
And, white with fear and hatred,
　Scowled at the narrow way　　　　440
Where, wallowing in a pool of blood,
　The bravest Tuscans lay.

LIII

But meanwhile axe and lever
　Have manfully been plied;
And now the bridge hangs tottering
　Above the boiling tide.
'Come back, come back, Horatius!'
　Loud cried the Fathers all.
'Back, Lartius! back, Herminius!
　Back, ere the ruin fall!'　　　　450

LIV

Back darted Spurius Lartius;
　Herminius darted back:
And, as they passed, beneath their feet
　They felt the timbers crack.
But when they turned their faces,
　And on the farther shore
Saw brave Horatius stand alone,
　They would have crossed once more.

LV

But with a crash like thunder
　Fell every loosened beam,　　　　460
And, like a dam, the mighty wreck
　Lay right athwart the stream:
And a long shout of triumph
　Rose from the walls of Rome,
As to the highest turret-tops
　Was splashed the yellow foam.

LVI

And, like a horse unbroken
　When first he feels the rein,
The furious river struggled hard,
　And tossed his tawny mane,　　　　470
And burst the curb, and bounded,
　Rejoicing to be free,
And whirling down, in fierce career,
Battlement, and plank, and pier,
　Rushed headlong to the sea.

LVII

Alone stood brave Horatius,
　But constant still in mind;
Thrice thirty thousand foes before,
　And the broad flood behind.
'Down with him!' cried false Sextus,　　　480
　With a smile on his pale face.
'Now yield thee,' cried Lars Porsena,
　'Now yield thee to our grace.'

LVIII

Round turned he, as not deigning
　Those craven ranks to see;
Nought spake he to Lars Porsena,
　To Sextus nought spake he;
But he saw on Palatinus
　The white porch of his home;
And he spake to the noble river　　　490
　That rolls by the towers of Rome:

LIX

'O, Tiber! father Tiber!
　To whom the Romans pray,
A Roman's life, a Roman's arms,
　Take thou in charge this day!'
So he spake, and speaking sheathed
　The good sword by his side,
And with his harness on his back,
　Plunged headlong in the tide.

LX

No sound of joy or sorrow　　　　500
　Was heard from either bank:

But friends and foes in dumb surprise,
With parted lips and straining eyes,
   Stood gazing where he sank;
And when above the surges
   They saw his crest appear,
All Rome sent forth a rapturous cry,
And even the ranks of Tuscany
   Could scarce forbear to cheer.

LXI

But fiercely ran the current,   510
   Swollen high by months of rain;
And fast his blood was flowing;
   And he was sore in pain,
And heavy with his armor,
   And spent with changing blows:
And oft they thought him sinking,
   But still again he rose.

LXII

Never, I ween, did swimmer,
   In such an evil case,
Struggle through such a raging flood   520
   Safe to the landing place:
But his limbs were borne up bravely
   By the brave heart within,
And our good father Tiber
   Bore bravely up his chin.[2]

LXIII

'Curse on him!' quoth false Sextus;
   'Will not the villain drown?
But for this stay, ere close of day
   We should have sacked the town!'
'Heaven help him!' quoth Lars Porsena,   530
   'And bring him safe to shore;
For such a gallant feat of arms
   Was never seen before.'

LXIV

And now he feels the bottom;
   Now on dry earth he stands;
Now round him throng the Fathers
   To press his gory hands;
And now, with shouts and clapping,
   And noise of weeping loud,
He enters through the River-Gate,   540
   Borne by the joyous crowd.

LXV

They gave him of the corn-land,
   That was of public right,
As much as two strong oxen
   Could plough from morn till night;
And they made a molten image,
   And set it up on high,
And there it stands unto this day
   To witness if I lie.

LXVI

It stands in the Comitium,   550
   Plain for all folk to see;
Horatius in his harness,
   Halting upon one knee:
And underneath is written,
   In letters all of gold,
How valiantly he kept the bridge
   In the brave days of old.

LXVII

And still his name sounds stirring
   Unto the men of Rome,
As the trumpet-blast that cries to them   560
   To charge the Volscian home;
And wives still pray to Juno
   For boys with hearts as bold
As his who kept the bridge so well
   In the brave days of old.

LXVIII

And in the nights of winter,
   When the cold north winds blow,
And the long howling of the wolves
   Is heard amidst the snow;
When round the lonely cottage   570
   Roars loud the tempest's din,
And the good logs of Algidus
   Roar louder yet within;

LXIX

When the oldest cask is opened,
   And the largest lamp is lit;
When the chestnuts glow in the embers,
   And the kid turns on the spit;
When young and old in circle
   Around the firebrands close;

---

2   'Our ladye bare upp her chinne.'
       Ballad of Childe Waters.

    'Never heavier man and horse
    Stemmed a midnight torrent's force;
          *

    Yet, through good heart and our Lady's grace,
    At length he gained the landing place.'
               Lay of the Last Minstrel, I.
               [Author's note]

When the girls are weaving baskets,   580
  And the lads are shaping bows;

            LXX
When the goodman mends his armor,
  And trims his helmet's plume;

When the goodwife's shuttle merrily
  Goes flashing though the loom;
    With weeping and with laughter
    Still is the story told,
How well Horatius kept the bridge
  In the brave days of old.   589

Lays of Ancient Rome *(1842; slightly revised, 1843). Text of 1888 reissue*
(Longmans, Green, & Co; illustrated by George Scharf, Junior).

William Barnes (1801–86)

William Barnes, philologist, antiquarian, and perhaps England's finest dialect poet, was born at Rushay in Dorset, the son of a tenant farmer, 20 March 1801. His mother, Grace Stott, was reputed a lover of poetry. Barnes left school to become a clerk in a solicitor's office in Sturminster, his nice handwriting his main qualification. But he was a classic self-improver – Philip Larkin in his fine appreciative essay 'The Poetry of William Barnes' (in *Required Writing*, 1983) called him 'a kind of successful Jude Fawley' – and soon he was borrowing books from the local rector, contributing verses to the local newspaper the *Dorset County Chronicle* (inspired by Julia Miles, who became his wife and remained his muse), beginning that process of acquiring languages and speculating in philology which lasted all his life. He learned French and Italian. In 1823 he turned schoolmaster in Wiltshire, travelled in Wales, became obsessed with the idea of linguistic purity, moved into Welsh studies, and learned Russian, Hebrew and Hindustani. In the early 1830s he began writing Dorset dialect poems. He became a key figure in the nineteenth-century movement to recover the so-called genesis of English in the languages of northern Europe, buoyed up by fantasies of the recoverability of the pure tongue of the Germanic races, and the language of Dorset became for him a strong case of the alleged original purity of English in its old northern European Saxon state before the corruptions from Latin, Greek and French invaded it. In the long 'Dissertation on the Dorset Dialect of the English Language' which prefaces his first volume, *Poems of Rural Life, in the Dorset Dialect* (1844), Barnes argued vigorously for the purity of Dorset diction against corrupted 'book English' – the voice of the country against the so-called elegance of the town, comparable in its 'pure and simple Saxon features', he wrote, with what can be found in 'the best compositions of many of the most polished languages.' 'If his verses should engage the happy mind of the dairymaid with her cow, promote the innocent evening cheerfulness of the family circle on the stone floor, or teach his rustic brethren to draw delight from the rich but frequently overlooked sources of nature within their own sphere of being, his fondest hopes will be realized.' Theological studies ran alongside the philological: in 1847 he was ordained as a Church of England minister; in 1849, after ten years on the books of St John's College, Cambridge, he gained his Cambridge BD. At the end of 1862, after some years living as a private scholar and journalist, he became rector of Came. A second batch of Dorset poems, *Hwomely Rhymes*, appeared in 1859, with a less rebarbative system of transcribing the Dorset speech, and *Poems of Rural Life in the Dorset Dialect: Third Collection* in 1862 – both of these volumes characteristically sandwiched by his extraordinary *Philological Grammar…Being an Introduction to the Science of Grammar in all Languages* (1854); by *Tiw; or, a View of the Roots and Stems of the English as a Teutonic Tongue* (1863); and *A Grammar and Glossary of the Dorset Dialect, with the History, Outspreading, and Bearings of South-Western English* (1863). It's noticeable that his *Poems of Rural Life in Common English* (1868) are as much thinned and purged of Latinate words as Barnes could manage. A comparison of his poems done in two versions, the Dorset and the Common or National English, shows where his linguistic beliefs and energies lay. In 1879 the three collections of Dorset dialect poems were collected up in one volume. Caroline Norton was a great help in promoting Barnes as a poet. Tennyson 'liked' his material. Coventry Patmore praised *Hwomely Rhymes* as doing us good, even though they mightn't look as flashy as 'the high-pressure poetry of the present day'. In his wonderfully astute and very Hardyesque Preface to his *Selection* of Barnes's poems (1908) – Barnes's internal rhymes, for instance, are admired as 'kindred lippings' – Thomas Hardy praised the 'singularly precise and beautiful definitions of what is signified'; 'such verbal dexterities, such searchings for the most cunning syllables, such satisfaction with the best phrase'. In other words, the best words (in the best order), as Coleridge said poetry should be – or, as Larkin's essay on Barnes has it, 'the natural words in their natural order'. Barnes died at Came rectory, 7 October 1886.

THE BLACKBIRD

Ov al the birds upon the wing
Between the zunny show'rs o' spring,
Var[1] al the lark, a-swingèn high,
Mid[2] zing sweet ditties to the sky,
An' sparrers, clus'tren roun' the bough,
Mid chatter to the men at plough;
The blackbird, hoppèn down along
The hedge, da zing the gâyest zong.

'Tis sweet, wi' yerly-wakèn eyes
To zee the zun when vust da rise,   10
Ar, hālen underwood an' lops
Vrom new-plēsh'd hedges[3] ar vrom copse,
To snatch oon's nammet[4] down below
A tree wher primruosen da grow,
But ther s noo time the whol dā long
Lik' evemen[5] wi' the blackbird's zong.

Var when my work is al a-done
Avore the zettèn o' the zun,
Then blushèn Jian da wā'k along
The hedge to mit me in the drong,[6]   20
An' stây till al is dim an' dark
Bezides the ashen tree's white bark,
An al bezides the blackbird's shill
An' runnèn evemen-whissle's still.

How in my buoyhood I did rove
Wi' pryèn eyes along the drove,[7]
Var blackbird's nestes in the quick-
Set hedges high, an' green, an' thick;
Ar clim' al up, wi' clingèn knees,
Var crows' nestes in swâyèn trees,   30
While frighten'd blackbirds down below
Did chatter o' ther well-know'd foe.

An' we da hear the blackbirds zing
Ther sweetest ditties in the spring,
When nippèn win's na muore da blow
Vrom narthern skies wi' sleet ar snow,
But drēve light doust along between
The cluose liane-hedges, thick an' green;
An' zoo the blackbird down along
The hedge da zing the gâyest zong.   40

First published, Dorset County Chronicle (DCC), *7 April 1842.* Poems of
Rural Life, in the Dorset Dialect: With a Dissertation and Glossary
(John Russell Smith, London; George Simonds, Dorchester, 1844).

THE BLACKBIRD
1 for (W.B.'s Glossary).
2 may or might (W.B.).
3 to plesh or plush: to lay a hedge (half-cutting and laying down stems) (W.B.).
4 lunch (noon-meat) (W.B.).
5 evening (W.B.).
6 narrow path between hedges (W.B.).
7 broad cattle-track between hedges (W.B.).

VELLEN THE TREE

Ees,[1] the girt elem tree out in little huome groun'
Wer a-stannen this marnen, an' now 's a-cut down.
Aye, the girt elem tree so big roun' an' so high,
Wher the mowers did goo to ther drink, an' did lie
A-yeazen[2] ther lims, var a zultery hour.
When the zun did strick down wi' his girtest o' pow'r.
Wher the hâymiakers put up ther picks an' ther riakes,
An' did squot down to snabble[3] ther cheese an' ther kiakes,
An' did vill vrom ther flaggons ther cups wi' ther yale,[4]
An' did miake therzelves merry wi' joke an wi' tiale.   10

Ees, we took up a ruope an' we tied en al roun'
At the top ō'n wi' oon end a-hangen to groun',
An' when we'd a-za'd[5] his girt stem a'most drough,
We gie'd the wold chap about oon tug ar two,
An' 'e swây'd āl his lims, an' 'e nodded his head,
Till 'e vell awoy down lik' a girt lump o' lead:
An' as we rinn'd awoy vrom 'en, cluose at our backs,
Oh! his boughs come a-whizzen an' gie-èn sich cracks;
An' his top wer so lofty that now's a-vell down
The stem ō'n da reach a'most auver the groun'.   20
Zoo the girt elem tree out in little huome groun'
Wer a-stannen this marnen, an' now 's a-cut down.

DCC, *14 June 1840*. Poems of Rural Life, in the Dorset Dialect *(1844)*.

CHRISTMAS INVITATION

Come down to marra night, an' mind
Don't leäve thy fiddle-bag behind.
We'll shiake a lag an' drink a cup
O' yal[1] to kip wold Chris'mas up.

An' let thy sister tiake thy yarm,
The wā'k woont do 'er any harm:
Ther's noo dirt now to spwile her frock,
Var 'tis a-vroze so hard's a rock.

Ther bēn't noo stranngers that 'ull come,
But only a vew nâighbours: zome   10
Vrom *Stowe*, an' *Combe*, an' two ar dree
Vrom uncles up at *Rookery*.

An' thee woot vine[2] a ruozy fiace,
An' pair ov eyes so black as sloos,
The pirtiest oones in al the pliace.
I'm sure I needen tell thee whose.

VELLEN THE TREE
1 yes (W.B.).
2 easing (W.B.).
3 eat up hastily or greedily (W.B.).
4 ale (W.B.).

5 sawn (W.B.).
CHRISTMAS INVITATION
1 ale (W.B.).
2 find (W.B.).

We got a back bran',[3] dree girt logs
So much as dree ov us can car:
We'll put 'em up a*th*irt[4] the dogs,
An' miake a vier to the bar,   20

An' ev'ry oone wull tell his tiale,
An' ev'ry oone wull zing his zong,
An' ev'ry oone wull drink his yal,
To love an' frien'ship al night long.

We'll snap the tongs,[5] we'll have a bal,
We'll shiake the house, we'll rise the ruf,
We'll romp an' miake the mâidens squal,
A catchèn ō'm at bline-man's buff.

Zoo come to marra night, an' mind
Don't leäve thy fiddle-bag behind: 30
We'll shiake a lag, and drink a cup
O' yal to kip wold Chris'mas up.

Poems of Rural Life, in the Dorset Dialect *(1844)*.

KEEPÈN UP O' CHRIS'MAS

An' zoo ya didden come a*th*irt
To have zome fun laste night. How wer't?
Var we'd a-work'd wi' al our might,
To scour the iron *th*ings up bright;
An' brush'd an' scrubb'd the house al droo,
An' brote in var a brand, a plock[1]
O' wood so big's an uppenstock,[2]
An' hung a bough o' misseltoo,
An' ax'd a merry friend ar too,
    To keepèn up o' Chris'mas.   10

An' ther wer wold an' young; an' *Bill*
Soon ā'ter dark stä'k'd up vrom mill,
An' when 'e wer a-comen near
'E whissled loud var I to hear;
An' roun' my head my frock I roll'd,
An' stood in archet[3] like a post,
To miake en *th*ink I wer a ghost;
But he wer up to't, an' did scuold,
To vine me stannen in the cuold,
    A keepèn up o' Chris'mas.   20

We plây'd at farfeits, an' we spun
The trencher[4] roun' an' miade sich fun!
An' had a giame o' dree-kiard loo,[5]
An' then begun to hunt the shoe.
An' al the wold[6] vo'ke zittèn near,

---

3   ? huge amount of fire-wood.
4   athwart, across (W.B.).
5   snappèn tongs. A game of forfeits (W.B.). A sort of musical chairs.
KEEPÈN UP O' CHRIS'MAS
1   block (W.B.).

2   horseblock (W.B.) – for mounting a horse from.
3   orchard (W.B.).
4   plate (game of spinning the plate).
5   3-card loo (card game).
6   old.

A-chattèn roun' the vier pliace,
Did smile in oone another's fiace,
An' shiake right han's wi' hearty cheer,
An' let ther left han's spill ther beer,
    A keepèn up o' Chris'mas. 30

Poems of Rural Life, in the Dorset Dialect (1844).

THE VÂICES THAT BE GONE

When evemen[1] shiades o' trees da hide
  A body by the hedge's zide,
An' twitt'ren birds, wi' plâysome flight,
Da vlee to roost at comen night,
Then I da sānter, out o' zight,
    In archet,[2] wher the pliace oonce rung
    Wi' lāfes[3] a-rised, an' zongs a-zung
      By vâices that be gone.

Ther's still the tree that bore our swing,
An' t'others wher the birds did zing; 10
But long-leav'd docks da auvergrow
The groun' we trampled biare below,
Wi' merry skippèns to an' fro,
    Bezide the banks wher *Jim* did zit
    A-plâyen o' the claranit
      To vâices that be gone.

How mother, when we us'd to stun
  Her head wi' al our nâisy fun,
Did wish us al a-gone vrom huome;
An' now that zome be dead, an' zome 20
Be gone, an' al the pliace is dum,
    How she da wish, wi' useless tears,
    To have agen about her ears
      The vâices that be gone.

Var al the mâidens an' the buoys
  But I, be marri'd off al woys,
Ar dead an' gone; but I da bide
At huome aluone at mother's zide,
An' of'en at the evemen-tide
    I still da sānter out wi' tears 30
    Down droo the archet wher my ears
      Da miss the vâices gone.

DCC, 19 August 1841. Poems of Rural Life, in the Dorset Dialect (1844).

RUSTIC CHILDHOOD

No city primness train'd my feet
To strut in childhood through the street,
But freedom let them loose to tread
The yellow cowslip's downcast head;

Or climb, above the twining hop
And ivy, to the elm-tree's top;
Where southern airs of blue-sky'd day
Breath'd o'er the daisy and the may.
  I knew you young, and love you now,
    O shining grass, and shady bough.   10

Far off from town, where splendour tries
To draw the looks of gather'd eyes,
And clocks, unheeded, fail to warn
The loud-tongued party of the morn,
We spent in woodland shades our day
In cheerful work or happy play,
And slept at night where rustling leaves
Threw moonlight shadows o'er my eaves.
  I knew you young, and love you now,
    O shining grass, and shady bough.   20

Or in the grassy drove by ranks
Of white-stemm'd ashes, or by banks
Of narrow lanes, in-winding round
The hedgy sides of shelving ground;
Where low-shot light struck in to end
Again at some cool-shaded bend,
Where we might see through darkleav'd boughs
The evening light on green hill-brows.
  I knew you young, and love you now,
    O shining grass, and shady bough.   30

Or on the hillock where I lay
At rest on some bright holyday;
When short noon-shadows lay below
The thorn in blossom white as snow;
And warm air bent the glist'ning tops
Of bushes in the lowland copse,
Before the blue hills swelling high
And far against the southern sky.
  I knew you young, and love you now,
    O shining grass, and shady bough.   40

Poems, Partly of Rural Life (In national English) *(John Russell Smith, 1846).*

MY ORCHET IN LINDEN LEA

'Ithin the woodlands, flow'ry gleäded,
  By the woak tree's mossy moot,
The sheenèn grass-bleädes, timber-sheäded,
  Now do quiver under voot;
An' birds do whissle auver head,
An' water's bubblèn in its bed,
An' there vor me the apple tree
Do leän down low in Linden Lea.

When leaves that leätely wer a-springèn
  Now do feäde 'ithin the copse,   10
An' päinted birds do hush their zingèn
  Up upon the timber's tops;

An' brown-leav'd fruit's a-turnèn red,
In cloudless zunsheen, auver head,
Wi' fruit vor me, the apple tree
Do leän down low in Linden Lea.

Let other vo'k meäke money vaster
    In the aïr o' dark-room'd towns,
I don't dread a peevish meäster;
    Though noo man do heed my frowns,   20
I be free to goo abrode,
Or teäke ageän my hwomeward road
To where, vor me, the apple tree
Do leän down low in Linden Lea.

DCC, *20 November 1856*. Hwomely Rhymes. A Second Collection of Poems
in The Dorset Dialect *(John Russell Smith, 1859)*. *['I have taken for this volume
of Dorset Poems, a mode of spelling which I believe is more intelligible than that
of the former one, inasmuch as it gives the lettered Dialect more of the book-form
of the national speech, and yet is so marked as to preserve, as correctly
as the other, the Dorset pronunciation.' Preface.]*

THE BEAN VIELD

'Twer' where the zun did warm the lewth,
An' win' did whiver in the sheäde,
The sweet-aïr'd beäns were out in blooth,
Down there 'ithin the elem gleäde;
A yollor-banded bee did come,
An' softly pitch, wi' hushèn hum,
Upon a beän, an' there did sip,
Upon a swaÿèn blossom's lip:
An' there cried he, 'Aye, I can zee,
This blossom's all a-zent vor me.'   10

A-jilted up an' down, astride
Upon a lofty hoss a-trot,
The meäster then come by wi' pride,
To zee the beäns that he'd a-got;
An' as he zot upon his hoss,
The hoss ageän did snort an' toss
His high-ear'd head, an' at the zight
Ov all the blossom, black an' white:
'Ah! ah!' thought he, the seäme's the bee,
'These beäns be all a-zent vor me.'   20

Zoo let the woorld's riches breed
A strife o' claïms, wi' weak an' strong,
Vor now what cause have I to heed
Who's in the right, or in the wrong;
Since there do come droo yonder hatch,
An' bloom below the house's thatch,
The best o' maïdens, an' do own
That she is mine, an' mine alwone:
Zoo I can zee that love do gi'e
The best ov all good gifts to me.   30

Vor whose be all the crops an' land
A-won an' lost, an' bought, an' zwold;

Or whose, a-roll'd vrom hand to hand,
The highest money that 's a-twold?
Vrom oone to t'other passèn on,
'Tis here to-day, to-morrow gone.
But there's a blessèn high above
It all – a soul o' stedvast love:
Zoo let it vlee, if God do gi'e
Sweet Jessie vor a gift to me.   40

Hwomely Rhymes (1859).

LWONESOMENESS

As I do zew, wi' nimble hand,
    In here avore the window's light,
How still do all the housegear stand
    Around my lwonesome zight.
How still do all the housegear stand
Since Willie now 've a-left the land.

The rwose-tree's window-sheädèn bow
    Do hang in leaf, an' win'-blow'n flow'rs
Avore my lwonesome eyes do show
    Theäse bright November hours.   10
Avore my lwonesome eyes do show
Wi' nwone but I to zee em blow.

The sheädes o' leafy buds, avore
    The peänes, do sheäke upon the glass,
An' stir in light upon the vloor,
    Where now vew veet do pass.
An' stir in light upon the vloor
Where there's a-stirrèn nothen mwore.

This wind mid dreve upon the maïn,
    My brother's ship, a-plowèn foam,   20
But not bring mother, cwold, nor raïn,
    At her now happy hwome.
But not bring mother, cwold, nor raïn,
Where she is out o' païn.

Zoo now that I'm a-mwopèn dumb,
    A-keepèn father's house, do you
Come often wi' your work vrom hwome,
    Vor company. Now do.
Come often wi' your work vrom hwome,
Up here a-while. Do come.

DCC, 17 April 1862. Poems of Rural Life in the Dorset Dialect.
Third Collection (John Russell Smith, 1862).

WINTER WEATHER

When elem stems do rise, in row,
Dark brown, vrom hangens under snow,
An' woods do reach as black as night

By slopen vields o' cleänest white,
The shooters by the snowy rick,
Where trees be high, an' wood is thick,
A-marken tracks the geäme do prick,
Do like the winter weather.

Or where do spread the grey-blue sheet
Ov ice, vor skeäter's gliden veet   10
That they do lift, vrom zide to zide,
Long yards, an' hit em down to slide;
Or sliders, one a-tott'ren slack
Ov limb, an' one upon his back,
An' one upright, do keep his track,
Ha' fun, in winter weather.

When we at night, in snow an' gloom,
Did seek some naïghbour's lighted room,
Though snow did show noo path avore,
Towards the house, we vound the door;   20
An' there, as round the brands, did spread
The creepen vire o' cherry red,
Our veet vrom snow, vrom wind our head,
Wer warm, in winter weather.

Wherever day mid give our road,
By knaps, or hollows over-snow'd,
By windy gaps, or lewer nooks,
Or bridged ice o' vrozen brooks;
Still mid we all, when night do come,
Know where we have a peacevul hwome,   30
An' glowen vire vor vingers numb
Wi' cwold, in winter weather.

Poems in the Dorset Dialect by the Late Rev. W. Barnes (1906).
(Poems mainly from 1867.) Text, Poems, ed. Bernard Jones, 2 vols
(Southern Illinois Press, Carbondale, 1962), I.

WINTER WEATHER

When stems of elms may rise in row,
Dark brown, from hillocks under snow,
And woods may reach as black as night,
By sloping fields of cleanest white.
If shooters by the snowy rick,
Where trees are high, and wood is thick,
Can mark the tracks the game may prick,
    They like the winter weather.

Or where may spread the grey-blue sheet
Of ice, for skaters' gliding feet,   10
That they uplift, from side to side,
Long yards, and hit them down to slide
Or sliders, one that totters slack
Of limb; and one that's on his back;
And one upright that keeps his track,
    Have fun in winter weather.

When we at night, in snow and gloom,
May seek some neighbour's lighted room,
Though snow may show no path before
The house, we still can find the door,   20
And there, as round the brands may spread
The creeping fire, of cherry red,
Our feet from snow, from wind our head,
   Are warm in winter weather.

Wherever day may give our road,
By hills or hollows oversnow'd,
By windy gaps, or shelter'd nooks,
Or bridgèd ice of frozen brooks,
Still may we all, as night may come,
Know where to find a peaceful home,   30
And glowing fire for fingers numb
   With cold, in winter weather.

Poems of Rural Life in Common English *(Macmillan and Co., 1868)*.

THE VIELD PATH

Here oonce did sound sweet words, a-spoke
   In wind that swum
   Where ivy clomb,
About the ribby woak;
An' still the words, though now a-gone,
Be dear to me, that linger on.

An' here, as comely vo'k did pass,
   Their sheädes did slide
   Below their zide,
Along the flow'ry grass,   10
An' though the sheädes be all a-gone,
Still dear's the ground they vell upon.

But could they come where then they stroll'd,
   However young
   Mid sound their tongue,
Their sheädes would show em wold;
But dear, though they be all a-gone,
Be sheädes o' trees that linger on.

O ashèn poles, a-sheenèn tall!
   You be too young
   To have a-sprung   20
In days when I wer small;
But you, broad woak, wi' ribby rind,
Wer here so long as I can mind.

DCC, *26 December 1867. Text (from MS),* Selected Poems, *ed. Andrew Motion
(Penguin, Harmondsworth, 1994).*

THE FIELD PATH

Here sounded words of dear old folk,
   Of this dear ground,
   Where ivy wound
About this ribbèd oak.
And still their words, their words now gone,
Are dear to me that linger on.

And here, as comely forms would pass,
   Their shades would slide
   Below their side,
Along the flow'ry grass.   10
And now, their shades, their shades now gone,
Still hallow ground they fell upon.

But could they come where then they stroll'd,
   However young
   Might sound their tongue,
Their shades would show them old.
So sweet are shades, the shades now shown,
The shades of trees they all have known.

These ashen poles that shine so tall,
   Are still too young   20
   To have upsprung
In days when I was small;
But you, stout oak, you, oak so stout,
Were here when my first moon ran out.

Poems of Rural Life in Common English *(1868)*.

John Henry Newman (1801–90)

John Henry Newman, Roman Catholic Cardinal, polemicist, novelist and poet, was born in the City of London, 21 February 1801, oldest child (he had two brothers and three sisters) of John Newman, a banker, and Jemima Foudrinier. The family was deeply Evangelical (mother was from a French Huguenot clan). John Henry went to private schools, fell in love with Walter Scott's novels, loved reading the Bible, and at the age of fifteen underwent an Evangelical conversion experience. The book which so influenced Dr Johnson and the Wesleys, William Law's *A Serious Call to a Devout and Holy Life* (1729), was a great factor in this teenage awakening. In 1817 he entered Trinity College, Oxford, won a Scholarship in 1818, but did badly (low down in the Second Class) in his final examinations in 1820. Still, the Scholarship helped him stay on in Oxford, teaching and reading, and in 1822 he won a Prize Fellowship at Oriel College. He was ordained Deacon, 13 June 1824, and became curate at St Clement's, Oxford. In March 1825 he became vice-principal of Alban Hall, then, in 1826, a tutor at Oriel. His Oriel friends included E. B. Pusey and R. H. Froude. In 1828 he became

Vicar of the University Church of St Mary. He was moving further and further away from Evangelicalism – faith in the inerrant rule of Scripture being replaced by faith in the inerrant rule of the Church of England. A quarrel over the nature of tutorships at Oriel led to his resignation from his College post in 1832. He and Froude went travelling about the Mediterranean (Rome was 'the most wonderful place in the world', despite its 'polytheistic, degrading, and idolatrous' religion). Becalmed for days in an orange-boat between Palermo and Marseilles in June 1833, Newman composed 'Lead, kindly light, amid the encircling gloom', which became one of the most popular Victorian hymns, for Christians of all stripes (it is very vague theologically) as well as for agnostics such as Thomas Hardy (its shadowy, half-lit border world between outright doubt and outright faith is where the imaginations of Victorian post-Christians liked to repose). It was by far the most popular hymn in the survey conducted by W. T. Stead for his book *Hymns That Have Helped* (1896) and appeared without strain in the Unitarian *Essex Hall Hymn Book* (1891) and in the first *Labour Church Hymnal* (1892).

Back in Oxford in July 1833 Newman became a key figure in the Oxford Movement to rub out the Protestant features of the Church of England, which was started by John Keble's Assize Sermon on 'National Apostasy', 14 July 1833, in St Mary's. The sensational *Tracts for the Times* by Newman and his allies, Newman's afternoon sermons at the University Church, his pamphlets promoting recovery of the Anglo-Catholic tradition (Lancelot Andrewes, for instance) electrified not just Oxford but the world. Newman gradually argued himself – and, of course, large numbers of other Anglicans, not least hordes of devout young men in Oxford University – into accepting the authority and infallibility of the Church of Rome as the only tenable ground of Christian being. In 1842 Newman set up an Anglican monastery in a few cottages at Littlemore on the edge of Oxford; in September 1843 he resigned from St Mary's; in October 1845 he was received into the Roman Catholic Church; a year later he was ordained a priest in Rome, and at Christmas 1847 he returned to England commissioned to set up Oratory Churches. From then on he was based in the Birmingham area, eventually at the Oratory in Edgbaston. In the great fifties agitation over the restoration of a Catholic hierarchy in England, the so-called Papal Aggression, Newman was found guilty of libelling Dr Achilli (an ex-Dominican monk), the Protestant agitator. For seven years, 1851–8, Newman worked as Rector of the new Catholic University in Dublin (his lectures on *The Idea of a University*, 1852, have become a classic of education theory). His response to Charles Kingsley's attacks in the early sixties on his shakiness about 'Truth for its own sake' led to the *Apologia pro Vita Sua* (1864), a classic of Victorian autobiography. Newman's fictionalized account of the reasons for Romanism, *Loss and Gain* (1848), is cumbersome by comparison with the same story told straight in the *Apologia*. Newman could not turn doctrine into novels. He could, however, do dogma in verse, as a succession of Hymn Books for the Birmingham Oratorians shows. Many of his verses and translations were assembled in *Verses on Various Occasions* (1868) – including material from the early *Lyra Apostolica* (1836), the *Verses for Penitents* (1860), and, of course, *The Dream of Gerontius* (1866). The *Dream* appeared first as a serial in the Catholic journal *The Month* in 1865. A death-bed scene done as a revived medieval psychomachia (oddly reminiscent of Marlowe's *Doctor Faustus*), the poem is as striking for its sense of the vastated abysses of non-faith as for its Catholic affirmations. The fifth set of Angelical verses in praise of God quickly entered the standard hymn repertoire as 'Praise to the Holiest in the Height'. Newman was made a Cardinal in 1879 (extremely late, many thought: but then he was openly contemptuous of continental Catholic excesses). He put his powerful and tireless intelligence at the service of general as well as narrowly Catholic apologetics (*The Grammar of Assent*, 1870, is an argument about belief that still packs a punch), but he was never un-slippery in his dialectics (Kingsley was not far wrong about his opponent's argumentative sleights-of-hand). Newman died at Edgbaston, 11 August 1890. Edward Elgar set *Gerontius* finely to music (1900). The Collected Works (1868–81) ran to thirty-six volumes.

THE PILLAR OF THE CLOUD[1]

Lead, Kindly Light, amid the encircling gloom,
  Lead Thou me on!
The night is dark, and I am far from home –
  Lead Thou me on!
Keep Thou my feet: I do not ask to see
The distant scene, – one step enough for me.

I was not ever thus, nor pray'd that Thou
  Shouldst lead me on;
I loved to choose and see my path, but now
  Lead Thou me on!
I loved the garish day, and, spite of fears,
Pride ruled my will: remember not past years.

So long Thy power hath blest me, sure it still
  Will lead me on,
O'er moor and fen, o'er crag and torrent, till
  The night is gone;

10

THE PILLAR OF THE CLOUD
1   in *Exodus*, Israelites are led by a (divinely provided) pillar of cloud.

And with the morn those angel faces smile
Which I have loved long since, and lost awhile.

At Sea: June 16, 1833

First published in volume form as 'Faith', in Lyra Apostolica *[High Church collection of poems by Keble, Newman, Froude, Williams, et al., from* British Magazine*] (Henry Mozley & Sons, Derby, 1836), with sub-title: 'Unto the godly there ariseth up light in the darkness'.* Verses On Various Occasions *(Burns, Oates, & Co., 1868).*

THE DREAM OF GERONTIUS

§ 1

Gerontius   Jesu, Maria – I am near to death,
     And Thou art calling me; I know it now.
Not by the token of this faltering breath,
     This chill at heart, this dampness on my brow, –
(Jesu, have mercy! Mary, pray for me!)
     'Tis this new feeling, never felt before,
(Be with me, Lord, in my extremity!)
     That I am going, that I am no more.
'Tis this strange innermost abandonment,
     (Lover of souls! great God! I look to Thee,)   10
This emptying out of each constituent
     And natural force, by which I come to be.
Pray for me, O my friends; a visitant
     Is knocking his dire summons at my door,
The like of whom, to scare me and to daunt,
     Has never, never come to me before;
'Tis death, – O loving friends, your prayers! – 'tis he!...
     As though my very being had given way,
     As though I was no more a substance now,
And could fall back on nought to be my stay,   20
     (Help, loving Lord! Thou my sole Refuge, Thou,)
And turn no whither, but must needs decay
     And drop from out the universal frame
Into that shapeless, scopeless, blank abyss,
     That utter nothingness, of which I came:
This is it that has come to pass in me;
O horror! this it is, my dearest, this;
So pray for me, my friends, who have not strength to pray.

Assistants
Kyrie eleïson, Christe eleïson, Kyrie eleïson.[1]
Holy Mary, pray for him.   30
All holy Angels, pray for him.
Choirs of the righteous, pray for him.
Holy Abraham, pray for him.
St John Baptist, St Joseph, pray for him.
St Peter, St Paul, St Andrew, St John,
All Apostles, all Evangelists, pray for him.

THE DREAM OF GERONTIUS
1   'Lord, have mercy, Christ, have mercy': opening words of Catholic
Mass.

All holy Disciples of the Lord, pray for him.
All holy Innocents, pray for him.
All holy Martyrs, all holy Confessors,
All holy Hermits, all Holy Virgins,   40
All ye Saints of God, pray for him.

Gerontius
Rouse thee, my fainting soul, and play the man;
   And through such waning span
Of life and thought as still has to be trod,
   Prepare to meet thy God.
And while the storm of that bewilderment
   Is for a season spent,
And, ere afresh the ruin on me fall,
   Use well the interval.

Assistants
Be merciful, be gracious; spare him, Lord.   50
Be merciful, be gracious; Lord, deliver him.
From the sins that are past;
   From Thy frown and Thine ire;
      From the perils of dying;
      From any complying
      With sin, or denying
      His God, or relying
   On self, at the last;
      From the nethermost fire;
From all that is evil;   60
From power of the devil;
Thy servant deliver,
For once and for ever.

By Thy birth, and by Thy Cross,
Rescue him from endless loss;
By Thy death and burial,
Save him from a final fall;
By Thy rising from the tomb,
   By Thy mounting up above,
   By the Spirit's gracious love,   70
Save him in the day of doom.

Gerontius
Sanctus fortis, Sanctus Deus,
   De profundis oro te,
Miserere, Judex meus,
   Parce mihi, Domine.[2]
Firmly I believe and truly
   God is Three, and God is One;
And I next acknowledge duly
   Manhood taken by the Son.
And I trust and hope most fully   80
   In that manhood crucified;
And each thought and deed unruly
   Do to death, as He has died.

2   'O strong and holy one, O Holy God, Out of the depths I pray
thee, Have mercy, O my Judge, Spare me, O Lord.'

Simply to His grace and wholly
   Light and life and strength belong,
And I love, supremely, solely,
   Him the holy, Him the strong.
Sanctus fortis, Sanctus Deus,
   De profundis oro te,
Miserere, Judex meus,   90
   Parce mihi, Domine.
And I hold in veneration,
   For the love of Him alone,
Holy Church, as His creation,
   And her teachings, as His own.
And I take with joy whatever
   Now besets me, pain or fear,
And with a strong will I sever
   All the ties which bind me here.
Adoration aye be given,   100
   With and through the angelic host,
To the God of earth and heaven,
   Father, Son, and Holy Ghost.
Sanctus fortis, Sanctus Deus,
   De profundis oro te,
Miserere, Judex meus,
   Mortis in discrimine.[3]

I can no more; for now it comes again,
That sense of ruin, which is worse than pain,
That masterful negation and collapse   110
Of all that makes me man; as though I bent
Over the dizzy brink
Of some sheer infinite descent;
Or worse, as though
Down, down for ever I was falling through
The solid framework of created things,
And needs must sink and sink
Into the vast abyss. And, crueller still,
A fierce and restless fright begins to fill
The mansion of my soul. And, worse and worse,   120
Some bodily form of ill
Floats on the wind, with many a loathsome curse
Tainting the hallow'd air, and laughs, and flaps
Its hideous wings,
And makes me wild with horror and dismay.
O Jesu, help! pray for me, Mary, pray!
Some Angel, Jesu! such as came to Thee
In Thine own agony.....
Mary, pray for me. Joseph, pray for me.
   Mary, pray for me.   130

Assistants
Rescue him, O Lord, in this his evil hour,
As of old so many by Thy gracious power: –
   (Amen.)
Enoch and Elias from the common doom;
   (Amen.)

3 'O strong and holy one, O Holy God, From the depths I pray thee,
Have mercy, O my Judge, in the critical moment of death.'

Noe from the waters in a saving home; (Amen.)
Abraham from th' abounding guilt of Heathenesse;
    (Amen.)
Job from all his multiform and fell distress;
    (Amen.)
Isaac, when his father's knife was raised to slay;
    (Amen.)
Lot from burning Sodom on its judgment-day;
    (Amen.)
Moses from the land of bondage and despair;
    (Amen.)
Daniel from the hungry lions in their lair;   140
    (Amen.)
And the Children Three amid the furnace-flame;
    (Amen.)
Chaste Susanna from the slander and the shame;
    (Amen.)
David from Golia and the wrath of Saul; (Amen.)
And the two Apostles from their prison-thrall;
    (Amen.)
Thecla from her torments; (Amen:)
    – so to show Thy power,
Rescue this Thy servant in his evil hour.

Gerontius   Novissima hora est;[4] and I fain would sleep.
The pain has wearied me.... Into Thy hands,
O Lord, into Thy hands....

The Priest   Proficiscere, anima Christiana, de hoc mundo![5]   150
Go forth upon thy journey, Christian soul!
Go from this world! Go, in the Name of God
The Omnipotent Father, who created thee!
Go, in the Name of Jesus Christ, our Lord,
Son of the Living God, who bled for thee!
Go, in the Name of the Holy Spirit, who
Hath been pour'd out on thee! Go, in the name
Of Angels and Archangels; in the name
Of Thrones and Dominations; in the name
Of Princedoms and of Powers; and in the name   160
Of Cherubim and Seraphim, go forth!
Go, in the name of Patriarchs and Prophets;
And of Apostles and Evangelists,
Of Martyrs and Confessors; in the name
Of holy Monks and Hermits; in the name
Of holy Virgins; and all Saints of God,
Both men and women, go! Go on thy course;
And may thy place to-day be found in peace,
And may thy dwelling be the Holy Mount
Of Sion: – through the Name of Christ, our Lord.   170

§ 2

Soul of Gerontius   I went to sleep; and now I am refresh'd,
A strange refreshment: for I feel in me
An inexpressive lightness, and a sense
Of freedom, as I were at length myself,

---

4 'This is my final hour.'   5 'Go forth, o Christian spirit, out of this world.'

And ne'er had been before. How still it is!
I hear no more the busy beat of time,
No, nor my fluttering breath, nor struggling pulse;
Nor does one moment differ from the next.
I had a dream; yes: – some one softly said
'He's gone;' and then a sigh went round the room.   180
And then I surely heard a priestly voice
Cry 'Subvenite[6];' and they knelt in prayer.
I seem to hear him still; but thin and low,
And fainter and more faint the accents come,
As at an ever-widening interval.
Ah! whence is this? What is this severance?
This silence pours a solitariness
Into the very essence of my soul;
And the deep rest, so soothing and so sweet,
Hath something too of sternness and of pain.   190
For it drives back my thoughts upon their spring
By a strange introversion, and perforce
I now begin to feed upon myself,
Because I have nought else to feed upon.

Am I alive or dead? I am not dead,
But in the body still; for I possess
A sort of confidence, which clings to me,
That each particular organ holds its place
As heretofore, combining with the rest
Into one symmetry, that wraps me round,   200
And makes me man; and surely I could move,
Did I but will it, every part of me.
And yet I cannot to my sense bring home,
By very trial, that I have the power.
'Tis strange; I cannot stir a hand or foot,
I cannot make my fingers or my lips
By mutual pressure witness each to each,
Nor by the eyelid's instantaneous stroke
Assure myself I have a body still.
Nor do I know my very attitude,   210
Nor if I stand, or lie, or sit, or kneel.

So much I know, not knowing how I know,
That the vast universe, where I have dwelt,
Is quitting me, or I am quitting it.
Or I or it is rushing on the wings
Of light or lightning on an onward course,
And we e'en now are million miles apart.
Yet . . . is this peremptory severance
Wrought out in lengthening measurements of space,
Which grow and multiply by speed and time?   220
Or am I traversing infinity
By endless subdivision, hurrying back
From finite towards infinitesimal,
Thus dying out of the expanded world?

Another marvel: some one has me fast
Within his ample palm; 'tis not a grasp

6 'O come to our aid.'

Such as they use on earth, but all around
Over the surface of my subtle being,
As though I were a sphere, and capable
To be accosted thus, a uniform   230
And gentle pressure tells me I am not
Self-moving, but borne forward on my way.
And hark! I hear a singing; yet in sooth
I cannot of that music rightly say
Whether I hear, or touch, or taste the tones.
Oh, what a heart-subduing melody!

     Angel
    My work is done,
      My task is o'er,
        And so I come,
          Taking it home,   240
    For the crown is won,
      Alleluia,
      For evermore.

    My Father gave
      In charge to me
        This child of earth
          E'en from its birth.
    To serve and save,
      Alleluia,
      And saved is he   250

    This child of clay
      To me was given,
        To rear and train
          By sorrow and pain
    In the narrow way,
      Alleluia.
      From earth to heaven.

Soul   It is a member of that family
Of wondrous beings, who, ere the worlds were made,
Millions of ages back, have stood around   260
The throne of God: – he never has known sin;
But through those cycles all but infinite,
Has had a strong and pure celestial life,
And bore to gaze on the unveil'd face of God,
And drank from the eternal Fount of truth,
And served Him with a keen ecstatic love.
Hark! he begins again.

Angel
O Lord, how wonderful in depth and height,
    But most in man, how wonderful Thou art!
With what a love, what soft persuasive might   270
    Victorious o'er the stubborn fleshly heart,
  Thy tale complete of saints Thou dost provide,
    To fill the throne which Angels lost through pride!

He lay a grovelling babe upon the ground,
    Polluted in the blood of his first sire,
With his whole essence shatter'd and unsound,

And coil'd around his heart a demon dire,
Which was not of his nature, but had skill
To bind and form his op'ning mind to ill.

Then was I sent from heaven to set right   280
    The balance in his soul of truth and sin,
And I have waged a long relentless fight,
    Resolved that death-environ'd spirit to win,
    Which from its fallen state, when all was lost,
    Had been repurchased at so dread a cost.

O what a shifting parti-colour'd scene
    Of hope and fear, of triumph and dismay,
Of recklessness and penitence, has been
    The history of that dreary, life-long fray!
    And O the grace to nerve him and to lead,   290
    How patient, prompt, and lavish at his need!

O man, strange composite of heaven and earth!
    Majesty dwarf'd to baseness! fragrant flower
Running to poisonous seed! and seeming worth
    Cloking corruption! weakness mastering power!
    Who never art so near to crime and shame,
    As when thou hast achieved some deed of name; –

How should ethereal natures comprehend
    A thing made up of spirit and of clay,
Were we not tasked to nurse it and to tend,   300
    Link'd one to one throughout its mortal day?
    More than the Seraph in his height of place,
    The Angel-guardian knows and loves the ransom'd race.

Soul   Now know I surely that I am at length
Out of the body; had I part with earth,
I never could have drunk those accents in,
And not have worshipp'd as a god the voice
That was so musical; but now I am
So whole of heart, so calm, so self-possess'd,
With such a full content, and with a sense   310
So apprehensive and discriminant,
As no temptation can intoxicate.
Nor have I even terror at the thought
That I am clasped by such a saintliness.

Angel
All praise to Him, at whose sublime decree
    The last are first, the first become the last;
By whom the suppliant prisoner is set free,
    By whom proud first-borns from their thrones are cast;
Who raises Mary to be Queen of heaven,
While Lucifer is left, condemn'd and unforgiven.   320

§ 3
Soul   I will address him. Mighty one, my Lord,
My Guardian Spirit, all hail!

Angel   All hail, my child!
My child and brother, hail! what wouldest thou?

Soul   I would have nothing but to speak with thee
For speaking's sake. I wish to hold with thee
Conscious communion; though I fain would know
A maze of things, were it but meet to ask,
And not a curiousness.

Angel   You cannot now
Cherish a wish which ought not to be wish'd.   330

Soul   Then I will speak. I ever had believed
That on the moment when the struggling soul
Quitted its mortal case, forthwith it fell
Under the awful Presence of its God,
There to be judged and sent to its own place
What lets[7] me now from going to my Lord?

Angel   Thou art not let; but with extremest speed
Art hurrying to the Just and Holy Judge:
For scarcely art thou disembodied yet.
Divide a moment, as men measure time,   340
Into its million-million-millionth part,
Yet even less than that the interval
Since thou didst leave the body; and the priest
Cried 'Subvenite,' and they fell to prayer;
Nay, scarcely yet have they begun to pray.

For spirits and men by different standards mete
The less and greater in the flow of time.
By sun and moon, primeval ordinances –
By stars which rise and set harmoniously –
By the recurring seasons, and the swing,   350
This way and that, of the suspended rod
Precise and punctual, men divide the hours,
Equal, continuous, for their common use.

Not so with us in the immaterial world;
But intervals in their succession
Are measured by the living thought alone
And grow or wane with its intensity.
And time is not a common property;
But what is long is short, and swift is slow,
And near is distant, as received and grasp'd   360
By this mind and by that, and by every one
Is standard of his own chronology.
And memory lacks its natural resting-points,
Of years, and centuries, and periods.
It is thy very energy of thought
Which keeps thee from thy God.

Soul   Dear Angel, say,
Why have I now no fear at meeting Him?
Along my earthly life, the thought of death
And judgment was to me most terrible.
I had it aye before me, and I saw   370
The Judge severe e'en in the Crucifix.

7   hinders.

Now that the hour is come, my fear is fled;
And at this balance of my destiny,
Now close upon me, I can forward look
With a serenest joy.

Angel   It is because
Then thou didst fear, that now thou dost not fear,
Thou hast forestall'd the agony, and so
For thee the bitterness of death is past.
Also, because already in thy soul
The judgment is begun. That day of doom,   380
One and the same for the collected world –
That solemn consummation for all flesh,
Is, in the case of each, anticipate
Upon his death; and, as the last great day
In the particular judgment is rehearsed,
So now, too, ere thou comest to the Throne,
A presage falls upon thee, as a ray
Straight from the Judge, expressive of thy lot.
That calm and joy uprising in thy soul
Is first-fruit to thee of thy recompense,   390
And heaven begun.

§ 4

Soul   But hark! upon my sense
Comes a fierce hubbub, which would make me fear,
Could I be frighted.

Angel   We are now arrived
Close on the judgment-court; that sullen howl
Is from the demons who assemble there.
It is the middle region, where of old
Satan appeared among the sons of God,
To cast his jibes and scoffs at holy Job.
So now his legions throng the vestibule,
Hungry and wild, to claim their property,   400
And gather souls for hell. Hist to their cry.

Soul   How sour and how uncouth a dissonance!

Demons
Low-born clods
    Of brute earth,
     They aspire
To become gods,
    By a new birth,
And an extra grace,
    And a score of merits,
       As if aught   410
Could stand in place
      Of the high thought,
     And the glance of fire
   Of the great spirits,
The powers blest,
    The lords by right,
     The primal owners,
      Of the proud dwelling
   And realm of light, –

Dispossessed,   420
Aside thrust,
          Chuck'd down,
By the sheer might,
Of a despot's will,
        Of a tyrant's frown,
    Who after expelling
    Their hosts, gave,
Triumphant still,
And still unjust,
        Each forfeit crown   430
    To psalm-droners,
    And canting groaners,
      To every slave,
    And pious cheat
      And crawling knave,
Who lick'd the dust
    Under his feet

Angel   It is the restless panting of their being;
Like beasts of prey, who, caged within their bars,
In a deep hideous purring have their life,   440
And an incessant pacing to and fro.

Demons
The mind bold
    And independent,
      The purpose free,
So we are told,
Must not think
    To have the ascendant.
        What's a saint?
    One whose breath
      Doth the air taint   450
    Before his death;
      A bundle of bones
    Which fools adore,
      Ha! ha!
    When life is o'er;

    Which rattle and stink,
    E'en in the flesh.
We cry his pardon!
    No flesh hath he;
    Ha! ha!   460
    For it hath died,
    'Tis crucified
    Day by day,
Afresh, afresh,
      Ha! ha!
    That holy clay,
      Ha! ha!
This gains guerdon,
    So priestlings prate,
      Ha! ha!   470
    Before the Judge,
      And pleads and atones
    For spite and grudge,

And bigot mood,

And envy and hate,

And greed of blood.

Soul   How impotent they are! and yet on earth
They have repute for wondrous power and skill;
And books describe, how that the very face
Of the Evil One, if seen, would have a force
Even to freeze the blood, and choke the life
Of him who saw it.

Angel   In thy trial-state
Thou hadst a traitor nestling close at home,
Connatural, who with the powers of hell
Was leagued, and of thy senses kept the keys,
And to that deadliest foe unlock'd thy heart.
And therefore is it, in respect of man,
Those fallen ones show so majestical.
But, when some child of grace, Angel or Saint,
Pure and upright in his integrity
Of nature, meets the demons on their raid,
They scud away as cowards from the fight.
Nay, oft hath holy hermit in his cell,
Not yet disburden'd of mortality,
Mocked at their threats and warlike overtures;
Or, dying, when they swarm'd, like flies, around,
Defied them, and departed to his Judge.

Demons
Virtue and vice,

  A knave's pretence,

    'Tis all the same;

      Ha! Ha!

        Dread of hell-fire,

      Of the venomous flame,

        A coward's plea.

Give him his price,

        Saint though he be,

Ha! Ha!

    From shrewd good sense

      He'll slave for hire;

    Ha! ha!

      And does but aspire

To the heaven above

    With sordid aim.

And not from love.

      Ha! ha!

Soul   I see not those false spirits; shall I see
My dearest Master, when I reach His throne?
Or hear, at least, His awful judgment-word
With personal intonation, as I now
Hear thee, not see thee, Angel? Hitherto
All has been darkness since I left the earth;
Shall I remain thus sight-bereft all through
My penance-time? If so, how comes it then
That I have hearing still, and taste, and touch,

480

490

500

510

520

Yet not a glimmer of that princely sense
Which binds ideas in one, and makes them live?

Angel   Nor touch, nor taste, nor hearing hast thou now;
Thou livest in a world of signs and types,
The presentations of most holy truths,   530
Living and strong, which now encompass thee.
A disembodied soul, thou hast by right
No converse with aught else beside thyself;
But, lest so stern a solitude should load
And break thy being, in mercy are vouchsaf'd
Some lower measures of perception,
Which seem to thee, as though through channels brought,
Through ear, or nerves, or palate, which are gone.
And thou art wrapp'd and swath'd around in dreams,
Dreams that are true, yet enigmatical;   540
For the belongings of thy present state,
Save through such symbols, come not home to thee.
And thus thou tell'st of space and time and size.
Of fragrant, solid, bitter, musical,
Or fire, and of refreshment after fire;
As (let me use similitude of earth,
To aid thee in the knowledge thou dost ask) –
As ice which blisters may be said to burn.
Nor hast thou now extension, with its parts
Correlative, – long habit cozens thee, –   550
Nor power to move thyself, nor limbs to move.
Hast thou not heard of those, who after loss
Of hand or foot, still cried that they had pains
In hand or foot, as though they had it still?
So is it now with thee, who hast not lost
Thy hand or foot, but all which made up man.
So will it be, until the joyous day
Of resurrection, when thou wilt regain
All thou hast lost, new-made and glorified.
How, even now, the consummated Saints   560
See God in heaven, I may not explicate;
Meanwhile, let it suffice thee to possess
Such means of converse as are granted thee,
Though, till that Beatific Vision, thou art blind;
For e'en thy purgatory, which comes like fire,
Is fire without its light.

Soul   His will be done!
I am not worthy e'er to see again
The face of day; far less His countenance,
Who is the very sun. Natheless in life,   570
When I look'd forward to my purgatory
It ever was my solace to believe,
That, ere I plunged amid the avenging flame,
I had one sight of Him to strengthen me.

Angel   Nor rash nor vain is that presentiment;
Yes, – for one moment thou shalt see thy Lord.
Thus will it be: what time thou art arraign'd
Before the dread tribunal, and thy lot
Is cast for ever, should it be to sit
On His right hand among His pure elect,   580

Then sight, or that which to the soul is sight,
As by a lightning-flash, will come to thee,
And thou shalt see, amid the dark profound,
Whom thy soul loveth, and would fain approach, –
One moment; but thou knowest not, my child,
What thou dost ask: that sight of the Most Fair
Will gladden thee, but it will pierce thee too.

Soul   Thou speakest darkly, Angel; and an awe
Falls on me, and a fear lest I be rash.

Angel   There was a mortal, who is now above   590
In the mid glory: he, when near to die,
Was given communion with the Crucified, –
Such, that the Master's very wounds were stamp'd
Upon his flesh; and, from the agony
Which thrill'd through body and soul in that embrace,
Learn that the flame of the Everlasting Love
Doth burn, ere it transform. . . .

§ 5
. . . Hark to those sounds
They come of tender beings angelical,
Least and most childlike of the sons of God.

> *First Choir of Angelicals*
> Praise to the Holiest in the height,   600
>   And in the depth be praise:
> In all His words most wonderful;
>   Most sure in all His ways!
>
> To us His elder race He gave
>   To battle and to win,
> Without the chastisement of pain,
>   Without the soil of sin.
>
> The younger son He will'd to be
>   A marvel in his birth:
> Spirit and flesh his parents were;   610
>   His home was heaven and earth.
>
> The Eternal bless'd His child, and arm'd,
>   And sent him hence afar,
> To serve as champion in the field
>   Of elemental war.
>
> To be His Viceroy in the world
>   Of matter, and of sense;
> Upon the frontier, towards the foe,
>   A resolute defence.

Angel   We now have pass'd the gate, and are within   620
The House of Judgment; and whereas on earth
Temples and palaces are form'd of parts
Costly and rare, but all material,
So in the world of spirits nought is found,
To mould withal and form into a whole,
But what is immaterial; and thus

The smallest portions of this edifice,
Cornice, or frieze, or balustrade, or stair,
The very pavement is made up of life –
Of holy, blessed, and immortal beings,   630
Who hymn their Maker's praise continually.

Second Choir of Angelicals
Praise to the Holiest in the height,
    And in the depth be praise:
In all His words most wonderful;
    Most sure in all His ways!

Woe to thee, man! for he was found
    A recreant in the fight;
And lost his heritage of heaven,
    And fellowship with light.

Above him now the angry sky,   640
    Around the tempest's din;
Who once had Angels for his friends,
    Had but the brutes for kin.

O man! a savage kindred they;
    To flee that monster brood
He scaled the seaside cave, and clomb
    The giants of the wood.

With now a fear, and now a hope,
    With aids which chance supplied,
From youth to eld, from sire to son,   650
    He lived, and toil'd, and died.

He dreed his penance age by age;
    And step by step began
Slowly to doff his savage garb,
    And be again a man.

And quicken'd by the Almighty's breath
    And chasten'd by His rod,
And taught by angel-visitings,
    At length he sought his God;

And learn'd to call upon His Name,   660
    And in His faith create
A household and a father-land,
    A city and a state.

Glory to Him who from the mire,
    In patient length of days,
Elaborated into life
    A people to His praise!

Soul   The sound is like the rushing of the wind –
The summer wind – among the lofty pines;
Swelling and dying, echoing round about,   670
Now here, now distant, wild and beautiful;
While, scatter'd from the branches it has stirr'd,
Descend ecstatic odours.

Third Choice of Angelicals
Praise to the Holiest in the height,
   And in the depth be praise:
In all His words most wonderful;
   Most sure in all His ways!

The Angels, as beseemingly
   To spirit-kind was given,
At once were tried and perfected,   680
   And took their seats in heaven.

For them no twilight or eclipse;
   No growth and no decay:
'Twas hopeless, all-ingulfing night,
   Or beatific day.

But to the younger race there rose
   A hope upon its fall;
And slowly, surely, gracefully,
   The morning dawn'd on all.

And ages, opening out, divide   690
   The precious and the base,
And from the hard and sullen mass
   Mature the heirs of grace.

O man! albeit the quickening ray,
   Lit from his second birth,
Makes him at length what once he was,
   And heaven grows out of earth;

Yet still between that earth and heaven –
   His journey and his goal –
A double agony awaits   700
   His body and his soul.

A double debt he has to pay –
   The forfeit of his sins:
The chill of death is past, and now
   The penance-fire begins.

Glory to Him; who evermore
   By truth and justice reigns;
Who tears the soul from out its case,
   And burns away its stains!

Angel They sing of thy approaching agony,   710
Which thou so eagerly didst question of:
It is the face of the Incarnate God
Shall smite thee with that keen and subtle pain;
And yet the memory which it leaves will be
A sovereign febrifuge[8] to heal the wound;
And yet withal it will the wound provoke,
And aggravate and widen it the more.

---

8 medicine to reduce fever.

Soul Thou speakest mysteries; still methinks I know
To disengage the tangle of thy words:
Yet rather would I hear thy angel voice,   720
Than for myself be thy interpreter.

Angel When then – if such thy lot – thou seest thy Judge,
The sight of Him will kindle in thy heart
All tender, gracious, reverential thoughts.
Thou wilt be sick with love, and yearn for Him,
And feel as though thou couldst but pity Him,
That one so sweet should e'er have placed Himself
At disadvantage such, as to be used
So vilely by a being so vile as thee.
There is a pleading in His pensive eyes   730
Will pierce thee to the quick, and trouble thee.
And thou wilt hate and loathe thyself; for, though
Now sinless, thou wilt feel that thou hast sinn'd,
As never thou didst feel; and wilt desire
To slink away, and hide thee from His sight:
And yet wilt have a longing aye to dwell
Within the beauty of His countenance.
And these two pains, so counter and so keen, –
The longing for Him, when thou seest Him not;
The shame of self at thought of seeing Him, –   740
Will be thy veriest, sharpest purgatory.

Soul My soul is in my hand: I have no fear, –
In His dear might prepared for weal or woe.
But hark! a grand, mysterious harmony:
It floods me, like the deep and solemn sound
Of many waters.

Angel   We have gain'd the stairs
Which rise towards the Presence-chamber; there
A band of mighty Angels keep the way
On either side, and hymn the Incarnate God.   750

Angels of the Sacred Stair
Father, whose goodness none can know, but they
    Who see Thee face to face,
By man hath come the infinite display
    Of Thy victorious grace;
But fallen man – the creature of a day –
    Skills not that love to trace.
It needs, to tell the triumph Thou hast wrought,
An Angel's deathless fire, an Angel's reach of thought.

It needs that very Angel, who with awe,
    Amid the garden shade,   760
The great Creator in His sickness saw,
    Soothed by a creature's aid,
And agonized, as victim of the Law
    Which He Himself had made;
For who can praise Him in His depth and height,
But he who saw Him reel amid that solitary fight.

Soul Hark! for the lintels of the presence-gate
Are vibrating and echoing back the strain.

Fourth Choir of Angelicals
Praise to the Holiest in the height,
   And in the depth be praise;
In all His words most wonderful;   770
   Most sure in all His ways!

The foe blasphemed the Holy Lord,
   As if He reckon'd ill,
In that He placed His puppet man
   The frontier place to fill.

For, even in his best estate,
   With amplest gifts endued,
A sorry sentinel was he,
   A being of flesh and blood.   780

As though a thing, who for his help
   Must needs possess a wife,
Could cope with those proud rebel hosts
   Who had angelic life.

And when, by blandishment of Eve,
   That earth-born Adam fell,
He shriek'd in triumph, and he cried,
   'A sorry sentinel;

'The Maker by His word is bound,
   Escape or cure is none;   790
He must abandon to his doom,
   And slay His darling son.'

Angel   And now the threshold, as we traverse it.
Utters aloud its glad responsive chant.

Fifth Choir of Angelicals
Praise to the Holiest in the height,
   And in the depth be praise:
In all His words most wonderful;
   Most sure in all His ways!

O loving wisdom of our God!
   When all was sin and shame,   800
   A second Adam to the fight
     And to the rescue came.

O wisest love! that flesh and blood
   Which did in Adam fail,
Should strive afresh against their foe,
   Should strive and should prevail;

And that a higher gift than grace
   Should flesh and blood refine,
God's Presence and His very Self,
   And Essence all-divine.   810

O generous love! that He who smote
   In man for man the foe,

The double agony in man
   For man should undergo;

And in the garden secretly,
   And on the cross on high,
Should teach His brethren and inspire
   To suffer and to die.

§ 6

Angel   Thy judgment now is near, for we are come
Into the veilèd presence of our God.   820

Soul   I hear the voices that I left on earth.

Angel   It is the voice of friends around thy bed,
Who say the 'Subvenite' with the priest.
Hither the echoes come; before the Throne
Stands the great Angel of the Agony,
The same who strengthen'd Him, what time He knelt
Lone in that garden shade, bedew'd with blood.
That Angel best can plead with Him for all
Tormented souls, the dying and the dead.

Angel of The Agony
Jesu! by that shuddering dread which fell on Thee;   830
Jesu! by that cold dismay which sicken'd Thee;
Jesu! by that pang of heart which thrill'd in Thee;
Jesu! by that mount of sins which crippled Thee;
Jesu! by that sense of guilt which stifled Thee;
Jesu! by that innocence which girdled Thee;
Jesu! by that sanctity which reign'd in Thee;
Jesu! by that Godhead which was one with Thee;
Jesu! spare these souls which are so dear to Thee,
Who in prison, calm and patient, wait for Thee;
Hasten, Lord, their hour, and bid them come to Thee,   840
To that glorious Home, where they shall ever gaze on Thee.

Soul   I go before my Judge. Ah!....

Angel   ....   Praise to His Name!
The eager spirit has darted from my hold,
And, with the intemperate energy of love,
Flies to the dear feet of Emmanuel;
But, ere it reach them, the keen sanctity,
Which with its effluence, like a glory, clothes
And circles round the Crucified, has seized,
And scorch'd, and shrivell'd it; and now it lies   850
Passive and still before the awful Throne.
O happy, suffering soul! for it is safe,
Consumed, yet quicken'd, by the glance of God.

Soul
Take me away, and in the lowest deep
   There let me be,
And there in hope the lone night-watches keep,
   Told out for me.
There, motionless and happy in my pain,
   Lone, not forlorn, –

There will I sing my sad perpetual strain,   860
   Until the morn.
There will I sing, and soothe my stricken breast,
   Which ne'er can cease
To throb, and pine, and languish, till possest
   Of its Sole Peace.
There will I sing my absent Lord and Love: –
   Take me away,
That sooner I may rise, and go above,
And see Him in the truth of everlasting day.

§ 7

Angel Now let the golden prison ope its gates,   870
   Making sweet music, as each fold revolves
   Upon its ready hinge. And ye, great powers,
   Angels of Purgatory, receive from me
   My charge, a precious soul, until the day,
   When, from all bond and forfeiture released,
   I shall reclaim it for the courts of light.

Souls in Purgatory

1 Lord, Thou hast been our refuge: in every generation;
2 Before the hills were born, and the world was: from age to age Thou art God.
3 Bring us not, Lord, very low: for Thou hast said, Come back again, ye sons of Adam.
4 A thousand years before Thine eyes are but as yesterday: and as a watch of the night which   880
   is come and gone.
5 The grass springs up in the morning: at evening-tide it shrivels up and dies.
6 So we fail in Thine anger: and in Thy wrath are we troubled.
7 Thou hast set our sins in Thy sight: and our round of days in the light of Thy countenance.
8 Come back, O Lord! how long: and be entreated for Thy servants.
9 In Thy morning we shall be filled with Thy mercy: we shall rejoice and be in pleasure all our
   days.
10 We shall be glad according to the days of our humiliation: and the years in which we have seen
   evil.
11 Look, O Lord, upon Thy servants and on Thy work: and direct their children.
12 And let the beauty of the Lord our God be upon us: and the work of our hands, establish
   Thou it.
Glory be to the Father, and to the Son: and to the Holy Ghost.
As it was in the beginning, is now, and ever shall be: world without end. Amen.   890

Angel
Softly and gently, dearly-ransom'd soul,
   In my most loving arms I now enfold thee,
And, o'er the penal waters, as they roll,
   I poise thee, and I lower thee, and hold thee.

And carefully I dip thee in the lake,
   And thou, without a sob or a resistance,
Dost through the flood thy rapid passage take,
   Sinking deep, deeper, into the dim distance.

Angels, to whom the willing task is given,
   Shall tend, and nurse, and lull thee, as thou liest;   900
And Masses on the earth, and prayers in heaven,
   Shall aid thee at the Throne of the Most Highest.

Farewell, but not for ever! brother dear,
    Be brave and patient on thy bed of sorrow;
Swiftly shall pass thy night of trial here,
    And I will come and wake thee on the morrow.

The Oratory: January, 1865.

First published in The Month *(April–May, 1865).* Verses on Various Occasions *(1868).*

L.E.L.: Letitia Elizabeth Landon (1802–38)

The racy life and sensational death of Letitia Landon haunted the Victorian poetical memory, especially of women poets such as Elizabeth Barrett Browning. She was born, 14 August 1802, into an ecclesiastical family of impoverished but fiercely loyal churchmen. One great-grandfather was said on his memorial stone to have used his pen 'to the utter confusion of all dissenters'. An uncle was Provost of Worcester College, Oxford. John Landon, her father, was a world traveller and an army recruiting agent. She attended the same Chelsea school as Mary Mitford and Caroline Lamb, and was taken up early by William Jerdan, editor of the *Literary Gazette* (who first set fascinated gaze on her when she was 'a plump girl bowling a hoop . . . with the hoop-stick in one hand and a book in the other, reading as she ran'). Her first poem appeared in Jerdan's *Gazette*, signed L., when she was only seventeen. Rapidly she became a mainstay of the paper, contributing numerous poems – now signed L.E.L. – and reviews. Her verses achieved instant popularity. Numerous volumes appeared through the 1820s. She also contributed widely to the popular albums and annuals of the day, wrote novels (*Ethel Churchill*, 1837, was thought the best of them) and joined the staff of *Fraser's Magazine.*

She needed the money – her family relied on her for financial support, which included keeping her brother at Oxford. She also needed the love of literary men. Scandalous rumours circulated about liaisons with Jerdan and with William Maginn, the editor of *Fraser's*, and also with Bulwer Lytton. Because of these stories an engagement – apparently to John Forster, future biographer of Dickens – was broken off, and in July 1838 she retreated to West Africa with a manifestly unsuitable husband, George Maclean, governor of Cape Coast Castle. He was said to have had a black mistress already in place, and when L.E.L. was found dead on 15 October 1838, an empty prussic acid bottle in her hand, no one knew for certain whether the cause was suicide, murder (the mistress succeeding as the vengeful black madwoman in the attic where Bertha Mason in *Jane Eyre* failed) or an accidental overdose (L.E.L. was taking prussic acid as medication). This sensational and sub-Byronic end seems only an apt apotheosis to her career as a precocious and gifted improviser (one of her best-selling poems was in fact 'The Improvisatrice', 1824) and to her writing's obsessive interest in heroic but doomed and deserted females.

Songs by L. E. L.

I

I loved her! and her azure eyes
Haunted me from sweet sunrise
To the dewy evening's close,
Dyeing rosier the rose.
    Yet I said, 'tis best to be
    Free – and I again was free.

But I changed – and auburn hair
Seem'd to float upon the air;
Till I thought the orange-flower
Breathed of nothing but her bower.   10
    Yet I said, 'tis best to be
    Free – and I again was free.

Next I loved a Moorish maid,
And her cheek of moonlit shade;

Pale and languid, left my sleep
Not a shade but her's to keep.
    Yet I said, 'tis best to be
    Free – and I again was free.

But there came a lovelier one;
She undid all they had done: 20
I loved – I love her – ah, how well!
Language has no power to tell.
    Now the wonder is to me
    How I ever lived while free?

II

A mouth that is itself a rose,
    And scatters roses too;
An eye that borrows from the sky
    Its sunshine and its blue;

A laugh, an echo from the song   30
  The lark at morning sings;
A voice – but that has sadder tones,
  And tells of tenderer things;

Auburn is her long dark hair
  With a golden shine:
Must I tell you more to know
  This true love of mine?

I might say she is so kind,
  Faithful, fond – but no!
My sweet maiden's hidden heart   40
  None but I may know.

III

I send back thy letters:
  Ah! would I could send
The memory that fetters,
  The dreams that must end.

I send back thy tresses,
  Thy long raven hair;
Could I send thy caresses,
  They too should be there.

But keep thou each token
  I lavished on thee;   50

Ring and chain are unbroken,
  Thou false one to me!

That my rival, – how bitter
  That word to my heart!
May read in their glitter
  How faithless thou art.

IV

As steals the dew along the flower,
  So stole thy smile on me;
I cannot tell the day, nor hour
  I first loved thee!   60

But now in every scene and clime,
  In change of grief or glee,
I only measure from the time
  I first loved thee!

I only think, – when fast and fair
  My good ship cuts the sea, –
I leave the lovely island where
  I first loved thee!

The wide world has one only spot
  Where I would wish to be;   70
Where, all the rest of life forgot,
  I first loved thee!

The New Monthly Magazine And Literary Journal, *47, Part II (1836), 29–30.*

SUBJECTS FOR PICTURES

The Banquet of Aspasia and Pericles[1]

Waken'd by the small white fingers,
  Which its chords obey,
On the air the music lingers
  Of a low and languid lay
    From a soft Ionian lyre; –
Purple curtains hang the walls,
And the dying daylight falls
O'er the marble pedestals
  Of the pillars that aspire,
    In honour of Aspasia,   10
  The bright Athenian bride.

There are statues white and solemn,
  Olden gods are they;
And the wreath'd Corinthian column
  Guardeth their array.
    Lovely that acanthus wreath,
Drooping round the graceful girth:

All the fairest things of earth,
Art's creations have their birth –
    Still from love and death.   20
    They are gather'd for Aspasia,
  The bright Athenian bride.

There are gold and silver vases
  Where carved victories shine;
While within the sunlight blazes
  Of the fragrant Teian wine,
    Or the sunny Cyprian isle.[2]
From the garlands on each brow
Take they early roses now;
And each rose-leaf bears a vow,   30
    As they pledge the radiant smile
  Of the beautiful Aspasia,
  The bright Athenian bride.

THE BANQUET OF ASPASIA AND PERICLES

1 Pericles, great Athenian leader; Aspasia, his beautiful, talented mistress; their home a centre of intellect and culture.

2 Teos, island celebrated for its wine (and erotic verse and drinking songs). Cyprus, associated with worship of Aphrodite, or Venus.

With the spoils of nations splendid
    Is that stately feast;
By her youthful slaves attended –
    Beauties from the East,
        With their large black dewy eyes.
Though their dark hair sweeps the ground,
Every heavy tress is wound   40
With the white sea-pearl around;
    For no queen in Persia vies
    With the proud Aspasia,
    The bright Athenian bride.

One hath caught mine eye – the fairest;
    'Tis a Theban girl:
Though a downcast look thou wearest,
    And nor flower nor pearl
        Winds thy auburn hair among:
With a white, unsandall'd foot,   50
Leaning languid on thy lute,
Weareth thy soft lip, though mute,
    Smiles yet sadder than thy song.
    Can grief come nigh Aspasia,
    The bright Athenian bride?

On an ivory couch reclining
    Doth the bride appear;
In her eyes the light is shining,
    For her chief is near; –
        And her smile grows bright to gaze   60
On the stately Pericles,

Lord of the Athenian seas,
And of Greece's destinies.
    Glorious, in those ancient days,
    Was the lover of Aspasia,
    The bright Athenian bride.

Round her small head, perfume-breathing
    Was a myrtle stem,
Fitter for her bright hair's wreathing
    Than or gold or gem;   70
        For the myrtle breathes of love.
O'er her cheek, so purely white,
From her dark eyes came such light
As is, on a summer night,
    With the moon above.
    Fair as moonlight was Aspasia,
    The bright Athenian bride.

These fair visions have departed,
    Like a poet's dream,
Leaving us pale and faint-hearted   80
    By life's common stream,
        Whence all lovelier light hath fled.
Not so: they have left behind
Memory to the kindling mind,
With bright fantasies combined.
    Still the poet's dream is fed
    By the beauty of Aspasia,
    The bright Athenian bride.

The New Monthly Magazine And Literary Journal, 47, Part II (1836), 176–8.

Calypso Watching the Ocean[1]

Years, years have passed away,
Since to yonder fated bay
    Did the Hero come.
Years, years have passed the while,
Since he left the lovely isle
    For his Grecian home.
He is with the dead – but She
Weepeth on eternally
    In the lone and lovely island
    Mid the far off southern seas.   10

Downwards floateth her bright hair,
Fair – how exquisitely fair!
    But it is unbound.
Never since that parting hour
Golden band or rosy flower
    In it has been wound;
There it droopeth sadly bright,

In the morning's sunny light,
    On the lone and lovely island
    In the far off southern seas.   20

Like a marble statue placed,
Looking o'er the watery waste,
    With its white fixed gaze;
There the Goddess sits, her eye
Raised to the unpitying sky:
    So uncounted days
Has she asked of yonder main.
Him it will not bring again
    To the lone and lovely island
    In the far off southern seas.   30

To that stately brow is given,
Loveliness that sprung from heaven –
    Is, like heaven, bright:

CALYPSO WATCHING THE OCEAN
1   Calypso, queen of island Ogygia, where Odysseus was wrecked, but
only stayed with her seven years.

Never there may time prevail,
But her perfect face is pale;
    And a troubled light
Tells of one who may not die,
Vex'd with immortality
    In the lone and lovely island
    Mid the far off southern seas.   40

Desolate beside that strand,
Bow'd upon her cold, white hand,
    Is her radiant head;
Silently she sitteth there,
While her large eyes on the air
    Trace the much-loved dead:
Eyes that know not tears nor sleep,
Would she not be glad to weep,
    In the lone and lovely island
    Mid the far off southern seas.   50

Far behind the fragrant pile,
Sends its odours through the isle;
    And the winds that stir
In the poplars, are imbued
With the cedar's precious wood,
    With incense and with myrrh,
Till the azure waves beneath
Bear away the scented breath
    Of the lone and lovely island
    In the far off southern seas.   60

But no more does that perfume
Hang around the purple loom
    Where Calypso wove
Threads of gold with curious skill,
Singing at her own sweet will
    Ancient songs of love:
Weary on the sea-wash'd shore,

She will sing those songs no more
    In the lone and lovely island
    Mid the far off southern seas.   70

From the large green leaves escape
Clusters of the blooming grape;
    Round the shining throne
Still the silver fountains play,
Singing on through night and day,
    But they sing alone:
Lovely in their early death,
No one binds a violet wreath,
    In the lone and lovely island
    Mid the far off southern seas.   80

Love and Fate – oh, fearful pair!
Terrible in strength ye are;
    Until ye had been,
Happy as a summer night,
Conscious of its own sweet light,
    Was that Island-queen.
Would she could forget to grieve,
Or that she could die and leave
    The lone and lovely island
    Mid the far off southern seas.   90

She is but the type of all,
Mortal or celestial,
    Who allow the heart,
In its passion and its power,
On some dark and fated hour,
    To assert its part.
Fate attends the steps of Love, –
Both brought misery from above
    To the lone and lovely island
    Mid the far off southern seas.   100

The New Monthly Magazine And Literary Journal, 47, Part III (1836), 20–1.

The Moorish Maiden's Vigil

Does she watch him, fondly watch him,
    Does the maiden watch in vain?
Do her dark eyes strain to catch him
    Riding o'er the moonlit plain,
        Stately, beautiful, and tall?
Those long eyelashes are gleaming
    With the tears she will not shed;
Still her patient hope is dreaming
    That it is his courser's tread,
        If an olive leaf but fall.   10
Woe for thee, my poor Zorayda,
    By the fountain's side;
Better, than this weary watching,
    Better thou hadst died.

Scarlet is the turban folded
　　Round the long black plaits of hair;
And the pliant gold is moulded
　　Round her arms that are as fair,
　　　　As the moonlight which they meet.
Little of their former splendour   20
　　Lingereth in her large dark eyes;
Ever sorrow maketh tender,
　　And the heart's deep passion lies
　　　　In their look so sad and sweet.
　　Woe for thee, my poor Zorayda,
　　　　By the fountain's side;
　　Better, than this weary watching,
　　　　Better thou hadst died.

Once the buds of the pomegranate
　　Paled beside her cheek's warm dye,   30
Now 'tis like the last sad planet
　　Waning in the morning sky –
　　　　She has wept away its red.
Can this be the Zegri maiden,
　　Whom Granada named its flower,
Drooping like a rose rain-laden? –
　　Heavy must have been the shower,
　　　　Bowing down its fragrant head.
　　Woe for thee, my poor Zorayda,
　　　　By the fountain's side;   40
　　Better, than this weary watching,
　　　　Better thou hadst died.

To the north her fancies wander,
　　There he dwells, her Spanish knight:
'Tis a dreadful thing to ponder,
　　Whether true love heard aright.
　　　　Did he say those gentle things
Over which fond memories linger,
　　And with which she cannot part?
Still his ring is on her finger,   50
　　Still his name is in her heart –
　　　　All around his image brings.
　　Woe for thee, my poor Zorayda,
　　　　By the fountain's side;
　　Better, than this weary watching,
　　　　Better thou hadst died.

Can the fond heart be forsaken
　　By the one who sought that heart?
Can there be who will awaken
　　All of life's diviner part,   60
　　　　For some vanity's cold reign.
Heavy is the lot of woman –
　　Heavy is her loving lot –
If it thus must share in common
　　Love with those who know it not –
　　　　With the careless and the vain.
　　Woe for thee, my poor Zorayda,
　　　　By the fountain's side;

Better, than this weary watching,
  Better thou hadst died.   70

Faithless Christian! – ere the blossom,
  Hanging on the myrtle bough,
Float on the clear fountain's bosom,
  She who listened to thy vow –
      She will watch for thee no more!
'Tis a tale of frequent sorrow
  Love seems fated to renew;
It will be again to-morrow
  Just as bitter and as true,
      As it aye has been of yore.   80
    Woe to thee, my poor Zorayda,
      By the fountain's wave;
  But the shade of rest is round thee –
      And it is the grave!

The New Monthly Magazine And Literary Journal, *47, Part III (1836), 24–5.*

A SUTTEE[1]

Gather her raven hair in one rich cluster,
Let the white champac[2] light it, as a star
Gives to the dusky night a sudden lustre,
      Shining afar.

Shed fragrant oils upon her fragrant bosom,
Until the breathing air around grows sweet;
Scatter the languid jasmine's yellow blossom
      Beneath her feet.

Those small white feet are bare – too soft are they
To tread on aught but flowers; and there is roll'd   10
Round the slight ankle, meet for such display,
      The band of gold.

Chains and bright stones are on her arms and neck;
What pleasant vanities are linked with them,
Of happy hours, which youth delights to deck
      With gold and gem.

She comes! So comes the Moon, when she has found
A silvery path wherein thro' heaven to glide.
Fling the white veil – a summer cloud – around;
      She is a bride!   20

And yet the crowd that gather at her side
Are pale, and every gazer holds his breath.
Eyes fill with tears unbidden, for the bride –
      The bride of Death!

A SUTTEE
1 Indian widow (Hindu) who immolates herself on husband's funeral
pyre.

2 fragrant Asian evergreen tree, sacred to Hindus.

She gives away the garland from her hair,
She gives the gems that she will wear no more;
All the affections, whose love-signs they were,
                              Are gone before.

The red pile blazes – let the bride ascend,
And lay her head upon her husband's heart,   30
Now in a perfect unison to blend –
                              No more to part.

The Zenana and Minor Poems of L. E. L. *(Fisher, Son, & Co., London; Quai d'Ecole,*
Paris, 1839).

FELICIA HEMANS

No more, no more – oh, never more returning,
    Will thy beloved presence gladden earth;
No more wilt thou with sad, yet anxious yearning
    Cling to those hopes which have no mortal birth.
Thou art gone from us, and with thee departed,
    How many lovely things have vanished too:
Deep thoughts that at thy will to being started,
    And feelings, teaching us our own were true.
Thou hast been round us, like a viewless spirit,
    Known only by the music on the air;   10
The leaf or flowers which thou hast named inherit
    A beauty known but from thy breathing there:
For thou didst on them fling thy strong emotion,
    The likeness from itself the fond heart gave;
As planets from afar look down on ocean,
    And give their own sweet image to the wave.

And thou didst bring from foreign lands their treasures,
    As floats thy various melody along;
We know the softness of Italian measures,
    And the grave cadence of Castilian song.   20
A general bond of union is the poet,
    By its immortal verse is language known,
And for the sake of song do others know it –
    One glorious poet makes the world his own.
And thou – how far thy gentle sway extended!
    The heart's sweet empire over land and sea;
Many a stranger and far flower was blended
    In the soft wreath that glory bound for thee.
The echoes of the Susquehanna's waters
    Paused in the pine-woods words of thine to hear;   30
And to the wide Atlantic's younger daughters
    Thy name was lovely, and thy song was dear.

Was not this purchased all too dearly? – never
    Can fame atone for all that fame hath cost.
We see the goal, but know not the endeavour,
    Nor what fond hopes have on the way been lost.
What do we know of the unquiet pillow,
    By the worn cheek and tearful eyelid prest,
When thoughts chase thoughts, like the tumultuous billow,

Whose very light and foam reveals unrest?   40
We say, the song is sorrowful, but know not
   What may have left that sorrow on the song;
However mournful words may be, they show not
   The whole extent of wretchedness and wrong
They cannot paint the long sad hours, passed only
   In vain regrets o'er what we feel we are.
Alas! the kingdom of the lute is lonely –
   Cold is the worship coming from afar.

Yet what is mind in woman, but revealing
   In sweet clear light the hidden world below,   50
By quicker fancies and a keener feeling
   Than those around, the cold and careless, know?
What is to feed such feeling, but to culture
   A soil whence pain will never more depart?
The fable of Prometheus and the vulture
   Reveals the poet's and the woman's heart.
Unkindly are they judged – unkindly treated –
   By careless tongues and by ungenerous words;
While cruel sneer, and hard reproach, repeated,
   Jar the fine music of the spirit's chords.   60
Wert thou not weary – thou whose soothing numbers
   Gave other lips the joy thine own had not?
Didst thou not welcome thankfully the slumbers
   Which closed around thy mourning human lot?

What on this earth could answer thy requiring,
   For earnest faith – for love, the deep and true,
The beautiful, which was thy soul's desiring,
   But only from thyself its being drew.
How is the warm and loving heart requited
   In this harsh world, where it awhile must dwell.   70
Its best affections wronged, betrayed, and slighted –
   Such is the doom of those who love too well.
Better the weary dove should close its pinion,
   Fold up its golden wings and be at peace;
Enter, O ladye, that serene dominion
   Where earthly cares and earthly sorrows cease.
Fame's troubled hour has cleared, and now replying,
   A thousand hearts their music ask of thine.
Sleep with a light, the lovely and undying
   Around thy grave – a grave which is a shrine.   80

The Zenana and Minor Poems of L. E. L. *(1839).*

THE FACTORY

'Tis an Accursed Thing!

There rests a shade above yon town,
   A dark funereal shroud:
'Tis not the tempest hurrying down,
   'Tis not a summer cloud.

The smoke that rises on the air
   Is as a type and sign;

A shadow flung by the despair
   Within those streets of thine.

That smoke shuts out the cheerful day
   The sunset's purple hues,   10
The moonlight's pure and tranquil ray,
   The morning's pearly dews.

Such is the moral atmosphere
   Around thy daily life;
Heavy with care, and pale with fear,
   With future tumult rife.

There rises on the morning wind
   A low appealing cry,
A thousand children are resign'd
   To sicken and to die!   20

We read of Moloch's sacrifice,[1]
   We sicken at the name,
And seem to hear the infant cries –
   And yet we do the same; –

And worse – 'twas but a moment's pain
   The heathen altar gave,
But we give years, – our idol, Gain,
   Demands a living grave!

How precious is the little one,
   Before his mother's sight,   30
With bright hair dancing in the sun,
   And eyes of azure light!

He sleeps as rosy as the south,
   For summer days are long;
A prayer upon the little mouth,
   Lull'd by his nurse's song.

Love is around him, and his hours
   Are innocent and free;
His mind essays its early powers
   Beside his mother's knee.   40

When afteryears of trouble come,
   Such as await man's prime,
How will he think of that dear home,
   And childhood's lovely time!

And such should childhood ever be,
   The fairy well; to bring
To life's worn, weary memory
   The freshness of its spring.

But here the order is reversed,
   And infancy, like age,   50
Knows of existence but its worst,
   One dull and darken'd page; –

Written with tears and stamp'd with toil,
   Crush'd from the earliest hour,
Weeds darkening on the bitter soil
   That never knew a flower.

Look on yon child, it droops the head,
   Its knees are bow'd with pain;
It mutters from its wretched bed,
   'O, let me sleep again!'   60

Alas! 'tis time, the mother's eyes
   Turn mournfully away;
Alas! 'tis time, the child must rise,
   And yet it is not day.

The lantern's lit – she hurries forth,
   The spare cloak's scanty fold
Scarce screens her from the snowy north,
   The child is pale and cold.

And wearily the little hands
   Their task accustom'd ply;   70
While daily, some 'mid those pale bands,
   Droop, sicken, pine, and die.

Good God! to think upon a child
   That has no childish days,
No careless play, no frolics wild,
   No words of prayer and praise!

Man from the cradle – 'tis too soon
   To earn their daily bread,
And heap the heat and toil of noon
   Upon an infant's head.   80

To labour ere their strength be come,
   Or starve, – such is the doom
That makes of many an English home
   One long and living tomb!

Is there no pity from above, –
   No mercy in those skies;
Hath then the heart of man no love,
   To spare such a sacrifice?

O, England! though thy tribute waves
   Proclaim thee great and free,   90
While those small children pine like slaves,
   There is a curse on thee!

First published in The Christian Lady's Magazine, *10 (1838), 219–22.*
Poetical Works, *ed. William Bell Scott (George Routledge, 1873).*

THE FACTORY
1   Canaanite deity to whose idol children were offered as burnt
sacrifice.

Winthrop Mackworth Praed (1802–39)

Winthrop Mackworth Praed, politician and poet, much renowned in his time and afterwards as a producer of somewhat glittering *vers de société*, was born 26 July 1802 at 35 St John Street, Bedford Row, London, the third son of William Mackworth Praed of Teignmouth, Devonshire. His mother was a Winthrop. She died when he was one year old and he was mainly cared for by an elder sister. He was a prodigious reader and chess-player before he was sent to Eton in March 1814. At that school he won prizes for English verse, edited the *Etonian* magazine and competed at the chess-board with E. B. Pusey. He went up to Trinity College, Cambridge, in Michaelmas 1821, was a great success as a classicist, became a friend of T. B. Macaulay, and was twice winner of the Chancellor's Medal for an English Poem (1823, 1824). After graduation in 1825 he tutored at Eton, won a Fellowship at Trinity (1827), was called to the Bar (1829), and entered Parliament (in 1830) as representative of St Germans, a rotten borough (the seat was his for £1,000). He naturally opposed the First Reform Bill of 1832, which abolished seats like his. He wrote much prose and verse for the conservative *Morning Post*. A strong political ally of the Duke of Wellington, he got into the Commons again in 1834, this time for Great Yarmouth, and he was Secretary to the Board of Control in Peel's administration (1834–5). In 1835 he married Helen Bogle, a woman of French extraction, daughter of a rich West Indian sugar-merchant, to whom he addressed several of his more feeling short poems. Her family opposed the marriage – which fired the love-plot of his long poem 'The Bridal of Belmont'. His verse lacked satirical venom, though, even when irked, like this, by greatly provoking circumstance. A touch for poetic elegance would always choke off extremities of feeling, and Praed's talent was always rather to amuse than to grip and destroy. He and his friend Derwent Coleridge successfully worked in the later thirties for a national education system. Never physically strong, Praed died youngish of a rapid consumption at Chester Square, London, 15 July 1839, leaving a widow and two daughters. His poems were collected first in American editions in 1844, 1850 and 1859, only subsequently appearing in the authorized English collection in two volumes (1864), with a memoir by Derwent Coleridge. This collection went into several editions. A volume of his essays appeared in Morley's Universal Library (1887) and a volume of *Political and Occasional Poems* appeared in 1888. Selections of his poems continued to be published throughout the century. They satisfied a taste not least for neatly packaged glimpses of high life.

LETTERS FROM TEIGNMOUTH

II: Private Theatricals

'Sweet, when actors first appear,
The loud collision of applauding gloves.'

Moultrie

Your labours, my talented brother,
    Are happily over at last:
They tell me – that, somehow or other,
    The Bill is rejected, – or past;
And now you'll be coming, I'm certain,
    As fast as your posters can crawl,
To help us to draw up our curtain,
    As usual, at Fustian Hall.

Arrangements are nearly completed;
    But still we've a Lover or two,
Whom Lady Albina entreated
    We'd keep, at all hazards, for you:

10

Sir Arthur makes horrible faces;
    Lord John is a trifle too tall;
And yours are the safest embraces
    To faint in, at Fustian Hall.

Come, Clarence; – it's really enchanting
    To listen and look at the rout:
We're all of us puffing and panting,
    And raving, and running about;   20
Here Kitty and Adelaide bustle;
    There Andrew and Anthony bawl;
Flutes murmur – chains rattle – robes rustle
    In chorus, at Fustian Hall.

By the bye, there are two or three matters
    We want you to bring us from Town:
The Inca's white plumes from the hatter's,
    A nose and a hump for the Clown;
We want a few harps for our banquet;
    We want a few masks for our ball;   30
And steal from your wise friend Bosanquet
    His white wig, for Fustian Hall!

Hunca Munca must have a huge sabre;
    Friar Tuck has forgotten his cowl;
And we're quite at a stand still with Weber
    For want of a lizard and owl:
And then, for our funeral procession,
    Pray get us a love of a pall, –
Or how shall we make an impression
    On feelings, at Fustian Hall?   40

And, Clarence, you'll really delight us,
    If you'll do your endeavour to bring,
From the Club, a young person to write us
    Our prologue, and that sort of thing;
Poor Crotchet, who did them supremely,
    Is gone for a Judge to Bengal;
I fear we shall miss him extremely
    This season, at Fustian Hall.

Come, Clarence! your idol Albina
    Will make a sensation, I feel;   50
We all think there never was seen a
    Performer so like the O'Neill:
At rehearsals, her exquisite fury
    Has deeply affected us all;
For one tear that trickles at Drury,
    There'll be twenty at Fustian Hall!

Dread objects are scattered before her
    On purpose to harrow her soul;
She stares, till a deep spell comes o'er her,
    At a knife, or a cross, or a bowl.   60
The sword never seems to alarm her
    That hangs on a peg to the wall;
And she doats on thy rusty old armour,
    Lord Fustian, of Fustian Hall.

She stabbed a bright mirror this morning, –
   (Poor Kitty was quite out of breath!) –
And trampled, in anger and scorning,
   A bonnet and feathers to death.
But hark! – I've a part in 'The Stranger,' –
   There's the Prompter's detestable call!   70
Come, Clarence – our Romeo and Ranger –
   We want you at Fustian Hall!

Written 1831. The Poems of Winthrop Mackworth Praed*, 2 vols*
(Edward Moxon & Co., 1864), II.

To Helen

With Crabbe's Poems, a Birthday Present

Give Crabbe, dear Helen, on your shelf,
A place by Wordsworth's mightier self;
In token that your taste, self wrought
From mines of independent thought,
And shaped by no exclusive rule
Of whim or fashion, sect or school,
Can honour Genius, whatsoe'er
The garb it chance or choose to wear.

Nor deem, dear Helen, unallied
The bards we station side by side;   10
Different their harps, – to each his own;
But both are true and pure of tone.
Brethren, methinks, in times like ours
Of misused gifts, perverted powers, –
Brethren are they, whose kindred song
Nor hides the Right, nor gilds the Wrong.

Dated 12 February 1837. Poems *(1864), I.*

To Helen

With Southey's Poems

A happy and a holy day
   Is this alike to soul and sight;
With cheerful love, and joyful lay
   Would I, dear Helen, greet its light.

But vain the purpose – very vain!
   I cannot play the minstrel's part,
When recent guilt and present pain
   Untune the lyre, unnerve the heart.

Yet prize these tomes of golden rhyme;
   And let them tell you, in far years,   10
When faint the record traced by Time
   Of brightest smiles or saddest tears,

As sunward rose the Persian's prayer,
   Though clouds might dim the votary's view,

So still, through doubt and grief and care,
My spirit, Helen, turned to you.

Dated 7 July 1838. Poems *(1864), I.*

TO HELEN

Dearest, I did not dream four years ago,
   When through your veil I saw your bright tears shine,
Caught your clear whisper, exquisitely low,
   And felt your soft hand tremble into mine,
That in so brief – so very brief a space,
   He, who in love both clouds and cheers our life,
Would lay on you, so full of light, joy, grace,
   The darker, sadder duties of the wife, –
Doubts, fears, and frequent toil, and constant care
   For this poor frame, by sickness sore bested;   10
The daily tendance on the fractious chair,
   The nightly vigil by the feverish bed.

Yet not unwelcomed doth this morn arise,
   Though with more gladsome beams it might have shone.
Strength of these weak hands, light of these dim eyes,
   In sickness, as in health, – bless you, My Own!

Dated Sudbury, 7 July 1839, Poems *(1864), I.*

Thomas Lovell Beddoes (1803–49)

Thomas Lovell Beddoes, poet and physician, was born in Clifton, near Bristol, 20 July 1803, eldest son of Dr Thomas Beddoes (chemist, quack-doctor, supporter of the French Revolution, friend of Southey and Coleridge, patron of the scientific genius Humphrey Davy) and Anna Edgeworth (sister of Maria Edgeworth, the Irish novelist). Dr Beddoes died when Thomas Lovell was five. The boy went to Bath Grammar School, then (1817) to Charterhouse, after that (May 1820) to Pembroke College, Oxford. He was a precociously literary youth – a novel and a play by the age of sixteen, a sonnet in the *Morning Post* at the same age (July 1819), a volume of verses *Improvisatore* while he was still a freshman (1821). The play *A Bride's Tragedy*, a mish-mash of Jacobean allegiances, was published in 1823, while Beddoes was still an undergraduate. He clearly thought he was heading for a theatrical career and projected, and wrote bits of, several plays. Meanwhile, still at Oxford, he was one of the backers for Shelley's *Posthumous Poems*. Like his father, he was rebellious and radical in his politics. The death of his mother in Florence (1824) interrupted his undergraduate career, but going out to Italy did mean he met Landor and Mary Shelley. He graduated in 1825, and began his greatly pre-occupying work on the big pseudo-medieval poem about the murder of a Silesian Duke by his court-jester, *Death's*

Jest-Book, or The Fool's Tragedy (published in final form only in 1850). After Oxford he became a medical student at several German universities, getting into his usual trouble with authorities over his democratic politics. He qualified as MD in 1832, practised in Zürich (where his appointment as professor of medicine was vetoed on political grounds), had to flee the city for his life in 1840 during a peasants' revolt, and became thereafter a peripatetic medical practitoner and physiological experimenter, mainly in Germany and Switzerland. His German translation of a standard work on the spinal cord appeared in 1838, and it is believed that large amounts of verse and political prose were published anonymously in German papers. His life did not conduce to great cheerfulness. Constantly on the move, he tinkered endlessly with *Death's Jest-Book*. Early in 1848 he almost died of an infection caught from a dead body in Frankfurt. Later that year he broke a leg falling from his horse near Basel; gangrene set in; the leg was amputated below the knee. He seemed to be recovering when he was found dying, 26 January 1849. There was a note directing all his MSS to the care of his friend Thomas Forbes Kelsall. 'I ought to have been among other things a better poet', it said. Kelsall saw *Death's Jest-Book* into print and brought out an edition of *Poems by the Late Thomas Lovell Beddoes*, with a memoir. People said Beddoes looked rather like Keats (he was indeed a tiny man) and also Shakespeare (he did, latterly, sport a beard). He died owning several Shropshire farms. Kelsall passed on his box of Beddoes papers to Robert Browning – who, like Tennyson, was an admirer.

SONG

By Female Voices

We have bathed, where none have seen us,
  In the lake and in the fountain,
    Underneath the charmed statue
Of the timid, bending Venus,
  When the water-nymphs were counting
In the waves the stars of night,
  And those maidens started at you,
Your limbs shone through so soft and bright.
  But no secrets dare we tell,
    For thy slaves unlace thee,   10
    And he, who shall embrace thee,
  Waits to try thy beauty's spell.

Death's Jest-Book, or The Fool's Tragedy *(William Pickering, 1850), Act IV, sc. iii.*

ATHULF'S SONG

A cypress-bough, and a rose-wreath sweet,
A wedding-robe, and a winding-sheet,
  A bridal-bed and a bier.
  Thine be the kisses, maid,
    And smiling Love's alarms;
  And thou, pale youth, be laid
    In the grave's cold arms.
  Each in his own charms,
    Death and Hymen[1] both are here;
      So up with scythe and torch,   10
      And to the old church porch,
    While all the bells ring clear:
  And rosy, rosy the bed shall bloom,
  And earthy, earthy heap up the tomb.

Now tremble dimples on your cheek,
Sweet be your lips to taste and speak,
  For he who kisses is near:
  By her the bridegod fair,
    In youthful power and force;
  By him the grizard bare,   20
    Pale knight on a pale horse,
    To woo him to a corpse.
    Death and Hymen both are here;
      So up with scythe and torch,
      And to the old church porch,
    While all the bells ring clear:
  And rosy, rosy the bed shall bloom,
  And earthy, earthy heap up the tomb.

Death's Jest-Book *(1850), Act IV, Sc. iii.*

ATHULF'S SONG
1 god of marriage.

A CROCODILE

Hard by the lilied Nile I saw
A duskish river-dragon stretched along,
The brown habergeon of his limbs enamelled
With sanguine almandines and rainy pearl:
And on his back there lay a young one sleeping,
No bigger than a mouse; with eyes like beads,
And a small fragment of its speckled egg
Remaining on its harmless, pulpy snout;
A thing to laugh at, as it gaped to catch
The baulking, merry flies. In the iron jaws   10
Of the great devil-beast, like a pale soul
Fluttering in rocky hell, lightsomely flew
A snowy troculus, with roseate beak
Tearing the hairy leeches from his throat.

The Poems Posthumous and Collected, *2 vols (William Pickering, 1851)*, I.
('Dramatic Scenes and Fragments', XI.)

INSIGNIFICANCE OF THE WORLD

Why what's the world and time? a fleeting thought
In the great meditating universe,
A brief parenthesis in chaos.

The Poems Posthumous and Collected *(1851)*, I.
('Dramatic Scenes and Fragments', XIX.)

SAD AND CHEERFUL SONGS CONTRASTED

Sing me no more such ditties: they are well
For the last gossips, when the snowy wind
Howls in the chimney till the very taper
Trembles with its blue flame, and the bolted gates
Rattle before old winter's palsied hand.
If you will sing, let it be cheerily
Of dallying love. There's many a one among you
Hath sung, beneath our oak trees to his maiden,
Light bird-like mockeries, fit for love in springtime.
Sing such a one.   10

The Poems Posthumous and Collected *(1851)*, I.
('Dramatic Scenes and Fragments', XXXVI.)

SONNET

To Tartar, a Terrier Beauty

Snowdrop of dogs, with ear of brownest dye,
Like the last orphan leaf of naked tree
Which shudders in bleak autumn; though by thee,
Of hearing careless and untutored eyes,
Not understood articulate speech of men,
Nor marked the artificial mind of books,
– The mortal's voice eternized by the pen, –
Yet hast thou thought and language all unknown
To Babel's scholars; oft intensest looks,
Long scrutiny o'er some dark-veined stone   10
Dost thou bestow, learning dead mysteries
Of the world's birth-day, oft in eager tone
With quick-tailed fellows bandiest prompt replies,
Solicitudes canine, four-footed amities.

The Poems Posthumous and Collected *(1851), I.*

James Clarence Mangan (1803–49)

James Clarence Mangan, Irish poet – archetypical drunken-Irish poet – was born James Mangan, 1 May 1803 – the Clarence he added later for poetic effect and in tribute to Shakespeare's unfortunate character of that name in *Richard III*. He was one of four children of a drunken and violent Dublin grocer and serial bankrupt, who may have actually killed one of the infant brothers. Mangan showed aptitude for the Romance languages at school but had to give up education early to help out the family finances. He worked in various ill-paid clerkly occupations – at a scrivener's, an accountant's, in the library of Trinity College, and in the office of the Irish Ordnance Survey. But alcohol (and the whiff of opium) kept him at menial levels. He taught himself German to read German philosophy, was animated by the cult of Werther and understudied the manner of the German Romantic poet (blue cloak, odd headgear, long golden unkempt hair, face a dissipated white). His work has a long streak of bad Romantic Gothicism in it. His literary contributions to Irish journals were numerous (he published only in Ireland). His forte was adaptation, pastiche, translation and pseudo-translation. He pretended knowledge of Turkish, Persian, Arabic, Coptic, but used German versions of writings from such languages. He was without Irish – a classic instance of the Irish writer whose tongue was utterly colonized by the English – and his adaptations from Irish came from versions available in English prose. He was a terse epigrammatist and satirist. A Catholic nationalist, his pen was closely involved with Thomas Davis's Young Ireland movement. He contributed variously to Charles Duffy's *Nation*, Mitchel's *United Irishman*, the *Irishman*, and *Duffy's Irish Catholic Magazine*. There was, clearly, a constant problem with identity, as Irishman and poet, which is part of his appeal to subsequent Irish nationalist writers such as Yeats. His pseudonyms were legion – Comet, Clarence, A Yankee, Manos, Lageniensis, von Baugtrotter, von Tutschemupp, The Mourne-r, The Man in the Cloak – and his life-work and identity are indeed still cloaked and shadowy. He was poor, weak, depressive, probably anorexic, lonely (he never married – his story was that he'd been monstrously jilted), a lost soul on James Thomson lines. He registered his sense of being a *poète maudit*, an outcast in the friendless city, not least in the autobiographical verse of *The Nameless One* (1848): 'trampled, derided, hated,/And worn by weakness, disease and wrong'. In and out of hospital at the end of the forties, he died, 20 June 1849, during a cholera epidemic, his general drunken debilitation and starvation assisting the cholera in its work on him. Dr Wilde – not yet Oscar's father – was the one who found him in 'the wretched hovel where he had retired to die': quite emaciated, 'in a state of indescribable misery and squalor'. His *German Anthology* appeared in two volumes in 1849. Thirty of his ballads were in Havelock Ellis's *Romances and Ballads of Ireland* (1850), and various collections and selections filtered slowly through in the years after his death. The vast extent of his oeuvre is only now becoming clear. Lionel Johnson's enthusiasm for Mangan's poetry was said to be a main reason for his adopting Irish nationality. The Ulsterman Louis MacNeice, by contrast, lacked sympathy ('all thump and swagger and syrupy self-pity'). For James Joyce, the magnetizing Mangan myth was probably a major inducement to get out of Ireland.

TWENTY GOLDEN YEARS AGO

O, the rain, the weary, dreary rain,
    How it plashes on the window-sill!
Night, I guess too, must be on the wane,
    Strass and Gass¹ around are grown so still.
Here I sit, with coffee in my cup –
    Ah! 'twas rarely I beheld it flow
In the taverns where I loved to sup
    Twenty golden years ago!

Twenty years ago, alas! – but stay,
    On my life, 'tis half-past twelve o'clock!   10
After all, the hours *do* slip away –
    Come, here goes to burn another block!
For the night, or morn, is wet and cold,
    And my fire is dwindling rather low: –
I had fire enough, when young and bold,
    Twenty golden years ago!

Dear! I don't feel well at all, somehow:
    Few in Weimar dream how bad I am;
Floods of tears grow common with me now,
    High-Dutch floods, that Reason cannot dam.   20
Doctors think I'll neither live nor thrive
    If I mope at home so – I don't know –
Am I living *now?* I *was* alive
    Twenty golden years ago.

Wifeless, friendless, flagonless, alone,
    Not quite bookless, though, unless I chuse,
Left with nought to do, except to groan,
    Not a soul to woo, except the Muse –
O! this, this is hard for *me* to bear,
    Me, who whilome lived so much *en haut*,   30
Me, who broke all hearts like chinaware
    Twenty golden years ago!

P'rhaps 'tis better: – Time's defacing waves
    Long have quenched the radiance of my brow –
They who curse me nightly from their graves
    Scarce could love me were they living now;
But my loneliness hath darker ills –
    Such dun-duns as Conscience, Thought and Co.,
Awful Gorgons! worse than tailors' bills
    Twenty golden years ago!   40

Did I paint a fifth of what I feel,
    O, how plaintive you would ween I was!
But I won't, albeit I have a deal
    More to wail about than Kerner² has!
Kerner's tears are wept for withered flowers,
    Mine for withered hopes; my Scroll of Woe

---

2   Andreas Justinus Kerner (1786–1862), occultist German physician
and poet.

Dates, alas! from Youth's deserted bowers,
   Twenty golden years ago!

Yet may Deutschland's bardlings flourish long!
   Me, I tweak no beak among them; – hawks   50
Must not pounce on hawks; besides, in song
   I could once beat all of them by chalks.
Though you find me, as I near my goal,
   Sentimentalising like Rousseau,[3]
Oh! I had a grand Byronian soul
   Twenty golden years ago!

Tick-tick, tick-tick! – Not a sound save Time's,
   And the windgust, as it drives the rain –
Tortured torturer of reluctant rhymes,
   Go to bed, and rest thine aching brain!   60
Sleep! – no more the dupe of hopes or schemes;
   Soon thou sleepest where the thistles blow –
Curious anticlimax to thy dreams
   Twenty golden years ago!

First published in Dublin University Magazine *(June 1840)*. Poems of
James Clarence Mangan (Many Hitherto Uncollected), *ed.*
D. J. O'Donoghue (O'Donoghue, & Co., M. H. Gill & Son,
Dublin; A. H. Bullen, London, 1903).

SIBERIA

In Siberia's wastes
   The Ice-wind's breath
Woundeth like the toothèd steel;
Lost Siberia doth reveal
   Only blight and death.

Blight and death alone.
   No Summer shines.
Night is interblent with Day.
In Siberia's wastes alway
   The blood blackens, the heart pines.   10

In Siberia's wastes
   No tears are shed,
For they freeze within the brain.
Nought is felt but dullest pain,
   Pain acute, yet dead;

Pain as in a dream,
   When years go by
Funeral-paced, yet fugitive,
When man lives, and doth not live,
   Doth not live – nor die.   20

3   Jean-Jacques Rousseau (1712–78), Genevan political philosopher,
educationalist, author of the influential *Confessions* (1781).

In Siberia's wastes
   Are sands and rocks.
Nothing blooms of green or soft,
But the snow-peaks rise aloft
   And the gaunt ice-blocks.

And the exile there
   Is one with those;
They are part, and he is part,
For the sands are in his heart,
   And the killing snows.   30

Therefore, in those wastes
   None curse the Czar.
Each man's tongue is cloven by
The North Blast, that heweth nigh
   With sharp scymitar.

And such doom each drees,
   Till, hunger-gnawn,
And cold-slain, he at length sinks there,
Yet scarce more a corpse than ere
   His last breath was drawn.   40

First published in The Nation *(18 April 1846).* Irish and Other Poems
(The O'Connell Press, M. H. Gill & Son, Dublin, 1886). Poems, *ed. O'Donoghue (1903).*

THE NIGHT IS FALLING

The night is falling in chill December,
   The frost is mantling the silent stream,
Dark mists are shrouding the mountain's brow;
My soul is weary: I now
         Remember
   The days of roses but as a dream.

The icy hand of the old Benumber,
   The hand of Winter is on my brain,
I try to smile, while I inly grieve;
I dare not hope or believe   10
         That Summer
   Will ever brighten the earth again,

So, gazing gravewards, albeit immortal,
   Man cannot pierce through the girdling Night
That sunders Time from Eternity,
Nor feel this death-valse to be
         The portal
   To realms of glory and Living Light.

First published in the Irish Monthly Magazine *(October 1845).*
Poems, *ed. O'Donoghue (1903).*

GONE IN THE WIND

Solomon! where is thy throne? It is gone in the wind.
Babylon! where is thy might? It is gone in the wind.
Like the swift shadows of Noon, like the dreams of the Blind,
Vanish the glories and pomps of the earth in the wind.

Man! canst thou build upon aught in the pride of thy mind?
Wisdom will teach thee that nothing can tarry behind;
Though there be thousand bright actions embalmed and enshrined,
Myriads and millions of brighter are snow in the wind.

Solomon! where is thy throne? It is gone in the wind.
Babylon! where is thy might? It is gone in the wind.   10
All that the genius of Man hath achieved or designed
Waits but its hour to be dealt with as dust by the wind.

Say, what is Pleasure? A phantom, a mask undefined;
Science? An almond, whereof we can pierce but the rind;
Honour and Affluence? Firmans that Fortune hath signed
Only to glitter and pass on the wings of the wind.

Solomon! where is thy throne? It is gone in the wind.
Babylon! where is thy might? It is gone in the wind.
Who is the Fortunate? He who in anguish hath pined!
He shall rejoice when his relics are dust in the wind!   20

Mortal! be careful with what thy best hopes are entwined;
Woe to the miners for Truth – where the Lampless have mined!
Woe to the seekers on earth for – what none ever find!
They and their trust shall be scattered like leaves on the wind.

Solomon! where is thy throne? It is gone in the wind.
Babylon! where is thy might? It is gone in the wind.
Happy in death are they only whose hearts have consigned
All Earth's affections and longings and cares to the wind.

Pity, thou, reader! the madness of poor Humankind,
Raving of Knowledge, – and Satan so busy to blind!   30
Raving of Glory, – like me, – for the garlands I bind
(Garlands of song) are but gathered, and – strewn in the wind!

Solomon! where is thy throne? It is gone in the wind.
Babylon! where is thy might? It is gone in the wind.
I, Abul-Namez, must rest; for my fire hath declined,
And I hear voices from Hades like bells on the wind.

First published in Dublin University Magazine *(1842).* Poems*, ed. O'Donoghue (1903).*

Edward (George Earle Lytton) Bulwer-Lytton (First Lord Lytton) (1803–73)

Edward Bulwer-Lytton – as he became; early on he was known as Lytton Bulwer – novelist, politician, occasional poet, was third and youngest son of a bullying military man, Colonel (later General) William Bulwer and Elizabeth Lytton of Knebworth Hall, Hertfordshire. He was born 25 May 1803 at 31 Baker Street, London, but not baptized until 1810, some time after his father died (in 1807). He was regarded as a prodigy, writing poems at the age of seven. He was educated privately (persuading his mother against sending him to Eton). His first volume, *Ismael and Other Poems*, appeared in 1820; his second, *Delmour, or the Tale of a Sylphid*, in 1823, while he was a Cambridge undergraduate. He was first at Trinity College, then Trinity Hall, where he read little and attended no lectures. He was a contemporary star of the Cambridge Debating Union along with Winthrop Mackworth Praed. He won the Chancellor's Medal for a poem *Sculpture* (1825), brought out the Byronic *Weeds and Flowers* volume (1825) and devoted himself after graduation to the life of the international dandy – racketing about between Paris and London, spreading fictionalized versions of grand passions, pursuing Lady Caroline Lamb, participating in a famous duel, winning lots of money gambling, becoming a devoted whist player, riding, fencing, boxing, acting the whole Byronic part (he was nicknamed 'Childe Harold'). He married the Irish beauty Rosina Doyle Wheeler in 1827, much against his mother's wishes, a marriage which ended in messy separation (she alleging violence, he getting her certified insane; she writing a novel, *Cheveley, or the Man of Honour* (1839) against him, pursuing him in the courts, attacking him before election crowds). He had to write to keep up an expensive mode of life, churning out journalism, much drama, and a chain of critically despised but popular novels, especially historical ones, such as *The Last Days of Pompeii* (1834). He was early on an associate of J. S. Mill, espousing certain Liberal causes such as anti-slavery, and working for authors' rights, but he became more and more hostile to extensions of the franchise after 1832. Upon his mother's death in 1843 he inherited Knebworth and assumed the name Bulwer-Lytton. He was in and out of Parliament, eventually as an outright Tory (he was Secretary for the Colonies in Lord Derby's ministry of 1858–9: there are towns in Australia named Lytton after him; and Derby created him Baron Lytton of Knebworth in 1866). He was a chum of Disraeli's and also close to Dickens. He wrote for Dickens's amateur acting troupe. They co-founded the Guild of Literature and Art to help indigent authors. Dickens named his son born in 1832 Edward Bulwer Lytton. Bulwer-Lytton edited the *New Monthly* (1831–2) and founded the *Monthly Chronicle* (1841). Several of his fictions were serialized in *Blackwood's Edinburgh Magazine*. As for poetry, he kept trying his hand at verse, especially narrative poems. *O'Neil, or the Rebel* appeared in 1827. There was the satirical *Siamese Twins* (1831), a *Collected Poems* (1831), an epic *King Arthur* (1848–9), *St Stephen's* (1860), *The Boatman* (1864), *The Lost Tales of Miletus* (1866). He translated Schiller (*Poems and Ballads*, 1844) and Horace (*Odes and Epodes*, 1869). He never indulged in self-doubt as either writer or critic, and his self-confident exuberance could lead to very interestingly mocking and meta-textual productions such as *My Novel* (1853 – by 'Pisistratus Caxton', a favourite pseudonym). But in all his work, including his non-fictional histories, such as *Athens, its Rise and Fall*, there's a bluff crudeness and vulgarity which prefers energy to, say, getting his facts right. His verse narrative *The New Timon* (1846), among other things, attacked Tennyson for ladylike verse ('Let School-Miss Alfred vent her chaste delight/On "darling little rooms so warm and bright"') and for the Civil List pension given to a 'wealthy' man. Tennyson replied with 'The New Timon, and the Poets', sent to *Punch* without his knowledge (he quickly regretted this: see his 'After-Thought'). With more truth, Tennyson's private opinion was that Lytton was a well-off wastrel, 'astride upon the nipple of Dandyism'. The striding dandy died at Torquay, 18 January 1873.

THE SOULS OF BOOKS

I

Sit here and muse! it is an antique room –
High roof'd with casements, through whose purple pane
Unwilling Daylight steals amidst the gloom,
Shy as a fearful stranger.
        There THEY reign,

In loftier pomp than waking life had known,
The Kings of Thought! not crown'd until the grave.
When Agamemnon[1] sinks into the tomb,
Homer takes back the royalties he gave,
And rules the nations from the Argive's throne.[2]   10
Ye ever-living and imperial Souls,
Lighting with undistinguished rays the air
We live and breathe in; who of us can tell
What he had been, if Cadmus[3] had not taught
The magic letters by which thought to thought
Bequeathes a wealth enlarged by every heir?
Had Plato's reasonings perished in his cell,
Leaving no trace on time-defying scrolls?
If, hush'd with Homer's harp his mighty line,
The world had lost 'the tale of Troy divine?'   20
There, loom the outlines vast of right and wrong.
Heroic force assuaged to human ruth;
Europe may date her history from the song
That gave the types of Homer to her youth.

II

Hark! while we muse, without the walls is heard
The various murmur of the labouring crowd,
How still, within those archive-cells interr'd,
The Calm Ones reign! and yet they rouse the loud
Passions and tumults of the circling world!
The peaceful temples they have built to Thought   30
Are the great arsenals of every war.
Thence, all the banners in gone time unfurl'd,
Ever again into fresh fields are brought,
Grace some new Cato's bier or some new Cæsar's car.[4]
They fire meek preachers with the zeal for truth,
And lift the looks of poets to the star;
To the old races they transmit their youth,
The Conscript Fathers of the men we are.

III

And now so still! Yet, Cicero,[5] heaves thy heart
In thy large language, sweet with measured swell.   40
Darling alike of Nature and of art,
Horace here smiles on life, and smiling sighs;
Reclined where Tyndaris, in the vale's cool dell
O'er Lesbian wine-cups chants her Teian lay;[6]
While on the mount which upward charms his eyes
Great Pan's free music[7] floats through summer skies!

O'er all our days reigns Thought's calm Yesterday
As out from books the guardian spirits rise.
Guiding our footsteps while upon our way
Their own fall noiseless.   50

THE SOULS OF BOOKS
1 Greek leader at siege of Troy.
2 Argive: Greek.
3 founder of Thebes, who introduced alphabet in Greece.
4 Cato (234–149 BC), fabled moral Roman censor; Caesar, generic
title of Roman emperors.

5 fabled Roman orator (106–43 BC).
6 Roman poet Horace (65–8 BC) wrote (*Odes* I.17) of Tyndaris (Helen
of Troy) singing her Teian lay (*fide teia*). Lytton is paraphrasing Horace.
The island of Teos was associated with erotic verse and drinking songs.
7 Pan, lustful, musical deity of all created things.

>   Hark! the world so loud,
>   And *they*, the movers of the world, so still!

    What robes the dead with glory? what can give
The regal purple to the funeral shroud?
We hunt some child of genius to the tomb,
And at its threshold hate and envy cease.
And what the charm that can such health distil
From wither'd leaves – oft poisons in their bloom?
We blame some books as harmful! *Do they live?*
If so, believe me, TIME hath made them pure.   60
In Books, the veriest wicked rest in peace –
God wills that nothing evil should endure;
The grosser parts fly off and leave the whole.
As the dust leaves the disembodied soul!
Come from thy niche, Lucretius![8] Thou didst teach
To man his wildest superstition – Chance,
Denied his grief the Jove whom prayer could reach.
And closed the pale Elysium[9] on his glance.
Dost thou make converts? No! thine art disproves
The creed which grants no planner to the plan;   70
As the contriving mind harmonious moves
Thro' every work attesting art in man,
So ev'n if Nature her First Cause conceal'd,
In man's contrivance God's would be reveal'd.
Go – bid the atoms into form combine,
And human art bear witness to Divine!

    Lo! that grim merriment of hatred;[10] born
Of him, the master-mocker of mankind,
Beside the grin of whose malignant spleen,
Lucian's[11] loud scoff seems pleasantry refined,   80
And Voltaire's[12] cynic sneer a smile serene.
Do we not place it in our children's hands,
Leading young Hope through Lemuel's fabled lands?
God's and man's libel in that foul Yahoo!
Well, and what mischief can the libel do?
O impotence of Genius to belie
Its glorious task – its mission from the sky!
Swift wrote this book to wreak a ribald scorn
On aught the Man should love or Priest should mourn;
And lo! the book, from all its ends beguiled,   90
A harmless wonder to some happy child!

                    IV
    All books grow sanctified by time; they are
Temples, at once, and landmarks. In them, we –
Who *but* for them, upon that inch of ground
We call 'THE PRESENT,' from the cell could see
No daylight trembling on the dungeon bar –
Turn, as we list, the globe's great axle round,
Traverse all space, and number every star,
And feel the Near less household than the Far!

---

8   Roman, anti-religious poet (98–*c*.55 BC).   11   Greek satirist (2nd century AD).
9   place of blissful after-life.   12   French ditto (1694–1778).
10 *Gulliver's Travels*. [Author's note]

There is no Past, so long as Books shall live!   100
A disinterr'd Pompeii wakes again
For him who seeks yon well; lost cities give
Up their untarnish'd wonders, and the reign
Of Jove revives and Saturn: – At our will
Rise dome and tower on Delphi's sacred hill;[13]
Bloom Cimon's[14] trees in Academe;[15] along
Leucadia's[16] headland sighs the Lesbian's song;
With Egypt's Queen once more we sail the Nile,[17]
And learn how worlds are barter'd for a smile:
Rise up, ye walls, with gardens blooming o'er;   110
Ope but that page – lo! Babylon once more!

V

Ye make the Past familiar as our home:
And is that all? No: in each prophet sage –
No; in each herald soul that Greece and Rome
Sent forth, ere yet to Bethlehem moved the Star,
In each bright guess illuming Tully's[18] page,
Or sparkling up from Plato's golden dreams,
Your earnest light converged the scatter'd beams,
Shot thro' the crannies of the silent portal
That spans the entrance of the Life to come.   120
And as yourselves have conquer'd death, ye are
Types of the truth that Thought must be immortal.

Apart from you, for not of human birth,
ONE BOOK, to hope and grief alike is given.
Mourner – love moulders not in graves of earth,
Read; and the lost smile down on thee from heaven.

Poems, *new edition, revised (John Murray, 1865)*.

Robert Stephen Hawker (1803–75)

The Revd Robert Stephen Hawker, antiquarian, poet, and antiquarian-poet, was a thorough West Countryman, born at Stoke Damerel, Devonshire, 3 December 1803, eldest son of Jane Elizabeth Drewitt from Plymouth and Jacob Stephen Hawker, a Plymouth doctor, who later became vicar of Stratton in Cornwall. Hawker went to Liskeard Grammar School; started work as a trainee solicitor in Plymouth; didn't like it and went to Cheltenham Grammar School instead. Aged nineteen he entered Pembroke College, Oxford, in April 1823. In November of that year he married a 41-year-old widow from Stratton, and migrated to Magdalen Hall, Oxford, from which he graduated in May 1828. In 1827 he won the Newgate Prize with a poem about Pompeii (largely lifted, it has been alleged, from Macaulay's Cambridge prize English Poem of 1819 on the same subject). Bishop Phillpots of Exeter liked Hawker's version, which assured Hawker of success in the Church of England. He became vicar of Morwenstow, Cornwall, in 1834, spending lavishly on the church fabric, the vicarage and the school he founded. He was a keen Tractarian. He started publishing early: his first book of poems was *Tendrils by Reuben* (1821). He brought out several volumes of religious verse, including *Reeds Shaken in the Wind* (1843) and *Reeds Shaken in the Wind: Second Cluster* (1844). A constant thread in his writing is retro-Cornish – both in poems (*Cornish Ballads*, 1869 and 1884) and in prose, for example the Cornish legends and Cornishness essays collected in *Footprints of Former Men in Cornwall*

---

13   Mount Parnassus; seat of poetry and Muses; with temple of Apollo (and Delphic oracle) at its foot.

14   Athenian general.

15   Athenian garden, where Plato taught.

16   Greek island, where Sappho was said to have hurled herself into the sea in unrequited love for Phaon (as in Ovid, *Heroides*, 15).

17   Cleopatra – as in Shakespeare's *Antony and Cleopatra*.

18   Cicero.

(1870). Hawker's wife, who published translations from German, died in 1863, aged 81. The following year Hawker married a Polish émigré's daughter, Pauline Anne Kuczynski. They had three daughters. Shortly before he died in Plymouth, 15 August 1875, he was formally received into the Roman Catholic Church. After his death there was much local debate about how long he had been, in effect, a Roman Catholic. And there are hints of covert activity about his writings, too, and not just his Pompeii

piece. The best-known of his Cornish revival ballads 'The Song of the Western Men' (first published anonymously in 1826) – 'And shall Trelawny die,/Here's twenty thousand Cornish men/Will see the reason why' – is of decidedly shady origin. Hawker only claimed it in 1832; many of his contemporaries thought it an ancient song. Hawker himself told people the chorus was genuinely old. Hawker is reputedly the original of Canon Tremaine in Mortimer Collins's novel *Sweet and Twenty* (1875).

TO ALFRED TENNYSON, LAUREATE, D.C.L.

On His 'Idylls of the King'

They told me in their shadowy phrase,
  Caught from a tale gone by,
That Arthur, King of Cornish praise,
  Died not, and would not die!

Dreams had they, that in fairy bowers,
  Their living warrior lies;
Or wears a garland of the flowers
  That grow in Paradise!

I read the Rune with deeper ken,
  And thus the myth I trace: –
A bard should rise, mid future men,
  The mightiest of his race.

He! – would great Arthur's deeds rehearse,
  On grey Dundagel's shore;
And so, the King! in laurelled verse,
  Shall live, and die no more!

August, 1859

The Poetical Works of Robert Stephen Hawker, Vicar of Morwenstow, Cornwall, Now First Collected and Arranged with A Prefatory Notice, *by J. G. Godwin (C. Kegan Paul & Co., 1879).*

A CROON ON HENNACLIFF

Thus said the rushing raven,
  Unto his hungry mate:
'Ho! gossip! for Bude Haven:
  There be corpses six or eight.
Cawk! cawk! the crew and skipper
  Are wallowing in the sea:
So there's a savoury supper
  For my old dame and me.'

'Cawk! gaffer! thou art dreaming,
  The shore hath wreckers bold;
Would rend the yelling seamen,
  From the clutching billows' hold.
Cawk! cawk! they'd bound for booty
  Into the dragon's den:

And shout, for "death or duty,"
    If the prey were drowning men.'

Loud laughed the listening surges,
    At the guess our grandame gave:
You might call them Boanerges,
    From the thunder of their wave.[1]   20
And mockery followed after
    The sea-bird's jeering brood:
That filled the skies with laughter,
    From Lundy Light to Bude.

'Cawk! cawk!' then said the raven,
    'I am fourscore years and ten:
Yet never in Bude Haven
    Did I croak for rescued men. –
They will save the Captain's girdle,
    And shirt, if shirt there be: 30
But leave their blood to curdle,
    For my old dame and me.'

So said the rushing raven
    Unto his hungry mate:
'Ho! gossip! for Bude Haven:
    There be corpses six or eight.
Cawk! cawk! the crew and skipper
    Are wallowing in the sea:
O what a savoury supper
    For my old dame and me.'   40

First published in All the Year Round, *10 September 1864.*
Poetical Works, ed. Godwin (1879).

R. E. (Rowland Eyles) Egerton-Warburton (1804–91)

R. E. Egerton-Warburton, sharp-eyed provider of gently satirical verse on modern subjects, not least sporting ones, was a Tory toff devoted to fox-hunting but with time enough on his hands for some breezy light-versifying – sometimes under the soubriquet 'Rambling Richard'. He was born near Chester, 14 September 1804. His father was the Revd Rowland Egerton, who tacked on the Warburton when he married Emma Croxton, sole inheritor of her grandfather Sir Peter Warburton's properties at Warburton and Arley in Cheshire. Peter Egerton Warburton, first white man to cross the central Australian desert, was R. E.'s younger brother. Young Rowland Egerton-Warburton went to Eton and then (in 1823) as a Gentleman-Commoner to Corpus Christi College, Oxford. After graduation he did the wealthy young man's Grand Tour of Europe before settling on the family estates at Arley where he lived as a provincial grandee. He married Mary Brooke, daughter of a neighbouring baronet, in 1831, and they had one son and heir. R. E. was High Sheriff of Cheshire in 1833. Being a keen Tory and High Churchman came with the territory. These principles caused a near rupture with his old friend Gladstone when the latter disestablished the Irish Church. R. E. bred horses, rode them hard to hounds, and wrote many songs for the Old Tarparley Club. His *Hunting Songs and Miscellaneous Verses* (1846) went into numerous editions. *Three Hunting Songs* appeared in 1855, Rambling Richard's *Epigrams and Humorous Verses* in 1867, *Poems, Epigrams and Sonnets* in 1877, and *Songs and Verses on Sporting Subjects* in 1879. Glaucoma caused him near-total blindness for the last seventeen years of his life. He died at Arley Hall, 6 December 1891.

A Croon on Hennacliff

1 Luke 9: James and John are called Boanerges, 'Sons of Thunder',
for wanting fire from heaven to consume sceptical Samaritans.

The Paper Knife

Belinda! deem not this, my shining blade,
A useless toy, alone for show display'd,
But let this verse instruct thee how to prize
A wand wherein such various magic lies.
   Peer'd at aslant, without my kindly aid,
The light of learning were but half display'd;
The Poet's song, pour'd forth in numbers sweet,
Would waste its rhythm in the folded sheet;
The march of intellect would lag behind,
And science fail to benefit mankind.   10
See 'neath my touch the sever'd leaves expand,
Diffusing knowledge o'er th' enlighten'd land;
I sweep the quarto with majestic stride,
Through duodecimos with ease I glide;
Hold in derision punctuation's laws,
Nor stop at colons, nor at commas pause;
While one bent figure questions, 'Why so fast?'
And one with admiration stands aghast!
To suit the action to the word my care,
Though oft *a passion into rags I tear!*   20
When hosts conflicting desperate warfare wage,
I cut and slash with all a hero's rage;
When heroines pine in sentimental grief,
With listless languor part the yielding leaf;
With ruthless step the lovers' bower invade,
And to rude eyes betray the blushing maid;
The course of true love cannot smoothly run
Through volumes three till my consent be won;
By mine the point in epigram is shown,
The edge of satire sharpen'd by my own;   30
'Tis mine to smooth the ruffled critic's spleen,
When authors quarrel mine to intervene.
Or true or false I let the secret out,
Give wings to wit, and scatter jokes about!
   Hard drudgery mine, the everlasting scrub
Of village news-room, and of London club;
Think through what columns, each succeeding day,
Both morn and eve, I pioneer the way;
Sun, Star, Globe, Herald, Chronicle, and *Post*,
My ivory baton marshals all the host;   40
To vulgar eyes reveals affairs of state,
Unfolds a tale or opens a debate.
Ye quidnuncs, patience! though the *Times* be due,
Ye needs must wait till I have skimm'd it through;
What though its pen the universe control,
It bides my pleasure ere its thunders roll.
Advertisements uncirculated lie,
Shows unannounced escape the public eye,
Puffs, like the winds in Æolus' cave,[1] are pent
In hidden corners, till I give them vent.   50
All sides alike my pliant labours fit,
'Twixt Whig and Tory I the difference split;

The Paper Knife
1   abode of Roman god of winds.

On every argument lay equal stress,
Promoting still the freedom of the press.
  Now with the swain through pastoral meads I stray,
Now through dull epics plod my weary way,
Now ghost-like glide before some tragic queen,
Now, ever varying, shift the comic scene;
Nor tear-drop falls, nor sides with laughter shake,
Till I my entrance and my exit make.   60

Poems, Epigrams and Sonnets *(Basil Montagu Pickering, 1877)*.

MODERN CHIVALRY

I

Time was, with sword and battle-axe,
  All clad in armour bright,
When cleaving skulls asunder
  Was the business of a knight.

II

Now chivalry means surgery,
  And spurs are won by him
Who can mend a skull when broken,
  Or piece a fractured limb.

III

Our knights of old couch'd lances,
  Drew long swords from the sheath,   10
Now knighthood couches eye-balls,
  And chivalry draws teeth.

IV

See! rescued from confinement,
  To charm our ravish'd sight,
Fair ladies are deliver'd
  By the arm of a true knight.

V

Behold! the knight chirurgeon
  To deeds of blood advance,
A bandage for a banner!
  And a lancet for a lance!   20

VI

To heroes of the hospital
  The 'bloody hand' is due,
But ye heralds bend the fingers,
  Or the fee may tumble through.

Poems, Epigrams and Sonnets *(1877)*.

A NEW DENOMINATION

Phœbe has lived a life of schism,
Been every '*ite*,' tried every '*ism*,'

Where rings the peal of pulpit thunder
Which she in turn has not sat under?
Each change of wind gives fresh occasion
For shifting to a new persuasion;
While wondering gossips, o'er their tea,
Each other ask, 'What will she be,
When next the *Times* shall as a convert quote her? –
A Plymouth Brother or a Yarmouth Bloater?'[1]   10

Poems, Epigrams and Sonnets *(1877)*.

A Lawyer's Bill

What a strange bill of costs do some lawyers indite!
I this item in mine discover –
'To lying awake in my bed at night,
And thinking your business over.'

Poems, Epigrams and Sonnets *(1877)*.

Past and Present

On four-horse coach, whose luggage pierced the sky,
    Perch'd on back seat, like clerk on office-stool,
    While wintry winds my dangling heels kept cool,
    In Whitney white envelop'd and blue tie,
Unpillow'd slumber from my half-closed eye
    Scared by the shrill tin horn; when welcome Yule
    Brought holiday season, it was thus from school
    I homeward came some forty years gone by.
Thus two long days and one long night I rode,
    Stage after stage, till the last change of team   10
    Stopp'd, splash'd and panting, at my fire's abode.
How nowaday from school comes home my son?
    Through duct and tunnel by a puff of steam,
    Shot like a pellet from his own pop-gun.

Poems, Epigrams and Sonnets *(1877)*.

'Il Sonnetto'

Would you a Sonnet pen you must confine
    The metre strictly to its rule of rhyme;
    Throughout the quatrains, in well-order'd time,
    Two rhymes alone their harmony combine.

These in two ways the verse may intertwine
    And vary thus in that Italian clime
    Whence sprung the sonnet, two alternate chime,
    Or one repeated links each central line.

Where ends each quatrain pause, and pause again
    Between the triplets; these, whichever best   10
    May please you, perfect with two rhymes or three;

A New Denomination
1   Plymouth Brethren: a millenarian sect; Yarmouth Bloater: a fish.

No rhyme must next its fellow, by your pen
    Misplac'd, fall jingling here. These rules transgress'd
Your fourteen lines will no true sonnet be.

Poems, Epigrams and Sonnets (1877).

My Dentist

In childhood who my first array
Of teeth pluck'd tenderly away,
For teeth like dogs have each their day?
                    My Dentist.

Who when my first had run their race,
And others had usurp'd their place,
When overcrowded gave them space?
                    My Dentist.

Whether the cavities were slight,
Or vast and deep, who stopp'd them tight,   10
Then made their polish'd surface white?
                    My Dentist.

When void of bone a gap was seen,
Who fix'd, the vacancy to screen,
An artificial one between?
                    My Dentist.

Who, when ambitious to be first
My horse fell headlong in the burst,
Replaced the ivories dispersed?
                    My Dentist.   20

Who 'Baily' left on parlour chair
With leaf turn'd down to show me where
Jack Russell's life was pictured there?
                    My Dentist.

Or reading in that doleful cell
Whyte-Melville's[1] verse, who knew full well
Its charm would every pang dispel?
                    My Dentist.

Who lull'd with laughing gas my fear
When conscious that a tug was near   30
For man's endurance too severe?
                    My Dentist.

And, lastly, when infirm I grew,
Who skilfully each relic drew,
And framed for me a mouth-piece new?
                    My Dentist.

Songs and Verses on Sporting Subjects (Pickering & Co., 1879)

My Dentist
1 G. J. Whyte-Melville (1821–78) wrote novels on field-sports.

Sarah (Fuller) Flower Adams (1805–48)

Sarah Flower Adams, radical poet, was born into a radical nonconformist, Unitarian family in Great Harlow in Essex, 22 February 1805. Her father Benjamin Flower, a crusading libertarian journalist, edited the *Cambridge Intelligencer*. Sarah and her sister Eliza were educated at home. After 1820 the family lived in London. Father died in 1827 and the girls moved in with the family of the Revd W. J. Fox, renowned Unitarian radical, minister of Finsbury Unitarian Chapel, a main member of the Anti-Corn Law League and editor of the *Monthly Repository*, to which, in the early thirties, Sarah Flower contributed articles. In 1834 she married fellow contributor William Bridges Adams, an engineer. She had a brief spell as an actress in the later thirties, but settled for writing as a career. She was very friendly with Robert Browning. Many of her poems were political ones for the Anti-Corn Law League. Her largest work was a blank verse play, *Vivia Perpetua* (1841), about a first-century woman who turns from Jupiter to Christ and is martyred for her faith. Sarah was an astute reviewer (in the *Westminster Review*, December 1844, she praised the passion but deplored the melancholy of Elizabeth Barrett Barrett's *Poems*, 1844). Her hymns were set to music by her sister and used in the Finsbury Chapel. 'Nearer, My God, to Thee' became known all over the English-speaking world – and became especially notorious as the theme said to have been played by the ship's orchestra as the liner *Titanic* went down in 1912. It first appeared in Fox's *Hymns and Anthems* (1841). Trinitarian compilers of hymn books were prone to counter any hint of Unitarianism or doubt in this hymn by bluntly orthodox emendation – adding a Doxology, for instance, to the 'Almighty Trinity', or substituting a verse of assurance in place of Mrs Adams's questioning last verse ('if...'), for example 'And when my Lord again/Glorious shall come,/Mine be a dwelling place/In thy bright home,/There evermore to be/Nearer to Thee, my God!/Nearer to Thee' – or simply leaving out the last verse altogether. Sarah Adams was never a well woman, had no children, and died, the *DNB* reports, 'of decline', in August 1848, aged 43. W. J. Fox celebrated her politics and her writing in one of his famous lectures to working people (*Lectures Addressed Chiefly to the Working Classes*, Lecture ix, vol. 4, 1849).

NEARER, MY GOD, TO THEE

Nearer, my God, to Thee,
    Nearer to Thee!
E'en though it be a cross
    That raiseth me:
Still all my song would be,
Nearer, my God! to Thee,
    Nearer to Thee!

Though like the wanderer,
    The sun gone down,
Darkness be over me,   10
    My rest a stone;
Yet in my dreams I'd be
Nearer, my God, to Thee,
    Nearer to Thee!

There let the way appear,
    Steps unto heaven;
All that Thou sendest me
    In mercy given:
Angels to beckon me
Nearer, my God, to Thee,   20
    Nearer to Thee!

Then with my waking thoughts
   Bright with Thy praise,
Out of my stony griefs
   Bethel I'll raise;
So by my woes to be
Nearer, my God, to Thee,
   Nearer to Thee!

Or if on joyful wing,
   Cleaving the sky,
Sun, moon, and stars forgot,
   Upward I fly;
Still all my song shall be,
Nearer, my God, to Thee,
   Nearer to Thee!

     30

First published Hymns and Anthems, *ed. W. J. Fox (Finsbury, 1841).*
Text, Vivia Perpetua: A Dramatic Poem in Five Acts: With
A Memoir of the Author [by E. F. Bridell-Fox] and Her Hymns
(privately printed, 1893). A re-doing of the story of Jacob at Bethel,
Genesis 28.

Thomas Cooper (1805–92)

Thomas Cooper, Chartist, lecturer and working-class polit-ical poet, was born in Leicester, 20 March 1805. His father, a dyer by trade, died when Cooper was three (in Exeter, where the family had moved). Back in the Midlands, in Gainsborough, Cooper's Methodist mother ran a fancy-box and dyeing business. Cooper attended a dame-school and then Gainsborough Bluecoat School. He was a pupil-teacher at 'Daddy Briggs's' private school. From an early age he was enraptured by literature – ballads especially and Bunyan's *The Pilgrim's Progress.* Aged thirteen he was attracted to Evangelical Christianity through Primitive Methodist open-air preachers, but the Primitives' stress on revivalistic salvationism was too ranting for his taste and he joined the Wesleyans, with whom he became active as a local preacher. He left school at the age of fifteen, tried the sea briefly and learned shoe-making. In the tradi-tional way of autodidactic cobblers he taught himself Latin, Greek and Hebrew, and read extensively in litera-ture, history, travel and theology, committing whole texts, such as *Hamlet,* to memory. In 1827 he set up as schoolmaster in Gainsborough, later on moving to a school in Lincoln. He became a journalist, working for various papers, first in London, then in Leicester. He fell out with the Wesleyans, and radical political activism dis-placed the Methodist kind when he became a Chartist in 1841. Leicester Chartism was run in fact very much like Primitive Methodism. There was a sort of chapel building or mechanics' institute where lectures, evening classes and a Sunday School took place, with the singing of Chartist hymns, open-air crusading, camp-meetings, and public processions with hymns. The former preacher now lec-tured on literary topics, and turned out verses and songs for the movement. Sacked from the *Leicester Mercury* for his politics, Cooper became editor of the Chartist *Midlands Counties Illuminator.* He was several times arrested for inflammatory speeches to strikers and in March 1843 was sentenced to two years in Stafford Gaol for 'sedition and conspiracy'. There he wrote his long and impassioned but determinedly dull ten-book epic in Spenserian stanzas, *The Purgatory of Suicides: A Prison Rhyme.* It was published in 1843 (dedicated to Carlyle) and sold very well, though it was probably more famous than actually read. Carlyle's response to the copy Cooper sent him was not simply to reciprocate with *Past and Present,* but to advise prose: 'Cer-tainly the *music* that is very traceable here might serve to irradiate into harmony for profitabler things than what are commonly called "Poems"...I always grudge to see any portion of a man's *musical talent* (which is the real intel-lect, the real vitality, or life of him) expended on making *words* rhyme.' (More practically, Carlyle twice gave Cooper five pounds when he was stuck for money.) Released from prison, having fallen out with the Chartist physical force party led by Feargus O'Connor, Cooper went on the stump as lecturer on historical and literary topics to radical and freethinking audiences. He published the short-lived *Cooper's Journal* in 1850, and from time to time tried his hand with other journals – the *Rushlight* and the *Extin-guisher.* In 1856 he surprised an audience by announcing his reconversion to Christianity, became a Christian Socia-list, and devoted himself to lecturing on Christian evid-ences. From 1867 he lived on an annuity got up by friends. He produced many volumes of moral and

Christian reflection, but his best-known book was his *Life of Thomas Cooper, Written by Himself* (1872), a minor Victorian classic in the self-help mode. His wife of forty-six years died in 1880; and he died, in Lincoln, 15 July 1892.

CHARTIST CHAUNT

Truth is growing – hearts are glowing
  With the flame of Liberty:
Light is breaking – Thrones are quaking –
  Hark! – the trumpet of the Free!
Long, in lowly whispers breathing,
  Freedom wandered drearily –
Still, in faith, her laurel wreathing
  For the day when there should be
  Freemen shouting – 'Victory!'

Now, she seeketh him that speaketh 10
  Fearlessly of lawless might;
And she speedeth him that leadeth
  Brethren on to win the Right.
Soon, the slave shall cease to sorrow –
  Cease to toil in agony;
Yea, the cry may swell to-morrow
  Over land and over sea –
  'Brethren, shout – ye all are free!'

Freedom bringeth joy that singeth
  All day long and never tires: 20
No more sadness – all is gladness
  In the hearts that she inspires:
For, she breathes a soft compassion
  Where the tyrant kindled rage;
And she saith to every nation –
  'Brethren, cease wild war to wage:
  Earth is your blest heritage.'

Though kings render their defender
  Titles, gold, and splendours gay –
Lo, thy glory – warrior gory – 30
  Like a dream shall fade away!
Gentle Peace her balm of healing
  On the bleeding world shall pour;
Brethren, love for brethren feeling,
  Shall proclaim, from shore to shore –
  'Shout – the sword shall slay no more!'

Poetical Works *(Hodder & Stoughton, 1877)*.

CHARTIST SONG

Air – Canadian Boat Song

The time shall come when Wrong shall end,
When peasant to peer no more shall bend –
When the lordly Few shall lose their sway,
And the Many no more their frown obey.

Toil, brothers, toil, till the work is done –
Till the struggle is o'er, and the Charter's won!

The time shall come when the artisan
Shall homage no more the titled man –
When the moiling men who delve the mine
By Mammon's decree no more shall pine.   10
   Toil, brothers, toil, till the work is done –
   Till the struggle is o'er and the Charter's won!

The time shall come when the weavers' band
Shall hunger no more, in their fatherland –
When the factory child can sleep till day,
And smile while it dreams of sport and play.
   Toil, brothers, toil, till the work is done –
   Till the struggle is o'er, and the Charter's won!

The time shall come when Man shall hold
His brother more dear than sordid gold –   20
When the Negro's stain his freeborn mind
Shall sever no more from human-kind.
   Toil, brothers, toil, till the world is free –
   Till Justice and Love hold jubilee!

The time shall come when kingly crown
And mitre for toys of the Past are shown –
When the Fierce and False alike shall fall,
And Mercy and Truth encircle all.
   Toil, brothers, toil, till the world is free –
   Till Mercy and Truth hold jubilee!   30

The time shall come when earth shall be
A garden of joy, from sea to sea –
When the slaughterous sword is drawn no more,
And goodness exults from shore to shore.
   Toil, brothers, toil, till the world is free –
   Till goodness shall hold high jubilee!

Poetical Works *(1877)*.

CHARTIST POETS: CHARTIST LIFE: 1842

I had not joined the ranks of the poor and the oppressed with the expectation of having those rough election scenes to pass through. And now I had passed through them, I began to turn my thoughts to something far more worthy of a man's earnestness. As soon as the Shaksperean Room was secured, I formed an adult Sunday-school, for men and boys who were at work on the week days. All the more intelligent in our ranks gladly assisted as teachers; and we soon had the room filled on Sunday mornings and afternoons. The Old and New Testaments, Channing's 'Self-culture,' and other tracts, of which I do not remember the names, formed our class-books. And we, fancifully, named our classes, not first, second, third, etc., but the 'Algernon Sydney Class,' 'Andrew Marvel Class,' 'John Hampden Class,' 'John Milton Class,' 'William Tell Class,' 'George Washington Class,' 'Major Cartwright Class,' 'William Cobbett Class,' and so on.

   I began also to teach Temperance more strongly than before. I became a teetotaler when I entered Leicester, and I kept my pledge, rigidly, for four years. We devised a new form of pledge, – 'I hereby promise to abstain, etc., until the People's Charter becomes the law of the land;' and I administered this pledge to several hundreds. I fear the majority of them kept their pledge but for a brief period, yet some persevered.

Next, I drew up a body of rules for our Chartist Association; and, as we so often indulged in singing, I proposed to two of our members who had occasionally shown me their rhymes, that they should compose hymns for our Sunday meetings. John Bramwich, the elder of these persons, was a stocking-weaver, and was now about fifty years old. He had been a soldier, and had seen service in the West Indies and America. He was a grave, serious man, the very heart of truth and sincerity. He died of sheer exhaustion, from hard labour and want, in the year 1846. William Jones, the other composer of rhymes I referred to, was a much younger man, of very pleasing manners and appearance. He was what is called a 'glove-hand,' and therefore earned better wages than a stockinger. He had been a hard worker, but had acquired some knowledge of music. He published a small volume of very excellent poetry, at Leicester, in 1853, and died in 1855, being held in very high respect by a large circle of friends.

The contributions of Bramwich and Jones to our hymnology, were published in my weekly *Extinguisher*, until we collected them in our 'Shaksperean Chartist Hymn Book.' The following is the most favourite hymn composed by Bramwich. – We sang it to the hymn tune 'New Crucifixion.'

> Britannia's sons, though slaves ye be,
> God, your Creator, made you free;
> He life and thought and being gave,
> But never, never made a slave!
>
> His works are wonderful to see,
> All, all proclaim the Deity;
> He made the earth, and formed the wave,
> But never, never made a slave!
>
> He made the sky with spangles bright,
> The moon to shine by silent night;   10
> The sun – and spread the vast concave,
> But never, never made a slave!
>
> The verdant earth, on which we tread,
> Was by His hand all carpeted;
> Enough for all He freely gave,
> But never, never made a slave!
>
> All men are equal in His sight,
> The bond, the free, the black, the white:
> He made them all, – them freedom gave;
> God made the man – Man made the slave!   20

Fourteen hymns were contributed by Bramwich to our 'Shaksperean Chartist Hymn Book,' and sixteen by William Jones. The following was our favourite hymn of those composed by Jones, and we usually sang it to the hymn tune called 'Calcutta.'

> Sons of poverty assemble,
>   Ye whose hearts with woe are riven,
> Let the guilty tyrants tremble,
>   Who your hearts such pain have given.
>   We will never
> From the shrine of truth be driven.
>
> Must ye faint – ah! how much longer?
>   Better by the sword to die

Than to die of want and hunger:
   They heed not your feeble cry: 10
      Lift your voices –
   Lift your voices to the sky!

Rouse them from their silken slumbers;
   Trouble them amidst their pride:
Swell your ranks, augment your numbers,
   Spread the Charter, far and wide!
      Truth is with us:
   God Himself is on our side.

See the brave, ye spirit broken,
   That uphold your righteous cause;   20
Who against them hath not spoken?
   They are, just as Jesus was,
      Persecuted
   By bad men and wicked laws.

Dire oppression, Heaven decrees it,
   From our land shall soon be hurled:
Mark the coming time and seize it –
   Every banner be unfurled!
      Spread the Charter!
   Spread the Charter through the world.   30

I venture to add one of the only two hymns that I contributed to our Hymn Book: we sang it in the noble air of the 'Old Hundredth.'[1]

God of the earth, and sea, and sky,
To Thee Thy mournful children cry:
Didst Thou the blue that bends o'er all
Spread for a general funeral pall?

Sadness and gloom pervade the land;
Death – famine – glare on either hand;
Didst Thou plant earth upon the wave
Only to form one general grave?

Father, why didst Thou form the flowers?
They blossom not for us, or ours: 10
Why didst Thou clothe the fields with corn?
Robbers from us our share have torn.

The ancients of our wretched race
Told of Thy sovereign power and grace,
That in the sea their foes o'erthrew –
Great Father! – is the record true?

Art Thou the same who, from all time,
O'er every sea, through every clime,
The stained oppressor's guilty head
Hast visited with vengeance dread?   20

1   old tune to metrical version of Psalm 100 ('All People that on Earth do dwell') – Geneva Psalter Version, 1551.

To us, – the wretched and the poor,
Whom rich men drive from door to door, –
To us, then, make Thy goodness known,
And we Thy lofty name will own.

Father, our frames are sinking fast:
Hast Thou our names behind Thee cast?
Our sinless babes with hunger die:
Our hearts are hardening! – Hear our cry!

Appear, as in the ancient days!
Deliver us from our foes, and praise   30
Shall from our hearts to Thee ascend –
To God our Father, and our Friend!

We now usually held one or two meetings in the Shaksperean Room on week nights, as well as on the Sunday night. Unless there were some stirring local or political topic, I lectured on Milton, and repeated portions of the 'Paradise Lost,' or on Shakespeare, and repeated portions of 'Hamlet,' or on Burns, and repeated 'Tam o' Shanter;' or I recited the history of England, and set the portraits of great Englishmen before young Chartists, who listened with intense interest; or I took up Geology, or even Phrenology, and made the young men acquainted, elementally, with the knowledge of the time.

Often, since the days of which I am speaking, some seeming stranger has stepped up to me, in one part of England or another – usually at the close of a lecture – and has said, 'You will not remember me. I was very young when I used to hear you in Leicester; but I consider that I owe a good deal to you. You gave me a direction of mind that I have followed,' – and so on. If events had not broken up the system I was forming, how much real good I might have effected in Leicester!

These thoughts have just brought to mind a pleasing incident which I ought to have mentioned earlier. I had been appealing strongly, one evening, to the patriotic feelings of young Englishmen, mentioning the names of Hampden and Sydney and Marvel; and eulogizing the grand spirit of dis-interestedness and self-sacrifice which characterised so many of our brave forerunners, when a handsome young man sprung upon our little platform and declared himself on the people's side, and desired to be enrolled as a Chartist. He did not belong to the poorest ranks; and it was the consciousness that he was acting in the spirit of self-sacrifice, as well as his fervid eloquence, that caused a thrilling cheer from the ranks of working men. He could not be more than fifteen at that time; he passed away from us too soon, with his father, who left Leicester, and I have never seen him but once, all these years. But the men of Sheffield have signalized their confidence in his patriotism by returning him to the House of Commons; and all England knows if there be a man of energy as well as uprightness in that house, it is Anthony John Mundella.

Our meetings were well attended, the number of our members increased greatly, and all went well until January, 1842, when the great hosiery houses announced that orders had ceased, and the greater number of the stocking and glove frames must stand still. The sale, not only of the *Northern Star*, but of my own *Extinguisher*, declined fearfully. Some of the working men began to ask me to let them have bread on credit; and I ventured to do it, trusting that all would be better in time. Our coffee-room was still filled, but not half the coffee was sold.

One afternoon, without counselling me, some five hundred of the men who were out of work formed a procession and marched through the town at a slow step, singing, and begging all the way they went. It wrung my heart to see a sight like that in England. They got but little, and I advised them never to repeat it.

While difficulties increased, I gave up both the sale of bread and the publication of my *Extin-guisher* for a few weeks. But several of the most necessitous men declared they must perish if I did not let them have bread. So I returned to the sale of bread – but had to give it to some to prevent them from starving. Of course I contracted debt by so doing; and I did it very foolishly. I would not do it again; at least, I hope I should not do it. I found also that our cause could not be held together without a paper. We had no organ for the exposure of wrongs – such as the attempts of some of the grinding 'masters' to establish the Truck System, extraordinary acts of 'docking' men's wages, and so on.

So I now issued another paper, and called it the *Commonwealthsman*, and inserted in it the lives of the illustrious Hampden, Pym, Sir John Eliot, Selden, Algernon Sydney, and others of their fellow-strugglers for freedom. I had a good sale for the earlier numbers – for they were sold for me by agents at Manchester, Sheffield, Birmingham, Wednesbury, Bilston, Stafford, and the Potteries. But trade grew bad in other towns; and the sale soon fell off.

In Leicester everything looked more hopeless. We closed the adult school – partly because the fine weather drew the men into the fields, and partly because they were too despairing to care about learning to read. Let some who read this mark what I am recording. We had not many pro-fane men in our ranks, but we had a few; and when I urged them not to forsake school their reply was, 'What the hell do we care about reading, if we can get nought to eat?'

A poor framework-knitter, whom I knew to be as true as steel, concealed the fact of his deep suffering from me for several weeks, though I saw the change in his dress, and knew that he must have pawned all but the mere rags he was wearing. He was frequently with me in the shop, render-ing kindly help. I spoke to him, one night, about his case; but some one came into the shop and interrupted me, and he suddenly retired. At eleven o'clock, just before we were about to close the shop, he came in hastily, laid a bit of paper on my desk, and ran out.

On the bit of paper he revealed his utter destitution, and the starvation and suffering of his young wife and child. On the previous morning, the note informed me, his wife awoke, saying, 'Sunday come again, and nothing to eat!' – and as the babe sought the breast there was no milk!

About the same time – I think it was in the same week – another poor stockinger rushed into my house, and, throwing himself wildly on a chair, exclaimed, with an execration, – 'I wish they would hang me! I have lived on cold potatoes that were given me these two days; and this morning I've eaten a raw potato for sheer hunger! Give me a bit of bread, and a cup of coffee, or I shall drop!' I should not like again to see a human face with the look of half insane despair which that poor man's countenance wore.

How fierce my discourses became now, in the market-place, on Sunday evenings! I wonder that I restrained myself at all. My heart often burned with indignation I knew not how to express. Nay – there was something worse. I began – from sheer sympathy – to feel a tendency to glide into the depraved thinkings of some of the stronger, but coarser spirits among the men. It is horrible to me to tell such a truth. But I must tell it. For if I be untruthful now, I had better not have begun my Life-story.

The real feeling of this class of men was fully expressed one day in the market-place when we were holding a meeting in the week. A poor religious stockinger said, – 'Let us be patient a little longer, lads. Surely, God Almighty will help us soon.'

'Talk no more about thy Goddle Mighty!' was the sneering rejoinder. 'There isn't one. If there *was* one, He wouldn't let us suffer as we do.'

Such was the feeling and language of the stronger and coarser spirits; and it was shared by such of the Socialists as we had among us. Not that there was ever any union of the Socialists with us, as a body. They had a room of their own in Leicester, and their leading men kept at a distance from us, and even protested against the reasonableness of our hopes. Indeed, to show us that we were wrong, they brought Alexander Campbell and Robert Buchanan (the father of Robert Buchanan the poet) to Leicester, to lecture on their scheme of 'Home Colonisation' and challenged us to answer them. I sustained the challenge myself, as the champion for the People's Charter.

During the summer of 1842, I often led the poor stockingers out into the villages, – sometimes on Sunday mornings, and sometimes on week day evenings, – and thus we collected the villagers of Anstey, and Wigston, and Glenn, and Countesthorpe, and Earl Shilton, and Hinckley, and Syston, and Mount Sorrel, and inducted them into some knowledge of Chartist principles. One Sunday we devoted entirely to Mount Sorrel, and I and Beedham stood on a pulpit of syenite, and addressed the hundreds that sat around and above us on the stones of a large quarry. It was a *Gwennap* – Wesley's grand Cornish preaching-place – on a small scale.

Our singing was enthusiastic; and the exhilaration of that Chartist 'camp-meeting' was often spoken of afterwards. Now and then, I preached Chartist sermons on Nottingham Forest, – where at that time there was another natural pulpit of rock; but it was seldom I had meetings there, though I liked the place, the open air, and the people, who were proud of their unenclosed 'Forest,' – unenclosed, now, no longer – but thickly built upon.

As the poor Leicester stockingers had so little work, they used to crowd the street, around my shop door, early in the evenings; and I had to devise some way of occupying them. Sometimes I would deliver them a speech; but more generally, on the fine evenings, we used to form a procession of four or five in a rank, and troop through the streets, singing the following triplet to the air of the chorus 'Rule Britannia:'

> 'Spread – spread the charter –
> Spread the Charter through the Land!
> Let Britons bold and brave join heart and hand!'

Or chanting the 'Lion of Freedom,' which I have already alluded to, – the words of which were as follows:

> The Lion of Freedom is come from his den;
> We'll rally around him, again and again:
> We'll crown him with laurel, our champion to be:
> O'Connor the patriot: for sweet Liberty!
>
> The pride of the people – He's noble and brave –
> A terror to tyrants – a friend to the slave:
> The bright star of Freedom – the noblest of men:
> We'll rally around him, again and again.
>
> Who strove for the patriots – was up night and day –
> To save them from falling to tyrants a prey?
> 'Twas fearless O'Connor was diligent then:
> We'll rally around him, again and again.
>
> Though proud daring tyrants his body confined,
> They never could conquer his generous mind:
> We'll hail our caged lion, now freed from his den:
> We'll rally around him, again and again.

The popularity of this song may serve to show how firmly O'Connor was fixed in the regard of a portion of the manufacturing operatives, as the incorruptible advocate of freedom. As a consequence, they immediately suspected the honesty of any local leader who did not rank himself under the banner of Feargus, the leader-in-chief.

The Life of Thomas Cooper, Written by Himself
(Hodder & Stoughton, 1872), ch. 16.

Elizabeth Barrett (Moulton-Barrett) Browning (1806–61)

Elizabeth Barrett Moulton-Barrett was born in County Durham, 6 March 1806, the eldest of the eleven children of Edward Barrett Moulton-Barrett and Mary Graham-Clarke. On both sides of the family the money came from slave-owning interests in the West Indies. Elizabeth grew up in extremely congenial circumstances at Hope End, near Ledbury, Herefordshire, precocious, adored, daddy's girl, learning Greek with her oldest brother (preparing for Charterhouse), producing at age eleven or so a huge epic on the Battle of Marathon, which papa had printed in four volumes. A sequence of catastrophes smashed up this idyllic existence – some sort of disabling spinal injury which made her bedridden for a year when she fell off her horse around the age of fifteen, mother's death in 1828, father's financial collapse after the abolition of slavery in 1834, and the consequent sale of Hope End. The climax of these disasters was the death by drowning in 1840 at Torquay of her favourite brother, Bro, after they'd had some minor squabble. She was by then an enfeebled recluse, temporarily at the seaside for her better health, away from the sick-room in the house in Wimpole Street in London to which a possessive father, lovingly tyrannical, had brought his family. Despite all these knocks and set-backs, however, she was establishing her name as a writer and poet. (She published as Elizabeth Barrett Barrett, or E.B.B.) Her *Essay on Mind* appeared in 1826, a translation of *Prometheus Unbound* in 1833, *The Seraphim and Other Poems* in 1838, and *Poems* in 1844. Her spaniel Flush, gift of the writer Mary Russell Mitford, greatly cheered her along, and Flush got into several of her poems; but the inspiration of Cowper, Felicia Hemans, L.E.L. and George Sand was undoubtedly more important. Friendship with the poet Richard Hengist Horne boosted her commitment to political radicalism. Her poem 'The Cry of the Children' was a loud voice in the great chorus of writerly anger provoked by the reports of the Children's Employment Commission of 1842. 'The Runaway Slave at Pilgrim's Point' would contribute powerfully to the American anti-slavery movement. And meanwhile Robert Browning was writing with love for 'your verses' and for 'you too'. Love for and elopement with Browning in 1846 undoubtedly transformed the life and writing of this tiny woman with the invalid's terribly pale face curtained by the grim 'black ringlets' which, as Nathaniel Hawthorne noted, 'cluster down into her neck and make her face look whiter'. She produced her best work – as E.B.B. still, but now Elizabeth Barrett Browning – with her husband in the healthier climate of Florence (the sun; the fruit and vegetables!), not least the frankly desirous *Sonnets From the Portuguese*, and the ambitious autobiographical epic *Aurora Leigh* (1856). Reviewers such as Coventry Patmore could not stomach this latter poem's attempts at 'woman's figures' – its steps towards what some feminist critics hail as an innovative discourse of the feminine. And even its fans might wish it – as with Robert Browning's *The Ring and the Book* – a bit shorter. The married life of the Brownings was not, of course, all smooth going. He particularly disliked her interest in spiritualism and didn't approve of her personal and political obsession with Napoleon III. But this love match of the Casa Guidi (their house in Florence) produced not only the one-time highly unforeseeable boon of a child, Penini, or Pen (after several miscarriages) – a doted-on infant, born in 1849, whose spelling lessons always took precedence over mama's writing – but also some of the most striking erotic poems by a woman in the whole period. When Wordsworth died in 1850 there was some move to have E.B.B. replace him as Poet Laureate. Tennyson was, of course, the better candidate, and settling back in England might well have shortened her life. As it was, she died, in Florence, 29 June 1861, aged only fifty-five.

FELICIA HEMANS

To L. E. L., Referring to Her Monody on That Poetess

Thou bay-crowned living One, that o'er the bay-crowned Dead art bowing,
And, o'er the shadeless moveless brow, the vital shadow throwing;
And, o'er the sighless songless lips, the wail and music wedding;
Dropping above the tranquil eyes, the tears not of their shedding! –

Take music from the silent Dead, whose meaning is completer;
Reserve thy tears for living brows, where all such tears are meeter;
And leave the violets in the grass, to brighten where thou treadest!
No flowers for her! no need of flowers – albeit 'bring flowers,' thou saidest.

Yes, flowers, to crown the 'cup and lute!' since both may come to breaking:
Or flowers, to greet the 'bride!' the heart's own beating works its aching: 10
Or flowers, to soothe the 'captive's' sight, from earth's free bosom gathered,
Reminding of his earthly hope, then withering as it withered!

But bring not near her solemn corse the type of human seeming!
Lay only dust's stern verity upon her dust undreaming.
And while the calm perpetual stars shall look upon it solely,
Her spherèd soul shall look on *them*, with eyes more bright and holy.

Nor mourn, O living One, because her part in life was mourning.
Would she have lost the poet's fire, for anguish of the burning? –

The minstrel harp, for the strained string? the tripod, for the afflated[1]
Woe? or the vision, for those tears, in which it shone dilated?   20

Perhaps she shuddered, while the world's cold hand her brow was wreathing,
But never wronged that mystic breath, which breathed in all her breathing;
Which drew from rocky earth and man, abstractions high and moving –
Beauty, if not the beautiful, and love, if not the loving.

Such visionings have paled in sight: the Saviour she descrieth,
And little recks *who* wreathed the brow which on His bosom lieth.
The whiteness of His innocence o'er all her garments flowing, –
There, learneth she the sweet 'new song,'[2] she will not mourn in knowing.

Be happy, crowned and living One! and, as thy dust decayeth,
May thine own England say for thee, what now for Her it sayeth –
'Albeit softly in our ears, her silver song was ringing,
The footfall of her parting soul is softer than her singing!'

First version, The Seraphim and Other Poems, *by Elizabeth B. Barrett (Saunders and Otley, 1838).*
Slightly revised, Poems, *by Elizabeth Barrett Browning, new edition, 2 vols (Chapman & Hall, 1850),*
II. Original title, 'Stanzas on the Death of Mrs Hemans, Written in Reference to Miss Landor's Poem
on the Same subject'. In 1838 there was an epigraph from William Habington, seventeenth-century poet:

> *Nor grieve this christall streame so soon did fall*
> *Into the ocean; since she perfumed all*
> *The banks she past –*

COWPER'S GRAVE

I

It is a place where poets crowned may feel the heart's decaying, –
It is a place where happy saints may weep amid their praying:
Yet let the grief and humbleness, as low as silence, languish!
Earth surely now may give her calm to whom she gave her anguish.

II

O poets! from a maniac's tongue, was poured the deathless singing!
O Christians! at your cross of hope, a hopeless hand was clinging!
O men! this man, in brotherhood, your weary paths beguiling,
Groaned inly while he taught you peace, and died while ye were smiling!

III

And now, what time ye all may read through dimming tears his story,
How discord on the music fell, and darkness on the glory,   10
And how, when one by one, sweet sounds and wandering lights departed,
He wore no less a loving face because so broken-hearted;

IV

He shall be strong to sanctify the poet's high vocation,
And bow the meekest Christian down in meeker adoration:
Nor ever shall he be, in praise, by wise or good forsaken;
Named softly, as the household name of one whom God hath taken.

FELICIA HEMANS   2   the new song sung in heaven, Revelation 5.9.
1   afflated (inspired) priestess delivered oracles at Delphos seated on a
three-legged bronze altar.

V

With quiet sadness and no gloom, I learn to think upon him,
With meekness, that is gratefulness to God whose heaven hath won him –
Who suffered once the madness-cloud, to His own love to blind him;
But gently led the blind along where breath and bird could find him;   20

VI

And wrought within his shattered brain, such quick poetic senses,
As hills have language for, and stars, harmonious influences!
The pulse of dew upon the grass, kept his within its number;
And silent shadows from the trees refreshed him like a slumber.

VII

Wild timid hares were drawn from woods to share his home-caresses,
Uplooking to his human eyes with sylvan tendernesses:
The very world, by God's constraint, from falsehood's ways removing,
Its women and its men became beside him, true and loving.

VIII

But while, in blindness he remained unconscious of the guiding,
And things provided came without the sweet sense of providing,   30
He testified this solemn truth, though phrenzy desolated –
Nor man, nor nature satisfy, whom only God created!

IX

Like a sick child that knoweth not his mother while she blesses
And drops upon his burning brow, the coolness of her kisses;
That turns his fevered eyes around – 'My mother! where's my mother?' –
As if such tender words and looks could come from any other! –

X

The fever gone, with leaps of heart, he sees her bending o'er him;
Her face all pale from watchful love, the unweary love she bore him! –
Thus, woke the poet from the dream, his life's long fever gave him,
Beneath those deep pathetic Eyes, which closed in death, to save him!   40

XI

Thus? oh, not *thus!* no type of earth could image that awaking,
Wherein he scarcely heard the chant of seraphs, round him breaking,
Or felt the new immortal throb of soul from body parted;
But felt *those eyes alone*, and knew '*My* Saviour! *not* deserted!'

XII

Deserted! who hath dreamt that when the cross in darkness rested
Upon the Victim's hidden face, no love was manifested?
What frantic hands outstretched have e'er the atoning drops averted,
What tears have washed them from the soul, that *one* should be deserted?

XIII

Deserted! God could separate from His own essence rather:
And Adam's sins *have* swept between the righteous Son and Father;   50
Yea, once, Immanuel's orphaned cry, His universe hath shaken –
It went up single, echoless, 'My God, I am forsaken!'

XIV

It went up from the Holy's lips amid his lost creation,
That, of the lost, no son should use those words of desolation;

That earth's worst phrenzies, marring hope, should mar not hope's fruition,
And I, on Cowper's grave, should see his rapture, in a vision!

First version in The Seraphim and other Poems *(1838). Revised,* Poems *(1850), II.*

TO GEORGE SAND

A Desire

Thou large-brained woman and large-hearted man,
Self-called George Sand! whose soul, amid the lions
Of thy tumultuous senses, moans defiance,
And answers roar for roar, as spirits can:
I would some mild miraculous thunder ran
Above the applauded circus, in appliance
Of thine own nobler nature's strength and science, –
Drawing two pinions, white as wings of swan,
From thy strong shoulders, to amaze the place
With holier light! That thou to woman's claim,   10
And man's, might join beside the angel's grace
Of a pure genius sanctified from blame;
Till child and maiden pressed to thine embrace,
To kiss upon thy lips a stainless fame.

Poems, *by Elizabeth Barrett Barrett, 2 vols (Edward Moxon, 1844), I.*

TO GEORGE SAND

A Recognition

True genius, but true woman! dost deny
Thy woman's nature with a manly scorn,
And break away the gauds and armlets worn
By weaker women in captivity?
Ah, vain denial! that revolted cry
Is sobbed in by a woman's voice forlorn: –
Thy woman's hair, my sister, all unshorn,
Floats back dishevelled strength in agony,
Disproving thy man's name. And while before
The world thou burnest in a poet-fire,   10
We see thy woman-heart beat evermore
Through the large flame. Beat purer, heart, and higher,
Till God unsex thee on the spirit-shore;
To which alone unsexing, purely aspire.

Poems *(1844), I.*

THE CRY OF THE CHILDREN

'φεῦ, φεῦ, τι προσδερκεσθε μ' ομμασιν, τεκνα.'
Medea[1]

Do ye hear the children weeping, O my brothers,
    Ere the sorrow comes with years?
They are leaning their young heads against their mothers, –
    And *that* cannot stop their tears.

THE CRY OF THE CHILDREN
1 'Alas, alas, why do you look at me like that, my children?' In   Euripides' *Medea*, Medea kills her children to avenge their father's desertion of her.

The young lambs are bleating in the meadows;
    The young birds are chirping in the nest;
The young fawns are playing with the shadows;
    The young flowers are blowing toward the west –
But the young, young children, O my brothers,
      They are weeping bitterly! –   10
They are weeping in the playtime of the others,
    In the country of the free.

Do you question the young children in the sorrow,
      Why their tears are falling so? –
The old man may weep for his to-morrow
      Which is lost in Long Ago –
The old tree is leafless in the forest –
    The old year is ending in the frost –
The old wound, if stricken, is the sorest –
    The old hope is hardest to be lost: 20
But the young, young children, O my brothers,
      Do you ask them why they stand
Weeping sore before the bosoms of their mothers,
    In our happy Fatherland?

They look up with their pale and sunken faces,
      And their looks are sad to see,
For the man's grief abhorrent, draws and presses
      Down the cheeks of infancy –
'Your old earth,' they say, 'is very dreary;'
    'Our young feet,' they say, 'are very weak!   30
Few paces have we taken, yet are weary –
    Our grave-rest is very far to seek!
Ask the old why they weep, and not the children,
      For the outside earth is cold, –
And we young ones stand without, in our bewildering,
      And the graves are for the old!

'True,' say the young children, 'it may happen
      That we die before our time!
Little Alice died last year – the grave is shapen
      Like a snowball, in the rime.   40
We looked into the pit prepared to take her –
    Was no room for any work in the close clay:
From the sleep wherein she lieth none will wake her,
    Crying, "Get up, little Alice! it is day".
If you listen by that grave, in sun and shower,
    With your ear down, little Alice never cries! –
Could we see her face, be sure we should not know her,
    For the smile has time for growing in her eyes, –
And merry go her moments, lulled and stilled in
      The shroud, by the kirk-chime!   50
It is good when it happens,' say the children,
      'That we die before our time!'

Alas, the wretched children! they are seeking
      Death in life, as best to have!
They are binding up their hearts away from breaking,
      With a cerement from the grave.
Go out, children, from the mine and from the city –
    Sing out, children, as the little thrushes do –

Pluck you handfuls of the meadow-cowslips pretty –
    Laugh aloud, to feel your fingers let them through!   60
But they answer, 'Are your cowslips of the meadows
    Like our weeds anear the mine?
Leave us quiet in the dark of the coal-shadows,
    From your pleasures fair and fine!

    'For oh,' say the children, 'we are weary,
        And we cannot run or leap –
If we cared for any meadows, it were merely
    To drop down in them and sleep.
Our knees tremble sorely in the stooping –
    We fall upon our faces, trying to go;   70
And, underneath our heavy eyelids drooping,
    The reddest flower would look as pale as snow.
For, all day, we drag our burden tiring,
    Through the coal-dark, underground –
Or, all day, we drive the wheels of iron
    In the factories, round and round.

    'For, all day, the wheels are droning, turning, –
        Their wind comes in our faces, –
Till our hearts turn, – our heads, with pulses burning,
    And the walls turn in their places –   80
Turns the sky in the high window blank and reeling –
    Turns the long light that droppeth down the wall –
Turn the black flies that crawl along the ceiling –
    All are turning, all the day, and we with all! –
And all day, the iron wheels are droning;
    And sometimes we could pray,
"O ye wheels," (breaking out in a mad moaning)
    "Stop! be silent for to-day!" '

    Ay! be silent! Let them hear each other breathing
        For a moment, mouth to mouth –   90
Let them touch each other's hands, in a fresh wreathing
    Of their tender human youth!
Let them feel that this cold metallic motion
    Is not all the life God fashions or reveals –
Let them prove their inward souls against the notion
    That they live in you, or under you, O wheels! –
Still, all day, the iron wheels go onward,
    As if Fate in each were stark;
And the children's souls, which God is calling sunward,
    Spin on blindly in the dark.   100

    Now tell the poor young children, O my brothers,
        That they look to Him and pray –
So the blessed One, who blesseth all the others,
    Will bless them another day.
They answer, 'Who is God that He should hear us,
    While the rushing of the iron wheels is stirred?
When we sob aloud, the human creatures near us
    Pass by, hearing not, or answer not a word!
And *we* hear not (for the wheels in their resounding)
    Strangers speaking at the door: 110
Is it likely God, with angels singing round Him,
    Hears our weeping any more?

'Two words, indeed, of praying we remember;
    And at midnight's hour of harm, –
"Our Father," looking upward in the chamber,
    We say softly for a charm.[2]
We know no other words, except "Our Father,"
    And we think that, in some pause of angels' song,
God may pluck them with the silence sweet to gather,
    And hold both within His right hand which is strong.   120
"Our Father!" If He heard us, He would surely
    (For they call Him good and mild)
Answer, smiling down the steep world very purely,
    "Come and rest with me, my child."

'But, no!' say the children, weeping faster,
    'He is speechless as a stone;
And they tell us, of His image is the master
    Who commands us to work on.
Go to!' say the children, – 'Up in Heaven,
    Dark, wheel-like, turning clouds are all we find!   130
Do not mock us; grief has made us unbelieving –
    We look up for God, but tears have made us blind.'
Do ye hear the children weeping and disproving,
    O my brothers, what ye preach?
For God's possible is taught by His world's loving –
    And the children doubt of each.

And well may the children weep before you;
    They are weary ere they run;
They have never seen the sunshine, nor the glory
    Which is brighter than the sun: 140
They know the grief of men, but not the wisdom;
    They sink in the despair, without the calm –
Are slaves, without the liberty in Christdom, –
    Are martyrs, by the pang without the palm, –
Are worn, as if with age, yet unretrievingly
    No dear remembrance keep, –
Are orphans of the earthly love and heavenly:
    Let them weep! let them weep!

They look up, with their pale and sunken faces,
    And their look is dread to see,   150
For you think you see their angels in their places,
    With eyes meant for Deity; –
'How long,' they say, 'how long, O cruel nation,
    Will you stand, to move the world, on a child's heart, –
Stifle down with a mailed heel its palpitation,
    And tread onward to your throne amid the mart?
Our blood splashes upward, O our tyrants,
    And your purple shews your path;

2   A fact rendered pathetically historical by Mr. Horne's report of his commission. The name of the poet of 'Orion' and 'Cosmo de' Medici' has, however, a change of associations; and comes in time to remind me (with other noble instances) that we have some brave poetic heat of literature still, – though open to the reproach, on certain points, of being somewhat gelid in our humanity. [Author's note] [Report of the Children's Employment Commission (1842) – full of instances of mangled memories of the Lord's Prayer among the unschooled proletarian young. R. H. Horne, E.B.B.'s friend, author of epic *Orion* (1843) and tragedy *Cosmo de' Medici* (1837).]

But the child's sob curseth deeper in the silence
    Than the strong man in his wrath!'   160

First published, Blackwood's Edinburgh Magazine, *54 (1843)*, 260–2. Poems *(1844)*, II.

L. E. L.'s Last Question

'Do you think of me as I think of you?'
    From her Poem written during the Voyage to the Cape

'Do you think of me as I think of you,
  My friends, my friends?' – She said it from the sea,
  The English minstrel in her minstrelsy;
While, under brighter skies than erst she knew,
  Her heart grew dark, – and groped there as the blind,
  To reach, across the waves, friends left behind –
'Do you think of me as I think of you?'

It seemed not much to ask – As *I* of *you?* –
  We all do ask the same. No eyelids cover
  Within the meekest eyes, that question over, –   10
And little, in the world, the Loving do,
  But sit (among the rocks?) and listen for
  The echo of their own love evermore –
'Do you think of me as I think of you?'

Love-learned, she had sung of love and love, –
  And, like a child, that, sleeping with dropt head
  Upon the fairy-book he lately read,
Whatever household noises round him move,
  Hears in his dream some elfin turbulence, –
  Even so, suggestive to her inward sense,   20
All sounds of life assumed one tune of love.

And when the glory of her dream withdrew, –
  When knightly gestes and courtly pageantries
  Were broken in her visionary eyes,
By tears the solemn seas attested true, –
  Forgetting that sweet lute beside her hand,
  She asked not, – Do you praise me, O my land? –
But, – 'Think ye of me, friends, as I of you?'

Hers was the hand that played for many a year
  Love's silver phrase for England, – smooth and well!   30
  Would God her heart's more inward oracle
In that lone moment might confirm her dear!
  For when her questioned friends in agony
  Made passionate response, – 'We think of *thee*,' –
Her place was in the dust, too deep to hear.

Could she not wait to catch their answering breath?
  Was she content – content – with ocean's sound,
  Which dashed its mocking infinite around
One thirsty for a little love? – beneath
  Those stars, content – where last her song had gone, –   40

They, mute and cold in radiant life, – as soon
Their singer was to be, in darksome death?[1]

Bring your vain answers – cry, 'We think of *thee!*'
How think ye of her? warm in long ago
Delights? – or crowned with budding bays? Not so.
None smile and none are crowned where lieth she, –
With all her visions unfulfilled, save one –
Her childhood's – of the palm-trees in the sun –
And lo! their shadow on her sepulchre!

'Do ye think of me as I think of you?' –   50
O friends, – O kindred, – O dear brotherhood
Of all the world! what are we, that we should
For covenants of long affection sue?
Why press so near each other, when the touch
Is barred by graves! Not much, and yet too much,
Is this 'Think of me as I think of you.'

But while on mortal lips I shape anew
A sigh to mortal issues, – verily
Above the unshaken stars that see us die
A vocal pathos rolls! and HE who drew   60
All life from dust, and for all, tasted death,
By death and life and love, appealing, saith,
Do you think of me as I think of you?

Poems *(1844)*, II.

THE RUNAWAY SLAVE AT PILGRIM'S POINT

I
I stand on the mark beside the shore
    Of the first white pilgrim's bended knee,
Where exile turned to ancestor,
    And God was thanked for liberty.
I have run through the night, my skin is as dark,
I bend my knee down on this mark . . .
    I look on the sky and the sea.

II
O pilgrim-souls, I speak to you!
    I see you come out proud and slow
From the land of the spirits pale as dew . . .   10
    And round me and round me ye go!
O pilgrims, I have gasped and run
All night long from the whips of one
    Who in your names works sin and woe.

L. E. L.'S LAST QUESTION
1 Her lyric on the polar star, came home with her latest papers.
[Author's note]

III

And thus I thought that I would come
  And kneel here where I knelt before,
And feel your souls around me hum
  In undertone to the ocean's roar:
And lift my black face, my black hand,
Here, in your names, to curse this land   20
  Ye blessed in freedom's evermore.

IV

I am black, I am black;[1]
And yet God made me, they say.
But if He did so, smiling back
  He must have cast His work away
Under the feet of His white creatures,
With a look of scorn, – that the dusky features
Might be trodden again to clay.

V

And yet He has made dark things
  To be glad and merry as light.
There's a little dark bird sits and sings;   30
  There's a dark stream ripples out of sight;
And the dark frogs chant in the safe morass,
And the sweetest stars are made to pass
  O'er the face of the darkest night.

VI

But *we* who are dark, we are dark!
  Ah God, we have no stars!
About our souls in care and cark
  Our blackness shuts like prison bars:
The poor souls crouch so far behind,   40
That never a comfort can they find
  By reaching through the prison-bars.

VII

Indeed, we live beneath the sky,...
  That great smooth Hand of God, stretched out
On all His children fatherly,
  To bless them from the fear and doubt,
Which would be, if, from this low place,
All opened straight up to His face
  Into the grand eternity.

VIII

And still God's sunshine and His frost,   50
  They make us hot, they make us cold,
As if we were not black and lost:
  And the beasts and birds, in wood and fold,
Do fear and take us for very men!
Could the weep-poor-will or the cat of the glen
  Look into my eyes and be bold?

THE RUNAWAY SLAVE AT PILGRIM'S POINT
1 cf. Song of Solomon 1.5: 'I am black, but comely.'

IX

I am black, I am black! –
  But, once, I laughed in girlish glee;
For one of my colour stood in the track
  Where the drivers drove, and looked at me –   60
And tender and full was the look he gave:
Could a slave look *so* at another slave? –
  I look at the sky and the sea.

X

And from that hour our spirits grew
  As free as if unsold, unbought:
Oh, strong enough, since we were two,
  To conquer the world, we thought!
The drivers drove us day by day;
We did not mind, we went one way,
  And no better a liberty sought.

XI

In the sunny ground between the canes,   70
  He said 'I love you' as he passed:
When the shingle-roof rang sharp with the rains,
  I heard how he vowed it fast:
While others shook, he smiled in the hut
As he carved me a bowl of the cocoa-nut
  Through the roar of the hurricanes.

XII

I sang his name instead of a song;
  Over and over I sang his name –
Upward and downward I drew it along
  My various notes; the same, the same!   80
I sang it low, that the slave-girls near
Might never guess from aught they could hear,
  It was only a name.

XIII

I look on the sky and the sea –
  We were two to love, and two to pray, –
Yes, two, O God, who cried to Thee,
  Though nothing didst Thou say.
Coldly Thou sat'st behind the sun!
And now I cry who am but one,
  How wilt Thou speak to-day? –   90

XIV

We were black, we were black!
  We had no claim to love and bliss:
What marvel, if each turned to lack?
  They wrung my cold hands out of his, –
They dragged him…where?…I crawled to touch
His blood's mark in the dust!…not much,
  Ye pilgrim-souls,…though plain as *this!*

XV

Wrong, followed by a deeper wrong!
  Mere grief's too good for such as I.   100
So the white men brought the shame ere long

To strangle the sob of my agony.
They would not leave me for my dull
Wet eyes! – it was too merciful
    To let me weep pure tears and die.

XVI

I am black, I am black!
    I wore a child upon my breast...
An amulet that hung too slack,
    And, in my unrest, could not rest:
Thus we went moaning, child and mother,
One to another, one to another,   110
    Until all ended for the best:

XVII

For hark! I will tell you low...low...
    I am black, you see, –
And the babe who lay on my bosom so,
    Was far too white...too white for me;
As white as the ladies who scorned to pray
Beside me at church but yesterday;
    Though my tears had washed a place for my knee.

XVIII

My own, own child! I could not bear
    To look in his face, it was so white.   120
I covered him up with a kerchief there;
    I covered his face in close and tight:
And he moaned and struggled, as well might be,
For the white child wanted his liberty –
    Ha, ha! he wanted his master right.

XIX

He moaned and beat with his head and feet,
    His little feet that never grew –
He struck them out, as it was meet,
    Against my heart to break it through.
I might have sung and made him mild –   130
But I dared not sing to the white-faced child
    The only song I knew.

XX

I pulled the kerchief very close:
    He could not see the sun, I swear,
More, then, alive, than now he does
    From between the roots of the mango... where?
...I know where. Close! a child and mother
Do wrong to look at one another,
    When one is black and one is fair.

XXI

Why, in that single glance I had   140
    Of my child's face,...I tell you all,
I saw a look that made me mad...
    The *master's* look, that used to fall
On my soul like his lash...or worse! –
And so, to save it from my curse,
    I twisted it round in my shawl.

XXII

And he moaned and trembled from foot to head,
   He shivered from head to foot;
Till, after a time, he lay instead
   Too suddenly still and mute.   150
I felt beside a stiffening cold...
I dared to lift up just a fold,...
   As in lifting a leaf of the mango-fruit.

XXIII

But *my* fruit...ha, ha! – there, had been
   (I laugh to think on't at this hour!...)
Your fine white angels, who have seen
   Nearest the secret of God's power,...
And plucked my fruit to make them wine,
And sucked the soul of that child of mine,
   As the humming-bird sucks the soul of the flower.   160

XXIV

Ha, ha, for the trick of the angels white!
   They freed the white child's spirit so.
I said not a word, but, day and night,
   I carried the body to and fro;
And it lay on my heart like a stone...as chill.
– The sun may shine out as much as he will:
   I am cold, though it happened a month ago.

XXV

From the white man's house, and the black man's hut,
   I carried the little body on.
The forest's arms did round us shut,   170
   And silence through the trees did run:
They asked no question as I went, –
They stood too high for astonishment, –
   They could see God sit on His throne.

XXVI

My little body, kerchiefed fast,
   I bore it on through the forest...on:
And when I felt it was tired at last,
   I scooped a hole beneath the moon.
Through the forest-tops the angels far,   180
With a white sharp finger from every star,
   Did point and mock at what was done.

XXVII

Yet when it was all done aright,...
   Earth, 'twixt me and my baby, strewed,...
All, changed to black earth,...nothing white,...
   A dark child in the dark, – ensued
Some comfort, and my heart grew young:
I sate down smiling there and sung
   The song I learnt in my maidenhood.

XXVIII

And thus we two were reconciled,
   The white child and black mother, thus: 190
For, as I sang it, soft and wild

The same song, more melodious,
Rose from the grave whereon I sate!
It was the dead child singing that,
    To join the souls of both of us.

XXIX

I look on the sea and the sky!
    Where the pilgrims' ships first anchored lay,
The free sun rideth gloriously;
    But the pilgrim-ghosts have slid away
Through the earliest streaks of the morn.   200
My face is black, but it glares with a scorn
    Which they dare not meet by day.

XXX

Ah! – in their stead, their hunter sons!
Ah, ah! they are on me – they hunt in a ring –
Keep off! I brave you all at once –
    I throw off your eyes like snakes that sting!
You have killed the black eagle at nest, I think:
Did you never stand still in your triumph, and shrink
    From the stroke of her wounded wing?

XXXI

(Man, drop that stone you dared to lift! –)   210
    I wish you, who stand there five abreast,
Each, for his own wife's joy and gift,
    A little corpse as safely at rest
As mine in the mangoes! – Yes, but *she*
May keep live babies on her knee,
    And sing the song she liketh best.

XXXII

I am not mad: I am black.
    I see you staring in my face –
I know you, staring, shrinking back –
    Ye are born of the Washington-race: 220
And this land is the free America:
And this mark on my wrist... (I prove what I say)
    Ropes tied me up here to the flogging-place.

XXXIII

You think I shrieked then? Not a sound!
    I hung, as a gourd hangs in the sun.
I only cursed them all around,
    As softly as I might have done
My very own child! – From these sands
Up to the mountains, lift your hands,
    O slaves, and end what I begun!   230

XXXIV

Whips, curses; these must answer those!
    For in this UNION, you have set
Two kinds of men in adverse rows,
    Each loathing each: and all forget
The seven wounds in Christ's body fair;
While HE sees gaping everywhere
    Our countless wounds that pay no debt.

XXXV

Our wounds are different. Your white men
    Are, after all, not gods indeed,   240
Nor able to make Christs again
    Do good with bleeding. *We* who bleed...
(Stand off!) *we* help not in our loss!
We are too heavy for our cross,
    And fall and crush you and your seed.

XXXVI

I fall, I swoon! I look at the sky:
    The clouds are breaking on my brain;
I am floated along, as if I should die
    Of liberty's exquisite pain –
In the name of the white child, waiting for me
In the death-dark where we may kiss and agree,   250
White men, I leave you all curse-free
    In my broken heart's disdain!

Poems *(1850), II.*

SONNETS FROM THE PORTUGUESE

VIII

What can I give thee back, O liberal
And princely giver,... who hast brought the gold
And purple of thine heart, unstained, untold,
And laid them on the outside of the wall,
For such as I to take, or leave withal,
In unexpected largesse? Am I cold,
Ungrateful, that for these most manifold
High gifts, I render nothing back at all?
Not so. Not cold! – but very poor instead!
Ask God who knows! for frequent tears have run   10
The colours from my life, and left so dead
And pale a stuff, it were not fitly done
To give the same as pillow to thy head.
Go farther! Let it serve to trample on.

XIII

And wilt thou have me fashion into speech
The love I bear thee, finding words enough,
And hold the torch out, while the winds are rough,
Between our faces, to cast light on each! –
I drop it at thy feet. I cannot teach
My hand to hold my spirit so far off
From myself...me...that I should bring thee proof
In words, of love hid in me out of reach.
Nay, let the silence of my womanhood
Commend my woman-love to thy belief, –   10
Seeing that I stand unwon, however wooed,
And rend the garment of my life, in brief,
By a most dauntless, voiceless fortitude,
Lest one touch of this heart convey its grief.

XVIII

I never gave a lock of hair away
To a man, Dearest, except this to thee,

Which now upon my fingers thoughtfully
I ring out to the full brown length and say
'Take it.' My day of youth went yesterday;
My hair no longer bounds to my foot's glee,
Nor plant I it from rose or myrtle-tree,
As girls do, any more. It only may
Now shade on two pale cheeks, the mark of tears,
Taught drooping from the head that hangs aside
Through sorrow's trick. I thought the funeral-shears
Would take this first; but Love is justified:
Take it, thou, ... finding pure, from all those years,
The kiss my mother left here when she died.

XXIV

Let the world's sharpness like a clasping knife,
Shut in upon itself and do no harm
In this close hand of Love, now soft and warm;
And let us hear no sound of human strife,
After the click of the shutting. Life to life –
I lean upon thee, Dear, without alarm,
And feel as safe as guarded by a charm,
Against the stab of worldlings who if rife
Are weak to injure. Very whitely still
The lilies of our lives may reassure
Their blossoms from their roots! accessible
Alone to heavenly dews that drop not fewer;
Growing straight, out of man's reach, on the hill.
God only, who made us rich, can make us poor.

XXVII

My own Beloved, who hast lifted me
From this drear flat of earth where I was thrown,
And in betwixt the languid ringlets, blown
A life-breath, till the forehead hopefully
Shines out again, as all the angels see,
Before thy saving kiss! My own, my own,
Who camest to me when the world was gone,
And I who looked for only God, found *thee!*
I find thee: I am safe, and strong, and glad.
As one who stands in dewless asphodel
Looks backward on the tedious time he had
In the upper life ... so I, with bosom-swell,
Make witness here between the good and bad,
That Love, as strong as Death, retrieves as well.

XXVIII

My letters! all dead paper, ... mute and white! –
And yet they seem alive and quivering
Against my tremulous hands, which loose the string
And let them drop down on my knee tonight.
This said, ... he wished to have me in his sight
Once, as a friend: this fixed a day in spring
To come and touch my hand ... a simple thing,
Yet I wept for it! – this, ... the paper's light ...
Said, *Dear, I love thee:* and I sank and quailed
As if God's future thundered on my past:
This said, *I am thine* – and so its ink has paled
With lying at my heart that beat too fast:

And this ... O Love, thy words have ill availed,
If, what this said, I dared repeat at last!

XXXVIII

First time he kissed me, he but only kissed
The fingers of this hand wherewith I write,
And ever since it grew more clean and white, ...
Slow to world-greetings ... quick with its 'Oh, list,'
When the angels speak. A ring of amethyst
I could not wear here plainer to my sight,
Than that first kiss. The second passed in height
The first, and sought the forehead, and half missed,
Half falling on the hair. O beyond meed!
That was the chrism[1] of love, which love's own crown,
With sanctifying sweetness, did precede.
The third, upon my lips, was folded down
In perfect, purple state! since when, indeed,
I have been proud and said, 'My Love, my own.'

XLII

How do I love thee? Let me count the ways.
I love thee to the depth and breadth and height[1]
My soul can reach, when feeling out of sight
For the ends of Being and Ideal Grace.
I love thee to the level of everyday's
Most quiet need, by sun and candlelight.
I love thee freely, as men strive for Right;
I love thee purely, as they turn from Praise;
I love thee with the passion put to use
In my old griefs, and with my childhood's faith;   10
I love thee with a love I seemed to lose
With my lost saints, – I love thee with the breath,
Smiles, tears, of all my life! – and, if God choose,
I shall but love thee better after death.

XLIII

Beloved, thou hast brought me many flowers
Plucked in the garden, all the summer through
And winter, and it seemed as if they grew
In this close room, nor missed the sun and showers.
So, in the like name of that love of ours,
Take back these thoughts, which here unfolded too,
And which on warm and cold days I withdrew
From my heart's ground. Indeed, those beds and bowers
Be overgrown with bitter weeds and rue,
And wait thy weeding: yet here's eglantine,   10
Here's ivy! – take them, as I used to do
Thy flowers, and keep them where they shall not pine:
Instruct thine eyes to keep their colours true,
And tell thy soul, their roots are left in mine.

Sonnets by E. B. B., Not For Publication *(Reading, 1847)*. Poems *(1850), II.*
(The sequence consists of 43 sonnets.)

SONNET XXXVIII
1 sacramental anointing oil mixed with balm.

SONNET XLII
1 'Nor height, nor depth, nor any other creature, shall be able to separate us from the love of God ...,' Romans 8. 39.

From: AURORA LEIGH

Dedication to John Kenyon, Esq.

The words 'cousin' and 'friend' are constantly recurring in this poem, the last pages of which have been finished under the hospitality of your roof, my own dearest cousin and friend; – cousin and friend, in a sense of less equality and greater disinterestedness than 'Romney''s.[1]

Ending, therefore, and preparing once more to quit England, I venture to leave in your hands this book, the most mature of my works, and the one into which my highest convictions upon Life and Art have entered: that as, through my various efforts in literature and steps in life, you have believed in me, borne with me, and been generous to me, far beyond the common uses of mere relationship or sympathy of mind, so you may kindly accept, in sight of the public, this poor sign of esteem, gratitude, and affection, from

your unforgetting
E. B. B.
39, Devonshire Place,
October 17, 1856

First Book

Of writing many books there is no end;[2]
And I who have written much in prose and verse
For others' uses, will write now for mine, –
Will write my story for my better self,
As when you paint your portrait for a friend,
Who keeps it in a drawer and looks at it
Long after he has ceased to love you, just
To hold together what he was and is.

I, writing thus, am still what men call young;
I have not so far left the coasts of life   10
To travel inland, that I cannot hear
That murmur of the outer Infinite
Which unweaned babies smile at in their sleep
When wondered at for smiling; not so far,
But still I catch my mother at her post
Beside the nursery-door, with finger up,
'Hush, hush – here's too much noise!' while her sweet eyes
Leap forward, taking part against her word
In the child's riot. Still I sit and feel
My father's slow hand, when she had left us both,   20
Stroke out my childish curls across his knee;
And hear Assunta's daily jest (she knew
He liked it better than a better jest)
Inquire how many golden scudi[3] went
To make such ringlets. O my father's hand
Stroke the poor hair down, stroke it heavily, –
Draw, press the child's head closer to thy knee!
I'm still too young, too young, to sit alone.

I write....

[· · ·]

AURORA LEIGH

1   Aurora's cousin in the poem.

2   Ecclesiastes 12.12: 'Of making many books there is no end.'

3   Italian coins.

The cygnet finds the water; but the man   30
Is born in ignorance of his element,
And feels out blind at first, disorganised
By sin i' the blood, – his spirit-insight dulled
And crossed by his sensations. Presently
We feel it quicken in the dark sometimes;
Then, mark, be reverent, be obedient, –
For those dumb motions of imperfect life
Are oracles of vital Deity
Attesting the Hereafter. Let who says
'The soul's a clean white paper,' rather say,   40
A palimpsest, a prophet's holograph
Defiled, erased and covered by a monk's, –
The apocalypse, by a Longus![4] poring on
Which obscene text, we may discern perhaps
Some fair, fine trace of what was written once,
Some upstroke of an alpha and omega
Expressing the old scripture.
                     Books, books, books!
I had found the secret of a garret-room
Piled high with cases in my father's name;   50
Piled high, packed large, – where, creeping in and out
Among the giant fossils of my past,
Like some small nimble mouse between the ribs
Of a mastodon, I nibbled here and there
At this or that box, pulling through the gap,
In heats of terror, haste, victorious joy,
The first book first. And how I felt it beat
Under my pillow, in the morning's dark,
An hour before the sun would let me read!
My books!   60
         At last, because the time was ripe,
I chanced upon the poets.
                As the earth
Plunges in fury, when the internal fires
Have reached and pricked her heart, and, throwing flat
The marts and temples, the triumphal gates
And towers of observation, clears herself
To elemental freedom – thus, my soul,
At poetry's divine first finger-touch,
Let go conventions and sprang up surprised,   70
Convicted of the great eternities
Before two worlds.
             What's this, Aurora Leigh,
You write so of the poets, and not laugh?
Those virtuous liars, dreamers after dark,
Exaggerators of the sun and moon,
And soothsayers in a tea-cup?
               I write so
Of the only truth-tellers, now left to God, –
The only speakers of essential truth,   80
Opposed to relative, comparative,
And temporal truths; the only holders by
His sun-skirts, through conventional grey glooms;

4   Longus wrote Greek prose romance *Daphnis and Chloe* (?3rd century
AD).

The only teachers who instruct mankind,
From just a shadow on a charnel-wall,
To find man's veritable stature out,
Erect, sublime, – the measure of a man,
And that's the measure of an angel, says
The apostle.[5] Ay, and while your common men
Build pyramids, gauge railroads, reign, reap, dine,   90
And dust the flaunty carpets of the world
For kings to walk on, or our senators,
The poet suddenly will catch them up
With his voice like a thunder... 'This is soul,
This is life, this word is being said in heaven,
Here's God down on us! what are you about?'
How all those workers start amid their work,
Look round, look up, and feel, a moment's space,
That carpet-dusting, though a pretty trade,
Is not the imperative labour after all.   100

My own best poets, am I one with you,
That thus I love you, – or but one through love?
Does all this smell of thyme about my feet
Conclude my visit to your holy hill
In personal presence, or but testify
The rustling of your vesture through my dreams
With influent odours? When my joy and pain,
My thought and aspiration, like the stops
Of pipe or flute, are absolutely dumb
If not melodious, do you play on me,   110
My pipers, – and if, sooth, you did not blow,
Would no sound come? or is the music mine,
As a man's voice or breath is called his own,
Inbreathed by the Life-breather? There's a doubt
For cloudy seasons!
                          But the sun was high
When first I felt my pulses set themselves
For concords; when the rhythmic turbulence
Of blood and brain swept outward upon words,
As wind upon the alders, blanching them   120
By turning up their under-natures till
They trembled in dilation. O delight
And triumph of the poet, – who would say
A man's mere 'yes,' a woman's common 'no,'
A little human hope of that or this,
And says the word so that it burns you through
With a special revelation, shakes the heart
Of all the men and women in the world,
As if one came back from the dead and spoke,
With eyes too happy, a familiar thing   130
Become divine i' the utterance! while for him
The poet, the speaker, he expands with joy;
The palpitating angel in his flesh
Thrills inly with consenting fellowship
To those innumerous spirits who sun themselves

5   Revelation 21.17. E. B. B. refers, apparently, to a theory of propor-
tion, based on this verse, by artist William Page, and explained to the
Brownings. It gets into R. B.'s 'Cleon'.

Outside of time.
                    O life, O poetry,
– Which means life in life! cognisant of life
Beyond this blood-beat, – passionate for truth
Beyond these senses, – poetry, my life, –   140
My eagle, with both grappling feet still hot
From Zeus's thunder, who has ravished me
Away from all the shepherds, sheep, and dogs,
And set me in the Olympian roar and round
Of luminous faces, for a cup-bearer,[6]
To keep the mouths of all the godheads moist
For everlasting laughters,[7] – I, myself,
Half drunk across the beaker, with their eyes!
How those gods look!
                    Enough so, Ganymede.   150
We shall not bear above a round or two –
We drop the golden cup at Heré's[8] foot
And swoon back to the earth, – and find ourselves
Face-down among the pine-cones, cold with dew,
While the dogs bark, and many a shepherd scoffs,
'What's come now to the youth?' Such ups and downs
Have poets.
                    Am I such indeed? The name
Is royal, and to sign it like a queen,
Is what I dare not, – though some royal blood   160
Would seem to tingle in me now and then,
With sense of power and ache, – with imposthumes[9]
And manias usual to the race. Howbeit
I dare not: 'tis too easy to go mad,
And ape a Bourbon in a crown of straws;[10]
The thing's too common.
                    Many fervent souls
Strike rhyme on rhyme, who would strike steel on steel
If steel had offered, in a restless heat
Of doing something. Many tender souls   170
Have strung their losses on a rhyming thread,
As children, cowslips: – the more pains they take,
The work more withers. Young men, ay, and maids,
Too often sow their wild oats in tame verse,
Before they sit down under their own vine[11]
And live for use. Alas, near all the birds
Will sing at dawn, – and yet we do not take
The chaffering swallow for the holy lark.

In those days, though, I never analysed
Myself even. All analysis comes late.   180
You catch a sight of Nature, earliest,
In full front sun-face, and your eyelids wink
And drop before the wonder of't; you miss
The form, through seeing the light. I lived, those days,
And wrote because I lived – unlicensed else:
My heart beat in my brain. Life's violent flood

---

6 Ganymede, shepherd-boy, was carried off to Mount Olympus by
Zeus (in form of an eagle), to become cup-bearer to the gods.
7 According to Homer the gods on Olympus laugh with inextin-
guishable laughters.

8 Heré: Hera, wife of Zeus, queen of the gods.
9 abscesses; moral corruptions.
10 Henri, last of the old Bourbon kings.
11 Place of Biblical retirement and security, as Micah 4.4.

Abolished bounds, – and, which my neighbour's field,
Which mine, what mattered? It is so in youth.
We play at leap-frog over the god Term;[12]
The love within us and the love without   190
Are mixed, confounded; if we are loved or love,
We scarce distinguish. So, with other power.
Being acted on and acting seem the same:
In that first onrush of life's chariot-wheels,
We know not if the forests move or we.

And so, like most young poets, in a flush
Of individual life, I poured myself
Along the veins of others, and achieved
Mere lifeless imitations of live verse,
And made the living answer for the dead,   200
Profaning nature. 'Touch not, do not taste,
Nor handle,'[13] – we're too legal, who write young:
We beat the phorminx[14] till we hurt our thumbs,
As if still ignorant of counterpoint;
We call the Muse . . . 'O Muse, benignant Muse!' –
As if we had seen her purple-braided head[15]
With the eyes in it, start between the boughs
As often as a stag's. What make-believe,
With so much earnest! what effete results,
From virile efforts! what cold wire-drawn odes,   210
From such white heats! – bucolics, where the cows
Would scare the writer if they splashed the mud
In lashing off the flies, – didactics, driven
Against the heels of what the master said;
And counterfeiting epics, shrill with trumps
A babe might blow between two straining cheeks
Of bubbled rose, to make his mother laugh;
And elegiac griefs, and songs of love,
Like cast-off nosegays picked up on the road,
The worse for being warm: all these things, writ   220
On happy mornings, with a morning heart,
That leaps for love, is active for resolve,
Weak for art only. Oft, the ancient forms
Will thrill, indeed, in carrying the young blood.
The wine-skins, now and then, a little warped,
Will crack even, as the new wine gurgles in.
Spare the old bottles! – spill not the new wine.[16]

By Keats's soul, the man who never stepped
In gradual progress like another man,
But, turning grandly on his central self,   230
Ensphered himself in twenty perfect years,
And died, not young, – (the life of a long life,
Distilled to a mere drop, falling like a tear
Upon the world's cold cheek to make it burn

12 Roman god of frontiers and borders.
13 Colossians 2.21.
14 ancient Greek stringed instrument, to accompany the voice.
15 According to Pindar, the Muses had purple, or violet, coloured hair.

16 'And no man putteth new wine into old bottles: else the new wine doth burst the bottles, and the wine is spilled . . . but new wine must be put into new bottles' (Mark 2.22).

For ever;) by that strong excepted soul,
I count it strange, and hard to understand,
That nearly all young poets should write old;
That Pope was sexagenarian at sixteen,
And beardless Byron academical,
And so with others. It may be, perhaps,   240
Such have not settled long and deep enough
In trance, to attain to clairvoyance, – and still
The memory mixes with the vision, spoils,
And works it turbid.
                Or perhaps, again,
In order to discover the Muse-Sphinx,
The melancholy desert must sweep round,
Behind you, as before. –
                For me, I wrote
False poems, like the rest, and thought them true,   250
Because myself was true in writing them.
I, peradventure, have writ true ones since
With less complacence.
                But I could not hide
My quickening inner life from those at watch.
They saw a light at a window now and then,
They had not set there. Who had set it there?
My father's sister started when she caught
My soul agaze in my eyes. She could not say
I had no business with a sort of soul,   260
But plainly she objected, – and demurred,
That souls were dangerous things to carry straight
Through all the spilt saltpetre of the world.

She said sometimes, 'Aurora, have you done
Your task this morning? – have you read that book?
And are you ready for the crochet here?' –
As if she said, 'I know there's something wrong;
I know I have not ground you down enough
To flatten and bake you to a wholesome crust
For household duties and properties,   270
Before the rain has got into my barn
And set the grains a-sprouting. What, you're green
With out-door impudence? you almost grow?'
To which I answered, 'Would she hear my task,
And verify my abstract of the book?
And should I sit down to the crochet work?
Was such her pleasure?'... Then I sate and teased
The patient needle till it split the thread,
Which oozed off from it in meandering lace
From hour to hour. I was not, therefore, sad;   280
My soul was singing at a work apart
Behind the wall of sense, as safe from harm
As sings the lark when sucked up out of sight,
In vortices of glory and blue air.

And so, through forced work and spontaneous work,
The inner life informed the outer life,
Reduced the irregular blood to settled rhythms,
Made cool the forehead with fresh-sprinkling dreams,
And, rounding to the spheric soul the thin
Pined body, struck a colour up the cheeks,   290

Though somewhat faint. I clenched my brows across
My blue eyes greatening in the looking-glass,
And said, 'We'll live, Aurora! we'll be strong.
The dogs are on us – but we will not die.'

Whoever lives true life, will love true love.
I learnt to love that England. Very oft,
Before the day was born, or otherwise
Through secret windings of the afternoons,
I threw my hunters off and plunged myself
Among the deep hills, as a hunted stag   300
Will take the waters, shivering with the fear
And passion of the course. And when, at last
Escaped, – so many a green slope built on slope
Betwixt me and the enemy's house behind,
I dared to rest, or wander, – like a rest
Made sweeter for the step upon the grass, –
And view the ground's most gentle dimplement,[17]
(As if God's finger touched but did not press
In making England!) such an up and down
Of verdure, – nothing too much up or down,   310
A ripple of land; such little hills, the sky
Can stoop to tenderly and the wheatfields climb;
Such nooks of valleys, lined with orchises,
Fed full of noises by invisible streams;
And open pastures, where you scarcely tell
White daisies from white dew, – at intervals
The mythic oaks and elm-trees standing out
Self-poised upon their prodigy of shade, –
I thought my father's land was worthy too
Of being my Shakspeare's.   320
                        Very oft alone,
Unlicensed; not unfrequently with leave
To walk the third with Romney and his friend
The rising painter, Vincent Carrington,
Whom men judge hardly, as bee-bonneted,
Because he holds that, paint a body well
You paint a soul by implication, like
The grand first Master.[18] Pleasant walks! for if
He said . . . 'When I was last in Italy' . . .
It sounded as an instrument that's played   330
Too far off for the tune – and yet it's fine
To listen.
          Ofter we walked only two,
If cousin Romney pleased to walk with me.
We read, or talked, or quarrelled, as it chanced:
We were not lovers, nor even friends well matched –
Say rather, scholars upon different tracks,
And thinkers disagreed; he, overfull
Of what is, and I, haply, overbold
For what might be.   340
                        But then the thrushes sang,
And shook my pulses and the elms' new leaves, –
And then I turned, and held my finger up,
And bade him mark that, howsoe'er the world

17   dimpling. An E. B. B. coinage.   18   a belief of Robert Browning, too. See his 'Fra Lippo Lippi'.

Went ill, as he related, certainly
The thrushes still sang in it. – At which word
His brow would soften, – and he bore with me
In melancholy patience, not unkind,
While, breaking into voluble ecstasy,
I flattered all the beauteous country round,   350
As poets use ... the skies, the clouds, the fields,
The happy violets hiding from the roads
The primroses run down to, carrying gold, –
The tangled hedgerows, where the cows push out
Impatient horns and tolerant churning mouths
'Twixt dripping ash-boughs, – hedgerows all alive
With birds and gnats and large white butterflies
Which look as if the May-flower had caught life
And palpitated forth upon the wind, –
Hills, vales, woods, netted in a silver mist,   360
Farms, granges, doubled up among the hills,
And cattle grazing in the watered vales,
And cottage chimneys smoking from the woods,
And cottage gardens smelling everywhere,
Confused with smell of orchards. 'See,' I said,
'And see! is God not with us on the earth?
And shall we put Him down by aught we do?
Who says there's nothing for the poor and vile
Save poverty and wickedness? behold!'
And ankle-deep in English grass I leaped,   370
And clapped my hands, and called all very fair.

In the beginning when God called all good,
Even then was evil near us, it is writ.[19]
But we, indeed, who call things good and fair,
The evil is upon us while we speak:
Deliver us from evil,[20] let us pray.

Aurora Leigh *(Chapman & Hall, 1856 [Title-page, 1857]). From the beginning
and the end of Book One. (The whole poem consists of 9 Books.)*

A MUSICAL INSTRUMENT

I
What was he doing, the great god Pan,[1]
   Down in the reeds by the river?
Spreading ruin and scattering ban,[2]
Splashing and paddling with hoofs of a goat,
And breaking the golden lilies afloat
   With the dragon-fly on the river.

II
He tore out a reed, the great god Pan,
   From the deep cool bed of the river:
The limpid water turbidly ran,

19 Genesis 1.31, 2.17.
20 Matthew 6.13 (phrase from the Lord's Prayer).

A MUSICAL INSTRUMENT
1 sexy rural deity, half-goat, who plays on pipes ('the pipes of Pan').
2 curse or execration.

And the broken lilies a-dying lay,   10
And the dragon-fly had fled away,
   Ere he brought it out of the river.

III

High on the shore sat the great god Pan
   While turbidly flowed the river;
And hacked and hewed as a great god can,
With his hard bleak steel at the patient reed,
Till there was not a sign of the leaf indeed
   To prove it fresh from the river.

IV

He cut it short, did the great god Pan,
   (How tall it stood in the river!)   20
Then drew the pith, like the heart of a man,
Steadily from the outside ring,
And notched the poor dry empty thing
   In holes, as he sat by the river.

V

'This is the way,' laughed the great god Pan
   (Laughed while he sat by the river),
'The only way, since gods began
To make sweet music, they could succeed.'
Then, dropping his mouth to a hole in the reed,
   He blew in power by the river.   30

VI

Sweet, sweet, sweet, O Pan!
   Piercing sweet by the river!
Blinding sweet, O great god Pan!
The sun on the hill forgot to die,
And the lilies revived, and the dragon-fly
   Came back to dream on the river.

VII

Yet half a beast is the great god Pan,
   To laugh as he sits by the river,
Making a poet out of a man:
The true gods sigh for the cost and pain, –   40
For the reed which grows nevermore again
   As a reed with the reeds in the river.

Last Poems *(Chapman & Hall, 1862).*

Frederick Tennyson (1807–98)

Alfred's Tennyson's oldest surviving brother, Frederick Tennyson, was born at Louth in Lincolnshire, 5 June 1807, second son of the Revd Dr George Clayton Tennyson, rector of Somersby, and his wife Elizabeth. As with his younger brother Charles, Frederick's poetic career was greatly outshone by the (for him) dispiriting greatness of Alfred. Frederick went to Eton; contributed (probably) four poems to Charles and Alfred's *Poems by Two Brothers* (1826); joined his two brothers at Trinity College, Cambridge in 1828 after a year at St John's; and won the Cambridge Browne Medal for Greek Verse (with an ode on the pyramids). He spent most of his life out of England. He was in Florence for twenty years (where he met Maria Giulotti, who became his wife in 1839, and knew the

Brownings well). In 1859 the pair moved to Jersey, where he stayed for the rest of his life. His *Days and Hours* came out in 1854. Charles Kingsley praised it, but in general the critics were unkind, and Frederick did not publish again until 1890 when his epic *The Isles of Greece* came out. His *Daphne* appeared the following year and in 1895 *Poems of the Day and Year* – recycling bits of the 1854 volume. Generously, Alfred said that Frederick's poems were 'organ-tones echoing among the mountains'. He was less kind to his brother's keen interest in levitation, table-rapping and other spiritualist manifestations ('I am convinced that God and ghosts of men would choose something other than mere table-legs through which to speak to the heart of man'). Frederick Tennyson died at the house of his son Captain Julius Tennyson in Kensington, London, 26 February 1898.

TEN YEARS AGO

Ten years are swiftly fled since yesterday –
    For yesterday it seems ten years ago –
    Ah! loveless Time, that lovest not to stay,
    But still to other years as swift as they
    Onward and on the unebbing moments flow:

What were ten years to me ten years ago?
    A breath upon the lip – a skylark's song –
    A path thro' vales where the wild-roses grow –
    A winding shore where morning breezes blow –
    A cloud where hopes like triple rainbows throng.   10

What are they? ah! what are those happy hours,
    The fair ten years that stept so laughingly
    Wreathed like a bridal company with flowers
    In virgin white, from forth their secret bowers
    Into the gray morn of Futurity?

Alas! into a gulf of weary cares
    I turn mine eyes – lo! pale and dead they lie,
    And with the lonely lamp my Sorrow bears
    I read the death-look each sweet phantom wears,
    Until fresh-springing anguish fills mine eye.   20

The roses on their brows so brightly braided,
    Are cast into the swift and silent river;
    The glossy love-locks that so richly shaded
    Their dimpling beauties all are gray and faded,
    The lovelight in their eyes is set for ever!

I'll sit beside your graves upon the shore,
    My songs shall murmur in your closed ears,
    No after years with smiles like those before
    Shall hear me breathe them love-vows any more,
    Since ye are not, O laughter-hearted years!   30

Shorter Poems, ed. Charles Tennyson (Macmillan, 1913).

PEACEFUL REST

If they shall say, 'He had no task on earth,'
And if no soul reanimate my dust,
No record like the memory of the Just
Circle my name – that is not of a worth

To claim renown or leave regret behind;
Then, Nature, mould thou of my broken clay
A little plot against the western wind
Not quite within, nor all apart from day;
Which violets blue may shadow with their bells:
And haply in some far millennial year,   10
When Hate hath fled away with Evil and Fear,
And War is dead, and Love among us dwells,
Haply, on some Spring morn of golden hours,
Thy gracious hand shall bid me gently forth
From painless slumbers underneath the flowers,
And show me the new Heaven, and promised Earth.

Shorter Poems *(1913)*.

OLD AGE

As when into the garden paths by night
One bears a lamp, and with its sickly glare
Scatters the burnished flowers a-dreaming there,
Palely they show like spectres in his sight,
Lovely no more, disfurnished of delight,
Some folded up and drooping o'er the way,
Their odours spent, their colour changed to gray,
Some that stood queen-like in the morning light
Fallen discrowned: so the low-burning loves
That tremble in the hearts of aged men   10
Cast their own light upon the world that moves
Around them, and receive it back again.
Old joys seem dead, old faces without joys;
Laughter is dead.   There is no mirth in boys.

Shorter Poems *(1913)*.

(The Honourable Mrs) Caroline (Elizabeth Sarah) Norton (1808–77)

Caroline Norton, famous as a beauty and rather infamous as a publicist for women's legal rights, was born in London in 1808 into a family of writers. Her grandfather was Richard Brinsley Sheridan, the playwright; her mother, Caroline Henrietta Sheridan, was a novelist; one of her sisters, Lady Helen Dufferin, wrote poems. They were extremely well connected socially. When Caroline's father Thomas Sheridan died in the colonial service in 1817, mother and daughters were given temporary royal accommodation at Hampton Court Palace. Caroline made much money by her writing, especially in the journals and annuals. Her work was exaggeratedly celebrated in its time as worthy of Byron for big-hearted pathos and rhetorical passion. She boasted she could make £1,400 in a single year. But her earnings went, of course, to her husband, the Hon. George Chapple Norton, a disgruntled no-hoper barrister, Tory MP for Guildford, who blatantly exploited his wife's earning power. Their marriage was, not surprisingly, unhappy. She left him in 1835, but returned because the law automatically afforded him custody of their three sons. The following year Norton took the Liberal Lord Melbourne to court on a charge of adultery with his wife – she was a Liberal and a supporter of the 1832 Reform Bill – in search of £10,000 damages. The jury unhesitatingly threw out the case (which apparently provided ammunition for 'Bardell v. Pickwick' in Dickens's *The Pickwick Papers*). Many people assumed it was anyway a put-up political job. Its notoriety lingered (the impetuous Diana Warwick in George Meredith's *Diana of the Crossways* is apparently based on Caroline Norton). After the trial, and by now highly aggrieved, Mrs Norton crusaded busily for changes in the laws about women's earnings, child custody and divorce. *A Plain Letter to the Lord Chancellor on the Infant Custody Bill* (1839), *English Laws for Women in the Nineteenth Century* (1854) and *Letter to the Queen on Lord Chancellor Cranworth's Marriage and Divorce Bill* (1857) helped not only to shift opinion but also, in the end, to effect legal change. The disadvantaged, too, were the subjects of her verses, for instance in *A Voice From the Factories* (1836) and *The Child of the Islands* (1845). She was undoubtedly inspired in such Condition-of-England texts by writers such as Carlyle and Disraeli, but, like them, was no egalitar-ian. 'Gradation' was the law of God, in her view – though the providentially strong and superior should protect the weak. Her novels, such as *Lost and Saved* (1863), feature strong-minded women with troubles greatly resembling her own. The slimy George Norton died in February 1875, and on 1 March 1877, though house-bound by illness, his widow married Sir William Stirling-Maxwell, an old friend. Three months later, 15 June 1877, she was dead, aged 69.

MY HEART IS LIKE A WITHERED NUT!

My heart is like a withered nut,
    Rattling within its hollow shell;
You cannot ope my breast, and put
    Any thing fresh with it to dwell.
The hopes and dreams that filled it when
    Life's spring of glory met my view,
Are gone! and ne'er with joy or pain
    That shrunken heart shall swell anew.

My heart is like a withered nut;
    Once it was soft to every touch,   10
But now 'tis stern and closely shut; –
    I would not have to plead with such.
Each light-toned voice once cleared my brow,
    Each gentle breeze once shook the tree
Where hung the sun-lit fruit, which now
    Lies cold, and stiff, and sad, like me!

My heart is like a withered nut –
    It once was comely to the view;
But since misfortune's blast hath cut,
    It hath a dark and mournful hue.   20
The freshness of its verdant youth
    Nought to that fruit can now restore;
And my poor heart, I feel in truth,
    Nor sun, nor smile shall light it more!

The Undying One, and Other Poems *(Henry Colburn & Richard Bentley, 1830).*

I WAS NOT FALSE TO THEE

I was not false to *thee*, and yet
My cheek alone looked pale;
My weary eye was dim and wet,
My strength began to fail.
Thou wert the same; thy looks were gay,
Thy step was light and free;
And yet, with truth, my heart can say,
I was not false to *thee!*

I was not false to thee, yet now
Thou hast a cheerful eye,   10

With flushing cheek and drooping brow
I wander mournfully.
I hate to meet the gaze of men,
I weep where none can see;
Why do *I* only suffer, when
I was not false to *thee?*

I was not false to thee; yet oh!
How scornfully they smile,
Who see me droop, who guess my woe,
Yet court thee all the while.   20
'Tis strange! but when long years are past,
Thou wilt remember me;
Whilst I can feel until the last,
I was not false to *thee!*

The Undying One, and Other Poems *(1830)*.

SONNET XIII

The Weaver

Little they think, the giddy and the vain,
  Wandering at pleasure 'neath the shady trees,
While the light glossy silk or rustling train
  Shines in the sun or flutters in the breeze,
How the sick weaver plies the incessant loom,
  Crossing in silence the perplexing thread,
Pent in the confines of one narrow room,
  Where droops complainingly his cheerless head: –
Little they think with what dull anxious eyes,
  Nor by what nerveless, thin, and trembling hands,   10
The devious mingling of those various dyes
  Were wrought to answer Luxury's commands:
But the day cometh when the tired shall rest, –
Where weary Lazarus leans his head on Abraham's breast![1]

The Dream, and Other Poems *(Henry Colburn, 1840)*.

Charles (Tennyson) Turner (1808–79)

Charles (Tennyson) Turner was the obscure elder brother of Alfred Tennyson. A prolific sonneteer, his life and career intersected curiously with, and were naturally overshadowed by, those of his far more famous brother, thirteen months his junior. Born 4 July 1808, second surviving son of the Revd Dr George Clayton Tennyson, rector of Somersby, Lincolnshire, and his wife Elizabeth, herself a vicar's daughter, Charles Tennyson was educated first at Louth Grammar School, then at home with Alfred (who had been earlier withdrawn from the school for unhappiness). Their first volume was a joint one, *Poems by Two Brothers* (1826), brought out by a Louth bookseller (they got £20 – most of it in credit at the bookseller's). The book probably also contained four poems by their older brother Frederick, who was at Eton. Charles and Alfred both went up to Trinity College, Cambridge, at the end of 1827, and matriculated together on the same day, 20 February 1828. They were joined in Trinity by Frederick,

SONNET XIII
1   i.e. in heaven: as Luke 16. 22, 'And it came to pass that the beggar [Lazarus] died, and was carried by angels into Abraham's bosom.'

who had spent his first year at St John's College. They made a striking trio, winning prizes, sharing a reputation as intellectuals and aesthetes. In 1830, while still undergraduates, Charles and Alfred both brought out individual volumes – Charles's *Sonnets and Fugitive Pieces*, Alfred's *Poems, Chiefly Lyrical*. Coleridge liked Charles's book, but unlike Alfred, Charles had no Hallam to launch his career into the public gaze, and hereabouts he embarked on the chain of mental problems and opium addiction which would dog him all his life. In 1833 he was ordained into the Church of England ministry. He took the curacy of Tealby, Lincolnshire (in the gift of his quarrelsome grandfather George Tennyson). In 1835 he changed his name to Turner in order to inherit from his great-uncle the Revd Samuel Turner – which included being vicar of Grasby and a large house at nearby Caistor (it had a 'watercloset with a recumbent Venus in it', according to Alfred). Charles never used the name of Tennyson again. In 1836 he married Louisa Sellwood of Horncastle (her elder sister Emily was a bridesmaid, and married Alfred in 1850). Being vicar of Grasby, while living some distance away, proved difficult (Nonconformists were a problem; Louisa disliked travel): they moved into the dilapidated vicarage; he took, as ever, to opium. Her efforts to get him off the drug helped Louisa herself become mentally ill, and soon the pair separated. He travelled about at home and abroad.

His wife returned to Grasby after ten years or so, and he got off the opium, thanks to his 'guardian angel' and, apparently, to the therapy of sonnet-writing. The black melancholia of the Tennysons was harder to shake off. After a publishing lapse of thirty-four years his *Sonnets* appeared (1864), dedicated to his brother, by now the Poet Laureate. Charles later attributed his long public silence to Alfred's deterring fame and 'perfect work'. *Small Tableaux* followed (1868) and *Sonnets, Lyrics and Translations* (1873). A *Collected Sonnets, Old and New* appeared in 1880, with many previously unpublished poems. Charles Turner died at Cheltenham, 25 April 1879 – undergoing treatment for mental illness. Unconsoled, religiously demented, his wife died within a month of her husband. His touch was for the contemporary anxieties which provoked him most – new theology, new technologies. At his best he made his small, tightly bound medium the vehicle for what he called small tableaux, featuring tiny things and persons. 'Letty's Globe' rightly became a favourite anthology piece; it had, Alfred thought, 'all the tenderness of Greek epigram'. 'I beg you, painter, not to despise these small pictures', exhorts the epigraph to *Small Tableaux*. And in an age of texts preoccupied with the dinky, the toy, the child, Charles Turner's acute small themes are indeed undespicable.

THE VACANT CAGE

Our little bird in his full day of health
With his gold-coated beauty made us glad,
But when disease approached with cruel stealth,
A sadder interest our smiles forbad.
How oft we watched him, when the night hours came,
His poor head buried near his bursting heart,
Which beat within a puft and troubled frame;
But he has gone at last, and played his part:
The seed-glass, slighted by his sickening taste,
The little moulted feathers, saffron-tipt,   10
The fountain, where his fever'd bill was dipt,
The perches, which his failing feet embraced,
All these remain – not even his bath removed –
But where's the spray and flutter that we loved?

THE VACANT CAGE (CONTINUED)

He shall not be cast out like wild-wood things!
We will not spurn those delicate remains;
No heat shall blanch his plumes, nor soaking rains
Shall wash the saffron from his little wings;
Nor shall he be incarthed – but in his cage
Stand, with his innocent beauty unimpair'd;
And all the skilled'st hand can do, to assuage
Poor Dora's grief, by more than Dora shared,
Shall here be done. What though these orbs of glass

Will feebly represent his merry look   10
Of recognition, when he saw her pass,
Or from her palm the melting cherry took –
Yet the artist's kindly craft shall not retain
The filming eye, and beak that gasped with pain.

Sonnets *(Macmillan & Co., London and Cambridge, 1864): 'To Alfred Tennyson these
Sonnets are Inscribed by his Affectionate Brother Charles Turner.'* Collected Sonnets,
Old and New, *Pref. Hallam Tennyson, Intro. Essay J. Spedding (C. Kegan Paul, 1880).*

THE CRITICS AT GETHSEMANE

Even here we meet the Critics. The deep grief,
Which all imaginative Art would faint
To express – the Angel's visit of relief –
The God bowed earthward like some mourning saint –
They tone down all in their unhappy way;
Distilling rose-tints from their Saviour's blood,
The God-man's sweat of anguish! to portray
Their sweet young Syrian – so divinely good,
'We must forgive His worshippers', they say;
Not so the Church! and tho' she needs must blush   10
At her own feeble handling, yet alway,
When she would paint her Master's darkest day,
She takes the full-hued life-drop on her brush,
And works, in simple faith, as best she may.

Sonnets *(1864);* Collected Sonnets *(1880).*

THE 'HIGHER CRITICISM'

O Sophistry! how many lips have kissed
And fondled thy puft hand, bedaub'd with ink
Of the 'higher criticism', which does not shrink
To substitute, for our sound faith in Christ,
A dreamy, hollow, unsubstantial creed:
Strikes its small penknife through the covenants
Both old and new, and, in a trice, supplants
Without replacing, all we love and need;
How blank will be thy scholarly regret
To see these blurred and shredded Gospels mount   10
Beyond the knives and ink-horns! – buoyant yet
With native strength, of which thou madest no count,
And, as heaven's lively oracles, confest
By all, disprove, perforce, each lying test.

Sonnets *(1864);* Collected Sonnets *(1880).*

LEBEN JESU AND VIE DE JÉSUS[1]

Hail, ancient creeds! that help us to disdain
These 'Lives of Jesus'; you, that boldly speak

LEBEN JESU AND VIE DE JÉSUS
1   David Friedrich Strauss, *Das Leben Jesu* (1835; trans. George Eliot,
1846). Ernest Renan, *Vie de Jésus* (1863).

Of an authentic Saviour, gracious, meek,
And wonderful, the Lamb for sinners slain;
Well, they may fret weak faith, make rebels glad,
But Oh! what honest soul can wish to see
These churches of the 'Leben' or the 'Vie'
Get themselves towers in Christendom? how sad
Is this wild masque of Christs, that flits athwart
The world, 'lo here! lo there!' from all the schools,   10
While the true Lord of glory stands apart,
And bides His welcome, as the madness cools,
When they shall greet Him with fond eyes and heart,
And test His slighted word by holier rules.

Sonnets *(1864)*; Collected Sonnets *(1880)*.

ALICE WADE VERSUS SMALL-POX

Thy golden hair is left – its silky mesh
The spoiler shall not mar, whate'er he takes;
Nor that still-brilliant eye, that sleeps and wakes
Among the flowing sores: but thy fair flesh,
All-confluent now, and molten by disease,
Must keep the stamp which this sick fortnight gave
Even till that latest fusion in the grave
Runs off our ingrained evils; but for these
Sweet relics of thyself, and what thou wert
A brief moon since, I should be half afraid   10
That Love might shrink, and merry Hymen flirt
His robe at thy lost hopes, my little maid!
Thou smilest! Ah! I see no power can hurt
The fortunes or the loves of Alice Wade!

Small Tableaux *(Macmillan & Co., 1868)*; Collected Sonnets *(1880)*.

ON SEEING A LITTLE CHILD SPIN A COIN OF ALEXANDER THE GREAT

This is the face of him, whose quick resource
Of eye and hand subdued Bucephalus,
And made the shadow of a startled horse
A foreground for his glory. It is thus
They hand him down; this coin of Philip's son
Recalls his life, his glories and misdeeds,
And that abortive court of Babylon,
Where the world's throne was left among the reeds.
His dust is lost among the ancient dead,
A coin his only presence: he is gone: 10
And all but this half mythic image fled –
A simple child may do him shame and slight;
'Twixt thumb and finger take the golden head,
And spin the horns of Ammon out of sight.

Collected Sonnets *(1880)*.

LETTY'S GLOBE

When Letty had scarce pass'd her third glad year,
And her young, artless words began to flow,
One day we gave the child a colour'd sphere
Of the wide earth, that she might mark and know,
By tint and outline, all its sea and land.
She patted all the world; old empires peep'd
Between her baby fingers; her soft hand
Was welcome at all frontiers. How she leap'd,
And laugh'd, and prattled in her world-wide bliss;
But when we turned her sweet unlearned eye   10
On our own isle, she raised a joyous cry,
'Oh! yes, I see it, Letty's home is there!'
And, while she hid all England with a kiss,
Bright over Europe fell her golden hair.

Collected Sonnets *(1880)*.

Edward FitzGerald (1809–83)

Edward ('Dotty') FitzGerald, writer and translator, was born at Bredfield Hall, Suffolk, 31 March 1809, into an immensely well-off Irish landowning family, seventh child of eight. His mother, Mary Frances FitzGerald, who also owned much land in England, was one of Ireland's wealthiest women. His father, John Purcell, had adopted her name when she came into her inheritance. FitzGerald saw little of his mother, absent most of the time, a classically aloof Bad Mother, and his misogyny set in early. He hated his birthplace so much he avoided it in later life. He hated his flogging tutors, too, and only took to education when he was sent as a boarder, aged nine, to King Edward VI Grammar School, Bury St Edmunds. From there he went in 1826 to Trinity College, Cambridge. W. M. Thackeray, his near-contemporary at Cambridge, became a close friend (Thackeray said FitzGerald was his 'best and oldest friend'). He got to know the Tennysons, who were also at Trinity – corresponding with Frederick all his life and apparently supporting Alfred early in his career with huge sums of money. He soon settled into a fairly reclusive way of life, first at Boulge, near Woodbridge, later in various rooms and houses in the locality. He preferred cramped quarters, a kind of perpetual undergraduate shabbiness and mess, and, of course, his boats. He became friends with Crabbe's son George (and his last work was his *Readings in Crabbe*). A dedicated homosexual eccentric, teetotal, vegetarian, he got into a tangle over the daughter of his friend Bernard Barton, the Quaker poet of Woodbridge (whose poems and letters he edited), and he married her unwillingly, unhappily, and very briefly in 1856. He much preferred the company of men – literary ones (Carlyle became another good friend in this category), but also beautiful young outdoor types, athletically muscular sorts, huntsmen, local fishermen and the

like – who tended, nonetheless, to end up with wives of their own. FitzGerald's (anonymous) *Euphranor: A Dialogue of Youth* (1851) attempts a kind of argued resolution between these two divergent male categories. From a literary perspective the most important friend was the muscled scholar Edward Cowell, who taught FitzGerald Persian and, crucially, supplied him with manuscript quatrains from the various writings attributed to the Persian Omar Khayyám (1048–1131), which he copied in Oxford's Bodleian Library. Cowell continued supplying manuscript from India, and extensively corresponded with FitzGerald about his English versions of these texts. FitzGerald had already produced 'free' translations of plays by the Spaniard Calderón (published 1853) and unpublished versions of Persian texts by Jámí and Attar, and he applied the free translation principle to Khayyám. His *Polonius: A Collection of Wise Saws and Modern Instances* (1852) had proved his touch for the aphoristic. Using heroic couplets was probably inspired by the orientalist William Jones's versions of the Persian Auhadi Kermáni. FitzGerald plundered Khayyám's Persian freely in the quest for readability – *mashing* was FitzGerald's word for his method; it was, he said, *tessellated* work. 'Better a live Sparrow than a stuffed Eagle', though. Rising to Khayyám's mixed mood of laconic wisdom, hedonism and scepticism, FitzGerald moulded his source materials into a sceptical, cynical even, exposition of an 'Eat, drink and be merry for tomorrow we die' nihilism – which was the exact opposite of Tennyson's *In Memoriam*. (That poem, FitzGerald thought, 'had the air of being evolved by a Poetical Machine of the highest order'.) A biddable colloquialism reminiscent of some Browning helped. Success came very slowly. Bernard Quaritch, the publisher, apparently sold no copies from publication in 1859 until 1861, when he rather desperately reduced the pamphlets from a shilling to one penny in the bargain bin outside his Leicester Square premises. The painter Whitley Stokes, happening by, picked up a few, gave copies to Dante Gabriel Rossetti and Richard Burton, and the Pre-Raphaelites rushed to buy and spread them about. Ruskin thought he'd never 'read anything so glorious, to my mind, as this poem'. Four further editions followed, in 1868, 1872, 1875 and (posthumously) 1889. The *Rubáiyát* became a cult poem, and one of the most popular English poems ever. Phrases from it entered the language: '*The Moving Finger writes*'; '*A Jug of Wine, a Loaf of Bread*', and so on. Housman's *A Shropshire Lad* shares marked affinities with it. FitzGerald died suddenly, 14 June 1883. He is buried at Boulge.

RUBÁIYÁT OF OMAR KHAYYÁM, THE ASTRONOMER-POET OF PERSIA

I

Awake! for Morning in the Bowl of Night
Has flung the Stone that puts the Stars to Flight:[1]
     And Lo! the Hunter of the East has caught
The Sultán's Turret in a Noose of Light.

II

Dreaming when Dawn's Left Hand was in the Sky
I heard a Voice within the Tavern cry,
     'Awake, my Little ones, and fill the Cup
'Before Life's Liquor in its Cup be dry.'

III

And, as the Cock crew, those who stood before
The Tavern shouted – 'Open then the Door!   10
     'You know how little while we have to stay,
'And, once departed, may return no more.'

IV

Now the New Year reviving old Desires,
The thoughtful Soul to Solitude retires,
     Where the WHITE HAND OF MOSES on the Bough
Puts out, and Jesus from the Ground suspires.[2]

V

Iram[3] indeed is gone with all its Rose,
And Jamshyd's Sev'n-ring'd Cup[4] where no one knows;
     But still the Vine her ancient Ruby yields,
And still a Garden by the Water blows.   20

VI

And David's Lips[5] are lock't; but in divine
High piping Pehlevi,[6] with 'Wine! Wine! Wine!
     '*Red* Wine!' – the Nightingale cries to the Rose
That yellow Cheek of hers to incarnadine.

RUBÁIYÁT OF OMAR KHAYYÁM

1 'Flinging a stone into a cup was the Signal for "To Horse" in the desert.' [Author's note]
2 Persian New Year begins in spring. In Exodus Moses tried to impress Pharaoh by turning his hand 'leprous as snow' – but [F.] 'not, according to the Persians, "*leprous as snow*" but *white* as our May blossom in spring perhaps! According to them also the Healing Power of Jesus resided in his Breath.'
3 fabled Arabian royal garden.
4 legendary king of ancient Iran, pre-Islam, alleged builder of city of Persepolis, whose seven-ringed cup was used for divination.
5 David the Psalmist.
6 ancient Iranian language.

VII

Come, fill the Cup, and in the Fire of Spring
The Winter Garment of Repentance fling:
    The Bird of Time has but a little way
To fly – and Lo! the Bird is on the Wing.

VIII

And look – a thousand Blossoms with the Day
Woke – and a thousand scatter'd into Clay: 30
    And this first Summer Month that brings the Rose
Shall take Jamshyd and Kaikobád[7] away.

IX

But come with old Khayyám, and leave the Lot
Of Kaikobád and Kaikhosru[8] forgot:
    Let Rustum[9] lay about him as he will,
Or Hátim Tai[10] cry Supper – heed them not.

X

With me along some Strip of Herbage strown
That just divides the desert from the sown,
    Where name of Slave and Sultán scarce is known,
And pity Sultán Mahmud on his Throne.   40

XI

Here with a Loaf of Bread beneath the Bough,
A Flask of Wine, a book of Verse – and Thou[11]
    Beside me singing in the Wilderness –
And Wilderness is Paradise enow.

XII

'How sweet is mortal Sovranty!' – think some:
Others – 'How blest the Paradise to come!'
    Ah, take the Cash in hand and wave the Rest;
Oh, the brave Music of a *distant* Drum!

XIII

Look to the Rose that blows about us – 'Lo,
'Laughing,' she says, 'into the World I blow: 50
    'At once the silken Tassel of my Purse
'Tear, and its Treasure on the Garden throw.'

XIV

The Worldly Hope men set their Hearts upon
Turns Ashes – or it prospers; and anon,
    Like Snow upon the Desert's dusty Face
Lightning a little Hour or two – is gone.

XV

And those who husbanded the Golden Grain,
And those who flung it to the Winds like Rain,
    Alike to no such aureate Earth are turn'd
As, buried once, Men want dug up again.   60

---

7 legendary pre-Islamic Iranian king.
8 another ancient Islamic king, celebrated in epic poem by Ferdowsi, *Sháh-námeh*.
9 most celebrated ancient Iranian hero: star of *Sháh-námeh*.

10 proverbially generous pre-Islamic Arab.
11 'A Book of Verses underneath the Bough,/A Jug of Wine, a Loaf of Bread – and Thou' (version of 5th edn, posthumously published, 1889).

XVI

Think, in this batter'd Caravanserai[12]
Whose Doorways are alternate Night and Day,
    How Sultán after Sultán with his Pomp
Abode his Hour or two, and went his way.

XVII

They say the Lion and the Lizard keep
The Courts where Jamshyd gloried and drank deep:
    And Bahrám, that great Hunter – the Wild Ass
Stamps o'er his Head, and he lies fast asleep.[13]

XVIII

I sometimes think that never blows so red
The Rose as where some buried Cæsar bled;   70
    That every Hyacinth the Garden wears
Dropt in its Lap from some once lovely Head.

XIX

And this delightful Herb whose tender Green
Fledges the River's Lip on which we lean –
    Ah, lean upon it lightly! for who knows
From what once lovely Lip it springs unseen!

XX

Ah, my Belovéd, fill the Cup that clears
To-DAY of past Regrets and future Fears –
    To-morrow? – Why, To-morrow I may be
Myself with Yesterday's Sev'n Thousand Years.   80

XXI

Lo! some we loved, the loveliest and best
That Time and Fate of all their Vintage prest,
    Have drunk their Cup a Round or two before,
And one by one crept silently to Rest.

XXII

And we, that now make merry in the Room
They left, and Summer dresses in new Bloom,
    Ourselves must we beneath the Couch of Earth
Descend, ourselves to make a Couch – for whom?

XXIII

Ah, make the most of what we yet may spend,
Before we too into the Dust descend;   90
    Dust into Dust, and under Dust, to lie,
Sans Wine, sans Song, sans Singer, and – sans End!

XXIV

Alike for those who for To-DAY prepare,
And those that after a To-MORROW stare,
    A Muezzin from the Tower of Darkness cries
'Fools! your Reward is neither Here nor There!'

12   an inn for overnight stay: metaphor for the transience of all things.
13   Bahrám Gur, fabled Persian king and hunter. *Gur* is a wild ass and
also the grave.

XXV

Why, all the Saints and Sages who discuss'd
Of the Two Worlds so learnedly, are thrust
   Like foolish Prophets forth; their Words to Scorn
Are scatter'd, and their Mouths are stopt with Dust.   100

XXVI

Oh, come with old Khayyám, and leave the Wise
To talk; one thing is certain, that Life flies;
   One thing is certain, and the Rest is Lies;
The Flower that once has blown for ever dies.

XXVII

Myself when young did eagerly frequent
Doctor and Saint, and heard great Argument
   About it and about: but evermore
Came out by the same Door as in I went.

XXVIII

With them the Seed of Wisdom did I sow,
And with my own hand labour'd it to grow: 110
   And this was all the Harvest that I reap'd –
'I came like Water, and like Wind I go.'

XXIX

Into this Universe, and *why* not knowing,
Nor *whence*, like Water willy-nilly flowing:
   And out of it, as Wind along the Waste,
I know not *whither*, willy-nilly blowing.

XXX

What, without asking, hither hurried *whence?*
And, without asking, *whither* hurried hence!
   Another and another Cup to drown
The Memory of this Impertinence!   120

XXXI

Up from Earth's Centre through the Seventh Gate
I rose, and on the Throne of Saturn sate,
   And many Knots unravel'd by the Road;
But not the Knot of Human Death and Fate.

XXXII

There was a Door to which I found no Key:
There was a Veil past which I could not see:
   Some little Talk awhile of ME and THEE
There seemed – and then no more of THEE and ME.

XXXIII

Then to the rolling Heav'n itself I cried,
Asking, 'What Lamp had Destiny to guide   130
   'Her little Children stumbling in the Dark?'
And – 'A blind Understanding!' Heav'n replied.

XXXIV

Then to this earthen Bowl did I adjourn
My Lip the secret Well of Life to learn:
   And Lip to Lip it murmur'd – 'While you live
'Drink! – for once dead you never shall return.'

XXXV

I think the Vessel, that with fugitive
Articulation answer'd, once did live,
   And merry-make; and the cold Lip I kiss'd
How many Kisses might it take – and give!   140

XXXVI

For in the Market-place, one Dusk of Day,
I watch'd the Potter thumping his wet Clay:
   And with its all obliterated Tongue
It murmur'd – 'Gently, Brother, gently, pray!'

XXXVII

Ah! fill the Cup: – what boots it to repeat
How Time is slipping underneath our Feet:
   Unborn TO-MORROW, and dead YESTERDAY,
Why fret about them if TO-DAY be sweet!

XXXVIII

One Moment in Annihilation's Waste,
One Moment, of the Well of Life to taste –   150
   The Stars are setting and the Caravan
Starts for the Dawn of Nothing – Oh, make haste!

XXXIX

How long, how long, in infinite Pursuit
Of This and That endeavour and dispute?
   Better be merry with the fruitful Grape
Than sadden after none, or bitter, Fruit.

XL

You know, my Friends, how long since in my House
For a new Marriage I did make Carouse:
   Divorced old barren Reason from my Bed,
And took the Daughter of the Vine to Spouse.   160

XLI

For 'Is' and 'Is-NOT' though *with* Rule and Line,
And 'UP-AND-DOWN' *without*, I could define,
   I yet in all I only cared to know,
Was never deep in anything but – Wine.

XLII

And lately, by the Tavern Door agape,
Came stealing through the Dusk an Angel Shape
   Bearing a Vessel on his Shoulder; and
He bid me taste of it; and 't was – the Grape!

XLIII

The Grape that can with Logic absolute
The Two-and-Seventy jarring Sects confute:[14]   170
   The subtle Alchemist that in a Trice
Life's leaden Metal into Gold transmute.

14   Islam was said to be divided into 72 differing parties.

XLIV

The mighty Mahmud,[15] the victorious Lord,
That all the misbelieving and black Horde
   Of Fears and Sorrows that infest the Soul
Scatters and slays with his enchanted Sword.

XLV

But leave the Wise to wrangle, and with me
The Quarrel of the Universe let be:
   And, in some corner of the Hubbub coucht,
Make Game of that which makes as much of Thee.   180

XLVI

For in and out, above, about, below,
'T is nothing but a Magic Shadow-show,
   Play'd in a Box whose Candle is the Sun,
Round which we Phantom Figures come and go.

XLVII

And if the Wine you drink, the Lip you press,
End in the Nothing all Things end in – Yes –
   Then fancy while Thou art, Thou art but what
Thou shalt be – Nothing – Thou shalt not be less.

XLVIII

While the Rose blows along the River Brink,
With old Khayyám the Ruby Vintage drink: 190
   And when the Angel with his darker Draught
Draws up to Thee – take that, and do not shrink.

XLIX

'T is all a Chequer-board of Nights and Days
Where Destiny with Men for Pieces plays:
   Hither and thither moves, and mates, and slays,
And one by one back in the Closet lays.

L

The Ball no Question makes of Ayes or Noes,
But Right or Left as strikes the Player goes;
   And He that toss'd Thee down into the Field,
He knows about it all – HE knows – HE knows![16]   200

LI

The Moving Finger writes; and, having writ,
Moves on: nor all thy Piety nor Wit
   Shall lure it back to cancel half a Line,
Nor all thy Tears wash out a Word of it.

LII

And that inverted Bowl we call The Sky,
Whereunder crawling coop't we live and die,
   Lift not thy hands to *It* for help – for It
Rolls impotently on as Thou or I.

15   Sultan Mahmud of Ghazna (reigned 998–1030), who conquered north-west India and had famous love-affair with his Turkish slave ('my friend Mahmud': F.).

16   refers to game of polo, invented in Persia (Persians said): emblem of Chance.

LIII

With Earth's first Clay They did the Last Man's knead,
And then of the Last Harvest sow'd the Seed:
   Yea, the first Morning of Creation wrote
What the Last Dawn of Reckoning shall read.

210

LIV

I tell Thee this – When, starting from the Goal,
Over the shoulders of the flaming Foal
   Of Heav'n Parwin and Mushtara[17] they flung,
In my predestin'd Plot of Dust and Soul

LV

The Vine had struck a Fibre; which about
If clings my Being – let the Sufi flout;
   Of my Base Metal may be filed a Key,
That shall unlock the Door he howls without.

220

LVI

And this I know: whether the one True Light,
Kindle to Love, or Wrath consume me quite,
   One Glimpse of It within the Tavern caught
Better than in the Temple lost outright.

LVII

Oh Thou, who didst with Pitfall and with Gin
Beset the Road I was to wander in,
   Thou wilt not with Predestination round
Enmesh me, and impute my Fall to Sin?

LVIII

Oh, Thou, who Man of baser Earth didst make,
And who with Eden didst devise the Snake;
   For all the Sin wherewith the Face of Man
Is blacken'd, Man's Forgiveness give – and take!

230

•

Kuza-Náma[18]

LIX

Listen again. One Evening at the Close
Of Ramazán, ere the better Moon arose,
   In that old Potter's Shop I stood alone
With the clay Population round in Rows.

LX

And, strange to tell, among the Earthen Lot
Some could articulate, while others not:
   And suddenly one more impatient cried –
'Who *is* the Potter, pray, and who the Pot?'

240

LXI

Then said another – 'Surely not in vain
'My Substance from the common Earth was ta'en,

---

17   Parwin: the Pleiades; Mushtara: planet Jupiter.   18   The Book of the Pots.

'That He who subtly wrought me into Shape
'Should stamp me back to common Earth again.'

LXII

Another said – 'Why, ne'er a peevish Boy,
'Would break the Bowl from which he drank in Joy;
   'Shall He that *made* the Vessel in pure Love
'And Fansy, in an after Rage destroy!'

LXIII

None answer'd this; but after Silence spake
A Vessel of a more ungainly Make:
   'They sneer at me for leaning all awry;
'What! did the Hand then of the Potter shake?'

250

LXIV

Said one – 'Folks of a surly Tapster tell,
'And daub his Visage with the Smoke of Hell;
   'They talk of some strict Testing of us – Pish!
'He's a Good Fellow, and 't will all be well.'

LXV

Then said another with a long-drawn Sigh,
'My Clay with long oblivion is gone dry:
   'But, fill me with the old familiar Juice,
'Methinks I might recover by-and-bye!'

260

LXVI

So while the Vessels one by one were speaking,
One spied the little Crescent all were seeking:
   And then they jogg'd each other, 'Brother! Brother!
'Hark to the Porter's Shoulder-knot a-creaking!'[19]

•

LXVII

Ah, with the Grape my fading Life provide,
And wash my Body whence the Life has died,
   And in a Windingsheet of Vine-leaf wrapt,
So bury me by some sweet Garden-side.

LXVIII

That ev'n my buried Ashes such a Snare
Of Perfume shall fling up into the Air,
   As not a True Believer passing by
But shall be overtaken unaware.

270

LXIX

Indeed the Idols I have loved so long
Have done my Credit in Men's Eye much wrong:
   Have drown'd my Honour in a shallow Cup,
And sold my Reputation for a Song.

19   the new moon – 'little Crescent' – heralds end of fasting month of
Ramadan, when drinking can begin again: 'Then it is that the Porter's
knot may be heard toward the *Cellar* perhaps' (F.'s note).

LXX

Indeed, indeed, Repentance oft before
I swore – but was I sober when I swore?
    And then and then came Spring, and Rose-in-hand
My thread-bare Penitence apieces tore.   280

LXXI

And much as Wine has play'd the Infidel,
And robb'd me of my Robe of Honour – well,
    I often wonder what the Vintners buy
One half so precious as the Goods they sell.

LXXII

Alas, that Spring should vanish with the Rose!
That Youth's sweet-scented Manuscript should close!
    The Nightingale that in the Branches sang,
Ah, whence, and whither flown again, who knows!

LXXIII

Ah Love! could thou and I with Fate conspire
To grasp this sorry Scheme of Things entire,   290
    Would not we shatter it to bits – and then
Re-mould it nearer to the Heart's Desire!

LXXIV

Ah, Moon of my Delight who know'st no wane,
The Moon of Heav'n is rising once again:
    How oft hereafter rising shall she look
Through this same Garden after me – in vain!

LXXV

And when Thyself with shining Foot shall pass
Among the Guests Star-scatter'd on the Grass,
    And in thy joyous Errand reach the Spot
Where I made one – turn down an empty Glass!   300

[TAMÁM SHUD][20]

Rubáiyát of Omar Khayyám, The Astronomer-Poet of Persia *(Bernard Quaritch,
Castle Street, Leicester Square, 1859). (Text of first – shorter – edition.)*

Fanny (Frances Anne) Kemble (Mrs Butler) (1809–93)

Fanny Kemble was an exuberant woman, a would-be wri-
ter and woman-of-letters, and a reluctant but famous
actress. She was born, 27 November 1809, into a very
famous London theatrical family. Her mother, Marie
Thérèse Kemble, was an actress; her father, Charles Kem-
ble, was actor-manager of Covent Garden Theatre; her
younger sister Adelaide became a famous opera singer;
their aunt was the distinguished actress Sarah Siddons.
Fanny was educated at French schools in Boulogne and
Paris. She began writing poems and plays early. But in
October 1829 she was forced onto the stage – which she
found 'utterly distasteful' – as part of her parents' desper-
ate efforts to prevent Covent Garden going bankrupt. Her
Juliet to her parents' Mercutio and Lady Capulet in *Romeo
and Juliet* was an instant hit. A string of female roles quickly
followed. These productions were so popular that £13,000
of the theatre's debts were rapidly wiped away. On an
American tour in 1833–4 Fanny met her future husband,
Pierce Mease Butler, a Georgia plantation owner, and she
tried settling down to domesticity. Her discomfort about

20 The End (literally, It is Ended).

slavery did not help; they separated; she came back to acting in England (and had great success with her Shakespeare readings); she was then only allowed to see her children for one month each year. For twenty years she lived under her maiden name at Lennox, Massachusetts, but came back to London for the last sixteen years of her life. Through all of this she was writing – plays, poems, translations of Schiller and Dumas, *Notes on Shakespeare's Plays* (1882), a novel *Far Away and Long Ago* (1889), several volumes of autobiography. Through her father's literary and theatrical connexions she knew Dickens and William Charles Macready. Through her brother John she met up with certain Cambridge Apostles including F. D. Maurice and Alfred Tennyson. Her poems – a side-show in a long and boisterous career – appeared first in America in 1844, and reappeared, variously revised and added to, in 1866 and 1883. She died in London, 15 January 1893, aged eighty-three, and is buried in Kensal Green Cemetery.

SONG

Pass thy hand through my hair, love;
    One little year ago,
In a curtain bright and rare, love,
    It fell golden o'er my brow.
But the gold has paled away, love,
    And the drooping curls are thin,
And cold threads of wintry gray, love,
    Glitter their folds within:
How should this be, in one short year?
It is not age – can it be care?   10

Fasten thine eyes on mine, love;
    One little year ago,
Midsummer's sunny shine, love,
    Had not a warmer glow.
But the light is there no more, love,
    Save in melancholy gleams,
Like wan moonlight wand'ring o'er, love,
    Dim lands in troubled dreams:
How should this be, in one short year?
It is not age – can it be care?   20

Lay thy cheek to my cheek, love;
    One little year ago
It was ripe, and round, and sleek, love,
    As the autumn peaches grow.
But the rosy hue has fled, love,
    Save a flush that goes and comes,
Like a flower born from the dead, love,
    And blooming over tombs:
How should this be, in one short year?
It is not age – can it be care?   30

Poems (Richard Bentley & Son, 1883).

SONNET

What is my lady like? thou fain wouldst know –
A rosy chaplet of fresh apple bloom,
Bound with blue ribbon, lying on the snow:
What is my lady like? the violet gloom
Of evening, with deep orange light below.

She's like the noonday smell of a pine wood,
She's like the sounding of a stormy flood,
She's like a mountain-top high in the skies,
To which the day its earliest light doth lend;
She's like a pleasant path without an end;   10
Like a strange secret, and a sweet surprise;
Like a sharp axe of doom, wreathed with blush roses,
A casket full of gems whose key one loses;
Like a hard saying, wonderful and wise.

Poems *(1883)*.

THE BLACK WALLFLOWER

I found a flower in a desolate plot,
Where no man wrought, – by a deserted cot,
Where no man dwelt; a strange, dark-colour'd gem,
Black heavy buds on a pale leafless stem;
I pluck'd it, wondering, and with it hied
To my brave May; and, showing it, I cried:
'Look, what a dismal flower! did ever bloom,
Born of our earth and air, wear such a gloom?
It looks as it should grow out of a tomb:
Is it not mournful?' 'No,' replied the child;   10
And, gazing on it thoughtfully, she smiled.
She knows each word of that great book of God,
Spread out between the blue sky and the sod:
'There are no mournful flowers – they are all glad;
This is a solemn one, but not a sad.'

Lo! with the dawn the black buds open'd slowly;
Within each cup a colour deep and holy,
As sacrificial blood, glow'd rich and red,
And through the velvet tissue mantling spread;
While in the midst of this dark crimson heat   20
A precious golden heart did throb and beat;
Through ruby leaves the morning light did shine,
Each mournful bud had grown a flow'r divine;
And bitter sweet to senses and to soul,
A breathing came from them, that fill'd the whole
Of the surrounding tranced and sunny air
With its strange fragrance, like a silent prayer.
Then cried I, 'From the earth's whole wreath I'll borrow
No flower but thee! thou exquisite type of sorrow!'

Poems *(1883)*.

Alfred (Lord) Tennyson (1809–92)

Alfred Tennyson, one of the two most important Victorian poets (the other is Robert Browning), was born, 6 August 1809, into a moody, contentious clan, greatly given to madness and epilepsy. He was the fourth son (and fourth of the twelve children) of the Revd Dr George Clayton Tennyson, rector of Somersby in northern Lincolnshire, and his wife, Elizabeth Fytche, a vicar's daughter. Dr Tennyson's rightful inheritance had been given to his younger brother Charles Tennyson D'Eyncourt by their wilful father, and this failure to receive the lands and riches they felt they deserved greatly vexed all the Tennyson children. Alfred lived with his grandmother and attended Louth Grammar School from age seven to eleven, but came home in 1820 to lessons with father and the freedom of father's large library. He was an avid reader and a precocious little producer of blank verse: hundreds of lines in imitation of Pope's Homer translation, thousands of epic lines after Walter Scott. In 1827 Alfred and his brother Charles followed their Old Etonian brother Frederick to Cambridge (Trinity College). The three brothers had collaborated on *Poems by Two Brothers*, published by a Louth bookseller the previous year. At Trinity Alfred won the Chancellor's medal for a poem on the subject of *Timbuctoo* (June 1829) and became a member of the Apostles club, getting friendly above all with Arthur Henry Hallam, the single most important influence on Tennyson's life and work. Hallam's long essay on Tennyson's *Poems, Chiefly Lyrical* (1830) in *The Englishman's Magazine* (August 1831) was a landmark in a friendship as well as being a crucial marker of critical enthusiasm for Tennyson in a sea of otherwise hostile early reactions to his poetry. In the summer vacation of 1830 Tennyson, Hallam and other Apostles went on an abortive expedition to Spain to assist General Torrijos's insurrection against Ferdinand II. Early in 1831 Tennyson left Cambridge without a degree, needed at home because his father lay dying. In July 1832 he visited the Rhineland with Hallam; in October his brother Edward went mad; in December *Poems* came out, to be savaged and derided by J. W. Croker in the *Quarterly Review* (April 1833). In September 1833, Hallam, by now engaged to Tennyson's sister Emily, died suddenly in Vienna. Tennyson, essentially widowed by this loss, began his years of terrible anguish – submerged in the great Victorian problems his grief prompted: questions of divine providence, of personal and universal purpose, of ends (is there life after death?) and origins (of the world, of Christianity). He was prone to mental upsets, and epilepsy, and spent time in asylum care (not least in Dr Matthew Allen's institution at High Beech, where John Clare was a patient, as also was Tennyson's brother Septimus). He began crafting his great cult of Arthur (and King Arthur), mooching about the country, gradually turning his grief into verse, assembling the 'elegies' that would appear eventually as his great master-work *In Memoriam A. H. H.* – structured, of course, around the Christmases that mark the foundational birth of Jesus and thus, for the Victorians, the greatly interrogated beginnings of the Christian Church. The Tennysons lost huge amounts of family money, cheated, essentially, by Dr Allen in a mechanized-wood-carving scam, but Tennyson never thought of working at anything but poetry. *Poems* (1842) in two volumes made Tennyson's name as the rising star of English verse. It rather heavily revised the earlier poems that it republished (Croker's jeers were a great prompt to the ever sensitive Tennyson to amend poems such as 'The Lady of Shallot'), as well as bringing wonderful new work, such as 'Ulysses', to public light. But Tennyson's moody glumness was not alleviated by recognition,

though his sense of financial security (he was never actually poor) was brightened by sales and a substantial Civil List Pension of £200 per year from September 1845. (The story is that Tennyson's Apostle friend Monckton Milnes read 'Ulysses' to Prime Minister Robert Peel to illustrate the poet's worth.) The publication of *In Memoriam* (May 1850) helped lay Arthur's ghost somewhat. In June 1850 Tennyson married Emily Sellwood, from then on his emotional mainstay; in November he succeeded Wordsworth as Poet Laureate. Elegy, though, would still command Tennyson's writing (*Ode on the Death of the Duke of Wellington*, which greatly upset public opinion, was published in November 1852), and the great Hamletian monodrama *Maud* (1855) – Tennyson's most extensive dramatic monologue – would be a story of gloomy introspection, madness, self-disgust and anger at the bad ways of the modern world (Tennyson's verse, as ever, greatly energized by its occasions of spleen). As Laureate, Tennyson was a zesty producer of jingoistic calls to armed alertness against the foreigner as well as indignant protests against military incompetence in the Crimea – especially in his most famous and much anthologized piece, 'The Charge of the Light Brigade' (9 December 1854). It was only appropriate that Francis Turner Palgrave's great national anthology, *The Golden Treasury of the Best Songs and Lyrical Poems in the English Language* (1861), should have been done with Tennyson's help and be dedicated to him. As the poetic voice of the nation, but especially as the nation's greatest elegist, he became increasingly close to Queen Victoria (one of whose houses, Osborne, Isle of Wight, was a neighbour, after all, of Tennyson's island home Farringford). A new edition of the Arthurian volume *Idylls of the King* was dedicated in 1862 to Victoria's husband, Prince Albert, who had recently died (December 1861). *In Memoriam* became the text which, the royal widow said, consoled her most after the Bible. Tennyson's later years were preoccupied with the nearly interminable, though popular, Arthurian books (his medievalist revivalism quite mesmerizing the Pre-Raphaelite painters), and with a lot of ill-judged dramas. (One of his plays, *The Promise of May*, 1882, was denounced from the stalls by the pugnacious Marquess of Queensberry, father of Oscar Wilde's Bosie, as a libel upon libertines!) Tennyson was given an Honorary Doctorate of Civil Law by Oxford University (1855) and eventually (after several earlier refusals) accepted a Baronetcy (from Gladstone) in 1883. His old age was a greatly feted one (he was visited rather than visiting). He and Emily had two sons, Hallam (August 1852) and Lionel (1854). Lionel died on his way back from India, April 1886. Tennyson died, 6 October 1892, at his second home, Aldworth, near Haslemere. His reputation was by then as huge as his sales were lucrative (£10,000 coming in the year of his death). Neither the Queen nor Gladstone turned up to the funeral, but still his coffin was carried to its resting place in Poets' Corner in Westminster Abbey, next to Browning, by the Chaucer monument, 12 October 1892, by an extraordinary collection of grandees – the Foreign Secretary Lord Rosebery, the Masters of Balliol and of

Trinity, Cambridge, the American Ambassador, the one-time Prime Minister and Chancellor of Oxford Lord Salisbury, J. A. Froude, the historian Lecky, Lord Dufferin the former Viceroy of India. Men of the Balaclava Light Brigade lined the nave. Always mindful of death and of his part as a great register of the period's sense of how problematized the Christian story of life after death had become,

the great Christian elegist had written his own ending-up hymn, 'Crossing the Bar': to be put, he desired, 'at the end of all editions of my poems'. It's the centrepiece of the wonderfully contrived Chapter XXIII ('The last Chapter') of Hallam Tennyson's great *Memoir* of his father (2 vols, 1897). Emily Tennyson died 10 August 1896. 'Crossing the Bar' was sung at her funeral, as at her husband's.

THE LADY OF SHALOTT

PART I

On either side the river lie
Long fields of barley and of rye,
That clothe the wold and meet the sky;
And thro' the field the road runs by
    To many-tower'd Camelot;
And up and down the people go,
Gazing where the lilies blow
Round an island there below,
    The island of Shalott.

Willows whiten, aspens quiver,   10
Little breezes dusk and shiver
Thro' the wave that runs for ever
By the island in the river
    Flowing down to Camelot.
Four gray walls, and four gray towers,
Overlook a space of flowers,
And the silent isle imbowers
    The Lady of Shalott.

By the margin, willow-veil'd,
Slide the heavy barges trail'd   20
By slow horses; and unhail'd
The shallop flitteth silken-sail'd
    Skimming down to Camelot:
But who hath seen her wave her hand?
Or at the casement seen her stand?
Or is she known in all the land,
    The Lady of Shalott?

Only reapers, reaping early
In among the bearded barley,
Hear a song that echoes cheerly   30
From the river winding clearly,
    Down to tower'd Camelot:
And by the moon the reaper weary,
Piling sheaves in uplands airy,
Listening, whispers ''Tis the fairy
    Lady of Shalott.'

PART II

There she weaves by night and day
A magic web with colours gay.

She has heard a whisper say,
A curse is on her if she stay[1]   40
    To look down to Camelot.
She knows not what the curse may be,
And so she weaveth steadily,
And little other care hath she,
    The Lady of Shalott.

And moving thro' a mirror clear
That hangs before her all the year,
Shadows of the world appear.
There she sees the highway near
    Winding down to Camelot: 50
There the river eddy whirls,
And there the surly village-churls,
And the red cloaks of market-girls,
    Pass onward from Shalott.

Sometimes a troop of damsels glad,
An abbot on an ambling pad,
Sometimes a curly shepherd-lad,
Or long-hair'd page in crimson clad,
    Goes by to tower'd Camelot;
And sometimes thro' the mirror blue   60
The knights come riding two and two:
She hath no loyal knight and true,
    The Lady of Shalott.

But in her web she still delights
To weave the mirror's magic sights,
For often thro' the silent nights
A funeral, with plumes and lights
    And music, went to Camelot:
Or when the moon was overhead,
Came two young lovers lately wed;   70
'I am half-sick of shadows,' said
    The Lady of Shalott.

PART III

A bow-shot from her bower-eaves,
He rode between the barley-sheaves,
The sun came dazzling thro' the leaves,
And flamed upon the brazen greaves[2]

THE LADY OF SHALOTT
1 stop.

2 shin armour.

Of bold Sir Lancelot.
A redcross knight for ever kneel'd
To a lady in his shield,
That sparkled on the yellow field,   80
　　Beside remote Shalott.

The gemmy bridle glitter'd free,
Like to some branch of stars we see
Hung in the golden Galaxy.
The bridle-bells rang merrily
　　As he rode down to Camelot:
And from his blazon'd baldric³ slung
A mighty silver bugle hung,
And as he rode his armour rung,
　　Beside remote Shalott.   90

All in the blue unclouded weather
Thick-jewell'd shone the saddle-leather,
The helmet and the helmet-feather
Burned like one burning flame together,
　　As he rode down to Camelot.
As often thro' the purple night,
Below the starry clusters bright,
Some bearded meteor, trailing light,
　　Moves over still Shalott.

His broad clear brow in sunlight glow'd;   100
On burnish'd hooves his war-horse trode;
From underneath his helmet flow'd
His coal-black curls as on he rode,
　　As he rode down to Camelot.
From the bank and from the river
He flash'd into the crystal mirror,
'Tirra lirra,' by the river
　　Sang Sir Lancelot.

She left the web, she left the loom,
She made three paces thro' the room,   110
She saw the water-lily bloom,
She saw the helmet and the plume,
　　She look'd down to Camelot.
Out flew the web and floated wide;
The mirror crack'd from side to side;
'The curse is come upon me,' cried
　　The Lady of Shalott.

PART IV
In the stormy east-wind straining,
The pale yellow woods were waning,
The broad stream in his banks complaining.   120
Heavily the low sky raining
　　Over towered Camelot;
Down she came and found a boat

Beneath a willow left afloat,
And round about the prow she wrote
　　The Lady of Shalott.

And down the river's dim expanse –
Like some bold seër in a trance,
Seeing all his own mischance –
With a glassy countenance   130
　　Did she look to Camelot.
And at the closing of the day
She loosed the chain, and down she lay;
The broad stream bore her far away,
　　The Lady of Shalott.

Lying, robed in snowy white
That loosely flew to left and right –
The leaves upon her falling light –
Thro' the noises of the night
　　She floated down to Camelot: 140
And as the boat-head wound along
The willowy hills and fields among,
They heard her singing her last song,
　　The Lady of Shalott.

Heard a carol, mournful, holy,
Chanted loudly, chanted lowly,
Till her blood was frozen slowly,
And her eyes were darken'd wholly,
　　Turn'd to towered Camelot.
For ere she reach'd upon the tide   150
The first house by the water-side,
Singing in her song she died,
　　The Lady of Shalott.

Under tower and balcony,
By garden-wall and gallery,
A gleaming-shape she floated by,
A corse between the houses high,
　　Silent into Camelot.
Out upon the wharfs they came,
Knight and burgher, lord and dame,   160
And round the prow they read her name,
　　The Lady of Shalott.

Who is this? and what is here?
And in the lighted palace near
Died the sound of royal cheer;
And they cross'd themselves for fear,
　　All the knights at Camelot:
But Lancelot mused a little space;
He said, 'She has a lovely face;
God in his mercy lend her grace,   170
　　The Lady of Shalott.'

Written by c. *May 1832.* Poems *(1832 [title page dated 1833]).* Poems, *2 vols
(Edward Moxon, 1842), I. 1842 text.*

3　belt; girdle.

The Palace of Art

I built my soul a lordly pleasure-house,
    Wherein at ease for aye to dwell.
I said, 'O Soul, make merry and carouse,
    Dear soul, for all is well.'

A huge crag-platform, smooth as burnished brass
    I chose. The ranged ramparts bright
From level meadow-bases of deep grass
    Suddenly scaled the light.

Thereon I built it firm. Of ledge or shelf
    The rock rose clear, or winding stair.   10
My soul would live alone unto herself
    In her high palace there.

And 'while the world runs round and round,' I said,
    'Reign thou apart, a quiet king,
Still as, while Saturn whirls, his steadfast shade
    Sleeps on his luminous ring.'

To which my soul made answer readily:
    'Trust me, in bliss I shall abide
In this great mansion, that is built for me,
    So royal-rich and wide.'   20

                    *   *   *   *

Four courts I made, East, West and South and North,
    In each a squared lawn, wherefrom
The golden gorge of dragons spouted forth
    A flood of fountain-foam.

And round the cool green courts there ran a row
    Of cloisters, branch'd like mighty woods,
Echoing all night to that sonorous flow
    Of spouted fountain-floods.

And round the roofs a gilded gallery
    That lent broad verge to distant lands,   30
Far as the wild swan wings, to where the sky
    Dipt down to sea and sands.

From those four jets four currents in one swell
    Across the mountain stream'd below
In misty folds, that floating as they fell
    Lit up a torrent-bow.

And high on every peak a statue seemed
    To hang on tiptoe, tossing up
A cloud of incense of all odour steam'd
    From out a golden cup.   40

So that she thought, 'And who shall gaze upon
    My palace with unblinded eyes,
While this great bow will waver in the sun
    And that sweet incense rise?'

For that sweet incense rose and never fail'd,
    And, while day sank or mounted higher,
The light aërial gallery, golden-rail'd,
    Burnt like a fringe of fire.
Likewise the deep-set windows, stain'd and traced,
    Would seem slow-flaming crimson fires   50
From shadow'd grots of arches interlaced,
    And tipt with frost-like spires.

                *   *   *   *

Full of long-sounding corridors it was,
    That over-vaulted grateful gloom,
Through which the livelong day my soul did pass,
    Well-pleased, from room to room.

Full of great rooms and small the palace stood,
    All various, each a perfect whole
From living Nature, fit for every mood
    And change of my still soul.   60

For some were hung with arras green and blue,
    Showing a gaudy summer-morn,
Where with puff'd cheek the belted hunter blew
    His wreathed bugle-horn.

One seem'd all dark and red – a tract of sand,
    And some one pacing there alone,
Who paced for ever in a glimmering land,
    Lit with a low large moon.

One show'd an iron coast and angry waves.
    You seem'd to hear them climb and fall   70
And roar rock-thwarted under bellowing caves,
    Beneath the windy wall.

And one, a full-fed river winding slow
    By herds upon an endless plain,
The ragged rims of thunder brooding low,
    With shadow-streaks of rain.

And one, the reapers at their sultry toil.
    In front they bound the sheaves. Behind
Were realms of upland, prodigal in oil,
    And hoary to the wind.   80

And one, a foreground black with stones and slags,
    Beyond, a line of heights, and higher
All barr'd with long white cloud the scornful crags,
    And highest, snow and fire.

And one, an English home – gray twilight poured
    On dewy pastures, dewy trees,
Softer than sleep – all things in order stored,
    A haunt of ancient Peace.

Nor these alone, but every landscape fair,
    As fit for every mood of mind,   90

Or gay, or grave, or sweet, or stern, was there
   Not less than truth design'd.

         *   *   *   *

Or the maid-mother by a crucifix,
   In tracts of pasture sunny-warm,
Beneath branch-work of costly sardonyx
   Sat smiling, babe in arm.

Or in a clear-wall'd city on the sea,
   Near gilded organ-pipes, her hair
Wound with white roses, slept St Cecily;
   An angel look'd at her.   100

Or thronging all one porch of Paradise
   A group of Houris bow'd to see
The dying Islamite, with hands and eyes
   That said, We wait for thee.

Or mythic Uther's deeply-wounded son[1]
   In some fair space of sloping greens
Lay, dozing in the vale of Avalon,
   And watched by weeping queens.

Or hollowing one hand against his ear,
   To listen for a footfall, ere he saw   110
The wood-nymph, stayed the Tuscan king to hear
   Of wisdom and of law.[2]

Or over hills with peaky tops engrail'd,
   And many a tract of palm and rice,
The throne of Indian Cama[3] slowly sailed
   A summer fanned with spice.

Or sweet Europa's mantle blew unclasp'd,
   From off her shoulder backward borne:
From one hand droop'd a crocus: one hand grasp'd
   The mild bull's golden horn.[4]   120

Or else flush'd Ganymede, his rosy thigh
   Half-buried in the Eagle's down,
Sole as a flying star shot through the sky
   Above the pillar'd town.[5]

Nor these alone: but every legend fair
   Which the supreme Caucasian[6] mind
Carved out of Nature for itself, was there,
   Not less than life, design'd.

         *   *   *   *

Then in the towers I placed great bells that swung,
   Moved of themselves, with silver sound;   130

THE PALACE OF ART
1 Arthur, son of Uther, legendary king, or Pendragon, of Britons.
2 Egeria, who gave laws to Numa Pompilius.
3 'Hindu God of young love, son of Brahma' (T).
4 Europa, abducted by Zeus in form of a bull.
5 beautiful Ganymede, carried off to Olympus, to become cup-bearer to the gods.
6 Indo-European.

And with choice paintings of wise men I hung
  The royal dais round.

For there was Milton like a seraph strong,
  Beside him Shakespeare bland and mild;
And there the world-worn Dante grasp'd his song,
  And somewhat grimly smiled.

And there the Ionian father of the rest;[7]
  A million wrinkles carved his skin;
A hundred winters snow'd upon his breast,
  From cheek and throat and chin.   140

Above, the fair hall-ceiling stately-set
  Many an arch high up did lift,
And angels rising and descending met
  With interchange of gift.

Below was all mosaic choicely plann'd
  With cycles of the human tale
Of this wide world, the times of every land
  So wrought, they will not fail.

The people here, a beast of burden slow,
  Toil'd onward, prick'd with goads and stings;   150
Here play'd, a tiger, rolling to and fro
  The heads and crowns of kings;

Here rose, an athlete, strong to break or bind
  All force in bonds that might endure,
And here once more like some sick man declined,
  And trusted any cure.

But over these she trod: and those great bells
  Began to chime. She took her throne:
She sat betwixt the shining oriels,
  To sing her songs alone.   160

And thro' the topmost oriels' colour'd flame
  Two godlike faces gazed below;
Plato the wise, and large-brow'd Verulam,[8]
  The first of those who know.

And all those names, that in their motion were
  Full-welling fountain-heads of change,
Betwixt the slender shafts were blazon'd fair
  In diverse raiment strange:

Through which the lights, rose, amber, emerald, blue,
  Flush'd in her temples and her eyes,   170
And from her lips, as morn from Memnon,[9] drew
  Rivers of melodies.

No nightingale delighteth to prolong
  Her low preamble all alone,

7 Homer.
8 Francis Bacon (Lord Verulam).

9 statue that made music when touched by rays of sun.

More than my soul to hear her echo'd song
    Throb thro' the ribbed stone;

Singing and murmuring in her feastful mirth,
    Joying to feel herself alive,
Lord over Nature, Lord of the visible earth,
    Lord of the senses five;   180

Communing with herself: 'All these are mine,
    And let the world have peace or wars,
'Tis one to me.' She – when young night divine
    Crown'd dying day with stars,

Making sweet close of his delicious toils –
    Lit light in wreaths and anadems,
And pure quintessences of precious oils
    In hollow'd moons of gems,

To mimic heaven; and clapt her hands and cried,
    'I marvel if my still delight   190
In this great house so royal-rich, and wide,
    Be flatter'd to the height.

'From shape to shape at first within the womb
    The brain is modell'd,' she began,
'And thro' all phases of all thought I come
    Into the perfect man.

'All nature widens upward. Evermore
    The simpler essence lower lies:
More complex is more perfect, owning more
    Discourse, more widely wise.'   200

Then of the moral instinct would she prate,
    And of the rising from the dead,
As hers by right of full-accomplish'd Fate;
    And at the last she said:

'I take possession of men's mind and deeds.
    I live in all things great and small.
I sit apart, holding no form of creeds,
    But contemplating all.'

                *   *   *   *

Full oft the riddle of the painful earth
    Flash'd thro' her as she sat alone,   210
Yet not the less held she her solemn mirth,
    And intellectual throne

Of full-spher'd contemplation. So three years
    She throve, but on the fourth she fell,
Like Herod, when the shout was in his ears,
    Struck thro' with pangs of hell.[10]

Lest she should fail and perish utterly,
    God, before whom ever lie bare

---

10 Acts 12.21–3.

The abysmal deeps of Personality,
    Plagued her with sore despair.   220

When she would think, where'er she turn'd her sight
    The airy hand confusion wrought,
Wrote, 'Mene, mene,' and divided quite
    The kingdom of her thought.[11]

Deep dread and loathing of her solitude
    Fell on her, from which mood was born
Scorn of herself; again, from out that mood
    Laughter at her self-scorn.

'What! is not this my place of strength,' she said,
    'My spacious mansion built for me,   230
Whereof the strong foundation-stones were laid
    Since my first memory?'

But in dark corners of her palace stood
    Uncertain shapes; and unawares
On white-eyed phantasms weeping tears of blood,
    And horrible nightmares,

And hollow shades enclosing hearts of flame,
    And, with dim fretted[12] foreheads all,
On corpses three-months-old at noon she came,
    That stood against the wall.   240

A spot of dull stagnation, without light
    Or power of movement, seem'd my soul,
'Mid onward-sloping motions infinite
    Making for one sure goal.

A still salt pool, lock'd in with bars of sand,
    Left on the shore; that hears all night
The plunging seas draw backward from the land
    Their moon-led waters white.

A star that with the choral starry dance
    Join'd not, but stood, and standing saw   250
The hollow orb of moving Circumstance
    Roll'd round by one fix'd law.

Back on herself her serpent pride had curl'd.
    'No voice,' she shriek'd in that lone hall,
'No voice breaks thro' the stillness of this world:
    One deep, deep silence all!'

She, mouldering with the dull earth's mouldering sod,
    Inwrapt tenfold in slothful shame,
Lay there exiled from eternal God,
    Lost to her place and name;   260

And death and life she hated equally,
    And nothing saw, for her despair,

11 the writing on the wall at Belshazzar's Feast, Daniel 5.23–7 (*Mene*.   12 'worm-fretted' (T).
'God hath numbered thy kingdom, and finished it').

But dreadful time, dreadful eternity,
    No comfort anywhere;

Remaining utterly confused with fears,
    And ever worse with growing time,
And ever unrelieved by dismal tears,
    And all alone in crime:

Shut up as in a crumbling tomb, girt round
    With blackness as a solid wall,   270
Far off she seem'd to hear the dully sound
    Of human footsteps fall.

As in strange lands a traveller walking slow,
    In doubt and great perplexity,
A little before moon-rise hears the low
    Moan of an unknown sea;

And knows not if it be thunder, or a sound
    Of rocks thrown down, or one deep cry
Of great wild beasts; then thinketh, 'I have found
    A new land, but I die.'   280

She howl'd aloud, 'I am on fire within.
    There comes no murmur of reply.
What is it that will take away my sin,
    And save me lest I die?'

So when four years were wholly finishèd,
    She threw her royal robes away.
'Make me a cottage in the vale,' she said,
    'Where I may mourn and pray.

'Yet pull not down my palace towers, that are
    So lightly, beautifully built: 290
Perchance I may return with others there
    When I have purged my guilt.'

Written by April 1832. Poems (1832); Poems (1842), I. 1842 text.

ST SIMEON STYLITES

Altho' I be the basest of mankind,
From scalp to sole one slough and crust of sin,
Unfit for earth, unfit for heaven, scarce meet
For troops of devils, mad with blasphemy,
I will not cease to grasp the hope I hold
Of saintdom, and to clamour, mourn and sob,
Battering the gates of heaven with storms of prayer,
Have mercy, Lord, and take away my sin.
   Let this avail, just, dreadful, mighty God,
This not be all in vain, that thrice ten years,   10
Thrice multiplied by superhuman pangs,
In hungers and in thirsts, fevers and cold,
In coughs, aches, stitches, ulcerous throes and cramps,
A sign betwixt the meadow and the cloud,

Patient on this tall pillar I have borne
Rain, wind, frost, heat, hail, damp, and sleet, and snow;
And I had hoped that ere this period closed
Thou wouldst have caught me up into thy rest,
Denying not these weather-beaten limbs
The meed of saints, the white robe and the palm. 20
    O take the meaning, Lord: I do not breathe,
Not whisper, any murmur of complaint.
Pain heaped ten-hundred-fold to this, were still
Less burthen, by ten-hundred-fold, to bear,
Than were those lead-like tons of sin that crush'd
My spirit flat before thee.
                        O Lord, Lord,
Thou knowest I bore this better at the first,
For I was strong and hale of body then;
And though my teeth, which now are dropt away,
Would chatter with the cold, and all my beard 30
Was tagged with icy fringes in the moon,
I drown'd the whoopings of the owl with sound
Of pious hymns and psalms, and sometimes saw
An angel stand and watch me, as I sang.
Now am I feeble grown; my end draws nigh –
I hope my end draws nigh: half deaf I am,
So that I scarce can hear the people hum
About the column's base, and almost blind,
And scarce can recognise the fields I know.
And both my thighs are rotted with the dew; 40
Yet cease I not to clamour and to cry,
While my stiff spine can hold my weary head,
Till all my limbs drop piecemeal from the stone,
Have mercy, mercy: take away my sin.
    O Jesus, if thou wilt not save my soul,
Who may be saved? who is it may be saved?[1]
Who may be made a saint, if I fail here?
Show me the man hath suffered more than I.
For did not all thy martyrs die one death?
For either they were stoned, or crucified, 50
Or burn'd in fire, or boil'd in oil, or sawn
In twain beneath the ribs; but I die here
To-day, and whole years long, a life of death.
Bear witness, if I could have found a way
(And heedfully I sifted all my thought)
More slowly-painful to subdue this home
Of sin, my flesh, which I despise and hate,[2]
I had not stinted practice, O my God.
    For not alone this pillar-punishment,
Not this alone I bore: but while I lived 60
In the white convent down the valley there,
For many weeks about my loins I wore
The rope that haled the buckets from the well,
Twisted as tight as I could knot the noose,
And spake not of it to a single soul,
Until the ulcer, eating through my skin,
Betray'd my secret penance, so that all

St Simeon Stylites
1 cf. Matthew 19.25: 'Who then can be saved?'

2 cf. Romans 7.17–18: 'sin…dwelleth in me…in me (that is, in my flesh) dwelleth no good thing.'

My brethren marvell'd greatly. More than this
I bore, whereof, O God, thou knowest all.
   Three winters, that my soul might grow to thee,   70
I lived up there on yonder mountain side.
My right leg chain'd into the crag, I lay
Pent in a roofless close of ragged stones,
Inswath'd sometimes in wandering mist, and twice
Black'd with thy branding thunder, and sometimes
Sucking the damps for drink, and eating not,
Except the spare chance-gift of those that came
To touch my body and be heal'd, and live.
And they say then that I work'd miracles,
Whereof my fame is loud amongst mankind,   80
Cured lameness, palsies, cancers. Thou, O God,
Knowest alone whether this was or no.
Have mercy, mercy! cover all my sin.
   Then, that I might be more alone with thee,
Three years I lived upon a pillar, high
Six cubits, and three years on one of twelve;
And twice three years I crouch'd on one that rose
Twenty by measure; last of all, I grew
Twice ten long weary weary years to this,
That numbers forty cubits from the soil.   90
   I think that I have borne as much as this –
Or else I dream – and for so long a time,
If I may measure time by yon slow light,
And this high dial, which my sorrow crowns –
So much – even so.
             And yet I know not well,
For that the evil ones come here, and say,
'Fall down, O Simeon: thou hast suffer'd long
For ages and for ages!' then they prate
Of penances I cannot have gone thro',
Perplexing me with lies; and oft I fall,   100
Maybe for months, in such blind lethargies
That Heaven, and Earth, and Time are choked.
                        But yet
Bethink thee, Lord, while thou and all the saints
Enjoy themselves in heaven, and men on earth
House in the shade of comfortable roofs,
Sit with their wives by fires, eat wholesome food,
And wear warm clothes, and even beasts have stalls,[3]
I, 'tween the spring and downfall of the light,
Bow down one thousand and two hundred times,
To Christ, the Virgin Mother, and the Saints;   110
Or in the night, after a little sleep,
I wake: the chill stars sparkle; I am wet
With drenching dews, or stiff with crackling frost.
I wear an undress'd goatskin on my back;
A grazing iron collar grinds my neck;
And in my weak, lean arms I lift the cross,
And strive and wrestle with thee till I die:[4]
O mercy, mercy! wash away my sin.
   O Lord, thou knowest what a man I am;

---

3   cf. Christ, Matthew 8.20, who 'hath not where to lay his head',   4   cf. wrestling Jacob, Genesis 32.
though the 'foxes have holes' etc.

A sinful man, conceived and born in sin:[5]   120
'Tis their own doing; this is none of mine;
Lay it not to me.[6] Am I to blame for this,
That here come those that worship me? Ha! ha!
They think that I am somewhat. What am I?
The silly people take me for a saint,
And bring me offerings of fruit and flowers:
And I, in truth (thou wilt bear witness here)
Have all in all endured as much, and more
Than many just and holy men, whose names
Are register'd and calendar'd for saints.   130
     Good people, you do ill to kneel to me.
What is it I can have done to merit this?
I am a sinner viler than you all.
It may be I have wrought some miracles,
And cured some halt[7] and maim'd; but what of that?
It may be, no one, even among the saints,
May match his pains with mine. But what of that?
Yet do not rise: for you may look on me,
And in your looking you may kneel to God.
Speak! is there any of you halt or maim'd?   140
I think you know I have some power with Heaven
From my long penance: let him speak his wish.
     Yes, I can heal him. Power goes forth from me.
They say that they are heal'd. Ah, hark! they shout
'St Simeon Stylites.' Why, if so,
God reaps a harvest in me. O my soul,
God reaps a harvest in thee. If this be,
Can I work miracles and not be saved?
This is not told of any. They were saints.
It cannot be but that I shall be saved;   150
Yea, crown'd a saint. They shout, 'Behold a saint!'
And lower voices saint me from above.
Courage, St Simeon! This dull chrysalis
Cracks into shining wings, and hope ere death
Spreads more and more and more, that God hath now
Sponged and made blank of crimeful record all
My mortal archives.
                    O my sons, my sons,
I, Simeon of the pillar, by surname
Stylites, among men; I, Simeon,
The watcher on the column till the end;   160
I, Simeon, whose brain the sunshine bakes;
I, whose bald brows in silent hours become
Unnaturally hoar with rime, do now
From my high nest of penance here proclaim
That Pontius and Iscariot[8] by my side
Show'd like fair seraphs. On the coals I lay,
A vessel full of sin: all hell beneath
Made me boil over. Devils plucked my sleeve,
Abaddon and Asmodeus[9] caught at me.

5   as Psalm 51.5.
6   cf. St Stephen, Acts 7.60, 'lay not this sin to their charge.'
7   lame.
8   Pontius Pilate, who washed his hands of Jesus, and Judas Iscariot
who betrayed Him.

9   Abaddon: 'bottomless pit,' Revelation 9.11; Asmodeus: 'the evil
spirit,' Tobit 3.8.

I smote them with the cross; they swarm'd again.   170
In bed like monstrous apes they crush'd my chest:
They flapp'd my light out as I read: I saw
Their faces grow between me and my book;
With colt-like whinny and with hoggish whine
They burst my prayer. Yet this way was left,
And by this way I 'scaped them. Mortify
Your flesh, like me, with scourges and with thorns;
Smite, shrink not, spare not. If it may be, fast
Whole Lents,[10] and pray. I hardly, with slow steps –
With slow, faint steps, and much exceeding pain –   180
Have scrambled past those pits of fire, that still
Sing in mine ears. But yield not me the praise:
God only thro' his bounty hath thought fit,
Among the powers and princes of this world,
To make me an example to mankind,
Which few can reach to. Yet I do not say
But that a time may come – yea, even now,
Now, now, his footsteps smite the threshold stairs
Of life – I say, that time is at the doors
When you may worship me without reproach;   190
For I will leave my relics in your land,
And you may carve a shrine about my dust,
And burn a fragrant lamp before my bones,
When I am gather'd to the glorious saints.
　　While I spake then, a sting of shrewdest pain
Ran shrivelling thro' me, and a cloudlike change,
In passing, with a grosser film made thick
These heavy, horny eyes. The end! the end!
Surely the end! What's here? a shape, a shade,
A flash of light. Is that the angel there   200
That holds a crown? Come, blessed brother, come.
I know thy glittering face. I waited long;
My brows are ready. What! deny it now?
Nay, draw, draw, draw nigh. So I clutch it. Christ!
'Tis gone: 'tis here again; the crown! the crown!
So now 'tis fitted on and grows to me,
And from it melt the dews of Paradise,
Sweet! sweet! spikenard, and balm, and frankincense.
Ah! let me not be fooled, sweet saints: I trust
That I am whole, and clean, and meet for Heaven.   210
　　Speak, if there be a priest, a man of God,
Among you there, and let him presently[11]
Approach, and lean a ladder on the shaft,
And climbing up into my airy home,
Deliver me the blessèd sacrament;
For by the warning of the Holy Ghost,
I prophesy that I shall die to-night,
A quarter before twelve.
　　　　　　　　But thou, O Lord,
Aid all this foolish people; let them take
Example, pattern: lead them to thy light.   220

Written by November 1833. Poems (1842), II.

---

10   40-day pre-Easter period when Christians traditionally fasted or   11   straightaway.
otherwise denied themselves.

ULYSSES

It little profits that an idle king,
By this still hearth, among these barren crags,
Match'd with an aged wife, I mete and dole
Unequal laws unto a savage race,
That hoard, and sleep, and feed, and know not me.
I cannot rest from travel: I will drink,
Life to the lees: all times I have enjoy'd
Greatly, have suffer'd greatly, both with those
That loved me, and alone; on shore, and when
Thro' scudding drifts the rainy Hyades[1]   10
Vext the dim sea; I am become a name;
For always roaming with a hungry heart
Much have I seen and known; cities of men
And manners, climates, councils, governments,
Myself not least, but honour'd of them all;
And drunk delight of battle with my peers,
Far on the ringing plains of windy Troy.
I am a part of all that I have met;
Yet all experience is an arch wherethro'
Gleams that untravell'd world, whose margin fades   20
For ever and for ever when I move.
How dull it is to pause, to make an end,
To rust unburnish'd, not to shine in use!
As tho' to breathe were life. Life piled on life
Were all too little, and of one to me
Little remains: but every hour is saved
From that eternal silence, something more,
A bringer of new things; and vile it were
For some three suns to store and hoard myself,
And this gray spirit yearning in desire   30
To follow knowledge like a sinking star,
Beyond the utmost bound of human thought.
    This is my son, mine own Telemachus,
To whom I leave the sceptre and the isle –
Well-loved of me, discerning to fulfil
This labour, by slow prudence to make mild
A rugged people, and thro' soft degrees
Subdue them to the useful and the good.
Most blameless is he, centred in the sphere
Of common duties, decent[2] not to fail   40
In offices of tenderness, and pay
Meet adoration to my household gods,
When I am gone. He works his work, I mine.
    There lies the port; the vessel puffs her sail:
There gloom the dark broad seas. My mariners,
Souls that have toiled, and wrought, and thought with me –
That ever with a frolic welcome took
The thunder and the sunshine, and opposed
Free hearts, free foreheads – you and I are old;
Old age hath yet his honour and his toil;   50
Death closes all: but something ere the end,
Some work of noble note, may yet be done,

ULYSSES   2   aware of what is fitting.
1   stars whose rising was thought to presage storms.

Not unbecoming men that strove with Gods.
The lights begin to twinkle from the rocks:
The long day wanes: the slow moon climbs: the deep
Moans round with many voices. Come, my friends,
'Tis not too late to seek a newer world.
Push off, and, sitting well in order, smite
The sounding furrows; for my purpose holds
To sail beyond the sunset, and the baths   60
Of all the western stars, until I die.
It may be that the gulfs will wash us down:
It may be we shall touch the Happy Isles,[3]
And see the great Achilles, whom we knew.
Tho' much is taken, much abides; and tho'
We are not now that strength which in old days
Moved earth and heaven; that which we are, we are;
One equal temper of heroic hearts,
Made weak by time and fate, but strong in will
To strive, to seek, to find, and not to yield.   70

*Written 20 October 1833, shortly after T. heard news of Arthur Hallam's death.
'It was more written with the feeling of his loss upon me than many poems in*
In Memoriam.' Poems *(1842), II. (Based on* Odyssey *xi. 100–137; and Dante,*
Inferno *xxvi. 90ff. – probably in H. F. Cary's translation (1805).)*

Morte d'Arthur

So all day long the noise of battle roll'd
Among the mountains by the winter sea;
Until King Arthur's table, man by man,
Had fall'n in Lyonness about their Lord,
King Arthur: then, because his wound was deep,
The bold Sir Bedivere uplifted him,
Sir Bedivere, the last of all his knights,
And bore him to a chapel nigh the field,
A broken chancel with a broken cross,
That stood on a dark strait of barren land.   10
On one side lay the Ocean, and on one
Lay a great water, and the moon was full.
    Then spake King Arthur to Sir Bedivere:
'The sequel of to-day unsolders all
The goodliest fellowship of famous knights
Whereof this world holds record. Such a sleep
They sleep – the men I loved. I think that we
Shall nevermore, at any future time,
Delight our souls with talk of knightly deeds,
Walking about the gardens and the halls   20
Of Camelot, as in the days that were.
I perish by this people which I made, –
Though Merlin sware that I should come again
To rule once more – but let what will be, be,
I am so deeply smitten through the helm
That without help I cannot last till morn.
Thou therefore take my brand Excalibur,
Which was my pride: for thou rememberest how

3 Isles of the Blest – beyond the Pillars of Hercules (i.e. Gibraltar).

In those old days, one summer noon, an arm
Rose up from out the bosom of the lake,   30
Clothed in white samite, mystic, wonderful,
Holding the sword – and how I row'd across
And took it, and have worn it, like a king:
And, wheresoever I am sung or told
In aftertime, this also shall be known:
But now delay not: take Excalibur,
And fling him far into the middle meer:
Watch what thou seëst, and lightly bring me word.'
    To him replied the bold Sir Bedivere:
'It is not meet, Sir King, to leave thee thus,   40
Aidless, alone, and smitten through the helm.
A little thing may harm a wounded man.
Yet I thy hest will all perform at full,
Watch what I see, and lightly bring thee word.'
    So saying, from the ruin'd shrine he stepp'd,
And in the moon athwart the place of tombs,
Where lay the mighty bones of ancient men,
Old knights, and over them the sea-wind sang
Shrill, chill, with flakes of foam. He, stepping down
By zigzag paths, and juts of pointed rock,   50
Came on the shining levels of the lake.
    There drew he forth the brand Excalibur,
And o'er him, drawing it, the winter moon,
Brightening the skirts of a long cloud, ran forth
And sparkled keen with frost against the hilt:
For all the haft twinkled with diamond sparks,
Myriads of topaz-lights, and jacinth-work
Of subtlest jewellery. He gazed so long
That both his eyes were dazzled, as he stood,
This way and that dividing the swift mind,   60
In act to throw: but at the last it seem'd
Better to leave Excalibur concealed
There in the many-knotted waterflags,
That whistled stiff and dry about the marge.
So strode he back slow to the wounded King.
    Then spake King Arthur to Sir Bedivere:
'Hast thou perform'd my mission which I gave?
What is it thou hast seen? or what hast heard?'
    And answer made the bold Sir Bedivere:
'I heard the ripple washing in the reeds,   70
And the wild water lapping on the crag.'
    To whom replied King Arthur, faint and pale:
'Thou hast betray'd thy nature and thy name,
Not rendering true answer, as beseem'd
Thy fëalty, nor like a noble knight:
For surer sign had follow'd, either hand,
Or voice, or else a motion of the meer.
This is a shameful thing for men to lie.
Yet now, I charge thee, quickly go again
As thou art lief and dear, and do the thing   80
I bad thee, watch, and lightly bring me word'.
    Then went Sir Bedivere the second time,
Counting the dewy pebbles, fix'd in thought;
But when he saw the wonder of the hilt,
How curiously and strangely chased, he smote
His palms together, and he cried aloud,

'And if indeed I cast the brand away,
Surely a precious thing, one worthy note,
Should thus be lost for ever from the earth,
Which might have pleased the eyes of many men.   90
What good should follow this, if this were done?
What harm, undone? deep harm to disobey,
Seeing obedience is the bond of rule.
Were it well to obey then, if a king demand
An act unprofitable, against himself?
The King is sick, and knows not what he does.
What record, or what relic of my lord
Should be to aftertime, but empty breath
And rumours of a doubt? but were this kept,
Stored in some treasure-house of mighty kings,   100
Some one might show it at a joust of arms,
Saying, "King Arthur's sword, Excalibur,
Wrought by the lonely maiden of the Lake.
Nine years she wrought it, sitting in the deeps
Upon the hidden bases of the hills."
So might some old man speak in the aftertime
To all the people, winning reverence.
But now much honour and much fame were lost.'
    So spake he, clouded with his own conceit,
And hid Excalibur the second time,   110
And so strode back slow to the wounded King.
    Then spoke King Arthur, breathing heavily:
'What is it thou hast seen? or what hast heard?'
    And answer made the bold Sir Bedivere:
'I heard the water lapping on the crag,
And the long ripple washing in the reeds.'
    To whom replied King Arthur, much in wrath:
'Ah, miserable and unkind, untrue,
Unknightly, traitor-hearted! Woe is me!
Authority forgets a dying king,   120
Laid widow'd of the power in his eye
That bowed the will. I see thee what thou art,
For thou, the latest-left of all my knights,
In whom should meet the offices of all,
Thou wouldst betray me for the precious hilt;
Either from lust of gold, or like a girl
Valuing the giddy pleasure of the eyes.
Yet, for a man may fail in duty twice,
And the third time may prosper, get thee hence:
But, if thou spare to fling Excalibur,   130
I will arise and slay thee with my hands.'
    Then quickly rose Sir Bedivere, and ran,
And, leaping down the ridges lightly, plunged
Among the bulrush-beds, and clutch'd the sword,
And strongly wheel'd and threw it. The great brand
Made lightnings in the splendour of the moon,
And flashing round and round, and whirled in an arch,
Shot like a streamer of the northern morn,
Seen where the moving isles of winter shock
By night, with noises of the northern sea.   140
So flash'd and fell the brand Excalibur:
But ere he dipt the surface, rose an arm
Clothed in white samite, mystic, wonderful,
And caught him by the hilt, and brandish'd him

Three times, and drew him under in the meer.
And lightly went the other to the King.
   Then spoke King Arthur, drawing thicker breath:
'Now see I by thine eyes that this is done.
Speak out: what is it thou hast heard, or seen?'
   And answer made the bold Sir Bedivere: 150
'Sir King, I closed mine eyelids, lest the gems
Should blind my purpose, for I never saw,
Nor shall see, here or elsewhere, till I die,
Not though I live three lives of mortal men,
So great a miracle as yonder hilt.
Then with both hands I flung him, wheeling him,
But when I look'd again, behold an arm,
Clothed in white samite, mystic, wonderful,
That caught him by the hilt, and brandish'd him
Three times, and drew him under in the meer.'   160
   And answer made King Arthur, breathing hard:
'My end draws nigh; 'tis time that I were gone.
Make broad thy shoulders to receive my weight,
And bear me to the margin; yet I fear
My wound hath taken cold, and I shall die.'
   So saying, from the pavement he half rose,
Slowly, with pain, reclining on his arm,
And looking wistfully with wide blue eyes
As in a picture. Him Sir Bedivere
Remorsefully regarded thro' his tears,   170
And would have spoken, but he found not words,
Then took with care, and kneeling on one knee,
O'er both his shoulders drew the languid hands,
And rising bore him thro' the place of tombs.
   But, as he walk'd, King Arthur panted hard,
Like one that feels a nightmare on his bed
When all the house is mute. So sigh'd the King,
Muttering and murmuring at his ear, 'Quick, quick!
I fear it is too late, and I shall die.'
But the other swiftly strode from ridge to ridge,   180
Clothed with his breath, and looking, as he walk'd,
Larger than human on the frozen hills.
He heard the deep behind him, and a cry
Before. His own thought drove him like a goad.
Dry clash'd his harness in the icy caves
And barren chasms, and all to left and right
The bare black cliff clang'd round him, as he based
His feet on juts of slippery crag that rang
Sharp-smitten with the dint of armed heels –
And on a sudden, lo! the level lake,   190
And the long glories of the winter moon.
   Then saw they how there hove a dusky barge,
Dark as a funeral scarf from stem to stern,
Beneath them; and descending they were ware
That all the decks were dense with stately forms
Black-stoled, black-hooded, like a dream – by these
Three Queens with crowns of gold – and from them rose
A cry that shiver'd to the tingling stars,
And, as it were one voice, an agony
Of lamentation, like a wind, that shrills   200
All night in a waste land, where no one comes,
Or hath come, since the making of the world.

Then murmur'd Arthur, 'Place me in the barge,'
And to the barge they came. There those three Queens
Put forth their hands, and took the King, and wept.
But she, that rose the tallest of them all
And fairest, laid his head upon her lap,
And loosed the shatter'd casque, and chafed his hands,
And call'd him by his name, complaining loud,
And dropping bitter tears against his brow   210
Striped with dark blood: for all his face was white
And colourless, and like the wither'd moon
Smote by the fresh beam of the springing east;
And all his greaves and cuisses[1] dash'd with drops
Of onset; and the light and lustrous curls –
That made his forehead like a rising sun
High from the daïs-throne – were parch'd with dust;
Or, clotted into points and hanging loose,
Mix'd with the knightly growth that fringed his lips.
So like a shatter'd column lay the King;   220
Not like that Arthur who, with lance in rest,
From spur to plume a star of tournament,
Shot thro' the lists at Camelot, and charged
Before the eyes of ladies and of kings.
        Then loudly cried the bold Sir Bedivere,
'Ah! my Lord Arthur, whither shall I go?
Where shall I hide my forehead and my eyes?
For now I see the true old times are dead,
When every morning brought a noble chance,
And every chance brought out a noble knight.   230
Such times have been not since the light that led
The holy Elders with the gift of myrrh.[2]
But now the whole ROUND TABLE is dissolved
Which was an image of the mighty world;
And I, the last, go forth companionless,
And the days darken round me, and the years,
Among new men, strange faces, other minds.'
        And slowly answer'd Arthur from the barge:
'The old order changeth, yielding place to new,
And God fulfils Himself in many ways,   240
Lest one good custom should corrupt the world.
Comfort thyself: what comfort is in me?
I have lived my life, and that which I have done
May He within Himself make pure! but thou –
If thou shouldst never see my face again,
Pray for my soul. More things are wrought by prayer
Than this world dreams of. Wherefore, let thy voice
Rise like a fountain for me night and day.
For what are men better than sheep or goats
That nourish a blind life within the brain,   250
If, knowing God, they lift not hands of prayer
Both for themselves and those who call them friend?
For so the whole round earth is every way
Bound by gold chains about the feet of God.
But now farewell. I am going a long way
With these thou seëst – if indeed I go –
(For all my mind is clouded with a doubt)

MORTE D'ARTHUR   2 the Magi, led by star to Jesus, baby in Bethlehem.
1 shin armour and thigh armour.

To the island-valley of Avilion;
Where falls not hail, or rain, or any snow,
Nor ever wind blows loudly; but it lies   260
Deep-meadow'd, happy, fair with orchard-lawns
And bowery hollows crowned with summer sea,
Where I will heal me of my grievous wound.'
    So said he, and the barge with oar and sail
Moved from the brink, like some full-breasted swan
That, fluting a wild carol ere her death,
Ruffles her pure cold plume, and takes the flood
With swarthy webs. Long stood Sir Bedivere
Revolving many memories, till the hull
Look'd one black dot against the verge of dawn,   270
And on the meer the wailing died away.

Here ended Hall, and our last light, that long
Had wink'd and threaten'd darkness, flared and fell:
At which the Parson, sent to sleep with sound,
And waked with silence, grunted 'Good!' but we
Sat rapt: it was the tone with which he read –
Perhaps some modern touches here and there
Redeem'd it from the charge of nothingness –
Or else we loved the man, and prized his work;
I know not: but we sitting, as I said,   280
The cock crew loud; as at that time of year
The lusty bird takes every hour for dawn:
Then Francis, muttering, like a man ill-used,
'There now – that's nothing!' drew a little back,
And drove his heel into the smoulder'd log,
That sent a blast of sparkles up the flue:
And so to bed; where yet in sleep I seem'd
To sail with Arthur under looming shores,
Point after point; till on to dawn, when dreams
Begin to feel the truth and stir of day,   290
To me, methought, who waited with a crowd,
There came a bark that, blowing forward, bore
King Arthur, like a modern gentleman
Of stateliest port; and all the people cried,
'Arthur is come again: he cannot die.'
Then those that stood upon the hills behind
Repeated – 'Come again, and thrice as fair;'
And, further inland, voices echoed – 'Come
With all good things, and war shall be no more.'
At this a hundred bells began to peal,   300
That with the sound I woke, and heard indeed
The clear church-bells ring in the Christmas-morn.

Written 1833–4. Poems *(1842), II. T's first big Arthurian poem, based closely on*
Thomas Malory's 15th-century Morte d'Arthur; *later incorporated into*
The Passing of Arthur *(1869), final part of T's longest work, the* Idylls of the King.

'BREAK, BREAK, BREAK'

Break, break, break,
   On thy cold gray stones, O Sea!
And I would that my tongue could utter
   The thoughts that arise in me.

O well for the fisherman's boy,
   That he shouts with his sister at play!
O well for the sailor lad,
   That he sings in his boat on the bay!

And the stately ships go on
  To their haven under the hill;   10
But O for the touch of a vanish'd hand,
  And the sound of a voice that is still!

Break, break, break,
  At the foot of thy crags, O Sea!
But the tender grace of a day that is dead
  Will never come back to me.

Written 'one spring' after Arthur Hallam's death, Sept. 1833:
probably spring 1834. Poems *(1842), II.*

LADY CLARA VERE DE VERE

Lady Clara Vere de Vere,
  Of me you shall not win renown;
You thought to break a country heart
  For pastime, ere you went to town.
At me you smiled, but unbeguiled
  I saw the snare, and I retired:
The daughter of a hundred Earls –
  You are not one to be desired.

Lady Clara Vere de Vere,
  I know you proud to bear your name,   10
Your pride is yet no mate for mine,
  Too proud to care from whence I came.
Nor would I break for your sweet sake
  A heart that doats on truer charms.
A simple maiden in her flower
  Is worth a hundred coats-of-arms.

Lady Clara Vere de Vere,
  Some meeker pupil you must find,
For were you queen of all that is,
  I could not stoop to such a mind.   20
You sought to prove how I could love,
  And my disdain is my reply.
The lion on your old stone gates
  Is not more cold to you than I.

Lady Clara Vere de Vere,
  You put strange memories in my head.
Not thrice your branching limes have blown
  Since I beheld young Laurence dead.
Oh your sweet eyes, your low replies:
  A great enchantress you may be;   30
But there was that across his throat
  Which you had hardly cared to see.

Lady Clara Vere de Vere,
  When thus he met his mother's view,
She had the passions of her kind,
  She spake some certain truths of you.

Indeed I heard one bitter word
  That scarce is fit for you to hear;
Her manners had not that repose
  Which stamps the caste of Vere de Vere.   40

Lady Clara Vere de Vere,
  There stands a spectre in your hall:
The guilt of blood is at your door.
  You changed a wholesome heart to gall.
You held your course without remorse,
  To make him trust his modest worth,
And, last, you fix'd a vacant stare,
  And slew him with your noble birth.

Trust me, Clara Vere de Vere,
  From yon blue heavens above us bent   50
The gardener Adam and his wife
  Smile at the claims of long descent.
Howe'er it be, it seems to me,
  'Tis only noble to be good.
Kind hearts are more than coronets,
  And simple faith than Norman blood.

I know you, Clara Vere de Vere,
  You pine among your halls and towers;
The languid light of your proud eyes
  Is wearied of the rolling hours.   60
In glowing health, with boundless wealth,
  But sickening of a vague disease,
You know so ill to deal with Time,
  You needs must play such pranks as these.

Clara, Clara Vere de Vere,
  If Time be heavy on your hands,
Are there no beggars at your gate,
  Nor any poor about your lands?
Oh! teach the orphan-boy to read,
  Or teach the orphan-girl to sew,   70
Pray Heaven for a human heart,
  And let the foolish yeoman go.

Written, perhaps, 1835. Poems *(1842), I. (Lady Clara was a fictional character,*
Tennyson said.)

THE POET'S SONG

The rain had fallen, the Poet arose,
   He pass'd by the town and out of the street;
A light wind blew from the gates of the sun,
   And waves of shadow went over the wheat,
And he sat him down in a lonely place,
   And chanted a melody loud and sweet,
That made the wild-swan pause in her cloud,
   And the lark drop down at his feet.

The swallow stopt as he hunted the bee,   10
   The snake slipt under a spray,
The wild hawk stood with the down on his beak,
   And stared, with his foot on the prey,
And the nightingale thought, 'I have sung many songs,
   But never a one so gay,
For he sings of what the world will be
   When the years have died away.'

Poems (1842), II (last poem in the book).

THE NEW TIMON, AND THE POETS

We know him, out of SHAKESPEARE'S art,
   And those fine curses which he spoke;
The old TIMON, with his noble heart,
   That, strongly loathing, greatly broke.

So died the Old: here comes the New.[1]
   Regard him: a familiar face:
I *thought* we knew him: What, it's you,
   The padded man – that wears the stays –

Who kill'd the girls and thrill'd the boys,
   With dandy pathos when you wrote,   10
A Lion, you, that made a noise,
   And shook a mane en papillotes.[2]

And once you tried the Muses too;
   You fail'd, Sir: therefore now you turn,
You fall on those who are to you,
   As Captain is to Subaltern.

But men of long-enduring hopes,
   And careless what this hour may bring,
Can pardon little would-be POPES
   And BRUMMELS,[3] when they try to sting.   20

An artist, Sir, should rest in Art,
   And waive a little of his claim;

To have the deep Poetic heart
   Is more than all poetic fame.

But you, Sir, you are hard to please;
   You never look but half content:
Nor like a gentleman at ease,
   With moral breadth of temperament.[4]

And what with spites and what with fears,
   You cannot let a body be: 30
It's always ringing in your ears,
   'They call this man as good as *me.*'

What profits now to understand
   The merits of a spotless shirt –
A dapper boot – a little hand –
   If half the little soul is dirt?

You talk of tinsel! why we see
   The old mark of rouge upon your cheeks.
You prate of Nature! you are he
   That spilt his life about the cliques.   40

A TIMON you! Nay, nay, for shame:
   It looks too arrogant a jest –
The fierce old man – to take *his* name
   You bandbox. Off, and let him rest.

*Punch, 28 February 1846 (signed 'Alcibiades'). In reply to Bulwer-Lytton's anonymous
attack on Tennyson and his Civil List Pension, in* The New Timon, *Part ii,
January 1846. (Alcibiades reads Timon's epitaph in Shakespeare's play.) Not reprinted by T.*

AFTER-THOUGHT

Ah, God! the petty fools of rhyme
   That shriek and sweat in pigmy wars
Before the stony face of Time,
   And look'd at by the silent stars; –

That hate each other for a song,
   And do their little best to bite,
That pinch their brothers in the throng,
   And scratch the very dead for spite, –

THE NEW TIMON, AND THE POETS
1   Edward Bulwer-Lytton.
2   in curl-papers.

3   dandies, after Beau Brummel, notorious Regency fashion-monger.
4   Lytton's novel *Pelham* (1828) is subtitled 'The Adventures of a Gentleman.'

And strain to make an inch of room
    For their sweet selves, and cannot hear   10
The sullen Lethe rolling doom
    On them and theirs, and all things here;

When one small touch of Charity
    Could lift them nearer Godlike State,

Than if the crowded Orb should cry
    Like those who cried DIANA[1] great:

And *I* too talk, and lose the touch
    I talk of. Surely, after all,
The noblest answer unto such
    Is kindly stillness when they brawl.   20

Punch, X (7 March 1846), 106. Signed 'Alcibiades'. Retitled 'Literary Squabbles'
(and slightly amended), Miniature Edition (1870).

From: THE PRINCESS; A MEDLEY

Tears, idle tears, I know not what they mean,
Tears from the depth of some divine despair
Rise in the heart, and gather to the eyes,
In looking on the happy Autumn-fields,
And thinking of the days that are no more.

Fresh as the first beam glittering on a sail,
That brings our friends up from the underworld,
Sad as the last which reddens over one
That sinks with all we love below the verge;
So sad, so fresh, the days that are no more.   10

Ah, sad and strange as in dark summer dawns
The earliest pipe of half-awakened birds
To dying ears, when unto dying eyes
The casement slowly grows a glimmering square;
So sad, so strange, the days that are no more.

Dear as remember'd kisses after death,
And sweet as those by hopeless fancy feign'd
On lips that are for others; deep as love,
Deep as first love, and wild with all regret;
O Death in Life, the days that are no more.[1]   20

    . . . .

Now sleeps the crimson petal, now the white;
Nor waves the cypress in the palace walk;
Nor winks the gold fin in the porphyry font:
The fire-fly wakens: waken thou with me.

    Now droops the milkwhite peacock like a ghost,
And like a ghost she glimmers on to me.
    Now lies the Earth all Danaë[2] to the stars,
And all thy heart lies open unto me.

    Now slides the silent meteor on, and leaves
A shining furrow, as thy thoughts in me.   10

    Now folds the lily all her sweetness up,
And slips into the bosom of the lake:

AFTER-THOUGHT
1 Acts 19.28–34: 'Great is Diana of the Ephesians' (anti-St Paul riot
at Ephesus).

FROM: THE PRINCESS
1 Part IV, lines 21–40. Written, Tintern Abbey.
2 impregnated by Zeus in form of a shower of gold.

So fold thyself, my dearest, thou, and slip
Into my bosom and be lost in me.[3]

. . . .

Come down, O maid, from yonder mountain height:
What pleasure lives in height (the shepherd sang)
In height and cold, the splendour of the hills?
But cease to move so near the Heavens, and cease
To glide a sunbeam by the blasted Pine,
To sit a star upon the sparkling spire;
And come, for Love is of the valley, come,
For Love is of the valley, come thou down
And find him; by the happy threshold, he,
Or hand in hand with Plenty in the maize,   10
Or red with spirted purple of the vats,
Or foxlike in the vine; nor cares to walk
With Death and Morning on the Silver Horns,
Nor wilt thou snare him in the white ravine,
Nor find him dropt upon the firths of ice,
That huddling slant in furrow-cloven falls
To roll the torrent out of dusky doors:
But follow; let the torrent dance thee down
To find him in the valley; let the wild
Lean-headed Eagles yelp alone, and leave   20
The monstrous ledges there to slope, and spill
Their thousand wreaths of dangling water-smoke,
That like a broken purpose waste in air:
So waste not thou; but come; for all the vales
Await thee; azure pillars of the hearth
Arise to thee; the children call, and I
Thy shepherd pipe, and sweet is every sound,
Sweeter thy voice, but every sound is sweet;
Myriads of rivulets hurrying thro' the lawn,
The moan of doves in immemorial elms,   30
And murmuring of innumerable bees.[4]

The Princess; A Medley *(Edward Moxon, 25 December 1847)*.

IN MEMORIAM

Strong Son of God, immortal Love,
  Whom we, that have not seen thy face,
  By faith, and faith alone, embrace,
Believing where we cannot prove;

Thine are these orbs of light and shade;
  Thou madest Life in man and brute;
  Thou madest Death; and lo, thy foot
Is on the skull which thou hast made.

Thou wilt not leave us in the dust:
  Thou madest man, he knows not why;   10
  He thinks he was not made to die;
And thou hast made him: thou art just.

Thou seemest human and divine,
  The highest, holiest manhood, thou:
  Our wills are ours, we know not how;
Our wills are ours, to make them thine.

Our little systems have their day;
  They have their day and cease to be:
  They are but broken lights of thee,
And thou, O Lord, art more than they.   20

We have but faith: we cannot know;
  For knowledge is of things we see;
  And yet we trust it comes from thee,
A beam in darkness: let it grow.

---

3 Part VII, lines 161–74. Imitates form of a Persian *ghazal* (though 'I don't read Persian': T.). Princess Ida reads from 'A volume of the Poets of her land.'

4 Part VII, lines 177–207. Written, Switzerland. Regarded by T. as one of his best poems for 'Simple rhythm and vowel music'.

Let knowledge grow from more to more,
   But more of reverence in us dwell;
   That mind and soul, according well,
May make one music as before,

But vaster. We are fools and slight;
   We mock thee when we do not fear: 30
   But help thy foolish ones to bear;
Help thy vain worlds to bear thy light.

Forgive what seem'd my sin in me;
   What seem'd my worth since I began;

For merit lives from man to man,
And not from man, O Lord, to thee.

Forgive my grief for one removed,
   Thy creature, whom I found so fair.
   I trust he lives in thee, and there
I find him worthier to be loved.   40

Forgive these wild and wandering cries,
   Confusions of a wasted youth;
   Forgive them where they fail in truth,
And in thy wisdom make me wise.

1849

IN MEMORIAM
A. H. H.
OBIIT MDCCCXXXIII[1]

I

I held it truth, with him[2] who sings
   To one clear harp in divers tones,
   That men may rise on stepping-stones
Of their dead selves to higher things.

But who shall so forecast the years
   And find in loss a gain to match?   50
   Or reach a hand thro' time to catch
The far-off interest of tears?

Let Love clasp Grief lest both be drown'd,
   Let darkness keep her raven gloss:
   Ah! sweeter to be drunk with loss,
To dance with death, to beat the ground;

Than that the victor Hours should scorn
   The long result of love, and boast:
   'Behold the man that loved and lost,
But all he was is overworn.'   60

II

Old Yew, which graspest at the stones
   That name the under-lying dead,
   Thy fibres net the dreamless head;
Thy roots are wrapt about the bones.

The seasons bring the flower again,
   And bring the firstling to the flock;
   And in the dusk of thee, the clock
Beats out the little lives of men.

O! not for thee the glow, the bloom,
   Who changest not in any gale!   70

Nor branding summer suns avail
To touch thy thousand years of gloom.

And gazing on the sullen tree,
   Sick for thy stubborn hardihood,
   I seem to fail from out my blood
And grow incorporate into thee.

III

O Sorrow, cruel fellowship!
   O Priestess in the vaults of Death!
   O sweet and bitter in a breath,
What whispers from thy lying lip?   80

'The stars,' she whispers, 'blindly run;
   A web is wov'n across the sky;
   From out waste places comes a cry,
And murmurs from the dying sun:

'And all the phantom, Nature, stands –
   With all the music in her tone,
   A hollow echo of my own, –
A hollow form with empty hands.'

And shall I take a thing so blind,
   Embrace her as my natural good;   90
   Or crush her, like a vice of blood,
Upon the threshold of the mind?

IV

To Sleep I give my powers away;
   My will is bondsman to the dark;
   I sit within a helmless bark,
And with my heart I muse and say:

IN MEMORIAM
1   Arthur Henry Hallam; died, Vienna, 15 September 1833.
2   Goethe.

O heart, how fares it with thee now,
    That thou should'st fail from thy desire,
    Who scarcely darest to inquire,
'What is it makes me beat so low?'   100

Something it is which thou hast lost,
    Some pleasure from thine early years.
    Break, thou deep vase of chilling tears,
That grief hath shaken into frost!

Such clouds of nameless trouble cross
    All night below the darken'd eyes;
    With morning wakes the will, and cries,
'Thou shalt not be the fool of loss.'

V

I sometimes hold it half a sin
    To put in words the grief I feel;   110
    For words, like nature, half reveal
And half conceal the Soul within.

But, for the unquiet heart and brain,
    A use in measur'd language lies;
    The sad mechanic exercise,
Like dull narcotics, numbing pain.

In words, like weeds, I'll wrap me o'er,
    Like coarsest clothes against the cold;
    But that large grief which these enfold
Is given in outline and no more.   120

VI

One writes, that 'Other friends remain,'
    That 'Loss is common to the race' –
    And common is the commonplace,
And vacant chaff well meant for grain.

That loss is common would not make
    My own less bitter, rather more:
    Too common! Never morning wore
To evening, but some heart did break.

O father, wheresoe'er thou be,
    That pledgest now thy gallant son;   130
    A shot, ere half thy draught be done
Hath still'd the life that beat from thee.

O mother, praying God will save
    Thy sailor, – while thy head is bowed,
    His heavy-shotted hammock-shroud
Drops in his vast and wandering grave.

Ye know no more than I who wrought
    At that last hour to please him well;
    Who mused on all I had to tell,
And something written, something thought;   140

Expecting still his advent home;
    And ever met him on his way
    With wishes, thinking, here today,
Or here tomorrow will he come.

O! somewhere, meek, unconscious dove,
    That sittest ranging golden hair;
    And glad to find thyself so fair,
Poor child, that waitest for thy love![3]

For now her father's chimney glows
    In expectation of a guest;   150
    And thinking 'this will please him best,'
She takes a riband or a rose;

For he will see them on to-night;
    And with the thought her colour burns;
    And, having left the glass, she turns
Once more to set a ringlet right;

And, even when she turn'd, the curse
    Had fallen, and her future Lord
    Was drowned in passing thro' the ford,
Or kill'd in falling from his horse.   160

O, what to her shall be the end?
    And what to me remains of good?
    To her, perpetual maidenhood,
And unto me no second friend.

VII

Dark house, by which once more I stand
    Here in the long unlovely street,
    Doors, where my heart was used to beat
So quickly, waiting for a hand,

A hand that can be clasp'd no more –
    Behold me, for I cannot sleep,   170
    And like a guilty thing I creep
At earliest morning to the door.

He is not here; but far away
    The noise of life begins again,
    And ghastly thro' the drizzling rain
On the bald street breaks the blank day.

VIII

A happy lover who has come
    To look on her that loves him well,
    Who lights[4] and rings the gateway bell,
And learns her gone and far from home;   180

He saddens, all the magic light
    Dies off at once from bower and hall,
    And all the place is dark, and all
The chambers emptied of delight;

---

3   first reference to T's sister Emily, engaged to be married to Hallam.   4   alights.

So find I every pleasant spot
  In which we two were wont to meet,
  The field, the chamber and the street,
For all is dark where thou art not.

Yet as that other, wandering there
  In those deserted walks, may find   190
  A flower beat with rain and wind,
Which once she fostered up with care;

So seems it in my deep regret,
  O my forsaken heart, with thee
  And this poor flower of poesy
Which little cared for fades not yet.

But since it pleased a vanish'd eye,
  I go to plant it on his tomb,
  That if it can it there may bloom,
Or dying, there at least may die.   200

IX

Fair ship, that from the Italian shore
  Sailest the placid ocean-plains
  With my lost Arthur's loved remains,
Spread thy full wings, and waft him o'er.

So draw him home to those that mourn
  In vain; a favourable speed
  Ruffle thy mirror'd mast, and lead
Thro' prosperous floods his holy urn.

All night no ruder air perplex
  Thy sliding keel, till Phosphor,[5] bright   210
  As our pure love, thro' early light
Shall glimmer on the dewy decks.

Sphere all your lights around, above;
  Sleep, gentle heavens, before the prow;
  Sleep, gentle winds, as he sleeps now,
My friend, the brother of my love;

My Arthur, whom I shall not see
  Till all my widowed race be run;
  Dear as the mother to the son,
More than my brothers are to me.   220

X

I hear the noise about thy keel;
  I hear the bell struck in the night:
  I see the cabin-window bright;
I see the sailor at the wheel.

Thou bringest the sailor to his wife,
  And travell'd men from foreign lands;
  And letters unto trembling hands;
And, thy dark freight, a vanish'd life.

So bring him: we have idle dreams:
  This look of quiet flatters thus   230
  Our home-bred fancies: O to us,
The fools of habit, sweeter seems

To rest beneath the clover sod,
  That takes the sunshine and the rains,
  Or where the kneeling hamlet drains
The chalice of the grapes of God;

Than if with thee the roaring wells
  Should gulf him fathom-deep in brine;
  And hands so often clasp'd in mine,
Should toss with tangle[6] and with shells.   240

XI

Calm is the morn without a sound,
  Calm as to suit a calmer grief,
  And only thro' the faded leaf
The chestnut pattering to the ground:

Calm and deep peace on this high wold,
  And on these dews that drench the furze,
  And all the silvery gossamers
That twinkle into green and gold:

Calm and still light on yon great plain
  That sweeps with all its autumn bowers,   250
  And crowded farms and lessening towers,
To mingle with the bounding main:

Calm and deep peace in this wide air,
  These leaves that redden to the fall;
  And in my heart, if calm at all,
If any calm, a calm despair:

Calm on the seas, and silver sleep,
  And waves that sway themselves in rest,
  And dead calm in that noble breast
Which heaves but with the heaving deep.   260

XII

Lo! as a dove when up she springs
  To bear thro' Heaven a tale of woe,
  Some dolorous message knit below
The wild pulsation of her wings;

Like her I go; I cannot stay;
  I leave this mortal ark behind,
  A weight of nerves without a mind,
And leave the cliffs, and haste away

O'er ocean-mirrors rounded large,
  And reach the glow of southern skies,   270
  And see the sails at distance rise,
And linger weeping on the marge,

---

5 'star of dawn' (T.).

6 'oar-weed' (T.).

And saying; 'Comes he thus, my friend?
    Is this the end of all my care?'
    And circle moaning in the air:
'Is this the end? Is this the end?'

And forward dart again, and play
    About the prow, and back return
    To where the body sits, and learn
That I have been an hour away.[7]   280

XIII

Tears of the widower, when he sees
    A late-lost form that sleep reveals,
    And moves his doubtful arms, and feels
Her place is empty, fall like these;

Which weep a loss for ever new,
    A void where heart on heart reposed;
    And, where warm hands have prest and closed,
Silence, till I be silent too.

Which weep the comrade of my choice,
    An awful thought, a life removed,   290
    The human-hearted man I loved,
A spirit, not a breathing voice.

Come Time, and teach me, many years,
    I do not suffer in a dream;
    For now so strange do these things seem,
Mine eyes have leisure for their tears;

My fancies time to rise on wing,
    And glance about the approaching sails,
    As tho' they brought but merchants' bales,
And not the burthen that they bring.   300

XIV

If one should bring me this report,
    That thou hadst touch'd the land to-day,
    And I went down unto the quay,
And found thee lying in the port,

And standing, muffled round with woe,
    Should see thy passengers in rank
    Come stepping lightly down the plank,
And beckoning unto those they know,

And if along with these should come
    The man I held as half-divine;   310
    Should strike a sudden hand in mine,
And ask a thousand things of home;

And I should tell him all my pain,
    And how my life had dropp'd of late,
    And he should sorrow o'er my state
And marvel what possess'd my brain;

And I perceived no touch of change,
    No hint of death in all his frame,
    But found him all in all the same,
I should not feel it to be strange.   320

XV

To-night the winds begin to rise
    And roar from yonder dropping day:
    The last red leaf is whirl'd away,
The rooks are blown about the skies;

The forest crack'd, the waters curl'd,
    The cattle huddled on the lea;
    And wildly dash'd on tower and tree
The sunbeam strikes along the world:

And but for fancies, which aver
    That all thy motions gently pass   330
    Athwart a plane of molten glass,
I scarce could brook the strain and stir

That makes the barren branches loud;
    And but for fear it is not so,
    The wild unrest that lives in woe
Would dote and pore on yonder cloud

That rises upward always higher,
    And onward drags a labouring breast,
    And topples round the dreary west,
A looming bastion fringed with fire.   340

XVI

What words are these have fall'n from me?
    Can calm despair and wild unrest
    Be tenants of a single breast,
Or sorrow such a changeling be?

Or doth she only seem to take
    The touch of change in calm or storm;
    But knows no more of transient form
In her deep self, than some dead lake

That holds the shadow of a lark
    Hung in the shadow of a heaven?   350
    Or has the shock, so harshly given,
Confus'd me like the unhappy bark

That strikes by night a craggy shelf,
    And staggers blindly ere she sink?
    And stunn'd me from my power to think
And all my knowledge of myself;

And made me that delirious man
    Whose fancy fuses old and new,
    And flashes into false and true,
And mingles all without a plan?   360

---

7 cf. Genesis 8.8–9, story of Noah's ark and messenger dove.

XVII

Thou comest, much wept for: such a breeze
    Compell'd thy canvas, and my prayer
    Was as the whisper of an air
To breathe thee over lonely seas.

For I in spirit saw thee move
    Thro' circles of the bounding sky;
    Week after week: the days go by:
Come quick, thou bringest all I love.

Henceforth, wherever thou may'st roam,
    My blessing, like a line of light,   370
    Is on the waters day and night,
And like a beacon guards thee home.

So may whatever tempest mars
    Mid-ocean, spare thee, sacred bark;
    And balmy drops in summer dark
Slide from the bosom of the stars.

So kind an office hath been done,
    Such precious relics brought by thee;
    The dust of him I shall not see
Till all my widow'd race be run.   380

XVIII

'Tis well; 'tis something, we may stand
    Where he in English earth is laid,
    And from his ashes may be made
The violet of his native land.[8]

'Tis little; but it looks in truth
    As if the quiet bones were blest
    Among familiar names to rest
And in the places of his youth.

Come then, pure hands, and bear the head
    That sleeps or wears the mask of sleep,   390
    And come, whatever loves to weep,
And hear the ritual of the dead.

Ah! yet, ev'n yet, if this might be,
    I, falling on his faithful heart,
    Would breathing thro' his lips impart
The life that almost dies in me:

That dies not, but endures with pain,
    And slowly forms the firmer mind,
    Treasuring the look it cannot find,
The words that are not heard again.   400

XIX

The Danube to the Severn gave[9]
    The darken'd heart that beat no more;

They laid him by the pleasant shore,
    And in the hearing of the wave.

There twice a day the Severn fills,
    The salt sea-water passes by,
    And hushes half the babbling Wye,
And makes a silence in the hills.

The Wye is hush'd nor moved along;
    And hush'd my deepest grief of all,   410
    When fill'd with tears that cannot fall,
I brim with sorrow drowning song.

The tide flows down, the wave again
    Is vocal in its wooded walls:
    My deeper anguish also falls,
And I can speak a little then.

XX

The lesser griefs that may be said,
    That breathe a thousand tender vows,
    Are but as servants in a house
Where lies the master newly dead;   420

Who speak their feeling as it is,
    And weep the fulness from the mind:
    'It will be hard,' they say, 'to find
Another service such as this.'

My lighter moods are like to these,
    That out of words a comfort win;
    But there are other griefs within,
And tears that at their fountain freeze;

For by the hearth the children sit
    Cold in that atmosphere of Death,   430
    And scarce endure to draw the breath.
Or like to noiseless phantoms flit:

But open converse is there none,
    So much the vital spirits sink
    To see the vacant chair, and think,
'How good! how kind! and he is gone.'

XXI

I sing to him that rests below,
    And, since the grasses round me wave,
    I take the grasses of the grave,
And make them pipes whereon to blow.   440

The traveller hears me now and then,
    And sometimes harshly will he speak;
    'This fellow would make weakness weak,
And melt the waxen hearts of men.'

---

8 T. was thinking of *Hamlet* V. i. 232–4 (violets to spring from the 'fair and unpolluted flesh' of Ophelia).

9 'He died at Vienna and was brought to Clevedon to be buried' (T.).

Another answers, 'Let him be,
   He loves to make parade of pain,
   That with his piping he may gain
The praise that comes to constancy.'

A third is wroth: 'Is this an hour
   For private sorrow's barren song,   450
   When more and more the people throng
The chairs and thrones of civil power?

'A time to sicken and to swoon,
   When science reaches forth her arms
   To feel from world to world, and charms
Her secret from the latest moon?'

Behold, ye speak an idle thing:
   Ye never knew the sacred dust:
   I do but sing because I must,
And pipe but as the linnets sing: 460

And one unto her note is gay,
   For now her little ones have ranged;
   And one unto her note is changed,
Because her brood is stol'n away.

XXII

The path by which we twain did go,
   Which led by tracts that pleased us well,
   Thro' four sweet years arose and fell,
From flower to flower, from snow to snow:

And we with singing cheer'd the way,
   And crown'd with all the season lent,   470
   From April on to April went,
And glad at heart from May to May:

But where the path we walk'd began
   To slant the fifth autumnal slope,
   As we descended following Hope,
There sat the Shadow fear'd of man;[10]

Who broke our fair companionship,
   And spread his mantle dark and cold;
   And wrapt thee formless in the fold,
And dull'd the murmur on thy lip;   480

And bore thee where I could not see
   Nor follow, tho' I walk in haste;
   And think that, somewhere in the waste,
The Shadow sits and waits for me.

XXIII

Now, sometimes in my sorrow shut,
   Or breaking into song by fits,
   Alone, alone, to where he sits,
The Shadow cloak'd from head to foot

Who keeps the keys of all the creeds,
   I wander, often falling lame,   490
   And looking back to whence I came,
Or on to where the pathway leads;

And crying, how changed from where it ran
   Thro' lands where not a leaf was dumb;
   But all the lavish hills would hum
The murmur of a happy Pan:

When each by turns was guide to each,
   And Fancy light from Fancy caught,
   And Thought leapt out to wed with Thought,
Ere thought could wed itself with Speech;   500

And all we met was fair and good,
   And all was good that Time could bring,
   And all the secret of the Spring
Moved in the chambers of the blood:

And many an old philosophy
   On Argive heights divinely sang,
   And round us all the thicket rang
To many a flute of Arcady.

XXIV

And was the day of my delight
   As pure and perfect as I say?   510
   The very source and fount of Day
Is dash'd with wandering isles of night.

If all was good and fair we met,
   This earth had been the Paradise
   It never look'd to human eyes
Since Adam left his garden yet.

And is it that the haze of grief
   Hath stretch'd my former joy so great?
   The lowness of the present state,
That sets the past in this relief?   520

Or that the past will always win
   A glory from its being far;
   And orb into the perfect star
We saw not, when we moved therein?

XXV

I know that this was Life, – the track
   Whereon with equal feet we fared;
   And then, as now, the day prepared
The daily burden for the back.

But this it was that made me move
   As light as carrier-birds in air;   530
   I loved the weight I had to bear,
Because it needed help of Love:

---

10   cf. the 'valley of the shadow of death', Psalm 23.4.

Nor could I weary, heart or limb,
　　When mighty Love would cleave in twain
　　The lading of a single pain,
And part it, giving half to him.

XXVI

Still onward winds the dreary way;
　　I with it; for I long to prove
　　No lapse of moons can canker Love,
Whatever fickle tongues may say.　　　　　　540

And if that eye which watches guilt
　　And goodness, and hath power to see
　　Within the green the moulder'd tree,
And towers fall'n as soon as built –

Oh, if indeed that eye foresee
　　Or see (in Him is no before)
　　In more of life true life no more
And Love the indifference to be,

So might I find, ere yet the morn
　　Breaks hither over Indian seas,　　　　　　550
　　That Shadow waiting with the keys,
To cloak me from my proper scorn.

XXVII

I envy not in any moods
　　The captive void of noble rage,
　　The linnet born within the cage
That never knew the summer woods:

I envy not the beast that takes
　　His license in the field of time,
　　Unfetter'd by the sense of crime,
To whom a conscience never wakes;　　　　　　560

Nor, what may count itself as blest,
　　The heart that never plighted troth
　　But stagnates in the weeds of sloth;
Nor any want-begotten rest.

I hold it true, whate'er befall;
　　I feel it, when I sorrow most;
　　'Tis better to have loved and lost
Than never to have loved at all.

XXVIII[11]

The time draws near the birth of Christ:
　　The moon is hid; the night is still;　　　　　　570
　　The Christmas bells from hill to hill
Answer each other in the mist.

Four voices of four hamlets round,
　　From far and near, on mead and moor,

Swell out and fail, as if a door
Were shut between me and the sound:

Each voice four changes on the wind,
　　That now dilate, and now decrease,
　　Peace and goodwill, goodwill and peace,
Peace and goodwill, to all mankind.　　　　　　580

This year I slept and woke with pain,
　　I almost wish'd no more to wake,
　　And that my hold on life would break
Before I heard those bells again:

But they my troubled spirit rule,
　　For they controll'd me when a boy;
　　They bring me sorrow touch'd with joy,
The merry merry bells of Yule.

XXIX

With such compelling cause to grieve
　　As daily vexes household peace,　　　　　　590
　　And chains regret to his decease,
How dare we keep our Christmas-eve;

Which brings no more a welcome guest
　　To enrich the threshold of the night
　　With shower'd largess of delight
In dance and song and game and jest.

Yet go, and while the holly boughs
　　Entwine the cold baptismal font,
　　Make one wreath more for Use and Wont
That guard the portals of the house;　　　　　　600

Old sisters of a day gone by,
　　Gray nurses, loving nothing new;
　　Why should they miss their yearly due
Before their time? They too will die.

XXX[12]

With trembling fingers did we weave
　　The holly round the Christmas hearth;
　　A rainy cloud possess'd the earth,
And sadly fell our Christmas-eve.

At our old pastimes in the hall
　　We gambol'd, making vain pretence　　　　　　610
　　Of gladness, with an awful sense
Of one mute Shadow watching all.

We paused: the winds were in the beech:
　　We heard them sweep the winter land;
　　And in a circle hand-in-hand
Sat silent, looking each at each.

11　one of the earliest sections, begun 1833.

12　dated 'Christmas Eve. 1833', in one MS.

Then echo-like our voices rang;
   We sung, tho' every eye was dim,
   A merry song we sang with him
Last year: impetuously we sang: 620

We ceased: a gentler feeling crept
   Upon us: surely rest is meet:
   'They rest,' we said, 'their sleep is sweet,'
And silence follow'd, and we wept.

Our voices took a higher range;
   Once more we sang: 'They do not die
   Nor lose their mortal sympathy,
Nor change to us, although they change;

Rapt from the fickle and the frail
   With gather'd power, yet the same,   630
   Pierces the keen seraphic flame
From orb to orb, from veil to veil.

Rise, happy morn, rise, holy morn,
   Draw forth the cheerful day from night:
   O Father! touch the east, and light
The light that shone when Hope was born.'

XXXI[13]

When Lazarus left his charnel-cave,
   And home to Mary's house return'd,
   Was this demanded – if he yearn'd
To hear her weeping by his grave?   640

'Where wert thou, brother, those four days?'
   There lives no record of reply,
   Which telling what it is to die
Had surely added praise to praise.

From every house the neighbours met,
   The streets were fill'd with joyful sound,
   A solemn gladness even crown'd
The purple brows of Olivet.

Behold a man raised up by Christ!
   The rest remaineth unreveal'd;   650
   He told it not; or something seal'd
The lips of that Evangelist.[14]

XXXII[15]

Her[16] eyes are homes of silent prayer,
   Nor other thought her mind admits
   But, he was dead, and there he sits,
And he that brought him back is there.

Then one deep love doth supersede
   All other, when her ardent gaze

   Roves from the living brother's face,
And rests upon the Life indeed.   660

All subtle thought, all curious fears,
   Borne down by gladness so complete,
   She bows, she bathes the Saviour's feet
With costly spikenard and with tears.

Thrice blest whose lives are faithful prayers,
   Whose loves in higher love endure;
   What souls possess themselves so pure,
Or is there blessedness like theirs?

XXXIII

O thou that after toil and storm
   Mayst seem to have reach'd a purer air,   670
   Whose faith has centre everywhere,
Nor cares to fix itself to form,

Leave thou thy sister when she prays,
   Her early Heaven, her happy views;
   Nor thou with shadow'd hint confuse
A life that leads melodious days.

Her faith thro' form is pure as thine,
   Her hands are quicker unto good.
   Oh, sacred be the flesh and blood
To which she links a truth divine!   680

See, thou that countest reason ripe
   In holding by the law within,
   Thou fail not in a world of sin,
And ev'n for want of such a type.

XXXIV

My own dim life should teach me this,
   That life shall live for evermore,
   Else earth is darkness at the core,
And dust and ashes all that is;

This round of green, this orb of flame,
   Fantastic beauty; such as lurks   690
   In some wild Poet, when he works
Without a conscience or an aim.

What then were God to such as I?
   'Twere hardly worth my while to choose
   Of things all mortal, or to use
A little patience ere I die;

'Twere best at once to sink to peace,
   Like birds the charming serpent draws,
   To drop head-foremost in the jaws
Of vacant darkness and to cease.   700

---

13   written 1833.
14   John 11 (the raised Lazarus was notoriously silent).
15   begun 1833.
16   Mary, sister of Lazarus. See John 12.

XXXV

Yet if some voice that man could trust
    Should murmur from the narrow house:
    The cheeks drop in; the body bows;
Man dies: nor is there hope in dust:

Might I not say, yet even here,
    But for one hour, O Love, I strive
    To keep so sweet a thing alive?
But I should turn mine ears and hear

The moanings of the homeless sea,
    The sound of streams that swift or slow   710
    Draw down Æonian hills, and sow
The dust of continents to be;

And Love would answer with a sigh,
    'The sound of that forgetful shore
    Will change my sweetness more and more,
Halfdead to know that I shall die.'

O me! what profits it to put
    An idle case? If Death were seen
    At first as Death, Love had not been,
Or been in narrowest working shut,   720

Mere fellowship of sluggish moods,
    Or in his coarsest Satyr-shape
    Had bruised the herb and crush'd the grape,
And bask'd and batten'd in the woods.

XXXVI

Tho' truths in manhood darkly join,
    Deep-seated in our mystic frame,
    We yield all blessing to the name
Of Him that made them current coin;

For Wisdom dealt with mortal powers,
    Where Truth in closest words shall fail,   730
    When Truth embodied in a tale
Shall enter in at lowly doors.

And so the Word had breath, and wrought
    With human hands the creed of creeds
    In loveliness of perfect deeds,
More strong than all poetic thought;

Which he may read that binds the sheaf,
    Or builds the house, or digs the grave,
    And those wild eyes that watch the wave
In roarings round the coral reef.   740

XXXVII

Urania[17] speaks with darkened brow:
    'Thou pratest here where thou art least;

This faith has many a purer priest,
    And many an abler voice than thou:

Go down beside thy native rill,
    On thy Parnassus set thy feet,
    And hear thy laurel whisper sweet
About the ledges of the hill.'

And my Melpomene[18] replies,
    A touch of shame upon her cheek: 750
    'I am not worthy but to speak
Of thy prevailing mysteries;

For I am but an earthly Muse,
    And owning but a little art
    To lull with song an aching heart,
And render human love his dues;

But brooding on the dear one dead,
    And all he said of things divine,
    (And dear to me as sacred wine
To dying lips is all he said),   760

I murmured, as I came along,
    Of comfort clasp'd in truth reveal'd;
    And loitered in the master's field,
And darken'd sanctities with song.'

XXXVIII

With weary steps I loiter on,
    Tho' always under alter'd skies
    The purple from the distance dies,
My prospect and horizon gone.

No joy the blowing season gives,
    The herald melodies of spring,   770
    But in the songs I love to sing
A doubtful gleam of solace lives.

If any care for what is here
    Survive in spirits render'd free,
    Then are these songs I sing of thee
Not all ungrateful to thine ear.

XXXIX

Could we forget the widow'd hour
    And look on Spirits breathed away,
    As on a maiden in the day
When first she wears her orange-flower![19]   780

When crown'd with blessing she doth rise
    To take her latest leave of home,
    And hopes and light regrets that come
Make April of her tender eyes;

---

17   Muse of Astronomy.
18   Muse of Tragedy, taken as Muse of Elegy.

19   traditional wedding flower.

And doubtful joys the father move,
    And tears are on the mother's face,
    As parting with a long embrace
She enters other realms of love;

Her office there to rear, to teach,
    Becoming as is meet and fit   790
    A link among the days, to knit
The generations each with each;

And, doubtless, unto thee is given
    A life that bears immortal fruit
    In such great offices as suit
The full-grown energies of heaven.

Ay me, the difference I discern!
    How often shall her old fireside
    Be cheer'd with tidings of the bride,
How often she herself return,   800

And tell them all they would have told,
    And bring her babe, and make her boast,
    Till even those that miss'd her most,
Shall count new things as dear as old:

But thou and I have shaken hands,
    Till growing winters lay me low;
    My paths are in the fields I know,
And thine in undiscover'd lands.

XL

Thy spirit ere our fatal loss
    Did ever rise from high to higher;   810
    As mounts the heavenward altar-fire,
As flies the lighter thro' the gross.

But thou art turn'd to something strange,
    And I have lost the links that bound
    Thy changes; here upon the ground;
No more partaker of thy change.

Deep folly! yet that this could be –
    That I could wing my will with might
    To leap the grades of life and light,
And flash at once, my friend, to thee: 820

For though my nature rarely yields
    To that vague fear implied in death;
    Nor shudders at the gulfs beneath,
The howlings from forgotten fields;

Yet oft when sundown skirts the moor
    An inner trouble I behold,
    A spectral doubt which makes me cold,
That I shall be thy mate no more,

Tho' following with an upward mind
    The wonders that have come to thee,   830
    Thro' all the secular to be,[20]
But evermore a life behind.

XLI

I vex my heart with fancies dim:
    He still outstript me in the race;
    It was but unity of place
That made me dream I ranked with him.

And so may Place retain us still,
    And he the much-beloved again,
    A lord of large experience, train
To riper growth the mind and will: 840

And what delights can equal those
    That stir the spirit's inner deeps,
    When one that loves but knows not, reaps
A truth from one that loves and knows?

XLII

If Sleep and Death be truly one,
    And every spirit's folded bloom
    Thro' all its intervital gloom
In some long trance should slumber on;

Unconscious of the sliding hour,
    Bare of the body, might it last,   850
    And silent traces of the past
Be all the colour of the flower:

So then were nothing lost to man;
    So that still garden of the souls
    In many a figured leaf enrolls
The total world since life began:

And love would last as pure and whole
    As when he loved me here in Time,
    And at the spiritual prime
Rewaken with the dawning soul.   860

XLIII

How fares it with the happy dead?
    For here the man is more and more;
    But he forgets the days before
God shut the doorways of his head.

The days have vanish'd, tone and tint,
    And yet perhaps the hoarding sense
    Gives out at times (he knows not whence)
A little flash, a mystic hint;

And in the long harmonious years
    (If Death so taste Lethean springs),[21]   870

20 'aeons of the future' (T.).
21 Lethe: classical river of underworld whose waters induce loss of
memory.

May some dim touch of earthly things
Surprise thee ranging with thy peers.

If such a dreamy touch should fall,
  O turn thee round, resolve the doubt;
  My guardian angel will speak out
In that high place, and tell thee all.

XLIV

The baby new to earth and sky,
  What time his tender palm is prest
  Against the circle of the breast,
Has never thought that 'this is I:'   880

But as he grows he gathers much,
  And learns the use of 'I', and 'me',
  And finds 'I am not what I see,
And other than the things I touch.'

So rounds he to a separate mind
  From whence clear memory may begin,
  As thro' the frame that binds him in
His isolation grows defined.

This use may lie in blood and breath,
  Which else were fruitless of their due,   890
  Had man to learn himself anew
Beyond the second birth of Death.

XLV

We ranging down this lower track,
  The path we came by, thorn and flower,
  Is shadow'd by the growing hour,
Lest life should fail in looking back.

So be it: there no shade can last
  In that deep dawn behind the tomb,
  But clear from marge to marge shall bloom
The eternal landscape of the past;   900

A lifelong tract of time reveal'd;
  The fruitful hours of still increase;
  Days order'd in a wealthy peace,
And those five years its richest field.

O Love! thy province were not large,
  A bounded field, nor stretching far,
  Look also, Love, a brooding star,
A rosy warmth from marge to marge.

XLVI

That each, who seems a separate whole,
  Should move his rounds, and fusing all   910
  The skirts of self again, should fall
Remerging in the general Soul,

Is faith as vague as all unsweet:
  Eternal form shall still divide

The eternal soul from all beside;
  And I shall know him when we meet:

And we shall sit at endless feast,
  Enjoying each the other's good;
  What vaster dream can hit the mood
Of Love on earth? He seeks at least   920

Upon the last and sharpest height,
  Before the spirits fade away,
  Some landing-place, to clasp and say,
'Farewell! We lose ourselves in light.'

XLVII

If these brief lays, of Sorrow born,
  Were taken to be such as closed
  Grave doubts and answers here proposed,
Then these were such as men might scorn:

Her care is not to part and prove;
  She takes, when harsher moods remit,   930
  What slender shade of doubt may flit,
And makes it vassal unto love:

And hence, indeed, she sports with words;
  But better serves a wholesome law,
  And holds it sin and shame to draw
The deepest measure from the chords:

Nor dare she trust a larger lay,
  But rather loosens from the lip
  Short swallow-flights of song, that dip
Their wings in tears, and skim away.   940

XLVIII

From art, from nature, from the schools,
  Let random influences glance,
  Like light in many a shiver'd lance
That breaks about the dappled pools:

The lightest wave of thought shall lisp,
  The fancy's tenderest eddy wreathe,
  The slightest air of song shall breathe
To make the sullen surface crisp.

And look thy look, and go thy way,
  But blame not thou the winds that make   950
  The seeming-wanton ripple break,
The tender-pencil'd shadow play.

Beneath all fancied hopes and fears
  Ay me! the sorrow deepens down,
  Whose muffled motions blindly drown
The bases of my life in tears.

XLIX

Be near me when my light is low,
  When the blood creeps, and the nerves prick

And tingle; and the heart is sick,
And all the wheels of Being slow.   960

Be near me when the sensuous frame
    Is racked with pangs that conquer trust,
    And time, a maniac, scattering dust,
And life, a Fury slinging flame.

Be near me when my faith is dry,
    And men the flies of latter spring,
    That lay their eggs, and sting and sing
And weave their petty cells and die.

Be near me when I fade away,
    To point the term of human strife,   970
    And on the low dark verge of life
The twilight of eternal day.

L[22]

Do we indeed desire the dead
    Should still be near us at our side?
    Is there no baseness we would hide?
No inner vileness that we dread?

Shall he for whose applause I strove,
    I had such reverence for his blame,
    See with clear eye some hidden shame
And I be lessen'd in his love?   980

I wrong the grave with fears untrue:
    Shall love be blamed for want of faith?
    There must be wisdom with great Death;
The dead shall look me thro' and thro'.

Be near us when we climb or fall:
    Ye watch, like God, the rolling hours
    With larger other eyes than ours,
To make allowance for us all.

LI

I cannot love thee as I ought,
    For love reflects the thing beloved;   990
    My words are only words, and moved
Upon the topmost froth of thought.

'Yet blame not thou thy plaintive song,'
    The Spirit of true love replied;
    'Thou canst not move me from thy side,
Nor human frailty do me wrong.

What keeps a spirit wholly true
    To that ideal which he bears?
    What record? not the sinless years
That breathed beneath the Syrian blue: 1000

So fret not, like an idle girl,
    That life is dash'd with flecks of sin.
    Abide: thy wealth is gathered in,
When Time hath sunder'd shell from pearl.'

LII

How many a father have I seen,
    A sober man, among his boys,
    Whose youth was full of foolish noise,
Who wears his manhood hale and green;

And dare we to this doctrine give,
    That had the wild oat not been sown,   1010
    The soil, left barren, scarce had grown
The grain by which a man may live?

Oh! if we held the doctrine sound
    For life outliving heats of youth,
    Yet who would preach it as a truth
To those that eddy round and round?

Hold thou the good: define it well:
    For fear divine Philosophy
    Should push beyond her mark, and be
Procuress to the Lords of Hell.   1020

LIII

Oh yet we trust that somehow good
    Will be the final goal of ill,
    To pangs of nature, sins of will,
Defects of doubt, and taints of blood;

That nothing walks with aimless feet;
    That not one life shall be destroy'd,
    Or cast as rubbish to the void,
When God hath made the pile complete;

That not a worm is cloven in vain;
    That not a moth with vain desire   1030
    Is shrivel'd in a fruitless fire,
Or but subserves another's gain.

Behold! we know not anything;
    I can but trust that good shall fall
    At last – far off – at last, to all,
And every winter change to spring.

So runs my dream: but what am I?
    An infant crying in the night:
    An infant crying for the light:
And with no language but a cry.[23]   1040

LIV[24]

The wish, that of the living whole
    No life may fail beyond the grave;

---

22   composed Christmas 1841.
23   *infant*, from *infans* (Latin), without speech.
24   LIV, LV, written, probably, under influence of C. Lyell, *Principles of*

Geology (1837); but added to poem's early versions to counter what T. thought over-assurances (?).

Derives it not from what we have
The likest God within the soul?

Are God and Nature then at strife,
    That Nature lends such evil dreams?
    So careful of the type she seems,
So careless of the single life;

That I, considering everywhere
    Her secret meaning in her deeds,   1050
    And finding that of fifty seeds
She often brings but one to bear;

I falter where I firmly trod,
    And falling with my weight of cares
    Upon the great world's altar-stairs
That slope thro' darkness up to God;

I stretch lame hands of faith, and grope,
    And gather dust and chaff, and call
    To what I feel is Lord of all,
And faintly trust the larger hope.   1060

LV
'So careful of the type?' but no.
    From scarped cliff and quarried stone
    She cries, 'A thousand types are gone:
I care for nothing, all shall go.

Thou makest thine appeal to me:
    I bring to life, I bring to death:
    The spirit does but mean the breath:
I know no more.' And he, shall he,

Man, her last work, who seem'd so fair,
    Such splendid purpose in his eyes,   1070
    Who roll'd the psalm to wintry skies,
Who built him fanes of fruitless prayer,

Who trusted God was love indeed
    And love Creation's final law –
    Tho' Nature, red in tooth and claw
With ravine, shriek'd against his creed –

Who loved, who suffer'd countless ills,
    Who battled for the True, the Just,
    Be blown about the desert dust,
Or seal'd within the iron hills?   1080

No more? A monster then, a dream,
    A discord. Dragons of the prime,
    That tare each other in their slime,
Were mellow music match'd with him.

O life as futile, then, as frail!
    O for thy voice to soothe and bless!
    What hope of answer, or redress?
Behind the veil, behind the veil.[25]

LVI
Peace, come away: the song of woe
    Is after all an earthly song: 1090
    Peace, come away: we do him wrong
To sing so wildly: let us go.

Come, let us go, your cheeks are pale,
    But half my life I leave behind;
    Methinks my friend is richly shrined,
But I shall pass; my work will fail.[26]

Yet in these ears till hearing dies,
    One set slow bell will seem to toll
    The passing of the sweetest soul
That ever looked with human eyes.   1100

I hear it now, and o'er and o'er,
    Eternal greetings to the dead;
    And 'Ave, Ave, Ave,' said,
'Adieu, adieu' for evermore!

LVII
In those sad words I took farewell:
    Like echoes in sepulchral halls,
    As drop by drop the water falls
In vaults and catacombs, they fell;

And, falling, idly broke the peace
    Of hearts that beat from day to day,   1110
    Half-conscious of their dying clay,
And those cold crypts where they shall cease.

The high Muse answer'd: 'Wherefore grieve
    Thy brethren with a fruitless tear?
    Abide a little longer here,
And thou shalt take a nobler leave.'

LVIII
He past; a soul of nobler tone:
    My spirit loved and loves him yet,
    Like some poor girl whose heart is set
On one whose rank exceeds her own.   1120

He mixing with his proper sphere,
    She finds the baseness of her lot;
    Half jealous of she knows not what,
And envying all that meet him there.

The little village looks forlorn;
    She sighs amid her narrow days,

25 'within the veil', Hebrews 6.19, where Christian mysteries are.
26 'The poet speaks of these poems. Methinks I have built a rich
shrine to my friend, but it will not last' (T.).

Moving about the household ways,
In that dark house where she was born.

The foolish neighbours come and go,
   And tease her till the day draws by;   1130
   At night she weeps, 'How vain am I!
How should he love a thing so low?'

LIX

If, in thy second state sublime,
   Thy ransom'd reason change replies
   With all the circle of the wise,
The perfect flower of human time;

And if thou cast thine eyes below,
   How dimly character'd and slight,
   How dwarf'd a growth of cold and night,
How blanch'd with darkness must I grow!   1140

Yet turn thee to the doubtful shore,
   Where thy first form was made a man;
   I loved thee, Spirit, and love, nor can
The soul of Shakspeare love thee more.

LX

Tho' if an eye that's downward cast
   Could make thee somewhat blench or fail,
   Then be my love an idle tale,
And fading legend of the past;

And thou, as one that once declined,
   When he was little more than boy,   1150
   On some unworthy heart with joy,
But lives to wed an equal mind;

   And breathes a novel world, the while
      His other passion wholly dies,
      Or in the light of deeper eyes
   Is matter for a flying smile.

LXI

Yet pity for a horse o'er-driven,
   And love in which my hound has part,
   Can hang no weight upon my heart
In its assumptions up to heaven;   1160

And I am so much more than these,
   As thou, perchance, art more than I,
   And yet I spare them sympathy,
And I would set their pains at ease.

So mayst thou watch me where I weep,
   As, unto vaster motions bound,
   The circuits of thine orbit round
A higher height, a deeper deep.

LXII[27]

Dost thou look back on what hath been,
   As some divinely gifted man,   1170
   Whose life in low estate began
And on a simple village green;

Who breaks his birth's invidious bar,
   And grasps the skirts of happy chance,
   And breasts the blows of circumstance,
And grapples with his evil star;

Who makes by force his merit known
   And lives to clutch the golden keys,
   To mould a mighty state's decrees,
And shape the whisper of the throne;   1180

And moving up from high to higher,
   Becomes on Fortune's crowning slope
   The pillar of a people's hope,
The centre of a world's desire;

Yet feels, as in a pensive dream,
   When all his active powers are still,
   A distant dearness in the hill,
A secret sweetness in the stream,

The limit of his narrower fate,
   While yet beside its vocal springs   1190
   He played at counsellors and kings,
With one that was his earliest mate;

Who ploughs with pain his native lea
   And reaps the labour of his hands,
   Or in the furrow musing stands;
'Does my old friend remember me?'

LXIII

Sweet soul! do with me as thou wilt;
   I lull a fancy trouble-tost
   With 'Love's too precious to be lost,
A little grain shall not be spilt.'   1200

And in that solace can I sing,
   Till out of painful phases wrought
   There flutters up a happy thought,
Self-balanced on a lightsome wing:

Since we deserved the name of friends,
   And thine effect so lives in me,
   A part of mine may live in thee
And move thee on to noble ends.

LXIV

You thought my heart too far diseased;
   You wonder when my fancies play   1210

27 'Composed by my father when he was walking up and down the
Strand and Fleet Street' (Hallam Tennyson).

To find me gay among the gay,
Like one with any trifle pleased.

The shade by which my life was crost,
   Which makes a desert in the mind,
   Has made me kindly with my kind,
And like to him whose sight is lost;

Whose feet are guided thro' the land,
   Whose jest among his friends is free,
   Who takes the children on his knee,
And winds their curls about his hand: 1220

He plays with threads, he beats his chair
   For pastime, dreaming of the sky;
   His inner day can never die,
His night of loss is always there.

LXV

When on my bed the moonlight falls,
   I know that in thy place of rest
   By that broad water of the west,
There comes a glory on the walls:

Thy marble bright in dark appears,
   As slowly steals a silver flame   1230
   Along the letters of thy name,
And o'er the number of thy years.

The mystic glory swims away;
   From off my bed the moonlight dies;
   And closing eaves of wearied eyes
I sleep till dusk is dipt in gray:

And then I know the mist is drawn
   A lucid veil from coast to coast,
   And in the chancel[28] like a ghost
Thy tablet glimmers to the dawn.   1240

LXVI

When in the down I sink my head,
   Sleep, Death's twin-brother, times my breath;
   Sleep, Death's twin-brother, knows not Death,
Nor can I dream of thee as dead:

I walk as ere I walk'd forlorn,
   When all our path was fresh with dew,
   And all the bugle breezes blew
Reveillée to the breaking morn.

But what is this? I turn about,
   I find a trouble in thine eye,   1250
   Which makes me sad I know not why,
Nor can my dream resolve the doubt:

But ere the lark hath left the lea
   I wake, and I discern the truth;
   It is the trouble of my youth
That foolish sleep transfers to thee.

LXVII

I dreamed there would be Spring no more,
   That Nature's ancient power was lost:
   The streets were black with smoke and frost,
They chatter'd trifles at the door: 1260

I wander'd from the noisy town,
   I found a wood with thorny boughs:
   I took the thorns to bind my brows,
I wore them like a civic crown:

I met with scoffs, I met with scorns
   From youth and babe and hoary hairs:
   They call'd me in the public squares
The fool that wears a crown of thorns.

They call'd me fool, they call'd me child:
   I found an angel of the night;   1270
   The voice was low, the look was bright,
He look'd upon my crown and smiled:

He reach'd the glory of a hand,
   That seem'd to touch it into leaf:
   The voice was not the voice of grief;
The words were hard to understand.

LXVIII

I cannot see the features right,
   When on the gloom I strive to paint
   The face I know; the hues are faint
And mix with hollow masks of night: 1280

Cloud-towers by ghostly masons wrought,
   A gulf that ever shuts and gapes,
   A hand that points, and palled shapes
In shadowy thoroughfares of thought;

And crowds that stream from yawning doors,
   And shoals of pucker'd faces drive;
   Dark bulks that tumble half alive,
And lazy lengths on boundless shores:

Till all at once beyond the will
   I hear a wizard music roll,   1290
   And through a lattice on the soul
Looks thy fair face and makes it still.

LXIX

Sleep, kinsman thou to death and trance
   And madness, thou hast forged at last

---

28   altered to *dark church* later, after T. actually visited Hallam's burial
place.

A night-long Present of the Past
In which we went through summer France.[29]

Hadst thou such credit with the soul?
　　Then bring an opiate trebly strong,
　　Drug down the blindfold sense of wrong
That thus my pleasure may be whole;　　　　1300

While now we talk as once we talk'd
　　Of men and minds, the dust of change,
　　The days that grow to something strange,
In walking as of old we walk'd

Beside the river's wooded reach,
　　The fortress, and the mountain ridge,
　　The cataract flashing from the bridge,
The breaker breaking on the beach.

LXX

Risest thou thus, dim dawn, again,
　　And howlest, issuing out of night,　　　　1310
　　With blasts that blow the poplar white,
And lash with storm the streaming pane?

Day, when my crowned estate begun
　　To pine in that reverse of doom,
　　Which sickened every living bloom,
And blurred the splendour of the sun;

Who usherest in the dolorous hour
　　With thy quick tears that make the rose
　　Pull sideways, and the daisy close
Her crimson fringes to the shower;　　　　1320

Who might'st have heaved a windless flame
　　Up the deep East, or, whispering, play'd
　　A chequer-work of beam and shade
From hill to hill, yet look'd the same.

As wan, as chill, as wild as now;
　　Day, mark'd as with some hideous crime,
　　When the dark hand struck down thro' time,
And cancell'd nature's best: but thou,

Lift as thou may'st thy burthen'd brows
　　Thro' clouds that drench the morning star,　　　　1330
　　And whirl the ungarner'd sheaf afar,
And sow the sky with flying boughs,

And up thy vault with roaring sound
　　Climb thy thick noon, disastrous day;
　　Touch thy dull goal of joyless gray,
And hide thy shame beneath the ground.

LXXI

So many worlds, so much to do,
　　So little done, such things to be,

How know I what had need of thee,
For thou wert strong as thou wert true?　　　　1340

The fame is quench'd that I foresaw,
　　The head hath miss'd an earthly wreath:
　　I curse not nature; no, nor death,
For nothing is that errs from law.

We pass; the path that each man trod
　　Is dim, or will be dim, with weeds:
　　What fame is left for human deeds
In endless age? It rests with God.

O hollow wraith of dying fame,
　　Fade wholly, while the soul exults,　　　　1350
　　And self-infolds the large results
Of force that would have forged a name.

LXXII

As sometimes in a dead man's face,
　　To those that watch it more and more,
　　A likeness hardly seen before
Comes out – to some one of his race:

So, dearest, now thy brows are cold,
　　I see thee what thou art, and know
　　Thy likeness to the wise below,
Thy kindred with the great of old.　　　　1360

But there is more than I can see,
　　And what I see I leave unsaid,
　　Nor speak it, knowing Death has made
His darkness beautiful with thee.

LXXIII

I leave thy praises unexpress'd
　　In verse that brings myself relief,
　　And by the measure of my grief
I leave thy greatness to be guess'd;

What practice howsoe'er expert
　　In fitting aptest words to things,　　　　1370
　　Or voice the richest-toned that sings,
Hath power to give thee as thou wert?

I care not in these fading days
　　To raise a cry that lasts not long,
　　And round thee with the breeze of song
To stir a little dust of praise.

Thy leaf has perish'd in the green,
　　And, while we breathe beneath the sun,
　　The world which credits what is done
Is cold to all that might have been.　　　　1380

So here shall silence guard thy fame;
　　But somewhere, out of human view,

29　1830 tour of T. and Hallam.

Whate'er thy hands are set to do
Is wrought with tumult of acclaim.

LXXIV

Take wings of fancy, and ascend,
   And in a moment set thy face
   Where all the starry heavens of space
Are sharpen'd to a needle's end;

Take wings of foresight; lighten thro'
   The secular abyss to come,   1390
   And lo! thy deepest lays are dumb
Before the mouldering of a yew;

And if the matin songs, that woke
   The darkness of our planet, last,
   Thine own shall wither in the vast,
Ere half the lifetime of an oak.

Ere these have clothed their branchy bowers
   With fifty Mays, thy songs are vain;
   And what are they when these remain
The ruined shells of hollow towers?   1400

LXXV

What hope is here for modern rhyme
   To him, who turns a musing eye
   On songs, and deeds, and lives, that lie
Foreshorten'd in the tract of time?

These mortal lullabies of pain
   May bind a book, may line a box,[30]
   May serve to curl a maiden's locks;
Or when a thousand moons shall wane

A man upon a stall may find,
   And, passing, turn the page that tells   1410
   A grief – then changed to something else,
Sung by a long-forgotten mind.

But what of that? My darken'd ways
   Shall ring with music all the same;
   To breathe my loss is more than fame,
To utter love more sweet than praise.

LXXVI

Again at Christmas did we weave
   The holly round the Christmas hearth;
   The silent snow possessed the earth,
And calmly fell our Christmas-eve;   1420

The yule-clog[31] sparkled keen with frost,
   No wing of wind the region swept,

But over all things brooding slept
The quiet sense of something lost.

As in the winters left behind,
   Again our ancient games had place,
   The mimic picture's breathing grace,[32]
And dance and song and hoodman-blind.[33]

Who show'd a token of distress?
   No single tear, no mark of pain: 1430
   O sorrow, then can sorrow wane?
O grief, can grief be changed to less?

O last regret, Regret can die!
   No – mixt with all this mystic frame,
   Her deep relations are the same,
But with long use her tears are dry.

LXXVII[34]

'More than my brothers are to me' –
   Let this not vex thee, noble heart!
   I know thee of what force thou art
To hold the costliest love in fee.   1440

But thou and I are one in kind,
   As moulded like in nature's mint;
   And hill and wood and field did print
The same sweet forms in either mind.

For us the same cold streamlet curl'd
   Through all his eddying coves; the same
   All winds that roam the twilight came
In whispers of the beauteous world.

At one dear knee we proffer'd vows,
   One lesson from one book we learn'd,   1450
   Ere childhood's flaxen ringlet turn'd
To black and brown on kindred brows.

And so my wealth resembles thine,
   But he was rich where I was poor,
   And he supplied my want the more
As his unlikeness fitted mine.

LXXVIII

If any vague desire should rise,
   That holy Death ere Arthur died
   Had moved me kindly from his side,
And dropt the dust on tearless eyes;   1460

Then fancy shapes, as fancy can,
   The grief my loss in him had wrought,
   A grief as deep as life or thought,
But stay'd in peace with God and man.

---

30 unwanted sheets of printed paper were used to stiffen book-spines
and line trunks.
31 Yule log: placed on fire on Christmas Eve.

32 'Tableaut vivants' (T.).
33 blind man's buff.
34 'Addressed to my brother Charles (Tennyson Turner)' (T.).

I make a picture in the brain;
  I hear the sentence that he speaks;
  He bears the burthen of the weeks,
But turns his burthen into gain.

His credit thus shall set me free;
  And, influence-rich to soothe and save,   1470
  Unused example from the grave,
Reach out dead hands to comfort me.

LXXIX

Could I have said while he was here,
'My love shall now no further range,
  There cannot come a mellower change,
For now is love mature in ear.'

Love, then, had hope of richer store:
  What end is here to my complaint?
  This haunting whisper makes me faint,
'More years had made me love thee more.'   1480

But Death returns an answer sweet:
  'My sudden frost was sudden gain,
  And gave all ripeness to the grain,
It might have drawn from after-heat.'

LXXX

I wage not any feud with Death
  For changes wrought on form and face;
  No lower life that earth's embrace
May breed with him, can fright my faith.

Eternal process moving on,
  From state to state the spirit walks;   1490
  And these are but the shatter'd stalks,
Or ruined chrysalis of one.

Nor blame I Death, because he bare
  The use of virtue out of earth;
  I know transplanted human worth
Will bloom to profit, otherwhere.

For this alone on Death I wreak
  The wrath that garners in my heart;
  He put our lives so far apart
We cannot hear each other speak.   1500

LXXXI

Dip down upon the northern shore,
  O sweet new-year delaying long;
  Thou doest expectant nature wrong;
Delaying long, delay no more.

What stays thee from the clouded noons,
  Thy sweetness from its proper place?

Can trouble live with April days,
  Or sadness in the summer moons?

Bring orchis, bring the foxglove spire,
  The little speedwell's darling blue,   1510
  Deep tulips dashed with fiery dew,
Laburnums, dropping-wells of fire.[35]

O thou, new-year, delaying long,
  Delayest the sorrow in my blood,
  That longs to burst a frozen bud
And flood a fresher throat with song.

LXXXII

When I contemplate all alone
  The life that had been thine below,
  And fix my thoughts on all the glow
To which thy crescent would have grown;   1520

I see thee sitting crowned with good,
  A central warmth diffusing bliss
  In glance and smile, and clasp and kiss,
On all the branches of thy blood;

Thy blood, my friend, and partly mine;
  For now the day was drawing on,
  When thou shouldst link thy life with one
Of mine own house, and boys of thine

Had babbled 'Uncle' on my knee;
  But that remorseless iron hour   1530
  Made cypress[36] of her orange flower,
Despair of Hope, and earth of thee.

I seem to meet their least desire,
  To clap their cheeks, to call them mine.
  I see their unborn faces shine
Beside the never-lighted fire.

I see myself an honour'd guest,
  Thy partner in the flowery walk
  Of letters, genial table-talk,
Or deep dispute, and graceful jest: 1540

While now thy prosperous labour fills
  The lips of men with honest praise,
  And sun by sun the happy days
Descend below the golden hills

With promise of a morn as fair;
  And all the train of bounteous hours
  Conduct by paths of growing powers,
To reverence and the silver hair;

Till slowly worn her earthly robe,
  Her lavish mission richly wrought,   1550

---

35   cf. (traditional-elegiac) flower passege in *Lycidas* 142–51, and Matthew Arnold's *Thyrsis* 61ff.

36   tree (and foliage) of mourning.

Leaving great legacies of thought,
Thy spirit should fail from off the globe;

What time mine own might also flee,
    As link'd with thine in love and fate,
    And, hovering o'er the dolorous strait
To the other shore, involved in thee,

Arrive at last the blessed goal,
    And he that died in Holy Land
    Would reach us out the shining hand,
And take us as a single soul.   1560

What reed was that on which I leant?
    Ah, backward fancy, wherefore wake
    The old bitterness again, and break
The low beginnings of content.

LXXXIII[37]

This truth came borne with bier and pall,
    I felt it, when I sorrow'd most,
    'Tis better to have loved and lost,
Than never to have loved at all –

O true in word, and tried in deed,
    Demanding, so to bring relief   1570
    To this which is our common grief,
What kind of life is that I lead;

And whether trust in things above
    Be dimmed of sorrow, or sustain'd;
    And whether love for him have drain'd
My capabilities of love;

Your words have virtue such as draws
    A faithful answer from the breast,
    Thro' light reproaches, half exprest,
And loyal unto kindly laws.   1580

My blood an even tenor kept,
    Till on mine ear this message falls,
    That in Vienna's fatal walls
God's finger touch'd him, and he slept.

The great Intelligences fair
    That range above our mortal state,
    In circle round the blessed gate,
Received and gave him welcome there;

And led him through the blissful climes,
    And show'd him in the fountain fresh   1590
    All knowledge that the sons of flesh
Shall gather in the cycled times.

But I remain'd, whose hopes were dim,
    Whose life, whose thoughts were little worth,

To wander on a darken'd earth,
Where all things round me breathed of him.

O friendship, equal-poised control,
    O heart, with kindliest motion warm,
    O sacred essence, other form,
O solemn ghost! O crownèd soul!   1600

Yet none could better know than I,
    How much of act at human hands
    The sense of human will demands,
By which we dare to live or die.

Whatever way my days decline,
    I felt and feel, though left alone,
    His being working in mine own,
The footsteps of his life in mine;

A life that all the Muses deck'd
    With gifts of grace that might express   1610
    All-comprehensive tenderness,
All-subtilising intellect:

And so my passion hath not swerved
    To works of weakness, but I find
    An image comforting the mind,
And in my grief a strength reserved.

Likewise the imaginative woe,
    That loved to handle spiritual strife,
    Diffused the shock through all my life,
But in the present broke the blow.   1620

My pulses therefore beat again
    For other friends that once I met;
    Nor can it suit me to forget
The mighty hopes that make us men.

I woo your love: I count it crime
    To mourn for any overmuch;
    I, the divided half of such
A friendship as had master'd Time;

Which masters Time indeed, and is
    Eternal, separate from fears.   1630
    The all-assuming months and years
Can take no part away from this:

But Summer on the steaming floods,
    And Spring that swells the narrow brooks,
    And Autumn, with a noise of rooks,
That gather in the waning woods,

And every pulse of wind and wave
    Recalls, in change of light or gloom,

---

37   Section dating from 1833, but revised after 1838(?) when T.
became engaged to Emily Sellwood.

My old affection of the tomb,
And my prime passion in the grave: 1640

My old affection of the tomb,
  A part of stillness, yearns to speak;
  'Arise, and get thee forth and seek
A friendship for the years to come.

I watch thee from the quiet shore;
  Thy spirit up to mine can reach;
  But in dear words of human speech
We two communicate no more.'

And I, 'Can clouds of nature stain
  The starry clearness of the free?   1650
  How is it? Canst thou feel for me
Some painless sympathy with pain?'

And lightly does the whisper fall;
  ''Tis hard for thee to fathom this;
  I triumph in conclusive bliss,
And that serene result of all.'

So hold I commerce with the dead;
  Or so methinks the dead would say;
  Or so shall grief with symbols play
And pining life be fancy-fed.   1660

Now looking to some settled end,
  That these things pass, and I shall prove
  A meeting somewhere, love with love,
I crave your pardon, O my friend;

If not so fresh, with love as true,
  I, clasping brother-hands, aver
  I could not, if I would, transfer
The whole I felt for him to you.

For which be they that hold apart
  The promise of the golden hours?   1670
  First love, first friendship, equal powers,
That marry with the virgin heart.

Still mine that cannot but deplore,[38]
  That beats within a lonely place,
  That yet remembers his embrace,
But at his footstep leaps no more,

My heart, tho' widowed, may not rest
  Quite in the love of what is gone,
  But seeks to beat in time with one
That warms another living breast.   1680

Ah, take the imperfect gift I bring,
  Knowing the primrose yet is dear,

The primrose of the later year,
  As not unlike to that of Spring.

LXXXIV

Sweet after showers, ambrosial air,
  That rollest from the gorgeous gloom
  Of evening over brake and bloom
And meadow, slowly breathing bare

The round of space, and rapt below
  Thro' all the dewy-tassell'd wood,   1690
  And shadowing down the horned flood
In ripples, fan my brows and blow

The fever from my cheek, and sigh
  The full new life that feeds thy breath
  Throughout my frame, till Doubt and Death,
Ill brethren, let the fancy fly

From belt to belt of crimson seas
  On leagues of odour streaming far,
  To where in yonder orient star
A hundred spirits whisper 'Peace.'   1700

LXXXV

I past beside the reverend walls
  In which of old I wore the gown;[39]
  I roved at random through the town,
And saw the tumult of the halls;

And heard once more in college fanes
  The storm their high-built organs make,
  And thunder-music, rolling, shake
The prophet blazon'd on the panes;

And caught once more the distant shout,
  The measured pulse of racing oars   1710
  Among the willows; paced the shores
And many a bridge, and all about

The same gray flats again, and felt
  The same, but not the same; and last
  Up that long walk of limes I past[40]
To see the rooms in which he dwelt.

Another name was on the door:
  I linger'd; all within was noise
  Of songs, and clapping hands, and boys
That crash'd the glass and beat the floor;   1720

Where once we held debate, a band
  Of youthful friends, on mind and art,
  And labour, and the changing mart,
And all the framework of the land;

---

38 mourn.
39 Trinity College, Cambridge.

40 Trinity College limes.

When one would aim an arrow fair,
   But send it slackly from the string;
   And one would pierce an outer ring,
And one an inner, here and there;

And last the master-bowman, he,
   Would cleave the mark. A willing ear   1730
   We lent him. Who, but hung to hear
The rapt oration flowing free

From point to point, with power and grace
   And music in the bounds of law,
   To those conclusions when we saw
The God within him light his face,

And seem to lift the form, and glow
   In azure orbits heavenly-wise;
   And over those ethereal eyes
The bar of Michael Angelo.[41]   1740

LXXXVI

Wild bird, whose warble, liquid sweet,
   Rings Eden through the budded quicks,
   O tell me where the senses mix,
O tell me where the passions meet,

Whence radiate: fierce extremes employ
   Thy spirits in the dusking leaf,
   And in the midmost heart of grief
Thy passion clasps a secret joy:

And I – my harp would prelude woe –
   I cannot all command the strings;   1750
   The glory of the sum of things
Will flash along the chords and go.

LXXXVII

Witch-elms that counterchange the floor
   Of this flat lawn with dusk and bright;
   And thou, with all thy breadth and height
Of foliage, towering sycamore;

How often, hither wandering down,
   My Arthur found your shadows fair,
   And shook to all the liberal air
The dust and din and steam of town: 1760

He brought an eye for all he saw;
   He mixt in all our simple sports;
   They pleased him, fresh from brawling courts
And dusty purlieus of the law.

O joy to him in this retreat,
   Immantled in ambrosial dark,

To drink the cooler air, and mark
The landscape winking through the heat:

O sound to rout the brood of cares,
   The sweep of scythe in morning dew,   1770
   The gust that round the garden flew,
And tumbled half the mellowing pears!

O bliss, when all in circle drawn
   About him, heart and ear were fed
   To hear him, as he lay and read
The Tuscan poets on the lawn:

Or in the all-golden afternoon
   A guest, or happy sister, sung,
   Or here she brought the harp and flung
A ballad to the brightening moon: 1780

Nor less it pleased in livelier moods,
   Beyond the bounding hill to stray,
   And break the livelong summer day
With banquet in the distant woods;

Whereat we glanced from theme to theme,
   Discuss'd the books to love or hate,
   Or touch'd the changes of the state,
Or threaded some Socratic dream;

But if I praised the busy town,
   He loved to rail against it still,   1790
   For 'ground in yonder social mill
We rub each other's angles down,

And merge' he said 'in form and gloss
   The picturesque of man and man.'
   We talk'd: the stream beneath us ran,
The wine-flask lying couch'd in moss,

Or cool'd within the glooming wave
   And last, returning from afar,
   Before the crimson-circled star
Had fall'n into her father's grave,   1800

And brushing ankle-deep in flowers,
   We heard behind the woodbine veil
   The milk that bubbl'd in the pail,
And buzzings of the honied hours.

LXXXVIII

He tasted love with half his mind,
   Nor ever drank the inviolate spring
   Where nighest heaven, who first could fling
This bitter seed among mankind;

---

41   T. remembers Hallam thinking the prominent ridge of forehead
bone over his eyes was like Michelangelo's ('surely I have the bar of
Michael Angelo!').

That could the dead, whose dying eyes
   Were closed with wail, resume their life,   1810
   They would but find in child and wife
An iron welcome when they rise:

'Twas well, indeed, when warm with wine,
   To pledge them with a kindly tear:
   To talk them o'er, to wish them here,
To count their memories half divine;

But if they came who past away,
   Behold their brides in other hands:
   The hard heir strides about their lands,
And will not yield them for a day.   1820

Yea, tho' their sons were none of these,
   Not less the yet-lov'd sire would make
   Confusion worse than death, and shake
The pillars of domestic peace.

Ah dear, but come thou back to me:
   Whatever change the years have wrought,
   I find not yet one lonely thought
That cries against my wish for thee.

LXXXIX

When rosy plumelets tuft the larch,
   And rarely pipes the mounted thrush;   1830
   Or underneath the barren bush
Flits by the sea-blue bird of March;

Come, wear the form by which I know
   Thy spirit in time among thy peers;
   The hope of unaccomplish'd years
Be large and lucid round thy brow.

When summer's hourly-mellowing change
   May breathe, with many roses sweet,
   Upon the thousand waves of wheat,
That ripple round the lonely grange;   1840

Come: not in watches of the night,
   But where the sunbeam broodeth warm,
   Come, beauteous in thine after form,
And like a finer light in light.

XC

If any vision should reveal
   Thy likeness, I might count it vain
   As but the canker of the brain;
Yea, though it spake and made appeal

To chances where our lots were cast
   Together in the days behind,   1850
   I might but say, I hear a wind
Of memory murmuring the past.

Yea, tho' it spake and bared to view
   A fact within the coming year;
   And tho' the months, revolving near,
Should prove the phantom-warning true,

They might not seem thy prophecies,
   But spiritual presentiments,
   And such refraction of events
As often rises ere they rise.   1860

XCI

I shall not see thee. Dare I say
   No spirit ever brake the band
   That stays him from the native land
Where first he walk'd when claspt in clay?

No visual shade of some one lost,
   But he, the Spirit himself, may come
   Where all the nerve of sense is numb;
Spirit to Spirit, Ghost to Ghost.

O, therefore from thy sightless range
   With gods in unconjectured bliss,   1870
   O, from the distance of the abyss
Of tenfold-complicated change,

Descend, and touch, and enter; hear
   The wish too strong for words to name;
   That in this blindness of the frame
My Ghost may feel that thine is near.

XCII

How pure at heart and sound in head,
   With what divine affections bold
   Should be the man whose thought would hold
An hour's communion with the dead.   1880

In vain shalt thou, or any, call
   The spirits from their golden day,
   Except, like them, thou too canst say,
My spirit is at peace with all.

They haunt the silence of the breast,
   Imaginations calm and fair,
   The memory like a cloudless air,
The conscience as a sea at rest:

But when the heart is full of din,
   And doubt beside the portal waits,   1890
   They can but listen at the gates,
And hear the household jar within.

XCIII[42]

By night we linger'd on the lawn,
   For underfoot the herb was dry;

---

42 possibly written 1841–2.

And genial warmth; and o'er the sky
The silvery haze of summer drawn;

And calm that let the tapers burn
   Unwavering: not a cricket chirr'd:
   The brook alone far-off was heard,
And on the board the fluttering urn: 1900

And bats went round in fragrant skies,
   And wheel'd or lit the filmy shapes
   That haunt the dusk, with ermine capes
And woolly breasts and beaded eyes;

While now we sang old songs that pealed
   From knoll to knoll, where, couch'd at ease,
   The white kine glimmer'd, and the trees
Laid their dark arms about the field.

But when those others, one by one,
   Withdrew themselves from me and night,   1910
   And in the house light after light
Went out, and I was all alone,

A hunger seized my heart; I read
   Of that glad year which once had been,
   In those fall'n leaves which kept their green,
The noble letters of the dead:

And strangely on the silence broke
   The silent-speaking words, and strange
   Was love's dumb cry defying change
To test his worth; and strangely spoke   1920

The faith, the vigour, bold to dwell
   On doubts that drive the coward back,
   And keen thro' wordy snares to track
Suggestion to her inmost cell.

So word by word, and line by line,[43]
   The dead man touch'd me from the past,
   And all at once it seem'd at last
His living soul was flash'd on mine,[44]

And mine in this was wound, and whirl'd
   About empyreal heights of thought,   1930
   And came on that which is, and caught
The deep pulsations of the world,

Æonian music measuring out
   The steps of Time – the shocks of Chance –
   The blows of Death. At length my trance
Was cancell'd, stricken through with doubt.

Vague words! but ah, how hard to frame
   In matter-moulded forms of speech,
   Or ev'n for intellect to reach
Thro' memory that which I became: 1940

Till now the doubtful dusk reveal'd
   The knolls once more where, couch'd at ease,
   The white kine glimmer'd, and the trees
Laid their dark arms about the field:

And suck'd from out the distant gloom
   A breeze began to tremble o'er
   The large leaves of the sycamore,
And fluctuate all the still perfume;

And gathering freshlier overhead,
   Rock'd the full-foliaged elms, and swung   1950
   The heavy-folded rose, and flung
The lilies to and fro, and said

'The dawn, the dawn,' and died away;
   And East and West, without a breath,
   Mixt their dim lights, like life and death,
To broaden into boundless day.

XCIV[45]

You say, but with no touch of scorn,
   Sweet-hearted, you, whose light-blue eyes
   Are tender over drowning flies,
You tell me, doubt is Devil-born.   1960

I know not: one indeed I knew[46]
   In many a subtle question versed,
   Who touched a jarring lyre at first,
But ever strove to make it true:

Perplext in faith, but pure in deeds,
   At last he beat his music out.
   There lives more faith in honest doubt,
Believe me, than in half the creeds.

He fought his doubts and gather'd strength,
   He would not make his judgment blind,   1970
   He faced the spectres of the mind
And laid them: thus he came at length

To find a stronger faith his own;
   And Power was with him in the night,
   Which makes the darkness and the light,
And dwells not in the light alone,

But in the darkness and the cloud,
   As over Sinaï's peaks of old,

43 cf. Isaiah 28.13: 'the word of the Lord … precept upon precept; line upon line'.

44 *His* later amended to *The* (T. troubled by blur of God and Hallam).

45 one of the poem's late, doubt-filled, additions.

46 Arthur Hallam.

While Israel made their gods of gold,
Altho' the trumpet blew so loud.   1980

XCV

My love has talk'd with rocks and trees;
  He finds on misty mountain-ground
  His own vast shadow glory-crown'd,
He sees himself in all he sees.

Two partners of a married life –
  I look'd on these and thought of thee
  In vastness and in mystery,
And of my spirit as of a wife.

These two – they dwelt with eye on eye,
  Their hearts of old have beat in tune,   1990
  Their meetings made December June,
Their every parting was to die.

Their love has never past away;
  The days she never can forget
  Are earnest[47] that he loves her yet,
Whate'er the faithless people say.

Her life is lone, he sits apart,
  He loves her yet, she will not weep,
  Tho' rapt in matters dark and deep
He seems to slight her simple heart.   2000

He thrids the labyrinth of the mind,
  He reads the secret of the star,
  He seems so near and yet so far,
He looks so cold: she thinks him kind.

She keeps the gift of years before,
  A wither'd violet is her bliss:
  She knows not what his greatness is,
For that, for all, she loves him more.

For him she plays, to him she sings
  Of early faith and plighted vows;   2010
  She knows but matters of the house,
And he, he knows a thousand things.

Her faith is fixt and cannot move,
  She darkly feels him great and wise,
  She dwells on him with faithful eyes,
'I cannot understand: I love.'

XCVI

You[48] leave us: you will see the Rhine,
  And those fair hills I sailed below,
  When I was there with him; and go
By summer belts of wheat and vine   2020

To where he breathed his latest breath,
  That City. All her splendour seems
  No livelier than the wisp that gleams
On Lethe in the eyes of Death.

Let her great Danube rolling fair
  Enwind her isles, unmarked of me:
  I have not seen, I will not see
Vienna; rather dream that there,

A treble darkness, evil haunts
  The birth, the bridal; friend from friend   2030
  Is oftener parted, fathers bend
Above more graves, a thousand wants

Gnarr[49] at the heels of men, and prey
  By each cold hearth, and sadness flings
  Her shadow on the blaze of kings:
And yet myself have heard him say,

That not in any mother town
  With statelier progress to and fro
  The double tides of chariots flow
By park and suburb under brown   2040

Of lustier leaves; nor more content,
  He told me, lives in any crowd,
  When all is gay with lamps, and loud
With sport and song, in booth and tent,

Imperial halls, or open plain;
  And wheels the circled dance, and breaks
  The rocket molten into flakes
Of crimson or in emerald rain.

XCVII

Risest thou thus, dim dawn, again,
  So loud with voices of the birds,   2050
  So thick with lowings of the herds,
Day, when I lost the flower of men;

Who tremblest thro' thy darkling red
  On you swoll'n brook that bubbles fast
  By meadows breathing of the past,
And woodlands holy to the dead;

Who murmurest in the foliaged eaves
  A song that slights the coming care,
  And Autumn laying here and there
A fiery finger on the leaves;   2060

Who wakenest with thy balmy breath
  To myriads on the genial earth,
  Memories of bridal, or of birth,
And unto myriads more, of death.

---

47 guarantee.
48 apparently, T.'s brother Charles (with reference to his Rhine
honeymoon, 1836).

49 'snarl' (T.).

O, wheresoever those may be,
   Betwixt the slumber of the poles,
   To-day they count as kindred souls;
They know me not, but mourn with me.

XCVIII

I wake, I rise: from end to end
   Of all the landscape underneath,   2070
   I find no place that does not breathe
Some gracious memory of my friend:

No gray old grange, or lonely fold,
   Or low morass and whispering reed,
   Or simple stile from mead to mead,
Or sheepwalk up the windy wold;

Nor hoary knoll of ash and haw
   That hears the latest linnet trill,
   Nor quarry trench'd along the hill
And haunted by the wrangling daw;   2080

Nor runlet tinkling from the rock;
   Nor pastoral rivulet that swerves
   To left and right thro' meadowy curves,
That feed the mothers of the flock;

But each has pleased a kindred eye,
   And each reflects a kindlier day;
   And, leaving these, to pass away,
I think once more he seems to die.

XCIX

Unwatch'd, the garden bough shall sway,
   The tender blossom flutter down,   2090
   Unloved that beech will gather brown,
This maple burn itself away;

Unloved, the sun-flower, shining fair,
   Ray round with flames her disk of seed,
   And many a rose-carnation feed
With summer spice the humming air;

Unloved, by many a sandy bar,
   The brook shall babble down the plain,
   At noon or when the lesser wain
Is twisting round the polar star;   2100

Uncared for, gird the windy grove,
   And flood the haunts of hern and crake;
   Or into silver arrows break
The sailing moon in creek and cove;

Till from the garden and the wild
   A fresh association blow,
   And year by year the landscape grow
Familiar to the stranger's child;

As year by year the labourer tills
   His wonted glebe, or lops the glades;   2110
   And year by year our memory fades
From all the circle of the hills.

C

We leave the well-beloved place
   Where first we gazed upon the sky;
   The roofs, that heard our earliest cry,
Will shelter one of stranger race.

We go, but ere we go from home,
   As down the garden-walks I move,
   Two spirits of a diverse love
Contend for loving masterdom.   2120

One whispers, here thy boyhood sung
   Long since its matin song, and heard
   The low love-language of the bird
In native hazels tassel-hung.

The other answers, 'Yea, but here
   Thy feet have stray'd in after hours
   With thy lost friend among the bowers,
And this hath made them trebly dear.'

These two have striven half the day,
   And each prefers his separate claim,   2130
   Poor rivals in a losing game,
That will not yield each other way.

I turn to go: my feet are set
   To leave the pleasant fields and farms;
   They mix in one another's arms
To one pure image of regret.

CI

On that last night before we went
   From out the doors where I was bred,
   I dream'd a vision of the dead,
Which left my after morn content.   2140

Methought I dwelt within a hall,
   And maidens with me: distant hills
   From hidden summits fed with rills
A river sliding by the wall.

The hall with harp and carol rang.
   They sang of what is wise and good
   And graceful. In the centre stood
A statue veiled, to which they sang;

And which, tho' veil'd, was known to me,
   The shape of him I loved, and love   2150
   For ever: then flew in a dove
And brought a summons from the sea:[50]

---

50   'eternity' (T.).

And when they learnt that I must go
  They wept and wail'd, but led the way
  To where a little shallop lay
At anchor in the flood below;

And on by many a level mead,
  And shadowing bluff that made the banks,
  We glided winding under ranks
Of iris, and the golden reed;   2160

And still as vaster grew the shore
  And roll'd the floods in grander space,
  The maidens gather'd strength and grace
And presence, lordlier than before;[51]

And I myself, who sat apart
  And watch'd them, waxed in every limb;
  I felt the thews of Anakim,[52]
The pulses of a Titan's heart;

As one would sing the death of war,
  And one would chant the history   2170
  Of that great race, which is to be,
And one the shaping of a star;[53]

Until the forward-creeping tides
  Began to foam, and we to draw
  From deep to deep, to where we saw
A great ship lift her shining sides.

The man we loved was there on deck,
  But thrice as large as man he bent
  To greet us. Up the side I went,
And fell in silence on his neck: 2180

Whereat those maidens with one mind
  Bewail'd their lot; I did them wrong:
  'We served thee here,' they said, 'so long,
And wilt thou leave us now behind?'

So rapt I was, they could not win
  An answer from my lips, but he
  Replying, 'Enter likewise ye
And go with us:' they entered in.

And while the wind began to sweep
  A music out of sheet and shroud,   2190
  We steer'd her toward a crimson cloud
That landlike slept along the deep.

CII

The time draws near the birth of Christ;
  The moon is hid, the night is still;

A single church below the hill[54]
Is pealing, folded in the mist.

A single peal of bells below,
  That wakens at this hour of rest
  A single murmur in the breast,
That these are not the bells I know.   220

Like strangers' voices here they sound,
  In lands where not a memory strays,
  Nor landmark breathes of other days,
But all is new unhallowed ground.[55]

CIII[56]

This holly by the cottage-eave,
  To night, ungather'd, shall it stand:
  We live within the stranger's land,
And strangely falls our Christmas-eve.

Our father's dust is left alone
  And silent under other snows: 2210
  There in due time the woodbine blows,
The violet comes, but we are gone.

No more shall wayward grief abuse
  The genial hour with mask and mime;
  For change of place, like growth of time,
Has broke the bond of dying use.

Let cares that petty shadows cast,
  By which our lives are chiefly proved,
  A little spare the night I loved,
And hold it solemn to the past.   2220

But let no footstep beat the floor,
  Nor bowl of wassail mantle warm;[57]
  For who would keep an ancient form
Through which the spirit breathes no more?

Be neither song, nor game, nor feast;
  Nor harp be touch'd, nor flute be blown;
  No dance, no motion, save alone
What lightens in the lucid east

Of rising worlds by yonder wood.
  Long sleeps the summer in the seed;   2230
  Run out your measur'd arcs, and lead
The closing cycle rich in good.

CIV

Ring out, wild bells, to the wild sky,
  The flying cloud, the frosty light:

---

51 'The progress of the Age' (T.).
52 the giants of Deuteronomy 2.10.
53 'The great hopes of humanity and science' (T.).
54 'Waltham Abbey church' (T.).

55 'High Beech, Epping Forest (where we were living)' (T.).
56 Christmas 1837 at High Beech.
57 i.e. don't bother to keep a bowl of Christmas punch warm.

The year is dying in the night;
Ring out, wild bells, and let him die.

Ring out the old, ring in the new,
　　Ring, happy bells, across the snow:
　　The year is going, let him go;
Ring out the false, ring in the true.　　　　　　2240

Ring out the grief that saps the mind,
　　For those that here we see no more;
　　Ring out the feud of rich and poor,
Ring in redress to all mankind.

Ring out a slowly dying cause,
　　And ancient forms of party strife;
　　Ring in the nobler modes of life,
With sweeter manners, purer laws.

Ring out the want, the care, the sin,
　　The faithless coldness of the times;　　　　2250
　　Ring out, ring out my mournful rhymes,
But ring the fuller minstrel in.

Ring out false pride in place and blood,
　　The civic slander and the spite;
　　Ring in the love of truth and right,
Ring in the common love of good.

Ring out old shapes of foul disease;
　　Ring out the narrowing lust of gold;
　　Ring out the thousand wars of old,
Ring in the thousand years of peace.[58]　　　2260

Ring in the valiant man and free,
　　The larger heart, the kindlier hand;
　　Ring out the darkness of the land,
Ring in the Christ that is to be.[59]

CV

It is the day when he was born,[60]
　　A bitter day that early sank
　　Behind a purple-frosty bank
Of vapour, leaving night forlorn.

The time admits not flowers or leaves
　　To deck the banquet. Fiercely flies　　　　2270
　　The blast of North and East, and ice
Makes daggers at the sharpen'd eaves,

And bristles all the brakes and thorns
　　To yon hard crescent, as she hangs
　　Above the wood which grides and clangs
Its leafless ribs and iron horns

Together, in the drifts that pass
　　To darken on the rolling brine

That breaks the coast. But fetch the wine,
Arrange the board and brim the glass;　　　　2280

Bring in great logs and let them lie,
　　To make a solid core of heat;
　　Be cheerful-minded, talk and treat
Of all things ev'n as he were by:

We keep the day. With festal cheer,
　　With books and music, surely we
　　Will drink to him, whate'er he be,
And sing the songs he loved to hear.

CVI

I will not shut me from my kind,
　　And, lest I stiffen into stone,　　　　　　2290
　　I will not eat my heart alone,
Nor feed with sighs a passing wind:

What profit lies in barren faith,
　　And vacant yearning, tho' with might
　　To scale the heaven's highest height,
Or dive below the wells of Death?

What find I in the highest place,
　　But mine own phantom chanting hymns?
　　And on the depths of death there swims
The reflex of a human face.　　　　　　　　2300

I'll rather take what fruit may be
　　Of sorrow under human skies:
　　'Tis held that sorrow makes us wise,
Whatever wisdom sleep with thee.

CVII

Heart-affluence in discursive talk
　　From household fountains never dry;
　　The critic clearness of an eye,
That saw thro' all the Muses' walk;

Seraphic intellect and force
　　To seize and throw the doubts of man;　　　2310
　　Impassion'd logic, which outran
The hearer in its fiery course;

High nature amorous of the good,
　　But touch'd with no ascetic gloom;
　　And passion pure in snowy bloom
Thro' all the years of April blood;

A love of freedom rarely felt,
　　Of freedom in her regal seat
　　Of England; not the schoolboy heat,
The blind hysterics of the Celt;　　　　　　2320

58　the millennium of Revelation 20.
59　'The broader Christianity of the future' (T.).

60　'February 1, 1811' (T.).

And manhood fused with female grace
   In such a sort, the child would twine
   A trustful hand, unasked, in thine,
And find his comfort in thy face;

All these have been, and thee mine eyes
   Have look'd on: if they look'd in vain,
   My shame is greater who remain,
Nor let thy wisdom make me wise.

CVIII

Thy converse drew us with delight,
   The men of rathe[61] and riper years: 2330
   The feeble soul, a haunt of fears,
Forgot his weakness in thy sight.

On thee the loyal-hearted hung,
   The proud was half disarm'd of pride,
   Nor cared the serpent at thy side
To flicker with his double tongue.

The stern were mild when thou wert by,
   The flippant put himself to school
   And heard thee, and the brazen fool
Was soften'd, and he knew not why;   2340

While I, thy nearest, sat apart,
   And felt thy triumph was as mine;
   And loved them more, that they were thine,
The graceful tact, the Christian art;

Nor mine the sweetness or the skill,
   But mine the love that will not tire,
   And, born of love, the vague desire
That spurs an imitative will.

CIX

The churl in spirit, up or down
   Along the scale of ranks, thro' all,   2350
   To who may grasp a golden ball
By blood a king, at heart a clown;

The churl in spirit, howe'er he veil
   His want in forms for fashion's sake,
   Will let his coltish nature break
At seasons thro' the gilded pale:

For who can always act? but he,
   To whom a thousand memories call,
   Not being less but more than all
The gentleness he seem'd to be,   2360

So wore his outward best, and join'd
   Each office of the social hour
   To noble manners, as the flower
And native growth of noble mind;

Nor ever narrowness or spite,
   Or villain fancy fleeting by,
   Drew in the expression of an eye,
Where God and Nature met in light,

And thus he bore without abuse
   The grand old name of gentleman,   2370
   Defamed by every charlatan,
And soiled with all ignoble use.

CX

High wisdom holds my wisdom less,
   That I, who gaze with temperate eyes
   On glorious insufficiencies,
Set light by narrower perfectness.

But thou, that fillest all the room
   Of all my love, art reason why
   I seem to cast a careless eye
On souls, the lesser lords of doom.   2380

For what wert thou? some novel power
   Sprang up for ever at a touch,
   And hope could never hope too much,
In watching thee from hour to hour,

Large elements in order brought,
   And tracts of calm from tempest made,
   And world-wide fluctuation sway'd
In vassal tides that followed thought.

CXI

'Tis held that sorrow makes us wise;
   Yet how much wisdom sleeps with thee   2390
   Which not alone had guided me,
But served the seasons that may rise;

For can I doubt, who knew thee keen
   In intellect, with force and skill
   To strive, to fashion, to fulfil –
I doubt not what thou wouldst have been:

A life in civic action warm,
   A soul on highest mission sent,
   A potent voice of Parliament,
A pillar steadfast in the storm,   2400

Should licensed boldness gather force,
   Becoming, when the time has birth,
   A lever to uplift the earth
And roll it in another course,

With many shocks that come and go,
   With agonies, with energies,
   With overthrowings, and with cries,
And undulations to and fro.

---

61   early.

CXII

Who loves not knowledge? Who shall rail
    Against her beauty? May she mix   2410
    With men and prosper! Who shall fix
Her pillars? Let her work prevail.

But on her forehead sits a fire:
    She sets her forward countenance
    And leaps into the future chance,
Submitting all things to desire.

Half-grown as yet, a child, and vain –
    She cannot fight the fear of death.
    What is she, cut from love and faith,
But some wild Pallas[62] from the brain   2420

Of Demons? fiery-hot to burst
    All barriers in her onward race
    For power. Let her know her place;
She is the second, not the first.

A higher hand must make her mild,
    If all be not in vain; and guide
    Her footsteps, moving side by side
With wisdom, like the younger child:

For she is earthly of the mind,
    But wisdom heavenly of the soul.   2430
    O, friend, who camest to thy goal
So early, leaving me behind,

I would the great world grew like thee,
    Who grewest not alone in power
    And knowledge, but by year and hour
In reverence and in charity.

CXIII

Now fades the last long streak of snow,
    Now burgeons every maze of quick
    About the flowering squares, and thick
By ashen roots the violets blow.   2440

Now rings the woodland loud and long,
    The distance takes a lovelier hue,
    And drown'd in yonder living blue
The lark becomes a sightless song.

Now dance the lights on lawn and lea,
    The flocks are whiter down the vale,
    And milkier every milky sail
On winding stream or distant sea;

Where now the seamew pipes, or dives
    In yonder greening gleam, and fly   2450

The happy birds, that change their sky
To build and brood; that live their lives

From land to land; and in my breast
    Spring wakens too; and my regret
    Becomes an April violet,
And buds and blossoms like the rest.

CXIV

Is it, then, regret for buried time
    That keenlier in sweet April wakes,
    And meets the year, and gives and takes
The colours of the crescent prime?   2460

Not all: the songs, the stirring air,
    The life re-orient out of dust,
    Cry thro' the sense to hearten trust
In that which made the world so fair.

Not all regret: the face will shine
    Upon me, while I muse alone;
    And that dear, dear voice that I have known
Still speak to me of me and mine:

Yet less of sorrow lives in me
    For days of happy commune dead;   2470
    Less yearning for the friendship fled,
Than some strong bond which is to be.

CXV

O days and hours, your work is this
    To hold me from my proper place,
    A little while from his embrace,
For fuller gain of after bliss:

That out of distance might ensue
    Desire of nearness doubly sweet;
    And unto meeting, when we meet,
Delight a hundredfold accrue,   2480

For every grain of sand that runs,
    And every span of shade that steals,
    And every kiss of toothed wheels,
And all the courses of the suns.

CXVI[63]

Contemplate all this work of Time,
    The giant labouring in his youth;
    Nor dream of human love and truth,
As dying Nature's earth and lime;

But trust that those we call the dead
    Are breathers of an ampler day   2490
    For ever nobler ends. They say,
The solid earth whereon we tread

---

62   or Minerva, Roman goddess of wisdom, arts, trades; fabled to
have sprung, fully armed, from head of Jupiter.

63   written after C. Lyell, *Principles of Geology* (1837), but before
R. Chambers, *Vestiges of Creation* (1844).

In tracts of fluent heat began,
  And grew to seeming-random forms,
  The seeming prey of cyclic storms,
Till at the last arose the man;

Who throve and branch'd from clime to clime,
  The herald of a higher race,
  And of himself in higher place,
If so he type this work of time   2500

Within himself, from more to more;
  Or, crown'd with attributes of woe
  Like glories, move his course, and show
That life is not as idle ore,

But iron dug from central gloom,
  And heated hot with burning fears,
  And dipp'd in baths of hissing tears,
And batter'd with the shocks of doom

To shape and use. Arise and fly
  The reeling Faun, the sensual feast;   2510
  Move upward, working out the beast,
And let the ape and tiger die.

CXVII

Doors, where my heart was used to beat
  So quickly, not as one that weeps
  I come once more; the city sleeps;
I smell the meadow in the street;

I hear a chirp of birds; I see
  Betwixt the black fronts long-withdrawn
  A light-blue lane of early dawn,
And think of early days and thee,   2520

And bless thee, for thy lips are bland,
  And bright the friendship of thine eye;
  And in my thoughts with scarce a sigh
I take the pressure of thine hand.

CXVIII

I trust I have not wasted breath:
  I think we are not wholly brain,
  Magnetic mockeries; not in vain,
Like Paul with beasts, I fought with Death;[64]

Not only cunning casts in clay:
  Let Science prove we are, and then   2530
  What matters Science unto men,
At least to me? I would not stay.

Let him, the wiser man who springs
  Hereafter, up from childhood shape

His action like the greater ape,
  But I was born to other things.

CXIX

Sad Hesper[65] o'er the buried sun
  And ready, thou, to die with him,
  Thou watchest all things ever dim
And dimmer, and a glory done: 2540

The team is loosen'd from the wain,[66]
  The boat is drawn upon the shore;
  Thou listenest to the closing door,
And life is darken'd in the brain.

Bright Phosphor,[67] fresher for the night,
  By thee the world's great work is heard
  Beginning, and the wakeful bird;
Behind thee comes the greater light:

The market boat is on the stream,
  And voices hail it from the brink;   2550
  Thou hear'st the village hammer clink,
And see'st the moving of the team.

Sweet Hesper-Phosphor, double name
  For what is one, the first, the last,
  Thou, like my present and my past,
Thy place is changed; thou art the same.

CXX

Oh, wast thou with me, dearest, then,
  While I rose up against my doom,
  And yearned to burst the folded gloom,
To bare the eternal Heavens again,   2560

To feel once more, in placid awe,
  The strong imagination roll
  A sphere of stars about my soul,
In all her motion one with law;

If thou wert with me, and the grave
  Divide us not, be with me now,
  And enter in at breast and brow,
Till all my blood, a fuller wave,

Be quicken'd with a livelier breath,
  And like an inconsiderate boy,   2570
  As in the former flash of joy,
I slip the thoughts of life and death;

And all the breeze of Fancy blows,
  And every dew-drop paints a bow,
  The wizard lightnings deeply glow,
And every thought breaks out a rose.

---

64 1 Corinthians 15.32.
65 Hesperus, Evening Star (planet Venus).

66 team of horses/oxen; wagon/cart.
67 Phosphorus, 'light-bringer', Greek morning-star (Roman Lucifer).

CXXI[68]

There rolls the deep where grew the tree.
　O earth, what changes hast thou seen!
　There where the long street roars, hath been
The stillness of the central sea.　　　　　　2580

The hills are shadows, and they flow
　From form to form, and nothing stands;
　They melt like mist, the solid lands,
Like clouds they shape themselves and go.

But in my spirit will I dwell,
　And dream my dream, and hold it true;
　For tho' my lips may breathe adieu,
I cannot think the thing farewell.

CXXII

That which we dare invoke to bless;
　Our dearest faith; our ghastliest doubt;　　　2590
　He, They, One, All; within, without;
The Power in darkness whom we guess;

I found Him not in world or sun,
　Or eagle's wing, or insect's eye;
　Nor thro' the questions men may try,
The petty cobwebs we have spun:

If e'er when faith had fall'n asleep,
　I heard a voice 'believe no more'
　And heard an ever-breaking shore
That tumbled in the Godless deep;　　　　　2600

A warmth within the breast would melt
　The freezing reason's colder part,
　And like a man in wrath the heart
Stood up and answered 'I have felt.'

No, like a child in doubt and fear:
　But that blind clamour made me wise;
　Then was I as a child that cries,
But, crying, knows his father near;

And what I seem beheld again
　What is, and no man understands;　　　　　2610
　And out of darkness came the hands
That reach thro' nature, moulding men.

CXXIII

Whatever I have said or sung,
　Some bitter notes my harp would give,
　Yea, tho' there often seem'd to live
A contradiction on the tongue,

Yet Hope had never lost her youth;
　She did but look thro' dimmer eyes;
　Or Love but play'd with gracious lies,
Because he felt so fix'd in truth:　　　　　2620

And if the song were full of care,
　He breathed the spirit of the song;
　And if the words were sweet and strong
He set his royal signet there;

Abiding with me till I sail
　To seek thee on the mystic deeps,
　And this electric force, that keeps
A thousand pulses dancing, fail.

CXXIV

Love is and was my Lord and King,
　And in his presence I attend　　　　　　2630
　To hear the tidings of my friend,
Which every hour his couriers bring.

Love is and was my King and Lord,
　And will be, tho' as yet I keep
　Within his court on earth, and sleep
Encompass'd by his faithful guard,

And hear at times a sentinel
　Who moves about from place to place,
　And whispers to the vast of space
Among the worlds, that all is well.　　　　　2640

CXXV

And all is well, tho' faith and form
　Be sunder'd in the night of fear;
　Well roars the storm to those that hear
A deeper voice across the storm,

Proclaiming social truth shall spread,
　And justice, ev'n tho' thrice again
　The red fool-fury of the Seine
Should pile her barricades with dead.

But ill for him that wears a crown,
　And him, the lazar, in his rags:　　　　　2650
　They tremble, the sustaining crags;
The spires of ice are toppled down,

And molten up, and roar in flood;
　The fortress crashes from on high,
　The brute earth lightens to the sky,
And the vast Æon sinks in blood,

And compass'd by the fires of Hell;
　While thou, dear spirit, happy star,
　O'erlook'st the tumult from afar,
And smilest, knowing all is well.　　　　　2660

CXXVI

The love that rose on stronger wings,
　Unpalsied when he met with Death,

68　see note to CXVI.

Is comrade of the lesser faith
That sees the course of human things.

No doubt vast eddies in the flood
   Of onward time shall yet be made,
   And throned races may degrade;
Yet O ye ministers of good,

Wild Hours that fly with Hope and Fear,
   If all your office had to do   2670
   With old results that look like new;
If this were all your mission here,

To draw, to sheathe a useless sword,
   To fool the crowd with glorious lies,
   To cleave a creed in sects and cries,
To change the bearing of a word,

To shift an arbitrary power,
   To cramp the student at his desk,
   To make old bareness picturesque
And tuft with grass a feudal tower;   2680

Why then my scorn might well descend
   On you and yours. I see in part
   That all, as in some piece of art,
Is toil cooperant to an end.

CXXVII

Dear friend, far off, my lost desire,
   So far, so near in woe and weal;
   O loved the most, when most I feel
There is a lower and a higher;

Known and unknown; human, divine!
   Sweet human hand and lips and eye;   2690
   Dear heavenly friend that canst not die,
Mine, mine, for ever, ever mine!

Strange friend, past, present, and to be,
   Loved deeplier, darklier understood;
   Behold I dream a dream of good,
And mingle all the world with thee.

CXXVIII

Thy voice is on the rolling air;
   I hear thee where the waters run;
   Thou standest in the rising sun,
And in the setting thou art fair.   2700

What art thou then? I cannot guess;
   But tho' I seem in star and flower
   To feel thee, some diffusive power,
I do not therefore love thee less:

My love involves the love before;
   My love is vaster passion now;
   Tho' mix'd with God and Nature thou,
I seem to love thee more and more.

Far off thou art, but ever nigh;
   I have thee still, and I rejoice;   2710
   I prosper, circled with thy voice;
I shall not lose thee though I die.

CXXIX

O living will that shalt endure
   When all that seems shall suffer shock,
   Rise in the spiritual rock,
Flow thro' our deeds and make them pure,

That we may lift from out of dust
   A voice as unto him that hears,
   A cry above the conquer'd years
To one that with us works, and trust   2720

With faith that comes of self-control,
   The truths that never can be proved
   Until we close with all we loved,
And all we flow from, soul in soul.

⸻

O true and tried, so well and long,[69]
   Demand not thou a marriage lay;
   In that it is thy marriage day
Is music more than any song.

Nor have I felt so much of bliss
   Since first he told me that he loved   2730
   A daughter of our house; nor proved
Since that dark day a day like this;

Tho' I since then have number'd o'er
   Some thrice three years: they went and came,
   Remade the blood and changed the frame,
And yet is love not less, but more;

No longer caring to embalm
   In dying songs a dead regret,
   But like a statue solid-set,
And moulded in colossal calm.   2740

Regret is dead, but love is more
   Than in the summers that are flown,
   For I myself with these have grown
To something greater than before;

Which makes appear the songs I made
   As echoes out of weaker times,

69 Section labelled 'Epilogue' by A. C. Bradley, later; originally
untitled. Describes marriage of T.'s sister Cecilia to his great friend
Edmund Lushington, 10 October 1842.

As half but idle brawling rhymes,
The sport of random sun and shade.

But where is she, the bridal flower,
   That must be made a wife ere noon?   2750
   She enters, glowing like the moon
Of Eden on its bridal bower:

On me she bends her blissful eyes
   And then on thee; they meet thy look
   And brighten like the star that shook
Betwixt the palms of paradise.

O when her life was yet in bud,
   He too foretold the perfect rose.
   For thee she grew, for thee she grows
For ever, and as fair as good.   2760

And thou[70] art worthy; full of power;
   As gentle; liberal-minded, great,
   Consistent; wearing all that weight
Of learning lightly like a flower.

But now set out: the noon is near,
   And I must give away the bride;
   She fears not, or with thee beside
And me behind her, will not fear:

For I that danced her on my knee,
   That watch'd her on her nurse's arm,   2770
   That shielded all her life from harm
At last must part with her to thee;

Now waiting to be made a wife,
   Her feet, my darling, on the dead;
   Their pensive tablets round her head,
And the most living words of life

Breathed in her ear. The ring is on,
   The 'wilt thou' answer'd, and again
   The 'wilt thou' ask'd, till out of twain
Her sweet 'I will' has made ye one.   2780

Now sign your names, which shall be read,
   Mute symbols of a joyful morn
   By village eyes as yet unborn;
The names are sign'd, and overhead

Begins the clash and clang that tells
   The joy to every wandering breeze;
   The blind wall rocks, and on the trees
The dead leaf trembles to the bells.

O happy hour, and happier hours
   Await them. Many a merry face   2790

Salutes them – maidens of the place,
That pelt us in the porch with flowers.

O happy hour, behold the bride
   With him to whom her hand I gave.
   They leave the porch, they pass the grave
That has today it's[71] sunny side.

Today the grave is bright for me,
   For them the light of life increas'd,
   Who stay to share the morning feast,
Who rest to-night beside the sea.   2800

Let all my genial spirits advance
   To meet and greet a whiter sun;
   My drooping memory will not shun
The foaming grape of eastern France.[72]

It circles round, and fancy plays,
   And hearts are warm'd and faces bloom,
   As drinking health to bride and groom
We wish them store of happy days.

Nor count me all to blame if I
   Conjecture of a stiller guest,   2810
   Perchance, perchance, among the rest,
And, tho' in silence, wishing joy.

But they must go, the time draws on,
   And those white-favour'd horses[73] wait;
   They rise, but linger; it is late;
Farewell, we kiss, and they are gone.

A shade falls on us like the dark
   From little cloudlets on the grass,
   But sweeps away as out we pass
To range the woods, to roam the park,   2820

Discussing how their courtship grew,
   And talk of others that are wed,
   And how she look'd and what he said,
And back we come at fall of dew.

Again the feast, the speech, the glee,
   The shade of passing thought, the wealth
   Of words and wit, the double health,
The crowning cup, the three times three,[74]

And last the dance; – till I retire:
   Dumb is that tower which spake so loud,   2830
   And high in heaven the streaming cloud,
And on the downs a rising fire:

And rise, O moon, from yonder down,
   Till over down and over dale

---

70 Lushington.
71 it's: *sic.*
72 champagne?

73 wearing white favours, i.e. ribbons.
74 'Hip-hip-hooray', three times.

All night the shining vapour sail
And pass the silent-lighted town,

The white-faced halls, the glancing rills,
   And catch at every mountain head,
   And o'er the friths that branch and spread
Their sleeping silver thro' the hills;   2840

And touch with shade the bridal doors,
   With tender gloom the roof, the wall;
   And breaking let the splendour fall
To spangle all the happy shores

By which they rest, and ocean sounds,
   And, star and system rolling past,
   A soul shall draw from out the vast
And strike his being into bounds,

And, moved thro' life of lower phase,[75]
   Result in man, be born and think,   2850

And act and love, a closer link
Betwixt us and the crowning race

Of those that, eye to eye, shall look
   On knowledge; under whose command
   Is Earth and Earth's, and in their hand
Is Nature like an open book;

No longer half-akin to brute,
   For all we thought and loved and did,
   And hoped, and suffer'd, is but seed
Of what in them is flower and fruit;   2860

Whereof the man, that with me trod
   This planet, was a noble type
   Appearing ere the times were ripe,
That friend of mine who lives in God,

That God, which ever lives and loves,
   One God, one law, one element,
   And one far-off divine event,
To which the whole creation moves.

Written October 1833–50. In Memoriam *(Anon.) (Edward Moxon, 1850).*
Text of first published edition. A few changes and additions were made subsequently.

ODE ON THE DEATH OF THE DUKE OF WELLINGTON[1]

I
Let us bury the Great Duke
   With an empire's lamentation,
Let us bury the Great Duke
   To the noise of the mourning of a mighty nation,

Mourning when their leaders fall,
Warriors carry the warrior's pall,
And sorrow darkens hamlet and hall.

II
Where shall we lay the man whom we deplore?[2]
He died on Walmer's lonely shore,
But here, in streaming London's central roar.   10
Let the sound of those he wrought for,
And the feet of those he fought for,
Echo round his bones for evermore.

III
Lead out the pageant: sad and slow,
As fits an universal woe,
Let the long long procession go,
And let the sorrowing crowd about it grow,

75 strong suggestions at the end of the poem of evolutionary optim-
ism – foetal, individual, tribal – of R. Chambers, *Vestiges of Creation*
(1844).

ODE ON THE DEATH OF THE DUKE OF WELLINGTON
1 died, 14 September 1852: buried, St Paul's Cathedral, 18 November
1852.
2 lament.

And let the mournful martial music blow;
The last great Englishman is low.

IV

Mourn, for to us he seems the last,   20
Remembering all his greatness in the Past.
No more in soldier fashion will he greet
With lifted hand the gazer in the street.
O friends, our chief state-oracle is mute:
Mourn for the man of long-enduring blood,
The statesman-warrior, moderate, resolute,
Whole in himself, a common good.
Mourn for the man of amplest influence,
Yet clearest of ambitious crime,
Our greatest yet with least pretence,   30
Great in council and great in war,
Foremost captain of his time,
Rich in saving common-sense,
And, as the greatest only are,
In his simplicity sublime.
O good gray head which all men knew,
O voice from which their omens all men drew,
O iron nerve to true occasion true,
O fallen at length that tower of strength
Which stood four-square to all the winds that blew!   40
Such was he whom we deplore.
The long self-sacrifice of life is o'er.
The great World-victor's victor[3] will be seen no more.

V

All is over and done:
Render thanks to the Giver,
England, for thy son.
Let the bell be toll'd.
Render thanks to the Giver,
And render him to the mould.
Under the cross of gold   50
That shines over city and river,
There he shall rest for ever
Among the wise and the bold.
Let the bell be toll'd:
And a reverent people behold
The towering car, the sable steeds:
Bright let it be with its blazon'd deeds,
Dark in its funeral fold.
Let the bell be toll'd:
And a deeper knell in the heart be knoll'd;   60
And the sound of the sorrowing anthem roll'd
Thro' the dome of the golden cross;[4]
And the volleying cannon thunder his loss;
He knew their voices of old.
For many a time in many a clime
His captain's-ear has heard them boom
Bellowing victory, bellowing doom;
When he with those deep voices wrought,

---

3   Wellington defeated Napoleon at Waterloo.   4   St Paul's Cathedral.

Guarding realms and kings from shame;
With those deep voices our dead captain taught
The tyrant, and asserts his claim
In that dread sound to the great name,
Which he has worn so pure of blame,
In praise and in dispraise the same,
A man of well-attemper'd frame.
O civic muse, to such a name,
To such a name for ages long,
To such a name,
Preserve a broad approach of fame,
And ever-ringing[5] avenues of song.

70

80

VI

Who is he that cometh, like an honour'd guest,
With banner and with music, with soldier and with priest,
With a nation weeping, and breaking on my rest?
Mighty seaman, this is he
Was great by land as thou by sea.[6]
Thine island loves thee well, thou famous man,
The greatest sailor since our world began.
Now, to the roll of muffled drums,
To thee the greatest soldier comes;
For this is he
Was great by land as thou by sea;
His foes were thine; he kept us free;
O give him welcome, this is he,
Worthy of our gorgeous rites,
And worthy to be laid by thee;
For this is England's greatest son,
He that gain'd a hundred fights,
Nor ever lost an English gun;
This is he that far away
Against the myriads of Assaye[7]
Clash'd with his fiery few and won;
And underneath another sun,
Warring on a later day,
Round affrighted Lisbon drew
The treble works, the vast designs
Of his labour'd rampart-lines,[8]
Where he greatly stood at bay,
Whence he issued forth anew,
And ever great and greater grew,
Beating from the wasted vines
Back to France her banded swarms,
Back to France with countless blows,
Till o'er the hills her eagles[9] flew
Beyond the Pyrenean pines,
Follow'd up in valley and glen
With blare of bugle, clamour of men,
Roll of cannon and clash of arms,
And England pouring on her foes.
Such a war had such a close.

90

100

110

---

5 ever-echoing (later edn).
6 Admiral Lord Nelson, victor of Trafalgar.
7 Hindoostan, 1803.
8 Torres Vedras, 1810.
9 Napoleon's banners.

He withdrew to brief repose.   120
Again their ravening eagle rose
In anger, wheel'd on Europe-shadowing wings,
And barking for the thrones of kings;
Till one that sought but Duty's iron crown
On that loud sabbath shook the spoiler down;[10]
A day of onsets of despair!
Dash'd on every rocky square
Their surging charges foam'd themselves away;
Last, the Prussian trumpet blew;
Thro' the long-tormented air   130
Heaven flash'd a sudden jubilant ray,
And down we swept and charged and overthrew.
So great a soldier taught us there,
What long-enduring hearts could do
In that world's-earthquake, Waterloo!
Mighty seaman, tender and true,
And pure as he from taint of craven guile,
O saviour of the silver-coasted isle,
O shaker of the Baltic and the Nile,[11]
If aught of things that here befall   140
Touch a spirit among things divine,
If love of country move thee there at all,
Be glad, because his bones are laid by thine!
And thro' the centuries let a people's voice
In full acclaim,
A people's voice,
The proof and echo of all human fame,
A people's voice, when they rejoice
At civic revel and pomp and game,
Attest their great commander's claim   150
With honour, honour, honour, honour to him,
Eternal honour to his name.

                           VII
A people's voice! we are a people yet.
Tho' all men else their nobler dreams forget,
Confused by brainless mobs and lawless Powers;
Thank Him who isled us here, and roughly set
His Saxon in blown seas and storming showers,
We have a voice, with which to pay the debt
Of boundless reverence and regret
To those great men who fought, and kept it ours.   160
And keep it ours, O God, from brute control;
O Statesmen, guard us, guard the eye, the soul
Of Europe, keep our noble England whole,
And save the one true seed of freedom sown
Betwixt a people and their ancient throne,
That sober freedom out of which there springs
Our loyal passion for our temperate kings;
For, saving that, ye help to save mankind
Till public wrong be crumbled into dust,
And drill the raw world for the march of mind,   170
 Till crowds be sane and crowns be just;

---

10   Battle of Waterloo, Sunday 18 June 1815.   11   Nelson's victory over Danes (1801), and French at Aboukir
                                                            (1798).

But wink no more in slothful overtrust.
Remember him who led your hosts;
Revere his warning; guard your coasts:
Your cannons moulder on the seaward wall;
His voice is silent in your council-hall
For ever; and whatever tempests lour
For ever silent; even if they broke
In thunder, silent; yet remember all
He spoke among you, and the Man who spoke;   180
Who never sold the truth to serve the hour,
Nor palter'd[12] with Eternal God for power;
Whose life was work, whose language rife
With rugged maxims hewn from life;
Whose eighty winters freeze with one rebuke
All great self-seekers trampling on the right:
Truth-teller was our England's Alfred[13] named;
Truth-lover was our English Duke;
Whatever record leap to light
He never shall be shamed.   190

VIII

Lo, the leader in these glorious wars
Now to glorious burial slowly borne,
Follow'd by the brave of other lands,
He, on whom from both her open hands
Lavish Honour shower'd all her stars,
And affluent Fortune emptied all her horn.
Yea, let all good things await
Him who cares not to be great,
But as he saves or serves the state.
Not once or twice in our rough island-story,   200
The path of duty was the way to glory:
He that walks it, only thirsting
For the right, and learns to deaden
Love of self, before his journey closes,
He shall find the stubborn thistle bursting
Into glossy purples, which outredden
All voluptuous garden-roses.
Not once or twice in our rough island-story,
The path of duty was the way to glory:
He, that ever following her commands,   210
On with toil of heart and knees and hands,
Thro' the long gorge to the far light has won
His path upward, and prevail'd,
Shall find the toppling crags of Duty scaled
Are close upon the shining table-lands
To which our God Himself is moon and sun.
Such was he: his work is done:
But while the races of mankind endure,
Let his great example stand
Colossal, seen of every land,   220
And keep the soldier firm, the statesman pure:
Till in all lands and thro' all human story
The path of duty be the way to glory:

12 prevaricated.   13 King Alfred the Great (after whom, of course, Tennyson is
named).

And let the land whose hearths he saved from shame
For many and many an age proclaim
At civic revel and pomp and game,
And when the long-illumined cities flame,
Their ever-loyal iron leader's fame,[14]
With honour, honour, honour, honour to him,
Eternal honour to his name.   230

IX

Peace, his triumph will be sung
By some yet unmoulded tongue
Far on in summers that we shall not see:
Peace, it is a day of pain
For one about whose patriarchal knee
Late the little children clung:
O peace, it is a day of pain
For one, upon whose hand and heart and brain
Once the weight and fate of Europe hung.
Ours the pain, be his the gain!   240
More than is of man's degree
Must be with us, watching here
At this, our great solemnity.
Whom we see not we revere;
We revere, and we refrain
From talk of battles loud and vain,
And brawling memories all too free
For such a wise humility
As befits a solemn fane:
We revere, and while we hear   250
The tides of Music's golden sea
Setting toward eternity,
Uplifted high in heart are we,
Until we doubt not that for one so true
There must be other nobler work to do
Than when he fought at Waterloo,
And Victor he must ever be.
For tho' the Giant Ages heave the hill
And break the shore, and evermore
Make and break, and work their will;   260
Tho' worlds on worlds in myriad myriads roll
Round us, each with different powers,
And other forms of life than ours,
What know we greater than the soul?
On God and Godlike men we build our trust.
Hush, the Dead March wails in the people's ears:
The dark crowd moves, and there are sobs and tears:
The black earth yawns: the mortal disappears;
Ashes to ashes, dust to dust;
He is gone who seem'd so great. –   270
Gone; but nothing can bereave him
Of the force he made his own
Being here, and we believe him
Something far advanced in State,
And that he wears a truer crown
Than any wreath that man can weave him.

---

14   Wellington was the 'Iron Duke'.

Speak no more of his renown,
Lay your earthly fancies down,
And in the vast cathedral leave him.
God accept him, Christ receive him.   280

Ode on the Death of the Duke of Wellington, *by Alfred Tennyson, Poet Laureate,*
first published, Edward Moxon, 16 November 1852. Text, 'A New Edition'
(Edward Moxon, 1853) – slightly revised. It was revised again, for Maud, and
Other Poems *(Edward Moxon, 1855); and tinkered with thereafter. (This poem was T's*
first separate publication as Poet Laureate.)

THE BROOK

An Idyl[1]

Here, by this brook, we parted; I to the East
And he for Italy – too late – too late:
One whom the strong sons of the world despise;
For lucky rhymes to him were scrip and share,
And mellow metres more than cent for cent;[2]
Nor could he understand how money breeds,
Thought it a dead thing; yet himself could make
The thing that is not as the thing that is.
O had he lived! In our schoolbooks we say,
Of those that held their heads above the crowd,   10
They flourish'd then or then; but life in him
Could scarce be said to flourish, only touch'd
On such a time as goes before the leaf,
When all the wood stands in a mist of green,
And nothing perfect: yet the brook he loved,
For which, in branding summers of Bengal,
Or even the sweet half-English Neilgherry[3] air
I panted, seems, as I re-listen to it,
Prattling the primrose fancies of the boy,
To me that loved him; for 'O brook,' he says,   20
'O babbling brook,' says Edmund in his rhyme,
'Whence come you?' and the brook, why not? replies.

   I come from haunts of coot and hern,
      I make a sudden sally,
   And sparkle out among the fern,
      To bicker down a valley.

   By thirty hills I hurry down,
      Or slip between the ridges,
   By twenty thorps, a little town,
      And half a hundred bridges.   30

   Till last by Philip's farm I flow
      To join the brimming river,
   For men may come and men may go,
      But I go on for ever.

THE BROOK
1 'Not the brook near Somersby' (T.).

2   100% return on investment.
3   mountains of Madras.

'Poor lad, he died at Florence, quite worn out,
Travelling to Naples. There is Darnley bridge,
It has more ivy; there the river; and there
Stands Philip's farm where brook and river meet.

I chatter over stony ways,
    In little sharps and trebles,   40
I bubble into eddying bays,
    I babble on the pebbles.

With many a curve my banks I fret
    By many a field and fallow,
And many a fairy foreland set
    With willow-weed and mallow.

I chatter, chatter, as I flow
    To join the brimming river,
For men may come and men may go,
    But I go on for ever.   50

'But Philip chatter'd more than brook or bird;
Old Philip; all about the fields you caught
His weary daylong chirping, like the dry
High-elbow'd grigs[4] that leap in summer grass.

I wind about, and in and out,
    With here a blossom sailing,
And here and there a lusty trout,
    And here and there a grayling,

And here and there a foamy flake
    Upon me, as I travel   60
With many a silvery waterbreak
    Above the golden gravel,

And draw them all along, and flow
    To join the brimming river,
For men may come and men may go,
    But I go on for ever.

'O darling Katie Willows, his one child!
A maiden of our century, yet most meek;
A daughter of our meadows, yet not coarse;
Straight, but as lissome as a hazel wand;   70
Her eyes a bashful azure, and her hair
In gloss and hue the chestnut, when the shell
Divides threefold to show the fruit within.

'Sweet Katie, once I did her a good turn,
Her and her far-off cousin and betrothed,
James Willows, of one name and heart with her.
For here I came, twenty years back – the week
Before I parted with poor Edmund; crost
By that old bridge which, half in ruins then,
Still makes a hoary eyebrow for the gleam   80

4   'crickets' (T.).

Beyond it, where the waters marry – crost,
Whistling a random bar of Bonny Doon,
And pushed at Philip's garden-gate. The gate,
Half-parted from a weak and scolding hinge,
Stuck; and he clamour'd from a casement, "run"
To Katie somewhere in the walks below,
"Run, Katie!" Katie never ran: she moved
To meet me, winding under woodbine bowers,
A little flutter'd, with her eyelids down,
Fresh apple-blossom, blushing for a boon.   90

    'What was it? less of sentiment than sense
Had Katie; not illiterate; nor of those
Who dabbling in the fount of fictive tears,
And nursed by mealy-mouthed philanthropies,
Divorce the Feeling from her mate the Deed.

    'She told me. She and James had quarrell'd. Why?
What cause of quarrel? None, she said, no cause;
James had no cause: but when I prest the cause,
I learnt that James had flickering jealousies
Which anger'd her. Who angered James? I said.   100
But Katie snatch'd her eyes at once from mine,
And sketching with her slender pointed foot
Some figure like a wizard pentagram
On garden gravel, let my query pass
Unclaim'd, in flushing silence, till I ask'd
If James were coming. "Coming every day,"
She answer'd, "ever longing to explain,
But evermore her father came across
With some long-winded tale, and broke him short;
And James departed vext with him and her."   110
How could I help her? "Would I – was it wrong?"
(Claspt hands and that petitionary grace
Of sweet seventeen subdued me ere she spoke)
"O would I take her father for one hour,
For one half-hour, and let him talk to me!"
And even while she spoke, I saw where James
Made toward us, like a wader in the surf,
Beyond the brook, waist-deep in meadow-sweet.

    'O Katie, what I suffer'd for your sake!
For in I went, and call'd old Philip out   120
To show the farm: full willingly he rose:
He led me thro' the short sweet-smelling lanes
Of his wheat-suburb, babbling as he went.
He praised his land, his horses, his machines;
He praised his ploughs, his cows, his hogs, his dogs;
He praised his hens, his geese, his guinea-hens;
His pigeons, who in session on their roofs
Approved him, bowing at their own deserts:
Then from the plaintive mother's teat he took
Her blind and shuddering puppies, naming each,   130
And naming those, his friends, for whom they were:
Then crost the common into Darnley chase
To show Sir Arthur's deer. In copse and fern
Twinkled the innumerable ear and tail.
Then, seated on a serpent-rooted beech,

He pointed out a pasturing colt, and said:
"That was the four-year-old I sold the Squire."
And there he told a long long-winded tale
Of how the Squire had seen the colt at grass,
And how it was the thing his daughter wish'd,   140
And how he sent the bailiff to the farm
To learn the price, and what the price he ask'd,
And how the bailiff swore that he was mad,
But he stood firm; and so the matter hung;
He gave them line: and five days after that
He met the bailiff at the Golden Fleece,
Who then and there had offer'd something more,
But he stood firm; and so the matter hung;
He knew the man; the colt would fetch its price;
He gave them line: and how by chance at last   150
(It might be May or April, he forgot,
The last of April or the first of May)
He found the bailiff riding by the farm,
And, talking from the point, he drew him in,
And there he mellow'd all his heart with ale,
Until they closed a bargain, hand in hand.

  'Then, while I breathed in sight of haven, he,
Poor fellow, could he help it? recommenced,
And ran thro' all the coltish chronicle,
Wild Will, Black Bess, Tantivy, Tallyho,   160
Reform, White Rose, Bellerophon, the Jilt,
Arbaces, and Phenomenon, and the rest,
Till, not to die a listener, I arose,
And with me Philip, talking still; and so
We turn'd our foreheads from the falling sun,
And following our own shadows thrice as long
As when they follow'd us from Philip's door,
Arrived, and found the sun of sweet content
Re-risen in Katie's eyes, and all things well.

     I steal by lawns and grassy plots,   170
        I slide by hazel covers;
     I move the sweet forget-me-nots
        That grow for happy lovers.

     I slip, I slide, I gloom, I glance,
        Among my skimming swallows;
     I make the netted sunbeam dance
        Against my sandy shallows.

     I murmur under moon and stars
        In brambly wildernesses;
     I linger by my shingly bars;   180
        I loiter round my cresses;

     And out again I curve and flow
        To join the brimming river,
     For men may come and men may go,
        But I go on for ever.

Yes, men may come and go; and these are gone,
All gone. My dearest brother, Edmund, sleeps,

Not by the well-known stream and rustic spire,
But unfamiliar Arno, and the dome
Of Brunelleschi;⁵ sleeps in peace: and he,   190
Poor Philip, of all his lavish waste of words
Remains the lean P. W. on his tomb:
I scraped the lichen from it: Katie walks
By the long wash of Australasian seas
Far off, and holds her head to other stars,
And breathes in April-autumns. All are gone.'

    So Lawrence Aylmer, seated on a stile
In the long hedge, and rolling in his mind
Old waifs of rhyme, and bowing o'er the brook
A tonsured head in middle age forlorn,   200
Mused, and was mute. On a sudden a low breath
Of tender air made tremble in the hedge
The fragile bindweed-bells and briony rings;
And he look'd up. There stood a maiden near,
Waiting to pass. In much amaze he stared
On eyes a bashful azure, and on hair
In gloss and hue the chestnut, when the shell
Divides threefold to show the fruit within:
Then, wondering, asked her 'Are you from the farm?'
'Yes' answer'd she. 'Pray stay a little: pardon me;   210
What do they call you?' 'Katie.' 'That were strange.
What surname?' 'Willows.' 'No!' 'That is my name.'
'Indeed!' and here he look'd so self-perplext,
That Katie laughed, and laughing blush'd, till he
Laugh'd also, but as one before he wakes,
Who feels a glimmering strangeness in his dream.
Then looking at her; 'Too happy, fresh and fair,
Too fresh and fair in our sad world's best bloom,
To be the ghost of one who bore your name
About these meadows, twenty years ago.'   220

    'Have you not heard?' said Katie, 'we came back.
We bought the farm we tenanted before.
Am I so like her? so they said on board.
Sir, if you knew her in her English days,
My mother, as it seems you did, the days
That most she loves to talk of, come with me.
My brother James is in the harvest-field:
But she – you will be welcome – O, come in!'

Begun 1854(?). Maud, and Other Poems, by Alfred Tennyson, D. C. L., Poet Laureate
(Edward Moxon, 1855).

THE CHARGE OF THE LIGHT BRIGADE¹

I

Half a league, half a league,
Half a league onward,

---

⁵ Brunelleschi's Cathedral, Florence.

THE CHARGE OF THE LIGHT BRIGADE
1 an incident of the Crimean War, 25 October 1854; British cavalry
stormed Russian cannon on misguided orders.

All in the valley of Death
   Rode the six hundred.
'Forward, the Light Brigade!
Charge for the guns!' he said:
Into the valley of Death
   Rode the six hundred.

II

'Forward, the Light Brigade!'
Was there a man dismay'd?   10
Not tho' the soldier knew
   Some one had blunder'd:
Their's not to make reply,
Their's not to reason why,
Their's but to do and die:
Into the valley of Death
   Rode the six hundred.

III

Cannon to right of them,
Cannon to left of them,
Cannon in front of them   20
   Volley'd and thunder'd;
Storm'd at with shot and shell,
Boldly they rode and well,
Into the jaws of Death,
Into the mouth of Hell
   Rode the six hundred.

IV

Flash'd all their sabres bare,
Flash'd as they turn'd in air
Sabring the gunners there,
Charging an army, while   30
   All the world wondered:
Plunged in the battery-smoke
Right thro' the line they broke;
Cossack and Russian
Reel'd from the sabre-stroke
   Shatter'd and sunder'd.
Then they rode back, but not
   Not the six hundred.

V

Cannon to right of them,
Cannon to left of them,   40
Cannon behind them
   Volley'd and thunder'd;
Storm'd at with shot and shell,
While horse and hero fell,
They that had fought so well
Came thro' the jaws of Death,
Back from the mouth of Hell,
All that was left of them,
   Left of six hundred.

VI

When can their glory fade?   50
O the wild charge they made!

All the world wonder'd.
Honour the charge they made!
Honour the Light Brigade,
Noble six hundred!

First published in The Examiner, *9 December 1854, signed A. T. Heavily*
revised in Maud, and Other Poems *(1855). ('Some one had blundered',*
e.g., was removed.) Earlier readings restored, in Maud, and other Poems,
A New Edition *(Edward Moxon, 1856). 1856 text.*

MAUD[1]

I

1

I hate the dreadful hollow behind the little wood,
Its lips in the field above are dabbled with blood-red heath,
The red-ribb'd ledges drip with a silent horror of blood,
And Echo there, whatever is ask'd her, answers 'Death.'

2

For there in the ghastly pit long since a body was found,
His who had given me life – O father! O God! was it well? –
Mangled, and flatten'd, and crush'd, and dinted into the ground:
There yet lies the rock that fell with him when he fell.

3

Did he fling himself down? who knows? for a vast speculation had fail'd,
And ever he mutter'd and madden'd, and ever wann'd with despair,   10
And out he walk'd when the wind like a broken worldling wail'd,
And the flying gold of the ruin'd woodlands drove thro' the air.

4

I remember the time, for the roots of my hair were stirr'd
By a shuffled step, by a dead weight trail'd, by a whisper'd fright,
And my pulses closed their gates with a shock on my heart as I heard
The shrill-edged shriek of a mother divide the shuddering night.

5

Villainy somewhere! whose? One says, we are villains all.
Not he: his honest fame should at least by me be maintained:
But that old man, now lord of the broad estate and the Hall,
Dropt off gorged from a scheme that had left us flaccid and drain'd.   20

6

Why do they prate of the blessings of Peace? we have made them a curse,
Pickpockets, each hand lusting for all that is not its own;
And lust of gain, in the spirit of Cain,[2] is it better or worse
Than the heart of the citizen hissing in war on his own hearthstone?

7

But these are the days of advance, the works of the men of mind,
When who but a fool would have faith in a tradesman's ware or his word?

MAUD   2   biblical brother-killer.
1   original title: *Maud or the Madness.* In 1875 *A Monodrama* was added
as subtitle.

Is it peace or war? Civil war, as I think, and that of a kind
The viler, as underhand, not openly bearing the sword.

8

Sooner or later I too may passively take the print
Of the golden age – why not? I have neither hope nor trust;   30
May make my heart as a millstone, set my face as a flint,
Cheat and be cheated, and die: who knows? we are ashes and dust.

9

Peace sitting under her olive, and slurring the days gone by,
When the poor are hovell'd and hustled together, each sex, like swine,
When only the ledger lives, and when only not all men lie;
Peace in her vineyard – yes! – but a company forges the wine.

10

And the vitriol madness flushes up in the ruffian's head,
Till the filthy by-lane rings to the yell of the trampled wife,
And chalk and alum and plaster are sold to the poor for bread,[3]
And the spirit of murder works in the very means of life,   40

11

And Sleep must lie down arm'd, for the villainous centre-bits[4]
Grind on the wakeful ear in the hush of the moonless nights,
While another is cheating the sick of a few last gasps, as he sits
To pestle a poison'd poison behind his crimson lights.

12

When a Mammonite mother kills her babe for a burial fee,[5]
And Timour-Mammon[6] grins on a pile of children's bones,
Is it peace or war? better, war! loud war by land and by sea,
War with a thousand battles, and shaking a hundred thrones.

13

For I trust if an enemy's fleet came yonder round by the hill,
And the rushing battle-bolt sang from the three-decker out of the foam,   50
That the smoothfaced snubnosed rogue would leap from his counter and till,
And strike, if he could, were it but with his cheating yardwand, home. –

14

What! am I raging alone as my father raged in his mood?
Must *I* too creep to the hollow and dash myself down and die
Rather than hold by the law that I made, nevermore to brood
On a horror of shatter'd limbs and a wretched swindler's lie?

15

Would there be sorrow for *me*? there was *love* in the passionate shriek,
Love for the silent thing that had made false haste to the grave –
Wrapt in a cloak, as I saw him, and thought he would rise and speak
And rave at the lie and the liar, ah God, as he used to rave.   60

3 adulterated food; notorious scandal attacked by reformers, such as Charles Kingsley in *Alton Locke*.
4 a drill (thieves' tool); and nickname for thief who uses it? (As in *Oliver Twist*.)

5 Mammon – biblical metaphor for unrighteousness and greed, much used by Thomas Carlyle.
6 Tamerlane the conqueror, in Matthew ('Monk') Lewis's Gothic novel *Timour* (1811).

16

I am sick of the Hall and the hill, I am sick of the moor and the main.
Why should I stay? can a sweeter chance ever come to me here?
O, having the nerves of motion as well as the nerves of pain,
Were it not wise if I fled from the place and the pit and the fear?

17

There are workmen up at the Hall: they are coming back from abroad;
The dark old place will be gilt by the touch of a millionaire:
I have heard, I know not whence, of the singular beauty of Maud;
I played with the girl when a child; she promised then to be fair.

18

Maud with her venturous climbings and tumbles and childish escapes,
Maud the delight of the village, the ringing joy of the Hall,   70
Maud with her sweet purse-mouth when my father dangled the grapes,
Maud the beloved of my mother, the moon-faced darling of all, –

19

What is she now? My dreams are bad. She may bring me a curse.
No, there is fatter game on the moor; she will let me alone.
Thanks, for the fiend best knows whether woman or man be the worse.
I will bury myself in myself, and the Devil may pipe to his own.

II

Long have I sigh'd for a calm: God grant I may find it at last!
It will never be broken by Maud, she has neither savour nor salt,
But a cold and clear-cut face, as I found when her carriage past,
Perfectly beautiful: let it be granted her: where is the fault?   80
All that I saw (for her eyes were downcast, not to be seen)
Faultily faultless, icily regular, splendidly null,
Dead perfection, no more; nothing more, if it had not been
For a chance of travel, a paleness, an hour's defect of the rose,
Or an underlip, you may call it a little too ripe, too full,
Or the least little delicate aquiline curve in a sensitive nose,
From which I escaped heart-free, with the least little touch of spleen.

III

Cold and clear-cut face, why come you so cruelly meek,
Breaking a slumber in which all spleenful folly was drowned,
Pale with the golden beam of an eyelash dead on the cheek,   90
Passionless, pale, cold face, star-sweet on a gloom profound;
Womanlike, taking revenge too deep for a transient wrong
Done but in thought to your beauty, and ever as pale as before
Growing and fading and growing upon me without a sound,
Luminous, gemlike, ghostlike, deathlike, half the night long
Growing and fading and growing, till I could bear it no more,
But arose, and all by myself in my own dark garden ground,
Listening now to the tide in its broad-flung shipwrecking roar,
Now to the scream of a maddened beach dragg'd down by the wave,
Walk'd in a wintry wind by a ghastly glimmer, and found   100
The shining daffodil dead, and Orion low in his grave.

IV

1

A million emeralds break from the ruby-budded lime
In the little grove where I sit – ah, wherefore cannot I be
Like things of the season gay, like the bountiful season bland,

When the far-off sail is blown by the breeze of a softer clime,
Half-lost in the liquid azure bloom of a crescent of sea,
The silent sapphire-spangled marriage ring of the land?

2

Below me, there, is the village, and looks how quiet and small!
And yet bubbles o'er like a city, with gossip, scandal, and spite;
And Jack on his ale-house bench has as many lies as a Czar;[7]
And here on the landward side, by a red rock, glimmers the Hall;
And up in the high Hall-garden I see her pass like a light;
But sorrow seize me if ever that light be my leading star!

3

When have I bow'd to her father, the wrinkled head of the race?
I met her to-day with her brother, but not to her brother I bow'd:
I bow'd to his lady-sister as she rode by on the moor;
But the fire of a foolish pride flash'd over her beautiful face.
O child, you wrong your beauty, believe it, in being so proud;
Your father has wealth well-gotten, and I am nameless and poor.

4

I keep but a man and a maid, ever ready to slander and steal;
I know it, and smile a hard-set smile, like a stoic, or like
A wiser epicurean, and let the world have its way:
For nature is one with rapine, a harm no preacher can heal;
The Mayfly is torn by the swallow, the sparrow spear'd by the shrike,
And the whole little wood where I sit is a world of plunder and prey.

5

We are puppets, Man in his pride, and Beauty fair in her flower;
Do we move ourselves, or are moved by an unseen hand at a game
That pushes us off from the board, and others ever succeed?
Ah yet, we cannot be kind to each other here for an hour;
We whisper, and hint, and chuckle, and grin at a brother's shame;
However we brave it out, we men are a little breed.

6

A monstrous eft[8] was of old the Lord and Master of Earth,
For him did his high sun flame, and his river billowing ran,
And he felt himself in his force to be Nature's crowning race.
As nine months go to the shaping an infant ripe for his birth,
So many a million of ages have gone to the making of man:
He now is first, but is he the last? is he not too base?

7

The man of science himself is fonder of glory, and vain,
An eye well-practised in nature, a spirit bounded and poor;
The passionate heart of the poet is whirl'd into folly and vice.
I would not marvel at either, but keep a temperate brain;
For not to desire or admire, if a man could learn it, were more
Than to walk all day like the sultan of old in a garden of spice.

8

For the drift of the Maker is dark, an Isis hid by the veil.
Who knows the ways of the world, how God will bring them about?

7 Nicholas I, provoker of Crimean War.   8 'The great old lizards of geology' (T.).

Our planet is one, the suns are many, the world is wide.
Shall I weep if a Poland fall? shall I shriek if a Hungary fail?[9]
Or an infant civilisation be ruled with rod or with knout?
I have not made the world, and He that made it will guide.

9

Be mine a philosopher's life in the quiet woodland ways,   150
Where if I cannot be gay let a passionless peace be my lot,
Far-off from the clamour of liars belied in the hubbub of lies;
From the long-neck'd geese of the world that are ever hissing dispraise
Because their natures are little, and, whether he heed it or not,
Where each man walks with his head in a cloud of poisonous flies.

10

And most of all would I flee from the cruel madness of love,
The honey of poison-flowers and all the measureless ill.
Ah Maud, you milkwhite fawn, you are all unmeet for a wife.
Your mother is mute in her grave as her image in marble above;
Your father is ever in London, you wander about at your will;   160
You have but fed on the roses and lain in the lilies of life.

V

1

A voice by the cedar tree
In the meadow under the Hall!
She is singing an air that is known to me,
A passionate ballad gallant and gay,
A martial song like a trumpet's call!
Singing alone in the morning of life,
In the happy morning of life and of May,
Singing of men that in battle array,
Ready in heart and ready in hand,   170
March with banner and bugle and fife
To the death, for their native land.

2

Maud with her exquisite face,
And wild voice pealing up to the sunny sky,
And feet like sunny gems on an English green,
Maud in the light of her youth and her grace,
Singing of Death, and of Honour that cannot die,
Till I well could weep for a time so sordid and mean,
And myself so languid and base.

3

Silence, beautiful voice!   180
Be still, for you only trouble the mind
With a joy in which I cannot rejoice,
A glory I shall not find.
Still! I will hear you no more,
For your sweetness hardly leaves me a choice
But to move to the meadow and fall before
Her feet on the meadow grass, and adore,
Not her, who is neither courtly nor kind,
Not her, not her, but a voice.

9   refers to Russian–Austrian occupation of Cracow, 1846, and defeat
of Hungarians, 1849.

VI

1

Morning arises stormy and pale,   190
No sun, but a wannish glare
In fold upon fold of hueless cloud,
And the budded peaks of the wood are bow'd
Caught and cuff'd by the gale:
I had fancied it would be fair.

2

Whom but Maud should I meet
Last night, when the sunset burn'd
On the blossom'd gable-ends
At the head of the village street,
Whom but Maud should I meet?   200
And she touch'd my hand with a smile so sweet
She made me divine amends
For a courtesy not return'd.

3

And thus a delicate spark
Of glowing and growing light
Thro' the livelong hours of the dark
Kept itself warm in the heart of my dreams,
Ready to burst in a coloured flame;
Till at last when the morning came
In a cloud, it faded, and seems   210
But an ashen-gray delight.

4

What if with her sunny hair
And smile as sunny as cold,
She meant to weave me a snare
Of some coquettish deceit,
Cleopatra-like as of old
To entangle me when we met,
To have her lion roll in a silken net
And fawn at a victor's feet.

5

Ah, what shall I be at fifty   220
Should Nature keep me alive,
If I find the world so bitter
When I am but twenty-five?
Yet, if she were not a cheat,
If Maud were all that she seem'd,
And her smile were all that I dream'd,
Then the world were not so bitter
But a smile could make it sweet.

6

What if tho' her eye seem'd full
Of a kind intent to me,   230
What if that dandy-despot, he,
That jewelled mass of millinery,
That oil'd and curl'd Assyrian Bull[10]

---

10 'with hair curled like that of bulls on Assyrian sculpture' (T.).

Smelling of musk and of insolence,
Her brother, from whom I keep aloof,
Who wants the finer politic sense
To mask, tho' but in his own behoof,
With a glassy smile his brutal scorn –
What if he had told her yestermorn
How prettily for his own sweet sake   240
A face of tenderness might be feign'd,
And a moist mirage in desert eyes,
That so, when the rotten hustings shake
In another month to his brazen lies,
A wretched vote may be gain'd.

7

For a raven ever croaks, at my side,
Keep watch and ward, keep watch and ward,
Or thou wilt prove their tool.
Yea, too, myself from myself I guard,
For often a man's own angry pride   250
Is cap and bells for a fool.

8

Perhaps the smile and tender tone
Came out of her pitying womanhood,
For am I not, am I not, here alone
So many a summer since she died,
My mother, who was so gentle and good?
Living alone in an empty house,
Here half-hid in the gleaming wood,
Where I hear the dead at midday moan,
And the shrieking rush of the wainscot mouse,   260
And my own sad name in corners cried,
When the shiver of dancing leaves is thrown
About its echoing chambers wide,
Till a morbid hate and horror have grown
Of a world in which I have hardly mixt,
And a morbid eating lichen fixt
On a heart half-turn'd to stone.

9

O heart of stone, are you flesh, and caught
By that you swore to withstand?
For what was it else within me wrought   270
But, I fear, the new strong wine of love,
That made my tongue so stammer and trip
When I saw the treasured splendour, her hand,
Come sliding out of her sacred glove,
And the sunlight broke from her lip?

10

I have play'd with her when a child;
She remembers it now we meet.
Ah well, well, well, I may be beguiled
By some coquettish deceit.   280
Yet, if she were not a cheat,
If Maud were all that she seem'd,
And her smile had all that I dream'd,
Then the world were not so bitter
But a smile could make it sweet.

VII

1

Did I hear it half in a doze
    Long since, I know not where?
Did I dream it an hour ago,
    When asleep in this arm-chair?

2

Men were drinking together,
    Drinking and talking of me;   290
'Well, if it prove a girl, the boy,
    Will have plenty: so let it be.'

3

Is it an echo of something
    Read with a boy's delight,
Viziers nodding together
In some Arabian night?[11]

4

Strange, that I hear two men,
    Somewhere, talking of me;
'Well, if it prove a girl, my boy
    Will have plenty: so let it be.'   300

VIII

She came to the village church,
And sat by a pillar alone;
An angel watching an urn
Wept over her, carved in stone;
And once, but once, she lifted her eyes,
And suddenly, sweetly, strangely blush'd
To find they were met by my own;
And suddenly, sweetly, my heart beat stronger
And thicker, until I heard no longer
The snowy-banded, dilettante,   310
Delicate-handed priest intone;
And thought, is it pride, and mused and sigh'd
'No surely, now it cannot be pride.'

IX

I was walking a mile,
More than a mile from the shore,
The sun look'd out with a smile
Betwixt the cloud and the moor,
And riding at set of day
Over the dark moor land,
Rapidly riding far away,   320
She waved to me with her hand.
There were two at her side,
Something flash'd in the sun,
Down by the hill I saw them ride,
In a moment they were gone:
Like a sudden spark

11 Narrator remembers overhearing his father and Maud's arranging
betrothal of their children – as in *Arabian Nights* story of Nourredin Ali
and Bedreddin Hassan.

Struck vainly in the night,
Then returns the dark
With no more hope of light.

X

1

Sick, am I sick of a jealous dread?   330
Was not one of the two at her side
This new-made lord, whose splendour plucks
The slavish hat from the villager's head?
Whose old grand-father has lately died,
Gone to a blacker pit, for whom
Grimy nakedness dragging his trucks
And laying his trams in a poison'd gloom
Wrought, till he crept from a gutted mine
Master of half a servile shire,
And left his coal all turn'd into gold   340
To a grandson, first of his noble line,
Rich in the grace all women desire,
Strong in the power that all men adore,
And simper and set their voices lower,
And soften as if to a girl, and hold
Awe-stricken breaths at a work divine,
Seeing his gewgaw castle shine,
New as his title, built last year,
There amid perky larches and pine,
And over the sullen-purple moor   350
(Look at it) pricking a cockney ear.

2

What, has he found my jewel out?
For one of the two that rode at her side
Bound for the Hall, I am sure was he:
Bound for the Hall, and I think for a bride.
Blithe would her brother's acceptance be.
Maud could be gracious too, no doubt
To a lord, a captain, a padded shape,
A bought commission, a waxen face,
A rabbit mouth that is ever agape –   360
Bought? what is it he cannot buy?
And therefore splenetic, personal, base,
A wounded thing with a rancourous cry,
At war with myself and a wretched race,
Sick, sick to the heart of life, am I.

3

Last week came one to the county town,
To preach our poor little army down,
And play the game of the despot kings,
Tho' the state has done it and thrice as well:
This broad-brim'd hawker of holy things,   370
Whose ear is stuff'd with his cotton, and rings
Even in dreams to the chink of his pence,
This huckster put down war! can he tell
Whether war be a cause or a consequence?
Put down the passions that make earth Hell!
Down with ambition, avarice, pride,
Jealousy, down! cut off from the mind

The bitter springs of anger and fear;
Down too, down at your own fireside,
With the evil tongue and the evil ear,   380
For each is at war with mankind.

4

I wish I could hear again
The chivalrous battle-song
That she warbled alone in her joy!
I might persuade myself then
She would not do herself this great wrong,
To take a wanton dissolute boy
For a man and leader of men.

5

Ah God, for a man with heart, head, hand,
Like some of the simple great ones gone   390
For ever and ever by,
One still strong man in a blatant[12] land,
Whatever they call him, what care I,
Aristocrat, democrat, autocrat – one
Who can rule and dare not lie.

6

And ah for a man to arise in me,
That the man I am may cease to be!

XI

1

O let the solid ground
    Not fail beneath my feet
Before my life has found   400
    What some have found so sweet;
Then let come what come may,
What matter if I go mad,
I shall have had my day.

2

Let the sweet heavens endure,
    Not close and darken above me
Before I am quite quite sure
    That there is one to love me;
Then let come what come may
To a life that has been so sad,   410
I shall have had my day.

XII

1

Birds in the high Hall-garden
    When twilight was falling,
Maud, Maud, Maud, Maud,
    They were crying and calling.

12   disposed to slandering the good and great (from Edmund Spenser's *blatant beast* in *The Fairie Queene*: with a hundred tongues and a poisonous sting, type of slander and calumny).

2

Where was Maud? in our wood;
    And I, who else, was with her,
Gathering woodland lilies,
    Myriads blow together.

3

Birds in our wood sang   420
    Ringing thro' the vallies,
Maud is here, here, here
    In among the lilies.

4

I kiss'd her slender hand,
    She took the kiss sedately;
Maud is not seventeen,
    But she is tall and stately.

5

I to cry out on pride
    Who have won her favour!
O Maud were sure of Heaven   430
    If lowliness could save her.

6

I know the way she went
    Home with her maiden posy,
For her feet have touch'd the meadows
    And left the daisies rosy.

7

Birds in the high Hall-garden
    Were crying and calling to her,
Where is Maud, Maud, Maud?
    One is come to woo her.

8

Look, a horse at the door,   440
    And little King Charles is snarling,[13]
Go back, my lord, across the moor,
    You are not her darling.

XIII

1

Scorn'd, to be scorn'd by one that I scorn,
Is that a matter to make me fret?
That a calamity hard to be borne?
Well, he may live to hate me yet.
Fool that I am to be vext with his pride!
I past him, I was crossing his lands;
He stood on the path a little aside;   450
His face, as I grant, in spite of spite,
Has a broad-blown comeliness, red and white,
And six feet two, as I think, he stands;
But his essences turn'd the live air sick,

<hr>

13   a King Charles spaniel.

And barbarous opulence jewel-thick
Sunn'd itself on his breast and his hands.

2

Who shall call me ungentle, unfair,
I long'd so heartily then and there
To give him the grasp of fellowship;
But while I past he was humming an air,   460
Stopt, and then with a riding whip
Leisurely tapping a glossy boot,
And curving a contumelious lip,
Gorgonised me from head to foot
With a stony British stare.

3

Why sits he here in his father's chair?
That old man never comes to his place:
Shall I believe him ashamed to be seen?
For only once, in the village street,
Last year, I caught a glimpse of his face,   470
A gray old wolf and a lean.
Scarcely, now, would I call him a cheat;
For then, perhaps, as a child of deceit,
She might by a true descent be untrue;
And Maud is as true as Maud is sweet:
Tho' I fancy her sweetness only due
To the sweeter blood by the other side;
Her mother has been a thing complete,
However she came to be so allied.
And fair without, faithful within,   480
Maud to him is nothing akin:
Some peculiar mystic grace
Made her only the child of her mother,
And heap'd the whole inherited sin
On the huge scapegoat of the race,
All, all upon the brother.

4

Peace, angry spirit, and let him be!
Has not his sister smiled on me?

XIV
1

Maud has a garden of roses
And lilies fair on a lawn;   490
There she walks in her state
And tends upon bed and bower,
And thither I climb'd at dawn
And stood by her garden-gate;
A lion ramps at the top,
He is claspt by a passion-flower.

2

Maud's own little oak-room
(Which Maud, like a precious stone
Set in the heart of the carven gloom,[14]

14   parody of John of Gaunt's description of England as 'This Pre-
cious stone set in the silver sea': *Richard II*, II. i. 46.

Lights with herself, when alone   500
She sits by her music and books
And her brother lingers late
With a roystering company) looks
Upon Maud's own garden-gate:
And I thought as I stood, if a hand, as white
As ocean-foam in the moon, were laid
On the hasp of the window, and my Delight
Had a sudden desire, like a glorious ghost, to glide,
Like a beam of the seventh Heaven, down to my side,
There were but a step to be made.   510

3

The fancy flatter'd my mind,
And again seem'd overbold;
Now I thought that she cared for me,
Now I thought she was kind
Only because she was cold.

4

I heard no sound where I stood
But the rivulet on from the lawn
Running down to my own dark wood;
Or the voice of the long sea-wave as it swell'd
Now and then in the dim-gray dawn;   520
But I look'd, and round, all round the house I beheld
The death-white curtain drawn;
Felt a horror over me creep,
Prickle my skin and catch my breath,
Knew that the death-white curtain meant but sleep,
Yet I shudder'd and thought like a fool of the sleep of death.

XV

So dark a mind within me dwells,
    And I make myself such evil cheer,
That if I be dear to some one else,
    Then some one else may have much to fear   530
But if I be dear to some one else,
    Then I should be to myself more dear.
Shall I not take care of all that I think,
Yea ev'n of wretched meat and drink,
If I be dear,
If I be dear to some one else.

XVI

I

This lump of earth has left his estate
The lighter by the loss of his weight;
And so that he find what he went to seek,
And fulsome Pleasure clog him, and drown   540
His heart in the gross mud-honey of town,
He may stay for a year who has gone for a week:
But this is the day when I must speak,
And I see my Oread coming down,
O this is the day!
O beautiful creature, what am I
That I dare to look her way;
Think I may hold dominion sweet,

Lord of the pulse that is lord of her breast,
And dream of her beauty with tender dread,   550
From the delicate Arab arch of her feet[15]
To the grace that, bright and light as the crest
Of a peacock, sits on her shining head,
And she knows it not: O, if she knew it,
To know her beauty might half undo it.
I know it the one bright thing to save
My yet young life in the wilds of Time,
Perhaps from madness, perhaps from crime,
Perhaps from a selfish grave.

2

What, if she be fasten'd to this fool lord,   560
Dare I bid her abide by her word?
Should I love her so well if she
Had given her word to a thing so low?
Shall I love her as well if she
Can break her word were it even for me?
I trust that it is not so.

3

Catch not my breath, O clamorous heart,
Let not my tongue be a thrall to my eye,
For I must tell her before we part,
I must tell her, or die.   570

XVII

Go not, happy day,[16]
    From the shining fields,
Go not, happy day,
    Till the maiden yields.
Rosy is the West,
    Rosy is the South,
Roses are her cheeks,
    And a rose her mouth
When the happy Yes
    Falters from her lips,   580
Pass and blush the news
    O'er the blowing ships;
Over blowing seas,
    Over seas at rest,
Pass the happy news,
    Blush it thro' the West;
Till the red man dance
    By his red cedar tree,
And the red man's babe
    Leap, beyond the sea.   590
Blush from West to East,
    Blush from East to West,
Till the West is East,
    Blush it thro' the West.
Rosy is the West,
    Rosy is the South,
Roses are her cheeks,
    And a rose her mouth.

15   ? like arched neck of Arab horse.   16   This lyric originally intended for *The Princess* (1847).

XVIII

1

I have led her home, my love, my only friend.
There is none like her, none.   600
And never yet so warmly ran my blood
And sweetly, on and on
Calming itself to the long-wish'd-for end,
Full to the banks, close on the promised good.

2

None like her, none.
Just now the dry-tongued laurels' pattering talk
Seem'd her light foot along the garden walk,
And shook my heart to think she comes once more;
But even then I heard her close the door,
The gates of Heaven are closed, and she is gone.   610

3

There is none like her, none.
Nor will be when our summers have deceased.
O, art thou sighing for Lebanon
In the long breeze that streams to thy delicious East,
Sighing for Lebanon,
Dark cedar, tho' thy limbs have here increased,
Upon a pastoral slope as fair,
And looking to the South, and fed
With honey'd rain and delicate air,
And haunted by the starry head   620
Of her whose gentle will has changed my fate,
And made my life a perfumed altar-flame;
And over whom thy darkness must have spread
With such delight as theirs of old, thy great
Forefathers of the thornless garden, there
Shadowing the snow-limb'd Eve from whom she came.

4

Here will I lie, while these long branches sway,
And you fair stars that crown a happy day
Go in and out as if at merry play,
Who am no more so all forlorn,   630
As when it seem'd far better to be born
To labour and the mattock-harden'd hand,
Than nursed at ease and brought to understand
A sad astrology,[17] the boundless plan
That makes you tyrants in your iron skies,
Innumerable, pitiless, passionless eyes,
Cold fires, yet with power to burn and brand
His nothingness into man.

5

But now shine on, and what care I,
Who in this stormy gulf have found a pearl   640
The countercharm of space and hollow sky,
And do accept my madness, and would die
To save from some slight shame one simple girl.

17   'modern astronomy...The stars are "cold fires"...no perceptible
warmth reaches us' (T.).

6

Would die; for sullen-seeming Death may give
More life to Love than is or ever was
In our low world, where yet 'tis sweet to live.
Let no one ask me how it came to pass;
It seems that I am happy, that to me
A livelier emerald twinkles in the grass,
A purer sapphire melts into the sea.   650

7

Not die; but live a life of truest breath,
And teach true life to fight with mortal wrongs.
O, why should Love, like men in drinking-songs,
Spice his fair banquet with the dust of death?
Make answer, Maud my bliss,
Maud made my Maud by that long lover's kiss,
Life of my life, wilt thou not answer this?
'The dusky strand of Death inwoven here
With dear Love's tie, makes Love himself more dear.'

8

Is that enchanted moan only the swell   660
Of the long waves that roll in yonder bay?
And hark the clock within, the silver knell
Of twelve sweet hours that past in bridal white,
And died to live, long as my pulses play;
But now by this my love has closed her sight
And given false death her hand, and stol'n away
To dreamful wastes where footless fancies dwell
Among the fragments of the golden day.
May nothing there her maiden grace affright!
Dear heart, I feel with thee the drowsy spell.   670
My bride to be, my evermore delight,
My own heart's heart, my ownest own, farewell;
It is but for a little space I go
And ye meanwhile far over moor and fell
Beat to the noiseless music of the night!
Has our whole earth gone nearer to the glow
Of your soft splendours that you look so bright?
I have climbed nearer out of lonely Hell.
Beat, happy stars, timing with things below,
Beat with my heart more blest than heart can tell,   680
Blest, but for some dark undercurrent woe
That seems to draw – but it shall not be so:
Let all be well, be well.

XIX

1

Her brother is coming back to-night,
Breaking up my dream of delight.

2

My dream? do I dream of bliss?
I have walk'd awake with Truth.
O when did a morning shine
So rich in atonement as this
For my dark-dawning youth,   690
Darken'd watching a mother decline

And that dead man at her heart and mine:
For who was left to watch her but I?
Yet so did I let my freshness die.

3

I trust that I did not talk
To gentle Maud in our walk
(For often in lonely wanderings
I have cursed him even to lifeless things)
But I trust that I did not talk,
Not touch on her father's sin: 700
I am sure I did but speak
Of my mother's faded cheek
When it slowly grew so thin,
That I felt she was slowly dying
Vext with lawyers and harass'd with debt:
For how often I caught her with eyes all wet,
Shaking her head at her son and sighing
A world of trouble within!

4

And Maud too, Maud was moved
To speak of the mother she loved   710
As one scarce less forlorn,
Dying abroad and it seems apart
From him who had ceased to share her heart,
And ever mourning over the feud,
The household Fury sprinkled with blood
By which our houses are torn:
How strange was what she said,
When only Maud and the brother
Hung over her dying bed –
That Maud's dark father and mine   720
Had bound us one to the other,
Betrothed us over their wine,
On the day when Maud was born;
Seal'd her mine from her first sweet breath.
Mine, mine by a right, from birth till death,
Mine, mine – our fathers have sworn.

5

But the true blood spilt had in it a heat
To dissolve the precious seal on a bond,
That, if left uncancell'd, had been so sweet;
And none of us thought of a something beyond,   730
A desire that awoke in the heart of the child,
As it were a duty done to the tomb,
To be friends for her sake, to be reconciled;
And I was cursing them and my doom,
And letting a dangerous thought run wild
While often abroad in the fragrant gloom
Of foreign churches – I see her there,
Bright English lily, breathing a prayer
To be friends, to be reconciled!

6

But then what a flint is he!   740
Abroad, at Florence, at Rome,

I find whenever she touch'd on me
This brother had laugh'd her down,
And at last, when each came home,
He had darken'd into a frown,
Chid her, and forbid her to speak
To me, her friend of the years before;
And this was what had redden'd her cheek
When I bow'd to her on the moor.

7

Yet Maud, altho' not blind   750
To the faults of his heart and mind,
I see she cannot but love him,
And says he is rough but kind,
And wishes me to approve him,
And tells me, when she lay
Sick once, with a fear of worse,
That he left his wine and horses and play,
Sat with her, read to her, night and day,
And tended her like a nurse.

8

Kind? but the deathbed desire   760
Spurn'd by this heir of the liar –
Rough but kind? yet I know
He has plotted against me in this,
That he plots against me still.
Kind to Maud? that were not amiss.
Well, rough but kind; why, let it be so:
For shall not Maud have her will?

9

For, Maud, so tender and true,
As long as my life endures
I feel I shall owe you a debt,   770
That I never can hope to pay;
And if ever I should forget
That I owe this debt to you
And for your sweet sake to yours;
O then, what then shall I say? –
If ever I *should* forget,
May God make me more wretched
Than ever I have been yet!

10

So now I have sworn to bury
All this dead body of hate,   780
I feel so free and so clear
By the loss of that dead weight,
That I should grow light-headed, I fear,
Fantastically merry;
But that her brother comes, like a blight
On my fresh hope, to the Hall to-night.

XX

1

Strange, that I felt so gay,
Strange, that I tried to-day

To beguile her melancholy;
The Sultan, as we name him, –
She did not wish to blame him –
But he vext her and perplext her
With his worldly talk and folly:
Was it gentle to reprove her
For stealing out of view
From a little lazy lover
Who but claims her as his due?
Or for chilling his caresses
By the coldness of her manners,
Nay, the plainness of her dresses?
Now I know her but in two,
Nor can pronounce upon it
If one should ask me whether
The habit, hat, and feather,
Or the frock and gipsy bonnet
Be the neater and completer;
For nothing can be sweeter
Than maiden Maud in either.

790

800

2

But tomorrow, if we live,
Our ponderous squire will give
A grand political dinner
To half the squirelings near;
And Maud will wear her jewels,
And the bird of prey will hover,
And the titmouse hope to win her
With his chirrup at her ear.

810

3

A grand political dinner
To the men of many acres,
A gathering of the Tory,
A dinner and then a dance
For the maids and marriage-makers,
And every eye but mine will glance
At Maud in all her glory.

820

4

For I am not invited,
But, with the Sultan's pardon,
I am all as well delighted,
For I know her own rose-garden,
And mean to linger in it
Till the dancing will be over;
And then, oh then, come out to me
For a minute, but for a minute,
Come out to your own true lover,
That your true lover may see
Your glory also, and render
All homage to his own darling,
Queen Maud in all her splendour.

830

XXI

Rivulet crossing my ground,
And bringing me down from the Hall

This garden-rose that I found,
Forgetful of Maud and me,   840
And lost in trouble and moving round
Here at the head of a tinkling fall,
And trying to pass to the sea;
O Rivulet, born at the Hall,
My Maud has sent it by thee
(If I read her sweet will right)
On a blushing mission to me,
Saying in odour and colour, 'Ah, be
Among the roses to-night.'

XXII

1

Come into the garden, Maud,   850
    For the black bat, night, has flown,
Come into the garden, Maud,
    I am here at the gate alone;
And the woodbine spices are wafted abroad,
    And the musk of the rose is blown.

2

For a breeze of morning moves,
    And the planet of Love is on high,
Beginning to faint in the light that she loves
    On a bed of daffodil sky,
To faint in the light of the sun she loves,   860
    To faint in his light, and to die.

3

All night have the roses heard
    The flute, violin, bassoon;
All night has the casement jessamine stirr'd
    To the dancers dancing in tune;
Till a silence fell with the waking bird,
    And a hush with the setting moon.

4

I said to the lily, 'There is but one
    With whom she has heart to be gay.
When will the dancers leave her alone?   870
    She is weary of dance and play.'
Now half to the setting moon are gone,
    And half to the rising day;
Low on the sand and loud on the stone
    The last wheel echoes away.

5

I said to the rose, 'The brief night goes
    In babble and revel and wine.
O young lord-lover, what sighs are those,
    For one that will never be thine?
But mine, but mine,' so I sware to the rose,   880
'For ever and ever, mine.'

6

And the soul of the rose went into my blood,
    As the music clash'd in the hall;

And long by the garden lake I stood,
 For I heard your rivulet fall
From the lake to the meadow and on to the wood,
 Our wood, that is dearer than all;

7

From the meadow your walks have left so sweet
 That whenever a March-wind sighs
He sets the jewel-print of your feet   890
 In violets blue as your eyes,
To the woody hollows in which we meet
 And the valleys of Paradise.

8

The slender acacia would not shake
 One long milk-bloom on the tree;
The white lake-blossom fell into the lake
 As the pimpernel dozed on the lea;
But the rose was awake all night for your sake,
 Knowing your promise to me;
The lilies and roses were all awake,   900
 They sigh'd for the dawn and thee.

9

Queen rose of the rosebud garden of girls,
 Come hither, the dances are done,
In gloss of satin and glimmer of pearls,
 Queen lily and rose in one;
Shine out, little head, sunning over with curls,
 To the flowers, and be their sun.

10

There has fallen a splendid tear
 From the passion-flower at the gate.
She is coming, my dove, my dear;   910
 She is coming, my life, my fate;
The red rose cries, 'She is near, she is near;'
 And the white rose weeps, 'She is late;'
The larkspur listens, 'I hear, I hear;'
 And the lily whispers, 'I wait.'

11

She is coming, my own, my sweet;
 Were it ever so airy a tread,
My heart would hear her and beat,
 Were it earth in an earthy bed;
My dust would hear her and beat,   920
 Had I lain for a century dead;
Would start and tremble under her feet,
 And blossom in purple and red.

XXIII

1

'The fault was mine, the fault was mine' –
Why am I sitting here so stunn'd and still,
Plucking the harmless wild-flower on the hill? –
It is this guilty hand! –
And there rises ever a passionate cry
From underneath in the darkening land –

What is it, that has been done?   930
O dawn of Eden bright over earth and sky,
The fires of Hell brake out of thy rising sun,
The fires of Hell and of Hate;
For she, sweet soul, had hardly spoken a word,
When her brother ran in his rage to the gate,
He came with the babe-faced lord;
Heap'd on her terms of disgrace,
And while she wept, and I strove to be cool,
He fiercely gave me the lie,
Till I with as fierce an anger spoke,   940
And he struck me, madman, over the face,
Struck me before the languid fool,
Who was gaping and grinning by:
Struck for himself an evil stroke;
Wrought for his house an irredeemable woe;
For front to front in an hour we stood,[18]
And a million horrible bellowing echoes broke
From the red-ribb'd hollow behind the wood,
And thunder'd up into Heaven the Christless code,
That must have life for a blow.   950
Ever and ever afresh they seem'd to grow.
Was it he lay there with a fading eye?
'The fault was mine,' he whisper'd, 'fly!'
Then glided out of the joyous wood
The ghastly Wraith of one that I know;
And there rang on a sudden a passionate cry,
A cry for a brother's blood:
It will ring in my heart and my ears, till I die, till I die.

                                    2
Is it gone? my pulses beat –
What was it? a lying trick of the brain?   960
Yet I thought I saw her stand,
A shadow there at my feet,
High over the shadowy land.
It is gone; and the heavens fall in a gentle rain,
When they should burst and drown with deluging storms
The feeble vassals of wine and anger and lust,
The little hearts that know not how to forgive:
Arise, my God, and strike, for we hold Thee just,
Strike dead the whole weak race of venomous worms,
That sting each other here in the dust;   970
We are not worthy to live.

                              XXIV
                                1
                    See what a lovely shell,[19]
                    Small and pure as a pearl,
                    Lying close to my foot,
                    Frail, but a work divine,
                    Made so fairily well
                    With delicate spire and whorl,
                    How exquisitely minute,
                    A miracle of design!

---

18   they fight a duel with pistols.   19   This lyric dates from the 1830s.

2

What is it? a learned man   980
Could give it a clumsy name.
Let him name it who can,
The beauty would be the same.

3

The tiny cell is forlorn,
Void of the little living will
That made it stir on the shore.
Did he stand at the diamond door
Of his house in a rainbow frill?
Did he push, when he was uncurl'd,
A golden foot or a fairy horn   990
Thro' his dim water-world?

4

Slight, to be crush'd with a tap
Of my finger-nail on the sand,
Small, but a work divine,
Frail, but of force to withstand,
Year upon year, the shock
Of cataract seas that snap
The three-decker's oaken spine
Athwart the ledges of rock,
Here on the Breton strand!   1000

5

Breton, not Briton; here
Like a shipwreck'd man on a coast
Of ancient fable and fear –
Plagued with a flitting to and fro,
A disease, a hard mechanic ghost
That never came from on high
Nor ever arose from below,
But only moves with the moving eye,
Flying along the land and the main –
Why should it look like Maud?   1010
Am I to be overawed
By what I cannot but know
Is a juggle born of the brain?

6

Back from the Breton coast,
Sick of a nameless fear,
Back to the dark sea-line
Looking, thinking of all I have lost;
An old song vexes my ear;
But that of Lamech is mine.[20]

7

For years, a measureless ill,   1020
For years, for ever, to part –
But she, she would love me still;

20   T. is thinking of Genesis 4.23, 'I have slain a man to my wounding,
and a young man to my hurt.'

And as long, O God, as she
Have a grain of love for me,
So long, no doubt, no doubt,
Shall I nurse in my dark heart,
However weary, a spark of will
Not to be trampled out.

8

Strange, that the mind, when fraught
With a passion so intense   1030
One would think that it well
Might drown all life in the eye, –
That it should, by being so overwrought,
Suddenly strike on a sharper sense
For a shell, or a flower, little things
Which else would have been past by!
And now I remember, I,
When he lay dying there,
I noticed one of his many rings
(For he had many, poor worm) and thought   1040
It is his mother's hair.

9

Who knows if he be dead?
Whether I need have fled?
Am I guilty of blood?
However this may be,
Comfort her, comfort her, all things good,
While I am over the sea!
Let me and my passionate love go by,
But speak to her all things holy and high,
Whatever happen to me!   1050
Me and my harmful love go by;
But come to her waking, find her asleep,
Powers of the height, Powers of the deep,
And comfort her tho' I die.

XXV

Courage, poor heart of stone!
I will not ask thee why
Thou canst not understand
That thou art left for ever alone:
Courage, poor stupid heart of stone. –
Or if I ask thee why,   1060
Care not thou to reply:
She is but dead, and the time is at hand
When thou shalt more than die.

XXVI[21]
1

O that 'twere possible
After long grief and pain
To find the arms of my true love
Round me once again!

21   This section (written 1833–4), published as part of 'Stanzas' in *The Tribute* (September 1837). The germ of 'Maud;' and a key part of the Hallam group of T. poems.

2

When I was wont to meet her
In the silent woody places
By the home that gave me birth,   1070
We stood tranced in long embraces
Mixt with kisses sweeter sweeter
Than any thing on earth.

3

A shadow flits before me,
Not thou, but like to thee:
Ah Christ, that it were possible
For one short hour to see
The souls we loved, that they might tell us
What and where they be.

4

It leads me forth at evening,   1080
It lightly winds and steals
In a cold white robe before me,
When all my spirit reels
At the shouts, the leagues of lights,
And the roaring of the wheels.

5

Half the night I waste in sighs,
Half in dreams I sorrow after
The delight of early skies;
In a wakeful doze I sorrow
For the hand, the lips, the eyes,   1090
For the meeting of the morrow,
The delight of happy laughter,
The delight of low replies.

6

'Tis a morning pure and sweet,
And a dewy splendour falls
On the little flower that clings
To the turrets and the walls;
'Tis a morning pure and sweet,
And the light and shadow fleet;
She is walking in the meadow,   1100
And the woodland echo rings;
In a moment we shall meet;
She is singing in the meadow
And the rivulet at her feet
Ripples on in light and shadow
To the ballad that she sings.

7

Do I hear her sing as of old,
My bird with the shining head,
My own dove with the tender eye?
But there rings on a sudden a passionate cry,   1110
There is some one dying or dead,
And a sullen thunder is roll'd;
For a tumult shakes the city,
And I wake, my dream is fled;

In the shuddering dawn, behold,
Without knowledge, without pity,
By the curtains of my bed
That abiding phantom cold.

8

Get thee hence, nor come again,
Mix not memory with doubt,   1120
Pass, thou deathlike type[22] of pain,
Pass and cease to move about!
'Tis the blot upon the brain
That *will* show itself without.

9

Then I rise, the eavedrops fall,
And the yellow vapours choke
The great city sounding wide;
The day comes, a dull red ball
Wrapt in drifts of lurid smoke
On the misty river-tide.   1130

10

Thro' the hubbub of the market
I steal, a wasted frame,
It crosses here, it crosses there,
Thro' all that crowd confused and loud,
The shadow still the same;
And on my heavy eyelids
My anguish hangs like shame.

11

Alas for her that met me,
That heard me softly call,
Came glimmering thro' the laurels   1140
At the quiet evenfall,
In the garden by the turrets
Of the old manorial hall.

12

Would the happy spirit descend,
From the realms of light and song,
In the chamber or the street,
As she looks among the blest,
Should I fear to greet my friend
Or to say 'forgive the wrong,'
Or to ask her, 'take me, sweet,   1150
To the regions of thy rest'?

13

But the broad light glares and beats,
And the shadow flits and fleets
And will not let me be;
And I loathe the squares and streets,
And the faces that one meets,
Hearts with no love for me:
Always I long to creep

22 archetype.

Into some still cavern deep,
There to weep, and weep, and weep   1160
My whole soul out to thee.

XXVII[23]

1

Dead, long dead,
Long dead!
And my heart is a handful of dust,
And the wheels go over my head,
And my bones are shaken with pain,
For into a shallow grave they are thrust,
Only a yard beneath the street,
And the hoofs of the horses beat, beat,
The hoofs of the horses beat,   1170
Beat into my scalp and my brain,
With never an end to the stream of passing feet,
Driving, hurrying, marrying, burying,
Clamour and rumble, and ringing and clatter,
And here beneath it is all as bad,
For I thought the dead had peace, but it is not so;
To have no peace in the grave, is that not sad?
But up and down and to and fro,
Ever about me the dead men go;
And then to hear a dead man chatter   1180
Is enough to drive one mad.

2

Wretchedest age, since Time began,
They cannot even bury a man;
And tho' we paid our tithes in the days that are gone,
Not a bell was rung, not a prayer was read;
It is that which makes us loud in the world of the dead;
There is none that does his work, not one;
A touch of their office might have sufficed,
But the churchmen fain would kill their church,
As the churches have kill'd their Christ.   1190

3

See, there is one of us sobbing,
No limit to his distress;
And another, a lord of all things, praying
To his own great self, as I guess;
And another, a statesman there, betraying
His party-secret, fool, to the press;
And yonder a vile physician, blabbing
The case of his patient – all for what?
To tickle the maggot born in an empty head,
And wheedle a world that loves him not,   1200
For it is but a world of the dead.

4

Nothing but idiot gabble!
For the prophecy given of old
And then not understood,

---

23   The 'mad scene', allegedly written in twenty minutes, February
1855.

Has come to pass as foretold;
Not let any man think for the public good,
But babble, merely for babble.
For I never whisper'd a private affair
Within the hearing of cat or mouse,
No, not to myself in the closet alone,
But I heard it shouted at once from the top of the house;[24]   1210
Everything came to be known.
Who told *him* we were there?

5

Not that gray old wolf, for he came not back
From the wilderness, full of wolves, where he used to lie;
He has gather'd the bones for his o'ergrown whelp to crack;
Crack them now for yourself, and howl, and die.

6

Prophet, curse me the blabbing lip,
And curse me the British vermin, the rat;
I know not whether he came in the Hanover ship,[25]   1220
But I know that he lies and listens mute
In an ancient mansion's crannies and holes:
Arsenic, arsenic, sure, would do it,
Except that now we poison our babes, poor souls!
It is all used up for that.

7

Tell him now: she is standing here at my head;
Not beautiful now, not even kind;
He may take her now; for she never speaks her mind,
But is ever the one thing silent here.
She is not of us, as I divine;   1230
She comes from another stiller world of the dead,
Stiller, not fairer than mine.

8

But I know where a garden grows,
Fairer than aught in the world beside,
All made up of the lily and rose
That blow by night, when the season is good,
To the sound of dancing music and flutes:
It is only flowers, they had no fruits,
And I almost fear they are not roses, but blood;
For the keeper was one, so full of pride,   1240
He linkt a dead man there to a spectral bride;
For he, if he had not been a Sultan of brutes,
Would he have that hole in his side?

9

But what will the old man say?
He laid a cruel snare in a pit
To catch a friend of mine one stormy day;
Yet now I could even weep to think of it;
For what will the old man say
When he comes to the second corpse in the pit?

---

24 Luke 12.3.

25 It was once thought the House of Hanover imported a brand of
rat into England.

10

Friend, to be struck by the public foe,   1250
Then to strike him and lay him low,
That were a public merit, far,
Whatever the Quaker holds, from sin;
But the red life spilt for a private blow –
I swear to you, lawful and lawless war
Are scarcely even akin.

11

O me, why have they not buried me deep enough?
Is it kind to have made me a grave so rough,
Me, that was never a quiet sleeper?
Maybe still I am but half-dead;   1260
Then I cannot be wholly dumb;
I will cry to the steps above my head
And somebody, surely, some kind heart will come
To bury me, bury me
Deeper, ever so little deeper.

XXVIII[26]

I

My life has crept so long on a broken wing
Thro' cells of madness, haunts of horror and fear,
That I come to be grateful at last for a little thing:
My mood is changed, for it fell at a time of year
When the face of night is fair on the dewy downs,   1270
And the shining daffodil dies, and the Charioteer
And starry Gemini hang like glorious crowns
Over Orion's grave low down in the west,
That like a silent lightning under the stars
She seem'd to divide in a dream from a band of the blest,
And spoke of a hope for the world in the coming wars –
'And in that hope, dear soul, let trouble have rest,
Knowing I tarry for thee,' and pointed to Mars
As he glowed like a ruddy shield on the Lion's breast.

2

And it was but a dream, yet it yielded a dear delight   1280
To have look'd, though but in a dream, upon eyes so fair,
That had been in a weary world my one thing bright;
And it was but a dream, yet it lighten'd my despair
When I thought that a war would arise in defence of the right,
That an iron tyranny now should bend or cease,
The glory of manhood stand on his ancient height,
Nor Britain's one sole God be the millionaire:
No more shall commerce be all in all, and Peace
Pipe on her pastoral hillock a languid note,
And watch her harvest ripen, her herd increase,   1290
Nor the cannon-bullet rust on a slothful shore,
And the cobweb woven across the cannon's throat
Shall shake its threaded tears in the wind no more.

3

And as months ran on and rumour of battle grew,
'It is time, O passionate heart,' said I

26   'Sane but shattered. Written when the cannon was heard booming
from the Solent before the Crimean War' (T.).

(For I cleaved to a cause that I felt to be pure and true),
'It is time, O passionate heart and morbid eye,
That old hysterical mock-disease should die.'
And I stood on a giant deck and mix'd my breath
With a loyal people shouting a battle cry,   1300
Till I saw the dreary phantom arise and fly
Far into the North, and battle, and seas of death.

4

Let it go or stay, so I wake to the higher aims
Of a land that has lost for a little her lust of gold,
And love of a peace that was full of wrongs and shames,
Horrible, hateful, monstrous, not to be told;
And hail once more to the banner of battle unroll'd!
Tho' many a light shall darken, and many shall weep
For those that are crush'd in the clash of jarring claims,
Yet God's just wrath shall be wreak'd on a giant liar;   1310
And many a darkness into the light shall leap,
And shine in the sudden making of splendid names,
And noble thought be freer under the sun,
And the heart of a people beat with one desire;
For the peace, that I deemed no peace, is over and done,
And now by the side of the Black[27] and the Baltic deep,
And deathful-grinning mouths of the fortress, flames
The blood-red blossom of war with a heart of fire.

5

Let it flame or fade, and the war roll down like a wind,
We have proved we have hearts in a cause, we are noble still,   1320
And myself have awaked, as it seems, to the better mind;
It is better to fight for the good than to rail at the ill;
I have felt with my native land, I am one with my kind,
I embrace the purpose of God, and the doom assigned.

Germ, 'Oh! that 'twere possible' (1833–4). Mainly written 1854–5. Final copy made 25 April 1855 ('last touch', 7 July). First published in Maud, and Other Poems *(1855). Revised, lengthened, improved, in* Maud, and other Poems, A New Edition *by Alfred Tennyson, D. C. L., Poet Laureate (Edward Moxon, 1856). (Divided, later, into 2 Parts, Part II beginning at Section XXIII; then into 3 Parts, Part III beginning at Section XXVIII.) 1856 text.*

PREFATORY POEM TO MY BROTHER'S SONNETS

Midnight, June 30, 1879

I

Midnight – in no midsummer tune
The breakers lash the shores:
The cuckoo of a joyless June
Is calling out of doors:
And thou hast vanish'd from thine own
To that which looks like rest,
True brother, only to be known
By those who love thee best.

II

Midnight – and joyless June gone by,
And from the deluged park   10

27 Black Sea.

The cuckoo of a worse July
Is calling thro' the dark:

But thou art silent underground,
And o'er thee streams the rain,
True poet, surely to be found
When Truth is found again.

III

And, now to these unsummer'd skies
The summer bird is still,
Far off a phantom cuckoo cries
From out a phantom hill;   20

And thro' this midnight breaks the sun
Of sixty years away,
The light of days when life begun,
The days that seem to-day,

When all my griefs were shared with thee,
As all my hopes were thine –
As all thou wert was one with me,
May all thou art be mine!

First published in Charles Tennyson Turner, Collected Sonnets, Old and New
(Kegan Paul & Co., 1880), with present sub-title as title. Text and title,
Tiresias and Other Poems, *by Alfred Lord Tennyson, D. C. L., P. L.*
(Macmillan & Co., 1885).

CROSSING THE BAR[1]

Sunset and evening star,
  And one clear call for me!
And may there be no moaning of the bar,
  When I put out to sea,

But such a tide as moving seems asleep,
  Too full for sound and foam,
When that which drew from out the boundless deep
  Turns again home.

Twilight and evening bell,
  And after that the dark!   10
And may there be no sadness of farewell,
  When I embark;

For tho' from out our bourne of Time and Place
  The flood may bear me far,
I hope to see my Pilot face to face[2]
  When I have crost the bar.

Demeter and Other Poems, *by Alfred Lord Tennyson, D. C. L., P. L.*
(Macmillan & Co., 1889). Last poem in the volume.

CROSSING THE BAR
1 written October 1889, crossing the Solent. A bar is a sandbank across a harbour mouth. 'Mind you put my *Crossing the Bar* at the end of all editions of my poems.'
2 1 Corinthians 13.12.

Hippolyte Adolphe Taine (1828–93)

Hippolyte Taine, critic, historian, philosopher, traveller, was born in the Ardennes, France, 21 April 1828. He studied in Paris, and made his name as a critic with a study of La Fontaine's *Fables* (1853). He was a Positivist, as appears in his study of French nineteenth-century philosophers (1857) and his *Philosophie de l'intelligence* (1870) and *Philosophie de l'art* (1881). His biggest work in every sense is his anti-revolutionary *Origines de la france contemporaine*

(1875–94). As a sociologist and sociological historian he often hits the nail on the head, even when, as in his *Notes sur l'Angleterre* (1871), he spent only ten weeks in the country he was observing. What's good about his remarks on Tennyson is the way his unabashed readiness to generalize about Englishness and English literature does that driving of nails home with such canny freshness as well as with such massive foreigner-cheek.

THE FAVOURITE POET OF A NATION

The favourite poet of a nation, it seems, is he whose works a man, setting out on a journey, prefers to put into his pocket. Now-a-days it would be Tennyson in England, and Alfred de Musset in France. The two publics differ: so do their modes of life, their reading, and their pleasures. Let us try to describe them; we shall better understand the flowers if we see them in the garden.

Here we are at Newhaven or at Dover, and we glide over the rails looking on either side. On both hands fly past country-houses; they exist everywhere in England, on the margin of lakes, on the edge of the bays, on the summit of the hill, in every picturesque point of view. They are the chosen abodes; London is but a business-place; men of the world live, amuse themselves, visit each other, in the country. How well ordered and pretty is this house! If near it there was some old edifice, abbey, or castle, it has been preserved. The new building has been suited to the old; even if detached and modern, it does not lack style; gable-ends, mullions, broad-windows, turrets perched at every corner, have a Gothic air in their newness. Even this cottage, modest as it is, suited to people with a very good income, is pleasant to see with its pointed roofs, its porch, its bright brown bricks, all covered with ivy. Doubtless grandeur is generally wanting; in these days the men who mould opinion are no longer great lords, but rich gentlemen, well brought up, and land-holders; it is pleasantness which appeals to them. But how they understand the word! All round the house is a lawn fresh and smooth as velvet, rolled every morning. In front, great rhododendrons form a bright thicket in which murmur swarms of bees; festoons of exotics creep and curve over the short grass; honeysuckles clamber up the trees; hundreds of roses, drooping over the windows, shed their rain of petals on the paths. Fine elms, yew-trees, great oaks, jealously tended, everywhere combine their leafage or rear their heads. Trees have been brought from Australia and China to adorn the thickets with the elegance or the singularity of their foreign shapes; the copper-beech stretches over the delicate verdure the shadow of its dark metallic-hued foliage. How delicious is the freshness of this verdure! How it glistens, and how it abounds in wild flowers brightened by the sun! What care, what cleanliness, how everything is arranged, kept up, refined, for the comfort of the senses and the pleasure of the eyes! If there is a slope, streams have been devised with little islets in the glen, peopled with tufts of roses; ducks of select breed swim in the pools, where the water-lilies display their satin stars. Fat oxen lie in the grass, sheep as white as if fresh from the washing, all kinds of happy and model animals, fit to delight the eyes of an amateur and a master. We return to the house, and before entering I look upon the view; decidedly the love of Englishmen for the country is innate; how comfortable it will be from that parlour window to look upon the setting sun, and the broad network of sunlight spread across the woods! And how cunningly they have disposed the house, so that the landscape may be seen at distance between the hills, and at hand between the trees! We enter. How nicely everything is got up, and how commodious! The least wants have been foreseen, provided for; there is nothing which is not correct and perfect; we imagine that all the objects have received a prize, or at least honourable mention, at some industrial exhibition. And the attendance of the servants is as good as the objects; cleanliness is not more scrupulous in Holland; Englishmen have, in proportion, three times as many servants as Frenchmen; not too many for the minute details of the service. The domestic machine acts without interruption, without shock, without hindrance; every wheel has its movement and its place, and the comfort which it dispenses falls on the mouth like honeydew, as true and as exquisite as the sugar of a model refinery when quite purified.

We converse with our host. We very soon find that his mind and soul have always been well balanced. When he left college he found his career shaped out for him; no need for him to revolt against the Church, which is half rational; nor against the Constitution, which is nobly liberal: the faith and law presented to him are good, useful, moral, liberal enough to maintain and employ all diversities of sincere minds. He became attached to them, he loves them, he has received from them the whole system of his practical and speculative ideas; he does not waver, he no longer doubts, he knows what he ought to believe and to do. He is not carried away by theories, dulled by sloth, checked by contradictions. Elsewhere youth is like a stagnant or scattering water; here there is a fine old channel which receives and directs to a useful and sure end the stream of its activities and passions. He acts, works, rules. He is married, has tenants, is a magistrate, becomes a politician. He improves and rules his parish, his estate, and his family. He founds societies, speaks at meetings, superintends schools, dispenses justice, introduces improvements; he employs his reading, his travels, his connections, his fortune, and his rank, to lead his neighbours and dependants amicably to some work which profits themselves and the public. He is influential and respected. He has the pleasures of self-esteem and the satisfaction of conscience. He knows that he has authority, and that he uses it loyally, for the good of others. And this healthy state of mind is supported by a wholesome life. His mind is beyond doubt cultivated and occupied; he is well-informed, knows several languages, has travelled, is fond of all precise information; he is kept by his newspaper conversant with all new ideas and discoveries. But, at the same time, he loves and practises all bodily exercises. He rides, takes long walks, hunts, yachts, follows closely and by himself all the details of breeding and agriculture; he lives in the open air, he withstands the encroachments of a sedentary life, which always elsewhere leads the modern man to agitation of the brain, weakness of the muscles, and excitement of the nerves. Such is this elegant and common-sense society, refined in comfort, regular in conduct, whose dilettante tastes and moral principles confine it within a sort of flowery border, and prevent it from having its attention diverted.

Does any poet suit such a society better than Tennyson? Without being a pedant, he is moral; he may be read in the family circle by night; he does not rebel against society and life; he speaks of God and the soul, nobly, tenderly, without ecclesiastical prejudice; there is no need to reproach him like Lord Byron; he has no violent and abrupt words, excessive and scandalous sentiments; he will pervert nobody. We shall not be troubled when we close the book; we may listen when we quit him, without contrast, to the grave voice of the master of the house, who repeats the evening prayers before the kneeling servants. And yet, when we quit him, we keep a smile of pleasure on our lips. The traveller, the lover of archæology, has been pleased by the imitations of foreign and antique sentiments. The sportsman, the lover of the country, has relished the little country scenes and the rich rural pictures. The ladies have been charmed by his portraits of women; they are so exquisite and pure! He has laid such delicate blushes on those lovely cheeks! He has depicted so well the changing expression of those proud or candid eyes! They like him because they feel that he likes them. More, he honours them, and rises in his nobility to the height of their purity. Young girls weep in listening to him; certainly when, a while ago, we heard the legend of 'Elaine' or 'Enid' read, we saw the fair heads drooping under the flowers which adorned them, and white shoulders heaving with furtive emotion. And how delicate was this emotion! He has not rudely trenched upon truth and passion. He has risen to the height of noble and tender sentiments. He has gleaned from all nature and all history what was most lofty and amiable. He has chosen his ideas, chiselled his words, equalled by his artifices, successes, and diversity of his style, the pleasantness and perfection of social elegance in the midst of which we read him. His poetry is like one of those gilt and painted stands in which flowers of the country and exotics mingle in artful harmony their stalks and foliage, their clusters and cups, their scents and hues. It seems made expressly for these wealthy, cultivated, free business men, heirs of the ancient nobility, new leaders of a new England. It is part of their luxury as of their morality; it is an eloquent confirmation of their principles, and a precious article of their drawing-room furniture.

We return to Calais, and travel towards Paris, without pausing on the road. There are on the way plenty of noblemen's castles, and houses of rich men of business. But we do not find amongst them, as in England, the thinking elegant world, which, by the refinement of its tastes and the superiority of its mind, becomes the guide of the nation and the arbiter of the beautiful. There are two peoples in France: the provinces and Paris; the one dining, sleeping, yawning, listening; the other thinking, daring, watching, and speaking: the first drawn by the second, as a snail by a butterfly, alternately amused and disturbed by the whims and the audacity of its guide. It is this guide we must look upon! Let us enter Paris! What a strange spectacle! It is evening, the streets are aflame, a luminous dust covers the busy noisy crowd, which jostles, elbows, crushes, and swarms in front of the theatres, behind the windows of the cafés. Have you remarked how all these faces are wrinkled, frowning, or pale; how anxious are their looks, how nervous their gestures? A violent brightness falls on these shining heads; most are bald before thirty. To find pleasure here, they must have plenty of excitement: the dust of the boulevard settles on the ice which they are eating; the smell of the gas and the steam of the pavement, the perspiration left on the walls dried up by the fever of a Parisian day, 'the human air full of impure rattle' – this is what they cheerfully breathe. They are crammed round their little marble tables, persecuted by the glaring light, the shouts of the waiters, the jumble of mixed talk, the monotonous motion of gloomy walkers, the flutter of loitering courtesans moving anxiously in the shadow. Doubtless their homes are unpleasing, or they would not change them for these bagmen's delights. We climb four flights, and find ourselves in a polished, gilded room, adorned with stuccoed ornaments, plaster statuettes, new furniture of old oak, with every kind of pretty knick-knack on the mantlepieces and the whatnots. 'It makes a good show'; you can give a good reception to envious friends and people of standing. It is an advertisement, nothing more; we pass half an hour there agreeably, and that is all. You will never make more than a house of call out of it; it is low in the ceiling, close, inconvenient, rented by the year, dirty in six months, serving to display a fictitious luxury. All the enjoyments of these people are factitious, and, as it were, snatched hurriedly; they have in them something unhealthy and irritating. They are like the cookery of their restaurants, the splendour of their cafés, the gaiety of their theatres. They want them too quick, too lively, too manifold. They have not cultivated them patiently, and culled them moderately; they have forced them on an artificial and heating soil; they grasp them in haste. They are refined and greedy; they need every day a stock of coloured words, broad anecdotes, biting railleries, new truths, varied ideas. They soon get bored, and cannot endure tedium, They amuse themselves with all their might, and find that they are hardly amused. They exaggerate their work and their expense, their wants and their efforts. The accumulation of sensations and fatigue stretches their nervous machine to excess, and their polish of social gaiety chips off twenty times a day, displaying a basis of suffering and ardour.

But how fine they are, and how free is their mind! How this incessant rubbing has sharpened them! How ready they are to grasp and comprehend everything! How apt this studied and manifold culture has made them to feel and relish tendernesses and sadnesses, unknown to their fathers, deep feelings, strange and sublime, which hitherto seemed foreign to their race! This great city is cosmopolitan; here all ideas may be born; no barrier checks the mind; the vast field of thought opens before them without a beaten or prescribed track. Use neither hinders nor guides them; an official Government and Church rid them of the care of leading the nation: the two powers are submitted to, as we submit to the beadle or the policeman, patiently and with chaff; they are looked upon as a play. In short, the world here seems but a melodrama, a subject of criticism and argument. And be sure that criticism and argument have full scope. An Englishman entering on life, finds to all great questions an answer ready made. A Frenchman entering on life finds to all great questions simply suggested doubts. In this conflict of opinions he must create a faith for himself, and, being mostly unable to do it, he remains open to every uncertainty, and therefore to every curiosity and to every pain. In this gulf, which is like a vast sea, dreams, theories, fancies, intemper-ate, poetic and sickly desires, collect and chase each other like clouds. If in this tumult of moving forms we seek some solid work to prepare a foundation for future opinions, we find only the slowly-rising edifices of the sciences, which here and there obscurely, like submarine polypes, con-struct of imperceptible coral the basis on which the belief of the human race is to rest.

Such is the world for which Alfred de Musset[1] wrote: in Paris he must be read. Read? We all know him by heart. He is dead, and it seems as if we daily hear him speak. A conversation among artists, as they jest in a studio, a beautiful young girl leaning over her box at the theatre, a street washed by the rain, making the black pavement shine, a fresh smiling morning in the woods of Fontainebleau, everything brings him before us, as if he were alive again. Was there ever a more vibrating and genuine accent? This man, at least, has never lied. He has only said what he felt, and he has said it, as he felt it. He thought aloud. He made the confession of every man. He was not admired, but loved; he was more than a poet, he was a man. Every one found in him his own feelings, the most transient, the most familiar; he did not restrain himself, he gave himself to all; he had the last virtues which remain to us, generosity and sincerity. And he had the most precious gift which can seduce an old civilisation, youth. As he said, 'that hot youth, a tree with a rough bark, which covers all with its shadow, prospect and path'. With what fire did he hurl onward love, jealousy, the thirst of pleasure, all the impetuous passions which rise with vir-gin blood from the depths of a young heart, and how did he make them clash together! Has any one felt them more deeply? He was too full of them, he gave himself up to them, was intoxicated with them. He rushed through life, like an eager racehorse in the country, whom the scent of plants and the splendid novelty of the vast heavens urge, breast foremost, in its mad career, which shat-ters all before him, and himself as well. He desired too much; he wished strongly and greedily to taste life in one draught, thoroughly; he did not glean or taste it; he tore it off like a bunch of grapes, pressed it, crushed it, twisted it; and he remains with stained hands, as thirsty as before.[2] Then broke forth sobs which found an echo in all hearts. What! so young, and already so wearied! So many precious gifts, so fine a mind, so delicate a tact, so rich and mobile a fancy, so precious a glory, such a sudden blossom of beauty and genius, and yet anguish, disgust, tears, and cries! What a mixture! With the same attitude he adores and curses. Eternal illusion, invincible experience, keep side by side in him to fight and tear him. He became old, and remained young; he is a poet, and he is a sceptic. The Muse and her peaceful beauty, Nature and her immortal freshness, Love and his happy smile, all the swarm of divine visions barely passed before his eyes, when we see approach-ing, with curses and sarcasms, all the spectres of debauchery and death. He is as a man in a festive scene, who drinks from a carven cup, standing up, in front, amidst applause and triumphal music, his eyes laughing, his heart full of joy, heated and excited by the generous wine descending in his breast, whom suddenly we see growing pale; there was poison in the cup; he falls, and the death-rattle is in his throat; his convulsed feet beat upon the silken carpet, and all the terrified guests look on. This is what we felt on the day when the most beloved, the most brilliant amongst us, suddenly quivered from an unseen attack, and was struck down, with the death-rattle in his throat, amid the lying splendours and gaieties of our banquet.

Well! such as he was, we love him for ever: we cannot listen to another; beside him, all seem cold or false. We leave at midnight the theatre in which he had heard Malibran, and we enter the gloomy *rue des Moulins*, where, on a hired bed, his Rolla[3] came to sleep and die. The lamps cast flickering rays on the slippery pavement. Restless shadows march past the doors, and trail along their dress of draggled silk to meet the passers-by. The windows are fastened; here and there a light pierces through a half-closed shutter, and shows a dead dahlia on the edge of a window-sill. Tomorrow an organ will grind before these panes, and the wan clouds will leave their droppings on these

THE FAVOURITE POET OF A NATION

1 1810–57.

2 'O médiocrité! celui qui pour tout bien
   T'apporte à ce tripot dégoûtant de la vie
   Est bien poltron au jeu s'il ne dit: Tout ou rien.'

[Author's note] [O mediocrity! the person who brings you for your own good to this disgusting gambling den of life is a cowardly gambler if he does not declare: All or nothing.]

3 hero of a de Musset poem. (Marie Malibran (1808–36): Spanish singer.)

dirty walls. From this wretched place came the most impassioned of his poems! These vilenesses and vulgarities of the stews and the lodging-house caused this divine eloquence to flow! it was these which at such a moment gathered in this bruised heart all the splendours of nature and history, to make them spring up in sparkling jets, and shine under the most glowing poetic sun that ever rose! We feel pity; we think of that other poet, away there in the Isle of Wight, who amuses himself by dressing up lost epics. How happy he is amongst his fine books, his friends, his honeysuckles and roses! No matter. De Musset, in this very spot, in this filth and misery, rose higher. From the heights of his doubt and despair, he saw the infinite, as we see the sea from a storm-beaten promontory. Religions, their glory and their decay, the human race, its pangs and its destiny, all that is sublime in the world, appeared there to him in a flash of lightning. He felt, at least this once in his life, the inner tempest of deep sensations, giant-dreams, and intense voluptuousness, whose desire enabled him to live, and whose lack forced him to die. He was no mere dilettante; he was not content to taste and enjoy; he left his mark on human thought; he told the world what was man, love, truth, happiness. He suffered, but he invented; he fainted, but he produced. He tore from his entrails with despair the idea which he had conceived, and showed it to the eyes of all, bloody but alive. That is harder and lovelier than to go fondling and gazing upon the ideas of others. There is in the world but one work worthy of a man, the production of a truth, to which we devote ourselves, and in which we believe. The people who have listened to Tennyson are better than our aristocracy of townsfolk and bohemians; but I prefer Alfred de Musset to Tennyson.

History of English Literature (Histoire de la littérature Anglaise, 1863–4), trans. H. van Laun (Edmonston & Douglas, Edinburgh, 1871), vol. II, bk v ('Modern Authors'), ch. 6 ('Poetry – Tennyson'), sect. VI, 535–41.

William Miller (1810–72)

William Miller, dubbed 'The Laureate of the Nursery' by Robert Buchanan, was born in Glasgow, August 1810. His first ambition to become a surgeon was frustrated through ill-health and he became a cabinet-maker instead. He carried on in this trade in Glasgow until November 1871 when an ulcerated leg forced him to give up manual work. His lyrics for children in the *Whistle-Binkie* anthology of Scottish songs (which began its long life in 1832) made him famous, and not only in Scotland. 'Wee Willie-Winkie' travelled the world, and was translated into several languages. It has become a standard item in the canon of British nursery rhymes. Something of its wide fame is indicated by the case of the Kipling character Percival William Williams in the story 'Wee Willie Winkie' (*Wee Willie Winkie and Other Child Stories*: Wheeler's Indian Railway Library, Allahabad, 1888), who got his Milleresque nickname from a 'nursery-book' – Miller's own, maybe, or perhaps Charles E. Leland's *Johnnykin and the Goblins* (1877), which has a Wee Willie Winkie in it. (*Winkle*, childish slang for a baby's penis, and *willy*, also slang for penis, perhaps found their stimulus hereabouts.) This poem alone is what keeps Miller's name alive in the world of nursery literature, but in his time Miller was widely popular for a roster of charmingly simple verses amounting to a whole mythology of childhood. His *Scottish Nursery Songs* appeared in 1863. His infected leg developed into 'a paralytic infection', and he died in Glasgow, 20 August 1872, having just reached the age of sixty-two. A monument was erected to him in the Glasgow Necropolis by a group of admirers.

WILLIE WINKIE[1]

A Nursery Rhyme

Wee Willie Winkie rins through the toon,
Up stairs an' doon stairs in his nicht-gown,

WILLIE WINKIE
1 The Scottish Nursery Morpheus. [Original footnote] [Morpheus: god of sleep]

Tirlin' at the window, crying at the lock,
'Are the weans in their bed, for it's now ten o'clock?'

'Hey Willie Winkie, are ye comin' ben?
The cat's singin' grey thrums to the sleepin' hen,
The dog's speldert on the floor and disna gie a cheep,
But here's a waukrife laddie, that *wunna fa' asleep*.'

Onything but sleep, you rogue, glow'ring like the moon,
Rattlin' in an airn jug wi' an airn spoon,   10
Rumblin', tumblin' roon about, crawin' like a cock,
Skirling like a kenna-what, waukenin' sleepin' fock.

'Hey Willie Winkie, the wean's in a creel,
Wamblin' aff a bodie's knee like a verra eel,
Ruggin' at the cat's lug, and ravelin' a' her thrums –
Hey Willie Winkie – see, there he comes.'

Wearit is the mither that has a stoorie wean,
A wee, stumpie, stoussie, that canna rin his lane,
That has a battle aye wi' sleep before he'll close an e'e –
But a kiss frae aff his rosy lips gies strength anew to me.   20

Whistle-Binkie, or the Piper of the Party: Being a Collection of Songs for the Social
Circle, Chiefly Original, *ed. Alexander Rodger, 3rd series (David Robertson, Glasgow, 1842).*

SPRING

The Spring comes linking and jinking through the woods,
Opening wi' gentle hand the bonnie green and yellow buds –
There's flowers and showers, and sweet sang o' little bird,
And the gowan wi' his red croon peeping thro' the yird.

The hail comes rattling and brattling snell and keen,
Dauding and blauding, though red set the sun at e'en;
In bonnet and wee loof the weans kep and look for mair,
Dancing thro'ther wi' the white pearls shining in their hair.

We meet wi' blythesome and kythesome cheerie weans,
Daffing and laughing far a-doon the leafy lanes,   10
Wi' gowans and buttercups busking the thorny wands,
Sweetly singing wi' the flower branch waving in their hands.

'Boon a' that's in thee, to win me, sunny Spring!
Bricht cluds and green buds, and sangs that the birdies sing;
Flower-dappled hill-side and dewy beech sae fresh at e'en;
Or the tappie-toorie fir-tree shining a' in green –

Bairnies, bring treasure and pleasure mair to me,
Stealing and speiling up to fondle on my knee!
In spring-time the young things are blooming sae fresh and fair,
That I canna, Spring, but love and bless thee evermair.   20

Scottish Nursery Songs and Other Poems *(William Machrone, Glasgow, 1863).*

NOVEMBER

Infant Winter, young November.
   Nursling of the glowing woods,
Lo! the sleep is burst that bound thee –
Lift thine eyes above, around thee,
   Infant sire of storm and floods.

Through the tangled green and golden
   Curtains of thy valley bed,
See the trees hath vied to woo thee,
And with homage to subdue thee –
   Show'ring bright leaves o'er thy head.   10

Let, oh! let their fading glories
   Grace the earth while still they may,
For the poplar's-orange, gleaming,
And the beech's ruddy beaming,
   Warmer seems to make the day.

Now the massy plane-leaf's twirling,
   Down the misty morning light,
And the saugh-tree's tinted treasure
Seems to seek the earth with pleasure –
   Show'ring down from morn till night.   20

Through the seasons, ever varying,
   Rapture fills the human soul;
Blessed dower! to mankind given,
All is perfect under heaven,
   In the part as in the whole.

Hush'd the golden flute of mavis,
   Silver pipe of little wren,
But the redbreast's notes are ringing,
And its 'weel-kent' breast is bringing
   Storied boyhood back again.   30

Woodland splendour of November,
   Did departing Autumn dye
All thy foliage, that when roamin'
We might pictur'd – see her gloamin'
   In thy woods as in her sky.

Scottish Nursery Songs *(1863)*.

Martin F. (Farquhar) Tupper (1810–89)

Martin F. Tupper, the greatly popular rhythmic moralist, was born in Marylebone, London, 17 July 1810, into a deeply Protestant tribe, full of Lutherans, Huguenots and Cromwellians, as well as army and navy officers. His father, Martin Tupper, was a medical doctor, his mother, Ellen Devis, the daughter of a landscape painter. Martin was sent to Charterhouse, 1821–6, and to Christ Church, Oxford (1828–32). He beat Gladstone to the Burton Theological Essay Prize in 1831. He was called to the Bar, but never practised, allegedly hampered by the strong stutter that had driven him to books from an early age. He began setting down his 'Proverbial Philosophy', jog-trot thoughts on all things great and small, from Life to the Lord's Prayer, while he was still in his teens. Endlessly moralizing in (more or less) iambic heptameters, his four series of *Proverbial Philosophy* (1838–69) ran to a million and a half copies sold. They did especially well in North America. He clearly touched a chord with the average Anglo-Saxon Christian reader. Oxford gave him an Honorary DCL in 1847; foreign honours reigned down (the Prussian gold medal for science and art, for instance, in 1844); he was a favourite at the English court in Prince Albert's time. In addition to the rhyming philosophy which made his name, Tupper poured out ballads, stories, travel writing, poems (for Rifle-clubs, for emigrants to Australia, against Ritualists, in favour of Orange Men), essays, reviews, volumes of Christian Evidences. Unlike its owner, his pen never stuttered. He made money lecturing in America once his speech impediment was under control. For all his popularity, though, he needed a Civil List Pension of £120 to get by on after 1873: an insurance office he'd invested in went bust. He married a second cousin, Isabella Devis, had large numbers of children, wrote the greatly self-serving *My Life As An Author* (1886), and died at Albury, 29 November 1889. He resented the charge of mongering trite commonplaces, but the critics on both sides of the Atlantic were merciless in repeating it. *Tupperism* and *Martin Tupper* entered the English language as synonyms for worthless commonplaces. Parodists like C. S. Calverley loved him for the opportunities for jibing he provided them ('Choose judiciously thy friends; for to discard them is undesirable,/ Yet it is better to drop thy friends, oh my daughter, than to drop thy "H's" ': 'Proverbial Philosophy. Of Friendship' in Calverley's *Verses and Translations* (1862), for example). And in the pages of *Punch* Tupper was for long the very by-word for versified commercially astute, windy sententiousness:

TUPPER for the Million the HATCHARDS advertise,
Celebrated TUPPER, the witty and the wise,
TUPPER the original, TUPPER the profound,
TUPPER for proverbial philosophy renowned,
SOLOMON and PLATO melted into one,
Though from end to end read ever, once begun;
Charmingly didactic, and never dull or slow,
TUPPER for the Million, at three-and-sixpence, O!
TUPPER will be CROESUS in case the Million pay;
Here's success to TUPPER, with hip, hip, hooray.

(*Punch*, vol. 45, 15 August 1863, 67)

OF THE BIBLE

It were seemly that a Scripture for all nations should be styled universally The Book,
That under one great Master-mind many scribes should write it,
That every letter of its text should have been well watched by warders,
And that one special people should conserve it for mankind.

It were not seemly that such Scripture, meant for duties here,
Should venture deep on other themes than morals and religion:
Science would be hinted, not exhausted; now and then a word,
Enough to prove its conscious Author chose the higher topics:
So then, worldly knowledge, albeit in no sort quenched,
Would thus be left to reason, as less worthy revelation;   10
And all we need to look for, or to learn from out The Book,
Are teachings of religion, not the secret things of science.
And yet how many gainsayers complain that man's great Guide
To holier thoughts, and better life, and higher worlds than ours,
Doth scantly condescend an ear to reason's curious tongue,
That asketh endless questions of small moment to man's soul.
Our record runneth: God made all. The how, the why, the when,
These are but idle queries, and the Maker doth not heed them.
Our knowledge is, that on a day He placed a man in Eden,
And gave him for his heritage the newly ordered globe;   20
Set him duties, tested him, and, when he fell, restored him,
And helped till now his children, whose children all are we.
Age after age, by tongue or symbol, records of our race
Were kept by holy men of old, obedient to high teaching;
And these primeval writings, with the like of later time,
Are come to us an heirloom, – the Scriptures of The Book.
Doubtless, though well guarded from great errors in the main,
It were not likely that no faults were dropt by many writers;

To conscience and his reason God leaveth freeborn man,
The twain enough for lower needs, though grace may help all higher.   30
So let those points and accents be, as some are right or wrong,
The strong root-words, the living thoughts, are God's own revelation;
And copiers and translators, with every care and skill,
May yet be somewhile found at fault, and well to be corrected.
And so the little (noways much) of failings in The Book
Is due to scribes who blotted what at first was fairly written.

How manifold the Bible! how majestic in variety!
History, poems, proverbs, parable, biography, and doctrine, –
How rich in all the ornaments and dignity of eloquence!
In annals as in prophecies how simple and sublime!   40
How full of quaint old stories, and of chivalrous adventure,
And whisperings of the birth of time, as mutterings of its death!
How fragrant is the incense of its praises and its prayers!
How comforting its promises, how precious are its precepts!
How wise, and kind, and pure, and good, its influence on the soul!
How strong its hold upon the heart, its power within the mind!
It speaketh peace to sinners, and high wisdom to the sage;
It is the traveller's guide-book, and the missionary's treasure;
The mother for her sailor-boy hath stored it in his locker,
The soldier at his foreign quarter poreth on its page,   50
The pious merchant's Bible will be posted near his ledger,
The very beggar sometimes hath it hidden in his rags.
It showeth in their action all the attributes of God,
His mercy, His omnipotence, His wisdom, and His justice;
It well displayeth every class and character of men,
Their guilt and their repentings, their happiness and woe.
No heroes equal Bible heroes – martyrs, captains, kings,
Joshua, David, Daniel, all the worthies of old time;
No stories are like Bible stories, exquisitely told, –
Isaac, Joseph, Ruth, and Job, and Samson, and Elijah.   60
Romance hath borrowed Bible exploits for its fabulous knights,
And Poesy from Bible wells hath drawn its richest nectar;
The minds of all our wisest have been moulded on its themes,
The hearts of all our purest have been chastened by its lessons:
And all the best of Adam's race that ever lived and died
Have lived in faith and died in hope through blessing from the Bible.
It is that truer tree of life, whose roots are in the Rock,
Whose trunk is strong as Lebanon, whose boughs outstretch the cedars;
Whose buds and flowers and fruits are for the healing of all nations,
Whose leaves shall never wither, but are green for evermore!   70

Well read out, with earnest voice, by one that understandeth,
The Word of God is eloquence beyond all human speech;
But common readers, slow of heart, and ignorant in mind,
Contrive to deaden half its life, to darken half its light;
And some, on silly system, still abjure dramatic effort,
With feeble tones and vulgar notes ensuring all things dull;
While, fairly spoken forth and with a feeling elocution,
The Scriptures have a might and a magnificence all their own.
And there is scanter need for long diluted exposition,
If he that readeth understandeth, and can read aright;   80
But slender learning in the Greek, and gross contempt for Hebrew,
And little knowledge of all knowledge far too often shown,
And lack of able utterance, and the lead-weight of routine,
These obscure the text so much they half excuse the sermon.

Also, there is some just need for wise and true revision,
Seeing our English tongue hath changed and grown by growth of years.
If one could 'eat damnation,'[1] who would tempt the terrible morsel?
The letters of Bellerophon[2] should ask to such a feast.
Yet how continually feeble souls, through that wrong phrase alone,
Are troubled all their lives as by a lion in the way.   90
Christ rested with the holy dead; His soul was never in 'hell:'
That word ill-rendered still confoundeth Hades with Gehenna.[3]
And other spotted places more might claim the Royal touch,
For close correction is a needbe of these searching times.
A flyleaf for our Bibles, with its list of mended texts,
A volume well compounded of all causes for amendment,
This were the simple wisdom for our heads in Church and State;
But, with no thought of change in style, – the solid English strength,
So statue-like, so graphic, and so simple and sublime, –
Only the lightest touch in phrase to heal up evil faults,   100
That were enough; all else as now unchanged for texts and teachings:
The dear old Family Bible should be still our champion volume,
The Medo-Persic law[4] to us, the standard of our Rights.

In this our day, an evil day of change and misbelief,
When craft and ignorance and sin are leagued against religion,
When every keen objector is hailed with guilty joy,
And shallow sceptics unabashed deny or doubt the Bible,
Great is the comfort where a man can feel his soul is strong
In simple trust on Scriptural truth, as simply as in childhood.
It is a joy, an honour, yea, a wisdom, to declare   110
A boundless and infantile faith in our dear English Bible!

The garden, and the apple, and the serpent, and the ark,
And every word in every verse, and in its literal meaning,
And histories and prophecies and miracles and visions,
In spite of learned unbelief, – we hold it all plain truth:
Not blindly, but intelligently, after search and study;
Hobbes and Paine considered well, and Germany and Colenso.[5]
The closer to the strict old text, the Bible still is clearer;
The more examined ever still more curiously exact:
Assyria, Edom, Petra, Zion, – from them all unearth   120
Whatever of old works ye will, these illustrate the Bible:
The sixty cities of Og are standing yet in Bashan;
The Pyramids, the Sculptured Wadys, and the Mount of Bel,
The marble slabs of Nineveh, and Tadmor in the desert,
All witness to its truth alike: Herodotus as Josephus.[6]

The Bible made us what we are, the mightiest Christian nation, –
The Bible buildeth in each man his character and mind,
From cradle hymns to wedlock, and through grey hairs to the grave,
At every step in life the Holy Bible is our helper:

OF THE BIBLE
1 1 Corinthians 11.29.
2 Corinthian hero, who carried a letter from jealous Proetus to his father-in-law, ordering B.'s death.
3 Acts 2.27, 31. Hades (Gr.) for Hebrew Sheol (place for souls after death); Gehenna, Hebrew for place of punishment after death.
4 'laws of the Persians and the Medes', Esther 1.19, proverbially unalterable.

5 Thomas Hobbes, 17th-century atheist; Thomas Paine, 18th-century radical deist; John Colenso, 19th-century Bishop of Natal, whose *The Pentateuch and the Book of Joshua Critically Examined* attacked biblical accuracy (1862–79).
6 Ancient Greek historian (5th century BC), and Jewish historian (1st century AD). Tupper exaggerates their biblical witness.

We have none other lamp to guide us through this darkling world,   130
No other staff, nor scrip, nor shoe, nor viand by the way,
No gentler nurse in sickness, no warmer friend in health,
No better comforter, companion, teacher than the Bible:
Every word within it hath been watered by saints' tears;
Every blessed page thereof been died-for by the martyrs:
To eyes that see, it shineth; to ears that hear, it speaketh;
To minds that know, it standeth out, as far before the age.
Modern science cannot find it obsolete or false,
Every new discovery but proving it more true.
The crusts of earth, the races, and the languages of men,   140
The laws of light and life, of chemistry and motion,
So wisely touched and hinted at, are wisely then passed by;
Man's reason would have nought to do, forerun by revelation.
And let them boast the Talmud:[7] should not Rabbis, Doctors, Scribes,
Have taught that Holy Child the very best of Jewish wisdom?
Yet, let them note, the Christ had left this world four hundred years,
Or ever from its oral state that Talmud was collected;
So then, Jews had caught from Christ those teachings in the Talmud
Some pundits are so quick to hint our Moral Teacher stole.

Yea, spite of all the learned zeal to prove the Bible false,   150
Their reckonings and disputings, and their eager hunt for errors, –
In spite of all their casuistry, discoveries, statistics,
And every sceptic effort of apostates, clerk and lay,
The Bible is but stablished by its gainsayers and assailants,
And all its difficulties die, though galvanised to live.
Their diggings in the mud of Egypt, and the caves of France,
Their searchings of old shellmounds and of pilestumps in the lakes,
Their scrutiny of languages, and chronicles, and races,
Their evil rage and scornful hate against the Blessed Book,
All corroborate old texts, and illustrate old truths,   160
Serving to prove that man on earth was last-born of creation,
Showing their scorching inquisition as a refiner's fire,
And with their burning-glasses testing still the unchanged gold.

The Bible, standing in its strength a pyramid foursquare,
The plain old English Bible, a gem with all its flaws,
That Bible, not the priest, nor the ordinance, nor the church,
(However sped by pastor, house of prayer, and simplest worship,)
That book of books, next to the Christ whereof it ever telleth,
Is still the heaven-blest fountain of conversion and salvation.
The peasant and the prince alike drink gladly of that well,   170
It comforteth with equal care the pauper and the statesman;
The widow and her orphans, from the palace to the cottage,
Are yearning on the Bible in glad reverence night and day;
The rough backwoodsman pondereth its pages in his cabin,
Thence going to his sturdy toil, a purer, stronger man;
Beneath its influence mutineers become an isle of saints,
And convicts in their prison-cells are changed to heirs of glory;
Its presence giveth evident peace and light to this Swiss Canton,
While its mere absence from that neighbour breedeth strife and sin;
It maketh Scotland great and good, blest with a shining Bible,   180
While Erin still is miserable, as hiding-up that light:
It is the voice of God to man, encouraging and warning,

7   the body of Jewish Law.

It is the speech of man to God, in sampled prayer and praise;
It is the golden thread of life, and strung with precious pearls,
Hung on each Christian infant's neck, its best baptismal birthright,
The amulet and anodyne and jewel of our race,
To soothe us in this vale of tears, and cheer our path to heaven.

Proverbial Philosophy, *4 series (1838–69). From Fourth Series, in* Proverbial Philosophy:
The Four Series Complete *(Cassell, Petter, Galpin & Co., [1881]).*

OF HOME

Infinitely varied, as with marriage, from heights to lowest depths,
From pleasantness and peace to miserable contentions,
For every heart the thought of Home will bring its special difference,
As varying truth may testify to sorrows or to joys.
An exile yearneth over Home in long romancing absence,
But oft his yearnings are fulfilled by realised disappointment;
The dreaming soldier longeth for his mother's wayside cottage,
The sailor museth on his watch about the wife ashore:
But what if crime and penury, if shame and sin be there?
How saddened into wormwood is the honied thought of Home!   10
With one man, all his memories will be piety and love,
A gentle mother's goodness, and a noble father's care;
With another, let him search the past as far back as he can,
It was an atmosphere of strife, all troubles and no comfort:

Here, is a soul that oweth all its wealth for heaven and earth
To pure affections, bright examples, wisdoms learnt of Home;
There, is a spirit ill-conditioned, outcast and rebellious from its birth,
Whose cruel parents in that Home had only taught it evil:
Some were born at a liberal hearth, warm with genial hospitalities,
Some at the board of meanness, amid sordid shifts and thrifts;   20
To those a recollected home were crowds of hearty friends,
To these penurious carefulness, a blank and frozen solitude:
One goeth Homeward from his toil to rest and peace and plenty,
Greeted on the threshold by his cleanly goodwife's kiss;
His neighbour meanwhile met by that old slattern left at home
With the quick hailstorm of her tongue in quarrelling and worry.

Joy for the happiness of Home! where peace, content, affection,
Shine a triple sun to bathe in bliss that little world:
There the good angel of the house, the mother, wife and mistress,
With gentle care and thoughtful love is ministering life;   30
There in firm wisdom ruleth well the father, husband, master,
Heaping it with prosperities, as guardian, guide and judge:
There the sons obey, diligently heeding duties,
There the cheerful daughters plan their charities for all,
There with no eyeservice, but in honest faith and truth,
The family domestics work, and worship with their betters;
While all the neighbours round about, and scores of friends far off,
Point to that house and praise it well, the happy Home of Christians.
O beautiful in essence is that angel in the house,
The gentle charitable wife, its pure presiding spirit,   40
So patient with all troubles, and so cheerful under changes,
So full of help to others, so forgetful of herself;
O husband, gladly praise her! O ye children, call her blessed!
For all her works and words shall hail her at the gates of heaven.

And, – woe for the wretchedness of Home! – where clamour, care and discord
Enwrap that desolate small sphere in whirlwinds of contention;
There, all rule is at an end; extravagance, disorder,
And discontented selfishness are harpies at each meal;
There the father is not honoured, neither is the master served,
There the husband pineth, disenchanted, without love;   50
There the thriftless brothers scorn to redeem young days,
But waste their chances in first years for afterlife-repentance;
There the pining sisters ever meditate escape,
Dreaming in hope of some calm home, far other than their father's;
Because the hearth they long to leave, curst by its evil angel,
Irascible and jealous, and unreasonably capricious,
Is ever hot with hatreds, and perilous from quarrels,
A married fury blighting there the slandered name of Mother!
So, the very hirelings will scoff, and scorn to take such service,
And neighbours whisper as they pass, and friends are scared away,   60
And Home, that was the name for peace, is synonymed with strife,
An earthly pandemonium through that termagant of wedlock.

Alas! the woeful change, – for once she had been worshipped,
In early years, ere sweet young Love had blown to bitter Marriage:
But now her image, long that idol in affection's temple,
Lieth as a broken Dagon[1] on its ruined floor;
For the contentions of a wife hath banned, instead of blessing,
The beauteous fane of Hymen, and the cheerful hearth of Home.
Who can estimate the torments worked by tongue and temper,
Those dislocations on the rack, of comfort and of love?   70
There be tortures, cruel as at Avignon,[2] wearing out saints of God,
Drop by drop maddening the brain with constant household worries;
There be moral harrowings and sawings, as David wrought at Rabbah,[3]
That lacerate the feeling heart year after year continually:
Silver weddings may have been, but more are forged of iron, –
Though few dare hint hard truths like these, and flatter or ignore them.
Let the adulteress be forgiven, let foolish extravagance go free,
But who can bear with temper and tongue to seventy times seven?
Changeable, passionate, and hateful, plagued with unreasoning animosities,
That bitter lawful-wife is still the bane and blight of Home;   80
Woe for that bed of nettles, woe for that nest of hornets,
Woe to the sensitive and gentle in their married lives!
Provocation, irritation, usurpation, iteration, vacillation, accusation,
Every phrase of malice in every note of harshness,
Prejudices, jealousies and strife, contention, hate, confusion,
Every phase of ill from weakness up to wickedness, –
All these have often cursed the Home, through ill-assorted marriage,
And many wives and husbands here will own they read their fates:
O noble hearts and generous minds! if still they smile unsoured,
Through lingering years of petty torment caused by such bad Homes: 90
For it is veritable martyrdom some best have had to bear,
That tyranny of wedlock with a wicked man, or woman.
Did not our glorious Milton feel it, tokened by his Doctrine of Divorce?[4]
Is not the matchless Shakspeare a like witness even in his testament?[5]

OF HOME
1 overthrown Philistine deity, 1 Samuel 5.
2 presumably a reference to French Protestant martyrs.
3 2 Samuel 12.31: David 'put' the people of Rabbah 'under saws, and
under harrows of iron … and made them pass through the brick-kiln'
(in forced labour).
4 John Milton, *The Doctrine and Discipline of Divorce* (1643).
5 Shakespeare notoriously bequeathed his 'second-best bed' to his
wife Anne Hathaway (1616).

Hooker was judicious in all else but a wife who burnt his books;[6]
And Palissy and Wesley were martyrs as to marriage;[7]
While Job, and Socrates, and Moses, justified of old,
The proverb of wise Solomon against a wife's contentions.

They mould each other, man and woman; make or mar each other:
If Una tamed her lion, Goneril tainted Alban:[8]   100
The man is made by gentleness, that meek and quiet spirit,
The holy conversation and obedience of the wife;
The man is marred by crossings and the nagging, vixen temper,
Night and day, by board and bed, embittered through that plague;
No escape, no respite; for the worm is at the core;
An exile cannot flee himself; nor hounds in leash run freely:
Who shall gauge the force of such a spiritual fetter,
Hindering all pursuit of good, and galling and injurious?
As who can guess the potency of woman's love and patience,
Her precious influence, her sweet strength, to bless a husband's Home?   110

And worse for you, O gentle wives! consorted with bad husbands,
The drunkard, the adulterer, the passionate, the mean;
How desolate your lots, – how steeped in grief your lives, –
How changed for you from peace to strife the sacred name of Home!
Not solely, and not chiefly, in the lowest haunts of life,
In cellars or in hovels is domestic discord seen;
Oft-times the dinner of herbs[9] hath quietness for seasoning,
And bitter want some sweet love-honey in its cup of gall:
But even with the richest in their palaces of pride,
Or where a midway competence hath all beside for comfort,   120
Not all their purple and fine linen, nor the stalled ox,
Can stay the hatreds that therewith have cursed too many a Home.

There is often a most miserable jealousy cankering domestic peace,
And gnawing at the narrow hearts of sundry men and women:
I touch not needfully the loathing that curseth criminal love,
And gladly would do murder for a wanton look or fashion;
But the meaner hatred and suspicion of each genial feeling,
And every kind of worth, by any innocently shown.
Pleasant neighbours, honest servants, good and clever children,
These are made the victims of that jealous lust for Self;   130
And chiefly nearest relatives, be they of wife or husband,
Are spoken against, and driven away, insulted and abused:
A brother near the throne is sure to get the bowstring;
Our monogamic firmament may hold no second sun;
Strait taxation, all for one, is rigidly exacted,
And good and wise men are but rivals to that morbid soul;
Without such close exclusion, is not married bliss too scarce?
Yet dearest friends not seldom thus are sacrificed to Hymen:
O ye bitter spoilers of the beauteous and the holy,
Married slaves to selfishness, ye jealous little minds,   140
It is you that fright from wedlock, beyond its common trials,
And put it to an open shame, degraded from due honour;
It is you that ban all blessing, and bring Satan into Eden,
Till Milton's Adam curse once more his selfish serpent Eve.[10]

---

6   Richard Hooker (1554–1600), Anglican apologist, made bad marriage to landlady's daughter.

7   Bernard Palissy (d. 1589), Huguenot glass-painter; John Wesley (1703–91), founder of Methodism.

8   Una, type of Protestant Church (the lion was England), in Edmund Spenser, *The Fairie Queene* (1593–6); wicked Goneril and (better) Albany in Shakespeare's *King Lear*.

9   Proverbs 15.17: 'Better is a dinner of herbs where love is, than a stalled ox and hatred therewith.'

10   in *Paradise Lost*.

But, O true paragons of marriage! – for thousands yet there be
Worthiest of honour and of love, though haply missing both,
How opposite are ye to those detestables, how patient and how kind,
The sweet Hermiones and Griseldas in too many a Home![11]
None can guess your sorrows, though religion soothe them still,
None can know the wretchedness that hideth in your bosoms: 150
Prayer and hope indeed are yours, and friends discreetly chosen;
But what shall compensate a wife for Home despoiled of love?
Home-love is a woman's very life; a man may live without it;
The mother-bird hath one poor nest; foxes have holes elsewhere.[12]
How often is there sadness and suspicion in the Home,
Where, like the barren figtree, unblest marriage hath no fruiting;[13]
Where woman's withering heart may never yearn on children,
And vainly year by year the father longed to kiss a son!
For mysterious Providence withholdeth in high wisdom
Full oft from those who wished it most the treasure of a child;   160
Giving, as with too liberal hand, to many who are thankless,
– Nay more, who grudge against the gift – that priceless wealth in offspring.
Yet hear this for your comfort, ye that are written childless,
Who grieved in disappointed youth that wedlock bore no fruit,
At least your tranquil age is saved from shame and sorrow
Too often heaped upon the Home by some ungrateful son;
Where are thy prayers and hopes, O father? where thy costs and cares?
And all thy love, O mother, – is but moonlight on that ruin.

Twice happy is the Home that is blest with children's children;
Thy sons and daughters were much care, but these be simple pleasures: 170
Another generation is responsible for these,
And so in every better sense is found thy second childhood.
Here be pretty playmates for thine innocent old age,
Full of hope and life and glee, and garrulous as thyself;
Here be keen-eyed comrades for thy wisdom to improve,
And friends to carry on thy praise, and talk of thee hereafter:
Nor only for amusement those dear little ones are seen,
Nor that thy sage experiences may help them in life's journey, –
But, since their angels always see the face of God their Father,[14]
These baby wards of heaven on earth can guide thy feet to Him!   180

Next after wife and husband, and the children young or old,
The happiness of Home shall much be made or marred by servants:
Whither are fled the faithful souls that loved through life one family,
In unsuspected honesty with dutiful heartservice?
Where are those models of economy, so diligent in their callings,
Showing good fidelity, not answering, not purloining?
An over-prevalent luxury, the strong desire for change,
With vanities of dress, and headiness and hardness,
And independent hate of rule, and class divorced from class,
And stilted thoughts of pride, bred from ill-digested schooling,   190
All these have worked their social harms, gnawing the heart of Home,
And well-nigh leave extinct the race of good and faithful servants.[15]

Ay, – but where too shall we find the wise and gracious housewife,
Whom royal Lemuel's mother sought as helpmate for her son?[16] –

---

11   Hermione, as in Shakespeare's *The Winter's Tale*; (Patient) Griselda,   14   Matthew 18.10.
as in Chaucer's *The Clerke's Tale*.   15   'good and faithful servant': Matthew 25.21.
12   Matthew 8.20.   16   as in proverbs 31.
13   Matthew 21.19–20.

All too little sympathy, and far too great exaction,
Nothing overlooked of fault, and seldom an indulgence, –
With these and worse, with silly pride, and poisonous airs of caste,
Too many a modern mistress will torment her women slaves.
On all sides is there blame; yet more with wives than husbands;
For man and master still work well together as good friends: 200
The genial word dropped now and then, of kindness or of caution,
Is oftener heard from man to man, than woman ruling woman:
And men have no proud prudery, but can wink at humble lovers,
Whereas the jealous housewife is affection's direst foe:
A master giveth counsel, as remembering his hot youth,
And is not set in frozen state so high above the servant;
Whereas the best a menial often heareth from her mistress
Is strict and harsh ascetic lore, with tartness of reproof.
Would that, as with Lemuel's queen, that tongue were ruled by kindness,
And, if she watch her household's ways, herself live not so idly!   210
A good and genial housewife secureth cheerful servants,
But our unkindly scolds are still the roots of discontent.

Who can make a monograph of such a theme as Home?
Who shall exhaust that field of thought, so thickly cropped with feelings?
Duty, interest, pleasure, pain, affections, fears and hopes,
Like cherubs flitting round each Home from nursery to the grave,
And recollections of old scenes, dim belike with sorrow,
And many disappointments, crowd about this pregnant theme.
How to paint young memories with panoramic power,
How to touch bereavements that have wrung the mourner's heart,   220
How to tell of birthday-feasts, of weddings and of deathbeds,
How to set before each mind the story of his Home?
It were easy, it were weary, to dilate at length,
And mould in full these features, barely outlined and suggested;
But let what I have written stand, faultily with omissions,
To sketch in light and shadow the romance and truth of Home.

Proverbial Philosophy, *Fourth Series (1869, [1881])*.

Arthur Henry Hallam (1811–33)

Arthur Henry Hallam, budding poet, and muse from beyond the grave of Alfred Tennyson, was born in Bedford Place, London, 1 February 1811. His father was Henry Hallam, the Whig historian. Hallam was linguistically precocious from an early age – though suffering at the same time, curiously, from a notorious bad memory. He became good at French, reportedly, by the age of seven. Foreign travel with his parents no doubt helped. After preparatory school in Putney he went to Eton, where he became friends with Gladstone and contributed to the *Eton Miscellany*. He'd already written 'several tragedies', according to the Memoir by his father. After school, in 1828, he toured Italy with his parents, and became fluent enough in Italian to produce many sonnets in that language. In October 1828 he went up to Trinity College, Cambridge, quickly fell in with the Apostles and formed the friendship with Alfred Tennyson that was to be not only the most important event in Tennyson's life but the most important influence on Tennyson's writing. Tennyson beat Hallam in the Chancellor's Prize Poem competition of 1829 (subject, *Timbuctoo*). Staying at Somersby Rectory with the Tennysons for Christmas 1829 Hallam met Tennyson's sister Emily and was soon in love with her. He wrote poems to her. His father forbade any public engagement before Hallam was twenty-one, and also poured cold water on a project for a joint book of poems with Tennyson. In 1830 the two friends were involved in the abortive intervention by the Apostles in the Spanish War of Independence (oddly proleptic, as later observers such as Graham Greene noted, of the support Cambridge men gave a century later to the Republican cause in the Spanish Civil War of 1936–9). Hallam staunchly and perceptively reviewed Tennyson's *Poems* (1830) in *The Englishman's Magazine* (August 1831). The religious thinking of his *Theodicoea Novissima* (1831) clearly influenced Tennyson's religious ideas. Hallam graduated in summer 1832, travelled along the Rhine with Tennyson, and began law studies in London. In 1833 his engagement to Emily Tennyson was made public. In Vienna, 15 September 1833, on a German tour with his father, he died, very suddenly, of a brain haemorrhage. His dying was a considerable surprise, even though he had never been physically strong. Tennyson was bereft. Hallam had been his spiritual and moral mainstay during a protracted time of dark family troubles, especially the melancholy madness of his father; in a period, too, when the *Poems* of 1830 and 1832 had been greatly abused by the reviewers. At a stroke Tennyson had lost his greatest love. Friends and relations talked inevitably of the biblical love of David and Jonathan – who would become gay icons in the twentieth century – a homosexual association clearly in the mind of Richard Le Gallienne, whose Introduction to the *Poems of Arthur Henry Hallam* (1893) is most anxious to make a kind of Decadent cult of the pair. They're celebrated as an exemplary aesthetico-homosexual couple whose love developed within the Apostolic band, or *comitatus*, of Cambridge brothers in which Hallam's 'manly beauty' was, of course, a key essence. The death of his friend became the great inspiration for most of Tennyson's poetry after 1833. It is the sub-text of his massive epic about King Arthur and his knights, *Idylls of the King*, and of course, the explicit occasion of the 'book of Elegies' that turned into *In Memoriam*, arguably the greatest Victorian poem of all. Hallam's death is thus, perhaps, the most significant event of all for Victorian poetry. He was buried in the chancel of the family church at Clevedon, Somerset, 3 January 1834. Henry Hallam's *Remains, in Verse and Prose, of Arthur Henry Hallam* was privately published (with the father's Memoir) in 1834. A second version, minus some of the poems, came out in 1862. Richard Le Gallienne's *Poems* reproduced all the poems of the *Remains* as well as Hallam's review of Tennyson's *Poems*. Another striking feature of Le Gallienne's Introduction is its opportunistic praise of the aesthetic emphasis of Hallam's review, as a way of intervening in the period's Tennyson–Browning debate: 'Unfortunately, nothing is rarer among critics, who are able to apply every test, philosophic, ethic, historic, save the one which is alone to the purpose. Hence so much wrong-headed injustice done to Tennyson's reputation from time to time, and so much (artistically) mistaken exaltation of Browning.'

A SCENE IN SUMMER

Alfred, I would that you beheld me now,
Sitting beneath a mossy ivied wall
On a quaint bench, which to that structure old
Winds an accordant curve. Above my head
Dilates immeasurable a wild of leaves,
Seeming received into the blue expanse
That vaults this summer noon: before me lies
A lawn of English verdure, smooth and bright,
Mottled with fainter hues of early hay,
Whose fragrance, blended with the rose perfume   10
From that white flowering bush, invites my sense
To a delicious madness – and faint thoughts
Of childish years are borne into my brain
By unforgotten ardours waking now.
Beyond, a gentle slope leads into shade
Of mighty trees, to bend whose eminent crown
Is the prime labour of the pettish winds,
That now in lighter mood are twirling leaves
Over my feet, or hurrying butterflies,
And the gay humming things that summer loves,   20
Thro' the warm air, or altering the bound
Where yon elm shadows in majestic line
Divide dominion with the abundant light.

June 1831

Remains, in Verse and Prose, of Arthur Henry Hallam *(W. Nicol, 51 Pall Mall, 1834)*. The Poems of Arthur Henry Hallam, Together With His Essay on the Lyrical Poems of Alfred Tennyson*, ed. Richard Le Gallienne (Elkin Mathews & John Lane, London, Macmillan & Co., New York, 1893).*

SONNET

Why throbbest thou, my heart, why thickly breathest?
  I ask no rich and splendid eloquence:
  A few words of the warmest and the sweetest
  Sure thou mayst yield without such coy pretence:
Open the chamber where affection's voice,
  For rare occasions is kept close and fine:
  Bid it but say, 'Sweet Emily, be mine,'[1]
  So for one boldness thou shalt aye rejoice.
Fain would I speak when the full music-streams
  Rise from her lips to linger on her face,   10
  Or like a form floating through Raffaelle's dreams,
Then fixed by him in ever living grace,
  She sits i' the silent worship of mine eyes.
  Courage, my heart: change thou for words thy sighs.

Remains (1834); Poems (1893).

SONNET

Still here – thou hast not faded from my sight,
  Nor all the music round thee from mine ear:
  Still grace flows from thee to the brightening year,
  And all the birds laugh out in wealthier light.
Still am I free to close my happy eyes,
  And paint upon the gloom thy mimic form,
  That soft white neck, that cheek in beauty warm,
  And brow half hidden where yon ringlet lies;
With, oh! the blissful knowledge all the while
  That I can lift at will each curvèd lid,   10
  And my fair dream most highly realise.
The time will come, 'tis ushered by my sighs,
  When I may shape the dark, but vainly bid
  True light restore that form, those looks, that smile.

Remains (1834); Poems (1893).

SONNET

Lady, I bid thee to a sunny dome
  Ringing with echoes of Italian song;
  Henceforth to thee these magic halls belong,
  And all the pleasant place is like a home.
Hark, on the right with full piano tone,
  Old Dante's voice encircles all the air;
  Hark yet again, like flute-tones mingling rare,
  Comes the keen sweetness of Petrarca's moan.
Pass thou the lintel freely: without fear
  Feast on the music: I do better know thee,   10
  Than to suspect this pleasure thou dost owe me
Will wrong thy gentle spirit, or make less dear
  That element whence thou must draw thy life; –
  An English maiden and an English wife.

Remains (1834); Poems (1893).

SONNET
1   Emily Tennyson, Alfred Tennyson's sister.

Alfred Domett (1811–87)

Chiefly remembered by literary history for his friendship with Robert Browning, Alfred Domett, poet and politician, was born in Camberwell, 20 May 1811, sixth of the nine children of a well-off ship-owner, Nathaniel Domett, and a ship-owner's daughter, Elizabeth Curling. He went to Stockwell Park House School (where he wrote verses – 'Mingling and mangling bits of rhyme') and then, October 1829, to St John's College, Cambridge. (An Anglican, unlike Browning, he was thus not debarred from Oxford and Cambridge.) He left without a degree, to become a man of leisure and letters in London and abroad (he travelled in Canada, the USA and Jamaica, 1833–5) and, eventually, a lawyer. His first volume of *Poems* (buoyantly youthful, imitative, bulky) appeared in 1833; his second, a slim-line celebration of Venice (*Venice*), in 1839. He produced the occasional poem for *Blackwood's Edinburgh Magazine* – including the once famous 'Christmas Hymn', later known as 'A Christmas Hymn (*Old Style, 1837*)'. Browning was his close friend, confidant and correspondent. They were both members of the Colloquials, a club of friends all from Camberwell. Another member was Joseph Arnould (Charterhouse; Wadham College, Oxford; First in Greats, 1836; Newdigate Prize, 1834), who went on to become Chief Justice in Bombay. Domett shared chambers with Arnould when he was called to the Bar at the Middle Temple in 1841. In May 1842 Domett purchased land from the New Zealand Company and left with great suddenness for the new colony ('Dear Browning, I return your books . . . God bless you for ever. Say goodbye for me to your family – I have not time to call'). Browning's surprise, shock and grief are expressed in the poem 'Waring'. Browning's 'The Guardian-Angel: A Picture at Fano', about a Barbieri painting seen with E. B. B. in Italy (July 1848), wonders where Domett is ('Where are you, dear old friend?/How rolls the Wairoa at your world's far end?'): they'd seen Barbieri's work together at Dulwich. Domett proved a hard-line, Might-is-Right, Carlylean colonist and took a strong pro-settler line in the Maori land-disputes. He was closely involved in administration of territory in New Zealand. He even served as Prime Minister, briefly, 1862–3. He married an English widow, Mrs George, became a stepfather and father, and eventually in 1872 returned to London and renewed closeness to Browning. *Ranolf and Amolia, a South Sea Day Dream*, his New Zealand epic, full of local topography and Browning-esque religiosity, was published in London in 1872. (Browning wrote that he 'ranked it under nothing – taken altogether – nothing that has appeared in my day and generation . . .': an exaggeration of its merits.) Domett's *Flotsam and Jetsam: Rhymes Old and New* (1877) is dedicated to Browning ('To (If Ever There Were One!) "A Mighty Poet and a Subtle-Souled Psychologist"'). He became a Vice-President of the Browning Society, 1881. He died 2 November 1887. He was Ernest Dowson's paternal great-uncle (!).

A Christmas Hymn

(Old Style. 1837)

I

It was the calm and silent night! –
   Seven hundred years and fifty-three
Had Rome been growing up to might,
   And now was Queen of land and sea!
No sound was heard of clashing wars;
   Peace brooded o'er the hushed domain;
Apollo, Pallas, Jove and Mars,
   Held undisturbed their ancient reign,
      In the solemn midnight
        Centuries ago!   10

II

'Twas in the calm and silent night! –
   The senator of haughty Rome

Impatient urged his chariot's flight,
   From lordly revel rolling home!
Triumphal arches gleaming swell
   His breast with thoughts of boundless sway;
What recked the ROMAN what befell
   A paltry province far away,
        In the solemn midnight
          Centuries ago!   20

III

Within that province far away
   Went plodding home a weary boor:
A streak of light before him lay,
   Fall'n through a half-shut stable door
Across his path. He passed – for nought
   Told what was going on within;
How keen the stars! his only thought;
   The air how calm and cold and thin,
        In the solemn midnight
          Centuries ago!   30

IV

O strange indifference! – low and high
   Drowsed over common joys and cares:
The earth was still – but knew not why;
   The world was listening – unawares!
How calm a moment may precede
   One that shall thrill the world for ever!
To that still moment none would heed,
   Man's doom was linked no more to sever
        In the solemn midnight
          Centuries ago!   40

V

It *is* the calm and solemn night!
   A thousand bells ring out, and throw
Their joyous peals abroad, and smite
   The darkness, charmed and holy *now!*
The night that erst no name had worn,
   To it a happy name is given;
For in that stable lay new-born
   The peaceful Prince of Earth and Heaven
        In the solemn midnight
          Centuries ago!   50

Flotsam and Jetsam: Rhymes Old and New *(Smith, Elder, & Co., 1877)*.

INVISIBLE SIGHTS

I

'So far away so long – and now
   Returned to England? – Come with me!
Some of our great "celebrities"
   You will be glad to see!'

II
Carlyle – the Laureate – Browning – *these!*
    These walking bipeds – Nay, you joke! –
Each wondrous power for thirty years
    O'er us head-downward folk

III
Wrapt skylike, at the Antipodes, –
    Those common limbs – that common trunk!   10
'Tis the Arab-Jinn who reached the clouds,
    Into his bottle shrunk.

IV
The flashing Mind – the boundless Soul
    We felt ubiquitous, that mash
Medullary or cortical –
    That six-inch brain-cube! – Trash!

1873

Flotsam and Jetsam *(1877)*.

FIREWORKS

I dreamt. There was a great crowd gazing
At fireworks set before them blazing.

The crowd were 'Missing Links';[1] Cambodia's
Great Temple shows no shapes more odious!;

Flat skulls, flat brows, yet convex noses,
Such as her ruined Fane discloses,

Men's heads in conflict fierce off-twisting,
Spite of tame elephants assisting; –

Such gibbering folk as grinned in ages
Long ere men lived o'er Lakes on stages;   10

Left shells on midden – flints in barrow,
Or split hyena-bones for marrow.

The Pyrotechnist was a creature
Of noblest presence – Greek in feature.

He sent a single cracker bouncing –
The Links' delight there's no pronouncing:

A single squib he showed them fizzing –
Their rapture drowned the small tube's whizzing:

One Roman candle fireball-shotted –
Down on their hams from fear they squatted: 20

1   hypothetical creatures, assumed to be evolutionary link between
man and anthropoid apes.

One Catherine-wheel's flame-petals playing –
Their gibbering hushed seemed almost praying:

A rocket skyward rushed up solely –
They shrieked him God – a Fetish wholly;

So wondrous fine his working – scheming;
He, too, so like themselves in seeming!

Then the good Pyrotechnist lastly
Brought one great work to please them vastly;

So grand, he felt in its ignition
The climax of his Exhibition.   30

He fixed it – lighted – set it whirling;
Squibs fizzed in streams from its unfurling:

It whirled away; in its progression,
Up flew fireballs in bright succession!

Still on it whirled; such gems emitting,
Such gold-thorns branching, fire-flowers flitting,

Such rings of flame, concentric, linking,
Such panting discs, expanding, shrinking;

The very Saint from whom they named it,
If such *her* wheel, could scarce have blamed it!   40

Still on it whirled – such rockets dashed up,
As if to heaven's keystone they flashed up;

Then split in melting stars and fine tails,
Long-stealing jewelled cats-o'-nine-tails;

You would have thought the Man-Ape nation
Must have gone mad with admiration!

But who can hit Men-Monkeys' notions?
Who guess a Missing-Link's emotions?

For up jumped one – lank, sly and shifty –
(His 'facial angle' well-nigh fifty)   50

Cries out, 'Pray stop your mopping, mowing;
He no more made the things he's showing –

'The toys by Time and Chance provided –
Made them no more than you or I did!

'Here is no skill – no trick needs solving;
'Tis all produced by that revolving!

'And powder's force – pasteboard's compression,
Cause that revolving, that progression;

'Until a squib that one could pocket,
Grows of itself into a rocket!'   60

This sudden light, first notions scattering,
Makes that swart tribe one sea of chattering;

Their flow of veneration staunches –
They can but blink and scratch their haunches:

Still more so when up danced a second,
(*His* brow some forty-five was reckoned)

Who mouthed at, mocked the placid showman:
'That Thing's a Phantom, friends, and *no* man!

'O Monkey-Men, 'tis clear; for seeing
The firework-making proved his Being,   70

'That myth of firework-making banished –
Argal,[2] his Being too has vanished:

'Your senses cheat you, in conclusion: –
Anthropo-Simian brain-illusion!'

His lofty scorn, his eyebrows twitching
High-raised, his logic so bewitching,

His lips protruded, red eyes leering,
Set all the mob the Showman jeering:

'Off with you, spectre! bogle flimsy,
Dissolving ghost, exploded whimsy!   80

You once packed off, that explanation
Leaves "*LINK*" the Lord of all Creation!' –

The Showman seemed at this reviling
To fade into the background, smiling:

Bedimmed by dust-clouds light-defying
Their antics kept about them flying:

Some Ape-Men who (quite mad reputed)
Still thought they saw him, were so hooted,

I woke – with admiration glowing
To find the Missing-Links so knowing.   90

March 1874

Flotsam and Jetsam *(1877)*.

2   therefore.

William Makepeace Thackeray (1811–63)

William Makepeace Thackeray – omni-competent man of letters: novelist, humorist, satirist, artist and balladeer, was born in Calcutta, 18 July 1811, into a large dynasty of British India's administrators and soldiers. Thackeray's father Richmond Thackeray, who had risen to a plum job as 'Collector of the 24 pergunnahs' (a pargana was an area comprising many villages), died in Calcutta, 13 September 1816 (the death-rate among the British in India was phenomenal), and his mother, Anne Becher (a 'reigning beauty' of Calcutta), soon after married Major Henry Smyth, author of a Hindustani dictionary and Hindustani jokebook. Aged five, William Makepeace was sent back to England, under the care of an aunt (until his mother and stepfather returned home in 1822). He attended assorted schools before going to the Charterhouse in the City of London – a notably brutal place which Thackeray later dubbed the Slaughterhouse, where he acquired a broken nose in one of the school's regular boxing bouts (George Stovin Venables, who stove in Thackeray's nose, remained a great friend of the once 'pretty, gentle' boy he'd rather de-prettified). Thackeray left Charterhouse in May 1828, was coached by Major Smyth at the Smyth's Devon home, entered Trinity College, Cambridge, in February 1829, did little work, became huge friends with Edward FitzGerald and Alfred Tennyson, who were also Trinity men, lost a lot of money gambling, and left without a degree at Easter 1830. He travelled about, spent time at Weimar (meeting Goethe), read a lot of novels on his sofa, settled in legal chambers in London in 1831, helped a friend's election campaign in 1832, and was lured away from the law by the writing and artistic life. In 1833 he put his inherited money into the *National Standard* journal, which soon folded, and he lost heavily too in financial speculations and gambling. In 1834 he went to Paris to turn himself into an artist (later he illustrated many of his novels and became a renowned caricaturist). He headed, though, more or less rapidly, driven by economic necessity, into writing for the journals – above all for *Punch*, *Fraser's Magazine* and the *Cornhill*, of which he was founder-editor, January 1860 to April 1862. His first major books sprang from his journalism, and it remained all his life a staple of income and a writing matrix for his fiction as well as non-fiction. Thackeray was a large man, 6′ 3″ tall, with a noticeably massive head. One of his jokier pseudonyms was The Fat Contributor. He followed the boxing Fancy, was a heavy gambler and a generally hard *sportif* type, on as good terms with racy low-life thugs, pimps and con-men as with the literary, political and genteel sorts he mixed enthusiastically with in his numerous clubs (not least the Athenaeum). A Liberal and radical, he stood for Parliament (losing Oxford narrowly in 1857). His notorious falling-out with Dickens in 1858 was over a satirical attack on himself by fellow Garrick Club member Edmund Yates. The great satirist, author of one of the sharpest satirical novels of the period, *Vanity Fair: A Novel Without a Hero* (1847–8), had quickly grown too sensitive to take the sort of rudeness he had himself frequently dished out to other writers. He and Dickens were, of course, the Big Two of the mid-century English novel (and they were reconciled just before Thackeray's death). Charlotte Brontë dedicated the second edition of *Jane Eyre* to Thackeray (he was widely rumoured to be an original for Mr Rochester). After *Vanity Fair* he made serious money from his journalism, his American lecture tours, and his novels – £1,200 from *The History of Henry Esmond* (1852), for instance, £4,000 from *The Newcomes: Memoirs of a Most Respectable Family* (1853–5). He needed to, for he lived as much beyond his means as he could manage. His wife Isabella Shawe, from Cork, started going mad after their third daughter was born, and was eventually confined to asylums, leaving Thackeray to look after the two surviving girls. Daughter Anne became the writer Anne Thackeray Ritchie. Harriet became the first Mrs Leslie Stephen. Thackeray died on Christmas Eve 1863, worn out by the long efforts of the writing life (which included, of course, the not inconsiderable rhymes and ballads). Dickens was lavish in the homage of his memorial address (in the *Cornhill*, February 1864) – talking of Thackeray's 'refined knowledge of human nature, of his subtle acquaintance with the weaknesses of human nature, of his delightful playfulness as an essayist, of his quaint and touching ballads' – but regretted 'that he too much feigned a want of earnestness, and that he made a pretence of under-valuing his art'.

THE BALLAD OF BOUILLABAISSE

A street there is in Paris famous,
   For which no rhyme our language yields,
Rue Neuve des Petits Champs its name is –
   The New Street of the Little Fields.

And here's an inn, not rich and splendid,
    But still in comfortable case;
The which in youth I oft attended,
    To eat a bowl of Bouillabaisse.

This Bouillabaisse a noble dish is –
    A sort of soup, or broth, or brew,   10
Or hotchpotch of all sorts of fishes,
    That Greenwich never could outdo;
Green herbs, red peppers, mussels, saffern,[1]
    Soles, onions, garlic, roach, and dace:
All these you eat at TERRÉ's tavern,
    In that one dish of Bouillabaisse.

Indeed, a rich and savoury stew 'tis;
    And true philosophers, methinks,
Who love all sorts of natural beauties,
    Should love good victuals and good drinks.   20
And Cordelier or Benedictine[2]
    Might gladly, sure, his lot embrace,
Nor find a fast-day too afflicting,
    Which served him up a Bouillabaisse.

I wonder if the house still there is?
    Yes, here the lamp is, as before;
The smiling red-cheeked écaillère[3] is
    Still opening oysters at the door.
Is TERRÉ still alive and able?
    I recollect his droll grimace: 30
He'd come and smile before your table,
    And hope you liked your Bouillabaisse.

We enter – nothing's changed or older.
    'How's Monsieur TERRÉ, waiter, pray?'
The waiter stares and shrugs his shoulder –
    'Monsieur is dead this many a day.'
'It is the lot of saint and sinner,
    So honest TERRÉ's run his race?'
'What will Monsieur require for dinner?'
    'Say, do you still cook Bouillabaisse?'   40

'Oh, oui, Monsieur,' 's the waiter's answer;
    'Quel vin Monsieur désire-t-il?'
'Tell me a good one.' 'That I can, sir:
    The Chambertin with yellow seal.'
'So TERRÉ's gone,' I say, and sink in
    My old accustomed corner-place;
'He's done with feasting and with drinking,
    With Burgundy and Bouillabaisse.'

My old accustomed corner here is,   50
    The table still is in the nook;
Ah! vanished many a busy year is
    This well-known chair since last I took.

THE BALLAD OF BOUILLABAISSE
1   saffron.

2   various kinds of monks.
3   girl who opens oysters.

When first I saw ye, *Cari luoghi*,[4]
   I'd scarce a beard upon my face,
And now a grizzled, grim old fogy,
   I sit and wait for Bouillabaisse.

Where are you, old companions trusty
   Of early days here met to dine?
Come, waiter! quick, a flagon crusty –   60
   I'll pledge them in the good old wine.
The kind old voices and old faces
   My memory can quick retrace;
Around the board they take their places,
   And share the wine and Bouillabaisse.

There's JACK has made a wondrous marriage;
   There's laughing TOM is laughing yet;
There's brave AUGUSTUS drives his carriage;
   There's poor old FRED in the *Gazette*;
On JAMES's head the grass is growing: 70
   Good Lord! the world has wagged apace
Since here we set the Claret flowing,
   And drank, and ate the Bouillabaisse.

Ah me! how quick the days are flitting!
   I mind me of a time that's gone,
When here I'd sit, as now I'm sitting,
   In this same place – but not alone.
A fair young form was nestled near me,
   A dear, dear face looked fondly up,
And sweetly spoke and smiled to cheer me   80
   – There's no one now to share my cup.

     *   *   *   *   *

I drink it as the Fates ordain it.
   Come, fill it, and have done with rhymes;
Fill up the lonely glass, and drain it
   In memory of dear old times.
Welcome the wine, whate'er the seal is;
   And sit you down and say your grace
With thankful heart, whate'er the meal is,
   – Here comes the smoking Bouillabaisse!

Ballads *(Ticknor & Fields, Boston, 1856).*

THE CANE-BOTTOMED CHAIR

In tattered old slippers that toast at the bars,
And a ragged old jacket perfumed with cigars,
Away from the world and its toils and its cares,
I've a snug little kingdom up four pair of stairs.

To mount to this realm is a toil, to be sure,
But the fire there is bright and the air rather pure;
And the view I behold on a sunshiny day
Is grand through the chimney-pots over the way.

4 dear places (Italian).

This snug little chamber is crammed in all nooks
With worthless old knicknacks and silly old books,   10
And foolish old odds and foolish old ends,
Cracked bargains from brokers, cheap keepsakes from friends.

Old armor, prints, pictures, pipes, china (all cracked),
Old rickety tables, and chairs broken-backed;
A twopenny treasury, wondrous to see;
What matter? 'tis pleasant to you, friend, and me.

No better divan need the sultan require,
Than the creaking old sofa that basks by the fire;
And 'tis wonderful, surely, what music you get
From the rickety, ramshackle, wheezy spinet.   20

That praying-rug came from a Turcoman's camp;
By Tiber once twinkled that brazen old lamp;
A Mameluke[1] fierce yonder dagger has drawn:
'Tis a murderous knife to toast muffins upon.

Long, long through the hours, and the night, and the chimes,
Here we talk of old books, and old friends, and old times;
As we sit in a fog made of rich Latakie[2]
This chamber is pleasant to you, friend, and me.

But of all the cheap treasures that garnish my nest,
There's one that I love and I cherish the best;   30
For the finest of couches that's padded with hair
I never would change thee, my cane-bottomed chair.

'Tis a bandy-legged, high-shouldered, worm-eaten seat,
With a creaking old back, and twisted old feet;
But since the fair morning when Fanny sat there,
I bless thee and love thee, old cane-bottomed chair.

If chairs have but feeling, in holding such charms,
A thrill must have passed through your withered old arms!
I looked, and I longed, and I wished in despair;
I wished myself turned to a cane-bottomed chair.   40

It was but a moment she sat in this place;
She'd a scarf on her neck, and a smile on her face!
A smile on her face, and a rose in her hair,
And she sat there, and bloomed in my cane-bottomed chair.

And so I have valued my chair ever since,
Like the shrine of a saint, or the throne of a prince;
Saint Fanny, my patroness sweet I declare,
The queen of my heart and my cane-bottomed chair.

When the candles burn low, and the company's gone
In the silence of night as I sit here alone –   50
I sit here alone, but we yet are a pair –
My Fanny I see in my cane-bottomed chair.

THE CANE-BOTTOMED CHAIR   2   Syrian tobacco.
1   member of Egyptian ruling caste.

She comes from the past and revisits my room;
She looks as she then did, all beauty and bloom;
So smiling and tender, so fresh and so fair,
And yonder she sits in my cane-bottomed chair.

Ballads *(1856)*. *[With unsympathetic allusion to Eliza Cook's 'The Old Arm-Chair'.]*

SORROWS OF WERTHER[1]

Werther had a love for Charlotte
    Such as words could never utter;
Would you know how first he met her?
    She was cutting bread and butter.

Charlotte was a married lady,
    And a moral man was Werther,
And for all the wealth of Indies,
    Would do nothing for to hurt her.

So he sighed and pined and ogled,
    And his passion boiled and bubbled,   10
Till he blew his silly brains out,
    And no more was by it troubled.

Charlotte, having seen his body
    Borne before her on a shutter,
Like a well-conducted person,
    Went on cutting bread and butter.

First published in Southern Literary Messenger *(November 1853)*. Ballads *(1856)*.

William Bell Scott (1811–90)

William Bell Scott, painter, poet, critic and memoirist, was born in Edinburgh, 12 September 1811, the seventh child of engraver Robert Scott and his wife Ross Bell, niece of a well-known sculptor. The parents had become Baptists after losing four children in infant deaths. Scott attended Edinburgh High School, studied and worked with his father, and had poems as early as 1834 in *Tait's Magazine* and the *Edinburgh University Souvenir*. In 1837 he moved to London, eking out a precarious existence as etcher, engraver and painter. From 1842 on he regularly exhibited at the Royal Academy. He married Letitia Margery Norquay, a High Church Anglican – despite an illness which was said to have caused her mental as well as facial impairment. In 1843 he moved to Newcastle-upon-Tyne where he spent twenty years organizing art education for the government schools of design, and also embellishing great houses with historical and balladic themes. His early verse – in *Hades; or The Transit: and The Progress of the Mind. Two Poems* (1838), and *The Year of the World: A Philosophical Poem on Redemption from the Fall* (1846) – was mystical and metaphysical, and Spasmodically inclined. Scott attracted the attention not least of Dante Gabriel Rossetti, who sent him his own poems, including *My Sister's Sleep* and *The Blessed Damozel*, in a package puzzlingly entitled *Songs of the Art Catholic*. A close liaison was established between Scott and the Rossettis, involving much to-ing and fro-ing between London and Newcastle, in a relationship helped as far as Christina Rossetti was concerned by Mrs Scott's sympathetic brand of Anglicanism, and not at all impaired, interestingly, by the Scotts' troilistic set-up after 1859 involving Alice Boyd, whose castle in Perthshire Scott decorated with murals. He was a contributor to the little

SORROWS OF WERTHER
1   Goethe's hero, in *The Sorrows of Young Werther* (1774–87): Hamletian Romantic icon.

Pre-Raphaelite flagship magazine *The Germ* and became 'Duns Scotus', or 'Scotus', even 'beloved Scotus', to the Rossettis. His poems, as well as their mode of production, acquired a Pre-Raphaelite hue. *Poems by William Bell Scott: Ballads, Studies from Nature, Sonnets, &c (1875)*, for instance, was a richly decorative book complete with seventeen etchings by Scott and Lawrence Alma-Tadema. Poetry is valuable only if it affects us 'like music or wine', Scott wrote in the Preface. In 1870 he bought an Adam house in Chelsea, not far from D. G. Rossetti, and commuted thereafter between London and Perthshire. In London he was intimate with main writers and artists, but especially with the Pre-Raphaelites around D. G. Rossetti and Swinburne, and the two volumes of his reminiscences (posthumously published in 1892) form a great source of information about artistic life in London, grudging and nasty-toned though Scott's line frequently is. Scott also produced many studies of painters and engravers, as well as editing a whole series of editions of English poets, including L.E.L. (1873). Christina Rossetti recalled her 'old admiration' when he sent her his last book of poems, *A Poet's Harvest Home: Being One Hundred Short Poems by William Bell Scott* (1882), just after Gabriel's death in that year. 'Accept this faint flash of a smouldering fun,/ The fun of a heavy old heart', she replied in verse to the man who, she said, could always rouse up her 'precarious sense of fun'. And Scott's fun was pretty smouldering, too, by then. In the eighties he suffered badly from angina, which finally killed him, 22 November 1890. He died at the Scottish castle of his devoted nurse Alice Boyd. Swinburne wrote some memorial verses for the *Athenaeum*, 28 February 1891.

To The Artists Called P.R.B.[1]

I thank you, brethren in Sincerity, –
   One who, within the temperate climes of Art,
   From the charmed circle humbly stands apart,
Scornfully also, with a listless eye
Watching old marionettes' vitality;
   For you have shown, with youth's brave confidence,
   The honesty of true speech and the sense
Uniting life with 'nature,' earth with sky.

In faithful hearts Art strikes its roots far down,
   And bears both flower and fruit with seeded core;
   When Truth dies out, the fruit appears no more,   10
But the flower hides a worm within its crown.
   God-speed you onward! once again our way
   Shall be made odorous with fresh flowers of May.

Written 1851. Poems by William Bell Scott: Ballads, Studies from
Nature, Sonnets, Etc., Illustrated by Seventeen Etchings,
by the Author & L. Alma-Tadema *(Longmans, Green, & Co., 1875)*.
Revises a version in Poems *(Smith, Elder, & Co., 1854)*.

A Rhyme of the Sun-Dial

The dial is dark, 'tis but half past-one:
But the crow is abroad, and the day's begun.

The dial is dim, 'tis but half-past two:
Fit the small foot with its neat first shoe.

The light gains fast, it is half-past three:
Now the blossom appears all over the tree.

To the Artists Called P.R.B.
1   Pre-Raphaelite Brotherhood.

The gnomon tells it is but half-past four:
Shut upon him the old school-door.

The sun is strong, it is half-past five:
Through this and through that let him hustle and strive.   10

Ha, thunder and rain! it is half-past six:
Hither and thither, go, wander and fix.

The shadows are sharp, it is half past-seven:
The Titan dares to scale even heaven!

The rain soon dries, it is half-past eight:
Time faster flies, but it is not late!

The sky now is clear, it is half-past nine:
Draw all the threads and make them entwine.

Clearer and calmer, 'tis half-past ten:
Count we the gains? not yet: try again.   20

The shadows lengthen, half-past eleven:
He looks back, alas! let the man be shriven!

The mist falls cold, it is half-past twelve:
Hark, the bell tolls! up, sexton, and delve!

> Poems *(1875). A version entitled 'A Rhyme of Life', with 4-line stanzas,*
> *appeared earlier in* Poems *(1854).*

THE WITCH'S BALLAD

O, I hae come from far away,
    From a warm land far away,
A southern land across the sea,
With sailor-lads about the mast,
Merry and canny, and kind to me.

And I hae been to yon town,
    To try my luck in yon town;
Nort, and Mysie, Elspie too.
Right braw we were to pass the gate,
Wi' gowden clasps on girdles blue.   10

Mysie smiled wi' miminy mouth,
    Innocent mouth, miminy mouth;[1]
Elspie wore her scarlet gown,
Nort's grey eyes were unco' gleg,[2]
My Castile comb was like a crown.

We walked abreast all up the street,
    Into the market up the street;
Our hair with marygolds was wound,

THE WITCH'S BALLAD   2   sharp.
1   cf. miminy-piminy: affected, over-refined (early 19th c. coinage)

Our bodices with love-knots laced,
Our merchandise with tansy bound.   20

Nort had chickens, I had cocks,
   Gamesome cocks, crowing cocks;
Mysie ducks, and Elspie drakes, –
For a wee groat or a pound;
We lost nae time wi' gives and takes.

– Lost nae time, for well we knew,
   In our sleeves full well we knew,
When the gloaming came that night,
Duck nor drake, nor hen nor cock
Would be found by candle light.   30

And when our chaffering all was done,
   All was paid for, sold and done,
We drew a glove on ilka hand,
We sweetly curtsied, each to each,
And deftly danced a saraband.

The market-lassies looked and laughed,
   Left their gear, and looked and laughed;
They made as they would join the game,
But soon their mithers, wild and wud,
With whack and screech they stopped the same.   40

Sae loud the tongues o' randles grew,
   The flytin' and the skirlin' grew,
At all the windows in the place,
Wi' spoons or knives, wi' needle or awl,
Was thrust out every hand and face.

And down each stair they thronged anon,
   Gentle, semple, thronged anon;
Souter[3] and tailor, frowsy Nan,
The ancient widow young again,
Simpering behind her fan.   50

Without a choice, against their will,
   Doited,[4] dazed, against their will,
The market lassie and her mither,
The farmer and his husbandman,
Hand in hand dance a' thegether.

Slow at first, but faster soon,
   Still increasing wild and fast,
Hoods and mantles, hats and hose,
Blindly doffed and cast away,
Left them naked, heads and toes.   60

They would have torn us limb from limb,
   Dainty limb from dainty limb;
But never one of them could win
Across the line that I had drawn
With bleeding thumb a-widdershin.

---

3   cobbler.   4   befuddled.

But there was Jeff the provost's son,
   Jeff the provost's only son;
There was Father Auld himsel',
The Lombard frae the hostelry,
And the lawyer Peter Fell.   70

All goodly men we singled out,
   Waled⁵ them well, and singled out,
And drew them by the left hand in;
Mysie the priest, and Elspie won
The Lombard, Nort the lawyer carle,
I mysel' the provost's son.

Then, with cantrip⁶ kisses seven,
   Three times round with kisses seven,
Warped and woven there spun we,
Arms and legs and flaming hair,   80
Like a whirlwind on the sea.

Like the wind that sucks the sea,
   Over and in and on the sea,
Good sooth it was a mad delight;
And every man of all the four
Shut his eyes and laughed outright.

Laughed as long as they had breath,
   Laughed while they had sense or breath;
And close about us coiled a mist
Of gnats and midges, wasps and flies,   90
Like the whirlwind shaft it rist.

Drawn up I was right off my feet,
   Into the mist and off my feet;
And, dancing on each chimney-top,
I saw a thousand darling imps
Keeping time with skip and hop.

And on the provost's brave ridge-tile,
   On the provost's grand ridge-tile,
The Blackamoor first to master me
I saw, – I saw that winsome smile,   100
The mouth that did my heart beguile,
And spoke the great Word over me,
In the land beyond the sea.

I called his name, I called aloud,
   Alas! I called on him aloud;
And then he filled his hand with stour,
And threw it towards me in the air;
My mouse flew out, I lost my pow'r!

My lusty strength, my power, were gone;
   Power was gone, and all was gone.   110
He will not let me love him more!
Of bell and whip and horse's tail
He cares not if I find a store.

---

5   chose.   6   witch's magic.

But I am proud if he is fierce!
　　I am as proud as he is fierce;
I'll turn about and backward go,
If I meet again that Blackmoor,
And he'll help us then, for he shall know
I seek another paramour.

And we'll gang once more to yon town,　　　　　　　　120
　　Wi' better luck to yon town;
We'll walk in silk and cramoisie,[7]
And I shall wed the provost's son,
My lady of the town I'll be.

For I was born a crowned king's child,
　　Born and nursed a king's child,
King o' a land ayont[8] the sea,
Where the Blackamoor kissed me first,
And taught me art and glamourie.[9]

Each one in her wame[10] shall hide　　　　　　　　130
　　Her hairy mouse, her wary mouse,
Fed on madwort and agramie, –
Wear amber beads between her breasts,
And blind-worm's skin about her knee.

The Lombard shall be Elspie's man,
　　Elspie's gowden husband-man;
Nort shall take the lawyer's hand;
The priest shall swear another vow:
We'll dance again the saraband!

Poems (1875).

THE NIGHTINGALE UNHEARD

Is that the much-desired, the wondrous wail
　　Of the brown bird by poets loved so long?
　　Nay, it is but the thrush's rich clear song
Through the red sunset rung; but down the vale,
Beneath the starlight, never do we fail
　　To hear the love-lorn singer: still and dark
　　Above our heads the black boughs arch; and, hark!
A wild short note – another – then a trail
Of loud clear song is drawn athwart the glow,
　　Filling the formless night with cheerfulness.　　　　　　　　10
　　But sure we know that melody full well, –
The dear old blackbird! Let's no further go;
　　There's no brown bird; – Ye poets all, confess
　　That Fancy only is your Philomel.[1]

Poems *(1875).*

7   crimson.
8   beyond.
9   magic.
10   belly; womb.

THE NIGHTINGALE UNHEARD
1   Athenian Philomela, raped by King Tereus, who cut out her tongue
to silence her: turned into nightingale.

MUSIC

Listless the silent ladies sit
About the room so gaily lit;
Madame Ions likes the cups or ray,
But thinks it scarce enough to say:
Mistress Cox is gone astray
To the night-light in her own nursery,
Wonders if little Maude was led
Without long coaxing into bed:
Miss Jemima Applewhite,
On a low stool by the fire,   10
Concentrates her confused desire, –
Perhaps will do so all the night,
On an unused rhyme for 'scan,'
And can but find the stiff word *man*:
Miss Temple pets the little hound,
That has a tendency to whine,
To-night its cushion can't be found;
And wonders when they'll leave the wine
Few take, but which men still combine
To linger over when they dine.   20

Indeed a frightful interval!
Madame Ions wants her game,
Or she must have her usual wink;
But now satiric Bertha Stahl
Jumps upon the music-stool,
And breaks into a sportive flame;
But what of all things do you think
She plays, that laughter-loving fool?
The funeral march, Dead March of Saul![1]

Oh, Lord of Hosts! their mailéd tread,   30
Bearing along the mailéd dead,
Makes me bow my stubborn head.
Never underneath the sun
With this heart-fathoming march be done;
Still, Lord of Hosts! to Thee we cry,
When our great ones, loved ones, die,
Still some grand lament we crave,
When we descend into the grave.

I turn, afraid that I may weep, –
Jemima's pestered wits still ran   40
After the unused rhyme for 'scan,'
Dear old Ions was asleep.

A Poet's Harvest Home: Being One Hundred Short Poems
(Elliot Stock, 1882). (Dedication: 'To W. M. Rossetti These Records of
a Season Are Inscribed In Memory of the Friendship of Half a Lifetime'.)

MUSIC
1 Dead March in G. F. Handel's Oratorio, *Saul* (1739).

Charles (John Huffam) Dickens (1812–70)

'Mr Popular Sentiment' in Trollope's telling phrase, Charles Dickens was born 9 February 1812 in Portsea, second child of eight in the family of John Dickens, a navy clerk, and Elizabeth, a naval lieutenant's daughter (interestingly, perhaps, John is the father's name of some of the biggest figures in British literature – Shakespeare, Wordsworth, Joyce). The family moved to London, via Chatham. Father's bad financial management landed him in the Marshalsea Prison for debt, and the young Dickens was put to work in the office of a blacking manufacturer at Hungerford Stairs, on the Thames. This traumatized him for life, but it also kickstarted into life his mightily productive lifelong black *imaginaire*. Beginning with *The Pickwick Papers* (1836–7) and ending with the unfinished *Edwin Drood*, his fifteen novels, numerous stories and travel books taught Victorian England how to imagine itself, not least in its urban dimensions. A loving satirist, Dickens is above all the gothic poet-in-prose of London. He also wrote the occasional poem. He was never not a reporter, a documentarist. Early on he trained and worked as a shorthand Parliamentary reporter; he wrote for the *Mirror of Parliament, True Sun* and *Morning Chronicle*. He edited *Bentley's Miscellany* (1837–9); founded the *Daily News* and was its first editor, January–February 1846; started up and edited *Household Words*, 1850–9; and edited its successor, *All the Year Round*, from 1859 until his death. A great dramatizer and theatricals-lover, his fiction always (to adapt the phrase from *Our Mutual Friend*, chapter 16, which T. S. Eliot wanted as title for the opening section of *The Waste Land*) does 'the police', or whatever characters are in question, 'in different voices'. Going on the road giving exciting and excited health-threatening readings based on his works helped kill him off. He fathered ten children – the boys all named after writers, Alfred Tennyson, Henry Fielding, and so on – but early in 1858 after twenty-four years of marriage he and his wife Catherine separated ('unhappy together, these two, good many years past', noted Dickens's great friend and inspiration Thomas Carlyle). In the wings and the shadows there was, of course, Dickens's mistress, the actress Ellen Ternan, inspiration for several gentle, lovely young women in the fiction (Dickens is never very good at imagining mature women). His emotional intensity, jeered at as sentimentalism, helped marginalize him for much of the twentieth century. But later twentieth-century criticism knows better, and no novelist is now more canonical. Dickens died 9 June 1870, and was buried in the national shrine of Westminster Abbey in London. *Household Words* was Dickens's special vehicle. He was joint proprietor with the publishers Bradbury and Evans, John Forster (consultant and adviser) and W. H. Wills, his co-editor. His editor's salary was £500 a year. He was paid extra as a contributor. He solicited contributions, read manuscripts, conferred weekly if possible with Wills about editorial matters, suggested topics for articles, revised and rewrote articles, corrected proofs and wrote much of the early numbers. *Household Words* had not heard of the Death of the Author. Dickens's name appeared all over it: 'CONDUCTED BY CHARLES DICKENS', declared the front-page masthead. The same words ran across every facing pair of pages. Advertisements and announcements commonly named Dickens, sometimes several times. He was omnipresent; he *was* *Household Words*, and *Household Words* was a main platform, built by him himself, for his educative programme of national truth-telling, which was also his project of satirical engagement with British social reality. The attack on the Pre-Raphaelites was thus no casual thing. Dickens's hostility to *detailism* in representation (to use George Henry Lewes's word: see pp. 498–510, below) is a most significant part of the period's intense and long debate about the nature and role of realism.

OLD LAMPS FOR NEW ONES

The Magician in 'Aladdin' may possibly have neglected the study of men, for the study of alchemical books; but it is certain that in spite of his profession he was no conjuror. He knew nothing of human nature, or the everlasting set of the current of human affairs. If, when he fraudulently sought to obtain possession of the wonderful Lamp, and went up and down, disguised, before the flying-palace, crying New Lamps for Old ones, he had reversed his cry, and made it Old Lamps for New ones, he would have been so far before his time as to have projected himself into the nineteenth century of our Christian Era.

This age is so perverse, and is so very short of faith – in consequence, as some suppose, of there having been a run on that bank for a few generations – that a parallel and beautiful idea, generally known among the ignorant as the Young England hallucination, unhappily expired before it could run alone, to the great grief of a small but a very select circle of mourners. There is something so fascinating, to a mind capable of any serious reflection, in the notion of ignoring all that has been done for the happiness and elevation of mankind during three or four centuries of slow and dearly-bought amelioration, that we have always thought it would tend soundly to the improvement of the general public, if any tangible symbol, any outward and visible sign, expressive of that admirable conception, could be held up before them. We are happy to have found such a sign at last; and although it would make a very indifferent sign, indeed, in the Licensed Victualling sense of the word, and would probably be rejected with contempt and horror by any Christian publican, it has our warmest philosophical appreciation.

In the fifteenth century, a certain feeble lamp of art arose in the Italian town of Urbino. This poor light, Raphael Sanzio by name, better known to a few miserably mistaken wretches in these later days, as Raphael (another burned at the same time, called Titian), was fed with a preposterous idea of Beauty – with a ridiculous power of etherealising, and exalting to the very Heaven of Heavens, what was most sublime and lovely in the expression of the human face divine on Earth – with the truly contemptible conceit of finding in poor humanity the fallen likeness of the angels of GOD, and raising it up again to their pure spiritual condition. This very fantastic whim effected a low revolution in Art, in this wise, that Beauty came to be regarded as one of its indispensable elements. In this very poor delusion, Artists have continued until this present nineteenth century, when it was reserved for some bold aspirants to 'put it down.'

The Pre-Raphael Brotherhood, Ladies and Gentlemen, is the dread Tribunal which is to set this matter right. Walk up, walk up; and here, conspicuous on the wall of the Royal Academy of Art in England, in the eighty-second year of their annual exhibition, you shall see what this new Holy Brotherhood, this terrible Police that is to disperse all Post-Raphael offenders, has 'been and done!'

You come – in this Royal Academy Exhibition, which is familiar with the works of WILKIE, COLLINS, ETTY, EASTLAKE, MULREADY, LESLIE, MACLISE, TURNER, STANFIELD, LANDSEER, ROBERTS, DANBY, CRESWICK, LEE, WEBSTER, HERBERT, DYCE, COPE, and others who would have been renowned as great masters in any age or country – you come, in this place, to the contemplation of a Holy Family.[1] You will have the goodness to discharge from your minds all Post-Raphael ideas, all religious aspirations, all elevating thoughts; all tender, awful, sorrowful, ennobling, sacred, graceful, or beautiful associations; and to prepare yourselves, as befits such a subject – Pre-Raphaelly considered – for the lowest depths of what is mean, odious, repulsive, and revolting.

You behold the interior of a carpenter's shop. In the foreground of that carpenter's shop is a hideous, wry-necked, blubbering, red-headed boy, in a bed-gown; who appears to have received a poke in the hand, from the stick of another boy with whom he has been playing in an adjacent gutter, and to be holding it up for the contemplation of a kneeling woman, so horrible in her ugliness, that (supposing it were possible for any human creature to exist for a moment with that dislocated throat) she would stand out from the rest of the company as a Monster, in the vilest cabaret in France, or the lowest ginshop in England. Two almost naked carpenters, master and journeyman, worthy companions of this agreeable female, are working at their trade; a boy, with some small flavor of humanity in him, is entering with a vessel of water; and nobody is paying any attention to a snuffy old woman who seems to have mistaken that shop for the tobacconist's next door, and to be hopelessly waiting at the counter to be served with half an ounce of her favourite mixture. Wherever it is possible to express ugliness of feature, limb, or attitude, you have it expressed. Such men as the carpenters might be undressed in any hospital where dirty drunkards, in a high state of varicose veins, are received. Their very toes have walked out of Saint Giles's.[2]

This, in the nineteenth century, and in the eighty-second year of the annual exhibition of the National Academy of Art, is the Pre-Raphael representation to us, Ladies and Gentlemen, of

OLD LAMPS FOR NEW ONES

1   John Everett Millais, *Christ in the Carpenter's Shop (Christ in the House of His Parents)*; exhibited untitled at the Royal Academy show of 1850, but with a biblical quotation subjoined: 'And one of you shall say unto him, what are those wounds in thine hands. Then he shall answer, Those with which I was wounded in the house of my friends' (Zechariah 13.6).

2   notorious London slum parish.

the most solemn passage which our minds can ever approach. This, in the nineteenth century, and in the eighty-second year of the annual exhibition of the National Academy of Art, is what Pre-Raphael Art can do to render reverence and homage to the faith in which we live and die! Consider this picture well. Consider the pleasure we should have in a similar Pre-Raphael rendering of a favourite horse, or dog, or cat; and, coming fresh from a pretty considerable turmoil about 'desecration' in connexion with the National Post Office, let us extol this great achievement, and commend the National Academy!

In further considering this symbol of the great retrogressive principle, it is particularly gratifying to observe that such objects as the shavings which are strewn on the carpenter's floor are admirably painted; and that the Pre-Raphael Brother is indisputably accomplished in the manipulation of his art. It is gratifying to observe this, because the fact involves no low effort at notoriety; everybody knowing that it is by no means easier to call attention to a very indifferent pig with five legs, than to a symmetrical pig with four. Also, because it is good to know that the National Academy thoroughly feels and comprehends the high range and exalted purposes of Art; distinctly perceives that Art includes something more than the faithful portraiture of shavings, or the skilful colouring of drapery – imperatively requires, in short, that it shall be informed with mind and sentiment; will on no account reduce it to a narrow question of trade-juggling with a palette, palette-knife, and paint-box. It is likewise pleasing to reflect that the great educational establishment foresees the difficulty into which it would be led, by attaching greater weight to mere handicraft, than to any other consideration – even to considerations of common reverence or decency; which absurd principle, in the event of a skilful painter of the figure becoming a very little more perverted in his taste, than certain skilful painters are just now, might place Her Gracious Majesty in a very painful position, one of these fine Private View Days.

Would it were in our power to congratulate our readers on the hopeful prospects of the great retrogressive principle, of which this thoughtful picture is the sign and emblem! Would that we could give our readers encouraging assurance of a healthy demand for Old Lamps in exchange for New ones, and a steady improvement in the Old Lamp Market! The perversity of mankind is such, and the untoward arrangements of Providence are such, that we cannot lay that flattering unction to their souls. We can only report what Brotherhoods, stimulated by this sign, are forming; and what opportunities will be presented to the people, if the people will but accept them.

In the first place, the Pre-Perspective Brotherhood will be presently incorporated, for the subversion of all known rules and principles of perspective. It is intended to swear every P. P. B. to a solemn renunciation of the art of perspective on a soup-plate of the willow pattern; and we may expect, on the occasion of the eighty-third Annual Exhibition of the Royal Academy of Art in England, to see some pictures by this pious Brotherhood, realising HOGARTH's idea of a man on a mountain several miles off, lighting his pipe at the upper window of a house in the foreground. But we are informed that every brick in the house will be a portrait; that the man's boots will be copied with the utmost fidelity from a pair of Bluchers, sent up out of Northamptonshire for the purpose; and that the texture of his hands (including four chilblains, a whitlow, and ten dirty nails) will be a triumph of the Painter's art.

A Society, to be called the Pre-Newtonian Brotherhood, was lately projected by a young gentleman, under articles to a Civil Engineer, who objected to being considered bound to conduct himself according to the laws of gravitation. But this young gentleman, being reproached by some aspiring companions with the timidity of his conception, has abrogated that idea in favour of a Pre-Galileo Brotherhood now flourishing, who distinctly refuse to perform any annual revolution round the Sun, and have arranged that the world shall not do so any more. The course to be taken by the Royal Academy of Art in reference to this Brotherhood is not yet decided upon; but it is whispered that some other large Educational Institutions in the neighbourhood of Oxford are nearly ready to pronounce in favour of it.

Several promising Students connected with the Royal College of Surgeons have held a meeting, to protest against the circulation of the blood, and to pledge themselves to treat all the patients they can get, on principles condemnatory of that innovation. A Pre-Harvey-Brotherhood is the result, from which a great deal may be expected – by the undertakers.

In literature, a very spirited effort has been made, which is no less than the formation of a P. G. A. P. C. B., or Pre-Gower and Pre-Chaucer-Brotherhood, for the restoration of the ancient English style of spelling, and the weeding out from all libraries, public and private, of those and all later pretenders, particularly a person of loose character named SHAKESPEARE. It having been suggested, however, that this happy idea could scarcely be considered complete while the art of printing was permitted to remain unmolested, another society, under the name of the Pre-Laurentius Brother-hood, has been established in connexion with it, for the abolition of all but manuscript books. These MR. PUGIN[3] has engaged to supply, in characters that nobody on earth shall be able to read. And it is confidently expected by those who have seen the House of Lords, that he will faith-fully redeem his pledge.

In Music, a retrogressive step, in which there is much hope, has been taken. The P. A. B., or Pre-Agincourt Brotherhood has arisen, nobly devoted to consign to oblivion Mozart, Beethoven, Han-del, and every other such ridiculous reputation, and to fix its Millennium (as its name implies) before the date of the first regular musical composition known to have been achieved in England. As this Institution has not yet commenced active operations, it remains to be seen whether the Royal Academy of Music will be a worthy sister of the Royal Academy of Art, and admit this enter-prising body to its orchestra. We have it on the best authority, that its compositions will be quite as rough and discordant as the real old original – that it will be, in a word, exactly suited to the pic-torial Art we have endeavoured to describe. We have strong hopes, therefore, that the Royal Acad-emy of Music, not wanting an example, may not want courage.

The regulation of social matters, as separated from the Fine Arts, has been undertaken by the Pre-Henry-the-Seventh Brotherhood, who date from the same period as the Pre-Raphael Brother-hood. This society, as cancelling all the advances of nearly four hundred years, and reverting to one of the most disagreeable periods of English History, when the Nation was yet very slowly emerging from barbarism, and when gentle female foreigners, come over to be the wives of Scottish Kings, wept bitterly (as well they might) at being left alone among the savage Court, must be regarded with peculiar favour. As the time of ugly religious caricatures (called mysteries), it is thoroughly Pre-Raphael in its spirit; and may be deemed the twin brother to that great society. We should be certain of the Plague among many other advantages, if this Brotherhood were properly encouraged.

All these Brotherhoods, and any other society of the like kind, now in being or yet to be, have at once a guiding star, and a reduction of their great ideas to something palpable and obvious to the senses, in the sign to which we take the liberty of directing their attention. We understand that it is in the contemplation of each Society to become possessed, with all convenient speed, of a collec-tion of such pictures; and that once, every year, to wit upon the first of April, the whole intend to amalgamate in a high festival, to be called the Convocation of Eternal Boobies.

Household Words, *no. 12, vol. I (15 June 1850), 265–7.*

Robert Browning (1812–89)

Alfred Tennyson's great rival for first place as chief Victor-ian poet, Robert Browning was born in Southampton Street, Camberwell, London, 7 May 1812, eldest child (his sister Sarianna was born in 1814) of Robert Browning, a scholarly and artistic banker who had given up more lucrative employment managing the family sugar planta-tions in St Kitts because of objections to slavery, and of Sarah Anna Wiedemann, a Scottish Congregationalist. The devout family attended York Street Congregationalist

Chapel in nearby Walworth. Browning had the run of his father's huge library from an early age; early on fell in love with Byron's poems; produced by about the age of twelve a Byronic volume *Incondita* (never published); aged fifteen fell even more dramatically in love with Shelley; was encouraged in his writing by the Unitarian Flower sisters (one of whom, as Sarah Flower Adams, became well known as the author of 'Nearer, my God, to Thee') and by the radical Unitarian preacher W. J. Fox. Browning

---

3 Augustus Welby Pugin (1812–52), Catholic convert and Gothic-revivalist architect (designed much of the new Houses of Parliament, 1836–7), key representative of the aesthetic retrogressions D. is mock-ing.

attended Nonconformist schools in Peckham, was taught privately at home, then enrolled in 1828 as only the sixteenth entrant to the brand-new London University, set up for students excluded by their non-Anglicanism from the Established Church-based Oxford and Cambridge. He lasted only a year: Shelley and private reading at home were more exciting. The extraordinary wide, if eclectic, reading Browning plunged into in his post-university period, 1829–33, made him almost the most learned of English poets – though he never escaped the scorn Oxbridge-educated critics heaped on this cultural and religious outsider. *Pauline: A Fragment of a Confession* appeared in March 1833, first move in Browning's lifelong play with dramatized selves, who would speak for, but not necessarily speak as, himself – the so-called 'dramatic monologue'. The first person to use the label 'Dramatic Monologue', was, it seems, George W. Thornbury in his *Songs of the Cavaliers and Roundheads, Jacobite Ballads & c* (Hurst and Blackett, 1857), to describe some of his poems (which lack, it must be said, the force Browning brings to the mode). 'Porphyria's Lover' and 'Johannes Agricola' (1833–4) were both published, under the heading 'Madhouse Cells', in W. J. Fox's *Monthly Repository* (January 1836), and Browning's career as poetic dramatizer of dubious self-exculpating, failed, doubting characters from the margins of morality, religion, art, intellect, society, history, had begun. The long poem *Paracelsus* (1835), dramatized story of a Carlylean mage, and *Sordello* (1840) – deliberately compressed and allusive – made Browning's reputation for cranky seriousness of subject, unmisgiving unsmoothness of diction, and overall obscurity. What, Walter Bagehot in his notorious comparison of Wordsworth, Tennyson and Browning – 'Pure, Ornate, and Grotesque Art in English Poetry' (1864) – would call Browning's 'grotesque realism', 'a taste for ugly reality', was already evident. *Strafford* (1837) began Browning's intermittent – and misguided – flirtation with the stage; the dramatic monologue, not the drama, was his great strength. *Dramatic Lyrics* (including 'My Last Duchess') came out in November 1842 as No. III in the series *Bells and Pomegranates* (all done at Browning's own expense). *Dramatic Romances and Lyrics* (*Bells and Pomegranates* VII, with such Browning standards as 'The Bishop Orders His Tomb') appeared in November 1845 – just a few months after Browning's first visit to the reclusive Elizabeth Barrett Moulton-Barrett, with whom he eloped to Italy after a secret marriage in September of the following year. In April 1847 the Brownings settled in Florence. Their only child, Robert Wiedemann Barrett Browning (Penini or Pen), was born in March 1849. *Christmas-Eve and Easter-Day*, Browning's magnificent exercise in grotesque comparative Christianity, was published in April 1850; the crucial 'Essay on Shelley' (Introduction to a volume of *Letters of Percy Bysshe Shelley*, quickly discovered to be forgeries) in 1852; *Men and Women* in 1855. This collection and *Dramatis Personae* (1864) have become the very centre of the Browning canon of mouth-full, anxious religious-agnostic, underdog-minded, bodily-realistic, hermeneutically-sceptical, self-conscious, self-doubting poems.

(In her review of *Men and Women* in the *Westminster Review*, January 1856, George Eliot declared that 'we would rather have "Fra Lippo Lippi" than any essay on Realism in Art'.) A large legacy of £11,000 at the end of 1856 from the Brownings' admirer – and her cousin – John Kenyon (who had been giving them an annual allowance of £100) solved the Brownings' financial difficulties. In June 1860 Browning picked up on a market-stall the 'Old Yellow Book' containing the Roman crime-story details that sparked his most extended dramatic monologue exercise, *The Ring and the Book* (1868–9). In Italy the Brownings were great friends with Isa Blagden, were visited by the likes of Burne-Jones, and looked after the aged Walter Savage Landor. On visits to London their acquaintance was cultivated by Carlyle, Ruskin, Coventry Patmore, Alfred Tennyson, Charles Kingsley, D. G. Rossetti. Elizabeth Barrett Browning died at their Florence house, Casa Guidi, 29 June 1861. A broken man, Browning quit Florence, never to return, and soon settled back in London. He became a seat-holder at the Bedford Chapel of the Welsh preacher-poet Thomas Jones. In 1863 he started the practice of dining out, visiting and concert-going, whenever opportunity presented, which made him a most prominent figure of the London literary and social scene. The forming of the Browning Society in 1881 set the seal on his distinction and fame. After *The Ring and the Book* his writing didn't really change, but it did mightily put on bulk ('His new poem has 15,000 lines: there's copiousness', awed Tennyson one time to William Allingham – and Tennyson was not especially anorexic himself). Volume after excellent volume poured out, all remaining stubbornly – and unaccountably – marginal to the canon. Honours accumulated: honorary degrees galore, an Honorary Fellowship at Balliol. Sixteen volumes of the *Poetical Works* were published in 1888–9. In later years Browning spent increasing time in Venice, and he died in the Palazzo Rezzonico there, 12 December 1889, the day the last of his now largely unread late volumes, *Asolando: Facts and Fancies*, came out. Browning's extraordinary verse – done, so to say, with 'This low-pulsed, forthright craftsman's hand of mine' ('Andrea del Sarto'): 'The better the uncouther', as he'd said in 'The Twins' in rhyming tribute to 'Grand rough old Martin Luther' – had outlived the snobbery and sneers of the cultural centrists, the anti-Dissenters, the Anglicans, the exquisites: Bagehot, Wilde ('Meredith is a prose Browning and so is Browning'), Hopkins ('a way of talking (and making his people talk) with the air and spirit of a man bouncing up from table with his mouth full of bread and cheese and saying that he meant to stand no blasted nonsense'). Ezra Pound and Henry James would rightly herald Browning as ur-modernist – relishing the scepticism of the dramatic monologue, the unreliability of its narrators, Browning's biblical insistence that while God might be true 'every man' is a liar, all as prophetic of modernistic things to come. His work *played* with knowledge, Henry James enthused. Pound specially liked Browning's gusto – 'Here's to you, Old Hippety-Hop o' the accents' ('Mesmerism').

MY LAST DUCHESS

Ferrara

That's my last Duchess painted on the wall,
Looking as if she were alive; I call
That piece a wonder, now: Frà Pandolf's hands
Worked busily a day, and there she stands.
Will't please you sit and look at her? I said
'Frà Pandolf' by design, for never read
Strangers like you that pictured countenance,
The depth and passion of its earnest glance,
But to myself they turned (since none puts by
The curtain I have drawn for you, but I)   10
And seemed as they would ask me, if they durst,
How such a glance came there; so not the first
Are you to turn and ask thus. Sir, 'twas not
Her husband's presence only, called that spot
Of joy into the Duchess' cheek: perhaps
Frà Pandolf chanced to say 'Her mantle laps
Over my lady's wrist too much,' or 'Paint
Must never hope to reproduce the faint
Half-flush that dies along her throat'; such stuff
Was courtesy, she thought, and cause enough   20
For calling up that spot of joy. She had
A heart.. how shall I say?.. too soon made glad,
Too easily impressed; she liked whate'er
She looked on, and her looks went everywhere.
Sir, 'twas all one! My favor at her breast,
The dropping of the daylight in the West,
The bough of cherries some officious fool
Broke in the orchard for her, the white mule
She rode with round the terrace – all and each
Would draw from her alike the forward speech,   30
Or blush, at least. She thanked men, – good; but thanked
Somehow.. I know not how.. as if she ranked
My gift of a nine hundred years old name
With anybody's gift. Who'd stoop to blame
This sort of trifling? Even had you skill
In speech – (which I have not) – to make your will
Quite clear to such an one, and say, 'Just this
Or that in you disgusts me; here you miss,
Or there exceed the mark' – and if she let
Herself be lessoned so, nor plainly set   40
Her wits to yours, forsooth, and made excuse,
– E'en then would be some stooping; and I chuse
Never to stoop. Oh, Sir, she smiled, no doubt,
Whene'er I passed her; but who passed without
Much the same smile? This grew; I gave commands;
Then all smiles stopped together. There she stands
As if alive. Will't please you rise? We'll meet
The company below then. I repeat,
The Count your Master's known munificence
Is ample warrant that no just pretence   50
Of mine for dowry will be disallowed;
Though his fair daughter's self, as I avowed
At starting, is my object. Nay, we'll go
Together down, Sir! Notice Neptune, tho',

Taming a sea-horse, thought a rarity,
Which Claus of Innsbruck cast in bronze for me.

Written, summer/ early autumn 1842. Bells and Pomegranates, No. III –
Dramatic Lyrics *(Edward Moxon, 1842), as 'Italy and France: I. Italy'.*
Present title in Poems, 2 vols *(Chapman & Hall, 1849), II. 1842 text.*

THE LOST LEADER

I

Just for a handful of silver he[1] left us,
    Just for a ribband to stick in his coat –
Got the one gift of which fortune bereft us,
    Lost all the others she lets us devote;
They, with the gold to give, doled him out silver,
    So much was their's who so little allowed:
How all our copper had gone for his service!
    Rags – were they purple, his heart had been proud!
We that had loved him so, followed him, honoured him,
    Lived in his mild and magnificent eye,   10
Learned his great language, caught his clear accents,
    Made him our pattern to live and to die!
Shakespeare was of us, Milton was for us,
    Burns, Shelley, were with us, – they watch from their graves!
He alone breaks from the van and the freemen,
    – He alone sinks to the rear and the slaves!

II

We shall march prospering, – not thro' his presence;
    Songs may excite us, – not from his lyre;
Deeds will be done, – while he boasts his quiescence,
    Still bidding crouch whom the rest bade aspire: 20
Blot out his name, then, – record one lost soul more,
    One task unaccepted, one footpath untrod,
One more devils'-triumph and sorrow for angels,
    One wrong more to man, one more insult to God!
Life's night begins: let him never come back to us!
    There would be doubt, hesitation and pain,
Forced praise on our part – the glimmer of twilight,
    Never glad confident morning again!
Best fight on well, for we taught him, – come gallantly,
    Strike our face hard ere we shatter his own;   30
Then let him get the new knowledge and wait us,
    Pardoned in Heaven, the first by the throne!

Bells and Pomegranates. No. VII. Dramatic Romances and Lyrics
(Edward Moxon, 6 November 1845).

THE LOST LEADER
1 Wordsworth; radical turned conservative; became Poet Laureate 4
April 1843.

SOLILOQUY OF THE SPANISH CLOISTER

I

GR-R-R – there go, my heart's abhorrence!
   Water your damned flower-pots, do!
If hate killed men, Brother Lawrence,
   God's blood, would not mine kill you!
What? your myrtle-bush wants trimming?
   Oh, that rose has prior claims –
Needs its leaden vase filled brimming?
   Hell dry you up with its flames!

II

At the meal we sit together:
   Salve tibi![1] I must hear   10
Wise talk of the kind of weather,
   Sort of season, time of year:
Not a plenteous cork-crop: scarcely
   Dare we hope oak-galls, I doubt:
What's the Latin name for 'parsley'?
   What's the Greek name for Swine's Snout?

III

Phew! We'll have our platter burnished,
   Laid with care on our own shelf!
With a fire-new spoon we're furnished,
   And a goblet for ourself,   20
Rinsed like something sacrificial
   Ere 'tis fit to touch our chaps –
Marked with L. for our initial!
   (He-he! There his lily snaps!)

IV

Saint, forsooth! While brown Dolores
   Squats outside the Convent bank
With Sanchicha, telling stories,
   Steeping tresses in the tank,
Blue-black, lustrous, thick like horsehairs,
   – Can't I see his dead eye grow,   30
Bright as 'twere a Barbary corsair's?
   That is, if he'd let it show!

V

When he finishes refection,
   Knife and fork across he lays
Never, to my recollection,
   As do I, in Jesu's praise.
I, the Trinity illustrate,
   Drinking watered orange-pulp;
In three sips the Arian[2] frustrate;
   While he drains his at one gulp!   40

SOLILOQUY OF THE SPANISH CLOISTER
1   'Your health!' (cod Latin).

2   heretic who denies the Trinity – school of Arius (d. 336).

VI

Oh, those melons? If he's able
  We're to have a feast; so nice!
One goes to the Abbot's table,
  All of us get each a slice.
How go on your flowers? None double?
  Not one fruit-sort can you spy?
Strange! – And I, too, at such trouble,
  Keep 'em close-nipped on the sly!

VII

There's a great text in Galatians,
  Once you trip on it, entails   50
Twenty-nine distinct damnations,
  One sure, if another fails:[3]
If I trip him just a-dying,
  Sure of Heaven as sure can be,
Spin him round and send him flying
  Off to hell a Manichee?[4]

VIII

Or, my scrofulous French novel
  On grey paper with blunt type!
Simply glance at it, you grovel
  Hand and foot in Belial's gripe.   60
If I double down its pages
  At the woeful sixteenth print,
When he gathers his greengages,
  Ope a sieve and slip it in't?

IX

Or, the Devil! – one might venture
  Pledge one's soul yet slily leave
Such a flaw in the indenture
  As he'd miss till, past retrieve,
Blasted lay that rose-acacia
  We're so proud of! *Hy, Zy, Hine* ...   70
St, there's Vespers! *Plena gratiâ*
  Ave, Virgo![5] Gr-r-r – you swine!

Dramatic Lyrics *(1842), as 'Camp and Cloister: II – Cloister (Spanish)'.*
Present title in Poems *(1849), II. 1842 text.*

PORPHYRIA'S LOVER

The rain set early in to-night,
  The sullen wind was soon awake,
It tore the elm-tops down for spite,
  And did its worst to vex the lake,
  I listened with heart fit to break,
When glided in Porphyria; straight
  She shut the cold out and the storm,
And kneeled and made the cheerless grate

---

3 There is no such text.
4 heretic who believed all matter under Devil's rule.

5 Hail, Virgin, full of grace.

Blaze up, and all the cottage warm;
 Which done, she rose, and from her form   10
Withdrew the dripping cloak and shawl,
 And laid her soiled gloves by, untied
Her hat and let the damp hair fall,
 And, last, she sat down by my side
 And called me. When no voice replied,
She put my arm about her waist,
 And made her smooth white shoulder bare,
And all her yellow hair displaced,
 And, stooping, made my cheek lie there,
 And spread o'er all her yellow hair,   20
Murmuring how she loved me; she
 Too weak, for all her heart's endeavour,
To set its struggling passion free
 From pride, and vainer ties dissever,
 And give herself to me for ever:
But passion sometimes would prevail,
 Nor could to-night's gay feast restrain
A sudden thought of one so pale
 For love of her, and all in vain;
 And she was come through wind and rain.   30
Be sure I looked up at her eyes
 Proud, very proud; at last I knew
Porphyria worshipped me; surprise
 Made my heart swell, and still it grew
 While I debated what to do.
That moment she was mine, mine, fair,
 Perfectly pure and good: I found
A thing to do, and all her hair
 In one long yellow string I wound
 Three times her little throat around,   40
And strangled her. No pain felt she;
 I am quite sure she felt no pain.
As a shut bud that holds a bee
 I warily oped her lids; again
 Laughed the blue eyes without a stain.
And I untightened next the tress
 About her neck; her cheek once more
Blushed bright beneath my burning kiss:
 I propped her head up as before,
 Only, this time my shoulder bore   50
Her head, which droops upon it still:
 The smiling rosy little head,
So glad it has its utmost will,
 That all it scorned at once is fled,
 And I, its love, am gained instead!
Porphyria's love: she guessed not how
 Her darling one wish would be heard.
And thus we sit together now,
 And all night long we have not stirred,
 And yet God has not said a word!   60

*Written, London, ? 1835. First published as 'Porphyria' in W. J. Fox's
Monthly Repository, n.s. X (January 1836), 43–4 (signed 'Z'). Dramatic Lyrics
(1842), as 'Madhouse Cells: II.' Present title in* Poems *(1849), II, as subtitle to 'II. —
Madhouse Cell'. 1842 text.*

HOME-THOUGHTS, FROM ABROAD

I

Oh, to be in England
Now that April's there,
And whoever wakes in England
Sees, some morning, unaware,
That the lowest boughs and the brush-wood sheaf
Round the elm-tree bole are in tiny leaf,
While the chaffinch sings on the orchard bough
In England – now!

II

And after April, when May follows,
And the whitethroat builds, and all the swallows –   10
Hark! where my blossomed pear-tree in the hedge
Leans to the field and scatters on the clover
Blossoms and dewdrops – at the bent spray's edge –
That's the wise thrush; he sings each song twice over,
Lest you should think he never could recapture
The first fine careless rapture!
And though the fields look rough with hoary dew,
All will be gay when noontide wakes anew
The buttercups, the little children's dower,
– Far brighter than this gaudy melon-flower!   20

*Dramatic Romances and Lyrics (1845), as first part of three-part poem. Separate existence,
with numbered stanzas,* Poems *(1849), II. Otherwise, 1845 text. (Browning's Italian visit of
1838 was in summer; his 1844 visit in autumn.)*

THE BISHOP ORDERS HIS TOMB AT SAINT PRAXED'S CHURCH[1]

Rome, 15—

Vanity, saith the preacher, vanity![2]
Draw round my bed: is Anselm keeping back?
Nephews – sons mine…ah God, I know not! Well –
She, men would have to be your mother once,
Old Gandolf envied me, so fair she was!
What's done is done, and she is dead beside,
Dead long ago, and I am Bishop since,
And as she died so must we die ourselves,
And thence ye may perceive the world's a dream.
Life, how and what is it? As here I lie   10
In this state-chamber, dying by degrees,
Hours and long hours in the dead night, I ask
'Do I live, am I dead?' Peace, peace seems all:
St Praxed's ever was the church for peace;
And so, about this tomb of mine. I fought
With tooth and nail to save my niche, ye know:
– Old Gandolf cozened[3] me, despite my care;
Shrewd was that snatch from out the corner South

THE BISHOP ORDERS HIS TOMB
1 Basilica of Santa Prassede, Rome (first visited by B., October 1844).
The Bishop probably not a particular historical one.
2 Ecclesiastes 1.2.
3 tricked.

He graced his carrion with, God curse the same!
Yet still my niche is not so cramp'd but thence   20
One sees the pulpit o' the epistle-side,[4]
And somewhat of the choir, those silent seats,
And up into the aery dome[5] where live
The angels, and a sunbeam's sure to lurk:
And I shall fill my slab of basalt there,
And 'neath my tabernacle[6] take my rest
With those nine columns round me, two and two,[7]
The odd one at my feet where Anselm stands:
Peach-blossom marble all, the rare, the ripe
As fresh-poured red wine of a mighty pulse.   30
– Old Gandolf with his paltry onion-stone,[8]
Put me where I may look at him! True peach,
Rosy and flawless: how I earned the prize!
Draw close: that conflagration of my church
– What then? So much was saved if aught were missed!
My sons, ye would not be my death? Go dig
The white-grape vineyard where the oil-press stood,
Drop water gently till the surface sinks,
And if ye find... Ah, God, I know not, I!...
Bedded in store of rotten figleaves soft,   40
And corded up in a tight olive-frail,[9]
Some lump, ah God, of *lapis lazuli*,
Big as a Jew's head cut off at the nape,[10]
Blue as a vein o'er the Madonna's breast...
Sons, all have I bequeathed you, villas, all,
That brave Frascati[11] villa with its bath,
So let the blue lump poise between my knees,
Like God the Father's globe on both his hands
Ye worship in the Jesu Church so gay,[12]
For Gandolf shall not choose but see and burst!   50
Swift as a weaver's shuttle fleet our years:[13]
Man goeth to the grave, and where is he?[14]
Did I say basalt for my slab, sons? Black –
'Twas ever antique-black I meant! How else
Shall ye contrast my frieze to come beneath?
The bas-relief in bronze ye promised me,
Those Pans[15] and Nymphs ye wot of, and perchance
Some tripod, thyrsus,[16] with a vase or so,
The Saviour at his sermon on the mount,[17]
St Praxed in a glory,[18] and one Pan   60
Ready to twitch the Nymph's last garment off,
And Moses with the tables[19]... but I know
Ye mark me not! What do they whisper thee,
Child of my bowels, Anselm? Ah, ye hope
To revel down my villas while I gasp

4   right side facing altar.
5   Santa Prassede's has two.
6   tomb canopy.
7   like the Hebrew tabernacle, Exodus 26.
8   *cipollino*: poor stone.
9   basket.
10 cf. John the Baptist, Salomé's victim.
11 town near Rome.
12 In Chiesa de Gesù, Rome, an angel holds globe of *lapis lazuli* in
Trinity altar-piece.

13 Job 7.6.
14 Job 7.9; 14.10.
15 Pan, sexy rural deity.
16 tripod – 3-legged stool for Apollo's priestesses; thyrsus – rod of
Bacchus (Dionysos), god of wine, sex, fertility.
17 Jesus: Matthew 5–7.
18 halo.
19 Tablets of the Law, Exodus 24–36.

Bricked o'er with beggar's mouldy travertine[20]
Which Gandolf from his tomb-top chuckles at!
Nay, boys, ye love me – all of jasper, then!
'Tis jasper[21] ye stand pledged to, lest I grieve
My bath must needs be left behind, alas!   70
One block, pure green as a pistachio-nut,
There's plenty jasper somewhere in the world –
And have I not St Praxed's ear to pray
Horses for ye, and brown Greek manuscripts,
And mistresses with great smooth marbly limbs?
– That's if ye carve my epitaph aright,
Choice Latin, picked phrase, Tully's every word,[22]
No gaudy ware like Gandolf's second line –
Tully, my masters? Ulpian[23] serves his need!
And then how I shall lie through centuries,   80
And hear the blessed mutter of the mass,
And see God made and eaten all day long,
And feel the steady candle-flame, and taste
Good strong thick stupifying incense-smoke!
For as I lie here, hours of the dead night,
Dying in state and by such slow degrees,
I fold my arms as if they clasped a crook,[24]
And stretch my feet forth straight as stone can point,
And let the bedclothes for a mortcloth[25] drop
Into great laps and folds of sculptor's-work: 90
And as yon tapers dwindle, and strange thoughts
Grow, with a certain humming in my ears,
About the life before this life I lived,
And this life too, Popes, Cardinals and Priests,
St Praxed at his sermon on the mount,
Your tall pale mother with her talking eyes,
And new-found agate urns as fresh as day,
And marble's language, Latin pure, discreet,
– Aha, ELUCESCEBAT[26] quoth our friend?
No Tully, said I, Ulpian at the best!   100
Evil and brief hath been my pilgrimage,[27]
All *lapis*, all, sons! Else I give the Pope
My villas: will ye ever eat my heart?
Ever your eyes were as a lizard's quick,
They glitter like your mother's for my soul,
Or ye would heighten my impoverished frieze,
Piece out its starved design, and fill my vase
With grapes, and add a vizor and a Term,[28]
And to the tripod ye would tie a lynx[29]
That in his struggle throws the thyrsus down,   110
To comfort me on my entablature[30]
Whereon I am to lie till I must ask
'Do I live, am I dead?' There, leave me, there!
For ye have stabbed me with ingratitude
To death – ye wish it – God, ye wish it! Stone –

20   limestone.
21   stone of Heavenly City wall.
22   Cicero, great Roman rhetorician.
23   Ulpianus – inferior Roman wordsmith.
24   a bishop's stick (and a villain).
25   pall.

26   'He was illustrious' (not the best Latin).
27   Genesis 47.9.
28   pedestal bust.
29   Dionysian pet.
30   top part of a column (misuse!).

Gritstone, a-crumble! Clammy squares which sweat
As if the corpse they keep were oozing through –
And no more *lapis* to delight the world!
Well go! I bless ye. Fewer tapers there,
But in a row: and, going, turn your backs   120
– Ay, like departing altar-ministrants,
And leave me in my church, the church for peace,
That I may watch at leisure if he leers –
Old Gandolf, at me, from his onion-stone,
As still he envied me, so fair she was!

Hood's Magazine, III (March 1845), 237–9, and Dramatic Romances and Lyrics
(1845), as 'The Tomb at St. Praxed's (Rome 15—)'. Retitled in Poems (1849), II.
1845 text. (Directed, B. said, against 'the Oxford business', i.e. the Tractarian movement.
Ruskin thought it summed up 'the Renaissance spirit' as well as did 30 pages of
The Stones of Venice – 'its worldliness, inconsistency, pride, hypocrisy,
ignorance of itself, love of art, of luxury, and of good Latin'.)

MEETING AT NIGHT

I

The grey sea and the long black land;
And the yellow half-moon large and low;
And the startled little waves that leap
In fiery ringlets from their sleep,
As I gain the cove with pushing prow,
And quench its speed in the slushy sand.

II

Then a mile of warm sea-scented beach;
Three fields to cross till a farm appears;
A tap at the pane, the quick sharp scratch
And blue spurt of a lighted match,   10
And a voice less loud, thro' its joys and fears,
Than the two hearts beating each to each!

PARTING AT MORNING

Round the cape of a sudden came the sea,
And the sun looked over the mountain's rim –
And straight was a path of gold for him,
And the need of a world of men for me.

Dramatic Romances and Lyrics (1845) as 'Night and Morning: I – Night. II –
Morning'. Present titles in Poems (1849), II. 1845 text.

LOVE AMONG THE RUINS

I

Where the quiet-coloured end of evening smiles,
  Miles and miles
On the solitary pastures where our sheep
  Half-asleep

Tinkle homeward thro' the twilight, stray or stop
  As they crop –

2

Was the site once of a city great and gay,[1]
  (So they say)
Of our country's very capital, its prince
  Ages since   10
Held his court in, gathered councils, wielding far
  Peace or war.

3

Now – the country does not even boast a tree,
  As you see,
To distinguish slopes of verdure, certain rills
  From the hills
Intersect and give a name to, (else they run
  Into one)

4

Where the domed and daring palace shot its spires[2]
  Up like fires   20
O'er the hundred-gated circuit of a wall[3]
  Bounding all,
Made of marble, men might march on nor be pressed,
  Twelve abreast.

5

And such plenty and perfection, see, of grass
  Never was!
Such a carpet as, this summer-time, o'erspreads
  And embeds
Every vestige of the city, guessed alone,
  Stock or stone –   30

6

Where a multitude of men breathed joy and woe
  Long ago;
Lust of glory pricked their hearts up, dread of shame
  Struck them tame;
And that glory and that shame alike, the gold
  Bought and sold.

7

Now, – the single little turret that remains
  On the plains,
By the caper over-rooted, by the gourd
  Overscored,   40
While the patching houseleek's head of blossom winks
  Through the chinks –

8

Marks the basement whence a tower in ancient time
  Sprang sublime,

LOVE AMONG THE RUINS

1 as in Edmund Spenser, *Ruines of Time*, 55–6.

2 as in Spenser, *Ruines of Rome*, 16.

3 like Babylon and Egyptian Thebes.

And a burning ring all round, the chariots traced
   As they raced,
And the monarch and his minions and his dames
   Viewed the games.

9

And I know, while thus the quiet-coloured eve
   Smiles to leave   50
To their folding, all our many-tinkling fleece
   In such peace,
And the slopes and rills in undistinguished grey
   Melt away —

10

That a girl with eager eyes and yellow hair
   Waits me there
In the turret whence the charioteers caught soul
   For the goal,
When the king looked, where she looks now, breathless, dumb
   Till I come.   60

11

But he looked upon the city, every side,
   Far and wide,
All the mountains topped with temples, all the glades'
   Colonnades,
All the causeys,[4] bridges, aqueducts, – and then,
   All the men!

12

When I do come, she will speak not, she will stand,
   Either hand
On my shoulder, give her eyes the first embrace
   Of my face,   70
Ere we rush, ere we extinguish sight and speech
   Each on each.

13

In one year they sent a million fighters forth
   South and North,
And they built their gods a brazen pillar high
   As the sky,
Yet reserved a thousand chariots in full force –
   Gold, of course.

14

Oh, heart! oh, blood that freezes, blood that burns!
   Earth's returns   80
For whole centuries of folly, noise and sin!
   Shut them in,
With their triumphs and their glories and the rest!
   Love is best.

Written, ? Florence, 1853? First poem in Men and Women, *2 vols
(Chapman & Hall, 10 November 1855), I. Seven-stanza form, first in the
6-volume edition of* The Poetical Works *(Smith, Elder, & Co., 1868).*

4 causeways.

FRA LIPPO LIPPI[1]

I am poor brother Lippo, by your leave!
You need not clap your torches to my face.
Zooks, what's to blame? you think you see a monk!
What, it's past midnight, and you go the rounds,
And here you catch me at an alley's end
Where sportive ladies leave their doors ajar.
The Carmine's my cloister:[2] hunt it up,
Do, – harry out, if you must show your zeal,
Whatever rat, there, haps on his wrong hole,
And nip each softling of a wee white mouse,   10
Weke, weke, that's crept to keep him company!
Aha, you know your betters! Then, you'll take
Your hand away that's fiddling on my throat,
And please to know me likewise. Who am I?
Why, one, sir, who is lodging with a friend
Three streets off – he's a certain . . . how d'ye call?
Master – a . . . Cosimo of the Medici,[3]
I' the house that caps the corner. Boh! you were best!
Remember and tell me, the day you're hanged,
How you affected such a gullet's-gripe!   20
But you, sir, it concerns you that your knaves
Pick up a manner nor discredit you.
Zooks, are we pilchards, that they sweep the streets
And count fair prize what comes into their net?
He's Judas to a tittle,[4] that man is!
Just such a face! why, sir, you make amends.
Lord, I'm not angry! Bid your hangdogs go
Drink out this quarter-florin to the health
Of the munificent House that harbours me
(And many more beside, lads! more beside!)   30
And all's come square again. I'd like his face –
His, elbowing on his comrade in the door
With the pike and lantern, – for the slave that holds
John Baptist's head a-dangle by the hair
With one hand ('Look you, now,' as who should say)[5]
And his weapon in the other, yet unwiped!
It's not your chance to have a bit of chalk,
A wood-coal or the like? or you should see!
Yes, I'm the painter, since you style me so.
What, brother Lippo's doings, up and down,   40
You know them and they take you? like enough!
I saw the proper twinkle in your eye –
'Tell you I liked your looks at very first.
Let's sit and set things straight now, hip to haunch.
Here's spring come, and the nights one makes up bands
To roam the town and sing out carnival,
And I've been three weeks shut within my mew,[6]
A-painting for the great man, saints and saints
And saints again. I could not paint all night –
Ouf! I leaned out of window for fresh air.   50

FRA LIPPO LIPPI
1 Fra Filippo Lippi (c.1406–69) – sourced in Giorgio Vasari's *Lives of the More Excellent Painters, Sculptors and Architects* (1550).
2 Carmelite monastery.
3 ruler of Florence; great patron of the arts.
4 small mark of punctuation in Hebrew: so 'in the smallest particular'.
5 the beheaded Baptist: a Victorian obsession.
6 enclosure; imprisoning place.

There came a hurry of feet and little feet,
A sweep of lute-strings, laughs, and whifts of song, –
Flower o' the broom,
Take away love, and our earth is a tomb!
Flower o' the quince,
I let Lisa go, and what good's in life since?
Flower o' the thyme[7] – and so on. Round they went.
Scarce had they turned the corner when a titter
Like the skipping of rabbits by moonlight, – three slim shapes –
And a face that looked up ... zooks, sir, flesh and blood,   60
That's all I'm made of! Into shreds it went,
Curtain and counterpane and coverlet,
All the bed-furniture – a dozen knots,
There was a ladder! down I let myself,
Hands and feet, scrambling somehow, and so dropped,
And after them. I came up with the fun
Hard by Saint Laurence,[8] hail fellow, well met, –
Flower o' the rose,
If I've been merry, what matter who knows?
And so as I was stealing back again   70
To get to bed and have a bit of sleep
Ere I rise up tomorrow and go work
On Jerome knocking at his poor old breast
With his great round stone to subdue the flesh,[9]
You snap[10] me of the sudden. Ah, I see!
Though your eye twinkles still, you shake your head –
Mine's shaved, – a monk, you say – the sting's in that!
If Master Cosimo announced himself,
Mum's the word naturally; but a monk!
Come, what am I a beast for? tell us, now!   80
I was a baby when my mother died
And father died and left me in the street.
I starved there, God knows how, a year or two
On fig-skins, melon-parings, rinds and shucks,
Refuse and rubbish. One fine frosty day,
My stomach being empty as your hat,
The wind doubled me up and down I went.
Old Aunt Lapaccia trussed me with one hand,
(Its fellow was a stinger as I knew)
And so along the wall, over the bridge,   90
By the straight cut to the convent. Six words, there,
While I stood munching my first bread that month:
'So, boy, you're minded,' quoth the good fat father
Wiping his own mouth, 'twas refection-time, –
'To quit this very miserable world?
Will you renounce' ... the mouthful of bread? thought I;
By no means! Brief, they made a monk of me;
I did renounce the world, its pride and greed,
Palace, farm, villa, shop and banking-house,
Trash, such as these poor devils of Medici   100
Have given their hearts to – all at eight years old.
Well, sir, I found in time, you may be sure,

7 a *stornello* (3-line Tuscan song).   10 grab.
8 San Lorenzo church.
9 ascetic saint: in Lippi's *Virgin Adoring the Child with Saint Hilarion* (a
Cosimo commission: now in Uffizi Gallery, Florence).

'Twas not for nothing – the good bellyful,
The warm serge and the rope that goes all round,
And day-long blessed idleness beside!
'Let's see what the urchin's fit for' – that came next.
Not overmuch their way, I must confess.
Such a to-do! they tried me with their books.
Lord, they'd have taught me Latin in pure waste!
Flower o' the clove,   110
All the Latin I construe is, 'amo' I love!
But, mind you, when a boy starves in the streets
Eight years together, as my fortune was,
Watching folk's faces to know who will fling
The bit of half-stripped grape-bunch he desires,
And who will curse or kick him for his pains –
Which gentleman processional and fine,
Holding a candle to the Sacrament,
Will wink and let him lift a plate and catch
The droppings of the wax to sell again,   120
Or holla for the Eight[11] and have him whipped, –
How say I? – nay, which dog bites, which lets drop
His bone from the heap of offal in the street!
– The soul and sense of him grow sharp alike,
He learns the look of things, and none the less
For admonitions from the hunger-pinch.
I had a store of such remarks, be sure,
Which, after I found leisure, turned to use:
I drew men's faces on my copy-books,
Scrawled them within the antiphonary's[12] marge,   130
Joined legs and arms to the long music-notes,
Found eyes and nose and chin for A.s and B.s,
And made a string of pictures of the world
Betwixt the ins and outs of verb and noun,
On the wall, the bench, the door. The monks looked black.
'Nay,' quoth the Prior, 'turn him out, d'ye say?
In no wise. Lose a crow and catch a lark.
What if at last we get our man of parts,
We Carmelites, like those Camaldolese[13]
And Preaching Friars,[14] to do our church up fine   140
And put the front on it that ought to be!'
And hereupon he bade me daub away.
Thank you! my head being crammed, their walls a blank,
Never was such prompt disemburdening.
First, every sort of monk, the black and white,
I drew them, fat and lean: then, folk at church,
From good old gossips waiting to confess
Their cribs[15] of barrel-droppings, candle-ends, –
To the breathless fellow at the altar-foot,
Fresh from his murder, safe[16] and sitting there   150
With the little children round him in a row
Of admiration, half for his beard and half
For that white anger of his victim's son
Shaking a fist at him with one fierce arm,
Signing himself with the other because of Christ

---

11 Florence's eight magistrates.
12 choral music book.
13 order of nuns in Florence region.

14 Dominicans.
15 little thefts.
16 the church is place of sanctuary.

(Whose sad face on the cross sees only this
After the passion of a thousand years)
Till some poor girl, her apron o'er her head
Which the intense eyes looked through, came at eve
On tip-toe, said a word, dropped in a loaf,   160
Her pair of ear-rings and a bunch of flowers
The brute took growling, prayed, and then was gone.
I painted all, then cried ''tis ask and have –
Choose, for more's ready!' – laid the ladder flat,
And showed my covered bit of cloister-wall.
The monks closed in a circle and praised loud
Till checked, (taught what to see and not to see,
Being simple bodies) 'that's the very man!
Look at the boy who stoops to pat the dog!
That woman's like the Prior's niece[17] who comes   170
To care about his asthma: it's the life!'
But there my triumph's straw-fire flared and funked;[18]
Their betters took their turn to see and say:
The Prior and the learned pulled a face
And stopped all that in no time. 'How? what's here?
Quite from the mark of painting, bless us all!
Faces, arms, legs and bodies like the true
As much as pea and pea! it's devil's-game!
Your business is not to catch men with show,
With homage to the perishable clay,   180
But lift them over it, ignore it all,
Make them forget there's such a thing as flesh.
Your business is to paint the souls of men –
Man's soul, and it's a fire, smoke .. no, it's not ..
It's vapour done up like a new-born babe –
(In that shape when you die it leaves your mouth)
It's .. well, what matters talking, it's the soul!
Give us no more of body than shows soul!
Here's Giotto,[19] with his Saint a-praising God,
That sets us praising, – why not stop with him?   190
Why put all thoughts of praise out of our heads
With wonder at lines, colours, and what not?
Paint the soul, never mind the legs and arms!
Rub all out, try at it a second time.
Oh, that white smallish female with the breasts,
She's just my niece ... Herodias, I would say, –
Who went and danced and got men's heads cut off![20]
Have it all out!' Now, is this sense, I ask?
A fine way to paint soul, by painting body
So ill, the eye can't stop there, must go further   200
And can't fare worse! Thus, yellow does for white
When what you put for yellow's simply black,
And any sort of meaning looks intense
When all beside itself means and looks nought.
Why can't a painter lift each foot in turn,
Left foot and right foot, go a double step,
Make his flesh liker and his soul more like,
Both in their order? Take the prettiest face,

---

17   euphemism for Prior's girlfriend.
18   gone up in smoke.
19   important Florentine painter and architect (1267–1337).

20   mistake for Salomé – Herodias' mother (Vasari's error). The obsessive John the Baptist story.

The Prior's niece...patron-saint – is it so pretty
You can't discover if it means hope, fear,   210
Sorrow or joy? won't beauty go with these?
Suppose I've made her eyes all right and blue,
Can't I take breath and try to add life's flash,
And then add soul and heighten them threefold?
Or say there's beauty with no soul at all –
(I never saw it – put the case the same –)
If you get simple beauty and nought else,
You get about the best thing God invents, –
That's somewhat. And you'll find the soul you have missed,
Within yourself, when you return Him thanks!   220
'Rub all out!' well, well, there's my life, in short,
And so the thing has gone on ever since.
I'm grown a man no doubt, I've broken bounds –
You should not take a fellow eight years old
And make him swear to never kiss the girls –
I'm my own master, paint now as I please –
Having a friend, you see, in the Corner-house!
Lord, it's fast holding by the rings in front –
Those great rings serve more purposes than just
To plant a flag in, or tie up a horse!   230
And yet the old schooling sticks, the old grave eyes
Are peeping o'er my shoulder as I work,
The heads shake still – 'It's Art's decline, my son!
You're not of the true painters, great and old:
Brother Angelico's the man, you'll find:[21]
Brother Lorenzo stands his single peer.[22]
Fag on at flesh, you'll never make the third!'
Flower o' the pine,
You keep your mistr...manners, and I'll stick to mine!
I'm not the third, then: bless us, they must know!   240
Don't you think they're the likeliest to know,
They, with their Latin? so, I swallow my rage,
Clench my teeth, suck my lips in tight, and paint
To please them – sometimes do and sometimes don't,
For, doing most, there's pretty sure to come
A turn – some warm eve finds me at my saints –
A laugh, a cry, the business of the world –
(*Flower o' the peach,*
Death for us all, and his own life for each!)
And my whole soul revolves, the cup runs o'er,[23]   250
The world and life's too big to pass for a dream,
And I do these wild things in sheer despite,
And play the fooleries you catch me at,
In pure rage! the old mill-horse, out at grass
After hard years, throws up his stiff heels so,
Although the miller does not preach to him
The only good of grass is to make chaff.
What would men have? Do they like grass or no –
May they or mayn't they? all I want's the thing
Settled for ever one way: as it is,   260
You tell too many lies and hurt yourself.
You don't like what you only like too much,

21   Fra Angelico (1387–1445) – very ethereal painter.
22   Lorenzo Monaco (d. *c.*1425): Fra Angelico's mentor.

23   Psalm 23.5.

You do like what, if given you at your word,
You find abundantly detestable.
For me, I think I speak as I was taught;
I always see the Garden and God there
A-making man's wife – and, my lesson learned,
The value and significance of flesh,
I can't unlearn ten minutes afterwards.

    You understand me: I'm a beast, I know.   270
But see, now – why, I see as certainly
As that the morning-star's about to shine,
What will hap some day. We've a youngster here
Comes to our convent, studies what I do,
Slouches and stares and lets no atom drop –
His name is Guidi[24] – he'll not mind the monks –
They call him Hulking Tom, he lets them talk –
He picks my practice up – he'll paint apace,
I hope so – though I never live so long,
I know what's sure to follow. You be judge!   280
You speak no Latin more than I, belike –
However, you're my man, you've seen the world
– The beauty and the wonder and the power,
The shapes of things, their colours, lights and shades,
Changes, surprises, – and God made it all!
– For what? do you feel thankful, ay or no,
For this fair town's face, yonder river's line,
The mountain round it and the sky above,
Much more the figures of man, woman, child,
These are the frame to? What's it all about?   290
To be passed o'er, despised? or dwelt upon,
Wondered at? oh, this last of course, you say.
But why not do as well as say, – paint these
Just as they are, careless what comes of it?
God's works – paint anyone, and count it crime
To let a truth slip. Don't object, 'His works
Are here already; nature is complete:
Suppose you reproduce her – (which you can't)
There's no advantage! you must beat her, then.'
For, don't you mark? we're made so that we love   300
First when we see them painted, things we have passed
Perhaps a hundred times nor cared to see;
And so they are better, painted – better to us,
Which is the same thing. Art was given for that –
God uses us to help each other so,
Lending our minds out. Have you noticed, now,
Your cullion's hanging face? A bit of chalk,
And trust me but you should, though! How much more,
If I drew higher things with the same truth!
That were to take the Prior's pulpit-place,   310
Interpret God to all of you! oh, oh,
It makes me mad to see what men shall do
And we in our graves! This world's no blot for us,
Nor blank – it means intensely, and means good:
To find its meaning is my meat and drink.
'Ay, but you don't so instigate to prayer'

24   Tomasso Guidi, Masaccio (1401–28?) – actually Lippi's master,
not pupil (mistake from footnotes in the Brownings' edition of Vasari).

Strikes in the Prior! 'when your meaning's plain
It does not say to folk – remember matins –
Or, mind you fast next Friday!' Why, for this
What need of art at all? A skull and bones,   320
Two bits of stick nailed cross-wise, or, what's best,
A bell to chime the hour with, does as well.
I painted a St Laurence six months since
At Prato,²⁵ splashed the fresco in fine style.
'How looks my painting, now the scaffold's down?'
I ask a brother: 'Hugely,' he returns –
'Already not one phiz²⁶ of your three slaves
Who turn the Deacon off his toasted side,
But's scratched and prodded to our heart's content,
The pious people have so eased their own   330
With coming to say prayers there in a rage.
We get on fast to see the bricks beneath.
Expect another job this time next year,
For pity and religion grow i' the crowd –
Your painting serves its purpose!' Hang the fools!

– That is – you'll not mistake an idle word
Spoke in a huff by a poor monk, Got wot,
Tasting the air this spicy night which turns
The unaccustomed head like Chianti wine!
Oh, the church knows! don't misreport me, now!   340
It's natural a poor monk out of bounds
Should have his apt word to excuse himself:
And hearken how I plot to make amends.
I have bethought me: I shall paint a piece
…There's for you! Give me six months, then go, see
Something in Sant' Ambrogio's!²⁷ (bless the nuns!
They want a cast of my office²⁸). I shall paint
God in the midst, Madonna and her babe,
Ringed by a bowery, flowery angel-brood,
Lilies and vestments and white faces, sweet   350
As puff on puff of grated orris-root
When ladies crowd to Church at midsummer.
And then in the front, of course a saint or two –
Saint John, because he saves the Florentines,²⁹
Saint Ambrose, who puts down in black and white
The convent's friends and gives them a long day,³⁰
And Job, I must have him there past mistake,
The man of Uz³¹ (and Us without the z,
Painters who need his patience). Well, all these
Secured at their devotions, up shall come   360
Out of a corner when you least expect,
As one by a dark stair into a great light
Music and talking, who but Lippo! I! –
Mazed, motionless and moon-struck – I'm the man!
Back I shrink – what is this I see and hear?

25 St Laurence, roasted to death 258. Lippi worked a lot at Prato,
near Florence; treated St Laurence at least twice; but this painting prob-
ably invented.
26 face (slangy).
27 St Ambrose, Florence convent, for which Lippi painted his *Coro-
nation of the Virgin* described here (now in Uffizi).
28 job sample.
29 patron saint of Florence.
30 confusion of St Ambrose and Cosimo's theologian friend
Ambrose.
31 biblical Job.

I, caught up with my monk's-things by mistake,
My old serge gown and rope that goes all round,
I, in this presence, this pure company!
Where's a hole, where's a corner for escape?
Then steps a sweet angelic slip of a thing[32]   370
Forward, puts out a soft palm – 'Not so fast!'
– Addresses the celestial presence, 'nay –
He made you and devised you, after all,
Though he's none of you! Could Saint John there, draw –
His camel-hair make up a painting-brush?[33]
We come to brother Lippo for all that,
Iste perfecit opus![34] So, all smile –
I shuffle sideways with my blushing face
Under the cover of a hundred wings
Thrown like a spread of kirtles when you're gay   380
And play hot cockles, all the doors being shut,
Till, wholly unexpected, in there pops
The hothead husband! Thus I scuttle off
To some safe bench behind, not letting go
The palm of her, the little lily thing
That spoke the good word for me in the nick,
Like the Prior's niece . . . Saint Lucy, I would say.[35]
And so all's saved for me, and for the church
A pretty picture gained. Go, six months hence!
Your hand, sir, and good bye: no lights, no lights!   390
The street's hushed, and I know my own way back –
Don't fear me! There's the grey beginning. Zooks!

Written, probably, Florence, first half of 1853. Men and Women *(1855), I.*

A Toccata of Galuppi's[1]

1

Oh Galuppi, Baldassaro, this is very sad to find!
I can hardly misconceive you; it would prove me deaf and blind;
But although I take your meaning, 'tis with such a heavy mind!

2

Here you come with your old music, and here's all the good it brings.
What, they lived once thus at Venice where the merchants were the kings,
Where Saint Mark's[2] is, where the Doges used to wed the sea with rings?

3

Ay, because the sea's the street there; and 'tis arched by . . . what you call
. . . Shylock's bridge with houses on it,[3] where they kept the carnival!
I was never out of England – it's as if I saw it all.

---

32   Santa Lucia, in the *Coronation* painting.
33   St John the Baptist dressed in camel-hair.
34   'This man arranged the work'. *Is perfect opus* – words attached to figure in the painting of its commissioner Maringhi – mistaken for Lippi.
35   Santa Lucia was a virgin. The Prior's 'niece', undoubtedly, wasn't.

A Toccata of Galuppi's
1   Baldassare Galuppi (1706–85), Venetian composer. Toccata: an exhibition piece for keyboards. B. owned Galuppi toccata-manuscripts.
2   Venice Cathedral.
3   the Rialto (as in *The Merchant of Venice*).

4

Did young people take their pleasure when the sea was warm in May?   10
Balls and masks begun at midnight, burning ever to mid-day,
When they made up fresh adventures for the morrow, do you say?

5

Was a lady such a lady, cheeks so round and lips so red, –
On her neck the small face buoyant, like a bell-flower on its bed,
O'er the breast's superb abundance where a man might base his head?

6

Well, (and it was graceful of them) they'd break talk off and afford
– She, to bite her mask's black velvet, he to finger on his sword,
While you sat and played Toccatas, stately at the clavichord?

7

What? Those lesser thirds so plaintive, sixths diminished, sigh on sigh,
Told them something? Those suspensions, those solutions[4] – 'Must we die?'   20
Those commiserating sevenths – 'Life might last! we can but try!'

8

'Were you happy?' – 'Yes.' – 'And are you still as happy?' – 'Yes – And you?'
– 'Then, more kisses' – 'Did *I* stop them, when a million seemed so few?'
Hark – the dominant's persistence, till it must be answered to!

9

So an octave struck the answer. Oh, they praised you, I dare say!
'Brave Galuppi! that was music! good alike at grave and gay!
I can always leave off talking when I hear a master play.'

10

Then they left you for their pleasure: till in due time, one by one,
Some with lives that came to nothing, some with deeds as well undone,
Death stepped tacitly[5] and took them where they never see the sun.   30

11

But when I sit down to reason, – think to take my stand nor swerve,
While I triumph o'er a secret wrung from nature's close reserve,
In you come with your cold music till I creep thro' every nerve.

12

Yes, you, like a ghostly cricket, creaking where a house was burned –
'Dust and ashes, dead and done with, Venice spent what Venice earned.
The soul, doubtless, is immortal – where a soul can be discerned.

13

'Yours for instance: you know physics, something of geology,
Mathematics are your pastime; souls shall rise in their degree;
Butterflies may dread extinction, – you'll not die, it cannot be!

14

'As for Venice and its people, merely born to bloom and drop,   40
Here on earth they bore their fruitage, mirth and folly were the crop.
What of soul was left, I wonder, when the kissing had to stop?

---

4 a resolution is a concord following a discord.   5 cf. *tacet* (Latin: 'it is silent'), indicating place in a score where an instrument doesn't play.

15

'Dust and ashes!' So you creak it, and I want[6] the heart to scold.
Dear dead women, with such hair, too – what's become of all the gold
Used to hang and brush their bosoms? I feel chilly and grown old.

Men and Women (1855), I.

'CHILDE ROLAND TO THE DARK TOWER CAME'

(See Edgar's song in 'Lear')[1]

1

My first thought was, he lied in every word,
    That hoary cripple, with malicious eye
    Askance to watch the working of his lie
On mine, and mouth scarce able to afford
Suppression of the glee that pursed and scored
    Its edge at one more victim gained thereby.

2

What else should he be set for, with his staff?
    What, save to waylay with his lies, ensnare
    All travellers who might find him posted there,
And ask the road? I guessed what skull-like laugh   10
Would break, what crutch 'gin write my epitaph
    For pastime in the dusty thoroughfare,

3

If at his counsel I should turn aside
    Into that ominous tract which, all agree,
    Hides the Dark Tower. Yet acquiescingly
I did turn as he pointed: neither pride
Nor hope rekindling at the end descried,
    So much as gladness that some end might be.

4

For, what with my whole world-wide wandering,
    What with my search drawn out thro' years, my hope   20
    Dwindled into a ghost not fit to cope
With that obstreperous joy success would bring, –
I hardly tried now to rebuke the spring
    My heart made, finding failure in its scope.

5

As when a sick man very near to death
    Seems dead indeed, and feels begin and end
    The tears and takes the farewell of each friend,
And hears one bid the other go, draw breath
Freelier outside, ('since all is o'er,' he saith,
    'And the blow fall'n no grieving can amend')   30

6

While some discuss if near the other graves
    Be room enough for this, and when a day

6   lack.

'CHILDE ROLAND TO THE DARK TOWER CAME'
    1   *King Lear*, III. iv. 187. Childe: a would-be knight.

Suits best for carrying the corpse away,
With care about the banners, scarves and staves, –
And still the man hears all, and only craves
    He may not shame such tender love and stay.

7

Thus, I had so long suffered in this quest,
    Heard failure prophesied so oft, been writ
    So many times among 'The Band' – to wit,
The knights who to the Dark Tower's search addressed   40
Their steps – that just to fail as they, seemed best,
    And all the doubt was now – should I be fit.

8

So, quiet as despair, I turned from him,
    That hateful cripple, out of his highway
    Into the path he pointed. All the day
Had been a dreary one at best, and dim
Was settling to its close, yet shot one grim
    Red leer to see the plain catch its estray.[2]

9

For mark! no sooner was I fairly found
    Pledged to the plain, after a pace or two,   50
    Than pausing to throw backward a last view
O'er the safe road, 'twas gone! grey plain all round!
Nothing but plain to the horizon's bound.
    I might go on; naught else remained to do.

10

So on I went. I think I never saw
    Such starved ignoble nature; nothing throve:
    For flowers – as well expect a cedar grove!
But cockle, spurge,[3] according to their law
Might propagate their kind, with none to awe,
    You'd think; a burr had been a treasure-trove.   60

11

No! penury, inertness and grimace,
    In some strange sort, were the land's portion. 'See
    Or shut your eyes' – said Nature peevishly –
'It nothing skills: I cannot help my case:
The Last Judgment's fire alone can cure this place,
    Calcine[4] its clods and set my prisoners free.'

12

If there pushed any ragged thistle-stalk
    Above its mates, the head was chopped – the bents[5]
    Were jealous else. What made those holes and rents
In the dock's harsh swarth leaves – bruised as to baulk   70
All hope of greenness? 'tis a brute must walk
    Pashing[6] their life out, with a brute's intents.

---

2 stray animal.
3 weeds.
4 burn to ash.

5 rough grass.
6 trampling.

13

As for the grass, it grew as scant as hair
    In leprosy – thin dry blades pricked the mud
    Which underneath looked kneaded up with blood.
One stiff blind horse, his every bone a-stare,
Stood stupefied, however he came there –
    Thrust out past service from the devil's stud!

14

Alive? he might be dead for aught I know,
    With that red gaunt and colloped[7] neck a-strain,   80
    And shut eyes underneath the rusty mane.
Seldom went such grotesqueness with such woe:
I never saw a brute I hated so –
    He must be wicked to deserve such pain.

15

I shut my eyes and turned them on my heart.
    As a man calls for wine before he fights,
    I asked one draught of earlier, happier sights,
Ere fitly I could hope to play my part.
Think first, fight afterwards – the soldier's art:
    One taste of the old time sets all to rights.   90

16

Not it! I fancied Cuthbert's reddening face
    Beneath its garniture of curly gold,
    Dear fellow, till I almost felt him fold
An arm in mine to fix me to the place,
That way he used. Alas! one night's disgrace!
    Out went my heart's new fire and left it cold.

17

Giles, then, the soul of honour – there he stands
    Frank as ten years ago when knighted first.
    What honest man should dare (he said) he durst.
Good – but the scene shifts – faugh! what hangman's hands   100
Pin to his breast a parchment? his own bands
    Read it. Poor traitor, spit upon and curst!

18

Better this present than a past like that –
    Back therefore to my darkening path again.
    No sound, no sight as far as eye could strain.
Will the night send a howlet[8] or a bat?
I asked: when something on the dismal flat
    Came to arrest my thoughts and change their train.

19

A sudden little river crossed my path
    As unexpected as a serpent comes.
    No sluggish tide congenial to the glooms –   110
This, as it frothed by, might have been a bath
For the fiend's glowing hoof – to see the wrath
    Of its black eddy bespate[9] with flakes and spumes.

7   meaty?   9   bespattered.
8   owl.

20

So petty yet so spiteful! All along,
    Low scrubby alders kneeled down over it;
    Drenched willows flung them headlong in a fit
Of mute despair, a suicidal throng:
The river which had done them all the wrong,
    Whate'er that was, rolled by, deterred no whit.   120

21

Which, while I forded, – good saints, how I feared
    To set my foot upon a dead man's cheek,
    Each step, or feel the spear I thrust to seek
For hollows, tangled in his hair or beard!
– It may have been a water-rat I speared,
    But, ugh! it sounded like a baby's shriek.

22

Glad was I when I reached the other bank.
    Now for a better country. Vain presage!
    Who were the strugglers, what war did they wage,
Whose savage trample thus could pad the dank   130
Soil to a plash¹⁰? toads in a poisoned tank,
    Or wild cats in a red-hot iron cage –

23

The fight must so have seemed in that fell cirque.
    What penned them there, with all the plain to choose?
    No foot-print leading to that horrid mews,¹¹
None out of it: mad brewage set to work
Their brains, no doubt, like galley-slaves the Turk
    Pits for his pastime, Christians against Jews.

24

And more than that – a furlong on – why, there!
    What bad use was that engine for, that wheel,   140
    Or brake,¹² not wheel – that harrow fit to reel
Men's bodies out like silk? with all the air
Of Tophet's tool,¹³ on earth left unaware,
    Or brought to sharpen its rusty teeth of steel.

25

Then came a bit of stubbed¹⁴ ground, once a wood,
    Next a marsh, it would seem, and now mere earth
    Desperate and done with; (so a fool finds mirth,
Makes a thing and then mars it, till his mood
Changes and off he goes!) within a rood –
    Bog, clay and rubble, sand and stark black dearth.   150

26

Now blotches rankling, coloured gay and grim,
    Now patches where some leanness of the soil's
    Broke into moss or substances like boils;
Then came some palsied oak, a cleft in him

10   puddle.
11   place of confinement.
12   heavy agricultural machine.

13   Tophet: biblical burning place (Hell).
14   stubby (? Browing's own adaptation – typical of much verbal idio-
syncrasy in this poem).

Like a distorted mouth that splits its rim
    Gaping at death, and dies while it recoils.

27

And just as far as ever from the end!
    Naught in the distance but the evening, nought
    To point my footstep further! At the thought,
A great black bird, Apollyon's bosom-friend,[15]
Sailed past, nor beat his wide wing dragon-penned[16]   160
    That brushed my cap – perchance the guide I sought.

28

For, looking up, aware I somehow grew,
    'Spite of the dusk, the plain had given place
    All round to mountains – with such name to grace
Mere ugly heights and heaps now stol'n in view.
How thus they had surprised me, – solve it, you!
    How to get from them was no plain case.

29

Yet half I seemed to recognize some trick
    Of mischief happened to me, God knows when –   170
    In a bad dream perhaps. Here ended, then,
Progress this way. When, in the very nick
Of giving up, one time more, came a click
    As when a trap shuts – you're inside the den!

30

Burningly it came on me all at once,
    This was the place! those two hills on the right,
    Crouched like two bulls locked horn in horn in fight –
While to the left, a tall scalped mountain . . . Dunce,
Fool, to be dozing at the very nonce,
    After a life spent training for the sight!   180

31

What in the midst lay but the Tower itself?
    The round squat turret, blind as the fool's heart,[17]
    Built of brown stone, without a counterpart
In the whole world. The tempest's mocking elf
Points to the shipman thus the unseen shelf
    He strikes on, only when the timbers start.[18]

32

Not see? because of night perhaps? – Why, day –
    Came back again for that! before it left,
    The dying sunset kindled through a cleft:
The hills, like giants at a hunting, lay –   190
    Chin upon hand, to see the game at bay, –
        'Now stab and end the creature – to the heft!'

15 Apollyon is the Devil in Bible's Apocalypse, and a demonic   17 'The fool hath said in his heart, There is no God', Psalm 14.1.
winged dragon-like creature in Bunyan's *The Pilgrim's Progress*.   18 split open.
16 penned: winged.

33

Not hear? when noise was everywhere! it tolled
   Increasing like a bell. Names in my ears,
   Of all the lost adventures my peers, –
How such a one was strong, and such was bold,
And such was fortunate, yet each of old
   Lost, lost! one moment knelled the woe of years.

34

There they stood, ranged along the hill-sides – met
   To view the last of me, a living frame   200
   For one more picture! in a sheet of flame
I saw them and I knew them all. And yet
Dauntless the slug-horn[19] to my lips I set,
   And blew. '*Childe Roland to the Dark Tower came.*'

Date of writing unknown – though B. claimed he finished it in one day. Men and Women
(1855), I. (A 'kind of dream'; 'only a fantasy'; 'no allegorical intention': B.)

MEMORABILIA

1

Ah, did you[1] once see Shelley plain,
   And did he stop and speak to you?
And did you speak to him again?
   How strange it seems, and new!

2

But you were living before that,
   And also you are living after,
And the memory I started at –
   My starting moves your laughter!

3

I crossed a moor[2] with a name of its own
   And a certain use in the world no doubt,   10
Yet a hand's-breadth of it shines alone
   'Mid the blank miles round about –

4

For there I picked up on the heather
   And there I put inside my breast
A moulted feather, an eagle-feather[3] –
   Well, I forget the rest.

Last poem in Men and Women *(1855), I.*

---

19   slogan. (B. misled by a Chatterton poem into thinking this a musical instrument – as blown by Roland at Ronces valles.)

MEMORABILIA

1   *you:* the man in Hodgson's bookshop, London, B. (startled, pale) overheard retailing a conversation with Shelley.

2   imaginary (B. said).

3   reference(?) to Shelley's *Ode to Liberty*, 5–8.

ANDREA DEL SARTO[1]

(Called 'The Faultless Painter')

But do not let us quarrel any more,
No, my Lucrezia; bear with me for once:
Sit down and all shall happen as you wish.
You turn your face, but does it bring your heart?
I'll work then for your friend's friend, never fear,
Treat his own subject after his own way,
Fix his own time, accept too his own price,
And shut the money into this small hand
When next it takes mine. Will it? tenderly?
Oh, I'll content him, – but tomorrow, Love!   10
I often am much wearier than you think,
This evening more than usual, and it seems
As if – forgive now – should you let me sit
Here by the window with your hand in mine
And look a half-hour forth on Fiesole,[2]
Both of one mind, as married people use,
Quietly, quietly the evening through,
I might get up to-morrow to my work
Cheerful and fresh as ever. Let us try.
To-morrow, how you shall be glad for this!   20
Your soft hand is a woman of itself,
And mine the man's bared breast she curls inside.
Don't count the time lost, either; you must serve
For each of the five pictures we require –
It saves a model. So! keep looking so –
My serpentining beauty, rounds on rounds!
– How could you ever prick those perfect ears,
Even to put the pearl there! oh, so sweet –
My face, my moon, my everybody's moon,
Which everybody looks on and calls his,   30
And, I suppose, is looked on by in turn,
While she looks – no one's: very dear, no less!
You smile? why, there's my picture ready made,
There's what we painters call our harmony!
A common greyness silvers everything,[3] –
All in a twilight, you and I alike
– You, at the point of your first pride in me
(That's gone you know), – but I, at every point;
My youth, my hope, my art, being all toned down
To yonder sober pleasant Fiesole.   40
There's the bell clinking from the chapel-top;
That length of convent-wall across the way
Holds the trees safer, huddled more inside;
The last monk leaves the garden; days decrease,
And autumn grows, autumn in everything.
Eh? the whole seems to fall into a shape
As if I saw alike my work and self
And all that I was born to be and do,

ANDREA DEL SARTO
1   Andrea the Tailor's Son. Written for John Kenyon, the Brownings'
patron – who wanted a copy of the Pitti Palace paired painting, sup-
posed to be of del Sarto and his wife Lucrezia, which Browning essen-

tially describes. Yet another poem sourced by Vasari's *Lives of the More
Excellent Painters*.
2   hill town near Florence.
3   more a case of the painting's ageing than any desired technique.

A twilight-piece. Love, we are in God's hand.
How strange now, looks the life he makes us lead!   50
So free we seem, so fettered fast we are:
I feel he laid the fetter: let it lie!
This chamber for example – turn your head –
All that's behind us! you don't understand
Nor care to understand about my art,
But you can hear at least when people speak;
And that cartoon, the second from the door
– It is the thing, Love! so such things should be –
Behold Madonna, I am bold to say.
I can do with my pencil what I know,   60
What I see, what at bottom of my heart
I wish for, if I ever wish so deep –
Do easily, too – when I say perfectly
I do not boast, perhaps: yourself are judge,
Who listened to the Legate's talk last week,
And just as much they used to say in France.
At any rate 'tis easy, all of it,
No sketches first, no studies, that's long past –
I do what many dream of all their lives
– Dream? strive to do, and agonise to do,   70
And fail in doing. I could count twenty such
On twice your fingers, and not leave this town,
Who strive – you don't know how the others strive
To paint a little thing like that you smeared
Carelessly passing with your robes afloat,
Yet do much less, so much less, some one[4] says,
(I know his name, no matter) so much less!
Well, less is more, Lucrezia! I am judged.
There burns a truer light of God in them,
In their vexed, beating stuffed and stopped-up brain,   80
Heart, or whate'er else, than goes on to prompt
This low-pulsed forthright craftsman's hand of mine.
Their works drop groundward, but themselves, I know,
Reach many a time a heaven that's shut to me,
Enter and take their place there sure enough,
Though they come back and cannot tell the world.
My works are nearer heaven, but I sit here.
The sudden blood of these men! at a word –
Praise them, it boils, or blame them, it boils too.
I, painting from myself and to myself,   90
Know what I do, am unmoved by men's blame
Or their praise either. Somebody remarks
Morello's[5] outline there is wrongly traced,
His hue mistaken; what of that? or else,
Rightly traced and well ordered; what of that?
Ah, but a man's reach should exceed his grasp,
Or what's a Heaven for? All is silver-grey
Placid and perfect with my art – the worse!
I know both what I want and what might gain –
And yet how profitless to know, to sigh   100
'Had I been two, another and myself,
Our head would have o'erlooked the world!' No doubt.
Yonder's a work now, of that famous youth

4   Michelangelo.   5   mountain to the north of Florence.

The Urbinate[6] who died five years ago.
('Tis copied, George Vasari sent it me.)
Well, I can fancy how he did it all,
Pouring his soul, with kings and popes to see,
Reaching, that Heaven might so replenish him,
Above and through his art – for it gives way;
That arm is wrongly put – and there again –   110
A fault to pardon in the drawing's lines,
Its body, so to speak! its soul is right,
He means right – that, a child may understand.
Still, what an arm! and I could alter it.
But all the play, the insight and the stretch –
Out of me! out of me! And wherefore out?
Had you enjoined them on me, given me soul,
We might have risen to Rafael, I and you.
Nay, Love, you did give all I asked, I think –
More than I merit, yes, by many times.   120
But had you – oh, with the same perfect brow,
And perfect eyes, and more than perfect mouth,
And the low voice my soul hears, as a bird
The fowler's pipe, and follows to the snare –
Had you, with these the same, but brought a mind!
Some women do so. Had the mouth there urged
'God and the glory! never care for gain.
The present by the future, what is that?
Live for fame, side by side with Angelo[7] –
Rafael is waiting: up to God, all three!'   130
I might have done it for you. So it seems –
Perhaps not. All is as God over-rules.
Beside, incentives come from the soul's self;
The rest avail not. Why do I need you?
What wife had Rafael, or has Angelo?
In this world, who can do a thing, will not –
And who would do it, cannot, I perceive:
Yet the will's somewhat – somewhat, too, the power –
And thus we half-men struggle. At the end,
God, I conclude, compensates, punishes.   140
'Tis safer for me, if the award be strict,
That I am something underrated here,
Poor this long while, despised, to speak the truth.
I dared not, do you know, leave home all day,
For fear of chancing on the Paris lords.
The best is when they pass and look aside;
But they speak sometimes; I must bear it all.
Well may they speak! That Francis, that first time,
And that long festal year at Fontainebleau![8]
I surely then could sometimes leave the ground,   150
Put on the glory,[9] Rafael's daily wear,
In that humane great monarch's golden look, –
One finger in his beard or twisted curl
Over his mouth's good mark that made the smile,
One arm about my shoulder, round my neck,

---

6 Raphael (1483–1520), from Urbino.   9 halo.
7 Michelangelo (Michel Agnolo Buonarroti).
8 del Sarto spent 1518–19 at Francis I's court of Fontainebleau, near
Paris.

The jingle of his gold chain in my ear,
You painting proudly with his breath on me,
All his court round him, seeing with his eyes,
Such frank French eyes, and such a fire of souls
Profuse, my hand kept plying by those hearts,–   160
And, best of all, this, this, this face beyond,
This in the back-ground, waiting on my work,
To crown the issue with a last reward!
A good time, was it not, my kingly days?
And had you not grown restless – but I know –
'Tis done and past; 'twas right, my instinct said;
Too live the life grew, golden and not grey –
And I'm the weak-eyed bat no sun should tempt
Out of the grange whose four walls make his world.
How could it end in any other way?   170
You called me, and I came home to your heart.
The triumph was to have ended there – then if
I reached it ere the triumph, what is lost?
Let my hands frame your face in your hair's gold,
You beautiful Lucrezia that are mine!
'Rafael did this, Andrea painted that;
The Roman's[10] is the better when you pray,
But still the other's Virgin was his wife –'
Men will excuse me. I am glad to judge
Both pictures in your presence; clearer grows   180
My better fortune, I resolve to think.
For, do you know, Lucrezia, as God lives,
Said one day Angelo, his very self,
To Rafael... I have known it all these years...
(When the young man was flaming out his thoughts
Upon a palace-wall for Rome to see,
Too lifted up in heart because of it)
'Friend, there's a certain sorry little scrub
Goes up and down our Florence, none cares how,
Who, were he set to plan and execute   190
As you are pricked on by your popes and kings,
Would bring the sweat into that brow of yours!'
To Rafael's! – And indeed the arm is wrong.
I hardly dare – yet, only you to see,
Give the chalk here – quick, thus the line should go!
Ay, but the soul! he's Rafael! rub it out!
Still, all I care for, if he spoke the truth,
(What he? why, who but Michel Angelo?
Do you forget already words like those?)
If really there was such a chance, so lost,   200
Is, whether you're – not grateful – but more pleased.
Well, let me think so. And you smile indeed!
This hour has been an hour! Another smile?
If you would sit thus by me every night
I should work better, do you comprehend?
I mean that I should earn more, give you more.
See, it is settled dusk now; there's a star;
Morello's gone, the watch-lights show the wall,
The cue-owls speak the name we call them by.[11]
Come from the window, Love, – come in, at last,   210

---

10   Raphael spent last 12 years of life at Rome.   11   *ciù* owls in Italian – the scops owl (B.'s own anglicization).

Inside the melancholy little house
We built to be so gay with. God is just.
King Francis may forgive me. Oft at nights
When I look up from painting, eyes tired out,
The walls become illumined, brick from brick
Distinct, instead of mortar fierce bright gold,
That gold of his I did cement them with!
Let us but love each other. Must you go?
That Cousin here again? he waits outside?
Must see you – you, and not with me? Those loans!   220
More gaming debts to pay? you smiled for that?
Well, let smiles buy me! have you more to spend?
While hand and eye and something of a heart
Are left me, work's my ware, and what's it worth?
I'll pay my fancy. Only let me sit
The grey remainder of the evening out,
Idle, you call it, and muse perfectly
How I could paint, were I but back in France,
One picture, just one more – the Virgin's face,
Not yours this time! I want you at my side   230
To hear them – that is, Michel Angelo –
Judge all I do and tell you of its worth.
Will you? To-morrow, satisfy your friend.
I take the subjects for his corridor,
Finish the portrait out of hand – there, there,
And throw him in another thing or two
If he demurs; the whole should prove enough
To pay for this same Cousin's freak. Beside,
What's better and what's all I care about,
Get you the thirteen scudi[12] for the ruff!   240
Love, does that please you? Ah, but what does he,
The Cousin! what does he to please you more?

    I am grown peaceful as old age to-night.
I regret little, I would change still less.
Since there my past life lies, why alter it?
The very wrong to Francis! it is true
I took his coin, was tempted and complied,
And built this house and sinned, and all is said.
My father and my mother died of want.
Well, had I riches of my own? you see   250
How one gets rich! Let each one bear his lot.
They were born poor, lived poor, and poor they died:
And I have laboured somewhat in my time
And not been paid profusely. Some good son
Paint my two hundred pictures – let him try!
No doubt, there's something strikes a balance. Yes,
You loved me quite enough, it seems to-night.
This must suffice me here. What would one have?
In heaven, perhaps, new chances, one more chance –
Four great walls in the New Jerusalem,   260
Meted on each side by the angel's reed,[13]
For Leonard,[14] Rafael, Angelo and me
To cover – the three first without a wife,

12   Roman coins.   14   Leonardo.
13   measured: Revelation 21. 10–21.

While I have mine! So – still they overcome
Because there's still Lucrezia, – as I choose.

Again the Cousin's whistle! Go, my Love.

Written, probably 1853. First poem in Men and Women *(1855), II.*

TWO IN THE CAMPAGNA

1

I wonder do you feel to-day
   As I have felt, since, hand in hand,
We sat down on the grass, to stray
   In spirit better through the land,
This morn of Rome and May?

2

For me, I touched a thought, I know,
   Has tantalised me many times,
(Like turns of thread the spiders throw
   Mocking across our path) for rhymes
To catch at and let go.   10

3

Help me to hold it: first it left
   The yellowing fennel, run to seed
There, branching from the brickwork's cleft,
   Some old tomb's ruin: yonder weed
Took up the floating weft,

4

Where one small orange cup amassed
   Five beetles, – blind and green they grope
Among the honey-meal, – and last
   Everywhere on the grassy slope
I traced it. Hold it fast!   20

5

The champaign¹ with its endless fleece
   Of feathery grasses everywhere!
Silence and passion, joy and peace,
   An everlasting wash of air –
Rome's ghost since her decease.

6

Such life there, through such lengths of hours,
   Such miracles performed in play,
Such primal naked forms of flowers,
   Such letting Nature have her way
While Heaven looks from its towers.   30

7

How say you? Let us, O my dove,
   Let us be unashamed of soul,
As earth lies bare to heaven above.²

TWO IN THE CAMPAGNA
1 campagna: open countryside.

2 cf. Danaë, seduced by Zeus in shower of gold: 'Now lies the Earth all Danaë to the stars' (Tennyson, *The Princess*, VII, 168).

How is it under our control
To love or not to love?

8

I would that you were all to me,
    You that are just so much, no more –
Nor yours, nor mine, – nor slave nor free!
    Where does the fault lie? what the core
Of the wound, since wound must be?   40

9

I would I could adopt your will,
    See with your eyes, and set my heart
Beating by yours, and drink my fill
    At your soul's springs, – your part my part
In life, for good and ill.

10

No. I yearn upward – touch you close,
    Then stand away. I kiss your cheek,
Catch your soul's warmth, – I pluck the rose
    And love it more than tongue can speak –
Then the good minute goes.   50

11

Already how am I so far
    Out of that minute? Must I go
Still like the thistle-ball, no bar,
    Onward, whenever light winds blow,
Fixed by no friendly star?

12

Just when I seemed about to learn!
    Where is the thread now? Off again!
The old trick! Only I discern –
    Infinite passion, and the pain
Of finite hearts that yearn.   60

Written, probably May 1854 (after 'some exquisite hours on the Campagna':
Elizabeth Barrett Browning). Men and Women *(1855), II.*

A GRAMMARIAN'S FUNERAL[1]

Time – Shortly after the Revival of Learning in Europe

Let us begin and carry up this corpse,
    Singing together.
Leave we the common crofts, the vulgar thorpes
    Each in its tether
Sleeping safe on the bosom of the plain,
    Cared-for till cock-crow:
Look out if yonder be not day again
    Rimming the rock-row!

A GRAMMARIAN'S FUNERAL
1   no certain model. One manuscript note labels the poem's last 12   lines 'In memoriam Johannis Conington' (great 19th-century Oxford Virgilian; Corpus Christi Professor of Latin).

That's the appropriate country – there, man's thought,
    Rarer, intenser,   10
Self-gathered for an outbreak, as it ought,
    Chafes in the censer.
Leave we the unlettered plain its herd and crop;
    Seek we sepulture
On a tall mountain, citied to the top,
    Crowded with culture!
All the peaks soar, but one the rest excels;
    Clouds overcome it;
No, yonder sparkle is the citadel's
    Circling its summit!   20
Thither our path lies – wind we up the heights –
    Wait ye the warning?
Our low life was the level's and the night's;
    He's for the morning!
Step to a tune, square chests, erect each head,
    'Ware the beholders!
This is our master, famous calm and dead,
    Borne on our shoulders.

Sleep, crop and herd! sleep, darkling thorpe and croft,
    Safe from the weather!   30
He, whom we convoy to his grave aloft,
    Singing together,
He was a man born with thy face and throat,
    Lyric Apollo!
Long he lived nameless: how should spring take note
    Winter would follow?
Till lo, the little touch, and youth was gone!
    Cramped and diminished,
Moaned he, 'New measures, other feet anon!
    My dance is finished?'   40
No, that's the world's way! (keep the mountain-side,
    Make for the city.)
He knew the signal, and stepped on with pride
    Over men's pity;
Left play for work, and grappled with the world
    Bent on escaping:
'What's in the scroll,' quoth he, 'thou keepest furled?
    Show me their shaping,
Theirs, who most studied man, the bard and sage, –
    Give!' – So, he gowned him,[2]   50
Straight got by heart that book to its last page:
    Learned, we found him!
Yea, but we found him bald too – eyes like lead,
    Accents uncertain:
'Time to taste life,' another would have said,
    'Up with the curtain!'
This man said rather, 'Actual life comes next?
    Patience a moment!
Grant I have mastered learning's crabbed text,
    Still there's the comment.[3]   60
Let me know all. Prate not of most or least,
    Painful or easy:
Even to the crumbs I'd fain eat up the feast,

2   put on academic robes.   3   the commentary on the text (still to do).

Ay, nor feel queasy!'
Oh, such a life as he resolved to live,
    When he had learned it,
When he had gathered all books had to give;
    Sooner, he spurned it!
Image the whole, then execute the parts –
    Fancy the fabric   70
Quite, ere you build, ere steel strike fire from quartz,
    Ere mortar dab brick!

(Here's the town-gate reached: there's the market-place
    Gaping before us.)
Yea, this in him was the peculiar grace
    (Hearten our chorus)
Still before living he'd learn how to live –
    No end to learning.
Earn the means first – God surely will contrive
    Use for our earning.   80
Others mistrust and say – 'But time escapes, –
    Live now or never!'
He said, 'What's Time? leave Now for dogs and apes!
    Man has For ever.'
Back to his book then: deeper drooped his head:
    Calculus[4] racked him:
Leaden before, his eyes grew dross of lead:
    Tussis[5] attacked him.
'Now, Master, take a little rest!' – not he!
    (Caution redoubled!   90
Step two a-breast, the way winds narrowly.)
    Not a whit troubled
Back to his studies, fresher than at first,
    Fierce as a dragon
He (soul-hydroptic[6] with a sacred thirst)
    Sucked at the flagon.
Oh, if we draw a circle premature,
    Heedless of far gain,
Greedy for quick returns of profit, sure
    Bad is our bargain!   100
Was it not great? did not he throw on God,
    (He loves the burthen[7]) –
God's task to make the heavenly period[8]
    Perfect the earthen?
Did not he magnify the mind, shew clear
    Just what it all meant?
He would not discount life, as fools do here,
    Paid by instalment!
He ventured neck or nothing – heaven's success
    Found, or earth's failure: 110
'Wilt thou trust death or not?' he answered 'Yes.
    'Hence with life's pale lure!'
That low man seeks a little thing to do,
    Sees it and does it:
This high man, with a great thing to pursue,
    Dies ere he knows it.

4 gallstones.
5 bronchial trouble.
6 thirsty in the soul.

7 chorus; repeated theme.
8 full stop, as well as period of time.

That low man goes on adding one to one,
   His hundred's soon hit:
This high man, aiming at a million,
   Misses an unit.[9]   120
That, has the world here – should he need the next,
   Let the world mind him!
This, throws himself on God, and unperplext
   Seeking shall find Him.
So, with the throttling hands of Death at strife,
   Ground he at grammar;
Still, through the rattle,[10] parts of speech were rife.
   While he could stammer
He settled *Hoti's* business – let it be! –
   Properly based *Oun* –   130
Gave us the doctrine of the enclitic *De*,[11]
   Dead from the waist down.
Well, here's the platform, here's the proper place:
   Hail to your purlieus
All ye highfliers of the feathered race,
   Swallows and curlews!
Here's the top-peak! the multitude below
   Live, for they can, there.
This man decided not to Live but Know –
   Bury this man there?   140
Here – here's his place, where meteors shoot, clouds form,
   Lightnings are loosened,
Stars come and go! let joy break with the storm –
   Peace let the dew send!
Lofty designs must close in like effects:
   Loftily lying,
Leave him – still loftier than the world suspects,
   Living and dying.

                                      Men and Women *(1855), II.*

CALIBAN UPON SETEBOS; OR, NATURAL THEOLOGY IN THE ISLAND[1]

       'Thou thoughtest that I was altogether such a one as thyself.'

['Will sprawl, now that the heat of day is best,
Flat on his belly in the pit's much mire,
With elbows wide, fists clenched to prop his chin.
And, while he kicks both feet in the cool slush,
And feels about his spine small eft-things[2] course,
Run in and out each arm, and make him laugh;
And while above his head a pompion-plant,[3]
Coating the cave-top as a brow its eye,
Creeps down to touch and tickle hair and beard,
And now a flower drops with a bee inside,   10

---

9 misses only by one.
10 death-rattle.
11 *Hoti* and *Oun*: Greek particles (*that* and *then*); enclitic *De*: Greek
suffix, *towards*: 'the biggest of the littlenesses' (B. to Tennyson).

CALIBAN UPON SETEBOS
1 Caliban, man-monster of Shakespeare's *The Tempest*; Setebos, god of
Caliban's witch-mother Sycorax.
2 newts and such.
3 pumpkin.

And now a fruit to snap at, catch and crunch:
He looks out o'er yon sea which sunbeams cross
And recross till they weave a spider-web,
(Meshes of fire, some great fish breaks at times)
And talks to his own self, howe'er he please,
Touching that other, whom his dam[4] called God.
Because to talk about Him, vexes – ha,
Could He but know! and time to vex is now,
When talk is safer than in winter-time.
Moreover Prosper and Miranda[5] sleep   20
In confidence he drudges at their task,
And it is good to cheat the pair, and gibe,
Letting the rank tongue blossom into speech.]

Setebos, Setebos, and Setebos!
'Thinketh, He dwelleth i' the cold o' the moon.

'Thinketh He made it, with the sun to match,
But not the stars; the stars came otherwise;
Only made clouds, winds, meteors, such as that:
Also this isle, what lives and grows thereon,
And snaky sea which rounds and ends the same.   30

'Thinketh, it came of being ill at ease:
He hated that He cannot change His cold,
Nor cure its ache. 'Hath spied an icy fish
That longed to 'scape the rock-stream where she lived,
And thaw herself within the lukewarm brine
O' the lazy sea her stream thrusts far amid,
A crystal spike 'twixt two warm walls of wave;
Only she ever sickened, found repulse
At the other kind of water, not her life,
(Green-dense and dim-delicious, bred o' the sun)   40
Flounced back from bliss she was not born to breathe,
And in her old bounds buried her despair,
Hating and loving warmth alike: so He.

'Thinketh, He made thereat the sun, this isle,
Trees and the fowls here, beast and creeping thing.
Yon otter, sleek-wet, black, lithe as a leech;
Yon auk, one fire-eye in a ball of foam,
That floats and feeds; a certain badger brown
He hath watched hunt with that slant white-wedge eye
By moonlight; and the pie with the long tongue   50
That pricks deep into oakwarts for a worm,
And says a plain word when she finds her prize,
But will not eat the ants; the ants themselves
That build a wall of seeds and settled stalks
About their hole – He made all these and more,
Made all we see, and us, in spite: how else?
He could not, Himself, make a second self
To be His mate; as well have made Himself.
He would not make what He mislikes or slights,
An eyesore to Him, or not worth His pains: 60
But did, in envy, listlessness or sport,

Make what Himself would fain, in a manner, be —
Weaker in most points, stronger in a few,
Worthy, and yet mere playthings all the while,
Things He admires and mocks too, — that is it.
Because, so brave, so better though they be,
It nothing skills if He begin to plague.
Look now, I melt a gourd-fruit into mash,
Add honeycomb and pods, I have perceived,
Which bite like finches when they bill and kiss, —   70
Then, when froth rises bladdery, drink up all,
Quick, quick, till maggots scamper through my brain;
Last, throw me on my back i' the seeded thyme,
And wanton, wishing I were born a bird.
Put case, unable to be what I wish,
I yet could make a live bird out of clay:
Would not I take clay, pinch my Caliban
Able to fly? — for, there, see, he hath wings,
And great comb like the hoopoe's to admire,
And there, a sting to do his foes offence,   80
There, and I will that he begin to live,
Fly to yon rock-top, nip me off the horns
Of grigs[6] high up that make the merry din,
Saucy through their veined wings, and mind me not.
In which feat, if his leg snapped, brittle clay,
And he lay stupid-like, — why, I should laugh;
And if he, spying me, should fall to weep,
Beseech me to be good, repair his wrong,
Bid his poor leg smart less or grow again, —
Well, as the chance were, this might take or else   90
Not take my fancy: I might hear his cry,
And give the manikin three legs for his one,
Or pluck the other off, leave him like an egg,
And lessoned he was mine and merely clay.
Were this no pleasure, lying in the thyme,
Drinking the mash, with brain become alive,
Making and marring clay at will? So He.

'Thinketh, such shows nor right nor wrong in Him,
Nor kind, nor cruel: He is strong and Lord.
'Am strong myself compared to yonder crabs   100
That march now from the mountain to the sea;
'Let twenty pass, and stone the twenty-first,
Loving not, hating not, just choosing so.
'Say, the first straggler that boasts purple spots
Shall join the file, one pincer twisted off;
'Say, this bruised fellow shall receive a worm,
And two worms he whose nippers end in red;
As it likes me each time, I do: so He.

Well then, 'supposeth He is good i' the main,
Placable if His mind and ways were guessed,   110
But rougher than His handiwork, be sure!
Oh, He hath made things worthier than Himself,
And envieth that, so helped, such things do more
Than He who made them! What consoles but this?

6 crickets.

That they, unless through Him, do naught at all,
And must submit: what other use in things?
'Hath cut a pipe of pithless elder-joint
That, blown through, gives exact the scream o' the jay
When from her wing you twitch the feathers blue:
Sound this, and little birds that hate the jay   120
Flock within stone's throw, glad their foe is hurt:
Put case such pipe could prattle and boast forsooth
'I catch the birds, I am the crafty thing,
I make the cry my maker cannot make
With his great round mouth; he must blow through mine!'
Would not I smash it with my foot? So He.

But wherefore rough, why cold and ill at ease?
Aha, that is a question! Ask, for that,
What knows, – the something over Setebos
That made Him, or He, may be, found and fought,   130
Worsted, drove off and did to nothing, perchance.
There may be something quiet o'er His head,
Out of His reach, that feels nor joy nor grief,
Since both derive from weakness in some way.
I joy because the quails come; would not joy
Could I bring quails here when I have a mind:
This Quiet, all it hath a mind to, doth.
'Esteemeth stars the outposts of its couch,
But never spends much thought nor care that way.
It may look up, work up, – the worse for those   140
It works on! 'Careth but for Setebos
The many-handed as a cuttle-fish,
Who, making Himself feared through what He does,
Looks up, first, and perceives He cannot soar
To what is quiet and hath happy life;
Next looks down here, and out of very spite
Makes this a bauble-world to ape yon real,
These good things to match those as hips do grapes.
'Tis solace making baubles, ay, and sport.
Himself peeped late, eyed Prosper at his books   150
Careless and lofty, lord now of the isle:
Vexed, 'stitched a book of broad leaves, arrow-shaped,
Wrote thereon, he knows what, prodigious words;
Has peeled a wand and called it by a name;
Weareth at whiles for an enchanter's robe
The eyed skin of a supple oncelot;[7]
And hath an ounce[8] sleeker than youngling mole,
A four-legged serpent he makes cower and couch,
Now snarl, now hold its breath and mind his eye,
And saith she is Miranda and my wife: 160
'Keeps for his Ariel[9] a tall pouch-bill crane
He bids go wade for fish and straight disgorge;
Also a sea-beast, lumpish, which he snared,
Blinded the eyes of, and brought somewhat tame,
And split its toe-webs, and now pens the drudge
In a hole o' the rock and calls him Caliban;
A bitter heart that bides its time and bites.

7   jaguar? ocelot?   9   Prospero's flyer-servant in Shakespeare's play.
8   cheetah? lynx?

'Plays thus at being Prosper in a way,
Taketh his mirth with make-believes: so He.

His dam held that the Quiet made all things   170
Which Setebos vexed only: 'holds not so.
Who made them weak, meant weakness He might vex.
Had He meant other, while His hand was in,
Why not make horny eyes no thorn could prick,
Or plate my scalp with bone against the snow,
Or overscale my flesh 'neath joint and joint,
Like an orc's armour? Ay, – so spoil His sport!
He is the One now: only He doth all.

'Saith, He may like, perchance, what profits Him.
Ay, himself loves what does him good; but why?   180
'Gets good no otherwise. This blinded beast
Loves whoso places flesh-meat on his nose,
But, had he eyes, would want no help, but hate
Or love, just as it liked him: He hath eyes.
Also it pleaseth Setebos to work,
Use all His hands, and exercise much craft,
By no means for the love of what is worked.
'Tasteth, himself, no finer good i' the world
When all goes right, in this safe summer time,
And he wants little, hungers, aches not much,   190
Than trying what to do with wit and strength.
'Falls to make something: 'piled yon pile of turfs,
And squared and stuck there squares of soft white chalk,
And, with a fish-tooth, scratched a moon on each,
And set up endwise certain spikes of tree,
And crowned the whole with a sloth's skull a-top,
Found dead i' the woods, too hard for one to kill.
No use at all i' the work, for work's sole sake;
'Shall some day knock it down again: so He.

'Saith He is terrible: watch His feats in proof!   200
One hurricane will spoil six good months' hope.
He hath a spite against me, that I know,
Just as He favours Prosper, who knows why?
So it is, all the same, as well I find.
'Wove wattles half the winter, fenced them firm
With stone and stake to stop she-tortoises
Crawling to lay their eggs here: well, one wave,
Feeling the foot of Him upon its neck,
Gaped as a snake does, lolled out its large tongue,
And licked the whole labour flat: so much for spite.   210
'Saw a ball flame down late (yonder it lies)
Where, half an hour before, I slept i' the shade:
Often they scatter sparkles: there is force!
'Dug up a newt He may have envied once
And turned to stone, shut up inside a stone.
Please Him and hinder this? – What Prosper does?
Aha, if He would tell me how! Not He!
There is the sport: discover how or die!
All need not die, for of the things o' the isle
Some flee afar, some dive, some run up trees;   220
Those at His mercy, – why, they please Him most
When . . when . . well, never try the same way twice!

Repeat what act has pleased, He may grow wroth.
You must not know His ways, and play Him off,
Sure of the issue. 'Doth the like himself:
'Spareth a squirrel that it nothing fears
But steals the nut from underneath my thumb,
And when I threat, bites stoutly in defence:
'Spareth an urchin[10] that, contrariwise,
Curls up into a ball, pretending death   230
For fright at my approach: the two ways please.
But what would move my choler more than this,
That either creature counted on its life
To-morrow and next day and all days to come,
Saying forsooth in the inmost of its heart,
'Because he did so yesterday with me,
And otherwise with such another brute,
So must he do henceforth and always.' – Ay?
'Would teach the reasoning couple what 'must' means!
'Doth as he likes, or wherefore Lord? So He.   240

'Conceiveth all things will continue thus,
And we shall have to live in fear of Him
So long as He lives, keeps His strength: no change,
If He have done His best, make no new world
To please Him more, so leave off watching this, –
If He surprise not even the Quiet's self
Some strange day, – or, suppose, grow into it
As grubs grow butterflies: else, here are we,
And there is He, and nowhere help at all.

'Believeth with the life, the pain shall stop.   250
His dam held different, that after death
He both plagued enemies and feasted friends:
Idly! He doth His worst in this our life,
Giving just respite lest we die through pain,
Saving last pain for worst, – with which, an end.
Meanwhile, the best way to escape His ire
Is, not to seem too happy. Sees, himself,
Yonder two flies, with purple films[11] and pink,
Bask on the pompion-bell above: kills both.
'Sees two black painful beetles roll their ball   260
On head and tail as if to save their lives:
Moves them the stick away they strive to clear.

Even so, 'would have Him misconceive, suppose
This Caliban strives hard and ails no less,
And always, above all else, envies Him.
Wherefore he mainly dances on dark nights,
Moans in the sun, gets under holes to laugh,
And never speaks his mind save housed as now:
Outside, 'groans, curses. If He caught me here,
O'erheard this speech, and asked 'What chucklest at?'   270
'Would, to appease Him, cut a finger off,
Or of my three kid yearlings burn the best,
Or let the toothsome apples rot on tree,
Or push my tame beast for the orc to taste:
While myself lit a fire, and made a song

10   hedgehog.   11   wings.

And sung it, '*What I hate, be consecrate*
To celebrate Thee and Thy state, no mate
For Thee; what see for envy in poor me?'
Hoping the while, since evils sometimes mend,
Warts rub away and sores are cured with slime,   280
That some strange day, will either the Quiet catch
And conquer Setebos, or likelier He
Decrepit may doze, doze, as good as die.

[What, what? A curtain o'er the world at once!
Crickets stop hissing; not a bird – or, yes,
There scuds His raven that has told Him all!
It was fool's play, this prattling! Ha! The wind
Shoulders the pillared dust, death's house o' the move,
And fast invading fires begin! White blaze –
A tree's head snaps – and there, there, there, there, there,   290
His thunder follows! Fool to gibe at Him!
Lo! 'Lieth flat and loveth Setebos!
'Maketh his teeth meet through his upper lip,
Will let those quails fly, will not eat this month
One little mess of whelks, so he may 'scape!]

Dramatis Personae *(Chapman & Hall, 28 May 1864).*

PISGAH-SIGHTS. I[1]

1

Over the ball of it,
    Peering and prying,
How I see all of it,
    Life there, outlying!
Roughness and smoothness,
    Shine and defilement,
Grace and uncouthness:
    One reconcilement.

2

Orbed as appointed,
    Sister with brother   10
Joins, ne'er disjointed
    One from the other.
All's lend-and-borrow;
    Good, see, wants evil,
Joy demands sorrow,
    Angel weds devil!

3

'Which things must – *why* be?'
    Vain our endeavour!
So shall things aye be
    As they were ever.   20

PISGAH-SIGHTS. I
1 old Moses viewed the Promised Land Jehovah prevented him
entering, from up Mount Pisgah: Deuteronomy 24.

'Such things should *so* be!'
　　Sage our desistence!
Rough-smooth let globe be,
　　Mixed – man's existence!

　　　　　4

Man – wise and foolish,
　　Lover and scorner,
Docile and mulish –
　　Keep each his corner!
Honey yet gall of it!
　　There's the life lying,　　　　　　　　　　　　　　　30
And I see all of it,
　　Only, I'm dying!

Pacchiarotto and How He Worked in Distemper: With Other
Poems *(Smith, Elder, 18 July 1876). MS dated 28 December 1875.*

PISGAH-SIGHTS. II

　　　　　1

Could I but live again,
　　Twice my life over,
Would I once strive again?
　　Would not I cover
Quietly all of it –
　　Greed and ambition –
So, from the pall of it,
　　Pass to fruition?

　　　　　2

'Soft!' I'd say, 'Soul mine!
　　Three-score and ten years,　　　　　　　　　　　　10
Let the blind mole mine
　　Digging out deniers!
Let the dazed hawk soar,
　　Claim the sun's rights too!
Turf 'tis thy walk's o'er,
　　Foliage thy flight's to.'

　　　　　3

Only a learner,
　　Quick one or slow one,
Just a discerner,
　　I would teach no one.　　　　　　　　　　　　　　20
I am earth's native:
　　No rearranging it!
I be creative,
　　Chopping and changing it?

　　　　　4

March, men, my fellows!
　　Those who, above me,
(Distance so mellows)
　　Fancy you love me:
Those who, below me,

(Distance makes great so)   30
Free to forego me,
    Fancy you hate so!

5

Praising, reviling,
    Worst head and best head,
Past me defiling,
    Never arrested,
Wanters, abounders,
    March, in gay mixture,
Men, my surrounders!
    I am the fixture.   40

6

So shall I fear thee,
    Mightiness yonder!
Mock-sun – more near thee,
    What is to wonder?
So shall I love thee,
    Down in the dark, – lest
Glowworm I prove thee,
    Star that now sparklest!

Pacchiarotto and How He Worked in Distemper (1876).
MS dated 19 February 1876.

NEVER THE TIME AND THE PLACE

Never the time and the place
    And the loved one all together!
This path – how soft to pace!
    This May – what magic weather!
Where is the loved one's face?
In a dream that loved one's face meets mine,
    But the house is narrow, the place is bleak
Where, outside, rain and wind combine
    With a furtive ear, if I strive to speak,
    With a hostile eye at my flushing cheek,   10
With a malice that marks each word, each sign!
O enemy sly and serpentine,
    Uncoil thee from the waking man!
        Do I hold the Past
        Thus firm and fast
Yet doubt if the Future hold I can?
This path so soft to pace shall lead
Thro' the magic of May to herself indeed!
Or narrow if needs the house must be,
Outside are the storms and strangers: we –   20
Oh, close, safe, warm sleep I and she,
    – I and she!

Jocoseria (Smith, Elder, 9 March 1883).

[RHYME FOR A CHILD VIEWING A NAKED VENUS IN A PAINTING OF 'THE JUDGEMENT OF PARIS']

He gazed and gazed and gazed and gazed,
Amazed, amazed, amazed, amazed.

*First published in Lady Laura Troubridge, Memories and Reflections
(Heinemann, 1925), 45. (1872, or thereabouts, 12-year-old Laura meets Browning at
Grosvenor Gallery in front of painting of 'entirely undraped' Venus:
'Well, let us make a funny rhyme about it, shall we?')*

Edward Lear (1812–88)

Edward Lear, painter and 'nonsense' writer, was a Londoner, born in Holloway into a large and poor family, 12 May 1812. He did odd-jobs of illustration work for shops, hospitals and doctors, before being taken on in 1831, aged nineteen, at the new London Zoo, where he drew birds. *The Family of the Psittacidae* (1832) was the result. Other similar work followed and his reputation as a highly talented bird and animal portraitist led to work (1832–6) for the Earl of Derby at Knowsley on the plates for *The Knowsley Menagerie*. At Knowsley he found out his great talent for amusing children with comic rhymes and sketches, and his *Book of Nonsense* (1846) was the result. It ran into at least twenty-six editions by the end of the century. In 1836 Lear left England to start the extraordinary existence he kept up for most of his life as a perpetual exile and nomad – trudging across Europe, the Middle East, the Balkans, India, Ceylon; inspired by a restless Pre-Raphaelite zeal for the real in exotic landscape; combining, as he put it, 'liberty, hard living and filth' (getting pelted with stones and screamed at as *Shaitan* (Satan) in Albania, being beaten and robbed by marauding Arabs, were all normal hazards). He had epileptic fits, was homosexual, and suffered from a large bulbous body and nose. Queen Victoria evidently enjoyed the twelve drawing lessons he gave her in 1846 ('teaches remarkably well', she wrote). His linguistic delight is everywhere evident in the chain of books that followed his first *Nonsense* volume. The key to his limericks' power is their arresting adjectival allegations – *umbrageous* old person of Spain, *illusive* old person of Woking, *abruptious* old man of Thames Ditton. Adjectives register the idiosyncratic descriptive power which makes his travel books, such as his various *Journals*

of a landscape painter, so arresting ('I read and felt that I was there', wrote Tennyson, a friend, of *Journals of a Landscape Painter in Albania and Illyria* (1851), in 'To E.L., on his Travels in Greece'. This idiosyncrasy of eye and words spills over onto the notes Lear made to himself on his landscape sketches (with their *rox* and *ski* and *4-ground*). The Turkish Bey who asked for repeats of Lear's performative description of a steam train – 'Tik-tok, tik-tok, tik-tok, tokka, tokka, tokka, tokka'; 'Squish-squash, squish-squash, thump-bump' – was catching the force of Lear's verbal infectiousness, which has never been limited to children. This 'nonsense' – onomatopoeia merging vertiginously into a disconcerting demonstration of the arbitrariness of names and signs – takes us close to the source of poetry's – and language's – incantatory magic. In the last years of his life Lear's base was in San Remo, where he died in January 1888. In 1889 an edition of three Tennyson poems, 'To E.L., on his Travels in Greece', 'The Daisy' and 'The Palace of Art', was published with Lear's illustrations, Tennyson breaking his usual practice and signing 100 copies out of affection for his old friend's memory. Lear's loneliness as a gay man in exile (unalleviated except in later years by his faithful man-servant Kokali, his grotesque physique (that nose...) and the devotion of generations of young readers for one of Britain's wittiest and most attractive of children's writers, are all deftly summed up in Auden's great elegiac sonnet, 'Edward Lear' (January 1939): '...he wept to himself in the night,/A dirty landscape-painter who hated his nose'; 'Words pushed him to the piano to sing comic songs;/And children swarmed to him like settlers. He became a land.'

There was an Old Person of Spain, who hated all trouble and pain;
So he sat on a chair, with his feet in the air,
That umbrageous Old Person of Spain.

*A Book of Nonsense (first version, 1846). Text of Fifth Edition, with Many New Pictures
and Verses (Routledge, Warne, & Routledge, 1862).*

There was an old person of Wick,
Who said, 'Tick-a-Tick, Tick-a-Tick;
Chickabee, Chickabaw.' And he said nothing more,
That laconic old person of Wick.

More Nonsense, Pictures, Rhymes, Botany, Etc. *(Robert John Bush, 1872)*.

There was an old man at a Station,
Who made a promiscuous oration;
But they said, 'Take some snuff! – You have talk'd quite enough
You afflicting old man at a Station!'

More Nonsense *(1872)*.

There was an old person of Woking,
Whose mind was perverse and provoking;
He sate on a rail, with his head in a pail,
That illusive old person of Woking.

More Nonsense *(1872)*.

There was an old person of Stroud,
Who was horribly jammed in a crowd;
Some she slew with a kick, some she scrunched with a stick,
That impulsive old person of Stroud.

More Nonsense *(1872)*.

There was an old man of Thames Ditton,
Who called out for something to sit on;
But they brought him a hat, and said – 'Sit upon that,
You abruptious old man of Thames Ditton!'

More Nonsense *(1872)*.

THE DONG WITH A LUMINOUS NOSE

When awful darkness and silence reign
  Over the great Gromboolian plain,
  Through the long, long wintry nights; –
When the angry breakers roar
As they beat on the rocky shore; –
  When Storm-clouds brood on the towering heights
Of the Hills of the Chankly Bore: –
Then, through the vast and gloomy dark,
There moves what seems a fiery spark,
  A lonely spark with silvery rays   10
  Piercing the coal-black night, –
  A Meteor strange and bright: –
Hither and thither the vision strays,
  A single lurid light.

Slowly it wanders, – pauses, – creeps, –
Anon it sparkles, – flashes and leaps;
And ever as onward it gleaming goes
A light on the Bong-tree stems it throws.
And those who watch at that midnight hour
From Hall or Terrace, or lofty Tower,   20

Cry, as the wild light passes along, –
  'The Dong! – the Dong!
 'The wandering Dong through the forest goes!
  'The Dong! the Dong!
 'The Dong with a luminous Nose!'

  Long years ago
  The Dong was happy and gay,
Till he fell in love with a Jumbly Girl
 Who came to those shores one day.
For the Jumblies came in a sieve, they did, –   30
Landing at eve near the Zemmery Fidd
  Where the Oblong Oysters grow,
 And the rocks are smooth and gray.
And all the woods and the valleys rang
With the Chorus they daily and nightly sang, –
  'Far and few, far and few,
  Are the lands where the Jumblies live;
  Their heads are green, and their hands are blue,
  And they went to sea in a sieve.'

Happily, happily passed those days!   40
 While the cheerful Jumblies staid;
 They danced in circlets all night long,
 To the plaintive pipe of the lively Dong,
  In moonlight, shine, or shade.
For day and night he was always there
By the side of the Jumbly Girl so fair,
With her sky-blue hands, and her sea-green hair.
Till the morning came of that hateful day
When the Jumblies sailed in their sieve away,
And the Dong was left on the cruel shore   50
Gazing – gazing for evermore, –
Ever keeping his weary eyes on
That pea-green sail on the far horizon, –
Singing the Jumbly Chorus still
As he sate all day on the grassy hill, –
  'Far and few, far and few,
  Are the lands where the Jumblies live;
  Their heads are green, and their hands are blue,
  And they went to sea in a sieve.'

But when the sun was low in the West,   60
 The Dong arose and said, –
 'What little sense I once possessed
 'Has quite gone out of my head!' –
And since that day he wanders still
By lake and forest, marsh and hill,
Singing – 'O somewhere, in valley or plain
'Might I find my Jumbly Girl again!
'For ever I'll seek by lake and shore
'Till I find my Jumbly Girl once more!'

 Playing a pipe with silvery squeaks,   70
 Since then his Jumbly Girl he seeks,
 And because by night he could not see,
 He gathered the bark of the Twangum Tree
  On the flowery plain that grows.

And he wove him a wondrous Nose, –
A Nose as strange as a Nose could be!
Of vast proportions and painted red,
And tied with cords to the back of his head.
    – In a hollow rounded space it ended
With a luminous lamp within suspended   80
        All fenced about
        With a bandage stout
        To prevent the wind from blowing it out; –
And with holes all round to send the light,
In gleaming rays on the dismal night.

And now each night, and all night long,
Over those plains still roams the Dong;
And above the wail of the Chimp and Snipe
You may hear the squeak of his plaintive pipe
While ever he seeks, but seeks in vain   90
To meet with his Jumbly Girl again;
Lonely and wild – all night he goes, –
The Dong with a luminous Nose!
And all who watch at the midnight hour,
From Hall or Terrace, or lofty Tower,
Cry, as they trace the Meteor bright,
Moving along through the dreary night, –
        'This is the hour when forth he goes,
        'The Dong with a luminous Nose!
        'Yonder – over the plain he goes;   100
          'He goes!
          'He goes;
        'The Dong with a luminous Nose!'

Laughable Lyrics: A Fourth Book of Nonsense Poems, Songs,
Botany, Music, Etc. *(Robert John Bush, [1877] 1876)*.

'How pleasant to know Mr. Lear!
    Who has written such volumes of stuff!
Some think him ill-tempered and queer,
    But a few think him pleasant enough.

His mind is concrete and fastidious,
    His nose is remarkably big;
His visage is more or less hideous,
    His beard it resembles a wig.

He has ears, and two eyes, and ten fingers,
    Leastways if you reckon two thumbs;   10
Long ago he was one of the singers,
    But now he is one of the dumbs.

He sits in a beautiful parlour,
    With hundreds of books on the wall;
He drinks a great deal of Marsala,
    But never gets tipsy at all.

He has many friends, laymen and clerical,
    Old Foss is the name of his cat:
His body is perfectly spherical,
    He weareth a runcible hat.   20

When he walks in a waterproof white,
   The children run after him so!
Calling out, 'He's come out in his night-
   gown, that crazy old Englishman, oh!'

He weeps by the side of the ocean,
   He weeps on the top of the hill;
He purchases pancakes and lotion,
   And chocolate shrimps from the mill.

He reads but he cannot speak Spanish,
   He cannot abide ginger-beer: 30
Ere the days of his pilgrimage vanish,
   How pleasant to know Mr. Lear!

From the Preface, 'By Way of Preface', Nonsense Songs and Stories *[6th edn] (1888).*

THE JUMBLIES

I

They went to sea in a Sieve, they did,
   In a Sieve they went to sea:
In spite of all their friends could say,
On a winter's morn, on a stormy day,
   In a Sieve they went to sea!
And when the Sieve turned round and round,
And every one cried, 'You'll all be drowned!'
They called aloud, 'Our Sieve ain't big,
   But we don't care a button! we don't care a fig!
     In a Sieve we'll go to sea!'   10
     Far and few, far and few,
       Are the lands where the Jumblies live;
       Their heads are green, and their hands are blue,
       And they went to sea in a Sieve.

II

They sailed away in a Sieve, they did,
   In a Sieve they sailed so fast,
With only a beautiful pea-green veil
Tied with a riband by way of a sail,
   To a small tobacco-pipe mast;
And every one said, who saw them go,   20
'O won't they be soon upset, you know!
   For the sky is dark, and the voyage is long,
And happen what may, it's extremely wrong
   In a Sieve to sail so fast!'
     Far and few, far and few,
       Are the lands where the Jumblies live;
       Their heads are green, and their hands are blue,
       And they went to sea in a Sieve.

III

The water it soon came in, it did,
   The water it soon came in;   30
So to keep them dry, they wrapped their feet
In a pinky paper all folded neat,
   And they fastened it down with a pin.

And they passed the night in a crockery-jar,
And each of them said, 'How wise we are!
  Though the sky be dark, and the voyage be long,
  Yet we never can think we were rash or wrong,
    While round in our Sieve we spin!'
  Far and few, far and few,
    Are the lands where the Jumblies live;   40
  Their heads are green, and their hands are blue,
    And they went to sea in a Sieve.

IV

And all night long they sailed away;
  And when the sun went down,
They whistled and warbled a moony song
To the echoing sound of a coppery gong,
  In the shade of the mountains brown.
'O Timballo! How happy we are,
When we live in a sieve and a crockery-jar.
And all night long in the moonlight pale,   50
We sail away with a pea-green sail,
  In the shade of the mountains brown!'
  Far and few, far and few,
    Are the lands where the Jumblies live;
  Their heads are green, and their hands are blue,
    And they went to sea in a Sieve.

V

They sailed to the Western Sea, they did,
  To a land all covered with trees,
And they bought an Owl, and a useful Cart,
And a pound of Rice, and a Cranberry Tart,   60
  And a hive of silvery Bees.
And they bought a Pig, and some green Jack-daws,
And a lovely Monkey with lollipop paws,
And forty bottles of Ring-Bo-Ree,
  And no end of Stilton Cheese.
  Far and few, far and few,
    Are the lands where the Jumblies live;
  Their heads are green, and their hands are blue,
    And they went to sea in a Sieve.

VI

And in twenty years they all came back,   70
  In twenty years or more,
And every one said, 'How tall they've grown!
  For they've been to the Lakes, and the Terrible Zone,
    And the hills of the Chankly Bore;'
And they drank their health, and gave them a feast
Of dumplings made of beautiful yeast;
And every one said, 'If we only live,
'We too will go to sea in a Sieve, –
  'To the hills of the Chankly Bore!'
  Far and few, far and few,   80
    Are the lands where the Jumblies live;
  Their heads are green, and their hands are blue,
    And they went to sea in a Sieve.

Nonsense Songs and Stories *[6th edn] (1888)*.

James R. (Reynolds) Withers (1812–92)

James Reynolds Withers was born, 24 May 1812, in the Cambridgeshire village of Weston Colville, near Newmarket, to aged and very poor parents (he had three older sisters). His father was a failed shoemaker. There was no money to send him to school, and his bare induction into the rudiments of reading and writing came from his mother. As a mere lad he was put to little boys' labour in the fields – picking stones, weeding corn, scaring birds, keeping watch over sheep. The interest in rural things evinced in his many sub-Wordsworthian verses thus began early. His awareness of poetry started, he said, by his reading a book of ballads and a copy of Isaac Watts's *Divine and Moral Songs for Children* (1720) out in the fields. Many of these verses he committed to memory. At the age of twelve he was apprenticed to a market-gardener at nearby Fordham; at fifteen he was a fully-fledged seven shillings a week gardener: a peasant, in fact. When he was nineteen he went as an under-porter at Magdalene College, Cambridge, but the pull of the countryside was too strong and he returned to gardening, despite that trade's regular lay-offs in bad winter weather. 'I could study nature in the day and books in the evening, and write my jingling verses without interruption.' In his mid-twenties Withers learned shoemaking, got married, and subsisted with difficulty on a mixture of shoemaking, casual agricultural labour and helping with the harvest. He and his wife had four children, two boys and two girls, one of whom died young, and is the subject of his touching poem 'On the Death of My Child'. (The surviving daughter belonged, in his words, to 'the "stitch, stitch, stitch" sisterhood' of poor women home-workers.) In the terrible winter of 1847 the family, deeply impoverished, had to go into the workhouse. For all this, Withers kept on writing. His talents were spotted by a Mrs R. D. Fyson, wife of a landowner whose harvests Withers helped garner in, and she helped him get published. His first volume, *Poems Upon Various Subjects*, appeared in 1854, a second volume of the same title in 1856, and a 'third edition' in 1864. *Rustic Songs and Wayside Musings* ran to four editions in 1867; and there was a further volume of *Poems* (1869). Dinah Mulock Craik wrote a fine, publicizing piece, 'A Hedge-Side Poet', in *Macmillan's Magazine* (April 1860), marvelling at the resilience, fine feeling and occasional poetic fire of this 'uneducated Hodge'. Would nobody with money raise 'into a position more suitable for him our hedge-side poet, James Reynolds Withers?' Nobody did. He died in January 1892, of that class of poets, in Mrs Craik's words, 'whom the muse finds at the plough, the loom, the forge, the tailor's board, or the cobbler's stall, – and leaves them there'. A memorial window was placed in Fordham Church, and in April 1898 a three-metre high Celtic Cross was set up in Withers's memory in Fordham church-yard.

ON THE DEATH OF MY CHILD

My child, thou art gone, thou art taken away;
    Thou now art consign'd to the cold silent tomb:
And shall I regret that so short was thy stay,
    When thou art remov'd from the evil to come?

I did hope that my troubles, my sorrows, and cares,
    Thou would'st soothe by thy fondness and gently assuage,
And have been to me all I could ask in my prayers,
    To cheer and support in the weakness of age.

How fondly I've look'd on those features delighted,
    When in childish simplicity sweetly she smiled;
But this flower, alas! by stern death was soon blighted,
    And green grass waves over the grave of my child.

I have stood by the bedside of friends when afflicted;
    I have seen a fond mother sink silent in death;
But could not, Oh! could not, feel half so affected,
    As when this belov'd one resign'd her last breath.

10

But she's gone from this world, where I'm still left to err,
    From its pains and false pleasures for ever she's free:
And this is my hope, I shall go unto her,
    For I know that she cannot return unto me.   20

'Thy will be done,'[1] Lord, I still wish to say,
    Though a task very hard for frail flesh and blood:
'Tis Thou that hast given and taken away,
    And blessed for ever be the name of the Lord.[2]

Poems Upon Various Subjects *(C. W. Naylor, Cambridge; Wertheim & Macintosh,*
London, 1854).

WHEN I WAS A BOY

When I was a boy, oh! when I was a boy,
And play'd with my hoop, or my top, or my toy,
In sunshine or pleasure my time pass'd away;
I lay down to sleep, and I wak'd up to play:
I knew not the care that on manhood attends,
But thought the whole world must be made up of friends;
And Hope spread her pictures my fancy to charm:
How bright were the prospects, the colours how warm.
With roses and flowers of every hue
She artfully hid all the thorns from my view: 10
Oh, Hope, thou deceiver, I cling to thee yet,
Though often have tried thee and found thee a cheat.
Thus into the future my thoughts often ran,
And painted the pleasures if I were a man!

When I grew a man, oh! when I grew a man,
And the lessons of life beginning to[1] scan,
The toils and the troubles of every day
Were lasting, though pleasures all melted away.
I found that the world had a mask on its face,
And long had I held but a shadow in chase;   20
And blight after blight made my roses all fade;
As they wither'd and fell, their thorns were display'd.
The idol I'd worship'd when gaily it shone,
Now stripp'd of its tinsel I found was but stone.
In youth I was counting the years coming on,
And now I look back to the days that are gone.
Past pleasures or future the present destroy,
And I sigh for the pleasures when I was a boy.

Poems Upon Various Subjects *(1854).*

ON THE DEATH OF MY CHILD
1 submissive words in the Lord's Prayer, 'Thy will be done in earth, as it is in heaven', Matthew 6.10.

2 'The Lord gave, and the Lord hath taken away; blessed be the Name of the Lord': words from the Burial Service in the Church of England's *Book of Common Prayer.*
WHEN I WAS A BOY
1 *so* in text, clearly a misprint.

INSENSIBILITY TO DEATH AROUND US

One day I sat in pensive mood
  Beside a gently flowing stream,
That wandered through a shady wood,
  Whose murmurs soothed my waking dream:
O'er the green leaves the zephyr played –
  A fragrant, cooling, wanton breeze –
And lulling sounds of music made
  Among the softly whispering trees.

Along the grassy margin grew
  Those plants which love a shady spot;   10
With eyes of softest, palest blue,
  Hung weeping the forget-me-not,
Still bending down with modest head,
  And gazing in the glassy wave –
That source[1] from whence its life is fed,
  And soon, alas! to be its grave.

I watched upon a willow tall
  A trembling leaf hang o'er my head;
At last I saw it silent fall,
  And float upon the watery bed.   20
'Gone – gone!' I cried, 'in summer's bloom,
  Whilst all around is fresh and gay;'
Like youth that finds an early tomb,
  I saw it slowly pass away.

I gathered many a shining stone,
  Which scattered lay within the wood,
Then tossed them from me one by one,
  And saw them sink into the flood:
A bubble rose, a circle spread,
  Enlarging faintly near the shore,   30
Soon every trace of them had fled –
  The waters glided as before.

And thus we see our neighbours die,
  And only feel a moment's pain;
We watch the sad procession by,
  Then turn to our pursuits again:
Insensible as heedless waves
  That sweep away the flow'rets' bloom,
We dance in sight of open graves,
  And sport with toys around the tomb.   40

Thus has it been for ages past,
  And so 'twill be when I am gone;
The world will hurry on as fast,
  Like water o'er the sunken stone.
When I return to parent earth,
  And mingle with forgotten clay,
It will not check a moment's mirth,
  Nor scarce be known a mile away.

Poems Upon Various Subjects, II (C. W. Naylor, Cambridge; Macintosh,
London, 1856).

LITTLE RILL

I know a rill, a little rill,
Gliding round the sloping hill,
Creeping under hollow ledges,
Playing bo-peep in the sedges;
Now rushing swiftly out of sight,
Now laughing in the sunny light,
Now hiding darkly, under bushes,
Now leaping over tufts of rushes;
And dancing o'er the shining stones,
To music of its silver tones.   10
  Little rill, merry rill,

Ever springing, little rill,
  Ever singing, never still –
Tinkle, tinkle, tinkle, tinkle;
Sprinkle, sprinkle, sprinkle, sprinkle;
  Never still, never still;
    Glancing, gliding,
    Skipping, sliding,
  Little rill, little rill,
  Sporting in thy wayward will,   20
  Never still, never still,
  Childhood is a little rill.

Poems Upon Various Subjects, II (1856).

INSENSIBILITY TO DEATH AROUND US
1 *scource* in original text, clearly a misprint.

THE POET

Deep in the rustic village shade,
Unknown to fame,
A simple, untaught urchin played,
Of humble name.

I knew him when an artless child,
Poor and obscure;
Before the world his heart defiled,
When thought was pure.

He'd wander in the woods for hours,
And leave his play;   10
He loved the trees, the fields, and flowers,
And wild bird's lay.

There was a time-warp'd willow tree
Beside a stream;
Beneath its shade at noon he'd be,
And sit and dream.

Under the chestnut's broad green crown,
On summer eves,
When silently the stars looked down,
Through trembling leaves;   20

He'd watch those gems that night'ly glow
Along the skies,
Smiling on all the world below,
Like angels' eyes.

He gave the airy clouds a form,
Of life and limb;
The hollow howling of the storm,
Was sweet to him.

He sought companionship with few –
A pensive lad;   30
Men called him, as he older grew,
Moon-struck and mad.

They did not know the calm delight
That filled his breast;
His wakeful musings in the night,
And they at rest;

The music floating on the breeze,
That soothed his ear;
The melody in sighing trees,
That he could hear.   40

At times in all the village glee
He took a part,
And forced himself to gaiety,
With aching heart:

But oft he sadly stole away,
Alone to weep;
When others in sweet slumbers lay,
He could not sleep.

Then would he read of champions bold,
By field and flood;   50
And wild romantic tales of old,
Which chilled his blood;

And the soft, witching, measured lines,
Whose numbers roll
O'er the young heart where feeling shrines,
And charm the soul.

Converse he held by Avon's stream,
With Nature's bard;[1]
Sighed o'er the melancholy theme,
Of Abelard;   60

With Milton scaled the heights of bliss,
In heaven's light,
And saw the dark, profound abyss,
Of endless night;

With Goldsmith traced the winding Po,
Or lazy Scheldt;[2]
In all the lonely wanderer's woe,
A portion felt;

O'er the 'Deserted Village' green
In fancy strayed;   70
Mused on each well depictured scene,
Of 'Auburn's' shade;[3]

Stood in wrapt awe at Byron's flight,
With daring wing;
And trembling saw the with'ring blight,
Of Passion's sting.

Himself had nursed a feeble fire,
In secret long;
At last he strung his rustic lyre,
And chimed a song.

Poems Upon Various Subjects, II (1856).

THE POET
1 Shakespeare.
2 'Or by the lazy Scheldt or wandering Po' (Belgian and Italian rivers): Oliver Goldsmith, 'The Traveller, or a Prospect of Society' (1764), line 2.
3 Oliver Goldsmith, 'The Deserted Village' (1770), about Irish village called Auburn.

Jemima Luke (1813–1906)

Jemima Luke, Evangelical Congregationalist hymn-writer, was born Jemima Thompson in Islington, London, 19 August 1813, the second child of the family (the first daughter died in infancy). Her father, Thomas Thompson, shared the same day of birth. He was a fairly well-off gent, deeply immersed in Christian endeavours – a founder of the Sunday School Union, on the committee of the London Missionary Society, a founder of the Home Missionary Society, and the originator of the first floating chapel for sailors. Her mother was quite an invalid. There were several brothers and sisters. Jemima was at first taught at home by a Miss Mason, then at a Miss Fry's in Dorset Street. She early on turned to verse, contributing precociously to the *Juvenile Friend*. The family moved about London – Brixton Hill, St John's Wood, Tavistock Square, Vanbrugh Fields on the edge of Blackheath. At one point they had a country house in Kent. Always they attended the local Congregationalist chapel, but also went to services at St John's, Bedford Row, where the Revd and Hon. Baptist Noel was minister. They were extremely involved in Missionary Society work, and held missionary meetings in their various houses. Mother died 29 May 1837. Father was soon married again, to the widowed sister of Baptist Noel – who had a grand estate, Poundsford

Park, in Somerset, to which the family moved. Jemima was all set to go to India as a missionary to work in female education when illness put a stop to her plans. In 1843 she married a Bristol Congregationalist minister, Samuel Luke. By then her best-known hymn, 'I think when I read that sweet story of old', had been written: two of its stanzas were jotted down in 1841, on the back of an envelope, in a coach, on the way to a meeting of the Society for Female Education in the East, near Poundsford. Her father sent it to the *Sunday School Magazine*. On the strength of the reputation this hymn engendered, she became editor of the *Missionary Reporter* for children. The hymn spread rapidly across the English-speaking world in hymn books for the young. In 1841 her *Memoirs of Female Missionaries* appeared; in 1851 a novel, *The Female Jesuit; or, The Spy in the Family*; and in 1856, *The Sequel to the Female Jesuit*. The Revd Samuel Luke died after twenty-five years of marriage. Jemima lived on alone, doing her good evangelical and missionary works, producing *The Pilgrim Boy, and Other Stories, by the Author of 'I think when I read that sweet story of old'* (1890). Her *Early Years of My Life, By the Author of 'I Think when I Read that Sweet Story of Old'* appeared in 1900. She died in 1906.

I think when I read that sweet story of old,
    When Jesus was here among men,
How He called little children, as lambs to His fold,
    I should like to have been with them then.
I wish that His hands had been placed on my head,
    That His arms had been thrown around me,
And that I might have seen His kind look when He said,
    'Let the little ones come unto Me.'

Yet still to His footstool in prayer I may go,
    And ask for a share in His love;
And if I now earnestly seek Him below,
    I shall see Him and hear Him above:
In that beautiful place He is gone to prepare
    For all who are washed and forgiven;
And many dear children are gathering there,
    'For of such is the kingdom of heaven.'

But thousands and thousands who wander and fall
    Never heard of that heavenly home, –
I should like them to know there is room for them all,
    And that Jesus has bid them to come.
I long for the joy of that glorious time,
    The sweetest, and brightest, and best,

When the dear little children of every clime
Shall crowd to His arms and be blessed.

Version in Early Years of my Life, By the Author of 'I Think when
I Read that Sweet Story of Old' *(Hodder & Stoughton, 1900).*

William Edmonstoune Aytoun (1813–65)

William Edmonstoune Aytoun, Scottish poet, lawyer, parodist, professor and critic, was born in Edinburgh, 21 June 1813, into a legal family with strong literary connexions. His father, Roger Aytoun, was a solicitor (what's known in Scotland as a writer to the signet), his mother a childhood friend of Walter Scott with a great knowledge of the Scottish ballad. One of his ancestors was the Robert Ayton who went to London with James I, was a friend of Ben Jonson and reputed author of the verses reworked by Burns as 'Auld Lang Syne' ('Should auld acquaintance be forgot'). Aytoun attended Edinburgh Academy and Edinburgh University, briefly tried legal studies in England, studied German literature for several months at Aschaffenburg, became a writer to the signet (1835), and was called to the Scottish Bar (1840). He'd published a precocious small volume of verses, *Poland, Homer, and Other Poems* in 1832, and took eagerly to various literary work: translations of Uhland and Homer, among others, in *Edinburgh Magazine*, 1836–40; *Lays of the Cavaliers* (1848: twenty-nine editions by 1883); collaborating with Theodore Martin on the popular *Bon Gaultier Ballads* (1855: thirteenth edition by 1877); *Poems and Ballads of Goethe* (1858), also with Theodore Martin; editing the two-volume *Ballads of Scotland* (1858). In 1845 he became Professor of Rhetoric and Belles Lettres at Edinburgh University. Much of his writing appeared in *Blackwood's*; he joined its staff in 1844; in 1849 he married the daughter of John Wilson, who as 'Christopher North' was one of the magazine's two mainstay writers (the other was John Gibson Lockhart).

Aytoun's novel of 1861, *Norman Sinclair*, appeared in *Blackwood's*; as did his sensational spoof review of a non-existent verse-drama, *Firmilian, or the Student of Badajoz: A Spasmodic Tragedy*, 'By T. Percy Jones'. The review, and the follow-up volume from Blackwood's, sought to mock the sensationalist rhetorical extravagances of the poets Aytoun dubbed the Spasmodic School – the long verse dramas of Philip James Bailey (*Festus*, 1839), Alexander Smith (*Life Drama*, 1853) and Sydney Dobell (his never-finished *Balder*, 1854). The review of *Firmilian* was taken seriously, despite its over-exuberant claims and its suspicious waivers ('It is, of course, utterly extravagant; but so are the whole of the writings of the poets of the Spasmodic school; and, in the eyes of a considerable body of modern critics, extravagance is regarded as a proof of extraordinary genius. It is, here and there, highly coloured; but that also is looked upon as a symptom of the divine afflatus, and rather prized than otherwise'), and so was the volume *Firmilian*, despite its jocularly giveaway preface, satirically modelled on Dobell's preface to the second edition of *Balder* ('It is my firm opinion that all high poetry is and must be spasmodic'). The success of these spoofs was all a rather salutary, even shaking, exercise for criticism and poetry – as such successful parodies tend to be. Aytoun was deeply upset by the death of his wife in 1859, and declined thereafter in health. He remarried in December 1863 but never recovered his old verve and cheerfulness and he died, childless, near Elgin, 4 August 1865.

FIRMILIAN: A TRAGEDY

*Firmilian: or, The Student of Badajoz: a Tragedy. By T. Percy Jones. Printed for Private
Circulation.*

We have great pleasure in announcing to our readers the fact, that we have at last discovered that long-expected phenomenon, the coming Poet, and we trust that his light will very soon become visible in the literary horizon. We cannot, however, arrogate to ourselves any large share of merit in this discovery – indeed, we must confess, with a feeling akin to shame, that we ought to have made it at a much earlier date. *Firmilian* is not altogether new to us. We have an indistinct recollection of having seen the tragedy in manuscript well-nigh two years ago; and, if we remember aright, a rather animated correspondence took place on the subject of the return of the papers. We had, by some untoward accident, allowed them to find their way into the Balaam-box, which girnel of genius was at that particular time full up to the very hinges. We felt confident that *Firmilian* lay under the weight of some twenty solid layers of miscellaneous literature; and we should as soon have thought of attempting to disinter an icthyosaurus from a slate-quarry, as of ransacking the bowels of the chest for that treasury of rare delights. However, we took care, on the occasion of the next incremation, to make search for the missing article, and had the pleasure of returning it to Mr Percy Jones, from whom we heard nothing further until we received his tragedy in print. Our first perusal having been rather of a cursory nature, we are not able to state with certainty whether the author has applied himself during the intervening period to the work of emendation; but we think it exceedingly probable that he has done so, as we now remark a degree of vivacity and force of expression, however extravagant many of the ideas may be, which had escaped our previous notice. We hope that, by a tardy act of justice, we shall offer no violence to that amiable modesty which has, in the mean time, restrained him from asking the verdict of the general public.

As to the actual amount of poetic genius and accomplishment which Mr Percy Jones possesses, there may, even among the circle of his friends, be considerable difference of opinion. Those who admire spasmodic throes and writings may possibly be inclined to exalt him to a very high pinnacle of fame; for certainly, in no modern work of poetry – and there have been several recently published which might have borne the *imprimatur* of Bedlam – have we found so many symptoms of unmistakable lunacy. Still there is a method in his madness – a rapidity of perception and originality of thought, which contrasts very favourably with the tedious drivellings of some other writers of the same school. His taste is not one whit better than theirs, but he brings a finer fancy and a more vivid imagination to the task; nor is he deficient in a certain rude exaggerated dramatic power, which has more than once reminded us of the early style of Marlowe and the other predecessors of Shakespeare.

It is not very easy to comprehend the exact creed and method of the new school of poets, who have set themselves to work upon a principle hitherto unknown, or at all events unproclaimed. This much we know from themselves, that they regard poetry not only as a sacred calling, but as the most sacred of any – that, in their opinion, every social relation, every mundane tie, which can interfere with the bard's development, must be either disregarded or snapped asunder – and that they are, to the fainting race of Adam, the sole accredited bearers of the Amreeta cup of immortality. Such is the kind of nonsense regarding the nature of his mission which each fresh poetaster considers it his duty to enunciate; and as there is nothing, however absurd, which will not become credited by dint of constant repetition, we need not be surprised that some very extraordinary views regarding the 'rights of genius' should of late years have been countenanced by men who ought to have known better. Poets are, like all other authors or artisans, valuable according to the quality of the article which they produce. If their handiwork be good, genuine, and true, it will pass at once into circulation and be prized – if the reverse, what title can they prefer to the name which they so proudly arrogate to themselves?

We do not, however, quarrel with a poet for having an exalted idea of his art – always supposing that he has taken any pains to acquire its rudiments. Without a high feeling of this kind, it would be difficult to maintain the struggle which must precede eminent success; nor would we have alluded to the subject but for the affectation and offensive swaggering of some who may indeed be rhymsters, but who never could be poets even if their days were to be prolonged to the extent of those of Methusaleh. When the painter of the tavern sign-post, whereon is depicted a beer-bottle voiding its cork, and spontaneously ejecting its contents right and left into a couple of convenient tumblers, talks to us of high art, Raphael, and the effects of *chiaroscuro*, it is utterly impossible to control the action of the risible muscles. And, in like manner, when one of our young poetical aspirants, on the strength of a trashy duodecimo filled with unintelligible ravings, asserts his claim to be considered as a prophet and a teacher, it is beyond the power of humanity to check the intolerable tickling of the midriff.

But, apart from their exaggerated notions of their calling, let us see what is the practice of the poets of the Spasmodic School. In the first place, they rarely, if ever, attempt anything like a plot. After you have finished the persual of their verses, you find yourself just as wise as when you began. You cannot tell what they would be at. You have a confused recollection of stars, and sunbeams, and moonbeams, as if you had been staring at an orrery; but sun, moon, and stars, were intended to give light to something – and what that something is, in the poet's page, you cannot, for the life of you, discover. In the second place, we regret to say that they are often exceedingly profane, not, we suppose, intentionally, but because they have not sense enough to see the limits which decency, as well as duty, prescribes. In the third place, they are occasionally very prurient. And, in the fourth place, they are almost always unintelligible.

Now, although we cannot by any means aver that Mr Percy Jones is entirely free from the faults which we have just enumerated, we look upon him as a decidedly favourable specimen of his tribe. There is, in *Firmilian*, if not a plot, at least some kind of comprehensible action; and in it he has portrayed the leading features of the poetical school to which he belongs with so much fidelity and effect, that we feel called upon to give an outline of his tragedy, with a few specimens from the more remarkable scenes.

The hero of the piece, Firmilian, is a student in the university of Badajoz, a poet, and entirely devoted to his art. He has been engaged for some time in the composition of a tragedy upon the subject of Cain, which is 'to win the world by storm;' but he unfortunately discovers, after he has proceeded a certain length in his task, that he has not yet thoroughly informed himself, by experience, of the real nature of the agonies of remorse. He finds that he cannot do justice to his subject without steeping his own soul in guilt, so as to experience the pangs of the murderer; and as, according to the doctrines of the spasmodic school of poetry, such investigations are not only permitted, but highly laudable, he sets himself seriously to ponder with what victim he should begin. All our spasmodic poets introduce us to their heroes in their studies, and Mr Percy Jones follows the tradition. He does not, however, like some of them, carry his imitative admiration of Goethe's *Faust* so far, as personally to evoke Lucifer or Mephistopheles – an omission for which we are really thankful. Firmilian begins by a soliloquy upon his frame of mind and feelings; and states himself to be grievously perplexed and hindered in his work by his comparative state of innocence. He then meditates whether he should commence his course of practical remorse by putting to death Mariana, a young lady to whom he is attached, or three friends and fellow-students of his, with whom he is to dine next day. After much hesitation, he decides on the latter view, and, after looking up 'Raymond Lullius' for the composition of a certain powder, retires to rest after a beautiful but somewhat lengthy apostrophe to the moon. There is nothing in this scene which peculiarly challenges quotation. The next is occupied by love-making; and certainly, if Mr Percy Jones had intended to exhibit his hero throughout in the most amiable and romantic light, nothing could be better than his appearance in the bower of Mariana. If, here and there, we encounter an occasional floridness, or even warmth of expression, we attribute that in a great measure to the sunny nature of the clime; just as we feel that the raptures of Romeo and Juliet are in accordance with the temperament of the land that gave them birth. But we presently find that Firmilian, though a poet, is a hypocrite and traitor in love. The next scene is laid in a tavern, where he and his friends, Garcia Perez, Alphonzo D'Aguilar, and Alonzo Olivarez are assembled, and there is a discussion, over the wine-cup, on the inexhaustible subject of knightly love. Alphonzo, claiming to be descended from the purest blood of Castile, asserts the superiority of European beauty over the rest of the universe; to which Firmilian, though known to be betrothed to Mariana, makes the following reply –

> *Firmilian*   I knew a poet once; and he was young,
> And intermingled with such fierce desires
> As made pale Eros veil his face with grief,
> And caused his lustier brother to rejoice.
> He was as amorous as a crocodile
> In the spring season, when the Memphian bank,
> Receiving substance from the glaring sun,
> Resolves itself from mud into a shore.
> And – as the scaly creature wallowing there,
> In its hot fits of passion, belches forth   10
> The steam from out its nostrils, half in love,
> And half in grim defiance of its kind;
> Trusting that either, from the reedy fen,
> Some reptile-virgin coyly may appear,
> Or that the hoary Sultan of the Nile

May make tremendous challenge with his jaws,
And, like Mark Anthony, assert his right
To all the Cleopatras of the ooze –
So fared it with the poet that I knew.

He had a soul beyond the vulgar reach,   20
Sun-ripened, swarthy. He was not the fool
To pluck the feeble lily from its shade
When the black hyacinth stood in fragrance by.
The lady of his love was dusk as Ind,
Her lips as plenteous as the Sphinx's are,
And her short hair crisp with Numidian curl.
She was a negress. You have heard the strains
That Dante, Petrarch, and such puling fools
As loved the daughters of cold Japhet's race,
Have lavished idly on their icicles.   30
As snow melts snow, so their unhasty fall
Fell chill and barren on a pulseless heart.
But, would you know what noontide ardour is,
Or in what mood the lion, in the waste,
All fever-maddened, and intent on cubs,
At the oasis waits the lioness –
That shall you gather from the fiery song
Which that young poet framed, before he dared
Invade the vastness of his lady's lips.

Judging from the implied character of the ditty in question, we are not sorry that we cannot lay it before our readers – indeed it does not appear in the volume, for D'Aguilar was so disgusted with the introduction that he openly reviled Firmilian as a pupil of Mahound, and bestowed a buffet on him, whereupon there was a flashing of swords. These, however, were sheathed, and the students again sate down amicably to drink. Firmilian, being suddenly called away, entreats his friends to amuse themselves, during his absence, with a special bottle of 'Ildefronso' – a vintage which we do not remember having seen in any modern list of wines. They comply – feel rather uncomfortable – and the scene concludes by the chaunt of a funeral procession beneath the window; an idea which we strongly suspect has been borrowed from Victor Hugo's tragedy of *Lucrèce Borgia*.

The next scene exhibits Firmilian pacing the cloisters. His three friends have died by poison, but he is not able by any means to conjure up a feeling of adequate remorse. He does not see that he is at all responsible in the matter. If he had poured out the wine into their glasses, and looked upon their dying agonies, then, indeed, he might have experienced the desired sensation of guilt. But he did nothing of the kind. They helped themselves, of their own free will and accord, and died when he was out of the way. On the whole, then, his first experiment was a blunder. During his reverie, an old preceptor of his, the Priest of St Nicholas, passes; and certain reminiscences of stripes suggest him as the next victim. The reader will presently see by what means this scheme is carried into execution. Suffice it to say, that the mere anticipation of it sheds a balm upon Firmilian's disappointed spirit, who, being now fully convinced that in a few days he will be able to realise the tortures of Cain, departs for an interview with Lilian, a young lady for whom he entertains a clandestine attachment. The next scene speaks for itself.

Exterior of the Cathedral of St Nicholas: Choir heard chaunting within. Enter Firmilian
How darkly hangs yon cloud above the spire!
There's thunder in the air –
                    What if the flash
Should rend the solid walls, and reach the vault
Where my terrestrial thunder lies prepared,
And so, without the action of my hand,

Whirl up those thousand bigots in its blaze,
And leave me guiltless, save in the intent?

That were a vile defraudment of my aim,
A petty larceny o' the element,
An interjection of exceeding wrong!   10
Let the hoarse thunder rend the vault of heaven,
Yea, shake the stars by myriads from their boughs,
As autumn tempests shake the fruitage down; –
Let the red lightning shoot athwart the sky,
Entangling comets by their spooming hair,
Piercing the zodiac belt, and carrying dread
To old Orion, and his whimpering hound; –
But let the glory of this deed be mine!

> *Organ and Choir*
> Sublimatus ad honorem
>   Nicholai presulis: 20
> Pietatis ante rorem
>   Cunctis pluit populis:
> Ut vix parem aut majorem
>   Habeat in seculis.[1]

Firmilian   Yet I could weep to hear the wretches sing!
There rolls the organ anthem down the aisle,
And thousand voices join in its acclaim.
All they are happy – they are on their knees;
Round and above them stare the images
Of antique saints and martyrs. Censers steam   30
With their Arabian charge of frankincense,
And every heart, with inward fingers, counts
A blissful rosary of pious prayer!
Why should they perish then? Is't yet too late?
    O shame, Firmilian, on thy coward soul!
What! thou, the poet! – thou, whose mission 'tis
To send vibration down the chord of time,
Until its junction with eternity –
Thou, who hast dared and pondered and endured,
Gathering by piecemeal all the noble thoughts   40
And fierce sensations of the mind – as one
Who in a garden culls the wholesome rose,
And binds it with the deadly nightshade up;
Flowers not akin, and yet, by contrast kind –
Thou, for a touch of what these mundane fools
Whine of as pity, to forego thine aim,
And never feel the gnawing of remorse,
Like the Promethean vulture on the spleen,
That shall instruct thee to give future voice
To the unuttered agonies of Cain!   50
Thou, to compare, with that high consequence
The breath of some poor thousand knights and knaves,
Who soaring, in the welkin, shall expire!
Shame, shame, Firmilian! on thy weakness, shame!

FIRMILIAN: A TRAGEDY
1 'Raised up to the honour of Bishop Nicholas: in times gone by when a whole people was awash with the dew of piety, to an extent scarcely bettered or even equalled in any age.'

Organ and Choir
Auro dato violari
  Virgines prohibuit:
Far in fame, vas in mari
  Servat et distribuit:
Qui timebant naufragari
  Nautis opem tribuit.[2]   60

Firmilian   A right good saint he seems, this Nicholas!
And over-worked too, if the praise be just,
Which these, his votaries, quaver as his claim.
Yet it is odd he should o'erlook the fact
That underneath this church of his are stored
Some twenty barrels of the dusky grain,
The secret of whose framing, in an hour
Of diabolic jollity and mirth,
Old Roger Bacon wormed from Belzebub!
He might keep better wardship for his friends;   70
But that to me is nothing. Now's the time!
Ha! as I take the matchbox in my hand,
A spasm pervades me, and a natural thrill
As though my better genius were at hand,
And strove to pluck me backwards by the hair.
I must be resolute. Lose this one chance,
Which bears me to th' Acropolis of guilt,
And this, our age, foregoes its noblest song.
I must be speedy –

Organ and Choir   80
A defunctis suscitatur
  Furtum qui commiserat:
Et Judæus baptizatur
  Furtum qui recuperat:
Illi vita restauratur,
  Hic ad fidem properat.[3]

Firmilian   No more was needed to confirm my mind!
That stanza blows all thoughts of pity off,
As empty straws are scattered by the wind!
For I have been the victim of the Jews,
Who, by vile barter, have absorbed my means.   90
Did I not pawn – for that same flagrant stuff,
Which only waits a spark to be dissolved,
And, having done its mission, must disperse
As a thin smoke into the ambient air –
My diamond cross, my goblet, and my books?
What! would they venture to baptise the Jew?
The cause assumes a holier aspect, then;
And, as a faithful son of Rome, I dare
To merge my darling passion in the wrong
That is projected against Christendom!   100
Pity, avaunt! I may not longer stay.

---

2 'With gifts of gold he prevents virgins from being violated: He saves up food in time of famine and spreads security across the seas: He offered help to sailors fearful of being shipwrecked.'

3 'The man who had carried out the robbery was raised up from among the dead: And the Jew who recovered the stolen object was baptized: To the first life was restored, the latter was propelled into the faith.'

Exit into the vaults. A short pause, after which he reappears.
'Tis done! I vanish like the lightning bolt!

>   *Organ and Choir*
>   Nicholai sacerdotum
>   Decus, honor, gloria:
>   Plebem omnem, clerum totum –[4]
>   (*The Cathedral is blown up*)

We back that scene, for intensity, against anything which has been written for the last dozen of years. Nay, we can even see in it traces of profound psychological observation. Firmilian, like Hamlet, is liable, especially on the eve of action, to fits of constitutional irresolution; and he requires, in order to nerve him to the deed, a more direct and plausible motive than that which originally prompted him. Hence we find him wavering, and almost inclined to abandon his purpose, until a casual passage in the choral hymn jars upon an excitable nerve, and urges him irresistibly forward. We shall presently find the same trait of character even more remarkably developed in another scene.

We then come to the obsequies of the students, which, being episodical, we may as well pass over. There are two ways of depicting grief – one quiet and impressive, the other stormy and clamorous. Mr Percy Jones, as might have been expected, adopts the latter method; and we are bound to say that we have never perused anything in print so fearful as the ravings of the bereaved Countess D'Aguilar, mother of the unfortunate Alphonzo. She even forgets herself so far as box the ears of the confessor who is officiously whispering consolation.

Meanwhile, where is the hero of the piece – the successful Guy Fawkes of the cathedral? Perched on a locality which never would have occurred to any but the most exalted imagination.

>   *Summit of the pillar of St Simeon Stylites*
>   *Firmilian* 'Twas a grand spectacle!   The solid earth
>   Seemed from its quaking entrails to eruct
>   The gathered lava of a thousand years,
>   Like an imposthume bursting up from hell!
>   In a red robe of flame, the riven towers,   110
>   Pillars and altar, organ-loft and screen,
>   With a singed swarm of mortals intermixed,
>   Were whirled in anguish to the shuddering stars,
>   And all creation trembled at the din.
>   It was my doing – mine alone! and I
>   Stand greater by this deed than the vain fool
>   That thrust his torch beneath Diana's shrine.
>   For what was it inspired Erostratus
>   But a weak vanity to have his name
>   Blaze out for arson in the catalogue?[5]   120
>   I have been wiser.   No man knows the name
>   Of me, the pyrotechnist who have given
>   A new apotheosis to the saint
>   With lightning blast, and stunning thunder knell!
>   And yet – and yet – what boots the sacrifice?
>   I thought to take remorse unto my heart,
>   As the young Spartan hid the savage fox
>   Beneath the foldings of his boyish gown,
>   And let it rive his flesh.   Mine is not riven –
>   My heart is yet unscarred.   I've been too coarse   130
>   And general in this business.   Had there been
>   Amongst that multitude a single man

---

4 'May the grace, honour, glory of the priests of Nicholas … All the people, the entire clergy …'

5 Erostratus, seeking fame, set fire to Diana's temple at Ephesus. Mention of his name was thereafter forbidden.

Who loved me, cherished me – to whom I owed
Sweet reciprocity for holy alms
And gifts of gentle import – had there been
Friend, – father, – brother, mingled in that crowd,
And I had slain him – then indeed my soul
Might have acquired fruition of its wish,
And shrieked delirious at the taste of sin!
But these – what were the victims unto me?   140
Nothing!   Mere human atoms, breathing clods,
Uninspired dullards, unpoetic slaves,
The rag, and tag, and bobtail of mankind;
Whom, having scorched to cinders, I no more
Feel ruth for what I did, than if my hand
Had thrust a stick of sulphur in the nest
Of some poor hive of droning humble-bees,
And smoked them into silence!
                              I must have
A more potential draught of guilt than this,
With more of wormwood in it!   150
                        Here I sit,
Perched like a raven on old Simeon's shaft,
With barely needful footing for my limbs –
And one is climbing up the inward coil,
Who was my friend and brother.   We have gazed
Together on the midnight map of heaven,
And marked the gems in Cassiopea's hair –
Together have we heard the nightingale
Waste the exuberant music of her throat,
And lull the flustering breezes into calm –
Together have we emulously sung   160
Of Hyacinthus, Daphne, and the rest,
Whose mortal weeds Apollo changed to flowers.
Also from him I have derived much aid
In golden ducats, which I fain would pay
Back with extremest usury, were but
Mine own convenience equal to my wish.
Moreover, of his poems he hath sold
Two full editions of a thousand each,
While mine remain neglected on the shelves!
Courage, Firmilian! for the hour has come   170
When thou canst know atrocity indeed,
By smiting him that was thy dearest friend.
And think not that he dies a vulgar death –
'Tis poetry demands the sacrifice!
Yet not to him be that revealment made.
He must not know with what a loving hand –
With what fraternal charity of heart
I do devote him to the infernal gods!
I dare not spare him one particular pang,
Nor make the struggle briefer!   Hush – he comes.   180

Haverillo, emerging from the staircase
How now, Firmilian! – I am scant of breath;
These steps have pumped the ether from my lungs,
And made the bead-drops cluster on my brow.
A strange, unusual, rendezvous is this –
An old saint's pillar, which no human foot
Hath scaled this hundred years!

Firmilian   Aye – it is strange!

Haverillo 'Faith, sir, the bats considered it as such:
They seem to flourish in the column here,
And are not over courteous.   Ha! I'm weary:
I shall sleep sound to-night.   190

Firmilian   You *shall* sleep sound!

Haverillo Either there is an echo in the place,
Or your voice is sepulchral.

Firmilian   Seems it so?

Haverillo Come, come, Firmilian – Be once more a man!
Leave off these childish tricks, and vapours bred
Out of a too much pampered fantasy.
What are we, after all, but mortal men,
Who eat, drink, sleep, need raiment and the like,
As well as any jolterhead alive?
Trust me, my friend, we cannot feed on dreams,   200
Or stay the hungry cravings of the maw
By mere poetic banquets.

Firmilian   Say you so?
Yet have I heard that by some alchemy
(To me unknown as yet) you have transmuted
Your verses to fine gold.

Haverillo   And all that gold
Was lent to you, Firmilian.

Firmilian   You expect,
Doubtless, I will repay you?   210

Haverillo   So I do.
You told me yesterday to meet you here,
And you would pay me back with interest.
Here is the note.

Firmilian   A moment. – Do you see
Yon melon-vender's stall down i' the square?
Methinks the fruit that, close beside the eye,
Would show as largely as a giant's head,
Is dwindled to a heap of gooseberries!
If Justice held no bigger scales than those
Yon pigmy seems to balance in his hands,   220
Her utmost fiat scarce would weigh a drachm!
How say you?

Haverillo   Nothing – 'tis a fearful height!
My brain turns dizzy as I gaze below,
And there's a strange sensation in my soles.

Firmilian Ay – feel you that?   Ixion felt the same
Ere he was whirled from heaven![6]

---

6   kin murderer, and rapist, bound to fiery wheel in underworld by
Zeus as punishment.

Haverillo   Firmilian!
You carry this too far. Farewell.   We'll meet
When you're in better humour.   230

Firmilian   Tarry, sir!
I have you here, and thus we shall not part.
I know your meaning well.   For that same dross,
That paltry ore of Mammon's mean device
Which I, to honour you, stooped to receive,
You'd set the Alguazils on my heels!
What! have I read your thought?   Nay, never shrink,
Nor edge towards the doorway!   You're a scholar!
How was't with Phaeton?

Haverillo   Alas! he's mad.
Hear me, Firmilian! Here is the receipt –   240
Take it – I grudge it not! If ten times more,
It were at your sweet service.

Firmilian   Would you do
This kindness unto me?

Haverillo   Most willingly.

Firmilian   Liar and slave!   There's falsehood in thine eye!
I read as clearly there, as in a book,
That, if I did allow you to escape,
In fifteen minutes you would seek the judge.
Therefore, prepare thee, for thou needs must die!   250

Haverillo   Madman – stand off!

Firmilian   There's but four feet of space
To spare between us.   I'm not hasty, I!
Swans sing before their death, and it may be
That dying poets feel that impulse too:
Then, prythee, be canorous.   You may sing
One of those ditties which have won you gold,
And my meek audience of the vapid strain
Shall count with Phœbus as a full discharge
For all your ducats.   Will you not begin?   260

Haverillo   Leave off this horrid jest, Firmilian!

Firmilian   Jest!   'Tis no jest!   This pillar's very high –
Shout, and no one can hear you from the square –
Wilt sing, I say?

Haverillo   Listen, Firmilian!
I have a third edition in the press,
Whereof the proceeds shall be wholly thine –
Spare me!

Firmilian   A third edition!   Atropos[7] –
Forgive me that I tarried!   270

Haverillo   Mercy! – Ah! –

Firmilian hurls him from the column.

---

7   third of the 'Cruel Fates' (she cut your thread of life).

There is a grand recklessness and savage energy displayed in this scene, which greatly increases our admiration of the author's abilities. He seems, indeed, in the fair way of making the spasmodic school famous in modern literature. With the death of Haverillo an ordinary writer would have paused – not so Percy Jones, who, with a fine aptitude for destruction, makes his hero, Firmilian, kill two birds with one stone. The manner in which he accomplishes this feat is most ingenious. He maintains the unity of the design by a very slight alteration of the locality. Whilst the two poets are ominously conversing on the summit of the pillar, a critic, affected by an intolerable itch for notoriety, is prowling in the square beneath –

Square below the pillar. Enter Apollodorus, a Critic.
Why do men call me a presumptuous cur,
A vapouring blockhead, and a turgid fool,
A common nuisance, and a charlatan?
I've dashed into the sea of metaphor
With as strong paddles as the sturdiest ship
That churns Medusæ into liquid light,
And hashed at every object in my way.
My ends are public.   I have talked of men
As my familiars, whom I never saw.   280
Nay – more to raise my credit – I have penned
Epistles to the great ones of the land,
When some attack might make them slightly sore,
Assuring them, in faith, it was not I.
What was their answer?   Marry – shortly this:
'Who, in the name of Zernebock, are you?'
I have reviewed myself incessantly –
Yea, made a contract with a kindred soul
For mutual interchange of puffery.
Gods – how we blew each other!   But, 'tis past –   290
Those halcyon days are gone; and, I suspect,
That, in some fit of loathing or disgust,
Mine ancient playmate hath deserted me.
And yet I am Apollodorus still!
I search for genius, having it myself,
With keen and earnest longings.   I survive
To disentangle, from the imping wings
Of our young poets, their crustaceous slough.
I watch them, as the watcher on the brook
Sees the young salmon wrestling from its egg,   300
And revels in its future bright career.
Ha! what seraphic melody is this?

Enter Sancho, a Costermonger, singing.
Down in the garden behind the wall,
    Merrily grows the bright-green leek;
The old sow grunts as the acorns fall,
    The winds blow heavy, the little pigs squeak.
One for the litter, and three for the teat –
Hark to their music, Juanna my sweet!

Apollodorus   Now, heaven be thanked! here is a genuine bard,
A creature of high impulse, one unsoiled   310
By coarse conventionalities of rule.
He labours not to sing, for his bright thoughts
Resolve themselves at once into a strain
Without the aid of balanced artifice.
All hail, great poet!

Sancho Save you, my merry master! Need you any leeks or onions? Here's the primest cauliflower, though I say it, in all Badajoz. Set it up at a distance of some ten yards, and I'll forfeit my ass if it does not look bigger than the Alcayde's wig.[8] Or would these radishes suit your turn? There's nothing like your radish for cooling the blood and purging distempered humours.

> *Apollodorus* I do admire thy vegetables much,
> But will not buy them.   Pray you, pardon me
> For one short word of friendly obloquy.
> Is't possible a being so endowed
> With music, song, and sun-aspiring thoughts,   320
> Can stoop to chaffer idly in the streets,
> And, for a huckster's miserable gain,
> Renounce the urgings of his destiny?
> Why, man, thine ass should be a Pegasus,
> A sun-reared charger snorting at the stars,
> And scattering all the Pleiads at his heels –
> Thy cart should be an orient-tinted car,
> Such as Aurora drives into the day,
> What time the rosy-fingered Hours awake –
> Thy reins –   330

Sancho Lookye, master, I've dusted a better jacket than yours before now, so you had best keep a civil tongue in your head. Once for all, will you buy my radishes?

Apollodorus No!

Sancho Then go to the devil and shake yourself!
Exit

> *Apollodorus* The foul fiend seize thee and thy cauliflowers!
> I was indeed a most egregious ass
> To take this lubber clodpole for a bard,
> And worship that dull fool. Pythian Apollo![9]
> Hear me – O hear! Towards the firmament
> I gaze with longing eyes; and, in the name
> Of millions thirsting for poetic draughts,
> I do beseech thee, send a poet down!   340
> Let him descend, e'en as a meteor falls,
> Rushing at noonday –
> *He is crushed by the fall of the body of Haverillo.*

We then find Firmilian wandering among the mountains, and lavishing a superfluity of apostrophe upon the rocks, forests, and cataracts around him. Whatever may be his moral deficiencies, we are constrained to admit that he must have studied the phenomena of nature to considerable purpose at the University of Badajoz, since he explains, in no fewer than twelve pages of blank verse, the glacier theory, entreating his own attention – for no one is with him – to the striated surface of rocks and the forcible displacement of boulders. He then, by way of amusement, works out a question in conic sections. But, notwithstanding these exercitations, he is obviously not happy. He is still as far as ever from his grand object, the thorough appreciation of remorse – for he can assign a distinct moral motive for each atrocity which he has committed. He at last reluctantly arrives at the conclusion that he is not the party destined –

> To shrine that page of history in song,
> And utter such tremendous cadences,

---

8 alcaide: governor of Spanish, Portuguese, or Moorish fortress.   9 deity of the oracle of Delphi.

That the mere babe who hears them at the breast,
Sans comprehension, or the power of thought,
Shall be an idiot to its dying hour!
I deemed my verse would make pale Hecate's orb[10]
Grow wan and dark; and into ashes change
The radiant star-dust of the milky-way.   350
I deemed that pestilence, disease, and death
Would follow every strophe – for the power
Of a true poet, prophet as he is,
Should rack creation!

If this view of the powers of poets and poetry be correct, commend us to the continuance of a lengthened period of prose!

Firmilian then begins to look about him for a new subject, and a new course of initiative discipline. Magic first occurs to him – but he very speedily abandons that idea, from a natural terror of facing the fiend, and a wholesome dread of the Inquisition. He admits having made already one or two experiments in that line, and narrates, with evident horror, how he drew a chalk circle in his apartments, kindled a brazier, and began an incantation, when suddenly a lurid light appeared in the sockets of a skull upon the shelf, and so nearly threw him into convulsions that he could barely mutter the exorcism. (It appears, from another part of the poem, that this exploit had been detected by his servant, a spy of the Inquisition, in consequence of his having neglected to erase the cabalistic markings in chalk, and was of course immediately reported.) At last he determines to fall back upon sensuality, and to devote his unexampled talents to a grand poem upon the amours of the Heathen deities. He states, with much show of truth, that the tone of morals which an exclusively classical education is apt to give, cannot but be favourable to an extensive and sublime erotic undertaking – and that the youthful appetite, early stimulated by the perusal of the Pantheon, and the works of Ovid, Juvenal, and Catullus, will eagerly turn to anything in the vernacular which promises still stronger excitement. We shall not venture, at the present, to apply ourselves seriously to that question.

That Firmilian – for we shall not say Mr Percy Jones – was well qualified for such an undertaking as he finally resolved to prosecute, must be evident to every one who has perused the earliest extract we have given; and we shall certainly hold ourselves excused from quoting the terms of the course of study which he now proposes to himself. Seriously, it is full time that the prurient and indecent tone which has liberally manifested itself in the writings of the young spasmodic poets should be checked. It is so far from occasional, that it has become a main feature of their school; and in one production of the kind, most shamefully bepuffed, the hero was represented as carrying on an intrigue with the kept-mistress of Lucifer! If we do not comment upon more recent instances of marked impurity, it is because we hope the offence will not be repeated. Meantime, let us back to Firmilian.

As he approaches the catastrophe, we remark, with infinite gratification, that Mr Percy Jones takes pains to show that he is not personally identified with the opinions of his hero. Up to the point which we have now reached, there has been nothing to convince us that Jones did not intend Firmilian to be admired – but we are thankful to say that before the conclusion we are undeceived. Jones, though quite as spasmodic as the best of them, *has* a sense of morals; and we do not know that we ever read anything better, in its way, than the following scene: –

A garden: Firmilian, Mariana

Firmilian   My Mariana!

Mariana   O my beautiful!
My seraph love – my panther of the wild –

10   the moon (Hecate a deity of the night and the ghost world).

My moon-eyed leopard – my voluptuous lord!
O, I am sunk within a sea of bliss,
And find no soundings!   360

Firmilian   Shall I answer back?
As the great Earth lies silent all the night,
And looks with hungry longing on the stars,
Whilst its huge heart beats on its granite ribs
With measured pulsings of delirious joy –
So look I, Mariana, on thine eyes!

Mariana   Ah, dearest! wherefore are we fashioned thus?
I cannot always hang around thy neck
And plant vermilion kisses on thy brow;
I cannot clasp thee, as yon ivy bush –   370
Too happy ivy! – holds, from year to year,
The stalwart oak within her firm embrace,
Mixing her tresses fondly up with his,
Like some young Jewish maid with Absalom's.[11]
Nay, hold, Firmilian! do not pluck that rose!

Firmilian   Why not? it is a fair one.

Mariana   Are fair things
Made only to be plucked? O fie on thee!
I did not think my lord a libertine!

Firmilian   Yet, sweetest, with your leave I'll take the rose,   380
For there's a moral in it. – Look you here.
'Tis fair, and sweet, and in its clustered leaves
It carries balmy dew: a precious flower,
And vermeil-tinctured, as are Hebe's lips.[12]
Yet say, my Mariana, could you bear
To gaze for ever only upon this,
And fling the rest of Flora's casket by?[13]

Mariana   No, truly – I would bind it up with more,
And make a fitting posy for my breast.
If I were stinted in my general choice,   390
I'd crop the lily, tender, fresh, and white, –
The shrinking pretty lily – and would give
Its modest contrast to the gaudier rose.
What next? some flower that does not love the day –
The dark, full-scented night-stock well might serve
To join the other two.

Firmilian   A sweet selection!
Think'st thou they'd bloom together on one breast
With a united fragrance?

Mariana   Wherefore not?   400
It is by union that all things are sweet.

Firmilian   Thou speakest well! I joy, my Mariana,
To find thy spirit overleaps the pale
Of this mean world's injurious narrowness!

---

11   biblical wild-boy prince Absalom had very long hair.   13   Flora: Roman goddess of flowers.
12   Hebe, goddess of youth; cup-bearer to (Greek) gods.

Never did Socrates proclaim a truth
More beautiful than welled from out thy lips –
'It is by union that all things are sweet.'
Thou, darling, art my rose – my dewy rose –
The which I'll proudly wear, but not alone.
Dost comprehend me?   410

Mariana   Ha! Firmilian –
How my eyes dazzle!

Firmilian   Let me show you now
The lily I have ta'en to bind with thee.
He brings Lilian from the summer-house.

Mariana   Is this a jest, Firmilian?

Firmilian   Could I jest
With aught so fair and delicate as this?
Nay, come – no coyness! Both of you embrace.
Then to my heart of hearts –

Mariana   Soft you a moment!   420
Methinks the posy is not yet complete.
Say, for the sake of argument, I share
My rights with this pale beauty – (for she's pretty;
Although so fragile and so frail a thing,
That a mere puff of April wind would mar her) –
Where is the night-stock?

Firmilian brings Indiana from the tool-house.
                              Here!

Mariana   A filthy negress!
Abominable!

Lilian   Mercy on me! what blubber lips she has!   430

Mariana, furiously to Firmilian
You nasty thing! Is this your poetry –
Your high soul-scheming and philosophy?
I hate and loathe you! (*To Indiana*). – Rival of my shoe,
Go, get thee gone, and hide thee from the day
That loathes thine ebon skin! Firmilian –
You'll hear of this! My brother serves the king.

Lilian   My uncle is the chief Inquisitor,
And he shall know of this ere curfew tolls!
What! Shall I share a husband with a coal?

Mariana   Right, girl! I love thee even for that word –   440
The Inquisition makes most rapid work,
And, in its books, that caitiff's name is down!

Firmilian   Listen one moment! When I was a babe,
And in my cradle puling for my nurse,
There fell a gleam of glory on the floor,
And in it, darkly standing, was a form –

Mariana   A negress, probably! Farewell awhile –
When next we meet – the faggot and the pile!

Come, Lillian!
Exeunt.

Indiana   I shake from head to foot with sore affright –   450
What will become of me?

Firmilian   Who cares? Good night!
Scene closes.

Bravo, Percy! The first part of that scene is managed with a dexterity which old Dekker[14] might have applauded, and the conclusion shows a perfect knowledge of womanly character and feeling. Firmilian is now cast beyond the pale of society, and in imminent danger, if apprehended, of taking a conspicuous part in an *auto-da-fé*. An author of inferior genius would probably have consigned him to the custody of the Familiars, in which case we should have had a dungeon and rack scene, if not absolute incremation as the catastrophe. But Jones knew better. He felt that such a cruel fate might, by the effect of contrast, revive some kind of sympathy in the mind of the reader for Firmilian, and he has accordingly adopted the wiser plan of depicting him as the victim of his own haunted imagination. The closing scene is so eminently graphic, and so perfectly original, that we give it entire.

> *A barren moor. Night – mist and fog. Enter Firmilian.*
> They're hot upon my traces!   Through the mist
> I heard their call and answer – and but now,
> As I was crouching 'neath a hawthorn bush,
> A dark Familiar swiftly glided by,
> His keen eyes glittering with the lust of death.
> If I am ta'en, the faggot and the pile
> Await me! Horror!   Rather would I dare,
> Like rash Empedocles, the Etna gulf,[15]   460
> Than writhe before the slaves of bigotry.
> Where am I?   If my mind deceives me not,
> Upon that common where, two years ago,
> An old blind beggar came and craved an alms,
> Thereby destroying a stupendous thought
> Just bursting in my mind – a glorious bud
> Of poesy, but blasted ere its bloom!
> I bade the old fool take the leftward path,
> Which leads to the deep quarry, where he fell –
> At least I deem so, for I heard a splash –   470
> But I was gazing on the gibbous moon,
> And durst not lower my celestial flight
> To care for such an insect-worm as he!
>   How cold it is!   The mist comes thicker on.
> Ha! – what is that?   I see around me lights
> Dancing and flitting, yet they do not seem
> Like torches either – and there's music too!
> I'll pause and listen.
>
> *Chorus of Ignes Fatui*
>   Follow, follow, follow!
>   Over hill and over hollow;   480
>   It is ours to lead the way,
>   When a sinner's footsteps stray –
>   Cheering him with light and song,

---

14   Thomas Dekker (*c.*1570–*c.*1641), London playwright.   15   Ancient Greek philosopher who reputedly threw himself into the crater of Mount Etna. Subject of a famous Matthew Arnold poem.

On his doubtful path along.
  Hark, hark!   The watch-dogs bark.
There's crash, and a splash, and a blind man's cry,
But the Poet looks tranquilly up at the sky!

Firmilian   Is it the echo of an inward voice,
Or spirit-words that make my flesh to creep,
And send the cold blood choking to my heart?   490
I'll shift my ground a little –

    Chorus of Ignes Fatui
    Flicker, flicker, flicker!
    Quicker still, and quicker.
    Four young men sate down to dine,
    And still they passed the rosy wine;
    Pure was the cask, but in the flask
    There lay a certain deadly powder –
    Ha! his heart is beating louder!
    Ere the day had passed away,
    Garcia Perez lifeless lay!   500
    Hark! his mother wails Alphonzo,
    Never more shall strong Alonzo
    Drink the wine of Ildefronso!

Firmilian   O horror! horror! 'twas by me they died!
I'll move yet farther on –

    Chorus of Ignes Fatui
    In the vaults under
    Bursts the red thunder;
    Up goes the cathedral,
    Priest, people, and bedral![16]
      Ho! ho! ho! ho!   510

Firmilian   My brain is whirling like a potter's wheel!
O Nemesis![17]

    Chorus of Ignes Fatui
    The Muses sing in their charmed ring,
    And Apollo weeps for him who sleeps,
    Alas! on a hard and a stony pillow –
    Haverillo! Haverillo!

Firmilian   I shall go mad!

    Chorus of Ignes Fatui
    Give him some respite – give him some praise –
    One good deed he has done in his days;
    Chaunt it, and sing it, and tell it in chorus –   520
    He has flattened the cockscomb of Apollodorus![18]

Firmilian   Small comfort that! The death of a shard-beetle,
Albeit the poorest and the paltriest thing
That crawls round refuse, cannot weigh a grain
Against the ponderous avalanche of guilt

---

16   church odd-job man (bellringer, sexton, gravedigger, etc.).   18   ?author of a prose treatise on the gods (just a cod rhyme).
17   Greek goddess who apportioned individual fate.

That hangs above me!   O me miserable!
I'll grope my way yet further.

> *Chorus of Ignes Fatui*
>   Firmilian! Firmilian!
>   What have you done to Lilian?
> There a cry from the grotto, a sob by the stream,   530
> A woman's loud wailing, a little babe's scream!
>   How fared it with Lilian,
>   In the pavilion,
>   Firmilian, Firmilian?

> *Firmilian*   Horror! I'm lost: –

> *Chorus of Ignes Fatui*
>   Ho! ho! ho!
>   Deep in the snow
> Lies a black maiden from Africa's shore!
>   Hasten, and shake her –
>   You never shall wake her –   540
> She'll roam through the glens of the Atlas no more!
>   Stay, stay, stay!
>   This way – this way –
> There's a pit before, and a pit behind,
> And the seeing man walks in the path of the blind!
> *Firmilian falls into the quarry. The Ignes Fatui dance as the curtain descends.*

And so ends the tragedy of Firmilian.

It is rather difficult to give a serious opinion upon the merits of such a production as this. It is, of course, utterly extravagant; but so are the whole of the writings of the poets of the Spasmodic school; and, in the eyes of a considerable body of modern critics, extravagance is regarded as a proof of extraordinary genius. It is, here and there, highly coloured; but that also is looked upon as a symptom of the divine afflatus, and rather prized than otherwise. In one point of proclaimed spasmodic excellence, perhaps it fails. You can always tell what Percy Jones is after, even when he is dealing with 'shuddering stars,' 'gibbous moons,' 'imposthumes of hell,' and the like; whereas you may read through twenty pages of the more ordinary stuff without being able to discern what the writers mean – and no wonder, for they really mean nothing. They are simply writing nonsense-verses; but they contrive, by blazing away whole rounds of metaphor, to mask their absolute poverty of thought, and to convey the impression that there must be something stupendous under so heavy a canopy of smoke. If, therefore, intelligibility, which is the highest degree of obscurity, is to be considered a poetic excellence, we are afraid that Jones must yield the palm to several of his contemporaries; if, on the contrary, perspicuity is to be regarded as a virtue, we do not hesitate in assigning the spasmodic prize to the author of *Firmilian*. To him the old lines on Marlowe, with the alteration of the name, might be applied –

> 'Next Percy Jones, bathed in the Thespian Springs,
> Had in him those brave sublunary Things
> That your first Poets had; his Raptures were
> All Air and Fire, which made his Verses clear;
> For that fierce Madness still he did retain,
> Which rightly should possess a Poet's Brain.'[19]

Blackwood's Magazine, *LXXV, no. 463 (May 1854), 533–51.*

---

19   Michael Drayton, (1563–1631), 'To My Most Dearely-Loved
Friend Henery Reynolds Esquire, of Poets and Poesie' (passage begin-
ning 'Neat Marlow bathed in the Thespian Springs').

Charlotte Brontë (1816–55)

Charlotte Brontë – one of the most important of Victorian novelists – was the third child of the Revd Patrick Brontë, Ulster-born Evangelical Anglican, and Maria Branwell, a Wesleyan Methodist from Penzance in Cornwall. Charlotte was born at Thornton, Yorkshire, 21 April 1816, in the heartland of Yorkshire Dissent, Methodism and Anglican Evangelicalism, and grew up in the vicarage of Haworth, to which parish her father was appointed in 1820. Her mother died in 1821, worn-out by child-bearing, and Methodist Aunt Branwell came up from Penzance to look after the large clutch of little ones – five sisters, Elizabeth, Maria, Charlotte, Emily, Anne, and brother Branwell. Patrick Brontë, crusty Tory patriot eccentrically given to firing his pistol of a morning across the graveyard next to the rectory (he kept it loaded by his bedside in case uprising workers, Luddites, and such, whom he'd preached against, should attack him in the night), was not as unkindly disposed as he is sometimes painted; nor was Aunt Branwell at all the prim Calvinist witch of the standard Winifred Gérin biographies of Charlotte and Emily, inspiring her charges with fears of Hell (she wasn't a Calvinist at all, but a Wesleyan Arminian who believed in the saving love of Christ for all humankind). A precocious motherless brood, the Brontë children's imaginations flourished in cultural isolation on tales of adventure and heroism fed by their father's Tory obsessions, the newspapers and local library books. Their invented plays were hot for the likes of the Duke of Wellington. After Maria and Elizabeth died in 1825, probably of fever contracted at the spartan Evangelical school for clergy daughters at Cowan Bridge to which all the girls were sent (featured as harsh Lowood School in Charlotte's *Jane Eyre*, 1847), the four remaining children huddled their fictional capacities together in celebration of the wastrel lives and loves of the extravagantly Byronic aristo inhabitants of Angria (Charlotte and Branwell) and Gondal (Emily and Anne) – set down in fetishistically tiny handwriting in extremely tiny hand-made books. These 'juvenilia' preoccupied the four Brontës for a surprisingly long time. Emily appears never to have given them up. Precocious immaturity was their persisting problem. Only Anne stuck it out as a working governess. Growing up and leaving would prove very hard for the others. None of Charlotte's spells away from Haworth as governess and schoolteacher were for very long. Intending to set up a school in the vicarage, Emily and Charlotte went to study French in 1842 at the Heger Pensionnat in Brussels. Their native Protestantism was deeply irked in Catholic Belgium. But still Charlotte returned there to teach in 1843. She stayed, though, barely a year, in yet one more failed attempt to get away from Haworth – driven out by Mme Heger's jealousy over Charlotte's obvious attraction to her husband (Charlotte's *Villette*, 1853, is the product of this episode). From an early age Charlotte and Branwell hankered for success in the outside literary world. He sent verses to Wordsworth, she to Robert Southey the Poet Laureate. Brush-offs never came more emphatically: Wordsworth never replied; Southey told Charlotte to beware 'day-dreams' and to go in for a woman's 'proper duties': 'Literature cannot be the business of a woman's life, and it ought not to be'. In later 1845 Charlotte found Emily's MS poems and the three surviving sisters then collaborated in *Poems by Currer, Ellis, and Acton Bell* (1846). The ambivalent pseudonyms were not so clearly male as actually to deceive (the sisters had 'a sort of conscientious scruple at assuming Christian names positively masculine'), but were still not clearly female ('we had a vague impression that authoresses are liable to be looked on with prejudice'). Publication cost them 30 guineas; they received only one review, and hardly any sales at all. Not at all encouraging; but they all started novels. Charlotte's first, *The Professor*, was widely rejected. Her second, *Jane Eyre: An Autobiography*, fared better: Smith, Elder brought it out in October 1847 to warm praise (G. H. Lewes reviewed it in *Fraser's Magazine*, contrasting it, a little obviously, with Jane Austen). As Branwell became wilder and drunker and more addicted to opium (he died in September 1848), the reclusive Emily faded away (dying December 1848), Anne sickened and died of consumption (May 1849) and her father grew more demanding, Charlotte continued with her novels *Shirley* (1849) and *Villette* – encouraged by Thackeray (to whom the second edition of *Jane Eyre* is dedicated), by Harriet Martineau, and by her eventual biographer Mrs Elizabeth Gaskell. Charlotte herself died, worn out, extremely nauseous, pregnant, at the end of March 1855 – seven months after her marriage to Patrick's curate Arthur Bell Nicolls, for which grudging parental permission had finally been granted. Of her verses in *Poems*, Charlotte told Mrs Gaskell they were 'chiefly juvenile productions, the restless effervescence of a mind that would not be still'. The poems are best seen as an adjunct to the fiction and part of Charlotte's grand narrative of the clash between yearning erotic temperaments desirous of emotional abandonment and fulfilment, and sterner disciplinary Protestant inclinations towards self-control and abnegation.

PRESENTIMENT

'Sister, you've sat there all the day,
    Come to the hearth a while;
The wind so wildly sweeps away,
    The clouds so darkly pile.
That open book has lain, unread,
    For hours upon your knee;
You've never smiled nor turned your head;
    What can you, sister, see?'

'Come hither, Jane, look down the field;
    How dense a mist creeps on!   10
The path, the hedge, are both concealed,
    Ev'n the white gate is gone;
No landscape through the fog I trace,
    No hill with pastures green;
All featureless is nature's face,
    All masked in clouds her mien.

'Scarce is the rustle of a leaf
    Heard in our garden now;
The year grows old, its days wax brief,
    The tresses leave its brow.   20
The rain drives fast before the wind,
    The sky is blank and grey;
O Jane, what sadness fills the mind
    On such a dreary day!'

'You think too much, my sister dear;
    You sit too long alone;
What though November days be drear?
    Full soon will they be gone.
I've swept the hearth, and placed your chair,
    Come, Emma, sit by me;   30
Our own fireside is never drear,
Though late and wintry wane the year,
    Though rough the night may be.'

'The peaceful glow of our fireside
    Imparts no peace to me:
My thoughts would rather wander wide
    Than rest, dear Jane, with thee.

I'm on a distant journey bound,
    And if, about my heart,
Too closely kindred ties were bound,   40
    'Twould break when forced to part.

'"Soon will November days be o'er" –
    Well have you spoken, Jane:
My own forebodings tell me more,
For me, I know by presage sure,
    They'll ne'er return again.
Ere long, nor sun nor storm to me
    Will bring or joy or gloom;
They reach not that Eternity
    Which soon will be my home.'   50

Eight months are gone, the summer sun
    Sets in a glorious sky;
A quiet field, all green and lone,
    Receives its rosy dye.
Jane sits upon a shaded stile,
    Alone she sits there now;
Her head rests on her hand the while
    And thought o'ercasts her brow.

She's thinking of one winter's day,
    A few short months ago,   60
When Emma's bier was borne away
    O'er wastes of frozen snow.
She's thinking how that drifted snow
    Dissolved in spring's first gleam,
And how her sister's memory now
    Fades, even as fades a dream.

The snow will whiten earth again,
    But Emma comes no more;
She left, 'mid winter's sleet and rain,
    This world for Heaven's far shore.   70
On Beulah's hills she wanders now,[1]
    On Eden's tranquil plain;[2]
To her shall Jane hereafter go,
    She ne'er shall come to Jane!

Written, May–11 July 1837. Poems by Currer, Ellis, and Acton Bell
(Aylott & Jones, May 1846).

THE MISSIONARY[1]

Plough, vessel, plough the British main,
Seek the free ocean's wider plain;
Leave English scenes and English skies,

Unbind, dissever English ties;
Bear me to climes remote and strange,
Where altered life, fast-following change,

PRESENTIMENT
1 Beulah Land: biblical pleasant place, became synonym for heaven in John Bunyan, *The Pilgrim's Progress*.

2 Eden: unfallen Paradise garden in Genesis (and Milton, *Paradise Lost*).
THE MISSIONARY
1 cf. St John Rivers in *Jane Eyre*: who goes as missionary to India.

Hot action, never-ceasing toil,
Shall stir, turn, dig, the spirit's soil;
Fresh roots shall plant, fresh seed shall sow,
Till a new garden there shall grow,   10
Cleared of the weeds that fill it now, –
Mere human love, mere selfish yearning,
Which, cherished, would arrest me yet.
I grasp the plough, there's no returning,
Let me, then, struggle to forget.

But England's shores are yet in view,
And England's skies of tender blue
Are arched above her guardian sea.
I cannot yet Remembrance flee;
I must again, then, firmly face   20
That task of anguish, to retrace.
Wedded to home – I home forsake;
Fearful of change – I changes make;
Too fond of ease – I plunge in toil;
Lover of calm – I seek turmoil:
Nature and hostile Destiny
Stir in my heart a conflict wild;
And long and fierce the war will be
Ere duty both has reconciled.

What other tie yet holds me fast   30
To the divorced, abandoned past?
Smouldering, on my heart's altar lies
The fire of some great sacrifice,
Not yet half quenched. The sacred steel
But lately struck my carnal will,
My life-long hope, first joy and last,
What I loved well, and clung to fast;
What I wished wildly to retain,
What I renounced with soul-felt pain;
What – when I saw it, axe-struck, perish –   40
Left me no joy on earth to cherish;
A man bereft – yet sternly now
I do confirm that Jephtha vow:[2]
Shall I retract, or fear, or flee?
Did Christ, when rose the fatal tree
Before Him, on Mount Calvary?
'Twas a long fight, hard fought, but won,
And what I did was justly done.

Yet, Helen! from thy love I turned,
When my heart most for thy heart burned;   50
I dared thy tears, I dared thy scorn –
Easier the death-pang had been borne.
Helen! thou mightst not go with me,
I could not – dared not stay for thee!
I heard afar, in bonds complain
The savage from beyond the main;
And that wild sound rose o'er the cry

Wrung out by passion's agony;
And even when, with the bitterest tear
I ever shed, mine eyes were dim,   60
Still, with the spirit's vision clear,
I saw Hell's empire, vast and grim,
Spread on each Indian river's shore,
Each realm of Asia covering o'er.
There, the weak, trampled by the strong,
Live but to suffer – hopeless die;
There pagan-priests, whose creed is Wrong,
Extortion, Lust, and Cruelty,
Crush our lost race – and brimming fill
The bitter cup of human ill;   70
And I – who have the healing creed,
The faith benign of Mary's Son,
Shall I behold my brother's need,
And selfishly to aid him shun?
I – who upon my mother's knees,
In childhood, read Christ's written word,
Received his legacy of peace,
His holy rule of action heard;
I – in whose heart the sacred sense
Of Jesus' love was early felt;   80
Of His pure full benevolence,
His pitying tenderness for guilt;
His shepherd-care for wandering sheep,
For all weak, sorrowing, trembling things,
His mercy vast, his passion deep
Of anguish for man's sufferings;
I – schooled from childhood in such lore –
Dared I draw back or hesitate,
When called to heal the sickness sore
Of those far off and desolate?   90
Dark, in the realm and shades of Death,
Nations and tribes and empires lie,
But even to them the light of Faith
Is breaking on their sombre sky:
And be it mine to bid them raise
Their drooped heads to the kindling scene,
And know and hail the sunrise blaze
Which heralds Christ the Nazarene.
I know how Hell the veil will spread
Over their brows and filmy eyes,   100
And earthward crush the lifted head
That would look up and seek the skies;
I know what war the fiend will wage
Against that soldier of the cross,
Who comes to dare his demon-rage,
And work his kingdom shame and loss.
Yes, hard and terrible the toil
Of him who steps on foreign soil,
Resolved to plant the gospel vine,
Where tyrants rule and slaves repine;   110
Eager to lift Religion's light

2   Jephtha, biblical type of promise-keeping unto death (his vow,
Judges ll. 30–40, led to his killing his daughter).

Where thickest shades of mental night
Screen the false god and fiendish rite;
Reckless that missionary blood,
Shed in wild wilderness and wood,
Has left, upon the unblest air,
The man's deep moan – the martyr's prayer.
I know my lot – I only ask
Power to fulfil the glorious task;
Willing the spirit, may the flesh   120
Strength for the day receive afresh.
May burning sun or deadly wind
Prevail not o'er an earnest mind;
May torments strange or direst death
Nor trample truth, nor baffle faith.
Though such blood-drops should fall from me
As fell in old Gethsemane,[3]
Welcome the anguish, so it gave
More strength to work – more skill to save.
And, oh! if brief must be my time,   130
If hostile hand or fatal clime
Cut short my course – still o'er my grave,
Lord, may Thy harvest whitening wave.
So I the culture may begin,
Let others thrust the sickle in;[4]

If but the seed will faster grow,
May my blood water what I sow!

What! have I ever trembling stood,
And feared to give to God that blood?
What! has the coward love of life   140
Made me shrink from the righteous strife?
Have human passions, human fears
Severed me from those Pioneers,
Whose task is to march first, and trace
Paths for the progress of our race?
It has been so; but grant me, Lord,
Now to stand steadfast by thy word!
Protected by salvation's helm,
Shielded by faith – with truth begirt,[5]
To smile when trials seek to whelm   150
And stand 'mid testing fires unhurt!
Hurling hell's strongest bulwarks down,
Even when the last pang thrills my breast,
When Death bestows the Martyr's crown,
And calls me into Jesus' rest.
Then for my ultimate reward –
Then for the world-rejoicing word –
The voice from Father – Spirit – Son:
'Servant of God, well hast thou done!'[6]

Poems by Currer, Ellis, and Acton Bell *(1846).*

The truest love that ever heart
  Felt at its kindled core
Did through each vein, in quickened start,
  The tide of being pour.

Her coming was my hope each day,
  Her parting was my pain;
The chance that did her steps delay,
  Was ice in every vein.

I dreamed it would be nameless bliss,
  As I loved, loved to be;   10
And to this object did I press
  As blind as eagerly.

But wide as pathless was the space
  That lay, our lives, between,
And dangerous as the foamy race
  Of ocean-surges green.

And haunted as a robber-path
  Through wilderness or wood;
For Might and Right, and Woe and Wrath,
  Between our spirits stood.   20

I dangers dared; I hindrance scorned;
  I omens did defy:
Whatever menaced, harassed, warned,
  I passed impetuous by.

On sped my rainbow, fast as light;
  I flew as in a dream;
For glorious rose upon my sight
  That child of Shower and Gleam.

Still bright on clouds of suffering dim
  Shines that soft, solemn joy;   30
Nor care I now, how dense and grim
  Disasters gather nigh:

I care not in this moment sweet,
  Though all I have rushed o'er
Should come on pinion, strong and fleet,
  Proclaiming vengeance sore:

Though haughty Hate should strike me down,
  Right, bar approach to me,
And grinding Might, with furious frown,
  Swear endless enmity.   40

---

3   Jesus 'sweat great drops of blood' in Gethsemane, Luke 22.44.
4   image from the Gospels of fields 'white already to harvest', waiting for reapers' sickle (conventionally read as metaphor for evangelistic effort).
5   biblical armour, Ephesians 6. 13–17.
6   cf. last words of *Jane Eyre.*

My love has placed her little hand
  With noble faith in mine,
And vowed that wedlock's sacred band
  Our natures shall entwine.

My love has sworn, with sealing kiss,
  With me to live – to die;
I have at last my nameless bliss:
  As I love – loved am I!

*Jane Eyre. An Autobiography, Edited by Currer Bell, 3 vols
(Smith, Elder, & Co., 1847), II, chapter LX (i.e. ch. 24). Rochester's Song.*

24 December

My darling,[1] thou wilt never know
The grinding agony of woe
  That we have borne for thee.
Thus may we consolation tear
E'en from the depth of our despair
  And wasting misery.

The nightly anguish thou art spared
When all the crushing truth is bared
  To the awakening mind,
When the galled heart is pierced with grief,   10
Till wildly it implores relief,
  But small relief can find.

Nor know'st thou what it is to lie
Looking forth with streaming eye
  On life's lone wilderness.
'Weary, weary, dark and drear,
How shall I the journey bear,
  The burden and distress?'

Then since thou art spared such pain
We will not wish thee here again;   20
  He that lives must mourn.
God help us through our misery
And give us rest and joy with thee
  When we reach our bourne!

Title as in MS. Text of Shakespeare Head edition, The Complete Poems of
Charlotte Brontë and Patrick Branwell Brontë, *ed. T. J. Wise and
J. A. Symington (Oxford, 1934).*

21 June 1849

There's little joy in life for me,
  And little terror in the grave;
I've lived the parting hour to see
  Of one I would have died to save.[1]

Calmly to watch the failing breath,
  Wishing each sigh might be the last;
Longing to see the shade of death
  O'er those belovèd features cast.

The cloud, the stillness that must part
  The darling of my life from me;   10
And then to thank God from my heart,
  To thank Him well and fervently;

Although I knew that we had lost
  The hope and glory of our life;
And now, benighted, tempest-tossed,
  Must bear alone the weary strife.

Title as in MS. Text of Shakespeare Head edition, Complete Poems *(1934).*

(Patrick) Branwell Brontë (1817–48)

Branwell Brontë, brother of the more famous sisters Brontë, and sad failure in his efforts to become a man of letters, dragged out his dismal progress as provincial rake mainly in the Yorkshire of his birth. He was born at Thornton, Yorkshire, 23 July 1817, fourth child and only son of the Evangelical Ulster-born perpetual curate, i.e.

24 December
1 Emily Brontë, who died 19 December 1848.

21 June 1849
1 Anne Brontë, who died, Scarborough, 28 May 1849, four days after leaving Haworth, with Charlotte – who returned to Haworth, 21 June.

vicar, of that parish, the Revd Patrick Brontë, and his wife, Penzance Methodist Maria Branwell. Mrs Brontë died of cancer, 15 September 1821, a few months after the family's move to the vicarage in Haworth and father's new post as perpetual curate of one of the strongest Dissenting and Methodist parishes in the land. The children were brought up by their Aunt Branwell, a woman erroneously painted by some biographers as harsh and Calvinist (she was neither), in a curious atmosphere of spartan domesticity, rough parental eccentricity (father firing his pistol, weapon against uprising radicals, across the graveyard first thing every morning), and a rather cultivated liberalism (they had drawing and music lessons, enjoyed the freedom of their father's books and the local Mechanics' Institute Library, and were left in peace to read the standard English poets, including the notorious Byron, as well as a strikingly mixed bag of journals, *Blackwood's*, *Fraser's*, and the *Methodist Magazine*). Unlike his sisters, Branwell was schooled at home by his father. Like his older sister, Charlotte, to whom he was closest, Branwell early on developed literary ambitions. In June 1826, momentously, Father brought home a set of twelve toy soldiers from Leeds, which instantly stimulated the precocious clutch of children to produce little plays and stories. Charlotte and Branwell collaborated on the twelve soldiers' African adventures, the Angrian stories. Soon Charlotte was moving her Angrian plots in the direction of love affairs, while Branwell, especially when left to himself while Charlotte was away at school, leaned more aggressively towards rebellion and warfare and the heroics of a character of his invention called at first, and proleptically no doubt, Rogue. In 1835 Branwell went down to London, apparently with ambitions to attend the Royal Academy as an art student (Charlotte had to leave home to work as a governess to help pay his fees). But after touring the taverns and watching some of the prize-fights he was keen on, Branwell slunk home, tail between his legs, in the first of his many open defeats

and retreats. Charlotte sent some of her poems to Poet Laureate Southey at the end of 1836, prompting Branwell to write to Wordsworth, 19 January 1837. Southey replied, albeit discouragingly; Wordsworth quite ignored Branwell's missive. From then on Branwell's career was manifestly on the skids. He made bits of money painting portraits; lived for a while in Bradford; attempted private tutoring; worked for a couple of dismal years as a clerk on the Leeds–Manchester railway (at Sowerby Bridge; then at Luddenden Foot), and was sacked for negligence in 1842. He became a tutor to the son of the Robinson family at Thorp Green where Anne was governess; said he was encouraged in passion for the mistress of the house ('daily troubled pleasure', for three years, he claimed), and was dismissed in July 1845, returning to Haworth thinking the older woman would marry him when her husband died (she didn't). (Later commentators, more sceptical than Charlotte's biographer Mrs Gaskell, have suggested that Branwell was detected in homosexual advances to young Edmund Robinson.) Back at home yet again, Branwell's intake of drink and laudanum zoomed; he had the DTs; became utterly trying to live with, the pain and bane of his father's and sisters' lives. He wrote verses to the last, and finished at least one volume of a three-decker novel. More and more deluded, hallucinating, raving and raging, sad, a rank failure in art as in life (rebukingly shut out of the collaborative volume of *Poems* by the 'Bell' sisters (May 1846), and galled no doubt at the success of his long-time literary collaborator Charlotte with *Jane Eyre*, 1847), he died, apparently of consumption, 26 September 1848, aged only thirty-one. The famous group portrait of his sisters is by him. The canvas has a curious smeary blank area in it which some people think is where he (or one of them) rubbed him out of the picture. The great hostility to alcoholic drink in Anne Brontë's *The Tenant of Wildfell Hall* (1848) undoubtedly owes much to her brother's excesses.

Why dost thou sorrow for the happy dead?
For if their life be lost, their toils are o'er
    And woe and want can trouble them no more,
Nor ever slept they in an earthly bed
So sound as now they sleep while, dreamless, laid
    In the dark chambers of the unknown shore
    Where Night and Silence seal each guarded door:
So, turn from such as these thy drooping head
And mourn the 'Dead alive' whose spirit flies –
    Whose life departs before his death has come –   10
Who finds no Heaven beyond Life's gloomy skies,
    Who sees no Hope to brighten up that gloom,
'Tis He who feels the worm that never dies –
    The REAL death and darkness of the tomb.

Composition began, 1837 (?). Published, Halifax Guardian, *14 May 1842.*
Text, The Poems of Patrick Branwell Brontë, *ed. Tom Winnifrith*
(published for the Shakespeare Head Press, by Basil Blackwell, 1983).

THORP GREEN

I sit, this evening, far away
   From all I used to know,
And nought reminds my soul to-day
   Of happy long ago.

Unwelcome cares, unthought-of fears,
   Around my room arise;
I seek for suns of former years,
   But clouds o'ercast my skies.

Yes – Memory, wherefore does thy voice
   Bring old times back to view,   10
As thou wouldst bid me not rejoice
   In thoughts and prospects new?

I'll thank thee, Memory, in the hour
   When troubled thoughts are mine –
For thou, like suns in April's shower,
   On shadowy scenes wilt shine.

I'll thank thee when approaching death
   Would quench life's feeble ember,
For thou wouldst even renew my breath
   With thy sweet word 'Remember'!   20

Dated 30 March 1843. Text, Poems*, ed. Winnifrith (1983).*

When all our cheerful hours seem gone for ever,
All lost that caused the body or the mind
To nourish love or friendship for our kind,
And Charon's boat, prepared, o'er Lethe's river
Our souls to waft, and all our thoughts to sever
From what was once life's Light; still there may be
Some well-loved bosom to whose pillow we
Could heartily our utter self deliver;
And if, toward her grave – Death's dreary road –
Our Darling's feet should tread, each step by her   10
Would draw our own steps to the same abode,
And make a festival of sepulture;
For what gave joy, and joy to us had owed,
Should Death affright us from, when he would her restore?

Dated (28) April 1846. Text, Poems*, ed. Winnifrith (1983).*

George Henry Lewes (1817–78)

George Henry Lewes (pronounced, and sometimes mis-spelt in his time, as Lew-*is*), biographer, philosophical and scientific speculator, editor, one of the shrewdest of Victorian critics as well as George Eliot's partner and agent, was born in 1817. His grandfather was Charles Lee Lewes, a comic actor of a certain reputation. His father was a literary man of some kind who disappeared when Lewes was young. His stepfather, a Captain Willim, Lewes disliked. The common word for Lewes's education was 'desultory' (Trollope used it; as did Leslie Stephen in the *DNB*). Lewes and his two brothers went to various schools in London, Jersey and France. Along the way Lewes's French became very good, and he wrote usefully on French authors like Dumas, Balzac and George Sand,

and became (briefly) a follower of Auguste Comte. He may well have studied medicine, and tried acting (later he joined Dickens's fund-raising troupe of actors; he also reviewed drama and wrote plays himself). A classic autodidact of the time, he was early on drawn into the radical freethinking Shelley-admiring world of old Leigh Hunt, a working-class intelligentsia on the fringes of heterodox Unitarian Christianity (a 'theological pariah', he called himself). These were people who met in a pub in Red Lion Square, Holborn (a traditionally radical part of London), to discuss philosophy (Spinoza, for example) at a Saturday night club of radicals and readers (a second-hand bookstall owner, a cobbler, a German Jewish watch-maker, Lewes himself, a student of anatomy, and all else). Lewes visited Germany in 1838, armed with introductions to Goethe's friends Eckermann and Von Ense, learned German, became a Goethe enthusiast (he produced the standard *Life and Works of Goethe*, in 1855). He became a key figure in radical literary London – a steady contributor to the *Westminster* and the *Edinburgh Review*, co-founder with Thornton Hunt (Leigh Hunt's son) of the *Leader* (1850), editor of the *Fortnightly Review* in its first year (1865–6), editorial adviser to Thackeray in the setting up of the *Cornhill Magazine* in 1860. He was simply omnipresent. He was polymathic too, producing in addition to his plays and a couple of bad novels, *Ranthorpe* (1847) and *Rose, Blanche, and Violet* (1848), hundreds of articles on everything from *Jane Eyre* (he greatly encouraged Charlotte Brontë) and table-rapping, to evolution and spontaneous combustion (this last the subject at the centre of a protracted quarrel with Dickens over the fiery death of Krook in *Bleak House*). True to his sexually liberated views, Lewes had condoned his wife Agnes's adultery with his friend Thornton Hunt, had registered Hunt's children by Agnes as his own, and thus forwent his legal right to claim a divorce when he would have liked to marry Marian Evans, the freethinking young assistant on John Chapman's *Westminster Review*, whom he first met in 1850. In 1854 Miss Evans and Lewes (the ugliest man in London, people said; though Charlotte Brontë thought he resembled her sister Emily) scandalously left for Weimar together as a pseudo-married couple. Lewes encouraged his new partner, the future George Eliot, into fiction, and fought hard both to keep her happy as a writer and also to ensure she received high advances and royalties. Some professionals sneered at his writings on psychology and physiology, but Darwin, T. H. Huxley and Pavlov were among admirers of his numerous scientific articles and books. Lewes gets into Raskolnikov's life and thought in Dostoevsky's *Crime and Punishment* (1866), chapter 2. As a critic Lewes often hits the nail on the head (George Bernard Shaw said he modelled his own drama criticism on Lewes's). Robert Browning's realism is 'rough' but truthful; Browning plays difficult rhymes 'as an Indian juggler plays with balls'. In Elizabeth Barrett Browning's verse 'The form of the vase is beautiful, and its arabesque tracery flatters the eye; but the material is fragile or indifferent'; she's not enough of 'our work-day world'. Unlike Milton in *Lycidas*, Tennyson in *In Memoriam* 'weeps himself'. And so on. Lewes's position in the Victorian realism debate – pro truth to 'the currents of life', but wary of detailism and ugliness ('Realism in Art has Truth as its Aim, Ugliness as a Pitfall', as he put it of Browning in the *Leader*, 27 April 1850) – is crucial. He became increasingly unwell in later years, but soldiered on, ever diligent, sceptical and versatile, greatly loved by his long-time companion. He died at their home, the Priory, St John's Wood, 28 November 1878.

THE PRINCIPLES OF SUCCESS IN LITERATURE

Ch. 3:   Of Vision in Art

I

There are many who will admit, without hesitation, that in Philosophy what I have called the Principle of Vision holds an important rank, because the mind must necessarily err in its speculations unless it clearly sees facts and relations; but there are some who will hesitate before admitting the principle to a similar rank in Art, because, as they conceive, Art is independent of the truth of facts, and is swayed by the autocratic power of Imagination.

It is on this power that our attention should first be arrested; the more so because it is usually spoken of in vague rhapsodical language, with intimations of its being something peculiarly mysterious. There are few words more abused. The artist is called a creator, which in one sense he is: and his creations are said to be produced by processes wholly unallied to the creations of Philosophy, which they are not. Hence it is a paradox to speak of the 'Principia',[1] as a creation demanding severe and continuous exercise of the imagination; but it is only a paradox to those who have never analysed the processes of artistic and philosophic creation.

THE PRINCIPLES OF SUCCESS IN LITERATURE
1   Sir Isaac Newton, *Philosophiae Naturalis Principia Mathematicae* (1687).

I am far from desiring to innovate in language, or to raise interminable discussions respecting the terms in general use. Nevertheless we have here to deal with questions that lie deeper than mere names. We have to examine processes, and trace, if possible, the methods of intellectual activity pursued in all branches of Literature; and we must not suffer our course to be obstructed by any confusion in terms that can be cleared up. We may respect the demarcations established by usage, but we must ascertain, if possible, the fundamental affinities. There is, for instance, a broad distinction between Science and Art, which, so far from requiring to be effaced, requires to be emphasised: it is that in Science the paramount appeal is to the Intellect – its purpose being instruction; in Art, the paramount appeal is to the Emotions – its purpose being pleasure. A work of Art must of course indirectly appeal to the Intellect, and a work of Science will also indirectly appeal to the Feelings; nevertheless a poem on the stars and a treatise on astronomy have distinct aims and distinct methods. But having recognised the broadly-marked differences, we are called upon to ascertain the underlying resemblances. Logic and Imagination belong equally to both. It is only because men have been attracted by the differences that they have overlooked the not less important affinities. Imagination is an intellectual process common to Philosophy and Art; but in each it is allied with different processes, and directed to different ends; and hence, although the 'Principia' demanded an imagination of not less vivid and sustained power than was demanded by 'Othello', it would be very false psychology to infer that the mind of Newton was competent to the creation of 'Othello', or the mind of Shakespeare capable of producing the 'Principia'. They were specifically different minds; their works were specifically different. But in both the imagination was intensely active. Newton had a mind predominantly ratiocinative: its movement was spontaneously towards the abstract relations of things. Shakespeare had a mind predominantly emotive, the intellect always moving in alliance with the feelings, and spontaneously fastening upon the concrete facts in preference to their abstract relations. Their mental Vision was turned towards images of different orders, and it moved in alliance with different faculties; but this Vision was the cardinal quality of both. Dr Johnson was guilty of a surprising fallacy in saying that a great mathematician might also be a great poet: 'Sir, a man can walk east as far as he can walk west.' True, but mathematics and poetry do not differ as east and west; and he would hardly assert that a man who could walk twenty miles could therefore swim that distance.

The real state of the case is somewhat obscured by our observing that many men of science, and some even eminent as teachers and reporters, display but slender claims to any unusual vigour of imagination. It must be owned that they are often slightly dull; and in matters of Art are not unfreqently blockheads. Nay, they would themselves repel it as a slight if the epithet 'imaginative' were applied to them; it would seem to impugn their gravity, to cast doubts upon their accuracy. But such men are the cisterns, not the fountains,[2] of Science. They rely upon the knowledge already organised; they do not bring accessions to the common stock. They are not investigators, but imitators; they are not discoverers – inventors. No man ever made a discovery (he may have stumbled on one) without the exercise of as much imagination as, employed in another direction and in alliance with other faculties, would have gone to the creation of a poem. Every one who has seriously investigated a novel question, who has really interrogated Nature with a view to a distinct answer, will bear me out in saying that it requires intense and sustained effort of imagination. The relations of sequence among the phenomena must be seen; they are hidden; they can only be seen mentally; a thousand suggestions rise before the mind, but they are recognised as old suggestions, or as inadequate to reveal what is sought; the experiments by which the problem may be solved have to be imagined; and to imagine a good experiment is as difficult as to invent a good fable, for we must have distinctly *present* – in clear mental vision – the known qualities and relations of all the objects, and must *see* what will be the effect of introducing some new qualifying agent. If any one thinks this is easy, let him try it: the trial will teach him a lesson respecting the methods of intellectual activity not without its use. Easy enough, indeed, is the ordinary practice of experiments already devised (as ordinary story-tellers re-tell the stories of others), or else a haphazard,

2   refers to Coleridge's image of original poets as 'fountains': 1816
preface to his poem *Christabel*.

blundering way of bringing phenomena together, to see what will happen. To invent is another process. The discoverer and the poet are inventors; and they are so because their mental vision detects the unapparent, unsuspected facts, almost as vividly as ocular vision rests on the apparent and familiar.

It is the special aim of Philosophy to discover and systematise the abstract *relations* of things; and for this purpose it is forced to allow the things themselves to drop out of sight, fixing attention solely on the quality immediately investigated, to the neglect of all other qualities. Thus the philosopher, having to appreciate the mass, density, refracting power, or chemical constitution of some object, finds he can best appreciate this by isolating it from every other detail. He abstracts this one quality from the complex bundle of qualities which constitute the object, and he makes this one stand for the whole. This is a necessary simplification. If all the qualities were equally present to his mind, his vision would be perplexed by their multiple suggestions. He may follow out the relations of each in turn, but he cannot follow them out together.

The aim of the poet is very different. He wishes to kindle the emotions by the suggestion of objects themselves; and for this purpose he must present images of the objects rather than of any single quality. It is true that he also must exercise a power of abstraction and selection. He cannot without confusion present all the details. And it is here that the fine selective instinct of the true artist shows itself, in knowing what details to present and what to omit. Observe this: the abstraction of the philosopher is meant to keep the object itself, with its perturbing suggestions, out of sight, allowing only one quality to fill the field of vision; whereas the abstraction of the poet is meant to bring the object itself into more vivid relief, to make it visible by means of the selected qualities. In other words, the one aims at abstract symbols, the other at picturesque effects. The one can carry on his deductions by the aid of colourless signs, x or y. The other appeals to the emotions through the symbols which will most vividly express the real objects in their relations to our sensibilities.

Imagination is obviously active in both. From known facts the philosopher infers the facts that are unapparent. He does so by an effort of imagination (hypothesis) which has to be subjected to verification: he makes a mental picture of the unapparent fact, and then sets about to prove that his picture does in some way correspond with the reality. The correctness of his hypothesis and verification must depend on the clearness of his vision. Were all the qualities of things apparent to Sense, there would be no longer any mystery. A glance would be Science. But only some of the facts are visible; and it is because we see little, that we have to imagine much. We see a feather rising in the air, and a quill, from the same bird, sinking to the ground: these contradictory reports of sense lead the mind astray; or perhaps excite a desire to know the reason. We cannot see, – we must imagine, – the unapparent facts. Many mental pictures may be formed, but to form the one which corresponds with the reality requires great sagacity and a very clear vision of known facts. In trying to form this mental picture we remember that when the air is removed the feather falls as rapidly as the quill, and thus we *see* that the air is the cause of the feather's rising; we mentally see the air pushing under the feather, and see it almost as plainly as if the air were a visible mass thrusting the feather upwards.

From a mistaken appreciation of the real process this would by few be called an effort of Imagination. On the contrary some 'wild hypothesis' would be lauded as imaginative in proportion as it departed from all suggestion of experience, i.e., real mental vision. To have imagined that the feather rose owing to its 'specific lightness' and that the quill fell owing to its 'heaviness', would to many appear a more decided effort of the imaginative faculty. Whereas it is no effort of that faculty at all; it is simply naming differently the facts it pretends to explain. To imagine – to form an image – we must have the numerous relations of things present to the mind, and see the objects in their actual order. In this we are of course greatly aided by the mass of organised experience, which allows us rapidly to estimate the relations of gravity or affinity just as we remember that fire burns and that heated bodies expand. But be the aid great or small, and the result victorious or disastrous, the imaginative process is always the same.

There is a slighter strain on the imagination of the poet, because of his greater freedom. He is not, like the philosopher, limited to the things which are, or were. His vision includes things which might be, and things which never were. The philosopher is not entitled to assume that Nature sympathises with man; he must prove the fact to be so if he intend making any use of it; – we admit no deductions from unproved assumptions. But the poet is at perfect liberty to assume this; and having done so, he paints what would be the manifestations of this sympathy. The naturalist who should describe a hippogriff would incur the laughing scorn of Europe; but the poet feigns its existence, and all Europe is delighted when it rises with Astolfo in the air.[3] We never pause to ask the poet whether such an animal exists. He has seen it, and we see it with his eyes. Talking trees do not startle us in Virgil and Tennyson. Puck and Titania, Hamlet and Falstaff, are as true for us as Luther and Napoleon, so long as we are in the realm of Art. We grant the poet a free privilege because he will use it only for our pleasure. In Science pleasure is not an object, and we give no licence.

Philosophy and Art both render the invisible visible by imagination. Where Sense observes two isolated objects, Imagination discloses two related objects. This relation is the nexus visible. We had not seen it before; it is apparent now. Where we should only see a calamity the poet makes us see a tragedy. Where we could only see a sunrise he enables us to see 'Day like a mighty river flowing in.'

Imagination is not the exclusive appanage of artists, but belongs in varying degrees to all men. It is simply the power of forming images. Supplying the energy of Sense where Sense cannot reach, it brings into distinctness the facts, obscure or occult, which are grouped round an object or an idea, but which are not actually present to Sense. Thus, at the aspect of a windmill, the mind forms images of many characteristic facts relating to it; and the kind of images will depend very much on the general disposition, or particular mood, of the mind affected by the object: the painter, the poet, and the moralist will have different images suggested by the presence of the windmill or its symbol. There are indeed sluggish minds so incapable of self-evolved activity, and so dependent on the immediate suggestions of Sense, as to be almost destitute of the power of forming distinct images beyond the immediate circle of sensuous associations; and these are rightly named unimaginative minds; but in all minds of energetic activity, groups and clusters of images, many of them representing remote relations, spontaneously present themselves in conjunction with objects or their symbols. It should, however, be borne in mind that Imagination can only recall what Sense has previously impressed. No man imagines any detail of which he has not previously had direct or indirect experience. Objects as fictitious as mermaids and hippogriffs are made up from the gatherings of Sense.

'Made up from the gatherings of Sense' is a phrase which may seem to imply some peculiar plastic power such as is claimed exclusively for artists: a power not of simple recollection, but of recollection and recombination. Yet this power belongs also to philosophers. To combine the half of a woman with the half of a fish, – to imagine the union as an existing organism, – is not really a different process from that of combining the experience of a chemical action with an electric action, and seeing that the two are one existing fact. When the poet hears the storm-cloud muttering, and sees the moonlight sleeping on the bank, he transfers his experience of human phenomena to the cloud and the moonlight: he personifies, draws Nature within the circle of emotion, and is called a poet. When the philosopher sees electricity in the storm-cloud, and sees the sunlight stimulating vegetable growth, he transfers his experience of physical phenomena to these objects, and draws within the circle of Law phenomena which hitherto have been unclassified. Obviously the imagination has been as active in the one case as in the other; the *differentia* lying in the purposes of the two, and in the general constitution of the two minds.

It has been noted that there is less strain on the imagination of the poet; but even his greater freedom is not altogether disengaged from the necessity of verification; his images must have at least subjective truth; if they do not accurately correspond with objective realities, they must correspond with our sense of congruity. No poet is allowed the licence of creating images inconsistent with our conceptions. If he said the moonlight *burnt* the bank, we should reject the image as untrue,

3   Duke Astolpho, and fabulous half-griffin half-horse creature, from
Ariosto's *Orlando Furioso* (1516), the great Italian epic poem.

inconsistent with our conceptions of moonlight; whereas the gentle repose of the moonlight on the bank readily associates itself with images of sleep.

The often mooted question, What is Imagination? thus receives a very clear and definite answer. It is the power of forming images; it reinstates, in a visible group, those objects which are invisible, either from absence or from imperfection of our senses. That is its generic character. Its specific character, which marks it off from Memory, and which is derived from the powers of selection and recombination, will be expounded further on. Here I only touch upon its chief characteristic, in order to disengage the term from that mysteriousness which writers have usually assigned to it, thereby rendering philosophic criticism impossible. Thus disengaged it may be used with more certainty in an attempt to estimate the imaginative power of various works.

Hitherto the amount of that power has been too frequently estimated according to the extent of *departure* from ordinary experience in the images selected. Nineteen out of twenty would unhesitatingly declare that a hippogriff was a greater effort of imagination than a well-conceived human character; a Peri[4] than a woman; Puck or Titania than Falstaff or Imogen. A description of Paradise extremely unlike any known garden must, it is thought, necessarily be more imaginative than the description of a quiet rural nook. It may be more imaginative; it may be less so. All depends upon the mind of the poet. To suppose that it must, because of its departure from ordinary experience, is a serious error. The muscular effort required to draw a cheque for a thousand pounds might as reasonably be thought greater than that required for a cheque of five pounds; and much as the one cheque seems to surpass the other in value, the result of presenting both to the bankers may show that the more modest cheque is worth its full five pounds, whereas the other is only so much waste paper. The description of Paradise may be a glittering farrago; the description of the landscape may be full of sweet rural images: the one having a glare of gaslight and Vauxhall[5] splendour; the other having the scent of new-mown hay.

A work is imaginative in virtue of the power of its images over our emotions; not in virtue of any rarity or surprisingness in the images themselves. A Madonna and Child by Fra Angelico is more powerful over our emotions than a Crucifixion by a vulgar artist; a beggar-boy by Murillo is more imaginative than an Assumption by the same painter; but the Assumption by Titian displays far greater imagination than either. We must guard against the natural tendency to attribute to the artist what is entirely due to accidental conditions. A tropical scene, luxuriant with tangled overgrowth and impressive in the grandeur of its phenomena, may more decisively arrest our attention than an English landscape with its green corn lands and plenteous homesteads. But this superiority of interest is no proof of the artist's superior imagination; and by a spectator familiar with the tropics, greater interest may be felt in the English landscape, because its images may more forcibly arrest his attention by their novelty. And were this not so, were the inalienable impressiveness of tropical scenery always to give the poet who described it a superiority in effect, this would not prove the superiority of his imagination. For either he has been familiar with such scenes, and imagines them just as the other poet imagines his English landscape – by an effort of mental vision, calling up the absent objects; or he has merely read the descriptions of others, and from these makes up his picture. It is the same with his rival, who also recalls and recombines. Foolish critics often betray their ignorance by saying that a painter or a writer 'only copies what he has seen, or puts down what he has known'. They forget that no man imagines what he has not seen or known, and that it is in the *selection of the characteristic details* that the artistic power is manifested. Those who suppose that familiarity with scenes or characters enables a painter or a novelist to 'copy' them with artistic effect, forget the well-known fact that the vast majority of men are painfully incompetent to avail themselves of this familiarity, and cannot form vivid pictures even to themselves of scenes in which they pass their daily lives; and if they could imagine these, they would need the delicate selective instinct to guide them in the admission and omission of details, as well as in the groupings of the images. Let any one try to 'copy' the wife or brother he knows so well, – to make a human image which shall speak and act so as to impress strangers with a belief in

4 middle-eastern fairy, originating in Persian myth.   5 London pleasure-garden.

its truth, – and he will then see that the much-despised reliance on actual experience is not the mechanical procedure it is believed to be. When Scott drew Saladin and Coeur de Lion[6] he did not really display more imaginative power than when he drew the Mucklebackits,[7] although the majority of readers would suppose that the one demanded a great effort of imagination, whereas the other formed part of his familiar experiences of Scottish life. The mistake here lies in confounding the sources from which the materials were derived with the plastic power of forming these materials into images. More conscious effort may have been devoted to the collection of the materials in the one case than in the other, but that this has nothing to do with the imaginative power employed may readily be proved by an analysis of the intellectual processes of composition. Scott had often been in fishermen's cottages and heard them talk; from the registered experience of a thousand details relating to the life of the poor, their feelings and their thoughts, he gained that material upon which his imagination could work; in the case of Saladin and Coeur de Lion he had to gain these principally through books and his general experience of life; and the images he formed – the vision he had of Mucklebackit and Saladin – must be set down to his artistic faculty, not to his experience or erudition.

It has been well said by a very imaginative writer,[8] that 'when a poet floats in the empyrean, and only takes a bird's-eye view of the earth, some people accept the mere fact of his soaring for sublimity, and mistake his dim vision of earth for proximity to heaven.' And in like manner, when a thinker frees himself from all the trammels of fact, and propounds a 'bold hypothesis', people mistake the vagabond erratic flights of guessing for a higher range of philosophic power. In truth, the imagination is most tasked when it has to paint pictures which shall withstand the silent criticism of general experience, and to frame hypotheses which shall withstand the confrontation with facts. I cannot here enter into the interesting question of Realism and Idealism in Art, which must be debated in a future chapter; but I wish to call special attention to the psychological fact, that fairies and demons, remote as they are from experience, are not created by a more vigorous effort of imagination than milk maids and poachers. The intensity of vision in the artist and of vividness in his creations are the sole tests of his imaginative power.

II

If this brief exposition has carried the reader's assent, he will readily apply the principle, and recognise that an artist produces an effect in virtue of the distinctness with which he sees the objects he represents, seeing them not vaguely as in vanishing apparitions, but steadily, and in their most characteristic relations. To this Vision he adds artistic skill with which to make us see. He may have clear conceptions, yet fails to make them clear to us: in this case he has imagination, but is not an artist. Without clear Vision no skill can avail. Imperfect Vision necessitates imperfect representation; words take the place of ideas.

In Young's 'Night Thoughts' there are many examples of the *pseudo*-imaginative, betraying an utter want of steady Vision. Here is one: –

> His hands the good man fixes on the skies,
> And bids earth roll, nor feels the idle whirl.[9]

'Pause for a moment,' remarks a critic, 'to realise the image, and the monstrous absurdity of a man's grasping the skies and hanging habitually suspended there, while he contemptuously bids earth roll, warns you that no genuine feeling could have suggested so unnatural a conception.'[10] It is obvious that if Young had imagined the position he assigned to the good man he would have seen its absurdity; instead of imagining, he allowed the vague transient suggestion of half-nascent images to shape themselves in verse.

---

6   Walter Scott, *The Talisman* (1825).
7   Scott, *The Antiquary* (1816).
8   George Eliot, in 'Worldliness and Other-Worldliness: the Poet Young', *Westminster Review* (January 1857).

9   Edward Young, *Night Thoughts*, IV (1743), 561–2.
10   George Eliot, again, in 'Worldliness and Other-Worldliness: the Poet Young.'

Now compare with this a passage in which imagination is really active. Wordsworth recalls how –

> In November days
> When vapours rolling down the valleys made
> A lonely scene more lonesome: among the woods
> At noon; and mid the calm of summer nights,
> When by the margin of the trembling lake
> Beneath the gloomy hills homeward I went
> In solitude, such intercourse was mine.

There is nothing very grand or impressive in this passage, and therefore it is a better illustration for my purpose. Note how happily the one image, out of a thousand possible images by which November might be characterised, is chosen to call up in us the feeling of the lonely scene; and with what delicate selection the calm of summer nights, the 'trembling lake' (an image in an epithet), and the gloomy hills, are brought before us. His boyhood might have furnished him with a hundred different pictures, each as distinct as this; power is shown in selecting this one – painting it so vividly. He continues: –

> 'Twas mine among the fields both day and night
> And by the waters, all the summer long.
> And in the frosty season, when the sun
> Was set, and, visible for many a mile
> The cottage windows through the twilight blazed,
> I heeded not the summons: happy time
> It was indeed for all of us; for me
> It was a time of rapture! Clear and loud
> The village clock tolled six – I wheeled about,
> Proud and exulting like an untired horse
> That cares not for his home. All shod with steel
> We hissed along the polished ice, in games
> Confederate, imitative of the chase
> And woodland pleasures – the resounding horn,
> The pack loud-chiming and the hunted hare.

There is nothing very felicitous in these lines; yet even here the poet, if languid, is never false. As he proceeds the vision brightens, and the verse becomes instinct with life: –

> So through the darkness and the cold we flew
> And not a voice was idle: with the din
> Smitten, the precipices rang aloud;
> *The leafless trees and every icy crag*
> *Tinkled like iron; while the distant hills*
> *Into the tumult sent an alien sound*
> *Of melancholy*, not unnoticed while the stars
> Eastwards were sparkling clear, and in the west
> The orange sky of evening died away.
> Not seldom from the uproar I retired
> Into a silent bay, or sportively
> Glanced sideway, leaving the tumultuous throng,
> *To cut across the reflex of a star;*
> *Image that flying still before me* gleamed
> Upon the glassy plain: and oftentime
> When we had given our bodies to the wind
> *And all the shadowy banks on either side*
> *Came creeping through the darkness,* spinning still
> The rapid line of motion, then at once
> Have I reclining back upon my heels

> Stopped short; yet still the solitary cliffs
> Wheeled by me – even as if the earth had rolled
> With visible motion her diurnal round!
> Behind me did they stretch in solemn train,
> Feebler and feebler, and I stood and watched
> Till all was tranquil as a summer sea.[11]

Every poetical reader will feel delight in the accuracy with which the details are painted, and the marvellous clearness with which the whole scene is imagined, both in its objective and subjective relations, i.e., both in the objects seen and the emotions they suggest.

What the majority of modern verse writers call 'imagery', is not the product of imagination, but a restless pursuit of comparison, and a lax use of language. Instead of presenting us with an image of the object, they present us with something which they tell us is like the object – which it rarely is. The thing itself has no clear significance to them, it is only a text for the display of their ingenuity. If, however, we turn from poetasters to poets, we see great accuracy in depicting the things themselves or their suggestions, so that we may be certain the things presented themselves in the field of the poet's vision, and were painted because seen. The images arose with sudden vivacity, or were detained long enough to enable their characters to be seized. It is this power of detention to which I would call particular notice, because a valuable practical lesson may be learned through a proper estimate of it. If clear Vision be indispensable to success in Art, all means of securing that clearness should be sought. Now one means is that of detaining an image long enough before the mind to allow of its being seen in all its characteristics. The explanation Newton gave of his discovery of the great law, points in this direction; it was by always thinking of the subject, by keeping it constantly before his mind, that he finally saw the truth. Artists brood over the chaos of their suggestions, and thus shape them into creations. Try and form a picture in your own mind of your early skating experience. It may be that the scene only comes back upon you in shifting outlines, you recall the general facts, and some few particulars are vivid, but the greater part of the details vanish again before they can assume decisive shape; they are but half nascent, or die as soon as born: a wave of recollection washes over the mind, but it quickly retires, leaving no trace behind. This is the common experience. Or it may be that the whole scene flashes upon you with peculiar vividness, so that you see, almost as in actual presence, all the leading characteristics of the picture. Wordsworth may have seen his early days in a succession of vivid flashes, or he may have attained to his distinctness of vision by a steadfast continuity of effort, in which what at first was vague became slowly definite as he gazed. It is certain that only a very imaginative mind could have seen such details as he has gathered together in the lines describing how he

> Cut across the reflex of a star;
> Image that flying still before me gleamed
> Upon the glassy plain.

The whole description may have been written with great rapidity, or with anxious and tentative labour: the memories of boyish days may have been kindled with a sudden illumination, or they may have grown slowly into the requisite distinctness, detail after detail emerging from the general obscurity, like the appearing stars at night. But whether the poet felt his way to images and epithets, rapidly or slowly, is unimportant; we have to do only with the result; and the result implies, as an absolute condition, that the images were distinct. Only thus could they serve the purposes of poetry, which must arouse in us memories of similar scenes and kindle emotions of pleasurable experience.

III

Having cited an example of bad writing consequent on imperfect Vision, I might consider that enough had been done for the immediate purpose of the present chapter; the many other illustra-

---

11   'Growth of Genius from the Influences of Natural Objects, on the Imagination in Boyhood, and Early Youth', *The Friend*, 28 December 1809. Incorporated into *The Prelude* (1850), 401–63.

tions which the Principle of Vision would require before it could be considered as adequately expounded, I must defer till I come to treat of the application of principles. But before closing this chapter it may be needful to examine some arguments which have a contrary tendency, and imply, or seem to imply, that distinctness of Vision is very far from necessary.

At the outset we must come to an understanding as to this word 'image', and endeavour to free the word 'vision' from all equivoque. If these words were understood literally there would be an obvious absurdity in speaking of an image of a sound, or of seeing an emotion. Yet if by means of symbols the effect of a sound is produced in us, or the psychological state of any human being is rendered intelligible to us, we are said to have images of these things which the poet has imagined. It is because the eye is the most valued and intellectual of our senses that the majority of metaphors are borrowed from its sensations. Language, after all, is only the use of symbols, and Art also can only affect us through symbols. If a phrase can summon a terror resembling that summoned by the danger which it indicates, a man is said to *see* the danger. Sometimes a phrase will awaken more vivid images of danger than would be called up by the actual presence of the dangerous object; because the mind will more readily apprehend the symbols of the phrase than interpret the indications of unassisted sense.

Burke in his 'Essay on the Sublime and Beautiful', lays down the proposition that distinctness of imagery is often injurious to the effect of art. 'It is one thing,' he says

> to make an idea clear, another to make it *affecting* to the imagination. If I make a drawing of a palace or a temple or a landscape, I present a very clear idea of those objects; but then (allowing for the effect of imitation, which is something) my picture can at most affect only as the palace, temple, or landscape would have affected in reality. On the other hand the most lively and spirited verbal description I can give raises a very obscure and imperfect *idea* of such objects; but then it is in my power to raise a stronger *emotion* by the description than I can do by the best painting. This experience constantly evinces. The proper manner of conveying the *affections* of the mind from one to the other is by words: there is great insufficiency in all other methods of communication; and so far is a clearness of imagery from being absolutely necessary to an influence upon the passions, that they may be considerably operated upon without presenting any image at all, by certain sounds adapted to that purpose.[12]

If by image is meant only what the eye can see, Burke is undoubtedly right. But this is obviously not our restricted meaning of the word when we speak of poetic imagery; and Burke's error becomes apparent when he proceeds to show that there 'are reasons in nature why an obscure idea, when properly conveyed, should be more affecting than the clear.' He does not seem to have considered that the idea of an indefinite object can only be properly conveyed by indefinite images; any image of Eternity or Death that pretended to visual distinctness would be false. Having overlooked this, he says, 'We do not anywhere meet a more sublime description than this justly celebrated one of Milton, wherein he gives the portrait of Satan with a dignity so suitable to the subject.

> He above the rest
> In shape and gesture proudly eminent
> Stood like a tower; his form had not yet lost
> All her original brightness, nor appeared
> Less than archangel ruined and the excess
> Of glory obscured: as when the sun new risen
> Looks through the horizontal misty air
> Shorn of his beams; or from behind the moon
> In dim eclipse disastrous twilight sheds
> On half the nations; and with fear of change
> Perplexes monarchs.[13]

12   Edmund Burke, *A Philosophical Enquiry Into the Origin of our Ideas of the Sublime and the Beautiful* ([1757] 2nd edn, 1759) Part II, Sect. IV, 'of the Difference Between Clearness and Obscurity with Regard to the Passions'.

13   *Paradise Lost*, I. 589–99.

Here is a very noble picture,' adds Burke, 'and in what does this poetical picture consist? In images of a tower, an archangel, the sun rising through mists, or an eclipse, the ruin of monarchs, and the revolution of kingdoms.' Instead of recognising the imagery here as the source of the power, he says, 'The mind is hurried out of itself [rather a strange result!] by a crowd of great and confused images; which affect because they are crowded and confused. For, separate them, and you lose much of the greatness; and join them, and you infallibly lose the clearness.' This is altogether a mistake. The images are vivid enough to make us feel the hovering presence of an awe-inspiring figure having the height and firmness of a tower, and the dusky splendour of a ruined archangel. The poet indicates only that amount of concreteness which is necessary for the clearness of the picture, – only the height and firmness of the tower and the brightness of the sun in eclipse. More concreteness would disturb the clearness by calling attention to irrelevant details. To suppose that these images produce the effect because they are crowded and confused (they are crowded and not confused) is to imply that any other images would do equally well, if they were equally crowded. 'Separate them, and you lose much of the greatness.'[14] Quite true: the image of the tower would want the splendour of the sun. But this much may be said of all descriptions which proceed upon details. And so far from the impressive clearness of the picture vanishing in the crowd of images, it is by these images that the clearness is produced: the details make it impressive, and affect our imagination.

It should be added that Burke came very near a true explanation in the following passage: –

> It is difficult to conceive how words can move the passions which belong to real objects without representing these objects clearly. This is difficult to us because we do not sufficiently distinguish between a clear expression and a strong expression. The former regards the understanding; the latter belongs to the passions. The one describes a thing as it is, the other describes it as it is felt. Now as there is a moving tone of voice, an impassioned countenance, an agitated gesture, which affect independently of the things about which they are exerted, so there are words and certain dispositions of words which being peculiarly devoted to passionate subjects, and always used by those who are under the influence of passion, touch and move us more than those which far more clearly and distinctly express the subject-matter.

Burke here fails to see that the tones, looks and gestures are the intelligible symbols of passion – the 'images' of the true sense – just as words are the intelligible symbols of ideas. The subject-matter is as clearly expressed by the one as by the other; for if the description of a Lion be conveyed in the symbols of admiration or of terror, the subject-matter is *then* a Lion passionately and zoologically considered. And this Burke himself was led to admit, for he adds,

> We yield to sympathy what we refuse to description. The truth is, all verbal description, merely as naked description, though never so exact, conveys so poor and insufficient an idea of the thing described, that it could scarcely have the smallest effect if the speaker did not call in to his aid those modes of speech that work a strong and lively feeling in himself. Then, by the contagion of our passions, we catch a fire already kindled in another.[15]

This is very true, and it sets clearly forth the fact that naked description, addressed to the calm understanding, has a different subject-matter from description addressed to the feelings, and the symbols by which it is made intelligible must likewise differ. But this in no way impugns the principle of Vision. Intelligible symbols (clear images) are as necessary in the one case as in the other.

IV

By reducing imagination to the power of forming images, and by insisting that no image can be formed except out of the elements furnished by experience, I do not mean to confound imagination with memory; indeed, the frequent occurrence of great strength of memory with comparative feebleness of imagination, would suffice to warn us against such a conclusion.

Its specific character, that which marks it off from simple memory, is its tendency to selection, abstraction, and recombination. Memory, as passive, simply recalls previous experiences of objects

---

14 Burke, *Of The Sublime*, Part II, Sect. V, 'The Same Subject Continued'.

15 *Of the Sublime*, Part V, Sect. VII, 'How Words Influence the Passions'.

and emotions; from these, imagination, as an active faculty, selects the elements which vividly symbolise the objects or emotions, and either by a process of abstraction allows these to do duty for the wholes, or else by a process of recombination creates new objects and new relations in which the objects stand to us or to each other (*invention*), and the result is an image of great vividness, which has perhaps no corresponding reality in the external world.

Minds differ in the vividness with which they recall the elements of previous experience, and mentally see the absent objects; they differ also in the aptitudes for selection, abstraction, and recombination: the fine selective instinct of the artist, which makes him fasten upon the details which will most powerfully affect us, without any disturbance of the harmony of the general impression, does not depend solely upon the vividness of his memory and the clearness with which the objects are seen, but depends also upon very complex and peculiar conditions of sympathy which we call genius. Hence we find one man remembering a multitude of details with a memory so vivid that it almost amounts at times to hallucination, yet without any artistic power; and we may find men – Blake was one – with an imagination of unusual activity, who are nevertheless incapable, from deficient sympathy, of seizing upon those symbols which will most affect us. Our native susceptibilities and acquired tastes determine which of the many qualities in an object shall most impress us, and be most clearly recalled. One man remembers the combustible properties of a substance, which to another is memorable for its polarising property; to one man a stream is so much water-power, to another a rendezvous for lovers.

In the close of the last paragraph we came face to face with the great difficulty which constantly arrests speculation on these matters – the existence of special aptitudes vaguely characterised as genius. These are obviously incommunicable. No recipe can be given for genius. No man can be taught how to exercise the power of imagination. But he can be taught how to aid it, and how to assure himself whether he is using it or not. Having once laid hold of the Principle of Vision as a fundamental principle of Art, he can always thus far apply it, that he can assure himself whether he does or does not distinctly *see* the cottage he is describing, the rivulet that is gurgling through his verses, or the character he is painting; he can assure himself whether he hears the voice of the speakers, and feels that what they say is true to their natures; he can assure himself whether he sees, as in actual experience, the emotion he is depicting; and he will know that if he does not see these things he must wait until he can, or he will paint them ineffectively. With distinct Vision he will be able to make the best use of his powers of expression; and the most splendid powers of expression will not avail him if his Vision be indistinct. This is true of objects that never were seen by the eye, that never could be seen. It is as true of what are called the highest flights of imagination as of the lowest flights. The mind must *see* the angel or the demon, the hippogriff or centaur, the pixie or the mermaid.

Ruskin notices how repeatedly Turner, – the most imaginative of landscape painters, – introduced into his pictures, after a lapse of many years, memories of something which, however small and unimportant, had struck him in his earlier studies.[16] He believes that all Turner's 'composition' was an arrangement of remembrances summoned just as they were wanted, and each in its fittest place. His vision was primarily composed of strong memory of the place itself, and secondarily of memories of other places associated in a harmonious, helpful way with the now central thought. He recalled and selected.

I am prepared to hear of many readers, especially young readers, protesting against the doctrine of this chapter as prosaic. They have been so long accustomed to consider imagination as peculiarly distinguished by its disdain of reality, and Invention as only admirable when its products are not simply new by selection and arrangement, but new in material, that they will reject the idea of involuntary remembrance of something originally experienced as the basis of all Art. Ruskin says of great artists,

> Imagine all that any of these men had seen or heard in the whole course of their lives, laid up accurately
> in their memories as in vast store-houses, extending with the poets even to the slightest intonations of

16   John Ruskin, *Modern Painters*, IV (1856), Part V, ch. 2.

syllables heard in the beginning of their lives, and with painters down to minute folds of drapery and shapes of leaves and stones; and over all this unindexed and immeasurable mass of treasure, the imagination brooding and wandering, but dream-gifted, so as to summon at any moment exactly such a group of ideas as shall justly fit each other.[17]

This is the explanation of their genius, as far as it can be explained.

Genius is rarely able to give any account of its own processes. But those who have had ample opportunities of intimately knowing the growth of works in the minds of artists, will bear me out in saying that a vivid memory supplies the elements from a thousand different sources, most of which are quite beyond the power of localisation, – the experience of yesterday being strangely intermingled with the dim suggestions of early years, the tones heard in childhood sounding through the diapason of sorrowing maturity; and all these kaleidoscopic fragments are recomposed into images that seem to have a corresponding reality of their own.

As all Art depends on Vision, so the different kinds of Art depend on the different ways in which minds look at things. The painter can only put into his pictures what he sees in Nature; and what he sees will be different from what another sees. A poetical mind sees noble and affecting suggestions in details which the prosaic mind will interpret prosaically. And the true meaning of Idealism is precisely this vision of realities in their highest and most affecting forms, not in the vision of something removed from or opposed to realities. Titian's grand picture of 'Peter the Martyr' is, perhaps, as instructive an example as could be chosen of successful Idealism; because in it we have a marvellous presentation of reality as seen by a poetic mind. The figure of the flying monk might have been equally real if it had been an ignoble presentation of terror – the superb tree, which may almost be called an actor in the drama, might have been painted with even greater minuteness, though not perhaps with equal effect upon us, if he had arrested our attention by its details – the dying martyr and the noble assassin might have been made equally real in more vulgar types – but the triumph achieved by Titian is that the mind is filled with a vision of poetic beauty which is felt to be real. An equivalent reality, without the ennobling beauty, would have made the picture a fine piece of realistic art. It is because of this poetic way of seeing things that one painter will give a faithful representation of a very common scene which shall nevertheless affect all sensitive minds as ideal, whereas another painter will represent the same with no greater fidelity, but with a complete absence of poetry. The greater the fidelity, the greater will be the merit of each representation; for if a man pretends to represent an object, he pretends to represent it accurately: the only difference is what the poetical or prosaic mind sees in the object.

Of late years there has been a reaction against conventionalism which called itself Idealism, in favour of *detailism* which calls itself Realism. As a reaction it has been of service; but it has led to much false criticism, and not a little false art, by an obtrusiveness of Detail and a preference for the Familiar, under the misleading notion of adherence to Nature. If the words Nature and Natural could be entirely banished from language about Art there would be some chance of coming to a rational philosophy of the subject; at present the excessive vagueness and shiftiness of these terms cover any amount of sophism. The pots and pans of Teniers and Van Mieris are natural; the passions and humours of Shakespeare and Molière are natural; the angels of Fra Angelico and Luini are natural; the Sleeping Fawn and Fates of Phidias are natural; the cows and misty marshes of Cuyp and the vacillations of Hamlet are equally natural. In fact the natural means *truth of kind*. Each kind of character, each kind of representation, must be judged by itself. Whereas the vulgar error of criticism is to judge of one kind by another, and generally to judge the higher by the lower, to remonstrate with Hamlet for not having the speech and manner of Mr Jones, to wish that Fra Angelico could have seen with the eyes of the Carracci, to wish verse had been prose, and that ideal tragedy were acted with the easy manner acceptable in drawing-rooms.

The rage for 'realism', which is healthy in as far as it insists on truth, has become unhealthy, in as far as it confounds truth with familiarity, and predominance of unessential details. There are other truths besides coats and waistcoats, pots and pans, drawing-rooms and suburban villas. Life has other aims besides those which occupy the conversation of 'Society'. And the painter who devotes years to a work representing modern life, yet calls for even more attention to a waistcoat than to the face of a philosopher, may exhibit truth of detail which will delight the tailor-mind, but he is defective in artistic truth, because he ought to be representing something higher than waistcoats, and because our thoughts on modern life fall very casually and without emphasis on waistcoats. In Piloty's much-admired picture of the 'Death of Wallenstein' (at Munich), the truth with which the carpet, the velvet, and all other accessories are painted, is certainly remarkable; but the falsehood of giving prominence to such details in a picture representing the dead Wallenstein – as if they were the objects which could possibly arrest our attention and excite our sympathies in such a spectacle – is a falsehood of the realistic school. If a man means to paint upholstery, by all means let him paint it so as to delight and deceive an upholsterer; but if it means to paint a human tragedy, the upholsterer must be subordinate, and velvet must not draw our eyes away from faces.

I have digressed a little from my straight route because I wish to guard the Principle of Vision from certain misconceptions which might arise on a simple statement of it. The principle insists on the artist assuring himself that he distinctly sees what he attempts to represent. *What* he sees, and *how* he represents it, depend on other principles. To make even this principle of Vision thoroughly intelligible in its application to all forms of Literature and Art, it must be considered in connection with the two other principles – Sincerity and Beauty, which are involved in all successful works. In the next chapter we shall treat of Sincerity.

Fortnightly Review *(ed. G. H. Lewes), I (15 July 1865), 562–89.*

John Mason Neale (1818–66)

John Mason Neale, the most influential of English Anglo-Catholic hymn-writers, was born 24 January 1818 at 40 Lamb's Conduit Street, London, the only son (he had three sisters) of the Revd Cornelius Neale and Susanna Neale, strongly Evangelical Anglicans. His father, a writer of allegories and poems as well as sermons, died when his son was five. The boy attended various private schools and tutors and entered Trinity College, Cambridge, in October 1836, as a classical scholar. While an undergraduate he became a strong follower of the Anglo-Catholic Oxford Movement. In 1839, still an undergraduate, he helped found the Cambridge Camden Society – later the Ecclesiological Society – to promote High Church liturgical practices, and not least the ancient Christian Latin hymns for particular services and seasons of the church year. The Society met regularly to sing in Latin. Upon graduation Neale became chaplain of Downing College, Cambridge. In 1845 he won the Seatonian Prize for a Sacred Poem – and won it altogether eleven times. He was ordained deacon in 1841 at St Margaret's, Westminster, already a High Anglican shrine. He married Sarah Norman Webster in July 1842. He became a very prominent and controversial Romanist, or Ritualist, in the jargon of the day. The only job in the Church of England he ever obtained after Cambridge was wardenship of Sackville College, East Grinstead, a kind of almshouse in the gift of two noble Anglo-Catholic ladies, daughters of the Duke of Dorset. The stipend never amounted to more than £30 a year; Neale had a wife and, eventually, five children to support;

so he needed to write prolifically – for the newspapers (three leaders a week at one stage for the *Morning Chronicle*), history books (he became a great expert on the Eastern Church), theological translations, biblical commentaries, children's stories and histories, editions of ballads and theological works, and of course, hymns. His first hymns were pastoral (*Hymns for the Sick*, 1843), and polemical (*Hymns for Children, in Accordance with the Catechism*, 1843: written 'to free our poor children from the yoke' of Evangelical Isaac Watts's kiddy hymn book, and full of such lines as 'I am a little Catholic,/And Christian is my name,/And I believe in Holy Church,/In every age the same'). But before long he had become the guiding light of Tractarian hymnodic research, recovery and translation. He was the chief personal agent in the Victorian recovery of ancient hymnody that was a main part of the Oxford Movement's antiquarian mission. His *Hymni Ecclesiae* (1851) is a scholarly edition of European hymns in original Latin. He produced four really major volumes of hymns either translated from or based on old originals: *Medieval Hymns and Sequences* (1851), *The Hymnal Noted* (1851 and 1854) – a major project of the Ecclesiological Society, involving music as well as words – and *Hymns of the Eastern Church* (1862). He published hymns for the cattle plague and invalids (both 1866). He brought out two volumes of carols: *Carols for Christmastide* (1853) – he's a major poet of Christmas (author of 'Good King Wenceslas'; 'Of the Father sole begotten': usually altered to 'Of the Father's heart [or love] begotten'; 'Good Christian men rejoice' –

and *Carols for Eastertide* (1854). Neale's writing made hymn-singing an Anglo-Catholic practice sufficient to rival the Evangelical and Nonconformist enthusiasm (both Thomas Hardy in *Under the Greenwood Tree* (1872) and Samuel Butler in *The Way of All Flesh* (1903) note the impact of the new Tractarian hymn-singing cult). He was the major contributor to *Hymns, Ancient and Modern, for Use in the Services of the Church*, which first appeared in December 1860 and rapidly became the standard Anglican hymn book. There were, for example, forty-eight contributions by him in the *A&M* edition of *1875* – over one-tenth of the whole. He's author not just of the standard Christmas carols named above, but of such canonical Anglican hymns as 'Christ is made the sure foundation' and 'Jerusalem the Golden'. All his life Neale had to contend with Protestant hostility to his Ritualism (his Bishop denounced the 'frippery' and 'spiritual haberdashery' he went in for), and he was occasionally the victim of mob violence. Protestant opposition closed down the home for fallen women in Aldershot, run by the Tractarian order of the Sisters of St Margaret, which Neale founded (the Sisters ran an orphanage and school for middle-class girls of East Grinstead as well). Neale's last public act was laying the foundation-stone for a new convent for the Sisters in July 1865. His health had never been strong. He died at East Grinstead after a severe illness, 6 August 1866, aged only forty-eight.

JERUSALEM THE GOLDEN

From: The Rhythm of Bernard de Morlaix[1]

Jerusalem the Golden,
    With milk and honey blest,
Beneath thy contemplation
    Sink heart and voice oppressed:
I know not, O I know not,
    What social joys are there;
What radiancy of glory,
    What light beyond compare!
And when I fain would sing them,
    My spirit fails and faints, –   10
And vainly would it image
    The assembly of the Saints.
They stand, those halls of Syon,
    Conjubilant with song,
And bright with many an angel,
    And all the martyr throng:
The Prince is ever in them;
    The daylight is serene;
The pastures of the blessed
    Are decked in glorious sheen.   20
There is the Throne of David, –
    And there, from care released,
The song of them that triumph,
    The shout of them that feast;
And they who, with their Leader,
    Have conquered in the fight,
For ever and for ever
    Are clad in robes of white.

O holy, placid harp-notes
    Of that eternal hymn!   30
O sacred, sweet refection,
    And peace of Seraphim!
O thirst, for ever ardent,
    Yet evermore content!

O true, peculiar vision
    Of GOD cunctipotent!
Ye know the many mansions
    For many a glorious name,
And divers retributions
    That divers merits claim: 40
For midst the constellations
    That deck our earthly sky,
This star than that is brighter, –
    And so it is on high.

Jerusalem the glorious!
    The glory of the Elect!
O dear and future vision
    That eager hearts expect:
Even now by faith I see thee:
    Even here thy walls discern: 50
To thee my thoughts are kindled,
    And strive and pant and yearn.
Jerusalem the onely,
    That look'st from heaven below,
In thee is all my glory;
    In me is all my woe;
And though my body may not,
    My spirit seeks thee fain,
Till flesh and earth return me
    To earth and flesh again.   60
O none can tell thy bulwarks,
    How gloriously they rise:

O none can tell thy capitals
    Of beautiful device:
Thy loveliness oppresses
    All human thought and heart:
And none, O peace, O Syon,

JERUSALEM THE GOLDEN
1   St Bernard of Cluny (fl. 1140), author of the 3,000-line *De Contemptu Mundi*, which Neale is adapting here.

Can sing thee as thou art.
New mansion of new people,
  Whom GOD's own love and light   70
Promote, increase, make holy,
  Identify, unite.
Thou City of the Angels!
  Thou City of the LORD!
Whose everlasting music
  Is the glorious decachord!
And there the band of Prophets
  United praise ascribes,
And there the twelvefold chorus
  Of Israel's ransomed tribes: 80
The lily-beds of virgins,
  The roses' martyr-glow,
The cohort of the Fathers
  Who kept the faith below.
And there the Sole-Begotten
  Is LORD in regal state;
He, Judah's mystic Lion,
  He, Lamb Immaculate.
O fields that know no sorrow!
  O state that fears no strife!   90
O princely bow'rs! O land of flow'rs!
  O Realm and Home of Life!

Jerusalem, exulting,
  On that securest shore,
I hope thee, wish thee, sing thee,
  And love thee evermore!
I ask not for my merit:
  I seek not to deny
My merit is destruction,
  A child of wrath am I: 100
But yet with Faith I venture
  And Hope upon my way;

For those perennial guerdons
  I labour night and day.
The Best and Dearest FATHER
  Who made me and Who saved,
Bore with me in defilement,
  And from defilement laved:
When in His strength I struggle,
  For very joy I leap;   110
When in my sin I totter,
  I weep, or try to weep:
And grace, sweet grace celestial,
  Shall all its love display,
And David's Royal Fountain
  Purge every sin away.

O mine, my golden Syon!
  O lovelier far than gold!
With laurel-girt battalions,
  And safe victorious fold: 120
O sweet and blessed Country,
  Shall I ever see thy face?
O sweet and blessed Country,
  Shall I ever win thy grace?
I *have* the hope within me
  To comfort and to bless!
Shall I ever win the prize itself?
  O tell me, tell me, Yes!

Exult, O dust and ashes!
  The LORD shall be thy part: 130
His only, His for ever,
  Thou shalt be, and thou art!
Exult, O dust and ashes!
  The LORD shall be thy part:
His only, His for ever,
  Thou shalt be, and thou art!

Originally published 1858. Text, Collected Hymns, Sequences and Carols
(Hodder & Stoughton, 1914).

THE PILGRIMS OF JESUS

After S. Joseph of the Studium

O happy band of pilgrims,
  If onward ye will tread
With JESUS as your Fellow
  To JESUS as your Head!

O happy, if ye labour
  As JESUS did for men:
O happy, if ye hunger
  As JESUS hunger'd then!

The Cross that JESUS carried
  He carried as your due: 10
The Crown that JESUS weareth
  He weareth it for you.

The Faith by which ye see Him,
  The Hope, in which ye yearn,
The Love that through all troubles
  To Him alone will turn, –

What are they, but vaunt-couriers
  To lead you to His Sight?
What are they, save the effluence
  Of Uncreated Light?   20

The trials that beset you,
  The sorrows ye endure,
The manifold temptations
  That Death alone can cure, –

What are they, but His jewels
   Of right celestial worth?
What are they but the ladder,
   Set up to Heav'n on earth?

O happy band of pilgrims,
   Look upward to the skies; –   30
Where such a light affliction
   Shall win you such a prize!

Hymns of the Eastern Church *(1862)*. *Text,* Collected Hymns,
Sequences and Carols *(1914)*.

Emily (Jane) Brontë (1818–48)

Emily Brontë was the fifth child of the Revd Patrick Brontë, Ulsterman, Evangelical, fierce Tory, and his Cornish Wesleyan wife, Maria Branwell. She was born at Thornton, Yorkshire, 20 August 1818, moving with the family to Haworth parsonage when she was two. Her mother died when Emily was only three. The young family was then looked after by their Cornish Methodist Aunt (who did not, contrary to Winifred's Gérin's *Life* of Emily, instil Calvinist fears of predestination and Hell into her charges – Wesleyan Methodism abhorred Calvinism). Emily was tough, 'stronger than a man' her sister Charlotte said, a good shot, at one time reputedly searing a bite from a rabid dog with heated fire-tongs, at another tearing her great mastiff Keeper away from the dog he was fighting. But she was never personally strong enough to stay away from Haworth for long, whether early on at the school for clergy daughters at Cowan Bridge when she was aged five (and where her sisters Maria and Elizabeth contracted fatal illnesses), or aged sixteen at the Roe Head school where Charlotte taught (four months), or as a teacher near Halifax three years later (six months), or in Brussels with Charlotte (ten months in 1842). Emily needed the moors above Haworth and the brusque homely mix of books ('I don't desire a school at all') and domesticity, jostling and shuttling between the privacy and freedom of her inner world of fantasy and imagination and the outer quotidian reality of ironing, baking bread, peeling potatoes, putting up with her father and drunken brother Branwell and with harsh-tongued Tabby the Yorkshire servant. She never abandoned the melodramatic world of the Gondal stories she shared in childhood and adolescence with her sister Anne. The juvenile passions of those kiddy stories (foot-stamping rages, hair-pulling revenges) are much visible in her great Gothic concoction *Wuthering Heights* (1847), as are the rough truths of the Haworth kitchen. Emily's poetry – oddly akin in form and tone to the contents of the religious and sentimental enthusiasm of the *Methodist Hymn Book* even while, as in 'No coward soul is mine', it was rejecting the vanity of any creed except faith in the personal 'God within my breast' – was sharply singled out by Sydney Dobell in the only review *Poems by Currer, Ellis, and Acton Bell* (1846) received (in the *Athenaeum*, July 1846) as the material most likely to 'yet find an audience in the outer world'. Charlotte Brontë published some of the poems in the deeply hagiographical, even if truth-telling, volume (1850) which contained *Wuthering Heights* and Anne Brontë's *Agnes Grey*. (Emily's poems, Charlotte's Biographical Notice declares, were surprisingly unlike 'the poetry women generally write. I thought them condensed and terse, vigorous and genuine'.) But that larger audience had to wait for a more complete picture of Emily's poetic output. She died at home in great agony in the later part of 1848, refusing to see a doctor until right at the very end.

What winter floods, what showers of spring
Have drenched the grass by night and day
And yet beneath that spectre ring
Unmoved and undiscovered lay

A mute remembrancer of crime
Long lost concealed forgot for years
It comes at last to cancel time
And waken unavailing tears

Dated 27 March 1832 in MS(?). First published, The Complete Poems of
Emily Brontë, *ed. Clement Shorter (Hodder & Stoughton, 1910).*
Text (and dating), Emily Jane Brontë, The Complete Poems
(ed. Janet Gezari, Penguin, Harmondsworth, 1992).

Long neglect has worn away
Half the sweet enchanting smile
Time has turned the bloom to grey
Mould and damp the face defile

But that lock of silky hair
Still beneath the picture twined
Tells what once those features were
Paints their image on the mind

Fair the hand that traced that line
'Dearest ever deem me true'   10
Swiftly flew the fingers fine
When the pen that motto drew

> *First published,* Poems of Charlotte, Emily, and Anne Brontë
> Now For the First Time Printed *(Dodd, Mead & Co, New York, 1902).*
> *Text,* Complete Poems *(1992).*

The night is darkening round me
The wild winds coldly blow
But a tyrant spell has bound me
And I cannot, cannot go

The giant trees are bending
Their bare boughs weighed with snow
And the storm is fast descending
And yet I cannot go

Clouds beyond cloud above me,
Wastes beyond wastes below,   10
But nothing drear can move me,
I will not, cannot go

> *Dated November 1837 in MS. First published,* Poems *(1902). Text,*
> Complete Poems *(1992).*

All hushed and still within the house
Without – all wind and driving rain
But something whispers to my mind
Through rain and [through the] wailing wind
       – Never again
Never again? Why not again?
Memory has power as real as thine

> *First published,* Complete Poems *(1910). Text,* Complete Poems *(1992).*

O Dream, where art thou now?
Long years have passed away
Since last from off thine angel brow
I saw the light decay –

Alas, alas for me
Thou wert so bright and fair
I could not think thy memory
Would yield me nought but care!

The sun-beam and the storm,
The summer-eve divine,   10
The silent night of solemn calm,
The full moon's cloudless shine

Were once entwined with thee
But now, with weary pain –
Lost vision! 'tis enough for me –
Thou canst not shine again.

Dated 5 November 1838 in MS. First published, Poems *(1902). Text,*
Complete Poems *(1992).*

How still, how happy! those are words
That once would scarce agree together
I loved the plashing of the surge –
The changing heaven, the breezy weather,

More than smooth seas and cloudless skies
And solemn, soothing, softened airs
That in the forest woke no sighs
And from the green spray shook no tears

How still, how happy! now I feel
Where silence dwells is sweeter far   10
Than laughing mirth's most joyous swell
However pure its raptures are

Come sit down on this sunny stone
'Tis wintery light o'er flowerless moors –
But sit – for we are all alone
And clear expand heaven's breathless shores

I could think in the withered grass
Spring's budding wreaths we might discern
The violet's eye might shyly flash
And young leaves shoot among the fern   20

It is but thought – full many a night
The snow shall clothe those hills afar
And storms shall add a drearier blight
And winds shall wage a wilder war

Before the lark may herald in
Fresh foliage twined with blossoms fair
And summer days again begin
Their glory-haloed crown to wear

Yet my heart loves December's smile
As much as July's golden beam   30
Then let us sit and watch the while
The blue ice curdling on the stream –

Dated 7 December 1838 in MS. First published, Poems *(1902). Text,*
Complete Poems *(1992).*

Mild the mist upon the hill
Telling not of storms tomorrow
No, the day has wept its fill
Spent its store of silent sorrow

Oh I'm gone back to the days of youth
I am a child once more
And 'neath my father's sheltering roof
And near the old hall door

I watch this cloudy evening fall
After a day of rain   10
Blue mists, sweet mists of summer pall
The horizon's mountain chain

The damp stands on the long green grass
As thick as morning's tears
And dreamy scents of fragrance pass
That breathe of other years

Dated 27 July 1839 in MS. First published, Complete Poems *(1910). Text,*
Complete Poems *(1992).*

Come, walk with me,
There's only thee
To bless my spirit now –
We used to love on winter nights
To wander through the snow;
Can we not woo back old delights?
The clouds rush dark and wild
They fleck with shade our mountain heights
The same as long ago
And on the horizon rest at last   10
In looming masses piled;
While moonbeams flash and fly so fast
We scarce can say they smiled –

Come walk with me, come walk with me;
We were not once so few
But Death has stolen our company
As sunshine steals the dew –
He took them one by one and we
Are left the only two;
So closer would my feelings twine   20
Because they have no stay but thine –

'Nay call me not – it may not be
Is human love so true?
Can Friendship's flower droop on for years
And then revive anew?
No, though the soil be wet with tears,
How fair soe'er it grew
The vital sap once perished
Will never flow again
And surer than that dwelling dread,   30
The narrow dungeon of the dead
Time parts the hearts of men –'

First published, Poems *(1902). 1902 text.*

TO IMAGINATION

When weary with the long day's care,
And earthly change from pain to pain,
And lost and ready to despair,
Thy kind voice calls me back again:

Oh, my true friend! I am not lone,
While thou canst speak with such a tone!

So hopeless is the world without;
The world within I doubly prize;
Thy world, where guile, and hate, and doubt,
And cold suspicion never rise;   10
Where thou, and I, and Liberty,
Have undisputed sovereignty.

What matters it, that, all around,
Danger, and guilt, and darkness lie,
If but within our bosom's bound
We hold a bright, untroubled sky,
Warm with ten thousand mingled rays
Of suns that know no winter days?

Reason, indeed, may oft complain
For Nature's sad reality   20
And tell the suffering heart how vain
Its cherished dreams must always be;
And Truth may rudely trample down
The flowers of Fancy, newly-blown:

But, thou art ever there, to bring
The hovering vision back, and breathe
New glories o'er the blighted spring
And call a lovelier Life from Death,
And whisper, with a voice divine,
Of real worlds, as bright as thine.   30

I trust not to thy phantom bliss,
Yet, still, in evening's quiet hour,
With never-failing thankfulness,
I welcome thee, Benignant Power;
Sure solacer of human cares,
And sweeter hope, when hope despairs!

> *Dated 3 September 1844 in MS.* Poems by Currer, Ellis, and Acton Bell
> *(Aylott & Jones, 1846). 1846 text.*

No coward soul is mine
No trembler in the world's storm-troubled sphere
I see Heaven's glories shine
And Faith shines equal arming me from Fear

O God within my breast
Almighty ever-present Deity
Life, that in me hast rest
As I Undying Life, have power in thee

Vain are the thousand creeds
That move men's hearts, unutterably vain,   10
Worthless as withered weeds
Or idlest froth amid the boundless main

To waken doubt in one
Holding so fast by thy infinity

So surely anchored on
The steadfast rock of Immortality

With wide-embracing love
Thy Spirit animates eternal years
Pervades and broods above,
Changes, sustains, dissolves, creates and rears   20

Though Earth and moon were gone
And suns and universes ceased to be
And thou wert left alone
Every Existence would exist in thee

There is not room for Death
Nor atom that his might could render void
Since thou are Being and Breath
And what thou art may never be destroyed

Dated 2 January 1846 in MS. First published in Currer Bell, ed., Wuthering Heights
and Agnes Grey *(Smith, Elder & Co., 1850). Text,* Complete Poems *(1992).*

OF DOUBTFUL AUTHORSHIP: PERHAPS BY EMILY JANE BRONTË, PERHAPS BY CHARLOTTE BRONTË

Often rebuked, yet always back returning
   To those first feelings that were born with me,
And leaving busy chase of wealth and learning
   For idle dreams of things which cannot be:

Today, I will seek not the shadowy region;
   Its unsustaining vastness waxes drear;
And visions rising, legion after legion,
   Bring the unreal world too strangely near.

I'll walk, but not in old heroic traces,
   And not in paths of high morality,   10
And not among the half-distinguished faces,
   The clouded forms of long-past history.

I'll walk where my own nature would be leading:
   It vexes me to choose another guide:
Where the grey flocks in ferny glens are feeding;
   Where the wild wind blows on the mountain side.

What have those lonely mountains worth revealing?
   More glory and more grief than I can tell:
The earth that wakes *one* human heart to feeling
   Can centre both the worlds of Heaven and Hell.   20

No MS exists. First published in Currer Bell, ed., Wuthering Heights and
Agnes Grey *(1850). 1850 text.*

Eliza Cook (1818–89)

Eliza Cook, the very popular poet, whose best-known poem 'The Old Arm-Chair', one of the most favourite of Victorian verses, was published (May 1837) when she was only eighteen, was born 24 December 1818, the youngest of eleven children of a Southwark 'brasier', Joseph Cook. How proletarian is a brasier? He's sometimes described as a mere working-class 'tinman', sometimes as a wealthy metal trader. At any rate, when he retired the family moved to a farm near Horsham in Sussex. There does not seem, though, to have been either money or inclination for Eliza's schooling, and she was entirely self-educated. Unschooled or not, her first volume of verses, *Lays of a Wild Harp*, came out when she was just seventeen (in 1835). William Jerdan, the editor with a keen eye for girl poets – cf. L.E.L. – took up Eliza's cause in his *Literary Gazette*. Elizabeth Barrett Barrett, like George Eliot, not given to being enthralled by females prettier than herself, took particular exception to the full-length 'poetical' picture of Eliza in her second, and greatly successful, volume *Melaia, and Other Poems* (1838) – the volume with 'The Old Arm-Chair' in it. Ordinary middle-class readers loved this writer. Always looking for fresh ways of earning, she started up her own monthly *Journal* in May 1849, a periodical written largely by herself – moralizing, chatty, bourgeois, domestic, with a feministic flavour on the subjects of marriage, education, clothing and property-owning. At only one-and-a-half pence a time *Eliza Cook's Journal* was within reach of most purses. It outsold even Dickens's *Household Words*, ran for five years, and was filletted for *Jottings from My Journal* (1860). After this Eliza's productivity rather slowed. *New Echoes, and Other Poems* appeared in 1864, a volume of tedious aphorisms *Diamond Dust* in 1865. But illness debilitated her. She took to living off her royalties, and needed a Civil List Pension of £100 a year (awarded in 1863). She never married, and rumours of lesbianism clustered about her name. She was certainly close friends with the actress Charlotte Cushman who moved in lesbian circles. And she did like wearing male clothing. Her writing, simple, clear, occasionally strong, was in general agreeably sentimental, patriotic, and intermittently radical. Her poem 'Poor Hood' led to the erection of a monument to him in Kensal Green Cemetery. She died at Wimbledon, 28 September 1889, after many years as a confirmed invalid, in her seventy-first year.

THE OLD ARM-CHAIR

I love it, I love it; and who shall dare
To chide me for loving that old arm-chair?
I've treasured it long as a sainted prize,
I've bedewed it with tears, and embalmed it with sighs;
'Tis bound by a thousand bands to my heart;
Not a tie will break, not a link will start.
Would ye learn the spell? a mother sat there,
And a sacred thing is that old arm-chair.

In childhood's hour I lingered near
The hallow'd seat with list'ning ear;   10
And gentle words that mother would give,
To fit me to die and teach me to live.
She told me shame would never betide,
With truth for my creed and God for my guide;
She taught me to lisp my earliest prayer,
As I knelt beside that old arm-chair.

I sat and watch'd her many a day,
When her eye grew dim, and her locks were grey:
And I almost worshipp'd her when she smil'd,
And turn'd from her Bible, to bless her child.   20
Years roll'd on, but the last one sped –
My idol was shatter'd, my earth-star fled;

I learnt how much the heart can bear,
When I saw her die in that old arm-chair.

'Tis past, 'tis past! but I gaze on it now
With quivering breath and throbbing brow:
'Twas there she nursed me; 'twas there she died;
And memory flows with lava tide.
Say it is folly, and deem me weak,
While the scalding drops start down my cheek;   30
But I love it, I love it, and cannot tear
My soul from a mother's old arm-chair.

First published, Weekly Dispatch (1837). Melaia, and Other Poems
(R. J. Wood, 1838). Text, Melaia (Charles Tilt, 1840).

SNOW

Brave Winter and I shall ever agree,
Though a stern and frowning gaffer is he.
I like to hear him, with hail and rain,
Come tapping against the window pane;
I like to see him come marching forth
Begirt with the icicle gems of the north;
But I like him best when he comes bedight
In his velvet robes of stainless white.

A cheer for the snow – the drifting snow!
Smoother and purer than beauty's brow!   10
The creature of thought scarce likes to tread
On the delicate carpet so richly spread.
With feathery wreaths the forest is bound,
And the hills are with glittering diadems crown'd:
'Tis the fairest scene we can have below.
Sing, welcome, then, to the drifting snow!

The urchins gaze with eloquent eye,
To see the flakes go dancing by.
In the thick of the storm how happy are they
To welcome the first deep snowy day.   20
Shouting and pelting – what bliss to fall
Half-smother'd beneath the well-aim'd ball!
Men of fourscore, did ye ever know
Such sport as ye had in the drifting snow?

I'm true to my theme, for I loved it well,
When the gossiping nurse would sit and tell
The tale of the geese – though, hardly believed –
I doubted and question'd the words that deceived.
I rejoice in it still, and love to see
The ermine mantle on tower and tree.   30
'Tis the fairest scene we can have below.
Hurrah! then, hurrah! for the drifting snow!

Melaia ([1838], 1840).

THE GALLANT ENGLISH TAR

There's one whose fearless courage yet has never fail'd in fight,
Who guards with zeal our country's weal, our freedom, and our right;
But though his strong and ready arm spreads havoc in its blow,
Cry 'Quarter!' and that arm will be the first to spare its foe.
He recks not though proud glory's shout may be the knell of death,
The triumph won, without a sigh he yields his parting breath.
He's Britain's boast, and claims a toast! 'In peace, my boys, or war,
Here's to the brave upon the wave, the gallant English Tar.'

Let but the sons of want come nigh, and tell their tale to him,
He'll chide their eyes for weeping, while his own are growing dim.   10
'Cheer up,' he cries, 'we all must meet the storm as well as calm;'
But, turning on his heel, Jack slips the guineas in their palm.
He'll hear no long oration, but tell you every man
Is born to act a brother's part, and do what good he can.
He's Britain's boast, and claims a toast! 'In peace, my boys, or war,
Here's to the brave upon the wave, the gallant English Tar.'

The dark blue jacket that enfolds the sailor's manly breast
Bears more of real honour than the star and ermine vest.
The tithe of folly in his head may wake the landsman's mirth,
But nature proudly owns him as her child of sterling worth.   20
His heart is warm, his hand is true, his word is frank and free;
And though he plays the ass on shore, he's lion of the sea.
He's Britain's boast, and claims a toast! 'In peace, my boys, or war,
Here's to the brave upon the wave, the gallant English Tar.'

Melaia ([1838], 1840).

A SONG FOR THE WORKERS

(Written for the Early Closing Movement.)

Let Man toil to win his living,
    Work is not a task to spurn;
Poor is gold of others' giving,
    To the silver that we earn.

Let Man proudly take his station
    At the smithy, loom, or plough;
The richest crown-pearls in a nation
    Hang from Labour's reeking brow.

Though her hand grows hard with duty,
    Filling up the common Fate,   10
Let fair Woman's cheek of beauty
    Never blush to own its state.

Let fond Woman's heart of feeling
    Never be ashamed to spread
Industry and honest dealing,
    As a barter for her bread.

Work on bravely, GOD's own daughters!
    Work on stanchly, GOD's own sons!

But when Life has too rough waters,
    Truth must fire her minute guns.   20

Shall ye be *unceasing* drudges?
    Shall the cry upon your lips
Never make your selfish judges
    Less severe with golden whips?

Shall the mercy that we cherish,
    As old England's primest boast,
See no slaves but those who perish
    On a far and foreign coast?

When we reckon hives of money,
    Owned by Luxury and Ease,   30
Is it just to grasp the honey
    While Oppression chokes the bees?

Is it just the poor and lowly
    Should be held as soulless things?
Have they not a claim as holy
    As rich men, to angels' wings?

Shall we burthen Boyhood's muscle?
  Shall the young Girl mope and lean,
Till we hear the dead leaves rustle
  On a tree that should be green?   40

Shall we bar the brain from thinking
  Of aught else than work and woe?
Shall we keep parched lips from drinking
  Where refreshing waters flow?

Shall we strive to shut out Reason,
  Knowledge, Liberty, and Health?
Shall all Spirit-light be treason
  To the mighty King of Wealth?

Shall we stint with niggard measure,
  Human joy and human rest?   50

Leave no profit – give no pleasure,
  To the toiler's human breast?

Shall our Men, fatigued to loathing,
  Plod on sickly, worn, and bowed?
Shall our Maidens sew fine clothing,
  Dreaming of their own white shroud?

No! for Right is up and asking
  Loudly for a juster lot;
And Commerce must not let her tasking
  Form a nation's canker spot.   60

Work on bravely, GOD's own daughters!
  Work on stanchly, GOD's own sons!
But till ye have smoother waters,
  Let Truth fire her minute guns!

Poems, vol. IV (Simpkin, Marshall, & Co., 1853).

SHAKESPEARE

(Written on Hearing of the Tercentenary Movement, 1864)

If Man *can* be immortal here,
  If Soul *can* stay when Life is done;
If Dust *can* brave the levelling spear,
  Thou, Shakespeare, art that mighty one.

Born 'neath the flag that never yields,
  Sprung from a people proudly free;
Whose Arms have won unnumbered fields,
  Whose Commerce spreads from Sea to Sea.

Son of the first and highest State,
  With noblest Rights that earth can hold,   10
Boasting the 'City of the Great,'
  Whose million highways teem with gold.

Truth-teller! whose illumined page
  Has never yet been laid aside;
Chief Prompter on Creation's stage,
  Our endless joy – our matchless pride.

At length rich England deigns to give
  Thy Genius a Memorial shrine,
And let her Shakespeare's image live,
  Recorded as the 'Soul divine!'   20

How many a pulse would throb and glow
  To see the marble pile uprear,
Which grants the Bard his late reward,
  A 'local habitation' here![1]

And 'mid the warmest mine will be,
  To laud the workers of the deed,
Which honours thee who shaped for me
  My simple Muse and trusting creed.

For less of fire had marked my lyre,
  And less of pleasing praise been mine;   30
Less earnest pains had marked *my* strains,
  If I had never worshipped *thine!*

In early youth I prized the Word
  That gently leads with Gospel rule;
Then, charmed by thee, I thought I heard
  A teacher in the self-same school.

And now when stricken Conscience calls
  For contrite heart and bended knee,
My meek and chastened spirit falls
  First to its God, and then to thee!   40

Kind Heaven has bounteously attuned
  A few sweet things within my breast,
And such blest things are those few strings,
  Their echo softens all the rest.

My song is weak – *my* chords are few,
  But faintest echoes only prove
That *all* bow down to hail and crown
  Our Poet-Priest with changeless love!

New Echoes, and Other Poems (Routledge, Warne, & Routledge, 1864).

SHAKESPEARE
1 the poet's pen 'gives to airy nothing/ A local habitation and a name',
A Midsummer Night's Dream, v.i.16–17.

'POOR HOOD'

(Written at Kensal-Green Cemetery)

What gorgeous cenotaphs arise,
    Of Parian shrine[1] and granite vault;
With blazoned claims on purer skies
    That shut out earthly flaw and fault!

Who lies below yon splendid tomb
    That stretches out so broad and tall?
The worms will surely ne'er exhume
    A sleeper locked within such wall.

And see, that other stately pile
    Of chiselled glory – staring out;   10
Come, Sexton, leave your work awhile,
    And tell us what we ask about.

So! one belongs to him who held
    A score of trained and tortured steeds;
Great Circus Hero – unexcelled,
    On what strange stuff Ambition feeds!

The other guards the last repose
    Of one who shone by juggling craft.
Methinks when such a Temple rose
    How Esculapius[2] must have laughed.   20

And see that tomb beneath yon tree! –
    But, Sexton, tell us where to find
The grave of him we came to see; –
    Is it not here, or are we blind?

We mean Poor Hood's – the man who made
    That Song about the 'Bridge of Sighs;'
– You know the Song – well, leave your spade,
    And please to show us where *he* lies.

What! there! without a single mark –
    Without a stone – without a line –   30
Does watchfire Genius leave no spark
    To note its ashes as divine?

Must strangers come to woo his shade,
    Scanning rare beauties as they pass;
And when they pause where *he* is laid,
    Stop at a trodden mound of grass?

And is it thus? Well, we suppose,
    England is far too poor to spare
A slab of white where Truth might write
    The title of her Poet Heir.   40

Let us adorn our city walks
    With senate form and soldier-chief –
Carve toga-folds and laurel stalks, –
    Let marble shine in robe and leaf.

But Hood; 'poor Hood!' – the Poet fool
    Who sung of Woman's woes and wrongs.
Who taught his Master's Golden Rule –
    Give *him* no statue for his *songs!*

Give him the dust beneath his head,
    Give him a grave – a grave alone –   50
In Life he dearly won his bread; –
    In Death he was not worth a stone.

Perhaps we rightly think that he
    Who flung God's light round lowly things,
Can soar above in Memory's love,
    Supported by his own, strong wings.

Our Shakespeare can be only met
    Within a narrow Playhouse Porch;
So, Hood, thy spirit need not fret;
    But hold its own immortal torch.   60

'Poor Hood!' for whom a people wreathes
    The heart-born flowers that never die.
'Poor Hood!' for whom a requiem breathes
    In every human Toil-wrung sigh.

Let the Horse-tamer's bed be known
    By the rich mausoleum-shrine;
Give the bold Quack his charnel throne –
    Their works were worthier far than thine.

And let thy Soul serenely sleep
    While pilgrims stand as I have stood;   70
To worship at a nameless heap,
    And fondly, sadly say, 'Poor Hood!'

New Echoes *(1864).*

'POOR HOOD'
1 constructed of finest marble, from island of Paros.

2 Aesculapius: god of medicine and healing arts.

Mrs C. F. (Cecil Frances) (Humphreys) Alexander (1818–95)

Cecil Frances Humphreys, who as Mrs C. F. Alexander was one of the most well-known of Victorian hymn-writers, was born into the Protestant Anglo-Irish ascendancy in County Wicklow in the south-east of Ireland in 1818. Her father, John Humphreys, a large landowner, was a British Army officer, as was her mother's father. She was educated at home with her three sisters (her two brothers went to Oxford), and was precociously given to writing at an early age – 'My Poems for Mama, C. F. H.', a weekly newspaper for the family, and so on. She became great friends with Lady Harriet Howard, daughter of the Earl of Wicklow. Together they came under the influence of the Oxford Movement, and in the early forties produced Anglo-Catholic tracts together, Lady Harriet doing the prose and Cecil Frances the verse (these writings were published in a volume, 1848). Cecil Frances's hymns and poems – more than 400 of them – were written with children specially in mind. Her *Verses for Holy Seasons* (1846) was dedicated to John Keble, inspirer of all Anglo-Catholic versifiers ('To the author of the *Christian Year*, this attempt to adapt the great principle of his immortal work to the exigencies of the school room...'). Keble wrote the Preface for her immensely popular *Hymns for Little Children by C. F. H.* (1848; 60th edition 1896), mainly written to illustrate the Prayer Book and Creed, and which contained some of the Christian world's best-known verse: 'All Things Bright and Beautiful', 'There is a green hill far away', 'Once in Royal David's City', 'Jesus calls us o'er the tumult'. When Gounod wrote the music for 'There is a green hill', the words, he said, seemed to set themselves: and there is indeed an extraordinary feel of ease, inevitability and aptness about her best lines. They stick in the memory. In October 1850 Cecil Humphreys married William Alexander, rector of Termonamangan in County Tyrone, six years her junior. They had four children. He rose high in the hierarchy of the Established Irish Church (Bishop of Derry and Raphoe, 1869; Archbishop of Armagh and Primate of All Ireland, 1896). She was everything a grand lady and clergy-wife was expected to be – catechizing the maids, superintending good works and schools (the profits from *Hymns for Little Children* went to a northern Irish school for the deaf and dumb), founding a home for fallen women. Her many volumes included *Moral Songs* (1849) and *Hymns, Descriptive and Devotional, for the Use of Schools* (1858). She compiled *The Sunday Book of Poetry* (1864). Her idea of a Christian society is evidenced in the verse of 'All Things Bright and Beautiful' normally excised from modern hymn books, about God ordering the estate of the rich man in his castle and of the poor man at his gate. Her poetry's social missionariness was indistinct from its theological mission – or, indeed, from its Protestant Ulster Unionism: 'Shall speech of any Fenians find an echo in the North'? 'Nay, not while Ulster's loyal yet, while Orangemen we see/Determined, brave, and peaceable, as Orangemen should be' (*The Loyalists of Ulster*, 1884). She died in the Bishop's Palace in Derry, 12 October 1895.

MAKER OF HEAVEN AND EARTH

All Things Bright and Beautiful

All things bright and beautiful,
    All creatures great and small,
All things wise and wonderful,
    The LORD GOD made them all.

Each little flower that opens,
    Each little bird that sings,
He made their glowing colours,
    He made their tiny wings.

The rich man in his castle,
    The poor man at his gate,   10
God made them, high or lowly,
    And ordered their estate.

The purple-headed mountain,
    The river running by,
The sunset, and the morning
    That brightens up the sky,

The cold wind in the winter,
    The pleasant summer sun,
The ripe fruits in the garden,
    He made them every one.   20

The tall trees in the greenwood,
    The meadows where we play,
The rushes by the water
    We gather every day; –

He gave us eyes to see them,
  And lips that we might tell,

How great is GOD Almighty,
  Who has made all things well.

Hymns for Little Children, by C. F. H. [i.e. Humphreys]
(Joseph Masters, 1848). Text, 5th edn (Joseph Masters, 1852).
The first stanza, originally 'bright and beauteous',
and 'wise and wondrous'.

WHO WAS CONCEIVED BY THE HOLY GHOST, BORN OF THE VIRGIN MARY

Once in Royal David's City

Once in royal David's City
  Stood a lowly cattle shed,
Where a mother laid her Baby
  In a manger for His bed.
Mary was that mother mild,
JESUS CHRIST her little child.

He came down to earth from Heaven,
  Who is God and LORD of all,
And His shelter was a stable,
  And His cradle was a stall;   10
With the poor, and mean, and lowly
Lived on earth our SAVIOUR Holy.

And through all His wondrous childhood
  He would honour and obey,
Love and watch the lowly maiden
  In whose gentle arms He lay.
Christian children all must be
Mild, obedient, good as He.

For He is our childhood's Pattern,
  Day by day like us He grew,   20
He was little, weak and helpless,
  Tears and smiles like us He knew,
And He feeleth for our sadness,
And He shareth in our gladness.

And our eyes at last shall see Him,
  Through His own redeeming love,
For that Child so dear and gentle
  Is our LORD in Heaven above;
And He leads His children on
To the place where He is gone.   30

Not in that poor lowly stable,
With the oxen standing by,
We shall see Him; but in Heaven,
Set at GOD's right Hand on high;
When like stars His children crowned,
All in white, shall wait around.

Hymns for Little Children ([1848], 1852).

SUFFERED UNDER PONTIUS PILATE, WAS CRUCIFIED, DEAD, AND BURIED

There is a Green Hill Far Away

There is a green hill far away,
  Without a city wall,
Where the dear LORD was crucified
  Who died to save us all.

We may not know, we cannot tell
  What pains He had to bear,
But we believe it was for us,
  He hung and suffered there.

He died that we might be forgiven,
  He died to make us good,   10

That we might go at last to Heaven.
  Saved by His precious Blood.

There was no other good enough
  To pay the price of sin,
He only could unlock the gate
  Of Heaven, and let us in.

O, dearly, dearly has He loved,
  And we must love Him too,
And trust in His redeeming blood,
  And try His works to do.   20

Hymns for Little Children ([1848], 1852).

Arthur Hugh Clough (1819–61)

Arthur Hugh Clough, the poet and educationalist known to the Tennysons as the 'child-angel', was born in Liverpool, 1 January 1819, second son of James Butler Clough, a cotton-trader, and his wife Anne Perfect. The family emigrated to Charleston, South Carolina, at the end of 1822, but the boys were brought back to attend English schools in 1828. In the summer of 1829 they entered Rugby School. Clough became a favourite pupil of the school's new headmaster, Thomas Arnold, and never shrugged off his spell. He edited the school magazine, in which his early poems appeared. In October 1837 he went up to Balliol College, Oxford, as a scholar. He became friends with Benjamin Jowett (later Balliol's famous master), Dean Stanley, and the Arnold brothers, Matthew and Thomas. The Anglo-Catholic Oxford Movement had been stirring busily since 1833 – its inspiration John Henry Newman was still vicar of the University Church of St Mary – and Clough was greatly caught up in the ecclesiastical debates which would, in his case, eventually lead to loss of Christian faith altogether. He missed obtaining a First Class in the examinations of 1841 (some people blaming his religious turmoils), but still went on to gain a prestigious Fellowship at Oriel (1842), where he remained as tutor until 1848. The undergraduate reading parties he led provided the frame for his long narrative poem *The Bothie of Tober-na-Vuolich* (originally titled *The Bothie of Toper-na-Fuosich*), a democratic Oxford undergraduate's radical love-story. The poem, written very fast, was published in November 1848 just after Clough resigned from Oriel, unable any longer to subscribe to the Church of England's Thirty-Nine Articles of Religion (then a condition of Oxford Fellowships). William Michael Rossetti's astute review of the *Bothie* in the first number of the Pre-Raphaelite magazine *The Germ* (January 1850) rightly praised its 'peculiar modernness', as well as its quotidian factuality. In May 1848 Clough had witnessed the Paris Revolution with Emerson, and the radical European fervours of the forties, as well as indignation over the Irish Potato Famine, clearly animate the politics of his poem. Shorter poems of the time, such as 'Epi-Strauss-ium', show Clough weighing too the sharp demythologizing force of D. F. Strauss's *Das Leben Jesu*, in the momentous 1845 translation of Mary Ann Evans, i.e. George Eliot. Apart from *Ambarvalia* (February 1849), a joint venture with Thomas Burbridge, the *Bothie* was the only volume of Clough's verse to appear in England in his lifetime. *Amours de Voyage*, his other big narrative, written at Rome in 1849, appeared only in the USA, serialized in the Boston

journal *Atlantic Monthly*. Clough's even more impressively radical and post-Christian piece of anguishing over modern poems, the Goethe-esque *Dipsychus* (worked on in Venice in 1850), was never finished. These long poems made convenient hold-alls, loose baggy monsters, much like the big omnivalent Victorian novels, for containing anything and everything that was on the writer's mind. (They are, as it were, the large formal mirror of the loose long line Clough favoured in the *Bothie* and *Amours*: his own accentual, ordinary-speech-based version – 'anglo-savage', Clough called it – of the Virgilian quantitative hexameter, or six-footed, line.) But for all his poetry's potent inclusiveness, Clough eschewed making poetry his main activity. He became Principal of University Hall, London, in 1849, and was Professor of English Literature there. Squeezed out in 1852 for religious unorthodoxy he went to Boston, Massachusetts, becoming great friends with Charles Eliot Norton, teaching, doing journalism, revising Dryden's translation of Plutarch's *Lives* (published 1859). In 1853 he returned to London to become an examiner in the Education Office. He married Blanche Smith (June 1854), found time to support his wife's cousin Florence Nightingale in her medical-charitable work, but settled deeply into a civil servant's bourgeois life, quite abandoning poetry (except for translating Homer) until ill health forced him in 1861 to travel around the Mediterranean and he started his ship-board version of *The Canterbury Tales*, entitled *Mari Magno*. He 'cried like a child' reading from this poem to Tennyson in the Pyrenees in September 1861. A few weeks later, 13 November 1861, he was dead, in Florence, having contracted a malarial infection. Matthew Arnold celebrated him in his poem 'Thyrsis' (and praised him unstintingly as man, poet, critic, translator in his essay 'On Translating Homer: Last Words', 1862). Encouraged by the widow, Clough's friend Frances Turner Palgrave (of *The Golden Treasury*) wrote a Memorial Introduction for her preliminary edition of Clough's *Poems* (1862, enlarged 1863). Mrs Clough then brought out for private circulation the *Letters and Remains* (1865) with all of *Dipsychus* for the first time. This material was supplemented in *Poems and Prose Remains*, edited by Mrs Clough, assisted by John Addington Symonds, in two volumes (1869). In the traditional manner of loyal but protective and manipulative Black Widows, she carefully bowdlerized and doctored many of the poems – sometimes missing the verbal point entirely (compare her *noise* for Clough's *poise* in *Amours de Voyage*, II. 175).

THE LATEST DECALOGUE[1]

Thou shalt have one God only; who
Would be at the expense of two?
No graven images may be
Worshipped, except the currency:
Swear not at all; for for thy curse
Thine enemy is none the worse:
At church on Sunday to attend
Will serve to keep the world thy friend:
Honour thy parents; that is, all
From whom advancement may befall: 10
Thou shalt not kill; but needst not strive
Officiously to keep alive:
Do not adultery commit;
Advantage rarely comes of it:
Thou shalt not steal; an empty feat,
When it's so lucrative to cheat:
Bear not false witness; let the lie
Have time on its own wings to fly:
Thou shalt not covet; but tradition
Approves all forms of competition.   20

The sum of all is, thou shalt love,
If any body, God above:
At any rate shall never labour
More than thyself to love thy neighbour.

First published, Poems *(Macmillan & Co., Cambridge and London, 1862).*
Lines 21–4, only in one MS version.

Say not the struggle naught availeth,
    The labor and the wounds are vain,
The enemy faints not nor faileth,
    And as things have been, things remain.

If hopes were dupes, fears may be liars;
    It may be, in yon smoke concealed,
Your comrades chase e'en now the fliers,
    And, but for you, possess the field.

For while the tired waves vainly breaking,
    Seem here no painful inch to gain,   10
Far back through creeks and inlets making
    Comes silent, flooding-in, the main,

And not by eastern windows only,
    When daylight comes, comes in the light,
In front the sun climbs slow, how slowly,
    But westward, look! the land is bright.

First published, The Crayon, *II, no. 5 (New York, 1 August 1855), 71.*
Poems *(1862).* Text, The Crayon.

THE LATEST DECALOGUE
1   Decalogue: the Ten Commandments.

To spend uncounted years of pain,
Again, again, and yet again,
In working out in heart and brain
    The problem of our being here;
To gather facts from far and near,
Upon the mind to hold them clear,
And, knowing more may yet appear,
Unto one's latest breath to fear
The premature result to draw –
Is this the object, end and law,   10
    And purpose of our being here?

First published, Putnam's Magazine, *II (1 July 1853), 73.* Poems, *2nd edn
(Macmillan & Co., London and Cambridge, 1863). In* The Poems and
Prose Remains *of Arthur Hugh Clough, ed. His Wife, 2 vols (Macmillan & Co.,
1869), II,* Poems, *this poem is titled 'Perchè Pensa Pensando S'Invecchia'.*

AMOURS DE VOYAGE

*Oh, you are sick of self-love, Malvolio,
And taste with a distempered appetite!*
                Shakespeare[1]

Il doutait de tout, même de l'amour.[2]
                French novel

Solvitur ambulando.
        Solutio Sophismatum[3]

*Flevit amores
Non elaboratum ad pedem.*
                Horace[4]

Canto I

*Over the great windy waters, and over the clear-crested summits,
    Unto the sun and the sky, and unto the perfecter earth,
Come, let us go, – to a land wherein gods of the old time wandered,
    Where every breath even now changes to ether divine.
Come, let us go; though withal a voice whisper, 'The world that we live in,
    Whithersoever we turn, still is the same narrow crib;
'Tis but to prove limitation, and measure a cord, that we travel;
    Let who would 'scape and be free go to his chamber and think;
'Tis but to change idle fancies for memories wilfully falser;
    'Tis but to go and have been.' – Come, little bark! let us go.*   10

            I.   *Claude to Eustace*
Dear Eustatio, I write that you may write me an answer,
Or at the least to put us again *en rapport* with each other.
Rome disappoints me much, – St. Peter's, perhaps, in especial;
Only the Arch of Titus and view from the Lateran please me:
This, however, perhaps, is the weather, which truly is horrid.
Greece must be better, surely; and yet I am feeling so spiteful,

---

AMOURS DE VOYAGE
1 *Twelfth Night,* I. v.85–6.
2 He doubted everything, even love.

3 It's solved by walking/as you go. *Sophistical Solution.*
4 *Epodes* xiv.10–11. He mourned his love(s) in simple metres.

That I could travel to Athens, to Delphi, and Troy, and Mount Sinai,
Though but to see with my eyes that these are vanity also.
    Rome disappoints me much; I hardly as yet understand, but
Rubbishy seems the word that most exactly would suit it.   20
All the foolish destructions, and all the sillier savings,
All the incongruous things of past incompatible ages,
Seem to be treasured up here to make fools of present and future.
Would to Heaven the old Goths had made a cleaner sweep of it!
Would to Heaven some new ones would come and destroy these churches!
However, one can live in Rome as also in London.
Rome is better than London, because it is other than London
It is a blessing, no doubt, to be rid, at least for a time, of
All one's friends and relations, – yourself (forgive me!) included, –
All the *assujettissement*[5] of having been what one has been,   30
What one thinks one is, or thinks that others suppose one;
Yet, in despite of all, we turn like fools to the English.
Vernon has been my fate; who is here the same that you knew him, –
Making the tour, it seems, with friends of the name of Trevellyn.

II.   *Claude to Eustace*

Rome disappoints me still; but I shrink and adapt myself to it.
Somehow a tyrannous sense of a superincumbent oppression
Still, wherever I go, accompanies ever, and makes me
Feel like a tree (shall I say?) buried under a ruin of brickwork.
Rome, believe me, my friend, is like its own Monte Testaceo,
Merely a marvellous mass of broken and castaway wine-pots.   40
Ye gods! what do I want with this rubbish of ages departed,
Things that nature abhors, the experiments that she has failed in?
What do I find in the Forum? An archway and two or three pillars.
Well, but St. Peter's? Alas, Bernini has filled it with sculpture!
No one can cavil, I grant, at the size of the great Coliseum.
Doubtless the notion of grand and capacious and massive amusement,
This the old Romans had; but tell me, is this an idea?
Yet of solidity much, but of splendour little is extant:
'Brickwork I found thee, and marble I left thee!' their Emperor vaunted;[6]
'Marble I thought thee, and brickwork I find thee!' the Tourist may answer.   50

III.   *Georgina Trevellyn to Louisa——*

At last, dearest Louisa, I take up my pen to address you.
Here we are, you see, with the seven-and-seventy boxes,
Courier, Papa and Mamma, the children, and Mary and Susan:
Here we all are at Rome, and delighted of course with St. Peter's,
And very pleasantly lodged in the famous Piazza di Spagna.
Rome is a wonderful place, but Mary shall tell you about it;
Not very gay, however; the English are mostly at Naples;
There are the A.s, we hear, and most of the W. party.
    George, however, is come; did I tell you about his mustachios?
Dear, I must really stop, for the carriage, they tell me, is waiting;   60
Mary will finish; and Susan is writing, they say, to Sophia.
Adieu, dearest Louise, – evermore your faithful Georgina.
Who can a Mr. Claude be whom George has taken to be with?
Very stupid, I think, but George says so *very* clever.

IV.   *Claude to Eustace*

No, the Christian faith, as at any rate I understood it,
With its humiliations and exaltations combining,

---

5 subjection.   6 Emperor Augustus.

Exaltations sublime, and yet diviner abasements,
Aspirations from something most shameful here upon earth and
In our poor selves to something most perfect above in the heavens, –
No, the Christian faith, as I, at least, understood it,   70
Is not here, O Rome, in any of these thy churches;
Is not here, but in Freiburg, or Rheims, or Westminster Abbey.
What in thy Dome I find, in all thy recenter efforts,
Is a something, I think, more *rational* far, more earthly,
Actual, less ideal, devout not in scorn and refusal,
But in a positive, calm, Stoic-Epicurean acceptance.
This I begin to detect in St. Peter's and some of the churches,
Mostly in all that I see of the sixteenth-century masters;
Overlaid of course with infinite gauds and gewgaws,
Innocent, playful follies, the toys and trinkets of childhood,   80
Forced on maturer years, as the serious one thing needful,
By the barbarian will of the rigid and ignorant Spaniard.
   Curious work, meantime, re-entering society: how we
Walk a livelong day, great Heaven, and watch our shadows!
What our shadows seem, forsooth, we will ourselves be.
Do I look like that? you think me that: then I *am* that.

V.   *Claude to Eustace*

Luther, they say, was unwise; like a half-taught German, he could not
See that old follies were passing most tranquilly out of remembrance;
Leo the Tenth was employing all efforts to clear out abuses;
Jupiter, Juno, and Venus, Fine Arts, and Fine Letters, the Poets,   90
Scholars, and Sculptors, and Painters, were quietly clearing away the
Martyrs, and Virgins, and Saints, or at any rate Thomas Aquinas:
He must forsooth make a fuss and distend his huge Wittenberg lungs, and
Bring back Theology once yet again in a flood upon Europe:
Lo you, for forty days from the windows of heaven it fell; the
Waters prevail on the earth yet more for a hundred and fifty;
Are they abating at last? the doves that are sent to explore are
Wearily fain to return, at the best with a leaflet of promise, –
Fain to return, as they went, to the wandering wave-tost vessel, –
Fain to re-enter the roof which covers the clean and the unclean, –   100
Luther, they say, was unwise; he didn't see how things were going;
Luther was foolish, – but, O great God! what call you Ignatius?
O my tolerant soul, be still! but you talk of barbarians,
Alaric, Attila, Genseric; – why, they came, they killed, they
Ravaged, and went on their way; but these vile, tyrannous Spaniards,
These are here still, – how long, O ye heavens, in the country of Dante?
These, that fanaticized Europe, which now can forget them, release not
This, their choicest of prey, this Italy; here you see them, –
Here, with emasculate pupils and gimcrack churches of Gesu,
Pseudo-learning and lies, confessional-boxes and postures, –   110
Here, with metallic beliefs and regimental devotions, –
Here, overcrusting with slime, perverting, defacing, debasing,
Michael Angelo's dome, that had hung the Pantheon in heaven,
Raphael's Joys and Graces, and thy clear stars, Galileo!

VI.   *Claude to Eustace*

Which of three Misses Trevellyn it is that Vernon shall marry
Is not a thing to be known; for our friend is one of those natures
Which have their perfect delight in the general tender-domestic,
So that he trifles with Mary's shawl, ties Susan's bonnet,
Dances with all, but at home is most, they say, with Georgina,
Who is, however, *too* silly in my apprehension for Vernon.   120

I, as before when I wrote, continue to see them a little;
Not that I like them much or care a *bajocco*[7] for Vernon,
But I am slow at Italian, have not many English acquaintance,
And I am asked, in short, and am not good at excuses.
Middle-class people these, bankers very likely, not wholly
Pure of the taint of the shop; will at table d'hôte and restaurant
Have their shilling's worth, their penny's pennyworth even:
Neither man's aristocracy this, nor God's, God knoweth!
Yet they are fairly descended, they give you to know, well connected;
Doubtless somewhere in some neighbourhood have, and are careful to keep, some   130
Threadbare-genteel relations, who in their turn are enchanted
Grandly among county people to introduce at assemblies
To the unpennied cadets our cousins with excellent fortunes.
Neither man's aristocracy this, nor God's, God knoweth!

VII.   *Claude to Eustace*

Ah, what a shame, indeed, to abuse these most worthy people!
Ah, what a sin to have sneered at their innocent rustic pretensions!
Is it not laudable really, this reverent worship of station?
Is it not fitting that wealth should tender this homage to culture?
Is it not touching to witness these efforts, if little availing,
Painfully made, to perform the old ritual service of manners?   140
Shall not devotion atone for the absence of knowledge? and fervour
Palliate, cover, the fault of a superstitious observance?
Dear, dear, what do I say? but, alas, just now, like Iago,
I can be nothing at all, if it is not critical wholly;
So in fantastic height, in coxcomb exultation,
Here in the Garden I walk, can freely concede to the Maker
That the works of his hand are all very good: his creatures,
Beast of the field and fowl, he brings them before me; I name them;
That which I name them, they are, – the bird, the beast, and the cattle.
But for Adam, – alas, poor critical coxcomb Adam!   150
But for Adam there is not found an help-meet for him.

VIII.   *Claude to Eustace*

No, great Dome of Agrippa, thou art not Christian! canst not,
Strip and replaster and daub and do what they will with thee, be so!
Here underneath the great porch of colossal Corinthian columns,
Here as I walk, do I dream of the Christian belfries above them?
Or on a bench as I sit and abide for long hours, till thy whole vast
Round grows dim as in dreams to my eyes, I repeople thy niches,
Not with the Martyrs, and Saints, and Confessors, and Virgins, and children,
But with the mightier forms of an older, austerer worship;
And I recite to myself, how   160
                    Eager for battle here
            Stood Vulcan, here matronal Juno,
                    And with the bow to his shoulder faithful
            He who with pure dew laveth of Castaly
            His flowing locks, who holdeth of Lycia
            The oak forest and the wood that bore him,
                    Delos' and Patara's own Apollo.[8]

---

7   small coin (I don't care *a bean*).

8   Hic avidus stetit
    Vulcanus, hic matrona Juno, et
        Nunquam humeris positurus arcum,
    Qui rore puro Castaliæ lavit

    Crines solutos, qui Lyciæ tenet
        Dumeta natalemque silvam,
            Delius et Patareus Apollo. [Author's note]
    [Horace, *Odes* III. iv.58–64. *Hinc . . . hinc*: 'on this side . . . on that', more usual.]

IX.   *Claude to Eustace*

Yet it is pleasant, I own it, to be in their company; pleasant,
Whatever else it may be, to abide in the feminine presence.
Pleasant, but wrong, will you say? But this happy, serene coexistence   170
Is to some poor soft souls, I fear, a necessity simple,
Meat and drink and life, and music, filling with sweetness,
Thrilling with melody sweet, with harmonies strange overwhelming,
All the long-silent strings of an awkward, meaningless fabric.
Yet as for that, I could live, I believe, with children; to have those
Pure and delicate forms encompassing, moving about you,
This were enough, I could think; and truly with glad resignation
Could from the dream of romance, from the fever of flushed adolescence,
Look to escape and subside into peaceful avuncular functions.
Nephews and nieces! alas, for as yet I have none! and, moreover,   180
Mothers are jealous, I fear me, too often, too rightfully; fathers
Think they have title exclusive to spoiling their own little darlings;
And by the law of the land, in despite of Malthusian doctrine,[9]
No sort of proper provision is made for that most patriotic,
Most meritorious subject, the childless and bachelor uncle.

X.   *Claude to Eustace*

Ye, too, marvellous Twain, that erect on the Monte Cavallo
Stand by your rearing steeds in the grace of your motionless movement,
Stand with your upstretched arms and tranquil regardant faces,
Stand as instinct with life in the might of immutable manhood, –
O ye mighty and strange, ye ancient divine ones of Hellas,   190
Are ye Christian too? to convert and redeem and renew you,
Will the brief form have sufficed, that a Pope has set up on the apex
Of the Egyptian stone that o'ertops you, the Christian symbol?[10]
   And ye, silent, supreme in serene and victorious marble,
Ye that encircle the walls of the stately Vatican chambers,
Juno and Ceres, Minerva, Apollo, the Muses and Bacchus,
Ye unto whom far and near come posting the Christian pilgrims,
Ye that are ranged in the halls of the mystic Christian Pontiff,
Are ye also baptized? are ye of the kingdom of Heaven?
Utter, O some one, the word that shall reconcile Ancient and Modern!   200
Am I to turn me for this unto thee, great Chapel of Sixtus?[11]

XI.   *Claude to Eustace*

These are the facts. The uncle, the elder brother, the squire (a
Little embarrassed, I fancy), resides in the family place in
Cornwall, of course; 'Papa is in business,' Mary informs me;
He's a good sensible man, whatever his trade is. The mother
Is – shall I call it fine? – herself she would tell you refined, and
Greatly, I fear me, looks down on my bookish and maladroit manners;
Somewhat affecteth the blue; would talk to me often of poets;
Quotes, which I hate, Childe Harold; but also appreciates Wordsworth;
Sometimes adventures on Schiller; and then to religion diverges;   210
Questions me much about Oxford; and yet, in her loftiest flights still
Grates the fastidious ear with the slightly mercantile accent.
   Is it contemptible, Eustace – I'm perfectly ready to think so, –
Is it, – the horrible pleasure of pleasing inferior people?
I am ashamed my own self; and yet true it is, if disgraceful,
That for the first time in life I am living and moving with freedom.

9   T. R. Malthus's notorious argument that population tended natur-
ally to outstrip means of sustenance (*Essay on the Principle of Population*,
1798, 1803).

10   reference to the statue of the Dioscuri – Castor and Pollux – and
the even huger Egyptian obelisk beside it.

11   the Sistine Chapel, built by 15th-century Pope Sixtus IV.

I, who never could talk to the people I meet with my uncle, –
I, who have always failed, – I, trust me, can suit the Trevellyns;
I, believe me, – great conquest, – am liked by the country bankers.
And I am glad to be liked, and like in return very kindly.   220
So it proceeds; *Laissez faire, laissez aller*, – such is the watchword.
Well, I know there are thousands as pretty and hundreds as pleasant,
Girls by the dozen as good, and girls in abundance with polish
Higher and manners more perfect than Susan or Mary Trevellyn.
Well, I know, after all, it is only juxtaposition, –
Juxtaposition, in short; and what is juxtaposition?

XII.   *Claude to Eustace*

But I am in for it now, – *laissez faire*, of a truth, *laissez aller*.
Yes, I am going, – I feel it, I feel and cannot recall it, –
Fusing with this thing and that, entering into all sorts of relations,
Tying I know not what ties, which, whatever they are, I know one thing,   230
Will, and must, woe is me, be one day painfully broken, –
Broken with painful remorses, with shrinkings of soul, and relentings,
Foolish delays, more foolish evasions, most foolish renewals.
But I have made the step, have quitted the ship of Ulysses;
Quitted the sea and the shore, passed into the magical island;
Yet on my lips is the *moly*, medicinal, offered of Hermes.[12]
I have come into the precinct, the labyrinth closes around me,
Path into path rounding slyly; I pace slowly on, and the fancy,
Struggling a while to sustain the long sequences, weary, bewildered,
Fain must collapse in despair; I yield, I am lost, and know nothing;   240
Yet in my bosom unbroken remaineth the clue;[13] I shall use it.
Lo, with the rope on my loins I descend through the fissure; I sink, yet
Inly secure in the strength of invisible arms up above me;
Still, wheresoever I swing, wherever to shore, or to shelf, or
Floor of cavern untrodden, shell-sprinkled, enchanting, I know I
Yet shall one time feel the strong cord tighten about me, –
Feel it, relentless, upbear me from spots I would rest in; and though the
Rope sway wildly, I faint, crags wound me, from crag unto crag re-
Bounding, or, wide in the void, I die ten deaths, ere the end I
Yet shall plant firm foot on the broad lofty spaces I quit, shall   250
Feel underneath me again the great massy strengths of abstraction,
Look yet abroad from the height o'er the sea whose salt wave I have tasted.

XIII.   *Georgina Trevellyn to Louisa* ——

Dearest Louisa, – Inquire, if you please, about Mr. Claude ——.
He has been once at R., and remembers meeting the H.s.
Harriet L., perhaps, may be able to tell you about him.
It is an awkward youth, but still with very good manners;
Not without prospects, we hear; and, George says, highly connected.
Georgy declares it absurd, but Mamma is alarmed and insists he has
Taken up strange opinions, and may be turning a Papist.
Certainly once he spoke of a daily service he went to.   260
'Where?' we asked, and he laughed and answered, 'At the Pantheon.'
This was a temple, you know, and now is a Catholic church; and
Though it is said that Mazzini has sold it for Protestant service,
Yet I suppose this change can hardly as yet be effected.
Adieu again, – evermore, my dearest, your loving Georgina.

---

12 magical herb *moly* given to Ulysses by Hermes as protection against Circe, who turned men into animals.

13 ball of thread, as given to Theseus by Ariadne to guide him through the Cretan labyrinth, to kill beastly Minotaur.

P.S. by Mary Trevellyn

I am to tell you, you say, what I think of our last new acquaintance.
Well, then, I think that George has a very fair right to be jealous.
I do not like him much, though I do not dislike being with him.
He is what people call, I suppose, a superior man, and
Certainly seems so to me; but I think he is terribly selfish.   270

———————

Alba,[14] *thou findest me still, and, Alba, thou findest me ever,*
    Now from the Capitol steps, now over Titus's Arch,
Here from the large grassy spaces that spread from the Lateran portal,
    Towering o'er aqueduct lines lost in perspective between,
Or from a Vatican window, or bridge, or the high Coliseum,
    Clear by the garlanded line cut of the Flavian ring.
Beautiful can I not call thee, and yet thou hast power to o'ermaster,
    Power of mere beauty; in dreams, Alba, thou hauntest me still.
Is it religion? I ask me; or is it a vain superstition?
    Slavery abject and gross? service, too feeble, of truth?   280
Is it an idol I bow to, or is it a god that I worship?
    Do I sink back on the old, or do I soar from the mean?
So through the city I wander and question, unsatisfied ever,
    Reverent so I accept, doubtful because I revere.

Canto II

Is it illusion? or does there a spirit from perfecter ages,
    Here, even yet, amid loss, change, and corruption abide?
Does there a spirit we know not, though seek, though we find, comprehend not,
    Here to entice and confuse, tempt and evade us, abide?
Lives in the exquisite grace of the column disjointed and single,
    Haunts the rude masses of brick garlanded gayly with vine,
E'en in the turret fantastic surviving that springs from the ruin,
    E'en in the people itself? is it illusion or not?
Is it illusion or not that attracteth the pilgrim transalpine,
    Brings him a dullard and dunce hither to pry and to stare?   10
Is it illusion or not that allures the barbarian stranger,
    Brings him with gold to the shrine, brings him in arms to the gate?

I.   *Claude to Eustace*

What do the people say, and what does the government do? – you
Ask, and I know not at all. Yet fortune will favour your hopes; and
I, who avoided it all, am fated, it seems, to describe it.
I, who nor meddle nor make in politics, – I who sincerely
Put not my trust in leagues nor any suffrage by ballot,
Never predicted Parisian millenniums, never beheld a
New Jerusalem coming down dressed like a bride out of heaven
Right on the Place de la Concorde, – I, nevertheless, let me say it,   20
Could in my soul of souls, this day, with the Gaul at the gates, shed
One true tear for thee, thou poor little Roman Republic!
What, with the German restored, with Sicily safe to the Bourbon,
Not leave one poor corner for native Italian exertion?
France, it is foully done! and you, poor foolish England, –
You, who a twelvemonth ago said nations must choose for themselves, you
Could not, of course, interfere, – you, now, when a nation has chosen——
Pardon this folly! *The Times* will, of course, have announced the occasion,
Told you the news of to-day; and although it was slightly in error

14   Rome.

When it proclaimed as a fact the Apollo[15] was sold to a Yankee,   30
You may believe when it tells you the French are at Civita Vecchia.

II.   *Claude to Eustace*

Dulce it is, and *decorum*, no doubt, for the country to fall, – to
Offer one's blood an oblation to Freedom, and die for the Cause;[16] yet
Still, individual culture is also something, and no man
Finds quite distinct the assurance that he of all others is called on,
Or would be justified, even, in taking away from the world that
Precious creature, himself. Nature sent him here to abide here,
Else why send him at all? Nature wants him still, it is likely.
On the whole, we are meant to look after ourselves; it is certain
Each has to eat for himself, digest for himself, and in general   40
Care for his own dear life, and see to his own preservation;
Nature's intentions, in most things uncertain, in this are decisive;
Which, on the whole, I conjecture the Romans will follow, and I shall.
  So we cling to our rocks like limpets; Ocean may bluster,
Over and under and round us; we open our shells to imbibe our
Nourishment, close them again, and are safe, fulfilling the purpose
Nature intended, – a wise one, of course, and a noble, we doubt not.
Sweet it may be and decorous, perhaps, for the country to die; but,
On the whole, we conclude the Romans won't do it, and I shan't.

III.   *Claude to Eustace*

Will they fight? They say so. And will the French? I can hardly,   50
Hardly think so; and yet – He is come, they say, to Palo,
He is passed from Monterone, at Santa Severa
He hath laid up his guns. But the Virgin, the Daughter of Roma,
She hath despised thee and laughed thee to scorn, – the Daughter of Tiber,
She hath shaken her head and built barricades against thee!
Will they fight? I believe it. Alas! 'tis ephemeral folly,
Vain and ephemeral folly, of course, compared with pictures,
Statues, and antique gems! – Indeed: and yet indeed too,
Yet, methought, in broad day did I dream, – tell it not in St. James's,
Whisper it not in thy courts, O Christ Church! – yet did I, waking,   60
Dream of a cadence that sings, *Si tombent nos jeunes héros, la*
Terre en produit de nouveaux contre vous tous prêts à se battre;[17]
Dreamt of great indignations and angers transcendental,
Dreamt of a sword at my side and a battle-horse underneath me.

IV.   *Claude to Eustace*

Now supposing the French or the Neapolitan soldier
Should by some evil chance come exploring the Maison Serny
(Where the family English are all to assemble for safety),
Am I prepared to lay down my life for the British female?
Really, who knows? One has bowed and talked, till, little by little,
All the natural heat has escaped of the chivalrous spirit.   70
Oh, one conformed, of course; but one doesn't die for good manners,
Stab or shoot, or be shot, by way of graceful attention.
No, if it should be at all, it should be on the barricades there;
Should I incarnadine ever this inky pacifical finger,

---

15   Belvidere Apollo (ancient marble statue in Vatican Belvidere
Gallery).
16   *Dulce et decorum est pro patria mori*: 'it is pleasant and right to die for
the fatherland'. Horace, *Odes* III. ii.13. The Cause is the shortlived
Roman Republic, led by Mazzini and Garibaldi, 1849.

17   'If our young heroes fall, the earth brings forth new ones eager to
fight against you': *The Marseillaise* (French revolutionary song, and
National Anthem).

Sooner far should it be for this vapour of Italy's freedom,
Sooner far by the side of the d——d and dirty plebeians.
Ah, for a child in the street I could strike; for the full-blown lady——
Somehow, Eustace, alas! I have not felt the vocation.
Yet these people of course will expect, as of course, my protection,
Vernon in radiant arms stand forth for the lovely Georgina,   80
And to appear, I suppose, were but common civility. Yes, and
Truly I do not desire they should either be killed or offended.
Oh, and of course you will say, 'When the time comes, you will be ready.'
Ah, but before it comes, am I to presume it will be so?
What I cannot feel now, am I to suppose that I shall feel?
Am I not free to attend for the ripe and indubious instinct?
Am I forbidden to wait for the clear and lawful perception?
Is it the calling of man to surrender his knowledge and insight
For the mere venture of what may, perhaps, be the virtuous action?
Must we, walking our earth, discerning a little, and hoping   90
Some plain visible task shall yet for our hands be assigned us, –
Must we abandon the future for fear of omitting the present,
Quit our own fireside hopes at the alien call of a neighbour,
To the mere possible shadow of Deity offer the victim?
And is all this, my friend, but a weak and ignoble refining,
Wholly unworthy the head or the heart of Your Own Correspondent?

V.   *Claude to Eustace*

Yes, we are fighting at last, it appears. This morning as usual,
Murray,[18] as usual, in hand, I enter the Caffè Nuovo;
Seating myself with a sense as it were of a change in the weather,
Not understanding, however, but thinking mostly of Murray,   100
And, for to-day is their day, of the Campidoglio Marbles,
Caffè-latte! I call to the waiter, – and *Non c' è latte,*[19]
This is the answer he makes me, and this the sign of a battle.
So I sit; and truly they seem to think anyone else more
Worthy than me of attention. I wait for my milkless *nero,*[20]
Free to observe undistracted all sorts and sizes of persons,
Blending civilian and soldier in strangest costume, coming in, and
Gulping in hottest haste, still standing, their coffee, – withdrawing
Eagerly, jangling a sword on the steps, or jogging a musket
Slung to the shoulder behind. They are fewer, moreover, than usual,   110
Much, and silenter far; and so I begin to imagine
Something is really afloat. Ere I leave, the Caffè is empty,
Empty too the streets, in all its length the Corso
Empty, and empty I see to my right and left the Condotti.
    Twelve o'clock, on the Pincian Hill, with lots of English,
Germans, Americans, French, – the Frenchmen, too, are protected, –
So we stand in the sun, but afraid of a probable shower;
So we stand and stare, and see, to the left of St. Peter's,
Smoke, from the cannon, white, – but that is at intervals only, –
Black, from a burning house, we suppose, by the Cavalleggieri;   120
And we believe we discern some lines of men descending
Down through the vineyard-slopes, and catch a bayonet gleaming.
Every ten minutes, however, – in this there is no misconception, –
Comes a great white puff from behind Michael Angelo's dome, and
After a space the report of a real big gun, – not the Frenchman's? –
That must be doing some work. And so we watch and conjecture.

18   guide-book.   20   black coffee.
19   'coffee with milk'; 'there's no milk'.

Shortly, an Englishman comes, who says he has been to St. Peter's,
Seen the Piazza and troops, but that is all he can tell us;
So we watch and sit, and, indeed, it begins to be tiresome. –
All this smoke is outside; when it has come to the inside,   130
It will be time, perhaps, to descend and retreat to our houses.
  Half-past one, or two. The report of small arms frequent,
Sharp and savage indeed; that cannot all be for nothing:
So we watch and wonder; but guessing is tiresome, very.
Weary of wondering, watching, and guessing, and gossiping idly,
Down I go, and pass through the quiet streets with the knots of
National Guards patrolling, and flags hanging out at the windows,
English, American, Danish, – and, after offering to help an
Irish family moving *en masse* to the Maison Serny,
After endeavouring idly to minister balm to the trembling   140
Quinquagenarian fears of two lone British spinsters,
Go to make sure of my dinner before the enemy enter.
But by this there are signs of stragglers returning; and voices
Talk, though you don't believe it, of guns and prisoners taken;
And on the walls you read the first bulletin of the morning. –
This is all that I saw, and all I know of the battle.

VI.   *Claude to Eustace*

Victory! Victory! – Yes! ah, yes, thou republican Zion,
Truly the kings of the earth are gathered and gone by together;
Doubtless they marvelled to witness such things, were astonished, and so forth.
Victory! Victory! Victory! – Ah, but it is, believe me,   150
Easier, easier far, to intone the chant of the martyr
Than to indite any pæan of any victory. Death may
Sometimes be noble; but life, at the best, will appear an illusion.
While the great pain is upon us, it is great; when it is over,
Why, it is over. The smoke of the sacrifice rises to heaven,
Of a sweet savour, no doubt, to Somebody; but on the altar,
Lo, there is nothing remaining but ashes and dirt and ill odour.
  So it stands, you perceive; the labial muscles that swelled with
Vehement evolution of yesterday Marseillaises,[21]
Articulations sublime of defiance and scorning, to-day col-   160
Lapse and languidly mumble, while men and women and papers
Scream and re-scream to each other the chorus of Victory. Well, but
I am thankful they fought, and glad that the Frenchmen were beaten.

VII.   *Claude to Eustace*

So, I have seen a man killed! An experience that, among others!
Yes, I suppose I have; although I can hardly be certain,
And in a court of justice could never declare I had seen it.
But a man was killed, I am told, in a place where I saw
Something; a man was killed, I am told, and I saw something.
  I was returning home from St. Peter's; Murray, as usual,
Under my arm, I remember; had crossed the St. Angelo bridge; and   170
Moving towards the Condotti, had got to the first barricade, when
Gradually, thinking still of St. Peter's, I became conscious
Of a sensation of movement opposing me, – tendency this way
(Such as one fancies may be in a stream when the wave of the tide is
Coming and not yet come, – a sort of poise and retention);
So I turned, and, before I turned, caught sight of stragglers
Heading a crowd, it is plain, that is coming behind that corner.

21   *The Marseillaise*: song of revolutionary France.

Looking up, I see windows filled with heads; the Piazza,
Into which you remember the Ponte St. Angelo enters,
Since I passed, has thickened with curious groups; and now the   180
Crowd is coming, has turned, has crossed that last barricade, is
Here at my side. In the middle they drag at something. What is it?
Ha! bare swords in the air, held up! There seem to be voices
Pleading and hands putting back; official, perhaps; but the swords are
Many, and bare in the air. In the air? They descend; they are smiting,
Hewing, chopping – At what? In the air once more upstretched! And
Is it blood that's on them? Yes, certainly blood! Of whom, then?
Over whom is the cry of this furor of exultation?
    While they are skipping and screaming, and dancing their caps on the points of
Swords and bayonets, I to the outskirts back, and ask a   190
Mercantile-seeming bystander, 'What is it?' and he, looking always
That way, makes me answer, 'A Priest, who was trying to fly to
The Neapolitan army,' – and thus explains the proceeding.
    You didn't see the dead man? No; – I began to be doubtful;
I was in black myself, and didn't know what mightn't happen; –
But a National Guard close by me, outside of the hubbub,
Broke his sword with slashing a broad hat covered with dust, – and
Passing away from the place with Murray under my arm, and
Stooping, I saw through the legs of the people the legs of a body.
    You are the first, do you know, to whom I have mentioned the matter.   200
Whom should I tell it to, else? – these girls? – the Heavens forbid it! –
Quidnuncs at Monaldini's? – idlers upon the Pincian?
    If I rightly remember, it happened on that afternoon when
Word of the nearer approach of a new Neapolitan army
First was spread. I began to bethink me of Paris Septembers,
Thought I could fancy the look of the old 'Ninety-two. On that evening
Three or four, or, it may be, five, of these people were slaughtered.
Some declare they had, one of them, fired on a sentinel; others
Say they were only escaping; a Priest, it is currently stated,
Stabbed a National Guard on the very Piazza Colonna: 210
History, Rumour of Rumours, I leave it to thee to determine!
    But I am thankful to say the government seems to have strength to
Put it down; it has vanished, at least; the place is most peaceful.
Through the Trastevere walking last night, at nine of the clock, I
Found no sort of disorder; I crossed by the Island-bridges,
So by the narrow streets to the Ponte Rotto, and onwards
Thence by the Temple of Vesta, away to the great Coliseum,
Which at the full of the moon is an object worthy a visit.

VIII.   *Georgina Trevellyn to Louisa——*
Only think, dearest Louisa, what fearful scenes we have witnessed! –

*   *   *   *   *   *   *   *   *   *   *

George has just seen Garibaldi, dressed up in a long white cloak, on   220
Horseback, riding by, with his mounted negro behind him:
This is a man, you know, who came from America with him,
Out of the woods, I suppose, and uses a *lasso* in fighting,
Which is, I don't quite know, but a sort of noose, I imagine;
This he throws on the heads of the enemy's men in a battle,
Pulls them into his reach, and then most cruelly kills them:
Mary does not believe, but we heard it from an Italian.
Mary allows she was wrong about Mr. Claude *being selfish*;
He was *most* useful and kind on the terrible thirtieth of April.
Do not write here any more; we are starting directly for Florence: 230
We should be off to-morrow, if only Papa could get horses;
All have been seized everywhere for the use of this dreadful Mazzini.

P.S.
    Mary has seen thus far. – I am really so angry, Louisa, –
Quite out of patience, my dearest! What can the man be intending?
I am quite tired; and Mary, who might bring him to in a moment,
Lets him go on as he likes, and neither will help nor dismiss him.

IX.   *Claude to Eustace*

It is most curious to see what a power a few calm words (in
Merely a brief proclamation) appear to possess on the people.
Order is perfect, and peace; the city is utterly tranquil;
And one cannot conceive that this easy and *nonchalant* crowd, that   240
Flows like a quiet stream through street and market-place, entering
Shady recesses and bays of church, *osteria*,²² and *caffè*,
Could in a moment be changed to a flood as of molten lava,
Boil into deadly wrath and wild homicidal delusion.
    Ah, 'tis an excellent race, – and even in old degradation,
Under a rule that enforces to flattery, lying, and cheating,
E'en under Pope and Priest, a nice and natural people.
Oh, could they but be allowed this chance of redemption! – but clearly
That is not likely to be. Meantime, notwithstanding all journals,
Honour for once to the tongue and the pen of the eloquent writer!   250
Honour to speech! and all honour to thee, thou noble Mazzini!

X.   *Claude to Eustace*

    I am in love, meantime, you think; no doubt you would think so.
I am in love, you say; with those letters, of course, you would say so.
I am in love, you declare. I think not so; yet I grant you
It is a pleasure indeed to converse with this girl. Oh, rare gift,
Rare felicity, this! she can talk in a rational way, can
Speak upon subjects that really are matters of mind and of thinking,
Yet in perfection retain her simplicity; never, one moment,
Never, however you urge it, however you tempt her, consents to
Step from ideas and fancies and loving sensations to those vain   260
Conscious understandings that vex the minds of man-kind.
No, though she talk, it is music; her fingers desert not the keys; 'tis
Song, though you hear in the song the articulate vocables sounded,
Syllabled singly and sweetly the words of melodious meaning.
    I am in love, you say: I do not think so, exactly.

XI.   *Claude to Eustace*

There are two different kinds, I believe, of human attraction:
One which simply disturbs, unsettles, and makes you uneasy,
And another that poises, retains, and fixes and holds you.
I have no doubt, for myself, in giving my voice for the latter.
I do not wish to be moved, but growing where I was growing,   270
There more truly to grow, to live where as yet I had languished.
I do not like being moved: for the will is excited; and action
Is a most dangerous thing; I tremble for something factitious,
Some malpractice of heart and illegitimate process;
We are so prone to these things with our terrible notions of duty.

XII.   *Claude to Eustace*

Ah, let me look, let me watch, let me wait, unhurried, unprompted!
Bid me not venture on aught that could alter or end what is present!
Say not, Time flies, and Occasion, that never returns, is departing!

22 hostelry; pub.

Drive me not out, ye ill angels with fiery swords, from my Eden,
Waiting, and watching, and looking! Let love be its own inspiration!   280
Shall not a voice, if a voice there must be, from the airs that environ,
Yea, from the conscious heavens, without our knowledge or effort,
Break into audible words? And love be its own inspiration?

XIII.   *Claude to Eustace*

Wherefore and how I am certain, I hardly can tell; but it *is* so.
She doesn't like me, Eustace; I think she never will like me.
Is it my fault, as it is my misfortune, my ways are not her ways?
Is it my fault, that my habits and modes are dissimilar wholly?
'Tis not her fault, 'tis her nature, her virtue, to misapprehend them:
'Tis not her fault, 'tis her beautiful nature, not ever to know me.
Hopeless it seems, – yet I cannot, though hopeless, determine to leave it: 290
She goes, – therefore I go; she moves, – I move, not to lose her.

XIV.   *Claude to Eustace*

Oh, 'tisn't manly, of course, 'tisn't manly, this method of wooing;
'Tisn't the way very likely to win. For the woman, they tell you,
Ever prefers the audacious, the wilful, the vehement hero;
She has no heart for the timid, the sensitive soul; and for knowledge, –
Knowledge, O ye Gods! – When did they appreciate knowledge?
Wherefore should they, either? I am sure I do not desire it.
  Ah, and I feel too, Eustace, she cares not a tittle about me!
(Care about me, indeed! and do I really expect it?)
But my manner offends; my ways are wholly repugnant;   300
Every word that I utter estranges, hurts, and repels her;
Every moment of bliss that I gain, in her exquisite presence,
Slowly, surely, withdraws her, removes her, and severs her from me.
Not that I care very much! – any way, I escape from the boy's own
Folly, to which I am prone, of loving where it is easy.
Not that I mind very much! Why should I? I am not in love, and
Am prepared, I think, if not by previous habit,
Yet in the spirit beforehand for this and all that is like it;
It is an easier matter for us contemplative creatures,
Us, upon whom the pressure of action is laid so lightly;   310
We, discontented indeed with things in particular, idle,
Sickly, complaining, by faith in the vision of things in general
Manage to hold on our way without, like others around us,
Seizing the nearest arm to comfort, help, and support us.
Yet, after all, my Eustace, I know but little about it,
All I can say for myself, for present alike and for past, is,
Mary Trevellyn, Eustace, is certainly worth your acquaintance.
You couldn't come, I suppose, as far as Florence to see her?

XV.   *Georgina Trevellyn to Louisa——*

. . . . . . To-morrow we're starting for Florence,
Truly rejoiced, you may guess, to escape from republican terrors;   320
Mr. C. and Papa to escort us; we by *vettura*[23]
Through Siena, and Georgy to follow and join us by Leghorn.
Then – Ah, what shall I say, my dearest? I tremble in thinking!
You will imagine my feelings, – the blending of hope and of sorrow!
How can I bear to abandon Papa and Mamma and my Sisters?
Dearest Louisa, indeed it is very alarming; but trust me
Ever, whatever may change, to remain your loving Georgina.

23 carriage.

P. S. by Mary Trevellyn

. . . . . . 'Do I like Mr. Claude any better?'
I am to tell you, – and, 'Pray, is it Susan or I that attract him?'
This he never has told, but Georgina could certainly ask him.   330
All I can say for myself is, alas! that he rather repels me.
There! I think him agreeable, but also a little repulsive.
So be content, dear Louisa; for one satisfactory marriage
Surely will do in one year for the family you would establish;
Neither Susan nor I shall afford you the joy of a second.

P. S. by Georgina Trevellyn

Mr. Claude, you must know, is behaving a little bit better;
He and Papa are great friends; but he really is too *shilly-shally*, –
So unlike George! Yet I hope that the matter is going on fairly.
I shall, however, get George, before he goes, to say something.
Dearest Louise, how delightful to bring young people together!   340

———————

Is it to Florence we follow, or are we to tarry yet longer,
    E'en amid clamour of arms, here in the city of old,
Seeking from clamour of arms in the Past and the Arts to be hidden,
    Vainly 'mid Arts and the Past seeking one life to forget?
Ah, fair shadow, scarce seen, go forth! for anon he shall follow, –
    He that beheld thee, anon, whither thou leadest, must go!
Go, and the wise, loving Muse, she also will follow and find thee!
    She, should she linger in Rome, were not dissevered from thee!

Canto III

Yet to the wondrous St. Peter's, and yet to the solemn Rotonda,
    Mingling with heroes and gods, yet to the Vatican walls,
Yet may we go, and recline, while a whole mighty world seems above us
    Gathered and fixed to all time into one roofing supreme;
Yet may we, thinking on these things, exclude what is meaner around us;
    Yet, at the worst of the worst, books and a chamber remain;
Yet may we think, and forget, and possess our souls in resistance. –
    Ah, but away from the stir, shouting, and gossip of war,
Where, upon Apennine slope, with the chestnut the oak-trees immingle,
    Where amid odorous copse bridle-paths wander and wind,   10
Where under mulberry-branches the diligent rivulet sparkles,
    Or amid cotton and maize peasants their water-works ply,
Where, over fig-tree and orange in tier upon tier still repeated,
    Garden on garden upreared, balconies step to the sky, –
Ah, that I were, far away from the crowd and the streets of the city,
    Under the vine-trellis laid, O my beloved, with thee!

I. *Mary Trevellyn to Miss Roper, – on the way to Florence*

Why doesn't Mr. Claude come with us? you ask. – We don't know.
You should know better than we. He talked of the Vatican marbles;
But I can't wholly believe that this was the actual reason, –
He was so ready before, when we asked him to come and escort us.   20
Certainly he is odd, my dear Miss Roper. To change so
Suddenly, just for a whim, was not quite fair to the party, –
Not quite right. I declare, I really almost am offended:
I, his great friend, as you say, have doubtless a title to be so.
Not that I greatly regret it, for dear Georgina distinctly
Wishes for nothing so much as to show her adroitness. But, oh, my
Pen will not write any more; – let us say nothing further about it.

    *   *   *   *   *   *   *   *   *   *   *

Yes, my dear Miss Roper, I certainly called him repulsive;
So I think him, but cannot be sure I have used the expression
Quite as your pupil should; yet he does most truly repel me.   30
Was it to you I made use of the word? or who was it told you?
Yes, repulsive; observe, it is but when he talks of ideas
That he is quite unaffected, and free, and expansive, and easy;
I could pronounce him simply a cold intellectual being. –
When does he make advances? – He thinks that women should woo him;
Yet, if a girl should do so, would be but alarmed and disgusted.
She that should love him must look for small love in return, – like the ivy
On the stone wall, must expect but a rigid and niggard support, and
E'en to get that must go searching all round with her humble embraces.

II.   *Claude to Eustace, – from Rome*

Tell me, my friend, do you think that the grain would sprout in the furrow,   40
Did it not truly accept as its *summum* and *ultimum bonum*[24]
That mere common and may-be indifferent soil it is set in?
Would it have force to develop and open its young cotyledons,
Could it compare, and reflect, and examine one thing with another?
Would it endure to accomplish the round of its natural functions,
Were it endowed with a sense of the general scheme of existence?
    While from Marseilles in the steamer we voyaged to Civita Vecchia,
Vexed in the squally seas as we lay by Capraja and Elba,
Standing, uplifted, alone on the heaving poop of the vessel,
Looking around on the waste of the rushing incurious billows,   50
'This is Nature,' I said: 'we are born as it were from her waters,
Over her billows that buffet and beat us, her offspring uncared-for,
Casting one single regard of a painful victorious knowledge,
Into her billows that buffet and beat us we sink and are swallowed.'
This was the sense in my soul, as I swayed with the poop of the steamer;
And as unthinking I sat in the hall of the famed Ariadne,
Lo, it looked at me there from the face of a Triton in marble.
It is the simpler thought, and I can believe it the truer.
Let us not talk of growth; we are still in our Aqueous Ages.

III.   *Claude to Eustace*

Farewell, Politics, utterly! What can I do? I cannot   60
Fight, you know; and to talk I am wholly ashamed. And although I
Gnash my teeth when I look in your French or your English papers,
What is the good of that? Will swearing, I wonder, mend matters?
Cursing and scolding repel the assailants? No, it is idle;
No, whatever befalls, I will hide, will ignore or forget it.
Let the tail shift for itself; I will bury my head. And what's the
Roman Republic to me, or I to the Roman Republic?
    Why not fight? – In the first place, I haven't so much as a musket;
In the next, if I had, I shouldn't know how I should use it;
In the third, just at present I'm studying ancient marbles;   70
In the fourth, I consider I owe my life to my country;
In the fifth, – I forget, but four good reasons are ample.
Meantime, pray, let 'em fight, and be killed. I delight in devotion.
So that I 'list not, hurrah for the glorious army of martyrs!
Sanguis martyrum semen Ecclesiæ;[25] though it would seem this
Church is indeed of the purely Invisible, Kingdom-come kind:
Militant here on earth! Triumphant, of course, then, elsewhere!
Ah, good Heaven, but I would I were out far away from the pother!

24   utter and final good.

25   famous Christian tag: 'The blood of the martyrs is the seed of the Church'.

IV.   *Claude to Eustace*

Not, as we read in the words of the olden-time inspiration,
Are there two several trees[26] in the place we are set to abide in;   80
But on the apex most high of the Tree of Life in the Garden,
Budding, unfolding, and falling, decaying and flowering ever,
Flowering is set and decaying the transient blossom of Knowledge, –
Flowering alone, and decaying, the needless, unfruitful blossom.
    Or as the cypress-spires by the fair-flowing stream Hellespontine,
Which from the mythical tomb of the godlike Protesilaüs
Rose sympathetic in grief to his love-lorn Laodamia,
Evermore growing, and, when in their growth to the prospect attaining,
Over the low sea-banks, of the fatal Ilian city,
Withering still at the sight which still they upgrow to encounter.[27]   90
    Ah, but ye that extrude from the ocean your helpless faces,
Ye over stormy seas leading long and dreary processions,
Ye, too, brood of the wind, whose coming is whence we discern not,
Making your nest on the wave, and your bed on the crested billow,
Skimming rough waters, and crowding wet sands that the tide shall return to,
Cormorants, ducks, and gulls, fill ye my imagination!
Let us not talk of growth; we are still in our Aqueous Ages.

V.   *Mary Trevellyn to Miss Roper, – from Florence*

Dearest Miss Roper, – Alas! we are all at Florence quite safe, and
You, we hear, are shut up! indeed, it is sadly distressing!
We were most lucky, they say, to get off when we did from the troubles.   100
Now you are really besieged! they tell us it soon will be over;
Only I hope and trust without any fight in the city.
Do you see Mr. Claude? – I thought he might do something for you.
I am quite sure on occasion he really would wish to be useful.
What is he doing? I wonder; – still studying Vatican marbles?
Letters, I hope, pass through. We trust your brother is better.

VI.   *Claude to Eustace*

Juxtaposition, in fine; and what is juxtaposition?
Look you, we travel along in the railway-carriage, or steamer,
And, *pour passer le temps*, till the tedious journey be ended,
Lay aside paper or book, to talk with the girl that is next one;   110
And, *pour passer le temps*, with the terminus all but in prospect,
Talk of eternal ties and marriages made in heaven.
    Ah, did we really accept with a perfect heart the illusion!
Ah, did we really believe that the Present indeed is the Only!
Or through all transmutation, all shock and convulsion of passion,
Feel we could carry undimmed, unextinguished, the light of our knowledge!
    But for his funeral train which the bridegroom sees in the distance,
Would he so joyfully, think you, fall in with the marriage-procession?
But for that final discharge, would he dare to enlist in that service?
But for that certain release, ever sign to that perilous contract?   120
But for that exit secure, ever bend to that treacherous doorway? –
Ah, but the bride, meantime, – do you think she sees it as he does?
    But for the steady fore-sense of a freer and larger existence,
Think you that man could consent to be circumscribed here into action?
But for assurance within of a limitless ocean divine, o'er
Whose great tranquil depths unconscious the wind-tost surface
Breaks into ripples of trouble that come and change and endure not, –

---

26   the Garden of Eden's Tree of Life and Tree of Knowledge of Good and Evil, Genesis 2.

27   Protesilaus: first Greek killed in siege of Troy; wife Laodamia killed herself after husband's brief, three-hour, return to life.

But that in this, of a truth, we have our being, and know it,
Think you we men could submit to live and move as we do here?
Ah, but the women, – God bless them! they don't think at all about it.   130
    Yet we must eat and drink, as you say. And as limited beings
Scarcely can hope to attain upon earth to an Actual Abstract,
Leaving to God contemplation, to His hands knowledge confiding,
Sure that in us if it perish, in Him it abideth and dies not,
Let us in His sight accomplish our petty particular doings, –
Yes, and contented sit down to the victual that He has provided.
Allah is great, no doubt, and Juxtaposition his prophet.
Ah, but the women, alas! they don't look at it in that way.
    Juxtaposition is great; – but, my friend, I fear me, the maiden
Hardly would thank or acknowledge the lover that sought to obtain her,   140
Not as the thing he would wish, but the thing he must even put up with, –
Hardly would tender her hand to the wooer that candidly told her
That she is but for a space, an *ad-interim* solace and pleasure, –
That in the end she shall yield to a perfect and absolute something,
Which I then for myself shall behold, and not another, –
Which, amid fondest endearments, meantime I forget not, forsake not.
Ah, ye feminine souls, so loving and so exacting,
Since we cannot escape, must we even submit to deceive you?
Since so cruel is truth, sincerity shocks and revolts you,
Will you have us your slaves to lie to you, flatter and – leave you?   150

VII.   *Claude to Eustace*

Juxtaposition is great, – but, you tell me, affinity greater.
Ah, my friend, there are many affinities, greater and lesser,
Stronger and weaker; and each, by the favour of juxtaposition,
Potent, efficient, in force, – for a time; but none, let me tell you,
Save by the law of the land and the ruinous force of the will, ah,
None, I fear me, at last quite sure to be final and perfect.
Lo, as I pace in the street, from the peasant-girl to the princess,
Homo sum, nihil humani a me alienum puto, –
Vir sum, nihil fæminei,[28] – and e'en to the uttermost circle,
All that is Nature's is I, and I all things that are Nature's.   160
Yes, as I walk, I behold, in a luminous, large intuition,
That I can be and become anything that I meet with or look at:
I am the ox in the dray, the ass with the garden-stuff panniers;
I am the dog in the doorway, the kitten that plays in the window,
On sunny slab of the ruin the furtive and fugitive lizard,
Swallow above me that twitters, and fly that is buzzing about me;
Yea, and detect, as I go, by a faint but a faithful assurance,
E'en from the stones of the street, as from rocks or trees of the forest,
Something of kindred, a common, though latent vitality, greets me;
And, to escape from our strivings, mistakings, misgrowths, and perversions,   170
Fain could demand to return to that perfect and primitive silence,
Fain be enfolded and fixed, as of old, in their rigid embraces.

VIII.   *Claude to Eustace*

And as I walk on my way, I behold them consorting and coupling;
Faithful it seemeth, and fond, very fond, very probably faithful;
All as I go on my way, with a pleasure sincere and unmingled.
    Life is beautiful, Eustace, entrancing, enchanting to look at;
As are the streets of a city we pace while the carriage is changing,

28   'I am a man, nothing human is, I consider, alien to me; I am a
man, nothing feminine…' [words from Roman playwright Terence].

As a chamber filled-in with harmonious, exquisite pictures,
Even so beautiful Earth; and could we eliminate only
This vile hungering impulse, this demon within us of craving,   180
Life were beatitude, living a perfect divine satisfaction.

IX.   *Claude to Eustace*

Mild monastic faces in quiet collegiate cloisters:
So let me offer a single and celibatarian phrase, a
Tribute to those whom perhaps you do not believe I can honour.
But, from the tumult escaping, 'tis pleasant, of drumming and shouting,
Hither, oblivious awhile, to withdraw, of the fact or the falsehood,
And amid placid regards and mildly courteous greetings
Yield to the calm and composure and gentle abstraction that reign o'er
Mild monastic faces in quiet collegiate cloisters.
   Terrible word, Obligation! You should not, Eustace, you should not,   190
No, you should not have used it. But, oh, great Heavens, I repel it!
Oh, I cancel, reject, disavow, and repudiate wholly
Every debt in this kind, disclaim every claim, and dishonour,
Yea, my own heart's own writing, my soul's own signature! Ah, no!
I will be free in this; you shall not, none shall, bind me.
No, my friend, if you wish to be told, it was this above all things,
This that charmed me, ah, yes, even this, that she held me to nothing.
No, I could talk as I pleased; come close; fasten ties, as I fancied;
Bind and engage myself deep; – and lo, on the following morning
It was all e'en as before, like losings in games played for nothing.   200
Yes, when I came, with mean fears in my soul, with a semi-performance
At the first step breaking down in its pitiful rôle of evasion,
When to shuffle I came, to compromise, not meet, engagements,
Lo, with her calm eyes there she met me and knew nothing of it, –
Stood unexpecting, unconscious. *She* spoke not of obligations,
Knew not of debt, – ah, no, I believe you, for excellent reasons.

X.   *Claude to Eustace*

Hang this thinking, at last! what good is it? oh, and what evil!
Oh, what mischief and pain! like a clock in a sick man's chamber,
Ticking and ticking, and still through each covert of slumber pursuing.
   What shall I do to thee, O thou Preserver of Men? Have compassion;   210
Be favourable, and hear! Take from me this regal knowledge;
Let me, contented and mute, with the beasts of the field, my brothers,
Tranquilly, happily lie, – and eat grass, like Nebuchadnezzar![29]

XI.   *Claude to Eustace*

Tibur is beautiful, too, and the orchard slopes, and the Anio
Falling, falling yet, to the ancient lyrical cadence;
Tibur and Anio's tide; and cool from Lucretilis ever,
With the Digentian stream, and with the Bandusian fountain,
Folded in Sabine recesses, the valley and villa of Horace: –
So not seeing I sang; so seeing and listening say I,
Here as I sit by the stream, as I gaze at the cell of the Sibyl,   220
Here with Albunea's home and the grove of Tiburnus beside me;[30]
Tivoli beautiful is, and musical, O Teverone,
Dashing from mountain to plain, thy parted impetuous waters!

29 Daniel 4.25, 32–3.
30   – domus Albuneæ resonantis,
     Et præceps Anio, et Tiburni lucus, et uda
       Mobilibus pomaria rivis.
       [Author's note]

[Horace, *Odes* I.vii.12–14. 'Albunea's echoing home and the headlong Anio and the grove of Tiburnus and the orchards watered by rushing streams'.]

Tivoli's waters and rocks; and fair unto Monte Gennaro
(Haunt even yet, I must think, as I wander and gaze, of the shadows,
Faded and pale, yet immortal, of Faunus, the Nymphs, and the Graces),
Fair in itself, and yet fairer with human completing creations,
Folded in Sabine recesses the valley and villa of Horace: –
So not seeing I sang; so now – Nor seeing, nor hearing,
Neither by waterfall lulled, nor folded in sylvan embraces,   230
Neither by cell of the Sibyl, nor stepping the Monte Gennaro,
Seated on Anio's bank, nor sipping Bandusian waters,
But on Montorio's height, looking down on the tile-clad streets, the
Cupolas, crosses, and domes, the bushes and kitchen-gardens,
Which, by the grace of the Tibur, proclaim themselves Rome of the Romans, –
But on Montorio's height, looking forth to the vapoury mountains,
Cheating the prisoner Hope with illusions of vision and fancy, –
But on Montorio's height, with these weary soldiers by me,
Waiting till Oudinot[31] enter, to reinstate Pope and Tourist.

XII.   *Mary Trevellyn to Miss Roper*

Dear Miss Roper, – It seems, George Vernon, before we left Rome, said   240
Something to Mr. Claude about what they call his attentions.
Susan, two nights ago, for the first time, heard this from Georgina.
It is *so* disagreeable and *so* annoying to think of!
If it could only be known, though we may never meet him again, that
It was all George's doing, and we were entirely unconscious,
It would extremely relieve – Your ever affectionate Mary.
P. S. (1)
     Here is your letter arrived this moment, just as I wanted.
So you have seen him, – indeed, – and guessed, – how dreadfully clever!
What did he really say? and what was your answer exactly?
Charming! – but wait for a moment, I haven't read through the letter.   250
P. S. (2)
     Ah, my dearest Miss Roper, do just as you fancy about it.
If you think it sincerer to tell him I know of it, do so.
Though I should most extremely dislike it, I know I could manage.
It is the simplest thing, but surely wholly uncalled for.
Do as you please; you know I trust implicitly to you.
Say whatever is right and needful for ending the matter.
Only don't tell Mr. Claude, what I will tell you as a secret,
That I should like very well to show him myself I forget it.
P. S. (3)
     I am to say that the wedding is finally settled for Tuesday.
Ah, my dear Miss Roper, you surely, surely can manage   260
Not to let it appear that I know of that odious matter.
It would be pleasanter far for myself to treat it exactly
As if it had not occurred: and I do not think he would like it.
I must remember to add, that as soon as the wedding is over
We shall be off, I believe, in a hurry, and travel to Milan,
There to meet friends of Papa's, I am told, at the Croce di Malta;
Then I cannot say whither, but not at present to England.

XIII.   *Claude to Eustace*

Yes, on Montorio's height for a last farewell of the city, –
So it appears; though then I was quite uncertain about it.
So, however, it was. And now to explain the proceeding.   270
     I was to go, as I told you, I think, with the people to Florence.

31   Nicolas Oudinot, Duke of Reggio, commander of expeditionary
force against Roman Republic, 1849.

Only the day before, the foolish family Vernon
Made some uneasy remarks, as we walked to our lodging together,
As to intentions, forsooth, and so forth. I was astounded,
Horrified quite; and obtaining just then, as it happened, an offer
(No common favour) of seeing the great Ludovisi collection,
Why, I made this a pretence, and wrote that they must excuse me.
How could I go? Great Heavens! to conduct a permitted flirtation
Under those vulgar eyes, the observed of such observers!
Well, but I now, by a series of fine diplomatic inquiries,   280
Find from a sort of relation, a good and sensible woman,
Who is remaining at Rome with a brother too ill for removal,
That it was wholly unsanctioned, unknown, – not, I think, by Georgina:
She, however, ere this, – and that is the best of the story, –
She and the Vernon, thank Heaven, are wedded and gone – honeymooning.
So – on Montorio's height for a last farewell of the city.
Tibur I have not seen, nor the lakes that of old I had dreamt of;
Tibur I shall not see, nor Anio's waters, nor deep en-
Folded in Sabine recesses the valley and villa of Horace;
Tibur I shall not see; – but something better I shall see.   290
   Twice I have tried before, and failed in getting the horses;
Twice I have tried and failed: this time it shall not be a failure.

>   *Therefore farewell, ye hills, and ye, ye envineyarded ruins!*
>   *Therefore farewell, ye walls, palaces, pillars, and domes!*
>   *Therefore farewell, far seen, ye peaks of the mythic Albano,*
>   *Seen from Montorio's height, Tibur and Æsula's hills!*
>   *Ah, could we once, ere we go, could we stand, while, to ocean descending,*
>   *Sinks o'er the yellow dark plain slowly the yellow broad sun,*
>   *Stand, from the forest emerging at sunset, at once in the champaign,*
>   *Open, but studded with trees, chestnuts umbrageous and old,*   300
>   *E'en in those fair open fields that incurve to thy beautiful hollow,*
>   *Nemi, imbedded in wood, Nemi, inurned in the hill! –*
>   *Therefore farewell, ye plains, and ye hills, and the City Eternal!*
>   *Therefore farewell! We depart, but to behold you again!*

Canto IV

>   *Eastward, or Northward, or West? I wander and ask as I wander,*
>   *Weary, yet eager and sure, Where shall I come to my love?*
>   *Whitherward hasten to seek her? Ye daughters of Italy, tell me,*
>   *Graceful and tender and dark, is she consorting with you?*
>   *Thou that out-climbest the torrent, that tendest thy goats to the summit,*
>   *Call to me, child of the Alp, has she been seen on the heights?*
>   *Italy, farewell I bid thee! for whither she leads me, I follow.*
>   *Farewell the vineyard! for I, where I but guess her, must go.*
>   *Weariness welcome, and labour, wherever it be, if at last it*
>   *Bring me in mountain or plain into the sight of my love.*   10

I.   *Claude to Eustace, – from Florence*
Gone from Florence; indeed; and that is truly provoking; –
Gone to Milan, it seems; then I go also to Milan.
Five days now departed; but they can travel but slowly; –
I quicker far; and I know, as it happens, the house they will go to. –
Why, what else should I do? Stay here and look at the pictures,
Statues, and churches? Alack, I am sick of the statues and pictures! –
No, to Bologna, Parma, Piacenza, Lodi, and Milan,
Off go we to-night, – and the Venus go to the Devil!

II.   *Claude to Eustace, – from Bellaggio*

Gone to Como, they said; and I have posted to Como.
There was a letter left; but the *cameriere*[32] had lost it.   20
Could it have been for me? They came, however, to Como,
And from Como went by the boat, – perhaps to the Splügen, –
Or to the Stelvio, say, and the Tyrol; also it might be
By Porlezza across to Lugano, and so to the Simplon
Possibly, or the St. Gothard, – or possibly, too, to Baveno,
Orta, Turin, and elsewhere. Indeed, I am greatly bewildered.

III.   *Claude to Eustace, – from Bellaggio*

I have been up the Splügen, and on the Stelvio also:
Neither of these can I find they have followed; in no one inn, and
This would be odd, have they written their names. I have been to Porlezza;
There they have not been seen, and therefore not at Lugano.   30
What shall I do? Go on through the Tyrol, Switzerland, Deutschland,
Seeking, an inverse Saul, a kingdom, to find only asses?[33]
    There is a tide, at least, in the *love* affairs of mortals,
Which, when taken at flood, leads on to the happiest fortune,[34] –
Leads to the marriage-morn and the orange-flowers and the altar,
And the long lawful line of crowned joys to crowned joys succeeding. –
Ah, it has ebbed with me! Ye gods, and when it was flowing,
Pitiful fool that I was, to stand fiddle-faddling in that way!

IV.   *Claude to Eustace, – from Bellaggio*

I have returned and found their names in the book at Como.
Certain it is I was right, and yet I am also in error.   40
Added in feminine hand, I read, *By the boat to Bellaggio.* –
So to Bellaggio again, with the words of her writing to aid me.
Yet at Bellaggio I find no trace, no sort of remembrance.
So I am here, and wait, and know every hour will remove them.

V.   *Claude to Eustace, – from Bellaggio*

I have but one chance left, – and that is going to Florence.
But it is cruel to turn. The mountains seem to demand me, –
Peak and valley from far to beckon and motion me onward.
Somewhere amid their folds she passes whom fain I would follow;
Somewhere among those heights she haply calls me to seek her.
Ah, could I hear her call! could I catch the glimpse of her raiment!   50
Turn, however, I must, though it seem I turn to desert her;
For the sense of the thing is simply to hurry to Florence,
Where the certainty yet may be learnt, I suppose, from the Ropers.

VI.   *Mary Trevellyn, from Lucerne, to Miss Roper, at Florence*

Dear Miss Roper, – By this you are safely away, we are hoping,
Many a league from Rome; ere long we trust we shall see you.
How have you travelled? I wonder; – was Mr. Claude your companion?
As for ourselves, we went from Como straight to Lugano;
So by the Mount St. Gothard; we meant to go by Porlezza,
Taking the steamer, and stopping, as you had advised, at Bellaggio,
Two or three days or more; but this was suddenly altered,   60
After we left the hotel, on the very way to the steamer.
So we have seen, I fear, not one of the lakes in perfection.
    Well, he is not come; and now, I suppose, he will not come.

---

32   male servant.
33   I Samuel 9: Saul, vainly searching for lost asses, met prophet
Samuel and was crowned King.

34   'There is a tide in the affairs of men,/Which, taken at the flood,
leads on to fortune': *Julius Caesar*, IV.iii. 217–18.

What will you think, meantime? – and yet I must really confess it; –
What will you say? I wrote him a note. We left in a hurry,
Went from Milan to Como, three days before we expected.
But I thought, if he came all the way to Milan, he really
Ought not to be disappointed: and so I wrote three lines to
Say I had heard he was coming, desirous of joining our party; –
If so, then I said, we had started for Como, and meant to   70
Cross the St. Gothard, and stay, we believed, at Lucerne, for the summer.
Was it wrong? and why, if it was, has it failed to bring him?
Did he not think it worth while to come to Milan? He knew (you
Told him) the house we should go to. Or may it, perhaps, have miscarried?
Any way, now, I repent, and am heartily vexed that I wrote it.

There is a home on the shore of the Alpine sea, that upswelling
   High up the mountain-sides spreads in the hollow between;
Wilderness, mountain, and snow from the land of the olive conceal it;
   Under Pilatus's hill low by its river it lies:
Italy, utter the word, and the olive and vine will allure not, –   80
   Wilderness, forest, and snow will not the passage impede;
Italy, unto thy cities receding, the clue to recover,
   Hither, recovered the clue, shall not the traveller haste?

Canto V

There is a city, upbuilt on the quays of the turbulent Arno,
   Under Fiesole's heights, – thither are we to return?
There is a city that fringes the curve of the inflowing waters,
   Under the perilous hill fringes the beautiful bay, –
Parthenope do they call thee? – the Siren, Neapolis, seated
   Under Vesevus's hill, – are we receding to thee? –
Sicily, Greece, will invite, and the Orient; – or are we to turn to
   England, which may after all be for its children the best?

I.   *Mary Trevellyn, at Lucerne, to Miss Roper, at Florence*

So you are really free, and living in quiet at Florence;
That is delightful news; you travelled slowly and safely;   10
Mr. Claude got you out; took rooms at Florence before you;
Wrote from Milan to say so; had left directly for Milan,
Hoping to find us soon; – *if he could, he would, you are certain.* –
Dear Miss Roper, your letter has made me exceedingly happy.
   You are quite sure, you say, he asked you about our intentions;
You had not heard as yet of Lucerne, but told him of Como. –
Well, perhaps he will come; however, I will not expect it.
Though you say you are sure, – *if he can, he will, you are certain.*
O my dear, many thanks from your ever affectionate Mary.

II.   *Claude to Eustace*

Florence
Action will furnish belief, – but will that belief be the true one?   20
This is the point, you know. However, it doesn't much matter.
What one wants, I suppose, is to predetermine the action,
So as to make it entail, not a chance-belief, but the true one.
Out of the question, you say; *if a thing isn't wrong, we may do it.*
Ah! but this *wrong,* you see – but I do not know that it matters.
Eustace, the Ropers are gone, and no one can tell me about them.

Pisa
Pisa, they say they think, and so I follow to Pisa,
Hither and thither enquiring. I weary of making enquiries.

I am ashamed, I declare, of asking people about it. –
Who are your friends? You said you had friends who would certainly know them.   30
Florence

But it is idle, moping, and thinking, and trying to fix her
Image more and more in, to write the old perfect inscription
Over and over again upon every page of remembrance.
   I have settled to stay at Florence to wait for your answer.
Who are your friends? Write quickly and tell me. I wait for your answer.

III.   *Mary Trevellyn to Miss Roper, at Lucca Baths*

You are at Lucca Baths, you tell me, to stay for the summer;
Florence was quite too hot; you can't move further at present.
Will you not come, do you think, before the summer is over?
   Mr. C. got you out with very considerable trouble;
And he was useful and kind, and seemed so happy to serve you.   40
Didn't stay with you long, but talked very openly to you;
Made you almost his confessor, without appearing to know it, –
What about? – and you say you didn't need his confessions.
O my dear Miss Roper, I dare not trust what you tell me!
   Will he come, do you think? I am really so sorry for him!
They didn't give him my letter at Milan, I feel pretty certain.
You had told him Bellaggio. We didn't go to Bellaggio;
So he would miss our track, and perhaps never come to Lugano,
Where we were written in full, *To Lucerne across the St. Gothard.*
But he could write to you; – you would tell him where you were going.   50

IV.   *Claude to Eustace*

Let me, then, bear to forget her. I will not cling to her falsely:
Nothing factitious or forced shall impair the old happy relation.
I will let myself go, forget, not try to remember;
I will walk on my way, accept the chances that meet me,
Freely encounter the world, imbibe these alien airs, and
Never ask if new feelings and thoughts are of her or of others.
Is she not changing, herself? – the old image would only delude me.
I will be bold, too, and change, – if it must be. Yet if in all things,
Yet if I do but aspire evermore to the Absolute only,
I shall be doing, I think, somehow, what she will be doing; –   60
I shall be thine, O my child, some way, though I know not in what way.
Let me submit to forget her; I must; I already forget her.

V.   *Claude to Eustace*

Utterly vain is, alas! this attempt at the Absolute, – wholly!
I, who believed not in her, because I would fain believe nothing,
Have to believe as I may, with a wilful, unmeaning acceptance.
I, who refused to enfasten the roots of my floating existence
In the rich earth, cling now to the hard, naked rock that is left me. –
Ah! she was worthy, Eustace, – and that, indeed, is my comfort, –
Worthy a nobler heart than a fool such as I could have given her.

———————

Yes, it relieves me to write, though I do not send, and the chance that   70
Takes may destroy my fragments. But as men pray, without asking
Whether One really exist to hear or do anything for them, –
Simply impelled by the need of the moment to turn to a Being
In a conception of whom there is freedom from all limitation, –
So in your image I turn to an *ens rationis*[35] of friendship,
Even so write in your name I know not to whom nor in what wise.

———————

35 a creature/being of the mind (an imaginary form of friendship).

There was a time, methought it was but lately departed,
When, if a thing was denied me, I felt I was bound to attempt it;
Choice alone should take, and choice alone should surrender.
There was a time, indeed, when I had not retired thus early,   80
Languidly thus, from pursuit of a purpose I once had adopted.
But it is over, all that! I have slunk from the perilous field in
Whose wild struggle of forces the prizes of life are contested.
It is over, all that! I am a coward, and know it.
Courage in me could be only factitious, unnatural, useless.

————————

Comfort has come to me here in the dreary streets of the city,
Comfort – how do you think? – with a barrel-organ to bring it.
Moping along the streets, and cursing my day, as I wandered,
All of a sudden my ear met the sound of an English psalm-tune.
Comfort me it did, till indeed I was very near crying.   90
Ah, there is some great truth, partial, very likely, but needful,
Lodged, I am strangely sure, in the tones of the English psalm-tune.
Comfort it was at least; and I must take without question
Comfort, however it come, in the dreary streets of the city.

————————

What with trusting myself and seeking support from within me,
Almost I could believe I had gained a religious assurance,
Formed in my own poor soul a great moral basis to rest on.
Ah, but indeed I see, I feel it factitious entirely;
I refuse, reject, and put it utterly from me;
I will look straight out, see things, not try to evade them;   100
Fact shall be fact for me, and the Truth the Truth as ever,
Flexible, changeable, vague, and multiform, and doubtful. –
Off, and depart to the void, thou subtle, fanatical tempter!

————————

I shall behold thee again (is it so?) at a new visitation,
O ill genius thou! I shall, at my life's dissolution,
(When the pulses are weak, and the feeble light of the reason
Flickers, an unfed flame retiring slow from the socket),
Low on a sick-bed laid, hear one, as it were, at the doorway,
And looking up see thee, standing by, looking emptily at me;
I shall entreat thee then, though now I dare to refuse thee, –   110
Pale and pitiful now, but terrible then to the dying. –
Well, I will see thee again: and while I can, will repel thee.

VI.   *Claude to Eustace*
Rome is fallen, I hear, the gallant Medici taken,
Noble Manara slain, and Garibaldi has lost *il Moro*;[36] –
Rome is fallen; and fallen, or falling, heroical Venice.
I, meanwhile, for the loss of a single small chit of a girl, sit
Moping and mourning here, – for her, and myself much smaller.
    Whither depart the souls of the brave that die in the battle,
Die in the lost, lost fight, for the cause that perishes with them?
Are they upborne from the field on the slumberous pinions of angels 120
Unto a far-off home, where the weary rest from their labour,
And the deep wounds are healed, and the bitter and burning moisture
Wiped from the generous eyes? or do they linger, unhappy,
Pining, and haunting the grave of their by-gone hope and endeavour?

36   the Moore (his black South American servant: *Canto* II, 220 ff).

All declamation, alas! though I talk, I care not for Rome, nor
Italy; feebly and faintly, and but with the lips, can lament the
Wreck of the Lombard youth, and the victory of the oppressor.
Whither depart the brave? – God knows; I certainly do not.

VII.   *Mary Trevellyn to Miss Roper*

He has not come as yet; and now I must not expect it.
You have written, you say, to friends at Florence, to see him,   130
If he perhaps should return; – but that is surely unlikely.
Has he not written to you? – he did not know your direction.
Oh, how strange never once to have told him where you were going!
Yet if he only wrote to Florence, that would have reached you.
If what you say he said was true, why has he not done so?
Is he gone back to Rome, do you think, to his Vatican marbles? –
O my dear Miss Roper, forgive me! do not be angry! –
You have written to Florence; – your friends would certainly find him.
Might you not write to him? – but yet it is so little likely!
I shall expect nothing more. – Ever yours, your affectionate Mary.   140

VIII.   Claude to Eustace

I cannot stay at Florence, not even to wait for a letter.
Galleries only oppress me. Remembrance of hope I had cherished
(Almost more than as hope, when I passed through Florence the first time)
Lies like a sword in my soul. I am more a coward than ever,
Chicken-hearted, past thought. The *caffès* and waiters distress me.
All is unkind, and, alas! I am ready for anyone's kindness.
Oh, I knew it of old, and knew it, I thought, to perfection,
If there is any one thing in the world to preclude all kindness,
It is the need of it, – it is this sad, self-defeating dependence.
Why is this, Eustace? Myself, were I stronger, I think I could tell you.   150
But it is odd when it comes. So plumb I the deeps of depression,
Daily in deeper, and find no support, no will, no purpose.
All my old strengths are gone. And yet I shall have to do something.
Ah, the key of our life, that passes all wards, opens all locks,
Is not *I will*, but *I must*. I must, – I must, – and I do it.

———————

After all, do I know that I really cared so about her?
Do whatever I will, I cannot call up her image;
For when I close my eyes, I see, very likely, St. Peter's,
Or the Pantheon façade, or Michael Angelo's figures,
Or at a wish, when I please, the Alban hills and the Forum, –   160
But that face, those eyes, – ah no, never anything like them;
Only, try as I will, a sort of featureless outline,
And a pale blank orb, which no recollection will add to.
After all perhaps there was something factitious about it;
I have had pain, it is true: I have wept; and so have the actors.

———————

At the last moment I have your letter, for which I was waiting;
I have taken my place, and see no good in enquiries.
Do nothing more, good Eustace, I pray you. It only will vex me.
Take no measures. Indeed, should we meet, I could not be certain;
All might be changed, you know. Or perhaps there was nothing to be changed.   170
It is a curious history, this; and yet I foresaw it;
I could have told it before. The Fates, it is clear, are against us;
For it is certain enough I met with the people you mention;
They were at Florence the day I returned there, and spoke to me even;
Stayed a week, saw me often; departed, and whither I know not.

Great is Fate, and is best. I believe in Providence partly.
What is ordained is right, and all that happens is ordered.
Ah, no, that isn't it. But yet I retain my conclusion.
I will go where I am led, and will not dictate to the chances.
Do nothing more, I beg. If you love me, forbear interfering.   180

IX.   Claude to Eustace

Shall we come out of it all, some day, as one does from a tunnel?
Will it be all at once, without our doing or asking,
We shall behold clear day, the trees and meadows about us,
And the faces of friends, and the eyes we loved looking at us?
Who knows? Who can say? It will not do to suppose it.

X.   Claude to Eustace, – *from Rome*

Rome will not suit me, Eustace; the priests and soldiers possess it;
Priests and soldiers: – and, ah! which is worst, the priest or the soldier?
    Politics, farewell, however! For what could I do? with inquiring,
Talking, collating the journals, go fever my brain about things o'er
Which I can have no control. No, happen whatever may happen,   190
Time, I suppose, will subsist; the earth will revolve on its axis;
People will travel; the stranger will wander as now in the city;
Rome will be here, and the Pope the *custode* of Vatican marbles.
    I have no heart, however, for any marble or fresco;
I have essayed it in vain; 'tis vain as yet to essay it:
But I may haply resume some day my studies in this kind;
Not as the Scripture says, is, I think, the fact. Ere our death-day,
Faith, I think, does pass, and Love; but Knowledge abideth.[37]
Let us seek Knowledge; – the rest may come and go as it happens.
Knowledge is hard to seek, and harder yet to adhere to.   200
Knowledge is painful often; and yet when we know, we are happy.
Seek it, and leave mere Faith and Love to come with the chances.
As for Hope, – to-morrow I hope to be starting for Naples.
Rome will not do, I see, for many very good reasons.
    Eastward, then, I suppose, with the coming of winter, to Egypt.

XI.   Mary Trevellyn to Miss Roper

You have heard nothing; of course, I know you can have heard nothing.
Ah, well, more than once I have broken my purpose, and sometimes,
Only too often, have looked for the little lake-steamer to bring him.
But it is only fancy, – I do not really expect it.
Oh, and you see I know so exactly how he would take it: 210
Finding the chances prevail against meeting again, he would banish
Forthwith every thought of the poor little possible hope, which
I myself could not help, perhaps, thinking only too much of;
He would resign himself, and go. I see it exactly.
So I also submit, although in a different manner.
    Can you not really come? We go very shortly to England.

_____

So go forth to the world, to the good report and the evil!
    Go, little book! [38] *thy tale, is it not evil and good?*
Go, and if strangers revile, pass quietly by without answer.
    Go, and if curious friends ask of thy rearing and age,   220
Say, 'I am flitting about many years from brain unto brain of
    Feeble and restless youths born to inglorious days:

_____

37   cf. 1 Corinthians 13, where faith, hope, and charity abide, while knowledge 'shall vanish away'.

38   'Go, litel bok, go, litel myn tragedye': Chaucer, *Troilus and Criseyde*, V, 1786. Traditional medieval *envoi*.

But,' so finish the word, 'I was writ in a Roman chamber,
When from Janiculan heights thundered the cannon of France.'

First published, Atlantic Monthly, I (February–May 1858). Poems (1862). Text, Poems, 2nd edn (1863).

FROM DIPSYCHUS

Scene IV

Spirit
As I sat at the café, I said to myself,   [130]
They may talk as they please about what they call pelf,
They may sneer as they like about eating and drinking,
But help it I cannot, I cannot help thinking
  How pleasant it is to have money, heigh ho!
  How pleasant it is to have money.

I sit at my table *en grand seigneur*,[1]
And when I have done, throw a crust to the poor;
Not only the pleasure, one's self, of good living,
But also the pleasure of now and then giving.   10
  So pleasant it is to have money, heigh ho!   [140]
  So pleasant it is to have money.

It was but last winter I came up to Town,
But already I'm getting a little renown;
I make new acquaintance where'er I appear;
I am not too shy, and have nothing to fear.
  So pleasant it is to have money, heigh ho!
  So pleasant it is to have money.

I drive through the streets, and I care not a d—mn;
The people they stare, and they ask who I am;   20
And if I should chance to run over a cad,   [150]
I can pay for the damage if ever so bad.
  So pleasant it is to have money, heigh ho!
  So pleasant it is to have money.

We stroll to our box and look down on the pit,
And if it weren't low should be tempted to spit;
We loll and we talk until people look up,
And when it's half over we go out and sup.
  So pleasant it is to have money, heigh ho!
  So pleasant it is to have money.   30

The best of the tables and best of the fare –   [160]
And as for the others, the devil may care;
It isn't our fault if they dare not afford
To sup like a prince and be drunk as a lord.
  So pleasant it is to have money, heigh ho!
  So pleasant it is to have money.

We sit at our tables and tipple champagne;
Ere one bottle goes, comes another again;

DIPSYCHUS
1   like a grand person.

The waiters they skip and they scuttle about,
And the landlord attends us so civilly out.   40
   So pleasant it is to have money, heigh ho!   [170]
   So pleasant it is to have money.

It was but last winter I came up to town,
But already I'm getting a little renown;
I get to good houses without much ado,
Am beginning to see the nobility too.
   So pleasant it is to have money, heigh ho!
   So pleasant it is to have money.

O dear! what a pity they ever should lose it!
For they are the gentry that know how to use it;   50
So grand and so graceful, such manners, such dinners,   [180]
But yet, after all, it is we are the winners.
   So pleasant it is to have money, heigh ho!
   So pleasant it is to have money.

Thus I sat at my table *en grand seigneur*,
And when I had done threw a crust to the poor;
Not only the pleasure, one's self, of good eating,
But also the pleasure of now and then treating.
   So pleasant it is to have money, heigh ho!
   So pleasant it is to have money.   60

They may talk as they please about what they call pelf,   [190]
And how one ought never to think of one's self,
And how pleasures of thought surpass eating and drinking –
My pleasure of thought is the pleasure of thinking
   How pleasant it is to have money, heigh ho!
   How pleasant it is to have money.

(Written in Venice, but for all parts true,
'Twas not a crust I gave him, but a sous.)

A gondola here, and a gondola there,
'Tis the pleasantest fashion of taking the air.   70
To right and to left; stop, turn, and go yonder,   [200]
And let us repeat, o'er the tide as we wander,
   How pleasant it is to have money, heigh ho!
   How pleasant it is to have money.

Come, leave your Gothic, worn-out story,
San Giorgio and the Redemptore;
I from no building, gay or solemn,
Can spare the shapely Grecian column.
'Tis not, these centuries four, for nought
Our European world of thought   80
Hath made familiar to its home   [210]
The classic mind of Greece and Rome;
In all new work that would look forth
To more than antiquarian worth,
Palladio's pediments and bases,
Or something such, will find their places:
Maturer optics don't delight
In childish dim religious light,
In evanescent vague effects
That shirk, not face, one's intellects;   90

They love not fancies fast betrayed,   [220]
And artful tricks of light and shade,
But pure form nakedly displayed,
And all things absolutely made.
The Doge's palace though, from hence,
In spite of Ruskin's d—d pretence,
The tide now level with the quay,
Is certainly a thing to see.
We'll turn to the Rialto soon;
One's told to see it by the moon.   100

A gondola here, and a gondola there,   [230]
'Tis the pleasantest fashion of taking the air.
To right and to left; stop, turn, and go yonder,
And let us repeat, o'er the flood as we wander,
    How pleasant it is to have money, heigh ho!
    How pleasant it is to have money.[2]

Scene V

Dipsychus
I dreamt a dream; till morning light
A bell rang in my head all night,
Tinkling and tinkling first, and then
Tolling; and tinkling; tolling again.   [10]
So brisk and gay, and then so slow!
O joy, and terror! mirth, and woe!
Ting, ting, there is no God; ting, ting –
Dong, there is no God; dong,
There is no God; dong, dong!   10

Ting, ting, there is no God; ting, ting;
Come dance and play, and merrily sing –
Ting, ting a ding; ting, ting a ding!
O pretty girl who trippest along,
Come to my bed – it isn't wrong.   [20]
Uncork the bottle, sing the song!
Ting, ting a ding: dong, dong.
Wine has dregs; the song an end;
A silly girl is a poor friend
And age and weakness who shall mend?   20
Dong, there is no God; Dong!

Ting, ting a ding! Come dance and sing!
Staid Englishmen, who toil and slave
From your first breeching to your grave,
And seldom spend and always save,   [30]
And do your duty all your life
By your young family and wife;
Come, be't not said you ne'er had known
What earth can furnish you alone.
The Italian, Frenchman, German even,   30
Have given up all thoughts of heaven;
And you still linger – oh, you fool! –

2   A version of stanzas 1, 2, [10], 11, appeared as Part One of 'Spec-
tator Ab Extra' in *Poems* (1862, 1863). One of the rough drafts of 'Spec-
tator' is entitled 'Philosophia Metropolitana'.

Because of what you learnt at school.
You should have gone at least to college,
And got a little ampler knowledge.   [40]
Ah well, and yet – dong, dong, dong:
Do, if you like, as now you do;
If work's a cheat, so's pleasure too;
And nothing's new and nothing's true;
Dong, there is no God; dong!   40

O Rosalie, my precious maid,
I think thou thinkest love is true;
And on thy fragrant bosom laid
I almost could believe it too.
O in our nook, unknown, unseen,   [50]
We'll hold our fancy like a screen,
Us and the dreadful fact between.
And it shall yet be long, aye, long,
The quiet notes of our low song
Shall keep us from that sad dong, dong.   50
Hark, hark, hark! O voice of fear!
It reaches us here, even here!
Dong, there is no God; dong!

Ring ding, ring ding, tara, tara,
To battle, to battle – haste, haste –   [60]
To battle, to battle – aha, aha!
On, on, to the conqueror's feast.
From east and west, and south and north,
Ye men of valour and of worth,
Ye mighty men of arms, come forth,   60
And work your will, for that is just;
And in your impulse put your trust,
Beneath your feet the fools are dust.
Alas, alas! O grief and wrong,
The good are weak, the wicked strong;   [70]
And O my God, how long, how long?
Dong, there is no God; dong!

Ring, ting; to bow before the strong,
There is a rapture too in this;
Speak, outraged maiden, in thy wrong   70
Did terror bring no secret bliss?
Were boys' shy lips worth half a song
Compared to the hot soldier's kiss?
Work for thy master, work, thou slave
He is not merciful, but brave.   [80]
Be't joy to serve, who free and proud
Scorns thee and all the ignoble crowd;
Take that, 'tis all thou art allowed,
Except the snaky hope that they
May some time serve, who rule to-day,   80
When, by hell-demons, shan't they pay?
O wickedness, O shame and grief,
And heavy load, and no relief!
O God, O God! and which is worst,
To be the curser or the curst,   [90]
The victim or the murderer? Dong
Dong, there is no God; dong!

Ring ding, ring ding, tara, tara,
Away, and hush that preaching – fagh!
Ye vulgar dreamers about peace,   90
Who offer noblest hearts, to heal
The tenderest hurts honour can feel,
Paid magistrates and the Police!
O piddling merchant justice, go,
Exacter rules than yours we know;   [100]
Resentment's rule, and that high law
Of whoso best the sword can draw.
Ah well, and yet – dong, dong, dong.
Go on, my friends, as now you do;
Lawyers are villains, soldiers too;
And nothing's new and nothing's true.   100
Dong, there is no God; dong!

O Rosalie, my lovely maid,
I think thou thinkest love is true;
And on thy faithful bosom laid   [110]
I almost could believe it too.
The villainies, the wrongs, the alarms
Forget we in each other's arms.
No justice here, no God above;
But where we are, is there not love?
What? what? thou also go'st? For how   110
Should dead truth live in lover's vow?
What, thou? thou also lost? Dong
Dong, there is no God; dong!

I had a dream, from eve to light   [120]
A bell went sounding all the night.
Gay mirth, black woe, thin joys, huge pain:
I tried to stop it, but in vain.
It ran right on, and never broke;
Only when day began to stream
Through the white curtains to my bed,   120
And like an angel at my head
Light stood and touched me – I awoke,
And looked, and said, 'It is a dream.'³

Scene V

Spirit
'There is no God,' the wicked saith,
    'And truly it's a blessing,
For what he might have done with us
    It's better only guessing.'

'There is no God,' a youngster thinks,
    'Or really, if there may be,
He surely didn't mean a man   [160]
    Always to be a baby.'

'There is no God, or if there is,'
    The tradesman thinks, ''twere funny   10

---

3   Much of Scene V appeared as 'The Lido' in *The Letters and Remains of
Arthur Hugh Clough* (Spottiswoode & Co., 1865), for private circulation
only.

If he should take it ill in me
   To make a little money.'

'Whether there be,' the rich man says,
   'It matters very little,
For I and mine, thank somebody,
   Are not in want of victual.'

Some others, also, to themselves   [170]
   Who scarce so much as doubt it,
Think there is none, when they are well,
   And do not think about it.   20

But country folks who live beneath
   The shadow of the steeple;
The parson and the parson's wife,
   And mostly married people;

Youths green and happy in first love,
   So thankful for illusion;
And men caught out in what the world   [180]
   Calls guilt, in first confusion;

And almost every one when age,
   Disease, or sorrows strike him,   30
Inclines to think there is a God,
   Or something very like Him.[4]

Scene X

Dipsychus

There have been times, not many, but enough
To quiet all repinings of the heart;
There have been times, in which my [tranquil] soul,
No longer nebulous, sparse, errant, seemed
Upon its axis solidly to move,
Centred and fast; no mere chaotic blank
For random rays to traverse unretained,
But rounding luminous its fair ellipse
Around its central sun.
               O happy hours!
O compensation ample for long days   10
Of what impatient tongues call wretchedness!
O beautiful, beneath the magic moon,
To walk the watery way of palaces!
O beautiful, o'ervaulted with gemmed blue,
This spacious court; with colour and with gold,
With cupolas, and pinnacles, and points,
And crosses multiplex, and tips and balls
(Wherewith the bright stars unreproving mix,
Nor scorn by hasty eyes to be confused);
Fantastically perfect this low pile   20
Of oriental glory; these long ranges
Of classic chiselling, this gay flickering crowd,

---

4 Published as separate poem, *Poems* (1862, 1863), with omission of
stanza 3, and with 'rich man thinks' (l. 13), 'and first confusion' (l.
28), 'sorrow' (l. 30).

And the calm Campanile. Beautiful!
O beautiful! and that seemed more profound,
This morning by the pillar when I sat
Under the great arcade, at the review,
And took, and held, and ordered on my brain
The faces, and the voices, and the whole mass
O' the motley facts of existence flowing by!
O perfect, if 'twere all! But it is not;   30
Hints haunt me ever of a More beyond:
I am rebuked by a sense of the incomplete,
Of a completion over-soon assumed,
Of adding up too soon. What we call sin,
I could believe a painful opening out
Of paths for ampler virtue. The bare field,
Scant with lean ears of harvest, long had mocked
The vext laborious farmer. Came at length
The deep plough in the lazy undersoil
Down-driving; with a cry earth's fibres crack,   40
And a few months, and lo! the golden leas,
And autumn's crowded shocks and loaded wains.
Let us look back on life. Was any change,
Any now blest expansion, but at first
A pang, remorse-like, shot to the inmost seats
Of moral being? To do anything,
Distinct on any one thing to decide,
To leave the habitual and the old, and quit
The easy-chair of use and wont, seems crime
To the weak soul, forgetful how at first   50
Sitting down seemed so too. Oh, oh these qualms,
And oh these calls! And, oh! this woman's heart,
Fain to be forced, incredulous of choice,
And waiting a necessity for God.
    Yet I could think, indeed, the perfect call
Should force the perfect answer. If the voice
Ought to receive its echo from the soul,
Wherefore this silence? If it *should* rouse my being,
Why this reluctance? Have not I thought o'ermuch
Of other men, and of the ways of the world?   60
But what they are, or have been, matters not.
To thine own self be true, the wise man says.
Are then my fears myself? O double self!
And I untrue to both. Oh, there are hours,
When love, and faith, and dear domestic ties,
And converse with old friends, and pleasant walks,
Familiar faces, and familiar books,
Study, and art, upliftings unto prayer,
And admiration of the noblest things,
Seem all ignoble only; all is mean,   70
And nought as I would have it. Then at others,
My mind is on her nest; my heart at home
In all around; my soul secure in place,
And the vext needle perfect to her poles.
Aimless and hopeless in my life I seem
To thread the winding byways of the town,
Bewildered, baffled, hurried hence and thence,
All at cross-purpose ever with myself,
Unknowing whence from whither. Then, in a moment,
At a step, I crown the Campanile's top,   80

And view all mapped below: islands, lagoon,
An hundred steeples and a million roofs,
The fruitful champaign, and the cloud-capt Alps,
And the broad Adriatic. Be it enough;
If I lose this, how terrible! No, no,
I am contented, and will not complain.
To the old paths, my soul! Oh, be it so!
I bear the workday burden of dull life
About these footsore flags of a weary world,
Heaven knows how long it has not been; at once,   90
Lo! I am in the Spirit on the Lord's day
With John in Patmos.[5] Is it not enough,
One day in seven? and if this should go,
If this pure solace should desert my mind,
What were all else? I dare not risk this loss.
To the old paths, my soul![6]

Dipsychus first published as a whole in Letters and Remains *(1865).*

That there are powers above us I admit;
It may be true too
That while we walk the troublous tossing sea,
That when we see the o'ertopping waves advance,
And when [we] feel our feet beneath us sink,
There are who walk beside us; and the cry
That rises so spontaneous to the lips,
The 'Help us or we perish,' is not nought,
An evanescent spectrum of disease.
It may be that in deed and not in fancy,   10
A hand that is not ours upstays our steps,
A voice that is not ours commands the waves,
Commands the waves, and whispers in our ear,
O thou of little faith, why didst thou doubt?
At any rate –
That there are beings above us, I believe,
And when we lift up holy hands of prayer,
I will not say they will not give us aid.

First published, The Poems and Prose Remains of Arthur Hugh Clough, *ed.
His Wife, 2 vols (Macmillan, 1869), II, Poems, entitled 'O Thou of Little Faith',
omitting the MS's opening line and 'too' (l.2). Scenario from Matthew 8.23–27.*

If to write, rewrite, and write again,
Bite now the lip and now the pen,
Gnash in a fury the teeth, and tear
Innocent paper or it may be hair,
In endless chases to pursue
That swift escaping word that would do,
Inside and out turn a phrase, and o'er,
Till all the little sense goes, it had before, –
If it be these things make one a poet,
I am one – Come and all the world may know it.   10

If to look over old poems and detest
What one once hugged as a child to one's breast,

5   Revelation l.9–10.
6   Lines 12–23, 72–84, published separately as part of 'At Venice',
Poems (1862, 1863), with 'lone ranges' (21), 'My mind is in her rest'
(72), 'Unknowing whence or whither. Then at once' (79). In *The Letters
and Remains of Arthur Hugh Clough* (1865), 'ever' (78) reads 'even'.

Find the things nothing that once had been so much,
The old noble forms gone into dust at a touch:
If to see oneself of one's fancied plumage stript,
If by one's faults as by furies to be whipt;
If to become cool and, casting for good away
All the old implements, take 'em up the next day;
If to be sane to-night and insane again to-morrow,
And salve up past pains with the cause of future sorrow, –   20
If to do these things make a man a poet,
I am one – Come and all the world may know it.

If nevertheless no other peace of mind,
No inward unity ever to find,
No calm, well-being, sureness or rest
Save when by that strange temper possest,
Out of whose kind sources in pure rhythm-flow
The easy melodious verse-currents go;
If to sit still while the world goes by,
Find old friends dull and new friends dry,   30
Dinners a bore and dancing worse,
Compared to the tagging of verse onto verse, –
If it be these things make one a poet,
I am one – Come and all the world may know it.

In one of Clough's '1851' Notebooks. First published, The Poems of
Arthur Hugh Clough, *ed. H. F. Lowry, A. L. P. Norrington
and F. L. Mulhauser (Oxford, 1951).*

Ernest (Charles) Jones (1819–68)

Ernest Jones, Chartist, novelist, democratic poet, was born in Berlin, 25 January 1819. His Welsh father, Major Charles Jones, was equerry to the Duke of Cumberland, with an estate in Holstein. Ernest was educated in Germany, had his ten-year-old's verses published by doting parents, and tried to run away at the age of eleven to assist the Polish insurgents. The family returned to England in 1838. Ernest was presented to Queen Victoria in 1841; married a Miss Atherley of Barfield, Cumberland; and in 1844 was called to the Bar. He did not practise law at the time, however; instead, in 1846, he joined the Chartists and almost overnight became a leader of the O'Connor faction – defending him against Thomas Cooper; editing O'Connor's monthly *The Labourer* (1847), writing for and then editing the *Northern Star*. He failed to get elected as a Radical MP for Halifax in 1847 (as he would fail again in Halifax in 1852, and in Nottingham in 1853 and 1855). He was second speaker after O'Connor at the great Chartist rally of April 1848 on Kennington Common, but parted company with O'Connor when he became a physical force revolutionary. After seditious speeches in May 1848 Jones was imprisoned for two years – Parliament affirming his right as a political prisoner not to pick oakum. Released, he started the paper *Notes to the People* where much of his best prose and verse appeared (including 'The Song of the Low', in March 1852). By this time he was politically a Communist. Marx and Engels thought him the best hope for Communism in Britain. He is apparently the model for the nasty workers' orator Slackbridge in Dickens's *Hard Times* (originally in *Household Words*, April–August 1854), a first version of whom was presented as Gruffshaw in Dickens's article about the Preston Lock-Out of 1854, 'On Strike', earlier in *Household Words*, 11 February 1854. Jones practised law, lectured widely on issues of labour and capital, and wrote hard, publishing numerous tales, sensation stories in prose and verse, as well as political pamphlets. His long poem *The Revolt of Hindostan* (1854) was rumoured to have been written in prison in his own blood on the pages of a prayer-book. Landor told Jones that Byron 'would have envied' his *The Battle-Day: and Other Poems* (1855), in which 'The Factory Town' appeared. *Corydon: A Tale of Faith and Chivalry and Other Poems* came out in 1860. Jones died suddenly, 26 January 1868, on the point of standing (and perhaps winning) as Radical parliamentary candidate for Manchester. He was buried in Ardwick cemetery on 30 January 1868, amidst great mourning crowds. He died a principled poor man having devoted all his inherited wealth to the people's cause. A public subscription raised money for his children.

THE FACTORY TOWN

The night had sunk along the city,
    It was a bleak and cheerless hour;
The wild winds sang their solemn ditty
    To cold grey wall and blackened tower.

The factories gave forth lurid fires
    From pent-up hells within their breast;
E'en Etna's burning wrath expires,
    But *man's* volcanoes never rest.

Women, children, men were toiling,
    Locked in dungeons close and black,   10
Life's fast-failing thread uncoiling
    Round the wheel, the *modern rack!*

E'en the very stars seemed troubled
    With the mingled fume and roar;
The city like a cauldron bubbled,
    With its poison boiling o'er.

For the reeking walls environ
    Mingled groups of death and life:
Fellow-workmen, flesh and iron,
    Side by side in deadly strife.   20

There, amid the wheels' dull droning
    And the heavy, choking air,
Strength's repining, labour's groaning,
    And the throttling of despair, –

With the dust around them whirling,
    And the white, cracked, fevered lips,
And the shuttle's ceaseless twirling,
    And the short life's toil eclipse –

Stood half-naked infants shivering
    With heart-frost amid the heat;   30
Manhood's shrunken sinews quivering
    To the engine's horrid beat!

Woman's aching heart was throbbing
    With her wasting children's pain,
While red Mammon's hand was robbing
    God's thought-treasure from their brain!

Yet their lord bids proudly wander
    Stranger eyes thro' factory scenes;
'Here are men, and engines yonder.'
    'I see nothing but *machines!*'   40

Hark! amid that bloodless slaughter
    Comes the wailing of despair:

'Oh! for but one drop of water!
    'Oh! for but one breath of air!

'One fresh touch of dewy grasses,
    'Just to cool this shrivelled hand!'[1]
'Just to catch one breeze that passes
    'From some shady forest land.'

No! though 'twas a night of summer
    With a scent of new mown hay   50
From where the moon, the fairies' mummer,
    On distant fields enchanted lay!

On the lealands slept the cattle,
    Freshness through the forest ran –
While, in Mammon's mighty battle,
    Man was immolating man!

While the rich, with power unstable,
    Crushed the pauper's heart of pain,
As though those rich were heirs of *Abel*,
    And the poor the sons of *Cain*.[2]   60

While the proud from drowsy riot,
    Staggered past his church unknown,
Where his God, in the great quiet,
    Preached the livelong night alone!

While the bloated trader passes,
    Lord of loom and lord of mill;
On his pathway rush the masses,
    Crushed beneath his stubborn will.

Eager slaves, a willing heriot,
    O'er their brethren's living road   70
Drive him in his golden chariot,
    Quickened by his golden goad.

Young forms – with their pulses stifled,
    Young heads – with the eldered brain,
Young hearts – of their spirit rifled,
    Young lives – sacrificed in vain:

There they lie – the withered corses,
    With not one regretful thought,
Trampled by thy fierce steam-horses,
    England's mighty *Juggernaut!*[3]   80

Over all the solemn heaven
    Arches, like a God's reproof
At the offerings man has driven
    To Hell's altars, loom and woof!

THE FACTORY TOWN
1 Cf. Jesus's parable of rich man who, in Hell torment, craves a drop
of water to cool his tongue.
2 In Genesis Cain killed his brother Abel. The poet is being ironic.

3 Hindu deity. Devotees were said to throw themselves under wheels
of the huge cart carrying the god's effigy in annual ceremony at Puri,
Orissa, India.

Hear ye not the secret sighing?
    And the tear drop thro' the night?
See ye not a nation dying
    For want of rest, and air, and light?

Perishing for want of *Nature!*
    Crowded in the stifling town –   90
Dwarfed in brain and shrunk' in stature –
    Generations growing *down!*

Thinner wanes the rural village,
    Smokier lies the fallow plain –
Shrinks the cornfields' pleasant tillage,
    Fades the orchard's rich domain;

And a banished population
    Festers in the fetid street: –
Give us, God, to save our nation,
    Less of *cotton*, more of *wheat*.   100

Take us back to lea and wild wood,
    Back to nature and to Thee!
To the child restore his childhood –
    To the man his dignity!

Lo! the night hangs o'er the city,
    And the hours in fever fly,
And the wild winds sing their ditty,
    And the generations die.

First published in The Labourer: A Monthly Magazine of Politics,
Literature, and Poetry, *I (1844), 49.* The Battle-Day: and
Other Poems *(G. Routledge & Co., 1855).*

THE SONG OF THE LOW

We're low – we're low – we're very, very low,
    As low as low can be;
The rich are high – for we make them so –
    And a miserable lot are we!
    And a miserable lot are we! are we!
    A miserable lot are we!

We plough and sow – we're so very, very low,
    That we delve in the dirty clay,
Till we bless the plain with the golden grain,
    And the vale with the fragrant hay.   10
Our place we know – we're so very low,
    'Tis down at the landlord's feet:
We're not too low – the bread to grow
    But too low the bread to eat.

    We're low, we're low, etc.

Down, down we go – we're so very, very low,
    To the hell of the deep sunk mines.
But we gather the proudest gems that glow,
    When the crown of a despot shines;
And whenever he lacks – upon our backs   20
    Fresh loads he deigns to lay,
We're far too low to vote the tax
    But we're not too low to pay.

    We're low, we're low, etc.

We're low, we're low – mere rabble, we know,
    But at our plastic power,

The mould at the lordling's feet will grow
    Into palace and church and tower –
Then prostrate fall – in the rich man's hall,
    And cringe at the rich man's door,   30
We're not too low to build the wall,
    But too low to tread the floor.

    We're low, we're low, etc.

We're low, we're low – we're very, very low
    Yet from our fingers glide
The silken flow – and the robes that glow,
    Round the limbs of the sons of pride.
And what we get – and what we give,
    We know – and we know our share.
We're not too low the cloth to weave –   40
    But too low the cloth to wear.

    We're low, we're low, etc.

We're low, we're low – we're very, very low,
    And yet when the trumpets ring,
The thrust of a poor man's arm will go
    Through the heart of the proudest king!
We're low, we're low – our place we know,
    We're only the rank and file,
We're not too low – to kill the foe,
    But too low to touch the spoil.   50

    We're low, we're low, etc.

Notes to the People, II (March 1852), 953. Text from Brian Maidment,
The Poorhouse Fugitives: Self-Taught Poets and Poetry in
Victorian Britain *(Carcanet, 1987).*

John Ruskin (1819–1900)

John Ruskin, artist, theorist, reformer, was the only child of protective mothering parents. Born 8 February 1819 in London, he was raised in very well-off circumstances – his father was the London end of the Domecq sherry business – but in an unrelenting regime of watchful Evangelical strictness: no frivolity, no toys, daily Bible readings with his mother, lots of Scottish Psalms. Until his father died in 1864, and his mother in 1871, Ruskin lived under parental scrutiny. When he went up to Christ Church, Oxford, in 1836, his mother camped in the nearby Mitre Hotel in the High Street and he had to go and read to her every night. Father joined them at weekends. For thirty years the three travelled Europe together. His father's bluntness about money ensured Ruskin's marriage to Effie Gray (1848) got off to a bad start. Illness (touches of consumption) made Ruskin abandon his undergraduate studies (he won the Newdigate Prize for poetry, and he was granted an honorary Double Fourth Class in 1842), but already his critical career was mapped out rather inevitably in his love for the repertoire of Romantic landscape – sea, sky, mountains – the latter especially in their Swiss varieties, and his devotion to Turner's paintings and drawings as the apogee of such enthusiasms. His ongoing celebration of these convictions, *Modern Painters: Their Superiority in the Art of Landscape Painting to all the Ancient Masters proved by Examples of the True, the Beautiful, and the Intellectual, from the Works of Modern Artists, especially from those of J. M. W. Turner, Esq. RA* (1843), was a great hit ('For a critic to be so much of a poet is a great thing', enthused Elizabeth Barrett Barrett). Artists should 'draw what was really there', and critics should celebrate this truthfulness. 'I feel now', said Charlotte Brontë, 'as if I had been walking blindfold: the book seems to give me eyes.' Ruskin had himself become a keen amateur geologist and mineralist, observing but also collecting great stores of rocks, stones, and other instructive specimens to reveal nature's aesthetic potential. Meanwhile, sadly, love of natural realism did not transfer easily to the body of his wife – and Ruskin's disgust at the pubic hair women did not have in paintings and sculpture meant his marriage was never consummated. (Effie obtained an annulment in 1853 and in 1855 married the Ruskins' mutual friend, the painter John Everett Millais.) Ruskin's aesthetic of a realism which was both moral and spiritual inevitably led to vocal support for the Pre-Raphaelites – Millais, Holman Hunt, D. G. Rossetti, G. F. Watts, Burne-Jones. His early polemics on their behalf, collected as *Pre-Raphaelitism* (1851) – 'they will draw', Ruskin wrote to *The Times*, 'either what they see, or what they suppose might have been the actual facts of the scene they desire to represent, irrespective of any conventional rules of picture-making' – would continue all his life. He became the generous patron of D. G. Rossetti and Lizzie Siddal. His parallel case for a moral Christianized aesthetic in architecture, inspired by Gothic cathedrals (set out in *The Seven Lamps of Architecture*, 1849), profoundly influenced the Victorian Gothic revival. Ruskin's meditations on the nature of the workers who built the Gothic buildings, in the great three-volume *Stones of Venice* (1851–3), greatly inspired William Morris's politico-moral aesthetic of democratic craftsmanship. Ruskin's continuing faith in truth to nature naturally fired his attack in *Modern Painters*, vol. III (1856) on the Pathetic Fallacy. The gibe at Whistler for not earning his fees in 1878, which landed Ruskin in the courts, followed logically from his lifelong stress on good art as moral labour. It's no surprise either that his later life should have focused so much on practical applications of his faith in the morality of beauty and labour – teaching at the Working Men's College in Great Ormond Street, London; founding his utopian Guild of St George, with its farms, co-ops, school-work and Sheffield Museum; inspiring the road-building at Hinksey when he was Slade Professor of the Arts at Oxford (daftly idealistic, but still greatly affecting the likes of Arnold Toynbee and the movement for university 'settlements' in the slums); opening a model tea-shop; employing the unemployed as street-cleaners; writing the astounding (rambling, tart, prophetic, polymathic) *Fors Clavigera*, his monthly letter 'to the workmen and labourers of Great Britain' (1871–84); lecturing all over the country. Ruskin worked himself into the ground. He put his money where his mouth was, disbursing his huge inherited fortune in vast charitable, educational and patronage activities – the inspiration of Tolstoy in his not dissimilar rich man's good works. Fearlessly, Ruskin took on the Mammon of Victorian Unrighteousness. The various proprietors curtailed the essays on political economy in Thackeray's *Cornhill* which became *Unto this Last* (1860), and the ones in J. A. Froude's *Fraser's Magazine* which became *Munera Pulveris* (1862). Ruskin was a main member of the prophetic and inspirational group of Victorian critics – others include Carlyle, Ruskin's great friend and ally, and Arnold and Morris – who argued powerfully for the moral and social function of art. *In Memoriam* and *Maud* were Ruskin's 'pet rhymes', he wrote to Tennyson in 1860, but *Idylls of the King* fell short as appropriate modern subject:

> And merely in the facts of modern life, not drawing-room formal life, but the far away and quite unknown growth of souls in and through any form of misery or servitude, there is an infinity of what men should be told, and what none but a poet can tell. I cannot but think that the intense

masterful and unerring transcript of an actuality, and the relation of a story of any real human life as a poet would watch and analyze it, would make all men feel more or less what poetry was, as they felt what Life and Fate were in their instant workings.

This seems to me the true task of the modern poet. And I think I have seen faces and heard voices by road and street side, which claimed or confessed as much as ever the loveliest or saddest of Camelot.

Ruskin's rejection by the strictly Evangelical Rose la Touche in 1872 and her death in 1875 greatly grieved him, and not long after that his intermittent mental breakdowns began to occur. He was forced to abandon his Oxford Professorship in 1884, and to retire to his estate at Brantwood. He still travelled and wrote – including his unfinished autobiography *Praeterita* (1885–1900) – but deliriums and fatigue of body and mind virtually blanked out his last decade. He died 20 January 1900, and was buried at Coniston as he requested, rather than in Westminster Abbey. The monumental Library Edition of his works, by E. T. Cook and A. D. O. Wedderburn (1902–12), runs to thirty-nine volumes.

[NATURE UNTENANTED]

With fingers light, the lingering breezes quiver
Over the flowing of the still, deep river,
Whose water sings among the reeds, and smiles
'Mid glittering forests and luxuriant isles.
The wooded plain extends its azure ocean –
Waves without voice, and surges without motion.
And the red sunset, through the silent air,
Wide o'er the landscape shakes its golden hair.
Bright flush the clouds, along the distance curled,
That stoop their lips to kiss the gladdened world,   10
Where the long ridges indistinct retire
And melt and mingle with the heaven of fire.
Far and more far the lines of azure sweep,
Faint as our thoughts when fading into sleep;
When pale and paler on the brain defined,
The distant dreamings die upon the mind.
Oh, widely seems yon narrow plain to swell, –
Then, oh! how far am I from thee, Adèle!
For many a broad champaign of summer green
And many a waving forest spreads between,   20
And many a wide-extended, surgy hill,
And sullen, rushing river, dark and chill;
And the deep dashing of the dreary sea
Is barrier between us constantly.
And here there is no dreaming of the past,
Here is no halo by remembrance cast, –
No light to linger o'er the lonely scene
With faint reflection, where thou hast not been.
Nature has lost her spirit stirring spell,
She has no voice, to murmur of Adèle.   30
There's nothing here, and nothing seems to be, –
And nought remembers, nothing mourns with me.
Here was thy voice unheard, thy face unknown,
And thy dear memory's in my heart alone.

Written, July 1836. Poems, *ed. W. G. Collingwood, 2 vols (George Allen, Sunnyside, Orpington, and Bell Yard, Temple Bar, London, 1891), II.*

La Madonna Dell' Acqua[1]

Around her shrine no earthly blossoms blow,
No footsteps fret the pathway to and fro;
No sign nor record of departed prayer,
Print of the stone, nor echo of the air;
Worn by the lip, nor wearied by the knee, –
Only a deeper silence of the sea:
For there, in passing, pause the breezes bleak,
And the foam fades, and all the waves are weak.
The pulse-like oars in softer fall succeed,
The black prow falters through the wild seaweed –   10
Where, twilight-borne, the minute thunders reach
Of deep-mouthed surf, that bays by Lido's beach,
With intermittent motion traversed far,
And shattered glancing of the western star,
Till the faint storm-bird on the heaving flow
Drops in white circles, silently like snow.
Not here the ponderous gem, nor pealing note,
Dim to adorn – insentient to adore –
But purple-dyed, the mists of evening float,
In ceaseless incense from the burning floor   20
Of ocean, and the gathered gold of heaven
Laces its sapphire vault, and, early given,
The white rays of the rushing firmament
Pierce the blue-quivering night through wreath or rent
Of cloud inscrutable and motionless,
Hectic and wan, and moon-companioned cloud!
Oh! lone Madonna – angel of the deep –
When the night falls, and deadly winds are loud,
Will not thy love be with us while we keep
Our watch upon the waters, and the gaze   30
Of thy soft eyes, that slumber not, nor sleep?[2]
Deem not thou, stranger, that such trust is vain;
Faith walks not on these weary waves alone,
Though weakness dread, or apathy disdain
The spot which God has hallowed for His own.
They sin who pass it lightly – ill divining
The glory of this place of bitter prayer;
And hoping against hope, and self-resigning,
And reach of faith, and wrestling with despair,
And resurrection of the last distress,   40
Into the sense of heaven, when earth is bare,
And of God's voice, when man's is comfortless.

First published in Heath's Book of Beauty *(1845), 18–19.* Poems, *by J. R.*
(Privately printed, 1850). Text, Poems, *ed. Collingwood, (1891), II.*

Of the Pathetic Fallacy

§ 1. German dulness, and English affectation, have of late much multiplied among us the use of two of the most objectionable words that were ever coined by the troublesomeness of metaphysicians, – namely, 'Objective' and 'Subjective'.

La Madonna dell' Acqua
1 'The Virgin of the Water'. ([Author's note]: In the centre of the lagoon between Venice and the mouths of the Brenta, supported on a few mouldering piles, stands a small shrine dedicated to the Madonna dell' Acqua, which the gondolier never passes without a prayer.)
2 like God, Psalm 121.4.

No words can be more exquisitely, and in all points, useless; and I merely speak of them that I may, at once and for ever, get them out of my way, and out of my reader's. But to get that done, they must be explained.

The word 'Blue', say certain philosophers, means the sensation of colour which the human eye receives in looking at the open sky, or at a bell gentian.

Now, say they farther, as this sensation can only be felt when the eye is turned to the object, and as, therefore, no such sensation is produced by the object when nobody looks at it, therefore the thing, when it is not looked at, is not blue; and thus (say they) there are many qualities of things which depend as much on something else as on themselves. To be sweet, a thing must have a taster; it is only sweet while it is being tasted, and if the tongue had not the capacity of taste, then the sugar would not have the quality of sweetness.

And then they agree that the qualities of things which thus depend upon our perception of them, and upon our human nature as affected by them, shall be called Subjective; and the qualities of things which they always have, irrespective of any other nature, as roundness or squareness, shall be called Objective.

From these ingenious views the step is very easy to a farther opinion, that it does not much matter what things are in themselves, but only what they are to us; and that the only real truth of them is their appearance to, or effect upon, us. From which position, with a hearty desire for mystification, and much egotism, selfishness, shallowness, and impertinence, a philosopher may easily go so far as to believe, and say, that everything in the world depends upon his seeing or thinking of it, and that nothing, therefore, exists, but what he sees or thinks of.

§ 2. Now, to get rid of all these ambiguities and troublesome words at once, be it observed that the word 'Blue' does *not* mean the *sensation* caused by a gentian on the human eye; but it means the *power* of producing that sensation; and this power is always there, in the thing, whether we are there to experience it or not, and would remain there though there were not left a man on the face of the earth. Precisely in the same way gunpowder has a power of exploding. It will not explode if you put no match to it. But it has always the power of so exploding, and is therefore called an explosive compound, which it very positively and assuredly is, whatever philosophy may say to the contrary.

In like manner, a gentian does not produce the sensation of blueness if you don't look at it. But it has always the power of doing so; its particles being everlastingly so arranged by its Maker. And, therefore, the gentian and the sky are always verily blue, whatever philosophy may say to the contrary; and if you do not see them blue when you look at them, it is not their fault but yours.

§ 3. Hence I would say to these philosophers: If, instead of using the sonorous phrase, 'It is objectively so,' you will use the plain old phrase, 'It *is* so;' and if instead of the sonorous phrase, 'It is subjectively so,' you will say, in plain old English, 'It does so,' or 'It seems so to me;' you will, on the whole, be more intelligible to your fellow-creatures: and besides, if you find that a thing which generally 'does so' to other people (as a gentian looks blue to most men), does *not* so to you, on any particular occasion, you will not fall into the impertinence of saying, that the thing is not so, or did not so, but you will say simply (what you will be all the better for speedily finding out), that something is the matter with you. If you find that you cannot explode the gunpowder, you will not declare that all gunpowder is subjective, and all explosion imaginary, but you will simply suspect and declare yourself to be an ill-made match. Which, on the whole, though there may be a distant chance of a mistake about it, is, nevertheless, the wisest conclusion you can come to until farther experiment.

§ 4. Now, therefore, putting these tiresome and absurd words quite out of our way, we may go on at our ease to examine the point in question, – namely, the difference between the ordinary, proper, and true appearances of things to us; and the extraordinary, or false appearances, when we are under the influence of emotion, or contemplative fancy; false appearances, I say, as being entirely unconnected with any real power or character in the object, and only imputed to it by us.

For instance –

The spendthrift crocus, bursting through the mould
Naked and shivering, with his cup of gold.[1]

This is very beautiful, and yet very untrue. The crocus is not a spendthrift, but a hardy plant; its yellow is not gold, but saffron. How is it that we enjoy so much the having it put into our heads that it is anything else than a plain crocus?

It is an important question. For, throughout our past reasonings about art, we have always found that nothing could be good, or useful, or ultimately pleasurable, which was untrue. But here is something pleasurable in written poetry which is nevertheless *un*true. And what is more, if we think over our favourite poetry, we shall find it full of this kind of fallacy, and that we like it all the more for being so.

§ 5. It will appear also, on consideration of the matter, that this fallacy is of two principal kinds. Either, as in this case of the crocus, it is the fallacy of wilful fancy, which involves no real expectation that it will be believed; or else it is a fallacy caused by an excited state of the feelings, making us, for the time, more or less irrational. Of the cheating of the fancy we shall have to speak presently; but, in this chapter, I want to examine the nature of the other error, that which the mind admits when affected strongly by emotion. Thus, for instance, in Alton Locke –

They rowed her in across the rolling foam –
The cruel, crawling foam.[2]

The foam is not cruel, neither does it crawl. The state of mind which attributes to it these characters of a living creature is one in which the reason is unhinged by grief. All violent feelings have the same effect. They produce in us a falseness in all our impressions of external things, which I would generally characterize as the 'Pathetic Fallacy'.

§ 6. Now we are in the habit of considering this fallacy as eminently a character of poetical description, and the temper of mind in which we allow it as one eminently poetical, because passionate. But, I believe, if we look well into the matter, that we shall find the greatest poets do not often admit this kind of falseness – that it is only the second order of poets who much delight in it.[3]

Thus, when Dante describes the spirits falling from the bank of Acheron 'as dead leaves flutter from a bough', he gives the most perfect image possible of their utter lightness, feebleness, passiveness, and scattering agony of despair, without, however, for an instant losing his own clear perception that *these* are souls, and *those* are leaves; he makes no confusion of one with the other. But when Coleridge speaks of

The one red leaf, the last of its clan,
That dances as often as dance it can,[4]

Of the Pathetic Fallacy

1 Oliver Wendel Holmes.
2 Charles Kingsley, 'The Sands of Dee,' *Alton Locke* (1850), ch. 26.
3 I admit two orders of poets, but no third; and by these two orders I mean the Creative (Shakespere, Homer, Dante), and Reflective or Perceptive (Wordsworth, Keats, Tennyson). But both of these must be *first*-rate in their range, though their range is different; and with poetry second-rate in *quality* no one ought to be allowed to trouble mankind. There is quite enough of the best, – much more than we can ever read or enjoy in the length of a life; and it is a literal wrong or sin in any person to encumber us with inferior work. I have no patience with apologies made by young pseudo-poets, 'that they believe there is *some* good in what they have written: that they hope to do better in time,' &c. *Some* good! If there is not *all* good, there is no good. If they ever hope to do better, why do they trouble us now? Let them rather courageously burn all they have done, and wait for the better days. There are few men, ordinarily educated, who in moments of strong feeling could not strike out a poetical thought, and afterwards polish it so as to be presentable. But men of sense know better than so to waste their time; and those who sincerely love poetry, know the touch of the master's hand on the chords too well to fumble among them after him. Nay, more than this; all inferior poetry is an injury to the good, inasmuch as it takes away the freshness of rhymes, blunders upon and gives a wretched commonalty to good thoughts; and, in general, adds to the weight of human weariness in a most woful and culpable manner. There are few thoughts likely to come across ordinary men, which have not already been expressed by greater men in the best possible way; and it is a wiser, more generous, more noble thing to remember and point out the perfect words, than to invent poorer ones, wherewith to encumber temporarily the world. [Author's note]
4 Samuel Taylor Coleridge, 'Christabel' (1816), Part I, 46.

he has a morbid, that is to say, a so far false, idea about the leaf: he fancies a life in it, and will, which there are not; confuses its powerlessness with choice, its fading death with merriment, and the wind that shakes it with music. Here, however, there is some beauty, even in the morbid passage; but take an instance in Homer and Pope. Without the knowledge of Ulysses, Elpenor, his youngest follower, has fallen from an upper chamber in the Circean palace, and has been left dead, unmissed by his leader, or companions, in the haste of their departure. They cross the sea to the Cimmerian land; and Ulysses summons the shades from Tartarus. The first which appears is that of the lost Elpenor. Ulysses, amazed, and in exactly the spirit of bitter and terrified lightness which is seen in Hamlet,[5] addresses the spirit with the simple, startled words: –

> Elpenor! How camest thou under the shadowy darkness? Hast thou come faster on foot than I in my black ship?

Which Pope renders thus: –

> O, say, what angry power Elpenor led
> To glide in shades, and wander with the dead?
> How could thy soul, by realms and seas disjoined,
> Outfly the nimble sail, and leave the lagging wind?[6]

I sincerely hope the reader finds no pleasure here, either in the nimbleness of the sail, or the laziness of the wind! And yet how is it that these conceits are so painful now, when they have been pleasant to us in the other instances?

§ 7. For a very simple reason. They are not a *pathetic* fallacy at all, for they are put into the mouth of the wrong passion – a passion which never could possibly have spoken them – agonized curiosity. Ulysses wants to know the facts of the matter; and the very last thing his mind could do at the moment would be to pause, or suggest in anywise what was *not* a fact. The delay in the first three lines, and conceit in the last, jar upon us instantly, like the most frightful discord in music. No poet of true imaginative power could possibly have written the passage.[7]

Therefore, we see that the spirit of truth must guide us in some sort, even in our enjoyment of fallacy. Coleridge's fallacy has no discord in it, but Pope's has set our teeth on edge. Without farther questioning, I will endeavour to state the main bearings of this matter.

§ 8. The temperament which admits the pathetic fallacy, is, as I said above, that of a mind and body in some sort too weak to deal fully with what is before them or upon them; borne away, or over-clouded, or over-dazzled by emotion; and it is a more or less noble state, according to the force of the emotion which has induced it. For it is no credit to a man that he is not morbid or inaccurate in his perceptions, when he has no strength of feeling to warp them; and it is in general a sign of higher capacity and stand in the ranks of being, that the emotions should be strong enough to vanquish, partly, the intellect, and make it believe what they choose. But it is still a grander condition when the intellect also rises, till it is strong enough to assert its rule against, or together with, the utmost efforts of the passions; and the whole man stands in an iron glow, white hot, perhaps, but still strong, and in no wise evaporating; even if he melts, losing none of his weight.

So, then, we have the three ranks: the man who perceives rightly, because he does not feel, and to whom the primrose is very accurately the primrose, because he does not love it. Then, secondly,

---

5   'Well said, old mole! can'st work i' the ground so fast?' [Author's note]. *Hamlet*, I.v.162.

6   Alexander Pope, Homer's *Odyssey*, XI, 71–4.

7   It is worth while comparing the way a similar question is put by the exquisite sincerity of Keats: –

>   He wept, and his bright tears
>   Went trickling down the golden bow he held.
>   Thus, with half-shut, suffused eyes, he stood:

>   While from beneath some cumb'rous boughs hard by,
>   With solemn step, an awful goddess came.
>   And there was purport in her looks for him,
>   Which he with eager guess began to read:
>   Perplexed the while, melodiously he said,
>   *'How cam'st thou over the unfooted sea?'*

[Author's note]. John Keats, *Hyperion. A Fragment* [1818–19], III, 42–50.

the man who perceives wrongly, because he feels, and to whom the primrose is anything else than a primrose: a star, or a sun, or a fairy's shield, or a forsaken maiden. And then, lastly, there is the man who perceives rightly in spite of his feelings, and to whom the primrose is for ever nothing else than itself – a little flower, apprehended in the very plain and leafy fact of it, whatever and how many soever the associations and passions may be, that crowd around it. And, in general, these three classes may be rated in comparative order, as the men who are not poets at all, and the poets of the second order, and the poets of the first; only however great a man may be, there are always some subjects which *ought* to throw him off his balance; some, by which his poor human capacity of thought should be conquered, and brought into the inaccurate and vague state of perception, so that the language of the highest inspiration becomes broken, obscure, and wild in metaphor, resembling that of the weaker man, overborne by weaker things.

§ 9. And thus, in full, there are four classes: the men who feel nothing, and therefore see truly; the men who feel strongly, think weakly, and see untruly (second order of poets); the men who feel strongly, think strongly, and see truly (first order of poets); and the men who, strong as human creatures can be, are yet submitted to influences stronger than they, and see in a sort untruly, because what they see is inconceivably above them. This last is the usual condition of prophetic inspiration.

§ 10. I separate these classes, in order that their character may be clearly understood; but of course they are united each to the other by imperceptible transitions, and the same mind, according to the influences to which it is subjected, passes at different times into the various states. Still, the difference between the great and less man is, on the whole, chiefly in this point of *alterability*. That is to say, the one knows too much, and perceives and feels too much of the past and future, and of all things beside and around that which immediately affects him, to be in anywise shaken by it. His mind is made up; his thoughts have an accustomed current; his ways are steadfast; it is not this or that new sight which will at once unbalance him. He is tender to impression at the surface, like a rock with deep moss upon it; but there is too much mass of him to be moved. The smaller man, with the same degree of sensibility, is at once carried off his feet; he wants to do something he did not want to do before; he views all the universe in a new light through his tears; he is gay or enthusiastic, melancholy or passionate, as things come and go to him. Therefore the high creative poet might even be thought, to a great extent, impassive (as shallow people think Dante stern), receiving indeed all feelings to the full, but having a great centre of reflection and knowledge in which he stands serene, and watches the feeling, as it were, from far off.

Dante, in his most intense moods, has entire command of himself, and can look around calmly, at all moments, for the image or the word that will best tell what he sees to the upper or lower world. But Keats and Tennyson, and the poets of the second order, are generally themselves subdued by the feelings under which they write, or, at least, write as choosing to be so, and therefore admit certain expressions and modes of thought which are in some sort diseased or false.

§ 11. Now so long as we see that the *feeling* is true, we pardon, or are even pleased by, the confessed fallacy of sight which it induces: we are pleased, for instance, with those lines of Kingsley's, above quoted, not because they fallaciously describe foam, but because they faithfully describe sorrow. But the moment the mind of the speaker becomes cold, that moment every such expression becomes untrue, as being for ever untrue in the external facts. And there is no greater baseness in literature than the habit of using these metaphorical expressions in cold blood. An inspired writer, in full impetuosity of passion, may speak wisely and truly of 'raging waves of the sea, foaming out their own shame'; but it is only the basest writer who cannot speak of the sea without talking of 'raging waves', 'remorseless floods', 'ravenous billows', &c.; and it is one of the signs of the highest power in a writer to check all such habits of thought, and to keep his eyes fixed firmly on the *pure fact*, out of which if any feeling comes to him or his reader, he knows it must be a true one.

To keep to the waves, I forget who it is who represents a man in despair, desiring that his body may be cast into the sea,

> *Whose changing mound, and foam that passed away,*
> Might mock the eye that questioned where I lay.

Observe, there is not a single false, or even overcharged, expression. 'Mound' of the sea wave is perfectly simple and true; 'changing' is as familiar as may be; 'foam that passed away', strictly literal; and the whole line descriptive of the reality with a degree of accuracy which I know not any other verse, in the range of poetry, that altogether equals. For most people have not a distinct idea of the clumsiness and massiveness of a large wave. The word 'wave' is used too generally of ripples and breakers, and bendings in light drapery or grass: it does not by itself convey a perfect image. But the word 'mound' is heavy, large, dark, definite; there is no mistaking the kind of wave meant, nor missing the sight of it. Then the term 'changing' has a peculiar force also. Most people think of waves as rising and falling. But if they look at the sea carefully, they will perceive that the waves do not rise and fall. They change. Change both place and form, but they do not fall; one wave goes on, and on, and still on; now lower, now higher, now tossing its mane like a horse, now building itself together like a wall, now shaking, now steady, but still the same wave, till at last it seems struck by something, and changes, one knows not how, – becomes another wave.

The close of the line insists on this image, and paints it still more perfectly, – 'foam that passed away'. Not merely melting, disappearing, but passing on, out of sight, on the career of the wave. Then, having put the absolute ocean fact as far as he may before our eyes, the poet leaves us to feel about it as we may, and to trace for ourselves the opposite fact, – the image of the green mounds that do not change, and the white and written stones that do not pass away; and thence to follow out also the associated images of the calm life with the quiet grave, and the despairing life with the fading foam:

> Let no man move his bones.
> As for Samaria, her king is cut off like the foam upon the water.[8]

But nothing of this is actually told or pointed out, and the expressions, as they stand, are perfectly severe and accurate, utterly uninfluenced by the firmly governed emotion of the writer. Even the word 'mock' is hardly an exception, as it may stand merely for 'deceive' or 'defeat', without implying any impersonation of the waves.

§ 12. It may be well, perhaps, to give one or two more instances to show the peculiar dignity possessed by all passages which thus limit their expression to the pure fact, and leave the hearer to gather what he can from it. Here is a notable one from the Iliad. Helen, looking from the Scaean gate of Troy over the Grecian host, and telling Priam the names of its captains, says at last:

> I see all the other dark-eyed Greeks; but two I cannot see, – Castor and Pollux, – whom one mother bore with me. Have they not followed from fair Lacedaemon, or have they indeed come in their sea-wandering ships, but now will not enter into the battle of men, fearing the shame and the scorn that is in Me?

Then Homer:

> So she spoke. But them, already, the life-giving earth possessed, there in Lacedaemon, in the dear fatherland.[9]

Note, here, the high poetical truth carried to the extreme. The poet has to speak of the earth in sadness, but he will not let that sadness affect or change his thoughts of it. No; though Castor and Pollux be dead, yet the earth is our mother still, fruitful, life-giving. These are the facts of the thing. I see nothing else than these. Make what you will of them.

§ 13. Take another very notable instance from Casimir de la Vigne's terrible ballad, *La Toilette de Constance*. I must quote a few lines out of it here and there, to enable the reader who has not the book by him, to understand its close.

8 Hosea 10.7.   9 *Iliad*, Book 3.

Vite, Anna, vite; au miroir
   Plus vite, Anna. L'heure s'avance,
Et je vais au bal ce soir
   Chez l'ambassadeur de France.

Y pensez-vous, ils sont fanés, ces nœuds,
   Ils sont d'hier, mon Dieu, comme tout passe!
Que du réseau qui retient mes cheveux
   Les glands d'azur retombent avec grâce.
Plus haut! Plus bas! Vous ne comprenez rien!
   Que sur mon front ce saphir étincelle: 10
Vous me piquez, maladroite. Ah, c'est bien.
   Bien, – chère Anna! Je t'aime, je suis belle.

Celui qu'en vain je voudrais oublier
   (Anna, ma robe) il y sera, j'espère.
(Ah, fi, profane, est-ce là mon collier?
   Quoi! ces grains d'or bénits par le Saint-Père!)
Il y sera; Dieu, s'il pressait ma main,
   En y pensant, à peine je respire;
Père Anselmo doit m'entendre demain.
   Comment ferai-je, Anna, pour tout lui dire?   20

   Vite un coup d'œil au miroir,
      Le dernier. – J'ai l'assurance
   Qu'on va m'adorer ce soir
      Chez l'ambassadeur de France.

Près du foyer, Constance s'admirait.
   Dieu! sur sa robe il vole une étincelle!
Au feu. Courez; Quand l'espoir l'enivrait,
   Tout perdre ainsi! Quoi! Mourir, – et si belle!
L'horrible feu ronge avec volupté
   Ses bras, son sein, et l'entoure, et s'élève,   30
Et sans pitié dévore sa beauté,
   Ses dixhuit ans, hélas, et son doux rêve!

   Adieu, bal, plaisir, amour!
      On disait, Pauvre Constance!
   Et on dansait, jusqu'au jour,
      Chez l'ambassadeur de France.[10]

Yes, that is the fact of it. Right or wrong, the poet does not say. What you may think about it, he does not know. He has nothing to do with that. There lie the ashes of the dead girl in her chamber. There they danced, till the morning, at the Ambassador's of France. Make what you will of it.

10 'Hurry up, Anna, hurry up; come on, over to the mirror, Anna. It's getting late, and tonight I'm going to the ball at the French ambassador's.

Just think, how they're wilted, these ribbons, yesterday's ribbons, my God, how everything fades. Just get the hair-net right, and make the blue tassels fall gracefully. Higher up! Lower! You don't understand anything! I want this sapphire to sparkle on my forehead: You annoy me, you're so clumsy. Ah, that's good, good – dear Anna! I love you, I am beautiful.

He'll be there, I hope, the one I'd like to forget (Anna, my frock). (Oh, you, is nothing sacred, isn't my necklace there? What! The one with the gold beads blessed by St Peter!) He'll be there; oh God, if he should squeeze my hand, I can scarcely breathe, just thinking of it.

Father Anselme will have to hear my confession tomorrow. How will I manage to tell him everything, Anna?

A quick glance in the mirror. One last time. – I'm sure they'll just adore me tonight at the French ambassador's.

By the fireplace, Constance admired herself. Oh God! A spark catches her dress. She's on fire! Over here! Just when she was drunk with high hopes, to lose everything like this! What! Dying – and so beautiful! The dreadful flame gnaws voluptuously at her arms, her breast, embraces her, climbs higher, devours her beauty without remorse, all her eighteen years, alas, and her sweet dream!

Farewell ball, pleasure, love! Poor Constance, they said. And they danced till dawn, at the French ambassador's.' (Jean François Casimir Delavigne (1793–1843))

If the reader will look through the ballad, of which I have quoted only about the third part, he will find that there is not, from beginning to end of it, a single poetical (so called) expression, except in one stanza. The girl speaks as simple prose as may be; there is not a word she would not have actually used as she was dressing. The poet stands by, impassive as a statue, recording her words just as they come. At last the doom seizes her, and in the very presence of death, for an instant, his own emotions conquer him. He records no longer the facts only, but the facts as they seem to him. The fire gnaws with *voluptuousness – without pity.* It is soon past. The fate is fixed for ever; and he retires into his pale and crystalline atmosphere of truth. He closes all with the calm veracity,

> They said, 'Poor Constance!'

§ 14. Now in this there is the exact type of the consummate poetical temperament. For, be it clearly and constantly remembered, that the greatness of a poet depends upon the two faculties, acuteness of feeling, and command of it. A poet is great, first in proportion to the strength of his passion, and then, that strength being granted, in proportion to his government of it; there being, however, always a point beyond which it would be inhuman and monstrous if he pushed this government, and, therefore, a point at which all feverish and wild fancy becomes just and true. Thus the destruction of the kingdom of Assyria cannot be contemplated firmly by a prophet of Israel. The fact is too great, too wonderful. It overthrows him, dashes him into a confused element of dreams. All the world is, to his stunned thought, full of strange voices. 'Yea, the fir-trees rejoice at thee, and the cedars of Lebanon, saying, "Since thou art gone down to the grave, no feller is come up against us." '[11] So, still more, the thought of the presence of Deity cannot be borne without this great astonishment. 'The mountains and the hills shall break forth before you into singing, and all the trees of the field shall clap their hands.'[12]

§ 15. But by how much this feeling is noble when it is justified by the strength of its cause, by so much it is ignoble when there is not cause enough for it; and beyond all other ignobleness is the mere affectation of it, in hardness of heart. Simply bad writing may almost always, as above noticed, be known by its adoption of these fanciful metaphorical expressions, as a sort of current coin; yet there is even a worse, at least a more harmful, condition of writing than this, in which such expressions are not ignorantly and feelinglessly caught up, but, by some master, skilful in handling, yet insincere, deliberately wrought out with chill and studied fancy; as if we should try to make an old lava stream look red-hot again, by covering it with dead leaves, or white-hot, with hoar-frost.

When Young is lost in veneration, as he dwells on the character of a truly good and holy man, he permits himself for a moment to be overborne by the feeling so far as to exclaim:

> Where shall I find him? angels, tell me where.
> You know him; he is near you; point him out.
> Shall I see glories beaming from his brow,
> Or trace his footsteps by the rising flowers?[13]

This emotion has a worthy cause, and is thus true and right. But now hear the cold-hearted Pope say to a shepherd girl –

> Where'er you walk, cool gales shall fan the glade;
> Trees, where you sit, shall crowd into a shade;
> Your praise the birds shall chant in every grove,
> And winds shall waft it to the powers above.
> But would you sing, and rival Orpheus' strain,

11   Isaiah 14.8.
12   Isaiah 55.12.

13   Edward Young, *Night Thoughts*, II (1742), 325–8.

> The wondering forests soon should dance again;
> The moving mountains hear the powerful call,
> And headlong streams hang, listening, in their fall.[14]

This is not, nor could it for a moment be mistaken for, the language of passion. It is simple false-hood, uttered by hypocrisy; definite absurdity, rooted in affectation, and coldly asserted in the teeth of nature and fact. Passion will indeed go far in deceiving itself; but it must be a strong passion, not the simple wish of a lover to tempt his mistress to sing. Compare a very closely parallel passage in Wordsworth, in which the lover has lost his mistress:

> Three years had Barbara in her grave been laid,
> When thus his moan he made: –
>
> 'Oh move, thou cottage, from behind yon oak,
>   Or let the ancient tree uprooted lie,
> That in some other way yon smoke
>   May mount into the sky.
> If still behind yon pine-tree's ragged bough,
>   Headlong, the waterfall must come,
>   Oh, let it, then, be dumb –
> Be anything, sweet stream, but that which thou art now.'[15]

Here is a cottage to be moved, if not a mountain, and a waterfall to be silent, if it is not to hang listening: but with what different relation to the mind that contemplates them! Here, in the extremity of its agony, the soul cries out wildly for relief, which at the same moment it partly knows to be impossible, but partly believes possible, in a vague impression that a miracle *might* be wrought to give relief even to a less sore distress, – that nature is kind, and God is kind, and that grief is strong: it knows not well what *is* possible to such grief. To silence a stream, to move a cottage wall, – one might think it could do as much as that!

§ 16. I believe these instances are enough to illustrate the main point I insist upon respecting the pathetic fallacy, – that so far as it *is* a fallacy, it is always the sign of a morbid state of mind, and comparatively of a weak one. Even in the most inspired prophet it is a sign of the incapacity of his human sight or thought to bear what has been revealed to it. In ordinary poetry, if it is found in the thoughts of the poet himself, it is at once a sign of his belonging to the inferior school; if in the thoughts of the characters imagined by him, it is right or wrong according to the genuineness of the emotion from which it springs; always, however, implying necessarily *some* degree of weakness in the character.

Take two most exquisite instances from master hands. The Jessy of Shenstone, and the Ellen of Wordsworth, have both been betrayed and deserted. Jessy, in the course of her most touching complaint, says:

> If through the garden's flowery tribes I stray,
>   Where bloom the jasmines that could once allure,
> 'Hope not to find delight in us,' they say,
>   'For we are spotless, Jessy; we are pure.'[16]

Compare with this some of the words of Ellen:

> 'Ah, why,' said Ellen, sighing to herself,
> 'Why do not words, and kiss, and solemn pledge,
> And nature, that is kind in woman's breast,

14 Alexander Pope, 'Summer. The Second Pastoral, or Alexis' (1709), 73–4, 79–84.
15 ''Tis said, that some have died for love', *Lyrical Ballads* (1800), 11–16, 33–6.
16 William Shenstone, Elegy XXVI, 'Describing the sorrow of an ingenuous mind, on the melancholy event of a licentious amour', *Poems Upon Various Occasions* (1737), 56–9.

And reason, that in man is wise and good,
And fear of Him who is a righteous Judge, –
Why do not these prevail for human life,
To keep two hearts together, that began
Their springtime with one love, and that have need
Of mutual pity and forgiveness, sweet
To grant, or be received; while that poor bird –
O, come and hear him! Thou who hast to me
Been faithless, hear him; – though a lowly creature,
One of God's simple children, that yet know not
The Universal Parent, *how* he sings!
As if he wished the firmament of heaven
Should listen, and give back to him the voice
Of his triumphant constancy and love.
The proclamation that he makes, how far
His darkness doth transcend our fickle light."[17]

The perfection of both these passages, as far as regards truth and tenderness of imagination in the two poets, is quite insuperable. But, of the two characters imagined, Jessy is weaker than Ellen, exactly in so far as something appears to her to be in nature which is not. The flowers do not really reproach her. God meant them to comfort her, not to taunt her; they would do so if she saw them rightly.

Ellen, on the other hand, is quite above the slightest erring emotion. There is not the barest film of fallacy in all her thoughts. She reasons as calmly as if she did not feel. And, although the singing of the bird suggests to her the idea of its desiring to be heard in heaven, she does not for an instant admit any veracity in the thought. 'As if,' she says, – 'I know he means nothing of the kind; but it does verily seem as if.' The reader will find, by examining the rest of the poem, that Ellen's character is throughout consistent in this clear though passionate strength.[18]

It then being I hope, now made clear to the reader in all respects that the pathetic fallacy is powerful only so far as it is pathetic, feeble so far as it is fallacious, and, therefore, that the dominion of Truth is entire, over this, as over every other natural and just state of the human mind, we may go on to the subject for the dealing with which this prefatory inquiry became necessary [i.e. landscape in poetry and painting] . . .

Modern Painters, *5 vols (George Allen, Sunnyside, Orpington, 1843–60); vol. III (Smith, Elder, & Co., 1856) (= Part 4, 'Of Many Things'), chapter xii, 'Of the Pathetic Fallacy'.*

'MY OWN ARTICLE ON WHISTLER'

It has long been alleged against me, with much indignation, that in criticism I do not help my friends. The sentiment that every expression of a man's opinions ought to help either himself, his friends, or his party, is now so completely the first commandment of English morality that I have ceased to be surprised when, if I say anybody's picture is good – though I don't know the painter from Noah – he immediately writes to thank me for my unexpected kindness; and if

---

17   Wordsworth, *The Excursion* (1814), Book 6, 869–87.
18   I cannot quit this subject without giving two more instances, both exquisite, of the pathetic fallacy, which I have just come upon, in *Maud*:

For a great speculation had fail'd;
And ever he mutter'd and madden'd, and ever wann'd with despair;
And out he walk'd, when the wind like a broken worldling wail'd,
And the *flying gold of the ruin'd woodlands drove thro' the air.*
[*Maud*, 9–12 (*vast* speculation).]

There has fallen a splendid tear
From the passion-flower at the gate.
The red rose cries, 'She is near, she is near!'
And the white rose weeps, 'She is late.'
The larkspur listens. 'I hear, I hear!'
And the lily whispers, 'I wait.'
[*Maud*, 908–9, 912–15.]

[Author's note]

I say it is bad, similarly writes to ask what he has done to offend me, or institutes an action for libel, in which the English law will politely estimate the force of my injurious opinion at a farthing, and make my friends pay it four hundred pounds[1] for the expression of its own opinion to that effect.

The function of the critic, in his relation to contemporary art, is of course the same as that of the critic with respect to contemporary literature; namely, to recommend 'authors' (the word is properly common to men of original power in both the arts) of merit to public attention, and to prevent authors of no merit from occupying it. All good critics delight in praising, as all bad ones in blaming (there is an interesting letter in Lockhart's *Life of Scott*, describing the vital difference between Scott and Jeffrey in this respect; and I am both proud and happy in being able to say of myself that the entire strength of my life has been spent in the praise of artists who among the ancients had remained unappreciated, or among the moderns, maligned or unknown.

I use the word 'maligned' deliberately and sorrowfully in thinking of the criticisms which first provoked me into literature; before I was old enough to learn with Horace and Turner '*Malignum spernere vulgus.*'[2] If attacks such as those I refer to (in *Blackwood's Magazine*, anonymous, and in recent periodicals by persons who even assert their ignorance for the pledge of their sincerity) could be repressed by the care and acumen of British Law, it would be well alike for the dignity of Literature and the interests of Art. But the Bench of honourable Criticism is as truly a Seat of Judgment as that of Law itself, and its verdicts, though usually kinder, must sometimes be no less stern. It has ordinarily been my privilege to extol, but occasionally my duty to condemn, the works of living painters. But no artist has ever been suspected of purchasing my praise, and this is the first attempt that has been made through the instrumentality of British Law to tax my blame. I do not know the sense attached, legally, to the word 'libel'; but the sense rationally attaching to it is that of a false description of a man's person, character, or work, made wilfully with the purpose of injuring him.

And the only answers I think it necessary to make to the charge of libel brought against me by the plaintiff, are first, that the description given of his work and character is accurately true so far as it reaches; and secondly, that it was calculated, so far as it was believed, to be extremely beneficial to himself and still more to the public. In the first place, the description given of him is absolutely true. It is my constant habit, while I praise without scruple, to weigh my words of blame in every syllable. I have spoken of the plaintiff as ill-educated and conceited, because the very first meaning of education in an artist is that he should know his true position with respect to his fellow-workmen, and ask from the public only a just price for his work. Had the plaintiff known either what good artists gave, habitually, of labour to their works, or received, contentedly, of pay for them, the price he set on his own productions would not have been coxcombry but dishonesty.

I have given him the full credit of his candid conceit, and supposed him to imagine his pictures to be really worth what he asks for them. And I did this with the more confidence, because the titles he gave them showed a parallel want of education. All well-informed painters and musicians are aware that there is analogy between painting and music. The public would at once recognize the coxcombry of a composer, who advertised a study in chiaroscuro for four voices, or a prismatic piece of colour in four flats, and I am only courteous in supposing nothing worse than coxcombry in an artist who offers them a symphony in green and yellow for two hundred pounds.

Nor is the final sentence, in which the plaintiff is spoken of as throwing his palette in the public's face, other than an accurate, though a brief, definition of a manner which is calculated to draw attention chiefly by its impertinence. The standard which I gave, thirty years ago, for estimate of the relative value of pictures, namely, that their preciousness depended ultimately on the greatness and the justice of the ideas they contained and conveyed,[3] has never been lost sight of by me since, and has been especially insisted on lately, in such resistance as I have been able to offer to the modern schools which suffer the object of art to be ornament rather than edification. It is true that

'MY OWN ARTICLE ON WHISTLER'

1 the amount of Ruskin's costs in the case; paid by a subscription among friends and admirers.

2 'To despise the malignant crowd': Horace, *Odes*, II. xvi, 39, 40.

3 in *Modern Painters*, vol. I; Cook and Wedderburn [C & W], III, 92.

there are many curious collectors of libraries, in whose eyes the binding of the volumes is of more importance than their contents; and there are many patrons of art who benevolently comply with the fashion of the day, without expecting to derive more benefit from the fronts of their pictures than from the backs of their books. But it is a critic's first duty in examining works proposed in public exhibition to distinguish the artist's work from the upholsterer's; and although it would be unreasonable to expect from the hasty and electric enlightenment of the nineteenth century, any pictorial elucidations of the Dispute of the Sacrament, or the School of Athens,[4] he may yet, without any severity of exaction, require of a young painter that he should work a little with his head as well as with his fingers; and may explain to the spectator, without libellous intention, the difference between Attic air and a London fog.

It gives me no little pain to be compelled to point out, as the essential grounds of the present action, the confusion between art and manufacture, which, lately encouraged in the public mind by vulgar economists, has at last, in no small manner, degraded the productions even of distinguished genius into marketable commodities, with the sale of which it is thought as unwarrantable to interfere as with the convenient dishonesties of popular trade.

This feeling has been still farther increased by the idea of many kindly persons that it is a delicate form of charity to purchase the feeble works of incompetent artists, and by the corresponding efforts of large numbers of the middle classes, under existing conditions of social pressure, to maintain themselves by painting and literature, without possessing the smallest natural faculties for either.

I will confine myself, with reference to this, in my estimate, infinitely mischievous tendency of the public mind, to the simple statement that in flourishing periods, whether of trade or art, the dignity, whether of operatives or artists, was held to consist in their giving, in every sense, good value for money and a fair day's work for a fair day's wages. The nineteenth century may perhaps economically pride itself on the adulteration of its products and the slackness of its industries. But it ought at least to instruct the pupils of its schools of Art, in the ancient code of the Artist's honour, that no piece of work should leave his hands, which his diligence could further complete, or his reflection further improve, and in the ancient decision of the Artist's pride, that his fame should be founded on what he had given, not on what he had received.

[Here the MS breaks off.]

(Unpublished, and probably unfinished, MS.) E. T. Cook and A. D. O. Wedderburn, eds, Works, vol. XXIX (1907), 585–7.

Charles Kingsley (1819–75)

Charles Kingsley, Christian Socialist clergyman, novelist, sanitary reformer, friend of working men, and poet, was born in Devon, 12 June 1819. His father, also Charles Kingsley, was vicar of Clovelly; his mother's father had made money in Barbados. Precocious, he was writing poems and sermons by the age of four. He went to school in Clifton, near Bristol, then to Helston Grammar School in Cornwall. The Kingsleys moved to London in 1836 when his father became rector of St Luke's, Chelsea, and Charles attended King's College, London. He entered Magdalene College, Cambridge, in Michaelmas 1838, and though he won a scholarship, and scraped a Classical First Class in 1842, he fully enacted the muscular part of what would later be called Muscular Christianity – rowing, riding, walking, boxing (taught by a black prize-fighter). Ordained in July 1842 he became first curate, then rector of Eversley in Hampshire, his parish for most of his life. He had taken strongly against the Oxford Movement (far too unmuscular and Queer): he worked all his life with and for young men, but was very heterosexual (the private papers, revealed only posthumously, are exuberantly bodily and erotic, but also highly uxorious: see Susan Chitty, *The Beast and the Monk: A Life of Charles Kingsley*, 1974). In 1844 he married Fanny Grenfell, and they had four children. Kingsley was greatly attracted to co-operative Christian Socialism, as well as to the Broad Church

---

4　Raphael's 'Dispute of the Sacrament' was 'the most perfect effort yet made by art to illustrate divine science,' Ruskin thought: *Eagle's Nest* (1872), § 46 (C & W, XXII, 156). 'School of Athens': C & W, V, 49, and XXII, 422.

Protestantism of the F. D. Maurice school. Sympathy for the labouring poor is the driving force of his first novel, *Yeast* (1848), and his second, *Alton Locke* (1850), which Carlyle recommended to Chapman & Hall, as it is of his later Rabelaisian, Shandeyesque children's classic *The Water-Babies* (1863) and his great late radical sermon on 'Human Soot', preached in Liverpool in June 1870 for the Kirkdale Ragged School (it is reported in *The Life and Letters, by His Wife* (1877), III, 322–6). As 'Parson Lot', Kingsley wrote energetically for the *Politics of the People* journal and the *Christian Socialist: A Journal of Association*, and published the wryly radical and bourgeois-scaring pamphlet *Cheap Clothes and Nasty* (1850), about the scandal of the sweated tailoring home-workers. He was an avid popular educator, as preacher and lecturer – to privileged audiences as Chaplain to the Queen (1859 on), as Professor of Modern Literature at Cambridge (1860–9), and as Cambridge tutor to the Prince of Wales, but also to his Eversley parishioners, to working men as Professor of Literature at Maurice's Queen's College, Harley Street, London, and to the ordinary audiences and Natural History classes he sought to enthuse with his own keen Darwinian interest in the life of the seashore, the geology of the bricks and slates of the city, and such-like phenomena (for which see, e.g., his *Glaucus, or the Wonders of the Shore* (1855) and *Town Geology* (1872)). His brusquely Protestant assertion in a review of A. J. Froude's *History of England* in *Macmillan's Magazine* (January 1860), that Roman Catholics, and John Henry Newman in particular, did not value truth for its own sake, provoked the public quarrel that resulted in Newman's *Apologia Pro Vita Sua*. Newman, arch dialectician, scored all the debating points, but Kingsley had indeed hit on Newman's casuistical tendencies. Kingsley preferred Englishmen uncontaminated by foreign ways – soldiers (*Brave Words to Brave Soldiers*, his tract for Crimean fighters, was distributed in thousands; the novel *Two Years Ago* (1857) praises war as a regenerating force); Rajah Brooke, the White Rajah of Sarawak (to whom his West Country heroizing novel *Westward Ho!* (1855) is dedicated); Governor Eyre, harsh repressor of the Jamaican slave revolt, 1865. Kingsley's evolutionary Darwinism put the English at the top of the evolutionary heap – well above the sub-species of blacks ('ape-like' African forebears haunt the actress Marie in *Two Years Ago*) and (in *The Water-Babies*) the Irish (subhuman potato-eating 'paddies') and Hindoos (too ape-like). In 1869 Kingsley was appointed a Canon of Chester Cathedral, and in 1873 of Westminster Abbey. His campaigns were numerous and persistent – for educational reform, women doctors, tobacco's pleasures, sanitation, a scientifically instructed theology. He kept on lecturing even as his health declined, even visiting the USA in 1874. His West Indian travels resulted in *At Last: A Christmas in the West Indies* (1870). Poetry did not occupy much of Kingsley's great output, but was a persistent interest. His first book was a poetic drama about St Elizabeth of Hungary, *The Saint's Tragedy* (1848). Poems seed the novels. *Andromeda, and Other Poems* came out in 1858. *Poems* (1872) gathers together most of his verse, including *The Saint's Tragedy*. Kingsley died 23 January 1875 at Eversley. His widow was granted a Civil List Pension, but turned down Queen Victoria's offer of an apartment in Hampton Court Palace (she died, near Leamington, at the end of 1891).

AIRLY BEACON

Airly Beacon, Airly Beacon;
  Oh the pleasant sight to see
Shires and towns from Airly Beacon,
  While my love climbed up to me!

Airly Beacon, Airly Beacon;
  Oh the happy hours we lay
Deep in fern on Airly Beacon,
  Courting through the summer's day!

Airly Beacon, Airly Beacon;
  Oh the weary haunt for me,   10
All alone on Airly Beacon,
  With his baby on my knee!

Written, 1847. Poems, Including The Saint's Tragedy, Andromeda,
Songs, Ballads, Etc*., Collected Edition (Macmillan & Co., 1872).*

THE SANDS OF DEE[1]

I

'O Mary, go and call the cattle home,
   And call the cattle home,
   And call the cattle home,
  Across the sands o' Dee;'
The western wind was wild and dank wi' foam,
  And all alone went she.

II

The western tide crept up along the sand,
   And o'er and o'er the sand,
   And round and round the sand,
  As far as eye could see;   10
The rolling mist came down and hid the land –
  And never home came she.

III

'Oh, is it weed, or fish, or floating hair –
   A tress o' golden hair,
   O' drowned maiden's hair,
  Above the nets at sea?
Was never salmon yet that shone so fair,
  Among the stakes on Dee.'

IV

They rowed her in across the rolling foam,
   The cruel crawling foam,
   The cruel hungry foam,   20
  To her grave beside the sea:
But still the boatmen hear her call the cattle home
  Across the sands o' Dee.

Written, Eversley, 1849. Alton Locke: Tailor and Poet: An Autobiography,
2 vols (Chapman & Hall, 1850), vol. II, ch. 5 (i.e. ch. 26 later), 'The Triumphant
Author.' (Poem untitled in the novel.) Poems (1872). Novel's text.

'MY LAST WORDS'

I

'Weep, weep, weep and weep,
  For pauper, dolt, and slave;
Hark! from wasted moor and fen,
Feverous alley, stifling den,
Swells the wail of Englishmen;
  "Work! or the grave!"

II

'Down, down, down, and down
  With idler, knave, and tyrant;
Why for sluggards stint and moil?

THE SANDS OF DEE
1 Scottish river: Aberdeen at its mouth.

He that will not live by toil   10
Has no right on English soil;
  God's word's our warrant!

III

'Up, up, up, and up!
  Face your game and play it!
The night is past – behold the sun! –
The cup is full, the web is spun,
The Judge is set, the doom begun;
  Who shall stay it?'

Written, on Torridge, May 1849. Alton Locke *(1850), vol. II, ch. 20
(i.e. ch. 41 later), 'Freedom, Equality and Brotherhood'.* Poems *(1872). Novel's text;
in* Poems *(1872) title is 'Alton Locke's Song. 1848.'*

THE TIDE RIVER

Clear and cool, clear and cool,
By laughing shallow, and dreaming pool;
  Cool and clear, cool and clear,
By shining shingle, and foaming wear;
Under the crag where the ouzel sings,
And the ivied wall where the church-bell rings,
    Undefiled, for the undefiled;
  Play by me, bathe in me, mother and child.

Dank and foul, dank and foul,
By the smoky town in its murky cowl;   10
  Foul and dank, foul and dank,
By wharf and sewer and slimy bank;
Darker and darker the further I go,
Baser and baser the richer I grow;
    Who dare sport with the sin-defiled?
  Shrink from me, turn from me, mother and child.

Strong and free, strong and free,
The floodgates are open, away to the sea.
  Free and strong, free and strong,
Cleansing my streams as I hurry along   20
To the golden sands, and the leaping bar,
And the taintless tide that awaits me afar,
As I lose myself in the infinite main,
Like a soul that has sinned and is pardoned again.
    Undefiled, for the undefiled;
  Play by me, bathe in me, mother and child.

Written, Eversley, 1862. The Water-Babies: A Fairy-Tale for a Land-Baby
(Macmillan & Co., London and Cambridge, 1863), ch. 1. (Untitled in the novel.)

YOUNG AND OLD

When all the world is young, lad,
  And all the trees are green;
And every goose a swan, lad,

And every lass a queen;
Then hey for boot and horse, lad,
And round the world away:
Young blood must have its course, lad,
And every dog his day.

When all the world is old, lad,
And all the trees are brown;
And all the sport is stale, lad,
And all the wheels run down;
Creep home, and take your place there,
The spent and maimed among:
God grant you find one face there,
You loved when all was young.

10

Written, 1862. The Water-Babies *(1863), ch. 2. (Untitled in the novel.)*

George Eliot (Mary Ann/Marian Evans) (1819–80)

Mary Ann, or Marian, Evans, born 22 November 1819, near Nuneaton in Warwickshire, was the fifth child, the third by his second wife, of a builder and carpenter who became agent for the Newdigate estates in Warwickshire and Derbyshire. An ordinary provincial girl, she grew up to be England's most formidable intellectual – critic, translator, humanist polemicist, novelist-of-ideas, poet – the equal, even the superior, of the greatest male minds of the time anywhere in Europe. Her first inclinations were devout and Evangelical, influenced by Miss Lewis, principal teacher at her school in Nuneaton, as well as by the Baptist Misses Franklin, whose school in Coventry she attended later, and by her Methodist preacher aunt Elizabeth Evans from Derby ('original' of the preacher Dinah Morris in Mary Ann's first full-length novel, *Adam Bede*, 1859). Her first publication was a poem in the *Christian Observer* (January 1840). After leaving school at Christmas 1835 she devoted herself to looking after her widowed father, to good works, and to learning Italian, German, Greek and Latin with private teachers. Falling in with the radical and freethinking circle around Charles Bray in Coventry led to her losing her Christian faith and refusing to attend church. Taking stands on principles was to be her trademark. So was acting the disciple to male scholars, intellectuals and men-of-letters – she tended to throw herself at them in the manner of what she recognized as her Dorothea Brooke complex, as in her greatest novel *Middlemarch* (1871–2). She was always in search of substitutes, it would appear, for the love and kindness her father and brother Isaac withdrew because of her freethinking ways. After Charles Bray came Dr Brabant (with his unfinished, Casaubon-like book undoing all theological dogmas, and his need for a secretary-researcher); John Chapman, editor of the *Westminster Review*, who took her into his house at 142 the Strand in London to do all the work on the paper; Herbert Spencer, the great social scientist, to whom she took the daring step of proposing marriage ('I could gather courage to work and make life valuable, if only I had you near me'); and, of course, George Henry Lewes, radical and scholar, editor of the *Leader*, with whom she lived for twenty happy years from 1854 to his death – the man who eased her gently into fiction writing, was her fierce literary agent (he drove a hard, greedy bargain) and loving counsellor. Only settling down with Lewes put an end to her repeated practice of going for other women's men-folk (Mrs Brabant put a stop to Mary Ann's visits to her husband; Mrs Chapman and Chapman's mistress combined to throw her out of the Strand home; she broke up Lewes's curious ménage with his admittedly unfaithful wife Agnes). It's no surprise that her sympathies for the cause of women were patchy (contributions to Girton College for women at Cambridge, and the Garrett Anderson hospital for women, but no keenness for action on women's suffrage). Intellectually and socially she was happiest in male company. It was men who mainly attended her and Lewes's fabled Sunday afternoons (respectable wives stayed away), men who worshipped the 'Sibyl in the Gloom'. Her mind's greatest eagerness was for male colouring. Her writing is manifestly the result, and bears the impress, of her reading in men's books, especially continental ones – Auguste Comte, father of positivism; Von Riehl, the great German sociologist, celebrated in the foundational review essay in the *Westminster Review*, July 1856, 'The Natural History of German Life'; and particularly those writers she actually translated from German – D. F. Strauss, author of the demythologizing *Life of Jesus* (1846), and Ludwig Feuerbach, whose great post-Protestant moral tractatus *The Essence of Christianity* she brought out in 1854. Under the pseudonym George Eliot – the name a homage to George Sand as well as to her own male-mindedness – her novels comprise the nineteenth century's greatest fictionalizing of liberal post-Christian humanist moralism. They also brought in huge sums of money. Her poems – mainly in

The Spanish Gipsy (1868) and *The Legend of Jubal and Other Poems* (1874) – come in a distinct, if still important, second, and are in fact interesting mainly as supplements to her fiction. Her closet-drama *Armgart* (1870), about an opera singer whose voice packs up, is not only a kind of reprise of Elizabeth Barrett Browning's *Aurora Leigh*, but bears in on George Eliot's fiction's continual concern with the life-problems of creative females, and recalls not least the singer Alchari in the last novel, *Daniel Deronda* (1876). The *Brother and Sister* sonnet sequence, George Eliot's own yearning meditation on her role as the biblical Canticles' 'little sister', is a retake of her lifelong brother–sister anxieties – her personal variant of the Antigone problematic, as it were, which finds its lengthiest expression in *The Mill on the Floss* (1860). After Lewes died, 28 November 1878, George Eliot turned, for the male support she could not survive without, to Johnnie Cross, twenty years her junior. Only the divorce laws had prevented her marrying Lewes (he'd condoned his wife's adulteries and so could not obtain a divorce); no such barrier existing now, she married Cross and in church, St George's Hanover Square, 6 May 1880. Brother Isaac came round immediately – after a quarter century of broken-off relations. On their honeymoon in Venice, Cross threw himself from an upper window into the Grand Canal (it was rumoured that he had a mad brother and that madness ran in the family). He did not drown. By the end of the year, 22 December 1880, George Eliot was dead – perhaps of a kidney complaint aggravated by some infection caught at a concert. Johnnie compiled the first, and distinctly hagiographical, *Life* (1884).

IN A LONDON DRAWINGROOM

The sky is cloudy, yellowed by the smoke.
For view there are the houses opposite
Cutting the sky with one long line of wall
Like solid fog: far as the eye can stretch
Monotony of surface & of form
Without a break to hang a guess upon.
No bird can make a shadow as it flies,
For all its shadow, as in ways o'erhung
By thickest canvass, where the golden rays
Are clothed in hemp. No figure lingering   10
Pauses to feed the hunger of the eye
Or rest a little on the lap of life.
All hurry on & look upon the ground,
Or glance unmarking at the passers by
The wheels are hurrying too, cabs, carriages
All closed, in multiplied identity.
The world seems one huge prison-house & court
Where men are punished at the slightest cost,
With lowest rate of colour, warmth & joy.

1865

MS poem. Bernard J. Paris, 'George Eliot's Unpublished Poetry', Studies in Philology, *56, no. 3 (July 1959), 539–58.*

'O MAY I JOIN THE CHOIR INVISIBLE'

Longum illud tempus, quum non ero, magis me movet, quam hoc exiguum'.
Cicero, Ad Att. xii. 18.[1]

O may I join the choir invisible
Of those immortal dead who live again

1   *Ad Atticum*: 'That long time, when I shall not exist, moves me more than this short (life).'

In minds made better by their presence: live
In pulses stirred to generosity,
In deeds of daring rectitude, in scorn
For miserable aims that end with self,
In thoughts sublime that pierce the night like stars,
And with their mild persistence urge man's search
To vaster issues.

      So to live is heaven: 10
To make undying music in the world,
Breathing as beauteous order that controls
With growing sway the growing life of man,
So we inherit that sweet purity
For which we struggled, failed, and agonised
With widening retrospect that bred despair.
Rebellious flesh that would not be subdued,
A vicious parent shaming still its child
Poor anxious penitence, is quick dissolved;
Its discords, quenched by meeting harmonies,   20
Die in the large and charitable air.
And all our rarer, better, truer self,
That sobbed religiously in yearning song,
That watched to ease the burthen of the world,
Laboriously tracing what must be,
And what may yet be better – saw within
A worthier image for the sanctuary,
And shaped it forth before the multitude
Divinely human, raising worship so
To higher reverence more mixed with love –   30
That better self shall live till human Time
Shall fold its eyelids, and the human sky
Be gathered like a scroll within the tomb
Unread for ever.

      This is life to come,
Which martyred men have made more glorious
For us who strive to follow. May I reach
That purest heaven, be to other souls
The cup of strength in some great agony,
Enkindle generous ardour, feed pure love,   40
Beget the smiles that have no cruelty –
Be the sweet presence of a good diffused,
And in diffusion ever more intense.
So shall I join the choir invisible
Whose music is the gladness of the world.

Dated 1867. The Legend of Jubal and Other Poems
(William Blackwood & Sons, Edinburgh, 1874).

BROTHER AND SISTER

I

I cannot choose but think upon the time
When our two lives grew like two buds that kiss
At lightest thrill from the bee's swinging chime,
Because the one so near the other is.

He was the elder and a little man
Of forty inches, bound to show no dread,

And I the girl that puppy-like now ran,
Now lagged behind my brother's larger tread.

I held him wise, and when he talked to me
Of snakes and birds, and which God loved the best,   10
I thought his knowledge marked the boundary
Where men grew blind, though angels knew the rest.

   If he said 'Hush!' I tried to hold my breath
   Wherever he said 'Come!' I stepped in faith.

II

Long years have left their writing on my brow,
But yet the freshness and the dew-fed beam
Of those young mornings are about me now,
When we two wandered toward the far-off stream

With rod and line. Our basket held a store
Baked for us only, and I thought with joy
That I should have my share, though he had more,
Because he was the elder and a boy.

The firmaments of daisies since to me
Have had those mornings in their opening eyes,   20
The bunchèd cowslip's pale transparency
Carries that sunshine of sweet memories,

   And wild-rose branches take their finest scent
   From those blest hours of infantine content.

III

Our mother bade us keep the trodden ways,
Stroked down my tippet, set my brother's frill,
Then with the benediction of her gaze
Clung to us lessening, and pursued us still

Across the homestead to the rookery elms,
Whose tall old trunks had each a grassy mound,
So rich for us, we counted them as realms
With varied products: here were earth-nuts found,

And here the Lady-fingers in deep shade;
Here sloping toward the Moat the rushes grew,   30
The large to split for pith, the small to braid;
While over all the dark rooks cawing flew,

   And made a happy strange solemnity,
   A deep-toned chant from life unknown to me.

IV

Our meadow-path had memorable spots:
One where it bridged a tiny rivulet,
Deep hid by tangled blue Forget-me-nots;
And all along the waving grasses met

My little palm, or nodded to my cheek,
When flowers with upturned faces gazing drew
My wonder downward, seeming all to speak
With eyes of souls that dumbly heard and knew.

Then came the copse, where wild things rushed unseen,
And black-scathed[1] grass betrayed the past abode   40
Of mystic gypsies, who still lurked between
Me and each hidden distance of the road.

    A gypsy once had startled me at play,
    Blotting with her dark smile my sunny day.

V

Thus rambling we were schooled in deepest lore,
And learned the meanings that give words a soul,
The fear, the love, the primal passionate store,
Whose shaping impulses make manhood whole.

Those hours were seed to all my after good;
My infant gladness, through eye, ear, and touch,
Took easily as warmth a various food
To nourish the sweet skill of loving much.

For who in age shall roam the earth and find
Reason for loving that will strike out love   50
With sudden rod from the hard year-pressed mind?
Were reasons sown as thick as stars above,

    'Tis love must see them, as the eye sees light:
    Day is but Number to the darkened sight.

VI

Our brown canal was endless to my thought;
And on its banks I sat in dreamy peace,
Unknowing how the good I loved was wrought,
Untroubled by the fear that it would cease.

Slowly the barges floated into view
Rounding a grassy hill to me sublime
With some Unknown beyond it, whither flew
The parting cuckoo toward a fresh spring time.

The wide-arched bridge, the scented elder-flowers,
The wondrous watery rings that died too soon,   60
The echoes of the quarry, the still hours
With white robe sweeping-on the shadeless noon,

    Were but my growing self, are part of me,
    My present Past, my root of piety.

VII

Those long days measured by my little feet
Had chronicles which yield me many a text;
Where irony still finds an image meet
Of full-grown judgements in this world perplext.

One day my brother left me in high charge,
To mind the rod, while he went seeking bait,

BROTHER AND SISTER
1 to scathe: to scorch.

And bade me, when I saw a nearing barge,
Snatch out the line, lest he should come too late.

Proud of the task, I watched with all my might
For one whole minute, till my eyes grew wide,   70
Till sky and earth took on a strange new light
And seemed a dream-world floating on some tide –

   A fair pavilioned boat for me alone
   Bearing me onward through the vast unknown.

VIII

But sudden came the barge's pitch-black prow,
Nearer and angrier came my brother's cry,
And all my soul was quivering fear, when lo!
Upon the imperilled line, suspended high,

A silver perch! My guilt that won the prey,
Now turned to merit, had a guerdon rich
Of hugs and praises, and made merry play,
Until my triumph reached its highest pitch

When all at home were told the wondrous feat,
And how the little sister had fished well.   80
In secret, though my fortune tasted sweet,
I wondered why this happiness befell.

   'The little lass had luck,' the gardener said:
   And so I learned, luck was with glory wed.

IX

We had the self-same world enlarged for each
By loving difference of girl and boy:
The fruit that hung on high beyond my reach
He plucked for me, and oft he must employ

A measuring glance to guide my tiny shoe
Where lay firm stepping-stones, or call to mind
'This thing I like my sister may not do,
For she is little, and I must be kind.'

Thus boyish Will the nobler mastery learned
Where inward vision over impulse reigns,   90
Widening its life with separate life discerned,
A Like unlike, a Self that self restrains.

   His years with others must the sweeter be
   For those brief days he spent in loving me.

X

His sorrow was my sorrow, and his joy
Sent little leaps and laughs through all my frame;
My doll seemed lifeless and no girlish toy
Had any reason when my brother came.

I knelt with him at marbles, marked his fling
Cut the ringed stem and make the apple drop,
Or watched him winding close the spiral string
That looped the orbits of the humming top.

Grasped by such fellowship my vagrant thought
Ceased with dream-fruit dream-wishes to fulfil;   100
My aëry-picturing fantasy was taught
Subjection to the harder, truer skill

That seeks with deeds to grave a thought-tracked line,
And by 'What is,' 'What will be' to define.

XI

School parted us; we never found again
That childish world where our two spirits mingled
Like scents from varying roses that remain
One sweetness, nor can evermore be singled.

Yet the twin habit of that early time
Lingered for long about the heart and tongue:
We had been natives of one happy clime,
And its dear accent to our utterance clung.

Till the dire years whose awful name is Change
Had grasped our souls still yearning in divorce,   110
And pitiless shaped them in two forms that range
Two elements which sever their life's course.

But were another childhood-world my share,
I would be born a little sister there.

Dated 1869. The Legend of Jubal and Other Poems *(1874).*

NOTES ON FORM IN ART

Abstract words and phrases which have an excellent genealogy are apt to live a little too much on their reputation and even to sink into dangerous impostors that should be made to show how they get their living. For this reason it is often good to consider an old subject as if nothing had yet been said about it; to suspend one's attention even to revered authorities and simply ask what in the present state of our knowledge are the facts which can with any congruity be tied together and labelled by a given abstraction.

For example, to any but those who are under the dire necessity of using the word and cannot afford to wait for a meaning, it must be more fruitful to ask, what relations of things can be properly included under the word 'Form' as applied to artistic composition, than to decide without any such previous inquiry that a particular work is wanting in form, or to take it for granted that the works of any one period or people are the examples of all that is admissible in artistic form.

Plain people, though indisposed to metaphysical subtleties, can yet understand that Form, as an element of human experience, must begin with the perception of separateness, derived principally from touch of which the other senses are modifications; and that things must be recognized as separate wholes before they can be recognized as wholes composed of parts, or before these wholes again can be regarded as relatively parts of a larger whole.

Form, then, as distinguished from merely massive impression, must first depend on the discrimination of wholes and then on the discrimination of parts. Fundamentally, form is unlikeness, as is seen in the philosophic use of the word 'Form' in distinction from 'Matter'; and in consistency with this fundamental meaning, every difference is Form. Thus, sweetness is a form of sensibility, rage is a form of passion, green is a form both of light and of sensibility. But with this fundamental discrimination is born in necessary antithesis the sense of wholeness or unbroken connexion in space and time: a flash of light is a whole compared with the darkness which precedes and follows it; the taste of sourness is a whole and includes parts or degrees as it subsides. And as knowledge continues to grow by its alternating processes of distinction and combination, seeing smaller and smaller unlikenesses and grouping or associating these under a common likeness, it arrives at the conception of wholes composed of parts more and more multiplied and highly differenced, yet more and more absolutely bound together by various conditions of common likeness or mutual dependence. And the fullest example of such a whole is the highest example of Form: in other words, the relation of multiplex interdependent parts to a whole which is itself in the most varied and therefore the fullest relation to other wholes. Thus, the human organism comprises things as diverse as the finger-nails and tooth-ache, as the nervous stimulus of muscle manifested in a shout, and the discernment of a red spot on a field of snow; but all its different elements or parts of experience are bound together in a more necessary wholeness or more inseparable group of common conditions than can be found in any other existence known to us. The highest Form, then, is the highest organism, that is to say, the most varied group of relations bound together in a wholeness which again has the most varied relations with all other phenomena.

It is only in this fundamental sense that the word 'Form' can be applied to Art in general. Boundary or outline and visual appearance are modes of Form which in music and poetry can only have a metaphorical presence. Even in the plastic arts Form obviously, in its general application, means something else than mere imitation of outline, more or less correctness of drawing or modelling – just as, with reference to descriptive poetry, it means something more than the bare delineation of landscape or figures. Even those who use the phrase with a very dim understanding, always have a sense that it refers to structure or composition, that is, to the impression from a work considered as a whole. And what is a structure but a set of relations selected and combined in accordance with the sequence of mental states in the constructor, or with the preconception of a whole which he has inwardly evolved? Artistic form, as distinguished from mere imitation, begins in sculpture and painting with composition or the selection of attitudes and the formation of groups, let the objects be of what order they may. In music it begins with the adjustment of tones and rhythm to a climax, apart from any direct imitation. But my concern is here chiefly with poetry which I take in its wider sense as including all literary production of which it is the prerogative and not the reproach that the choice and sequence of images and ideas – that is, of relations and groups of relations – are more or less not only determined by emotion but intended to express it. I say more or less; for even the ravings of madness include multitudinous groups and sequences which are parts of common experience; and in the range of poetry we see wide distances of degree in the combination of emotive force with sequences that are not arbitrary and individual but true and universal, just as the guiding emotion varies from an idiosyncrasy only short of madness to a profoundly human passion which is or must come to be the heritage of all mankind. Sometimes the wider signification of poetry is taken to be fiction or invention as opposed to ascertained external fact or discovery. But what is fiction other than an arrangement of events or feigned correspondences according to predominant feeling? We find what destiny pleases; we make what pleases us – or what we think will please others.

Even taken in its derivative meaning of outline, what is Form but the limit of that difference by which we discriminate one object from another? – a limit determined partly by the intrinsic relations or composition of the object, and partly by the extrinsic action of other bodies upon it. This is true whether the object is a rock or a man; but in the case of the inorganic body, outline is the result of a nearly equal struggle between inner constitution and the outer play of forces; while in the human organism the outline is mainly determined by the intrinsic relation of its parts, and what is called fitness, beauty, or harmony in its outline and movements is dependent on the inward balance. The muscular strength which hurls, the muscular grace which gives a rhythmic movement to half a dozen balls, show a moving outline of which the chief factors are relations within the body; but the line with which a rock cuts the sky, or the shape of a boulder, may be more due to outer forces than to inner constitution. In ordinary language, the form of a stone is accidental. But the true expression of the difference is, that the wholeness of the stone depends simply on likeness of crystallization and is merely a wholeness of mass which may be broken up into other wholes; whereas the outline defining the wholeness of the human body is due to a consensus or constant interchange of effects among its parts. It is wholeness not merely of mass but of strict and manifold dependence. The word 'consensus' expresses that fact in a complex organism by which no part can suffer increase or diminution without a participation of all other parts in the effect produced and a consequent modification of the organism as a whole.

By this light, forms of art can be called higher or lower only on the same principle as that on which we apply these words to organisms; viz. in proportion to the complexity of the parts bound up into an indissoluble whole. In Poetry – which has this superiority over all the other arts, that its medium, language, is the least imitative, and is in the most complex relation with what it expresses – Form begins in the choice of rhythms and images as signs of a mental state, for this is a process of grouping or association of a less spontaneous and more conscious order than the grouping or association which constitutes the very growth and natural history of mind. *Poetry* begins when passion weds thought by finding expression in an image; but *Poetic Form* begins with a choice of elements, however meagre, as the accordant expression of emotional states. The most monotonous burthen chanted by an Arab boatman on the Nile is still a beginning of poetic form.

Poetic Form was not begotten by thinking it out or framing it as a shell which should hold emotional expression, any more than the shell of an animal arises before the living creature; but emotion, by its tendency to repetition, i.e., rhythmic persistence in proportion as diversifying thought is absent, creates a form by the recurrence of its elements in adjustment with certain given conditions of sound, language, action, or environment. Just as the beautiful expanding curves of a bivalve shell are not first made for the reception of the unstable inhabitant, but grow and are limited by the simple rhythmic conditions of its growing life.

It is a stale observation that the earliest poetic forms arose in the same spontaneous unreflecting way – that the rhythmic shouts with clash of metal accompanying the huntsman's or conqueror's course were probably the nucleus of the ballad epic; that the funeral or marriage sing-song, wailing or glad, with more or less violent muscular movement and resonance of wood or metal made the rude beginnings of lyric poetry. But it is still worth emphasis that this spontaneous origin is the most completely demonstrated in relation to a form of art which ultimately came to be treated more reflectively than any other – the tragic and comic drama.

A Form being once started must by and by cease to be purely spontaneous: the form itself becomes the object and material of emotion, and is sought after, amplified and elaborated by discrimination of its elements till at last by the abuse of its refinement it preoccupies the room of emotional thinking; and poetry, from being the fullest expression of the human soul, is starved into an ingenious pattern-work, in which tricks with vocables take the place of living words fed with the blood of relevant meaning, and made musical by the continual intercommunication of sensibility and thought.

The old phrases should not give way to scientific explanation, for speech is to a great extent like sculpture, expressing observed phenomena and remaining true in spite of Harvey and Bichat.[1] In the later development of poetic fable the ἀναγνώρισις[2] tends to consist in the discernment of a previously unrecognized *character*, and this may also form the περιπέτεια,[3] according to Aristotle's notion that in the highest form the two coincide.

Written 1868. Unpublished MS notebook, now in Yale University Library (Beinecke Rare Book and Manuscript collection).

NOTES ON FORM IN ART
1　William Harvey (1578–1657), discovered circulation of the blood. Marie François Xavier Bichat (1771–1802) explained laws of bodily 'tissues' (he's Lydgate's idol in *Middlemarch*).

2　*anagnorisis*: recognition. Moment of realizing in Greek tragedy (Aristotle, *Poetics*).

3　*peripeteia*: reversal of fortune in Greek tragedy (Aristotle). Misspelt as peripateia in MS.

Ebenezer Jones (1820–60)

Ebenezer Jones, Chartist and post-Romantic, whose poetry was highly disregarded in his own lifetime, was born in Islington, 20 January 1820, into a comfortably off and religiously strict Calvinist family. The death of his father brought financial ruin and Ebenezer had to take up employment as a clerk with a City of London tea-trading firm, working twelve hours a day. He steeped himself in the radical authors and politics of his youth – Shelley, Carlyle, Robert Owen socialism, Chartism. The strenuousness of his writing is manifestly influenced by Carlyle. His ill-fated collection *Studies of Sensation and Event* was produced (1843) in a storm of unrequited love. In 1844 he married Caroline Atherstone, niece of Edwin Atherstone, author of the massive and turgid epic *The Fall of Nineveh* (1847), but continued to be unhappy in love. They soon separated; he became an accountant, dabbled in political journalism, and gave up poetry, only to return to it as he lay dying of consumption. He died early at the age of forty, 14 September 1860, dispirited and forgotten as a poet. His recuperation began with Dante Gabriel Rossetti's piece in *Notes and Queries*, 1870 ('vivid disorderly power'), and continued with a brochure about him and his work by R. H. Shepherd (1878), papers by Theodore Watts in the *Athenaeum* (September and October 1878), an edition by Shepherd of *Studies of Sensation and Event* (1879) with various memoirs, and an article by William Bell Scott (*Academy*, November 1879). The verdict of the poet John Leicester Warren, Lord de Tabley (quoted in the *DNB*), is extreme in both directions, but not too much so: 'When Jones writes a bad line, he writes one with a vengeance. It is hardly possible to say how excruciatingly bad he is now and then. And yet, at his best, in organic rightness, beauty, and, above all, spontaneity, we must go among the very highest poetic names to match him.'

HIGH SUMMER

I never wholly feel that summer is high,
However green the trees, or loud the birds,
However movelessly eye winking herds,
Stand in field ponds, or under large trees lie, –
Till I do climb all cultured pastures by,
That hedged by hedgerows studiously fretted trim,
Smile like a lady's face with lace laced prim,
And on some moor or hill that seeks the sky
Lonely and nakedly, – utterly lie down,
And feel the sunshine throbbing on body and limb,   10
My drowsy brain in pleasant drunkenness swim,
Each rising thought sink back, and dreamily drown,
Smiles creep o'er my face, and smother my lips, and cloy,
Each muscle sink to itself, and separately enjoy.

Studies of Sensation and Event *(Charles Fox, 1843)*.

EYEING THE EYES OF ONE'S MISTRESS

When down the crowded aisle, my wandering eyes
'Lighted on thine fixed scanningly on my face,
They struck not passion fire, but in their place
Did settlingly fix themselves, contemplative wise,
Thine eyes to fathom; – for as one that lies
On mountain side where thick leaved branches vein
'Twixt him and the sun, and gazes o'er the plain
That wide beneath him variedly amplifies;

I think my being was elevatedly lain
On its own thought, and in thy being gazing   10
With tranquil speculation, that did gain
Singular delight: thus mine eyes thine appraising,
By dial reckoning, only a moment spent;
Whole ages, by the heart's right measurement.

But when thine eyelids bent into thy gaze
Nearing regard, and instigating light;
Their lashes narrowing o'er the dewy blaze
That suddenly thine eyes did appetite;
Narrowing as if thou fear'dst to invite
Too utterly, but truly that their motion   20
Caressingly closing faintly, might excite
My tranquil gaze to passionate devotion; –
Then, suddenly seemed I an infinite life;
Infinitely falling down before thy shrine;
Infinitely praying thy descent; the strife
Of the aisle's crowd seemed gone; thine eyes and mine,
Devouring distance, into each other grew;
While thine unfeigning lids gloriously upward flew.

Studies of Sensation and Event (1843).

A COMING CRY

The few to whom popes' kings have given the earth God gives to all,
Do tell us that for them alone its fruits increase and fall;
They tell us, that by labour, we may earn our daily bread;
But they take the labour for their engines that work on unfed;
And so we starve; and now the few have published a decree, –
Starve on, or eat in workhouses, the crumbs of charity;
Perhaps it's better than starvation, – once we'll pray, and then,
We'll all go building workhouses, million, million men!

We'll all go building workhouses, – million, million hands,
So jointed wondrously by God, to work love's wise commands;   10
We'll all go building workhouses, – million, million minds,
By great God chartered to condemn whatever harms or binds;
The God-given mind shall image, the God-given hand shall build
The prisons for God's children by the earth-lords willed;
Perhaps it's better than starvation, once we'll pray, and then,
We'll all go building workhouses, – million, million men.

What'll we do with the workhouses? million, million men!
Shall we all lie down, and madden, each in his lonely den?
What! we whose sires made Cressy! we, men of Nelson's mould!
We, of the Russel's country, – God's Englishmen the bold!   20
Will we, at earth's lords' bidding, build ourselves dishonoured graves?
Will we who've made this England, endure to be its slaves?
Thrones totter before the answer! – once we'll pray, and then,
We'll all go building workhouses, – million, million men.

Studies of Sensation and Event (1843).

Jean Ingelow (1820–97)

Jean Ingelow was, like Tennyson (who was one of her admirers), a poet whose verses seem never to forget their author's native Lincolnshire landscapes for very long. She was born, 17 March 1820, in Boston, oldest child of a large brood (four sisters, five brothers), compelled to retreat from Boston, eventually to London, when the bank of which her father was the manager failed. She never went to school and never lived away from the family home. Her first volume of verses, *A Rhyming Chronicle of Incidents and Feelings*, came out in 1850, her first novel, *Allerton and Dreux*, in 1851, but fame and financial success only came with *Poems* (1863). This contained her most renowned verses, including the finely naturalistic, even Hardyesque, 'Divided' and the mawkish pseudo-antique ballad 'The High Tide on the Coast of Lincolnshire (1571)', and it sold hugely, particularly in the USA (200,000 copies, it was said). Nothing after it matched the success of this volume, but it certainly established her as a distinct figure in the literary life of central London. In 1860 she joined the Portfolio Society, founded by Barbara Leigh Smith (Bodichon) and Bessie Rayner Parkes, which overlapped with the Langham Place group. She knew Isa Craig Knox and Adelaide Anne Procter – as well as the satirist Charles Stuart Calverley (his parody of 'Divided' appeared in his *Fly Leaves*, 1872), and Dora Greenwell and Christina Rossetti. Rossetti felt 'envy and humiliation' when in 1865 she was given the eighth edition of Ingelow's *Poems* (1863). Ingelow also knew Browning and Ruskin, and Edward FitzGerald was yet another admirer of her work. Her fiction was at its best when done for children, and *Mopsa the Fairy* (1869), about a boy who crosses wonderingly into fairyland (and not unakin, though the motif is pretty common, to Charles Kingsley's *The Water-Babies*, 1863), has become a classic of the mode. John Everett Millais illustrated her *Stories Told to a Child* (1865). She never married, and died in Kensington, 20 July 1897, aged seventy-seven. She is buried in Brompton Cemetery.

DIVIDED

I

An empty sky, a world of heather,
    Purple of foxglove, yellow of broom;
We two among them wading together,
    Shaking out honey, treading perfume.

Crowds of bees are giddy with clover,
    Crowds of grasshoppers skip at our feet,
Crowds of larks at their matins hang over,
    Thanking the Lord for a life so sweet.

Flusheth the rise with her purple favour,
    Gloweth the cleft with her golden ring,
'Twixt the two brown butterflies waver,
    Lightly settle, and sleepily swing.

We two walk till the purple dieth
    And short dry grass under foot is brown,
But one little streak at a distance lieth
    Green like a ribbon to prank the down.

II

Over the grass we stepped unto it,
    And God He knoweth how blithe we were!
Never a voice to bid us eschew it:
    Hey the green ribbon that showed so fair!

10

20

Hey the green ribbon! we kneeled beside it,
    We parted the grasses dewy and sheen;
Drop over drop there filtered and slided,
    A tiny bright beck that trickled between.

Tinkle, tinkle, sweetly it sung to us,
    Light was our talk as of faëry bells;
Faëry wedding-bells faintly rung to us
    Down in their fortunate parallels.

Hand in hand, while the sun peered over,
    We lapped the grass on that youngling spring;   30
Swept back its rushes, smoothed its clover,
    And said, 'Let us follow it westering.'

III

A dappled sky, a world of meadows,
    Circling above us the black rooks fly
Forward, backward; lo their dark shadows
    Flit on the blossoming tapestry.

Flit on the beck, for her long grass parteth
    As hair from a maid's bright eyes blown back;
And, lo, the sun like a lover darteth
    His flattering smile on her wayward track.   40

Sing on! we sing in the glorious weather
    Till one steps over the tiny strand,
So narrow, in sooth, that still together
    On either brink we go hand in hand.

The beck grows wider, the hands must sever.
    On either margin, our songs all done,
We move apart, while she singeth ever,
    Taking the course of the stooping sun.

He prays, 'Come over' – I may not follow;
    I cry, 'Return' – but he cannot come:
We speak, we laugh, but with voices hollow;   50
    Our hands are hanging, our hearts are numb.

IV

A breathing sigh, a sigh for answer,
    A little talking of outward things;
The careless beck is a merry dancer,
    Keeping sweet time to the air she sings.

A little pain when the beck grows wider;
    'Cross to me now – for her wavelets swell:'
'I may not cross' – and the voice beside her
    Faintly reacheth, though heeded well.   60

No backward path; ah! no returning;
    No second crossing that ripple's flow:
'Come to me now, for the west is burning;
    Come ere it darkens;' – 'Ah, no! ah, no!'

Then cries of pain, and arms outreaching –
    The beck grows wider and swift and deep:

Passionate words as of one beseeching –
    The loud beck drowns them; we walk, and weep.

V

A yellow moon in splendour drooping,
    A tired queen with her state oppressed,   70
Low by rushes and swordgrass stooping,
    Lies she soft on the waves at rest.

The desert heavens have felt her sadness;
    Her earth will weep her some dewy tears;
The wild beck ends her tune of gladness,
    And goeth stilly as soul that fears.

We two walk on in our grassy places
    On either marge of the moonlit flood,
With the moon's own sadness in our faces,
    Where joy is withered, blossom and bud.   80

VI

A shady freshness, chafers whirring,
    A little piping of leaf-hid birds;
A flutter of wings, a fitful stirring,
    A cloud to the eastward snowy as curds.

Bare grassy slopes, where kids are tethered,
    Round valleys like nests all ferny-lined;
Round hills, with fluttering tree-tops feathered,
    Swell high in their freckled robes behind.

A rose-flush tender, a thrill, a quiver,
    When golden gleams to the tree-tops glide;   90
A flashing edge for the milk-white river,
    The beck, a river – with still sleek tide.

Broad and white, and polished as silver,
    On she goes under fruit-laden trees;
Sunk in leafage cooeth the culver,
    And 'plaineth of love's disloyalties.

Glitters the dew and shines the river,
    Up comes the lily and dries her bell;
But two are walking apart for ever,
    And wave their hands for a mute farewell.   100

VII

A braver swell, a swifter sliding;
    The river hasteth, her banks recede:
Wing-like sails on her bosom gliding
    Bear down the lily and drown the reed.

Stately prows are rising and bowing
    (Shouts of mariners winnow the air),
And level sands for banks endowing
    The tiny green ribbon that showed so fair.

While, O my heart! as white sails shiver,
    And crowds are passing, and banks stretch wide,   110

How hard to follow, with lips that quiver,
    That moving speck on the far-off side.

Farther, farther – I see it – know it –
    My eyes brim over, it melts away:
Only my heart to my heart shall show it
    As I walk desolate day by day.

VIII

And yet I know past all doubting, truly –
    A knowledge greater than grief can dim –
I know, as he loved, he will love me duly –
    Yea better – e'en better than I love him.   120

And as I walk by the vast calm river,
    The awful river so dread to see,
I say, 'Thy breadth and thy depth for ever
    Are bridged by his thoughts that cross to me.'

Poems (Longman, Roberts, & Green, 1863).

THE LONG WHITE SEAM

As I came round the harbour buoy,
    The lights began to gleam,
No wave the land-locked water stirred,
    The crags were white as cream;
And I marked my love by candle-light
    Sewing her long white seam.
        It's aye sewing ashore, my dear,
            Watch and steer at sea,
        It's reef and furl, and haul the line,
            Set sail and think of thee.   10

I climbed to reach her cottage door;
    O sweetly my love sings!
Like a shaft of light her voice breaks forth,
    My soul to meet it springs
As the shining water leaped of old,
    When stirred by angel wings.
        Aye longing to list anew,
            Awake and in my dream,
        But never a song she sang like this,
            Sewing her long white seam.   20

Fair fall the lights, the harbour lights,
    That brought me in to thee,
And peace drop down on that low roof
    For the sight that I did see,
And the voice, my dear, that rang so clear
    All for the love of me.
        For O, for O, with brows bent low
            By the candle's flickering gleam,
        Her wedding gown it was she wrought,
            Sewing the long white seam.   30

Poems, 2 vols (Longmans, Green, & Co., 1880), II.

Anne Brontë (1820–49)

The youngest daughter of the Revd Patrick Brontë, Anglican Evangelical Ulsterman, and of Cornish Methodist Maria Branwell, born 15 March 1820, in Thornton, Yorkshire, Anne Brontë was the most mature of the Brontë children, at least in terms of coping with life away from home. Where the others kept retreating home, she held down a governessing post with the Robinson family of Thorp Green for five years until her brother Branwell arrived briefly to tutor the son of the family and broke up her life by having some sort of affair with Mrs Robinson. (The Mrs Robinson story was Branwell's: it's been suggested that the problem might have been homosexual advances to young Edmund Robinson.) Little Anne studied at home with brother Branwell while the other sisters were away at the Cowan Bridge Clergy Daughters School – disastrously for them, as it turned out (even if its spartan regime did provide much material for Charlotte's *Jane Eyre*), because Maria and Elizabeth contracted fatal illnesses there. Anne's Latin was far better than Charlotte's and Emily's. When she went later, on a free place, to the school at Roe Head where Charlotte briefly taught, and from which Emily left too homesick to stay, Anne flourished. And she was the family member who freed her writing most positively from the imaginative grip of the Gothic 'juvenilia', leaving Emily behind to live and die as lone citizen of Gondal. Anne's poems in the sisters' collaborative and shyly and cryptically named *Poems by Currer, Ellis, and Acton Bell.* (1846) were, discouragingly, singled out in what was virtually the volume's only review, by Sydney Dobell in the *Athenaeum*, July 1846, as needing 'indulgences of affection' to be thought well of. *Asineum* once again, would have been Swinburne's vexed response, but he was far less well brought up than 'Acton Bell'. Her poems, greatly haunted by William Cowper's, are personally un-soft and theologically argumentative – rather like her second novel, *The Tenant of Wildfell Hall* (1848), angry about the kind of dissoluteness and alcoholism that finally killed off Branwell, and hostile to the Calvinist doctrine of divinely ordained eternal punishment. Charlotte's Biographical Notice of Ellis and Acton Bell attached to the 1850 reprint edition of the 1847 volume containing Anne's first novel, *Agnes Grey*, and Emily's *Wuthering Heights*, talks of Anne's mournfulness, morbidity, and religious melancholy ('it subdued her mood and bearing to a perpetual pensiveness; the pillar of a cloud glided constantly before her eyes'). But all that seems wide of her poems' mark. Anne's affinity with the despondent Calvinist William Cowper is charitably resistant to his despairs in herself. Different from and more resolute than any of the others right to her end ('Take courage, Charlotte, *take courage*', she exhorted her sister, as her verses exhorted herself), she determined, though ill, to revisit Scarborough, where she had been happy with the Robinsons, and she died there, 28 May 1849, away from Haworth and the moors Emily mythicized in *Wuthering Heights*. She is buried in Scarborough – though, greatly ironically, Matthew Arnold's fond memorial poem, 'Haworth Churchyard: April 1855', imagines her lying back home with her sisters.

'Oh, they have robbed me of the hope,
　My spirit held so dear;
They will not let me hear that voice
　My soul delights to hear.

'They will not let me see that face
　I so delight to see;

And they have taken all thy smiles,
　And all thy love from me.

'Well, let them seize on all they can; –
　One treasure still is mine, –　　　　　　10
A heart that loves to think on thee,
　And feels the worth of thine.'

Undated (? 1840). In Agnes Grey: A Novel, by Acton Bell, *vol. III of*
Wuthering Heights, A Novel, by Ellis Bell, *in Three Volumes*
(Thomas Cantley Newby, 1847), ch. XVII, 'Confessions'.

LINES WRITTEN AT THORP GREEN

That summer sun whose genial glow
Now cheers my drooping spirit so
　Must cold and distant be,
And only light our northern clime
With feeble ray, before the time
　I long so much to see.

And this soft whispering breeze that now
So gently cools my fevered brow,
　This too, alas, must turn –
To a wild blast whose icy dart　　　　　　10
Pierces and chills me to the heart,
　Before I cease to mourn.

And these bright flowers I love so well,
Verbena, rose and sweet bluebell,
   Must droop and die away.
Those thick green leaves with all their shade
And rustling music, they must fade
   And every one decay.

But if the sunny summer time
And woods and meadows in their prime   20
   Are sweet to them that roam –
Far sweeter is the winter bare
With long dark nights and landscape drear
   To them that are at home!

19 August 1841. First published, Poems, *by Charlotte, Emily and Anne Brontë (New York, 1902). Text,* The Poems of Anne Brontë, *ed. Edward Chitham (1979).*

To Cowper

Sweet are thy strains, celestial Bard,
   And oft in childhood's years,
I've read them o'er and o'er again,
   With floods of silent tears.

The language of my inmost heart,
   I traced in every line;
My sins, *my* sorrows, hopes, and fears,
   Were there – and only mine.

All for myself the sigh would swell,
   The tear of anguish start;   10
I little knew what wilder woe
   Had filled the poet's heart.

I did not know the nights of gloom,
   The days of misery;
The long, long years of dark despair,
   That crushed and tortured thee.

But they are gone; from earth at length
   Thy gentle soul is pass'd,
And in the bosom of its God
   Has found its home at last.   20

It must be so, if God is love,
   And answers fervent prayer;

Then surely thou shalt dwell on high,
   And I may meet thee there.

Is he the source of every good,
   The spring of purity?
Then in thine hours of deepest woe,
   Thy God was still with thee.

How else, when every hope was fled,
   Couldst thou so fondly cling   30
To holy things and holy men?
   And how so sweetly sing,

Of things that God alone could teach?
   And whence that purity,
That hatred of all sinful ways –
   That gentle charity?

Are these the symptoms of a heart
   Of heavenly grace bereft:
For ever banished from its God,
   To Satan's fury left?   40

Yet, should thy darkest fears be true,
   If Heaven be so severe
That such a soul as thine is lost, –
   O! how shall *I* appear?

10 November 1842. Text, Poems by Currer, Ellis, and Acton Bell *(Aylott & Jones, 1846).*

Monday Night May 11th 1846

Why should such gloomy silence reign,
And why is all the house so drear,
When neither danger, sickness, pain,
Nor death, nor want have entered here?

We are as many as we were
That other night, when all were gay,
And full of hope, and free from care;
Yet, is there something gone away.

The moon without as pure and calm,
Is shining as that night she shone;   10
But now, to us, she brings no balm,
For something from our hearts is gone.

Something whose absence leaves a void –
A cheerless want in every heart;
Each feels the bliss of all destroyed,
And mourns the change – but each apart.

The fire is burning in the grate
As redly as it used to burn;
But still the hearth is desolate,
Till mirth and love with *peace* return.   20

'Twas *peace* that flowed from heart to heart,
With looks and smiles that spoke of heaven,

And gave us language to impart
The blissful thoughts itself had given.

Domestic peace! best joy of earth,
When shall we all thy value learn?
White angel, to our sorrowing hearth,
Return – oh, graciously return!

First published in Wuthering Heights and Agnes Grey, by Ellis and Acton Bell,
A New Edition, Revised, with a Biographical Notice of the Authors, a Selection
from their Literary Remains, and a Preface, by Currer Bell *(Smith, Elder, & Co.,
1850). Text, 'Selections from Poems by Acton Bell', in Currer Bell (Charlotte Brontë),*
The Professor *(Smith, Elder, & Co., 1860). 'Domestic Peace' is 1850 and 1860 title.*

THE NARROW WAY

Believe not those who say
    The upward path is smooth,
Lest thou shouldst stumble in the way,
    And faint before the truth.

It is the only road
    Unto the realms of joy;
But he who seeks that blest abode
    Must all his powers employ.

Bright hopes and pure delight
    Upon his course may beam,   10
And there, amid the sternest heights,
    The sweetest flowerets gleam.

On all her breezes borne,
    Earth yields no scents like those;
But he that dares not grasp the thorn
    Should never crave the rose.

Arm – arm thee for the fight!
    Cast useless loads away;
Watch through the darkest hours of night;
    Toil through the hottest day.   20

Crush pride into the dust,
    Or thou must needs be slack;
And trample down rebellious lust,
    Or it will hold thee back.

Seek not thy honour here;
    Waive pleasure and renown;
The world's dread scoff undaunted bear,
    And face its deadliest frown.

To labour and to love,
    To pardon and endure,   30
To lift thy heart to God above,
    And keep thy conscience pure;

Be this thy constant aim,
    Thy hope, thy chief delight:
What matter who should whisper blame,
    Or who should scorn or slight?

What matter if thy God approve,
    And if, within thy breast,
Thou feel the comfort of His love,
    The earnest of His rest.   40

24 April 1848. First published in Wuthering Heights, Etc. *(1850).*
Text of 'Selections' in The Professor *(1860). Untitled in MS.*

Frederick Locker (later Locker-Lampson) (1821–95)

Frederick Locker, book-collector, friend of writers, and poet, was born 29 May 1821 at Greenwich Hospital, London, of which his father, Edward Hawke Locker, was the civil commissioner. His mother, Eleanor Boucher, was daughter of a vicar at Epsom who knew George Washington. Locker's younger brother, Arthur, joined the Australian gold-rush after Charterhouse and Oxford and wrote several Australian adventure stories for boys. After various schools, in and around London, Frederick went into the City of London as a clerk at a colonial broker's office, then became a clerk in the Admiralty. He was exceedingly bored there, as his posthumous autobiography makes clear. He much preferred versifying the documents he handled for his naval masters to summarizing them in regular fashion, and, on grounds of ill-health, he started in 1849 a long leave of absence. In 1850 he married Lady Charlotte Bruce, whose father was the Lord Elgin who brought the Elgin Marbles to England. In 1857 the first volume of *London Lyrics* came out, inaugurating a series of books with that title, much reprinted, rejigged, and in effect his only poetic work. *London Lyrics* (1876) claims to be 'A New Edition, Enlarged, and Finally Revised'. Locker became a collector of other men's flowers – in *Lyra Elegantiarum* (1867), 'some of the best specimens of *vers de société* and *vers d'occasion* in the English language', and *Patchwork* (1879), a collection of literary extracts (Locker's Commonplace Book was always at the ready for a fine literary *mot*) – as well as of books (the catalogue of his collection, *The Rowfant Library*, was published in 1886), and of literary acquaintances. He was friends with many of the most important writers of his time – Tennyson, Thackeray, George Eliot, Dickens, Trollope, Bulwer-Lytton. It was said there was nobody significant in London whom he had not at least met. He went travelling to Paris and Switzerland with Tennyson in the sixties. Tennyson acquired a London apartment in Victoria Street precisely to be near Locker. Locker's memories of Tennyson in Hallam Tennyson's *Memoir* of his father (II.66–80) are among that great work's liveliest and most intimate. Locker's verse, never far from the comic mode, often hits off its Victorian grown-up's obsession with little things and people (the Lit-tle Nell–Letty's Globe syndrome) with some force, despite Locker's particular tendency for the dinky to become merely the itsy-bitsy. At the wedding of John Simeon's daughter, Tennyson and Locker noticed a five-year-old bridesmaid, 'and as she knelt before us in unconscious reverence, she displayed the soles of her little white shoes. These, and her little face and her general adornment were altogether very engaging, and Tennyson whispered to me: "She and her shoes remind me of one of your poems".' Doubtless 'My Mistress's Boots'. The frontispiece of the 1868 limited (private) presentation edition of *London Lyrics* (entitled *Poems* simply) has an illustration of this poem by Locker's friend George Cruikshank, showing pixies making the boots. An edition of 1881 has an endpiece ('Little Dinky') by the still well-known children's book illustrator Kate Greenaway. Locker's first wife died in 1872; in 1874 he married Hannah Jane Lampson from Rowfant, Sussex, and moved there permanently. He altered his name to Locker-Lampson in 1885. One of his daughters from the first marriage, Eleanor, married Tennyson's younger son Lionel (1878), then (1888) Augustine Birrell. Locker-Lampson died at Rowfant, 30 May 1895. Augustine Birrell edited his memoir, *My Confidences* (1896).

THE BEAR PIT

At the Zoological Gardens

We liked the bear's serio-comical face,
As he loll'd with a lazy, a lumbering grace;
Said Slyboots to me (just as if *she* had none),
'Papa, let's give Bruin a bit of your bun.'

Says I, 'A plum bun might please wistful old Bruin,
He can't eat the stone that the cruel boy threw in;
Stick *yours* on the point of mama's parasol,
And then he will climb to the top of the pole.

'Some bears have got two legs, some have got more,
Be good to old bears if they've no legs or four;   10
Of duty to age you should never be careless,
My dear, I am bald, and I soon shall be hairless.

'The strangest aversion exists among bears
From rude forward persons who give themselves airs,
We know how some graceless young people were maul'd
For plaguing Elisha, and calling him bald.'

'Strange ursine devotion! Their dancing-days ended,
Bears die to "remove" what, in life, they defended:
They succour'd the Prophet, and, since that affair,
The bald have a painful regard for the bear.'   20

My Moral – Small People may read it, and run.
(The child has my moral, the bear has my bun), –

THE BEAR PIT
1   2 Kings 2.23–4.

Forbear to give pain, if it's only in jest,
And care to think pleasure a phantom at best.
A paradox too – none can hope to attach it,
Yet if you pursue it you'll certainly catch it.

London Lyrics *(Basil Montagu Pickering, 1862). The following epigraph appeared in*
London Lyrics *(Henry S. King & Co., 1876):*

It seems that poor Bruin has never had peace
'Twixt bald men in Bethel, and wise men in grease.
Old Adage

A TERRIBLE INFANT

I recollect a nurse call'd Ann,
    Who carried me about the grass,
And one fine day a fine young man
    Came up, and kiss'd the pretty lass:
She did not make the least objection!
        Thinks I, 'Aha!
When I can talk I'll tell Mamma' –
And that's my earliest recollection.

London Lyrics*, 'Fifth Edition' (Strahan & Co., 1872).*

MY MISTRESS'S BOOTS

They nearly strike me dumb, –
I tremble when they come
        Pit-a-pat:
This palpitation means
These Boots are Geraldine's –
        Think of that!

O, where did hunter win
So delicate a skin
        For her feet?
You lucky little kid,   10
You perish'd, so you did,
        For my sweet.

The faery stitching gleams
On the toes, and in the seams,
        And reveals
That the Pixies were the wags
Who tipt these funny tags,
        And these heels.

What soles to charm an elf! –
Had Crusoe, sick of self,   20
        Chanced to view
One printed near the tide,
O, how hard he would have tried
        For the two!¹

MY MISTRESS'S BOOTS
1   allusion to Robinson Crusoe finding a single footprint on his
island's beach in Defoe's novel *Robinson Crusoe* (1719–20).

For Gerry's debonair,
And innocent, and fair
    As a rose:
She's an angel in a frock, –
With a fascinating cock
    To her hose!   30

Those simpletons who squeeze
Their pretty toes to please
    Mandarins,
Would positively flinch
From venturing to pinch
    Geraldine's!

Cinderella's *lefts and rights*
To Geraldine's were frights:
    And, in truth,
The damsel, deftly shod,   40
Has dutifully trod
    From her youth.

Come, Gerry, since it suits
Such a busy puss in boots
    To be gone,
Set your dainty hand awhile
On my shoulder, dear, and I'll
    Put them on.

Albury, June 29, 1864

Poems *[private edition]* (*John Wilson, 1868*). (*London Lyrics, 'Fifth Edition'*
(*1872*) *claims this poem first published 1865.*) *The following epigraph appeared in*
London Lyrics (*1876*):

She has dancing eyes and ruby lips,
Delightful boots – and away she skips.

Dora (Dorothy) Greenwell (1821–82)

Dora Greenwell, devotional poet and essayist as well as a polemical journalist, was born into a landed Durham family, the only daughter of five children, 6 December 1821. The estate had to be sold up in 1848 to pay off huge debts and the family moved in an unsettled fashion around the north of England. When her father died in 1854, Dora settled with her mother, apparently an awkward customer, in Durham. They lived together for eighteen years, the daughter never marrying, increasingly religious, during which time she wrote most of her verses. Her several volumes of Christian verse, including *Carmina Crucis* (1869) and *Songs of Salvation* (1873), are never gloomy, but still profoundly meditative, preaching up Christian resignation as well as hope – 'road-side songs', she called them, 'with both joy and sorrow in them.' It's no surprise that her name as a poet was sometimes associated with Christina Rossetti. (When they met in 1875 Rossetti liked Greenwell for her large-mindedness, but was struck by how much more 'dilapidated' she was 'than myself, poor thing'.) Poetically Greenwell greatly admired Elizabeth Barrett Browning, to whom *Poems* (1867) is dedicated. (Most of Greenwell's many poems of intense friendship, desire, love, suggest a female object – even the ones with no obvious pronouns to prove it.) Politically, Greenwell was drawn rather to the side of her acquaintance Josephine Butler, famous crusader against the Contagious Diseases Act. On that feistier side of her writing are her essays on the education of imbeciles, on women's education and work and suffrage, and her attacks on the slave trade, vivisection, and prejudice against spinsters. Her now famous essay 'Our Single Women' (*North British Review*, February 1864; in her *Essays*, 1866) is critical of the idea of a distinct sphere of activity for women, but also defends fiction as the place where 'the secret of a woman's soul' can be uniquely expressed. Art and poetry, she believed (*Two Friends*, 2nd edn, 1867), were not only good as instruments of moral elevation, but good in themselves. As well as her devotional prose works – principally *The Patience of Hope*

(1860), *A Present Heaven* (1855: retitled *The Covenant of Life and Peace*, 1867), *Two Friends* and its sequel *Colloquia Crucis* (1871) – she also wrote *Lives* of Lacordaire and of the Quaker John Woolman. Never a sectarian Christian, she may even have joined the Society of Friends after her mother's death in 1871 gave her back her freedom. She certainly quit Durham then to live near her brothers in London and Bristol. In 1881 some sort of accident made her an invalid and she died in Bristol, 29 March 1882. On her tombstone in Arno's Vale cemetery are carved a hand holding a cross and the words 'Et Teneo et Teneor' – 'I both hold and am held'. This was the apt frontispiece to several of her books.

A PICTURE

It was in autumn that I met
   Her whom I love; the sunflowers bold
Stood up like guards around her set,
And all the air with mignonette
   Was warm within the garden old;
   Beside her feet the marigold
Glowed star-like, and the sweet-pea sent
A sigh to follow as she went
Slowly adown the terrace; – there
I saw thee, oh my love! and thou wert fair.   10

She stood in the full noonday, unafraid,
   As one beloved of sunlight; for awhile
She leant upon the timeworn balustrade;
The white clematis wooed her, and the clove
   Hung all its burning heart upon her smile;
And on her cheek and in her eyes was love;
And on her lips that, like an opening rose,
Seemed parting some sweet secret to disclose,
The soul of all the summer lingered; – there
I saw thee, oh my love! and thou wert fair.   20

Poems (Alexander Strachan, 1867).

TO ELIZABETH BARRETT BROWNING IN 1851

I lose myself within thy mind – from room
   To goodly room thou leadest me, and still
   Dost show me of thy glory more, until
My soul like Sheba's Queen faints, overcome,
And all my spirit dies within me, numb,[1]
   Sucked in by thine, a larger star, at will;
   And hasting like thy bee, my hive to fill,
I 'swoon for very joy' amid thy bloom;
Till – not like that poor bird (as poets feign)
   That tried against the Lutanist's her skill,   10
   Crowding her thick precipitate notes, until
Her weak heart brake above the contest vain –
   Did not thy strength a nobler thought instil,
I feel as if I ne'er could sing again!

Poems (Alexander Strachan & Co., Edinburgh, 1861),
as 'To Elizabeth Barrett Browning'. Poems (Alexander Strachan, 1867), with this title.

TO ELIZABETH BARRETT BROWNING IN 1851
1 'there was no more spirit in her': the Queen of Sheba's overawed
reaction to King Solomon's splendours and wisdom, 1 Kings 10.5.

TO ELIZABETH BARRETT BROWNING IN 1861

I praised thee not while living; what to thee
   Was praise of mine? I mourned thee not when dead;
   I only loved thee, – love thee! oh thou fled
Fair spirit, free at last where all are free,
I only love thee, bless thee, that to me
   For ever thou hast made the rose more red,
   More sweet each word by olden singers said
In sadness, or by children in their glee;
   Once, only once in life I heard thee speak,
   Once, only once I kissed thee on the cheek,   10
And met thy kiss and blessing; scarce I knew
Thy smile, I only loved thee, only grew
   Through wealth, through strength of thine, less poor, less weak;
Oh what hath death with souls like thine to do?

Poems (1867).

A SCHERZO (A SHY PERSON'S WISHES)

With the wasp at the innermost heart of a peach,
On a sunny wall out of tip-toe reach,
With the trout in the darkest summer pool,
With the fern-seed clinging behind its cool
Smooth frond, in the chink of an aged tree,
In the woodbine's horn with the drunken bee,
With the mouse in its nest in a furrow old,
With the chrysalis wrapt in its gauzy fold;
With things that are hidden, and safe, and bold,
With things that are timid, and shy, and free,   10
Wishing to be;
With the nut in its shell, with the seed in its pod,
With the corn as it sprouts in the kindly clod,
Far down where the secret of beauty shows
In the bulb of the tulip, before it blows;
With things that are rooted, and firm, and deep,
Quiet to lie, and dreamless to sleep;
With things that are chainless, and tameless, and proud,
With the fire in the jagged thunder-cloud,
With the wind in its sleep, with the wind in its waking,   20
With the drops that go to the rainbow's making,
Wishing to be with the light leaves shaking,
Or stones on some desolate highway breaking;
Far up on the hills, where no foot surprises
The dew as it falls, or the dust as it rises;
To be couched with the beast in its torrid lair,
Or drifting on ice with the polar bear,
With the weaver at work at his quiet loom;
Anywhere, anywhere, out of this room!

Poems (1867).

VENI, VENI, EMMANUEL![1]

And art Thou come with us to dwell,
Our Prince, our Guide, our Love, our Lord?
And is thy name Emmanuel,
God present with His world restored?

The world is glad for Thee! the rude
Wild moor, the city's crowded pen;
Each waste, each peopled solitude,
Becomes a home for happy men.

The heart is glad for Thee! it knows
None now shall bid it err or mourn; 10
And o'er its desert breaks the rose
In triumph o'er the grieving thorn.

Thou bringest all again; with Thee
Is light, is space, is breadth and room
For each thing fair, beloved, and free,
To have its hour of life and bloom.

Each heart's deep instinct unconfess'd;
Each lowly wish, each daring claim;
All, all that life hath long repress'd,
Unfolds, undreading blight or blame. 20

Thy reign eternal will not cease;
Thy years are sure, and glad, and slow;
Within Thy mighty world of peace
The humblest flower hath leave to blow,

And spread its leaves to meet the sun,
And drink within its soul the dew;
The child's sweet laugh like light may run
Through life's long day, and still be true;

The maid's fond sigh, the lover's kiss,
The firm warm clasp of constant friend; 30
And nought shall fail, and nought shall miss
Its blissful aim, its blissful end.

The world is glad for Thee! the heart
Is glad for Thee! and all is well,
And fixed, and sure, because THOU ART,
Whose name is call'd Emmanuel.

Carmina Crucis (Bell & Daldy, 1869). Last poem of a small group under this title.
(A shorter version got into The Methodist Hymn Book.*)*

Matthew Arnold (1822–88)

Matthew Arnold, poet, editor, social-, religious-, literary-critic, and Victorian England's most dandified Jeremiah, was born at Laleham-on-Thames near Staines, 24 December 1822, eldest son of Mary (Penrose) and Dr Thomas Arnold, schoolmaster and Broad Church Anglican, soon to become famous as the headmaster of Rugby School (celebrated in Thomas Hughes's *Tom Brown's Schooldays*, 1857), and then as Regius Professor of Modern History at Oxford. Family vacations were spent at the Arnolds' house at Fox How, Ambleside, in the Lake District, which Wordsworth helped design, and where of an evening the young Arnolds might hear Wordsworth or Southey read a poem or two. Matthew Arnold was at Winchester for a year, then four years at Rugby, before going up as a Classical Scholar to Balliol College, Oxford, in 1841. At Oxford he won the Newdigate Prize, 1843 (poem on 'Cromwell'), resisted being swept along on the fashionable Tractarian, Anglo-Catholic current, and formed his great friendship with another Old Rugbeian Arthur Hugh Clough. Disappointing everyone but his coach Clough by netting only a Second Class in his Classics finals (1844) – but then he had been quite idle – he became in quick succession a Fellow of Oriel College, a Rugby master, and private secretary to Lord Landsdowne (1847). In 1848 he visited Switzerland and met his 'Marguerite' – though she may be more fantasy than reality. In 1851 Landsdowne appointed him an Inspector of Schools. From then on Arnold's literary and critical activities had to co-exist (as his *Times* obituary put it) with 'the task of examining national schoolchildren in spelling, the rules of arithmetic, and plain sewing'. This work as a civil servant enabled him to marry Frances Lucy Wightman, a judge's daughter, though the expense of children would also keep him hard at work writing, for money, in the journals (*Fraser's*, the *Cornhill*, the *Fortnightly* especially), and taking on assorted literary jobs. School inspecting took him all over the country and abroad, and informed his polemical interest in education practice particularly in continental Europe (*The Popular Education of France*, 1861; *A French Eton*, 1864; *Schools and Universities on the Continent*, 1868). His first published collection of poems was *The Strayed Reveller and Other Poems* (1849). *Empedocles on Etna, and Other Poems* followed (1852). *Poems* (1853) and *Poems* (1854) came with important Prefaces, laying down what would be his characteristic dissatisfaction with English poetry within a problematic modernity, the modern period of 'doubts' and 'discouragement', in particular poetry's failure to provide 'guidance' and 'morals' amidst the great 'confusion of the present times', the bewildering 'multitude of voices counselling different things' (Keats is 'incoherent'; elsewhere Arnold accused Keats and Browning of a 'confused multitudinousness'). The 1853 Preface admires Shakespeare, but looks more to Goethe as a model of architectonic coherence. Arnold's critical inspiration came particularly from France (he would model himself on Saint-Beuve). In 1857 he began his ten-year spell as Oxford's (elected) Professor of Poetry, which set him up as a main force in the development of critical thought in England. In his lectures, his essays in the journals, and the volumes they turned into (the first series of *Essays in Criticism* came out in 1865, the second posthumously in 1888) he explained 'the function of criticism at the present time': to be traditional and classical, to use canonical poetic 'touchstones' as a guide to knowing 'the best' that has been thought and known in the world, to see 'the object as in itself it really is', to use poetry as 'a criticism of life'. England should have an Academy on French lines to control literary waywardness. These themes from Arnold's literary criticism would merge readily into the more obviously social criticism – focused particularly in *Culture and Anarchy* (1869), the greatest of Arnold's assaults on Philistinism, parochialism, provincialism, Hebraism, the politics and education of religious Dissenters, radicals and all 'Our Liberal Practitioners': all this in the name of Hellenism, 'sweetness and light', the 'tone of the centre', and other elitist, centrist features of an aestheticized Rugbeian–Oxonian conservatism – as well as into the Anglican-biblical critiques, *St Paul and Protestantism* (1870) and *Literature and Dogma* (1873). The poetry, melancholy, elegiac, bereft, yearningly suffused with the sense of numerous losses – faith, of course, but also loves, dogs, friends, poets ('The last poetic voice is dumb', he wrote of Wordsworth's death in 1850) – eventually got rather submerged by the urgency of producing prose threnodies for the lostness of culture generally. Tennyson told his son Hallam to 'Tell Mat not to write any more of those prose things, like *Literature and Dogma*, but to give us something like his "Thyrsis", "Scholar-Gipsy" or "Forsaken Merman"'; but the public, prosing life had taken firm command. 'Thyrsis', Arnold's elegy for Clough (in *New Poems*, 1867), was probably his last great poem. The first Collected Edition of his *Poems* came out in two volumes in 1869. In 1870 Arnold became a Senior Inspector of Schools, and received an Honorary DCL from Oxford. Twice, in 1877 and again in 1885, he refused re-nomination as Professor of Poetry. He selected Wordsworth's *Poems* (1879), was awarded a Civil List Pension of £250 per annum by Gladstone (1883), lectured in America (1883–4; 1886), brought out various editions of his poems, *Selected* (1878) and *Collected* (3 vols, 1885), and became Chief Inspector of Schools (1884–6). He died suddenly of heart failure (it ran in the family) in Liverpool, 15 April 1888. Browning attended his funeral at Laleham; Tennyson sent flowers.

Preface to the First Edition of *Poems* (1853)

In two small volumes of Poems, published anonymously, one in 1849 the other in 1852, many of the Poems which compose the present volume have already appeared. The rest are now published for the first time.

I have, in the present collection, omitted the Poem from which the volume published in 1852 took its title. I have done so, not because the subject of it was a Sicilian Greek born between two and three thousand years ago,[1] although many persons would think this a sufficient reason. Neither have I done so because I had, in my own opinion, failed in the delineation which I intended to effect. I intended to delineate the feelings of one of the last of the Greek religious philosophers, one of the family of Orpheus and Musaeus, having survived his fellows, living on into a time when the habits of Greek thought and feeling had begun fast to change, character to dwindle, the influence of the Sophists to prevail. Into the feelings of a man so situated there entered much that we are accustomed to consider as exclusively modern; how much, the fragments of Empedocles himself which remain to us are sufficient at least to indicate. What those who are familiar only with the great monuments of early Greek genius suppose to be its exclusive characteristics, have disappeared; the calm, the cheerfulness, the disinterested objectivity have disappeared: the dialogue of the mind with itself has commenced; modern problems have presented themselves; we hear already the doubts, we witness the discouragement, of Hamlet and of Faust.[2]

The representation of such a man's feelings must be interesting, if consistently drawn. We all naturally take pleasure, says Aristotle, in any imitation or representation whatever: this is the basis of our love of Poetry; and we take pleasure in them, he adds, because all knowledge is naturally agreeable to us; not to the philosopher only, but to mankind at large.[3] Every representation therefore which is consistently drawn may be supposed to be interesting, inasmuch as it gratifies this natural interest in knowledge of all kinds. What is *not* interesting, is that which does not add to our knowledge of any kind; that which is vaguely conceived and loosely drawn; a representation which is general, indeterminate, and faint, instead of being particular, precise, and firm.

Any accurate representation may therefore be expected to be interesting; but, if the representation be a poetical one, more than this is demanded. It is demanded, not only that it shall interest, but also that it shall inspirit and rejoice the reader; that it shall convey a charm, and infuse delight. For the Muses, as Hesiod says, were born that they might be a 'forgetfulness of evils, and a truce from cares':[4] and it is not enough that the Poet should add to the knowledge of men, it is required of him also that he should add to their happiness. 'All art,' says Schiller, 'is dedicated to Joy,[5] and there is no higher and no more serious problem, than how to make men happy. The right art is that alone, which creates the highest enjoyment.'

A poetical work, therefore, is not yet justified when it has been shown to be an accurate, and therefore interesting representation; it has to be shown also that it is a representation from which men can derive enjoyment. In presence of the most tragic circumstances, represented in a work of Art, the feeling of enjoyment, as is well known, may still subsist; the representation of the most utter calamity, of the liveliest anguish, is not sufficient to destroy it; the more tragic the situation, the deeper becomes the enjoyment; and the situation is more tragic in proportions as it becomes more terrible.

What then are the situations, from the representation of which, though accurate, no poetical enjoyment can be derived? They are those in which the suffering finds no vent in action; in which a continuous state of mental distress is prolonged, unrelieved by incident, hope, or resistance; in which there is everything to be endured, nothing to be done. In such situations there is inevitably something morbid, in the description of them something monotonous. When they occur in actual life, they are painful, not tragic; the representation of them in poetry is painful also.

Preface to the First Edition of *Poems*
1 'Empedocles on Etna'.
2 Shakespeare's Hamlet, Goethe's Faust.
3 *Poetics* iv, 2–4.

4 *Theogony* 53–5.
5 'Über den Gebrauch des Chors in der Tragödie', *Die Braut von Messina* (1803).

To this class of situations, poetically faulty as it appears to me, that of Empedocles, as I have endeavoured to represent him, belongs; and I have therefore excluded the Poem from the present collection.

And why, it may be asked, have I entered into this explanation respecting a matter so unimportant as the admission or exclusion of the Poem in question? I have done so, because I was anxious to avow that the sole reason for its exclusion was that which has been stated above; and that it has not been excluded in deference to the opinion which many critics of the present day appear to entertain against subjects chosen from distant times and countries: against the choice, in short, of any subjects but modern ones.

'The Poet,' it is said, and by an intelligent critic, 'the Poet who would really fix the public attention must leave the exhausted past, and draw his subjects from matters of present import, and *therefore* both of interest and novelty.'[6]

Now this view I believe to be completely false. It is worth examining, inasmuch as it is a fair sample of a class of critical dicta everywhere current at the present day, having a philosophical form and air, but no real basis in fact; and which are calculated to vitiate the judgment of readers of poetry, while they exert, so far as they are adopted, a misleading influence on the practice of those who write it.

What are the eternal objects of Poetry, among all nations and at all times? They are actions; human actions; possessing an inherent interest in themselves, and which are to be communicated in an interesting manner by the art of the Poet.[7] Vainly will the latter imagine that he has everything in his own power; that he can make an intrinsically inferior action delightful with a more excellent one by his treatment of it: he may indeed compel us to admire his skill, but his work will possess, within itself, an incurable defect.

The Poet, then, has in the first place to select an excellent action; and what actions are the most excellent? Those, certainly, which most powerfully appeal to the great primary human affections: to those elementary feelings which subsist permanently in the race, and which are independent of time. These feelings are permanent and the same; that which interests them is permanent and the same also. The modernness or antiquity of an action, therefore, has nothing to do with its fitness for poetical representation; this depends upon its inherent qualities. To the elementary part of our nature, to our passions, that which is great and passionate is eternally interesting; and interesting solely in proportion to its greatness and to its passion. A great human action of a thousand years ago is more interesting to it than a smaller human action of to-day, even though upon the representation of this last the most consummate skill may have been expended, and though it has the advantage of appealing by its modern language, familiar manners, and contemporary allusions, to all our transient feelings and interests. These, however, have no right to demand of a poetical work that it shall satisfy them; their claims are to be directed elsewhere. Poetical works belong to the domain of our permanent passions: let them interest these, and the voice of all subordinate claims upon them is at once silenced.

Achilles, Prometheus, Clytemnestra, Dido[8] – what modern poem presents personages as interesting, even to us moderns, as these personages of an 'exhausted past'? We have the domestic epic dealing with the details of modern life which pass daily under our eyes; we have poems representing modern personages in contact with the problems of modern life, moral, intellectual, and social; these works have been produced by poets the most distinguished of their nation and time; yet I fearlessly assert that Hermann and Dorothea, Childe Harold, Jocelyn, The Excursion,[9] leave the reader cold in comparison with the effect produced upon him by the latter books of the Iliad, by the Oresteia, or by the episode of Dido. And why is this? Simply because in the three latter cases the action is greater, the personages nobler, the situations more intense: and this is the true basis of the interest in a poetical work, and this alone.

6   *Spectator*, 2 April 1853, 325. Anon. review of Edwin Arnold, *Poems*.
7   Aristotle, *Poetics* ix, 9.
8   Achilles (*Iliad*); Prometheus (Aeschylus, *Prometheus Unbound*); Clytemnestra (Aeschylus, *Agamemnon*); Dido (Virgil, *Aeneid* iv).
9   Titles of works by Goethe (1797); Byron (1812–18); Lamartine (1835); Wordsworth (1814).

It may be urged, however, that past actions may be interesting in themselves, but that they are not to be adopted by the modern Poet, because it is impossible for him to have them clearly present to his own mind, and he cannot therefore feel them deeply, nor represent them forcibly. But this is not necessarily the case. The externals of a past action, indeed, he cannot know with the precision of a contemporary; but his business is with its essentials. The outward man of Oedipus or of Macbeth, the houses in which they lived, the ceremonies of their courts, he cannot accurately figure to himself; but neither do they essentially concern him. His business is with their inward man;[10] with their feelings and behaviour in certain tragic situations, which engage their passions as men; these have in them nothing local and casual; they are as accessible to the modern Poet as to a contemporary.

The date of an action, then, signifies nothing: the action itself, its selection and construction, this is what is all-important. This the Greeks understood far more clearly than we do. The radical difference between their poetical theory and ours consists, as it appears to me, in this: that, with them, the poetical character of the action in itself, and the conduct of it, was the first consideration;[11] with us, attention is fixed mainly on the value of the separate thoughts and images which occur in the treatment of an action.[12] They regarded the whole; we regard the parts. With them, the action predominated over the expression of it; with us, the expression predominates over the action. Not that they failed in expression, or were inattentive to it; on the contrary, they are the highest models of expression, the unapproached masters of the *grand style*.[13] But their expression is so excellent because it is so admirably kept in its right degree of prominence; because it is so simple and so well subordinated; because it draws its force directly from the pregnancy of the matter which it conveys. For what reason was the Greek tragic poet confined to so limited a range of subjects? Because there are so few actions which unite in themselves, in the highest degree, the conditions of excellence: and it was not thought that on any but an excellent subject could an excellent Poem be constructed. A few actions, therefore, eminently adapted for tragedy, maintained almost exclusive possession of the Greek tragic stage; their significance appeared inexhaustible; they were as permanent problems, perpetually offered to the genius of every fresh poet.[14] This too is the reason of what appears to us moderns a certain baldness of expression in Greek tragedy; of the triviality with which we often reproach the remarks of the chorus, where it takes part in the dialogue: that the action itself, the situation of Orestes, or Merope, or Alcamaeon, was to stand the central point of interest, unforgotten, absorbing, principal; that no accessories were for a moment to distract the spectator's attention from this; that the tone of the parts was to be perpetually kept down, in order not to impair the grandiose effect of the whole. The terrible old mythic story on which the drama was founded stood, before he entered the theatre, traced in its bare outlines upon the spectator's mind; it stood in his memory, as a group of statuary, faintly seen, at the end of a long and dark vista: then came the Poet, embodying outlines, developing situations, not a word wasted, not a sentiment capriciously thrown in: stroke upon stroke, the drama proceeded: the light deepened upon the group: more and more it revealed itself to the rivetted gaze of the spectator: until at last, when the final words were spoken, it stood before him in broad sunlight, a model of immortal beauty.

This was what a Greek critic demanded; this was what a Greek poet endeavoured to effect. It signified nothing to what time an action belonged; we do not find that the Persae occupied a particularly high rank among the dramas of Aeschylus, because it represented a matter of contemporary interest: this was not what a cultivated Athenian required; he required that the permanent elements of his nature should be moved; and dramas of which the action, though taken from a long-distant mythic time, yet was calculated to accomplish this in a higher degree than that of the Persae, stood higher in his estimation accordingly. The Greeks felt, no doubt, with their exquisite sagacity of taste, that an action of present times was too near them, too much mixed up with

10 'inner man': Ephesians 3.16.
11 Aristotle, *Poetics* vi, 10.
12 'exquisite bits and images': M.A., to Clough, 28 October 1852.
13 phrase from Goethe: *grosser Styl, hoher Styl.*
14 Aristotle, *Poetics* xiii, 5.

what was accidental and passing, to form a sufficiently grand, detached, and self-subsistent object for a tragic poem: such objects belonged to the domain of the comic poet, and of the lighter kinds of poetry. For the more serious kinds, for *pragmatic* poetry,[15] to use an excellent expression of Polybius, they were more difficult and severe in the range of subjects which they permitted. But for all kinds of poetry alike there was one point on which they were rigidly exacting; the adaptability of the subject to the kind of poetry selected, and the careful construction of the poem. Their theory and practice alike, the admirable treatise of Aristotle,[16] and the unrivalled works of their poets, exclaim with a thousand tongues – 'All depends upon the subject; choose a fitting action, penetrate yourself with the feeling of its situations; this done, everything else will follow.'

How different a way of thinking from this is ours! We can hardly at the present day understand what Menander meant, when he told a man who inquired as to the progress of his comedy that he had finished it, not having yet written a single line, because he had constructed the action of it in his mind.[17] A modern critic would have assured him that the merit of his piece depended on the brilliant things which arose under his pen as he went along. We have poems which seem to exist merely for the sake of single lines and passages; not for the sake of producing any total-impression. We have critics who seem to direct their attention merely to detached expressions, to the language about the action, not to the action itself.[18] I verily think that the majority of them do not in their hearts believe that there is such a thing as a total-impression to be derived from a poem at all, or to be demanded from a poet; they think the term a commonplace of metaphysical criticism. They will permit the Poet to select any action he pleases, and to suffer that action to go as it will, provided he gratifies them with occasional bursts of fine writing, and with a shower of isolated thoughts and images. That is, they permit him to leave their poetical sense ungratified, provided that he gratifies their rhetorical sense and their curiosity. Of his neglecting to gratify these, there is little danger; he needs rather to be warned against the danger of attempting to gratify these alone; he needs rather to be perpetually reminded to prefer his action to everything else; so to treat this, as to permit its inherent excellences to develope themselves, without interruption from the intrusion of his personal peculiarities; most fortunate, when he most entirely succeeds in effacing himself, and in enabling a noble action to subsist as it did in nature.

But the modern critic not only permits a false practice; he absolutely prescribes false aims. 'A true allegory of the state of one's own mind in a representative history,' the Poet is told, 'is perhaps the highest thing that one can attempt in the way of poetry' – and accordingly he attempts it.[19] An allegory of the state of one's own mind, the highest problem of an art which imitates actions! No assuredly, it is not, it never can be so; no great poetical work has ever been produced with such an aim. Faust itself, in which something of the kind is attempted, wonderful passages as it contains, and in spite of the unsurpassed beauty of the scenes which relate to Margaret, Faust itself, judged as a whole, and judged strictly as a poetical work, is defective: its illustrious author, the greatest poet of modern times, the greatest critic of all times, would have been the first to acknowledge it; he only defended his work, indeed, by asserting it to be 'something incommensurable'.[20]

The confusion of the present times is great, the multitude of voices counselling different things bewildering, the number of existing works capable of attracting a young writer's attention and of becoming his models, immense: what he wants is a hand to guide him through the confusion, a voice to prescribe to him the aim which he should keep in view, and to explain to him that the value of the literary works which offer themselves to his attention is relative to their power of helping him forward on his road towards this aim. Such a guide the English writer at the present day will nowhere find. Failing this, all, that can be looked for, all indeed that can be desired, is, that his attention should be fixed on excellent models; that he may reproduce, at any rate, something of their excellence, by penetrating himself with their works and by catching their spirit, if he cannot be taught to produce what is excellent independently.

---

15 phrase of Goethe, rather than Polybius.

16 Aristotle's *Poetics*.

17 in Plutarch, *Moralia* 347E–F.

18 A. is thinking of Anon. praise for Spasmodic Alexander Smith's *A Life Drama* (1853) in *North British Review* (August 1853).

19 *North British Review* (August 1853), 338.

20 Goethe, in Eckermann, *Conversations* (3 January 1830).

Foremost among these models for the English writer stands Shakspeare: a name the greatest perhaps of all poetical names; a name never to be mentioned without reverence. I will venture, however, to express a doubt, whether the influence of his works, excellent and fruitful for the readers of poetry, for the great majority, has been of unmixed advantage to the writers of it. Shakspeare indeed chose excellent subjects; the world could afford no better than Macbeth, or Romeo and Juliet, or Othello: he had no theory respecting the necessity of choosing subjects of present import, or the paramount interest attaching to allegories of the state of one's own mind; like all great poets, he knew well what constituted a poetical action; like them, wherever he found such an action, he took it; like them, too, he found his best in past times. But to these general characteristics of all great poets he added a special one of his own; a gift, namely, of happy, abundant, and ingenious expression, eminent and unrivalled: so eminent as irresistibly to strike the attention first in him, and even to throw into comparative shade his other excellences as a poet. Here has been the mischief. These other excellences were his fundamental excellences *as a poet*; what distinguishes the artist from the mere amateur, says Goethe, is *Architectonicè*[21] in the highest sense; that power of execution, which creates, forms, and constitutes: not the profoundness of single thoughts, not the richness of imagery, not the abundance of illustration. But these attractive accessories of a poetical work being more easily seized than the spirit of the whole, and these accessories being possessed by Shakspeare in an unequalled degree, a young writer having recourse to Shakspeare as his model runs great risk of being vanquished and absorbed by them, and, in consequence, of reproducing, according to the measure of his power, these, and these alone. Of this preponderating quality of Shakspeare's genius, accordingly, almost the whole of modern English poetry has, it appears to me, felt the influence. To the exclusive attention on the part of his imitators to this it is in a great degree owing, that of the majority of modern poetical works the details alone are valuable, the composition worthless. In reading them one is perpetually reminded of that terrible sentence on a modern French poet: – *il dit tout ce qu'il veut, mais malheureusement il n'a rien à dire.*[22]

Let me give an instance of what I mean. I will take it from the works of the very chief among those who seem to have been formed in the school of Shakspeare: of one whose exquisite genius and pathetic death render him for ever interesting. I will take the poem of Isabella, or the Pot of Basil, by Keats. I choose this rather than the Endymion, because the latter work (which a modern critic has classed with the Fairy Queen!)[23] although undoubtedly there blows through it the breath of genius, is yet as a whole so utterly incoherent, as not strictly to merit the name of a poem at all. The poem of Isabella, then, is a perfect treasure-house of graceful and felicitous words and images; almost in every stanza there occurs one of those vivid and picturesque turns of expression, by which the object is made to flash upon the eye of the mind, and which thrill the reader with a sudden delight. This one short poem contains, perhaps, a greater number of happy single expressions which one could quote than all the extant tragedies of Sophocles. But the action, the story? The action in itself is an excellent one; but so feebly is it conceived by the poet, so loosely constructed, that the effect produced by it, in and for itself, is absolutely null. Let the reader, after he has finished the poem of Keats, turn to the same story in the Decameron:[24] he will then feel how pregnant and interesting the same action has become in the hands of a great artist, who above all things delineates his object; who subordinates expression to that which it is designed to express.

I have said that the imitators of Shakspeare, fixing their attention on his wonderful gift of expression, have directed their imitation to this, neglecting his other excellences. These excellences, the fundamental excellences of poetical art, Shakspeare no doubt possessed them – possessed many of them in a splendid degree; but it may perhaps be doubted whether even he himself did not sometimes give scope to his faculty of expression to the prejudice of a higher poetical duty. For we must never forget that Shakspeare is the great poet he is from his skill in discerning and firmly conceiving an excellent action, from his power of intensely feeling a situation, of intimately

21   *Architektonik.*
22   'He says everything that he wants to, but unfortunately he has nothing to say' (Gautier?).
23   of Edmund Spenser. *North British Review* critic again (August 1853, 332).
24   by Boccaccio: 5th novel, 4th day.

associating himself with a character; not from his gift of expression, which rather even leads him astray, degenerating sometimes into a fondness for curiosity of expression, into an irritability of fancy, which seems to make it impossible for him to say a thing plainly, even when the press of the action demands the very directest language, or its level character the very simplest. Mr. Hallam, than whom it is impossible to find a saner and more judicious critic, has had the courage (for at the present day it needs courage) to remark, how extremely and faultily difficult Shakspeare's language often is.[25] It is so: you may find main scenes in some of his greatest tragedies, King Lear for instance, where the language is so artificial, so curiously tortured, and so difficult, that every speech has to be read two or three times before its meaning can be comprehended. This over-curiousness of expression is indeed but the excessive employment of a wonderful gift – of the power of saying a thing in a happier way than any other man; nevertheless, it is carried so far that one understands what M. Guizot meant, when he said that Shakspeare appears in his language to have tried all styles except that of simplicity.[26] He has not the severe and scrupulous self-restraint of the ancients, partly no doubt, because he had a far less cultivated and exacting audience: he has indeed a far wider range than they had, a far richer fertility of thought; in this respect he rises above them: in his strong conception of his subject, in the genuine way in which he is penetrated with it, he resembles them, and is unlike the moderns: but in the accurate limitation of it, the conscientious rejection of superfluities, the simple and rigorous development of it from the first line of his work to the last, he falls below them, and comes nearer to the moderns. In his chief works, besides what he has of his own, he has the elementary soundness of the ancients; he has their important action and their large and broad manner: but he has not their purity of method. He is therefore a less safe model; for what he has of his own is personal, and inseparable from his own rich nature; it may be imitated and exaggerated, it cannot be learned or applied as an art; he is above all suggestive; more valuable, therefore, to young writers as men than as artists. But clearness of arrangement, rigour of development, simplicity of style – these may to a certain extent be learned: and these may, I am convinced, be learned best from the ancients, who although infinitely less suggestive than Shakspeare, are thus, to the artist, more instructive.

What, then, it will be asked, are the ancients to be our sole models? the ancients with their comparatively narrow range of experience, and their widely different circumstances? Not, certainly, that which is narrow in the ancients, nor that in which we can no longer sympathize. An action like the action of the Antigone of Sophocles, which turns upon the conflict between the heroine's duty to her brother's corpse and that to the laws of her country, is no longer one in which it is possible that we should feel a deep interest. I am speaking too, it will be remembered, not of the best sources of intellectual stimulus for the general reader, but of the best models of instruction for the individual writer. This last may certainly learn of the ancients, better than anywhere else, three things which it is vitally important for him to know: – the all-importance of the choice of a subject; the necessity of accurate construction; and the subordinate character of expression. He will learn from them how unspeakably superior is the effect of the one moral impression left by a great action treated as a whole, to the effect produced by the most striking single thought or by the happiest image. As he penetrates into the spirit of the great classical works, as he becomes gradually aware of their intense significance, their noble simplicity, and their calm pathos, he will be convinced that it is this effect, unity and profoundness of moral impression, at which the ancient Poets aimed; that it is this which constitutes the grandeur of their works, and which makes them immortal. He will desire to direct his own efforts towards producing the same effect. Above all, he will deliver himself from the jargon of modern criticism, and escape the danger of producing poetical works conceived in the spirit of the passing time, and which partake of its transitoriness.

The present age makes great claims upon us: we owe it service, it will not be satisfied without our admiration. I know not how it is, but their commerce with the ancients appears to me to produce, in those who constantly practise it, a steadying and composing effect upon their judgment,

25   Henry Hallam, *Introduction to the Literature of Europe in the Fifteenth,*   26   phrase from Guizot, *Shakespeare et son temps* (1852).
Sixteenth, and Seventeenth Centuries (1837–9; 1876 edn), III. 315–16.

not of literary works only, but of men and events in general. They are like persons who have had a very weighty and impressive experience; they are more truly than others under the empire of facts, and more independent of the language current among those with whom they live. They wish neither to applaud nor to revile their age: they wish to know what it is, what it can give them, and whether this is what they want. What they want, they know very well; they want to educe and cultivate what is best and noblest in themselves: they know, too, that this is no easy task – χαλεπὸν, as Pittacus said, χαλεπὸν ἐσθλὸν ἔμμεναι[27] – and they ask themselves sincerely whether their age and its literature can assist them in the attempt. If they are endeavouring to practise any art, they remember the plain and simple proceedings of the old artists, who attained their grand results by penetrating themselves with some noble and significant action, not by inflating themselves with a belief in the pre-eminent importance and greatness of their own times. They do not talk of their mission, nor of interpreting their age, nor of the coming Poet; all this, they know, is the mere delirium of vanity;[28] their business is not to praise their age, but to afford to the men who live in it the highest pleasure which they are capable of feeling. If asked to afford this by means of subjects drawn from the age itself, they ask what special fitness the present age has for supplying them: they are told that it is an era of progress, an age commissioned to carry out the great ideas of industrial development and social amelioration. They reply that with all this they can do nothing; that the elements they need for the exercise of their art are great actions, calculated powerfully and delightfully to affect what is permanent in the human soul; that so far as the present age can supply such actions, they will gladly make use of them; but that an age wanting in moral grandeur can with difficulty supply such, and an age of spiritual discomfort with difficulty be powerfully and delightfully affected by them.

A host of voices will indignantly rejoin that the present age is inferior to the past neither in moral grandeur nor in spiritual health. He who possesses the discipline I speak of will content himself with remembering the judgements passed upon the present age, in this respect, by the men of strongest head and widest culture whom it has produced; by Goethe and by Niebuhr.[29] It will be sufficient for him that he knows the opinions held by these two great men respecting the present age and its literature; and that he feels assured in his own mind that their aims and demands upon life were such as he would wish, at any rate, his own to be; and their judgement as to what is impeding and disabling such as he may safely follow. He will not, however, maintain a hostile attitude towards the false pretensions of his age; he will content himself with not being overwhelmed by them. He will esteem himself fortunate if he can succeed in banishing from his mind all feelings of contradiction, and irritation, and impatience; in order to delight himself with the contemplation of some noble action of a heroic time, and to enable others, through his representation of it, to delight in it also.

I am far indeed from making any claim, for myself, that I possess this discipline; or for the following Poems, that they breathe its spirit. But I say, that in the sincere endeavour to learn and practise, amid the bewildering confusion of our times, what is sound and true in poetical art, I seemed to myself to find the only sure guidance, the only solid footing, among the ancients. They, at any rate, knew what they wanted in Art, and we do not. It is this uncertainty which is disheartening, and not hostile criticism. How often have I felt this when reading words of disparagement or of cavil: that it is the uncertainty as to what is really to be aimed at which makes our difficulty, not the dissatisfaction of the critic, who himself suffers from the same uncertainty. *Non me tua turbida terrent Dicta: Dii me terrent, et Jupiter hostis.*[30]

Two kinds of *dilettanti*, says Goethe, there are in poetry: he who neglects the indispensable mechanical part, and thinks he has done enough if he shows spirituality and feeling; and he who seeks to arrive at poetry merely by mechanism, in which he can acquire an artisan's readiness, and is

---

27 Diogenes Laertius, *Life of Pittacus*: 'It's difficult to be good.'

28 riposte to passage about coming Poet in Alexander Smith, *A Life Drama*, quoted in *North British Review*.

29 B. G. Niebuhr, German historian (1776–1831).

30 'It's not your disturbed words that frighten me: it's the Gods who make me afraid, and Jupiter my enemy': Virgil, *Aeneid* xii, 894–5. A. misremembered V.'s *fervida* (fervent) as *turbida* (corrected in *Poems*, 1854).

without soul and matter. And he adds, that the first does most harm to Art, and the last to himself.[31] If we must be *dilettanti*: if it is impossible for us, under the circumstances amidst which we live, to think clearly, to feel nobly, and to delineate firmly: if we cannot attain to the mastery of the great artists – let us, at least, have so much respect for our Art as to prefer it to ourselves: let us not bewilder our successors: let us transmit to them the practice of Poetry, with its boundaries and wholesome regulative laws, under which excellent works may again, perhaps, at some future time, be produced, not yet fallen into oblivion through our neglect, not yet condemned and cancelled by the influence of their eternal enemy, Caprice.

FOX HOW, AMBLESIDE,
October 1, 1853

Poems. A New Edition *(Longman, Brown, Green, & Longmans, 1853).*

PREFACE TO SECOND EDITION OF *POEMS* (1854)

I have allowed the Preface to the former edition of these Poems to stand almost without change, because I still believe it to be, in the main, true. I must not, however, be supposed insensible to the force of much that has been alleged against portions of it, or unaware that it contains many things incompletely stated, many things which need limitation. It leaves, too, untouched the question, how far and in what manner the opinions there expressed respecting the choice of subjects apply to lyric poetry; that region of the poetical field which is chiefly cultivated at present.[1] But neither have I time now to supply these deficiencies, nor is this the proper place for attempting it: on one or two points alone I wish to offer, in the briefest possible way, some explanation.

An objection has been ably urged to the classing together, as subjects equally belonging to a past time, Oedipus and Macbeth.[2] And it is no doubt true that to Shakspeare, standing on the verge of the middle ages, the epoch of Macbeth was more familiar than that of Oedipus. But I was speaking of actions as they presented themselves to us moderns: and it will hardly be said that the European mind, since Voltaire, has much more affinity with the times of Macbeth than with those of Oedipus. As moderns, it seems to me, we have no longer any direct affinity with the circumstances and feelings of either; as individuals, we are attracted towards this or that personage, we have a capacity for imagining him, irrespective of his times, solely according to a law of personal sympathy; and those subjects for which we feel this personal attraction most strongly, we may hope to treat successfully. Prometheus or Joan of Arc, Charlemagne or Agamemnon – one of these is not really nearer to us now than another; each can be made present only by an act of poetic imagination; but this man's imagination has an affinity for one of them, and that man's for another.

It has been said that I wish to limit the Poet in his choice of subjects to the period of Greek and Roman antiquity: but it is not so: I only counsel him to choose for his subjects great actions, without regarding to what time they belong. Nor do I deny that the poetic faculty can and does manifest itself in treating the most trifling action, the most hopeless subject. But it is a pity that power should be wasted; and that the Poet should be compelled to impart interest and force to his subject, instead of receiving them from it, and thereby doubling his impressiveness. There is, it has been excellently said, an immortal strength in the stories of great actions: the most gifted poet, then, may well be glad to supplement with it that mortal weakness, which, in presence of the vast spectacle of life and the world, he must for ever feel to be his individual portion.

Again, with respect to the study of the classical writers of antiquity; it has been said that we should emulate rather than imitate them. I make no objection: all I say is, let us study them.

31 A. is referring here as elsewhere in the Preface, to Goethe's essay 'Über den sogenannten Dilettantismus' (on the so-called Dilettantism).
PREFACE TO SECOND EDITION OF *POEMS*
1 Arnold is thinking of W. C. Roscoe, *Prospective Review* x (1854), who pointed out the limitation of Aristotle's limiting representation to human action: 'We have poems to the Lesser Celandine, to a Mouse, to the Skylark ... which ... are purely descriptive of natural objects.'
2 In *Spectator*, 3 December 1853, Supplement, 5.

They can help to cure us of what is, it seems to me, the great vice of our intellect, manifesting itself in our incredible vagaries in literature, in art, in religion, in morals: namely, that it is *fantastic*, and wants *sanity*. Sanity – that is the great virtue of the ancient literature; the want of that is the great defect of the modern, in spite of all its variety and power. It is impossible to read carefully the great ancients, without losing something of our caprice and eccentricity; and to emulate them we must at least read them.

London, June 1, 1854

Poems. Second Edition (Longman, Brown, Green, & Longmans, 1854).

To Marguerite

In Returning a Volume of the Letters of Ortis[1]

Yes: in the sea of life enisl'd,
With echoing straits between us thrown,
Dotting the shoreless watery wild,
We mortal millions live *alone*.
The islands feel the enclasping flow,
And then their endless bounds they know.

But when the moon their hollows lights,
And they are swept by balms of spring,
And in their glens, on starry nights,
The nightingales divinely sing,   10
And lovely notes, from shore to shore,
Across the sounds and channels pour;

Oh then a longing like despair
Is to their farthest caverns sent;
– For surely once, they feel, we were
Parts of a single continent.
Now round us spreads the watery plain –
Oh might our marges meet again!

Who order'd, that their longing's fire
Should be, as soon as kindled, cool'd?   20
Who renders vain their deep desire?
A God, a God their severance rul'd!
And bade betwixt their shores to be
The unplumb'd, salt, estranging sea.

Written, probably, Sept.–Oct. 1849. Empedocles on Etna, and Other Poems,
By A. (B. Fellowes, 1852).

Self-Dependence

Weary of myself, and sick of asking
What I am, and what I ought to be,
At this vessel's prow I stand, which bears me
Forwards, forwards, o'er the starlit sea.

To Marguerite
1 Marguerite: unidentified Swiss girl Arnold met, 1848–9, in Switzer- land. Ortis: unhappy lover in Ugo Foscolo, *Ultime Lettere di Jacopo Ortis* (1802), trans. Alexandre Dumas (1839).

And a look of passionate desire
O'er the sea and to the stars I send:
'Ye who from my childhood up have calm'd me,
Calm me, ah, compose me to the end.

'Ah, once more,' I cried, 'ye Stars, ye Waters,
On my heart your mighty charm renew: 10
Still, still let me, as I gaze upon you,
Feel my soul becoming vast like you.'

From the intense, clear, star-sown vault of heaven,
Over the lit sea's unquiet way,
In the rustling night-air came the answer –
'Wouldst thou *be* as these are? *Live* as they.

'Unaffrighted by the silence round them,
Undistracted by the sights they see,
These demand not that the things without them
Yield them love, amusement, sympathy.   20

'And with joy the stars perform their shining,
And the sea its long moon-silver'd roll;
For alone they live, nor pine with noting
All the fever of some differing soul.

'Bounded by themselves, and unobservant
In what state God's other works may be,
In their own tasks all their powers pouring,
These attain the mighty life you see.'

O air-born Voice! long since, severely clear,
A cry like thine in mine own heart I hear.
'Resolve to be thyself; and know that he,
Who finds himself, loses his misery!'

Written,(?) late 1849–early 1850. Empedocles on Etna, and Other Poems (1852).

DOVER BEACH

The sea is calm to-night.
The tide is full, the moon lies fair
Upon the Straits; on the French coast, the light
Gleams, and is gone; the cliffs of England stand,
Glimmering and vast, out in the tranquil bay.
Come to the window, sweet is the night air!
Only, from the long line of spray
Where the ebb meets the moon-blanch'd land,
Listen! you hear the grating roar
Of pebbles which the waves suck back, and fling,   10
At their return, up the high strand,
Begin, and cease, and then again begin,
With tremulous cadence slow, and bring
The eternal note of sadness in.

Sophocles long ago
Heard it on the Ægæan, and it brought
Into his mind the turbid ebb and flow

Of human misery; we
Find also in the sound a thought,
Hearing it by this distant northern sea.   20

The sea of faith
Was once, too, at the full, and round earth's shore
Lay like the folds of a bright girdle furl'd;
But now I only hear
Its melancholy, long withdrawing roar,
Retreating to the breath
Of the night-wind, down the vast edges drear
And naked shingles of the world.

Ah, love, let us be true
To one another! for the world, which seems   30
To lie before us like a land of dreams,
So various, so beautiful, so new,
Hath really neither joy, nor love, nor light,
Nor certitude, nor peace, nor help for pain;
And we are here as on a darkling plain
Swept with confused alarms of struggle and flight,
Where ignorant armies clash by night.[1]

Written, probably, June 1851. New Poems *(Macmillan & Co., 1867).*

THE SCHOLAR-GIPSY

'There was very lately a lad in the University of Oxford, who was by his poverty forced to leave his studies there; and at last to join himself to a company of vagabond gipsies. Among these extravagant people, by the insinuating subtilty of his carriage, he quickly got so much of their love and esteem as that they discovered to him their mystery. After he had been a pretty while well exercised in the trade, there chanced to ride by a couple of scholars, who had formerly been of his acquaintance. They quickly spied out their old friend among the gipsies; and he gave them an account of the necessity which drove him to that kind of life, and told them that the people he went with were not such impostors as they were taken for, but that they had a traditional kind of learning among them, and could do wonders by the power of imagination, their fancy binding that of others: that himself had learned much of their art, and when he had compassed the whole secret, he intended, he said, to leave their company, and give the world an account of what he had learned.' – *Glanvil's Vanity of Dogmatizing,* 1661.[1]

Go, for they call you, Shepherd,[2] from the hill;
    Go, Shepherd, and untie the wattled cotes:
        No longer leave thy wistful flock unfed,
    Nor let thy bawling fellows rack their throats,
        Nor the cropp'd herbage shoot another head.
            But when the fields are still,
    And the tired men and dogs all gone to rest,
        And only the white sheep are sometimes seen
        Cross and recross the strips of moon-blanch'd green;
    Come, Shepherd, and again renew the quest.   10

DOVER BEACH
1 reference to nighttime Battle of Epipolae, Thucydides, *Peloponnesian War,* vii, ch.44.

THE SCHOLAR-GIPSY
1 Joseph Glanvil. A patchwork of quotations.
2 Clough.

Here, where the reaper was at work of late,
  In this high field's dark corner, where he leaves
    His coat, his basket, and his earthen cruise,[3]
  And in the sun all morning binds the sheaves,
    Then here, at noon, comes back his stores to use;
      Here will I sit and wait,
  While to my ear from uplands far away
    The bleating of the folded flocks is borne;
    With distant cries of reapers in the corn –
All the live murmur of a summer's day.   20

Screen'd is this nook o'er the high, half-reap'd field,
  And here till sun-down, Shepherd, will I be.
    Through the thick corn the scarlet poppies peep
  And round green roots and yellowing stalks I see
    Pale pink convolvulus in tendrils creep:
      And air-swept lindens yield
  Their scent, and rustle down their perfum'd showers
    Of bloom on the bent grass where I am laid,
    And bower me from the August sun with shade;
And the eye travels down to Oxford's towers.   30

And near me on the grass lies Glanvil's book[4] –
  Come, let me read the oft-read tale again,
    The story of the Oxford scholar poor
  Of pregnant parts and quick inventive brain,
    Who, tired of knocking at Preferment's door,
      One summer-morn forsook
  His friends, and went to learn the Gipsy lore,
    And roam'd the world with that wild brotherhood,
    And came, as most men deem'd, to little good,
But came to Oxford and his friends no more.   40

But once, years after, in the country lanes
  Two scholars, whom at college erst he knew
    Met him, and of his way of life enquir'd.
  Whereat he answer'd, that the Gipsy crew,
    His mates, had arts to rule as they desir'd
      The workings of men's brains;
  And they can bind them to what thoughts they will:
    'And I,' he said, 'the secret of their art,
    When fully learn'd, will to the world impart:
But it needs happy moments for this skill.'   50

This said, he left them, and return'd no more.
  But rumours hung about the country side,
    That the lost Scholar long was seen to stray,
  Seen by rare glimpses, pensive and tongue-tied,
    In hat of antique shape, and cloak of grey,
      The same the Gipsies wore.
  Shepherds had met him on the Hurst[5] in spring;
    At some lone alehouse in the Berkshire moors,
    On the warm ingle bench, the smock-frock'd boors
Had found him seated at their entering,   60

3 pot for water.   5 Cumnor Hurst.
4 Joseph Glanvil, *The Vanity of Dogmatizing* (1661).

But, mid their drink and clatter, he would fly:
  And I myself seem half to know thy looks,
    And put the shepherds, Wanderer, on thy trace;
  And boys who in lone wheatfields scare the rooks
    I ask if thou hast pass'd their quiet place;
      Or in my boat I lie
  Moor'd to the cool bank in the summer heats,
    Mid wide grass meadows which the sunshine fills,
    And watch the warm green muffled Cumner hills,
  And wonder if thou haunt'st their shy retreats.   70

For most, I know, thou lov'st retired ground.
  Thee, at the ferry, Oxford riders blithe,
    Returning home on summer nights, have met
  Crossing the stripling Thames at Bab-lock-hithe,
    Trailing in the cool stream thy fingers wet,
      As the slow punt swings round:
  And leaning backward in a pensive dream,
    And fostering in thy lap a heap of flowers
    Pluck'd in shy fields and distant woodland bowers,
  And thine eyes resting on the moonlit stream   80

And then they land, and thou art seen no more.
  Maidens, who from the distant hamlets come
    To dance around the Fyfield elm in May,
  Oft through the darkening fields have seen thee roam,
    Or cross a stile into the public way.
      Oft thou hast given them store
  Of flowers – the frail-leaf'd, white anemone –
    Dark bluebells drench'd with dews of summer eves –
    And purple orchises with spotted leaves –
  But none hath words she can report of thee.   90

And, above Godstow Bridge, when hay-time's here
  In June, and many a scythe in sunshine flames,
    Men who through those wide fields of breezy grass
  Where black-wing'd swallows haunt the glittering Thames,
    To bathe in the abandon'd lasher[6] pass,
      Have often pass'd thee near
  Sitting upon the river bank o'ergrown:
    Mark'd thy outlandish garb, thy figure spare,
    Thy dark vague eyes, and soft abstracted air;
  But, when they came from bathing, thou wert gone.   100

At some lone homestead in the Cumner hills,
  Where at her open door the housewife darns,
    Thou hast been seen, or hanging on a gate
  To watch the threshers in the mossy barns.
    Children, who early range these slopes and late
      For cresses from the rills,
  Have known thee watching, all an April day,
    The springing pastures and the feeding kine;
    And mark'd thee, when the stars come out and shine,
  Through the long dewy grass move slow away.   110

6 pool near a weir.

In Autumn, on the skirts of Bagley Wood
    Where most the Gipsies by the turf-edg'd way
        Pitch their smok'd tents, and every bush you see
    With scarlet patches tagg'd and shreds of grey,
        Above the forest ground call'd Thessaly –
            The blackbird picking food
    Sees thee, nor stops his meal, nor fears at all;
        So often has he known thee past him stray
        Rapt, twirling in thy hand a wither'd spray,
    And waiting for the spark from Heaven to fall.   120

And once, in winter, on the causeway chill
    Where home through flooded fields foot-travellers go,
        Have I not pass'd thee on the wooden bridge,
    Wrapt in thy cloak and battling with the snow,
        Thy face towards Hinksey and its wintry ridge?
            And thou hast climb'd the hill,
    And gain'd the white brow of the Cumner range,
        Turn'd once to watch, while thick the snow-flakes fall,
        The line of festal light in Christ-Church hall –
    Then sought thy straw in some sequester'd grange.   130

But what – I dream! Two hundred years are flown
    Since first thy story ran through Oxford halls,
        And the grave Glanvil did the tale inscribe
    That thou wert wander'd from the studious walls
        To learn strange arts, and join a Gipsy tribe:
            And thou from earth art gone
    Long since, and in some quiet churchyard laid;
        Some country nook, where o'er thy unknown grave
        Tall grasses and white flowering nettles wave,
    Under a dark, red-fruited yew-tree's shade.   140

– No, no, thou hast not felt the lapse of hours.
    For what wears out the life of mortal men?
        'Tis that from change to change their being rolls:
    'Tis that repeated shocks, again, again,
        Exhaust the energy of strongest souls,
            And numb the elastic powers.
    Till having us'd our nerves with bliss and teen,[7]
        And tir'd upon a thousand schemes our wit,
        To the just-pausing Genius we remit
    Our worn-out life, and are – what we have been.   150

Thou hast not liv'd, why should'st thou perish, so?
    Thou hadst *one* aim, *one* business, *one* desire:
        Else wert thou long since number'd with the dead –
    Else hadst thou spent, like other men, thy fire.
        The generations of thy peers are fled,
            And we ourselves shall go;
    But thou possessest an immortal lot,
        And we imagine thee exempt from age
        And living as thou liv'st on Glanvil's page,
    Because thou hadst – what we, alas, have not.   160

7   grief; woe.

For early didst thou leave the world, with powers
  Fresh, undiverted to the world without,
    Firm to their mark, not spent on other things;
  Free from the sick fatigue, the languid doubt,
    Which much to have tried, in much been baffled, brings.
      O life unlike to ours!
  Who fluctuate idly without term or scope,
    Of whom each strives, nor knows for what he strives,
    And each half lives a hundred different lives;
  Who wait like thee, but not, like thee, in hope.   170

Thou waitest for the spark from Heaven and we,
  Light half-believers of our casual creeds,
    Who never deeply felt, nor clearly will'd,
  Whose insight never has borne fruit in deeds,
    Whose vague resolves never have been fulfill'd;
      For whom each year we see
  Breeds new beginnings, disappointments new;
    Who hesitate and falter life away,
    And lose to-morrow the ground won to-day —
  Ah! do not we, Wanderer, await it too?   180

Yes, we await it, but it still delays,
  And then we suffer and amongst us One,[8]
    Who most has suffer'd, takes dejectedly
  His seat upon the intellectual throne;
    And all his store of sad experience he
      Lays bare of wretched days;
  Tells us his misery's birth and growth and signs,
    And how the dying spark of hope was fed,
    And how the breast was sooth'd, and how the head,
  And all his hourly varied anodynes.   190

This for our wisest: and we others pine,
  And wish the long unhappy dream would end,
    And waive all claim to bliss, and try to bear
  With close-lipped Patience for our only friend,
    Sad Patience, too near neighbour to Despair:
      But none has hope like thine.
  Thou through the fields and through the woods dost stray,
    Roaming the country side, a truant boy,
    Nursing thy project in unclouded joy,
  And every doubt long blown by time away.   200

O born in days when wits were fresh and clear,
  And life ran gaily as the sparkling Thames;
    Before this strange disease of modern life,
  With its sick hurry, its divided aims,
    Its heads o'ertax'd, its palsied hearts, was rife —
      Fly hence, our contact fear!
  Still fly, plunge deeper in the bowering wood!
    Averse, as Dido did with gesture stern
    From her false friend's approach in Hades turn,[9]
  Wave us away, and keep thy solitude!   210

8 Tennyson?   9 *Aeneid* vi, 469–73.

Still nursing the unconquerable hope,
  Still clutching the inviolable shade,
    With a free onward impulse brushing through,
  By night, the silver'd branches of the glade –
    Far on the forest skirts, where none pursue,
      On some mild pastoral slope
  Emerge, and resting on the moonlit pales,
    Freshen thy flowers, as in former years,
    With dew, or listen with enchanted ears,
  From the dark dingles, to the nightingales.   220

But fly our paths, our feverish contact fly!
  For strong the infection of our mental strife,
    Which, though it gives no bliss, yet spoils for rest;
  And we should win thee from thy own fair life,
    Like us distracted, and like us unblest.
      Soon, soon thy cheer would die,
  Thy hopes grow timorous, and unfix'd thy powers,
    And thy clear aims be cross and shifting made:
    And then thy glad perennial youth would fade,
  Fade, and grow old at last and die like ours.   230

Then fly our greetings, fly our speech and smiles!
  – As some grave Tyrian[10] trader, from the sea,
    Descried at sunrise an emerging prow
  Lifting the cool-hair'd creepers stealthily,
  The fringes of a southward-facing brow
      Among the Ægean isles;
  And saw the merry Grecian coaster come,
    Freighted with amber grapes, and Chian wine,
    Green bursting figs, and tunnies steep'd in brine;
  And knew the intruders on his ancient home,   240

The young light-hearted Masters of the waves;
  And snatch'd his rudder, and shook out more sail,
    And day and night held on indignantly
  O'er the blue Midland waters with the gale,
    Betwixt the Syrtes[11] and soft Sicily,
      To where the Atlantic raves
  Outside the Western Straits, and unbent sails
    There, where down cloudy cliffs, through sheets of foam,
    Shy traffickers, the dark Iberians come;
  And on the beach undid his corded bales.   250

Written, (?) 1852–3, perhaps May–Aug. 1853. Poems. A New Edition *(1853). Early titles*
considered by Arnold: 'The First Mesmerist', 'The Wandering Mesmerist'.

HAWORTH CHURCHYARD

April, 1855

Where, under Loughrigg, the stream
Of Rotha sparkles through fields
Vested for ever with green,

---

10   from Tyre; a Phoenician.   11   North African coastal quicksands.

Four years since, in the house
Of a gentle spirit now dead,
Wordsworth's son-in-law, friend[1] –
I saw the meeting of two
Gifted women.[2] The one,
Brilliant with recent renown,
Young, unpractised, had told   10
With a master's accent her feign'd
Story of passionate life;[3]
The other, maturer in fame,
Earning, she too, her praise
First in fiction, had since
Widen'd her sweep, and surveyed
History, politics, mind.

The two held converse; they wrote
In a book which of world-famous souls
Kept the memorial; – bard,   20
Warrior, statesman, had sign'd
Their names; chief glory of all,
Scott had bestow'd there his last
Breathings of song, with a pen
Tottering, a death-stricken hand.

Hope at that meeting smiled fair.
Years in number, it seem'd,
Lay before both, and a fame
Heighten'd, and multiplied power. –
Behold! The elder, to-day,   30
Lies expecting from death,
In mortal weakness, a last
Summons! the younger is dead![4]

First to the living we pay
Mournful homage; – the Muse
Gains not an earth-deafen'd ear.

Hail to the steadfast soul,
Which, unflinching and keen,
Wrought to erase from its depth
Mist and illusion and fear!   40
Hail to the spirit which dared
Trust its own thoughts, before yet
Echoed her back by the crowd!
Hail to the courage which gave
Voice to its creed, ere the creed
Won consecration from time!

Turn we next to the dead. –
How shall we honour the young,
The ardent, the gifted? how mourn?

HAWORTH CHURCHYARD
1 Edward Quillinan (1791–1851), minor poet.
2 Charlotte Brontë, and Harriet Martineau (the novelist): 21 December 1850.
3 *Jane Eyre* (1847).
4 Charlotte Brontë died 31 March 1855.

Console we cannot, her ear   50
Is deaf. Far northward from here,
In a churchyard high 'mid the moors
Of Yorkshire, a little earth
Stops it for ever to praise.

Where behind Keighley the road
Up to the heart of the moors
Between heath-clad showery hills
Runs, and colliers' carts
Poach the deep ways coming down,
And a rough, grimed race have their homes –   60
There on its slope is built
The moorland place. But the church
Stands on the crest of the hill,
Lonely and bleak; – at its side
The parsonage-house and the graves.

Strew with laurel the grave
Of the early-dying! Alas,
Early she goes on the path
To the silent country, and leaves
Half her laurels unwon,   70
Dying too soon! yet green
Laurels she had, and a course
Short, but redoubled by fame.

And not friendless, and not
Only with strangers to meet,
Faces ungreeting and cold,
Thou, O mourn'd one, to-day
Enterest the house of the grave!
Those of thy blood, whom thou lov'dst,
Have preceded thee – young,   80
Loving, a sisterly band;
Some in art, some in gift
Inferior – all in fame.
They, like friends, shall receive
This comer, greet her with joy;
Welcome the sister, the friend;
Hear with delight of thy fame!

Round thee they lie – the grass
Blows from their graves to thy own!⁵
She, whose genius, though not   90
Puissant like thine, was yet
Sweet and graceful; – and she
(How shall I sing her?) whose soul
Knew no fellow for might,
Passion, vehemence, grief,
Daring, since Byron died,
That world-famed son of fire – she, who sank
Baffled, unknown, self-consumed;

5   not so: Anne Brontë is buried at Scarborough; Charlotte, Emily
(and Branwell) *inside* Haworth church.

Whose too bold dying song
Stirred, like a clarion-blast, my soul.   100

Of one, too, I have heard,
A brother – sleeps he here?
Of all that gifted race
Not the least gifted; young,
Unhappy, eloquent – the child
Of many hopes, of many tears.
O boy, if here thou sleep'st, sleep well!
On thee too did the Muse
Bright in thy cradle smile;
But some dark shadow came   110
(I know not what), and interposed.

Sleep, O cluster of friends,
Sleep! – or only when May,
Brought by the west-wind, returns
Back to your native heaths,
And the plover is heard on the moors,
Yearly awake to behold
The opening summer, the sky,
The shining moorland – to hear
The drowsy bee, as of old,   120
Hum o'er the thyme, the grouse
Call from the heather in bloom!
Sleep, or only for this
Break your united repose!

Epilogue

So I sang; but the Muse,
Shaking her head, took the harp –
Stern interrupted my strain,
Angrily smote on the chords.

April showers
Rush o'er the Yorkshire moors.   130
Stormy, through driving mist,
Loom the blurred hills; the rain
Lashes the newly-made grave.[6]

Unquiet souls!
In the dark fermentation of earth –
In the never idle workshop of nature –
In the eternal movement –
Ye shall find yourselves again!

First published, in a larger version, Fraser's Magazine *(May 1855).*
This version, first in Poems, New and Complete Edition, *2 vols*
(Macmillan & Co., 1877), II.

6   hardly: unless the church roof was leaking.

THYRSIS[1]

A Monody,[2] to Commemorate the Author's Friend, Arthur Hugh Clough, who Died at Florence, 1861[3]

How changed is here each spot man makes or fills!
   In the two Hinkseys nothing keeps the same;
     The village-street its haunted mansion lacks,
   And from the sign is gone Sibylla's name,
     And from the roofs the twisted chimney-stacks;
     Are ye too changed, ye hills?
   See, 'tis no foot of unfamiliar men
     To-night from Oxford up your pathway strays!
   Here came I often, often, in old days;
Thyrsis and I; we still had Thyrsis then.   10

Runs it not here, the track by Childsworth[4] Farm,
   Up past the wood, to where the elm-tree crowns
     The hill behind whose ridge the sunset flames?
   The signal-elm, that looks on Ilsley Downs,
     The Vale, the three lone wears,[5] the youthful
       Thames? –
     This winter-eve is warm,
   Humid the air; leafless, yet soft as spring,
     The tender purple spray on copse and briers;
     And that sweet City with her dreaming spires,
She needs not June for beauty's heightening,   20

Lovely all times she lies, lovely to-night!
   Only, methinks, some loss of habit's power
     Befalls me wandering through this upland dim;
   Once pass'd I blindfold here, at any hour,
     Now seldom come I, since I came with him.
     That single elm-tree bright
   Against the west – I miss it! is it gone?
     We prized it dearly; while it stood, we said,
     Our friend, the Scholar-Gipsy, was not dead;
While the tree lived, he in these fields lived on.   30

Too rare, too rare, grow now my visits here!
   But once I knew each field, each flower, each stick;
     And with the country-folk acquaintance made
   By barn in threshing-time, by new-built rick.
   Here, too, our shepherd-pipes we first assay'd.
     Ah me! this many a year
   My pipe is lost, my shepherd's-holiday!
     Needs must I lose them, needs with heavy heart
     Into the world and wave of men depart;
But Thyrsis of his own will went away.   40

It irk'd him to be here, he could not rest.
   He loved each simple joy the country yields,

THYRSIS
1 pastoral name taken from Greek pastoral poet Theocritus, *Idylls*, and from Virgil's *Eclogues*, vii.
2 claiming affinity with Milton's 'Monody' on the death of *his* friend, *Lycidas*.
3 'Throughout this Poem there is reference to another piece, *The Scholar-Gipsy*, printed in the first volume of the Author's Poems' [original footnote].
4 Chilswell.
5 weirs.

He loved his mates; but yet he could not keep,
   For that a shadow lower'd on the fields,
     Here with the shepherds and the silly sheep.
      Some life of men unblest
   He knew, which made him droop, and filled his head.
    He went; his piping took a troubled sound
    Of storms that rage outside our happy ground;
   He could not wait their passing, he is dead!   50

So, some tempestuous morn in early June,
   When the year's primal burst of bloom is o'er,
    Before the roses and the longest day –
   When garden-walks and all the grassy floor,
     With blossoms, red and white, of fallen May
      And chestnut-flowers are strewn –
   So have I heard the cuckoo's parting cry,
    From the wet field, through the vext garden-trees,
    Come with the volleying rain and tossing breeze:
   The bloom is gone, and with the bloom go I.   60

Too quick despairer, wherefore wilt thou go?
   Soon will the high Midsummer pomps come on,
    Soon will the musk carnations break and swell,
   Soon shall we have gold-dusted snapdragon,
    Sweet-William with his homely cottage-smell,
     And stocks in fragrant blow;
   Roses that down the alleys shine afar,
    And open, jasmine-muffled lattices,
    And groups under the dreaming garden-trees,
   And the full moon, and the white evening-star.[6]   70

He hearkens not! light comer, he is flown!
   What matters it? next year he will return,
    And we shall have him in the sweet spring-days,
   With whitening hedges, and uncrumpling fern,
    And blue-bells trembling by the forest-ways,
     And scent of hay new-mown.
   But Thyrsis never more we swains shall see!
    See him come back, and cut a smoother reed,
    And blow a strain the world at last shall heed –
   For Time, not Corydon, hath conquer'd thee![7]   80

Alack, for Corydon no rival now! –
   But when Sicilian shepherds lost a mate,
    Some good survivor with his flute would go,
   Piping a ditty sad for Bion's fate,[8]
    And cross the unpermitted ferry's flow,
     And relax Pluto's brow,
   And make leap up with joy the beauteous head
    Of Proserpine, among whose crownéd hair
    Are flowers first opened on Sicilian air,
   And flute his friend, like Orpheus, from the dead.   90

---

6 pastoral elegies go in for floral listings, as *Lycidas*, 133–51.
7 Corydon outdoes Thyrsis in singing-contest, Virgil, *Eclogues*, vii.
8 hero of the Greek elegy 'Lament for Bion' (died of poison) – which referred, as such poems tended to, to Orpheus's attempt to get his Eurydice back from the Underworld by wooing its rulers, Pluto and Proserpine, with his music.

O easy access to the hearer's grace
  When Dorian shepherds sang to Proserpine!
    For she herself had trod Sicilian fields,
  She knew the Dorian water's gush divine,
    She knew each lily white which Enna yields,
      Each rose with blushing face;
  She loved the Dorian pipe, the Dorian strain.
    But ah, of our poor Thames she never heard!
    Her foot the Cumner cowslips never stirr'd;
And we should tease her with our plaint in vain.   100

Well! wind-dispers'd and vain the words will be,
  Yet, Thyrsis, let me give my grief its hour
    In the old haunt, and find our tree-topp'd hill!
  Who, if not I, for questing here hath power?
    I know the wood which hides the daffodil,
      I know the Fyfield tree,
  I know what white, what purple fritillaries
    The grassy harvest of the river-fields,
    Above by Ensham,⁹ down by Sandford, yields,
And what sedg'd brooks are Thames's tributaries;   110

I know these slopes; who knows them if not I? –
  But many a dingle on the loved hill-side,
    With thorns once studded, old, white-blossom'd trees,
  Where thick the cowslips grew, and far described
    High tower'd the spikes of purple orchises,
      Hath since our day put by
  The coronals of that forgotten time.
    Down each green bank hath gone the ploughboy's team,
    And only in the hidden brookside gleam
Primroses, orphans of the flowery prime.   120

Where is the girl, who, by the boatman's door,
  Above the locks, above the boating throng,
    Unmoor'd our skiff, when, through the Wytham flats,
  Red loosestrife and blond meadow-sweet among
    And darting swallows and light water-gnats,
      We track'd the shy Thames shore?
  Where are the mowers, who, as the tiny swell
    Of our boat passing heav'd the river-grass,
    Stood with suspended scythe to see us pass? –
They all are gone, and thou art gone as well.   130

Yes, thou art gone! and round me too the night
  In ever-nearing circle weaves her shade.
    I see her veil draw soft across the day,
  I feel her slowly chilling breath invade
    The cheek grown thin, the brown hair sprent¹⁰ with grey;
      I feel her finger light
  Laid pausefully upon life's headlong train;
    The foot less prompt to meet the morning dew,
    The heart less bounding at emotion new,
And hope, once crush'd, less quick to spring again.   140

9 Eynsham.   10 sprinkled.

And long the way appears, which seemed so short
  To the less practis'd eye of sanguine youth;
    And high the mountain-tops, in cloudy air,
The mountain-tops where is the throne of Truth,
    Tops in life's morning-sun so bright and bare!
      Unbreachable the fort
      Of the long-batter'd world uplifts its wall.
        And strange and vain the earthly turmoil grows,
        And near and real the charm of thy repose,
    And night as welcome as a friend would fall.   150

But hush! the upland hath a sudden loss
  Of quiet; – Look! adown the dusk hillside,
    A troop of Oxford hunters going home,
As in old days, jovial and talking, ride!
    From hunting with the Berkshire hounds they come –
      Quick, let me fly, and cross
    Into yon farther field! – 'Tis done; and see,
      Back'd by the sunset, which doth glorify
      The orange and pale violet evening-sky,
    Bare on its lonely ridge, the Tree! the Tree!   160

I take the omen! Eve lets down her veil,
  The white fog creeps from bush to bush about,
    The west unflushes, the high stars grow bright,
And in the scatter'd farms the lights come out.
    I cannot reach the Signal-Tree to-night,
      Yet, happy omen, hail!
    Hear it from thy broad lucent Arno vale[11]
      (For there thine earth-forgetting eyelids keep
      The morningless and unawakening sleep
    Under the flowery oleanders pale),   170

Hear it, O Thyrsis, still our tree is there! –
  Ah, vain! These English fields, this upland dim,
    These brambles pale with mist engarlanded,
That lone, sky-pointing tree, are not for him.
    To a boon southern country he is fled,
      And now in happier air,
    Wandering with the great Mother's[12] train divine
      (And purer or more subtle soul than thee,
      I trow, the mighty Mother doth not see!)
    Within a folding of the Apennine,   180

Thou hearest the immortal chants of old.
  Putting his sickle to the perilous grain
    In the hot cornfield of the Phrygian king,
For thee the Lityerses song again
    Young Daphnis with his silver voice doth sing;
      Sings his Sicilian fold,
    His sheep, his hapless love, his blinded eyes;
      And how a call celestial round him rang,

---

11 Clough is buried in the Protestant Cemetery, Florence.   12 Demeter, mother of Proserpine.

And heavenward from the fountain-brink he sprang,
And all the marvel of the golden skies.[13]   190

There thou art gone, and me thou leavest here
    Sole in these fields; yet will I not despair;
        Despair I will not, while I yet descry
    'Neath the mild canopy of English air
        That lonely Tree against the western sky.
            Still, still these slopes, 'tis clear,
    Our Gipsy-Scholar haunts, outliving thee!
        Fields where soft sheep from cages pull the hay,
        Woods with anemones in flower till May,
    Know him a wanderer still; then why not me?   200

A fugitive and gracious light he seeks,
    Shy to illumine; and I seek it too.
        This does not come with houses or with gold,
    With place, with honour, and a flattering crew;
        'Tis not in the world's market bought and sold.
            But the smooth-slipping weeks
    Drop by, and leave its seeker still untired;
        Out of the heed of mortals he is gone,
        He wends unfollow'd, he must house alone;
    Yet on he fares, by his own heart inspired.   210

Thou too, O Thyrsis, on like quest wert bound;
    Thou wanderedst with me for a little hour;
        Men gave thee nothing, but this happy quest,
    If men esteem'd thee feeble, gave thee power,
        If men procured thee trouble, gave thee rest.
            And this rude Cumner ground,
    Its fir-topped Hurst, its farms, its quiet fields,
        Here cam'st thou in thy jocund youthful time,
        Here was thine height of strength, thy golden prime;
    And still the haunt beloved a virtue yields.   220

What though the music of thy rustic flute
    Kept not for long its happy, country tone;
        Lost it too soon, and learnt a stormy note
    Of men contention-tossed, of men who groan,
        Which task'd thy pipe too sore, and tired thy throat –
            It fail'd, and thou wast mute;
    Yet hadst thou alway visions of our light,
        And long with men of care thou couldst not stay,
        And soon thy foot resumed its wandering way,
    Left human haunt, and on alone till night.   230

Too rare, too rare, grow now my visits here!
    'Mid city-noise, not, as with thee of yore,
        Thyrsis, in reach of sheep-bells is my home!
    Then through the great town's harsh, heart-wearying roar,
        Let in thy voice a whisper often come,
            To chase fatigue and fear:
    Why faintest thou? I wandered till I died.

13   Daphnis, ideal Sicilian shepherd in Greek pastoral tradition, went to Phrygia to rescue his beloved Piplea from King Lityerses, who chal-lenged all-comers to reaping contests. Hercules saved Daphnis, killed Lityerses.

Roam on! The light we sought is shining still.
Dost thou ask proof? Our tree yet crowns the hill,
Our Scholar travels yet the loved hill-side.   240

Mainly written, probably, 1864–5; finished by late Jan. 1866. First published in USA,
Every Saturday (10 March 1866); then Macmillan's Magazine (April 1866).
Text, New Poems (1867), with flown (line 71) for Macmillan's gone, relax (86)
for M's unbend. In 1867 Arnold inserted an epigraph:

'Thus yesterday, to-day, to-morrow come,
They hustle one another and they pass;
But all our hustling morrows only make
The smooth to-day of God.
From Lucretius, an unpublished Tragedy.'

[Not specially relevant to Thyrsis, but put in because Arnold had heard Tennyson was
working on 'Lucretius' – pipping Arnold to the post, after twenty years' preoccupation
with this subject. Arnold never finished his 'Lucretius'.]

GROWING OLD

What is it to grow old?
Is it to lose the glory of the form,
The lustre of the eye?
Is it for beauty to forego her wreath?
Yes, but not this alone.

Is it to feel our strength –
Not our bloom only, but our strength – decay?
Is it to feel each limb
Grow stiffer, every function less exact,
Each nerve more weakly strung?   10

Yes, this, and more; but not
Ah, 'tis not what in youth we dream'd 'twould be!
'Tis not to have our life
Mellow'd and soften'd as with sunset-glow,
A golden day's decline.

'Tis not to see the world
As from a height, with rapt prophetic eyes,
And heart profoundly stirr'd;
And weep, and feel the fullness of the past,
The years that are no more.   20

It is to spend long days
And not once feel that we were ever young;
It is to add, immured
In the hot prison of the present, month
To month with weary pain.

It is to suffer this,
And feel but half, and feebly, what we feel.
Deep in our hidden heart
Festers the dull remembrance of a change,
But no emotion – none.   30

It is – last stage of all –
When we are frozen up within, and quite

The phantom of ourselves,
To hear the world applaud the hollow ghost
Which blamed the living man.

New Poems *(1867). Written, probably, in reply to Browning's 'Rabbi Ben Ezra' –
'Grow old along with me / The best is yet to be' – in* Dramatis Personae *(1864).*

THE PROGRESS OF POESY

A Variation

Youth rambles on life's arid mount,
And strikes the rock, and finds the vein,
And brings the water from the fount,[1]
The fount which shall not flow again.

The man mature with labour chops
For the bright stream a channel grand,
And sees not that the sacred drops
Ran off and vanish'd out of hand.

And then the old man totters nigh,
And feebly rakes among the stones.   10
The mount is mute, the channel dry;
And down he lays his weary bones.

New Poems *(1867)*.

THE LAST WORD

Creep into thy narrow bed,
Creep, and let no more be said!
Vain thy onset! all stands fast;
Thou thyself must break at last.

Let the long contention cease!
Geese are swans, and swans are geese.
Let them have it how they will!
Thou art tired; best be still.

They out-talk'd thee, hiss'd thee, tore thee.
Better men fared thus before thee;   10
Fired their ringing shot and pass'd,
Hotly charged – and broke at last.

Charge once more, then, and be dumb!
Let the victors, when they come,
When the forts of folly fall,
Find thy body by the wall!

New Poems *(1867)*.

THE PROGRESS OF POESY
1 like Moses, in the biblical wilderness.

The Superior Adequacy of Poetry

The men who are the flower and glory of our race are to pass here before us, the highest manifestations, whether on this line or on that, of the force which stirs in every one of us – the chief poets, artists, religious founders, philosophers, historians, scholars, orators, warriors, statesmen, voyagers, leaders in mechanical invention and industry, who have appeared amongst mankind. And the poets are to pass first. Why? Because, of the various modes of manifestation through which the human spirit pours its force, theirs is the most adequate and happy.

The fact of this superior adequacy of poetry is very widely felt; and, whether distinctly seized or no, is the root of poetry's boundless popularity and power. The reason for the fact has again and again been made an object of inquiry. Partial explanations of it have been produced. Aristotle declared poetry to be more philosophical and of more serious worth than history, because poetry deals with generals, history with particulars. Aristotle's idea is expanded by Bacon, after his own fashion, who extols poetry as 'submitting the shews of things to the desires of the mind,' to the desires for 'a more ample greatness, a more exact goodness, and a more absolute variety, than can be found in the nature of things.' No man, however, can fully draw out the reasons why the human spirit feels itself to attain to a more adequate and satisfying expression in poetry than in any other of its modes of activity. For to draw them out fully we should have to go behind our own nature itself, and that we can none of us do. Portions of them we may seize, but not more; Aristotle and Bacon themselves have not succeeded in seizing more than portions of them. And at one time, probably, and to one set of observers, one ground of the primordial and incontestable fact before us comes clearest into light; at another, and to other observers, another.

For us to-day, what ground for the superiority of poetry is the most evident, the most notable? Surely its solidity. Already we have seen Aristotle prefer it to history on this very ground. Poetry has, says he, a higher wisdom and a more serious worth than history. Compare poetry with other efforts of the human spirit besides history. Compare it with art. It is more intellectual than art, more interpretative. Along with the plastic representation it utters the idea, it thinks. Poetry is often called art, and poets are classed with painters and sculptors as artists. But Goethe has with profound truth insisted on the difference between them. 'Poetry is held to be art,' he says, 'and yet it is not, as art is, mechanism, mechanical. I deny poetry to be an art. Neither is it a science. Poetry is to be called neither art nor science, but genius.' Poetry is less artistic than the arts, but in closer correspondence with the intelligential nature of man, who is defined, as we know, to be 'a thinking animal;' poetry thinks, and the arts do not.

But it thinks emotionally, and herein it differs from science, and is more of a stay to us. Poetry gives the idea, but it gives it touched with beauty, heightened by emotion. This is what we feel to be interpretative for us, to satisfy us – thought, but thought invested with beauty, with emotion. Science thinks, but not emotionally. It adds thought to thought, accumulates the elements of a synthesis which will never be complete until it is touched with beauty and emotion; and when it is touched with these, it has passed out of the sphere of science, it has felt the fashioning hand of the poet. So true is this, that the more the follower of science is a complete man, the more he will feel the refreshment of poetry as giving him a satisfaction which our nature is always desiring, but to which his science can never bring him. And the more an artist, on the other hand, is a complete man, the higher he will appreciate the reach and effectualness which poetry gains by being, in Goethe's words, not art but genius; by being from its very nature forbidden to limit itself to the sphere of plastic representation, by being forced to talk and to think.

Poetry, then, is more of a stay to us than art or science. It is more explicative than art, and it has the emotion which to science is wanting. But the grand sources of explication and emotion, in the popular opinion, are philosophy and religion. Philosophy – the love of wisdom – is indeed a noble and immortal aspiration in man. But the philosophies, the constructions of systematic thought which have arisen in the endeavour to satisfy this aspiration, are so perishable that to call up the memory of them is to pass in review man's failures. We have mentioned Goethe, the poet of that land of philosophies, Germany. What a series of philosophic systems has Germany seen since the birth of Goethe! and what sort of a stay is any one of them compared with the poetry of

Germany's one great poet? So necessary, indeed, and so often shown by experience, is the want of solidity in constructions of this kind, that it argues, one may say, a dash of the pedant in a man to approach them, except perhaps in the ardour of extreme youth, with any confidence. And the one philosopher who has known how to give to such constructions, not indeed solidity, but charm, is Plato, the poet among philosophers, who produces his abstractions like the rest, but produces them more than half in play and with a smile.

And religion? The reign of religion as morality touched with emotion is indeed indestructible. But religion as men commonly conceive it – religion depending on the historicalness of certain supposed facts, on the authority of certain received traditions, on the validity of certain accredited dogmas – how much of this religion can be deemed unalterably secure? Not a dogma that does not threaten to dissolve, not a tradition that is not shaken, not a fact which has its historical character free from question. Compare the stability of Shakspeare with the stability of the Thirty-Nine Articles! Our religion has materialised itself in the fact – the supposed fact; it has attached its emotion to the fact. For poetry the idea is everything; the rest is its world of illusion, of divine illusion; it attaches its emotion to the idea, the idea *is* the fact. The strongest part of our religion to-day is its unconscious poetry. The future of poetry is immense, because in conscious poetry, where it is worthy of its high destinies, our race, as time goes on, will find an ever surer and surer stay.

Preface, The Hundred Greatest Men: Portraits of the One Hundred Greatest Men of History, *vol. I,* Poetry: Poets, Dramatists, Novelists *(Sampson Low, Marston, Searle, & Rivington, 1879). The ending was rewritten for the opening of Arnold's essay 'The Study of Poetry' (1880).*

Eliza Keary (?1822–?1889)

The details of Eliza Keary's life are obscure. Her father, William Keary, was an Irishman from Galway who moved to England when he was compelled to sell up in Ireland. His wife, Lucy Plumer, came from Wetherby in Yorkshire. Eliza may have been born in England and is known to have lived as a young girl in Yorkshire – in Nunnington and Hull. William Keary was some kind of preacher. Eliza's brother Charles F. Keary published things and her younger sister Annie wrote novels and poems for children. Eliza brought out a kiddy novel, *The Magic Valley* (1877); published verse for children (as in *At Home Again* and *Pets and Playmates* (both 1887)); was co-author with her sister of *Early Egyptian History For the Young* (1861); edited her sister's letters (1883), and wrote the *Memoir of Annie Keary* (1882). Her most important work is *Little Seal-Skin and Other Poems* (1874) – confessional, Christian, and with a tendency towards being nicely discomposed as to form.

OLD AGE

Such a wizened creature,
   Sitting alone;
     Every kind of ugliness thrown
Into each feature.

'I wasn't always so,'
   Said the wizened
     One; 'sweet motions unimprisoned
Were mine long ago.'

And again, 'I shall be –
   At least something
     Out of this outside me, shall wing
Itself fair and free.'

    10

Little Seal-Skin and Other Poems *(George Bell & Son, 1874).*

LUCY

I found her sitting among the toys,
On a low stool with idle fingers on her knees,
While the slant sunlight crowned her, and as it streamed
Along the shop through tiers of shelves,
Touched the quaint toys with life.   I came to her,
And put my hand upon her arm, saying,
'What is it, Lucy?   The clean floor quiet
From pattering feet, and these smooth shelves, and you
Alone!   No children peering up and down?
Only bright motes swimming upon the dusty air!'   10
She said, 'The children will not come again
To buy, nor I stay here to sell.'   'But why?'
I asked her trembling, for the sweet head drooped
So low.   'Is it some trouble, Lucy – ruin?
May I know?'   Then she looked up at me
With her clear eyes, and said, 'No trouble, madam,
Only a change that breaks my life in two.
Perhaps, one liker to me, one as poor
As all my kin are poor, and one with years
Few as my own – this had been more my dream: 20
I never thought of love in golden guise,
Though I have dreamed one should be this and this,
And all for me – not what *he* is, madam,
He who has come to break my life in two.
Yes, let him break it; he has taken me
With love and tenderness like a father's –'
'But is not your young dream, my Lucy?'   'No,'
The sweet voice made answer; and the drooping head
Drooped lower till it fell on trembling hands.
I sighed, 'Weak woman, who cannot keep
Whole-hearted till her one supreme has come.'

Little Seal-Skin *(1874).*

INCOMPLETE – COMPLETE

I've lived my life some seventy weary years,
And, gathered up on my extreme verge of Time,
Lie looking with blind eyes on the dark sea.
When I looked first at life as now at death
My eyes were like two suns shining in strength
That pierced with sudden glory all they saw.
And 'I will live a glorious life,' I said,
'I will climb heights, I will shine out afar.
My "meant to be" complete in my "I am."'
I am – what am I? weary, sad, and old,   10
I've failed, am weary, failed, and sad, and old;
My light is quenched, 'tis dark, all dark within,
I look at death and death glooms back on me.
Father, what is't? a voice – does it come from Thee,
Dost Thou remember?   Canst Thou pity me?

'Each shall be all I meant in My great day,
Thou hast not failed,' God, do I hear Thee say,
'But seven times purified, art sevenfold dear,
And I've ten cities waiting for thee here.'[1]

Little Seal-Skin *(1874)*.

William (Johnson) Cory (1823–92)

William Johnson, later William Cory, schoolmaster and poet, was born in Torrington, Devon, 9 January 1823, second son of Charles Johnson and his wife Theresa Furse, a vicar's daughter (and a great-niece of Sir Joshua Reynolds). His brother Charles became well known as canon and archdeacon of Westminster Abbey, under the name Charles Furse. William Johnson was a King's Scholar and Newcastle Scholar at Eton, and a Scholar of King's College, Cambridge. At Cambridge he won the Chancellor's Medal in 1843 for an English Poem (on Plato), won the Craven Classical Scholarship in 1844, and became a Fellow of King's in 1845. In the autumn of 1845 he returned to Eton as a teacher of classics and in his twenty-six years there achieved both fame and notoriety for his teaching and for the kind of close interest in his boy charges which characterized many homosexual boarding-school masters, especially high-minded Classicist gays. His pupils remembered him (as Robert Bridges, for example, did) for besottedly preaching up the merits of Tennyson (Cory went in for disparaging Shakespeare, Goethe, Dante). He was also besotted by the passing soldiery – 'Brats, the British army', he'd cry, leading his pupils into the street to watch the Guards going by on their way to Windsor Castle – as well, naturally, as by any beautiful brat who showed literary promise. He copied out his pupil Digby Mackworth Dolben's verses, for instance ('better than Newman', Cory thought). He wrote the words of the 'Eton Boating Song' (mailing the first draft to a former pupil

who was by then a subaltern at Lahore). *Ionica*, Cory's main volume of verse, a not-so-crypto homoerotic handbook from a teacher who drooled over his boys (dedicated to Old Etonian Charles Wood, later Lord Halifax), was published piecemeal (1858, 1877, 1891: *Ionica* II, 1897, being entirely anonymous). It became a cult-book for Etonians and for others pederastically inclined in the Johnson circle. In 1872 Cory abruptly departed Eton (and resigned his King's Fellowship), because, it's thought, of having allowed his erotic interests to carry him even further than usual, and he changed his name to Cory. He had a private income, so money was no problem. He'd published *Nuces* (1869–70), notes on the Latin Primer, and *Lucretius* (1871), a guide to writing Latin lyrics, and he carried on with such-like classical projects. *Iophon*, his manual on writing Greek iambics, appeared in 1873. His slashingly unreliable *Guide to Modern English History* was never completed. In 1878, at Madeira, where he had retreated for his better health, he married a local vicar's daughter, Rosa Caroline de Carteret Guille, and fathered a son. He ended up a private classics teacher to ladies in Hampstead, where he died, 16 June 1892. In the (posthumous) *Extracts from the Letters and Journals of William Cory*, printed by the Oxford University Press for private subscribers (1897), a pleasing sharpness is commonly overwhelmed by a bitching egotism. A. C. Benson introduced an edition of *Ionica* in 1905. Reginald Viscount Esher's memoir *Ionicus* – mainly Cory's letters – appeared in 1923.

AN INVOCATION

I never prayed for Dryads,[1] to haunt the woods again;
More welcome were the presence of hungering, thirsting men,
Whose doubts we could unravel, whose hopes we could fulfil,
Our wisdom tracing backward, the river to the rill,
Were such beloved forerunners one summer day restored,
Then, then we might discover the Muse's mystic hoard.

Oh, dear divine Comatas,[2] I would that thou and I
Beneath this broken sunlight this leisure day might lie;

INCOMPLETE – COMPLETE
1　cf. Luke 8.2: 'Mary Magdalene, out of whom went seven devils'; and Luke 19.7: 'because thou hast been faithful in a very little, have thou authority over ten cities'.

AN INVOCATION
1　tree nymphs (female, of course).
2　name of a fictional (male) pastoral singer in Theocritus, *Idylls*, VII.

Where trees from distant forests, whose names were strange to thee,
Should bend their amorous branches within thy reach to be,   10
And flowers thine Hellas[3] knew not, which art hath made more fair,
Should shed their shining petals upon thy fragrant hair.

Then thou shouldst calmly listen with ever-changing looks
To songs of younger minstrels and plots of modern books,
And wonder at the daring of poets later born,
Whose thoughts are unto thy thoughts as noon-tide is to morn;
And little shouldst thou grudge them their greater strength of soul,
Thy partners in the torch-race, though nearer to the goal.

As when ancestral portraits look gravely from the walls
Upon the youthful baron who treads their echoing halls;   20
And whilst he builds new turrets, the thrice ennobled heir
Would gladly wake his grandsire his home and feast to share;
So from Ægean laurels that hide thine ancient urn
I fain would call thee hither, my sweeter lore to learn.

Or in thy cedarn prison thou waitest for the bee:
Ah, leave that simple honey, and take thy food from me.
My sun is stooping westward. Entrancèd dreamer, haste:
There's fruitage in my garden, that I would have thee taste.
Now lift the lid a moment: now, Dorian shepherd, speak:
Two minds shall flow together, the English and the Greek.   30

Ionica (Smith, Elder, 1858).

HERSILIA[1]

I see her stand with arms a-kimbo,
A blue and blonde *sub aureo nimbo;*[2]
She scans her literary limbo,
The reliques of her teens;
Things like the chips of broken stilts,
Or tatters of embroidered quilts,
Or nosegays tossed away by jilts,
Notes, ballads, tales, and scenes.

Soon will she gambol like a lamb,
Fenced, but not tethered, near the Cam.   10
Maybe she'll swim where Byron swam,
And chat beneath the limes,
Where Arthur, Alfred, Fitz, and Brooks[3]
Lit thought by one another's looks,
Embraced their jests and kicked their books,
In England's happier times;

Ere magic poets felt the gout,
Ere Darwin whelmed the Church in doubt,
Ere Apologia had found out
The round world must be right;   20
When Gladstone, bluest of the blue,

3 Greece.
HERSILIA
1 name of the wife of Romulus, one of Rome's mythical founders.
2 'under a golden (god-like) halo'; a Cambridge (sporting) 'blue' (?).

3 all Trinity College, Cambridge, men – Byron, Arthur Hallam, Alfred Tennyson, FitzGerald – except (?) Brooks (Charles Brooks (?), editor of *Punch*, who did not attend a university).

Read all Augustine's folios through;
When France was tame, and no one knew
We and the Czar would fight.[4]

'Sixty years since' (said dear old Scott;
We're bound, you know, to quote Sir Wat)
This isle had not a sweeter spot
Than Neville's Court by Granta;[5]
No Newnham[6] then, no kirtled scribes,
No Clelia to harangue the tribes,   30
No race for girls, no apple bribes
To tempt an Atalanta.[7]

We males talked fast, we meant to be
World-betterers all at twenty-three,
But somehow failed to level thee,
Oh, battered fort of Edom![8]
Into the breach our daughters press,
Brave patriots in unwarlike dress,
Adepts at thought-in-idleness,
Sweet devotees of freedom.   40

And now it is your turn, fair soul,
To see the fervent car-wheels roll,
Your rivals clashing past the goal,
Some sly Milanion leading
Ah! with them may your Genius bring
Some Celia, some Miss Mannering;
For youthful friendship is a thing
More precious than succeeding.

Ionica *(George Allen, 1891).*

Anna Laetitia Waring (1823–1910)

Anna Laetitia Waring, Welsh hymn-writer, was born at Plas-y-velin, Neath, 19 April 1823, eldest daughter of Elijah and Deborah Waring, cultivated Quakers. There were seven brothers and sisters all told. Anna's favourite younger sister Clara died at the age of twelve, when Anna was eighteen. This traumatic death seems not unconnected with Anna's decision to abandon Quaker practices for the sacramentalism of the Church of England, into which church she was baptized, in Winchester, 15 May 1842, when she was just turned nineteen. This move was encouraged by an uncle who had also turned Anglican, and who wrote hymns. Anna Waring was said, paradoxically, to be both humorously inclined but also grave; passionate but, as Mary S. Talbot, author of the little book *In Remembrance of Anna Letitia [sic] Waring* (1911), put it, with feelings 'kept under strict control'. Verse-writing was her

persistent pastime. In her verses her love of animals is granted unabashed rein ('I like my cat'; 'My little rough dog and I') and her love of Jesus Christ gets almost as free expression. A classic Evangelical spinster of independent means, retiring, pious, learned in her way (she read the Old Testament in Hebrew), but one who also spent much time visiting prisoners in the jails of Bristol, her adopted city ('It is like watching by a filthy gutter to pick out a jewel here and there, as the foul stream goes by'), she blended her intense love of her Saviour with (apparently) love for another woman. This proved rather awkward for her memoirist. 'Her friendships were few, but as might be expected of such a nature, of singular depth and intensity. With one gifted friend for years she maintained an intimate correspondence.' 'Before her death, and after that of this dear friend, A. L. Waring, in

4 Charles Darwin, evolutionist; Newman's *Apologia pro Vita Sua* (1864) ?; Gladstone, Prime Minister; St Augustine; Crimean War.
5 a court in Trinity College, Cambridge, on the River Cam, or Granta.
6 Cambridge college for women, founded 1871.

7 Atalanta, speedy huntress who would only marry man who outpaced her, was tricked by Hippomenes (Milanion) into losing (he dropped 3 distracting golden apples).
8 longstanding biblical enemy of Children of Israel.

accordance with her great natural reserve, destroyed almost all letters and records of these deep affections. Of the few which remain, none are suitable for publication.' Thus, intriguingly, Mary S. Talbot. Waring's *Hymns and Meditations* (1850) sold well, reaching its eleventh thousand by 1870. Her verses were especially liked by American congregations. Her hymn of quiet submission, 'Father, I know that all my life/Is portioned out for me', was, it's claimed, particularly appreciated by hymn-singers everywhere.

Arrestingly, Hymn No. XVIII of *Hymns and Meditations*, 'To———, about leaning on our Saviour's breast' and meeting there with the unnamed friend, was dropped in the volume's later editions. Anna Waring outlived all her siblings, surviving to a grand, if finally extremely painful, old age. She died in Bristol, 10 May 1910, aged 87, bearing 'the gentle pain of patience to the end'. She remains a significant presence in English hymnody.

'I will fear no evil, for Thou art with me.'
Psalm xxiii. 4

In Heavenly Love abiding,
   No change my heart shall fear,
And safe is such confiding,
   For nothing changes here.
The storm may roar without me,
   My heart may low be laid,
But God is round about me,
   And can I be dismayed?

Wherever He may guide me,
   No want shall turn me back;   10
My Shepherd is beside me,
   And nothing can I lack.
His wisdom ever waketh,
   His sight is never dim, –
He knows the way he taketh,
   And I will walk with Him.

Green pastures are before me,
   Which yet I have not seen,
Bright skies will soon be o'er me,
   Where the dark clouds have been.   20
My hope I cannot measure,
   My path to life is free,
My Saviour has my treasure,
   And He will walk with me.

Hymns and Meditations, *by A.L.W. (C. Gilpin, 1850).*

'I believe in the communion of saints.'

'Are they not all ministering spirits, sent forth to minister for them who shall be heirs of salvation.'
Hebrews 1.14

O loving spirit do not go!
   Thy presence is a precious thing;
It makes my tears more softly flow,
   And sweetens every song I sing.
My heart with heavenly comfort fill,
And bring me joyful tidings still.

It soothes my soul to have thee near,
   And I believe that thou wilt stay, –
Because the Lord, thy life, is here,
   And He will never go away.   10

And blest will our communion be,
With thee in Him and Him in thee.

I love to have thee by my side,
    With thy sweet face so pure and bright,
While in my Saviour's robe I hide,
    A robe like thine, exceeding white;
Blest with the blessed ones above,
Seen by His light, and with His love.

Thy soul, to heavenly bliss restored,
    Mine through a sacred veil will see, –   20
That glorious body of our Lord
    Wherein He died for thee and me.
I like that thou shouldst live within,
And know my heart without its sin.

Oft in my secret communings
    With thoughts of those who count thee dear,
I speak to thee of many things
    That others would not care to hear;
Now that no pain thy love can share,
I like to think that *thou* wilt care.   30

I hear thee in the song of birds,
    Thee in the gladdening flowers I see,
And earth has music for the words
    That came to us from heaven through thee.
Hope, joy, the good that God has willed,
Thy hope confirmed – thy joy fulfilled.

I do not bid thee now farewell,
    (A prayer unmeet for life like thine,)
With thy beloved in heaven I dwell,
    And thy beloved on earth are mine.   40
My heart with them, and theirs with thee,
How canst thou, dear one, distant be?

We tarry still upon the road,
    Our path goes on, we know not where,
But God is always our abode,
    And we are sure to meet thee there:
Our life His charge, our work His will,
To love thee is delightful still.

Soon, yes, it must be soon, we know,
    Our work of faith and love complete,   50
We to thy happy home shall go,
    And find thee at our Father's feet.
There His Beloved prepares our place,
And we shall see thee face to face.

Meanwhile, to thee with whom we live
    A hidden life by night and day,
Pain we are sure we cannot give,
    But pleasure I believe we may:
And this belief henceforth shall be
New life, new strength, new joy to me.   60

Hymns and Meditations, *by A.L.W. (1850).*

Coventry (Kersey Dighton) Patmore (1823–96)

Coventry Patmore, eulogist of 'The Angel in the House', was born in Woodford, Essex, 23 July 1823, eldest son of P. G. Patmore, critic and novelist, friend of Leigh Hunt, Hazlitt, Lamb, and editor of the *New Monthly Magazine*. Patmore's schooling was private, mixed, and occasionally French (in 1839), and no doubt helped shape him as a lifelong dabbler – in chemistry, maths, astronomy, farming, architectural theory, prosody. He always made the family fireworks for Guy Fawkes Day. He thought at one time of becoming an Anglican clergyman. His first volume of *Poems* was in 1844. A year later, his father's losses in failed railway investments meant Coventry had to go out to work, in the Printed Books department of the British Museum. In 1847 he married Emily Augusta Andrews, daughter of the Congregationalist minister who taught Ruskin Greek. Patmore contributed two poems and a curious article on *Macbeth* to the Pre-Raphaelite magazine *The Germ*, and it was apparently at his prompting that Ruskin wrote his famous letter to *The Times* in defence of Pre-Raphaelite art. He was not an easy friend, his relation with Tennyson being the great exception. It was Patmore who was sent to search for the mislaid manuscript book of *In Memoriam* verses at Tennyson's old Mornington Street lodgings – and found it in the food cupboard. Emily Patmore was the inspiration for what became Patmore's long verse sequence *The Angel in the House* – a sort of mood music of married life, aphoristic, domesticated (Ruskin liked its 'sparkling humilities'). The origins of the sequence are in the *Tamerton Church Tower and Other Poems* volume (1853). Its two books appeared separately as *The Betrothal*, anonymously, in 1854 and *The Espousals* (1856). Patmore's verse stories of love continued in *Faithful for Ever* (1860) and *The Victories of Love* (1862), the latter written while his wife was dying of consumption. They had three sons and three daughters. Her Protestantism held him back from turning Roman Catholic, but once she died he soon converted, in Rome, in 1864, helped on by the woman who became his second wife, Marianne Caroline Byles. Patmore retired from the Museum to farm in Sussex, before settling in Hastings in The Mansion, which he had admired as a boy. He brought out *The Unknown Eros, and Other Odes* (1877 and 1878) and *Amelia* (1878). One of his closest literary relationships was with Gerard Manley Hopkins, conducted mainly by correspondence, with Hopkins being extremely critical, tetchy, high-handed, tactless, about almost everything of Patmore's – poems, poetics, ideas of religion, women, politics. But then Patmore's poetics were often mocked (Tennyson, for example, sneered at the dicta on metre that appeared in the *North British Review*, 1857). Patmore's second wife died in 1880, and is commemorated in the Roman Catholic church in Hastings which Patmore commissioned from Basil Champneys (later Patmore's biographer). In 1881 he married his daughter's governess Harriet Robson and they had a son. But his poetry-writing days were virtually over. His favourite daughter Emily died in 1882, and his son Henry in 1883. On Christmas Day 1887 he burned his big MS of *Sponsa Dei*, meditations on love, physical and spiritual, accumulated over ten years, blaming Hopkins, who'd suggested they might lead 'the general reading public' astray. He went on writing prose. Critical collections appeared as *Principle in Art* (1889) and *Religio Poetae* (1893). A volume of meditations and aphorisms, many of them religious, *Rod, Root, and Flower* came out in 1895. In his last years Patmore was friendly with W. E. Henley, Francis Thompson and the Meynells. He died at Lymington, after a bout of pneumonia, 26 November 1896.

FROM: THE ANGEL IN THE HOUSE

The Paragon

When I behold the skies aloft
    Passing the pageantry of dreams,
The cloud whose bosom, cygnet-soft,
    A couch for nuptial Juno seems;
The ocean broad, the mountains bright,
    The shadowy vales with feeding herds,
I from my lyre the music smite,
    Nor want for justly matching words.
All powers of the sea and air,
    All interests of hill and plain,

I so can sing, in seasons fair,
   That who hath felt may feel again.
Elated oft by such free songs,
   I think with utterance free to raise
That hymn for which the whole world longs,
   A worthy hymn in woman's praise;
A hymn bright-noted like a bird's,
   Arousing these song-sleepy times
With rhapsodies of perfect words,
   Ruled by returning kiss of rhymes.   20
But when I look on her and hope
   To tell with joy what I admire,
My thoughts lie cramp'd in narrow scope,
   Or in the feeble birth expire;
No mystery of well-woven speech,
   No simplest phrase of tenderest fall,
No liken'd excellence can reach
   Her, the most excellent of all,
The best half of creation's best,
   Its heart to feel, its eye to see,   30
The crown and complex of the rest,
   Its aim and its epitome.
Nay, might I utter my conceit,
   'Twere after all a vulgar song,
For she's so simply, subtly sweet,
   My deepest rapture does her wrong.
Yet is it now my chosen task
   To sing her worth as Maid and Wife;
Nor happier post than this I ask,
   To live her laureate all my life.   40
On wings of love uplifted free,
   And by her gentleness made great,
I'll teach how noble man should be
   To match with such a lovely mate;
And then in her may move the more
   The woman's wish to be desired,
(By praise increased,) till both shall soar,
   With blissful emulations fired.
And, as geranium, pink, or rose
   Is thrice itself through power of art,   50
So may my happy skill disclose
   New fairness even in her fair heart;
Until that churl shall nowhere be
   Who bends not, awed, before the throne
Of her affecting majesty,
   So meek, so far unlike our own;
Until (for who may hope too much
   From her who wields the powers of love?)
Our lifted lives at last shall touch
   That happy goal to which they move;   60
Until we find, as darkness rolls
   Away, and evil mists dissolve,
The nuptial contrasts are the poles
   On which the heavenly spheres revolve.

The Angel in the House, Poems, *vol. 2 (George Bell & Sons, 1879), Bk I Canto II,
'Mary and Mildred, Preludes, I'. First version, The Angel in the House, The Betrothal
(John W. Parker, 1854), II. 'Mary and Mildred, The Accompaniments. I. The Paragon'.*

The Wife's Tragedy

Man must be pleased; but him to please
　　Is woman's pleasure; down the gulf
Of his condoled necessities
　　She casts her best, she flings herself.
How often flings for nought, and yokes
　　Her heart to an icicle or whim,
Whose each impatient word provokes
　　Another, not from her, but him;
While she, too gentle even to force
　　His penitence by kind replies,　　　　　　　　　　　　10
Waits by, expecting his remorse,
　　With pardon in her pitying eyes;
And if he once, by shame oppress'd,
　　A comfortable word confers,
She leans and weeps against his breast,
　　And seems to think the sin was hers;
And whilst his love has any life,
　　Or any eye to see her charms,
At any time, she's still his wife,
　　Dearly devoted to his arms;　　　　　　　　　　　　20
She loves with love that cannot tire;
　　And when, ah woe, she loves alone,
Through passionate duty love springs higher,
　　As grass grows taller round a stone.

　　　　　　　　The Angel in the House, Poems, *vol. 2 (1879), Bk I, Canto IX,*
'Sahara. Preludes, I'. First version, The Angel in the House, The Betrothal
(1854), Canto IX. 'The Railway. The Accompaniments. 2. The Wife's Tragedy'.

The Foreign Land

A woman is a foreign land,
　　Of which, though there he settle young,
A man will ne'er quite understand
　　The customs, politics, and tongue.
The foolish hie them post-haste through,
　　See fashions odd, and prospects fair,
Learn of the language, 'How d'ye do,'
　　And go and brag they have been there.
The most for leave to trade apply,
　　For once, at Empire's seat, her heart,　　　　　　　　10
Then get what knowledge ear and eye
　　Glean chancewise in the life-long mart.
And certain others, few and fit,
　　Attach them to the Court, and see
The Country's best, its accent hit,
　　And partly sound its polity.

　　　　　　　　The Angel in the House, Poems, *vol. 2 (1879), Bk II, Canto IX,*
'The Friends, Preludes, 2'. Not in earlier editions/ versions of the poem.

Felicity

To marry her and take her home!
　　The poet, painting pureness, tells

Of lilies; figures power by Rome;
  And each thing shows by something else!
But through the songs of poets look,
  And who so lucky to have found
In universal nature's book
  A likeness for a life so crown'd!
Here they speak best who best express
  Their inability to speak,   10
And none are strong, but who confess
  With happy skill that they are weak.

The Angel in the House, Poems, *vol. 2 (1879), Bk II, Canto X, 'The Epitaph.*
Preludes, 2'. Earlier version, The Angel in the House, *2nd edn*
(John W. Parker & Son, 1857), The Espousals, *Bk II, Canto X, 'The Epitaph,*
Preludes, 3'. Not in The Espousals, The Angel in the House, *Bk II*
(John W. Parker, 1856).

The Married Lover

Why, having won her, do I woo?
  Because her spirit's vestal grace
Provokes me always to pursue,
  But, spirit-like, eludes embrace;
Because her womanhood is such
  That, as on court-days subjects kiss
The Queen's hand, yet so near a touch
  Affirms no mean familiarness,
Nay, rather marks more fair the height
  Which can with safety so neglect   10
To dread, as lower ladies might,
  That grace could meet with disrespect,
Thus she with happy favour feeds
  Allegiance from a love so high
That thence no false conceit proceeds
  Of difference bridged, or state put by;
Because, although in act and word
  As lowly as a wife can be,
Her manners, when they call me lord,
  Remind me 'tis by courtesy;   20
Not with her least consent of will,
  Which would my proud affection hurt,
But by the noble style that still
  Imputes an unattain'd desert;
Because her gay and lofty brows,
  When all is won which hope can ask,
Reflect a light of hopeless snows
  That bright in virgin ether bask;
Because, though free of the outer court
  I am, this Temple keeps its shrine   30
Sacred to Heaven; because, in short,
  She's not and never can be mine.

The Angel in the House, Poems, *vol. 2 (1879), Bk II, Canto XII,*
'Husband and Wife. Preludes, 1'. Earlier version, The Angel in the House, *2nd edn,*
The Espousals, *Bk II, Canto XII, 'Husband and Wife. Preludes, 1'. Not in*
The Espousals *(1856).*

WINTER

I, singularly moved
To love the lovely that are not beloved,
Of all the Seasons, most
Love Winter, and to trace
The sense of the Trophonian pallor on her face.[1]
It is not death, but plenitude of peace;
And the dim cloud that does the world enfold
Hath less the characters of dark and cold
Than warmth and light asleep,
And correspondent breathing seems to keep   10
With the infant harvest, breathing soft below
Its eider coverlet of snow;
Nor is in field or garden anything
But, duly look'd into, contains serene
The substance of things hoped for, in the Spring,
And evidence of Summer not yet seen.[2]
On every chance-mild day
That visits the moist shaw,
The honeysuckle, 'sdaining to be crost
In urgence of sweet life by sleet or frost,   20
'Voids the time's law
With still increase
Of leaflet new, and little, wandering spray;
Often, in sheltering brakes,
As one from rest disturb'd in the first hour,
Primrose or violet bewilder'd wakes,
And deems 'tis time to flower;
Though not a whisper of her voice he hear,
The buried bulb does know
The signals of the year,   30
And hails far Summer with his lifted spear.
The gorse-field dark, by sudden, gold caprice,
Turns, here and there, into a Jason's fleece;[3]
Lilies, that soon in Autumn slipp'd their gowns of green,
And vanish'd into earth,
And came again, ere Autumn died, to birth,
Stand full-array'd, amidst the wavering shower,
And perfect for the Summer, less the flower;
In nook of pale or crevice of crude bark,
Thou canst not miss,   40
If close thou spy, to mark
The ghostly chrysalis,
That, if thou touch it, stirs in its dream dark;
And the flush'd Robin, in the evenings hoar,
Does of Love's Day, as if he saw it, sing;
But sweeter yet than dream or song of Summer or Spring
Are Winter's sometime smiles, that seem to well
From infancy ineffable;
Her wandering, languorous gaze,
So unfamiliar, so without amaze,   50

WINTER
1 Trophonius, builder of Temple of Apollo at Delphi; after death became oracle (cave at Lebadeia): so awesome nobody smiled after consulting it.

2 Faith is 'the substance of things hoped for, the evidence of things not seen', Hebrews 11.1.

3 Jason, ancient Greek saga hero, led Argonaut expedition to recover Golden Fleece.

On the elemental, chill adversity,
The uncomprehended rudeness; and her sigh
And solemn, gathering tear,
And look of exile from some great repose, the sphere
Of ether, moved by ether only, or
By something still more tranquil.

'The Unknown Eros', *Bk I. III. In* The Unknown Eros, Poems, *4 vols*
(George Bell & Sons, 1879), vol. IV.

THE TOYS

My little Son, who look'd from thoughtful eyes
And moved and spoke in quiet grown-up wise,
Having my law the seventh time disobey'd,
I struck him, and dismiss'd
With hard words and unkiss'd,
His Mother, who was patient, being dead.
Then, fearing lest his grief should hinder sleep,
I visited his bed,
But found him slumbering deep,
With darken'd eyelids, and their lashes yet   10
From his late sobbing wet.
And I, with moan,
Kissing away his tears, left others of my own;
For, on a table drawn beside his head,
He had put, within his reach,
A box of counters and a red-vein'd stone,
A piece of glass abraded by the beach
And six or seven shells,
A bottle with bluebells
And two French copper coins, ranged there with careful art,   20
To comfort his sad heart.
So when that night I pray'd
To God, I wept, and said:
Ah, when at last we lie with tranced breath,
Not vexing Thee in death,
And Thou rememberest of what toys
We made our joys,
How weakly understood,
Thy great commanded good,
Then, fatherly not less   30
Than I whom Thou hast moulded from the clay,
Thou'lt leave Thy wrath, and say,
'I will be sorry for their childishness.'

Pall Mall Gazette *(30 November 1876).* The Unknown Eros, and Other Odes
(George Bell & Sons, 1877), Ode XI. The Unknown Eros *(1879), Bk I. X.*

ARBOR VITAE[1]

With honeysuckle, over-sweet, festoon'd;
With bitter ivy bound;

ARBOR VITAE
1 Tree of Life.

Terraced with funguses unsound;
Deform'd with many a boss
And closed scar, o'ercushion'd deep with moss;
Bunch'd all about with pagan mistletoe;
And thick with nests of the hoarse bird
That talks, but understands not his own word;
Stands, and so stood a thousand years ago,
A single tree.   10
Thunder has done its worst among its twigs,
Where the great crest yet blackens, never pruned,
But in its heart, alway
Ready to push new verdurous boughs, whene'er
The rotting saplings near it fall and leave it air,
Is all antiquity and no decay.
Rich, though rejected by the forest-pigs,
Its fruit, beneath whose rough, concealing rind
They that will break it find
Heart-succouring savour of each several meat,   20
And kernell'd drink of brain-renewing power,
With bitter condiment and sour,
And sweet economy of sweet,
And odours that remind
Of haunts of childhood and a different day.
Beside this tree,
Praising no Gods nor blaming, sans a wish,
Sits, Tartar-like,[2] the Time's civility,
And eats its dead-dog off a golden dish.

The Week (5 January 1878). The Unknown Eros (1879), Bk II. III.

To The Body

Creation's and Creator's crowning good;
Wall of infinitude;
Foundation of the sky,
In Heaven forecast
And long'd for from eternity,
Though laid the last;
Reverberating dome,
Of music cunningly built home
Against the void and indolent disgrace
Of unresponsive space;   10
Little, sequester'd pleasure-house
For God and for His Spouse;
Elaborately, yea, past conceiving, fair,
Since, from the graced decorum of the hair,
Ev'n to the tingling, sweet
Soles of the simple, earth-confiding feet,
And from the inmost heart
Outward unto the thin
Silk curtains of the skin,
Every least part   20
Astonish'd hears

2   like Tartarus: Hell? Like a Tartar: a rough oppressor?

And sweet replies to some like region of the spheres;
Form'd for a dignity prophets but darkly name,
Lest shameless men cry 'Shame!'
So rich with wealth conceal'd
That Heaven and Hell fight chiefly for this field;
Clinging to everything that pleases thee
With indefectible fidelity;
Alas, so true
To all thy friendships that no grace   30
Thee from thy sin can wholly disembrace;
Which thus 'bides with thee as the Jebusite,
That, maugre all God's promises could do,
The chosen People never conquer'd quite;
Who therefore lived with them,
And that by formal truce and as of right,
In metropolitan Jerusalem.[1]
For which false fealty
Thou needs must, for a season, lie
In the grave's arms, foul and unshriven,   40
Albeit, in Heaven,
Thy crimson-throbbing Glow
Into its old abode aye pants to go,
And does with envy see
Enoch, Elijah, and the Lady, she
Who left the lilies in her body's lieu.[2]
O, if the pleasures I have known in thee
But my poor faith's poor first-fruits be,
What quintessential, keen, ethereal bliss
Then shall be his   50
Who has thy birth-time's consecrating dew
For death's sweet chrism retain'd,
Quick, tender, virginal, and unprofaned!

The Unknown Eros (1879), Bk II. VII.

THE GIRL OF ALL PERIODS

An Idyll

'And even our women,' lastly grumbles Ben,
'Leaving their nature, dress and talk like men!'
A damsel, as our train stops at Five Ashes,
Down to the station in a dog-cart dashes.
A footman buys her ticket, 'Third class, parly;'
And, in huge-button'd coat and 'Champagne Charley'[1]
And such scant manhood else as use allows her,
Her two shy knees bound in a single trouser,[2]
With, 'twixt her shapely lips, a violet
Perch'd as a proxy for a cigarette,   10
She takes her window in our smoking carriage,

TO THE BODY
1 Joshua 15.63.
2 biblical Enoch and Elijah, plus the Virgin Mary: who went to hea-
ven (Catholic doctrine – of Assumption of Blessed Virgin Mary) with-
out dying.

THE GIRL OF ALL PERIODS
1 a hat? named after ritzy man-about-town (a 'Champagne Charley')?
2 ? tight skirt?

And scans us, calmly scorning men and marriage.
Ben frowns in silence; older, I know better
Than to read ladies 'haviour in the letter.
This aping man is crafty Love's devising
To make the woman's difference more surprising;
And, as for feeling wroth at such rebelling
Who'd scold the child for now and then repelling
Lures with 'I won't!' or for a moment's straying
In its sure growth towards more full obeying?   20
'Yes, she had read the "Legend of the Ages,"[3]
'And George Sand[4] too, skipping the wicked pages.'
And, whilst we talk'd, her protest firm and perky
Against mankind, I thought, grew lax and jerky;
And, at a compliment, her mouth's compressure
Nipt in its birth a little laugh of pleasure;
And smiles, forbidden her lips, as weakness horrid,
Broke, in grave lights, from eyes and chin and forehead;
And, as I push'd kind 'vantage 'gainst the scorner,
The two shy knees press'd shier to the corner;   30
And Ben began to talk with her, the rather
Because he found out that he knew her father,
Sir Francis Applegarth, of Fenny Compton,
And danced once with her sister Maude at Brompton;
And then he stared until he quite confused her,
More pleased with her than I, who but excused her;
And, when she got out, he, with sheepish glances,
Said he'd stop too, and call on old Sir Francis.

Amelia, Tamerton Church Tower, Etc. *(George Bell & Sons, 1878).*

William Brighty Rands (also 'Matthew Browne' and 'Henry Holbeach') (1823–82)

William Brighty Rands, poet, journalist, writer of novels and hymns and for children, was born in Keppel Street, Chelsea, on Christmas Eve 1823, son of a candle-maker. He obtained work variously in a warehouse, as an actor, as an attorney's clerk, then (May 1857 to August 1875) as a parliamentary reporter. He wrote prose and verse prolifically under an array of pseudonyms as well as in his own name – Henry Holbeach, Matthew Browne, Timon Fieldmouse. From October 1855 until June 1871 he was 'The Literary Lounger' of the *Illustrated Times*. He appeared in the *Contemporary Review* as both Henry Holbeach and Matthew Browne. *Chain of Lilies and Other Poems* (1857) appears to be his first volume of verse. He made his name, if that is the word, as a children's writer, one of the large group of writers powerfully entering the miniaturized world of the Victorian child, with *Lilliput Levee* (1864 – illustrated by John Everett Millais and G. J. Pinwell; it went into several editions), *Lilliput Revels* (1871), *Lilliput Lectures* (1871) and *Lilliput Legends* (1872) – all by Anon. His novel *Henry Holbeach, Student in Life and Philosophy*, by Henry Holbeach, was published in 1865, followed by Holbeach's *Shoemaker's Village* (1871). Matthew Browne's *Verses and Opinions* came out in 1861, followed by his *Chaucer's England* (2 vols, 1869). William Brighty Rands died at his home, Luton Villa, Ondine Road, East Dulwich, 23 April 1882.

3   presumably Victor Hugo's long poem *La Légende des Siècles* (1859)   4   French novelist deemed naughtily emancipatory.

DOLL POEMS

I

The Picture

This is her picture – Dolladine –
The beautifullest doll that ever was seen!
Oh, what nosegays! Oh, what sashes!
Oh, what beautiful eyes and lashes!

Oh, what a precious perfect pet!
On each instep a pink rosette;
Little blue shoes for her little blue tots;
Elegant ribbons in bows and knots.

Her hair is powdered; her arms are straight,
Only feel – she is quite a weight!   10
Her legs are limp, though; – stand up, miss! –
What a beautiful buttoned-up mouth to kiss!

II

The Love Story

This is the doll with respect to whom
A story is told that ends in gloom;
For there was a sensitive little sir
Went out of his mind for love of her!

They pulled a wire, she moved her eye;
They squeezed the bellows, they made her cry;
But the boy could never be persuaded
That these were really things which *they* did.

'My Dolladine,' he said, 'has life;
I love her, and she shall be my wife;   10
Dainty delicate Dolladine,
The prettiest girl that ever was seen!'

To give his passion a chance to cool,
They sent the lover to boarding-school.
But absence only made it worse –
He never learnt anything, prose or verse!

He drew her likeness on his slate;
His Grammar was in a *dreadful* state,
With Dolladine all over the edges,
And true-love knots, and vows, and pledges.   20

What was the consequence? – Doctor Whack
Begged of his parents to take him back.
When his condition, poor boy, was seen,
Too late, they sent for Dolladine.

And now he will never part with her:
He calls her lily, and rose, and myrrh,
Dolly-o'-diamonds, precious lamb,
Humming-bird, honey-pot, jewel, jam,

Darling, delicate-dear-delight,
Angel-o'-red, angel-o'-white,   30
Queen of beauty, and suchlike names;
In fact all manner of darts and flames!

Of course, while he keeps up this wooing
His education goes to ruin:
What are his prospects in future life,
With only a doll for his lawful wife?

It is feared his parents' hearts will break!
And there's one remark I wish to make:
I may be wrong, but it seems a pity
For a movable doll to be made too pretty.   40

An old-fashioned doll, that is not like nature,
Can never pass for a human creature;
It is in a doll that moves her eyes
That the danger of these misfortunes lies!

The lover's name must be suppressed
For obvious reasons. He lives out west,
And if I call him Pygmalion Pout,
I don't believe you will find him out!

III

Dressing Her

This is the way we dress the Doll: –
You may make her a shepherdess, the Doll,
If you give her a crook with a pastoral hook,
But this is the way we dress the Doll.

Chorus
Bless the Doll, you may press the Doll,
But do not crumple and mess the Doll!
This is the way we dress the Doll.

First, you observe her little chemise,
As white as milk, with ruches of silk;
And the little drawers that cover her knees,   10
As she sits or stands, with golden bands,
And lace in beautiful filagrees.

Chorus
Bless the Doll, you may press the Doll,
But do not crumple or mess the Doll!
This is the way we dress the Doll.

Now these are the bodies: she has two,
One of pink, with ruches of blue,
And sweet white lace; be careful, do!
And one of green, with buttons of sheen,
Buttons and bands of gold, I mean,   20
With lace on the border in lovely order,
The most expensive we can afford her!

Chorus

Bless the Doll, you may press the Doll,
But do not crumple or mess the Doll!
This is the way we dress the Doll.

Then, with black at the border, jacket;
And this – and this – she will not lack it;
Skirts? Why, there are skirts, of course,
And shoes and stockings we shall enforce,
With a proper bodice, in the proper place   30
(Stays that lace have had their days
And made their martyrs); likewise garters,
All entire. But our desire

Is to show you her night attire,
At least a part of it. Pray admire
This sweet white thing that she goes to bed in!
It's not the one that's made for her wedding;
That is special, a new design,
Made with a charm and a countersign,
Three times three and nine times nine: 40
These are only her usual clothes:
Look, *there's* a wardrobe! gracious knows
It's pretty enough, as far as it goes!

So you see the way we dress the Doll:
You might make her a shepherdess, the Doll,
If you gave her a crook with a pastoral hook,
With sheep, and a shed, and a shallow brook,
And all that, out of the poetry-book.

Chorus

Bless the Doll, you may press the Doll,
But do not crumple or mess the Doll!
This is the way we dress the Doll;
If you had not seen, could you guess the Doll?

Lilliput Lyrics *(John Lane the Bodley Head, 1899).*

William Allingham (also 'D. Pollex' and 'Patricius Walker') (1824–89)

William Allingham, Irish poet, editor, and Boswell to Alfred Tennyson's Dr Johnson, was born in a little house next to the harbour in Ballyshannon, County Donegal, 19 March 1824. The Protestant Allinghams had been in Ireland since Elizabethan times. Allingham's father was a timber importer with a small fleet of ships. The boy was taken from school to become a clerk in the Ballyshannon Provincial Bank at the age of fourteen, but educated himself by hard reading. Aged twenty-two he left banking to become a customs officer, serving variously in Belfast (where he 'preached Tennyson' to the clerks), Donegal Town, Ramsey on the Isle of Man, Coleraine and Ballyshannon. He developed literary ambitions, corresponded with Leigh Hunt, began regular lionizing pilgrimages to England, where through Hunt he met Carlyle and, through Coventry Patmore, got on very good terms with D. G. Rossetti (who illustrated several of Allingham's volumes) and with Alfred Tennyson. A poem of his, 'The Wayside Well', appeared in the very first number of *Household Words*. He contributed to that journal for several years, and thought that poems of his had given things to *Great Expectations* and *A Tale of Two Cities*. He sent his first volume of *Poems* to Tennyson, first met the great man in 1851, and fell into a devoted discipular posture from which he never straightened up.

When Tennyson read some of Allingham's work aloud, it 'never seemed to me so good before or since'. *Day and Night Songs* (1854) made Allingham's name. A subsequent edition was illustrated by Rossetti and Millais. Volumes of his verse appeared every few years, many of them containing revised versions of poems published earlier. He was very popular: his verses were hawked about by ballad-sellers. In 1863 he moved from Ballyshannon Customs House to the one at Lymington – rather nearer to Tennyson, and his *Diary* (published 1907) is second to none as a revealing record of the sharp-tongued Laureate's words and doings from 1863 until 1889. What Allingham thought of as his own greatest work, an epic of kindly Irish landlordism, *Laurence Bloomfield in Ireland*, appeared in 1864. Turgenev is reported as saying upon reading it that he 'never understood Ireland before'. Yeats's view, though, was that Allingham 'sang Ballyshannon not Ireland'. The fame of *Bloomfield* earned its author a Civil List Pension of £60, later raised to £200. In 1870, egged on by Carlyle, Allingham retired from the customs service to become sub-editor, under J. A. Froude, of *Fraser's Magazine*, to which he had long contributed. Patricius Walker's *Rambles* appeared in 1873. In 1874 Allingham succeeded Froude as editor of *Fraser's* and married Helen Paterson (half his age). The inspiration who replaced Ballyshannon, so to say, as muse, she became a well-known water-colourist and illustrator (for example, she illustrated Hardy's *Far From the*

Madding Crowd in the *Cornhill*, 1874). Allingham went on editing *Fraser's* for five years. A fall from a horse greatly impaired his well-being. In 1884 he brought out a volume of unusually waspish, cynical poetic jottings, *Blackberries*, in the name of D. Pollex ('England! Leave Asia, Africa, alone/And mind this little country of thine own', *et si qua alia*). He died at his home in Hampstead, 18 November 1889. His last words, 'I am seeing things you know nothing of', were a great consolation to the ageing Tennyson, who reported them often. This did nothing, however, for Allingham's reputation. The English critics tended to denigrate him, not least for Irishness. ('He has the fluency and ease of verse which has been again and again noticed as common in Irish poets; but he has been allowed by competent critics to be dull, tame and uninventive': thus George Saintsbury in his *Cambridge History of English Literature* – before proceeding to misquote 'Up the airy mountain'.) A definitive collection of Allingham's verse appeared in six volumes, 1888–93. Yeats edited *Sixteen Poems* for his sister's Dun Emer Press (1905). Allingham's widow Helen edited a selection of his *Poems* (1912) and a collection of remains (*By the Way*, also 1912). The Ulster poet John Hewitt wrote a fine introduction to his selection (Dolmen Press, 1967). Yeats said Allingham was a 'minor immortal', and told Mrs Allingham he was 'sometimes inclined to believe that he was my own master in Irish verse, starting me in the way I have gone whether for good or ill'.

THE FAIRIES

A Nursery Song

Up the airy mountain,
    Down the rushy glen,
We daren't go a hunting
    For fear of little men;
Wee folk, good folk,
    Trooping all together;
Green jacket, red cap,
    And grey-cock's feather!

Down along the rocky shore
    Some make their home,   10
They live on crispy pancakes
    Of yellow tide-foam;
Some in the reeds
    Of the black mountain-lake,
With frogs for their watch-dogs,
    All night awake.

High on the hill-top
    The old King sits;
He is now so old and grey
    He's nigh lost his wits.   20
With a bridge of white mist
    Columbkill he crosses,
On his stately journeys

From Slieveleague to Rosses;[1]
Or going up with music
    On cold starry nights,
To sup with the Queen
    Of the gay Northern Lights.

They stole little Bridget
    For seven years long;   30
When she came down again
    Her friends were all gone.
They took her lightly back,
    Between the night and morrow,
They thought that she was fast asleep,
    But she was dead with sorrow.
They have kept her ever since
    Deep within the lakes,
On a bed of flag-leaves,
    Watching till she wakes.   40

By the craggy hill-side,
    Through the mosses bare,
They have planted thorn-trees
    For pleasure here and there.
Is any man so daring
    As dig up one in spite,
He shall find the thornies set
    In his bed at night.

Up the airy mountain,
    Down the rushy glen,   50
We daren't go a hunting
    For fear of little men;
Wee folk, good folk,
    Trooping all together;
Green jacket, red cap,
    And grey-cock's feather!

Written 1849. Version in Poems *(Chapman & Hall, 1850).*

THE WINDING BANKS OF ERNE

Or, The Emigrant's Adieu to Ballyshannon (A Local Ballad)

I

Adieu to Ballyshannon! where I was bred and born;
Go where I may, I'll think of you, as sure as night and morn,
The kindly spot, the friendly town, where every one is known,
And not a face in all the place but partly seems my own;
There's not a house or window, there's not a field or hill,
But, east or west, in foreign lands, I'll recollect them still.
I leave my warm heart with you, though my back I'm forced to turn –
So adieu to Ballyshannon, and the winding banks of Erne!

THE FAIRIES
1   Glenn Columbkill, Slieveleague, Rosses: places in western Donegal.

2

No more on pleasant evenings we'll saunter down the Mall,
When the trout is rising to the fly, the salmon to the fall.   10
The boat comes straining on her net, and heavily she creeps,
Cast off, cast off! – she feels the oars, and to her berth she sweeps;
Now fore and aft keep hauling, and gathering up the clue,[1]
Till a silver wave of salmon rolls in among the crew.
Then they may sit, with pipes a-lit, and many a joke and 'yarn'; –
Adieu to Ballyshannon, and the winding banks of Erne!

3

The music of the waterfall, the mirror of the tide,
When all the green-hill'd harbour is full from side to side –
From Portnasun to Bulliebawns, and round the Abbey Bay,
From rocky Inis Saimer to Coolnargit sandhills grey;   20
While far upon the southern line, to guard it like a wall,
The Leitrim mountains, clothed in blue, gaze calmly over all,
And watch the ship sail up or down, the red flag at her stern; –
Adieu to these, adieu to all the winding banks of Erne!

4

Farewell to you, Kildoney lads, and them that pull an oar,
A lug-sail set, or haul a net, from the Point to Mullaghmore;
From Killybegs to bold Slieve-League, that ocean-mountain steep,
Six hundred yards in air aloft, six hundred in the deep;
From Dooran to the Fairy Bridge, and round by Tullen strand,
Level and long, and white with waves, where gull and curlew stand; – 30
Head out to sea when on your lee the breakers you discern! –
Adieu to all the billowy coast, and winding banks of Erne!

5

Farewell Coolmore, – Bundoran! and your summer crowds that run
From inland homes to see with joy th' Atlantic-setting sun:
To breathe the buoyant salted air, and sport among the waves;
To gather shells on sandy beach, and tempt the gloomy caves;
To watch the flowing, ebbing tide, the boats, the crabs, the fish;
Young men and maids to meet and smile, and form a tender wish;
The sick and old in search of health, for all things have their turn –
And I must quit my native shore, and the winding banks of Erne!   40

6

Farewell to every white cascade from the Harbour to Belleek,
And every pool where fins may rest, and ivy-shaded creek;
The sloping fields, the lofty rocks, where ash and holly grow,
The one split yew-tree gazing on the curving flood below;
The Lough, that winds through islands under Turaw mountain green;
And Castle Caldwell's stretching woods, with tranquil bays between;
And Breesie Hill, and many a pond among the heath and fern, –
For I must say adieu – adieu to the winding banks of Erne!

7

The thrush will call through Camlin groves the live-long summer day;
The waters run by mossy cliff, and bank with wild flowers gay;   50
The girls will bring their work and sing beneath a twisted thorn,

THE WINDING BANKS OF ERNE
1 or clew: ball of string, twine, rope.

Or stray with sweethearts down the path among the growing corn;
Along the river side they go, where I have often been, –
O, never shall I see again the days that I have seen!
A thousand chances are to one I never may return, –
Adieu to Ballyshannon, and the winding banks of Erne!

8

Adieu to evening dances, when merry neighbours meet,
And the fiddle says to boys and girls, 'Get up and shake your feet!'
To 'shanachus'[2] and wise old talk of Erin's days gone by –
Who trench'd the rath on such a hill, and where the bones may lie   60
Of saint, or king, or warrior chief; with tales of fairy power,
And tender ditties sweetly sung to pass the twilight hour.
The mournful song of exile is now for me to learn –
Adieu, my dear companions on the winding banks of Erne!

9

Now measure from the Commons down to each end of the Purt,
Round the Abbey, Moy, and Knather, – I wish no one any hurt;
The Main Street, Back Street, College Lane, the Mall, and Portnasun,
If any foes of mine are there, I pardon every one.
I hope that man and womankind will do the same by me;
For my heart is sore and heavy at voyaging the sea.   70
My loving friends I'll bear in mind, and often fondly turn
To think of Ballyshannon, and the winding banks of Erne.

10

If ever I'm a money'd man, I mean, please God, to cast
My golden anchor in the place where youthful years were pass'd;
Though heads that now are black and brown must meanwhile gather grey,
New faces rise by every hearth, and old ones drop away –
Yet dearer still that Irish hill than all the world beside;
It's home, sweet home, where'er I roam, through lands and waters wide.
And if the Lord allows me, I surely will return
To my native Ballyshannon, and the winding banks of Erne.   80

*Fifty Modern Poems (Bell & Daldy, 1865). In Songs Ballads and Stories
(George Bell & Sons, 1877), Ballyshannon becomes Ballyshanny – 'The vernacular, and more correct,
form of the name' (author's note), and a longer note explains the etymology and refers to Rambles,
by Patricius Walker (1873), i.e. Allingham himself. Ballyshannon Harbour is where the
River Erne enters Donegal Bay.*

The Boy from his bedroom-window
    Look'd over the little town,
And away to the bleak black upland
    Under a clouded moon.

The moon came forth from her cavern,
    He saw the sudden gleam
Of a tarn in the swarthy moorland;
    Or perhaps the whole was a dream.

For I never could find that water
    In all my walks and rides: 10
Far-off, in the Land of Memory,
    That midnight pool abides.

2   old stories, – histories, genealogies. [Author's note]

Many fine things had I glimpse of,
    And said, 'I shall find them one day.'
Whether within or without me
    They were, I cannot say.

Songs Ballads and Stories (1877).

Everything passes and vanishes;
    Everything leaves its trace;
And often you see in a footstep
    What you could not see in a face.

Evil May-Day (Longmans & Co., 1883).

No funeral gloom, my dears, when I am gone,
Corpse-gazing, tears, black raiment, graveyard grimness;
Think of me as withdrawn into the dimness,
Yours still, you mine; remember all the best
Of our past moments, and forget the rest;
    And so, to where I wait, come gently on.

Evil May-Day (1883).

THREE SISTERS

Three sisters, Charlotte, Emily and Anne,
Afar in Yorkshire wolds they live together;
Names that I keep like any sacristan;
The human registry of souls as pure
As sky in hermit waters on a moor,
Those liquid islands of dark seas of heather;
Voices that reach my solitude from theirs;
Hands that I kiss a thousand miles away,
And send a thousand greetings of my own –
But these, alas! only the west wind bears.   10
– Nay, they are gone. The hills and vales are lone
Where Earth once knew them. What is now to say?
Three strangers dead – 'tis little to endure:
Great crowds of strangers vanish every day.
Yet will I see those gravestones if I can.

Evil May-Day (1883).

Four ducks on a pond,
A grass-bank beyond,
A blue sky of spring,
White clouds on the wing;
What a little thing
To remember for years –
To remember with tears!

Evil May-Day (1883).

WRITING

A man who keeps a diary, pays
Due toll to many tedious days;

But life becomes eventful – then
His busy hand forgets the pen.
Most books, indeed, are records less
Of fulness than of emptiness.

Blackberries, Picked off Many Bushes, By D. Pollex and Others, Put in a
Basket by W. Allingham *(G. Philip & Son, 1884).*

I will not be a critic where I love.
Love must love or not love –
So long as he's my sweetheart I will love him.
What care I what the world call this or that?
Have I such reason, that it cannot err,
Like God's? I am a poor weak human soul,
And love or hate, I cannot tell you why –
Friends have I, real, or they seem so now,
And while I'm in that notion I am theirs
Through good and evil –   10
If friendship, love, are nothing, what's life worth?
Some may endure to play at chilly chess
With men and women – I must hate and love!

By the Way, Verses, Fragments, and Notes, *arranged by Helen Allingham*
(Longmans, Green & Co., 1912).

Sydney (Thompson) Dobell (also Sydney Yendys) (1824–74)

Sydney Dobell, wine merchant and 'Spasmodic' poet, was born into a religiously radical family in Cranbrook, Kent, 5 April 1824. His father, John Dobell, was a hide trader turned wine merchant. His mother was a daughter of Samuel Thornton, founder at the end of the eighteenth century of a congregation of Unitarian Christians (admirers of the Primitive Church, apocalyptic in interest), meeting in Old Change, London. Sydney Dobell was 'kept from the world', so never went to school or university, read widely on his own, and was soon marked out for intellectual eccentricity. The family moved to Cheltenham in 1836, and eventually the son was put in charge of the Gloucester branch of the family wine business. He married in 1844. Dobell was keenly wrought up over the cause of the freedom of nations – Italian, Spanish, Hungarian. *The Roman* (1850), by Sydney Yendys, written in the cause of Italian liberation, was greatly admired by Mazzini. Dobell's enthusiastic-ish piece about the Brontës in the *Athenaeum* resulted in a warm correspondence with Charlotte Brontë. She was clearly rather stunned by *Balder: Part the First* ('By the Author of "The Roman" '), Dobell's verbally extremist, Gothic, slamming and banging dramatic poem about a poet's life and work (she felt 'a certain horror', she said, at the character of Balder, and her letter of 3 February 1854 is full of words like *inflated, wild* and *frantic*). Balder was a main target of William Aytoun's long spoof dramatic poem *Firmilian; or, the Student of Badajoz: A Spasmodic Tragedy* of 1854 and of Aytoun's earlier send-up review in *Blackwood's Magazine* (May 1854). After that Dobell never eluded the label Spasmodic. In 1854 he went to Edinburgh in search of medical treatment for his wife, and he lived there for three years, getting to know Aytoun as well as Alexander Smith, another of Aytoun's Spasmodic targets, with whom Dobell collaborated in *Sonnets on the War* (1855). Dobell's *England in Time of War* came out in 1856. Dobell's strong biblical interest in Armageddon found a distinct focus in the Crimea (he thought Sebastopol etymologically related to Armageddon). His poor health drove him to winter on the Isle of Wight, in Cannes, in Spain and Italy, but he kept returning to Gloucestershire. He was active in good works in Gloucester, was a pioneer in the Co-operative Movement, and wrote in favour of parliamentary reform – though he was no friend of what he called 'mob-rule'. He ended up living near Nailsworth on the upper edges of the Stroud Valley, and died there in 1874. He's buried in Painswick cemetery. His *Collected Poems* appeared in two volumes in 1875, with a one-volume selection following in 1887. A collection of prose came out in 1876, and the *Life and Letters* in two volumes in 1875, edited by 'E. J.'.

THE WOUNDED

'Thou canst not wish to live,' the surgeon said.
He clutched him, as a soul thrust forth from bliss
Clings to the ledge of Heaven! 'Would'st thou keep this
Poor branchless trunk?' 'But she would lean my head
Upon her breast; oh, let me live!' 'Be wise.'
'I could be very happy; both these eyes
Are left me; I should see her; she would kiss
My forehead: only let me live.' – He dies
Even in the passionate prayer. 'Good Doctor, say
If thou canst give more than another day   10
Of life?' 'I think there may be hope.' 'Pass on.
I will not buy it with some widow's son!'
'Help,' 'help,' 'help,' 'help!' 'God curse thee!' 'Doctor, stay,
Yon Frenchman went down earlier in the day.'

Sonnets on the War, by Alexander Smith & The Author of 'Balder' and
'The Roman' (David Bogue, 1855).

DESOLATE

From the sad eaves the drip-drop of the rain!
The water washing at the latchel door;
A slow step plashing by upon the moor;
A single bleat far from the famished fold;
The clicking of an embered hearth and cold;
The rainy Robin tic-tac at the pane.

'So as it is with thee
Is it with me,
So as it is and it used not to be,
With thee used not to be,   10
Nor me.'
So singeth Robin on the willow tree,
The rainy Robin tic-tac at the pane.

Here in this breast all day
The fire is dim and low,
Within I care not to stay,
Without I care not to go.

A sadness ever sings
Of unforgotten things,
And the bird of love is patting at the pane;   20
But the wintry water deepens at the door,
And a step is plashing by upon the moor
Into the dark upon the darkening moor,
And alas, alas, the drip-drop of the rain!

England in Time of War (Smith, Elder & Co., 1856).

WHERE ARE YOU, POETS[1]

Where are you, Poets, that a Hero dies
Unsung? He who, when Duty brought too soon
His billet of rest toiled on till he had won
The countersign of Glory? There he lies,
And in the silence of your poesies
He looks a Poem; yea, so made and done
As if the Bardic Heavens had thrown him down
In model to your making. Close his eyes,
That yours may learn him. To fulfil the Law
In Gospel, force the seeds of use to flower   10
In Beauty, to enman invisible Truth
And then transfigure – this is Poetry.
And this the World and his dear Country saw
Hymned unawares in that unconquer'd youth
Who, scorning to give less than all his power,
Having bled for us, then aspired to die;
And, dying thus, left one more pledge behind
That England may again deserve to lead Mankind.

Poetical Works *(Smith, Elder, & Co., 1875), II.*

SONG OF A MAD GIRL, WHOSE LOVER HAS DIED AT SEA[1]

Under the green white blue of this and that and the other,
That and the other, and that and the other, for ever and ever,
Under the up and down and the swaying ships swing-swonging,
There they flung him to sleep who will never come back to my longing.
The Father comes back to his child and the son comes back to his Mother,
But neither by land or sea
Will he ever come back to me,
Never, never, never
Will he come back to me.
All day I run by the Cliff, all night I stand in the sand,   10
All day I furrow and burrow the holmes and the heights,
But whether by night or day
There's never a trace or a track,
Never a word or a breath,
In the swill and the swoop and the flash and the foam and the wind,
Never a fleck or a speck
Coming, coming my way.
The mew comes back to the strand and the ship comes back to the land,
But he will never come back
To all the prayers that I pray thro' the scorching black of the day   20
And the freezing black of the nights,
Never, never come back
To the ear that harks itself deaf and the eye that strains itself blind,
And the heart that is starving to death.

WHERE ARE YOU, POETS
1   This Poem, on the death, in the Ashantee War, of Eardley Wilmot,
'who, early in the day, received a wound that entitled him to leave off
fighting, but continued to lead his men till killed by a second wound' –
is the last work of the writer, who, probably, intended to condense it
into a Sonnet. [Author's note]

SONG OF A MAD GIRL
1   (This Song was written...in the Isle of Wight, at a house almost
overhanging the sea.) [Author's note]

He was chill and they threw him to cold,
He was dead and they threw him to drown,
He was weary and wanted rest –
They should have laid him on my breast,
He would have slept on my breast,
But they threw him into the boiling boil and bubble,   30
The wheel and the whirl, the driff and the draff
Of the everlasting trouble.
I swear to you he was mine! I swear to you he was my own.
Madam, if I may make so bold,
Do you know what the dead men do
In the black and blue, in the green and brown?
Deep, deep, you think they sleep
Where the mermen moan and the mermaids weep?
Ah, ah, you make me laugh!
I'm not yet twenty years old,   40
But lean your ear
And you shall hear
A little thing that I know.
Up and up they come to the top,
Down and down they go down.
To and fro the finny fish go,
But slow and slow, and so and so,
Low over high, high under low,
Up and up they come to the top,
Down and down they go down: 50
When the sun comes up they come to the top,
When the sun sinks they go down.

Poetical Works (1875), II.

George MacDonald (1824–1905)

George MacDonald, Scottish preacher, novelist, children's writer and poet, was born, the youngest of five sons, on the farm of his father George MacDonald at Huntly, Aberdeenshire, 10 December 1824. The MacDonalds were old Jacobites and Gaelic speakers. MacDonald's mother, Helen MacKay, was sister of a renowned Gaelic scholar, Mackintosh MacKay. The parents were Congregationalists. George was a poor but academically successful scholarship boy at King's College, Aberdeen (graduating MA in 1845). He tutored in London, entered Highbury Congregational College in 1848 to prepare for the ministry, and became pastor of Trinity Congregational Chapel, Arundel, in 1850. In 1851 he married Louisa Powell (they would have eleven children all told). MacDonald was too biblically modernist and theologically experimental for his congregation (too 'German' – he believed in the salvation of animals and of the devil). He resigned in 1853 and went to Manchester to become a man of letters. In the great Victorian tradition of fraught Christians, he set up in a rented room as preacher and religious mentor to a group of working men. He was greatly influenced by the Christianized free-thought of Henry Septimus Sutton, the

Nottingham-born poet and Manchester journalist. The Browningesque religious poetic tragedy *Within and Without* (1855), much of it written at Arundel, was admired by Tennyson and won MacDonald the close friendship and support of Byron's widow. The *Poems* of 1857 and the fairy romance *Phantastes* (1858) confirmed him as a writer to watch. In his autobiography *Surprised by Joy*, C. S. Lewis said that *Phantastes* baptized his imagination, and MacDonald was a cult author for Lewis and his fellow Inklings. G. K. Chesterton said that *The Princess and the Goblin* (1872) made a difference to his whole existence. Among MacDonald's many adult novels, *David Elginbrod* (1863), *Alec Forbes* (1865) and *Robert Falconer* (1868) are main examples of the Victorian quest for a moral and religious perspective free of the rigidities of traditional Christian orthodoxy – especially of Scottish Calvinism. After a health-restoring stay in Algiers and several years in Hastings, the MacDonalds settled down in London in 1860, first in Bloomsbury, then near Regent's Park. He was especially close to Browning (they both attended the sermons of the Welsh preacher-poet Thomas Jones) and to Ruskin; but he also knew all the other heavyweights of Victorian writing –

the likes of Carlyle, Tennyson, Morris, Arnold. He became an Anglican layman through his friendship with F. D. Maurice but he never lost his strong Nonconformist connections, and preached often in the chapels of Dissent. He edited *Good Words for the Young* (1872–3), lectured widely on literature, not least at King's College, London, and in the USA (1872). Queen Victoria arranged him a Civil List Pension of £100 in 1877. He and his wife (and children) apparently helped on the movement that revived the performance of Mystery Plays by their appearance in her stage adaptation of *The Pilgrim's Progress*. In his last twenty years or so the MacDonalds spent much time in Italy for the sake of his health (Mrs MacDonald died there, 1902). And still the writings poured out, especially the verse and stories for children. Of MacDonald's poem *The Diary of an Old Soul* (1880), Ruskin said it helped to confirm the 'age not destitute of religious poetry' (the other evidence was Keble's hymns and Longfellow's *Hiawatha*). MacDonald's *Works of Fancy and Imagination* were collected in ten volumes in 1871; his *Poetical Works* in two volumes in 1893. There was a new edition of *The Fairy Tales* in 1904, and *Phantastes* appeared yet again in 1905, in an edition illustrated by MacDonald's friend Arthur Hughes. MacDonald died after a long illness at Ashtead, home of his youngest daughter, and his ashes were buried next to his wife in the English Cemetery at Bordighera, their Italian home. Five of their six sons and two of their daughters survived him.

What Professor Owl *Knows*

Nobody knows the world but me.
The rest go to bed: I sit up to see.
I'm a better student than any of you all,
For I never begin till the darkness fall,
And I never read without my glasses;
But that's not how my wisdom passes.

I have learning, I say – but that's not it:
I observe. I have seen the white moon sit
On her nest, the sea, like a second owl,
Hatching the boats and the long-legged fowl!   10
When the oysters gape – you may make a note –
She drops a pearl into every throat.

I can see the wind: now can you do that?
I see the dreams he carries in his hat;
I see him snorting them out as he goes;
I see them rush in at the snoring nose.
Ten thousand things you could not *think*,
I can write them down with pen and ink.

You see I know: you may pull off your hat,
Whether round and lofty, or square and flat.   20
You cannot do better than trust in me;
You may shut your eyes in fact – *I* see.
Lifelong I will lead you, and then – I'm the owl –
I will bury you nicely with my spade and showl.

Version in Works of Fancy and Imagination, *10 vols (Strahan & Co., 1871), III;*
greatly revising earlier version, 'What the Owl Knows', in The Disciple and
Other Poems *(Strahan & Co., 1867); and in turn heavily rewritten in*
Poetical Works, *2 vols (Chatto & Windus, 1893), II, as 'Professor Noctutus'.*

A Manchester Poem

'Tis a poor drizzly morning, dark and sad.
The cloud has fallen, and filled with fold on fold
The chimneyed city; and the smoke is caught,

And spreads diluted in the cloud, and sinks,
A black precipitate, on miry streets.
And faces gray glide through the darkened fog.

   Slave engines utter again their ugly growl,
And soon the iron bands and blocks of stone
That prison them to their task, will strain and quiver
Until the city tremble. The clamour of bells,   10
Importunate, keeps calling pale-faced forms
To gather and feed those Samsons' groaning strength
With labour; and among the many come
A man and woman – the woman with her gown
Drawn over her head, the man with bended neck
Submissive to the rain. Amid the jar,
And clash, and shudder of the awful force,
They enter and part – each to a different task,
But each a soul of knowledge to brute force,
Working a will through the organized whole   20
Of cranks and belts and levers, pinions and screws
Wherewith small man has eked his body out,
And made himself a mighty, weary giant.
   In labour close they pass the murky day,
'Mid floating dust of swift-revolving wheels,
And filmy spoil of quick contorted threads,
Which weave a sultry chaos all about;
Until, at length, old darkness, swelling slow
Up from the caves of night to make an end,
Chokes in its tide the clanking of the looms,   30
The monster-engines, and the flying gear.
'Tis Earth that draws her curtains, and calls home
Her little ones, and sets her down to nurse
Her tired children – like a mother-ghost
With her neglected darlings in the dark.
So out they walk, with sense of glad release,
And home – to a dreary place! Unfinished walls,
Earth-heaps, and broken bricks, and muddy pools
Lie round it like a rampart against the spring,
The summer, and all sieges of the year.   40

   But, lo, the dark has opened an eye of fire!
The room reveals a temple, witnessed by signs
Seen in the ancient place! Lo, here is light,
Yea, burning fire, with darkness on its skirts;
Pure water, ready to baptize; and bread;
And in the twilight edges of the light,
A book; and, for the cunning-woven veil,
Their faces – hiding God's own holiest place!
Even their bed figures the would-be grave
Where One arose triumphant, slept no more!   50
So at their altar-table they sit down
To eat their Eucharist; for, to the heart
That reads the live will in the dead command,
He is the bread, yea, all of every meal.
   But as, in weary rest, they silent sit,
They gradually grow aware of light
That overcomes their lamp, and, through the blind,
Casts from the window-frame two shadow-glooms
That make a cross of darkness on the white.

The woman rises, eagerly looks out: 60
Lo, some fair wind has mown the earth-sprung fog,
And, far aloft, the white exultant moon,
From her blue window, curtained all with white,
Looks greeting them – God's creatures they and she!
Smiling she turns; he understands the smile:
To-morrow will be fair – as holy, fair!
And lying down, in sleep they die till morn,
While through their night throb low aurora-gleams
Of resurrection and the coming dawn.
   They wake: 'tis Sunday. Still the moon is there,   70
But thin and ghostly – clothed upon with light,
As if, while they were sleeping, she had died.
They dress themselves, like priests, in clean attire,
And, through their lowly door, enter God's room.
   The sun is up, the emblem on his shield.
One side the street, the windows all are moons
To light the other side that lies in shade.
See, down the sun-side, an old woman come
In a red cloak that makes the whole street glad!
A long-belated autumn-flower she seems,   80
Dazed by the rushing of the new-born life
Up hidden stairs to see the calling sun,
But in her cloak and smile they know the spring,
And haste to meet her through slow dissolving streets
Widening to larger glimmers of growing green.
Oh, far away the streets repel the spring!
Yet every stone in the dull pavement shares
The life that thrills anew the outworn earth,
A right Bethesda angel[1] – for all, not some!

   A street unfinished leads them forth at length   90
Where green fields bask, and hedgerow trees, apart,
Stand waiting in the air as for some good,
And the sky is broad and blue – and there is all!
No peaceful river meditates along
The weary flat to the less level sea!
No forest brown, on pillared stems, its boughs
Meeting in gothic arches, bears aloft
A groined vault, fretted with tremulous leaves!
No mountains lift their snows, and send their brooks
Down babbling with the news of silent things!   100
But love itself is commonest of all,
And loveliest of all, in all the worlds!
And he that hath not forest, brook, or hill,
Must learn to read aright what commoner books
Unfold before him. If ocean solitudes –
Then darkness dashed with glory, infinite shades,
And misty minglings of the sea and sky.
If only fields – the humble man of heart
Will revel in the grass beneath his foot,
And from the lea lift his glad eye to heaven,   110
God's palette, where his careless painter-hand
Sweeps comet-clouds that net the gazing soul;

A MANCHESTER POEM
1 Bethesda: Jerusalem pool, where angel occasionally disturbed the   water – and first one in was cured: John 5 (*impotent man* waits 38 years in
                                                                        vain for cure).

Streaks endless stairs, and blots half-sculptured blocks;
Curves filmy pallors; heaps huge mountain-crags;
Nor touches where it leaves not beauty's mark.
　　To them the sun and air are feast enough,
As through field-paths and lanes they slowly walk;
But sometimes, on the far horizon dim
A veil is lifted, and they spy the hills,
Cloudlike and faint, yet sharp against the sky;   120
Then wakes an unknown want, which asks and looks
As for some thing forgot – loved long ago,
But on the hither verge of childhood dropt:
'Tis but home-sickness roused in the soul by Spring!
Fresh birth and eager growth, reviving life,
Which *is* because it *would be*, fill the world;
The very light is new-born with the grass;
The stones themselves are warm; the brown earth swells,
Filled, sponge-like, with dark beams, which nestle close
And brood unseen and shy, and potent warm   130
In every little corner, nest, and crack
Where buried lurks a blind and sleepy seed
Waiting the touch of the finger of the sun.
The mossy stems and boughs, where yet no life
Oozes exuberant in brown and green,
Are clad in golden splendours, crossed and lined
With shuttle-shadows weaving lovely change.
Through the tree-tops the west wind rushing goes,
Calling and rousing the dull sap within:
The fine jar down the stem sinks tremulous,   140
From airy root thrilling to earthy branch.
And though as yet no buddy baby dots
Sparkle the darkness of the hedgerow twigs,
The smoke-dried bark appears to spread and swell
In the soft nurture of the warm light-bath.
　　The sun had left behind him the keystone
Of his low arch half-way when they turned home,
Filled with pure air, and light, and operant spring:
Back, like the bees, they went to their dark house
To store their innocent spoil in honeyed thought.   150

　　But on their way, crossing a field, they chanced
Upon a spot where once had been a home,
And roots of walls still peered out, grown with moss.
'Twas a dead cottage, mouldered quite, where yet
Lay the old shadow of a vanished care;
The little garden's blunt, half-blotted map
Was yet discernible by thinner grass
Upon the walks. There, in the midst of dry
Bushes, dead flowers, rampant, uncomely weeds,
A single snowdrop drooped its snowy drop,   160
The lonely remnant of a family
That in the garden dwelt about the home –
Reviving with the spring when home was gone:
They see; its spiritual counterpart
Wakes up and blossoms white in their meek souls –
A longing, patient, waiting hopefulness,
The snowdrop of the heart; a heavenly child,
That, pale with the earthly cold, hangs its fair head
As it had nought to say 'gainst any world;

While they in whom it dwells, nor knows itself,   170
Inherit in their meekness all the worlds.

    I love thee, flower, as a slow lingerer
Upon the verge of my humanity.
Lo, on thine inner leaves and in thy heart
The loveliest green, acknowledging the grass –
White-minded memory of lowly friends!
But almost more I love thee for the earth
Which clings to thy transfigured radiancy,
Uplifted with thee from thine abandoned grave;
Say rather the soiling of thy garments pure   180
Upon thy road into the light and air,
The heaven of thy new birth. Some gentle rain
Will one day wash thee white, and send the earth
Back to the earth; but, sweet friend, while it clings,
I love the cognizance of our family.

    With careful hands uprooting it, they bore
The little plant a willing captive home –
Fearless of dark abode, because secure
In its own tale of light. As once of old
The angel of the annunciation shone,   190
Bearing all heaven into a common house,
It brings in with it field and sky and air.
A pot of mould its one poor tie to earth,
Its heaven an ell of blue 'twixt chimney-tops,
Its world the priests of that small temple-room,
It takes its prophet-place with fire and book,
Type of primeval spring, whose mighty arc
Hath not yet drawn the summer up the sky.
At night, when the dark shadow of the cross
Will enter, clothed in moonlight, still and wan   200
Like a pale mourner at its foot the flower
Will, drooping, wait the dawn. Then the dark bird
Which holds breast-caged the secret of the sun,
And therefore hangs himself a prisoner caged,
Will break into its song – Lo, God is light!

    Weary and hopeful, to their sleep they go;
And all night long the snowdrop glimmers white
Thinning the dark, unknowing it, and unseen.

    Out of my verse I woke, and saw my room,
My precious books, the cherub-forms above,   210
And rose, and walked abroad, and sought the woods;
And roving odours met me on my way.
    I entered Nature's church, a shimmering vault
Of boughs, and clouded leaves – filmy and pale
Betwixt me and the sun, while at my feet
Their shadows, dark and seeming solid, lay
Like tombstones o'er the vanished flowers of Spring.
The place was silent, save for the broken song
Of some Memnonian,[2] glory-stricken bird

---

2   Theban statue of Memnon, said to make music when first struck by
dawn rays of sun.

That burst into a carol and was still;   220
It was not lonely: golden beetles crept,
Green goblins, in the roots; and squirrel things
Ran, wild as cherubs, through the tracery;
And here and yonder a flaky butterfly
Was doubting in the air, scarlet and blue.
    But 'twixt my heart and summer's perfect grace,
Drove a dividing wedge, and far away
It seemed, like voice heard loud yet far away
By one who, waking half, soon sleeps outright: –
Where was the snowdrop? where the flower of hope?   230
In me the spring was throbbing; round me lay
Resting fulfilled, the odour-breathing summer!
My heart heaved swelling like a prisoned bud,
And summer crushed it with its weight of light!

    Winter is full of stings and sharp reproofs,
Healthsome, not hurtful, but yet hurting sore;
Summer is too complete for growing hearts –
Too idle its noons, its morns too triumphing,
Too full of slumberous dreams its dusky eves;
Autumn is full of ripeness and the grave;   240
We need a broken season, where the cloud
Is ruffled into glory, and the dark
Falls rainful o'er the sunset; need a world
Whose shadows ever point away from it;
A scheme of cones abrupt, and flattened spheres,
And circles cut, and perfect laws the while
That marvellous imperfection ever points
To higher perfectness than heart can think;
Therefore to us, a flower of harassed Spring,
Crocus, or primrose, or anemone,   250
Is lovely as was never rosiest rose;
A heath-bell on a waste, lonely and dry,
Says more than lily, stately in breathing white;
A window through a vaulted roof of rain
Lets in a light that comes from farther away,
And, sinking deeper, spreads a finer joy
Than cloudless noon-tide splendorous o'er the world:
Man seeks a better home than Paradise;
Therefore high hope is more than deepest joy,
A disappointment better than a feast,   260
And the first daisy on a wind-swept lea
Dearer than Eden-groves with rivers four.

Version in Poetical Works *(1893), I: greatly revising earlier version, in* Works of Fancy
and Imagination *(1871), III.*

THE SHORTEST AND SWEETEST OF SONGS

Come
Home.

Poetical Works *(1893), II.*

Henry S. (Septimus) Sutton (1825–1901)

Henry Septimus Sutton, newspaperman, religiose and early 'Green' poet, was born in Nottingham in 1825, son of Richard Sutton, the proprietor of the weekly *Nottingham Register*. He was intended for a career as a chemist and druggist, but hated that; was articled to a surgeon; then became a journalist. He was active in Mechanics' Institute work. In the later forties he moved to Manchester, where he became chief reporter on the *Manchester Examiner and Times* (1853). He was a considerable religious influence on George MacDonald in the mid-fifties when the latter was running his freelance post-Christian group for Manchester working men. He edited the *Alliance News* for forty years, and was also editor of *Meliora*, a magazine of 'social science'. His first volume of poems was *The Evangel of Love Interpreted* (Nottingham, 1847). *Clifton Grove Garland* followed (Nottingham, 1848), then *Rose's Diary* (Manchester, 1854). His *Quinquenergia: or Proposals For a New Practical Theology* was also published in 1854. He was a friend of Philip James Bailey, the Nottingham poet who wrote the notoriously terrible Spasmodic poem *Festus* (1839), and of Coventry Patmore – the Catholic poet who was not disposed to turn any religious brooder from his door. Sutton's poems are gentle things, built on a mixture of cheerfulness ('How happy is our case/How beautiful it is to be alive'), Christianized ethicity ('Unless I strive these people dear to bless,/I do not love my God') and gentle ironies about human awfulness. A collected *Poems* appeared in Glasgow in 1886, with some revisions of previously published verses.

MAN

Man doth usurp all space,
Stares thee in rock, bush, river, in the face.
Never yet thine eyes beheld a tree;
'Tis no sea thou seest in the sea,
'Tis but a disguised humanity.
To avoid thy fellow, vain thy plan;
All that interests a man is man.

Poems (*David M. Main, Glasgow, 1886*).

WHO SHALL DELIVER?

He spake; – from vanity, it seem'd to be;
Was silent; still he saw 'twas vanity.
He own'd his vainness; vanity took possession
Of that most sad confession.
He vow'd to kill the weed, and strove to do 't,
And hew'd and hack'd down to the very root:
Alas, rank vanity would still be thriving
And prosp'ring even in that very striving.
Then fell he down and pray'd: – *Lord, take my breath,*
And save me from the body of this death.[1]   10

Poems (*1886*).

WHO SHALL DELIVER?
1 cf. Romans 7.24: 'O wretched man that I am! who shall deliver me from the body of this death?'

THE EARTH DEFACED

How wonderful, how beautiful, the world!
   At its continual creation, Thou,
O Lord, art present Maker; – fashioned thus
Because it is a dwelling-place to be
Of them who shall be dwelling-place for Thee.

Thou, Father, build'st this palace for Thy child;
A surface river-marbled, flower-emboss'd,
Scribed with old-time inscriptions in its floor;
Close-clustered trees for its arched columns tall,
And sun, and moon, and stars, high over all.   10

'Tis we who shear the lustre from the sun,
And glory from the flowers. Wigwams of mud
We build within thy lofty Parthenon,
Between the noble pillars, and deface
With our mean uses the majestic place.

Poems (1886).

William McGonagall (1825–1902)

William McGonagall, Scotland's most notorious doggerel poet, was born in the slummy Grassmarket district of Edinburgh in March 1825, the youngest child of Irish parents. His father did whatever work he could as a weaver and pedlar around Scotland and in the Orkneys. By his own account in 'A Summary History of Poet McGonagall', William grew up admiring beautiful scenery, 'great men such as Shakespeare', 'great preachers, such as the Rev. George Gilfillan', and 'Great Poets such as Burns'. He worked in a cotton factory in Dundee, delighted in acting Shakespearean parts in the Theatre Royal at Dundee, and 'discovered himself to be a poet'. He read in public houses, and circuses – anywhere he could in fact, published broadsheets, and achieved local fame around Dundee as 'the Poet Laureate of the Tay Bridge'. He celebrated disasters in the Tay Bridge collapse mode, funerals, battles, local and national heroes, all the stuff of thrilling newspaper stories, with a charming naivety and unmisgiving colloquial vigour. He sent verses to Queen Victoria and received some sort of royal reply – though he was turned away when he sought to meet her at Balmoral, July 1878 ('You are not Poet to Her Majesty; Tennyson's the real poet to Her Majesty', said the constable on guard). In 1887 he travelled to New York but soon returned, having failed to get anywhere as a public entertainer. He has entered the popular British canon as a likeably good–bad poet, the Grandma Moses of British verse, an inspiration to innocent rhymesters everywhere. He pays constant artless tribute to the misguided faith in the archetypal equation between the poetic and mere rhyming. He claimed to have been given in 1894 the title Sir William Topaz McGonagall, Grand Knight of the Holy Order of the Burmese White Elephant. (He did enjoy sending himself up.) He died in Edinburgh, 29 September 1902.

THE TAY BRIDGE DISASTER

Beautiful Railway Bridge of the Silv'ry Tay!
Alas! I am very sorry to say
That ninety lives have been taken away
On the last Sabbath day of 1879,
Which will be remember'd for a very long time.

'Twas about seven o'clock at night,
And the wind it blew with all its might,
And the rain came pouring down,
And the dark clouds seem'd to frown,

And the Demon of the air seem'd to say –   10
'I'll blow down the Bridge of Tay.'

When the train left Edinburgh
The passengers' hearts were light and felt no sorrow,
But Boreas blew a terrific gale,
Which made their hearts for to quail,
And many of the passengers with fear did say –
'I hope God will send us safe across the Bridge of Tay.'

But when the train came near to Wormit Bay,
Boreas he did loud and angry bray,
And shook the central girders of the Bridge of Tay   20
On the last Sabbath day of 1879,
Which will be remember'd for a very long time.

So the train sped on with all its might,
And Bonnie Dundee soon hove in sight,
And the passengers' hearts felt light,
Thinking they would enjoy themselves on the New Year,
With their friends at home they lov'd most dear,
And wish them all a happy New Year.

So the train mov'd slowly along the Bridge of Tay,
Until it was about midway,   30
Then the central girders with a crash gave way,
And down went the train and passengers into the Tay
The Storm Fiend did loudly bray,
Because ninety lives had been taken away,
On the last Sabbath day of 1879,
Which will be remember'd for a very long time.

As soon as the catastrophe came to be known
The alarm from mouth to mouth was blown,
And the cry rang out all o'er the town,
Good Heavens! the Tay Bridge is blown down,   40
And a passenger train from Edinburgh,
Which fill'd all the people's hearts with sorrow,
And made them for to turn pale,
Because none of the passengers were sav'd to tell the tale
How the disaster happen'd on the last Sabbath day of 1879
Which will be remember'd for a very long time.

It must have been an awful sight,
To witness in the dusky moonlight,
While the Storm Fiend did laugh, and angry did bray,
Along the Railway Bridge of the Silv'ry Tay.   50
Oh! ill-fated Bridge of the Silv'ry Tay,
I must now conclude my lay
By telling the world fearlessly without the least dismay,
That your central girders would not have given way,
At least many sensible men do say,
Had they been supported on each side with buttresses,
At least many sensible men confesses,
For the stronger we our houses do build,
The less chance we have of being killed.

Text, Poetic Gems: Selected from the Works of William McGonagall,
Poet and Tragedian *(David Winter & Son, Dundee, 1947)*.

DEATH AND BURIAL OF LORD TENNYSON

Alas! England now mourns for her poet that's gone –
The late and the good Lord Tennyson.
I hope his soul has fled to heaven above,
Where there is everlasting joy and love.

He was a man that didn't care for company,
Because company interfered with his study,
And confused the bright ideas in his brain,
And for that reason from company he liked to abstain.

He has written some fine pieces of poetry in his time,
Especially the May Queen, which is really sublime;   10
Also the gallant charge of the Light Brigade –
A most heroic poem, and beautifully made.

He believed in the Bible, also in Shakespeare,
Which he advised young men to read without any fear;
And by following the advice of both works therein,
They would seldom or never commit any sin.

Lord Tennyson's works are full of the scenery of his boyhood,
And during his life all his actions were good;
And Lincolnshire was closely associated with his history,
And he has done what Wordsworth did for the Lake Country.   20

His remains now rest in Westminster Abbey,
And his funeral was very impressive to see;
It was a very touching sight, I must confess,
Every class, from the Queen, paying a tribute to the poet's greatness.

The pall-bearers on the right of the coffin were Mr W. E. H. Lecky,
And Professor Butler, Master of Trinity, and the Earl of Rosebery;
And on the left were Mr J. A. Froude and the Marquis of Salisbury,
Also Lord Selborne, which was an imposing sight to see.

There were also on the left Professor Jowett,
Besides Mr Henry Whyte and Sir James Paget,   30
And the Marquis of Dufferin and the Duke of Argyll,
And Lord Salisbury, who seemed melancholy all the while.

The chief mourners were all of the Tennyson family,
Including the Hon. Mr and Mrs Hallam Tennyson, and Masters Lionel and Aubrey,
And Mr Arthur Tennyson, and Mr and Mrs Horatio Tennyson;
Also Sir Andrew Clark, who was looking woe begone.

The bottom of the grave was thickly strewn with white roses,
And for such a grave kings will sigh where the poet now reposes;
And many of the wreaths were much observed and commented upon,
And conspicuous amongst them was one from Mrs Gladstone.   40

The Gordon boys were there looking solemn and serene,
Also Sir Henry Ponsonby to represent the Queen;
Likewise Henry Irving, the great tragedian,
With a solemn aspect, and driving his brougham.

And, in conclusion, I most earnestly pray,
That the people will erect a monument for him without delay,

To commemorate the good work he has done,
And his name in gold letters written thereon!

Text, *Last Poetic Gems*: Selected from the Works of William McGonagall, Poet and Tragedian,
ed. *James L. Smith (David Winter & Son, Dundee; Gerald Duckworth & Co., London, 1968).*

Adelaide Anne Procter (1825–64)

Adelaide Anne Procter, born 30 October 1825 at 25 Bedford Square, London, was the first child and eldest daughter of parents with high cultural pretensions – friends of Dickens and Thackeray and more or less everybody else in literary London. Anne Skepper Procter was the life and soul of many an evening of literati; Bryan Waller Procter was a solicitor, amateur pugilist, Commissioner for Lunacy, encourager of young talent (such as Robert Browning and Swinburne), who enjoyed considerable though temporary fame in the 1820s as the poet and song-writer Barry Cornwall. 'Child of my heart! My sweet beloved First-born!' was 'golden-tressed' Adelaide's poetic welcome into the world – rather setting the tone for her own effusions. Her doting parents pampered her into literariness. In the Memoir he wrote at the parents' suggestion for the posthumous edition (1866) of her collected *Legends and Lyrics*, Dickens dwells fetishistically on the tiny album of poems her mother made for her which, treasured now as memento of a dead daughter, 'looks as if she had carried it about like another little girl might have carried a doll'. (The little Brontës, more sternly raised, had to make their own midget books, and wrote all their contents themselves.) Adelaide's first published poem was 'Ministering Angels' in *Heath's Book of Beauty* (1843), one of the many prettified annuals put out for women. She got into *Household Words* when she sent a batch of verses to its conductor Charles Dickens – posing as 'Mary Berwick', with the honourable wish not to exploit the family connexion. Almost all her verses appeared in *Household Words* or Dickens's other journal *All the Year Round*. Miss Berwick's real identity was soon outed and, her verses being so often flat and unmemorable, it is difficult to explain their continued presence in those papers except as illustration of Dickens's extreme partiality to the pleasant young daughters of friends. Roughly a sixth of all the *Household Words* poems are by Adelaide Procter. Elizabeth Barrett Browning's surprise at this public success is understandable. In fact, while Dickens in his Memoir declares that Miss Procter's effusions had far more merit than the 'shoal of verses' constantly sent in, and that 'The Seven Poor Travellers' was 'very pretty', back-stage he was harsher. For publishing her 'Beyond', in *Household Words*, 2 October 1858, he sharply rapped co-editor W. H. Wills's knuckles: 'Pray, *pray* don't have Poems unless they are good...Beyond is really Beyond anything I ever saw, in utter badness.' Still, *Legends and Lyrics*, which gathered up these poems into Adelaide Procter's main collection, went on being reprinted. 'A Lost Chord', piously dreaming about a sad person's heavenly prospects, became something of a Victorian classic, not least because Arthur Sullivan's setting made it available as a theologically undemanding secular hymn – right up Dickens's street, of course. Around 1851 she converted to Rome along with her two sisters (one of whom became a nun). She was forever busy in good works – sick visiting, education of the poor, shelters for the homeless. The proceeds of *A Chaplet of Verses* (1862) went to what its money-raising Foreword describes as the first ever Roman Catholic Night Shelter in England or Ireland, the Providence Row Night Refuge for Homeless Women and Children ('In this country, as we all know, the very poorest and most destitute are in many cases Catholics'). She was a main member of the Langham Place group of feminist writers and artists. In 1859 she was appointed to the Committee of the National Association for the Promotion of Social Science, investigating employment for women. Her association with the women-run Victoria Press of women compositors and book-binders, set up by Bessie Rayner Parkes and Emily Faithful, led to her editing *Victoria Regia* (1861), an anthology – including Isa Blagden, Dinah Mulock, Caroline Norton, Tennyson, Arnold, Thackeray – to show off the typesetting and bookbinding skills of the Victoria Press's women workers. The first book of *Legends and Lyrics* was dedicated to the lesbian actress Matilde Hays (she dressed, Elizabeth Barrett Browning reported with some amaze from Rome, as a man from the waist up – and Mrs Browning seems to have been relieved that the second volume was not also dedicated to 'Miss Hays'). Always delicate in health, Adelaide Anne Procter died of TB, 2 February 1864, after months confined to her room. She is buried in Kensal Green cemetery.

A WOMAN'S QUESTION

Before I trust my Fate to thee,
Or place my hand in thine,

Before I let thy Future give
   Colour and form to mine,
Before I peril all for thee, question thy soul to-night for me.

I break all slighter bonds, nor feel
   A shadow of regret:
Is there one link within the Past,
   That holds thy spirit yet?
Or is thy Faith as clear and free as that which I can pledge to thee?   10

Does there within thy dimmest dreams
   A possible future shine,
Wherein thy life could henceforth breathe,
   Untouched, unshared by mine?
If so, at any pain or cost, oh, tell me before all is lost.

Look deeper still. If thou canst feel
   Within thy inmost soul,
That thou hast kept a portion back,
   While I have staked the whole;
Let no false pity spare the blow, but in true mercy tell me so.   20

Is there within thy heart a need
   That mine cannot fulfil?
One chord that any other hand
   Could better wake or still?
Speak now – lest at some future day my whole life wither and decay.

Lives there within thy nature hid
   The demon-spirit Change,
Shedding a passing glory still
   On all things new and strange? –   30
It may not be thy fault alone – but shield my heart against thy own.

Couldst thou withdraw thy hand one day
   And answer to my claim,
That Fate, and that to-day's mistake,
   Not thou – had been to blame?
Some soothe their conscience thus: but thou, O, surely, thou wilt warn me now.

Nay, answer not – I dare not hear,
   The words would come too late;
Yet I would spare thee all remorse,
   So, comfort thee, my Fate: –
Whatever on my heart may fall – remember, I *would* risk it all!   40

Household Words *(6 February 1858)*. Legends and Lyrics: A Book of Verses *(Bell & Daldy, 1858)*.

THANKFULNESS

I thank Thee, oh my God, who made
   The Earth so bright;
So full of splendour and of joy,
   Beauty and light;
So many glorious things are here,
   Noble and right.

I thank Thee, too, that Thou hast made
  Joy to abound;
So many gentle thoughts and deeds
  Circling us round,   10
That in the darkest spot of Earth
  Some love is found.

I thank Thee *more* that all our joy
  Is touched with pain;
That shadows fall on brightest hours,
  That thorns remain;
So that Earth's bliss may be our guide,
  And not our chain.

For Thou who knowest, Lord, how soon
  Our weak heart clings,   20
Hast given us joys, tender and true,
  Yet all with wings,
So that we see, gleaming on high,
  Diviner things!

I thank Thee, Lord, that Thou hast kept
  The best in store;
We have enough, yet not too much
  To long for more:
A yearning for a deeper peace
  Not known before.   30

I thank Thee, Lord, that here our souls,
  Though amply blest,
Can never find, although they seek,
  A perfect rest –
Nor ever shall, until they lean
  On Jesus' breast.

                                    Legends and Lyrics (1858).

A LOST CHORD

Seated one day at the Organ,
  I was weary and ill at ease,
And my fingers wandered idly
  Over the noisy keys.

I do not know what I was playing,
  Or what I was dreaming then;
But I struck one chord of music,
  Like the sound of a great Amen.

It flooded the crimson twilight
  Like the close of an Angel's Psalm,   10
And it lay on my fevered spirit
  With a touch of infinite calm.

It quieted pain and sorrow,
  Like love overcoming strife;

It seemed the harmonious echo
  From our discordant life.

It linked all perplexed meanings
  Into one perfect peace,
And trembled away into silence
  As if it were loth to cease.   20

I have sought, but I seek it vainly,
  That one lost chord divine,
Which came from the soul of the Organ,
  And entered into mine.

It may be that Death's bright angel
  Will speak in that chord again,
It may be that only in Heaven
  I shall hear that grand Amen.

English Woman's Journal, *5 (1860), 36*. Legends and Lyrics:
A Book of Verses, Second Volume *(Bell & Daldy, 1861)*.

A WOMAN'S ANSWER

I will not let you say a Woman's part
  Must be to give exclusive love alone;
Dearest, although I love you so, my heart
  Answers a thousand claims besides your own.

I love – what do I not love? earth and air
  Find space within my heart, and myriad things
You would not deign to heed, are cherished there,
  And vibrate on its very inmost strings.

I love the summer with her ebb and flow
  Of light, and warmth, and music that have nurst   10
Her tender buds to blossoms . . . and you know
  It was in summer that I saw you first.

I love the winter dearly too, ... but then
  I owe it so much; on a winter's day,
Bleak, cold, and stormy, you returned again,
  When you had been those weary months away.

I love the Stars like friends; so many nights
  I gazed at them, when you were far from me,
Till I grew blind with tears . . . those far off lights
  Could watch you, whom I longed in vain to see.   20

I love the Flowers; happy hours lie
  Shut up within their petals close and fast:
You have forgotten, dear: but they and I
  Keep every fragment of the golden Past.

I love, too, to be loved; all loving praise
  Seems like a crown upon my Life, – to make
It better worth the giving, and to raise
  Still nearer to your own the heart you take.

I love all good and noble souls; – I heard
    One speak of you but lately, and for days   30
Only to think of it, my soul was stirred
    In tender memory of such generous praise.

I love all those who love you; all who owe
    Comfort to you: and I can find regret
Even for those poorer hearts who once could know,
    And once could love you, and can now forget.

Well, is my heart so narrow – I, who spare
    Love for all these? Do I not even hold
My favourite books in special tender care,
    And prize them as a miser does his gold?   40

The Poets that you used to read to me
    While summer twilights faded in the sky;
But most of all I think Aurora Leigh,
    Because – because – do you remember why?

Will you be jealous? Did you guess before
    I loved so many things? – Still you the best: –
Dearest, remember that I love you more,
    Oh, more a thousand times than all the rest!

Legends and Lyrics, Second Volume *(1861)*.

Walter Bagehot (1826–77)

Walter Bagehot, influential economist, constitutional expert, and critic, was born in the Langport, Somerset, branch of Stuckey's Bank, 3 February 1826, son of Thomas Watson Bagehot, a Unitarian banker (who was also a water-colourist and great reader), and the vivacious Edith Estlin, widow of a Bristol Unitarian and niece of Samuel Stuckey, the bank founder. She was subject to periods of delusions and insanity. One of her sons by her first marriage was an imbecile. She was a devout Anglican: her slim volume of verses *An Echo* (1841) was published to raise money for a village church she sponsored. At her wish Walter Bagehot attended the Church of England service in the afternoon after morning service with the Unitarians. He was early on introduced to the pleasures of literature when governesses read him Scott and Dickens. After Langport Grammar School, he went to the Unitarian Bristol College, then (1842) to the Nonconformist's University College, London, where he graduated with a First Class degree in 1846 (and won a maths scholarship). He gained an MA and a Gold Medal in Moral and Intellectual Philosophy in 1848. He was on very close terms with R. H. Hutton (future editor of the *Spectator*) and with A. H. Clough, whom he met through Oxford friends. He helped Clough get the post of Principal of University Hall, London. In 1851 he saw at first hand the Paris *coup d'état* – which put him off uprising politics for life. In the fifties he was very active indeed in literary journalism, producing a stream of long reviews and essays. He was on the editorial staff of the *National Review*. He joined his father's bank in 1852, having abandoned reading for the Bar. In 1858 he married the eldest daughter of James Wilson, founder of the anti-Corn Law free-trade newspaper the *Economist*, and for the last seventeen years of his life he was the *Economist*'s editor. The pressures of editing, and of writing about political and money matters – his classic book on the *English Constitution* (1862), his attempt to apply Darwinism to politics in *Physics and Politics* (1872), his money market study *Lombard Street* (1875) – led to a thinning of literary critical work in the sixties. He enjoyed immense prestige in the money world. Chancellors of the Exchequer sat at his feet. His two volumes of *Literary Studies* gathered up his critical essays (1878). In politics he was a sort of gentle reformer (advocating a dilution of the hereditary element in the House of Lords, for example), but was wary of 'hungry and ignorant men' dictating politics. What is good about the English, he thinks, is their steady dullness – less exciting than French cleverness and reflectiveness, of course, but a lot safer for people's heads. As a critic he is clear, though often wrong-headed – too deprecatory about Dickens's characters, for example, too down on Browning's 'grotesquerie'. What is good about Bagehot the critic is his granting literature the seriousness to be taken seriously. He's a startlingly memorable phrasemaker – 'Tacitus wrote like a pair of stays'; Swift is 'a detective in a Dean's wig'; you can tell writers from their writing because 'people do not keep tame steam-engines to write their books'. At such moments of verbal sharpness and fun one recognizes why he was regarded as an extraordinarily amenable conversationalist. He is credited with first using the word *padding* for superfluous spoken or written matter. He died at his birthplace, 24 March 1877. He never resorted to padding.

WORDSWORTH, TENNYSON, AND BROWNING; OR PURE, ORNATE, AND GROTESQUE ART IN ENGLISH POETRY

Enoch Arden, & c. By Alfred Tennyson, D. C. L., Poet Laureate; Dramatis Personae. *By Robert Browning.[1]*

We couple these two books together, not because of their likeness, for they are as dissimilar as books can be, nor on account of the eminence of their authors, for in general two great authors are too much for one essay, but because they are the best possible illustration of something we have to say upon poetical art – because they may give to it life and freshness. The accident of contemporaneous publication has here brought together two books, very characteristic of modern art, and we want to show how they are characteristic.

[...]

We are disposed to believe that no very sharp definition can be given – at least in the present state of the critical art – of the boundary line between poetry and other sorts of imaginative delineation. Between the undoubted dominions of the two kinds there is a debateable land; everybody is agreed that the *Oedipus at Colonus is* poetry: every one is agreed that the wonderful appearance of Mrs. Veal is *not* poetry.[2] But the exact line which separates grave novels in verse like *Aylmer's Field* or *Enoch Arden*, from grave novels not in verse like *Silas Marner* or *Adam Bede*, we own we cannot draw with any confidence. Nor, perhaps, is it very important; whether a narrative is thrown into verse or not certainly depends in part on the taste of the age, and in part on its mechanical helps. Verse is the only mechanical help to the memory in rude times, and there is little writing till a cheap something is found to write upon, and a cheap something to write with. Poetry – verse at least – is the literature of *all work* in early ages; it is only later ages which write in what *they* think a natural and simple prose. There are other casual influences in the matter too; but they are not material now. We need only say here that poetry, because it has a more marked rhythm than prose, must be more intense in meaning and more concise in style than prose. People expect a 'marked rhythm' to imply something worth marking; if it fails to do so they are disappointed. They are displeased at the visible waste of a powerful instrument; they call it 'doggerel,' and rightly call it, for the metrical expression of full thought and eager feeling – the burst of metre – incident to high imagination, should not be wasted on petty matters which prose does as well, – which it does better – which it suits by its very limpness and weakness, whose small changes it follows more easily, and to whose lowest details it can fully and without effort degrade itself. Verse, too, should be *more concise*, for long-continued rhythm tends to jade the mind, just as brief rhythm tends to attract the attention. Poetry should be memorable and emphatic, intense, and *soon over*.

The great divisions of poetry, and of all other literary art, arise from the different modes in which these *types* – these characteristic men, these characteristic feelings – may be variously described. There are three principal modes which we shall attempt to describe – the *pure*, which is sometimes, but not very wisely, called the classical; the *ornate*, which is also unwisely called romantic; and the *grotesque*, which might be called the mediaeval.

[...]

The definition of *pure* literature is that it describes the type in its simplicity, we mean, with the exact amount of accessory circumstance which is necessary to bring it before the mind in finished

WORDSWORTH, TENNYSON, AND BROWNING
1 both published 1864. *Enoch Arden* written November 1861–April 1862.

2 Sophocles, *Oedipus at Colonus* (406–5 BC); Daniel Defoe, *A True Relation of The Apparition of One Mrs Veal* (1706).

perfection, and *no more* than that amount. The *type* needs some accessories from its nature – a picturesque landscape does not consist wholly of picturesque features. There is a setting of surroundings – as the Americans would say, of *fixings* – without which the reality is not itself. By a traditional mode of speech, as soon as we see a picture in which a complete effect is produced by detail so rare and so harmonized as to escape us, we say how 'classical'. The whole which is to be seen appears at once and through the detail, but the detail itself is not seen: we do not think of that which gives us the idea; we are absorbed in the idea itself. Just so in literature the pure art is that which works with the fewest strokes; the fewest, that is, for its purpose, for its aim is to call up and bring home to men an idea, a form, a character, and if that idea be twisted, that form be involved, that character perplexed, many strokes of literary art will be needful. Pure art does not mutilate its object: it represents it as fully as is possible with the slightest effort which is possible: it shrinks from no needful circumstances, as little as it inserts any which are needless. The precise peculiarity is not merely that no incidental circumstance is inserted which does not tell on the main design: no art is fit to be called *art* which permits a stroke to be put in without an object; but that only the minimum of such circumstance is inserted at all. The form is sometimes said to be bare, the accessories are sometimes said to be invisible, because the appendages are so choice that the shape only is perceived.

The English literature undoubtedly contains much impure literature; impure in its style if not in its meaning: but it also contains one great, one nearly perfect, model of the pure style in the literary expression of typical *sentiment*; and one not perfect, but gigantic and close approximation to perfection in the pure delineation of objective character. Wordsworth, perhaps, comes as near to choice purity of style in sentiment as is possible; Milton, with exceptions and conditions to be explained, approaches perfection by the strenuous purity with which he depicts character.

[…]

It is not unremarkable that we should find in Milton and in *Paradise Lost* the best specimen of pure style. He was schoolmaster in a pedantic age, and there is nothing so unclassical – nothing so impure in style – as pedantry. The out-of-door conversational life of Athens was as opposed to bookish scholasticism as a life can be. The most perfect books have been written not by those who thought much of books, but by those who thought little, by those who were under the restraint of a sensitive talking world, to which books had contributed something, and a various eager life the rest. Milton is generally unclassical in spirit where he is learned, and naturally, because the purest poets do not overlay their conceptions with book knowledge, and the classical poets, having in comparison no books, were under little temptation to impair the purity of their style by the accumulation of their research. Over and above this, there is in Milton, and a little in Wordsworth also, one defect which is in the highest degree faulty and unclassical, which mars the effect and impairs the perfection of the pure style. There is a want of *spontaneity*, and a sense of effort. It has been happily said that Plato's words must have *grown* into their places. No one would say so of Milton or even of Wordsworth. About both of them there is a taint of duty; a vicious sense of the good man's task. Things seem right where they are, but they seem to be put where they are. *Flexibility* is essential to the consummate perfection of the pure style because the sensation of the poet's efforts carries away our thoughts from his achievements. We are admiring his labours when we should be enjoying his words. But this is a defect in those two writers, not a defect in pure art. Of course it *is* more difficult to write in few words than to write in many; to take the best adjuncts, and those only, for what you have to say, instead of using all which comes to hand; it *is* an additional labour if you write verses in a morning, to spend the rest of the day in *choosing*, or making those verses fewer. But a perfect artist in the pure style is as effortless and as natural as in any style, perhaps is more so.

[…]

The extreme opposite to this pure art is what may be called ornate art. This species of art aims also at giving a delineation of the typical idea in its perfection and its fullness, but it aims at so doing in a manner most different. It wishes to surround the type with the greatest number of circumstances which it will *bear*. It works not by choice and selection, but by accumulation and aggregation. The idea is not, as in the pure style, presented with the least clothing which it will endure, but with the richest and most involved clothing that it will admit.

We are fortunate in not having to hunt out of past literature an illustrative specimen of the ornate style. Mr. Tennyson has just given one admirable in itself, and most characteristic of the defects and the merits of this style. The story of Enoch Arden, as he has enhanced and presented it, is a rich and splendid composite of imagery and illustration. Yet how simple that story is in itself. A sailor who sells fish, breaks his leg, gets dismal, gives up selling fish, goes to sea, is wrecked on a desert island, stays there some years, on his return finds his wife married to a miller, speaks to a landlady on the subject, and dies. Told in the pure and simple, the unadorned and classical style, this story would not have taken three pages, but Mr. Tennyson has been able to make it the principal – the largest tale in his new volume. He has done so only by giving to every event and incident in the volume an accompanying commentary. He tells a great deal about the torrid zone which a rough sailor like Enoch Arden certainly would not have perceived; and he gives to the fishing village, to which all the characters belong, a softness and a fascination which such villages scarcely possess in reality.

The description of the tropical island on which the sailor is thrown, is an absolute model of adorned art:

> The mountain wooded to the peak, the lawns
> And winding glades high up like ways to Heaven,
> The slender coco's drooping crown of plumes,
> The lightning flash of insect and of bird,
> The lustre of the long convolvuluses
> That coil'd around the stately stems, and ran
> Ev'n to the limit of the land, the glows
> And glories of the broad belt of the world,
> All these he saw; but what he fain had seen
> He could not see, the kindly human face,
> Nor ever hear a kindly voice, but heard
> The myriad shriek of wheeling ocean-fowl,
> The league-long roller thundering on the reef,
> The moving whisper of huge trees that branch'd
> And blossom'd in the zenith, or the sweep
> Of some precipitous rivulet to the wave,
> As down the shore he ranged, or all day long
> Sat often in the seaward-gazing gorge,
> A shipwreck'd sailor, waiting for a sail:
> No sail from day to day, but every day
> The sunrise broken into scarlet shafts
> Among the palms and ferns and precipices;
> The blaze upon the waters to the east;
> The blaze upon his island overhead;
> The blaze upon the waters to the west;
> Then the great stars that globed themselves in Heaven,
> The hollower-bellowing ocean, and again
> The scarlet shafts of sunrise – but no sail.[3]

No expressive circumstance can be added to this description, no enhancing detail suggested. A much less happy instance is the description of Enoch's life before he sailed:

> While Enoch was abroad on wrathful seas.
> Or often journeying landward; for in truth
> Enoch's white horse, and Enoch's ocean spoil
> In ocean-smelling osier, and his face,
> Rough-redden'd with a thousand winter gales,

3   lines 568–95.

> Not only to the market-cross were known,
> But in the leafy lanes behind the down,
> Far as the portal-warding lion-whelp,
> And peacock yew-tree of the lonely Hall,
> Whose Friday fare was Enoch's ministering.[4]

So much has not often been made of selling fish.

The essence of ornate art is in this manner to accumulate round the typical object, everything which can be said about it, every associated thought that can be connected with it without impairing the essence of the delineation.

The first defect which strikes a student of ornate art – the first which arrests the mere reader of it – is what is called a want of simplicity. Nothing is described as it is, everything has about it an atmosphere of *something else*. The combined and associated thoughts, though they set off and heighten particular ideas and aspects of the central conception, yet complicate it: a simple thing – 'a daisy by the river's brim' – is never left by itself, something else is put with it; something not more connected with it than 'lion-whelp' and the 'peacock yew-tree' are with the 'fresh fish for sale' that Enoch carries past them. Even in the highest cases ornate art leaves upon a cultured and delicate taste, the conviction that it is not the highest art, that it is somehow excessive and over-rich, that it is not chaste in itself or chastening to the mind that sees it – that it is in an unexplained manner unsatisfactory, 'a thing in which we feel there is some hidden want!'

That want is a want of 'definition'. We must all know landscapes, river landscapes especially, which are in the highest sense beautiful, which when we first see them give us a delicate pleasure; which in some – and these the best cases – give even a gentle sense of surprise that such things should be so beautiful, and yet when we come to live in them, to spend even a few hours in them, we seem stifled and oppressed. On the other hand there are people to whom the sea-shore is a companion, an exhilaration; and not so much for the brawl of the shore as for the *limited* vastness, the finite infinite of the ocean as they see it. Such people often come home braced and nerved, and if they spoke out the truth, would have only to say, 'We have seen the horizon line'; if they were let alone indeed, they would gaze on it hour after hour, so great to them is the fascination, so full the sustaining calm, which they gain from that union of form and greatness. To a very inferior extent, but still, perhaps, to an extent which most people understand better, a common arch will have the same effect. A bridge completes a river landscape; if of the old and many-arched sort it regulates by a long series of defined forms the vague outline of wood and river which before had nothing to measure it; if of the new scientific sort it introduces still more strictly a geometrical element; it stiffens the scenery which was before too soft, too delicate, too vegetable. Just such is the effect of pure style in literary art. It calms by conciseness; while the ornate style leaves on the mind a mist of beauty, an excess of fascination, a complication of charm, the pure style leaves behind it the simple, defined, measured idea, as it is, and by itself. That which is chaste chastens; there is a poised energy – a state half thrill, and half tranquillity – which pure art gives, which no other can give; a pleasure justified as well as felt; an ennobled satisfaction at what ought to satisfy us, and must ennoble us.

Ornate art is to pure art what a painted statue is to an unpainted. It is impossible to deny that a touch of colour *does* bring out certain parts, does convey certain expressions, does heighten certain features, but it leaves on the work as a whole, a want, as we say, 'of something'; a want of that inseparable chasteness which clings to simple sculpture, an impairing predominance of alluring details which impairs our satisfaction with our own satisfaction; which makes us doubt whether a higher being than ourselves will be satisfied even though we are so. In the very same manner, though the *rouge* of ornate literature excites our eye, it also impairs our confidence.

[...]

The essence of pure art consists in its describing what is as it is, and this is very well for what can bear it, but there are many inferior things which will not bear it, and which nevertheless

---

4   lines 91–100.

ought to be described in books. A certain kind of literature deals with illusions, and this kind of literature has given a colouring to the name romantic. A man of rare genius, and even of poetical genius, has gone so far as to make these illusions the true subject of poetry – almost the sole subject. 'Without,' says Father Newman, of one of his characters, 'being himself a poet, he was in the season of poetry, in the sweet spring-time, when the year is most beautiful because it is new. Novelty was beauty to a heart so open and cheerful as his; not only because it was novelty, and had its proper charm as such, but because when we first see things, we see them in a gay confusion, which is a principal element of the poetical. As time goes on, and we number and sort and measure things, – as we gain views, – we advance towards philosophy and truth, but we recede from poetry.

'When we ourselves were young, we once on a time walked on a hot summer-day from Oxford to Newington – a dull road, as any one who has gone it knows; yet it was new to us; and we protest to you, reader, believe it or not, laugh or not, as you will, to us it seemed on that occasion quite touchingly beautiful; and a soft melancholy came over us, of which the shadows fall even now, when we look back upon that dusty, weary journey. And why? because every object which met us was unknown and full of mystery. A tree or two in the distance seemed the beginning of a great wood, or park, stretching endlessly; a hill implied a vale beyond, with that vale's history; the bye-lanes, with their green hedges, wound on and vanished, yet were not lost to the imagination. Such was our first journey; but when we had gone it several times, the mind refused to act, the scene ceased to enchant, stern reality alone remained; and we thought it one of the most tiresome, odious roads we ever had occasion to traverse.'[5]

That is to say, that the function of the poet is to introduce a 'gay confusion', a rich medley which does not exist in the actual world – which perhaps could not exist in any world – but which would seem pretty if it did exist. Everyone who reads *Enoch Arden* will perceive that this notion of all poetry is exactly applicable to this one poem. Whatever be made of Enoch's 'Ocean spoil in ocean-smelling osier,' of the 'portal-warding lion-whelp, and peacock yew-tree', every one knows that in himself Enoch could not have been charming. People who sell fish about the country (and that is what he did, though Mr. Tennyson won't speak out, and wraps it up) never are beautiful. As Enoch was and must be coarse, in itself the poem must depend for its charm on a 'gay confusion' – on a splendid accumulation of impossible accessories.

Mr. Tennyson knows this better than many of us – he knows the country world; he has proved it that no one living knows it better; he has painted with pure art – with art which describes what is a race perhaps more refined, more delicate, more conscientious, than the sailor – the 'Northern Farmer', and we all know what a splendid, what a living thing, he has made of it. He could, if he only would, have given us the ideal sailor in like manner – the ideal of the natural sailor we mean – the characteristic present man as he lives and is. But this he has not chosen. He has endeavoured to describe an exceptional sailor, at an exceptionally refined port, performing a graceful act, an act of relinquishment. And with this task before him, his profound taste taught him that ornate art was a necessary medium – was the sole effectual instrument – for his purpose. It was necessary for him if possible to abstract the mind from reality, to induce us *not* to conceive or think of sailors as they are while we are reading of his sailors, but to think of what a person who did not know might fancy sailors to be. A casual traveller on the sea-shore, with the sensitive mood and the romantic imagination Mr. Newman has described, might fancy, would fancy, a seafaring village to be like that. Accordingly, Mr. Tennyson has made it his aim to call off the stress of fancy from real life, to occupy it otherwise, to bury it with pretty accessories; to engage it on the 'peacock yew-tree', and the 'portal-warding lion-whelp'. Nothing, too, can be more splendid than the description of the tropics as Mr. Tennyson delineates them, but a sailor would not have felt the tropics in that manner. The beauties of nature would not have so much occupied him. He would have known little of the scarlet shafts of sunrise and nothing of the long convolvuluses. As in *Robinson Crusoe*, his own petty contrivances and his small ailments would have been the principal subject to him. 'For three years', he might have said, 'my back was bad, and then I put two

5   John Henry Newman, *Loss and Gain: The Story of a Convert* (1848), ch. 3.

pegs into a piece of drift wood and so made a chair, and after that it pleased God to send me a chill.' In real life his piety would scarcely have gone beyond that.

It will indeed be said, that though the sailor had no words for, and even no explicit conscious-ness of the splendid details of the torrid zone, yet that he had, notwithstanding, a dim latent inex-pressible conception of them: though he could not speak of them or describe them, yet they were much to him. And doubtless such is the case. Rude people are impressed by what is beautiful – deeply impressed – though they could not describe what they see, or what they feel. But what is absurd in Mr. Tennyson's description – absurd when we abstract it from the gorgeous additions and ornaments with which Mr. Tennyson distracts us – is, that his hero feels nothing else but these great splendours. We hear nothing of the physical ailments, the rough devices, the low super-stitions, which really would have been the *first* things, the favourite and principal occupations of his mind. Just so when he gets home he *may* have had such fine sentiments, though it is odd, and he *may* have spoken of them to his landlady, though that is odder still – but it is incredible that his whole mind should be made up of fine sentiments. Beside those sweet feelings, if he had them, there must have been many more obvious, more prosaic, and some perhaps more healthy. Mr. Tennyson has shown a profound judgement in distracting us as he does. He has given us a classic delineation of the 'Northern Farmer' with no ornament at all – as bare a thing as can be – because he then wanted to describe a true type of real men: he has given us a sailor crowded all over with ornament and illustration, because he then wanted to describe an unreal type of fan-cied men, not sailors as they are, but sailors as they might be wished.

Another prominent element in *Enoch Arden* is yet more suitable to, yet more requires the aid of, ornate art. Mr. Tennyson undertook to deal with *half belief*. The presentiments which Annie feels are exactly of that sort which everybody has felt, and which every one has half believed – which hardly any one has more than half believed. Almost every one, it has been said, would be angry if any one else reported that he believed in ghosts; yet hardly any one, when thinking by himself, wholly disbelieves them. Just so such presentiments as Mr. Tennyson depicts, impress the inner mind so much that the outer mind – the rational understanding – hardly likes to consider them nicely or to discuss them sceptically. For these dubious themes an ornate or complex style is need-ful. Classical art speaks out what it has to say plainly and simply. Pure style cannot hesitate; it describes in concisest outline what is, as it is. If a poet really believes in presentiments he can speak out in pure style. One who could have been a poet – one of the few in any age of whom one can say certainly that they could have been, and have not been – has spoken thus:

> When Heaven sends sorrow,
>   Warnings go first,
>   Lest it should burst
>   With stunning might
>   On souls too bright
>   To fear the morrow.
>
> Can science bear us
>   To the hid springs
>   Of human things?
>   Why may not dream,
>   Or thought's day-gleam,
>   Startle, yet cheer us?
>
> Are such thoughts fetters,
>   While faith disowns
>   Dread of earth's tones,
>   Recks but Heaven's call,
>   And on the wall,
>   Reads but Heaven's letters?[6]

6 John Henry Newman, 'Warnings' (1833), in *Hymns* (1876).

But if a poet is not sure whether presentiments are true or not true; if he wishes to leave his readers in doubt; if he wishes an atmosphere of indistinct illusion and of moving shadow, he must use the romantic style, the style of miscellaneous adjunct, the style 'which shirks, not meets' your intellect, the style which as you are scrutinizing disappears.

Nor is this all, or even the principal lesson, which *Enoch Arden* may suggest to us, of the use of ornate art. That art is the appropriate art for an *unpleasing type*. Many of the characters of real life, if brought distinctly, prominently, and plainly before the mind, as they really are, if shown in their inner nature, their actual essence, are doubtless very unpleasant. They would be horrid to meet and horrid to think of. We fear it must be owned that Enoch Arden is this kind of person. A dirty sailor who did *not* go home to his wife is not an agreeable being: a varnish must be put on him to make him shine. It is true that he acts rightly; that he is very good. But such is human nature that it finds a little tameness in mere morality. Mere virtue belongs to a charity school-girl, and has a taint of the catechism. All of us feel this, though most of us are too timid, too scrupulous, too anxious about the virtue of others, to speak out. We are ashamed of our nature in this respect, but it is not the less our nature. And if we look deeper into the matter there are many reasons why we should not be ashamed of it. The soul of man, and as we necessarily believe of beings greater than man, has many parts beside its moral part. It has an intellectual part, an artistic part, even a religious part, in which mere morals have no share. In Shakespeare or Goethe, even in Newton or Archimedes, there is much which will not be cut down to the shape of the commandments. They have thoughts, feelings, hopes – immortal thoughts and hopes – which have influenced the life of men, and the souls of men, ever since their age, but which the 'whole duty of man', the ethical compendium, does not recognize. Nothing is more unpleasant than a virtuous person with a mean mind. A highly developed moral nature joined to an undeveloped intellectual nature, an undeveloped artistic nature, and a very limited religious nature, is of necessity repulsive. It represents a bit of human nature – a good bit, of course, but a bit only – in disproportionate, unnatural, and revolting prominence; and, therefore, unless an artist use delicate care, we are offended. The dismal act of a squalid man needed many condiments to make it pleasant, and therefore Mr. Tennyson was right to mix them subtly and to use them freely.

A mere act of self-denial can indeed scarcely be pleasant upon paper. An heroic struggle with an external adversary, even though it end in a defeat, may easily be made attractive. Human nature likes to see itself look grand, and it looks grand when it is making a brave struggle with foreign foes. But it does not look grand when it is divided against itself. An excellent person striving with temptation is a very admirable being in reality, but he is not a pleasant being in description. We hope he will win and overcome his temptation, but we feel that he would be a more interesting being, a higher being, if he had not felt that temptation so much. The poet must make the struggle great in order to make the self-denial virtuous, and if the struggle be too great, we are apt to feel some mixture of contempt. The internal metaphysics of a divided nature are but an inferior subject for art, and if they are to be made attractive, much else must be combined with them. If the excellence of *Hamlet* had depended on the ethical qualities of Hamlet, it would not have been the masterpiece of our literature. He acts virtuously of course, and kills the people he ought to kill, but Shakespeare knew that such goodness would not much interest the pit. He made him a handsome prince, and a puzzling meditative character; these secular qualities relieve his moral excellence, and so he becomes 'nice'. In proportion as an artist has to deal with types essentially imperfect, he must disguise their imperfections; he must accumulate around them as many first-rate accessories as may make his readers forget that they are themselves second-rate. The sudden *millionaires* of the present day hope to disguise their social defects by buying old places, and hiding among aristocratic furniture; just so a great artist who has to deal with characters artistically imperfect will use an ornate style, will fit them into a scene where there is much else to look at.

For these reasons ornate art is within the limits as legitimate as pure art. It does what pure art could not do. The very excellence of pure art confines its employment. Precisely because it gives the best things by themselves and exactly as they are, it fails when it is necessary to describe inferior things among other things, with a list of enhancements and a crowd of accompaniments that in reality do not belong to it. Illusion, half belief, unpleasant types, imperfect types, are as much the proper sphere of ornate art, as an inferior landscape is the proper sphere for the true efficacy of moonlight. A really great landscape needs sunlight and bears sunlight; but moonlight is an equalizer of beauties; it gives a romantic unreality to what will not stand the bare truth. And just so does romantic art.

There is, however, a third kind of art which differs from these on the point in which they most resemble one another. Ornate art and pure art have this in common, that they paint the types of literature in as good perfection as they can. Ornate art, indeed, uses undue disguises and unreal enhancements; it does not confine itself to the best types; on the contrary it is its office to make the best of imperfect types and lame approximations; but ornate art, as much as pure art, catches its subject in the best light it can, takes the most developed aspect of it which it can find, and throws upon it the most congruous colours it can use. But grotesque art does just the contrary. It takes the type, so to say, *in difficulties*. It gives a representation of it in its minimum development, amid the circumstances least favourable to it, just while it is struggling with obstacles, just where it is encumbered with incongruities. It deals, to use the language of science, not with normal types but with abnormal specimens; to use the language of old philosophy, not with what nature is striving to be, but with what by some lapse she has happened to become.

This art works by contrast. It enables you to see, it makes you see, the perfect type by painting the opposite deviation. It shows you what ought to be by what ought not to be, when complete it reminds you of the perfect image, by showing you the distorted and imperfect image. Of this art we possess in the present generation one prolific master. Mr. Browning is an artist working by incongruity. Possibly hardly one of his most considerable efforts can be found which is not great because of its odd mixture. He puts together things which no one else would have put together, and produces on our minds a result which no one else would have produced, or tried to produce. His admirers may not like all we may have to say of him. But in our way we too are among his admirers. No one ever read him without seeing not only his great ability but his great *mind*. He not only possesses superficial useable talents, but the strong something, the inner secret something which uses them and controls them; he is great, not in mere accomplishments, but in himself. He has applied a hard strong intellect to real life; he has applied the same intellect to the problems of his age. He has striven to know what *is*: he has endeavoured not to be cheated by counterfeits, not to be infatuated with illusions. His heart is in what he says. He has battered his brain against his creed till be believes it. He has accomplishments too, the more effective because they are mixed. He is at once a student of mysticism, and a citizen of the world. He brings to the club sofa distinct visions of old creeds, intense images of strange thoughts: he takes to the bookish student tidings of wild Bohemia, and little traces of the *demi-monde*. He puts down what is good for the naughty and what is naughty for the good. Over women his easier writings exercise that imperious power which belongs to the writings of a great man of the world upon such matters. He knows women, and therefore they wish to know him. If we blame many of Browning's efforts, it is in the interest of art, and not from a wish to hurt or degrade him.

If we wanted to illustrate the nature of grotesque art by an exaggerated instance we should have selected a poem which the chance of late publication brings us in this new volume. Mr. Browning has undertaken to describe what may be called *mind in difficulties* – mind set to make out the universe under the worst and hardest circumstances. He takes 'Caliban', not perhaps exactly Shakespeare's Caliban, but an analogous and worse creature; a strong thinking power, but a nasty creature – a gross animal, uncontrolled and unelevated by any feeling of religion or duty. The delineation of him will show that Mr. Browning does not wish to take undue advantage of his readers by a choice of nice subjects.

[Quotes 'Caliban upon Setebos', lines 1–11 and 24–58.]

It may seem perhaps to most readers that these lines are very difficult, and that they are unpleasant. And so they are. We quote them to illustrate, not the *success* of grotesque art, but the *nature* of grotesque art. It shows the end at which this species of art aims, and if it fails, it is from over-boldness in the choice of a subject by the artist, or from the defects of its execution. A thinking faculty more in difficulties – a great type, – an inquisitive, searching intellect under more disagreeable conditions, with worse helps, more likely to find falsehood, less likely to find truth, can scarcely be imagined. Nor is the mere description of the thought at all bad: on the contrary, if we closely examine it, it is very clever. Hardly any one could have amassed so many ideas at once nasty and suitable. But scarcely any readers – any casual readers – who are not of the sect of Mr. Browning's admirers will be able to examine it enough to appreciate it. From a defect, partly of subject, and partly of style, many of Mr. Browning's works make a demand upon the reader's zeal and sense of duty to which the nature of most readers is unequal. They have on the turf the convenient expression 'staying power': some horses can hold on and others cannot. But hardly any reader not of especial and peculiar nature can hold on through such composition. There is not enough of 'staying power' in human nature. One of his greatest admirers once owned to us that he seldom or never began a new poem without looking on in advance, and foreseeing with caution what length of intellectual adventure he was about to commence. Whoever will work hard at such poems will find much mind in them: they are a sort of quarry of ideas, but whoever goes there will find these ideas in such a jagged, ugly, useless shape that he can hardly bear them.

[…]

It is very natural that a poet whose wishes incline, or whose genius conducts him to a grotesque art, should be attracted towards mediaeval subjects. There is no age whose legends are so full of grotesque subjects, and no age where real life was so fit to suggest them. Then, more than at any other time, good principles have been under great hardships. The vestiges of ancient civilization, the germs of modern civilization, the little remains of what had been, the small beginnings of what is, were buried under a cumbrous mass of barbarism and cruelty. Good elements hidden in horrid accompaniments are the special theme of grotesque art, and these mediaeval life and legends afford more copiously than could have been furnished before Christianity gave its new elements of good, or since modern civilization has removed some few at least of the old elements of destruction. A *buried* life like the spiritual mediaeval was Mr. Browning's natural element, and he was right to be attracted by it. His mistake has been, that he has not made it pleasant; that he has forced his art to topics on which no one could charm, or on which he, at any rate, could not; that on these occasions and in these poems he has failed in fascinating men and women of sane taste.

We say 'sane' because there is a most formidable and estimable *insane* taste. The will has great though indirect power over the taste, just as it has over the belief. There are some horrid beliefs from which human nature revolts, from which at first it shrinks, to which, at first, no effort can force it. But if we fix the mind upon them they have a power over us just because of their natural offensiveness. They are like the sight of human blood: experienced soldiers tell us that at first men are sickened by the smell and newness of blood almost to death and fainting, but that as soon as they harden their hearts and stiffen their minds, as soon as they *will* bear it, then comes on appetite for slaughter, a tendency to gloat on carnage, to love blood, at least for the moment, with a deep eager love. It is a principle that if we put down a healthy instinctive aversion, nature avenges herself by creating an unhealthy insane attraction. For this reason the most earnest truth-seeking men fall into the worst delusions; they will not let their mind alone; they force it towards some ugly thing, which a crotchet of argument, a conceit of intellect recommends, and nature punishes their disregard of her warning by subjection to the ugly one, by belief in it. Just so the most industrious critics get the most admiration. They think it unjust to rest in their instinctive natural horror: they overcome it, and angry nature gives them over to ugly poems and marries them to detestable stanzas.

Mr. Browning possibly, and some of the worst of Mr. Browning's admirers certainly, will say that these grotesque objects exist in real life, and therefore they ought to be, at least may be, described in art. But though pleasure is not the end of poetry, pleasing is a condition of poetry. An exceptional monstrosity of horrid ugliness cannot be made pleasing, except it be made to suggest – to recall – the perfection, the beauty, from which it is a deviation. Perhaps in extreme cases no art is equal to this; but then such self-imposed problems should not be worked by the artist; these out-of-the-way and detestable subjects should be let alone by him. It is rather characteristic of Mr. Browning to neglect this rule. He is the most of a realist, and the least of an idealist of any poet we know. He evidently sympathizes with some part at least of Bishop Blougram's apology.[7] Anyhow this world exists. 'There *is* good wine – there *are* pretty women – there *are* comfortable benefices – there *is* money, and it is pleasant to spend it. Accept the creed of your age and you get these, reject that creed and you lose them. And for what do you lose them? For a fancy creed of your own, which no one else will accept, which hardly any one will call a "creed", which most people will consider a sort of unbelief.' Again, Mr. Browning evidently loves what we may call the realism, the grotesque realism, of orthodox christianity. Many parts of it in which great divines have felt keen difficulties are quite pleasant to him. He must *see* his religion, he must have an 'object-lesson' in believing. He must have a creed that will *take*, which wins and holds the miscellaneous world, which stout men will heed, which nice women will adore. The spare moments of solitary religion – the 'obdurate questionings', the high 'instincts', the 'first affections', the 'shadowy recollections',

> Which, do they what they may,
> Are yet the fountain-light of all our day –
> Are yet a master-light of all our seeing;

the great but vague faith – the unutterable tenets seem to him worthless, visionary; they are not enough immersed in matter; they move about 'in worlds not realized'. We wish he could be tried like the prophet once; he would have found God in the earthquake and the storm; he would have deciphered from them a bracing and a rough religion: he would have known that crude men and ignorant women felt them too, and he would accordingly have trusted them; but he would have distrusted and disregarded the 'still small voice'; he would have said it was 'fancy' – a thing you thought you heard to-day, but were not sure you had heard to-morrow: he would call it a nice illusion, an immaterial prettiness; he would ask triumphantly 'How are you to get the mass of men to heed this little thing?' he would have perserved and insisted '*My wife* does not hear it'.[8]

But although a suspicion of beauty, and a taste for ugly reality, have led Mr. Browning to exaggerate the functions, and to caricature the nature of grotesque art, we own or rather we maintain that he has given many excellent specimens of that art within its proper boundaries and limits. Take an example, his picture of what we may call the *bourgeois* nature in *difficulties*, in the utmost difficulty, in contact with magic and the supernatural. He has made of it something homely, comic, true; reminding us of what *bourgeois* nature really is. By showing us the type under abnormal conditions, he reminds us of the type under its best and most satisfactory conditions – [Quotes extensively from 'The Pied Piper of Hamelin,' *Dramatic Lyrics* (1842).]

Something more we had to say of Mr. Browning, but we must stop. It is singularly characteristic of this age that the poems which rise to the surface should be examples of ornate art, and grotesque art, not of pure art. We live in the realm of the *half* educated. The number of readers grows daily, but the quality of readers does not improve rapidly. The middle class is scattered, headless; it is well-meaning but aimless; wishing to be wise, but ignorant how to be wise. The aristocracy of England never was a literary aristocracy, never even in the days of its full power, of its unquestioned predominance, did it guide – did it even seriously try to guide – the taste of England. Without guidance young men and tired men are thrown amongst a mass of books; they have to choose which they like; many of them would much like to improve their culture, to chasten their taste, if they knew how. But left to themselves they take, not pure art, but showy art; not that which permanently relieves the eye and makes it happy whenever it looks, and as long as it looks, but *glaring* art which catches and arrests the eye for a moment, but which in the end fatigues it. But before the wholesome remedy of nature – the fatigue – arrives, the hasty reader has passed on to some new excitement, which in its turn stimulates for an instant, and then is passed by for ever. These conditions are not favourable to the due appreciation of pure art – of that art which

---

7 'Bishop Blougram's Apology', *Men and Women* (1855).
8 allusion to prophet Elijah, who learns God is not in earthquake, wind, fire, but in 'a still small voice', 1 Kings 19. 11–12.

must be known before it is admired – which must have fastened irrevocably on the brain before you appreciate it – which you must love ere it will seem worthy of your love. Women too, whose voice in literature counts as well as that of men – and in a light literature counts for more than that of men – women, such as we know them, such as they are likely to be, ever prefer a delicate un-reality to a true or firm art. A dressy literature, an exaggerated literature seem to be fated to us. These are our curses, as other times had theirs.

The National Review, *November 1864. [Full essay in* Collected Works of Walter Bagehot, *ed. Norman St John Stevas, 8 vols (The Economist, 1965), Literary Essays (2 vols), I, 318–66.]*

Dinah Maria Mulock (Mrs Craik) (1826–87)

Dinah Mulock was born 20 April 1826, the oldest child of the pastor of a small Baptist chapel in Stoke-on-Trent, Thomas Mulock, and his schoolmistress wife Dinah. The family and chapel atmosphere was bookish as well as Non-conformist. Young Dinah's Latin was good enough by the age of thirteen for her to teach it to her mother's pupils. Her first published poem, on the birth of the Princess Royal, appeared in the *Staffordshire Advertiser* when she was sixteen. Her father becoming increasingly unstable and neglectful – he was compelled to resign his pastorate – around 1846 the aspiring author took her invalid mother and young brother away to London, in hopes of making enough money there by writing to keep them. She was greatly helped at the moral end of the book trade by Alexander Macmillan, the publisher, and Charles Mudie of the notoriously restrictive Circulating Library. The righteously inclined journals *Good Words* and *Once A Week* were natural homes for her stories and poems. Her first three-decker novel for right-minded adults, *The Ogilvies* (about marriage),

appeared in 1849. Her fictions flowed abundantly; she moved to Hampstead; she was a popular writer. True fame indeed arrived with the huge-selling *John Halifax, Gentleman* (1856), a moving story of Christian middle-class ideals in the from-rags-to-riches mode. Numerous other fictions followed, including the even huger selling *A Life for a Life* (1859). Very prosperous, she had William Morris design her house at Shortlands, near Bromley, in Kent (1869). In 1864 she had been granted a Civil List Pension and a year after that she married George Lillie Craik, one of the Macmillan partners. There were no children. Her scores of books include several volumes of poetry as well as translations and volumes of cultural comment. Her warm description of women artists in Paris in *About Money And Other Things* (1886) is characteristic of the gentle radicalism which marks other writings such as *A Woman's Thoughts About Women* (1858) – women will get on, as she had done, in areas such as the arts. She died suddenly, 12 October 1887.

TO ELIZABETH BARRETT BROWNING ON HER LATER SONNETS. 1856

I know not if the cycle of strange years
    Will ever bring thy human face to me,
Sister! – I say this, not as of thy peers,
    But like as those who their own grief can see
In the large mirror of another's tears.

Comforter! many a time thy soul's white feet
    Stole on the silent darkness where I lay
With voice of distant singing – solemn sweet –
    'Be of good cheer, I too have trod that way;'
And I rose up and walked in strength complete.   10

Oft, as amidst the furnace of fierce woe
    My own will lit, I writhing stood, yet calm,
I saw thee moving near me, meek and low,
    Not speaking, – only chaunting the one psalm,
'God's love suffices when all world-loves go.'

Year after year have I, in passion strong,
    Clung to thy garments when my soul was faint, –

Touching thee, all unseen amid the throng;[1]
  But now, thou risest to joy's heaven – my saint!
And I look up – and cannot hear thy song.   20

Or hearing, understand not; save as those
  Who from without list to the bridegroom-strain
They might have sung – but that the dull gates close –[2]
  And so they smile a blessing through their pain,
Then, turning, lie and sleep among the snows.

So, go thou in, saint – sister – comforter!
  Of this, thy house of joy, heaven keep the doors!
And sometimes through the music and the stir
  Set thy lamp shining from the upper floors,
That we without may say – 'Bless God – and her!'   30

Poems by the Author of 'John Halifax, Gentleman'
(Longman, Green, Longman & Roberts, 1862).

Mortimer Collins (1827–76)

Mortimer Collins, comic poet, essayist, novelist, was born in Plymouth, 29 June 1827. His father, Francis Collins, was a solicitor, mathematician and author of a volume of *Spiritual Songs* (1824). Collins was persuaded into schoolmastering by his mother, and he taught maths at Queen Elizabeth's College, Guernsey, but his heart was in writing, and gradually he turned himself into a full-time literary man, editing journals, producing numerous comic poems, satires, parodies (he especially admired Aristophanes), as well as more earnest verse, especially love poems, several novels and volumes of essays. He contributed widely to papers such as *Fun, Punch, Temple Bar* and *Tinsley's Magazine.* His first volume of verses was *Idylls and Rhymes* (1855); eventually he produced over twenty books of various kinds. His first wife, Susannah Hubbard, widow of a Revd J. H. Crump, died in 1867 after eighteen years of marriage, and he married Frances Cotton a year later – she is the F. C. to whom several poems are addressed. Women feature greatly in his verses – often satirically (like Chloe the Cambridge graduate who stars in several squibs, and prefers, for instance, Cambridge π to cooking puddings), but not always satirically (some of his words about kisses and sweethearts in his Penny Readings mater-

ial for the locals caused a rumpus with the vicar in his village of Knowl Hill, Berkshire). He was a large man, an outdoors type, liking dogs and walking, who contributed many letters about bird-life to the *Times.* A Tory bohemian (notably careless about his clothes), he was old-fashioned in religion (there are poems in *The British Birds, from the Ghost of Aristophanes,* 1872, mocking freethinkers and positivists). Swinburne poured his usual invective on Collins for having satirically targeted the offensive 'pigmy poet' in *Two Plunges for a Pearl* (1872: originally in *London Society,* January–November 1871): 'blatant pothouse parasite', 'a scurrilous newspaper scribber'. Collins moved to Knowl Hill in 1862, rarely spending a night away from it. He wrote hard for much of the day, and again from ten until two at night, but still managed to have lots of literary friends – R. H. Horne, Frederick Locker-Lampson (who introduced him to Swinburne), Edmund Yates, and in particular the novelist R. D. Blackmore. Collins died of a bad heart, 28 July 1876. His friends edited various posthumous volumes. His second wife Frances (who died 17 March 1886) co-operated on several of his books and published a novel of her own, *A Broken Lily,* in 1882.

From: A LETTER TO THE RIGHT HON. BENJAMIN DISRAELI, M. P.

The statesman comes not: will the poet come?
Since Byron died, the Muses have been dumb.   [100]
Wordsworth was great, you tell me. Yes, of course;

TO ELIZABETH BARRETT BROWNING ON HER LATER SONNETS
1 as Jesus was touched by the woman ill with the 'issue of blood', Mark 5. 24–34.

2 the 'foolish virgins' excluded from the marriage feast, Matthew 25. 1–12.

But Byron was an elemental force –
Not an Apollo, such as Stratford sees,
But a fierce dauntless fighting Hercules;
English in brain and fibre, power and pique –
(Browning's Italian, and the Laureate Greek).
English that epic in the octave rhyme,
On whose wide canvas he has sketched the time: 10
English the wild eccentric course he ran –
He was a poet…ay, and more, a man.   [110]

Is Tennyson no poet? Yes, indeed,
'Miss Alfred's' are delicious books to read:
In summer tide, when all the woods are still,
Pleasant to wander at one's own sweet will,
Dream of the amorous gossiping that broke
The eternal silence of a garrulous oak,
Dream of the Princess who was buried deep
In an unfathomed century of sleep,
Dream of the savage adjectives that fall   20
From the loud lunatic of *Locksley Hall.*   [120]
Sweet singer of the madrigal melodious
Why did he make King Arthur's story odious?
Why, with a flattery at which men wince,
Compare the Hero to a blameless Prince?
Why send the old figures to a modern school,
Turn Vivian harlot, Merlin sensual fool?[1]

Lovely and lucid are the Laureate's pearls:
A perfect poet, sir, for little girls.   30
Soft flows his rhymeless verse, constructed well,
And sweetly matched each soothing syllable.   [130]
But where's the passion a great poet knows
When the hot blood in every artery flows?
Not his the satire even fools can feel,
When each strong line is a keen blade of steel;
Not his the lyric love that has unlaced
The cestus,[2] warm from Aphrodite's waist;
But if you like a smooth Virgilian style,
A very proper moral, free from bile,   40
Ethics of Dr. Watts', Colenso's creed,[3]
Those nice green volumes give you all you need.   [140]

Greater and less is Browning: greater far
He will be, dwelling in some future star.
This world's his nursery: well we know his tune –
A baby-giant, crying for the moon.
If he were only English! if he could
But think in English it would do him good.
Now, in Italian subtlety immersed,
His last and longest poem is his worst;[4]   50
He tells a tale whose actors would delight
Charles Reade or Wilkie Collins, men of might,[5]   [150]

A LETTER TO THE RIGHT HON. B. DISRAELI, M. P.

1 reference to Tennyson's *Idylls of the King* poems.

2 Roman boxing glove, made from bull-hide thongs and reinforced
by metal.

3 Isaac Watts, 18th-century hymn-writer; Colenso, controversial
modernist Bishop.

4 *The Ring and the Book* (1869).

5 macabre novelists.

A tale the Adelphi would receive with joy[6] –
And makes it longer than the tale of Troy.

Arnold is English. On the Berkshire marge
Of Thames, I see him watch the tardy barge,
While the swift swallow in endless cycle flies,
While the scythed hay in swathes of summer lies.
Ah! and he muses, wandering thus alone,
On one pure spirit, now in realms unknown.   60
Has that true poet, quick-departing guest,
In other regions found perpetual rest?[7]   [160]
I can forgive who saw the Reveller stray
To where Odysseus in Aiaie lay –
Who watched the Gipsy Scholar's mazy path
Over wild wold and solitary strath –
I can forgive him, that mysterious haze
Shrouds every vision of his later days,
That life is lost in melancholy mist…
But why the deuce did he turn essayist?   70

Swinburne, a singer perfect as the birds,
Poet spontaneous, demigod of words,   [170]
Too fond, no doubt, of blood and filth and foam,
With the hetaira[8] far too much at home,
Yet rises to the height of the highest bard,
Pourtraying Mary with her Chastelard.[9]
Learned historians, prodigies of toil,
Ne'er touched his picture of the Harlot Royal.
They could not know her chamber's faint perfume,
Or how lamps flickered in that amorous room,   80
Or how she kissed, or how white throat and breast
Throbbed through the midnight's exquisite unrest,   [180]
Or how her serpent nature, sensuous, cruel,
Made of what men call love a deadly duel –
Wherein the opponent always fell we know,
Dauphin or Darnley, Bothwell, Rizzio.[10]
Heartless and shameless, perfect form and face,
The poison-blossom of the Stuart's wild race,
Knowledge of her was Swinburne's fame and fate:
Behold, I crown him Mary's Laureate.   90

Nothing I know, and nothing will I say,
Of Morris – Chaucer of the modern day: [190]
Thus much I learn from various reviews –
He's the husband now of Chaucer's widowed Muse.
Of Locker what? Apollo in the fashion –
Humour and pathos mild, no touch of passion.
From Suckling, Lovelace, Prior, Luttrel, Praed,[11]
Locker inherits his inspiring Maid:
Not nude and passionate, not fast and flighty,
Like Swinburne's rosy-bosomed Aphrodite: 100
Not icy cold as Parian[12] sculpture is,

---

6   *Adelphi* magazine.
7   A. H. Clough.
8   concubine; prostitute.
9   *Chastelard* (1865), verse drama about Mary, Queen of Scots
(1542–87), and French admirer.

10   Mary's two husbands, her lover and her adviser: all come to sticky
ends.
11   17th- and 18th-century poets, plus Winthrop Mackworth Praed.
12   marble.

Like Tennyson's blue-stockinged Artemis: [200]
Not erudite and sapient, grimly frowning,
Like the Athena that's adored by Browning:
But just the Period's Girl, a pretty creature,
Of dainty style though inexpressive feature,
Who carefully reserves her choice opinions
For length of petticoats and bulk of chignons,
In whom no tragic impulse ever rankles,
Who always says her prayers and shows her ankles.[13]   110

A Letter to the Right Hon. Benjamin Disraeli, M. P. *(John Camden Hotten, 1869),
lines 99–208. (First published, anon. pamphlet.)*

To F. C.

20TH *February 1875*

Fast falls the snow, O lady mine,
Sprinkling the lawn with crystals fine,
But by the gods we won't repine
   While we're together,
We'll chat and rhyme and kiss and dine,
   Defying weather.

So stir the fire and pour the wine,
And let those sea-green eyes divine
Pour their love-madness into mine:
   I don't care whether   10
'Tis snow or sun or rain or shine
   If we're together.

Athenaeum *(2 September 1876).* Selections from the Poetical Works of
Mortimer Collins, *ed. F. Percy Cotton (Richard Bentley, 1886).*

SONNET TO F.C.

Women there are who say the world is slow
   To recognise their scientific power;
   Wherefore they fill with heat the flying hour,
And let the beauty of their sweet life go
Like water thro' a child's frail fingers. So
   Might the tree murmur not to be a tower,
   Might envy of the strong storm vex the shower
That wakes sweet blossoms and makes brooklets flow.
The lady whom I love has no such thought;
   No stolid strength of mind shall make her weak,   10
   No folly sink her in the sad abyss
Where these same scientific souls are caught.
   She knows a kiss befits a lovely cheek,
Ay, and that rosy lips were made to kiss.

Selections from the Poetical Works *(1886).*

---

13   See Frederick Locker-Lampson, 'My Mistress's Boots'.

SEA SONNET

II

I saw my Lady spring into the sea,
    And the sea loved her, and with wooing tide
    Touched her soft bosom and fair, fluttering side
And all the secrets that are sweet to me.
Next day old Ocean was awake with glee.
    Who wonders at his sudden strengthful pride,
    Having embraced my beauty and my bride
And felt her on his wild wave floating free?
Ocean, thou art a very ancient god,
    And I have tried thee in thy happiest hour,   10
    And won from thee an ecstasy divine;
Yet, though a man is moulded from a clod,
    And though a lady's only just a flower,
    Thou canst not know the glory that is mine.

Selections from the Poetical Works *(1886)*.

MARTIAL[1] IN LONDON

Exquisite wines and comestibles,
    From Slater, and Fortnum and Mason;[2]
Billiards, *écarté*,[3] and chess-tables;
    Water in vast marble basin;
Luminous books (not voluminous)
To read under beech-trees cacuminous;[4]
One friend who is fond of a distich,
And doesn't get too syllogistic;
A valet, who knows the complete art
Of service; – a maiden, his sweetheart;   10
Give me these, in some rural pavilion,
And I'll envy no Rothschild his million.

Selections from the Poetical Works *(1886)*.

George Meredith (1828–1909)

George Meredith, a wild and unconstrained novelist who also wrote poems, was born in Portsmouth, 12 February 1828, the son and grandson of tailors and naval outfitters. Under his father's management the family shop failed while G. M. was a boy and from an early age there began the cycle of reducing circumstances relieved by occasional accesses of funds from here and there. On his mother's money he went to a local boarding-school. On some kind of legacy he was sent for several months to the Moravian school at Neuwied near Coblenz in Germany. He came away at the end of 1844 knowing German at least. Early in 1845 he was articled to a solicitor in the City of London. Exceedingly poor – surviving, it's said, on a bowl of porridge a day – he turned to writing for a living that would never substantially materialize. He started on his lifelong career of contributing widely to the journals; became an intimate of the circle around the satirist Thomas Love Peacock; married at the age of twenty-one Peacock's daughter, Mary Ellen Nicolls, a writer and poet who was a widow several years older than him; they had a son.

MARTIAL IN LONDON
1   satirical and epigrammatical Roman poet, died *c.* AD 104.
2   posh food vendors.
3   a card game.
4   with high tops (jokey word).

He sent poems to *Household Words* – though he actively despised Dickens as 'the incarnation of Cockneydom', and when *Once A Week* was started up in 1859 to rival Dickens's *All the Year Round*, Meredith joined with it against 'the enemy'. His *Poems* appeared in 1851, dedicated to Peacock. He began writing novels (*The Shaving of Shagpat*) with the debt-collectors at the door, and was heavily dependent on Peacock for money and lodging. In 1856 he was model for the figure of the poet in the minor Pre-Raphaelite Henry Wallis's painting *The Death of Chatterton*. Two years later Mary Ellen ran off with Wallis to the island of Capri. The bitterness of the affair gets into Meredith's novel *The Ordeal of Richard Feverel* (1859), and, of course, the poetic sequence *Modern Love* (1862), which came out after his wife's fatal illness and death (Meredith hard-heartedly refusing to see her or attend the funeral), was a direct result of these marital troubles. Despite critical support from the Pre-Raphaelites – in 1862 Meredith lodged with Dante Gabriel Rossetti and Swinburne in Cheyne Walk, and Swinburne was particularly enthusiastic about his writing – Meredith never made money from literature. He produced numerous novels, *The Egoist* (1879) and *Diana of the Crossways* (1885) being the best known, but relied on hack-work for a living – his twice-weekly column in the *Ipswich Journal*, for example; reading manuscripts for Chapman and Hall for over thirty years (on which he gave judgement with his usual opinionated vehemence: Samuel Butler's *Erewhon* 'Will not do'; 'No' to G. B. Shaw's *Immaturity*). In 1864 he married the half-French

Marie Vulliamy, and they soon set up home in Jane Austen country at Box Hill, where Meredith could indulge his passion for the Surrey outdoors. Journalism (in the later sixties he travelled in Europe for the *Morning Post*) and other writing flowed profusely. He was a torrential talker too. He was also congenitally flatulent, but then so is his prose. His best-known critical work, the lecture *On the Idea of Comedy and the Uses of the Comic Spirit* (1877), is eloquent without force. His novels shriek with linguistic overdoing, an excessive torrent of baroque superabundance ('the effort is prodigious, and the confusion often chaotic', as Virginia Woolf puts it in her wonderfully apt essay 'On Re-Reading Meredith'). He mastered everything but language, thought Oscar Wilde, with point. His ego was monster-sized (the Book of the Earth, the earth he adored as an optimistic naturalist and Home Counties pantheist, is, *The Egoist* alleges, the Book of Egoism). He particularly thought women needed mastering – a 'brutal sex mastery' hovers about him, as G. K. Chesterton notes astutely in *The Victorian Age in English Literature*. Hardy relished Meredith's support and felt his force ('George Meredith (1828–1909)' is a poem of staunch tribute). D. H. Lawrence's nature writing is not uninfluenced by Meredith's. Robert Lowell's sequences of sonnets and expanded sonnets might be thought descendants of *Modern Love*. Meredith ended up deaf and paralysed, wheeled about in a bath-chair. He died 18 May 1909, a very late Victorian. His last letter was one of condolence to Watts-Dunton over the death of Swinburne, a month or so before.

From: MODERN LOVE

I

By this he knew she wept with waking eyes:
That, at his hand's light quiver by her head,
The strange low sobs that shook their common bed,
Were called into her with a sharp surprise,
And strangled mute, like little gaping snakes,
Dreadfully venomous to him. She lay
Stone-still, and the long darkness flow'd away
With muffled pulses. Then, as midnight makes
Her giant heart of Memory and Tears
Drink the pale drug of silence, and so beat   10
Sleep's heavy measure, they from head to feet
Were moveless, looking thro' their dead black years,
By vain regret scrawl'd over the blank wall.
Like sculptured effigies they might be seen
Upon their marriage-tomb, the sword between;
Each wishing for the sword that severs all.

V

A message from her set his brain aflame.
A world of household matters fill'd her mind,
Wherein he saw hypocrisy design'd:
She treated him as something that is tame,
And but at other provocation bites.

Familiar was her shoulder in the glass,
Through that dark rain: yet it may come to pass
That a changed eye finds such familiar sights,
More keenly tempting than new loveliness.
The 'What has been' a moment seem'd his own: 10
The splendours, mysteries, dearer because known,
Nor less divine: Love's inmost sacredness,
Called to him, 'Come!' – In that restraining start,
Eyes nurtured to be look'd at, scarce could see
A wave of the great waves of Destiny
Convulsed at a check'd impulse of the heart.

VI

It chanced his lips did meet her forehead cool.
She had no blush, but slanted down her eye.
Shamed nature, then, confesses love can die:
And most she punishes the tender fool
Who will believe what honours her the most!
Dead! is it dead? She has a pulse, and flow
Of tears, the price of blood-drops, as I know,
For whom the midnight sobs around Love's ghost,
Since then I heard her, and so will sob on.
The love is here; it has but changed its aim.   10
O bitter barren woman! what's the name?
The name, the name, the new name thou hast won?
Behold me striking the world's coward stroke!
That will I not do, though the sting is dire.
– Beneath the surface this, while by the fire
They sat, she laughing at a quiet joke.

VII

She issues radiant from her dressing-room,
Like one prepared to scale an upper sphere:
– By stirring up a lower, much I fear!
How deftly that oil'd barber lays his bloom!
That long-shank'd dapper Cupid with frisk'd curls,
Can make known women torturingly fair;
The gold-eyed serpent dwelling in rich hair,
Awakes beneath his magic whisks and twirls.
His art can take the eyes from out my head,
Until I see with eyes of other men;   10
While deeper knowledge crouches in its den,
And sends a spark up: – is it true we're wed?
Yea! filthiness of body is most vile,
But faithlessness of heart I do hold worse.
The former, it were not so great a curse
To read on the steel-mirror of her smile.

VIII

Yet it was plain she struggled, and that salt
Of righteous feeling made her pitiful.
O abject worm, so queenly beautiful!
Where came the cleft between us? whose the fault?
My tears are on thee, that have rarely dropp'd
As balm for any bitter wound of mine:
My breast will open for thee at a sign!
But, no: we are two reed-pipes, coarsely stopp'd:
The God once fill'd them with his mellow breath;

And they were music till he flung them down,   10
Used! used! Hear now the discord-loving clown
Puff his gross spirit in them, worse than death!
I do not know myself without thee more:
In this unholy battle I grow base:
If the same soul be under the same face,
Speak, and a taste of that old time restore!

IX

He felt the wild beast in him betweenwhiles
So masterfully rude, that he would grieve
To see the helpless delicate thing receive
His guardianship through certain dark defiles.
Had he not teeth to rend, and hunger too?
But still he spared her. Once: 'Have you no fear?'
He said: 't was dusk; she in his grasp; none near.
She laughed: 'No, surely; am I not with you?'
And uttering that soft starry 'you,' she lean'd
Her gentle body near him, looking up;   10
And from her eyes, as from a poison-cup,
He drank until the flittering eyelids screen'd.
Devilish malignant witch! and oh, young beam
Of heaven's circle-glory! Here thy shape
To squeeze like an intoxicating grape –
I might, and yet thou goest safe, supreme.

XIV

What soul would bargain for a cure that brings
Contempt the nobler agony to kill?
Rather let me bear on the bitter ill,
And strike this rusty bosom with new stings!
It seems there is another veering fit,
Since on a gold-hair'd lady's eyeballs pure,
I look'd with little prospect of a cure,
The while her mouth's red bow loos'd shafts of wit
Just Heaven! can it be true that jealousy
Has deck'd the woman thus? and does her head   10
Whirl giddily for what she forfeited?
Madam! you teach me many things that be.
I open an old book, and there I find,
That 'Women still may love whom they deceive.'
Such love I prize not, Madam: by your leave,
The game you play at is not to my mind.

XVI

In our old shipwreck'd days there was an hour,
When in the firelight steadily aglow,
Join'd slackly, we beheld the red chasm grow
Among the clicking coals. Our library-bower
That eve was left to us: and hush'd we sat
As lovers to whom Time is whispering.
From sudden-open'd doors we heard them sing:
The nodding elders mix'd good wine with chat.
Well knew we that Life's greatest treasure lay
With us, and of it was our talk. 'Ah, yes!   10
Love dies!' I said: I never thought it less.
She yearn'd to me that sentence to unsay.
Then when the fire domed blackening, I found

Her cheek was salt against my kiss, and swift
Up the sharp scale of sobs her breast did lift: –
Now am I haunted by that taste! that sound!

XVII

At dinner, she is hostess, I am host.
Went the feast ever cheerfuller? She keeps
The Topic over intellectual deeps
In buoyancy afloat. They see no ghost.
With sparkling surface-eyes we ply the ball:
It is in truth a most contagious game:
HIDING THE SKELETON, shall be its name.
Such play as this the devils might appal!
But here's the greater wonder; in that we
Enamour'd of our acting and our wits,   10
Admire each other like true hypocrites.
Warm-lighted looks, Love's Ephemerae,
Shoot gaily o'er the dishes and the wine.
We waken envy of our happy lot.
Fast, sweet, and golden, shows the marriage-knot.
Dear guests, you now have seen Love's corpse-light shine!

XXIII

'T is Christmas weather, and a country house
Receives us: rooms are full: we can but get
An attic-crib. Such lovers will not fret
At that, it is half-said. The great carouse
Knocks hard upon the midnight's hollow door,
But when I knock at hers, I see the pit.
Why did I come here in that dullard fit?
I enter, and lie couch'd upon the floor.
Passing, I caught the coverlet's quick beat: –
Come, Shame, burn to my soul! and Pride, and Pain –   10
Foul demons that have tortured me, sustain!
Out in the freezing darkness the lambs bleat.
The small bird stiffens in the low starlight.
I know not how, but shuddering as I slept,
I dream'd a banished Angel to me crept:
My feet were nourish'd on her breasts all night.

XXIV

The misery is greater, as I live!
To know her flesh so pure, so keen her sense,
That she does penance now for no offence,
Save against Love. The less can I forgive!
The less can I forgive, though I adore
That cruel lovely pallor which surrounds
Her footsteps; and the low vibrating sounds
That come on me, as from a magic shore.
Low are they, but most subtle to find out
The shrinking soul. Madam, 't is understood   10
When women play upon their womanhood.
It means, a Season gone. And yet I doubt
But I am duped. That nun-like look waylays
My fancy. Oh! I do but wait a sign!
Pluck out the eyes of Pride! thy mouth to mine!
Never! though I die thirsting. Go thy ways!

XXV

You like not that French novel? Tell me why.
You think it quite unnatural. Let us see.
The actors are, it seems, the usual three:
Husband, and wife, and lover. She – but fie!
In England we'll not hear of it. Edmond,
The lover, her devout chagrin doth share;
Blanc-mange and absinthe are his penitent fare,
Till his pale aspect makes her overfond:
So, to preclude fresh sin, he tries rosbif.
Meantime the husband is no more abused: 10
Auguste forgives her ere the tear is used.
Then hangeth all on one tremendous If: –
IF she will choose between them. She does choose;
And takes her husband, like a proper wife.
Unnatural? My dear, these things are life:
And life, they say, is worthy of the Muse.

XXIX

Am I failing? for no longer can I cast
A glory round about this head of gold.
Glory she wears, but springing from the mould;
Not like the consecration of the Past!
Is my soul beggar'd? Something more than earth
I cry for still: I cannot be at peace
In having Love upon a mortal lease.
I cannot take the woman at her worth!
Where is the ancient wealth wherewith I clothed
Our human nakedness, and could endow   10
With spiritual splendour a white brow
That else had grinn'd at me the fact I loath'd?
A kiss is but a kiss now! and no wave
Of a great flood that whirls me to the sea.
But, as you will! we'll sit contentedly,
And eat our pot of honey on the grave.

XXXI

This golden head has wit in it. I live
Again, and a far higher life, near her.
Some women like a young philosopher;
Perchance because he is diminutive.
For woman's manly god must not exceed
Proportions of the natural nursing size.
Great poets and great sages draw no prize
With women: but the little lap-dog breed,
Who can be hugg'd, or on a mantel-piece
Perch'd up for adoration, these obtain   10
Her homage. And of this we men are vain?
Of this! 'T is order'd for the world's increase!
Small flattery! Yet she has that rare gift
To beauty, Common Sense. I am approved.
It is not half so nice as being loved,
And yet I do prefer it. What's my drift?

XXXIV

Madam would speak with me. So, now it comes:
The Deluge, or else Fire! She's well; she thanks
My husbandship. Our chain on silence clanks.

Time leers between us, twiddling his thumbs.
Am I quite well? Most excellent in health!
The journals, too, I diligently peruse.
Vesuvius is expected to give news:
Niagara is no noisier. By stealth
Our eyes dart scrutinizing snakes. She's glad
I'm happy, says her quivering under-lip.   10
'And are not you?' 'How can I be?' 'Take ship!
For happiness is somewhere to be had.'
'Nowhere for me!' Her voice is barely heard.
I am not melted, and make no pretence.
With truisms I freeze her, tongue and sense.
Niagara, or Vesuvius, is deferr'd.

XXXV

It is no vulgar nature I have wived.
Secretive, sensitive, she takes a wound
Deep to her soul, as if the sense had swoon'd,
And not a thought of vengeance had survived.
No confidences has she: but relief
Must come to one whose suffering is acute.
O have a care of natures that are mute!
They punish you in acts: their steps are brief.
What is she doing? What does she demand
From Providence, or me? She is not one   10
Long to endure this torpidly, and shun
The drugs that crowd about a woman's hand.
At Forfeits during snow we play'd, and I
Must kiss her. 'Well perform'd!' I said: then she:
''T is hardly worth the money, you agree?'
Save her? What for? To act this wedded lie!

XLII

I am to follow her. There is much grace
In woman when thus bent on martyrdom.
They think that dignity of soul may come,
Perchance, with dignity of body. Base!
But I was taken by that air of cold
And statuesque sedateness, when she said
'I'm going'; lit a taper, bow'd her head,
And went, as with the stride of Pallas[1] bold.
Fleshly indifference horrible! The hands
Of Time now signal: O, she's safe from me!   10
Within those secret walls what do I see?
Where first she set the taper down she stands:
Not Pallas: Hebe[2] shamed! Thoughts black as death,
Like a stirr'd pool in sunshine break. Her wrists
I catch: she faltering, as she half resists,
'You love...? love...? love...?' all in an indrawn breath.

XLVII

We saw the swallows gathering in the sky,
And in the osier-sile we heard them noise.
We had not to look back on summer joys,

Modern Love
1 Athene, patron goddess of Athens: an un-soft female.

2 goddess of youth; cup-bearer of the gods.

Or forward to a summer of bright dye:
But in the largeness of the evening earth
Our spirits grew as we went side by side.
The hour became her husband, and my bride.
Love that had robb'd us so, thus bless'd our dearth!
The pilgrims of the year wax'd very loud
In multitudinous chatterings, as the flood   10
Full brown came from the west, and like pale blood
Expanded to the upper crimson cloud.
Love that had robb'd us of immortal things,
This little moment mercifully gave,
And still I see across the twilight wave,
The swan sail with her young beneath her wings.

XLVIII

Their sense is with their senses all mix'd in,
Destroy'd by subtleties these women are!
More brain, O Lord, more brain! or we shall mar
Utterly this fair garden we might win.
Behold! I looked for peace, and thought it near.
Our inmost hearts had open'd, each to each.
We drank the pure daylight of honest speech.
Alas! that was the fatal draught, I fear.
For when of my lost Lady came the word,
This woman, O this agony of flesh!   10
Jealous devotion bade her break the mesh,
That I might seek that other like a bird.
I do adore the nobleness! despise
The act! She has gone forth, I know not where.
Will the hard world my sentience of her share?
I feel the truth; so let the world surmise.

XLIX

He found her by the ocean's moaning verge,
Nor any wicked change in her discern'd;
And she believed his old love had return'd,
Which was her exultation, and her scourge.
She took his hand, and walked with him, and seem'd
The wife he sought, tho' shadow-like and dry.
She had one terror, lest her heart should sigh,
And tell her loudly she no longer dream'd.
She dared not say, 'This is my breast: look in.'
But there's a strength to help the desperate weak.   10
That night he learned how silence best can speak
The awful things when Pity pleads for Sin.
About the middle of the night her call
Was heard, and he came wondering to the bed.
'Now kiss me, dear! it may be, now!' she said.
Lethe had passed those lips, and he knew all.[3]

L

Thus piteously Love closed what he begat:
The union of this ever-diverse pair!
These two were rapid falcons in a snare,

---

3   Lethe: death drink (dead souls drank waters of this river of Hell to
forget past lives).

Condemned to do the flitting of the bat.
Lovers beneath the singing sky of May,
They wander'd once; clear as the dew on flowers:
But they fed not on the advancing hours:
Their hearts held cravings for the buried day.
Then each applied to each that fatal knife,
Deep questioning, which probes to endless dole.   10
Ah, what a dusty answer gets the soul
When hot for certainties in this our life! –
In tragic hints here see what evermore
Moves dark as yonder midnight ocean's force,
Thundering like ramping hosts of warrior horse,
To throw that faint thin line upon the shore!

Modern Love, and Poems of the English Roadside, with Poems
and Ballads *(Chapman & Hall, 1862).*

LUCIFER IN STARLIGHT

On a starred night Prince Lucifer uprose.
Tired of his dark dominion swung the fiend
Above the rolling ball in cloud part screened,
Where sinners hugged their spectre of repose.
Poor prey to his hot fit of pride were those.
And now upon his western wing he leaned,
Now his huge bulk o'er Afric's sands careened,
Now the black planet shadowed Arctic snows.
Soaring through wider zones that pricked his scars
With memory of the old revolt from Awe,   10
He reached a middle height, and at the stars,
Which are the brain of heaven, he looked, and sank.
Around the ancient track marched rank on rank,
The army of unalterable law.

Poems and Lyrics of the Joy of the Earth *(Macmillan & Co., 1883).*

THE POINT OF TASTE

Unhappy poets of a sunken prime!
You to reviewers are as ball to bat.
They shadow you with Homer, knock you flat
With Shakespeare: bludgeons brainingly sublime
On you the excommunicates of Rhyme,
Because you sing not in the living Fat.
The wiry whizz of an intrusive gnat
Is verse that shuns their self-producing time.
Sound them their clocks, with loud alarum trump,
Or watches ticking temporal at their fobs,   10
You win their pleased attention. But, bright God
O' the lyre, what bully-drawlers they applaud!
Rather for us a tavern-catch, and bump
Chorus where Lumpkin with his Giles hobnobs.

Poems and Lyrics of the Joy of the Earth *(1883).*

SOCIETY

Historic be the survey of our kind,
And how their brave Society took shape.
Lion, wolf, vulture, fox, jackal and ape,
The strong of limb, the keen of nose, we find,
Who, with some jars in harmony, combined,
Their primal instincts taming, to escape
The brawl indecent, and hot passions drape.
Convenience pricked conscience, that the mind.
Thus entered they the field of milder beasts,
Which in some sort of civil order graze,   10
And do half-homage to the God of Laws.
But are they still for their old ravenous feasts,
Earth gives the edifice they build no base:
They spring another flood of fangs and claws.

A Reading of the Earth *(Macmillan & Co., 1888)*.

ENGLAND BEFORE THE STORM

I

The day that is the night of days,
With cannon-fire for sun ablaze,
We spy from any billow's lift;
And England still this tidal drift!
Would she to sainted forethought vow
A space before the thunders flood,
That martyr of its hour might now
    Spare her the tears of blood.

II

Asleep upon her ancient deeds,
She hugs the vision plethora breeds,   10
And counts her manifold increase
Of treasure in the fruits of peace.
What curse on earth's improvident,
When the dread trumpet shatters rest,
Is wreaked, she knows, yet smiles content
    As cradle rocked from breast.

III

She, impious to the Lord of Hosts,
The valour of her offspring boasts,
Mindless that now on land and main
His heeded prayer is active brain.   20
No more great heart may guard the home,
Save eyed and armed and skilled to cleave
Yon swallower wave with shroud of foam,
    We see not distant heave.

IV

They stand to be her sacrifice,
The sons this mother flings like dice,
To face the odds and brave the Fates;

As in those days of starry dates,
When cannon cannon's counterblast
Awakened, muzzle muzzle bowled,   30
And high in swathe of smoke the mast
Its fighting rag outrolled.

Poems, The Empty Purse, With Odes to the Comic Spirit,
To Youth in Memory, And Verses *(Macmillan & Co., 1892)*.

Dante Gabriel (Gabriel Charles Dante) Rossetti (1828–82)

Dante Gabriel Rossetti – actually Gabriel Charles Dante Rossetti – poet and painter, hinge-figure of two generations of Pre-Raphaelite artists, inspirer of Decadent poets, was born, 12 May 1828, at 38 Charlotte Street (now Hallam Street) in London. His father was Gabriele Rossetti, Italian Republican refugee poet and crackpot Dante scholar (Professor of Italian at London University from 1831), who read Dante's *Divine Comedy* as a prophetic anti-papal cryptogram. His mother was Frances Mary Lavinia Polidori, sister of John Polidori, Byron's doctor and author of *The Vampyre*. The Rossetti children – D. G.'s younger brother William Michael, sisters Maria and Christina G., were as aesthetically precocious as their lively and artistic circumstances would suggest. Little Dante Gabriel was soon steeped in Shakespeare, Byron and Scott, composing infantile dramas, having an adolescent Scott-like ballad published by doting grandfather Gaetano (who did similarly for young Christina). Dante Gabriel left school at fourteen, studied at Sass's Drawing Academy (which Edward Lear also attended: the one portrayed as Gandish's in Thackeray's novel *The Newcomes*) and entered the Royal Academy Schools in 1844. Fellow students included Holman Hunt and John Everett Millais. From the mid-forties he was doing translations of Dante (Tennyson advising revisions). He illustrated Poe and Goethe's *Faust*, fell in love with Browning (copying out all of *Pauline* in the British Museum); purchased a notebook of Blake's; sought advice on being a painter and poet from William Bell Scott and Leigh Hunt. His letter to Ford Madox Brown asking for painting lessons was so egregiously flattering that it was taken as an insult and Brown went round with a cudgel to beat Rossetti up. In 1848 he took a studio in Cleveland Street with Holman Hunt and that year, around the time his translation of Dante's *Vita Nuova* was finished, the Pre-Raphaelite Brotherhood, with Rossetti, Hunt, Millais and Thomas Woolner as its main members, was formed. Programmatically medievalizing, anti-industrialist, fringe Anglo-Catholic, they were against 'slosh' and in favour of a colourful hard-edgedness of regard. 'These Pre-Raffelites they talk of', wrote Carlyle, 'are said to copy the thing as it is or invent it as they believe it must have been. . . . It's the only way of doing anything fit to

be seen.' Rossetti's first major oil painting, *The Girlhood of Mary Virgin*, was exhibited at the Free Exhibition of March 1849. He probably met Lizzie Siddal, first of many proletarian female muses, in 1849 – she'd been spotted in a hat-shop near Leicester Square by his friend from Sass's and the Royal Academy, Walter Deverell. Rossetti was a main driving-force in the short-lived Pre-Raphaelite journal *The Germ*, January–April 1850, his poem 'The Blessed Damozel' appearing in the second number. Ruskin's letter to *The Times*, 25 May 1854, defending Pre-Raphaelite painting ('Painting taking its proper place beside literature') brought him close to the group. He was a generous patron of the fractious Rossetti (he funded the *Early Italian Poets* volume of Rossetti translations). Rossetti became friends with the admired Browning, 1855–6. In the illustrated Moxon Tennyson of 1857 Rossetti had five engravings, including 'The Lady of Shalott'. He was a prime mover in the abortive 1857 Long Vacation frescoes project in the Oxford Union building – which brought him into active association with the second Pre-Raphaelite wave and the Oxford gang of Ted (Burne-) Jones, William Morris and Swinburne. He had poems in *The Oxford and Cambridge Magazine*. He married Lizzie Siddal on 23 May 1860, after protracted delaying. There was a still-born child. Lizzie died of an overdose of laudanum, probably suicidally, 11 February 1862, and Rossetti impetuously deposited his manuscript poems in her coffin. He settled at 16 Cheyne Walk, sharing the house with Swinburne and George Meredith, getting to know Whistler, and Fantin-Latour (who showed him round Parisian studios in November 1864). In the sixties his main model and mistress was big proley Fanny Cornforth ('funny old elephant', Rossetti called her). She modelled the fallen woman in *Found* (begun 1854) – the visual equivalent of the poem 'Jenny'. The small portrait of Fanny (1859), *Bocca Baciata* (the Kissed Mouth: words from a Boccaccio sonnet) – 'gross sensuality of a revolting kind': Holman Hunt; 'more stunning than can be decently expressed': Swinburne – marks a landmark in Pre-Raphaelite Aestheticism, and in Rossetti's obsessive engagement with the dangerous female mouth ('burnt red', as the poem 'Nuptial Sleep' has it). Fanny became a main inspiration for Rossetti's 'whoppers', his big rawly sexy paintings, all big hair and big lips, on themes of dangerously attractive mythic women, such as *Lady Lilith* (1864–8), which sent Swinburne into the usual raptures ('the idea incarnate of faultless fleshly beauty and peril of pleasure unavoidable'), but his accompanying and parallel poems (in this case the poem entitled 'Body's Beauty') provoked Robert Buchanan's notorious attack on Rossetti as the 'grotesque' acme of 'The Fleshly School of Poetry' (*Contemporary Review*, October 1871). Buchanan wasn't at all mistaken in his sense of the Browningesque bodily revolution going on in and around Rossetti, only wrong in thinking it *morbid, nasty, trash*. At the end of the sixties, Rossetti began his affair with Janey Morris — yet one more in the long train of disposable female objects of desire and fantasy. (*Proserpine*, 1873, a late triumph in the *femme fatale* mode, has Mrs Morris as the wonderfully moody empress of Hades, with the customary big hair and great red lips, holding the hellish pomegranate – its cut-out slice making it another pronounced mouth, its white seeds the teeth of a *vagina dentata* – biting which has locked her in the Underworld; Rossetti's Italian sonnet on the subject is painted on the picture,

the translation inscribed on the frame.) Rossetti had his poems dug up macabrely from Lizzie's coffin in October 1869. They bulked out his *Poems* published the following year. His poetic reputation was now that of third-place holder after Tennyson and Browning. But his eyes were getting worse, toothache was terrible, he was taking more and more chloral and whisky, and paranoia was increasing. The Buchanan attack tipped him right over the edge, and in June 1872 he was committed to Dr Hake's asylum. He almost died of a laudanum overdose. William Morris looked after him intermittently at Kelmscott Manor in the early seventies, but he was a very tiresome patient – rude, thoughtless, selfish. He still painted and wrote, though, and brought out a new edition of the *Poems* (1881) along with *Ballads and Sonnets*. His 101-sonnet cycle *The House of Life* appeared complete for the first time, and he found help and consolation with new friends, especially Theodore Watts (-Dunton) and Hall Caine. He died at Birchington-on-Sea, Kent, 10 April 1882. The *Collected Works* were edited by William Michael Rossetti – keeper of the Rossetti-clan fame – in two volumes (1890), with a long, mainly biographical, preface.

THE BLESSED DAMOZEL

The blessed Damozel leaned out
  From the gold bar of Heaven:
Her blue grave eyes were deeper much
  Than a deep water, even.
She had three lilies in her hand,
  And the stars in her hair were seven.

Her robe, ungirt from clasp to hem,
  No wrought flowers did adorn,
But a white rose of Mary's gift
  On the neck meetly worn;   10
And her hair, lying down her back,
  Was yellow like ripe corn.

Herseemed she scarce had been a day
  One of God's choristers;
The wonder was not yet quite gone
  From that still look of hers;
Albeit to them she left, her day
  Had counted as ten years.

(To *one* it is ten years of years:
  ......Yet now, here in this place   20
Surely she leaned o'er me, – her hair
  Fell all about my face.......
Nothing: the Autumn-fall of leaves.
  The whole year sets apace.)

It was the terrace of God's house
  That she was standing on, –
By God built over the sheer depth

  In which Space is begun;
So high, that looking downward thence,
  She could scarce see the sun.   30

It lies from Heaven across the flood
  Of ether, as a bridge.
Beneath, the tides of day and night
  With flame and blackness ridge
The void, as low as where this earth
  Spins like a fretful midge.

But in those tracts, with her, it was
  The peace of utter light
And silence. For no breeze may stir
  Along the steady flight   40
Of seraphim; no echo there,
  Beyond all depth or height.

Heard hardly, some of her new friends,
  Playing at holy games,
Spake, gentle-mouthed, among themselves,
  Their virginal chaste names;
And the souls, mounting up to God,
  Went by her like thin flames.

And still she bowed herself, and stooped
  Into the vast waste calm;   50
Till her bosom's pressure must have made
  The bar she leaned on warm,
And the lilies lay as if asleep
  Along her bended arm.

From the fixt lull of heaven, she saw
   Time, like a pulse, shake fierce
Through all the worlds. Her gaze still strove,
   In that steep gulph, to pierce
The swarm: and then she spake, as when
   The stars sang in their spheres.   60

'I wish that he were come to me,
   For he will come,' she said.
'Have I not prayed in solemn heaven?
   On earth, has he not prayed?
Are not two prayers a perfect strength?
   And shall I feel afraid?

'When round his head the aureole clings,
   And he is clothed in white,
I'll take his hand, and go with him
   To the deep wells of light,   70
And we will step down as to a stream
   And bathe there in God's sight.

'We two will stand beside that shrine,
   Occult, withheld, untrod,
Whose lamps tremble continually
   With prayer sent up to God;
And where each need, revealed, expects
   Its patient period.

'We two will lie i' the shadow of
   That living mystic tree   80
Within whose secret growth the Dove
   Sometimes is felt to be,
While every leaf that His plumes touch
   Saith His name audibly.

'And I myself will teach to him –
   I myself, lying so, –
The songs I sing here; which his mouth
   Shall pause in, hushed and slow,
Finding some knowledge at each pause
   And some new thing to know.'   90

(Alas! to *her* wise simple mind
   These things were all but known
Before: they trembled on her sense, –
   Her voice had caught their tone.
Alas for lonely Heaven! Alas
   For life wrung out alone!

Alas, and though the end were reached?......
   Was *thy* part understood
Or borne in trust? And for her sake
   Shall this too be found good? –   100
May the close lips that knew not prayer
   Praise ever, though they would?)

'We two,' she said, 'will seek the groves
   Where the lady Mary is,
With her five handmaidens, whose names
   Are five sweet symphonies: –
Cecily, Gertrude, Magdalen,
   Margaret, and Rosalys.

'Circle-wise sit they, with bound locks
   And bosoms covered;   110
Into the fine cloth, white like flame,
   Weaving the golden thread,
To fashion the birth-robes for them
   Who are just born, being dead.

'He shall fear haply, and be dumb.
   Then I will lay my cheek
To his, and tell about our love,
   Not once abashed or weak:
And the dear Mother will approve
   My pride, and let me speak.   120

'Herself shall bring us, hand in hand,
   To Him round whom all souls
Kneel – the unnumber'd solemn heads
   Bowed with their aureoles:
And Angels, meeting us, shall sing
   To their citherns and citoles.

'There will I ask of Christ the Lord
   Thus much for him and me: –
To have more blessing than on earth
   In nowise; but to be   130
As then we were, – being as then
   At peace. Yea, verily.

'Yea, verily; when he is come
   We will do thus and thus:
Till this my vigil seem quite strange
   And almost fabulous;
We two will live at once, one life;
   And peace shall be with us.'

She gazed, and listened, and then said,
   Less sad of speech than mild: 140
   'All this is when he comes.' She ceased;
   The light thrilled past her, filled
With Angels, in strong level lapse.
   Her eyes prayed, and she smiled.

(I saw her smile.) But soon their flight
   Was vague 'mid the poised spheres.
And then she cast her arms along
   The golden barriers,
And laid her face between her hands,
   And wept. (I heard her tears.)   150

Written 1847. Version of first publication, in The Germ: Thoughts Towards
Nature in Poetry, Literature, and Art, *no. 2 (Aylott & Jones,
February 1850). Much revised, and shortened, in* Poems *(F. S. Ellis, 1870).*

JENNY

'Vengeance of Jenny's case! Fie on her! Never name her, child!'
(Mrs. Quickly)[1]

Lazy laughing languid Jenny,
Fond of a kiss and fond of a guinea,
Whose head upon my knee to-night
Rests for a while, as if grown light
With all our dances and the sound
To which the wild tunes spun you round:
Fair Jenny mine, the thoughtless queen
Of kisses which the blush between
Could hardly make much daintier;
Whose eyes are as blue skies, whose hair   10
Is countless gold incomparable:
Fresh flower, scarce touched with signs that tell
Of Love's exuberant hotbed: – Nay,
Poor flower left torn since yesterday
Until to-morrow leave you bare;
Poor handful of bright spring-water
Flung in the whirlpool's shrieking face;
Poor shameful Jenny, full of grace
Thus with your head upon my knee; –
Whose person or whose purse may be   20
The lodestar of your reverie?

    This room of yours, my Jenny, looks
A change from mine so full of books,
Whose serried ranks hold fast, forsooth,
So many captive hours of youth, –
The hours they thieve from day and night
To make one's cherished work come right,
And leave it wrong for all their theft,
Even as to-night my work was left:
Until I vowed that since my brain   30
And eyes of dancing seemed so fain,
My feet should have some dancing too: –
And thus it was I met with you.
Well, I suppose 'twas hard to part,
For here I am. And now, sweetheart,
You seem too tired to get to bed.

    It was a careless life I led
When rooms like this were scarce so strange
Not long ago. What breeds the change, –
The many aims or the few years?   40
Because to-night it all appears
Something I do not know again.

    The cloud's not danced out of my brain, –
The cloud that made it turn and swim
While hour by hour the books grew dim.

Why, Jenny, as I watch you there, –
For all your wealth of loosened hair,
Your silk ungirdled and unlac'd
And warm sweets open to the waist,
All golden in the lamplight's gleam, –   50
You know not what a book you seem,
Half-read by lightning in a dream!
How should you know, my Jenny? Nay,
And I should be ashamed to say: –
Poor beauty, so well worth a kiss!
But while my thought runs on like this
With wasteful whims more than enough,
I wonder what you're thinking of.

    If of myself you think at all,
What is the thought? – conjectural   60
On sorry matters best unsolved? –
Or inly is each grace revolved
To fit me with a lure? – or (sad
To think!) perhaps you're merely glad
That I'm not drunk or ruffianly
And let you rest upon my knee.

    For sometimes, were the truth confess'd,
You're thankful for a little rest, –
Glad from the crush to rest within,
From the heart-sickness and the din
Where envy's voice at virtue's pitch   70
Mocks you because your gown is rich;
And from the pale girl's dumb rebuke,
Whose ill-clad grace and toil-worn look
Proclaim the strength that keeps her weak,
And other nights than yours bespeak;
And from the wise unchildish elf,
To schoolmate lesser than himself
Pointing you out, what thing you are: –
Yes, from the daily jeer and jar,
From shame and shame's outbraving too,   80
Is rest not sometimes sweet to you? –
But most from the hatefulness of man,
Who spares not to end what he began,
Whose acts are ill and his speech ill,
Who, having used you at his will,
Thrusts you aside, as when I dine
I serve the dishes and the wine.

    Well, handsome Jenny mine, sit up:
I've filled our glasses, let us sup,

JENNY
1 Shakespeare, *The Merry Wives of Windsor*, IV.i.56 [malapropism for 'genitive case']. Mistress Quickly continues: 'Never name her, child, if she be a whore.'

And do not let me think of you,   90
Lest shame of yours suffice for two.
What, still so tired? Well, well then, keep
Your head there, so you do not sleep;
But that the weariness may pass
And leave you merry, take this glass.
Ah! lazy lily hand, more bless'd
If ne'er in rings it had been dress'd
Nor ever by a glove conceal'd!

    Behold the lilies of the field,
They toil not neither do they spin;   100
(So doth the ancient text begin,[2] –
Not of such rest as one of these
Can share.) Another rest and ease
Along each summer-sated path
From its new lord the garden hath,
Than that whose spring in blessings ran
Which praised the bounteous husbandman,
Ere yet, in days of hankering breath,
The lilies sickened unto death.

    What, Jenny, are your lilies dead?   110
Aye, and the snow-white leaves are spread
Like winter on the garden-bed.
But you had roses left in May, –
They were not gone too. Jenny, nay,
But must your roses die, and those
Their purfled buds that should unclose?
Even so; the leaves are curled apart,
Still red as from the broken heart,
And here's the naked stem of thorns.

    Nay, nay, mere words. Here nothing warns   120
As yet of winter. Sickness here
Or want alone could waken fear, –
Nothing but passion wrings a tear.
Except when there may rise unsought
Haply at times a passing thought
Of the old days which seem to be
Much older than any history
That is written in any book;
When she would lie in fields and look
Along the ground through the blown grass,   130
And wonder where the city was,
Far out of sight, whose broil and bale
They told her then for a child's tale.

    Jenny, you know the city now.
A child can tell the tale there, how
Some things which are not yet enroll'd
In market-lists are bought and sold
Even till the early Sunday light,
When Saturday night is market-night

Everywhere, be it dry or wet,   140
And market-night in the Haymarket.
Our learned London children know,
Poor Jenny, all your mirth and woe;
Have seen your lifted silken skirt
Advertize dainties through the dirt;
Have seen your coach-wheels splash rebuke
On virtue; and have learned your look
When, wealth and health slipped past, you stare
Along the streets alone, and there,
Round the long park, across the bridge,   150
The cold lamps at the pavement's edge
Wind on together and apart,
A fiery serpent for your heart.

    Let the thoughts pass, an empty cloud!
Suppose I were to think aloud, –
What if to her all this were said?
Why, as a volume seldom read
Being opened halfway shuts again,
So might the pages of her brain
Be parted at such words, and thence   160
Close back upon the dusty sense.
For is there hue or shape defin'd
In Jenny's desecrated mind,
Where all contagious currents meet,
A Lethe[3] of the middle street?
Nay, it reflects not any face,
Nor sound is in its sluggish pace,
But as they coil those eddies clot,
And night and day remember not.

    Why, Jenny, you're asleep at last! –   170
Asleep, poor Jenny, hard and fast, –
So young and soft and tired; so fair,
With chin thus nestled in your hair,
Mouth quiet, eyelids almost blue
As if some sky of dreams shone through!

    Just as another woman sleeps!
Enough to throw one's thoughts in heaps
Of doubt and horror, – what to say
Or think, – this awful secret sway,
The potter's power over the clay![4]   180
Of the same lump (it has been said)
For honour and dishonour made,
Two sister vessels.[5] Here is one.

    My cousin Nell is fond of fun,
And fond of dress, and change, and praise,
So mere a woman in her ways:
And if her sweet eyes rich in youth
Are like her lips that tell the truth,
My cousin Nell is fond of love.

---

2 Matthew 6.28.
3 river of the classical Underworld whose waters induce forgetful-
ness.

4 Jeremiah 18.1ff.
5 2 Timothy 2.20.

And she's the girl I'm proudest of.   190
Who does not prize her, guard her well?
The love of change, in cousin Nell,
Shall find the best and hold it dear:
The unconquered mirth turn quieter
Not through her own, through others' woe:
The conscious pride of beauty glow
Beside another's pride in her,
One little part of all they share.
For Love himself shall ripen these
In a kind soil to just increase   200
Through years of fertilizing peace.

    Of the same lump (as it is said)
For honour and dishonour made,
Two sister vessels. Here is one.

    It makes a goblin of the sun.

    So pure, – so fall'n! How dare to think
Of the first common kindred link?
Yet, Jenny, till the world shall burn
It seems that all things take their turn;
And who shall say but this fair tree   210
May need, in changes that may be,
Your children's children's charity?
Scorned then, no doubt, as you are scorn'd!
Shall no man hold his pride forewarn'd
Till in the end, the Day of Days,
At Judgment, one of his own race,
As frail and lost as you, shall rise, –
His daughter, with his mother's eyes?

    How Jenny's clock ticks on the shelf!
Might not the dial scorn itself   220
That has such hours to register?
Yet as to me, even so to her
Are golden sun and silver moon,
In daily largesse of earth's boon,
Counted for life-coins to one tune.
And if, as blindfold fates are toss'd,
Through some one man this life be lost,
Shall soul not somehow pay for soul?

    Fair shines the gilded aureole
In which our highest painters place   230
Some living woman's simple face.
And the stilled features thus descried
As Jenny's long throat droops aside, –
The shadows where the cheeks are thin,
And pure wide curve from ear to chin, –
With Raffael's or Da Vinci's hand
To show them to men's souls, might stand,
Whole ages long, the whole world through,
For preachings of what God can do.

What has man done here? How atone,   240
Great God, for this which man has done?
And for the body and soul which by
Man's pitiless doom must now comply
With lifelong hell, what lullaby
Of sweet forgetful second birth
Remains? All dark. No sign on earth
What measure of God's rest endows
The many mansions of his house.[6]

    If but a woman's heart might see
Such erring heart unerringly   250
For once! But that can never be.

    Like a rose shut in a book
In which pure women may not look,
For its base pages claim control
To crush the flower within the soul;
Where through each dead rose-leaf that clings,
Pale as transparent psyche-wings,[7]
To the vile text, are traced such things
As might make lady's cheek indeed
More than a living rose to read;   260
So nought save foolish foulness may
Watch with hard eyes the sure decay;
And so the life-blood of this rose,
Puddled with shameful knowledge, flows
Through leaves no chaste hand may unclose:
Yet still it keeps such faded show
Of when 'twas gathered long ago,
That the crushed petals' lovely grain,
The sweetness of the sanguine stain,
Seen of a woman's eyes, must make   270
Her pitiful heart, so prone to ache,
Love roses better for its sake: –
Only that this can never be: –
Even so unto her sex is she.

    Yet, Jenny, looking long at you,
The woman almost fades from view.
A cipher of man's changeless sum
Of lust, past, present, and to come,
Is left. A riddle that one shrinks   280
To challenge from the scornful sphinx.

    Like a toad within a stone
Seated while Time crumbles on;
Which sits there since the earth was curs'd
For Man's transgression at the first;
Which, living through all centuries,
Not once has seen the sun arise;
Whose life, to its cold circle charmed,
The earth's whole summers have not warmed;
Which always – whitherso the stone
Be flung – sits there, deaf, blind, alone; –   290

---

6 'In my father's house are many mansions', John 14.2.

7 Psyche: beloved of Cupid.

Aye, and shall not be driven out
Till that which shuts him round about
Break at the very Master's stroke,
And the dust thereof vanish as smoke,
And the seed of Man vanish as dust: –
Even so within this world is Lust.

Come, come, what use in thoughts like this?
Poor little Jenny, good to kiss, –
You'd not believe by what strange roads
Thought travels, when your beauty goads   300
A man to-night to think of toads!
Jenny, wake up.... Why, there's the dawn!

And there's an early waggon drawn
To market, and some sheep that jog
Bleating before a barking dog;
And the old streets come peering through
Another night that London knew;
And all as ghostlike as the lamps.

So on the wings of day decamps
My last night's frolic. Glooms begin   310
To shiver off as lights creep in
Past the gauze curtains half drawn-to,
And the lamp's doubled shade grows blue, –
Your lamp, my Jenny, kept alight,
Like a wise virgin's, all one night!⁸
And in the alcove coolly spread
Glimmers with dawn your empty bed;
And yonder your fair face I see
Reflected lying on my knee,
Where teems with first foreshadowings   320
Your pier-glass scrawled with diamond rings.

And now without, as if some word
Had called upon them that they heard,
The London sparrows far and nigh
Clamour together suddenly;
And Jenny's cage-bird grown awake
Here in their song his part must take,
Because here too the day doth break.

And somehow in myself the dawn
Among stirred clouds and veils withdrawn   330
Strikes greyly on her. Let her sleep.
But will it wake her if I heap
These cushions thus beneath her head
Where my knee was? No, – there's your bed,
My Jenny, while you dream. And there
I lay among your golden hair
Perhaps the subject of your dreams,
These golden coins.
                    For still one deems

That Jenny's flattering sleep confers
New magic on the magic purse, –   340
Grim web, how clogged with shrivelled flies!
Between the threads fine fumes arise
And shape their pictures in the brain.
There roll no streets in glare and rain,
Nor flagrant man-swine whets his tusk;
But delicately sighs in musk
The homage of the dim boudoir;
Or like a palpitating star
Thrilled into song, the opera-night
Breathes faint in the quick pulse of light;   350
Or at the carriage-window shine
Rich wares for choice; or, free to dine,
Whirls through its hour of health (divine
For her) the concourse of the Park.
And though in the discounted dark
Her functions there and here are one,
Beneath the lamps and in the sun
There reigns at least the acknowledged belle
Apparelled beyond parallel.
Ah Jenny, yes, we know your dreams.   360

For even the Paphian Venus⁹ seems
A goddess o'er the realms of love,
When silver-shrined in shadowy grove:
Aye, or let offerings nicely placed
But hide Priapus¹⁰ to the waist,
And whoso looks on him shall see
An eligible deity.

Why, Jenny, waking here alone
May help you to remember one,
Though all the memory's long outworn   370
Of many a double-pillowed morn.
I think I see you when you wake,
And rub your eyes for me, and shake
My gold, in rising, from your hair,
A Danaë for a moment there.¹¹

Jenny, my love rang true! for still
Love at first sight is vague, until
That tinkling makes him audible.

And must I mock you to the last,
Ashamed of my own shame, – aghast   380
Because some thoughts not born amiss
Rose at a poor fair face like this?
Well, of such thoughts so much I know:
In my life, as in hers, they show,
By a far gleam which I may near,
A dark path I can strive to clear.

Only one kiss. Good-bye, my dear.

Written 1848–69; mainly 1858–69. Poems *(1870).*

---

8   parable of wise (and foolish) virgins, Matthew 25.1–13.
9   prostitute (from Paphos, Cyprus city, devoted to Venus).

10   chief deity of lust and obscenity.
11   seduced by Zeus in form of a shower of gold.

THE WOODSPURGE

The wind flapped loose, the wind was still,
Shaken out dead from tree and hill:
I had walked on at the wind's will, –
I sat now, for the wind was still.

Between my knees my forehead was, –
My lips, drawn in, said not Alas!
My hair was over in the grass,
My naked ears heard the day pass.

My eyes, wide open, had the run   10
Of some ten weeds to fix upon;
Among those few, out of the sun,
The woodspurge flowered, three cups in one.

From perfect grief there need not be
Wisdom or even memory:
One thing then learnt remains to me, –
The woodspurge has a cup of three.

Written 1856. Song No. VIII of 'Sonnets and Songs, towards a work to be called
"The House of Life"', Poems (1870).

EVEN SO

So it is, my dear.
All such things touch secret strings
   For heavy hearts to hear.
So it is, my dear.

   Very like indeed:
Sea and sky, afar, on high,
   Sand and strewn seaweed, –
Very like indeed.

   But the sea stands spread
As one wall with the flat skies,   10
Where the lean black craft like flies

Seem well-nigh stagnated,
Soon to drop off dead.

   Seemed it so to us
When I was thine and thou wast mine,
   And all these things were thus,
   But all our world in us?

   Could we be so now?
Not if all beneath heaven's pall
   Lay dead but I and thou,   20
   Could we be so now!

Written 1859. Poems (1870).

FOR *THE WINE OF CIRCE* BY EDWARD BURNE JONES[1]

Dusk-haired and gold-robed o'er the golden wine
   She stoops, wherein, distilled of death and shame,
   Sink the black drops; while, lit with fragrant flame,
Round her spread board the golden sunflowers shine.
Doth Helios here with Hecatè combine[2]
   (O Circe, thou their votaress?) to proclaim
   For these thy guests all rapture in Love's name,
Till pitiless Night give Day the countersign?

Lords of their hour, they come. And by her knee
   Those cowering beasts, their equals heretofore,   10
Wait; who with them in new equality
   To-night shall echo back the unchanging roar
   Which sounds forever from the tide-strown shore
Where the dishevelled seaweed hates the sea.

Written 1869. Poems (1870).

FOR *THE WINE OF CIRCE*
1 large watercolour, 1863–9. Crouching Circe puts potion in jar, as new ships put into her harbour; black panthers, ex-sailors, earlier potion drinkers, snuffle about their female bewitcher. Exhibited 1869.
2 Helios, sun god; Hecate, queen of darkness.

From: THE HOUSE OF LIFE: A SONNET-SEQUENCE (1881)

Part I: Youth and Change

Sonnet VI: The Kiss[1]

What smouldering senses in death's sick delay
   Or seizure of malign vicissitude
   Can rob this body of honour, or denude
This soul of wedding-raiment worn to-day?
For lo! even now my lady's lips did play
   With these my lips such consonant interlude
   As laurelled Orpheus longed for when he wooed
The half-drawn hungering face with that last lay.[2]

I was a child beneath her touch, – a man
   When breast to breast we clung, even I and she, –   10
   A spirit when her spirit looked through me, –
A god when all our life-breath met to fan
Our life-blood, till love's emulous ardours ran,
   Fire within fire, desire in deity.

Sonnet VII: Supreme Surrender[1]

To all the spirits of Love that wander by
   Along his love-sown harvest-field of sleep
   My lady lies apparent; and the deep
Calls to the deep;[2] and no man sees but I.
The bliss so long afar, at length so nigh,
   Rests there attained. Methinks proud Love must weep
   When Fate's control doth from his harvest reap
The sacred hour for which the years did sigh.

First touched, the hand now warm around my neck
   Taught memory long to mock desire: and lo!   10
   Across my breast the abandoned hair doth flow,
Where one shorn tress long stirred the longing ache:
And next the heart that trembled for its sake
   Lies the queen-heart in sovereign overthrow.

Sonnet XI: The Love-Letter[1]

Warmed by her hand and shadowed by her hair
   As close she leaned and poured her heart through thee,
   Whereof the articulate throbs accompany
The smooth black stream that makes thy whiteness fair, –
Sweet fluttering sheet, even of her breath aware, –
   Oh let thy silent song disclose to me
   That soul wherewith her lips and eyes agree
Like married music in Love's answering air.

THE KISS

1 Written 1869. Sonnet No. IV of 'Sonnets and Songs, towards a work to be called "The House of Life"', *Poems* (1870).
2 Orpheus, using song to get wife Eurydice out of Underworld.

SUPREME SURRENDER

1 Written 1870. No. VI (1870).
2 Psalm 42.7.

THE LOVE-LETTER

1 Written 1870. No. X (1870).

Fain had I watched her when, at some fond thought,
  Her bosom to the writing closelier press'd,   10
  And her breast's secrets peered into her breast;
When, through eyes raised an instant, her soul sought
My soul, and from the sudden confluence caught
  The words that made her love the loveliest.

Sonnet XXVI: Mid-Rapture[1]

Thou lovely and beloved, thou my love;
  Whose kiss seems still the first; whose summoning eyes,
  Even now, as for our love-world's new sunrise,
Shed very dawn; whose voice, attuned above
All modulation of the deep-bowered dove,
  Is like a hand laid softly on the soul;
  Whose hand is like a sweet voice to control
Those worn tired brows it hath the keeping of: –

What word can answer to thy word, – what gaze
  To thine, which now absorbs within its sphere   10
  My worshiping face, till I am mirrored there
Light-circled in a heaven of deep-drawn rays?
What clasp, what kiss mine inmost heart can prove,
O lovely and beloved, O my love?

Sonnet LIII: Without Her[1]

What of her glass[2] without her? The blank grey
  There where the pool is blind of the moon's face.
  Her dress without her? The tossed empty space
Of cloud-rack whence the moon has passed away.
Her paths without her? Day's appointed sway
  Usurped by desolate night. Her pillowed place
  Without her? Tears, ah me! for love's good grace,
And cold forgetfulness of night or day.

What of the heart without her? Nay, poor heart,
  Of thee what word remains ere speech be still?   10
  A wayfarer by barren ways and chill,
Steep ways and weary, without her thou art,
Where the long cloud, the long wood's counterpart,
  Sheds doubled darkness up the labouring hill.

Sonnet LIV: Love's Fatality[1]

Sweet Love, – but oh! most dread Desire of Love
  Life-thwarted. Linked in gyves[2] I saw them stand,
  Love shackled with Vain-longing, hand to hand:
And one was eyed as the blue vault above:
But hope tempestuous like a fire-cloud hove
  I' the other's gaze, even as in his whose wand

MID-RAPTURE
1 Written 1871.
WITHOUT HER
1 Written 1871.
2 mirror.

LOVE'S FATALITY
1 Written 1871.
2 fetters.

Vainly all night with spell-wrought power has spann'd
The unyielding caves of some deep treasure-trove.

Also his lips, two writhen flakes of flame,
   Made moan: 'Alas O love, thus leashed with me!
   Wing-footed thou, wing-shouldered, once born free:
And I, thy cowering self, in chains grown tame, –
Bound to thy body and soul, named with thy name, –
   Life's iron heart, even Love's Fatality.'

10

Part II: Change and Fate [Sonnet LX onwards]

Sonnet LXIX: Autumn Idleness[1]

This sunlight shames November where he grieves
   In dead red leaves, and will not let him shun
   The day, though bough with bough be over-run.
But with a blessing every glade receives
High salutation; while from hillock-eaves
   The deer gaze calling, dappled white and dun,
   As if, being foresters of old, the sun
Had marked them with the shade of forest-leaves.

Here dawn to-day unveiled her magic glass;
   Here noon now gives the thirst and takes the dew;
Till eve bring rest when other good things pass.
   And here the lost hours the lost hours renew
While I still lead my shadow o'er the grass,
   Nor know, for longing, that which I should do.

10

Sonnet LXXVII: Soul's Beauty[1]

Under the arch of Life, where love and death,
   Terror and mystery, guard her shrine, I saw
   Beauty enthroned; and though her gaze struck awe,
I drew it in as simply as my breath.
Hers are the eyes which, over and beneath,
   The sky and sea bend on thee, – which can draw,
   By sea or sky or woman, to one law,
The alloted bondman of her palm and wreath.

This is that Lady Beauty, in whose praise
   Thy voice and hand shake still, – long known to thee
     By flying hair and fluttering hem, – the beat
     Following her daily of thy heart and feet,
   How passionately and irretrievably,
In what fond flight, how many ways and days!

10

Sonnet LXXVIII: Body's Beauty[1]

Of Adam's first wife, Lilith, it is told
   (The witch he loved before the gift of Eve,)
   That, ere the snake's, her sweet tongue could deceive,

AUTUMN IDLENESS
1 Written 1850.
SOUL'S BEAUTY
1 Written 1867.

BODY'S BEAUTY
1 Written 1867.

And her enchanted hair was the first gold.
And still she sits, young while the earth is old,
  And, subtly of herself contemplative,
  Draws men to watch the bright web she can weave,
Till heart and body and life are in its hold.

The rose and poppy are her flowers; for where
  Is he not found, O Lilith, whom shed scent
And soft-shed kisses and soft sleep shall snare?
  Lo! as that youth's eyes burned at thine, so went
  Thy spell through him, and left his straight neck bent
And round his heart one strangling golden hair.

10

Sonnet LXXXI: Memorial Thresholds[1]

What place so strange, – though unrevealèd snow
  With unimaginable fires arise
  At the earth's end, – what passion of surprise
Like frost-bound fire-girt scenes of long ago?
Lo! this is none but I this hour; and lo!
  This is the very place which to mine eyes
  Those mortal hours in vain immortalize,
'Mid hurrying crowds, with what alone I know.

City, of thine a single simple door,
  By some new Power reduplicate, must be
  Even yet my life-porch in eternity,
Even with one presence filled, as once of yore:
Or mocking winds whirl round a chaff-strown floor
  Thee and thy years and these my words and me.

10

Sonnet LXXXII: Hoarded Joy[1]

I said: 'Nay, pluck not, – let the first fruit be:
  Even as thou sayest, it is sweet and red,
  But let it ripen still. The tree's bent head
Sees in the stream its own fecundity
And bides the day of fulness. Shall not we
  At the sun's hour that day possess the shade,
  And claim our fruit before its ripeness fade,
And eat it from the branch and praise the tree?'

I say: 'Alas! our fruit hath wooed the sun
  Too long, – 'tis fallen and floats adown the stream.
Lo, the last clusters! Pluck them every one,
  And let us sup with summer; ere the gleam
Of autumn set the year's pent sorrow free,
And the woods wail like echoes from the sea.'

10

Sonnet XCVII: A Superscription[1]

Look in my face; my name is Might-have-been;
  I am also called No-more, Too-late, Farewell;

MEMORIAL THRESHOLDS
1 Written 1873.
HOARDED JOY
1 Written 1870. No. XXXVIII (1870).

A SUPERSCRIPTION
1 Written 1868. No. XLVI (1870).

Unto thine ear I hold the dead-sea shell
Cast up thy Life's foam-fretted feet between;
Unto thine eyes the glass where that is seen
   Which had Life's form and Love's, but by my spell
   Is now a shaken shadow intolerable,
Of ultimate things unuttered the frail screen.

Mark me, how still I am! But should there dart
   One moment through thy soul the soft surprise   10
   Of that winged Peace which lulls the breath of sighs, –
Then shalt thou see me smile, and turn apart
Thy visage to mine ambush at thy heart
   Sleepless with cold commemorative eyes.

Sonnet CI: The One Hope[1]

When vain desire at last and vain regret
   Go hand in hand to death, and all is vain,
   What shall assuage the unforgotten pain
And teach the unforgetful to forget?
Shall Peace be still a sunk stream long unmet, –
   Or may the soul at once in a green plain
   Stoop through the spray of some sweet life-fountain
And cull the dew-drenched flowering amulet?

Ah! when the wan soul in that golden air
   Between the scriptured petals softly blown   10
   Peers breathless for the gift of grace unknown, –
Ah! let none other alien spell soe'er
But only the one Hope's one name be there, –
   Not less nor more, but even that word alone.

The whole sequence was separately published as The House of Life, A Sonnet-Sequence,
'The Siddal Edition' (Ellis & Elvey, 1898).

NUPTIAL SLEEP

At length their long kiss severed, with sweet smart:
   And as the last slow sudden drops are shed
   From sparkling eaves when all the storm has fled,
So singly flagged the pulses of each heart.
Their bosoms sundered, with the opening start
   Of married flowers to either side outspread
   From the knit stem; yet still their mouths, burnt red,
Fawned on each other where they lay apart.

Sleep sank them lower than the tide of dreams,
   And their dreams watched them sink, and slid away.   10
Slowly their souls swam up again, through gleams
   Of watered light and dull drowned waifs of day;

THE ONE HOPE
1 Written 1870. No. L (1870). *Ballads and Sonnets* (Ellis & White, 1881).
Final sonnet in the extended sequence.

Till from some wonder of new woods and streams
He woke, and wondered more: for there she lay.

Written 1869. 'Sonnets and Songs, towards a work to be called "The House of Life"',
Poems (1870). Suppressed in Ballads and Sonnets (1881) and The House of Life:
A Sonnet Sequence, 'The Siddal Edition' (1898). Restored as No. VIa in
The Works of Dante Gabriel Rossetti, ed. W. M. Rossetti (Ellis, 1911). 1870 text.

'FOUND'[1]

(For a Picture)

'There is a budding morrow in midnight:'[2] –
  So sang our Keats, our English nightingale.
  And here, as lamps across the bridge turn pale
In London's smokeless resurrection-light,
Dark breaks to dawn. But o'er the deadly blight
  Of Love deflowered and sorrow of none avail
  Which makes this man gasp and this woman quail,
Can day from darkness ever again take flight?

Ah! gave not these two hearts their mutual pledge,
Under one mantle sheltered 'neath the hedge   10
  In gloaming courtship? And, O God! to-day
He only knows he holds her; – but what part
Can life now take? She cries in her locked heart, –
'Leave me – I do not know you – go away!'

Written 1881. Ballads and Sonnets (1881).

Gerald Massey (1828–1907)

Gerald Massey was born, 29 May 1828, in a stone hut on the canal near Tring, Hertfordshire, into the large family of William and Mary Massey. His father was a canal boatman. Both parents were illiterate. Gerald went briefly to a penny-school, but was soon employed, aged eight, at a local silk-mill, getting up at 5 a.m., working until 6.30 p.m., for a weekly wage of pennies. When the mill burned down, the boy turned to straw-plaiting, but soon fell ill with the plaiters' ague, brought on by working in marshy surroundings. 'I never knew what childhood meant', he declared later. He read whatever he could – the Bible, Bunyan, *Robinson Crusoe*, Methodist tracts. Aged fifteen he drifted to London, got work as an errand boy, fell in love with books, reading anything that came to hand, scouring bookstalls, going without food to buy reading matter – history books, Cobbett's *French Without a Master*, *Lloyd's Penny Times*. Eventually he started versifying. A Tring bookseller

brought out his *Poems and Chansons* (1848), which sold 250 copies. Meanwhile revolutions in Europe and Chartism at home were exciting him. He was reading Tom Paine and Constantin Volney. He and an Uxbridge Chartist printer started up a working-men's paper, *The Spirit of Freedom*. Massey got himself sacked from several jobs because of his literary work and his politics. He contributed to Chartist Thomas Cooper's *Cooper's Journal* (1850), but in the same year he joined the Christian Socialists, became secretary to their Board, contributed to the *Christian Socialist* journal, and brought out his second volume, *Voices of Freedom and Lyrics of Love*. F. D. Maurice wrote to Charles Kingsley that while Massey was 'not quite an Alton Locke' (the working-class self-helper of Kingsley's novel of that name) he did have 'some of the real stuff in him'. *The Ballad of Babe Christabel, with Other Lyrical Poems* (1854), with a Biographic Sketch detailing Massey's early life and struggles,

'FOUND'
1 Rossetti's unfinished picture (started 1854): countryman finds fallen-woman sweetheart on London's Blackfriars Bridge (a white calf in net on his drover's cart; woman gorgeously clothed; on knees;

rebuffing rescuer).
2 Keats, 'To Homer', *Life, Letters and Literary Remains of John Keats* (1848).

really made his name as libertarian poet of the people. Alexander Smith compared him with Burns, Walter Savage Landor with Keats and Shakespeare. Tennyson thanked Massey effusively for the book: he thought Massey made 'our good old English tongue crack and sweat for it occasionally', but still expressed great joy at 'thus suddenly coming on a poet of such fine lyrical impulse'. Ruskin thought Massey's writing 'a helpful and precious gift to the working-classes'. Sydney Dobell came to admire and stayed on as a great friend (he liked the 'fine flushing enthusiasm' of Massey's *War Waits* – there was a lot of Spasmodic affinity in this author). For a time Massey assisted John Chapman, the radical publisher in the Strand in London, and George Eliot, Chapman's right-hand woman, was thought by some to have based features of her workingman hero in *Felix Holt, the Radical* (1866) on Massey. He contributed to the *Athenaeum*, the *Leader, All the Year Round* and *Good Words*. In 1854, short of money, he moved to Edinburgh, lecturing on art, poetry and politics, writing for *Chambers' Journal* and the *Witness*. Massey's verses became extremely patriotic, obsessed with the Crimean War and the Indian Mutiny. Isa Knox beat him and five other finalists for the Crystal Palace Burns Centenary Prize

Poem in 1859. He was one of the main working-class exhibits in Samuel Smiles's *Self Help* (1859). Around this time he shuttled about the country, acquiring eventually a most useful patron in Lady Marian Alford, whose son Lord Brownlow gave him a house on his estate, Ward's Hurst, near Little Gaddesden. Massey lived there from 1862 until 1877 – developing his cranky interests in the secret meanings of Shakespeare, mystical readings of the Bible, spiritualism and mesmerism. These were his themes on several lecture tours to North America and Australasia in the seventies and eighties. He obtained a Civil List Pension in 1863, augmented in 1887. His later years, at New Southgate, Dulwich and South Norwood, were spent cracking the mystic codes of ancient Egypt, and publishing the results of these researches in massive tomes, culminating in *Ancient Egypt the Light of the World, In Twelve Books* (1907). He was married twice (Rosina Jane Knowles, 1850; Eva Byron, 1868) and had a total of nine children. He died in South Norwood, 29 October 1907, survived by two daughters. His daughter Christabel assembled his main poems in two volumes, *My Lyrical Life: Poems Old and New* (1889).

SONG OF THE RED REPUBLICAN

Fling out the red Banner! its fiery front under,
 Come, gather ye, gather ye, Champions of Right!
And roll round the world, with the voice of God's thunder,
 The Wrongs we've to reckon, oppressions to smite.
They deem that we strike no more like the old Hero-band,
 Victory's own battle-hearted and brave:
Blood of Christ! brothers mine, it were sweet but to see ye stand,
 Triumph or Tomb welcome, Glory or Grave!

Fling out the red Banner in mountain and valley!
 Let Earth feel the tread of the free once again;   10
Now soldiers of Freedom, for love of God, rally,
 Old Earth yearns to know that her children are Men.
We are nerved by a thousand wrongs, burning and bleeding,
 Bold Thoughts leap to birth, but the bold Deeds must come;
And wherever Humanity's yearning and pleading,
 One battle for Liberty strike we heart-home.

Fling out the red Banner! achievements immortal
 Have yet to be won by the hands labour-brown;
And few, few may enter the proud promise-portal,
 Yet wear it in thought like a glorious Crown!   20
And O joy of the onset! sound trumpet, array us;
 True hearts would leap up were all hell in our path.
Up, up from the Slave-land; who stirreth to stay us,
 Shall fall, as of old, in a Red Sea of wrath.[1]

SONG OF THE RED REPUBLICAN
1   Pharaoh's army, pursuing biblical Israelites escaping Egyptian slavery, drowned in Red Sea.

Fling out the red Banner, O Sons of the morning!
    Young spirits abiding to burst into wings, –
We stand shadow-crown'd, but sublime is the warning,
    All heaven's grimly husht, and the Bird of Storm sings!
    'All's well,' saith the Sentry on Tyranny's tower,
While Hope by his watch-fire is grey and tear-blind;   30
Ay, all's well! Freedom's Altar burns, hour by hour,
    Live brands for the fire-damp with which ye are mined.

Fling out the red Banner! the patriots perish,
    But where their bones whiten the seed striketh root:
Their blood hath run red the great harvest to cherish:
    Now gather ye, Reapers, and garner the fruit.
Victory! victory! Tyrants are quaking!
    The Titan of Toil from the bloody thrall starts;
The slaves are awaking, the dawn-light is breaking,
    The foot-fall of Freedom beats quick at our hearts!   40

First version of this much rewritten poem, 'The Red Banner', The Red Republican, no. 1 (1850).
Text, The Ballad of Babe Christabel, with Other Lyrical Poems (David Bogue, 1854).

THEY ARE BUT GIANTS WHILE WE KNEEL

Good People! put no faith in Kings, nor in your Princes trust,
Who break your hearts for bread, and grind your faces in the dust:
The Palace Paupers look from lattice high and mock your prayer:
The Champions of the Christ are dumb, or golden bit they wear.
O but to see ye bend no more to earth's crime-cursèd things –
Ye are God's Oracles: stand forth! be Nature's Priests and Kings!
Ye fight and bleed, while Fortune's darlings slink in splendid lair;
With lives that crawl, like worms through buried Beauty's golden hair! –
A tale of lives wrung out in tears their Grandeur's garb reveals,
And the last sobs of breaking hearts sound in their Chariot-wheels!   10
O league ye – crush the things that kill all love and liberty!
They are but Giants while we kneel: ONE LEAP, AND UP GO WE.

Trust not the Priests, whose tears are lies, their hearts are hard and cold;
They lead ye to sweet pastures, where they fleece the foolish fold!
The Church and State are linkt and sworn to desolate the land.
Good people, 'twixt these Foxes' tails, We'll fling a fiery brand.[1]
Up, if ye will be free, to golden calves no longer bow:[2]
The Nations yearn for Liberty – the world grows earnest now.
Your bent-knee is half-way to hell! – Up, Serviles, from the dust!
The Harvest of the free red-ripens for the sickle-thrust.   20
They're quaking now, and shaking now, who wrought the hurtling sorrow,
To-day the desolators, but the desolate To-morrow!
Loud o'er their murder's menace wakes the watch-word of the Free:
They are but Giants while we kneel: ONE LEAP, AND UP GO WE!

Some bravest patriot-hearts have gone, to break beyond the Sea,
And many in the Dungeon have died for you and me!
And still we glut the Merciless – give all Life's glory up,
That stars of flame, and winking eyes, may crown their revel-cup!

THEY ARE BUT GIANTS WHILE WE KNEEL
1 reference, one of biblical Samson's tricks against Philistines' corn-fields, Judges 15.

2 Israelites worshipped Golden Calf instead of Jehovah (traditional emblem of money worship), Exodus 32.

Back, tramplers on the Many! Death and Danger ambusht lie;
 Beware ye, or the blood may run! the patient people cry: 30
Ah! shut not out the light of hope, or we may blindly dash,
Like Samson with his strong death-grope, and whelm ye in the crash.
Think how they spurred the People mad, that old Régime of France,
Whose heads, like poppies from Death's Scythe fell in a bloody dance.
Ye plead in vain, ye bleed in vain, ah! Blind! when will ye see
They are but Giants while we kneel? ONE LEAP, AND UP GO WE.

The merry flowers are springing from our last-year Martyrs' mould,
As if their dreams had taken blossom telling what they would have told;
Of all our rainbowed Future: and what this earth shall be,
When we have bartered blows and bonds for life and liberty.   40
Ah! what a face of glory shall the weary world put on,
When Love is crownèd, and shall king the heart its royal throne!
O we shall see our darlings smile, – who meet us tearful now, –
Ere the Eternal morn breaks grey, on the Beloved's brow:
And Love shall give the kiss of Death no more to those we love,
And pride, not shame, shall flush the face of our heart-nestling Dove.
Rouse, Titans, scale th'Olympus where the hindering Tyrants be:
They are but Giants while we kneel: ONE LEAP, AND UP GO WE!

First version of this much revised poem, in The Friend of the People *(8 March 1851).*
Text, The Ballad of Babe Christabel *(1854).*

O LAY THY HAND IN MINE, DEAR!

O lay thy hand in mine, dear!
  We're growing old, we're growing old;
But Time hath brought no sign, dear,
  That hearts grow cold, that hearts grow cold.
'Tis long, long since our new love
  Made life divine, made life divine;
But age enricheth true love,
  Like noble wine, like noble wine.

And lay thy cheek to mine, dear,
  And take thy rest, and take thy rest;   10
Mine arms around thee twine, dear,
  And make thy nest, and make thy nest.
A many cares are pressing
  On this dear head, on this dear head;
But Sorrow's hands in blessing
  Are surely laid, are surely laid.

O lean thy life on mine, dear!
  'Twill shelter thee, 'twill shelter thee.
Thou wert a winsome vine, dear,
  On my young tree, on my young tree: 20
And so, till boughs are leafless,
  And Song-birds flown, and Song-birds flown,
We'll twine, then lay us, griefless,
  Together down, together down.

The Poetical Works of Gerald Massey, *A New Edition (Routledge, Warne, & Routledge, 1861).*

MY LOVE

My Love is true and tender,
    Her eyes are rich with rest;
Her hair of dappled splendour,
    The colour I love best;
So sweet, so gay, so odorous-warm,
    She nestles here, heart-high,
A bounteous aspect, beauteous form,
    But, just a wee bit sly.

My Love is no light Dreamer,
    A-floating with the foam;   10
But a brave life-sea swimmer,
    With footing found in Home.
My winsome Wife, she's bright without,
    And beautiful within;
But – I would not say quite without
    The least wee touch of sin.

My Love is not an Angel
    In one or two small things:
But just a wifely woman
    With other wants than wings.   20
You have some little leaven
    Of earth, you darling dear;
If you were fit for Heaven,
    You might not nestle here.

My Lyrical Life, Poems Old and New, *two series ([1869] Kegan Paul,*
Trench & Co., 1889), 1st series.

ONLY A DREAM

As proper mode of quenching legal lust,
    A Roué takes unto Himself a Wife:
'Tis Cheaper when the bones begin to rust,
And there's no other Woman you can trust:
But, mind you, in return, Law says you must
    Provide her with the physical means of life:
And then the blindest beast may wallow and roll;
The twain are One flesh, never mind the Soul:
You may not cruelly beat her, but are free
To violate the life in sanctuary;   10
In virgin soil renew old seeds of Crime
To blast eternity as well as time:
    She must show black and blue, or no divorce
    Is granted by the Law of Physical Force.

My Lyrical Life *(1889), 1st series. Epigraph to 'Only A Dream' –*
earlier version of which, sans *epigraph,* The Poetical Works *(1861).*

WOMANKIND

Dear things! we would not have you learn too much –
   Your Ignorance is so charming! We've a notion
That greater knowledge might not lend you such
   Sure aid to blind obedience and devotion.

My Lyrical Life (1889), 1st series.

A VERY EARLY RISER

At the Last Day while all the rest
   Are soundly sleeping underground,
He will be up clean-shaved and dressed
   An hour before the Trumpets sound.

My Lyrical Life (1889), 1st series.

AN ANGEL IN THE HOUSE

You have your Angel in the House! but look
On this, her likeness, mirrored in a book,
If but to learn how shadowy the Ideal
In presence of the living, loving Real.

My Lyrical Life (1889), 1st series.

ON A WEDDING-DAY

Thus, hand in hand, and heart in heart,
   Face nestling unto face,
Forgotten things like Spirits start
   From many a hiding-place!
There is no sound of Babe or Bird,
   And all the stillness seems
Sweet as the music only heard
   Adown the land of dreams.

And if, because it is so proud,
   My heart will find a voice,   10
And in its dear dream love aloud,
   And speak of sweet still joys,
It is no genuine gift of God,
   But only Goblin Gold,
That withers into dead leaves, should
   The secret tale be told.

Nine years ago you came to me,
   And nestled on my breast,
A soft and wingèd mystery
   That settled here to rest;   20
And my heart rocked its Babe of bliss,
   And soothed its child of air,
With something 'twixt a song and kiss,
   To keep it nestling there.

At first I thought the fairy form
   Too spirit-soft and good

To fill my poor, low nest with warm
   And wifely womanhood.
But such a cozy peep of home
   Did your dear eyes unfold;   30
And in their deep and dewy gloom
   What tales of love were told!

In dreamy curves your beauty drooped,
   As tendrils lean to twine,
And very graciously they stooped
   To bear their fruit, my Vine!
To bear such blessed fruit of love
   As tenderly increased
Among the ripe vine-branches of
   Your balmy-breathing breast.   40

We cannot boast to have bickered not
   Since you and I were wed;
We have not lived the smoothest lot,
   Nor made the downiest bed!
Time has not passed o'erhead in Stars,
   And underfoot in flowers,
With wings that slept on fragrant airs
   Through all the happy hours.

It is our way, more fate than fault,
   Love's cloudy fire to clear,   50
To find some virtue in the salt
   That sparkles in a tear!
Pray God it all come right at last,
   Pray God it so befall,
That when our day of life is past
   The end may crown it all.

Ah, Dear! though lives may pull apart
   Down to the roots of love,
One thought will bend us heart to heart,
   Till lips re-wed above!   60
 One thought the knees of pride will bow
   Down to the grave-yard sod;
 You are the Mother of Angels now!
   We have two babes with God.

Cling closer, closer, for their loss,
   About our darlings left,
And let their memories grow like moss
   That healeth rent and rift; –
For his dear sake, our Soldier Boy,
   For whom we nightly plead   70
That he may live for God, and die
   For England in her need, –

For her, who like a dancing boat
   Leaps o'er life's solemn waves,
Our little Lightheart who can float
   And frolic over graves;
And Grace, who making music goes,
   As in some shady place

A Brooklet, prattling to the boughs,
    Looks up with its bright face.   80

Cling closer, closer, life to life,
    Cling closer, heart to heart;
The time will come, my own wed Wife,
    When you and I must part!
Let nothing break our band but Death,
    For in the worlds above
'Tis the breaker Death that soldereth
    Our ring of Wedded Love.

My Lyrical Life *(1889), 2nd series.*

J. (John) Stanyan Bigg (1828–65)

John Stanyan Bigg, journalist and poet, was born in Ulverston, Lancashire, 14 July 1828. He was educated locally, then at a boarding-school in Warwickshire. After working for his father, he turned to journalism, became editor of the *Ulverston Advertiser*, then went to the north of Ireland to edit the *Downshire Protestant*. He married a Miss R. A. H. Pridham at Downpatrick. In 1860 he returned to England to become proprietor as well as editor of the *Ulverston Advertiser*. He was said to have been turned on as a boy to literature – and to making a profit from it – by reading the *Arabian Nights* and reciting the stories to friends for cash. His first book, *The Sea King* (1848), is a long verse romance based on Sharon Turner's *History of the Anglo-Saxons. Night and the Soul* – a work with Spasmodic inclinations – appeared in 1854; *Shifting Scenes and Other Poems* in 1862, with a rather cloudy Preface 'On the Importance of "Action" in Poetry'. Bigg contributed widely to journals like the *London Quarterly Review*, the *Eclectic Review*, and *Dublin University Magazine*. He was one of the six runners-up for the Crystal Palace Burns Centenary Prize in 1859, which Isa Knox won. His one-volume novel *Alfred Staunton* (1860) had readers. He died, prematurely, at Ulverston, 19 May 1865, aged thirty-six.

HARTLEY PIT CATASTROPHE

Prologue

Written by J. Stanyan Bigg, and delivered by T. Town, Esq., Ulverston, at the Concert held there February 11th, 1862, on behalf of those who are bereaved by the accident.

Death in the Palace; Death within the Cot,
Death in all ranks! 'Tis but the common lot;
He comes with stealthy steps, and in the night,
Taketh our cherished treasure from our sight;
He tracks our steps, through hamlet, tower, and town,
And, with sure instinct, brings his victim down;
And smites the pauper as he smites the crown.
With pallid face he leaps into his car,
And flames out ruddy in the sweat of war;
He comes unto the cottage door and knocks,   10
And then, in spite of bars, and bolts, and locks,
Some one gets up and goes, – and is not seen –
Only another hillock on the green
Of the Sabbatic churchyard; – all is done,
And one more mortal shall not see the sun!

But seldom to a village doth he come,
Wringing all hearts, and hushing all the hum
Of its glad voices. Seldom is he seen
Wrapping in shadow *all* the village green;
Seldom he enters in at *every* door,   20
And writes the fearful legend up – 'No more,'
Over the mantel-piece, and on the floor.
No more a father's shadow on the wall;
No more a husband's step, a brother's call,
No more the ruddy child with sunny hair,
Coming into the house – a psalm and prayer.
No more the eager hand upon the door,
For father, husband, brother, are no more.

Thus has it been at Hartley. Every room
Of every cottage hath its special gloom,   30
Some one is missing – husband, father, son,
Shall fill their place no more. Their day is done;
And there is night, and woe, and wail, and gloom,
And saddest shadows fill up all the room
Of the dear lost ones, – each one in his place;
Death hath washed white each bronzed and ruddy face;
And so of all the dearest ties an end,
Of father, husband, brother, child, and friend:
Husbands have said their last 'Good-morn,' and boys
Have set aside for ever childish toys,   40
And with the morning breeze upon their breath
Have gone into the mysteries of death,
Their mothers' pleading arms not heeding; – So
Went the grey-headed, so the strong men go
When the dread Angel makes the sign of woe.

A village has been stricken: – On the door
Of every cottage are the words 'No more;'
No more the sturdy hands that won the bread,
Husband, and brother, child, and friend are dead.
And we, who come before you thus, to-night,   50
Cannot bring back the lost ones to the light;
Cannot refill the lorn and empty chair,
Cannot bring back the earnest evening prayer;
Cannot unto the mother give her son,
Nor to the wife her husband – all is done!
But still, amid this holocaust of dead,
The living need what we can give them – Bread!

Shifting Scenes and Other Poems *(William Freeman, 1862).*

AN IRISH PICTURE

A smoking swamp before a cottage door;
A drowned dog bobbing to a soleless shoe;
A broken wash-tub, with its ragged staves
Swimming and ducking to a battered hat,
Whenever the wind stirs the reedy slime;
A tumbled peat-stack, dripping in the rain;
A long, lank pig, with dissipated eyes,
Leading a vagrant life among the moors;

A rotting paling, and a plot of ground,
With fifteen cabbage-stalks amid lush weeds;   10
A moss-grown pathway, and a worn-out gate,
Its broken bars down-dangling from the nails;
A windy cottage, with a leaky thatch,
And two dim windows set like eyes asquint;
A bulging doorway, with a drunken lean;
Two half-nude children dabbling in the mire,
And scrambling eagerly for bottle-necks;
A man akimbo at the open door,
His battered hat slouched o'er his sottish eyes,
Smoking contented in the falling rain.   20

Shifting Scenes *(1862)*.

Arthur J. (Joseph) Munby (1828–1910)

Arthur J. Munby, poet and lawyer, was born in 1828 in York, oldest child (he had five brothers and a sister) of Joseph Munby, a solicitor, and Caroline Eleanor Forth. He attended St Peter's School, York, before going up to Trinity College, Cambridge (BA, 1851; MA, 1856). He entered Lincoln's Inn in June 1851, and was called to the Bar in November 1855. From 1858 until retirement thirty years later he worked in the Ecclesiastical Commissioner's Office. *Benoni*, his first volume of verses, appeared in 1852. He was one of the six also-rans when Isa Knox carried off the Crystal Palace Burns Centenary Prize in 1859. *Verses, New and Old* (1865) collected his poems from magazines such as *Fraser's, Macmillan's, Temple Bar*. The anonymously published *Dorothy* (1880), dedicated to his friend the novelist R. D. Blackmore, was rather a hit in the scenes-from-rural-life mode (Robert Browning praised its 'exquisiteness of observation'). *Vestigia Retrorsum* appeared in 1891, *Poems, Chiefly Lyrical and Elegiac* in 1901, and his last volume, *Relicta*, in 1909. As 'Jones Brown' he brought out *Vulgar*

Verses (1891) – pieces about ordinary people done in 'dialect' and colloquial speech. There was also *Susan, a Poem of Degrees* (1893) and *Ann Morgan's Love, a Pedestrian Poem* (1896). Munby had antiquarian interests – he was a Fellow of the Society of Antiquarians – and contributed a great deal to the journal *Notes and Queries*. He strongly supported the cause of ordinary people's education, and for ten years, 1860–70, taught a Latin class at the Working Men's College in Great Ormond Street, London. A keynote of his writing is a recognition of and sympathy with manual labourers, especially working women. One reason for this appeared when his Will was read after his death (at Pyrford in Surrey, 29 January 1910) and the existence of a wife was revealed – Hannah Cullwick, his servant, whom he had married secretly, 14 January 1873, but who, the Will claimed, had refused to give up her servant status. She died not long before Munby, in July 1909. One of his compilations was a volume of epitaphs and obituaries entitled *Faithful Servants*.

SCENT AND JEWELS

Lady, why blend these dying sweets
With that immortal sweetness all thine own?
    Why ask of Art her counterfeits –
Her languid cloying odours – but to crown
        That ever-deepening, ever-mellowing bloom
        Whose very presence is perfume?

    Dost thou mistrust thine ardent eyes
And that deep glow of soul indwelling there,
    That with these rival galaxies
Of glimmering gems thou hast bedew'd thy hair?   10
        Or dost thou stoop to those who equal deem
        The innate lustre and the surface-gleam?

The clear starr'd purple overhead
Brooks not her virgin trueness should be soil'd
   With false and fever'd glare and red
Of mocking meteors; of their thrones despoiled
     She shoots them down in scorn, to find i' the Earth
     Some miry home more level with their birth:

   So do thou ever prize, like her,
The simple majesty of maidenhood;   20
   And in calm wrath the odours tear
And soulless jewels from thee: upstart brood
     Unblest! and only let thy cool white brow
     For ever wear the light of its own stainless snow.

Benoni: Poems *(John Ollivier, 1852)*.

The Sexes

O, you are fair – you have soft turtle-eyes,
   Not flush'd with vulgar passion, clouded not
With stains of folly, – whose transparent lymph
   No shadows dull, no fretful eddies blot:

Your souls are precious oratories, closed
   And curtain'd in from all things not divine;
Where smoothest sounds enrich the loving air,
   And moons alone and silver cressets shine.

You dwell in peace among your pleasant hours –
   You hear no echoes from the far-off strife;   10
You lift your shining eyes, and all the place
   Feels happier – feels the magic of your life.

But we – for us in the thick thronging days
   No shrine, no bower, no oasis appears;
No path is left whereby we might have climb'd
   Back for a moment to the better years:

We have forgotten all – we hear not now
   Our mothers' teachings, – see not in the land
Its ancient beauties, – look on you as dreams
   Too fair to love, too high to understand: 20

We are uncover'd – the rank, stagnant air
   Infects our breath – our curdled souls endure
A press of crawling horrors – and vile sounds
   Hiss in our dull ears: how can we be pure?

Benoni: Poems *(1852)*.

The Serving Maid

When you go out at early morn,
   Your busy hands, sweet drudge, are bare;
   For you must work, and none are there
To see with scorn – to feel with scorn.

And when the weekly wars begin,
 Your arms are naked to the hilt,
 And many a sturdy pail's a-tilt
To sheathe them in – to plunge them in.

For you at least can understand
 That daily work is hard and stern,   10
 That those who toil for bread must learn
To bare the hand – to spoil the hand.

But in the evening, when they dine,
 And you behind each frequent chair
 Are flitting lightly here and there
To bring them wine – to pour them wine;

Oh then, from every dainty eye
 That may not so be shock'd or grieved,
 Your hands are hid, your arms are sleeved:
We ask not why – we tell not why.   20

Ah fools! Though you for workday scours,
 And they for show, unveil their charms,
 Love is not bound to snowy arms,
He thinks of yours – he speaks of yours:

To me his weighted shaft has come;
 Though hand and arm are both unseen,
 Your rosy wrist peeps out between
And sends it home – and speeds it home.

       Verses, New and Old *(Bell & Daldy, 1865)*.

POST MORTEM

I lay in my coffin under the sod;
But the rooks they caw'd, and the sheep they trod
And munch'd and bleated, and made such a noise –
What with the feet of the charity boys
Trampling over the old grave-stones –
That it loosen'd my inarticulate bones,
 And chased my sleep away.

So I turn'd (for the coffin is not so full
As it was, you know) my aching skull;
And said to my wife – and it's not my fault   10
If she *does* lie next to me in the vault –
Said to her kindly, 'My love, my dear,
How do you like these sounds we hear
 Over our heads to-day?'

My wife had always a good strong voice;
But I'm not so sure that I did rejoice
When I found it as strong as it used to be,
And so unexpectedly close to me: 20
I thought, if her temper *should* set in,
Why, the boards between us are very thin,
And whenever the bearers come one by one

To deposit the corpse of my eldest son,
Who is spending the earnings of his papa
With such sumptuous ease and such great *éclât*,[1]
They may think it more pleasant, perhaps, than I did,
To find that in death we were not divided.[2]   30
However, I trusted to time and the worms;
And I kept myself to the mildest terms
   Of a conjugal How d'ye do.

'John,' said my wife, 'you're a Body, like me;
At least if you ain't, why you ought to be;
And I really don't think, when I reflect,
That I ought to pay as much respect
To a rattling prattling skeleton   40
As I did to a man of sixteen stone.
However (says she), I shall just remark
That this here place is so cool and dark,
I'm certain sure, if you hadn't have spoke,
My slumber'd never have thus been broke;
So I wish you'd keep your — voice in your head;
For I don't see the good of being dead,
   If one mayn't be quiet too.'   50

She spoke so clear and she spoke so loud,
I thank'd my stars that a linen shroud
And a pair of boards (though they *were* but thin)
Kept out some part of that well-known din:
And, talking of shrouds, the very next word
That my empty echoing orbits heard
Was, 'Gracious me, I can tell by the feel
That I'm all over rags from head to heel!   60
Here's jobs for needle and thread without ending,
For there's ever-so-many holes wants mending!'
'My love,' I ventured to say, 'I fear
It's not much use, your mending 'em here;
For, as fast as you do, there's worse than moth,
And worse than mice, or rats, or both,
Will eat up the work of your cotton ball
And leave you never a shroud at all –   70
   No more than they have to me.'

Now, whether it was that she took it ill
My seeming to question her feminine skill,
Or whether 'twas simply that we were wedded –
The very thing happen'd that most I dreaded:
For, by way of reply, on the coffin-side,
Just where the planks had started wide,
There came a blow so straight and true   80
That it shook my vertebral column in two;
And what more might have follow'd I cannot tell,
But that very minute ('twas just as well)
The flagstone was lifted overhead,
And the red-nosed buriers of the dead
Let down a load on my coffin-plate
That stunn'd me quite with the shock of its weight.

POST MORTEM
1 flare, splendour, brilliance.

2 parodic use of famous phrase from David and Jonathan story,
2 Samuel 1.23, 'and in their death they were not divided'.

'Twas the corpse, of course, of my eldest son,   90
Who had injured his brain (a little one)
By many a spirituous brain-dissolver,
And finish'd it off with a Colt's revolver.
Well – when they had gone and the noise had ceased,
I look'd for one other attack, at least:
But, would you believe it? The place was quiet,
And the worms had resumed their usual diet!
Nay, everything else was silent too;   100
The rooks they neither caw'd nor flew,
And the sheep slept sound by footstone and head,
And the charity boys had been whipp'd to bed.

So I turn'd again, and I said to myself –
'Now, as sure as I'm laid on this sordid shelf
Away from the living that smile or weep,
I'll sleep if I can, and let *her* too sleep:
And I will not once, for pleasure or pain,   110
Unhinge my jaws to speak again,
    No, not if she speaks to me.'

                                    Verses, New and Old *(1865)*.

CHRISTMAS

Our Christmas is a time of make-believe:
    We carol still, we who are growing old,
    Beside the grave wherein lies stark and cold
All that once warm'd and gladden'd Christmas Eve.
Ah, yes! We do it that we may not grieve
    Our children; lest they also should behold,
    Through mirth and music, amid gifts and gold,
The one sad face that never can deceive –
The face of Sorrow. For on Christmas Day
    Sorrow was born; who came on earth to die   10
Vainly: *how* vainly, none, alas! can say
    Who hath not heard believers strive and cry;
Who hath not felt, on this bright bitter morn,
That if our God can fail, we too were best unborn.

                Vestigia Retrorsum: Poems *(Eden, Remington & Co., 1891)*.

A DEATHBED: JULY 1ST, 18—

This is the very room in which she died:
I know it well; and when the moonlight falls,
As now it falls, upon her little bed,
How white the bed looks – like her own frail form
When she was dying!
                    Yet she did not die
By moonlight, like our leader, Tennyson:
He, after so much waiting, so much grief
And glory, and such happiest renown
Of blessing others as himself was blest,   10
And making sorrow fruitfuller than joy,
He, with the milder radiance round his head,
Pass'd to that gracious Country whence he came.

But she went thither on a summer's morn;
Round her fair dwelling all the garden rang
With songs of birds, and fragrant odours breathed
From many a flower to soothe her, and the sun
Lighted her onward to that place of rest
Wherein her husband stood awaiting her.

She did not say a word, before she died;   20
But she look'd up, and with her soft blue eyes
She saw him, clad already in the glow
Of such a state of Being as to her
Was new and most transcendent, but to him
Familiar now; and thus he welcomed her,
His lifelong wife, to that still fairer home.

We too, perchance, shall join her at the last;
If we are like her, or in any wise
Can compass such a journey, such an end.
Meanwhile, she still is with us; and abides,   30
A charming Presence, in the faithful hearts
Of many folk, and most of all in mine.

Poems, Chiefly Lyrical and Elegiac *(Kegan, Paul, Trench, Trübner, 1901).*

Bessie Rayner Parkes (Mme Belloc) (1829–1925)

Bessie Rayner Parkes was born in Birmingham ('Dear smoky Birmingham' in her poem 'To Birmingham'), into a great radical Unitarian Midlands dynasty – her great-grandfather was Joseph Priestley; her father, Joseph Parkes, was one of the founders of the Reform Club. Liberalism was in her blood. She was educated at a Unitarian school for girls in Warwickshire. From the age of eighteen, her closest friend was Barbara Leigh Smith (later Bodichon); in their thirties they travelled Europe together without chaperone, which was then not normal; they worked together to reform the law on married women's property; they co-founded the *English Woman's Journal* (1858–62). Parkes's *Remarks Upon the Education of Girls* (1854) and *Essays on Women's Work* (1865) indicate her distance from the likes of Coventry Patmore and his vision of women as merely Angels in the House. Bessie learned typesetting to help further the all-women Victoria Press. She knew George Eliot, Mrs Gaskell, Elizabeth Barrett Browning. A great friend was Adelaide Anne Procter, whose poetry and work as a poet she greatly preferred to her own. Which is not to say she lacked poetic ambition for herself.

She was a main member of the Langham Place group and the Portfolio Society – key groups encouraging women writers, which included Procter, Isa Craig Knox, Dora Greenwell, Jean Ingelow, and on whose fringes was Christina Rossetti. Her *Poems* (1852) – by B. R. Parkes – was brought out by John Chapman, the radical editor and publisher (and George Eliot's colleague – and lover?), as was the second (amended) edition of 1855 (this time under the name of Bessie Rayner Parkes). Both volumes are dedicated to Barbara Leigh Smith. In 1864 she converted to Roman Catholicism and in 1867 married Louis Belloc, an Irish-Frenchman, and moved to France. When Belloc died in 1872 she returned to England, but though her friendship with Barbara Bodichon continued and she lived to the ripe old age of ninety-six, her radical days were over. Perhaps her Catholicism had something to do with this. Her daughter, Marie Belloc-Lowndes, became an author, as did Belloc-Lowndes's more famous brother, Hilaire Belloc (born 1870). His reactionary anti-Semitic and anti-feminist politics were rather far removed from what his mother had once canvassed.

To Elizabeth Barrett Browning

I was a child when first I read your books,
And lov'd you dearly, so far as I could see
Your obvious meanings, your more subtle depths
Being then (as still, perhaps,) a mystery.

I had no awe of you, so much does love,
In simple daring, all shy fears transcend;
And when they told me, 'You shall travel south',
I chiefly thought, 'In Florence dwells my friend!'
In those first days I seldom heard your name,
You seem'd in my strange fancy all my own,   10
Or else as if you were some saint in Heaven
Whose image took my bookcase for a throne.
As time went on, your words flew far and wide,
I heard them quoted, critically scann'd
With grave intentness, learnt, half mournfully,
That you were *a great Poet in the land,*
So far, so far from me, who lov'd you so,
And never might one human blessing claim;
Yet oh! how I rejoic'd that you were great,
And all my heart exulted in your fame;   20
A woman's fame, and *yours!* I use no words
Of any careful beauty, being plain
As earnestness, and quiet as that Truth
Which shrinks from any flattering speech with pain.
Indeed, I should not dare – but that this love,
Long nurs'd, demands expression, and alone
Seeks by love's dear strength – to approach near you
In words so weak and poor beside your own.

Poems, *by B. R. Parkes (John Chapman, 1852), as 'To *****'. Present title in* Poems,
2nd edn, by Bessie Rayner Parkes (John Chapman, 1855). 1852 text.

FOR ADELAIDE

Who is the Poet? He who sings
    Of high, abstruse, and hidden things,
Or rather he who with a liberal voice
Does with the glad hearts of all earth rejoice?
O sweetest Singer! rather would I be
Gifted with thy kind melody
Than weave mysterious rhymes and such as seem
Born in the dim depths of some sage's dream:
But I have no such art; they will not choose
The utterance of my harsh ungenial muse   10
For any cradle chant; I shall not aid
The mournful mother or the loving maid
To find relief in song. I shall not be
Placed side by side, O Poet dear, with thee
In any grateful thoughts, yet be it known
By all who read how much thou hast mine own!
When, with bent brow and all too anxious heart,
I walk with hurrying step the crowded mart,
And look abroad on men with faithless eyes,
Then do sweet snatches of thy song arise,   20
And float into my heart like melodies
Down dropping from the far blue deeps of heaven,
Or sweet bells wafted over fields at even.
Therefore, if thanks for any gifts be due,
If any service be esteemèd true,
If any virtues do to verse belong,
Take thou the Poet's name, by right of song!

Suffer that I, who never yet did give
False words to that dear art by which I live,
Pluck down bright bay-leaves from the eternal tree,   30
And place them where they have true right to be!¹

Poems, *2nd edn (1855). Adelaide is, presumably, Adelaide Anne Procter.*

Elizabeth Eleanor (Lizzie) Siddal (1829–62)

Lizzie Siddal was a beautiful working-class Londoner, with wonderful red hair, whose Sheffield-born father ran some sort of cutlery business off London's Old Kent Road. She fell, so to say, among thieves – in her case the Pre-Raphaelite Brotherhood and their cronies – picked out and picked up as a model by the twenty-year-old painter Walter Howell Deverell while serving in a milliner's shop near Leicester Square. The Brotherhood liked slumming for their 'Stunners' (Janey Morris, William Morris's wife, daughter of a livery-stable keeper in Oxford, was such another). Lizzie Siddal became a quintessence of Pre-Raphaelite womanhood, the face that launched a huge tranche of medievalizing portraiture. She sat for Holman Hunt's *A Persecuted British Family Rescuing a Christian From Persecution by the Druids.* She was John Everett Millais's Ophelia (kept lying in a bath of cold water, she contracted a terrible cold and her father threatened legal action), and Dante Gabriel Rossetti's Beatrice and Virgin Mary. She and Swinburne, another high-spirited little red-head, romped together, it was said, like brother and sister (forever reading to people, he read Elizabethan plays to her). She drew, tutored probably by Rossetti. It is likely they were lovers. The Brotherhood and the feminists she met through them, Bessie Rayner Parkes and Barbara Leigh Smith, encouraged her into thinking she had more talent than she had. Ruskin bought her drawings and gave her an annual allowance. Having genius demanded of her was no help to her tendency to fraughtfulness. Rossetti's reluctance to marry her seems to have aggravated her stressed condition. She was heavily addicted to laudanum. Rossetti did eventually marry his 'Guggums', but they were notoriously unhappy together. A still-born daughter in

May 1861 was massively perturbing to her. In February 1862 she died of an overdose of laudanum. Wilde's story was that after a ructious dinner with Swinburne at the Sablonière Hotel in Leicester Square, the Rossettis had quarrelled over her drug addiction; he'd shoved a whole bottle of laudanum at her saying 'There, take the lot'; and after he had left with Swinburne (kinder interpreters think to attend the Working Men's College; less kind ones, to visit one of his other women), she had indeed taken the lot. Rossetti seems to have feared a manslaughter charge but, as Swinburne described the Inquest at which he gave evidence: 'Happily there was no difficulty in proving that illness had quite deranged her mind.' Accidental death was the verdict; she was buried in Highgate Cemetery. Guiltily, Rossetti put his manuscript notebook of poems in the coffin; farcically, after seven years, he had them dug up again. Gothically, Lizzie's hair (the Pre-Raphaelites, like most Victorians, were obsessed by hair) was reported to have grown so as to quite fill the coffin. Her friends did not think of her 'genius' as extending much to poetry. A suggestion by Christina Rossetti after Lizzie's death of a joint volume of verses (during her life she'd felt Lizzie as a too potent rival for her brother's affections) fell through – after all Lizzie's poems proved 'almost too hopelessly sad for publication'. Dante Gabriel Rossetti copied out and titled six of her pieces, but that was all. William Michael Rossetti published some of her poems in his end-of-century gatherings of Pre-Raphaelite materials, *Ruskin: Rossetti: Pre-Raphaelitism* (1899), *Dante Gabriel Rossetti: His Family Letters* (1895), and *Some Reminiscences* (1906). The first edition of her *Poems and Drawings* was not until 1978 in Canada.

A SILENT WOOD

O silent wood, I enter thee
With a heart so full of misery
For all the voices from the trees
And the ferns that cling about my knees.

FOR ADELAIDE
1   wreaths of bay (laurel) leaves were used to crown (Roman) conquerors and poets.

In thy darkest shadow let me sit
When the grey owls about thee flit;
There will I ask of thee a boon,
That I may not faint or die or swoon.

Gazing through the gloom like one
Whose life and hopes are also done,   10
Frozen like a thing of stone
I sit in thy shadow – but not alone.

Can God bring back the day when we two stood
Beneath the clinging trees in that dark wood?

Written summer 1857? First published in Burlington Magazine, *I (May 1903), 291–2.*
Text in Lizzie Siddal, Poems and Drawings, *ed. Roger C. Lewis and Mark S. Lasner*
(The Wombat Press, Wolfville, Nova Scotia, 1978).

LORD MAY I COME?

Life and night are falling from me,
Death and day are opening on me,
Wherever my footsteps come and go,
Life is a stony way of woe.
    Lord, have I long to go?

Hollow hearts are ever near me,
Soulless eyes have ceased to cheer me:
    Lord, may I come to thee?

Life and youth and summer weather
To my heart no joy can gather.   10
    Lord, lift me from life's stony way!
Loved eyes long closed in death watch for me:
Holy death is waiting for me –
    Lord, may I come to-day?

My outward life feels sad and still
Like lilies in a frozen rill;
I am gazing upwards to the sun,
Lord, Lord, remembering my lost one.
    O Lord, remember me!

How is it in the unknown land?   20
Do the dead wander hand in hand?
    God, give me trust in thee.

Do we clasp dead hands and quiver
With an endless joy for ever?
Do tall white angels gaze and wend
Along the banks where lilies bend?
Lord, we know not how this may be:
Good Lord we put our faith in thee –
    O God, remember me.

Written early 1862. First published in W. M. Rossetti, Some Reminiscences, *2 vols*
(Scribner's Sons, New York, 1906), I, 199–200. Text, Poems and Drawings *(1978).*

DEAD LOVE

Oh never weep for love that's dead
   Since love is seldom true
But changes his fashion from blue to red,
   From brightest red to blue,
And love was born to an early death
   And is so seldom true.

Then harbour no smile on your bonny face
   To win the deepest sigh.
The fairest words on truest lips
   Pass on and surely die,   10
And you will stand alone, my dear,
   When wintry winds draw nigh.

Sweet, never weep for what cannot be,
   For this God has not given.
If the merest dream of love were true
   Then, sweet, we should be in heaven,
And this is only earth, my dear,
   Where true love is not given.

Written autumn 1859? First published in W. M. Rossetti, Ruskin: Rossetti:
Pre-Raphaelitism *(George Allen, 1899). Text,* Poems and Drawings *(1978).*
(Christina Rossetti's favourite: 'piquant as it is with cool bitter sarcasm'.)

WORN OUT

Thy strong arms are around me, love,
   My head is on thy breast;
Low words of comfort come from thee
   Yet my soul has no rest.

For I am but a startled thing
   Nor can I ever be
Aught save a bird whose broken wing
   Must fly away from thee.

I cannot give to thee the love
   I gave so long ago,   10
The love that turned and struck me down
   Amid the blinding snow.

I can but give a failing heart
   And weary eyes of pain,
A faded mouth that cannot smile
   And may not laugh again.

Yet keep thine arms around me, love,
   Until I fall to sleep;
Then leave me, saying no goodbye
   Lest I might wake, and weep.   20

Written spring 1856? First published in W. M. Rossetti, Ruskin: Rossetti:
Pre-Raphaelitism *(1899). Text,* Poems and Drawings *(1978).*

William Michael Rossetti (1829–1919)

William Michael Rossetti, keeper of the Pre-Raphaelite flame and the Rossetti family memory, was born into the radical, cultured, noisily Italian Rossetti household, in Charlotte Street, just off Portland Place, in central London, 25 September 1829, younger than his only brother Dante Gabriel, older than his second sister Christina. He was educated, like Dante Gabriel, at King's College School, London. For all of his professional working life he was a tax-man, entering the Excise Office when he was sixteen, staying with what turned into the Inland Revenue Board until retirement (as a Senior Assistant Secretary) in 1894. He carried on as the person who assessed pictures and drawings for estate duty well into his official retirement. He dabbled in paint, though only a bit; wrote poems, though not many; did a certain amount of translation from Italian (the *Inferno* (1865) – almost obligatory in his family); but his considerable energies went into advertising and garnering the work of the Pre-Raphaelite movement. He has been aptly dubbed its general secretary. He edited and wrote much of their magazine *The Germ* (1850) – he turned in a notable review of Clough's *Bothie*, for example – and was official keeper of the *PRB Journal*. For a time he lived communally with Dante Gabriel, Swinburne and Meredith in Cheyne Walk, Chelsea. He defended Swinburne in print against Robert Buchanan's 'Fleshly School' accusations. He was art critic for the *Spectator* and other papers (writing pieces gathered as *Fine Art, Chiefly Contemporary*, 1867, a good illustration of Pre-Raphaelite standards in criticism). His selection of Whitman (1868) was the first in Britain. He edited Moxon's Popular Poets series (1870–3), edited Shelley (1870) and Blake (1874), did a *Life* of Keats (1887), wrote widely on Shelley. After his brother's death in 1882 he became simply his brother's voice, and after his sister's death in 1894, hers too – assiduously editing their poems in numerous volumes, writing criticism of their work, doing the *Memoir* of Dante Gabriel (1895), compiling the *Family Letters* (1908). William Bell Scott quarrelled with him over his suppressions and hagiographical inclinations – he'd quite emasculated 'the dear old pagan D. G. R.', Scott thought. Edmund Gosse called him 'the terrible W. M. Rossetti, that giant of mediocrity, grinding the family annals to dust in the dark' and 'squeezing the last sixpence out of his dead brother's body'. He worked for the *Oxford English Dictionary*, edited texts for the Early English Text Society, did a Chaucer Society joint edition of Chaucer's *Troilus* and Boccaccio's *Filostrato* (1883), and wrote a study of Dante (1910). W. M. was as republican as his father and Dante Gabriel, and as anti-clerical as Swinburne. For fear their sentiments might lose him his Civil Service post D. G. advised against the publication in 1881 of his *Democratic Sonnets* (they were held back until 1907). In March 1874, a bachelor in his mid-forties, he married Lucy, daughter of the painter Ford Madox Brown, a painter herself and an agnostic – whose lively presence in the Rossetti ménage in Euston Road deeply upset Christina and her mother and eventually caused their flight to live with aunts in Torrington Place. The W. M. Rossettis had two sons and three daughters. She died in 1894. He died at home in Primrose Hill, London, the Grand Old Man of Pre-Raphaelite letters, 5 February 1919.

PRÆRAPHAELITISM [1851]

Non pas que je sois l'adversaire de ce qui se fait maintenant dans la peinture en Angleterre; j'ai été frappé même de cette prodigieuse conscience que ce peuple peut apporter même dans les choses d'imagination. Il semble même qu'en revenant au rendu excessif des détails ils sont plus dans leur génie que quand ils imitent les peintres italiens, et surtout les coloristes flamands.

Delacroix, 1858[1]

The rules of art may be broadly divided into two classes, the positive and the conventional. We say conventional, not here in the invidious sense in which the term is more currently used, but merely to imply the presence of general consent. The rules of perspective, of anatomy, are positive rules;

PRÆRAPHAELITISM

1 'Not that I'm against what's going on now in painting in England: I've been struck, rather, by this prodigious feeling that this people can bring, in fact, to the things of the imagination. Their national genius seems to show even in their excessive commitment to detailism – much more than when they imitate Italian painters and – especially – the Flemish colourists.'

there are both positive and conventional rules of light and shade, and of colour; those of composition, as teachable under any system, are wholly conventional. And the reason of this distinction is too obvious to need being more than alluded to. Nature is always in perspective, and any conspicuous departure from her ordinary plan of anatomy is a monstrosity; there are natural facts and harmonies of colour, and uniform effects of light and shade, as well as combinations and proportions of these, generally adopted, but not constantly visible in nature; while no certain means exist for determining the relation of position in which a given event or emotion will place those affected by it.

To the positive rules obedience is imperative, though not of equal importance in all cases – he is not a correct artist who violates them: obedience to the conventional rules can rationally be based only on conviction of their value as conductive to truth or beauty. No man is born into the world under obligation to subscribe to the opinions, or see according to the perceptions, of another; least of all is the artist bound to do so. Art – except such as consists in the mere collection of materials through the medium of strict copyism – represents individual mind and views working from absolute data of fact. Turn and twist it as we may, nature and the man are the two halves of every true work of art. The imitation of natural objects as speciments, unblended, unsubordinated, with no purpose save imitation, is confessedly a low branch of art: but the imitation of another man's perception of natural objects? The imitation of the form of a face through which you are incompetent to trace or pourtray the character is a laborious imbecility: but the imitation of Phidias's or Raphael's preference in feature, because Phidias or Raphael liked that, while you prefer Miss Smith?[2]

The conventional rules of painting are, and must ever be, matter of opinion: they are not fact, but belief of the best adaptability of fact. Of such are the rules of a principal light and a principal shadow in certain definite proportions, of the balance of colour, and of specific forms of grouping – as the pyramidal, for instance. The faith in these or the like of these as imperative dogmas in art, the non-observance of which is heresy, has been the result of one of two causes; either that general opinion, and consequently that of the artists who first acted on and promulgated them, was in their favour, or that the public taste was indoctrinated by the artists. There can be little doubt that the second supposition represents the true state of the case; it being difficult to believe that, on questions of the practical management of nature by art, the public should have been in advance of its professors, or that any but floating notions, waiting to be put into shape but incapable of guiding, should have been abroad on the subject. We may assume, then, that the public was educated into these principles successively by their visible influence in renowned works or the direct authority of the painter; and that they have come down to late generations insisted upon, magnified from methodic practice perhaps into tradition and formal rule, with all the additional weight derived first from admiring disciples, then from unquestioning scholars, lastly from drowsy and comfortable imitators. It is so pleasant to learn what you have to do, instead of studying and discovering it.

On enquiry, the artist of the nineteenth century finds that conventional rules rest on some one's ipse dixit or ipse fecit; and, reflecting further on the point, it may possibly occur to him that he too is endowed, or, to be an artist, ought to be endowed, with the faculties of observation and analysis, and might exercise those faculties for the confirmation or otherwise of the axioms he has been taught. Perhaps he will walk out into the sunlight, and be struck with the teasing fact that, so far as his unaided perceptions testify, there is no principal shadow occupying one third of the space, and that really the background declines to recede in that accommodating ratio which he knows it is bound to abide by. Or perhaps he will mix with the intellectual and the beautiful, and, finding a hardly appreciable leaven of Greek ideal, be compelled to lapse into the notion that mind can speak through homely features, and loveliness be English as well as Hellenic. Or he will come across groups of endless variety, consistency, and interest, which by rights do not compose at all.

It is now three years ago that three young artists asserted in concert through their pictures that such was their deliberate conviction. They informed the general body of artists and the public at

---

2   Phidias, greatest sculptor of ancient Greece; Raphael, Italian painter
(1483–1520).

large, in the language of practical demonstration, that, in fact, they intended to divest themselves of not a little of the academical arraying supplied to them, and would replace it from their own resources to the best of their ability: that what they saw, that they would paint – all of it, and all fully; and what they did not see they would try to do without. And they called themselves Præ-raphaelites.

The painters before Raphael had worked in often more than partial ignorance of the positive rules of art, and unaffected by conventional rules. These were not known of in their days; and they neither invented nor discovered them. It is to the latter fact, and not the former, that the adoption of the name 'Præraphaelites' by the artists in question is to be ascribed. Præraphaelites truly they are – but of the nineteenth century. Their aim is the same – truth; and their process the same – exactitude of study from nature: but their practice is different, for their means are enlarged. Nor is it in direction, but in tone, of mind – in earnestness and thoroughness – that they are otherwise identified with their prototypes.

Such we understand to be the character of the protest which the 'P. R. B.s'[3] have devoted them-selves to record, – investigation for themselves on all points which have hitherto been settled by example or unproved precept, and unflinching avowal of the result of such investigation; to which is added the absolute rejection of all meretricious embellishment – of all which might be intro-duced to heighten effect or catch the eye to the disregard or overlaying of actual or presumable fact. It is in the nature of conventional rules that their true authority diminishes in proportion as their factitious sway extends itself; for they come to be looked on as inherent and necessary ele-ments in pictorial practice, instead of what they really are, means to a certain end, useful only in so far as they subserve that. But this end may be, and often must be, one not germane to the true purpose of the work in hand, when its introduction and all that ministers to it are but so much excrescence. Thus it is that the pernicious use to which rules of this kind are applied has narrowed the word 'conventional' into an epithet of reproach. The artist is taught to rely not on fact, but on another's use or combination of fact. He puts his eyes to school. He takes results, and not materials, as his ways and means for working in a creative and imitative art; and rejoices to find that his secondary creation is like a previous secondary – comparatively careless whether either resembles the primary.

The main dangers incidental to Præraphaelitism are threefold. First, that, in the effort after un-adulterated truth, the good of conventional rules should be slighted, as well as their evil avoided. Certainly it is not the first glance at any aspect of nature which will inform the artist of its most essential qualities, and indicate the mode of setting to work which will be calculated to produce the noblest as well as the closest representation possible. Minute study, however, such as the Præ-raphaelite artists bestow on their renderings from nature, cannot but result in the attainment of one order of truth. Besides this, it is a practical education; an apprenticeship to the more accurate learn-ing of structure, to the more eclectic appreciation of effect; and tends in a more thorough manner to answer the purpose contemplated by the cramming education which they set aside. To the dis-advantage under notice the Præraphaelite method of study from nature is liable, as are the execu-tive and manipulative parts of a picture under any system – and for the same reason, that, in all, experience is required for perfect mastery; with this difference in its favour, that it has an absolute value of sincerity and faithfulness.

The second danger is that detail and accessory should be insisted on to a degree detracting from the importance of the chief subject and action. But this does not naturally, much less of necessity, follow from the Præraphaelite principle; which contemplates the rendering of nature as it is, – in other words, as it seems to the artist from his point of view, material and intellectual (for there is no separating the two things), and the principal, therefore, in its supremacy, the subordinate in its subordination. The contrary mistake is one to which only a low estimate, a semi-comprehension, of his own principles, can lead the Præraphaelite. It can scarcely, under any circumstances, be fallen into by a man of original or inventive power.

---

3   Pre-Raphaelite Brothers, or Brotherhood.

Thirdly, there remains the danger of an injudicious choice of model; a danger of whose effect the Præraphaelite pictures offer more than one instance. All artists, indeed, unless they have emancipated themselves into so imaginative an altitude, far from the gross region of fact, as to dispense with models altogether, are exposed to it; for Virgin Maries and Cleopatras are not to be found for the wanting: but he who believes that 'ideal beauty consists partly in a Greek outline of nose, partly in proportions expressible in decimal fractions between the lips and chin, but partly also in that degree of improvement which he is to bestow upon God's works in general,'[4] will find the difficulty yielding enough under the influence of idealism by rote. The Præraphaelite dares not 'improve God's works in general.' His creed is truth; which in art means appropriateness in the first place, scrupulous fidelity in the second. If true to himself, he will search diligently for the best attainable model; whom, when obtained, he must render as conformably as possible with his conception, but as truly as possible also to the fact before him. Not that he will copy the pimples or the freckles; but transform, disguise, 'improve,' he may not. His work must be individual too – expressive of *me* no less than of *not-me*. He cannot learn off his ideal, and come prepared to be superior to the mere real. It is indeed a singular abuse to call that idealism which is routine and copy; a solecism which cries aloud to common sense for extinction. A young artist cannot enter the lists armed with an ideal prepense, though he may flaunt as his pennant the tracing-paper scored with fac-similes of another man's ideal. If he *will* have one, properly so called, he must work for it; and his own will not be born save through a long and laborious process of comparison, sifting, and meditation. The single-minded artist must, in the early part of his career, work according to his existing taste in actual living beauty, whether or not he means eventually to abide on principle by unidealized fact; and tastes in beauty differ notoriously. The prescription-artist corrects his by Raphael and the Greeks. For the other there is nothing but watchfulness, study, and self-reliance. He is working arduously not to self-expression only, but to development.

Modern Præraphaelitism is distinct from mediævalism equally in thought and in practice, so far as the latter depends on education, skill of hand, and acquaintance with the principles of design or perspective. Even in the works which bring the originators of this 'totally independent and sincere method of study' within the same lines of thought or of period with the predecessors of Raphael, the points of variance are essential and decisive. Yet more alien are they from that important section of the modern German school which is said to have recurred to a past phasis of art with the view of reaching by gradual stages to their ideal. This ideal, to judge by the chief works of the separatists, seems beyond doubt to be the Raphaelesque. The works of Overbeck, of Steinle, and in a less degree of Cornelius and Bendemann,[5] bear a strong affinity to the Raphaelesque standard of form and sentiment – sometimes to that of Raphael's later period, seldom to his earliest. Other painters, such as Fuhrich[6] in the compositions which display himself most vividly, can hardly be said to have reverted to any previous school; the character of conception and invention being with these, where not markedly original, German and national to the fullest extent, similarly with the quality of form; for the sources of which characteristics it would be futile to refer back from the artists themselves. Historically, however, some of this subdivision also may be counted in the same class; and, in the works of all, a standard, a preconception of some kind, is equally and unmistakeably evident. But the German and the English cases present this important difference. The former was an academic revival: the principles of an unquestioned dogma had fallen into degradation, and the aim has been constantly after the highest issue of the school which announced it. In England the Raphaelesque dogma is not only a convention but a cant; few, if any, enforce it systematically in practice. It is held in terrorem over the heads of students; but

4 As Mr. Ruskin phrases it in his pamphlet, *Præraphaelitism* [1851]. His main principle, however – that our artists should, and that the Præraphaelites do, 'select nothing' – would in truth, as it appears to us, while it assumes to beg too much in their favour, carry their condemnation in it, could its application to them be verified. This we believe not to be the case; and that, indeed, strict non-selection cannot, in the nature of things, be taken as the rule in a picture of character or

incident. But perhaps Mr. Ruskin intended his exhortation in a much more limited sense than it bears, thus broadly put. [Author's note]
5 J. F. Overbeck (1789–1869), E. J. von Steinle (1810–86), P. von Cornelius (1783–1867): German 'Nazarene' artists. E. J. F. Bendemann (1811–89): Düsseldorf School painter.
6 J. von Führich (1800–76): late Nazarene.

such is the almost unlimited range of subject and attempt recognized in England that little beyond fragments of precept, intended to enhance the telling attractiveness of a picture, are seriously laid to heart. These are enough to restrain the student from launching out unfettered on the study of nature, but do not suffice to create a school even academically correct. The English innovation corresponds with the German in no other sense than this. The English revivalists recur to the one primary school – nature, as interpreted by their own eyes and feelings; the Germans, to the purest form of a school ready-organized for them. The English, starting with the acquired knowledge of the day, and having before them an unbounded horizon, may be expected to work out such faculties as are in them to original and progressive results; the Germans, with the same advantages, but a rigorously fixed goal to aspire towards, may at best rival their most cherished prescriptions. Actual consonance between the outcomings of the two systems there is none.

The Præraphaelites have been working bravely and without compromise for three years, and have fought their way into public disfavour, – a gain perhaps, as art goes. We hold them to be in the right path: not only because they have achieved unique excellence in imitative execution, nor that we consider their system exceptional, and as such specially needed at the present moment (though these would be grounds of rational approbation); but because we believe it to be intrinsically the true one, capable, and best capable, of leading its adherents each to the highest point of attainment his mental faculties will permit him to reach. It is of secondary importance, yet matter for satisfaction and of good omen, that the young men who have set the first example in this course of study are, unless we mistake, of power themselves to work out the process to worthy intellectual results.

From: Fine Art, Chiefly Contemporary: Notices Reprinted, with Revisions *(Macmillan & Co., London and Cambridge, 1867). Originally in* The Spectator, *1851.*

T. E. (Thomas Edward) Brown (1830–97)

T. E. Brown, schoolmaster and Manx poet, was born in Douglas, Isle of Man, in 1830, fifth son of Robert Brown, vicar of Kirk Braddon on the island, and his wife Dorothy Thomson. One of T. E.'s brothers became a well-known Baptist, minister of Myrtle Street Chapel, Liverpool. T. E. was a pupil at King William's College, Isle of Man, before entering Christ Church, Oxford, in 1849, where he obtained Double First Classes in Classics and in Law and History. He became a Fellow of Oriel College in 1854, was ordained into the Church of England in 1855, and got his MA in 1856. He married Amelia Stowell of Ramsey, Isle of Man, in 1857, so had to resign his Fellowship since married Fellows were not permitted at Oxford and Cambridge at the time. The pair had many children. He returned to the Isle of Man to become Vice Principal of King William's and, very keen on Manx traditions and people, is reputed to have cultivated acquaintance with Manx sailors, fishermen, and the like. In September 1861 he moved to Gloucester as headmaster of the Crypt School, where W. E. Henley was one of the boys in his charge. In 1864 he moved to Clifton College School, Bristol, to become second master and head of the 'modern',

i.e. non-Classical, side. From 1884 to 1893 he was also curate at St Barnabas Church in Bristol. Brown was a terse, rugged versifier, manifestly influenced by Robert Browning (it's no surprise that Browning was an admirer), and, not unmindful of Crabbe's Aldeburgh stories in verse, was anxious to promote Manx themes and Manx 'dialect'. The first of his tales in verse to be published was 'Betsy Lee', in *Macmillan's Magazine*, April 1873. It got into book form, with other Manx narrative poems, in *Fo'c'sle Yarns* (1881). *The Doctor and Other Poems* came out in 1887, *The Manx Witch and Other Poems* in 1889, *Old John* in 1893. Brown's old pupil W. E. Henley published him in the *Scots* (later *National*) *Observer* and the *New Review*, and was a prime mover for Brown's *Collected Poems* (1900), as well as contributing an Introduction to the 1901 reprint. Henley celebrated Brown in a sonnet ('cynic, saint,/Salt, humourist, Christian, poet; with a free/Far-glancing, luminous utterance'). The opening line of Brown's 'My Garden' ('A garden is a lovesome thing, God wot!') has entered the language. Brown retired to Ramsey in 1893, but died suddenly, 30 October 1897, whilst addressing the boys of Clifton College. He is buried in Redland Green, Bristol.

Clevedon Verses

VIII: The Bristol Channel

I

The sulky old gray brute!
But when the sunset strokes him,
Or twilight shadows coax him,
He gets so silver-milky,
He turns so soft and silky,
He'd make a water-spaniel for King Knut.[1]

II

This sea was Lazarus, all day
At Dives' gate he lay,
And lapped the crumbs.
Night comes;   10
The beggar dies –
Forthwith the Channel, coast to coast,
Is Abraham's bosom; and the beggar lies
A lovely ghost.[2]

Written, probably, 1878. Old John, and Other Poems *(Macmillan & Co., 1893).*

'Ne Sit Ancillæ'[1]

Poor little Teignmouth slavey,
Squat, but rosy!
Slatternly, but cosy,
A humble adjunct of the British navy,
A fifth-rate dabbler in the British gravy –
How was I mirrored? In what spiritual dress
Appeared I to your struggling consciousness?

Thump! bump!
A dump
Of first a knife and then a fork!   10
Then plump
A mustard-pot, then slump, stump, frump,
The plates
Like slates –
And lastly fearful wrestling with a cork.
And so I thought – 'Poor thing!
She has not any wing
To waft her from the grease,
To give her soul release
From this dull sphere   20
Of baccy, beef, and beer.'

But, as it happed,
I spoke of Chagford, Chagford by the moor,

CLEVEDON VERSES
1 eleventh-century King of England, Norway, Denmark, fabled to have ordered incoming tide to withdraw (to prove flatterers silly who said he had that power).
2 reference to story of rich man and beggar, Luke 16 (rich man Dives goes to hell; poor man Lazarus to 'Abraham's bosom').

'NE SIT ANCILLAE'
1 title from opening of Horace, *Odes*, II.4 – addressed to man who loves a slave girl, 'Ne sit ancillae tibi amor pudori': Don't let love of your slave girl seem shameful.

Sweet Chagford town. Then pure
And bright as Burton tapped[2]
By master hand,
Then, red as is a peach,
My little maid found speech –
Gave me to understand
She knew 'them parts' –   30
And to our several hearts
We stood elate,
As each revealed to each
A mate –
She stood, I sate,
And saw within her eyes
The folly of an infinite surprise.

Old John *(1893)*.

MY GARDEN

A garden is a lovesome thing, God wot!
Rose plot,
Fringed pool,
Ferned grot –
The veriest school
Of peace; and yet the fool
Contends that God is not –
Not God! in gardens! when the eve is cool?
Nay, but I have a sign;
'Tis very sure God walks in mine.   10

MS dated 8 July 1875. Old John *(1893)*.

THE WELL

I am a spring –
Why square me with a kerb?
Ah, why this measuring
Of marble limit? Why this accurate vault
Lest day assault,
Or any breath disturb?
And why this regulated flow
Of what 'tis good to feel, and what to know?
You have no right
To take me thus, and bind me to your use,   10
Screening me from the flight
Of all great wings that are beneath the heaven,
So that to me it is not given
To hold the image of the awful Zeus,
Nor any cloud or star
Emprints me from afar.
O cruel force,
That gives me not a chance

2   Burton beer.

To fill my natural course;
With mathematic rod   20
Economising God;
Calling me to pre-ordered circumstance
Nor suffering me to dance
Over the pleasant gravel,
With music solacing my travel –
With music, and the baby buds that toss
In light, with roots and sippets of the moss!
A fount, a tank:
Yet through some sorry grate
A driblet faulters, till around the flank   30
Of burly cliffs it creeps; then, silver-shooting,
Threads all the patient fluting
Of quartz, and violet-dappled slate:
A puny thing, on whose attenuate ripples
No satyr stoops to see
His broken effigy,
No naiad leans the languor of her nipples.
One faith remains –
That through what ducts soe'er,
What metamorphic strains,   40
What chymic filt'rings, I shall pass
To where, O God, Thou lov'st to mass
Thy rains upon the crags, and dim the sphere.
So, when night's heart with keenest silence thrills,
Take me, and weep me on the desolate hills!

MS dated March 1870. Posthumously published, Collected Poems, *ed. H. F. Brown,*
H. G. Dakyns and W. E. Henley (Macmillan & Co., 1900).

A SERMON AT CLEVEDON

Good Friday

Go on! Go on!
Don't wait for me!
Isaac was Abraham's son –
Yes, certainly –
And as they clomb Moriah –
I know! I know!
A type of the Messiah –
Just so! just so!
Perfectly right; and then the ram
Caught in the – *listening?* Why of course I am!   10
Wherefore, my brethren, that was counted – yes –
To Abraham for righteousness –
Exactly, so I said –
At least – but go a-head!
Now mark
The conduct of the Patriarch –
'Behold the wood!'
Isaac exclaimed – By Jove, an Oxford hood!
'But where' –
What long straight hair!   20
'Where is the lamb?'
You mean – the ram:

No, no! I beg you pardon!
There's the Churchwarden,
In the Clerk's pew –
Stick tipped with blue –
Now Justification –
'By Faith?' I fancy; Aye, the old equation;
Go it, Justice! Go it, Mercy!
Go it, Douglas! Go it, Percy!   30
I back the winner,
And have a vague conception of the sinner –
Limbs nude,
Horatian attitude,
Nursing his foot in Sublapsarian mood –
More power
To you my friend! you're good for half-an-hour.
Dry bones! dry bones!
But in my ear the long-drawn west wind moans,
Sweet voices seem to murmur from the wave;   40
And I can sit, and look upon the stones
That cover Hallam's grave.[1]

Posthumously published, Collected Poems *(1900).*

DARTMOOR

Sunset at Chagford

Homo Loquitur[1]

Is it ironical, a fool enigma,
This sunset show?
The purple stigma,
Black mountain cut upon a saffron glow –
Is it a mammoth joke,
A riddle put for me to guess,
Which having duly honoured, I may smoke,
And go to bed,
And snore,
Having a soothing consciousness   10
Of something red?
Or is it more?
Ah, is it, is it more?

A dole, perhaps?
The scraps
Tossed from the table of the revelling gods? –
What odds!

I taste them – Lazarus
Was nourished thus!
But, all the same, it surely is a cheat –   20
Is this the stuff they eat?

A SERMON AT CLEVEDON
1   Arthur Henry Hallam, buried in the chancel of Clevedon Church.
The poem's sermon is from Genesis 22, with allusions to Galatians 3.6,
and Romans 5.

DARTMOOR
1   'the man speaks'.

A cheat! a cheat!
Then let the garbage be –
Some pig-wash! let it vanish down the sink
Of night! 'tis not for me.
I will not drink
Their draff,
While, throned on high, they quaff
The fragrant sconce –
Has Heaven no cloaca for the nonce?   30

Say 'tis an anodyne –
It never shall be mine.
I want no opiates –
The best of all their cates
Were gross to balk the meanest sense;
I want to be co-equal with their fates;
I will not be put off with temporal pretence:
I want to be awake, and know, not stand
And stare at waving of a conjuror's hand.

But is it speech   40
Wherewith they strive to reach
Our poor inadequate souls?
The round earth rolls;
I cannot hear it hum –
The stars are dumb –
The voices of the world are in my ear
A sensuous murmur. Nothing speaks
But man, my fellow – him I hear,
And understand; but beasts and birds
And winds and waves are destitute of words.   50
What is the alphabet
The gods have set?
What babbling! what delusion!
And in these sunset tints
What gay confusion!
Man prints
His meaning, has a letter
Determinate. I know that it is better
Than all this cumbrous hieroglyph –
The *For*, the *If*   60
Are growth of man's analysis:
The gods in bliss
Scrabble a baby jargon on the skies
For us to analyse!
Cumbrous? nay, idiotic –
A party-coloured symbolism,
The fragments of a shivered prism:
Man gives the swift demotic.

'Tis good to see
The economy   70
Of poor upstriving man!
Since time began,
He has been sifting
The elements; while God, on chaos drifting,
Sows broadcast all His stuff.
Lavish enough,

No doubt; but why this waste?
See! of these very sunset dies
The virgin chaste
Takes one, and in a harlot's eyes   80
Another rots. They go by billion billions:
Each blade of grass
Ignores them as they pass;
The spiders in their foul pavilions,
Behold this vulgar gear,
And sneer;
Dull frogs
In bogs
Catch rosy gleams through rushes,
And know that night is near;   90
Wrong-headed thrushes
Blow bugles to it;
And a wrong-headed poet
Will strut, and strain the cogs
Of the machine, he blushes
To call his Muse, and maunder;
And, marvellous to relate!
These pseudo-messengers of state
Will wander
Where there is no intelligence to meet them,   100
Nor even a sensorium to greet them.
The very finest of them
Go where there's nought to love them
Or notice them: to cairns, to rocks
Where ravens nurse their young,
To mica-splints from granite-boulders wrung
By channels of the marsh, to stocks
Of old dead willows in a pool as dead.
Can anything be said
To these? The leech   110
Looks from its muddy lair,
And sees a silly something in the air –
Call you this *speech?*
O God, if it be speech,
Speak plainer,
If Thou would'st teach
That I shall be a gainer!
The age of picture-alphabets is gone:
We are not now so weak;
We are too old to con   120
The horn-book of our youth. Time lags –
O, rip this obsolete blazon into rags!
And speak! O, speak!

But, if I be a spectacle
In Thy great theatre, then do Thy will:
Arrange Thy instruments with circumspection;
Summon Thine angels to the vivisection!
But quick! O, quick!
For I am sick,
And very sad.   130
Thy pupils will be glad.
'See,' Thou exclaim'st, 'this ray!
How permanent upon the retina!

How odd that purple hue!
The pineal gland is blue.
I stick this probe
In the posterior lobe –
Behold the cerebellum
A smoky yellow, like old vellum!
Students will please observe   140
The structure of the optic nerve.
See! nothing could be finer –
That film of pink
Around the hippocampus minor.
Behold!
I touch it, and it turns bright gold.
Again! – as black as ink.
Another lancet – thanks!
That's Manx –
Yes, the delicate pale sea-green   150
Passing into ultra-marine –
A little blurred – in fact
This brain seems packed
With sunsets. Bring
That battery here; now put your
Negative pole beneath the suture –
That's just the thing.
Now then the other way –
I say! I say!
More chloroform!   160
(A little more will do no harm)
Now this is the most instructive of all
The phenomena, what in fact we may call
The most obvious justification
Of vivisection in general.
Observe (once! twice!
That's very nice) –
Observe, I say, the incipient relation
Of a quasi-moral activity
To this physical agitation!   170
Of course, you see....'
Yes, yes, O God,
I feel the prod
Of that dissecting knife.
Instructive, say the pupil angels, *very:*
And some take notes, and some take sandwiches and sherry;
And some are prying
Into the very substance of my brain –
I feel their fingers!   180
(My life! my life!)
Yes, yes! it lingers!
The sun, the sun –
Go on! go on!
Blue, yellow, red!
But please remember that I am not dead,
Nor even dying.

Posthumously published, Collected Poems *(1900).*

Christina G. (Georgina) Rossetti (1830–94)

Christina Georgina – or Christina G. as she came to prefer it – Rossetti was the best woman poet of her time and indeed, one of the greatest of Victorian poets *tout court*. Devoutly yearning, melancholically resigned, the apparent quietism of her heaven-minded verses keeps surprising by its lack of innocence, its unmisgivingness about misgivings, its clear-eyedness about love and life and death, by its wittiness, the sinewy grip on its formal means, and its spry readerly entrapments. No wonder she took to Emily Dickinson's poems when she encountered them near the end of her life. She was born into an impoverished, boisterous, Italian ménage, highly cultivated, politically radical, in Charlotte Street (now Hallam Street), London, 5 December 1830. Her father, Gabriele Rossetti, was an Italian poet and revolutionary in exile who taught Italian at King's College, London. Her mother, Frances Mary Lavinia, was a Polidori – her brother John Polidori was Byron's doctor and the author of *The Vampyre*. The family had rejected Roman Catholicism (too Bourbon by far). Christina's devoted, even repressive, High Anglican Christianity was to become the centre of her being (her sister Maria became an Anglican nun), but her earliest years are marked rather by temper tantrums (the famous episode of cutting her arm with scissors to get back at her mother) and by urgent poetic precocity. Grandfather Gaetano Polidori privately printed her twelve-year-old's verses to her mother (1842) and a whole little volume (1847). At the age of nineteen she was contributing to the Pre-Raphaelite paper *The Germ*, founded by her brothers Dante Gabriel and William Michael and their friends. She lived at home, unmarried. At least two suitors were rebuffed – the Pre-Raphaelite painter James Collinson and the poet and translator Charles Bagot Cayley – on a mixture of grounds including religious ones. Christina's reputation was as the quiet one in the corner, 'the most unobtrusive of all' – and she did gradually lapse into a classic Victorian female invalidism, and her brand of Christianity did indeed counsel submission and loss of self (her mid-teen religious crisis involved giving up the pleasures of chess and the theatre). But early on she taught Italian to help out the family finances, volunteered to go as one of Florence Nightingale's nurses to the Crimea (rejected on grounds of youth), worked for years with fallen women at the Highgate Penitentiary, made two journeys to Europe, and was little enough suppressed not to feel jealousy over Lizzie Siddal's hold over her brother D. G. and envy over Jean Ingelow's successes, to fight with Augusta Webster over women's suffrage (it wasn't biblical), to be sharp about Lewis Carroll's kind of writing in *Speaking Likenesses* (1874), and to tease D. G. about her work – her so-called death-centred 'bogieism', it might be, or his casually wanting to alter her lines as if she were just another Eliza Cook. Reputation came with her first real collection, *Goblin Market and Other Poems* (1862). Numerous other volumes of poems followed, lyrics and sonnets especially; and there were also the nursery rhymes of *Sing-Song* (1879; 1893), as well as devotional prose in fat volumes for the Society for the Promotion of Christian Knowledge. Like her sister Maria, Christina published expertly on the poetry of Dante. She almost died of Graves' Disease in the period 1871–3 and the discoloured face which that illness left her with discouraged her from public appearances. She nursed her brother D. G. through his last illness (1882), and her mother through hers (1886). By then she was living with her aunts. In 1892 she had an operation to remove breast cancer, which, however, recurred. Her death-bed was not at all free from anxieties about sin and her prospects in an afterlife. She died in considerable bodily pain – her screams caused a neighbour to send in a complaining note – in Torrington Square, London, 29 December 1894, aged sixty-four, her great later-twentieth-century acclaim still far in the future.

Song

She sat and sang alway
  By the green margin of a stream,
Watching the fishes leap and play
  Beneath the glad sunbeam.

I sat and wept alway
  Beneath the moon's most shadowy beam,

Watching the blossoms of the May
  Weep leaves into the stream.

I wept for memory:
  She sang for hope that is so fair: 10
My tears were swallowed by the sea;
  Her songs died on the air.

Written 26 November 1848. Goblin Market and Other Poems,
by Christina Rossetti (Macmillan Co., 1862).

SONG

When I am dead, my dearest,
   Sing no sad songs for me;
Plant thou no roses at my head,
   Nor shady cypress tree:
Be the green grass above me
   With showers and dewdrops wet;
And if thou wilt, remember,
   And if thou wilt, forget.

I shall not see the shadows,
   I shall not feel the rain;   10
I shall not hear the nightingale
   Sing on, as if in pain:
And dreaming through the twilight
   That doth not rise nor set,
Haply I may remember,
   And haply may forget.

Written 12 December 1848. Goblin Market *(1862).*

'A BRUISED REED SHALL HE NOT BREAK'[1]

I will accept thy will to do and be,
   Thy hatred and intolerance of sin,
   Thy will at least to love, that burns within
      And thirsteth after Me:
So will I render fruitful, blessing still,
   The germs and small beginnings in thy heart,
   Because thy will cleaves to the better part.[2] –
      Alas, I cannot will.

Dost not thou will, poor soul? Yet I receive
   The inner unseen longings of the soul,   10
   I guide them turning towards Me; I control
      And charm hearts till they grieve:

If thou desire, it yet shall come to pass,
   Though thou but wish indeed to choose My love;
   For I have power in earth and heaven above. –
      I cannot wish, alas!

What, neither choose nor wish to choose? and yet
   I still must strive to win thee and constrain:
   For thee I hung upon the cross in pain,
      How then can I forget?   20
If thou as yet dost neither love, nor hate,
   Nor choose, nor wish, – resign thyself, be still
   Till I infuse love, hatred, longing, will. –
      I do not deprecate.

Written 13 June 1852. Goblin Market *(1862).*

ECHO

Come to me in the silence of the night;
   Come in the speaking silence of a dream;
Come with soft rounded cheeks and eyes as bright
   As sunlight on a stream;
      Come back in tears,
O memory, hope, love of finished years.

Oh dream how sweet, too sweet, too bitter sweet,
   Whose wakening should have been in Paradise,
Where souls brimfull of love abide and meet;

Where thirsting longing eyes   10
   Watch the slow door
That opening, letting in, lets out no more.

Yet come to me in dreams, that I may live
   My very life again though cold in death:
Come back to me in dreams, that I may give
   Pulse for pulse, breath for breath:
      Speak low, lean low,
As long ago, my love, how long ago.

Written 18 December 1854. Goblin Market *(1862).*

IN AN ARTIST'S STUDIO

One face looks out from all his canvases,
   One selfsame figure sits or walks or leans:

We found her hidden just behind those screens,
That mirror gave back all her loveliness.

'A BRUISED REED SHALL HE NOT BREAK'
1 Isaiah 42.3.

2 Luke 10.38–42: Mary chooses 'good part', i.e. better one than domestic sister Martha.

A queen in opal or in ruby dress,
  A nameless girl in freshest summer greens,
  A saint, an angel – every canvas means
The same one meaning, neither more nor less.
He feeds upon her face by day and night,

And she with true kind eyes looks back on him,   10
Fair as the moon and joyful as the light:
  Not wan with waiting, not with sorrow dim;
  Not as she is, but was when hope shone bright;
  Not as she is, but as she fills his dream.

Written 24 December 1856. New Poems by Christina Rossetti, Hitherto Unpublished
and Uncollected, *ed W. M. Rossetti (Macmillan & Co., 1896).*

A Better Resurrection

I have no wit, no words, no tears;
  My heart within me like a stone
Is numbed too much for hopes or fears;
  Look right, look left, I dwell alone;
I lift mine eyes, but dimmed with grief
  No everlasting hills[1] I see;
My life is in the falling leaf:
  O Jesus, quicken me.

My life is like a faded leaf,
  My harvest dwindled to a husk;   10
Truly my life is void and brief
  And tedious in the barren dusk;

My life is like a frozen thing,
  No bud nor greenness can I see:
Yet rise it shall – the sap of Spring;
  O Jesus, rise in me.

My life is like a broken bowl,
  A broken bowl that cannot hold
One drop of water for my soul
  Or cordial in the searching cold;   20
Cast in the fire the perished thing,
  Melt and remould it, till it be
A royal cup for Him my King:
  O Jesus, drink of me.

Written 30 June 1857. Goblin Market *(1862).*

Another Spring

If I might see another Spring
  I'd not plant summer flowers and wait:
I'd have my crocuses at once,
My leafless pink mezereons,
  My chill-veined snowdrops, choicer yet
  My white or azure violet,
Leaf-nested primrose; anything
  To blow at once not late.

If I might see another Spring
  I'd listen to the daylight birds   10
That build their nests and pair and sing,
Nor wait for mateless nightingale;

I'd listen to the lusty herds,
  The ewes with lambs as white as snow,
I'd find out music in the hail
  And all the winds that blow.

If I might see another Spring –
  Oh stinging comment on my past
That all my past results in 'if' –
  If I might see another Spring   20
I'd laugh to-day, to-day is brief;
  I would not wait for anything:
I'd use to-day that cannot last,
  Be glad to-day and sing.

Written 15 September 1857. Goblin Market *(1862).*

A Birthday

My heart is like a singing bird
  Whose nest is in a watered shoot;
My heart is like an appletree

Whose boughs are bent with thickset fruit;
My heart is like a rainbow shell
  That paddles in a halcyon sea;

A Better Resurrection
1 Genesis 49.26.

My heart is gladder than all these
   Because my love is come to me.

Raise me a dais of silk and down;
   Hang it with vair and purple dyes;   10
Carve it in doves and pomegranates,

And peacocks with a hundred eyes;
Work it in gold and silver grapes,
   In leaves and silver fleurs-de-lys;
Because the birthday of my life
   Is come, my love is come to me.

Written 18 November 1857. Macmillan's Magazine, *III (April 1861), 49.* Goblin Market *(1862).*

AN APPLE GATHERING

I plucked pink blossoms from mine apple tree
   And wore them all that evening in my hair:
Then in due season when I went to see
   I found no apples there.

With dangling basket all along the grass
   As I had come I went the selfsame track:
My neighbours mocked me while they saw me pass
   So empty-handed back.

Lilian and Lilias smiled in trudging by,
   Their heaped-up basket teazed me like a jeer;   10
Sweet-voiced they sang beneath the sunset sky,
   Their mother's home was near.

Plump Gertrude passed me with her basket full,
   A stronger hand than hers helped it along;

A voice talked with her through the shadows cool
   More sweet to me than song.

Ah Willie, Willie, was my love less worth
   Than apples with their green leaves piled above?
I counted rosiest apples on the earth
   Of far less worth than love.   20

So once it was with me you stooped to talk
   Laughing and listening in this very lane:
To think that by this way we used to walk
   We shall not walk again!

I let my neighbours pass me, ones and twos
   And groups; the latest said the night grew chill,
And hastened: but I loitered, while the dews
   Fell fast I loitered still.

Written 23 November 1857. Macmillan's Magazine, *IV (August 1861), 329.*
Goblin Market *(1862).*

WHAT WOULD I GIVE?

What would I give for a heart of flesh to warm me through,
Instead of this heart of stone ice-cold whatever I do;
Hard and cold and small, of all hearts the worst of all.[1]

What would I give for words, if only words would come;
But now in its misery my spirit has fallen dumb:

Oh, merry friends, go your way, I have never a word to say.

What would I give for tears, not smiles but scalding tears,
To wash the black mark clean, and to thaw the frost of years,
To wash the stain ingrain and to make me clean again.

Written 14 April 1858. The Prince's Progress and Other Poems, *by Christina Rossetti*
(Macmillan & Co., 1866).

UP-HILL

Does the road wind up-hill all the way?
   Yes, to the very end.
Will the day's journey take the whole long day?
   From morn to night, my friend.

But is there for the night a resting-place?
   A roof for when the slow dark hours begin.
May not the darkness hide it from my face?
   You cannot miss that inn.

WHAT WOULD I GIVE?
1 cf. 2 Corinthians 3.3: 'Ye are … the epistle of Christ … written not

with ink, but with the Spirit of the Living God; not in tables of stone,
but in the fleshy tables of the heart.'

Shall I meet other wayfarers at night?
   Those who have gone before.   10
Then must I knock, or call when just in sight?
   They will not keep you standing at that door.

Shall I find comfort, travel-sore and weak?
   Of labour you shall find the sum.
Will there be beds for me and all who seek?
   Yea, beds for all who come.

Written 29 June 1858. Macmillan's Magazine, III (February 1861), 325.
Goblin Market (1862).

WINTER RAIN

Every valley drinks,
   Every dell and hollow:
Where the kind rain sinks and sinks,
   Green of Spring will follow.

Yet a lapse of weeks
   Buds will burst their edges,
Strip their wool-coats, glue-coats, streaks,
   In the woods and hedges;

Weave a bower of love
   For birds to meet each other,   10
Weave a canopy above
   Nest and egg and mother.

But for fattening rain
   We should have no flowers,
Never a bud or leaf again
   But for soaking showers;

Never a mated bird
   In the rocking tree-tops,
Never indeed a flock or herd
   To graze upon the lea-crops.   20

Lambs so woolly white,
   Sheep the sun-bright leas on,
They could have no grass to bite
   But for rain in season.

We should find no moss
   In the shadiest places,
Find no waving meadow grass
   Pied with broad-eyed daisies:

But miles of barren sand,
   With never a son or daughter,   30
Not a lily on the land,
   Or lily on the water.

Written 31 January 1859. Goblin Market (1862).

GOBLIN MARKET

Morning and evening
Maids heard the goblins cry:
'Come buy our orchard fruits,
Come buy, come buy:
Apples and quinces,
Lemons and oranges,
Plump unpecked cherries,
Melons and raspberries,
Bloom-down-cheeked peaches,
Swart-headed mulberries,   10
Wild free-born cranberries,
Crab-apples, dewberries,
Pine-apples, blackberries,
Apricots, strawberries; –
All ripe together
In summer weather, –
Morns that pass by,
Fair eves that fly;
Come buy, come buy: 20
Our grapes fresh from the vine,
Pomegranates full and fine,
Dates and sharp bullaces,

Rare pears and greengages,
Damsons and bilberries,
Taste them and try:
Currants and gooseberries,
Bright-fire-like barberries,
Figs to fill your mouth,
Citrons from the South,
Sweet to tongue and sound to eye;   30
Come buy, come buy.'

   Evening by evening
Among the brookside rushes,
Laura bowed her head to hear,
Lizzie veiled her blushes:
Crouching close together
In the cooling weather,
With clasping arms and cautioning lips,
With tingling cheeks and finger tips.
'Lie close,' Laura said,   40
Pricking up her golden head:
'We must not look at goblin men,
We must not buy their fruits:

Who knows upon what soil they fed
Their hungry thirsty roots?'
'Come buy,' call the goblins
Hobbling down the glen.
'Oh,' cried Lizzie, 'Laura, Laura,
You should not peep at goblin men.'
Lizzie covered up her eyes,   50
Covered close lest they should look;
Laura reared her glossy head,
And whispered like the restless brook:
'Look, Lizzie, look, Lizzie,
Down the glen tramp little men.
One hauls a basket,
One bears a plate,
One lugs a golden dish
Of many pounds weight.
How fair the vine must grow   60
Whose grapes are so luscious;
How warm the wind must blow
Through those fruit bushes.'
'No,' said Lizzie: 'No, no, no;
Their offers should not charm us,
Their evil gifts would harm us.'
She thrust a dimpled finger
In each ear, shut eyes and ran:
Curious Laura chose to linger
Wondering at each merchant man.   70
One had a cat's face,
One whisked a tail,
One tramped at a rat's pace,
One crawled like a snail,
One like a wombat prowled obtuse and furry,
One like a ratel tumbled hurry skurry.
She heard a voice like voice of doves
Cooing all together:
They sounded kind and full of loves
In the pleasant weather.   80

Laura stretched her gleaming neck
Like a rush-imbedded swan,
Like a lily from the beck,
Like a moonlit poplar branch,
Like a vessel at the launch
When its last restraint is gone.

Backwards up the mossy glen
Turned and trooped the goblin men,
With their shrill repeated cry,
'Come buy, come buy.'   90
When they reached where Laura was
They stood stock still upon the moss,
Leering at each other,
Brother with queer brother;
Signalling each other,

Brother with sly brother.
One set his basket down,
One reared his plate;
One began to weave a crown
Of tendrils, leaves, and rough nuts brown   100
(Men sell not such in any town);
One heaved the golden weight
Of dish and fruit to offer her:
'Come buy, come buy,' was still their cry.
Laura stared but did not stir,
Longed but had no money:
The whisk-tailed merchant bade her taste
In tones as smooth as honey,
The cat-faced purr'd,
The rat-paced spoke a word   110
Of welcome, and the snail-paced even was heard;
One parrot-voiced and jolly
Cried 'Pretty Goblin' still for 'Pretty Polly;' –
One whistled like a bird.

But sweet-tooth Laura spoke in haste:
'Good folk, I have no coin;
To take were to purloin:
I have no copper in my purse,
I have no silver either,
And all my gold is on the furze   120
That shakes in windy weather
Above the rusty heather.'
'You have much gold upon your head,'
They answered all together:
'Buy from us with a golden curl.'
She clipped a precious golden lock,
She dropped a tear more rare than pearl,
Then sucked their fruit globes fair or red:
Sweeter than honey from the rock,[1]
Stronger than man-rejoicing wine,   130
Clearer than water flowed that juice;
She never tasted such before,
How should it cloy with length of use?
She sucked and sucked and sucked the more
Fruits which that unknown orchard bore;
She sucked until her lips were sore;
Then flung the emptied rinds away
But gathered up one kernel-stone,
And knew not was it night or day
As she turned home alone.   140

Lizzie met her at the gate
Full of wise upbraidings:
'Dear, you should not stay so late,
Twilight is not good for maidens;
Should not loiter in the glen
In the haunts of goblin men.
Do you not remember Jeanie,

GOBLIN MARKET
1 Psalm 81.16.

How she met them in the moonlight,
Took their gifts both choice and many,
Ate their fruits and wore their flowers   150
Plucked from bowers
Where summer ripens at all hours?
But ever in the moonlight
She pined and pined away;
Sought them by night and day,
Found them no more but dwindled and grew grey;
Then fell with the first snow,
While to this day no grass will grow
Where she lies low:
I planted daisies there a year ago   160
That never blow.
You should not loiter so.'
'Nay, hush,' said Laura:
'Nay, hush, my sister:
I ate and ate my fill,
Yet my mouth waters still;
To-morrow night I will
Buy more:' and kissed her:
'Have done with sorrow;
I'll bring you plums to-morrow   170
Fresh on their mother twigs,
Cherries worth getting;
You cannot think what figs
My teeth have met in,
What melons icy-cold
Piled on a dish of gold
Too huge for me to hold,
What peaches with a velvet nap,
Pellucid grapes without one seed:
Odorous indeed must be the mead   180
Whereon they grow, and pure the wave they drink
With lilies at the brink,
And sugar-sweet their sap.'

  Golden head by golden head,
Like two pigeons in one nest
Folded in each other's wings,
They lay down in their curtained bed:
Like two blossoms on one stem,
Like two flakes of new-fall'n snow,
Like two wands of ivory   190
Tipped with gold for awful kings.
Moon and stars gazed in at them,
Wind sang to them lullaby,
Lumbering owls forbore to fly,
Not a bat flapped to and fro
Round their nest:
Cheek to cheek and breast to breast
Locked together in one nest.

  Early in the morning
When the first cock crowed his warning,   200
Neat like bees, as sweet and busy,
Laura rose with Lizzie:
Fetched in honey, milked the cows,

Aired and set to rights the house,
Kneaded cakes of whitest wheat,
Cakes for dainty mouths to eat,
Next churned butter, whipped up cream,
Fed their poultry, sat and sewed;
Talked as modest maidens should:
Lizzie with an open heart,   210
Laura in an absent dream,
One content, one sick in part;
One warbling for the mere bright day's delight,
One longing for the night.

  At length slow evening came:
They went with pitchers to the reedy brook;
Lizzie most placid in her look,
Laura most like a leaping flame.
They drew the gurgling water from its deep;
Lizzie plucked purple and rich golden flags,   220
Then turning homewards said: 'The sunset flushes
Those furthest loftiest crags;
Come, Laura, not another maiden lags,
No wilful squirrel wags,
The beasts and birds are fast asleep.'
But Laura loitered still among the rushes
And said the bank was steep.

  And said the hour was early still,
The dew not fall'n, the wind not chill:
Listening ever, but not catching   230
The customary cry,
'Come buy, come buy,'
With its iterated jingle
Of sugar-baited words:
Not for all her watching
Once discerning even one goblin
Racing, whisking, tumbling, hobbling;
Let alone the herds
That used to tramp along the glen,
In groups or single,   240
Of brisk fruit-merchant men.

  Till Lizzie urged, 'O Laura, come;
I hear the fruit-call but I dare not look:
You should not loiter longer at this brook:
Come with me home.
The stars rise, the moon bends her arc,
Each glowworm winks her spark,
Let us get home before the night grows dark:
For clouds may gather
Though this is summer weather,   250
Put out the lights and drench us through;
Then if we lost our way what should we do?'

  Laura turned cold as stone
To find her sister heard that cry alone,
That goblin cry,
'Come buy our fruits, come buy.'
Must she then buy no more such dainty fruits?

Must she no more such succous pasture find,
Gone deaf and blind?
Her tree of life drooped from the root: 260
She said not one word in her heart's sore ache;
But peering thro' the dimness, nought discerning,
Trudged home, her pitcher dripping all the way;
So crept to bed, and lay
Silent till Lizzie slept;
Then sat up in a passionate yearning,
And gnashed her teeth for baulked desire, and wept
As if her heart would break.

    Day after day, night after night,
Laura kept watch in vain   270
In sullen silence of exceeding pain.
She never caught again the goblin cry:
'Come buy, come buy;' –
She never spied the goblin men
Hawking their fruits along the glen:
But when the noon waxed bright
Her hair grew thin and grey;
She dwindled, as the fair full moon doth turn
To swift decay and burn
Her fire away.   280

    One day remembering her kernel-stone
She set it by a wall that faced the south;
Dewed it with tears, hoped for a root,
Watched for a waxing shoot,
But there came none;
It never saw the sun,
It never felt the trickling moisture run:
While with sunk eyes and faded mouth
She dreamed of melons, as a traveller sees
False waves in desert drouth   290
With shade of leaf-crowned trees,
And burns the thirstier in the sandful breeze.

    She no more swept the house,
Tended the fowls or cows,
Fetched honey, kneaded cakes of wheat,
Brought water from the brook:
But sat down listless in the chimney-nook
And would not eat.

    Tender Lizzie could not bear
To watch her sister's cankerous care   300
Yet not to share.
She night and morning
Caught the goblins' cry:
'Come buy our orchard fruits,
Come buy, come buy:' –
Beside the brook, along the glen,
She heard the tramp of goblin men,
The voice and stir
Poor Laura could not hear;
Longed to buy fruit to comfort her,   310
But feared to pay too dear.
She thought of Jeanie in her grave,

Who should have been a bride;
But who for joys brides hope to have
Fell sick and died
In her gay prime,
In earliest Winter time,
With the first glazing rime,
With the first snow-fall of crisp Winter time.

    Till Laura dwindling   320
Seemed knocking at Death's door:
Then Lizzie weighed no more
Better and worse;
But put a silver penny in her purse,
Kissed Laura, crossed the heath with clumps of furze
At twilight, halted by the brook:
And for the first time in her life
Began to listen and look.

    Laughed every goblin
When they spied her peeping: 330
Came towards her hobbling,
Flying, running, leaping,
Puffing and blowing,
Chuckling, clapping, crowing,
Clucking and gobbling,
Mopping and mowing,
Full of airs and graces,
Pulling wry faces,
Demure grimaces,
Cat-like and rat-like,   340
Ratel- and wombat-like,
Snail-paced in a hurry,
Parrot-voiced and whistler,
Helter skelter, hurry skurry,
Chattering like magpies,
Fluttering like pigeons,
Gliding like fishes, –
Hugged her and kissed her:
Squeezed and caressed her:
Stretched up their dishes,   350
Panniers, and plates:
'Look at our apples
Russet and dun,
Bob at our cherries,
Bite at our peaches,
Citrons and dates,
Grapes for the asking,
Pears red with basking
Out in the sun,
Plums on their twigs;   360
Pluck them and suck them,
Pomegranates, figs.' –

    'Good folk,' said Lizzie,
Mindful of Jeanie:
'Give me much and many:' –
Held out her apron,
Tossed them her penny.

'Nay, take a seat with us,
Honour and eat with us,'
They answered grinning: 370
'Our feast is but beginning.
Night yet is early,
Warm and dew-pearly,
Wakeful and starry:
Such fruits as these
No man can carry;
Half their bloom would fly,
Half their dew would dry,
Half their flavour would pass by.
Sit down and feast with us,   380
Be welcome guest with us,
Cheer you and rest with us.' –
'Thank you,' said Lizzie: 'But one waits
At home alone for me:
So without further parleying,
If you will not sell me any
Of your fruits though much and many,
Give me back my silver penny
I tossed you for a fee.' –
They began to scratch their pates,   390
No longer wagging, purring,
But visibly demurring,
Grunting and snarling.
One called her proud,
Cross-grained, uncivil;
Their tones waxed loud,
Their looks were evil.
Lashing their tails
They trod and hustled her,
Elbowed and jostled her,   400
Clawed with their nails,
Barking, mewing, hissing, mocking,
Tore her gown and soiled her stocking,
Twitched her hair out by the roots,
Stamped upon her tender feet,
Held her hands and squeezed their fruits
Against her mouth to make her eat.

White and golden Lizzie stood,
Like a lily in a flood, –
Like a rock of blue-veined stone   410
Lashed by tides obstreperously, –
Like a beacon left alone
In a hoary roaring sea,
Sending up a golden fire, –
Like a fruit-crowned orange-tree
White with blossoms honey-sweet
Sore beset by wasp and bee, –
Like a royal virgin town
Topped with gilded dome and spire
Close beleaguered by a fleet   420
Mad to tug her standard down.

One may lead a horse to water,
Twenty cannot make him drink.

Though the goblins cuffed and caught her,
Coaxed and fought her,
Bullied and besought her,
Scratched her, pinched her black as ink,
Kicked and knocked her,
Mauled and mocked her,
Lizzie uttered not a word;   430
Would not open lip from lip
Lest they should cram a mouthful in:
But laughed in heart to feel the drip
Of juice that syrupped all her face,
And lodged in dimples of her chin,
And streaked her neck which quaked like curd.
At last the evil people
Worn out by her resistance
Flung back her penny, kicked their fruit
Along whichever road they took,   440
Not leaving root or stone or shoot;
Some writhed into the ground,
Some dived into the brook
With ring and ripple,
Some scudded on the gale without a sound,
Some vanished in the distance.

In a smart, ache, tingle,
Lizzie went her way;
Knew not was it night or day;
Sprang up the bank, tore thro' the furze,   450
Threaded copse and dingle,
And heard her penny jingle
Bouncing in her purse, –
Its bounce was music to her ear.
She ran and ran
As if she feared some goblin man
Dogged her with gibe or curse
Or something worse:
But not one goblin skurried after,
Nor was she pricked by fear;   460
The kind heart made her windy-paced
That urged her home quite out of breath with haste
And inward laughter.

She cried 'Laura,' up the garden,
'Did you miss me?
Come and kiss me.
Never mind my bruises,
Hug me, kiss me, suck my juices
Squeezed from goblin fruits for you,
Goblin pulp and goblin dew.   470
Eat me, drink me, love me;
Laura, make much of me:
For your sake I have braved the glen
And had to do with goblin merchant men.'

Laura started from her chair,
Flung her arms up in the air,
Clutched her hair:
'Lizzie, Lizzie, have you tasted

For my sake the fruit forbidden?[2]
Must your light like mine be hidden,[3]   480
Your young life like mine be wasted,
Undone in mine undoing
And ruined in my ruin,
Thirsty, cankered, goblin-ridden?' –
She clung about her sister,
Kissed and kissed and kissed her:
Tears once again
Refreshed her shrunken eyes,
Dropping like rain
After long sultry drouth;   490
Shaking with aguish fear, and pain,
She kissed and kissed her with a hungry mouth.

    Her lips began to scorch,
That juice was wormwood to her tongue,
She loathed the feast:
Writhing as one possessed she leaped and sung,
Rent all her robe, and wrung
Her hands in lamentable haste,
And beat her breast.
Her locks streamed like the torch   500
Borne by a racer at full speed,
Or like the mane of horses in their flight,
Or like an eagle when she stems the light
Straight toward the sun,
Or like a caged thing freed,
Or like a flying flag when armies run.

    Swift fire spread through her veins, knocked at her
heart,
Met the fire smouldering there
And overbore its lesser flame;
She gorged on bitterness without a name: 510
Ah! fool, to choose such part
Of soul-consuming care!
Sense failed in the mortal strife:
Like the watch-tower of a town
Which an earthquake shatters down,
Like a lightning-stricken mast,
Like a wind-uprooted tree
Spun about,
Like a foam-topped waterspout
Cast down headlong in the sea,   520
She fell at last;
Pleasure past and anguish past,

Is it death or is it life?

    Life out of death.
That night long Lizzie watched by her,
Counted her pulse's flagging stir,
Felt for her breath,
Held water to her lips, and cooled her face
With tears and fanning leaves:
But when the first birds chirped about their eaves,   530
And early reapers plodded to the place
Of golden sheaves,
And dew-wet grass
Bowed in the morning winds so brisk to pass,
And new buds with new day
Opened of cup-like lilies on the stream,
Laura awoke as from a dream,
Laughed in the innocent old way,
Hugged Lizzie but not twice or thrice;
Her gleaming locks showed not one thread of grey,   540
Her breath was sweet as May
And light danced in her eyes.

    Days, weeks, months, years
Afterwards, when both were wives
With children of their own;
Their mother-hearts beset with fears,
Their lives bound up in tender lives;
Laura would call the little ones
And tell them of her early prime,
Those pleasant days long gone   550
Of not-returning time:
Would talk about the haunted glen,
The wicked, quaint fruit-merchant men,
Their fruits like honey to the throat
But poison in the blood;
(Men sell not such in any town:)
Would tell them how her sister stood
In deadly peril to do her good,
And win the fiery antidote:
Then joining hands to little hands   560
Would bid them cling together,
'For there is no friend like a sister
In calm or stormy weather;
To cheer one on the tedious way,
To fetch one if one goes astray,
To lift one if one totters down,
To strengthen whilst one stands.'

Composed by 22 April 1859. Originally titled 'A Peep at Goblins'.
Goblin Market *(1862).*

PROMISES LIKE PIE-CRUST

Promise me no promises,
    So will I not promise you;

Keep we both our liberties,
    Never false and never true:

2   as Eve did in Garden of Eden, Genesis 2.3.

3   Matthew 5.15.

Let us hold the die uncast,
　　Free to come as free to go:
For I cannot know your past,
　　And of mine what can you know?

You, so warm, may once have been
　　Warmer towards another one:　　　　　　　10
I, so cold, may once have seen
　　Sunlight, once have felt the sun:
Who shall show us if it was
　　Thus indeed in time of old?

Fades the image from the glass
　　And the fortune is not told.

If you promised, you might grieve
　　For lost liberty again:
If I promised, I believe
　　I should fret to break the chain:　　　　　20
Let us be the friends we were,
　　Nothing more but nothing less:
Many thrive on frugal fare
　　Who would perish of excess.

Written 20 April 1861. New Poems, Hitherto Unpublished and
Uncollected, ed. W. M. Rossetti (1896).

THE LOWEST PLACE

Give me the lowest place: not that I dare
　　Ask for that lowest place, but Thou hast died
That I might live and share
　　Thy glory by Thy side.

Give me the lowest place: or if for me
　　That lowest place too high, make one more low
Where I may sit and see
　　My God and love Thee so.

Written 25 July 1863. The Prince's Progress and Other Poems (1866).
Last poem in the volume.

TWICE

I took my heart in my hand
　　(O my love, O my love),
I said: Let me fall or stand,
　　Let me live or die,
But this once hear me speak –
　　(O my love, O my love) –
Yet a woman's words are weak;
　　You should speak, not I.

You took my heart in your hand
　　With a friendly smile,　　　　　　　　　10
With a critical eye you scanned,
　　Then set it down,
And said: It is still unripe,
　　Better wait awhile;
Wait while the skylarks pipe,
　　Till the corn grows brown.

As you set it down it broke –
　　Broke, but I did not wince;
I smiled at the speech you spoke,
　　At your judgment that I heard:　　　　　20
But I have not often smiled
　　Since then, nor questioned since,

Nor cared for corn-flowers wild,
　　Nor sung with the singing bird.

I take my heart in my hand,
　　O my God, O my God,
My broken heart in my hand:
　　Thou hast seen, judge Thou.
My hope was written on sand,
　　O my God, O my God:　　　　　　　　　30
Now let Thy judgment stand –
　　Yea, judge me now.

This contemned of a man,
　　This marred one heedless day,
This heart take Thou to scan
　　Both within and without:
Refine with fire[1] its gold,
　　Purge Thou its dross away[2] –
Yea, hold it in Thy hold,
　　Whence none can pluck it out.　　　　　40

I take my heart in my hand –
　　I shall not die, but live –
Before Thy face I stand;

TWICE
1　Malachi 3.2.

2　Isaiah 1.25.

I, for Thou callest such:
   All that I have I bring,
     All that I am I give,

Smile Thou and I shall sing,
   But shall not question much.

Written June 1864. The Prince's Progress *(1866).*

'SUMMER IS ENDED'[1]

To think that this meaningless thing was ever a rose,
   Scentless, colourless, *this*!
   Will it ever be thus (who knows?)
     Thus with our bliss,
   If we wait till the close?

Though we care not to wait for the end, there comes the end
     Sooner, later, at last,
   Which nothing can mar, nothing mend:
     An end locked fast,
   Bent we cannot re-bend.   10

Date of writing not known. A Pageant and Other Poems *(Macmillan & Co., 1881).*

From: LATER LIFE: A DOUBLE SONNET OF SONNETS

26

This Life is full of numbness and of balk,
   Of haltingness and baffled short-coming,
   Of promise unfulfilled, of everything
That is puffed vanity and empty talk:
Its very bud hangs cankered on the stalk,
   Its very song-bird trails a broken wing,
   Its very Spring is not indeed like Spring,

But sighs like Autumn round an aimless walk.
This Life we live is dead for all its breath;
   Death's self it is, set off on pilgrimage,   10
   Travelling with tottering steps the first short stage:
     The second stage is one mere desert dust
     Where Death sits veiled amid creation's rust: –
Unveil thy face, O Death who art not Death.

Date of writing not known. A Pageant *(1881). Titled 'Veiled Death' in MS.*

27

I have dreamed of Death: – what will it be to die
   Not in a dream, but in the literal truth
   With all Death's adjuncts ghastly and uncouth,
The pang that is the last and the last sigh?
Too dulled, it may be, for a last good-bye,
   Too comfortless for any one to soothe,
   A helpless charmless spectacle of ruth

Through long last hours, so long while yet they fly.
So long to those who hopeless in their fear
   Watch the slow breath and look for what they dread: 10
While I supine with ears that cease to hear,
     With eyes that glaze, with heart pulse running down
   (Alas! no saint rejoicing on her bed),
     May miss the goal at last, may miss a crown.

Date of writing not known. A Pageant *(1881). Titled 'Memento Mori' in MS.*

A CHRISTMAS CAROL

In the bleak mid-winter
   Frosty wind made moan,
Earth stood hard as iron,
   Water like a stone;
Snow has fallen, snow on snow,
   Snow on snow,

In the bleak mid-winter
   Long ago.

Our God, Heaven cannot hold Him,
   Nor earth sustain;   10
Heaven and earth shall flee away

SUMMER IS ENDED
1 Jeremiah 8.2.: 'The harvest is past, the summer is ended, and we are
not saved'.

When He comes to reign:
In the bleak mid-winter
  A stable-place sufficed
The Lord God Almighty
  Jesus Christ.

Enough for Him whom cherubim
  Worship night and day,
A breastful of milk
  And a mangerful of hay;   20
Enough for Him whom angels
  Fall down before,
The ox and ass and camel
  Which adore.

Angels and archangels
  May have gathered there,

Cherubim and seraphim
  Throng'd the air,
But only His mother
  In her maiden bliss   30
Worshipped the Beloved
  With a kiss.

What can I give Him,
  Poor as I am?
If I were a shepherd
  I would bring a lamb,
If I were a wise man
  I would do my part, –
Yet what I can I give Him,
  Give my heart.   40

Date of writing not known (no MS). Scribner's Monthly, *III (January 1872),*
278. Goblin Market, The Prince's Progress, and Other Poems, *by*
Christina G. Rossetti (Macmillan & Co., 1875).

TOUCHING 'NEVER'

Because you never yet have loved me, dear,
  Think you you never can nor ever will?
  Surely while life remains hope lingers still,
Hope the last blossom of life's dying year.
Because the season and mine age grow sere,
  Shall never Spring bring forth her daffodil,
  Shall never sweeter Summer feast her fill

Of roses with the nightingales they hear?
If you had loved me, I not loving you,
  If you had urged me with the tender plea   10
Of what our unknown years to come might do
(Eternal years, if Time should count too few),
  I would have owned the point you pressed on me,
Was possible, or probable, or true.

Date of writing not known. A Pageant *(1881).*

YET A LITTLE WHILE

I dreamed and did not seek: to-day I seek
  Who can no longer dream;
But now am all behindhand, waxen weak,
  And dazed amid so many things that gleam
    Yet are not what they seem.

I dreamed and did not work: to-day I work
  Kept wide awake by care
And loss, and perils dimly guessed to lurk;

I work and reap not, while my life goes bare
  And void in wintry air.   10

I hope indeed; but hope itself is fear
  Viewed on the sunny side;
I hope, and disregard the world that's here,
  The prizes drawn, the sweet things that betide;
    I hope, and I abide.

Date of writing not known. A Pageant *(1881).*

Alexander Smith (1830–67)

Alexander Smith, 'Spasmodic' poet, was born in Kilmarnock, Scotland, 31 December 1830, son of Peter Smith, a lace-pattern designer, and Helen Murray, who sang him Gaelic songs and told him Ossianic legends. He grew up in Paisley and Glasgow. At twelve he was apprenticed to the lace-pattern business, but read ardently in his spare time, not least in the Romantic poets. His own poems were first published in the Glasgow *Evening Citizen*. He was promoted, like several other local proletarian poets, by the Revd Thomas Gilfillian. *Life Drama* (1853), a long, sub-Keatsian poem about a budding poet called Walter – portions of which were published by Gilfillian in the *Critic* and the *Eclectic Review* – was so successful that Smith was able to give up the fabric trade. He travelled to London (calling in on Philip James Bailey in Nottingham, author of the notorious *Festus* (1839), the long 'Spasmodic' verse-drama about a poet-figure inspired by Goethe's *Faust* and which had no doubt inspired *Life Drama*). In the metropolis he made the acquaintance of George Henry Lewes, who promoted Smith in the *Leader*. Back in Glasgow, Smith edited the *Glasgow Miscellany*. He became Secretary to the University of Edinburgh in 1854 (and rose to become Registrar). In the winter of 1854 he began a friendship with Sydney Dobell, up in Edinburgh for the sake of his wife's medical treatment. They co-operated in *Sonnets on the Crimean War* (1855), thus confirming the poetic alliance between them suggested by William Aytoun's parodic lampooning of the 'Spasmodic' Bailey–Dobell–Smith syndrome in *Firmilian; or, The Student of Badajoz: A Spasmodic Tragedy* (1854) and in the spoof review which preceded it from the pen of the mischievous Aytoun in *Blackwood's Edinburgh Magazine*, May 1854. Aytoun's rich merriment over the verbal spasms of Smith & Co. did not, however, prevent a deep admiration for Smith, and

it was through Aytoun that Smith came to write for *Blackwood's*. *City Poems*, which featured Smith's best, though still rather hectic poem, 'Glasgow' (shortest in a gathering of long narrative poems), came out in 1857 – the year Smith married a Flora Macdonald (descended, apparently, from *the* Flora Macdonald). Smith was accused of plagiarism in this volume (it contained the 'mutilated property of other bards, strewn about the life-wrecks of noble vessels thrown upon a wild Scotch coast', snorted the *Athenaeum* in December 1857) – a mite unfairly since Smith is no more intensely imitative than the average second-hand poet. A reputation for literary thieving stuck to him, and his *Edwin of Deira* (1861) was accused of imitating Tennyson's Arthurian manner (*Idylls of the King* had started to appear in public in 1859). Smith contributed massively to newspapers and journals and to *Chambers' Encyclopedia* and the *Encyclopedia Britannica*. He published two novels, *Alfred Hagart's Household* (1866) and *Miss Dora M'Quarrie* (1867), edited Burns (1865), and brought out a book of essays, *Dreamthorp: A Book of Essays Written in the Country* (1863), and a travel book, *A Summer in Skye* (1865). He fell ill in the latter part of 1866 and died 5 January 1867. *Last Leaves*, a gathering of essays, appeared posthumously in 1868, edited with a memoir by Patrick Procter Alexander. It includes a self-serving essay on Sydney Dobell, pointing hintfully to the qualities of his fellow Spasmodic ('The reader capable of appreciating beauty, passion, pathos, cannot fail to recognise all these' in Dobell – and by implication in Smith). He is buried in Warriston Cemetery in Edinburgh. Of *Life Drama*, Matthew Arnold said that Smith 'has certainly an extraordinary faculty, although I think that he is a phenomenon of a very dubious character'. Even his friends might have agreed with that judgement of Spasmodic Smith.

GLASGOW

Sing, Poet, 'tis a merry world;
That cottage smoke is rolled and curled
   In sport, that every moss
Is happy, every inch of soil; –
Before *me* runs a road of toil
   With my grave cut across.
Sing, trailing showers and breezy downs –
I know the tragic hearts of towns.

City! I am true son of thine;
Ne'er dwelt I where great mornings shine   10
   Around the bleating pens;

Ne'er by the rivulets I strayed,
And ne'er upon my childhood weighed
   The silence of the glens.
Instead of shores where ocean beats,
I hear the ebb and flow of streets.

Black Labour draws his weary waves,
Into their secret-moaning caves;
   But with the morning light,
That sea again will overflow   20
With a long weary sound of woe,
   Again to faint in night.

Wave am I in that sea of woes,
Which, night and morning, ebbs and flows.

I dwelt within a gloomy court,
Wherein did never sunbeam sport;
    Yet there my heart was stirr'd –
My very blood did dance and thrill,
When on my narrow window-sill,
    Spring lighted like a bird.   30
Poor flowers – I watched them pine for weeks,
With leaves as pale as human cheeks.

Afar, one summer, I was borne;
Through golden vapours of the morn,
    I heard the hills of sheep:
I trod with a wild ecstasy
The bright fringe of the living sea:
    And on a ruined keep
I sat, and watched an endless plain
Blacken beneath the gloom of rain.   40

O fair the lightly sprinkled waste,
O'er which a laughing shower has raced!
    O fair the April shoots!
O fair the woods on summer days,
While a blue hyacinthine haze
    Is dreaming round the roots!
In thee, O City! I discern
Another beauty, sad and stern.

Draw thy fierce streams of blinding ore,
Smite on a thousand anvils, roar   50
    Down to the harbour-bars;
Smoulder in smoky sunsets, flare
On rainy nights, with street and square
    Lie empty to the stars.
From terrace proud to alley base
I know thee as my mother's face.

When sunset bathes thee in his gold,
In wreaths of bronze thy sides are rolled,
    Thy smoke is dusky fire;   60
And, from the glory round thee poured,
A sunbeam like an angel's sword
    Shivers upon a spire.
Thus have I watched thee, Terror! Dream!
While the blue Night crept up the stream.

The wild Train plunges in the hills,
He shrieks across the midnight rills;
    Streams through the shifting glare,
The roar and flap of foundry fires,
That shake with light the sleeping shires;
    And on the moorlands bare,   70
    He sees afar a crown of light
Hang o'er thee in the hollow night.

At midnight, when thy suburbs lie
As silent as a noonday sky,

    When larks with heat are mute,
I love to linger on thy bridge,
All lonely as a mountain ridge,
    Disturbed but by my foot;
While the black lazy stream beneath,
Steals from its far-off wilds of heath.   80

And through thy heart, as through a dream,
Flows on that black disdainful stream;
    All scornfully it flows,
Between the huddled gloom of masts,
Silent as pines unvexed by blasts –
    'Tween lamps in streaming rows.
O wondrous sight! O stream of dread!
O long dark river of the dead!

Afar, the banner of the year
Unfurls: but dimly prisoned here,   90
    'Tis only when I greet
A dropt rose lying in my way,
A butterfly that flutters gay
    Athwart the noisy street,
I know the happy Summer smiles
Around thy suburbs, miles on miles.

'Twere neither pæan now, nor dirge,
The flash and thunder of the surge
    On flat sands wide and bare;
No haunting joy or anguish dwells   100
In the green light of sunny dells,
    Or in the starry air.
Alike to me the desert flower,
The rainbow laughing o'er the shower.

While o'er thy walls the darkness sails,
I lean against the churchyard rails;
    Up in the midnight towers
The belfried spire, the street is dead,
I hear in silence over head
    The clang of iron hours: 110
It moves me not – I know her tomb
Is yonder in the shapeless gloom.

All raptures of this mortal breath,
Solemnities of life and death,
    Dwell in thy noise alone:
Of me thou hast become a part –
Some kindred with my human heart
    Lives in thy streets of stone;
For we have been familiar more
Than galley-slave and weary oar.   120

The beech is dipped in wine; the shower
Is burnished; on the swinging flower
    The latest bee doth sit.
The low sun stares through dust of gold,
And o'er the darkening heath and wold
    The large ghost-moth doth flit.

In every orchard Autumn stands,
With apples in his golden hands.

But all these sights and sounds are strange;
Then wherefore from thee should I range?   130
  Thou hast my kith and kin:

My childhood, youth, and manhood brave;
Thou hast that unforgotten grave
  Within thy central din.
A sacredness of love and death
Dwells in thy noise and smoky breath.

City Poems (Macmillan & Co., Cambridge, 1857).

(Mrs) Isa (Craig) Knox (1831–1903)

Isa Knox, a self-taught Christian poet, was born 17 October 1831, the only child of an Edinburgh hosier and glove-maker. Her parents died when she was a young child and she was brought up by her grandmother. She left school when she was only nine, but she read much, formed literary aspirations, and eventually contributed many poems to the *Scotsman*, signed *Isa*. Her first volume, *Poems by Isa*, came out in 1856, published by the distinguished Edinburgh firm of Blackwood's. In 1857 she travelled south to London where she became, controversially, the first woman secretary of the National Association for the Promotion of Social Science. She was, with Adelaide Anne Procter (who also worked for the Association), close to the Langham Place group of feminist literary activists. She married her cousin John Knox in May 1866. In 1859 she won the £50 Prize for the Burns Centenary Poem at the Crystal Palace, beating hundreds of entrants, including Gerald Massey and A. J. Munby. She contributed widely to the journals, especially the Christian and family ones like *Good Words*, edited the *Argosy* magazine for a time, did a book on slavery (1863), published poems in further volumes such as *Songs of Consolation* (1874), brought out a much reprinted novel, *Esther West* (1874), and produced some popular instructive tomes for the young, *Little Folk's History of England* (1872), *Easy History for Upper Standards* (1884), and two series of *Tales of the Parables* (1872–7). A *Selection from Mrs Knox's Poems* appeared in 1892, but by then her writing career had tapered off. She died at Brockley in Suffolk, 23 December 1903, aged seventy-two.

THE BOX

St. Mark xiv.3.[1]

She brake the box, and on his head
The costly spikenard freely shed:
  Its fragrance filled the place;
And he on whom it was bestowed,
Who knew the gift from love had flowed,
  Approved the lavish grace.

He murmured at the waste, whose heart
Already played the traitor's part:[2]
  The others murmured too;
They nursed their small economies,   10
They kept the bag before their eyes,
  And hid their lord from view.

Hid from their hearts that more and more
He could increase the precious store
  From which such gifts are shed –
Freely the sweets of nature grow,

THE BOX
1 'And being in Bethany in the house of Simon the leper, as he sat at meat, there came a woman having an alabaster box of ointment of spikenard very precious; and she broke the box, and poured it on his head.'
2 Judas (though not in St. Mark's version).

But love must bid their fragrance flow,
   And love the ointment spread.

Look at the liberal world, and see
Each blessing lavished boundlessly!   20
   What, dost thou call it waste?
The beauty of the wayside flower,
The sweetness scattered every hour,
   That all alike may taste?

They who the costliest gifts have given,
Raising the fair-wrought towers to heaven,
   Whose precious stones endure,
Filling the place with prayer and psalm,
Anointing hearts with beauty's balm,
   Have most enriched the poor.   30

While they each gen'rous use who chide –
Whether they seek their greed to hide,
   Or but of sight too near,
Would save the cistern's scant supply,
And let the feeding fount run dry –
   Rob God's poor souls of cheer.

O generous heart, thy need fulfil,
Spend if thou wilt more freely still,
   And love's rich odours raise;
If all for love, and not for pride,   40
Surely thy Lord will take thy side,
   And crown thee with his praise.

Songs of Consolation *(Macmillan & Co., 1874).*

Unto This Last[1]

St. Matthew xx.16.[2]

They murmured when they came,
To take the promised pay;
They murmured – not that some had more,
That none had less than they.

Ah! with our hearts too well
That murmuring accords –
But if at their poor grudge we smile,
What mean the Master's words?

This lesson of our Lord's,
Think you it would convey   10
A pretext for the privilege
Of idling all the day?

Unto this Last
1   Title of John Ruskin's anti-capitalist book, 1860.
2   'So the last shall be first, and the first last: for many be called but few chosen' (conclusion of Jesus's parable of vineyard labourers who all earn the same day's wage, even if they started work late in the day).

Because the end may be
The same some ages hence;
Because our liberal Master means
To make no difference?

The end! When will it be?
What know'st thou of the end?
Which giving all thy promised good
Must all thy thought transcend.   20

What if indeed the Lord
Will give to all the same?
Surely thine inmost heart must own
Not more, but less thy claim.

Thou couldst not think for shame
Thy work or service hard!
Was not that heavenly service still
Its own too great reward?

Nay, in thy vineyard, Lord,
This were enough to win   30
To serve thee first, and serve thee last,
By early entering in.

Songs of Consolation (1874).

C. S. (Charles Stuart) (Blayds) Calverley (1831–84)

C. S. Calverley, translator and parodist, was born Charles Stuart Blayds, 22 December 1831, at Martley, Worcestershire, where his father the Revd Henry Blayds was vicar. These Blayds reverted to the old family name of Calverley (which they'd dropped at the beginning of the nineteenth century) only in 1852, so it was as Blayds that Calverley attended Marlborough (briefly) and Harrow School (which he left in 1850) and Balliol College, Oxford (from which he was sent down at the beginning of 1852). At school he was renowned as an athlete, was lazy in his studies but gifted and very smart, and he seems to have won his Balliol scholarship by improvising the required Latin verses on the spot in the oral examination. In 1851 he won the Oxford Chancellor's Prize for Latin Verse, but was expelled shortly thereafter in a culmination of a career of rule-breaking. Under his new name of Calverley he entered Christ's College, Cambridge, was a terrific success in his Classical studies, won prize after prize, became a Craven Scholar, came second in the classical Tripos of 1856, and was elected a Fellow of his College in 1858. His *Verses and Translations* appeared in 1862; he taught; but gave up his Fellowship to marry a first cousin from Yorkshire, Ellen Calverley. He studied Law; joined the

Inner Temple (1865); and practised as a barrister on the northern circuit. *Translations into English and Latin* appeared in 1866. He was severely concussed while ice-skating at his father-in-law's place, Oulton Hall, near Leeds, in the winter of 1866–7, and after that grew so enfeebled he had to abandon legal work. His Theocritus translations appeared in 1869 and his *Fly Leaves* in 1872; but he was a slowing-down man, as Bright's Disease and depression took over. He died 17 February 1884 and is buried in Folkestone. His translations from Virgil, Homer, Horace, Theocritus and Lucretius are terribly dated; his numerous translations of standard poems from English into Latin have interest but read like undergraduate exercises and private pleasures only. His parodies do, however, live still. Which of them 'is emphatically the best it would be difficult to say; they are all of them so uniformly good': thus William Davenport Adams in his anthology *The Comic Poets of the Nineteenth Century: Poems of Wit and Humour by Living Writers* (1876), with what was clearly a widespread feeling. Leslie Stephen, who wrote Calverley's *DNB* entry, thought him 'perhaps the best parodist in the language'. Perhaps is the key-word. He is certainly among the better parodists.

CHARADES NO. VI

Sikes, housebreaker, of Houndsditch,[1]
  Habitually swore;
But so surpassingly profane
  He never was before,
As on a night in winter,
  When – softly as he stole
In the dim light from stair to stair,
Noiseless as boys who in her lair
Seek to surprise a fat old hare –
He barked his shinbone, unaware   10
  Encountering *my whole*.

As pours the Anio plainward,
  When rains have swollen the dykes,
So, with such noise, poured down *my first*
  Stirred by the shins of Sikes.
The Butler Bibulus heard it;
  And straightway ceased to snore,
And sat up, like an egg on end,
  While men might count a score:
Then spake he to Tigerius,   20
  A Buttons bold was he:
'Buttons, I think there's thieves about;
Just strike a light and tumble out;
If you can't find one, go without,
  And see what you may see.'

But now was all the household,
  Almost, upon its legs,
Each treading carefully about
  As if they trod on eggs.
With robe far-streaming issued   30
  Paterfamilias forth;
And close behind him, – stout and true
  And tender as the North, –
Came Mrs. P., supporting
  On her broad arm her fourth.[2]

Betsy the nurse, who never
  From largest beetle ran,
And – conscious p'raps of pleasing caps –
  The housemaids, formed the van:
And Bibulus the butler,   40
  His calm brows slightly arched;
(No mortal wight had ere that night
  Seen him with shirt unstarched;)

And Bob, the shockhaired knifeboy,
  Wielding two Sheffield blades,
And James Plush of the sinewy legs,
  The love of lady's maids:
And charwoman and chaplain
  Stood mingled in a mass,
And 'Things,' thought he of Houndsditch,   50
  'Is come to a pretty pass.'

Beyond all things a baby
  Is to the schoolgirl dear;
Next to herself the nursemaid loves
  Her dashing grenadier;
Only with life the sailor
  Parts from the British flag;
While one hope lingers, the cracksman's fingers
  Drop not his hard-earned 'swag'

But, as hares do *my second*   60
  Thro' green Calabria's copses,[3]
As females vanish at the sight
  Of short-horns and of wopses;
So, dropping forks and tea-spoons,
  The pride of Houndsditch fled,
Dumbfoundered by the hue and cry
  He'd raised up overhead.

*   *   *   *   *

They gave him – did the judges –
  As much as was his due.
And, Saxon, shouldst thou e'er be led   70
  To deem this tale untrue;
Then – any night in winter,
  When the cold north wind blows,
And bairns are told to keep out cold
  By tallowing the nose:
When round the fire the elders
  Are gathered in a bunch,
And the girls are doing crochet,
  And the boys are reading Punch: –
Go thou and look in Leech's book;[4]   80
  There haply shalt thou spy
A stout man on a staircase stand,
With aspect anything but bland,
And rub his right shin with his hand,
  To witness if I lie.

Verses and Translations, by C.S.C. (Deighton, Bell, & Co., Cambridge; Bell & Daldy, London, 1862). Draws parodically on T. B. Macaulay's 'Horatius.' Dickens has a famous robber called Bill Sikes in Oliver Twist. All Calverley's 'Charades' are little riddles (my whole, my first, my second . . .): answer here, coal-scuttle (apparently!).

CHARADES NO. VI
1 proletarian quarter of London, in eastern part of the city.
2 child.
3 Calabria: region of southern Italy, right at the toe of the country.

4 presumably John Leech (1817–64), famous comic illustrator and cartoonist (a mainstay of *Punch*), whose *Pictures of Life and Character . . . from the Collection of Mr Punch* started to appear in 1854 (3 series by 1860).

CONTENTMENT

After the Manner of Horace

Friend, there be they on whom mishap
  Or never or so rarely comes,
That, when they think thereof, they snap
  Derisive thumbs:

And there be they who lightly lose
  Their all, yet feel no aching void;
Should aught annoy them, they refuse
  To be annoyed:

And fain would I be e'en as these!
  Life is with such all beer and skittles;   10
They are not difficult to please
  About their victuals:

The trout, the grouse, the early pea,
  By such, if there, are freely taken;
If not, they munch with equal glee
  Their bit of bacon:

And when they wax a little gay
  And chaff the public after luncheon,
If they're confronted with a stray
  Policeman's truncheon,   20

They gaze thereat with outstretch'd necks,
  And laughter which no threats can smother,
And tell the horror-stricken X
  That he's another.

In snowtime if they cross a spot
  Where unsuspected boys have slid,

They fall not down – though they would not
  Mind if they did:

When the spring rosebud which they wear
  Breaks short and tumbles from its stem,   30
No thought of being angry e'er
  Dawns upon them;

Though 'twas Jemima's hand that placed,
  (As well you ween) at evening's hour,
In the loved button-hole that chaste
  And cherished flower.

And when they travel, if they find
  That they have left their pocket-compass
Or Murray[1] or thick boots behind,
  They raise no rumpus,   40

But plod serenely on without:
  Knowing it's better to endure
The evil which beyond all doubt
  You cannot cure.

When for that early train they're late,
  They do not make their woes the text
Of sermons in the Times,[2] but wait
  On for the next;

And jump inside, and only grin
  Should it appear that that dry wag,   50
The guard, omitted to put in
  Their carpet-bag.

Fly Leaves, *by C.S.C. (Deighton, Bell, & Co., Cambridge; Bell & Daldy,
London, 1872). The metre imitates Horace's* Sapphic Odes.

'FOREVER'

Forever!   'Tis a single word!
  Our rude forefathers deemed it two:
Can you imagine so absurd
  A view?

Forever!   What abysms of woe
  The word reveals, what frenzy, what
Despair!   For ever (printed so)
  Did not.

It looks, ah me! how trite and tame!
  It fails to sadden or appal   10
Or solace – it is not the same
  At all.

O thou to whom it first occurred
  To solder the disjoined, and dower
Thy native language with a word
  Of power:

CONTENTMENT
1   John Murray, publisher, issued a prolific series of *Handbooks for Tra-
vellers* in Europe.

2   newspaper (readers' letters?).

We bless thee!   Whether far or near
  Thy dwelling, whether dark or fair
Thy kingly brow, is neither here
       Nor there.   20

But in men's hearts shall be thy throne,
  While the great pulse of England beats
Thou coiner of a word unknown
       To Keats!

And nevermore must printer do
  As men did longago; but run

'For' into 'ever,' bidding two
       Be one.

Forever! passion-fraught, it throws
  O'er the dim page a gloom, a glamour: 30
It's sweet, it's strange; and I suppose
       It's grammar.

Forever!   'Tis a single word!
  And yet our fathers deemed it two:
Nor am I confident they erred;
       Are you?

                               Fly Leaves *(1872)*.

LOVERS, AND A REFLECTION

In moss-prankt dells which the sunbeams flatter
  (And heaven it knoweth what that may mean;
Meaning, however, is no great matter)
  Where woods are a-tremble, with rifts atween;

Thro' God's own heather we wonn'd together,
  I and my Willie (O love my love):
I need hardly remark it was glorious weather,
  And flitterbats wavered alow, above:

Boats were curtseying, rising, bowing,
  (Boats in that climate are so polite),   10
And sands were a ribbon of green endowing,
  And O the sundazzle on bark and bight!

Thro' the rare red heather we danced together,
  (O love my Willie!) and smelt for flowers:
I must mention again it was gorgeous weather,
  Rhymes are so scarce in this world of ours: –

By rises that flushed with their purple favours,
  Thro' becks that brattled o'er grasses sheen,
We walked and waded, we two young shavers,
  Thanking our stars we were both so green.   20

We journeyed in parallels, I and Willie,
  In fortunate parallels! Butterflies,
Hid in weltering shadows of daffodilly
  Or marjoram, kept making peacock eyes:

Songbirds darted about, some inky
  As coal, some snowy (I ween) as curds;
Or rosy as pinks, or as roses pinky –
  They reck of no eerie To-come, those birds!

But they skim over bents which the millstream washes,
  Or hang in the lift 'neath a white cloud's hem;   30
They need no parasols, no goloshes;
  And good Mrs. Trimmer she feedeth them.

Then we thrid God's cowslips (as erst His heather)
   That endowed the wan grass with their golden blooms;
And snapt – (it was perfectly charming weather) –
   Our fingers at Fate and her goddess-glooms:

And Willie 'gan sing (O, his notes were fluty;
   Wafts fluttered them out to the white-wing'd sea) –
Something made up of rhymes that have done much duty,
   Rhymes (better to put it) of 'ancientry:'   40

Bowers of flowers encounted showers
   In William's carol – (O love my Willie!)
Then he bade sorrow borrow from blithe to-morrow
   I quite forget what – say a daffodily:

A nest in a hollow, 'with buds to follow,'
   I think occurred next in his nimble strain;
And clay that was 'kneaden' of course in Eden –
   A rhyme most novel, I do maintain:

Mists, bones, the singer himself, love-stories,
   And all least furlable things got 'furled;'   50
Not with any design to conceal their glories,
   But simply and solely to rhyme with 'world.'

          *   *   *   *   *

O if billows and pillows and hours and flowers,
   And all the brave rhymes of an elder day,
Could be furled together, this genial weather,
   And carted, or carried on wafts away,
Nor ever again trotted out – ay me!
How much fewer volumes of verse there'd be!

Fly Leaves *(1872). (A parody of Jean Ingelow,* Poems *(1863), which included 'Divided' in this anthology.)*

April

Or, The New Hat

[In deference to a prevalent taste this Poem is also a Double Acrostic]

Prologue
My Boots had been wash'd – well wash'd – in a show'r;
   But little I griev'd about that:
What I felt was the havock a single half-hour
   Had made with my costly new Hat.

For the Boot, tho' its lustre be dimm'd, shall assume
   Fresh sprightliness after a while:
But what art may restore its original bloom,
   When once it hath flown, to the Tile?

I clomb to my perch, and the Horses (a bay
   And a brown) trotted off with a clatter: 10
The Driver look'd round in his affable way
   And said huskily 'Who is your hatter?'

I was pleas'd that he'd notic'd its shape and its shine,
    And as soon as we reached the *Old Druid*
I begg'd that he'd drink to my new Four-and-nine
    In a glass of his favourite Fluid.

A gratified smile sat, I own, on my lips
    When the Landlady called to the Master
(He was standing hard by with his hands on his hips)
    To 'look at the gentleman's Castor!'[1]
                           20

I laugh'd, as an Organ-man paus'd in mid-air
    ('Twas an air that I happen'd to know
By a great foreign Maestro) expressly to stare
    At *ze gent wiz ze joli chapeau.*

Yet how swift is the transit from laughter to tears!
    Our glories, how fleeting are they!
That Hat might (with care) have adorned me for years;
    But 'twas ruin'd, alack, in a Day!

How I lov'd thee, my Bright One! I wrench in Remorse
    My hands from my Coat-tail and wring 'em:
'Why did not I, why, as a matter of course,
    When I purchas'd thee, purchase a Gingham!'[2]
                           30

First published, Punch *(16 April 1881). Text,* The Complete Works
(George Bell & Sons, 1901).

Lewis Carroll (Charles Lutwidge Dodgson) (1832–98)

Charles Lutwidge Dodgson, the future Lewis Carroll, Oxford mathematician, pioneer photographer, with Edward Lear one of the leading pair of Victorian 'Nonsense' writers, was born, 27 January 1832, third child of eleven, oldest boy of four, in the rectory of Daresbury, near Warrington, Lancashire. He was taught religious principles by his mother Frances Lutwidge and maths, classics and literature by his father, the Revd Charles Dodgson. His love of little creatures, puppets and gadgets began early (he collected snails and wrote puppet plays). Aged twelve he was sent to school at Richmond, Yorkshire, then, in 1846, to Rugby School. At the beginning of 1851 – in the year his mother died – he entered Christ Church, Oxford, to read Classics and Mathematics. From his schools and college he organized family magazines – *Useful and Instructive Poetry* ('Never stew your sister' was one of his verse contributions), the *Rectory Magazine*, the *Rectory Umbrella*. He did well in his studies, especially in maths, graduated in 1854, and began his career as Christ Church maths lecturer. At the end of 1861 he was ordained deacon in the Church of England, but never went on to become a fully fledged priest (he had fashionable doubts about the Creeds as well as a sermon-stymying stammer – he preferred giving Bible talks to children with lantern slides and a mechanical Humpty Dumpty). His last family magazine was the *Mischmasch* (1855–62) – comic juvenilia when he was hardly juvenile (as with the Brontës, the edge between so-called juvenilia and so-called adult material is very blurred: and that was probably a help to the Nonsense author). The first stanza of 'Jabberwocky' ("Twas bryllyg and ye slythy toves') first appeared in *Mischmasch* in pseudo-runic script. Meanwhile, Dodgson was sending parodies, mock rules and regulations, funny stories to *Comic Times* (1855), then to its successor the *Train*. The *Train*'s editor, Edmund Yates, picked out the name Lewis Carroll from four possible pseudonyms Dodgson offered him. Carroll was obsessed with photography and with photographing little children, especially little girls, preferably naked. He photographed many of the most distinguished writers and artists of his time – George MacDonald, Alfred Tennyson, Millais, D. G. Rossetti, and also their child relations. They stare out from these

1 Castor: slang for hat (originally beaver-fur); as is 'tile', line 8.

2 umbrella, especially one covered in gingham (more slang).

photographs, these tiny tots, now dressed up as waifs, or fictional people, now nude – shrewd-seeming miniature adults, as calculating and knowing as the street-wise steet-arabs in Dr Barnado's charity shots. It was the miniaturized sexiness of Victorian fairy painters that magnetized Carroll, the dinky-toy and gadget lover: he 'counted 165 fairies' in Joseph Noel Paton's *The Quarrel of Oberon and Titania* in 1857. Doing Tennyson's niece Agnes Grace Weld as Little Red Riding Hood led to his photographing Tennyson and the golden-ringleted sons of the poet, Hallam and Lionel – who besotted other unmarried men too, male tutors, A. J. A. Symonds, and the like. Most fruitful for literature were Carroll's dealings with the little ones of the Dean of Christ Church's family – especially Alice Liddell, the second daughter. *Alice in Wonderland* began in stories to amuse three of the Liddell girls on a picnic-outing along the Thames, 4 July 1862. *Alice's Adventures in Wonderland* was published in 1865 by Macmillan, anxious for a follow-up in the kiddy market to Kingsley's *The Water-Babies*. *Through the Looking Glass and What Alice Found There* followed at Christmas 1871. The illustrations of John Tenniel capture not only the whimsy and the chaos of Alice's *fausse-naïve* encounters but also their horror, violence and implicit sexual danger. It's a nightmare being enmeshed in the sadistically disarranged games and tangled logics of the clerical child lover with the blackened hands (black from photographic chemicals: he wore gloves in public). Mrs Liddell eventually broke off the relationship with her daughters out of worry (and there are some pages enticingly razored out of Carroll's diaries). (Mrs Tennyson had her anxieties too when Carroll sent a knife to young Hallam for Christmas with encouragement to cut himself and his brother with it.) Dodgson's article in defence of

girl actors on the public stage (in the *Theatre*, 1889) pooh-poohs the very idea of sexual danger. Child actresses, like little Ellen Ternan, were just one source of the friendships this (so to say) active-repressed paedophile made all over the country. His long mock-travel ballad, *The Hunting of the Snark* (1876), was dedicated to the nine-year-old Gertrude Chataway, encountered on the beach on the Isle of Wight in 1871. Whether the poem is an allegory used to be much debated. (In his paranoid moments Carroll's old friend D. G. Rossetti imagined it as a cryptic denigration of himself.) The dedicatory poem to *Sylvie and Bruno*, Carroll's odd mixed book for adults and children (1889–93), is a double-acrostic to Isa Bowman, the first stage Alice (1886). Nor was Carroll's pen idle. He wrote textbooks in geometry and mathematical logic, promulgated games such as the Wonderland Postage-Stamp Game (1890), turned out lots of minor satirical pamphlets on once burning issues such as university politics, campaigned against vivisection, wrote over 100,000 letters (all carefully logged in his usual manic way). His poems were gathered as *Phantasmagoria and Other Poems* (1876), expanded into *Rhyme? And Reason?* (1883). They are not all comic poems. Carroll never married – and nor did the six sisters he installed in Guildford after their father's death in 1868. He resigned his Christ Church Lectureship in 1881, but carried on living in the college. He died of bronchitis on a visit to his sisters, 14 January 1898, with his last volume of verse, *Three Sunsets and Other Poems*, at the printers. The intensity of his 'Nonsense' work substantially redefined the English nursery canon. His nonce formations – *galumphing, brillig, mimsy, frabjous, beamish*, and so forth – entered the language in numbers.

How doth the little crocodile
  Improve his shining tail,
And pour the waters of the Nile
  On every golden scale!

How cheerfully he seems to grin,
  How neatly spreads his claws,
And welcomes little fishes in,
  With gently smiling jaws!

Alice's Adventures in Wonderland *(Macmillan & Co., 1865).*

'You are old, Father William,' the young man said
  'And your hair has become very white;
And yet you incessantly stand on your head –
  Do you think, at your age, it is right?'

'In my youth', Father William replied to his son,
  'I feared it might injure the brain;
But, now that I'm perfectly sure I have none,
  Why, I do it again and again.'

'You are old,' said the youth, 'as I mentioned before,
  And have grown most uncommonly fat;

10

Yet you turned a back-somersault in at the door –
    Pray, what is the reason of that?'

'In my youth', said the sage, as he shook his grey locks,
    'I kept all my limbs very supple
By the use of this ointment – one shilling the box –
    Allow me to sell you a couple?'

'You are old,' said the youth, 'and your jaws are too weak
    For anything tougher than suet;
Yet you finished the goose, with the bones and the beak –
    Pray, how did you manage to do it?'   20

'In my youth,' said his father, 'I took to the law,
    And argued each case with my wife;
And the muscular strength, which it gave to my jaw
    Has lasted the rest of my life.'

'You are old,' said the youth, 'one would hardly suppose
    That your eye was as steady as ever;
Yet you balanced an eel on the end of your nose –
    What made you so awfully clever?'

'I have answered three questions, and that is enough,'
    Said his father, 'Don't give yourself airs!   30
Do you think I can listen all day to such stuff?
    Be off, or I'll kick you down-stairs!'

Alice's Adventures in Wonderland *(1865)*.

JABBERWOCKY

'Twas brillig, and the slithy toves
    Did gyre and gimble in the wabe:
All mimsy were the borogoves,
    And the mome raths outgrabe.

'Beware the Jabberwock, my son!
    The jaws that bite, the claws that catch!
Beware the Jubjub bird, and shun
    The frumious Bandersnatch!'

He took his vorpal sword in hand:
    Long time the manxome foe he sought –   10
So rested he by the Tumtum tree,
    And stood awhile in thought.

And, as in uffish thought he stood,
    The Jabberwock, with eyes of flame,
Came whiffling through the tulgey wood,
    And burbled as it came!

One, two! One, two! And through and through
    The vorpal blade went snicker-snack!
He left it dead, and with its head
    He went galumphing back.   20

'And hast thou slain the Jabberwock?
    Come to my arms, my beamish boy!
O frabjous day! Callooh! Callay!'
    He chortled in his joy.

'Twas brillig, and the slithy toves
    Did gyre and gimble in the wabe:
All mimsy were the borogoves,
    And the mome raths outgrabe.

Through the Looking-Glass and What Alice Found There
(Macmillan & Co., 1871: dated 1872).

In winter, when the fields are white,
I sing this song for your delight –

In spring, when woods are getting green,
I'll try and tell you what I mean:

In summer, when the days are long,
Perhaps you'll understand the song:

In autumn, when the leaves are brown,
Take pen and ink, and write it down.

I sent a message to the fish:
I told them 'This is what I wish.'   10

The little fishes of the sea,
They sent an answer back to me.

The little fishes' answer was
'We cannot do it, Sir, because –'

I sent to them again to say
'It will be better to obey'.

The fishes answered, with a grin,
'Why, what a temper you are in!'

I told them once, I told them twice:
They would not listen to advice.   20

I took a kettle large and new,
Fit for the deed I had to do.

My heart went hop, my heart went thump:
I filled the kettle at the pump.

Then some one came to me and said
'The little fishes are in bed.'

I said to him, I said it plain,
'Then you must wake them up again.'

I said it very loud and clear:
I went and shouted in his ear.   30

But he was very stiff and proud:
He said, 'You needn't shout so loud!'

And he was very proud and stiff:
He said 'I'd go and wake them, if –'

I took a corkscrew from the shelf:
I went to wake them up myself.

And when I found the door was locked,
I pulled and pushed and kicked and knocked.

And when I found the door was shut,
I tried to turn the handle, but –   40

Through the Looking Glass and What Alice Found There *(1871: dated 1872).*

THE HUNTING OF THE SNARK

An Agony in Eight Fits[1]

Fit the First

The Landing

'Just the place for a Snark!' the Bellman cried,
    As he landed his crew with care;
Supporting each man on the top of the tide
    By a finger entwined in his hair.

'Just the place for a Snark! I have said it twice:
    That alone should encourage the crew.
Just the place for a Snark! I have said it thrice:
    What I tell you three times is true.'

The crew was complete: it included a Boots –
    A maker of Bonnets and Hoods –   10
A Barrister, brought to arrange their disputes –
    And a Broker, to value their goods.

A Billiard-marker, whose skill was immense,
    Might perhaps have won more than his share –
But a Banker, engaged at enormous expense,
    Had the whole of their cash in his care.

There was also a Beaver, that paced on the deck,
    Or would sit making lace in the bow:
And had often (the Bellman said) saved them from wreck
    Though none of the sailors knew how.   20

There was one who was famed for the number of things
    He forgot when he entered the ship:
His umbrella, his watch, all his jewels and rings,
    And the clothes he had bought for the trip.

He had forty-two boxes, all carefully packed,
    With his name painted clearly on each:
But, since he omitted to mention the fact,
    They were all left behind on the beach.

THE HUNTING OF THE SNARK
1   fit: a section of a poem.

The loss of his clothes hardly mattered, because
    He had seven coats on when he came,
With three pair of boots – but the worst of it was,
    He had wholly forgotten his name.   30

He would answer to 'Hi' or to any loud cry,
    Such as 'Fry me!' or 'Fritter my wig!'
To 'What-you-may-call-um!' or 'What-was-his-name!'
    But especially 'Thing-um-a-jig!'

While, for those who preferred a more forcible word,
    He had different names from these:
His intimate friends called him 'Candle-ends',
    And his enemies 'Toasted-cheese'.   40

'His form is ungainly – his intellect small –'
    (So the Bellman would often remark)
'But his courage is perfect! And that, after all,
    Is the thing that one needs with a Snark.'

He would joke with hyænas, returning their stare
    With an impudent wag of the head:
And he once went a walk, paw-in-paw, with a bear,
    'Just to keep up its spirits,' he said.

He came as a Baker: but owned, when too late –
    And it drove the poor Bellman half-mad –   50
He could only bake Bridecake – for which, I may state,
    No materials were to be had.

The last of the crew needs especial remark,
    Though he looked an incredible dunce:
He had just one idea – but, that one being 'Snark',
    The good Bellman engaged him at once.

He came as a Butcher: but gravely declared,
    When the ship had been sailing a week,
He could only kill Beavers. The Bellman looked scared,
    And was almost too frightened to speak: 60

But at length he explained, in a tremulous tone,
    There was only one Beaver on board;
And that was a tame one he had of his own,
    Whose death would be deeply deplored.

The Beaver, who happened to hear the remark,
    Protested, with tears in its eyes,
That not even the rapture of hunting the Snark
    Could atone for that dismal surprise!

It strongly advised that the Butcher should be
    Conveyed in a separate ship: 70
But the Bellman declared that would never agree
    With the plans he had made for the trip:

Navigation was always a difficult art,
    Though with only one ship and one bell:
And he feared he must really decline, for his part,
    Undertaking another as well.

The Beaver's best course was, no doubt, to procure
    A second-hand dagger-proof coat –
So the Baker advised it – and next, to insure
    Its life in some Office of note: 80

This the Baker suggested, and offered for hire
    (On moderate terms), or for sale,
Two excellent Policies, one Against Fire
    And one Against Damage From Hail.

Yet still, ever after that sorrowful day,
    Whenever the Butcher was by,
The Beaver kept looking the opposite way,
    And appeared unaccountably shy.

Fit the Second

The Bellman's Speech

The Bellman himself they all praised to the skies –
    Such a carriage, such ease and such grace!
Such solemnity, too! One could see he was wise,
    The moment one looked in his face!

He had bought a large map representing the sea,
    Without the least vestige of land:
And the crew were much pleased when they found it to be
    A map they could all understand.

'What's the good of Mercator's North Poles and Equators,
    Tropics, Zones, and Meridian Lines?'   10
So the Bellman would cry: and the crew would reply
    'They are merely conventional signs!

'Other maps are such shapes, with their islands and capes!
    But we've got our brave Captain to thank'
(So the crew would protest) 'that he's bought us the best –
    A perfect and absolute blank!'

This was charming, no doubt: but they shortly found out
    That the Captain they trusted so well
Had only one notion for crossing the ocean,
    And that was to tingle his bell.   20

He was thoughtful and grave – but the orders he gave
    Were enough to bewilder a crew.
When he cried 'Steer to starboard, but keep her head larboard!'
    What on earth was the helmsman to do?

Then the bowsprit got mixed with the rudder sometimes:
    A thing, as the Bellman remarked,
That frequently happens in tropical climes,
    When a vessel is, so to speak, 'snarked'.

But the principal failing occurred in the sailing,
    And the Bellman, perplexed and distressed,   30
Said he *had* hoped, at least, when the wind blew due East,
    That the ship would *not* travel due West!

But the danger was past – they had landed at last,
    With their boxes, portmanteaus, and bags:

Yet at first sight the crew were not pleased with the view
    Which consisted of chasms and crags.

The Bellman perceived that their spirits were low,
    And repeated in musical tone
Some jokes he had kept for a season of woe –
    But the crew would do nothing but groan.   40

He served out some grog with a liberal hand,
    And bade them sit down on the beach:
And they could not but own that their Captain looked grand,
    As he stood and delivered his speech.

'Friends, Romans, and countrymen, lend me your ears!'[2]
    (They were all of them fond of quotations:
So they drank to his health, and they gave him three cheers,
    While he served out additional rations).

'We have sailed many months, we have sailed many weeks,
    (Four weeks to the month you may mark),   50
But never as yet ('tis your Captain who speaks)
    Have we caught the least glimpse of a Snark!

'We have sailed many weeks, we have sailed many days,
    (Seven days to the week I allow),
But a Snark, on the which we might lovingly gaze,
    We have never beheld till now!

'Come, listen, my men, while I tell you again
    The five unmistakable marks
By which you may know, wheresoever you go,
    The warranted genuine Snarks.   60

'Let us take them in order. The first is the taste,
    Which is meagre and hollow, but crisp:
Like a coat that is rather too tight in the waist,
    With a flavour of Will-o-the-Wisp.

'Its habit of getting up late you'll agree
    That it carries too far, when I say
That it frequently breakfasts at five-o'clock tea,
    And dines on the following day.

'The third is its slowness in taking a jest.
    Should you happen to venture on one,   70
It will sigh like a thing that is deeply distressed:
    And it always looks grave at a pun.

'The fourth is its fondness for bathing-machines,
    Which it constantly carries about,
And believes that they add to the beauty of scenes –
    A sentiment open to doubt.

'The fifth is ambition. It next will be right
    To describe each particular batch:
Distinguishing those that have feathers, and bite,
    From those that have whiskers, and scratch.   80

---

2 Marc Antony in Shakespeare's *Julius Caesar*, III. ii. 74.

'For, although common Snarks do no manner of harm,
    Yet I feel it my duty to say
Some are Boojums –' The Bellman broke off in alarm,
    For the Baker had fainted away.

Fit the Third

The Baker's Tale

They roused him with muffins – they roused him with ice –
    They roused him with mustard and cress –
They roused him with jam and judicious advice –
    They set him conundrums to guess.

When at length he sat up and was able to speak,
    His sad story he offered to tell;
And the Bellman cried 'Silence! Not even a shriek!'
    And excitedly tingled his bell.

There was silence supreme! Not a shriek, not a scream,
    Scarcely even a howl or a groan,   10
As the man they called 'Ho!' told his story of woe
    In an antediluvian tone.

'My father and mother were honest, though poor –'
    'Skip all that!' cried the Bellman in haste.
'If it once becomes dark, there's no chance of a Snark –
    We have hardly a minute to waste!'

'I skip forty years,' said the Baker in tears,
    'And proceed without further remark
To the day when you took me aboard of your ship
    To help you in hunting the Snark.   20

'A dear uncle of mine (after whom I was named)
    Remarked, when I bade him farewell –'
'Oh, skip your dear uncle!' the Bellman exclaimed,
    As he angrily tingled his bell.

'He remarked to me then,' said that mildest of men,
    '"If your Snark be a Snark, that is right:
Fetch it home by all means – you may serve it with greens,
    And it's handy for striking a light.

'"You may seek it with thimbles – and seek it with care;
    You may hunt it with forks and hope;   30
You may threaten its life with a railway-share;
    You may charm it with smiles and soap –"'

('That's exactly the method,' the Bellman bold
    In a hasty parenthesis cried,
'That's exactly the way I have always been told
    That the capture of Snarks should be tried!')

'"But oh, beamish nephew, beware of the day,
    If your Snark be a Boojum! For then
You will softly and suddenly vanish away,
    And never be met with again!"   40

'It is this, it is this that oppresses my soul,
    When I think of my uncle's last words:

And my heart is like nothing so much as a bowl
    Brimming over with quivering curds!

'It is this, it is this –' 'We have had that before!'
    The Bellman indignantly said.
And the Baker replied 'Let me say it once more.
    It is this, it is this that I dread!

'I engage with the Snark – every night after dark –
    In a dreamy delirious fight: 50
I serve it with greens in those shadowy scenes,
    And I use it for striking a light:

'But if ever I meet with a Boojum, that day,
    In a moment (of this I am sure),
I shall softly and suddenly vanish away –
    And the notion I cannot endure!'

Fit the Fourth

The Hunting

The Bellman looked uffish, and wrinkled his brow.
    'If only you'd spoken before!
It's excessively awkward to mention it now,
    With the Snark, so to speak, at the door!

'We should all of us grieve, as you well may believe,
    If you never were met with again –
But surely, my man, when the voyage began,
    You might have suggested it then?

'It's excessively awkward to mention it now –
    As I think I've already remarked.'   10
And the man they called 'Hi!' replied, with a sigh,
    'I informed you the day we embarked.

'You may charge me with murder – or want of sense –
    (We are all of us weak at times):
But the slightest approach to a false pretence
    Was never among my crimes!

'I said it in Hebrew – I said it in Dutch –
    I said it in German and Greek:
But I wholly forgot (and it vexes me much)
    That English is what you speak!'   20

' 'Tis a pitiful tale,' said the Bellman, whose face
    Had grown longer at every word:
'But, now that you've stated the whole of your case,
    More debate would be simply absurd.

'The rest of my speech' (he exclaimed to his men)
    'You shall hear when I've leisure to speak it.
But the Snark is at hand, let me tell you again!
    'Tis your glorious duty to seek it!

'To seek it with thimbles, to seek it with care;
    To pursue it with forks and hope;   30
To threaten its life with a railway-share;
    To charm it with smiles and soap!

'For the Snark's a peculiar creature, that won't
    Be caught in a commonplace way.
Do all that you know, and try all that you don't:
    Not a chance must be wasted to-day!

'For England expects – I forbear to proceed:
    'Tis a maxim tremendous, but trite:
And you'd best be unpacking the things that you need
    To rig yourselves out for the fight.'   40

Then the Banker endorsed a blank cheque (which he crossed),
    And changed his loose silver for notes:
The Baker with care combed his whiskers and hair,
    And shook the dust out of his coats:

The Boots and the Broker were sharpening a spade –
    Each working the grindstone in turn:
But the Beaver went on making lace, and displayed
    No interest in the concern:

Though the Barrister tried to appeal to its pride,
    And vainly proceeded to cite   50
A number of cases, in which making laces
    Had been proved an infringement of right.

The maker of Bonnets ferociously planned
    A novel arrangement of bows:
While the Billiard-marker with quivering hand
    Was chalking the tip of his nose.

But the Butcher turned nervous, and dressed himself fine,
    With yellow kid gloves and a ruff –
Said he felt it exactly like going to dine,
    Which the Bellman declared was all 'stuff'.   60

'Introduce me, now there's a good fellow,' he said,
    'If we happen to meet it together!'
And the Bellman, sagaciously nodding his head,
    Said 'That must depend on the weather.'

The Beaver went simply galumphing about,
    At seeing the Butcher so shy:
And even the Baker, though stupid and stout,
    Made an effort to wink with one eye.

'Be a man!' said the Bellman in wrath, as he heard
    The Butcher beginning to sob.   70
'Should we meet with a Jubjub, that desperate bird,
    We shall need all our strength for the job!'

Fit the Fifth

The Beaver's Lesson
They sought it with thimbles, they sought it with care;
    They pursued it with forks and hope;
They threatened its life with a railway-share;
    They charmed it with smiles and soap.

Then the Butcher contrived an ingenious plan
    For making a separate sally;

And had fixed on a spot unfrequented by man,
   A dismal and desolate valley.

But the very same plan to the Beaver occurred:
   It had chosen the very same place: 10
Yet neither betrayed, by a sign or a word,
   The disgust that appeared in his face.

Each thought he was thinking of nothing but 'Snark'
   And the glorious work of the day;
And each tried to pretend that he did not remark
   That the other was going that way.

But the valley grew narrow and narrower still,
   And the evening got darker and colder,
Till (merely from nervousness, not from good will)
   They marched along shoulder to shoulder.   20

Then a scream, shrill and high, rent the shuddering sky
   And they knew that some danger was near:
The Beaver turned pale to the tip of its tail,
   And even the Butcher felt queer.

He thought of his childhood, left far behind –
   That blissful and innocent state –
The sound so exactly recalled to his mind
   A pencil that squeaks on a slate!

' 'Tis the voice of the Jubjub!' he suddenly cried.
   (This man, that they used to call 'Dunce'.)   30
'As the Bellman would tell you,' he added with pride,
   'I have uttered that sentiment once.

' 'Tis the note of the Jubjub! Keep count, I entreat.
   You will find I have told it you twice.
'Tis the song of the Jubjub! The proof is complete.
   If only I've stated it thrice.'

The Beaver had counted with scrupulous care,
   Attending to every word:
But it fairly lost heart, and outgrabe in despair,
   When the third repetition occurred.   40

It felt that, in spite of all possible pains,
   It had somehow contrived to lose count,
And the only thing now was to rack its poor brains
   By reckoning up the amount.

'Two added to one – if that could but be done',
   It said, 'with one's fingers and thumbs!'
Recollecting with tears how, in earlier years,
   It had taken no pains with its sums.

'The thing can be done,' said the Butcher, 'I think.
   The thing must be done, I am sure.   50
The thing shall be done! Bring me paper and ink,
   The best there is time to procure.'

The Beaver brought paper, portfolio, pens,
   And ink in unfailing supplies:

While strange creepy creatures came out of their dens,
    And watched them with wondering eyes.

So engrossed was the Butcher, he heeded them not,
    As he wrote with a pen in each hand,
And explained all the while in a popular style
    Which the Beaver could well understand.   60

'Taking Three as the subject to reason about –
    A convenient number to state –
We add Seven, and Ten, and then multiply out
    By One Thousand diminished by Eight.

'The result we proceed to divide, as you see,
    By Nine Hundred and Ninety and Two:
Then subtract Seventeen, and the answer must be
    Exactly and perfectly true.

'The method employed I would gladly explain,
    While I have it so clear in my head,   70
If I had but the time and you had but the brain –
    But much yet remains to be said.

'In one moment I've seen what has hitherto been
    Enveloped in absolute mystery,
And without extra charge I will give you at large
    A Lesson in Natural History.'

In his genial way he proceeded to say
    (Forgetting all laws of propriety,
And that giving instruction, without introduction,
    Would have caused quite a thrill in Society),   80

'As to temper the Jubjub's a desperate bird.
    Since it lives in perpetual passion:
Its taste in costume is entirely absurd –
    It is ages ahead of the fashion:

'But it knows any friend it has met once before:
    It never will look at a bribe:
And in charity-meetings it stands at the door,
    And collects – though it does not subscribe.

'Its flavour when cooked is more exquisite far
    Than mutton, or oysters, or eggs: 90
(Some think it keeps best in an ivory jar,
    And some, in mahogany kegs:)

'You boil it in sawdust: you salt it in glue:
    You condense it with locusts and tape:
Still keeping one principal object in view –
    To preserve its symmetrical shape.'

The Butcher would gladly have talked till next day,
    But he felt that the Lesson must end,
And he wept with delight in attempting to say
    He considered the Beaver his friend: 100

While the Beaver confessed, with affectionate looks
    More eloquent even than tears,

It had learned in ten minutes far more than all books
   Would have taught it in seventy years.

They returned hand-in-hand, and the Bellman, unmanned
   (For a moment) with noble emotion,
Said 'This amply repays all the wearisome days
   We have spent on the billowy ocean!'

Such friends, as the Beaver and Butcher became,
   Have seldom if ever been known;   110
In winter or summer, 'twas always the same –
   You could never meet either alone.

And when quarrels arose – as one frequently finds
   Quarrels will, spite of every endeavour –
The song of the Jubjub recurred to their minds,
   And cemented their friendship for ever!

Fit the Sixth

The Barrister's Dream

They sought it with thimbles, they sought it with care;
   They pursued it with forks and hope;
They threatened its life with a railway-share;
   They charmed it with smiles and soap.

But the Barrister, weary of proving in vain
   That the Beaver's lace-making was wrong,
Fell asleep, and in dreams saw the creature quite plain
   That his fancy had dwelt on so long.

He dreamed that he stood in a shadowy Court,
   Where the Snark, with a glass in its eye,   10
Dressed in gown, bands, and wig, was defending a pig
   On the charge of deserting its sty.

The Witnesses proved, without error or flaw,
   That the sty was deserted when found:
And the Judge kept explaining the state of the law
   In a soft under-current of sound.

The indictment had never been clearly expressed,
   And it seemed that the Snark had begun,
And had spoken three hours, before any one guessed
   What the pig was supposed to have done.   20

The Jury had each formed a different view
   (Long before the indictment was read),
And they all spoke at once, so that none of them knew
   One word that the others had said.

'You must know –' said the Judge: but the Snark exclaimed 'Fudge!
   That statute is obsolete quite!
Let me tell you, my friends, the whole question depends
   On an ancient manorial right.

'In the matter of Treason the pig would appear
   To have aided, but scarcely abetted: 30
While the charge of Insolvency fails, it is clear,
   If you grant the plea "never indebted".

'The fact of Desertion I will not dispute:
　　But its guilt, as I trust, is removed
(So far as relates to the costs of this suit)
　　By the Alibi which has been proved.

'My poor client's fate now depends on your votes.'
　　Here the speaker sat down in his place,
And directed the Judge to refer to his notes
　　And briefly to sum up the case.　　　　　　　　　　　　40

But the Judge said he never had summed up before;
　　So the Snark undertook it instead,
And summed it so well that it came to far more
　　Than the Witnesses ever had said!

When the verdict was called for, the Jury declined,
　　As the word was so puzzling to spell;
But they ventured to hope that the Snark wouldn't mind
　　Undertaking that duty as well.

So the Snark found the verdict, although, as it owned,
　　It was spent with the toils of the day:　　　　　　　　50
When it said the word 'GUILTY!' the Jury all groaned
　　And some of them fainted away.

Then the Snark pronounced sentence, the Judge being quite
　　Too nervous to utter a word:
When it rose to its feet, there was silence like night,
　　And the fall of a pin might be heard.

'Transportation for life' was the sentence it gave,
　　'And *then* to be fined forty pound.'
The Jury all cheered, though the Judge said he feared
　　That the phrase was not legally sound.　　　　　　　　60

But their wild exultation was suddenly checked
　　When the jailer informed them, with tears,
Such a sentence would have not the slightest effect,
　　As the pig had been dead for some years.

The Judge left the Court, looking deeply disgusted:
　　But the Snark, though a little aghast,
As the lawyer to whom the defence was intrusted,
　　Went bellowing on to the last.

Thus the Barrister dreamed, while the bellowing seemed
　　To grow every moment more clear:　　　　　　　　　70
Till he woke to the knell of a furious bell,
　　Which the Bellman rang close at his ear.

Fit the Seventh

The Banker's Fate

They sought it with thimbles, they sought it with care;
　　They pursued it with forks and hope;
They threatened its life with a railway-share;
　　They charmed it with smiles and soap.

And the Banker, inspired with a courage so new
　　It was matter for general remark,

Rushed madly ahead and was lost to their view
    In his zeal to discover the Snark.

But while he was seeking with thimbles and care,
    A Bandersnatch swiftly drew nigh   10
And grabbed at the Banker, who shrieked in despair,
    For he knew it was useless to fly.

He offered large discount – he offered a cheque
    (Drawn 'to bearer') for seven-pounds-ten:
But the Bandersnatch merely extended its neck
    And grabbed at the Banker again.

Without rest or pause – while those frumious jaws
    Went savagely snapping around –
He skipped and he hopped, and he floundered and flopped,
    Till fainting he fell to the ground.   20

The Bandersnatch fled as the others appeared
    Led on by that fear-stricken yell:
And the Bellman remarked 'It is just as I feared!'
    And solemnly tolled on his bell.

He was black in the face, and they scarcely could trace
    The least likeness to what he had been:
While so great was his fright that his waistcoat turned white –
    A wonderful thing to be seen!

To the horror of all who were present that day,
    He uprose in full evening dress,   30
And with senseless grimaces endeavoured to say
    What his tongue could no longer express.

Down he sank in a chair – ran his hands through his hair –
    And chanted in mimsiest tones
Words whose utter inanity proved his insanity,
    While he rattled a couple of bones.

'Leave him here to his fate – it is getting so late!'
    The Bellman exclaimed in a fright.
'We have lost half the day. Any further delay,
    And we sha'n't catch a Snark before night!'   40

Fit the Eighth

The Vanishing

They sought it with thimbles, they sought it with care;
    They pursued it with forks and hope;
They threatened its life with a railway-share;
    They charmed it with smiles and soap.

They shuddered to think that the chase might fail,
    And the Beaver, excited at last,
Went bounding along on the tip of its tail,
    For the daylight was nearly past.

'There is Thingumbob shouting!' the Bellman said.
    'He is shouting like mad, only hark!   10

He is waving his hands, he is wagging his head,
  He has certainly found a Snark!'

They gazed in delight, while the Butcher exclaimed
  'He was always a desperate wag!'
They beheld him – their Baker – their hero unnamed –
  On the top of a neighbouring crag,

Erect and sublime, for one moment of time,
  In the next, that wild figure they saw
(As if stung by a spasm) plunge into a chasm,
  While they waited and listened in awe.   20

'It's a Snark!' was the sound that first came to their ears,
  And seemed almost too good to be true.
Then followed a torrent of laughter and cheers:
  Then the ominous words 'It's a Boo—'

Then, silence. Some fancied they heard in the air
  A weary and wandering sigh
That sounded like '—jum!' but the others declare
  It was only a breeze that went by.

They hunted till darkness came on, but they found
  Not a button, or feather, or mark,   30
By which they could tell that they stood on the ground
  Where the Baker had met with the Snark.

In the midst of the word he was trying to say,
  In the midst of his laughter and glee,
He had softly and suddenly vanished away –
  For the Snark *was* a Boojum, you see.

      The Hunting of the Snark: An Agony in Eight Fits *(Macmillan & Co., 1876).*

POETA FIT, NON NASCITUR[1]

'How shall I be a poet?
  How shall I write in rhyme?
You told me once "the very wish
  Partook of the sublime".
Then tell me how! Don't put me off
  With your "another time"!'

The old man smiled to see him,
  To hear his sudden sally;
He liked the lad to speak his mind
  Enthusiastically;   10
And thought 'There's no hum-drum in him,
  Nor any shilly-shally.'

'And would you be a poet
  Before you've been to school?

POETA FIT, NON NASCITUR
1 'A poet is made, not born.' (Has a classical ring to it, but has no
classical source.)

Ah, well! I hardly thought you
    So absolute a fool.
First learn to be spasmodic –
    A very simple rule.

'For first you write a sentence,
    And then you chop it small;   20
Then mix the bits, and sort them out
    Just as they chance to fall:
The order of the phrases makes
    No difference at all.

'Then, if you'd be impressive,
    Remember what I say,
That abstract qualities begin
    With capitals alway:
The True, the Good, the Beautiful –
    Those are the things that pay!   30

'Next, when you are describing
    A shape, or sound, or tint;
Don't state the matter plainly,
    But put it in a hint;
And learn to look at all things
    With a sort of mental squint.'

'For instance, if I wished, Sir,
    Of mutton-pies to tell,
Should I say "dreams of fleecy flocks
    Pent in a wheaten cell"?'   40
'Why, yes,' the old man said: 'that phrase
    Would answer very well.

'Then fourthly, there are epithets
    That suit with any word –
As well as Harvey's Reading Sauce
    With fish, or flesh, or bird –
Of these, "wild", "lonely", "weary", "strange",
    Are much to be preferred.'

'And will it do, O will it do
    To take them in a lump –   50
As "the wild man went his weary way
    To a strange and lonely pump"?'
'Nay, nay! You must not hastily
    To such conclusions jump.

'Such epithets, like pepper,
    Give zest to what you write;
And, if you strew them sparely,
    They whet the appetite:
But if you lay them on too thick,
    You spoil the matter quite!   60

'Last, as to the arrangement:
    Your reader, you should show him,
Must take what information he
    Can get, and look for no im-

mature disclosure of the drift
    And purpose of your poem.

'Therefore, to test his patience –
    How much he can endure –
Mention no places, names, or dates,
    And evermore be sure   70
Throughout the poem to be found
    Consistently obscure.

'First fix upon the limit
    To which it shall extend:
Then fill it up with "Padding"[2]
    (Beg some of any friend):
Your great SENSATION-STANZA
    You place towards the end.'

'And what is a Sensation,
    Grandfather, tell me, pray?   80
I think I never heard the word
    So used before to-day:
Be kind enough to mention one
    "*Exempli gratiâ*".'[3]

And the old man, looking sadly
    Across the garden-lawn,
Where here and there a dew-drop
    Yet glittered in the dawn,
Said 'Go to the Adelphi,
    And see the "Colleen Bawn".[4]   90

'The word is due to Boucicault –
    The theory is his,
Where life becomes a Spasm,
    And History a Whiz:
If that is not Sensation,
    I don't know what it is.

'Now try your hand, ere Fancy
    Have lost its present glow –'
'And then,' his grandson added,
    'We'll publish it, you know: 100
Green cloth – gold-lettered at the back –
    In duodecimo!'

Then proudly smiled that old man
    To see the eager lad
Rush madly for his pen and ink
    And for his blotting-pad –
But, when he thought of *publishing*,
    His face grew stern and sad.

Rhyme? And Reason? *(Macmillan & Co., 1883)*.

2 a usage coined, apparently, by Walter Bagehot.   4 play by Dion Boucicault (1820?–90), Irish dramatist (1860).
3 for example (usually abbreviated to 'e.g.').

Joseph Skipsey (1832–1903)

Joseph Skipsey, the collier poet, was born, 17 March 1832, in a parish of Tynemouth, Northumberland, youngest of a coalminer's eight children. His father, Cuthbert Skipsey, was shot dead by special constables during a coal-strike. Joseph went down the mine at the age of seven, never attended school, but taught himself to write and read – at first only the Bible, then Milton, Shakespeare, Burns and translations, particularly of Goethe's *Faust* and Heine. At the age of twenty he walked to London, worked in railway construction, married (1854) his boarding-house landlady Sara Ann Headley, and moved back north to the Durham coalfield. A volume of *Poems* (1859) brought him to the attention of James Clepham, editor of the *Gateshead Observer*, who got him lighter work, including a spell as assistant librarian to the Newcastle Literary and Philosophical Society. He was encouraged in his writing by Thomas Dixon, a Sunderland working-man who was in Ruskin's ambit. Over the years the volumes of verse appeared in considerable numbers – *Poems, Songs and Ballads* (1862), *The Collier Lad, and Other Lyrics* (1864), *Poems* (1871), *A Book of Miscellaneous Lyrics* (1878) – reissued, amended, as *A Book of Lyrics* (1881), *Carols from the Coalfields* (1886), *Songs and Lyrics* (1892). Skipsey wrote prefaces to reprints of poets like Burns, Shelley and Blake, and lectured (1883) on 'The Poet as Seer and Singer' to the Newcastle Literary and Philosophical Society ('the poet who would sing his thoughts into the hearts and souls of his fellow-men, must to some extent live the lives of these men…Like the most prosaic of these, he will have his ups and downs in the great battle of human life, and, like them, he will have its manifold duties to perform; for though he is born with a golden bell in his soul, he may not be born with a silver spoon in his mouth'). The lecture was published in *Igdrasil – Journal of the Ruskin Reading Guild* in 1890. Literary London, especially the Pre-Raphaelites, warmed to Skipsey's verses. D. G. Rossetti was especially keen on this coalminer-poet. Theodore Watts-Dunton enthused in the *Athenaeum* (November 1878) over the *Book of Miscellaneous Lyrics*. Through Thomas Dixon, Skipsey met Burne-Jones in London – who campaigned to get Skipsey a small Civil List Pension. Oscar Wilde compared *Carols from the Coalfields* with Blake. When Skipsey gave up mining for good, he worked as a school caretaker in Newcastle (1882–5), then as a janitor at Armstrong College in Durham (1888–9). In June 1889, supported by the cultural glitterati (Browning, Alfred Tennyson, John Morley, William Morris, D. G. Burne-Jones and others) Skipsey and his wife became custodians of Shakespeare's Birthplace in Stratford-upon-Avon. They resigned in October 1891, fed up with ministering to tourists, and returned to northern retirement. The germ of Henry James's story 'The Birthplace' came from reports of Skipsey's experiences in Stratford. Sara Ann died, August 1902; Skipsey himself died, in Gateshead, 3 September 1903.

MOTHER WEPT

Mother wept, and father sighed;
  With delight a-glow
Cried the lad, 'to-morrow,' cried,
  'To the pit I go.'

Up and down the place he sped, –
  Greeted old and young;
Far and wide the tidings spread;
  Clapt his hands and sung.

Came his cronies; some to gaze
  Wrapt in wonder; some
Free with counsel; some with praise;
  Some with envy dumb.

'May he,' many a gossip cried,
  'Be from peril kept;'

Father hid his face and sighed,
   Mother turned and wept.

A Book of Lyrics, Including Songs, Ballads, and Chants,
new edition, revised (David Bogue, 1881).

'GET UP!'

'Get up!' the caller calls, 'Get up!'
   And in the dead of night,
To win the bairns their bite and sup,
   I rise a weary wight.

My flannel dudden donn'd, thrice o'er
   My birds are kiss'd, and then
I with a whistle shut the door,
   I may never ope again.

A Book of Lyrics (1881).

THE COLLIER LAD

My lad he is a Collier Lad,
   And ere the lark awakes,
He's up and away to spend the day
   Where daylight never breaks;
But when at last the day has pass'd,
   Clean washed and cleanly clad,
He courts his Nell who loveth well
   Her handsome Collier Lad.

      Chorus
There's not his match in smoky Shields;
   Newcastle never had   10
A lad more tight, more trim, nor bright
   Than is my Collier Lad.

Tho' doomed to labour under ground,
   A merry lad is he;
And when a holiday comes round,
   He'll spend that day in glee;
He'll tell his tale o'er a pint of ale,
   And crack his joke, and bad
Must be the heart who loveth not
   To hear the Collier Lad.   20

At bowling matches on the green
   He ever takes the lead,
For none can swing his arm and fling
   With such a pith and speed:
His bowl is seen to skim the green,
   And bound as if right glad
To hear the cry of victory
   Salute the Collier Lad.

When 'gainst the wall they play the ball,
    He's never known to lag,   30
But up and down he gars it bound,
    Till all his rivals fag;
When deftly – lo! he strikes a blow
    Which gars them all look sad,
And wonder how it came to pass
    They play'd the Collier Lad.

The quoits are out, the hobs are fix'd,
    The first round quoit he flings
Enrings the hob; and lo! the next
    The hob again enrings;   40
And thus he'll play the summer day,
    The theme of those who gad;
And youngsters shrink to bet their brass
    Against the Collier Lad.

When in the dance he doth advance,
    The rest all sigh to see
How he can spring and kick his heels,
    When they a-wearied be;
Your one-two-three, with either knee
    He'll beat, and then, glee-mad,   50
A heel-o'er-head leap crowns the dance
    Danced by the Collier Lad.

Besides a will and pith and skill,
    My laddie owns a heart
That never once would suffer him
    To act a cruel part;
That to the poor would ope the door
    To share the last he had;
And many a secret blessing's pour'd
    Upon my Collier Lad.   60

He seldom goes to church, I own,
    And when he does, why then,
He with a leer will sit and hear,
    And doubt the holy men;
This very much annoys my heart;
    But soon as we are wed,
To please the priest, I'll do my best
    To tame my Collier Lad.

Songs and Lyrics, collected and revised (Walter Scott, 1892).
Revised and expanded version of text in A Book of Lyrics,
Including Songs, Ballads, and Chants *(1881).*

The Revd R. W. (Richard Watson) Dixon (1833–1900)

R. W. Dixon, church historian, poet and friend of poets, was born, 5 May 1833, in Islington, eldest child of a cultured family of Methodists who kept up their traditional Anglican connexions after the fashion originally approved by John Wesley. Dixon's father, the Revd Dr James Dixon, was a distinguished Wesleyan preacher; his mother, Mary Watson, herself the daughter of a Wesleyan minister, was a good musician and excellent linguist (well up in Latin,

Greek, French and Italian). Dixon went to King Edward's School, Birmingham, where he was friends with Charles Faulkner, later a key Morrisian Socialist, and Edward (Ted) Jones – later Burne-Jones, the famous Pre-Raphaelite painter. At Oxford from 1853 Dixon was a key figure in the second-wave Pre-Raphaelite group, that is the 'Birmingham Group' of friends – William Fulford, Faulkner, Cormell Price (who later founded Kipling's school, the United Services College, and got into *Stalky & Co.*), all, like Dixon, at Pembroke College; and Jones at Exeter College, afforced by the only non-Birmingham boy among them, Exeter College's William Morris. They were all Anglo-Catholic Tractarians (most of them intending at the time to take Holy Orders), devoted medievalizers, Tennyson fans ('Poetry was the thing'; 'it was felt with justice that this was due to Tennyson, Tennyson had invented a new poetry, a new poetic English: his use of words was new, and every piece that he wrote was a conquest of a new region. This lasted till "Maud", in 1855'), devotees too of Ruskin's *The Stones of Venice*. After Oxford (BA in Classics, 1857), Dixon lived for a while with Morris and Jones in Red Lion Square in London. He was part of Rossetti's gang of enthusiasts who amateurishly adorned the new and fashionably Gothic Oxford Union building with Arthurian frescoes in the summer vacation of 1857. In 1858 he was ordained to a Lambeth curacy, and shortly after, April 1859, he officiated at William Morris's wedding in Oxford to Janey (and, as everyone thought he might, did indeed address the couple as 'William and Mary'). His church career shuffled along very tardily indeed, and he never obtained the large preferments – and salaries – his friends thought he deserved, despite the vast *History of the Church of England from the Abolition of the Roman Jurisdiction* which he became renowned for. He spent most of his life as a shabby, hard-worked parish priest, his promotions consisting of a couple of rural deanships and an honorary canonry at Carlisle Cathedral. For several years he was a schoolmaster, in London, later in Carlisle. At Highgate School he taught Gerard Manley Hopkins, who out of the blue sent his old schoolmaster a fan letter (June 1878), praising his volume *Christ's Company and Other Poems* (1861) as worthy of Keats, and regretting Dixon's lack of fame. Thus began a devoted friendship and literary-critical correspondence (published only in 1935) with the poet whose genius Dixon was one of the very few to know about, let alone recognize. Dixon's better poems are indeed the early ones of the *Christ's Company* volume – highly coloured and textured, as well as devout, in a recognizably Pre-Raphaelite idiom. *Historical Odes* appeared in 1863, and there were later volumes and pamphlets of verse, including the narrative poem *Mano* (1883), but the later writing energy really went into his father's *Life* (1874), sermons, and the big *History*. Dixon was married twice: in 1861 to Maria Sturgeon, a widow with daughters, who died in 1876; and in 1882 to Matilda Routledge. He had no children of his own. In December 1891 he was severely weakened by influenza, and he died in January 1900 after a short bout of the flu.

St Mary Magdalene

Kneeling before the altar step,
    Her white face stretched above her hands;
In one great line her body thin
Rose robed right upwards to her chin;
Her hair rebelled in golden bands,
    And filled her hands;

Which likewise held a casket rare
    Of alabaster at that tide;
Simeon was there and looked at her,
Trancedly kneeling, sick and fair;
Three parts the light her features tried,   10
    She rest implied.

Strong singing reached her from within,
    Discordant, but with weighty rhymes;
Her swaying body kept the stave;
Then all the woods about her wave,
She heard, and saw, in mystic mimes,
    Herself three times.

Once, in the doorway of a house,
    With yellow lintels painted fair,
Very far off, where no men pass,   20

Green and red banners hung in mass
Above scorched woodwork wormed and bare,
    And spider's snare.

She, scarlet in her form and gold,
    Fallen down upon her hands and knees,
Her arms and bosom bare and white,
Her long hair streaming wild with light,
Felt all the waving of the trees,
    And hum of bees.   30

A rout of mirth within the house,
    Upon the ear of madness fell,
Stunned with its dread, yet made intense;
A moment, and might issue thence
Upon the prey they quested well,
    Seven fiends of hell.

She grovelled on her hands and knees,
    She bit her breath against that rout;
Seven devils inhabited within,
Each acting upon each his sin,   40
Limb locked in limb, snout turning snout,
    And these would out.

Twice, and the woods lay far behind,
    Gold corn spread broad from slope to slope
The copses rounded in faint light,
Far from her pathway gleaming white,
Which gleamed and wound in narrow scope,
    Her narrow hope.

She on the valley stood and hung,
    Then downward swept with steady haste;   50
The steady wind behind her sent
Her robe before her as she went;
Descending on the wind, she chased
    The form she traced.

She, with her blue eyes blind with flight,
    Rising and falling in their cells,
Hands held as though she played a harp,
Teeth glistening as in laughter sharp,
Flew ghostly on, a strength like hell's,
    When it rebels.   60

Behind her, flaming on and on,
    Rushing and streaming as she flew;
Moved over hill as if through vale,
Through vale as if o'er hill, no fail;
Her bosom trembled as she drew
    Her long breath through.

Thrice, with an archway overhead,
    Beneath, what might have seemed a tomb;
White garments fallen fold on fold,
As if limbs yet were in their hold,   70
Drew the light further in the gloom,
    Of the dark room.

She, fallen without thought or care,
   Heard, as it were, a ceaseless flow
Of converse muttered in her ear,
Like waters sobbing wide and near,
About things happened long ago
   Of utter woe.

Christ's Company and Other Poems *(Smith, Elder, 1861)*.

DREAM

I

With camel's hair I clothed my skin,
   I fed my mouth with honey wild;
And set me scarlet wool to spin,
   And all my breast with hyssop filled;
Upon my brow and cheeks and chin
   A bird's blood spilled.

I took a broken reed to hold,
   I took a sponge of gall to press;
I took weak water-weeds to fold
   About my sacrificial dress.   10

I took the grasses of the field,
   The flax was bolled upon my crine;[1]
And ivy thorn and wild grapes healed
   To make good wine.

I took my scrip of manna sweet,
   My cruse of water did I bless;
I took the white dove by the feet,
   And flew into the wilderness.

II

The tiger came and played;
Uprose the lion in his mane;   20
The jackal's tawny nose
And sanguine dripping tongue
Out of the desert rose
And plunged its sands among;
The bear came striding o'er the desert plain.

Uprose the horn and eyes
And quivering flank of the great unicorn,
And galloped round and round;
Uprose the gleaming claw
Of the leviathan, and wound   30
In steadfast march did draw
Its course away beyond the desert's bourn.

I stood within a maze
Woven round about me by a magic art,

DREAM
1 boll: pod; crine: hair.

And ordered circle-wise:
The bear more near did tread,
And with two fiery eyes,
And with a wolfish head,
Did close the circle round in every part.

III

With scarlet corded horn, 40
With frail wrecked knees and stumbling pace,
The scapegoat came:
His eyes took flesh and spirit dread in flame
At once, and he died looking towards my face.

Christ's Company *(1861)*.

SONNET

Give me the darkest corner of a cloud,
  Placed high upon some lonely mountain's head,
Craggy and harsh with ruin; let me shroud
  My life in horror, for I wish me dead.
No gentle lowland known and loved of old,
  Lure me to life back through the gate of tears;
But long time drenched with rain and numb with cold,
  May I forget the solace of the years:
No trees by streams, no light and warmth of day,
  No white clouds pausing o'er the happy town; 10
But wind and rain, and fogbanks slow and gray,
  And stony wastes, and uplands scalped and brown;
No life, but only death in life: a grave
As cold and bleak as thine, dear soul, I crave.

Christ's Company *(1861)*.

William Morris (1834–96)

Painter, poet, craftsman, entrepreneur, environmentalist, revolutionary international socialist, William Morris was a big man in every sense: fat, a huge lover of food and wine; a gargantuan producer of original verses, verse translations, prose romances, utopian fiction and politico-aesthetic polemic; a tireless reviver of decayed handicraft techniques (stained-glass, calligraphy, fabric dyeing, hand-weaving); an inspirer of the world-wide Arts and Crafts movement; a crusader for the political rights of the poor and powerless and for the availability to ordinary people of aesthetically pleasing domestic objects at affordable prices. He was born, 24 March 1834, near Walthamstow, eldest son and third child of William Morris, City money-broker, and Emma Shelton, a music-teacher's daughter from Worcester. Much of his pampered, idyllic and strictly Evangelical childhood was spent at his father's large house, Woodfall Hall, on the edge of Epping Forest. He had a child-sized suit of armour to ride about in on his pony.

Formidably precocious, he is said to have read all of Scott's novels by the age of seven. He was at Marlborough College from 1848 to 1851, had private tuition, and entered Exeter College, Oxford, January 1853. At Exeter he became great friends with Ted Jones, who ended up as the celebrated Pre-Raphaelite painter Sir Edward Burne-Jones, and other boys from Birmingham up at Oxford – Charles Faulkner, Richard Watson Dixon, William Fulford, Cormell Price. Hugely influenced by the medievalizing tendencies of the time – religious Tractarianism, Keats, Tennyson, Browning, Charles Kingsley's novel *Yeast*, Ruskin's cult-book *The Stones of Venice* (whose section on the nature and the makers of Gothic remained a lifelong touchstone for Morris) – Morris and his friends became the second wave of Pre-Raphaelitism. Well-off on his inherited shares, and with lifelong thoughts of co-operative communities setting in this early, Morris contemplated funding a monastery for his 'Brotherhood' of friends. He did not, in the event, join the Roman Catholic Church (his perennial tendency to short-lived bouts of enthusiasm was marked thus early too). He began writing poetry at university; decided after Finals (December 1855) to become an architect (he was greatly moved by the Gothic cathedrals of northern France), and was articled, January 1856, to the Gothic Revivalist George Edmund Street, Oxford diocesan architect. In Street's Beaumont Street office in Oxford, Morris started his lifelong friendship with Philip Webb. Morris paid for all twelve issues of the *Oxford and Cambridge Magazine* of 1856 (beginning thus his career as paymaster-general of radical causes), as well as contributing eight prose tales, five poems, two articles (one on Amiens Cathedral) and a review of Browning's *Men and Women*. After less than a year with Street, latterly in the London office, Morris abandoned architecture and moved into D. G. Rossetti's old studio at 17 Red Lion Square, with Rossetti and Ted Jones, to paint. He wrote poems (*The Defence of Guenevere, and Other Poems* – revivalist and medievalist – appeared in March 1858), and was active in the larky 1857 summer vacation project to decorate the walls and ceilings of the Oxford Union Debating Hall with Arthurian frescoes. In this Oxford interlude he fell in love with Janey Burden, daughter of a stable-man in Holywell Street, one of the Pre-Raphaelites' long slate of 'stunners', young proletarian women assiduously picked up in shops and off the street to become models, girlfriends and wives. Morris and Janey were married, 26 April 1859, in St Michael's, Oxford, by the (now) Revd R. W. Dixon. In the early sixties Morris's colossal energies went into creating the Red House, Bexleyheath, Kent (designed by Webb) as a revolutionary model of retro-medieval hand-working applied to a domestic building, and also into forming at 8 Red Lion Square the interior decorating firm of Morris, Marshall, Faulkner, & Co. (the partners included Webb, D. G. Rossetti, Jones, and Madox Brown the painter), which firm produced hand-crafted stained-glass, metalwork, woodwork, tapestries, wallpaper, carpets, all the hallmarks of Morris's great revivalist vision, for churches and for homes. In 1865 Morris moved in over the firm's workshops in Queen Square, Bloomsbury. Here he turned again to poetry, turning out in the late sixties his extremely long verse narrative *The Earthly Paradise* (1868–70), a kind of Chaucerian odyssey, built around Jason and his Argonauts, in which Keats meets Christian Socialism and Morris could express his mixed feelings about women (what C. S. Lewis called 'the endless hithering and thithering' of desire) – dismay and lusts sponsored not least by Janey's burgeoning affair with D. G. Rossetti. In the seventies Morris took up the production of illuminated manuscripts (his work included manuscript versions of FitzGerald's *Omar Khayyám* and the *Aeneid*), and turned his imagination northwards to Iceland and its sagas (the *Volsunga-saga*, translated by Morris and Erikr Magnusson, appeared in 1870; he travelled to Iceland, 1871, 1873). In 1871 he acquired Kelmscott Manor House, Lechlade (which soon turned into yet one more of his showcases for Arts and Crafts principles), and in 1878 he moved

into his permanent London home at Kelmscott House, Hammersmith. *Love is Enough*, a pseudo-medieval alliterative poem, appeared in 1872, his Old Norse translations *Three Northern Love Stories* and his translation of the *Aeneid* in 1875, and in 1876 his huge epic *The Story of Sigurd and Volsung and the Fall of the Niblungs*. In the mid-1870s Morris spent much time in a vat (as Burne-Jones put it) in Staffordshire, learning how to renew the arts of vegetable, especially indigo, dyeing. After that, ever curious and restless, he took up carpet-weaving. His designs, the textiles and fittings, were on sale in Morris & Co.'s shop in Oxford Street, in London's West End. In 1881 the furniture makers, weavers and dyers moved to restored workshops at Merton Abbey near Wimbledon. Morris's fabric designing moved into high gear in the 1880s, not least in the great intricate floral patterns named after tributaries of the Thames, which show him (in the words of his 1994 biographer Fiona MacCarthy) 'the brother of Darwin in his botanical precision' and 'the cousin of Browning in his build-up of complexities of meaning'. Towards the end of the seventies Morris turned his unstoppable vitality to public crusading and political agitation – becoming treasurer of the Eastern Question Association (November 1876), which protested Turkish atrocities in the Balkans (subject of Oscar Wilde's sonnet, 'On the Recent Massacres of Christians in Bulgaria'); founding 'Anti-Scrape', the Society for the Protection of Ancient Buildings (March 1877); becoming treasurer of the National Liberal League (1879); hardening his radicalism into Socialism to join the Democratic Federation (subsequently the Social-Democratic Federation), writing for its journal *Justice*, breaking away (December 1884) to lead the Socialist League (and edit its paper the *Commonweal*). The busy lecturer on liberal-radical aesthetics turned into the lecturer on revolutionary socialism and aesthetics ('What business have we with art unless all can share it?'), tirelessly stumping up and down the country (the *Odyssey* he was translating always in his knapsack), preaching in the open air several times every Sunday (with the likes of G. B. Shaw), getting arrested for defiant street demos, providing songs for insurrectionist working men, such as 'The March of the Workers' (sung to the tune of 'John Brown's Body', with Gustav Holst it might be, on the harmonium). *A Dream of John Ball*, a prose dream-work about human fellowship, was serialized in *Commonweal* (1886–7). *Chants for Socialists* appeared as a volume in 1885. *News From Nowhere* (1891), a Utopian satire which became a twentieth-century Socialist Bible, was another *Commonweal* serial (1890). In November 1890, having finished *News From Nowhere*, Morris left the Socialist League because of its increasing anarchist tendencies and founded the Hammersmith Socialist Society. That year he also set up the Kelmscott Press at Hammersmith, designing types and ornamental lettering and publishing the finest printed books known in England, certainly up until then, perhaps ever. The fifty or so Kelmscott volumes included his own *Poems by the Way* (1891) and *The Story of Beowulf* (1895), his loose rhyming-up of A. J. Wyatt's prose translations of the Anglo-Saxon poem, and culminated in the great *Chaucer* of 1896. Beginning in 1889 Morris poured out a sequence of prose romances, the most crafted of which is *The Well at the World's End* (1896). Janey's second big affair, with the poet Wilfrid Scawen Blunt, was conducted under Morris's very nose in the Hammersmith house. Morris himself was active in socialist politics – speeches, rallies – to the end. As he lay dying in Hammersmith in September 1896, rare manuscripts were brought for him to fondle, while Alfred Dolmetsch played him sixteenth-century English music on the virginal. Morris died, 3 October 1896, survived by Janey and their two daughters, epileptic unhappy Jenny, and May, her father's right-hand woman (and the 'Mystic Bride' of G. B. Shaw). Morris had become the renowned Grand Old Man of British Socialism, the inspiring dreamer of post-industrial work satisfactions and of beauty and aesthetic delight in all environments and for all people, as well as the guru of the Arts and Crafts people who carried on his vision across the globe. When Morris heard that Ruskin had called him 'the ablest man of his time', he celebrated, characteristically, with a bottle of his favourite Imperial Tokay. He was buried at Kelmscott in the presence of Socialist Leaguers, workmen from Merton Abbey, and sales personnel from Morris & Co., Oxford Street.

THE DEFENCE OF GUENEVERE

But, knowing now that they would have her speak,
She threw her wet hair backward from her brow,
Her hand close to her mouth touching her cheek,

As though she had had there a shameful blow,
And feeling it shameful to feel ought but shame
All through her heart, yet felt her cheek burned so,

She must a little touch it; like one lame
She walked away from Gauwaine, with her head
Still lifted up; and on her cheek of flame

The tears dried quick; she stopped at last and said: 10
'O knights and lords, it seems but little skill
To talk of well-known things past now and dead.

'God wot I ought to say, I have done ill,
And pray you all forgiveness heartily!
Because you must be right such great lords – still

'Listen, suppose your time were come to die,
And you were quite alone and very weak;
Yea, laid a dying while very mightily

'The wind was ruffling up the narrow streak
Of river through your broad lands running well: 20
Suppose a hush should come, then some one speak:

'"One of these cloths is heaven, and one is hell,
Now choose one cloth for ever, which they be,
I will not tell you, you must somehow tell

'"Of your own strength and mightiness; here, see!"
Yea, yea, my lord, and you to ope your eyes,
At foot of your familiar bed to see

'A great God's angel standing, with such dyes,
Not known on earth, on his great wings, and hands,
Held out two ways, light from the inner skies   30

'Showing him well, and making his commands
Seem to be God's commands, moreover, too,
Holding within his hands the cloths on wands;

'And one of these strange choosing cloths was blue,
Wavy and long and one cut short and red;
No man could tell the better of the two.

'After a shivering half-hour you said,
"God help! heaven's colour, the blue"; and he said, "hell."
Perhaps you then would roll upon your bed,

'And cry to all good men that loved you well,   40
"Ah Christ! if only I had known, known, known";
Launcelot went away, then I could tell,

'Like wisest man how all things would be, moan,
And roll and hurt myself, and long to die,
And yet fear much to die for what was sown.

'Nevertheless you, O Sir Gauwaine, lie,
Whatever may have happened through these years,
God knows I speak truth, saying that you lie.'

Her voice was low at first, being full of tears,
But as it cleared, it grew full loud and shrill,   50
Growing a windy shriek in all men's ears,

A ringing in their startled brains, until
She said that Gauwaine lied, then her voice sunk,
And her great eyes began again to fill,

Though still she stood right up, and never shrunk,
But spoke on bravely, glorious lady fair!
Whatever tears her full lips may have drunk,

She stood, and seemed to think, and wrung her hair,
Spoke out at last with no more trace of shame,
With passionate twisting of her body there: 60

'It chanced upon a day that Launcelot came
To dwell at Arthur's court: at Christmas-time
This happened; when the heralds sung his name,

'"Son of King Ban of Benwick," seemed to chime
Along with all the bells that rang that day,
O'er the white roofs, with little change of rhyme.

'Christmas and whitened winter passed away,
And over me the April sunshine came,
Made very awful with black hail-clouds, yea

'And in the Summer I grew white with flame,   70
And bowed my head down – Autumn, and the sick
Sure knowledge things would never be the same,

'However often Spring might be most thick
Of blossoms and buds, smote on me, and I grew
Careless of most things, let the clock tick, tick,

'To my unhappy pulse, that beat right through
My eager body; while I laughed out loud,
And let my lips curl up at false or true,

'Seemed cold and shallow without any cloud,
Behold my judges, then the cloths were brought: 80
While I was dizzied thus, old thoughts would crowd,

'Belonging to the time ere I was bought
By Arthur's great name and his little love,
Must I give up for ever then, I thought,

'That which I deemed would ever round me move
Glorifying all things; for a little word,
Scarce ever meant at all, must I now prove

'Stone-cold for ever? Pray you, does the Lord
Will that all folks should be quite happy and good?
I love God now a little, if this cord   90

'Were broken,¹ once for all what striving could
Make me love anything in earth or heaven.
So day by day it grew, as if one should

'Slip slowly down some path worn smooth and even,
Down to a cool sea on a summer day;
Yet still in slipping was there some small leaven

'Of stretched hands catching small stones by the way,
Until one surely reached the sea at last,
And felt strange new joy as the worn head lay

'Back, with the hair like sea-weed; yea all past   100
Sweat of the forehead, dryness of the lips,
Washed utterly out by the dear waves o'ercast

'In the lone sea, far off from any ships!
Do I not know now of a day in Spring?
No minute of that wild day ever slips

'From out my memory; I hear thrushes sing,
And wheresoever I may be, straightway
Thoughts of it all come up with most fresh sting;

'I was half mad with beauty on that day,
And went without my ladies all alone,   110
In a quiet garden walled round every way;

'I was right joyful of that wall of stone,
That shut the flowers and trees up with the sky,
And trebled all the beauty: to the bone,

'Yea right through to my heart, grown very shy
With weary thoughts, it pierced, and made me glad;
Exceedingly glad, and I knew verily,

'A little thing just then had made me mad;
I dared not think, as I was wont to do,
Sometimes, upon my beauty; if I had   120

THE DEFENCE OF GUENEVERE
1 cf. Ecclesiastes 12.6. 'Or ever the silver cord be loosed, or the
golden bowl be broken...'

'Held out my long hand up against the blue,
And, looking on the tenderly darken'd fingers,
Thought that by rights one ought to see quite through,

'There, see you, where the soft still light yet lingers,
Round by the edges; what should I have done,
If this had joined with yellow spotted singers,

'And startling green drawn upward by the sun?
But shouting, loosed out, see now! all my hair,
And trancedly stood watching the west wind run

'With faintest half-heard breathing sound – why there   130
I lose my head e'en now in doing this;
But shortly listen – In that garden fair

'Came Launcelot walking; this is true, the kiss
Wherewith we kissed in meeting that spring day,
I scarce dare talk of the remember'd bliss,

'When both our mouths went wandering in one way,
And aching sorely, met among the leaves;
Our hands being left behind strained far away.

'Never within a yard of my bright sleeves
Had Launcelot come before – and now, so nigh!   140
After that day why is it Guenevere grieves?

'Nevertheless you, O Sir Gauwaine, lie,
Whatever happened on through all those years,
God knows I speak truth, saying that you lie.

'Being such a lady could I weep these tears
If this were true? A great queen such as I
Having sinn'd this way, straight her conscience sears;

'And afterwards she liveth hatefully,
Slaying and poisoning, certes never weeps, –
Gauwaine be friends now, speak me lovingly.   150

'Do I not see how God's dear pity creeps
All through your frame, and trembles in your mouth?
Remember in what grave your mother sleeps,

'Buried in some place far down in the south,
Men are forgetting as I speak to you;
By her head sever'd in that awful drouth

'Of pity that drew Agravaine's fell blow,
I pray your pity! let me not scream out
For ever after, when the shrill winds blow

'Through half your castle-locks! let me not shout   160
For ever after in the winter night
When you ride out alone! in battle-rout

'Let not my rusting tears make your sword light!
Ah! God of mercy how he turns away!
So, ever must I dress me to the fight,

'So – let God's justice work! Gauwaine, I say,
See me hew down your proofs: yea all men know
Even as you said how Mellyagraunce one day,

'One bitter day in *la Fausse Garde*, for so
All good knights held it after, saw –   170
Yea, sirs, by cursed unknightly outrage; though

'You, Gauwaine, held his word without a flaw,
This Mellyagraunce saw blood upon my bed –
Whose blood then pray you? is there any law

'To make a queen say why some spots of red
Lie on her coverlet? or will you say,
"Your hands are white, lady, as when you wed,

' "Where did you bleed?" and must I stammer out – "Nay,
I blush indeed, fair lord, only to rend
My sleeve up to my shoulder, where there lay   180

' "A knife-point last night": so must I defend
The honour of the lady Guenevere?
Not so, fair lords, even if the world should end

'This very day, and you were judges here
Instead of God. Did you see Mellyagraunce
When Launcelot stood by him? What white fear

'Curdled his blood, and how his teeth did dance,
His side sink in? as my knight cried and said,
"Slayer of unarm'd men, here is a chance!

' "Setter of traps, I pray you guard your head,   190
By God I am so glad to fight with you,
Stripper of ladies, that my hand feels lead

' "For driving weight; hurrah now! draw and do,
For all my wounds are moving in my breast,
And I am getting mad with waiting so."

'He struck his hands together o'er the beast,
Who fell down flat, and grovell'd at his feet,
And groan'd at being slain so young – "at least."

'My knight said, "Rise you, sir, who are so fleet
At catching ladies, half-arm'd will I fight,   200
My left side all uncovered!" then I weet,

'Up sprang Sir Mellyagraunce with great delight
Upon his knave's face; not until just then
Did I quite hate him, as I saw my knight

'Along the lists look to my stake and pen
With such a joyous smile, it made me sigh
From agony beneath my waist-chain, when

'The fight began, and to me they drew nigh;
Ever Sir Launcelot kept him on the right,
And traversed warily, and ever high   210

'And fast leapt caitiff's sword, until my knight
Sudden threw up his sword to his left hand,
Caught it, and swung it; that was all the fight.

'Except a spout of blood on the hot land;
For it was hottest summer; and I know
I wonder'd how the fire, while I should stand,

'And burn, against the heat, would quiver so,
Yards above my head; thus these matters went;
Which things were only warnings of the woe

'That fell on me. Yet Mellyagraunce was shent,   220
For Mellyagraunce had fought against the Lord;
Therefore, my lords, take heed lest you be blent

'With all this wickedness; say no rash word
Against me, being so beautiful; my eyes,
Wept all away to grey, may bring some sword

'To drown you in your blood; see my breast rise,
Like waves of purple sea, as here I stand;
And how my arms are moved in wonderful wise,

'Yea also at my full heart's strong command,
See through my long throat how the words go up   230
In ripples to my mouth; how in my hand

'The shadow lies like wine within a cup
Of marvellously colour'd gold; yea now
This little wind is rising, look you up,

'And wonder how the light is falling so
Within my moving tresses: will you dare,
When you have looked a little on my brow,

'To say this thing is vile? or will you care
For any plausible lies of cunning woof,
When you can see my face with no lie there   240

'For ever? am I not a gracious proof –
"But in your chamber Launcelot was found" –
Is there a good knight then would stand aloof,

'When a queen says with gentle queenly sound:
"O true as steel come now and talk with me,
I love to see your step upon the ground

'"Unwavering, also well I love to see
That gracious smile light up your face, and hear
Your wonderful words, that all mean verily

'"The thing they seem to mean: good friend, so dear   250
To me in everything, come here to-night,
Or else the hours will pass most dull and drear;

'"If you come not, I fear this time I might
Get thinking over much of times gone by,
When I was young, and green hope was in sight;

' "For no man cares now to know why I sigh;
And no man comes to sing me pleasant songs,
Nor any brings me the sweet flowers that lie

' "So thick in the gardens; therefore one so longs
To see you, Launcelot; that we may be   260
Like children once again, free from all wrongs

' "Just for one night." Did he not come to me?
What thing could keep true Launcelot away
If I said "come"? there was one less than three

'In my quiet room that night, and we were gay;
Till sudden I rose up, weak, pale, and sick,
Because a bawling broke our dream up, yea

'I looked at Launcelot's face and could not speak,
For he looked helpless too, for a little while;
Then I remember how I tried to shriek,   270

'And could not, but fell down; from tile to tile
The stones they threw up rattled o'er my head,
And made me dizzier; till within a while

'My maids were all about me, and my head
On Launcelot's breast was being soothed away
From its white chattering, until Launcelot said –

'By God! I will not tell you more to-day,
Judge any way you will – what matters it?
You know quite well the story of that fray,

'How Launcelot still'd their bawling, the mad fit   280
That caught up Gauwaine – all, all, verily,
But just that which would save me; these things flit.

'Nevertheless you, O Sir Gauwaine, lie,
Whatever may have happen'd these long years,
God knows I speak truth, saying that you lie!

'All I have said is truth, by Christ's dear tears.'
She would not speak another word, but stood
Turn'd sideways; listening, like a man who hears

His brother's trumpet sounding through the wood
Of his foes' lances. She lean'd eagerly,   290
And gave a slight spring sometimes, as she could

At last hear something really; joyfully
Her cheek grew crimson, as the headlong speed
Of the roan charger drew all men to see,
The knight who came was Launcelot at good need.

The Defence of Guenevere, and Other Poems (Bell & Daldy, 1858).
Volume dedicated 'To my Friend, Dante Gabriel Rossetti, Painter.'

THE HAYSTACK IN THE FLOODS

Had she come all the way for this,
To part at last without a kiss?
Yea, had she borne the dirt and rain
That her own eyes might see him slain
Beside the haystack in the floods?

Along the dripping leafless woods,
The stirrup touching either shoe,
She rode astride as troopers do;
With kirtle kilted to her knee,
To which the mud splash'd wretchedly;   10
And the wet dripp'd from every tree
Upon her head and heavy hair,
And on her eyelids broad and fair;
The tears and rain ran down her face.
By fits and starts they rode apace,
And very often was his place
Far off from her; he had to ride
Ahead, to see what might betide
When the roads cross'd; and sometimes, when
There rose a murmuring from his men,   20
Had to turn back with promises;
Ah me! she had but little ease;
And often for pure doubt and dread
She sobb'd, made giddy in the head
By the swift riding; while, for cold,
Her slender fingers scarce could hold
The wet reins; yea, and scarcely, too,
She felt the foot within her shoe
Against the stirrup: all for this,
To part at last without a kiss   30
Beside the haystack in the floods.

For when they near'd that old soak'd hay,
They saw across the only way
That Judas, Godmar, and the three
Red running lions dismally
Grinn'd from his pennon, under which,
In one straight line along the ditch,
They counted thirty heads.

                    So then,
While Robert turn'd round to his men,   40
She saw at once the wretched end,
And, stooping down, tried hard to rend
Her coif the wrong way from her head,
And hid her eyes; while Robert said:
'Nay, love, 'tis scarcely two to one,
At Poictiers where we made them run
So fast – why, sweet my love, good cheer.
The Gascon frontier is so near,
Nought after this.'

                    But, 'O,' she said,
'My God! my God! I have to tread   50
The long way back without you; then

The court at Paris; those six men;
The gratings of the Chatelet;
The swift Seine on some rainy day
Like this, and people standing by,
And laughing, while my weak hands try
To recollect how strong men swim,
All this, or else a life with him,
For which I should be damned at last,
Would God that this next hour were past!'   60

He answer'd not, but cried his cry,
'St. George for Marny!' cheerily;
And laid his hand upon her rein.
Alas! no man of all his train
Gave back that cheery cry again;
And, while for rage his thumb beat fast
Upon his sword-hilts, some one cast
About his neck a kerchief long,
And bound him.

        Then they went along   70
To Godmar; who said: 'Now, Jehane,
You lover's life is on the wane
So fast, that, if this very hour
You yield not as my paramour,
He will not see the rain leave off –
Nay, keep your tongue from gibe and scoff,
Sir Robert, or I slay you now.'

She laid her hand upon her brow,
Then gazed upon the palm, as though
She thought her forehead bled, and – 'No,'   80
She said, and turn'd her head away,
As there were nothing else to say,
And everything were settled: red
Grew Godmar's face from chin to head:
'Jehane, on yonder hill there stands
My castle, guarding well my lands:
What hinders me from taking you,
And doing that I list to do
To your fair wilful body, while
Your knight lies dead?'   90

        A wicked smile
Wrinkled her face, her lips grew thin,
A long way out she thrust her chin:
'You know that I should strangle you
While you were sleeping; or bite through
Your throat, by God's help – ah!' she said,
'Lord Jesus, pity your poor maid!
For in such wise they hem me in,
I cannot choose but sin and sin,
Whatever happens: yet I think   100
They could not make me eat or drink,
And so should I just reach my rest.'

'Nay, if you do not my behest,
O Jehane! though I love you well,'

Said Godmar, 'would I fail to tell
All that I know.' 'Foul lies,' she said.
'Eh? lies my Jehane? by God's head,
At Paris folks would deem them true!
Do you know, Jehane, they cry for you,
"Jehane the brown! Jehane the brown!   110
Give us Jehane to burn or drown!" –
Eh – gag me Robert! – sweet my friend,
This were indeed a piteous end
For those long fingers, and long feet,
And long neck, and smooth shoulders sweet;
An end that few men would forget
That saw it – So, an hour yet:
Consider, Jehane, which to take
Of life or death!'

          So, scarce awake,   120
Dismounting, did she leave that place,
And totter some yards: with her face
Turn'd upward to the sky she lay,
Her head on a wet heap of hay,
And fell asleep: and while she slept,
And did not dream, the minutes crept
Round to the twelve again; but she,
Being waked at last, sigh'd quietly,
And strangely childlike came, and said:
'I will not.' Straightway Godmar's head,   130
As though it hung on strong wires, turn'd
Most sharply round, and his face burn'd.

For Robert – both his eyes were dry,
He could not weep, but gloomily
He seem'd to watch the rain; yea, too,
His lips were firm; he tried once more
To touch her lips; she reach'd out, sore
And vain desire so tortured them,
The poor grey lips, and now the hem
Of his sleeve brush'd them.   140

          With a start
Up Godmar rose, thrust them apart;
From Robert's throat he loosed the bands
Of silk and mail; with empty hands
Held out, she stood and gazed, and saw,
The long bright blade without a flaw
Glide out from Godmar's sheath, his hand
In Robert's hair; she saw him bend
Back Robert's head; she saw him send
The thin steel down; the blow told well,   150
Right backward the knight Robert fell,
And moan'd as dogs do, being half dead,
Unwitting, as I deem: so then
Godmar turn'd grinning to his men,
Who ran, some five or six, and beat
His head to pieces at their feet.

Then Godmar turn'd again, and said:
'So, Jehane, the first fitte is read!

Take note, my lady, that your way
Lies backward to the Chatelet!'   160
She shook her head and gazed awhile
At her cold hands with a rueful smile,
As though this thing had made her mad.

This was the parting that they had
Beside the haystack in the floods.

The Defence of Guenevere (1858).

SUMMER DAWN

Pray but one prayer for me 'twixt thy closed lips,
    Think but one thought of me up in the stars.
The summer night waneth, the morning light slips,
    Faint and grey 'twixt the leaves of the aspen,
        betwixt the cloud-bars,
That are patiently waiting there for the dawn:
    Patient and colourless, though Heaven's gold
Waits to float through them along with the sun.
Far out in the meadows, above the young corn,
    The heavy elms wait, and restless and cold   10
The uneasy wind rises; the roses are dun;
Through the long twilight they pray for the dawn,
Round the lone house in the midst of the corn.
    Speak but one word to me over the corn,
    Over the tender, bow'd locks of the corn.

The Defence of Guenevere (1858).

THE MARCH OF THE WORKERS

What is this, the sound and rumour? What is this that all men hear,
Like the wind in hollow valleys when the storm is drawing near,
Like the rolling on of ocean in the eventide of fear?
                            'Tis the people marching on.

Whither go they, and whence come they? What are these of whom ye tell?
In what country are they dwelling 'twixt the gates of heaven and hell?
Are they mine or thine for money? Will they serve a master well?
                            Still the rumour's marching on.

    Hark the rolling of the thunder!
    Lo the sun! and lo thereunder   10
    Riseth wrath, and hope, and wonder,
                    And the host comes marching on.

Forth they come from grief and torment; on they wend toward health and mirth,
All the wide world is their dwelling, every corner of the earth.
Buy them, sell them for thy service! Try the bargain what 'tis worth,
                    For the days are marching on.

These are they who build thy houses, weave thy raiment, win thy wheat,
Smooth the rugged, fill the barren, turn the bitter into sweet,

All for thee this day – and ever. What reward for them is meet
                              Till the host comes marching on?   20

        Hark the rolling of the thunder!
        Lo the sun! and lo thereunder
        Riseth wrath, and hope, and wonder,
                      And the host comes marching on.

Many a hundred years passed over have they laboured deaf and blind;
Never tidings reached their sorrow, never hope their toil might find.
Now at last they've heard and hear it, and the cry comes down the wind,
                      And their feet are marching on.

O ye rich men hear and tremble! for with words the sound is rife:
'Once for you and death we laboured; changed henceforward is the strife.   30
We are men, and we shall battle for the world of men and life;
                      And our host is marching on.'

        Hark the rolling of the thunder!
        Lo the sun! and lo thereunder
        Riseth wrath, and hope, and wonder,
                      And the host comes marching on.

'Is it war, then? Will ye perish as the dry wood in the fire?
Is it peace? Then be ye of us, let your hope be our desire.
Come and live! for life awaketh, and the world shall never tire;
                      And hope is marching on.'   40

'On we march then, we the workers, and the rumour that ye hear
Is the blended sound of battle and deliv'rance drawing near;
For the hope of every creature is the banner that we bear,
                      And the world is marching on.'

        Hark the rolling of the thunder!
        Lo the sun! and lo thereunder
        Riseth wrath, and hope, and wonder,
                      And the host comes marching on.

Chants for Socialists *(Socialist League, 1885)*. *To be sung to the tune of*
'John Brown's Body'.

A GARDEN BY THE SEA

    I know a little garden-close,
    Set thick with lily and red rose,
    Where I would wander if I might
    From dewy morn to dewy night,
    And have one with me wandering.

    And though within it no birds sing,
    And though no pillared house is there,
    And though the apple-boughs are bare
    Of fruit and blossom, would to God
    Her feet upon the green grass trod,   10
    And I beheld them as before.

    There comes a murmur from the shore,
    And in the close two fair streams are,

Drawn from the purple hills afar,
Drawn down unto the restless sea:
Dark hills whose heath-bloom feeds no bee,
Dark shore no ship has ever seen,
Tormented by the billows green
Whose murmur comes unceasingly
Unto the place for which I cry.   20

For which I cry both day and night,
For which I let slip all delight,
Whereby I grow both deaf and blind,
Careless to win, unskilled to find,
And quick to lose what all men seek.

Yet tottering as I am and weak,
Still have I left a little breath
To seek within the jaws of death
An entrance to that happy place,
To seek the unforgotten face,   30
Once seen once kissed, once reft from me
Anigh the murmuring of the sea.

Poems by the Way (Kelmscott Press, 1891).

VERSES FOR PICTURES: POMONA

I am the ancient Apple-Queen,
As once I was so am I now.
For evermore a hope unseen,
Betwixt the blossom and the bough.

Ah, where's the river's hidden Gold!
And where the windy grave of Troy?
Yet come I as I came of old,
From out the heart of Summer's joy.

Poems by the Way (1891). Words written for the Pomona *tapestry, 300 × 210 cm,*
designed by Burne-Jones, executed 1884–5 at Morris & Co.'s Merton Abbey Works.
Stanza 1 along the tapestry's top; stanza 2 along the bottom.

THE END OF MAY

How the wind howls this morn
About the end of May,
And drives June on apace
To mock the world forlorn
And the world's joy passed away
And my unlonged-for face!
The world's joy passed away;
For no more may I deem
That any folk are glad
To see the dawn of day   10
Sunder the tangled dream
Wherein no grief they had.
Ah, through the tangled dream

Where others have no grief
Ever it fares with me
That fears and treasons stream
And dumb sleep slays belief
Whatso therein may be.
Sleep slayeth all belief
Until the hopeless light   20
Wakes at the birth of June
More lying tales to weave,
More love in woe's despite,
More hope to perish soon.

Poems by the Way *(1891)*.

How I Became a Socialist

I am asked by the Editor to give some sort of a history of the above conversion, and I feel that it may be of some use to do so, if my readers will look upon me as a type of a certain group of people, but not so easy to do clearly, briefly and truly. Let me, however, try. But first, I will say what I mean by being a Socialist, since I am told that the word no longer expresses definitely and with certainty what it did ten years ago. Well, what I mean by Socialism is a condition of society in which there should be neither rich nor poor, neither master nor master's man, neither idle nor overworked, neither brain-sick brain workers, nor heart-sick hand workers, in a word, in which all men would be living in equality of condition, and would manage their affairs unwastefully, and with the full consciousness that harm to one would mean harm to all – the realization at last of the meaning of the word COMMONWEALTH.

Now this view of Socialism which I hold to-day, and hope to die holding, is what I began with; I had no transitional period, unless you may call such a brief period of political radicalism during which I saw my ideal clear enough, but had no hope of any realization of it. That came to an end some months before I joined the (then) Democratic Federation, and the meaning of my joining that body was that I had conceived a hope of the realization of my ideal. If you ask me how much of a hope, or what I thought we Socialists then living and working would accomplish towards it, or when there would be effected any change in the face of society, I must say, I do not know. I can only say that I did not measure my hope, nor the joy that it brought me at the time. For the rest, when I took that step I was blankly ignorant of economics; I had never so much as opened Adam Smith, or heard of Ricardo, or of Karl Marx. Oddly enough, I *had* read some of Mill, to wit, those posthumous papers of his (published, was it in the *Westminster Review* or the *Fortnightly?*) in which he attacks Socialism in its Fourierist guise.[1] In those papers he put the arguments, as far as they go, clearly and honestly, and the result, so far as I was concerned, was to convince me that Socialism was a necessary change, and that it was possible to bring it about in our own days. Those papers put the finishing touch to my conversion to Socialism. Well, having joined a Socialist body (for the Federation soon became definitely Socialist), I put some conscience into trying to learn the economical side of Socialism, and even tackled Marx, though I must confess that, whereas I thoroughly enjoyed the historical part of 'Capital,' I suffered agonies of confusion of the brain over reading the pure economics of that great work. Anyhow, I read what I could, and will hope that some information stuck to me from my reading; but more, I must think, from continuous conversation with such friends as Bax and Hyndman and Scheu,[2] and the brisk course of

How I Became a Socialist
1   Adam Smith, David Ricardo, Karl Marx: economic theorists of right and left. John Stuart Mill: libertarian. François Fourier: French social theorist.
2   Ernest Belfort Bax (1804–67), founder with Morris of Socialist League. Henry Mayers Hyndman, author of *England for All*, founder of Democratic Federation, foundational English Marxist. Andreas Scheu, refugee Viennese anarchist and furniture designer; close associate of W.M. in Democratic Federation and Socialist League.

propaganda meetings which were going on at the time, and in which I took my share. Such finish to what of education in practical Socialism as I am capable of I received afterwards from some of my Anarchist friends, from whom I learned, quite against their intention, that Anarchism was impossible, much as I learned from Mill against *his* intention that Socialism was necessary.

But in this telling how I fell into *practical* Socialism I have begun, as I perceive, in the middle, for in my position of a well-to-do man, not suffering from the disabilities which oppress a working-man at every step, I feel that I might never have been drawn into the practical side of the question if an ideal had not forced me to seek towards it. For politics as politics, *i.e.*, not regarded as a necessary if cumbersome and disgustful means to an end, would never have attracted me, nor when I had become conscious of the wrongs of society as it now is, and the oppression of poor people, could I have ever believed in the possibility of a *partial* setting right of those wrongs. In other words, I could never have been such a fool as to believe in the happy and 'respectable' poor.

If, therefore, my ideal forced me to look for practical Socialism, what was it that forced me to conceive of an ideal? Now, here comes in what I said (in this paper) of my being a type of a certain group of mind.

Before the uprising of *modern* Socialism almost all intelligent people either were, or professed themselves to be, quite contented with the civilization of this century. Again, almost all of these really were thus contented, and saw nothing to do but to perfect the said civilization by getting rid of a few ridiculous survivals of the barbarous ages. To be short, this was the *Whig* frame of mind, natural to the modern prosperous middle-class men, who, in fact, as far as mechanical progress is concerned, have nothing to ask for, if only Socialism would leave them alone to enjoy their plentiful style.

But besides these contented ones there were others who were not really contented, but had a vague sentiment of repulsion to the triumph of civilization, but were coerced into silence by the measureless power of Whiggery. Lastly, there were a few who were in open rebellion against the said Whiggery – a few, say two, Carlyle and Ruskin. The latter, before my days of practical Socialism, was my master towards the ideal aforesaid, and, looking backward, I cannot help saying, by the way, how deadly dull the world would have been twenty years ago but for Ruskin! It was through him that I learned to give form to my discontent, which I must say was not by any means vague. Apart from the desire to produce beautiful things, the leading passion of my life has been and is hatred of modern civilization. What shall I say of it now, when the words are put into my mouth, my hope of its destruction – what shall I say of its supplanting by Socialism?

What shall I say concerning its mastery of and its waste of mechanical power, its commonwealth so poor, its enemies of the commonwealth so rich, its stupendous organization – for the misery of life! Its contempt of simple pleasures which everyone could enjoy but for its folly? Its eyeless vulgarity which has destroyed art, the one certain solace of labour? All this I felt then as now, but I did not know why it was so. The hope of the past times was gone, the struggles of mankind for many ages had produced nothing but this sordid, aimless, ugly confusion; the immediate future seemed to me likely to intensify all the present evils by sweeping away the last survivals of the days before the dull squalor of civilization had settled down on the world. This was a bad look-out indeed, and, if I may mention myself as a personality and not as a mere type, especially so to a man of my disposition, careless of metaphysics and religion, as well as of scientific analysis, but with a deep love of the earth and the life on it, and a passion for the history of the past of mankind. Think of it! Was it all to end in a counting-house on the top of a cinder-heap, with Podsnap's[3] drawing-room in the offing, and a Whig committee dealing out champagne to the rich and margarine to the poor in such convenient proportions as would make all men contented together, though the pleasure of the eyes was gone from the world, and the place of Homer was to be taken by Huxley?[4] Yet, believe me, in my heart, when I really forced myself to look towards the future, that is what I saw in it, and, as far

3   Podsnap, in Dickens's *Our Mutual Friend* (1864–5): a type of purita-
nical self-satisfaction. (The cinder-heaps are Mr Boffin's dust-heaps –
and source of wealth, also in *OMF*.)

4   T. H. Huxley, famous Victorian agnostic and Darwinian.

as I could tell, scarce anyone seemed to think it worth while to struggle against such a consummation of civilization. So there I was in for a fine pessimistic end of life, if it had not somehow dawned on me that amidst all this filth of civilization the seeds of a great chance, what we others call Social-Revolution, were beginning to germinate. The whole face of things was changed to me by that discovery, and all I had to do then in order to become a Socialist was to hook myself on to the practical movement, which, as before said, I have tried to do as well as I could.

To sum up, then, the study of history and the love and practice of art forced me into a hatred of the civilization which, if things were to stop as they are, would turn history into inconsequent nonsense, and make art a collection of the curiosities of the past which would have no serious relation to the life of the present.

But the consciousness of revolution stirring amidst our hateful modern society prevented me, luckier than many others of artistic perceptions, from crystallizing into a mere railer against 'progress' on the one hand, and on the other from wasting time and energy in any of the numerous schemes by which the quasi-artistic of the middle classes hope to make art grow when it has no longer any root, and thus I became a practical Socialist.

A last word or two. Perhaps some of our friends will say, what have we to do with these matters of history and art? We want by means of Social-Democracy to win a decent livelihood, we want in some sort to live, and that at once. Surely any one who professes to think that the question of art and cultivation must go before that of the knife and fork (and there are some who do propose that) does not understand what art means, or how that its roots must have a soil of a thriving and unanxious life. Yet it must be remembered that civilization has reduced the workman to such a skinny and pitiful existence, that he scarcely knows how to frame a desire for any life much better than that which he now endures perforce. It is the province of art to set the true ideal of a full and reasonable life before him, a life to which the perception and creation of beauty, the enjoyment of real pleasure that is, shall be felt to be as necessary to man as his daily bread, and that no man, and no set of men, can be deprived of this except by mere opposition, which should be resisted to the utmost.

Justice *(16 June 1894)*. Collected Works, *ed. May Morris, vol. XXIII (Longmans, Green & Co., 1915), 277–81.*

James Thomson (also 'B.V.': Bysshe Vanolis) (1834–82)

James Thomson, the so-called 'laureate of pessimism', self-proclaimed 'Ishmael' and 'child of the devil', was born, 23 November 1834, in Port Glasgow, Scotland. His father, James Thomson, ship's officer, was disabled by a stroke. A sister died of measles caught from James. Their mother, Sarah Kennedy, was a devotee of Edward Irving and a member of the Irvingite apocalyptic and glossolalic Catholic Apostolic Church. The family had moved to London by 1842, by which time the mother had died. Young James was educated at the Royal Caledonian Asylum for sons of poor Scottish soldiers and sailors in Islington. In 1850 he entered the school of the Military Asylum, Chelsea, to train as an army schoolmaster, serving at first in Ireland, near Cork ('Pumping muddy information into unretentive sieves'). There he became friends with enlisted man Charles Bradlaugh (who would be Victorian England's most famous atheist) and fell in love with the young Matilda Weller (who soon died, and became Thomson's lifelong ghostly muse). In October 1862 Thomson was dis-

honourably discharged from the army after an incident involving a prohibited bathing-place – but probably also because of increasing addiction to drink. He was becoming a cyclical melancholic and binge drinker. He probably also took opium. He lodged in London with the Bradlaughs (Bradlaugh having bought himself out of the military) and wrote for the journals, especially Bradlaugh's *National Reformer* (1860–75), as B.V. (Bysshe Vanolis: the admired Shelley's second name, coupled with an anagram of the name of German writer Novalis). In 1866 Thomson was given his marching orders from Bradlaugh's home as a too tiresome drunk, and began his drawn-out existence as an impoverished one-room lodging-house exile and haunter of the British Museum Reading Room – a sort of embryo George Gissing character. In November 1869 he burnt many of his papers, clearing the decks for writing the pessimistic urban nightmares of *The City of Dreadful Night*, eventually serialized in the *National Reformer*, March–May 1874. In 1872 Thomson's self-consciously

Satanic wanderings took him to Colorado as an inspector of mines; in 1873 to Spain to report the civil war there for the *New York World*. Edith Simcox reviewed *The City of Dreadful Night* enthusiastically in the *Academy*. George Eliot wanted 'a wider embrace of human fellowship' in the poem. When he read it in adolescence Kipling was shaken to his 'unformed core', as he put it. *The City of Dreadful Night and Other Poems* (1880) sold unexpectedly well and won Thomson Meredith's friendship. The subsequent *Vane's Story and Other Poems* (1881) fared less well, though.

Drink brought an end to a marriage prospect with the secularist Miss Barrs of Leicester. Thomson was finally thrown out of his digs – a book thief, filthy, drunk, his old carpet-slippers no use in the wet of the street. He was sent to prison for two weeks for setting fire to his landlady's kitchen. On 1 June 1882 he collapsed with a stomach haemorrhage in the room of Philip Bourke Marston, the blind poet and his friend. He died two days later in University College Hospital. He was buried with secularist rituals in Highgate Cemetery.

A REAL VISION OF SIN

Like a soaking blanket overhead
Spongy and lax the sky was spread,
Opaque as the eye of a fish long dead.

Like trees in a drawing gummed together
Some trees stood dim in the drizzling weather;
Sweating mere blood-flowers gloomed the heather.

Like a festering gash left gaping wide
That foul canal, long swooned from tide,
The marshy moorland did divide.

In a slushy hollow near its bank,   10
Where noisome weeds grew thick and dank,
And the very soil like an old corpse stank,

They cowered together, the man and crone,
Two old bags of carious bone;
They and a mangy cur alone:

Ragged, haggard, filthy, both;
Viewing each the other loath;
Growling now and then an oath.

She at length with a spasm raised
Her strong grey eyes, still strong tho' glazed;   20
And thus her meditations phrased:

'No mite left of all our treasure;
Sin itself has no more pleasure:
Drained out, drained out our full measure!'

He quavered back: 'It does seem so:
The sun 'e died out long ago;
The earth and the sky are a-rottin' slow.'

She writhed her thick brows, dirty grey:
'Then take at once my easy way
Of swamping misery from our clay.   30

'No trembling, dear red-rat-eyes! Come!
We slip together through that green scum,
And then with the world here rot on dumb.'

He sat still, nipping spiteful blows
On the snarling cur's amorphous nose;
Relishing faintly her propose.

'Well *you* look lovely, so you do,
To call *me* names: a-drowndin' you
Would go to spoil this pleasant view!

'This 'ere damned life is bad enough;
But, say we smother in that stuff,
Our next life's only worse, you muff!'   40

The woman thereto coldly sneered:
'Of course, as usual all afeared,
Old slaver-dewy stubble-beard.

'Idiot and coward! hell-flames feed
On certain fuel; but, indeed,
A used-up soul won't sate their greed.

'When Earth once gets us cold and stark
She'll keep us safely in the dark: 50
No fear of rousing with the lark!

'Full long ago in grim despair,
She growled, *How those two witch-fires flare!*
They'll get no second chance I swear!'

She laught this truth out 'gainst the man;
Who shuffling, ill at ease, began:
'You can be devilish sore, you can.

'Suppose you're right; this life's a one
That's cursèd bad, but better than none....
I wish they'd light another Sun.   60

'We used to spree and we don't spree now;
A screw is loose in the world, allow,
We didn't make it, anyhow.

'Say Life's hard-up, No-life's more glum:
Just think – a lashing lot of rum,
And a night with you and a cool old chum!'

She fingered a toad from its love-work sweet,
And flung to the cur with a 'mangy, eat;
They say there's poison in the meat;

'And so the next time you bite this dear   70
He'll die off mad; for else I fear
He'd fester for ever and ever here.'

Its loose fangs squashed through the nectarous lump;
Then it went and crouched on a doddered stump,
With an evil eye on the Male Sin's hump.

He blinked and shuffled and swore and groaned:
Rasping the bristly beard she owned,
She thought drear thoughts until she too moaned.

'I see the truth,' with a scornful laugh,
'I have starved abroad on the swine-fouled draff,   80
While sleek at home sucked the fatt'ning calf.

'Too late, too late! Yet it's good to see,
If only damnation, thoroughly;
My Life has never met with me.

'And *you*, you never loved me, *you!*
A heart that never once beat true,
How could it love? I loved for two.

'This dirty crumpled rag of a breast
Was globed with milk once; I possest
The means of being grandly blest!   90

'Did the babe of mine suck luscious sips,
Soothing the nipple with rose-soft lips
While her eyes drooped mild in a dear eclipse?

'A babe! – could I now squeeze out three drops
Between that poor cur's ulcerous chaps,
He'd die as livid as yon tree-tops.

'You know where it rests, that child-dream gone?
Come, grope in this charming water-lawn,
Through ooze and slime and filth and spawn:

'Perhaps we shall find a shudderous feel,   100
Neither of eft,¹ nor toad, nor eel;
May hear a long long stifled squeal:

'Touch the rotten bones of a murdered brat
Whose flesh was daint to the water-rat, –
If it *does* gnaw flesh, it would relish that!'

He ventured, 'Curse all memory!
It's more than thirty years' – but she
Continued fierce, unheedingly –

'Come, and this loathsome life out-smother,
No fear that we'll ever have another: 110
The rain may beat and the wind may wuther,

'But we shall rot with the rotting soil,
Safe in sleep from the whole sad coil;
Sleep's better than corn and wine and oil.

'Here's a kiss; now at once!' effused the witch,
And dragged the wildered male to the ditch,
And plunged there prone by a bladdery bitch.

Drowned dead, stone dead, and still her grasp
Clawed *him*: but with a frenzied gasp
He shuddered off the scranny clasp.   120

A REAL VISION OF SIN
1 newt.

Up the soddened bank in a fury of funk
He sprawled: 'She's awful! but she's sunk;
I daren't die except dead drunk.'

He managed at length the hollow to win;
And was gulping down with a pang-writhed grin
The black bottle's last of vitriol gin,

When his gorge was choked by a sudden blight:
The cur growled mad with venom and fright,
And its blotches of hair all bristled upright.

Its frenzy burst out in a wolfish yell;   130
It leapt at his throat like an imp of hell;
In a spasm of horror the bottle fell:

It griped up his flaccid throat with a force
That made his terrorment gurgle hoarse,
While he turned as blue as a cholera-corse.

It haled him into the festering dike;
So all sank dead in its clam alike, –
The Man, the Woman, the virtuous Tyke.

And the dense rain crooned in its sullen flow
From the sodden sky-stretch drooping low   140
To the sodden earth; and to and fro

Crept a maundering wind too weak to blow;
And the dim world murmured dismal woe:
For the earth and the sky *were* a-rotting slow.

> MS dated 4 March 1859. Progress (November 1884). Poetical Works, 2 vols
> (Reeves & Turner, and Bertram Dobell, 1895), II. 'Written in disgust at Tennyson's,
> which is very pretty and clever and silly and truthless' (actually aimed more at T.'s
> 'Two Voices' than 'The Vision of Sin').

Once in a Saintly Passion

Once in a saintly passion
    I cried with desperate grief,
O Lord, my heart is black with guile,
    Of sinners I am chief.
Then stooped my guardian angel
    And whispered from behind:
'Vanity, my little man,
    You're nothing of the kind.'

> One MS is dated 28 May 1865. First published in the 'Memoir of Thomson',
> by Bertram Dobell, in A Voice from the Nile, and Other Poems
> (Reeves & Turner, 1884); then in Dobell's memoir in Poetical Works (1895), I.

ART

I

What precious thing are you making fast
    In all these silken lines?
And where and to whom will it go at last?
    Such subtle knots and twines!

I am tying up all my love in this,
    With all its hopes and fears,
With all its anguish and all its bliss,
    And its hours as heavy as years.

I am going to send it afar, afar,
    To I know not where above;   10
To that sphere beyond the highest star
    Where dwells the soul of my Love.

But in vain, in vain, would I make it fast
    With countless subtle twines;
For ever its fire breaks out at last,
    And shrivels all the lines.

II

If you have a carrier-dove
    That can fly over land and sea;
And a message for your Love,
    'Lady, I love but thee!'   20

And this dove will never stir
    But straight from her to you,
And straight from you to her;
    As you know and she knows too.

Will you first ensure, O sage,
    Your dove that never tires
With your message in a cage,
    Though a cage of golden wires?

Or will you fling your dove:
    'Fly, darling, without rest,   30
Over land and sea to my Love,
    And fold your wings in her breast'?

III

Singing is sweet; but be sure of this,
Lips only sing when they cannot kiss.

Did he ever suspire a tender lay
While her presence took his breath away?

Had his fingers been able to toy with her hair
Would they then have written the verses fair?

Had she let his arm steal round her waist
Would the lovely portrait yet be traced?   40

Since he could not embrace it flushed and warm
He has carved in stone the perfect form.

Who gives the fine report of the feast?
He who got none and enjoyed it least.

Were the wine really slipping down his throat
Would his song of the wine advance a note?

Will you puff out the music that sways the whirl,
Or dance and make love with a pretty girl?

Who shall the great battle-story write?
Not the hero down in the thick of the fight.   50

Statues and pictures and verse may be grand,
But they are not the Life for which they stand.

*MS dated 18 June 1865 (cancelled title: 'Elementary Philosophy of Love Poems').
National Reformer (17 Feb. 1867). The City of Dreadful Night and
Other Poems (Reeves & Turner, 1880), 1880 text.*

IN THE ROOM

'Ceste insigne Fable et tragicque comedie.'
                    Rabelais[1]

I

The sun was down, and twilight grey
    Filled half the air; but in the room,
Whose curtain had been drawn all day,
    The twilight was a dusky gloom:
Which seemed at first as still as death,
    And void; but was indeed all rife
With subtle thrills, the pulse and breath
    Of multitudinous lower life.

II

In their abrupt and headlong way
    Bewildered flies for light had dashed   10
Against the curtain all the day,
    And now slept wintrily abashed;
And nimble mice slept, wearied out
    With such a double night's uproar;
But solid beetles crawled about
    The chilly hearth and naked floor.

III

And so throughout the twilight hour
    That vaguely murmurous hush and rest
There brooded; and beneath its power
    Life throbbing held its throbs supprest: 20
Until the thin-voiced mirror sighed,
    I am all blurred with dust and damp,

IN THE ROOM
1 'This notable fable and tragic comedy'.

So long ago the clear day died,
   So long has gleamed nor fire nor lamp.

IV

Whereon the curtain murmured back,
   Some change is on us, good or ill;
Behind me and before is black
   As when those human things lie still:
But I have seen the darkness grow
   As grows the daylight every morn;   30
Have felt out there long shine and glow,
   In here long chilly dusk forlorn.

V

The cupboard grumbled with a groan,
   Each new day worse starvation brings:
Since *he* came here I have not known
   Or sweets or cates or wholesome things:
But now! a pinch of meal, a crust,
   Throughout the week is all I get.
I am so empty; it is just
   As when they said we were to let.   40

VI

What is become, then, of our Man?
   The petulant old glass exclaimed;
If all this time he slumber can,
   He really ought to be ashamed.
I wish we had our Girl again,
   So gay and busy, bright and fair:
The girls are better than these men,
   Who only for their dull selves care.

VII

It is so many hours ago –
   The lamp and fire were both alight –   50
I saw him pacing to and fro,
   Perturbing restlessly the night.
His face was pale to give one fear,
   His eyes when lifted looked too bright;
He muttered; what, I could not hear:
   Bad words though; something was not right.

VIII

The table said, He wrote so long
   That I grew weary of his weight;
The pen kept up a cricket song,   60
   It ran and ran at such a rate:
And in the longer pauses he
   With both his folded arms downpressed,
And stared as one who does not see,
   Or sank his head upon his breast.

IX

The fire-grate said, I am as cold
   As if I never had a blaze;
The few dead cinders here I hold,
   I held unburned for days and days.

Last night he made them flare; but still
    What good did all his writing do?   70
Among my ashes curl and thrill
    Thin ghosts of all those papers too.

X

The table answered, Not quite all;
    He saved and folded up one sheet,
And sealed it fast, and let it fall;
    And here it lies now white and neat.
Whereon the letter's whisper came,
    My writing is closed up too well;
Outside there's not a single name,
    And who should read me I can't tell.   80

XI

The mirror sneered with scornful spite
    (That ancient crack which spoiled her looks
Had marred her temper), Write and write!
    And read those stupid, worn-out books!
That's all he does, read, write, and read,
    And smoke that nasty pipe which stinks:
He never takes the slightest heed
    How any of us feels or thinks.

XII

But Lucy fifty times a day
    Would come and smile here in my face,   90
Adjust a tress that curled astray,
    Or tie a ribbon with more grace:
She looked so young and fresh and fair,
    She blushed with such a charming bloom,
It did one good to see her there,
    And brightened all things in the room.

XIII

She did not sit hours stark and dumb
    As pale as moonshine by the lamp;
To lie in bed when day was come,
    And leave us curtained chill and damp.   100
She slept away the dreary dark,
    And rose to greet the pleasant morn;
And sang as gaily as a lark
    While busy as the flies sun-born.

XIV

And how she loved us every one;
    And dusted this and mended that,
With trills and laughs and freaks of fun,
    And tender scoldings in her chat!
And then her bird, that sang as shrill
    As she sang sweet; her darling flowers   110
That grew there in the window-sill,
    Where she would sit at work for hours.

XV

It was not much she ever wrote;
    Her fingers had good work to do;

Say, once a week a pretty note;
   And very long it took her too.
And little more she read, I wis;
   Just now and then a pictured sheet,
Besides those letters she would kiss
   And croon for hours, they were so sweet.   120

XVI

She had her friends too, blithe young girls,
   Who whispered, babbled, laughed, caressed,
And romped and danced with dancing curls,
   And gave our life a joyous zest.
But with this dullard, glum and sour,
   Not one of all his fellow-men
Has ever passed a social hour;
   We might be in some wild beast's den.

XVII

This long tirade aroused the bed,
   Who spoke in deep and ponderous bass,   130
Befitting that calm life he led,
   As if firm-rooted in his place:
In broad majestic bulk alone,
   As in thrice venerable age,
He stood at once the royal throne,
   The monarch, the experienced sage:

XVIII

I know what is and what has been;
   Not anything to me comes strange,
Who in so many years have seen
   And lived through every kind of change.   140
I know when men are good or bad,
   When well or ill, he slowly said;
When sad or glad, when sane or mad,
   And when they sleep alive or dead.

XIX

At this last word of solemn lore
   A tremor circled through the gloom,
As if a crash upon the floor
   Had jarred and shaken all the room:
For nearly all the listening things
   Were old and worn, and knew what curse   150
Of violent change death often brings,
   From good to bad, from bad to worse;

XX

They get to know each other well,
   To feel at home and settled down;
Death bursts among them like a shell,
   And strews them over all the town.
The bed went on, This man who lies
   Upon me now is stark and cold;
He will not any more arise,
   And do the things he did of old.   160

XXI

But we shall have short peace or rest;
   For soon up here will come a rout,
And nail him in a queer long chest,
   And carry him like luggage out.
They will be muffled all in black,
   And whisper much, and sigh and weep:
But he will never more come back,
   And some one else in me must sleep.

XXII

Thereon a little phial shrilled,
   Here empty on the chair I lie: 170
I heard one say, as I was filled,
   With half of this a man would die.
The man there drank me with slow breath,
   And murmured, Thus ends barren strife:
O sweeter, thou cold wine of death,
   Than ever sweet warm wine of life.

XXIII

One of my cousins long ago,
   A little thing, the mirror said,
Was carried to a couch to show
   Whether a man was really dead.   180
Two great improvements marked the case:
   He did not blur her with his breath,
His many-wrinkled, twitching face
   Was smooth old ivory: verdict, Death.

XXIV

It lay, the lowest thing there, lulled
   Sweet-sleep-like in corruption's truce;
The form whose purpose was annulled,
   While all the other shapes meant use.
It lay, the *he* become now *it*,
   Unconscious of the deep disgrace,   190
Unanxious how its parts might flit
   Through what new forms in time and space.

XXV

It lay and preached, as dumb things do,
   More powerfully than tongues can prate;
Though life be torture through and through,
   Man is but weak to plain of fate:
The drear path crawls on drearier still
   To wounded feet and hopeless breast?
Well, he can lie down when he will,
   And straight all ends in endless rest.   200

XXVI

And while the black night nothing saw,
   And till the cold morn came at last,
That old bed held the room in awe
   With tales of its experience vast.
It thrilled the gloom; it told such tales
   Of human sorrows and delights,

Of fever moans and infant wails,
    Of births and deaths and bridal nights.

*Written 1867–8. National Reformer (19 May 1872). The City of Dreadful Night
and Other Poems (1880). 1880 text. (National Reformer headnote: 'This room is
believed to have been situate in Grub Street...', followed by quotation from Johnson's
Dictionary (actually 'Contradictionary', on 'Grub Street'.)*

From: THE CITY OF DREADFUL NIGHT

Per me si va nella città dolente.
                Dante[1]

*Poi di tanto adoprar, di tanti moti
D'ogni celeste, ogni terrena cosa,
Girando senza posa,
Per tornar sempre là donde son mosse;
Uso alcuno, alcun frutto
Indovinar non so.[2]*

*Sola nel mondo eterna, a cui si volve
Ogni creata cosa,
In te, morte, si posa
Nostra ignuda natura;
Lieta no, ma sicura*

*Dell' antico dolor...
Però ch' esser beato
Nega ai mortali e nega a' morti il fato.[3]*
                Leopardi

Proem

Lo, thus, as prostrate, 'In the dust I write
    My heart's deep languor and my soul's sad tears.'
Yet why evoke the spectres of black night
    To blot the sunshine of exultant years?
Why disinter dead faith from mouldering hidden?
Why break the seals of mute despair unbidden,
    And wail life's discords into careless ears?

Because a cold rage seizes one at whiles
    To show the bitter old and wrinkled truth
Stripped naked of all vesture that beguiles,   10
    False dreams, false hopes, false masks and modes of youth;
Because it gives some sense of power and passion
In helpless impotence to try to fashion
    Our woe in living words howe'er uncouth.

THE CITY OF DREADFUL NIGHT
1 *Inferno*, Canto III. i. 'This way for the sorrowful city.' (Inscription at
the entrance of Hell.)
2 Leopardi, Canto XXIII, 'Canto Notturno di un Pastore errante dell'
Asia': 'In so much acting, so much motion of every celestial and earthly
thing, gyrating without pause to return whence they came, I can detect
no point nor profit.'

3 Leopardi, 'Coro di Morti' – chorus of Mummies in the Laboratory
of Frederick Ruysch: 'In thee, O death, the only eternal thing in the uni-
verse, to whom all created things turn, our naked selfhood rests. Not
happy, but secure the ancient grief.... For fate denies the state of bles-
sedness both to the living and to the dead.'

Surely I write not for the hopeful young,
    Or those who deem their happiness of worth,
Or such as pasture and grow fat among
    The shows of life and feel nor doubt nor dearth,
Or pious spirits with a God above them
To sanctify and glorify and love them,
    Or sages who foresee a heaven on earth.   20

For none of these I write, and none of these
    Could read the writing if they deigned to try:
So may they flourish, in their due degrees,
    On our sweet earth and in their unplaced sky.
If any cares for the weak words here written,
It must be some one desolate, Fate-smitten,
    Whose faith and hope are dead, and who would die.

Yes, here and there some weary wanderer
    In that same city of tremendous night,   30
Will understand the speech, and feel a stir
    Of fellowship in all-disastrous fight;
'I suffer mute and lonely, yet another
Uplifts his voice to let me know a brother
    Travels the same wild paths though out of sight.'

O sad Fraternity, do I unfold
    Your dolorous mysteries shrouded from of yore?
Nay, be assured; no secret can be told
    To any who divined it not before:
None uninitiate by many a presage   40
Will comprehend the language of the message,
    Although proclaimed aloud for evermore.

                        I
The City is of Night; perchance of Death,
    But certainly of Night; for never there
Can come the lucid morning's fragrant breath
    After the dewy dawning's cold grey air;
The moon and stars may shine with scorn or pity;
The sun has never visited that city,
    For it dissolveth in the daylight fair.

Dissolveth like a dream of night away;
    Though present in distempered gloom of thought
And deadly weariness of heart all day.   10
    But when a dream night after night is brought
Throughout a week, and such weeks few or many
Recur each year for several years, can any
    Discern that dream from real life in aught?

For life is but a dream whose shapes return,
    Some frequently, some seldom, some by night
And some by day, some night and day: we learn,
    The while all change and many vanish quite,
In their recurrence with recurrent changes
A certain seeming order; where this ranges   20
    We count things real; such is memory's might.

A river girds the city west and south,
    The main north channel of a broad lagoon,

Regurging with the salt tides from the mouth;
   Waste marshes shine and glister to the moon
For leagues, then moorland black, then stony ridges;
Great piers and causeways, many noble bridges,
   Connect the town and islet suburbs strewn.

Upon an easy slope it lies at large,
   And scarcely overlaps the long curved crest
Which swells out two leagues from the river marge.
   A trackless wilderness rolls north and west,
Savannahs, savage woods, enormous mountains,
Bleak uplands, black ravines with torrent fountains;
   And eastward rolls the shipless sea's unrest.

The city is not ruinous, although
   Great ruins of an unremembered past,
With others of a few short years ago
   More sad, are found within its precincts vast.
The street-lamps always burn; but scarce a casement
In house or palace front from roof to basement
   Doth glow or gleam athwart the mirk air cast.

The street-lamps burn amidst the baleful glooms,
   Amidst the soundless solitudes immense
Of rangèd mansions dark and still as tombs.
   The silence which benumbs or strains the sense
Fulfils with awe the soul's despair unweeping:
Myriads of habitants are ever sleeping,
   Or dead, or fled from nameless pestilence!

Yet as in some necropolis you find
   Perchance one mourner to a thousand dead,
So there; worn faces that look deaf and blind
   Like tragic masks of stone. With weary tread,
Each wrapt in his own doom, they wander, wander,
Or sit foredone and desolately ponder
   Through sleepless hours with heavy drooping head.

Mature men chiefly, few in age or youth,
   A woman rarely, now and then a child:
A child! If here the heart turns sick with ruth
   To see a little one from birth defiled,
Or lame or blind, as preordained to languish
Through youthless life, think how it bleeds with anguish
   To meet one erring in that homeless wild.

They often murmur to themselves, they speak
   To one another seldom, for their woe
Broods maddening inwardly and scorns to wreak
   Itself abroad; and if at whiles it grow
To frenzy which must rave, none heeds the clamour,
Unless there waits some victim of like glamour,
   To rave in turn, who lends attentive show.

The City is of Night, but not of Sleep;
   There sweet sleep is not for the weary brain;
The pitiless hours like years and ages creep,
   A night seems termless hell. This dreadful strain
Of thought and consciousness which never ceases,

Or which some moments' stupor but increases,
　　This, worse than woe, makes wretches there insane.

They leave all hope behind who enter there:[4]
　　One certitude while sane they cannot leave,
One anodyne for torture and despair;
　　The certitude of Death, which no reprieve
Can put off long; and which, divinely tender,
But waits the outstretched hand to promptly render
　　That draught whose slumber nothing can bereave.[5]

VII

Some say that phantoms haunt those shadowy streets,
　　And mingle freely there with sparse mankind;
And tell of ancient woes and black defeats,
　　And murmur mysteries in the grave enshrined:
But others think them visions of illusion,
Or even men gone far in self-confusion;
　　No man there being wholly sane in mind.

And yet a man who raves, however mad,
　　Who bares his heart and tells of his own fall,
Reserves some inmost secret good or bad:
　　The phantoms have no reticence at all: 10
The nudity of flesh will blush though tameless,
The extreme nudity of bone grins shameless,
　　The unsexed skeleton mocks shroud and pall.

I have seen phantoms there that were as men
　　And men that were as phantoms flit and roam;
Marked shapes that were not living to my ken,
　　Caught breathings acrid as with Dead Sea foam:
The City rests for man so weird and awful,
That his intrusion there might seem unlawful,   20
　　And phantoms there may have their proper home.

IX

It is full strange to him who hears and feels,
　　When wandering there in some deserted street,
The booming and the jar of ponderous wheels,
　　The trampling clash of heavy ironshod feet:
Who in this Venice of the Black Sea rideth?
Who in this city of the stars abideth
　　To buy or sell as those in daylight sweet?

The rolling thunder seems to fill the sky
　　As it comes on; the horses snort and strain,
The harness jingles, as it passes by;   10
　　The hugeness of an overburthened wain:
A man sits nodding on the shaft or trudges
Three parts asleep beside his fellow-drudges:
　　And so it rolls into the night again.

---

4 *Lasciata ogni speranza voi ch'entrate!* 'Abandon all hope, you who
enter.' Part of inscription at entrance to Hell, Dante, *Inferno*, Canto
III. i.

5 Though the Garden of thy Life be wholly waste, the sweet flowers
withered, the fruit-trees barren, over its wall hang ever the rich dark
clusters of the Vine of Death, within easy reach of thy hand, which
may pluck of them when it will. [Original footnote]

What merchandise? whence, whither, and for whom?
　　Perchance it is a Fate-appointed hearse,
Bearing away to some mysterious tomb
　　Or Limbo of the scornful universe
The joy, the peace, the life-hope, the abortions
Of all things good which should have been our portions,   20
　　But have been strangled by that City's curse.

XI

What men are they who haunt these fatal glooms,
　　And fill their living mouths with dust of death,
And make their habitations in the tombs,[6]
　　And breathe eternal sighs with mortal breath,
And pierce life's pleasant veil of various error
To reach that void of darkness and old terror
　　Wherein expire the lamps of hope and faith?

They have much wisdom yet they are not wise,
　　They have much goodness yet they do not well,
(The fools we know have their own Paradise,   10
　　The wicked also have their proper Hell);
They have much strength but still their doom is stronger,
Much patience but their time endureth longer,
　　Much valour but life mocks it with some spell.

They are most rational and yet insane:
　　An outward madness not to be controlled;
A perfect reason in the central brain,
　　Which has no power, but sitteth wan and cold,
And sees the madness, and foresees as plainly
The ruin in its path, and trieth vainly   20
　　To cheat itself refusing to behold.

And some are great in rank and wealth and power,
　　And some renowned for genius and for worth;
And some are poor and mean, who brood and cower
　　And shrink from notice, and accept all dearth
Of body, heart and soul, and leave to others
All boons of life: yet these and those are brothers,
　　The saddest and the weariest men on earth.

XIV

Large glooms were gathered in the mighty fane,
　　With tinted moongleams slanting here and there;
And all was hush: no swelling organ-strain,
　　No chant, no voice or murmuring of prayer;
No priests came forth, no tinkling censers fumed,
And the high altar space was unillumed.

Around the pillars and against the walls
　　Leaned men and shadows; others seemed to brood
Bent or recumbent in secluded stalls.
　　Perchance they were not a great multitude
Save in that city of so lonely streets
Where one may count up every face he meets.[7]

---

6 cf. man with 'unclean spirit', who dwells 'among the tombs', Mark 5.1ff.

7 cf. T. S. Eliot's *Prufrock* ('. . . time/To prepare a face to meet the faces that you meet').

All patiently awaited the event
    Without a stir or sound, as if no less
Self-occupied, doomstricken while attent.
    And then we heard a voice of solemn stress
From the dark pulpit, and our gaze there met
Two eyes which burned as never eyes burned yet:

Two steadfast and intolerable eyes
    Burning beneath a broad and rugged brow;   20
The head behind it of enormous size.
    And as black fir-groves in a large wind bow,
Our rooted congregation, gloom-arrayed,
By that great sad voice deep and full were swayed: –

O melancholy Brothers, dark, dark, dark!
O battling in black floods without an ark!
    O spectral wanderers of unholy Night!
My soul hath bled for you these sunless years,
With bitter blood-drops running down like tears:
    Oh, dark, dark, dark, withdrawn from joy and light!   30

My heart is sick with anguish for your bale;
Your woe hath been my anguish; yea, I quail
    And perish in your perishing unblest.
And I have searched the highths and depths, the scope
Of all our universe, with desperate hope
    To find some solace for your wild unrest.

And now at last authentic word I bring,
Witnessed by every dead and living thing;
    Good tidings of great joy for you, for all:[8]
There is no God; no Fiend with names divine   40
Made us and tortures us; if we must pine,
    It is to satiate no Being's gall.

It was the dark delusion of a dream,
That living Person conscious and supreme,
    Whom we must curse for cursing us with life;
Whom we must curse because the life He gave
Could not be buried in the quiet grave,
    Could not be killed by poison or by knife.[9]

This little life is all we must endure,
The grave's most holy peace is ever sure,   50
    We fall asleep and never wake again;
Nothing is of us but the mouldering flesh,
Whose elements dissolve and merge afresh
    In earth, air, water, plants, and other men.

We finish thus; and all our wretched race
Shall finish with its cycle, and give place
    To other beings, with their own time-doom:
Infinite æons ere our kind began;

8   cf. Angel to shepherds at birth of Jesus: 'behold, I bring you good tidings of great joy, which shall be to all people': Luke 2.10.
9   cf. Job 2.9–3.3: 'Then said his wife unto him…curse God, and die. But he said, thou speakest as one of the foolish women speaketh… After this opened Job his mouth, and cursed his day…'

Infinite æons after the last man
    Has joined the mammoth in earth's tomb and womb.   60

We bow down to the universal laws,
Which never had for man a special clause
    Of cruelty or kindness, love or hate:
If toads and vultures are obscene to sight,
If tigers burn with beauty and with might,[10]
    Is it by favour or by wrath of Fate?

All substance lives and struggles evermore
Through countless shapes continually at war,
    By countless interactions interknit:
If one is born a certain day on earth,   70
All times and forces tended to that birth,
    Not all the world could change or hinder it.

I find no hint throughout the Universe
Of good or ill, of blessing or of curse;
    I find alone Necessity Supreme;
With infinite Mystery, abysmal, dark,
Unlighted ever by the faintest spark
    For us the flitting shadows of a dream.

O Brothers of sad lives! they are so brief;
A few short years must bring us all relief: 80
    Can we not bear these years of labouring breath?
But if you would not this poor life fulfil,
Lo, you are free to end it when you will,
    Without the fear of waking after death. –

The organ-like vibrations of his voice
    Thrilled through the vaulted aisles and died away;
The yearning of the tones which bade rejoice
    Was sad and tender as a requiem lay:
Our shadowy congregation rested still
As brooding on that 'End it when you will.'   90

XVIII

I wandered in a suburb of the north,
    And reached a spot whence three close lanes led down,
Beneath thick trees and hedgerows winding forth
    Like deep brook channels, deep and dark and lown:
The air above was wan with misty light,
The dull grey south showed one vague blur of white.

I took the left-hand lane and slowly trod
    Its earthen footpath, brushing as I went
The humid leafage; and my feet were shod
    With heavy languor, and my frame downbent,   10
With infinite sleepless weariness outworn,
So many nights I thus had paced forlorn.

After a hundred steps I grew aware
    Of something crawling in the lane below;

10   cf. Blake's 'The Tyger': 'burning bright/In the forests of the
night'.

It seemed a wounded creature prostrate there
    That sobbed with pangs in making progress slow,
The hind limbs stretched to push, the fore limbs then
    To drag; for it would die in its own den.

But coming level with it I discerned
    That it had been a man; for at my tread   20
It stopped in its sore travail and half-turned,
    Leaning upon its right, and raised its head,
And with the left hand twitched back as in ire
Long grey unreverend locks befouled with mire.

A haggard filthy face with bloodshot eyes,
    An infamy for manhood to behold.
He gasped all trembling, What, you want my prize?
    You leave, to rob me, wine and lust and gold
And all that men go mad upon, since you
Have traced my sacred secret of the clue?   30

You think that I am weak and must submit;
    Yet I but scratch you with this poisoned blade,
And you are dead as if I clove with it
    That false fierce greedy heart. Betrayed! betrayed!
I fling this phial if you seek to pass,
And you are forthwith shrivelled up like grass.

And then with sudden change, Take thought! take thought!
    Have pity on me! it is mine alone.
If you could find, it would avail you naught;
    Seek elsewhere on the pathway of your own: 40
For who of mortal or immortal race
The lifetrack of another can retrace?

Did you but know my agony and toil!
    Two lanes diverge up yonder from this lane;
My thin blood marks the long length of their soil;
    Such clue I left, who sought my clue in vain:
My hands and knees are worn both flesh and bone;
I cannot move but with continual moan.

But I am in the very way at last
    To find the long-lost broken golden thread   50
Which reunites my present with my past,
    If you but go your own way. And I said,
I will retire as soon as you have told
Where unto leadeth this lost thread of gold.

And so you know it not! he hissed with scorn;
    I feared you, imbecile! It leads me back
From this accursed night without a morn,
    And through the deserts which have else no track,
And through vast wastes of horror-haunted time,
To Eden innocence in Eden's clime: 60

And I become a nursling soft and pure,
    An infant cradled on its mother's knee,
Without a past, love-cherished and secure;
    Which if it saw this loathsome present Me,

Would plunge its face into the pillowing breast,
And scream abhorrence hard to lull to rest.

He turned to grope; and I retiring brushed
   Thin shreds of gossamer from off my face,
And mused, His life would grow, the germ uncrushed;
   He should to antenatal night retrace,   70
And hide his elements in that large womb
Beyond the reach of man-evolving Doom.

And even thus, what weary way were planned,
   To seek oblivion through the far-off gate
Of birth, when that of death is close at hand!
   For this is law, if law there be in Fate:
What never has been, yet may have its when;
The thing which has been, never is again.

XIX

The mighty river flowing dark and deep,
   With ebb and flood from the remote sea-tides
Vague-sounding through the City's sleepless sleep,
   Is named the River of the Suicides;
For night by night some lorn wretch overweary,
And shuddering from the future yet more dreary,
   Within its cold secure oblivion hides.

One plunges from a bridge's parapet,
   As by some blind and sudden frenzy hurled;
Another wades in slow with purpose set   10
   Until the waters are above him furled;
Another in a boat with dreamlike motion
Glides drifting down into the desert ocean,
   To starve or sink from out the desert world.

They perish from their suffering surely thus,
   For none beholding them attempts to save,
The while each thinks how soon, solicitous,
   He may seek refuge in the self-same wave;
Some hour when tired of ever-vain endurance
Impatience will forerun the sweet assurance   20
   Of perfect peace eventual in the grave.

When this poor tragic-farce has palled us long,
   Why actors and spectators do we stay? –
To fill our so-short *rôles* out right or wrong;
   To see what shifts are yet in the dull play
For our illusion; to refrain from grieving
Dear foolish friends by our untimely leaving:
   But those asleep at home, how blest are they!

Yet it is but for one night after all:
   What matters one brief night of dreary pain?   30
When after it the weary eyelids fall
   Upon the weary eyes and wasted brain;
And all sad scenes and thoughts and feelings vanish
In that sweet sleep no power can ever banish,
   That one best sleep which never wakes again.

XXI

Anear the centre of that northern crest
　　Stands out a level upland bleak and bare,
From which the city east and south and west
　　Sinks gently in long waves; and thronèd there
An Image sits, stupendous, superhuman,
The bronze colossus of a wingèd Woman,
　　Upon a graded granite base foursquare.

Low-seated she leans forward massively,
　　With cheek on clenched left hand, the forearm's might
Erect, its elbow on her rounded knee;   10
　　Across a clasped book in her lap the right
Upholds a pair of compasses; she gazes
With full set eyes, but wandering in thick mazes
　　Of sombre thought beholds no outward sight.[11]

Words cannot picture her; but all men know
　　That solemn sketch the pure sad artist wrought
Three centuries and threescore years ago,
　　With phantasies of his peculiar thought:
The instruments of carpentry and science
Scattered about her feet, in strange alliance   20
　　With the keen wolf-hound sleeping undistraught;

Scales, hour-glass, bell, and magic-square above;
　　The grave and solid infant perched beside,
With open winglets that might bear a dove,
　　Intent upon its tablets, heavy-eyed;
Her folded wings as of a mighty eagle,
But all too impotent to lift the regal
　　Robustness of her earth-born strength and pride;

And with those wings, and that light wreath which seems
　　To mock her grand head and the knotted frown   30
Of forehead charged with baleful thoughts and dreams,
　　The household bunch of keys, the housewife's gown
Voluminous, indented, and yet rigid
As if a shell of burnished metal frigid,
　　The feet thick-shod to tread all weakness down;

The comet hanging o'er the waste dark seas,
　　The massy rainbow curved in front of it
Beyond the village with the masts and trees;
　　The snaky imp, dog-headed, from the Pit,
Bearing upon its batlike leathern pinions
Her name unfolded in the sun's dominions,   40
　　The 'MELENCOLIA' that transcends all wit.[12]

Thus has the artist copied her, and thus
　　Surrounded to expound her form sublime,
Her fate heroic and calamitous;

11   cf. Milton's argumentative devils, *Paradise Lost*, ii, 561, who 'found no end in wand'ring mazes lost'.

12   cf. Dürer's 1514 engraving 'Melencolia', and Thomson's poem 'The "Melencolia" of Albrecht Dürer' (not published in T.'s lifetime).

In a letter to her, T. compared George Eliot to 'that grand and awful Melancholy of Albert Dürer which dominates the City of my poem'.

Fronting the dreadful mysteries of Time,
Unvanquished in defeat and desolation,
Undaunted in the hopeless conflagration
    Of the day setting on her baffled prime.

Baffled and beaten back she works on still,   50
    Weary and sick of soul she works the more,
Sustained by her indomitable will:
    The hands shall fashion and the brain shall pore,
And all her sorrow shall be turned to labour,
Till Death the friend-foe piercing with his sabre
    That mighty heart of hearts ends bitter war.

But as if blacker night could dawn on night,
    With tenfold gloom on moonless night unstarred,
A sense more tragic than defeat and blight,
    More desperate than strife with hope debarred,[13]   60
More fatal than the adamantine Never
Encompassing her passionate endeavour,
    Dawns glooming in her tenebrous regard:

The sense that every struggle brings defeat
    Because Fate holds no prize to crown success;
That all the oracles are dumb[14] or cheat
    Because they have no secret to express;
That none can pierce the vast black veil uncertain
Because there is no light beyond the curtain;[15]
    That all is vanity and nothingness.   70

Titanic from her high throne in the north,
    That City's sombre Patroness and Queen,
In bronze sublimity she gazes forth
    Over her Capital of teen and threne,[16]
Over the river with its isles and bridges,
The marsh and moorland, to the stern rock-ridges,
    Confronting them with a coëval mien.

The moving moon and stars from east to west
    Circle before her in the sea of air;
Shadows and gleams glide round her solemn rest.   80
    Her subjects often gaze up to her there:
The strong to drink new strength of iron endurance,
The weak new terrors; all, renewed assurance
    And confirmation of the old despair.

Written, 16 Jan. 1870–29 Oct. 1873. National Reformer *(22 March–17 May 1874).*
The City of Dreadful Night and Other Poems *(1880). 1880 text. The 1880*
volume is dedicated 'To the Memory of The Younger Brother of Dante GIACOMO
LEOPARDI A Spirit as Lofty A Genius as Intense With a Yet More Tragic Doom'.

13   cf. Proverbs 13.12: 'Hope deferred maketh the heart sick.'
14   Milton, 'Ode on the Morning of Christ's Nativity' (1629), 173:
'The oracles are dumb'.
15   cf. the *veil* in Tennyson's *In Memoriam*, LV (and Hebrews 6.19).
16   *teen*: woe. *threne*: a lamentation, or dirge.

DESPOTISM TEMPERED BY DYNAMITE

There is no other title in the world
So proud as mine, who am no law-cramped king,
No mere imperial monarch absolute,
The WHITE TSAR worshipped as a visible God,
As Lord of Heaven no less than Lord of Earth –
   I look with terror to my crowning day.

Through half of Europe my dominions spread,
And then through half of Asia to the shores
Of Earth's great ocean washing the New World;
And nothing bounds them to the Northern Pole,   10
They merge into the everlasting ice –
   I look with terror to my crowning day.

Full eighty million subjects worship me –
Their father, high priest, monarch, God on earth;
My children who but hold their lives with mine
For our most Holy Russia dear and great,
Whose might is concentrated in my hands –
   I look with terror to my crowning day.

I chain and gag with chains and gags of iron
The impious hands and mouths that dare express   20
A word against my sacred sovranty;
The half of Asia is my prison-house,
Myriads of convicts lost in its Immense –
   I look with terror to my crowning day.

I cannot chain and gag the evil thoughts
Of men and women poisoned by the West,
Frenzied in soul by the anarchic West;
These thoughts transmute themselves to dynamite;
My sire was borne all shattered to his tomb –
   I look with terror to my crowning day.   30

My peasants rise to their unvarying toil,
And go to sleep outwearied by their toil,
Without the hope of any better life.
But with no hope they have no deadly fear,
They sleep and eat their scanty food in peace –
   I look with terror to my crowning day.

My palaces are prisons to myself;
I taste no food that may not poison me;
I plant no footstep sure it will not stir
Instant destruction of explosive fire;   40
I look with terror to each day and night –
   With tenfold terror to my crowning day.

*MS dated 1 May 1882 (Thomson's last poem). Weekly Dispatch (4 June 1882 –
the day after his death). A Voice from The Nile (1884). 1884 text.*

Ellen Johnston (?1835–?1874)

Ellen Johnston, 'The Factory Girl', was born in Hamilton, Scotland, around 1835. Her father, James Johnston, a stonemason who wrote verses, seems to have deserted his wife Mary Bilsford and his young daughter by going off to America. Little Ellen lived with her grandparents. Thinking, wrongly, her husband dead, mother married again. Ellen was 'dragged' from the grandparents, and was badly beaten by her mother and stepfather. Self-taught in books, she was put to work in a Glasgow weaving mill at the age of eleven, and made many attempts to run away from home, probably (by the sound of her autobiographical story) to escape her stepfather's sexual abuse. Johnston's autobiographical account in her only volume of poems (1867) is, though, throughout, adoring and condoning of the man. She became pregnant while still a teenager, and was abandoned by her lover to bring up her daughter by herself. She worked around Glasgow, perennially isolated by her literariness from factory colleagues; spent two years in Belfast factories (1857–9); moved to Dundee to work in a jute mill, where she proved herself calamitously unpopular with her female colleagues over some unfair-dismissal appeal. All told she spent almost a quarter of a century in factory labour. Unhappy, she was taken up as a poet by Alex Campbell, editor of the *Glasgow Sentinel* and the (Glasgow) *Penny Post*. Campbell, a political radical, and a keen encourager of working-class bards, helped her make the Poet's Corner of his *Penny Post* into her forum, where she published her own verses and conducted rhymed debates with fellow contributors. Her poems are about the Crimean War ('Lord Raglan's Address to the Allied Armies' made her name throughout Britain), democratic European struggles in Italy and Poland, the plight of the poor and the worker in Scotland, and her patent yearning for handsome young male lovers. Her openly desirous verses have even been allied with the 'Fleshly School' mode attacked by Robert Buchanan (curiously, the son of the *Glasgow Sentinel*'s founder). Alex Campbell appealed in the *Penny Post* of 27 January 1866 for subscribers to a collection of Johnston's verses. The volume *Autobiography, Poems and Songs of Ellen Johnston, 'The Factory Girl'* eventually appeared nearly two years later in 1867, prefaced by a Testimonial from one of her backers, the Revd George Gilfillan (friend of Scottish proletarian poets), talking, though, condescendingly of her fluent and sweet rhymes which 'have attracted the notice and warm praise of many of her own class', despite the lack of a cultivated mind: 'I hope she will be encouraged by this to cultivate her mind, to read to correct the faults in her style – arising from her limited opportunities.' A second, expanded edition was published in 1869 – but with the story of her seduction and pregnancy toned down because of readers' objections. Johnston and Campbell worked hard to promote her work through readings and benefit concerts. By 1869 the book had sold 800 copies. On the strength of rather promising early sales Johnston resigned from factory work, hoping to live by her writing; but she could not. In June 1868 she appealed to Prime Minister Disraeli for financial aid from the Royal Bounty Fund ('after working as a power-loom weaver for upwards of twenty years with a very delicate state of health – left work about six months ago and since then has been obtaining a very limited and precarious subsistence by the sale of her book and the aid of some friends': thus her petition). She received £50, with, apparently, an extra £5 from Queen Victoria herself. Her patron Alex Campbell died early in 1870, and her corner in Poet's Corner ceased. In April 1873 the *Penny Post* reported the illness and 'distressing circumstances' of 'our old contributor', suggesting 'her old admirers' might give money to assist her. She seems to have died in the workhouse. The literary historian Gustav Klaus thinks she was probably the pauper 'Helen Johnston' who died, 20 April 1874, in the Barnhill Poorhouse, Springburn, Glasgow, of anasarca – a form of dropsy caused by kidney malfunction due to malnutrition.

THE LAST SARK[1]

(Written in 1859)

Gude guide me, are you hame again, an' ha'e ye got nae wark,
We've naething noo tae put awa' unless yer auld blue sark;
My head is rinnin' roon about far lichter than a flee –
What care some gentry if they're weel though a' the puir wad dee!

THE LAST SARK
1 dress.

Our merchants an' mill masters they wad never want a meal,
Though a' the banks in Scotland wad for a twelvemonth fail;
For some o' them have far mair goud than ony ane can see –
What care some gentry if they're weel though a' the puir wad dee!

This is a funny warld, John, for it's no divided fair,
And whiles I think some o' the rich have got the puir folk's share,   10
Tae see us starving here the nicht wi' no ae bless'd bawbee –
What care some gentry if they're weel though a' the puir wad dee!

Oor hoose ance bean an' cosey, John; oor beds ance snug an warm
Feels unco cauld an' dismal noo, an' empty as a barn;
The weans sit greeting² in oor face, and we ha'e noucht to gie –
What care some gentry if they're weel though a' the puir wad dee!

It is the puir man's hard-won toil that fills the rich man's purse;
I'm sure his gouden coffers they are het wi' mony a curse;
Were it no for the working men what wad the rich men be?
What care some gentry if they're weel though a' the puir wad dee!   20

My head is licht, my heart is weak, my een are growing blin';
The bairn is faen' aff my knee – oh! John, catch haud o' him,
You ken I hinna tasted meat for days far mair than three;
Were it no for my helpless bairns I wadna care to dee.

Written in 1859. Autobiography, Poems and Songs of Ellen Johnston,
The 'Factory Girl' *(William Love, Glasgow, 1867).*

AN ADDRESS TO NATURE ON ITS CRUELTY

O Nature, thou to me was cruel,
That made me up so small a jewel;
I am so small I cannot shine
Amidst the great that read my rhyme.
When men of genius pass me by,
I am so small they can't descry
One little mark or single trace
Of Burns' science in my face.
Those publications that I sold,
Some typed in blue and some on gold,   10
Learned critics who have seen them
Say origin dwells within them;
But when myself perchance they see,
They laugh and say, 'O is it she?
Well, I think the little boaster
Is nothing but a fair impostor;
She looks so poor-like and so small,
She's next unto a nought-at-all;
Such wit and words quite out-furl
The learning of "A Factory Girl."'   20
At first they do my name exalt,
And with my works find little fault;
But when upon myself they gaze,

2   crying.

They say some other claims the praise.
O Nature, had'st thou taken time
And made me up somewhat sublime,
With handsome form and pretty face,
And eyes of language – smiles of grace;
With snowy brow and ringlets fair,
A beauty quite beyond compare;   30
Winning the charms of fortune's smile,
Still dressed in grandeur all the while;
Then those who see me would believe
I never tried for to deceive
By bringing out a publication
Of borrowed lines or yet quotation.
But those who see me in this dress,
So small and thin I must confess,
Well may they dare the words to use.
Can such a vase distil Love's muse;   40
Well may they ask dare I profess
The talent of an authoress?
Oh who could deem to gaze on me,
That e'er I mused on land or sea,
That I have sat in shady bower
Musing on thy fairest flower;
That I have sought the silvery stream
At midnight hour, calm and serene,
When skies of diamond sparkling flame
Shed pearly tears of heartsick shame,   50
To see me bound in hardship's blight,
Whilst man did rob me of my right,
And critics read my simple rhyme
And dared to say it was not mine?
Imperfect though my lays may be,
Still they belong to none but me.
My blighted breast is their abode,
They were placed there by nature's God;
And though my years are spent in pain,
Still seeking fortune's smiles in vain,   60
Still sighing youth's sweet years away,
Changing life's light into clay;
Hard toiling for my daily bread
With burning heart and aching head.
A vision of delusion's dream,
Hastening downward death's dark stream;
Yet nature between you and I,
Beneath the universal sky,
Who dares to say I have bereft
Another genius of their gift.   70

Autobiography, Poems and Songs *(1867)*.

John (Byrne) Leicester Warren, Lord de Tabley (also 'G. F. Preston', 'George F. Preston', 'W. P. Lancaster', 'William Lancaster', 'William P. Lancaster', 'M.A.') (1835–95)

John Byrne Leicester Warren, Third Baron de Tabley – numismatist, book-plate collector, rubiologist (i.e. expert on brambles) and none-too-successful gentleman-of-letters – was born at Tabley House, the family's grand pile in Cheshire, 26 April 1835. The Warrens wintered in style abroad, mainly in Italy, during John Byrne's childhood. In 1847 he was sent to Eton, thence to Christ Church, Oxford (second classes in Classics Moderations and History Finals). He studied German in Dresden. Retiring by nature, he was nonetheless well acquainted with the men at the centre of politics and literature. At Oxford he 'knew the best men of his time'. Gladstone was an old family friend. Warren would become friends with Browning, Swinburne, William Bell Scott, W. J. Courthope, Tennyson, Burne-Jones. After Oxford he went to Constantinople as Lord Stratford de Redcliffe's diplomatic attaché, then studied the law and was called to the Bar with an eye (as commonly in his class) to serving in Parliament, but literature distracted him from both politics and law. He took to writing reviews for the *Saturday Review*. His first volume of verses appeared in 1859 as *Poems by G. F. Preston*. He was phenomenally unsure as to his preferred literary identity. G. F., or George F., Preston fathered four volumes of verse, all told, each one of which sank without making any impact. After that, Warren tried his luck as W. P. Lancaster, or William Lancaster, or William P. Lancaster, M. A. (first shot *Praeterita*, 1863). As M. A. he did rather better with his Swinburnean *Philoctetes: A Metrical Drama after the Antique* (1866), many readers thinking it was by Matthew Arnold. This smidgin of success prompted M. A.'s *Orestes: A Metrical Drama* (1867), which flopped (though this didn't stop Warren becoming a rather obsessive versifier of past lives – Nimrod, Ophelia, Pandora, Jael, Napoleon). There was evidently no money for him in poetry – and in fact he lost money backing his own volumes – so he turned to fiction, publishing four novels anonymously, pot-boilers all. In every way Warren was a great accumulator: coins (he produced a monograph on Greek Federal coinage), sea-shells, book-plates, flora, poetic forms. He tried Browningesque monologues and a kind of Fleshly decadence after Swinburne and D. G. Rossetti in his *Rehearsals* (1870) and *Searching the Net* (1873) – by J. B. L. Warren; went in for fashionable Circe poems galore; did a long verse tragedy, *The Soldier of Fortune* (1876 – a gorgeousness too far, which was drubbed by the critics and mocked for being in what critics described as the Spasmodic vein of Aytoun's *Firmilian*). Warren seems to have retreated after this rebuff from London literary life to his various country places in Cheshire, the Isle of Wight, Bournemouth, Poole, and a life of collecting things (his *Guide to Book-Plates* (1880) was a great success), ice-skating (he could cut his initials in the ice), tramping about in search of plant-life (the posthumous *Flora of Cheshire* (1899) is clearly a countryside classic: 'Life is short and brambles are interminable'), and sending scores of articles to *Notes and Queries* under assorted names. Warren was rediscovered as a poet through the warmed-over contents of the volumes entitled *Poems, Dramatic and Lyrical* (Elkin Mathews and John Lane, 1893) and *Poems, Dramatic and Lyrical, Second Series* (John Lane, 1895). He was, of course, by then the third Baron (he succeeded his father in 1887) and John Leicester Warren (Lord) de Tabley was evidently an attractive title-page lure for a time when glossy decadence of the Mathews–Lane sort was not unrelated to mere snobbery. His trained eye for natural phenomena generates better verse than his second-hand decadence. Getting nature right was one of his critical criteria (Keats 'is a mere Cockney as to country matters. Even Tennyson now and then goes wrong'). He suffered latterly from gouts and rheums, and he died at Ryde, Isle of Wight, 22 November 1895. He was buried at St Oswald's, Little Poover, in his ancestral Cheshire. The author of the Biographical Note in *The Flora of Cheshire*, Sir Mountstuart Grant Duff, reports that no literary men turned up for the burial, though the tenantry were out in force. Duff blamed Warren's morbid and reclusive later years. His sister, and literary executor, Lady Leighton, 'was anxious that, as he had been christened with water brought from the Jordan, so he should be buried in earth brought from the Holy Land; and accordingly...we all threw some of it into the grave'. A *Collected Poems* was brought out in 1904, and John Drinkwater edited a Selection in 1924.

'MAGA CIRCE'[1]

A Picture at Rome

This is her island squared in cypress lines;
With cedar ranks about her alley walks
Set frequent, and the faces of their boles
Are crimson deep as sunset stains of cloud.
The floor between them, rank and overgrown,
Is tangled with luxuriant heads of bloom
All in a mat together, mixed with grass.
There are the bells of some wide wine-deep flowers,
Great apple fruits and tawny orange globes;
And bunchy cactus tipped in fire-bright buds,   10
Gray aloe spikes and heavy curling vines,
And speckled poison berries intertwined.

Her groves lead down upon the light free waves;
Here foam-heads dance and ripple into sound.
The laughter of many birds is in her elms,
Jays, owls, sea-crows, larks, lapwings, nightingales,
As jumbled as the flowers beneath their notes.
The Isle-grove ends abruptly on the sea,
A stranded star-fish neighbours by the turf
Where the snail toils beneath his painted walls.   20
Small seaward gusts irresolute breathe near;
And sweeter waftings, sent from middle brine,
Stir the deep grasses at her perfect feet,
Where Circe, shining down the gaudy flowers,
Leans centre-light of all this paradise.
One ankle gleams against the margin turf
Just beyond where the wave-teeth cease to bite.
And sea-pinks grow less rosy near her feet.

But this enchantress, island-queen, herself
Bears on her head a bright tire marvellous,   30
And for a girdle one of many dyes
Woven and traced with curious pattern-spells.
Her face is not at first so beautiful,
That one should say, 'Fear her, she will slay men
And draw them into deaths by her strange ways,
And some soft snare hid under all of her.'
We must consider well upon her face,
And then the silent beauty of it all,
Begins upon us, grows and greatens on,
Like sweet increasing music, chord on chord,   40
Till all our being falters overthrown;
And she lures out our soul into her hands,
As faint and helpless as a newborn babe,
To have her way and will with all of it.

O, she this Circe mage, is strange and great,
And deadlier than those terrible bright forms,

'MAGA CIRCE'
1   'Sorceress Circe': Circe, the witch who turned Odysseus's compan-
ions into swine, an her island of Aeaea.

That beam out on us obviously divine,
And at a flash content us with their grace.
Her love eats deeper to the core of men,
Scathing and killing, fierce and unappeased;   50
Until not only the divine in us,
But all the human also (which indeed
Are one tho' this less perfect) fade and change,
And fall corrupted into alien forms.
Till we resemble those strange-headed things
Herded away behind her island throne,
Chimeras, tiger-apes, and wolfish swine.

Rehearsals: A Book of Verses *(Strahan & Co., 1870)*.

THE POWER OF INTERVAL

A fair girl tripping out to meet her love,
Trimmed in her best, fresh as a clover-bud.
An old crone leaning at an ember'd fire,
Short-breath'd in sighs and moaning to herself –
And all the interval of stealing years
To make that this, and one by one detach
Some excellent condition, till Despair,
Faint at the vision, sadly, fiercely blinds
Her burning eyes on her forgetful hands.

Rehearsals *(1870), and* Poems, Dramatic and Lyrical, *Illus. C. Ricketts
(Elkin Mathews & John Lane: at the Sign of the Bodley Head, 1893).*

CIRCE

This the house of Circe, queen of charms –
A kind of beacon-cauldron poised on high,
Hooped round with ember-clasping iron bars,
Sways in her palace porch, and smoulderingly
Drips out in blots of fire and ruddy stars;
But out behind that trembling furnace air,
The lands are ripe and fair,
Hush are the hills and quiet to the eye.
The river's reach goes by
With lamb and holy tower and squares of corn,   10
And shelving interspace
Of holly bush and thorn
And hamlets happy in an Alpine morn,
And deep-bowered lanes with grace
Of woodbine newly born.

But inward o'er the hearth a torch-head stands
Inverted, slow green flames of fulvous hue,
Echoed in wave-like shadows over her.
A censer's swing-chain set in her fair hands
Dances up wreaths of intertwisted blue   20
In clouds of fragrant frankincense and myrrh.
A giant tulip head and two pale leaves
Grew in the midmost of her chamber there,
A flaunting bloom, naked and undivine,

Rigid and bare,
Gaunt as a tawny bond-girl born to shame,
With freckled cheeks and splotched side serpentine,
A gipsy among flowers,
Unmeet for bed or bowers,
Virginal where pure-handed damsels sleep: 30
Let it not breathe a common air with them,
Lest when the night is deep,
And all things have their quiet in the moon,
Some birth of poison from its leaning stem
Waft in between their slumber-parted lips,
And they cry out or swoon,
Deeming some vampire sips,
Where riper Love may come for nectar boon!

And near this tulip, reared across a loom,
Hung a fair web of tapestry half done,   40
Crowding with folds and fancies half the room:
Men eyed as gods and damsels still as stone,
Pressing their brows alone,
In amethystine robes,
Or reaching at the polished orchard globes,
Or rubbing parted love-lips on their rind,
While the wind
Sows with sere apple leaves their breast and hair.
And all the margin there
Was arabesqued and bordered intricate   50
With hairy spider things
That catch and clamber,
And salamander in his dripping cave
Satanic ebon-amber;
Blind worm, and asp, and eft of cumbrous gait,
And toads who love rank grasses near a grave,
And the great goblin moth, who bears
Between his wings the ruined eyes of death;
And the enamelled sails
Of butterflies, who watch the morning's breath.   60
And many an emerald lizard with quick ears
Asleep in rocky dales.
And for an outer fringe embroidered small,
A ring of many locusts, horny-coated,
A round of chirping tree-frogs merry-throated,
And sly, fat fishes sailing, watching all.

Poems, Dramatic and Lyrical *(1893)*.

THE STUDY OF A SPIDER

From holy flower to holy flower
Thou weavest thine unhallowed bower.
The harmless dewdrops, beaded thin,
Ripple along thy ropes of sin.
Thy house a grave, a gulf thy throne
Affright the fairies every one.
Thy winding sheets are gray and fell,
Imprisoning with nets of hell
The lovely births that winnow by,

Winged sisters of the rainbow sky: 10
Elf-darlings, fluffy, bee-bright things,
And owl-white moths with mealy wings,
And tiny flies, as gauzy thin
As e'er were shut electrum[1] in.
These are thy death spoils, insect ghoul,
With their dear life thy fangs are foul.
Thou felon anchorite of pain
Who sittest in a world of slain.
Hermit, who tunest song unsweet
To heaving wing and writhing feet.   20
A glutton of creation's sighs,
Miser of many miseries.
Toper, whose lonely feasting chair
Sways in inhospitable air.
The board is bare, the bloated host
Drinks to himself toast after toast.
His lip requires no goblet brink
But like a weazel must he drink.
The vintage is as old as time
And bright as sunset, pressed and prime.   30

Ah, venom mouth and shaggy thighs
And paunch grown sleek with sacrifice,
Thy dolphin back and shoulders round
Coarse-hairy, as some goblin hound
Whom a hag rides to sabbath on,
While shuddering stars in fear grow wan.
Thou palace priest of treachery,
Thou type of selfish lechery,
I break the toils around thy head
And from their gibbets take thy dead.   40

Poems, Dramatic and Lyrical *(1893)*.

Thomas Ashe (1836–89)

Thomas Ashe was born in Stockport, near Manchester, in 1836, son of John Ashe, a Manchester manufacturer who became a priest in the Church of England late in life (prepared for ordination, in fact, by his own son). Thomas went to Stockport Grammar School, then to St John's College, Cambridge. His first volume of verses, *Poems* (1859), appeared in the year of his graduation. He was ordained into the Church of England ministry, served as curate at Silverstone, but did not like the work and became a schoolmaster instead. He went to Leamington College to teach modern subjects in 1865, after that to Queen Elizabeth School, Ipswich. At the end of the seventies he moved to Paris, where he lived for two years, returning in 1881 to London and a life of literary labour. He edited Coleridge's writings steadily through the eighties. A stream of his own poems also appeared over the years – *Dryope,*

and Other Poems (1861), *Pictures, and Other Poems* (1865), *The Sorrows of Hipsipyle: A Poem* (1867), *Poems* (1871), *Edith, or Love and Life in Cheshire: A Poem* (1873), *Songs Now and Then* (1876). A 'Complete Edition' of his *Poems* came out in 1886, followed by *Songs of a Year* in the year before his death, 18 December 1889. He never became well known as a poet. At longer or shorter length he preferred telling stories in verse, especially about far-off female beloveds – Plectrude, Hildegard, Yseult. He is fond of poeticizing girls, particularly pubescent ones – Ettie, Annette, Fay, Avice, Ethel, Elfin, Kattie, Marit, Pansie. His narratives are high on charm, and achieve, at their best, a kind of moody Hardyesque force. He was a man for prevailing poetic winds (his *Sorrows of Hipsipyle* follows, for example, the dramatic-antique path of Swinburne's *Atalanta in Calydon*). He died in London, but was buried in

THE STUDY OF A SPIDER
1 amber.

St James's churchyard, Sutton, Macclesfield. Havelock Ellis rather promoted Ashe – writing an article on his poems in *Westminster Review* (April 1886), and contributing a selection of his verse, with a critical introduction, to Alfred H. Miles, *The Poets and the Poetry of the Century*, vol. 6, *William Morris to Robert Buchanan* (1892).

COUSIN CARRIE

This is the stile where Carrie lean'd: –
   My sister Liv and I
Came through the summer woods with her,
   And could not pass it by.
We lean'd among the leafy green,
   And stay'd to chat awhile:
The happy morn was happier
   With Cousin Carrie's smile.

The woody thickets closed us round;
   But sun-beams, slim and fair,   10
They gleam'd on Carrie's cheek and neck,
   And loops of yellow hair.
I see her just as then: – I sit
   Here on the stile alone:
And sadder with the setting day
   The woods and I are grown.

Pictures, and Other Poems *(Bell & Daldy,* 1865*).*

PALL-BEARING

I remember, they sent
   Some one to me, who said,
'You were his friend while he lived:
   Be so now he is dead.'

So I went next day to the house;
   And a woman nodded to me,
As I sat alone in thought: –
   Said, 'Sir, would you like to see

The poor dead body upstairs,
   Before we rivet the lid?'   10
But I said, 'I would rather not:
   For the look would never be hid

'From my sight, day after day,
   From my soul, year after year.
Enough to look on the pall:
   Enough to follow the bier.'

So the mourners gather'd at last;
   And the poor dead body was put
In a hearse with mournful plumes,
   And the door of the hearse was shut.   20

And when the mourners were all
   In the coaches, ready to start,
The sorrowing parent came
   To me, and whisper'd apart.

He smiled as well as he could;
    And the import of what he said
Was, that I should bear at the feet,
    And his son would bear at the head.

He was ever my friend;
    And I was happy to be   30
Of ever so little use
    To one who had so loved me.

But, what a weight, O God!
    Was that one coffin to bear!
Like a coffin of lead!
    And I carry it everywhere

About, wherever I go!
    If I lift the slightest thing,
That requires an effort to lift,
    The effort at once will bring   40

The whole weight into my hands,
    And I carry the corpse at the feet;
And feel as if it would drop,
    And slip out of its winding-sheet.

I have made a vow in my heart,
    Whatever the friends may say,
Never to carry a corpse
    Again, to my dying day.

Poems, A New Edition (H. Knights, Printer, Ipswich, [1871]).
Later, revised version, titled 'Corpse-Bearing', Poems, Complete Edition
(George Bell & Sons, 1886).

REMEMBER

You said you'd write ere the year was over,
    And winter's come and the year near end: –
O not as lover writes unto lover,
    But just, you know, as a friend to friend.
This line is only to say my home is
    The same old village: I feel, somehow,
You could not fail me or break a promise: –
    Remember, now!

Still, while the skurry of snows sun-smitten
    Flush'd-up the rivers and swell'd the rills;   10
And summer's blossoms, and rose love-litten,
    Grew pale, and died as the daffodils;
And hedgerows glisten'd adrip, and whiten'd,
    And brambles redden'd with hips again;
For your word given how my heart lighten'd! –
    Remember, then!

Through blind ill-hiding a window, that is
    Alit and ruddy in front of me,
I, at my blacken'd and frost-scrawl'd lattice,
    See fair hands trimming a Christmas-tree: 20

> For New Year's on us, – I trust, a better.
>   You will not dally? you will be true?
>   You'll keep your promise, and write the letter? –
>   Remember, do!

Poems (1886).

W. S. (William Schwenk) Gilbert (1836–1911)

W. S. Gilbert, one of the funniest and, probably, the most financially well-off of writers for the Victorian theatre, was born in London, in Southampton Street, just off the Strand, 18 November 1836, the son of William Gilbert (an East India Company physician turned novelist) and Anne Morris. His Germanic middle name came from a grandfather. At the age of two he was kidnapped by crooks in Naples and held to ransom for £25. He took his pseudonym Bab from his childhood pet-name. He went to assorted schools in Boulogne and West London; studied at King's College, London; failed in his ambition to go to the Crimean War as an officer when the fighting ended too soon for him (he became an enthusiastic Militia officer instead). He worked as a clerk (1857–62) in the Privy Council office. With a legacy he bought his way into the Law, but he obtained very little work as a barrister, and grew increasingly dependent on his contributions – drawings as well as words – to *Fun* magazine. *Punch*'s editor Mark Lemon did not much care for Gilbert's work and *Fun* was where his wonderfully witty series of 'Bab Ballads' appeared. *Bab Ballads* came out in volume form in 1871. *More Bab Ballads* followed in 1873, *Fifty Bab Ballads* in 1884. And so on. He contributed widely to the *Cornhill, Temple Bar, Tinsley's Magazine*, et al., and turned himself into a formidably prolific writer for the stage – particularly comic stuff, farces, travesties, 'fairy comedy', opera bouffe, which were generally great hits, and serious blank verse dramas, which were not. He first teamed up with the composer Arthur Seymour Sullivan in the opera *Trial by Jury* in March 1875 (at the Royalty Theatre, owned by Richard D'Oyly Carte). This led to the great sequence of operas done by the D'Oyly Carte Company, which came to be known as the Savoy Operas after Gilbert's satire on the new aestheticism, *Patience* (1881), transferred to D'Oyly Carte's new opera house, the Savoy, specially built for Gilbert and Sullivan. There followed some of the most famous pieces in the light operatic repertoire: *Iolanthe* (1882), *Princess Ida* (1884: based on Gilbert's earlier comedy *The Princess*, 1870, after Tennyson's poem of that name), *The Mikado* (1885), *Ruddigore* (1887), *The Yeomen of the Guard* (1888), *The Gondoliers* (1889). D'Oyly Carte, Sullivan and Gilbert made fabulous sums for the time – reputedly £30,000 each for *The Mikado* alone – and they fell out over money. Their last Gilbert and Sullivan collaboration was *The Grand Duke* (1896) and after that Gilbert's work fell rapidly out of popular esteem. He was a meticulous composer and a dictatorial director. He built and owned the Garrick Theatre in London's Charing Cross Road (1889) and acquired a large Norman Shaw designed house in Middlesex. He died from a heart attack, 29 May 1911, after rescuing a young woman from drowning in his open-air swimming lake. He gave his name to a style – the Gilbertian – that mode of gibing, pat, spryly and ludicrously rhyming verses with which he turned current fads and preoccupations upside down.

(THE ÆSTHETE)

If you're anxious for to shine in the high æsthetic line as a man of culture rare,
You must get up all the germs of the transcendental terms, and plant them everywhere.
You must lie upon the daisies and discourse in novel phrases of your complicated state of mind
The meaning doesn't matter if it's only idle chatter of a transcendental kind.
  And every one will say,
  As you walk your mystic way,
'If this young man expresses himself in terms too deep for *me*,
Why what a very singularly deep young man this deep young man must be!'

Be eloquent in praise of the very dull old days which have long since passed away,
And convince 'em, if you can, that the reign of good Queen Anne was Culture's palmiest day. 10
Of course you will pooh-pooh whatever's fresh and new, and declare it's crude and mean,
For Art stopped short in the cultivated court of the Empress Josephine.
  And every one will say,

As you walk your mystic way,
'If that's not good enough for him which is good enough for *me*,
Why what a very cultivated kind of youth this kind of youth must be!'

Then a sentimental passion of a vegetable fashion must excite your languid spleen,
An attachment *à la* Plato for a bashful young potato, or a not-too-French French bean!
Though the Philistines may jostle, you will rank as an apostle in the high æsthetic band,   20
If you walk down Piccadilly with a poppy or a lily in your mediæval hand.
   And every one will say,
   As you walk your flowery way,
'If he's content with a vegetable love which would certainly not suit *me*,
Why, what a most particularly pure young man this pure young man must be!'

> *Song of Reginald Bunthorne (A Fleshly Poet), in* Patience; or, Bunthorne's Bride!
> *(Chappell & Co., 1881), Act I. First produced at Opéra Comique, 23 April 1881.*

(ANGLICIZED UTOPIA)

Society has quite forsaken all her wicked courses,
   Which empties our police courts, and abolishes divorces.
      (Divorce is nearly obsolete in England.)
No tolerance we show to undeserving rank and splendour;
For the higher his position is, the greater the offender.
      (That's a maxim that is prevalent in England.)
No Peeress at our Drawing Room before the Presence passes
Who wouldn't be accepted by the lower-middle classes.
Each shady dame, whatever be her rank, is bowed out neatly.
(In short, this happy country has been Anglicized completely!   10
      It really is surprising
      What a thorough Anglicizing
   We have brought about – Utopia's quite another land;
      In her enterprising movements,
      She is England – with improvements,
   Which we dutifully offer to our mother-land!)

Our city we have beautified – we've done it willy-nilly –
And all that isn't Belgrave Square is Strand and Piccadilly.[1]
      (We haven't any slummeries in England!)
We have solved the labour question with discrimination polished,   20
So poverty is obsolete and hunger is abolished –
      (We are going to abolish it in England.)
The Chamberlain our native stage has purged, beyond a question,
Of 'risky' situation and indelicate suggestion:[2]
No piece is tolerated if it's costumed indiscreetly –
(In short, this happy country has been Anglicized completely!
      It really is surprising, *etc.*)

Our Peerage we've remodelled on an intellectual basis,
Which certainly is rough on our hereditary races –
      (We are going to remodel it in England.)   30
The Brewers and the Cotton Lords no longer seek admission,
And Literary Merit meets with proper recognition –
      (As Literary Merit does in England!)

ANGLICIZED UTOPIA   2 Lord Chamberlain: responsible for stage censorship.
1 smart districts of London.

Who knows but we may count among our intellectual chickens
Like them an Earl of Thackeray and p'raps a Duke of Dickens[3] –
Lord Fildes and Viscount Millais (when they come) we'll welcome sweetly[4] –
(And then, this happy country will be Anglicized completely!
    It really is surprising, *etc.*)

King Paramount the First (King of Utopia), and Chorus (chorus parts in brackets), in
Utopia (Limited); or, The Flowers of Progress *(Chappell & Co., 1893), Act II.*
First produced at the Savoy Theatre, 7 October 1893.

Frances Ridley Havergal (1836–79)

Frances Ridley Havergal – her middle name a tribute to the kind of Protestant martyr she herself aspired to be – was the youngest child of the Revd William Havergal and his first wife Jane. She was born in the rectory at Astley in Worcestershire. William Havergal was, like Frances's brother Henry, a composer of church music. An Evangelical Anglican, he keenly supported the Church Missionary Society (one of his settings was Bishop Heber's famous 'From Greenland's Icy Mountains'). He passed on his brand of Evangelical Christianity to his daughter, who became scrupulously pietistic and sturdily missionary after she had passed in her teens through the sort of typically anxious religious crisis that, for example, Christina Rossetti also experienced. 'I committed my soul to the Saviour, and earth and heaven seemed brighter from that moment.' She was well educated. She studied in Germany; she knew Hebrew. But worldly delights, even of an innocuous sort, like secular musical pleasures and books for their own sake, must be abandoned in the demanding cause of Christ. 'I love, I love my Master,/I will not go out free' was one characteristically submissive poem; 'Master, speak! Thy servant heareth!' another. 'Who is on the Lord's side, who will serve the king?': the challenge to Christian servitude could be most peremptory. Like 'Take my life, and let it be/Consecrated, Lord, to Thee', 'I am trusting Thee, Lord Jesus', and 'Lord, speak to me that I may speak,/In living echoes of Thy tone': such verses, set to memorable music and sung repeatedly in church and chapel, became a main part of the discourse, the consciousness, the imagination of the Evangelical world. Even on holiday Frances must speak for Jesus – the posthumous *Swiss Letters and Alpine Poems*, edited by her sister J. Miriam Crane (1881), for example, is not only a lively record of scrambles in the mountains ('we soon found it necessary to *peel*, and actually went up in our petticoats! You can't think how hot one gets climbing, even among the snow'), but is full of zealous daily encounters with those she must witness to about her Protestant and Evangelical faith ('We had only a few leaflets left,

with "Rock of Ages" in French and German, and these they accepted eagerly. I have since regretted that it did not occur to me at the moment to *sing* it'). The glowing affectivity of Frances Havergal's religious writing ('Oh, I *can* say now that Jesus *is* "to me a living bright Reality", and that He really and truly *is* "more dear, more intimately nigh, than e'en the sweetest earthly tie." No friendship could be what I find his to be') and her almost mythic reputation – established through her first collection, *The Ministry of Song* (1871), and its many successors, through the two-volume posthumous collection edited by her sister Maria V. G. Havergal (1884), and through the numerous reprints, collections, and the many singletons on cards ('Take My Life', for example, was much reprinted as a leaflet or tract for use in services of Christian dedication and for enclosing in letters) – as well as through her magazine appearances (in *Good Words*, and so on), and her sister's *Memorials* (second edition 1886) and its numerous successors from other hands, but above all through the hymn book in the pew and words and tunes constantly on the lips of congregations – all this made Frances Havergal a sort of Low Church Victorian saint. The proceeds of her writing went to the Church Missionary Society and the YMCA. From 1846 to 1860 she was a devoted Sunday School teacher. She lived at home with her father and mother (who died in 1848) and then her stepmother. For many years the family lived in Leamington Spa, her father dying there in 1870, his second wife following him in 1878, after which Frances moved to South Wales. She had never been entirely well. Early on she had to leave her English school because of erysipelas (nervous inflammation of the face). She wrote often from her sick-bed (one of her best-known hymns, 'Like a river glorious/Is God's perfect love', is titled 'Perfect Peace. In Illness'). She scarcely recovered at all from her typhoid fever of 1874 and died after an attack of peritonitis, 3 June 1879. She was forty-two. As Evangelical tradition and myth required, she was rejoicing in her Master's love and singing hymns to the very end.

---

3 W. M. Thackeray and Charles Dickens, writers.

4 Luke Fildes and John Everett Millais, painters.

THE MINISTRY OF SONG

In God's great field of labour
    All work is not the same;
He hath a service for each one
    Who loves His holy name.
And you to whom the secrets
    Of all sweet sounds are known,
Rise up! for He hath called you
    To a mission of your own.
And rightly to fulfil it,
    His grace can make you strong,   10
Who to your charge hath given
    The Ministry of Song.

Sing to the little children,
    And they will listen well;
Sing grand and holy music,
    For they can feel its spell.
Tell them the tale of Jephthah;[1]
    Then sing them what he said, –
'Deeper and deeper still,' and watch
    How the little cheek grows red,   20
And the little breath comes quicker;
    They will ne'er forget the tale,
Which the song has fastened surely,
    As with a golden nail.

I remember, late one evening,
    How the music stopped, for, hark!
Charlie's nursery door was open,
    He was calling in the dark, –
'Oh no! I am not frightened,
    And I do not want a light;   30
But I cannot sleep for thinking
    Of the song you sang last night.
Something about a "valley,"
    And "make rough places plain,"
And "Comfort ye";[2] so beautiful!
    Oh, sing it me again!'

Sing at the cottage bedside;
    They have no music there,
And the voice of praise is silent
    After the voice of prayer.   40
Sing of the gentle Saviour
    In the simplest hymns you know,
And the pain-dimmed eye will brighten
    As the soothing verses flow.
Better than loudest plaudits
    The murmured thanks of such,
For the King will stoop to crown them
    With His gracious 'Inasmuch.'[3]

Sing, where the full-toned organ
    Resounds through aisle and nave,   50
And the choral praise ascendeth
    In concord sweet and grave.
Sing, where the village voices
    Fall harshly on your ear,
And, while more earnestly you join,
    Less discord you will hear.
The noblest and the humblest
    Alike are 'common praise',
And not for human ear alone
    The psalm and hymn we raise.   60

Sing in the deepening twilight,
    When the shadow of eve is nigh,
And her purple and golden pinions
    Fold o'er the western sky.
Sing in the silver silence,
    While the first moonbeams fall;
So shall your power be greater
    Over the hearts of all.
Sing till you bear them with you
    Into a holy calm,   70
And the sacred tones have scattered
    Manna, and myrrh, and balm.

Sing! that your song may gladden;
    Sing like the happy rills,
Leaping in sparkling blessing
    Fresh from the breezy hills.
Sing! that your song may silence
    The folly and the jest,
And the 'idle word' be banished
    As an unwelcome guest.   80
Sing! that your song may echo
    After the strain is past,
A link of the love-wrought cable
    That holds some vessel fast.

Sing to the tired and anxious;
    It is yours to fling a ray,
Passing indeed, but cheering,
    Across the rugged way.
Sing to God's holy servants,
    Weary with loving toil,   90
Spent with their faithful labour
    On oft ungrateful soil.
The chalice of your music
    All reverently bear,
For with the blessèd angels
    Such ministry you share.

THE MINISTRY OF SONG

1   whose sacred vow led to his daughter's killing, Judges 11.30 ff.
2   Isaiah 40. 1–4: 'Comfort ye ... my people, saith your God. ... Every valley shall be exalted ... and the crooked shall be made straight, and the rough places plain.'
3   'Inasmuch as ye have done it unto one of the least of these my brethren, ye have done it unto me', Matthew 25.40.

When you long to bear the Message
   Home to some troubled breast,
Then sing with loving fervour,
   'Come unto Him, and rest.'[4]   100
Or would you whisper comfort,
   Where words bring no relief,
Sing how 'He was despised,
   Acquainted with our grief.'[5]
And, aided by His blessing,
   The song may win its way
Where speech had no admittance,
   And change the night to day.

Sing, when His mighty mercies
   And marvellous love you feel,   110
And the deep joy of gratitude
   Springs freshly as you kneel;
When words, like morning starlight,
   Melt powerless, – rise and sing!

And bring your sweetest music
   To Him, your gracious King.
Pour out your song before Him
   To whom our best is due;
Remember, He who hears your prayer
   Will hear your praises too.   120

Sing on in grateful gladness!
   Rejoice in this good thing
Which the Lord thy God hath given thee,
   The happy power to sing.
But yield to Him, the Sovereign,
   To whom all gifts belong,
In fullest consecration,
   Your ministry of song.
Until His mercy grant you
   That resurrection voice,   130
Whose only ministry shall be
   To praise Him and rejoice.

The Ministry of Song (James Nisbet & Co., 1871).

A WORKER'S PRAYER

Lord, speak to me, that I may speak
   In living echoes of Thy tone;
As Thou hast sought, so let me seek
   Thy erring children, lost and lone.

O lead me, Lord, that I may lead
   The wandering and the wavering feet;
O feed me, Lord, that I may feed
   Thy hungering ones with manna sweet.[1]

O strengthen me, that while I stand
   Firm on the Rock[2] and strong in Thee,   10
I may stretch out a loving hand
   To wrestlers with the troubled sea.

O teach me, Lord, that I may teach
   The precious things Thou dost impart;

And wing my words, that they may reach
   The hidden depths of many a heart.

O give Thine own sweet rest to me,
   That I may speak with soothing power
A word in season[3], as from Thee,
   To weary ones in needful hour.   20

O fill me with Thy fulness, Lord,
   Until my very heart o'erflow
In kindling thought and glowing word,
   Thy love to tell, Thy praise to show.

O use me, Lord, use even me,
   Just *as* Thou wilt, and *when*, and *where*;
Until Thy blessèd Face I see,
   Thy rest, Thy joy, Thy glory share.

Written April 1872. Text of Poetical Works, *2 vols, ed. Maria V. G. Havergal*
(James Nisbet & Co., 1884), II.

---

4 Matthew 11.28: 'Come unto me, all ye that labour and are heavy laden and I will give you rest.'
5 Isaiah 53.3: 'He is despised and rejected of men; a man of sorrows and acquainted with grief.'

A WORKER'S PRAYER
1 manna: divinely provided food for ancient Israelites in wilderness wanderings.
2 Jesus Christ.
3 2 Timothy 4.2: 'Preach the word: be instant in season, out of season...'

CONSECRATION HYMN

'Here we offer and present unto Thee, O Lord, ourselves, our souls and bodies, to be a reasonable, holy, and lively sacrifice unto Thee.'[1]

Take my life, and let it be
Consecrated, Lord, to Thee.

Take my moments and my days;
Let them flow in ceaseless praise.

Take my hands, and let them move
At the impulse of Thy love.

Take my feet, and let them be
Swift and 'beautiful' for Thee.[2]

Take my voice, and let me sing
Always, only, for my King.   10

Take my lips, and let them be
Filled with messages from Thee.

Take my silver and my gold;
Not a mite would I withhold.[3]

Take my intellect, and use
Every power as Thou shalt choose.

Take my will, and make it Thine;
It shall be no longer mine.

Take my heart, it *is* Thine own;
It shall be Thy royal throne.   20

Take my love; my Lord, I pour
At Thy feet its treasure-store.[4]

Take myself, and I will be
Ever, *only*, ALL for Thee.

Written 1874. Text of Poetical Works *(1884), II.*

MY MASTER

'I love my master;...I will not go out free. And he shall serve him for ever.'
Ex. xxi. 5, 6

I
I love, I love my Master,
    I will not go out free,
For He is my Redeemer,
    He paid the price for me.

II
I would not leave His service,
    It is so sweet and blest;
And in the weariest moments
    He gives the truest rest.

III
I would not halve my service,
    His only it must be, –   10
His *only*, who so loved me
    And gave Himself for me.

IV
My Master shed His life-blood
    My vassal life to win,

And save me from the bondage
    Of tyrant self and sin.

V
He chose me for His service,
    And gave me power to choose
That blessèd, 'perfect freedom'
    Which I shall never lose: 20

VI
For He hath met my longing
    With word of golden tone,
That I shall serve for ever
    Himself, Himself alone.

VII
'Shall serve Him' hour by hour,
    For He will show me how;
My Master is fulfilling
    His promise even now!

CONSECRATION HYMN
1 words from the minister's prayer of oblation at Holy Communion – in Church of England's Book of Common Prayer.
2 'How beautiful...are the feet of him that bringeth good tidings', Isaiah 52.7.
3 the widow's mite, Mark 12.42.
4 like Mary Magdalene, who anointed Jesus's feet from her 'alabaster box of ointment', having washed them with her tears and dried them with her hair: Luke 7.37–8.

VIII
'Shall serve Him,' and 'for ever;'
   O hope most sure, most fair!   30
The perfect love outpouring
   In perfect service there!

IX
Rejoicing and adoring,
   Henceforth my song shall be:
I love, I love my Master,
   I will not go out free!

Text of Poetical Works *(1884), II.*

H. (Henry) Cholmondeley Pennell (1836–?)

Henry Cholmondeley Pennell, civil servant, fisherman and wit, was born in 1836, son of Sir Charles Henry Pennell. He entered government service in 1853, was seconded (1865) to Egypt as reformist head of the Department of Internal Commerce, and became a Royal Inspector of Fisheries (1866). He wrote a lot for *Punch*, making his name as a writer of zestful light verse with *Puck on Parnassus* (1861). Much of his writing is light if exuberant and energetic *vers de société*, occasional stuff, and so on, as in *Pegasus Re-saddled* (1877). But darker satirical engagements are undertaken in *Crescent and Other Lyrics* (1864) and *The Modern Babylon* (1872). His own selection of his verses appeared as '*From Grave to Gay*' (1884), a title which indicates his pitch and range. He also produced several books about fish and fishing – *The Book of the Pike* (1865), *The Modern Practical Angler* (1870), and many more – as well as for a time editing the *Fisherman's Magazine and Review* (1864).

LITTLE BO-PEEP

'Little Bo-peep has lost her sheep,'[1]
And some one or other's lost little Bo-peep –
Or she'd never be wand'ring at twelve o'clock
With a golden crook, and a velvet frock,
In a diamond necklace, in such a rout, –
In diamond buckles, and high-heel'd shoes
(And a dainty wee foot in them too, if you choose,
And an ankle a sculptor might rave about....)
But I think she's a little witch, you know,
With her broomstick-crook and her high-heel'd shoe   10
And the mischievous fun that flashes thro'
The wreaths of her amber hair – don't you?
No wonder the flock follows little Bo-peep, –
Such a shepherd would turn all the world into sheep,
To trot at her heels and look up in the face
Of their pastor for – goodness knows what, say for grace? –
Her face that recalls in its reds and its blues,
And its setting of gold, 'Esmeralda' by Greuze....[2]

There you've Little Bo-peep, dress, diamonds, and all,
As I met her last night at the Fancy Ball.   20

'From Grave to Gay': Selections from the Complete Poems *(Longmans, Green, 1884).*

LITTLE BO-PEEP
1 opening line of well-known nursery rhyme.

2 Jean Baptiste Greuze (1725–1805), painter of pretty girls.

'Faite à Peindre'

'Made to be painted' – a Millais[1] might give
A fortune to study that exquisite face –
The face is a fortune – a Lawrence[2] might live
Anew in each line of that figure's still grace.

The pose is perfection, a model each limb,
From the delicate foot to the classical head;
But the almond blue eyes, with their smiling, look dim,
And lips to be *loved* want a trifle more red.

Statuesque? no, a Psyche, let's say, in repose, –
A Psyche whose Cupid beseeches in vain,[3] –   10
We sigh as the nightingale sighs to the rose
That declines (it's averred) to give sighs back again....

If the wind shook the rose? then a shower would fall
Of sweet-scented petals to gather who list;
If a sigh shook my Psyche? she'd yawn, that is all,
She's made to be painted – and not to be kist.

'From Grave to Gay' *(1884).*

The Night Mail North

(Euston Square, 1840)[1]

Now then, take your seats! for Glasgow and the North;
Chester! – Carlisle! – Holyhead, – and the wild Frith of Forth;
'Clap on the steam and sharp's the word,
'You men in scarlet cloth: –

'Are there any more pas..sengers,
'For the Night..Mail..to the North!'

Are there any more passengers?
Yes three – but they can't get in, –
Too late, too late! – How they bellow and knock,
They might as well try to soften a rock   10
As the heart of that fellow in green.

For the Night Mail North? what ho –
(No use to struggle, you can't get thro'
My young and lusty one) –
Whither away from the gorgeous town? –

'For the lake and the stream and the heather brown,
'And the double-barrelled gun!'

For the Night Mail North, I say?
You, with the eager eyes –
You with the haggard face and pale? –   20

'Faite à Peindre'
1   John Everett Millais, painter (1829–96).
2   Thomas Lawrence, painter (1769–1830).

3   In Pysche and Cupid story in Apuleius's *Golden Ass* (2nd century),
it's the woman Psyche who beseeches – or searches – in vain.
The Night Mail North
1   site of Great Central London railway station.

'From a ruined hearth and a starving brood,
   'A Crime and a felon's gaol!'

For the Night Mail North, old man? –
   Old statue of despair –
Why tug and strain at the iron gate?
'*My daughter!!*'

   Ha! too late, too late,
 She is gone, you may safely swear;
 She has given you the slip, d'you hear?
 She has left you alone in your wrath, –   30
And she's off and away, with a glorious start,
To the home of her choice, with the man of her heart,
   By the Night Mail North!
    . . . . .
     . . . . .

Wh———ish, R———ush,
Wh———ish, R———ush . . .
   'What's all that hullabaloo?
'Keep fast the gates there – who is this
   'That insists on bursting thro'?'

A desperate man whom none may withstand,
For look, there is something clench'd in his hand –   40
   Tho' the bearer is ready to drop –
   He waves it wildly to and fro,
 And hark! how the crowd are shouting below –
     'Back!'
   And back the opposing barriers go,
'*A reprieve for the Cannongate murderer, Ho!*
   '*In the Queen's name* –
     'STOP.
   '*Another has confessed the crime.*'

   Whish – rush – whish – rush . . .   50

The Guard has caught the flutt'ring sheet,
Now forward and northward! fierce and fleet,
Thro' the mist and the dark and the driving sleet,
   As if life and death were in it;
    'Tis a splendid race! a race against Time, –
   And a thousand to one we win it:
    Look at those flitting ghosts –
    The white-arm'd finger-posts –
If we're moving the eighth of an inch, I say,
   We're going a mile a minute!   60
A mile a minute – for life or death –
Away, away! though it catches one's breath,
 The man shall not die in his wrath:

   The quivering carriages rock and reel –
Hurrah! for the rush of the grinding steel!
The thundering crank, and the mighty wheel! –

   Are there any more pas . . sengers
For the Night . . Mail . . to the North?

'From Grave to Gay' *(1884)*.

(Mrs Julia) Augusta Webster (also 'Cecil Home') (1837–94)

Augusta Webster was born at Poole, Dorset, 30 January 1837. Her father, Vice-Admiral George Davies, was an officer in the coastguard service; her mother's father, Alexander Hume, had been an intimate of Lamb, Hazlitt and William Godwin. Augusta was brought up on a ship in Chichester Harbour before her father's work took her to Banff in Scotland, where she went to school, and then to Cambridge (he was Chief Constable of Huntingdonshire). She attended courses at Cambridge School of Art, studied Greek – to help her younger brother – and taught herself Italian and Spanish. She became fluent in French while living in Paris and Geneva. She published her first and second poetry volumes, *Blanche Lisle and Other Poems* (1860) and *Lilian Gray* (1864), as well as her three-decker novel *Lesley's Guardians* (1864), under the gender-ambivalent name of Cecil Home. At the end of 1863 she married Thomas Webster, a Fellow and Lecturer in Law at Trinity College, Cambridge. Their only child is celebrated in the incomplete sonnet sequence *Mother and Daughter* (1895), introduced by W. M. Rossetti. Augusta did Greek translations – Aeschylus' *Prometheus Bound* (1866), Euripides' *Medea* (1868) – which male Greek scholars praised. Her own work came truly alive, as in *Dramatic Studies* (1866), *A Woman Sold and Other Poems* (1867) and *Portraits* (1870), when she adapted the dramatic monologue of Tennyson and Browning to women's voices and personae. Not surprisingly, she was also drawn to verse drama – *The Auspicious Day* (1872), *Disguises* (1879), *In a Day* (1882: the only one actually acted), *The Sentence* (1887 – greatly admired by Christina Rossetti). She liked the Italian song form known as *rispetti*, and experimented with English versions in *A Book of Rhyme* (1881) – where, oddly enough, they're mistakenly called *stornelli*. In the seventies and eighties, after she and her husband moved to London, she was active in education, twice elected (1879, 1885) to the London School Board. She theorized and politicized widely in print – writing about, for example, translation and poetic selfhood, women's clothing and 'Matrimony as a Means of Livelihood', in the essays collected in *A Housewife's Opinions* (1879). Her *Parliamentary Franchise for Women Ratepayers* (1878) sticks up for the logic of allowing women rate-payers to vote. Her claim to poetic importance is in her development of the womanly dramatic monologue, and her astute insistence on the importance of material factors – money, class, power – in all questions of social, political and moral life. She died at Kew, 5 September 1894, aged fifty-seven.

DEAD AMY

Do I weep because she is dead?
Ah no, it is very calm in the grave,
And she needed calm, for storms were wild
And my darling was never very brave:
Now she smiles in sleep like a little child
    Dreaming at night in its happy bed:
    Why should I weep for her dead?

She was very young and bright,
But she could not laugh her sorrows away
As I, who am stronger and harder, could do,
Though the brown of my locks grew dimmed with grey:
But she, her heart was too simple and true
    To jest with grief, and her cheek grew white –
    It was once so fair and bright.

Perhaps it was all for the best
For both, though it leaves me so very lone,
I could hardly have borne so much distress,
If it had not been all and only my own.
Ah well! her smile was a thing to bless

My sharpest pain, but nought pains her rest,   20
So I think it is all for the best.

For I think I must have gone mad
Had I seen her grow worn and early old
With the care and the burden of toilsome days.
To see her pallid with hunger and cold
And pained by want in a thousand ways,
    To see her sweet face grow rigid and sad,
    Surely I must have gone mad!

But she would have borne it all
And still have smiled, but she could not bear   30
All the shame and the loathing that others draw
On our name, and our burden of lonely care –
For we had not many friends that were true,
    So had small love-comfortings in our fall,
    And she could not bear it at all.

She did not often weep
But grew more silent and still every day,
And seldom moved, but sat white and sad;
So when I saw she must pass away
I had almost the courage to be glad –   40
    Ah well! my darling has happy sleep,
    And so I do not weep.

A Woman Sold and Other Poems *(Macmillan & Co., 1867)*.

From: MARJORY: ENGLISH STORNELLI[1]

Summer

The Heart that Lacks Room

I love him, and I love him, and I love:
    Oh heart, my love goes welling o'er the brim.
He makes my light more than the sun above,
    And what am I save what I am to him?
All will, all hope I have, to him belong;
Oh heart, thou art too small for love so strong:
    Oh heart, grow large, grow deeper for his sake;
    Oh love him better, heart, or thou wilt break!

The Lovers

And we are lovers, lovers he and I:
    Oh sweet dear name that angels envy us;
Lovers for now, lovers for by and by,
    And God to hear us call each other thus.
Flow softly, river of our life, and fair;
We float together to the otherwhere:
    Storm, river of our life, if storm must be,
    We brunt thy tide together to that sea.

A Book of Rhyme *(Macmillan & Co., 1881)*.

MARJORY: ENGLISH STORNELLI
1 Italian. Mistake for *rispetti*. 8-line stanzas, as here, lines 1–4 rhyming   alternately, lines 5–8 rhyming in pairs. *Stornelli* are 3-line ditties, with 1st line of 5 syllables.

IN THE PAMFILI-DORIA GARDENS[1]

Brown stagnant dawn, forgotten of the sun,
   And then wan noon beneath white pools of sky,
Mists blackening, and the long harsh night begun.
   What bird could know to bid the day goodbye?
      No sun to rise, no sun to sink:
      At noon birds chirped 'Day's near, we think,'
And 'twas the night-fall had begun.

Dawns thus, noons thus, nights thus, with never a change,
   This leaden while of weeks of the young year;
A snowdrop, if one struggles forth, looks strange,   10
   A birth unnatural in a world so drear,
      And keeps its stem within the mould,
      Afraid and parching in the cold:
Poor flower, in such a world too strange.

No pulse of Spring's revival beats and thrills;
   Beneath the narrow vault of cloud and rime,
Beneath the thick and bitter air that kills,
   The rigid earth lies sere . . . in budding time.
      No vernal rush in blade and tree
      And us that makes us glad to be: 20
We breathe the thick bleak air that kills.

But all the while I know where, too far hence,
   Through earth's flushed pores the year's young life leaps forth;
Where air is drunken with Spring's quickening sense;
   Where infinite sky is east, west, south, and north,
      Bluer than any sapphire's light;
      Where dawn and noon and fostering night
Instil Spring's subtle quickening sense,

Where ruby, rose, white flushing at the marge,
   Pearl, and shell-pink, and grey, and amethyst,
Crowded upon their sunshine acres large,   30
   (Posies at will and next day none be missed)
      Blow, born of light and Spring's soft breeze,
      The shyly sweet anemones:
Sunshine and blossom acres large.

Oh, star anemones, whose fragrance coy,
   Close at the heart like a young maiden's hope,
Gave me its secret, and your radiance joy,
   Ye are blowing now, and on the bosky slope,
      The emerald and shadowy gloom
      Is shot with purple wefts of bloom,   40
For violets breathe the spring-time joy.

Pleased children, greedy for the flowers, make haste;
   With nosegay both hands big must add and add –
Their world is full enough of flowers for waste.
   Someone that being older is more sad
      Hides, maybe, where a stillness is

IN THE PAMFILI-DORIA GARDENS
1   at Rome.

To feel the exquisite Spring bliss,
And but one flower's too much to waste.

Ah well, 'tis black and barren here to-day;
   My life lags numbed: and yet there is for me   50
Some part in sunshine and birds' welcoming song,
   Who know the Spring that's where far strangers see,
     And am the happier in my home
     Because of violets at Rome,
Of wind-flowers 'neath Rome's Spring-birds' song.

Selections from the Verse *(Macmillan & Co., 1893).*

Henry S. (Sambrooke) Leigh (1837–83)

Henry Sambrooke Leigh, comic writer, was born in London, 29 March 1837. His grandfather had a bookshop in the Strand; his father, James Mathews Leigh (who died in 1860), was a playwright of sorts, and a painter who ran a well-known painting school off London's Oxford Street. Henry was skilled in French, Portuguese and Spanish. His main work was for the stage, especially in the seventies and eighties. He translated many French comic operas; wrote, adapted and produced large numbers of comic operas, opera bouffes, and musical shows for the London theatres. He edited *Jeux d'Esprit Written and Spoken by French and English Wits and Humorists* (1877). And he produced a fine handful of volumes of considerable mocking, witty, satirical light verses and lyrics: *Carols of Cockayne* (1869) – 'Dedicated to Tom Hood, Esq., By His Friend and Workfellow' – which went into several editions; *Gillott and Goosequill* (1871); *A Town Garland: A Collection of Lyrics* (1878); *Strains from the Strand: Trifles in Verse* (1882). He was known as a brilliant talker and an amusing singer of comic songs. He lived in Lowther's Private Hotel in the Strand, and died there, 16 June 1883. He is buried in Brompton Cemetery.

CROOKED ANSWERS

(Dedicated to the Laureate)

No. 1 – Vere de Vere

The Lady Clara V. de V.
   Presents her very best regards
To that misguided Alfred T.
   (With one of her enamell'd cards).
Though uninclin'd to give offence,
   The Lady Clara begs to hint
That Master Alfred's common sense
   Deserts him utterly in print.

The Lady Clara can but say,
   That always from the very first   10
She snubb'd in her decisive way
   The hopes that silly Alfred nurs'd.
The fondest words that ever fell
   From Lady Clara, when they met,
Were 'How d'ye do? I hope you're well!'
   Or else 'The weather's very wet.'

To show a disregard for truth
   By penning scurrilous attacks,
Appears to Lady C. in sooth
   Like stabbing folks behind their backs.   20

The age of chivalry, she fears,
    Is gone for good, since noble dames
Who irritate low sonneteers
    Get pelted with improper names.

The Lady Clara cannot think
    What kind of pleasure can accrue
From wasting paper, pens, and ink,
    On statements the reverse of true.
If Master Launcelot, one fine day,
    (Urged on by madness or by malt,)   30
Destroy'd himself – can Alfred say
    The Lady Clara was in fault?

Her Ladyship needs no advice
    How time and money should be spent,
And can't pursue at any price
    The plan that Alfred T. has sent.
She does not in the least object
    To let the 'foolish yeoman' go,
But wishes – let him recollect –
    That he should move to Jericho.   40

No. 2 – Maud

Nay, I cannot come into the garden just now,
    Tho' it vexes me much to refuse:
But I *must* have the next set of waltzes, I vow,
    With Lieutenant de Boots of the Blues.

I am sure you'll be heartily pleas'd when you hear
    That our ball has been quite a success.
As for *me* – I've been looking a monster, my dear,
    In that old-fashion'd guy of a dress.

You had better at once hurry home, dear, to bed:
    It is getting so dreadfully late.   10
You may catch the bronchitis or cold in the head
    If you linger so long at our gate.

Don't be obstinate, Alfy; come, take my advice –
    For I know you're in want of repose.
Take a basin of gruel (you'll find it *so* nice)
    And remember to tallow your nose.

No, I tell you I can't and I shan't get away,
    For De Boots has implor'd me to sing.
As to *you* – if you like it, of course you can stay;
    You were always an obstinate thing.   20

If you feel it a pleasure to talk to the flow'rs
    About 'babble and revel and wine,'
When you might have been snoring for two or three hours,
    Why, it's not the least business of mine.

Carols of Cockayne *(James Camden Hotten, 1869). Volume dedicated 'to Tom Hood, Esq., By His Friend and Workfellow'. (Preface says volume title suggested by Frederick Locker, author of* London Lyrics'.)

WEATHERBOUND IN THE SUBURBS

The air is damp, the skies are leaden;
   The ominous lull of impending rain
Presses upon me, and seems to deaden
   Every sense but a sense of pain.

Hopes of getting again to London
   Lapse into utter and grim despair;
Shall I do my verses or leave them *un*done?
   I don't know, and I don't much care.

I sit in a silence broken only
   Now and again by the wandering breeze,   10
A breeze in the garden, wandering lonely,
   Or playing the fool with shivering trees.

I have slept all night – should I call it sleeping? –
   Out of all sound but the pattering drops
Against the pane, and the wild wind keeping
   Revelry up in the chimney-tops.

I want the hum of my working brothers –
   London bustle and London strife –
To count as one in three million others; –
   How can I *live* away from life?   20

                        Carols of Cockayne *(1869)*.

SONGS OF THE SICK ROOM

No. 1 – Cod-Liver Oil

On the bleak shore of Norway, I've lately been told,
   Large numbers of cod-fish are found,
And the animals' livers are afterwards sold
   At so many 'pfennigs' per pound;
From which is extracted, with infinite toil,
A villainous fluid called cod-liver oil!

Now, I don't mind a powder, a pill, or a draught –
   Though I mingle the former with jam –
And many's the mixture I've cheerfully quaff'd,
   And the pill I have gulp'd like a lamb.   10
But then I envelop my pills in tin-foil,
And I can't do the same with my cod-liver oil!

In the course of my lifetime I've swallow'd enough
   To have floated a ship of the line,
And it's purely the fault of this horrible stuff
   That I've ceased to enjoy ginger wine.
For how can you wonder to see me recoil
From a liquor I mix'd with my cod-liver oil?

There are few deeds of daring from which I should quail –
   There are few things I'd tremble to do –   20
But there's one kind of tonic that makes me turn pale,
   And quite spoils my appetite, too;
But, you see, just at present, I've got none to spoil –
So I don't mind alluding to cod-liver oil!

                        Carols of Cockayne *(1869)*.

Algernon Charles Swinburne (1837–1909)

Algernon Charles Swinburne, tiny producer of unstoppably vast amounts of poetry and criticism, in his youth the fiercest Victorian épateur of the bourgeoisie, in later years the mildest of beprammed-baby adorers, was born into the English aristocracy in Chester Street, Grosvenor Place, London, 5 April 1837. His father, Admiral Charles Henry Swinburne, was second son of a Northumberland baronet; his mother, Lady Jane, was daughter of an earl. Algernon, eldest son, had a pampered, devout, Anglo-Catholic childhood. He read intensely, though family piety forbade novels, at the same time as spending much time out of doors, particularly swimming in the sea. The sea became a constant reference point for his poems' intense moodiness, especially their many gloomings about love and loneliness. His growth was stunted except for his huge hydrocephalic head, made the more prominent by his great mass of bright carroty hair. At Eton, which he entered at Easter 1849, this 'little elf' sported the school's largest-sized hat, read everything (especially Dickens and Shakespeare), started collecting rare editions of Elizabethan and Jacobean dramatists, and acquired a perverse taste for the sado-masochistic pleasures of being flogged. Characteristically of an extremely supportive family, his parents introduced him to Wordsworth at the age of twelve, and had him blessed by old Samuel Rogers (he who refused the Laureateship in 1850). His mother got his childhood verses into *Fraser's Magazine*. (The Admiral would fund his son's first volumes.) He left Eton under some cloud; was prepared privately for Oxford; went up to Balliol College in January 1856, where his lifelong friendship with Benjamin Jowett was formed, and his life-long devotion to Mazzini and the causes of European republicanism grew as he dropped his Anglo-Catholicism for a strongly atheistic democratism. He met Ruskin (who would think as highly of his poems as of Turner's paintings), fell in with Ted Jones (the future painter Burne-Jones) and William Morris, and became friends with D. G. Rossetti through the abortive 1857 frescoes project at the Oxford Union. In his second Oxford year Swinburne dined with Tennyson – another sign of his well-connectedness – and Tennyson read him *Maud*. He got a Second in Classical Moderations, won the Taylor scholarship for French and Italian, gained a reputation for boisterous behaviour and wild republican politics, and was encouraged to leave without a degree. He was, however, writing hard, and took London lodgings to be near the Joneses, resolved to lead the bohemian literary life (funded, of course, by the Admiral). Summers were spent at his grandfather's place in Northumberland, and in the North Sea. When his grandfather died Swinburne lived for a time with the William Bell Scotts in Newcastle,

before moving to London in 1861. He became very close to D. G. Rossetti, lodging with him and Meredith in Cheyne Walk from 1862. He was a key witness at the inquest on Lizzie Siddal in February 1862. That year he swam in the Lac de Gaube on a family trip to the Pyrenees. In the early 1860s he travelled widely in Europe, meeting Whistler and Landor and Mrs Gaskell, writing 'Itylus' and 'Dolores' in Fiesole (1864). It was London that was bad for him. Richard Burton introduced him disastrously to brandy. Verbena Lodge in St John's Wood, a brothel for flagellants, was too enticingly handy. His reputation flourished as a daemonically unstoppable talker with an aweing memory, dazzling wit, inspired reciter of his own verses, who was also a foul-mouthed satirist, blasphemer and drunk. He was obviously in a bad way in many respects. His hands shook uncontrollably, he was subject to fits, drank himself into stupors. At the same time *Atalanta in Calydon* (1865), in a cover decorated by Rossetti, was hailed by Ruskin as 'the grandest thing ever done by a youth – though he is a Demoniac youth'. *Poems and Ballads* (April 1866) made such a tremendous scandal, not least because of its celebrations of sado-masochism and necrophilia, that its publisher Moxon withdrew it within weeks. Swinburne shared his flagellation fantasies with Burne-Jones and Simeon ('Jew jube') Solomon – the painter jailed for soliciting in public lavatories. Sade was 'ce bon Marquis'. Swinburne would swoon over the dangerous females in Rossetti's paintings – Lilith, Proserpine. His verses adore Our Lady of Pain. He loved contemplating the potential of female teeth for drawing blood – the 'sharp indenture' of the kiss. When his friends arranged for the American circus horse-rider Adah Mencken to help him lose his virginity (his first love, his cousin Mary Gordon, having preferred a big one-armed hero of the Indian Mutiny to 'little Carrots') she couldn't make him understand 'that biting's no use'. Swinburne preferred the goings-on at George Powell's place in Normandy – plenty of drink, much fawning over beautiful boy servants and obscene photos of German youths, in an atmosphere dense with speculation about bestialism with monkeys. Swinburne's erotic textualizings cultivate a suspiciously distinct vagueness. Browning complained of the 'fuzz of words'. Robert Buchanan's notorious 1871 attack on the 'Fleshly School' includes 'the little mad boy' Swinburne in the collective accusations of 'spasmodic ramifications in the erotic direction' and poems 'lost in a whirl of aesthetic terminology'. (Swinburne rose to the occasion with his usual verve in a letter, referring to the excremental stink of the piece and of 'the dwellings inhabited by the critical tribe so beautifully defined by Rabelais as the "turdilousifartishittical buggeraminous ballockwaggers"'.)

Swinburne did at least have the grace, as in 'Poeta Loqui-tur' (published 1918), to parody his own 'maze of monoto-nous murmur'. Much of his poetic energy also went into celebrating European republican causes. (Housman did not care for the politics of *Songs Before Sunrise*: Aphrodite was a much more interesting goddess of poetry than Lib-erty, he thought; you might as well write an Ode to Elbow-room as to Liberty.) The Admiral died 4 March 1877. The second series of *Poems and Ballads* appeared in 1878. By this time Swinburne's dissoluteness was so extreme his mother and brother stepped in to fix him up with a steady income and a safe haven away from London under the tutelage of a poetical lawyer, Theodore (Watts-)Dunton, at the Pines in Putney. Here, once weaned off the Burtonian brandy, and onto Shakespearian brown ale (via Tennysonian port), Swinburne, now considerably deaf, settled down to a leisurely, dull regime of single lunchtime bottles of Bass, walks in the park patting babies (one of those was Robert Graves), and much mazy criticism and versifying. His later verses were helped even less than his earlier ones by his explicit eschewing of any search for 'sharp-eyed prettinesses, shining surprises', 'striking accidents', 'intrusive and singular and exceptional beauties'. He died of pneumonia, 10 April 1909, and was buried in the family plot at Bonchurch on the Isle of Wight.

ITYLUS[1]

Swallow, my sister, O sister swallow,
  How can thine heart be full of the spring?
    A thousand summers are over and dead.
What hast thou found in the spring to follow?
  What hast thou found in thine heart to sing?
    What wilt thou do when the summer is shed?

O swallow, sister, O fair swift swallow,
  Why wilt thou fly after spring to the south,
    The soft south whither thine heart is set?
Shall not the grief of the old time follow?   10
  Shall not the song thereof cleave to thy mouth?
    Hast thou forgotten ere I forget?

Sister, my sister, O fleet sweet swallow,
  Thy way is long to the sun and the south;
    But I, fulfilled of my heart's desire,
Shedding my song upon height, upon hollow,
  From tawny body and sweet small mouth
    Feed the heart of the night with fire.

I the nightingale all spring through,
  O swallow, sister, O changing swallow,   20
    All spring through till the spring be done,
Clothed with the light of the night on the dew,
  Sing, while the hours and the wild birds follow,
    Take flight and follow and find the sun.

Sister, my sister, O soft light swallow,
  Though all things feast in the spring's guest-chamber,
    How hast thou heart to be glad thereof yet?
For where thou fliest I shall not follow,
  Till life forget and death remember,
    Till thou remember and I forget.   30

Swallow, my sister, O singing swallow,
  I know not how thou hast heart to sing.
    Hast thou the heart? is it all past over?

ITYLUS
1 in Greek mythology, the son who was mistakenly killed by his mother Aedon, who, grieving greatly, was turned into a nightingale. Aedon, the poem's speaker, addresses Philomela, the woman who, raped by Tereus, had her tongue ripped out, and turned into a swallow.

Thy lord the summer is good to follow,
   And fair the feet of thy lover the spring:
      But what wilt thou say to the spring thy lover?

O swallow, sister, O fleeting swallow,
   My heart in me is a molten ember
      And over my head the waves have met.
But thou wouldst tarry or I would follow,   40
   Could I forget or thou remember,
      Couldst thou remember and I forget.

O sweet stray sister, O shifting swallow,
   The heart's division divideth us.
      Thy heart is light as a leaf of a tree;
But mine goes forth among sea-gulfs hollow
   To the place of the slaying of Itylus,
      The feast of Daulis, the Thracian sea.²

O swallow, sister, O rapid swallow,
   I pray thee sing not a little space.   50
      Are not the roofs and the lintels wet?
The woven web that was plain to follow,
   The small slain body, the flower-like face,
      Can I remember if thou forget?

O sister, sister, thy first-begotten!
   The hands that cling and the feet that follow,
      The voice of the child's blood crying yet
Who hath remembered me? who hath forgotten?
   Thou hast forgotten, O summer swallow,
      But the world shall end when I forget.   60

Poems and Ballads (Edward Moxon & Co., April 1866). The 'First Series'.
'To My Friend Edward Burne-Jones These Poems are Affectionately and
Admiringly Dedicated.'

ANACTORIA¹

; τίνος αὖ τὺ πειθοῖ
μὰψ σαγηνεύσας φιλότατα;
Sappho²

My life is bitter with thy love; thine eyes
Blind me, thy tresses burn me, thy sharp sighs
Divide my flesh and spirit with soft sound,
And my blood strengthens, and my veins abound.
I pray thee sigh not, speak not, draw not breath;
Let life burn down, and dream it is not death.
I would the sea had hidden us, the fire
(Wilt thou fear that, and fear not my desire?)
Severed the bones that bleach, the flesh that cleaves,
And let our sifted ashes drop like leaves.   10

---

2   Daulis was the setting for the story of Philomela's rape and its con-
sequences.
ANACTORIA
1   woman addressee of a Sappho poem.

2   Aphrodite addresses Sappho: 'Whose friendship have you suddenly
netted by persuasion?' (Problematic lines in Greek. Swinburne follows
19th-century editorial restorations, now thought controversial.)

I feel thy blood against my blood: my pain
Pains thee, and lips bruise lips, and vein stings vein.
Let fruit be crushed on fruit, let flower on flower,
Breast kindle breast, and either burn one hour.
Why wilt thou follow lesser loves? are thine
Too weak to bear these hands and lips of mine?
I charge thee for my life's sake, O too sweet
To crush love with thy cruel faultless feet,
I charge thee keep thy lip from hers or his,
Sweetest, till theirs be sweeter than my kiss: 20
Lest I too lure, a swallow for a dove,
Erotion or Erinna[3] to my love.
I would my love could kill thee; I am satiated
With seeing thee live, and fain would have thee dead.
I would earth had thy body as fruit to eat,
And no mouth but some serpent's found thee sweet.
I would find grievous ways to have thee slain,
Intense device, and superflux of pain;
Vex thee with amorous agonies, and shake
Life at thy lips, and leave it there to ache;   30
Strain out thy soul with pangs too soft to kill,
Intolerable interludes, and infinite ill;
Relapse and reluctation[4] of the breath,
Dumb tunes and shuddering semitones of death.
I am weary of all thy words and soft strange ways,
Of all love's fiery nights and all his days,
And all the broken kisses salt as brine
That shuddering lips make moist with waterish wine,
And eyes the bluer for all those hidden hours
That pleasure fills with tears and feeds from flowers,   40
Fierce at the heart with fire that half comes through,
But all the flower-like white stained round with blue;
The fervent underlid, and that above
Lifted with laughter or abashed with love;
Thine amorous girdle, full of thee and fair,
And leavings of the lilies in thine hair.
Yea, all sweet words of thine and all thy ways,
And all the fruit of nights and flower of days,
And stinging lips wherein the hot sweet brine
That Love was born of burns and foams like wine,   50
And eyes insatiable of amorous hours,
Fervent as fire and delicate as flowers,
Coloured like night at heart, but cloven through
Like night with flame, dyed round like night with blue,
Clothed with deep eyelids under and above –
Yea, all thy beauty sickens me with love;
Thy girdle empty of thee and now not fair,
And ruinous lilies in thy languid hair.
Ah, take no thought for Love's sake; shall this be,
And she who loves thy lover not love thee?   60
Sweet soul, sweet mouth of all that laughs and lives,
Mine is she, very mine; and she forgives.
For I beheld in sleep the light that is

3   Erotion: 5-year-old whose death is lamented by Martial. Name   4   struggle; resistance.
means 'little Love'. Erinna: female lyric poet of 4th century BC; famed
for poem 'The Distaff'.

In her high place in Paphos,⁵ heard the kiss
Of body and soul that mix with eager tears
And laughter stinging through the eyes and ears;
Saw Love, as burning flame from crown to feet,
Imperishable, upon her storied seat;
Clear eyelids lifted toward the north and south,
A mind of many colours, and a mouth   70
Of many tunes and kisses; and she bowed,
With all her subtle face laughing aloud,
Bowed down upon me, saying, 'Who doth thee wrong,
Sappho?' but thou – thy body is the song,
Thy mouth the music; thou art more than I,
Though my voice die not till the whole world die;
Though men that hear it madden; though love weep,
Though nature change, though shame be charmed asleep.
Ah, wilt thou slay me lest I kiss thee dead?
Yet the queen laughed from her sweet heart and said: 80
'Even she that flies shall follow for thy sake,
And she shall give thee gifts that would not take,
Shall kiss that would not kiss thee' (yea, kiss me)
'When thou wouldst not' – when I would not kiss thee!
Ah, more to me than all men as thou art,
Shall not my songs assuage her at the heart?
Ah, sweet to me as life seems sweet to death,
Why should her wrath fill thee with fearful breath?
Nay, sweet, for is she God alone? hath she
Made earth and all the centuries of the sea,   90
Taught the sun ways to travel, woven most fine
The moonbeams, shed the starbeams forth as wine,
Bound with her myrtles, beaten with her rods,
The young men and the maidens and the gods?
Have we not lips to love with, eyes for tears,
And summer and flower of women and of years?
Stars for the foot of morning, and for noon
Sunlight, and exaltation of the moon;
Waters that answer waters, fields that wear
Lilies, and languor of the Lesbian⁶ air?   100
Beyond those flying feet of fluttered doves,
Are there not other gods for other loves?
Yea, though she scourge thee, sweetest, for my sake,
Blossom not thorns and flowers not blood should break.
Ah that my lips were tuneless lips, but pressed
To the bruised blossom of thy scourged white breast!
Ah that my mouth for Muses' milk were fed
On the sweet blood thy sweet small wounds had bled!
That with my tongue I felt them, and could taste
The faint flakes from thy bosom to the waist!   110
That I could drink thy veins as wine, and eat
Thy breasts like honey! that from face to feet
Thy body were abolished and consumed,
And in my flesh thy very flesh entombed!
Ah, ah, thy beauty! like a beast it bites,
Stings like an adder, like an arrow smites.
Ah sweet, and sweet again, and seven times sweet,
The paces and the pauses of thy feet!

5   city of Cyprus, where Venus was worshipped. A Paphian: a prosti-   6   from Lesbos: Sappho's island.
tute.

Ah sweeter than all sleep or summer air
The fallen fillets fragrant from thine hair!　　　　　　　　120
Yea, though their alien kisses do me wrong,
Sweeter thy lips than mine with all their song;
Thy shoulders whiter than a fleece of white,
And flower-sweet fingers, good to bruise or bite
As honeycomb of the inmost honey-cells,
With almond-shaped and roseleaf-coloured shells
And blood like purple blossom at the tips
Quivering; and pain made perfect in thy lips
For my sake when I hurt thee; O that I
Durst crush thee out of life with love, and die,　　　　　130
Die of thy pain and my delight, and be
Mixed with thy blood and molten into thee!
Would I not plague thee dying overmuch?
Would I not hurt thee perfectly? not touch
Thy pores of sense with torture, and make bright
Thine eyes with bloodlike tears and grievous light?
Strike pang from pang as note is struck from note,
Catch the sob's middle music in thy throat,
Take thy limbs living, and new-mould with these
A lyre of many faultless agonies?　　　　　　　　　140
Feed thee with fever and famine and fine drouth,
With perfect pangs convulse thy perfect mouth,
Make thy life shudder in thee and burn afresh,
And wring thy very spirit through the flesh?
Cruel? but love makes all that love him well
As wise as heaven and crueller than hell.
Me hath love made more bitter toward thee
Than death toward man; but were I made as he
Who hath made all things to break them one by one,
If my feet trod upon the stars and sun　　　　　　　150
And souls of men as his have alway trod,
God knows I might be crueller than God.
For who shall change with prayers or thanksgivings
The mystery of the cruelty of things?
Or say what God above all gods and years
With offering and blood-sacrifice of tears,
With lamentation from strange lands, from graves
Where the snake pastures, from scarred mouths of slaves,
From prison, and from plunging prows of ships
Through flamelike foam of the sea's closing lips –　　　160
With thwartings of strange signs, and wind-blown hair
Of comets, desolating the dim air,
When darkness is made fast with seals and bars,
And fierce reluctance of disastrous stars,
Eclipse, and sound of shaken hills, and wings
Darkening, and blind inexpiable things –
With sorrow of labouring moons, and altering light
And travail of the planets of the night,
And weeping of the weary Pleiads seven,
Feeds the mute melancholy lust of heaven?　　　　　170
Is not his incense bitterness, his meat
Murder? his hidden face and iron feet
Hath not man known, and felt them on their way
Threaten and trample all things and every day?
Hath he not sent us hunger? who hath cursed
Spirit and flesh with longing? filled with thirst

Their lips who cried unto him? who bade exceed
The fervid will, fall short the feeble deed,
Bade sink the spirit and the flesh aspire,
Pain animate the dust of dead desire,   180
And life yield up her flower to violent fate?
Him would I reach, him smite, him desecrate,
Pierce the cold lips of God with human breath,
And mix his immortality with death.
Why hath he made us? what had all we done
That we should live and loathe the sterile sun,
And with the moon wax paler as she wanes,
And pulse by pulse feel time grow through our veins?
Thee too the years shall cover; thou shalt be
As the rose born of one same blood with thee,   190
As a song sung, as a word said, and fall
Flower-wise, and be not any more at all,
Nor any memory of thee anywhere;
For never Muse has bound above thine hair
The high Pierian⁷ flower whose graft outgrows
All summer kinship of the mortal rose
And colour of deciduous days, nor shed
Reflex and flush of heaven about thine head,
Nor reddened brows made pale by floral grief
With splendid shadow from that lordlier leaf.   200
Yea, thou shalt be forgotten like spilt wine,
Except these kisses of my lips on thine
Brand them with immortality; but me –
Men shall not see bright fire nor hear the sea,
Nor mix their hearts with music, nor behold
Cast forth of heaven with feet of awful gold
And plumeless wings that make the bright air blind,
Lightning, with thunder for a hound behind
Hunting through fields unfurrowed and unsown –
But in the light and laughter, in the moan   210
And music, and in grasp of lip and hand
And shudder of water that makes felt on land
The immeasurable tremor of all the sea,
Memories shall mix and metaphors of me.
Like me shall be the shuddering calm of night,
When all the winds of the world for pure delight
Close lips that quiver and fold up wings that ache;
When nightingales are louder for love's sake,
And leaves tremble like lute-strings or like fire;
Like me the one star swooning with desire   220
Even at the cold lips of the sleepless moon,
As I at thine; like me the waste white noon,
Burnt through with barren sunlight; and like me
The land-stream and the tide-stream in the sea.
I am sick with time as these with ebb and flow,
And by the yearning in my veins I know
The yearning sound of waters; and mine eyes
Burn as that beamless fire which fills the skies
With troubled stars and travailing things of flame;
And in my heart the grief consuming them   230
Labours, and in my veins the thirst of these,

7 Pieria, on slopes of Mount Olympus – birthplace of the Muses and
Orpheus.

And all the summer travail of the trees
And all the winter sickness; and the earth,
Filled full with deadly works of death and birth,
Sore spent with hungry lusts of birth and death,
Has pain like mine in her divided breath;
Her spring of leaves is barren, and her fruit
Ashes; her boughs are burdened, and her root
Fibrous and gnarled with poison; underneath
Serpents have gnawn it through with tortuous teeth   240
Made sharp upon the bones of all the dead,
And wild birds rend her branches overhead.
These, woven as raiment for his word and thought,
These hath God made, and me as these, and wrought
Song, and hath lit it at my lips; and me
Earth shall not gather though she feed on thee.
As a shed tear shalt thou be shed; but I –
Lo, earth may labour, men live long and die,
Years change and stars, and the high God devise
New things, and old things wane before his eyes   250
Who wields and wrecks them, being more strong than they –
But, having made me, me he shall not slay.
Nor slay nor satiate, like those herds of his
Who laugh and live a little, and their kiss
Contents them, and their loves are swift and sweet,
And sure death grasps and gains them with slow feet,
Love they or hate they, strive or bow their knees –
And all these end; he hath his will of these.
Yea, but albeit he slay me, hating me –
Albeit he hide me in the deep dear sea   260
And cover me with cool wan foam, and ease
This soul of mine as any soul of these,
And give me water and great sweet waves, and make
The very sea's name lordlier for my sake,
The whole sea sweeter – albeit I die indeed
And hide myself and sleep and no man heed,
Of me the high God hath not all his will.
Blossom of branches, and on each high hill
Clear air and wind, and under in clamorous vales
Fierce noises of the fiery nightingales,   270
Buds burning in the sudden spring like fire,
The wan washed sand and the waves' vain desire,
Sails seen like blown white flowers at sea, and words
That bring tears swiftest, and long notes of birds
Violently singing till the whole world sings –
I Sappho shall be one with all these things,
With all high things for ever; and my face
Seen once, my songs once heard in a strange place,
Cleave to men's lives, and waste the days thereof
With gladness and much sadness and long love.   280
Yea, they shall say, earth's womb has borne in vain
New things, and never this best thing again;
Borne days and men, borne fruits and wars and wine,
Seasons and songs, but no song more like mine.
And they shall know me as ye who have known me here,
Last year when I loved Atthis,[8] and this year

8   a woman; or, Attis, the Phrygian shepherd who became a priest of
Cybele and castrated himself when he broke his vow of chastity.

When I love thee; and they shall praise me, and say
'She hath all time as all we have our day,
Shall she not live and have her will' – even I?
Yea, though thou diest, I say I shall not die.   290
For these shall give me of their souls, shall give
Life, and the days and loves wherewith I live,
Shall quicken me with loving, fill with breath,
Save me and serve me, strive for me with death.
Alas, that neither moon nor snow nor dew
Nor all cold things can purge me wholly through,
Assuage me nor allay me nor appease,
Till supreme sleep shall bring me bloodless ease;
Till time wax faint in all his periods;
Till fate undo the bondage of the gods,   300
And lay, to slake and satiate me all through,
Lotus and Lethe⁹ on my lips like dew,
And shed around and over and under me
Thick darkness and the insuperable sea.

Poems and Ballads *(1866)*.

ILICET¹

There is an end of joy and sorrow;
Peace all day long, all night, all morrow,
    But never a time to laugh or weep.
The end is come of pleasant places,
The end of tender words and faces,
    The end of all, the poppied sleep.

No place for sound within their hearing,
No room to hope, no time for fearing,
    No lips to laugh, no lids for tears.
The old years have run out all their measure;   10
No chance of pain, no chance of pleasure,
    No fragment of the broken years.

Outside of all the worlds and ages,
There where the fool is as the sage is,
    There where the slayer is clean of blood,
No end, no passage, no beginning,
There where the sinner leaves off sinning,
    There where the good man is not good.

There is not one thing with another,
But Evil saith to Good: My brother,
    My brother, I am one with thee: 20
They shall not strive nor cry for ever:
No man shall choose between them: never
    Shall this thing end and that thing be.

Wind wherein seas and stars are shaken
Shall shake them, and they shall not waken;

---

9   lotus: fruit inducing forgetfulness and happy dream state. Lethe,
water of forgetfulness.

ILICET

1   (Latin) 'it's all over, all up, finished, time to depart' (the word used,
e.g., at the end of funeral ceremonies).

None that has lain down shall arise;
The stones are sealed across their places;
One shadow is shed on all their faces,
   One blindness cast on all their eyes.   30

Sleep, is it sleep perchance that covers
Each face, as each face were his lover's?
   Farewell; as men that sleep fare well.
The grave's mouth laughs unto derision
Desire and dread and dream and vision,
   Delight of heaven and sorrow of hell.

No soul shall tell nor lip shall number
The names and tribes of you that slumber;
   No memory, no memorial.
'Thou knowest' – who shall say thou knowest?   40
There is none highest and none lowest:
   An end, an end, an end of all.

Good night, good sleep, good rest from sorrow
To these that shall not have good morrow;
   The gods be gentle to all these.
Nay, if death be not, how shall they be?
Nay, is there help in heaven? it may be
   All things and lords of things shall cease.

The stooped urn, filling, dips and flashes;
The bronzèd brims are deep in ashes;   50
   The pale old lips of death are fed.
Shall this dust gather flesh hereafter?
Shall one shed tears or fall to laughter,
   At sight of all these poor old dead?

Nay, as thou wilt; these know not of it;
Thine eyes' strong weeping shall not profit,
   Thy laughter shall not give thee ease;
Cry aloud, spare not,[2] cease not crying,
Sigh, till thou cleave thy sides with sighing,
   Thou shalt not raise up one of these.   60

Burnt spices flash, and burnt wine hisses,
The breathing flame's mouth curls and kisses
   The small dried rows of frankincense;
All round the sad red blossoms smoulder,
Flowers coloured like the fire, but colder,
   In sign of sweet things taken hence;

Yea, for their sake and in death's favour
Things of sweet shape and of sweet savour
   We yield them, spice and flower and wine;
Yea, costlier things than wine or spices,   70
Whereof none knoweth how great the price is,
   And fruit that comes not of the vine.

From boy's pierced throat and girl's pierced bosom
Drips, reddening round the blood-red blossom,

2   Isaiah 58.1.

The slow delicious bright soft blood,
Bathing the spices and the pyre,
Bathing the flowers and fallen fire,
　　Bathing the blossom by the bud.

Roses whose lips the flame has deadened
Drink till the lapping leaves are reddened　　　　　　　　　　　　　80
　　And warm wet inner petals weep;
The flower whereof sick sleep gets leisure,
Barren of balm and purple pleasure,
　　Fumes with no native steam of sleep.

Why will ye weep? what do ye weeping?
For waking folk and people sleeping,
　　And sands that fill and sands that fall,
The days rose-red, the poppied hours,
Blood, wine, and spice and fire and flowers,
　　There is one end of one and all.　　　　　　　　　　　　　　　90

Shall such an one lend love or borrow?
Shall these be sorry for thy sorrow?
　　Shall these give thanks for words or breath?
Their hate is as their loving-kindness;
The frontlet of their brows is blindness,
　　The armlet of their arms is death.

Lo, for no noise or light of thunder
Shall these grave-clothes be rent in sunder;
　　He that hath taken, shall he give?
He hath rent them: shall he bind together?　　　　　　　　　　　100
He hath bound them: shall he break the tether?
　　He hath slain them: shall he bid them live?

A little sorrow, a little pleasure,
Fate metes us from the dusty measure
　　That holds the date of all of us;
We are born with travail and strong crying,
And from the birth-day to the dying
　　The likeness of our life is thus.

One girds himself to serve another,
Whose father was the dust, whose mother　　　　　　　　　　　110
　　The little dead red worm therein;
They find no fruit of things they cherish;
The goodness of a man shall perish,
　　It shall be one thing with his sin.

In deep wet ways by grey old gardens
Fed with sharp spring the sweet fruit hardens;
　　They know not what fruits wane or grow;
Red summer burns to the utmost ember;
They know not, neither can remember,
　　The old years and flowers they used to know.　　　　　　　120

Ah, for their sakes, so trapped and taken,
For theirs, forgotten and forsaken,
　　Watch, sleep not, gird thyself with prayer.
Nay, where the heart of wrath is broken,
Where long love ends as a thing spoken,
　　How shall thy crying enter there?

Though the iron sides of the old world falter,
The likeness of them shall not alter
   For all the rumour of periods,
The stars and seasons that come after,   130
The tears of latter men, the laughter
   Of the old unalterable gods.

Far up above the years and nations,
The high gods, clothed and crowned with patience,
   Endure through days of deathlike date;
They bear the witness of things hidden;
Before their eyes all life stands chidden,
   As they before the eyes of Fate.

Not for their love shall Fate retire,
Nor they relent for our desire,   140
   Nor the graves open for their call.
The end is more than joy and anguish,
Than lives that laugh and lives that languish,
   The poppied sleep, the end of all.

Poems and Ballads (1866).

HERMAPHRODITUS[1]

I

Lift up thy lips, turn round, look back for love,
   Blind love that comes by night and casts out rest;
   Of all things tired thy lips look weariest,
Save the long smile that they are wearied of.
Ah sweet, albeit no love be sweet enough,
   Choose of two loves and cleave unto the best;
   Two loves at either blossom of thy breast
Strive until one be under and one above.
Their breath is fire upon the amorous air,
   Fire in thine eyes and where thy lips suspire: 10
And whosoever hath seen thee, being so fair,
   Two things turn all his life and blood to fire;
A strong desire begot on great despair,
   A great despair cast out by strong desire.

II

Where between sleep and life some brief space is,
   With love like gold bound round about the head,
   Sex to sweet sex with lips and limbs is wed,
Turning the fruitful feud of hers and his
To the waste wedlock of a sterile kiss;
   Yet from them something like as fire is shed   20
   That shall not be assuaged till death be dead,
Though neither life nor sleep can find out this.
Love made himself of flesh that perisheth
   A pleasure-house for all the loves his kin;
But on the one side sat a man like death,

HERMAPHRODITUS
1 a Greek statue in the Louvre Museum, Paris, which inspired this poem – as it inspired Théophile Gautier's poem 'Contralto' (which Swinburne draws on). Hermaphroditus, son of Hermes and Aphrodite, became one body with Salmacis, (female) water nymph, after her desirous embrace, i.e. the lovely boy acquired womanly breasts.

And on the other a woman sat like sin.
So with veiled eyes and sobs between his breath
Love turned himself and would not enter in.

III

Love, is it love or sleep or shadow or light
   That lies between thine eyelids and thine eyes?   30
   Like a flower laid upon a flower it lies,
Or like the night's dew laid upon the night.
Love stands upon thy left hand and thy right,
   Yet by no sunset and by no moonrise
   Shall make thee man and ease a woman's sighs,
Or make thee woman for a man's delight.
To what strange end hath some strange god made fair
   The double blossom of two fruitless flowers?
Hid love in all the folds of all thy hair,
   Fed thee on summers, watered thee with showers,   40
Given all the gold that all the seasons wear
   To thee that art a thing of barren hours?

IV

Yea, love, I see; it is not love but fear.
   Nay, sweet, it is not fear but love, I know;
   Or wherefore should thy body's blossom blow
So sweetly, or thine eyelids leave so clear
Thy gracious eyes that never made a tear –
   Though for their love our tears like blood should flow,
   Though love and life and death should come and go,
So dreadful, so desirable, so dear?   50
Yea, sweet, I know; I saw in what swift wise
   Beneath the woman's and the water's kiss
   Thy moist limbs melted into Salmacis,
And the large light turned tender in thine eyes,
And all thy boy's breath softened into sighs;
   But Love being blind, how should he know of this?

Au Musée du Louvre, Mars 1863

Poems and Ballads *(1866).*

FRAGOLETTA[1]

O Love! what shall be said of thee?
The son of grief begot by joy?
Being sightless, wilt thou see?
Being sexless, wilt thou be
Maiden or boy?

I dreamed of strange lips yesterday
And cheeks wherein the ambiguous blood
Was like a rose's – yea,
A rose's when it lay
Within the bud.   10

FRAGOLETTA
1 Fragoletta (Italian: 'little strawberry'): name of the cross-dressing lesbian heroine of Henri de Latouche's novel *Fragoletta* (1829) inspired by the Greek statue 'Hermaphroditus' in the Louvre Museum, Paris – which also inspired Swinburne's poem 'Hermaphroditus'.

What fields have bred thee, or what groves
Concealed thee, O mysterious flower,
O double rose of Love's,
With leaves that lure the doves
From bud to bower?

I dare not kiss it, lest my lip
Press harder than an indrawn breath,
And all the sweet life slip
Forth, and the sweet leaves drip,
Bloodlike, in death.   20

O sole desire of my delight!
O sole delight of my desire!
Mine eyelids and eyesight
Feed on thee day and night
Like lips of fire.

Lean back thy throat of carven pearl,
Let thy mouth murmur like the dove's;
Say, Venus hath no girl,
No front of female curl,
Among her Loves.   30

Thy sweet low bosom, thy close hair,
Thy strait soft flanks and slenderer feet,
Thy virginal strange air,
Are these not over fair
For Love to greet?

How should he greet thee? what new name,
Fit to move all men's hearts, could move
Thee, deaf to love or shame,
Love's sister, by the same
Mother as Love?   40

Ah sweet, the maiden's mouth is cold,
Her breast-blossoms are simply red,
Her hair mere brown or gold,
Fold over simple fold
Binding her head.

Thy mouth is made of fire and wine,
Thy barren bosom takes my kiss
And turns my soul to thine
And turns thy lip to mine,
And mine it is.   50

Thou hast a serpent in thine hair,
In all the curls that close and cling;
And ah, thy breast-flower!
Ah love, thy mouth too fair
To kiss and sting!

Cleave to me, love me, kiss mine eyes.
Satiate thy lips with loving me;
Nay, for thou shalt not rise;
Lie still as Love that dies
For love of thee.   60

Mine arms are close about thine head,
My lips are fervent on thy face,
And where my kiss hath fed
Thy flower-like blood leaps red
To the kissed place.

O bitterness of things too sweet!
O broken singing of the dove!
Love's wings are over fleet,
And like the panther's feet
The feet of Love.   70

Poems and Ballads *(1866)*.

A Cameo

There was a graven image of Desire
    Painted with red blood on a ground of gold
    Passing between the young men and the old,
And by him Pain, whose body shone like fire,
And Pleasure with gaunt hands that grasped their hire.
    Of his left wrist, with fingers clenched and cold,
    The insatiable Satiety kept hold,
Walking with feet unshod that pashed the mire.
The senses and the sorrows and the sins,
    And the strange loves that suck the breasts of Hate   10
Till lips and teeth bite in their sharp indenture,[1]
Followed like beasts with flap of wings and fins.
    Death stood aloof behind a gaping grate,
Upon whose lock was written *Peradventure*.

Poems and Ballads *(1866)*.

The Garden of Proserpine[1]

Here, where the world is quiet;
    Here, where all trouble seems
Dead winds' and spent waves' riot
    In doubtful dreams of dreams;
I watch the green field growing
For reaping folk and sowing,
For harvest-time and mowing,
    A sleepy world of streams.

I am tired of tears and laughter,
    And men that laugh and weep;   10
Of what may come hereafter
    For men that sow to reap:
I am weary of days and hours,
Blown buds of barren flowers,
Desires and dreams and powers
    And everything but sleep.

A Cameo
1 contract (punning noun): based on toothed cut dividing the two
halves of ancient written contracts.

The Garden of Proserpine
1 Empress of Hades: obsessively painted by D. G. Rossetti.

Here life has death for neighbour,
    And far from eye or ear
Wan waves and wet winds labour,
    Weak ships and spirits steer;   20
They drive adrift, and whither
They wot not who make thither;
But no such winds blow hither,
    And no such things grow here.

No growth of moor or coppice,
    No heather-flower or vine,
But bloomless buds of poppies,
    Green grapes of Proserpine,
Pale beds of blowing rushes
Where no leaf blooms or blushes   30
Save this whereout she crushes
    For dead men deadly wine.

Pale, without name or number,
    In fruitless fields of corn,
They bow themselves and slumber
    All night till light is born;
And like a soul belated,
In hell and heaven unmated,
By cloud and mist abated
    Comes out of darkness morn.   40

Though one were strong as seven,
    He too with death shall dwell,
Nor wake with wings in heaven,
    Nor weep for pains in hell;
Though one were fair as roses,
His beauty clouds and closes;
And well though love reposes,
    In the end it is not well.

Pale, beyond porch and portal,
    Crowned with calm leaves, she stands   50
Who gathers all things mortal
    With cold immortal hands;
Her languid lips are sweeter
Than love's who fears to greet her
To men that mix and meet her
    From many times and lands.

She waits for each and other,
    She waits for all men born;
Forgets the earth her mother,
    The life of fruits and corn;   60
And spring and seed and swallow
Take wing for her and follow
Where summer song rings hollow
    And flowers are put to scorn.

There go the loves that wither,
    The old loves with wearier wings;
And all dead years draw thither,
    And all disastrous things;

Dead dreams of days forsaken,
Blind buds that snows have shaken,   70
Wild leaves that winds have taken,
　　Red strays of ruined springs.

We are not sure of sorrow,
　　And joy was never sure;
To-day will die to-morrow;
　　Time stoops to no man's lure;
And love, grown faint and fretful,
With lips but half regretful
Sighs, and with eyes forgetful
　　Weeps that no loves endure.   80

From too much love of living,
　　From hope and fear set free,
We thank with brief thanksgiving
　　Whatever gods may be
That no life lives for ever;
That dead men rise up never;
That even the weariest river
　　Winds somewhere safe to sea.

Then star nor sun shall waken,
　　Nor any change of light: 90
Nor sound of waters shaken,
　　Nor any sound or sight:
Nor wintry leaves nor vernal,
Nor days nor things diurnal;
Only the sleep eternal
　　In an eternal night.

Poems and Ballads *(1866)*.

LOVE AND SLEEP

Lying asleep between the strokes of night
　　I saw my love lean over my sad bed,
　　Pale as the duskiest lily's leaf or head,
Smooth-skinned and dark, with bare throat made to bite,
Too wan for blushing and too warm for white,
　　But perfect-coloured without white or red.
　　And her lips opened amorously, and said –
I wist not what, saving one word – Delight.
And all her face was honey to my mouth,
　　And all her body pasture to mine eyes;   10
　　The long lithe arms and hotter hands than fire,
The quivering flanks, hair smelling of the south,
　　The bright light feet, the splendid supple thighs
　　And glittering eyelids of my soul's desire.

Poems and Ballads *(1866)*.

'NON DOLET'[1]

It does not hurt. She looked along the knife
   Smiling, and watched the thick drops mix and run
   Down the sheer blade; not that which had been done
Could hurt the sweet sense of the Roman wife,
But that which was to do yet ere the strife
   Could end for each for ever, and the sun:
   Nor was the palm yet nor was peace yet won
While pain had power upon her husband's life.

It does not hurt, Italia. Thou art more
   Than bride to bridegroom; how shalt thou not take   10
   The gift love's blood has reddened for thy sake?
Was not thy lifeblood given for us before?
   And if love's heartblood can avail thy need,
   And thou not die, how should it hurt indeed?

            Songs Before Sunrise (F. S. Ellis, 1871). The volume is dedicated (in a poem)
            'To Joseph Mazzini,' Italian republican. Swinburne's sado-masochism goes political.

THE LAKE OF GAUBE

The sun is lord and god, sublime, serene,
   And sovereign on the mountains: earth and air
Lie prone in passion, blind with bliss unseen
   By force of sight and might of rapture, fair
   As dreams that die and know not what they were.
The lawns, the gorges, and the peaks, are one
Glad glory, thrilled with sense of unison
In strong compulsive silence of the sun.

Flowers dense and keen as midnight stars aflame
   And living things of light like flames in flower   10
That glance and flash as though no hand might tame
   Lightnings whose life outshone their stormlit hour
   And played and laughed on earth, with all their power
Gone, and with all their joy of life made long
And harmless as the lightning life of song,
Shine sweet like stars when darkness feels them strong.

The deep mild purple flaked with moonbright gold
   That makes the scales seem flowers of hardened light,
The flamelike tongue, the feet that noon leaves cold,
   The kindly trust in man, when once the sight   20
   Grew less than strange, and faith bade fear take flight,
Outlive the little harmless life that shone
And gladdened eyes that loved it, and was gone
Ere love might fear that fear had looked thereon.

Fear held the bright thing hateful, even as fear
   Whose name is one with hate and horror, saith
That heaven, the dark deep heaven of water near,

'NON DOLET'
1 'It does not hurt.'

Is deadly deep as hell and dark as death.
 The rapturous plunge that quickens blood and breath
With pause more sweet than passion, ere they strive   30
To raise again the limbs that yet would dive
Deeper, should there have slain the soul alive.

As the bright salamander in fire of the noonshine exults and is glad of his day,
The spirit that quickens my body rejoices to pass from the sunlight away,
To pass from the glow of the mountainous flowerage, the high multitudinous bloom,
Far down through the fathomless night of the water, the gladness of silence and gloom.
Death-dark and delicious as death in the dream of a lover and dreamer may be,
It clasps and encompasses body and soul with delight to be living and free:
Free utterly now, though the freedom endure but the space of a perilous breath,
And living, though girdled about with the darkness and coldness and strangeness of death: 40
Each limb and each pulse of the body rejoicing, each nerve of the spirit at rest,
All sense of the soul's life rapture, a passionate peace in its blindness blest.
So plunges the downward swimmer, embraced of the water unfathomed of man,
The darkness unplummeted, icier than seas in midwinter, for blessing or ban;
And swiftly and sweetly, when strength and breath fall short, and the dive is done,
Shoots up as a shaft from the dark depth shot, sped straight into sight of the sun;
And sheer through the snow-soft water, more dark than the roof of the pines above,
Strikes forth, and is glad as a bird whose flight is impelled and sustained of love.
As a sea-mew's love of the sea-wind breasted and ridden for rapture's sake
Is the love of his body and soul for the darkling delight of the soundless lake: 50
As the silent speed of a dream too living to live for a thought's space more
Is the flight of his limbs through the still strong chill of the darkness from shore to shore.
Might life be as this is and death be as life that casts off time as a robe,
The likeness of infinite heaven were a symbol revealed of the lake of Gaube.

Whose thought has fathomed and measured
 The darkness of life and of death,
The secret within them treasured,
 The spirit that is not breath?
Whose vision has yet beholden
 The splendour of death and of life?   60
Though sunset as dawn be golden,
 Is the word of them peace, not strife?
Deep silence answers: the glory
 We dream of may be but a dream,
And the sun of the soul wax hoary
 As ashes that show not a gleam.
But well shall it be with us ever
 Who drive through the darkness here,
If the soul that we live by never,
 For aught that a lie saith, fear.

A Channel Passage and Other Poems *(Chatto & Windus, 1899). Volume 'In Memory of William Morris
and Edward Burne Jones'* [sic].

Walter (Horatio) Pater (1839–94)

The critical influence of Walter Pater, cultural historian, journalist, novelist, don, repressed poet and repressed homosexual, and the most important aestheticist critic England produced, has persisted through the twentieth century. His is a key voice for aesthetic impressionism; his beatific vision of the artist and the reader as agonized solipsists is a main force in modernism; his persistent assumption that the readerly gaze is male and that the passionately regarded beautiful object is a male body – the 'form' grown 'perfect in hand or face', 'the face of one's friend' – has made him an iconic presence in Gay or Queer studies. He was born, 4 August 1839, in Shadwell in East London's dockland, a proletarian region, to Maria Hill Pater and Dr Richard Glade Pater, who worked, as did Pater's physician uncle, as a medic for the poor. Walter's older brother William became a medical doctor in turn. His father died when Pater was four, the uncle when he was six, his mother when he was fourteen. At thirteen he entered the King's School, Canterbury, where his classically inspired cult of male friendships was strongly instated in a 'Triumvirate' of chums. In June 1858, already a keen Ruskin reader, he entered The Queen's College, Oxford, to study Classics. He had tutorials with Jowett of Balliol, but only managed a Second Class in his Literae Humaniores finals, 1862. Vacations were often spent in Heidelberg and Dresden where his aunt and sisters resided. His plans to enter the Church of England priesthood were scotched when his Triumvirate friend, John Rainier McQueen of Balliol, reported him, presumably for unorthodoxy, to the Bishop of London. He hung on in Oxford, living by hack tutoring, until in 1865 he netted the first non-clerical Fellowship (in Classics) at Brasenose College. Around this time Pater burnt his poems. One of his pupils was Gerard Manley Hopkins. Pater spent much time mooning over muddied oafs and flannelled fools at the university's sports fields. In 1862 he started writing for the *Westminster Review*, in 1869 for the *Fortnightly*, in 1876 for *Macmillan's*. That year he became associated with the Pre-Raphaelites, especially Swinburne, as well as moving to 2 Bradmore Road with his two unmarried sisters Hester and Clara. (Ten years later Clara was one of the founders of Somerville College for Women in Oxford.) His essays on painters and painting became his first book, *Studies in the History of the Renaissance* (1873). This book, and especially its Conclusion – a version of the conclusion to his 1868 review of some William Morris poems, which was omitted from the second edition of *Studies* in 1881 lest it 'mislead' young men – confirmed the great attraction of his ideas and person for aesthetic and homosexual males, young and old. (Pater's old tutor the Revd W. W. Capes preached against the new 'humanitarian culture' of *Studies* in November 1873.) He was a close friend of the painter Simeon Solomon, imprisoned in 1873 for sex in a public lavatory. In 1874 love letters between Solomon and W. M. Hardinge, the 'Balliol Bugger' (allegedly filthy sonneteer, and future novelist), were passed to Jowett, perhaps through W. H. Mallock (whose Mr Rose in the novel *The New Republic* is Pater), which led to the rustication of Hardinge, and Pater's ticking off by Jowett as well as getting Pater's Proctorship blackballed at Brasenose. In 1875, Pater's friend Oscar Browning – he was given to fondling undergraduates at Bradmore Road – lost his teaching post at Eton in a boy-sex scandal. Oscar Wilde, Lionel Johnson, Richard Le Gallienne, Marc-André Raffalovich (great friend of John Gray, who was allegedly the model for Wilde's Dorian Gray) were all drawn to Pater's hard gem-like flame. So were the lesbian writers 'Vernon Lee' (Violet Paget) and 'Michael Field' (Katherine Bradley and Edith Cooper). Mrs Humphrey Ward, author of the smash-hit novel *Robert Elsmere*, was a good Oxford neighbour. Pater shamelessly plugged his friends in reviews (Arthur Symons, George Moore, Mrs Ward) – it was one inevitable result of his cult of friendship. He was an assiduous walker, travelled much, especially in France, wintered in Rome in 1882, reviewed and wrote hard. His great pro-epicurean novel *Marius the Epicurean* came out in 1885, his *Imaginary Portraits* in 1887, his *Appreciations: With an Essay on Style* in 1893. The insistent interest in pain and suffering and 'love's inversion into cruelty' (a 'characteristic of our late day', as he put it in his 1889 review of Symon's *Nights and Days*) strengthened, some observers think, as a result of difficulties at Oxford. In 1886 the Paters moved to Kensington in London, then back to Oxford (64 St Giles) in 1893. Charlotte Green, sister of J. A. Symonds, widow of the philosopher T. H. Green, a colleague of Clara Pater at Somerville, nursed Pater in his final illness, rheumatic fever and pleurisy, in 1894. He died, 30 July 1894, and is buried in Holywell cemetery, Oxford (next door, appropriately, to Oxford's English Faculty Building).

CONCLUSION[1] TO THE RENAISSANCE (1873, 1888)

Λέγει που 'Ηράκλειτος ὅτι πάντα χωρεῖ καὶ οὐδὲν μένει[2]

To regard all things and principles of things as inconstant modes or fashions has more and more become the tendency of modern thought. Let us begin with that which is without – our physical life. Fix upon it in one of its more exquisite intervals, the moment, for instance, of delicious recoil from the flood of water in summer heat. What is the whole physical life in that moment but a combination of natural elements to which science gives their names? But those elements, phosphorus and lime and delicate fibres, are present not in the human body alone: we detect them in places most remote from it. Our physical life is a perpetual motion of them – the passage of the blood, the waste and repairing of the lenses of the eye, the modification of the tissues of the brain under every ray of light and sound – processes which science reduces to simpler and more elementary forces. Like the elements of which we are composed, the action of these forces extends beyond us: it rusts iron and ripens corn. Far out on every side of us those elements are broadcast, driven in many currents; and birth and gesture and death and the springing of violets from the grave[3] are but a few out of ten thousand resultant combinations. That clear, perpetual outline of face and limb is but an image of ours, under which we group them – a design in a web, the actual threads of which pass out beyond it. This at least of flame-like our life has, that it is but the concurrence, renewed from moment to moment, of forces parting sooner or later on their ways.

Or if we begin with the inward world of thought and feeling, the whirlpool is still more rapid, the flame more eager and devouring. There it is no longer the gradual darkening of the eye, the gradual fading of colour from the wall – movements of the shore-side, where the water flows down indeed, though in apparent rest – but the race of the midstream, a drift of momentary acts of sight and passion and thought. At first sight experience seems to bury us under a flood of external objects, pressing upon us with a sharp and importunate reality, calling us out of ourselves in a thousand forms of action. But when reflexion begins to play upon those objects they are dissipated under its influence; the cohesive force seems suspended like some trick of magic; each object is loosed into a group of impressions – colour, odour, texture – in the mind of the observer. And if we continue to dwell in thought on this world, not of objects in the solidity with which language invests them, but of impressions, unstable, flickering, inconsistent, which burn and are extinguished with our consciousness of them, it contracts still further: the whole scope of observation is dwarfed into the narrow chamber of the individual mind. Experience, already reduced to a group of impressions, is ringed round for each one of us by that thick wall of personality through which no real voice has ever pierced on its way to us, or from us to that which we can only conjecture to be without. Every one of those impressions is the impression of the individual in his isolation, each mind keeping as a solitary prisoner its own dream of a world. Analysis goes a step further still, and assures us that those impressions of the individual

---

CONCLUSION TO THE RENAISSANCE

1 This brief 'Conclusion' was omitted in the second edition of this book, as I conceived it might possibly mislead some of those young men into whose hands it might fall. On the whole, I have thought it best to reprint it here, with some slight changes which bring it closer to my original meaning. I have dealt more fully in *Marius the Epicurean* with the thoughts suggested by it. [Pater's footnote to *The Renaissance: Studies in Art and Poetry*, 4th Thousand, revised and enlarged (Macmillan & Co., 1888). The 'Conclusion' is a version of the ending of Pater's review of William Morris's *The Defence of Guenevere* (1858), *The Life and Death of Jason* (1867) and *The Earthly Paradise* (1868), in the *Westminster Review*, XXXIV, n.s. (October 1868, 300–12). In the *WR* (p. 309), this paragraph preceded the one Pater begins his conclusion with: 'One characteristic of the pagan spirit these new poems have which is on their surface – the continual suggestion, pensive or passionate, of the shortness of life; this is contrasted with the bloom of the world and gives new seduction to it; the sense of death and the desire of beauty;

the desire of beauty quickened by the sense of death. "*Arrieré!*" you say, "here in a tangible form we have the defect of all poetry like this. The modern world is in possession of truths; what but a passing smile can it have for a kind of poetry which, assuming artistic beauty of form to be an end in itself, passes by those truths and the living interests which are connected with them, to spend a thousand cares in telling once more these pagan fables as if it had but to choose between a more and a less beautiful shadow?" It is a strange transition from the earthly paradise to the sad-coloured world of abstract philosophy. But let us accept the challenge; let us see what modern philosophy, when it is sincere, really does say about human life and the truth we can attain in it, and the relation of this to the desire of beauty.']

2 'Heraclitus says "All things give way: nothing remaineth"': Pater's trans. of Socrates' words in Plato, *Cratylus*, 402A; in his *Plato and Platonism*, *Works*, VI (1910).

3 *Hamlet*, V.i: Laertes hopes violets may spring from sister Ophelia's grave.

mind to which, for each one of us, experience dwindles down, are in perpetual flight; that each of them is limited by time, and that as time is infinitely divisible, each of them is infinitely divisible also; all that is actual in it being a single moment, gone while we try to apprehend it, of which it may ever be more truly said that it has ceased to be than that it is. To such a tremulous wisp constantly re-forming itself on the stream, to a single sharp impression, with a sense in it, a relic more or less fleeting, of such moments gone by, what is real in our life fines itself down. It is with this movement, with the passage and dissolution of impressions, images, sensations, that analysis leaves off – that continual vanishing away, that strange, perpetual, weaving and unweaving of ourselves.[4]

Philosophiren, says Novalis, *ist dephlegmatisiren, vivificiren.*[5] The service of philosophy,[6] of speculative culture, towards the human spirit, is to rouse, to startle it to a life of constant and eager observation. Every moment some form grows perfect in hand or face; some tone on the hills or the sea is choicer than the rest; some mood of passion or insight or intellectual excitement is irresistibly real and attractive to us, – for that moment only. Not the fruit of experience, but experience itself, is the end. A counted number of pulses only is given to us of a variegated, dramatic life. How may we see in them all that is to be seen in them by the finest senses? How shall we pass most swiftly from point to point, and be present always at the focus where the greatest number of vital forces unite in their purest energy?

To burn always with this hard, gem-like flame, to maintain this ecstasy, is success in life. In a sense it might even be said that our failure is to form habits: for, after all, habit is relative to a stereotyped world, and meantime it is only the roughness of the eye that makes any two persons, things, situations, seem alike. While all melts under our feet, we may well grasp at any exquisite passion, or any contribution to knowledge that seems by a lifted horizon to set the spirit free for a moment, or any stirring of the senses, strange dyes, strange colours, and curious odours, or work of the artist's hands, or the face of one's friend. Not to discriminate every moment some passionate attitude in those about us, and in the very brilliancy of their gifts some tragic dividing of forces on their ways, is, on this short day of frost and sun, to sleep before evening. With this sense of the splendour of our experience and of its awful brevity, gathering all we are into one desperate effort to see and touch, we shall hardly have time to make theories about the things we see and touch. What we have to do is to be for ever curiously testing new opinions and courting new impressions, never acquiescing in a facile orthodoxy, of Comte, or of Hegel, or of our own. Philosophical theories or ideas, as points of view, instruments of criticism, may help us to gather up what might otherwise pass unregarded by us. 'Philosophy is the microscope of thought.'[7] The theory or idea or system which requires of us the sacrifice of any part of this experience, in consideration of some interest into which we cannot enter, or some abstract theory we have not identified with ourselves, or of what is only conventional, has no real claim upon us.

One of the most beautiful passages of Rousseau is that in the sixth book of the *Confessions*, where he describes the awakening in him of the literary sense.[8] An undefinable taint of death had clung always about him, and now in early manhood he believed himself smitten by mortal disease. He asked himself how he might make as much as possible of the interval that remained; and he was not biassed by anything in his previous life when he decided that it must be by intellectual excitement, which he found just then in the clear, fresh writings of Voltaire. Well! we are all *condamnés*, as Victor Hugo says: we are all under sentence of death but with a sort of indefinite reprieve – *les hommes sont tous condamnés à mort avec des sursis indéfinis.*[9] we have an interval, and then our place knows us no more. Some spend this interval in listlessness, some in high passions, the wisest, at

4   *WR* version, p. 311, adds a paragraph: 'Such thoughts seem desolate at first; at times all the bitterness of life seems concentrated in them. They bring the image of one washed out beyond the bar in a sea at ebb, losing even his personality, as the elements of which he is composed pass into new combinations. Struggling, as he must, to save himself, it is himself that he loses at every moment.'
5   'To philosophise...is to clear away phlegm, to vivify' (Novalis is Baron Friedrich von Hardenberg (1772–1801), German poet and novelist).

6   *WR* version, p. 311, and *The Renaissance*, 1st edn, continue this sentence with: 'and of religion and culture as well, to the human spirit, is to startle it into a sharp and eager observation.'
7   Victor Hugo, in *Les Misérables* (1862).
8   Jean-Jacques Rousseau, *Confessions* (1781), Part i, Bk 6.
9   'Men are all condemned to death with indefinite stays of execution': Hugo, *Le Dernier Jour d'un Condamné* (1836).

least among 'the children of this world,' in art and song.[10] For our one chance lies in expanding that interval, in getting as many pulsations as possible into the given time. Great passions may give us this quickened sense of life, ecstasy and sorrow of love, the various forms of enthusiastic activity, disinterested or otherwise, which come naturally to many of us. Only be sure it is passion – that it does yield you this fruit of a quickened, multiplied consciousness. Of such wisdom, the poetic passion, the desire of beauty, the love of art for its own sake,[11] has most. For art comes to you proposing frankly to give nothing but the highest quality to your moments as they pass, and simply for those moments' sake.

> Studies in the History of the Renaissance *(Macmillan & Co., 1873)*. Text, The Renaissance: Studies in Art and Poetry, *4th Thousand, revised and enlarged (Macmillan & Co., 1888) – the so-called third edition.*

(Henry) Austin Dobson (1840–1921)

Austin Dobson, belle-lettriste and light-versifier, was born the eldest son of a Plymouth civil engineer, 18 January 1840. He was educated at schools in Beaumaris, Coventry and Strasbourg. At the age of sixteen he entered the Board of Trade and remained there, a lifelong civil servant, until retirement in 1901. One of his colleagues was the poet William Cosmo Monkhouse. With Edmund Gosse working as a translator in the commercial department, the Board of Trade was known as a 'nest of singing birds'. (Lord Farrer, a head of the Department, spoke less warmly of 'certain civil servants who would have been excellent administrators if they had not been indifferent poets'.) Dobson was not utterly indifferent as a poet, and his poetic contributions to the magazines (*St Paul's, Good Words, Belgravia, Harper's,* and so on), and the consequent volumes of verse, abounded. His first volume, *Vignettes in Rhyme and Vers de Société* (1873), was dedicated to Anthony Trollope in whose *St Paul's* magazine many of the book's pieces first appeared. *Proverbs in Porcelain and Other Verses* followed (1875). The two volumes, combined and added to, appeared in the USA as *Vignettes in Rhyme and Other Verses*

in 1880, and rearranged, in England in 1883 as *Old World Idylls.* This volume went into many editions, as did *At the Sign of the Lyre* (1885) – which had many new poems for a change. Various re-assortments and selections followed, as well as the first of several *Collected Poems* in 1895, but Dobson was running out of steam as a poet, in quantity as well as quality, and his heart, certainly from 1879 on, when his *William Hogarth* appeared, was really in his numerous studies of eighteenth-century artists and writers – Fielding, Bewick, Walpole, Fanny Burney, Richardson, Hogarth again. His final score of such work included fifty-odd Introductions for reprinted eighteenth-century texts, eight biographies and ten volumes of collected essays. The Civil Service was evidently less demanding then than now. Dobson married a civil engineer's daughter, Frances Mary Beardmore, in 1865, and fathered five sons and five daughters. He died in Ealing, west of London, 2 September 1921. His *Complete Poetical Works* appeared from the Oxford University Press in 1923, edited by Alban Dobson, with a very useful list of its contents' first places of publication.

Love in Winter

Between the berried holly-bush
The Blackbird whistled to the Thrush:
'Which way did bright-eyed Bella go?
Look, Speckle-breast, across the snow, –
Are those her dainty tracks I see,
That wind toward the shrubbery?'

The Throstle pecked the berries still.
'No need for looking, Yellow-bill;
Young Frank was there an hour ago,
Half frozen, waiting in the snow;　　　　　　　　10

10　Luke 16.8, parable of unjust steward, 'commended...because he had done wisely: for the children of this world are in their generation wiser than the children of light'.

11　All earlier editions had 'art for art's sake': the phrase which caught on as characterizing Pater and his school.

His callow beard was white with rime, –
'Tchuck, – 'tis a merry pairing-time!'

'What would you?' twittered in the Wren;
'These are the reckless ways of men.
I watched them bill and coo as though
They thought the sign of Spring was snow;
If men but timed their loves as we,
'Twould save this inconsistency.'

'Nay, Gossip,' chirped the Robin, 'nay;
I like their unreflective way.   20
Besides, I heard enough to show
Their love is proof against the snow: –
Why wait, he said, *why wait for May,*
When love can warm a winter's day?

Good Words *(February 1871). Text,* Vignettes in Rhyme and Vers de Société
(Now First Collected) *(Henry S. King & Co., 1873).*

THE BALLAD OF PROSE AND RHYME

(Ballade à Double Refrain)

When the ways are heavy with mire and rut,
    In November fogs, in December snows,
When the North Wind howls, and the doors are shut, –
    There is place and enough for the pains of prose;
    But whenever a scent from the whitethorn blows,
And the jasmine-stars at the casement climb,
    And a Rosalind-face at the lattice shows,
Then hey! – for the ripple of laughing rhyme!

When the brain gets dry as an empty nut,
    When the reason stands on its squarest toes,   10
When the mind (like a beard) has a 'formal cut,' –
    There is place and enough for the pains of prose;
    But whenever the May-blood stirs and glows,
And the young year draws to the 'golden prime,'
    And Sir Romeo sticks in his ear a rose, –
Then hey! – for the ripple of laughing rhyme!

In a theme where the thoughts have a pedant-strut,
    In a changing quarrel of 'Ayes' and 'Noes,'
In a starched procession of 'If' and 'But,' –
    There is place and enough for the pains of prose;   20
    But whenever a soft glance softer grows
And the light hours dance to the trysting-time,
    And the secret is told 'that no one knows,' –
Then hey! – for the ripple of laughing rhyme!

Envoy

In the work-a-day world, – for its needs and woes,
There is place and enough for the pains of prose;
But whenever the May-bells clash and chime,
Then hey! – for the ripple of laughing rhyme!

Belgravia *(January 1878). Text,* Old World Idylls and Other Verses
(Kegan Paul, Trench & Co., 1883).

THE BALLAD OF IMITATION

(Ballade)

'C'est imiter quelqu'un que de planter des choux.'[n]
Alfred de Musset

If they hint, O Musician, the piece that you played
  Is nought but a copy of Chopin or Spohr;
That the ballad you sing is but merely 'conveyed'
  From the stock of the Arnes and the Purcells of yore;
  That there's nothing, in short, in the words or the score
That is not as out-worn as the 'Wandering Jew';
  Make answer – Beethoven could scarcely do more –
That the man who plants cabbages imitates, too!

If they tell you, Sir Artist, your light and your shade
  Are simply 'adapted' from other men's lore;   10
That – plainly to speak of a 'spade' as a 'spade' –
  You've 'stolen' your grouping from three or from four;
  That (however the writer the truth may deplore),
'Twas Gainsborough painted *your* 'Little Boy Blue';
  Smile only serenely – though cut to the core –
For the man who plants cabbages imitates, too!

And you too, my Poet, be never dismayed
  If they whisper your Epic – 'Sir Éperon d'Or' –
Is nothing but Tennyson thinly arrayed
  In a tissue that's taken from Morris's store;   20
  That no one, in fact, but a child could ignore
That you 'lift' or 'accommodate' all that you do;
  Take heart – though your Pegasus' withers be sore –
For the man who plants cabbages imitates, too!

POSTSCRIPTUM. – And you, whom we all so adore,
  Dear Critics, whose verdicts are always so new! –
One word in your ear. There were Critics before...
  And the man who plants cabbages imitates, too!

Belgravia *(March 1878). Text,* Old World Idylls *(1883).*

ON THE HURRY OF THIS TIME

(To F. G.)

With slower pen men used to write,
  Of old, when 'letters' were 'polite;'
  In ANNA's, or in GEORGE's days,
  They could afford to turn a phrase,
Or trim a straggling theme aright.

They knew not steam; electric light
Not yet had dazed their calmer sight; –

THE BALLAD OF IMITATION
1 'Imitating someone is just planting cabbages.'

They meted out both blame and praise
   With slower pen.

Too swiftly now the Hours take flight!   10
What's read at morn is dead at night:
   Scant space have we for Art's delays,
   Whose breathless thought so briefly stays,
We may not work – ah! would we might! –
   With slower pen.

      Eighteenth Century Essays, selected Austin Dobson (Kegan Paul, Trench,
      Trübner & Co., Ltd., 1882): untitled. Text of Collected Poems, *2 vols*
      (Dodd, Mead & Co., New York, 1895), I.

(William) Cosmo Monkhouse (1840–1901)

Cosmo Monkhouse, poet and art critic, son of a solicitor father and a mother of French Huguenot descent, was born in London, 18 March 1840. He was a pupil at St Paul's School, 1848–65, after which he entered the Civil Service as a clerk. He was one of the notorious 'nest of singing birds' at the Board of Trade along with his contemporaries Austin Dobson and Edmund Gosse. He rose through departmental ranks, travelled for the Board in South America, and ended up as Assistant Secretary to the Finance Department. He wrote verse at school and was soon an assiduous contributor of poems to the journals – *Temple Bar*, the *Argosy*, the *Englishman's Magazine*. His first volume, *A Dream of Idleness, and Other Poems*, was published by Moxon in 1865, but did not catch on, and

Monkhouse turned rather to literary and art criticism, producing a great stream of books and articles on Hogarth, Turner, English water-colourists, Leigh Hunt, John Tenniel, Reynolds, the National Gallery collections, and the like. His second volume of poems, *Corn and Poppies*, came out in 1890. There were also posthumous volumes, including *Nonsense Rhymes* (1902), illustrated by G. K. Chesterton, and consisting of limericks of a merely conventional and not at all filthy kind ('There was an old monk of Basing', and so on: though *that*, of course, might lead to anything!). Monkhouse's dramatic monologue mode was not at all bad. He married twice and had two sons and six daughters. He died, still a civil servant, at Skegness, 2 July 1901.

Any Soul to Any Body

So we must part, my body, you and I
   Who've spent so many pleasant years together.
'Tis sorry work to lose your company
   Who clove to me so close, whate'er the weather,
From winter unto winter, wet or dry;
   But you have reached the limit of your tether,
And I must journey on my way alone,
And leave you quietly beneath a stone.

They say that you are altogether bad
   (Forgive me, 'tis not my experience),   10
And think me very wicked to be sad
   At leaving you, a clod, a prison, whence
To get quite free I should be very glad.
   Perhaps I may be so, some few days hence,
But now, methinks, 'twere graceless not to spend
A tear or two on my departing friend.

Now our long partnership is near completed,
   And I look back upon its history;
I greatly fear I have not always treated

You with the honesty you showed to me. 20
And I must own that you have oft defeated
   Unworthy schemes by your sincerity,
And by a blush or stammering tongue have tried
To make me think again before I lied.

'Tis true you're not so handsome as you were,
   But that's not your fault and is partly mine.
You might have lasted longer with more care,
   And still looked something like your first design;
And even now, with all your wear and tear,
   'Tis pitiful to think I must resign 30
You to the friendless grave, the patient prey
Of all the hungry legions of Decay.

But you must stay, dear body, and I go.
   And I was once so very proud of you;
You made my mother's eyes to overflow
   When first she saw you, wonderful and new.
And now, with all your faults, 'twere hard to find
   A slave more willing or a friend more true.
Ay – even they who say the worst about you
Can scarcely tell what I shall do without you. 40

Corn and Poppies *(Elkin Matthews, 1890). Separately published by R. and R. Clark,*
Edinburgh, 1890. Title alludes to R. Browning's poem 'Any Wife to Any Husband',
Men and Women *(1855).*

RECOLLECTIONS OF ALFRED TENNYSON

A Day Dream (1869)

I had a holiday down by the sea,
And I said to the Present 'Away with thee,'
And suffered the tide of Memory
   To wash me away from Place and Time.
And many a morn, as I lay afloat,
I smoked and dreamed in my little boat,
Of fields of barley and of rye
That either side the river lie
   That ever flows to Camelot.
   For I was full of the golden rhyme 10
     Of Tennyson, the Laureate.

And oft, as I lay at my length, afloat,
Faces I never had seen before
(But I knew them well though they knew not me),
Sweet faces came and peeped over the boat,
Madeline, Adeline, Eleänore,
And often at eve, when the light was wan,
Afar I heard the gathering glee
Of the jubilant voice of the Dying Swan;
   For little had I to do with time, 20
   And my soul was steeped in the golden rhyme
     Of Tennyson, the Laureate.

And once my slow keel gently grazed
A loamy marge, and I arose

And passed into a little close
Where on a blooming bank there lay
The fainting form of Fatima,
Stung to the soul with sharp desire,
And when her face I gently raised
Her breath was on my cheek as fire, –   30
   (Beside me lay, uncut, the *Times*,
     For I chewed the cud of the golden rhymes
       Of Tennyson, the Laureate).

Not long, for suddenly the breath
Failed, and she slid from my lax clasp,
And quick night came and quenched the day
In her bright orbs.   I wondered, while
She gave her life up with a smile
And cry of 'Antony'; and death,
Clothed in the semblance of an asp,   40
Writhed from her robe and slunk away.
   Ay me, it was a pleasant time
     When I was borne upon the rhyme
       Of Tennyson, the Laureate.

Behind, a sweet voice whispered, 'Look!'
I turning soon beheld a maid,
Her hair in many a chestnut braid,
And at her feet a noisy Brook.
'You will be welcome, sir,' she said.
And led the way to a near Mill,   50
With mignonette upon the sill
Of a neat window o'er my head.
   Alas, that it should end, this time,
     When I breathed the breath of the golden rhyme
       Of Tennyson, the Laureate.

We entered in.   The room was foul –
A vinous fume hung in the air;
Knee by knee, and cheek by jowl,
Two topers old were bibbing there.
I knew the place, I knew the men,   60
I knew it was the House of Sin; –
But cried 'Where hast thou brought me then?'
She answered with a toothless grin.
   Oblivious of the feet of Time,
     I flowed on with the golden rhyme
       Of Tennyson, the Laureate.

When suddenly there rose a din,
And in there strode a Red-Cross Knight,
With armour bright, and visage sad,
Who, with a clean sweep of his sword,   70
Swept flask and flagon from the board,
And cried 'My name is Galahad';
And out into the darkness dim,
And through the world I followed him.
   For I was free from the trammels of Time,
     And lived in the spacious world of rhyme
       Of Tennyson, the Laureate.

And after many a day we came
Where, on a tall cliff firmly set,
A Palace rose up like a flame,   80
As fairylike and delicate,
Built of a stone that hath no name.
'I surely know, or I forget,'
I said, 'Sir Knight, but truly this
Of Art, I think, the Palace is.'
   I sang this to the silver chime
    That rings for ever through the rhyme
      Of Tennyson, the Laureate.

'Not Art, but Arthur,' cried the Knight,
And soon in a great hall we found   90
The blameless King, and Table Round,
Engirt with knights, – a goodly sight.
Then cried the King, and smote the oak,
'Love, Truth, and Beauty, one, but three,
This is the Artist's Trinity!'
And lo, 'twas Tennyson who spoke.
   For this shall be through endless time
    The burden of the golden rhyme
      Of Tennyson, our Laureate.

Corn and Poppies *(1890)*.

Thomas Hardy (1840–1928)

Thomas Hardy was born into a respectable rural working-class family (his father, also Thomas, was a builder) in the Dorset hamlet of Higher Bockhampton, in the parish of Stinsford, not far from Dorchester, 2 June 1840. He was eldest of four children – two sons, two daughters. Hardy was proud of his family connexion with Vice-Admiral Sir Thomas Masterman Hardy, Horatio Nelson's flag-captain and subject of Nelson's mythical dying request to 'Kiss me, Hardy'. Hardy's father and grandfather were famous local musicians, accompanying the hymns in Stinsford parish church's musicians' gallery and playing a lot at local celebrations, sacred and secular (as described in Hardy's second published novel, *Under the Greenwood Tree*, 1872). He attended a Nonconformist school in Dorchester (acquiring Latin as well as French). From 1856 he trained as an architect in the Dorchester firm of John Hinks, continued his studies (learning Greek), wrote poems, became great friends with Horace Moule, an embryo poet and critic, member of a distinguished Anglican family, who encouraged Hardy's literary interests and later, most disturbingly for Hardy, committed suicide. As an architect Hardy was employed in the fashionable replacement of ancient church buildings by modern Gothic ones – work he later greatly regretted. From 1862 to 1867 he worked in London in Arthur Blomfield's popular architectural practice. He continued to write poems, fed intensely on the cultural life of the capital (theatres, the National Gal-

lery, Dickens's readings, Exeter Hall concerts), and fell, as was his wont, into the most Gothic of experiences (he was Blomfield's man, for instance, supervising by night the removal of the contents of the old St Pancras graveyard to make way for St Pancras railway station). In 1867 he returned to Lower Bockhampton to do occasional architectural work but mainly to live as a writer – which meant novels, rather than poems. Greatly encouraged by Meredith, Chapman & Hall's reader (who urged on him the importance of plot), and by Leslie Stephen (who published *Far From the Madding Crowd* as a *Cornhill Magazine* serial in 1874), he turned himself into one of the major Victorian novelists and short-story writers. In 1874 he married Emma Lavinia Gifford, whom he'd met working on church restoration in St Juliot, Cornwall. They moved around, living variously in London and the West Country, until they settled finally in 1885 in Max Gate, the rather grim house Hardy designed for them, near Dorchester. The marriage became increasingly unhappy; there was an unrequited love affair with the Hon Mrs Arthur Henniker (Hardy loved the titled and the posh); his two great novels – *Tess of the D'Urbervilles* (1891) and *Jude the Obscure* (1895), though immensely popular, were sniped at for immorality – and so Hardy abandoned the novel for the old privities of lyric poetry. At the age of fifty-eight he published *Wessex Poems and Other Verses*, and embarked on his extraordinary late flowering as one of England's most distinguished poets. *Poems of the Past and the Present* followed in 1901. From 1902 until 1908 he worked on his most ambitious poetic project, the Napoleonic epic *The Dynasts* (1904–8). His most important work remained, though, the small poem, especially in *Satires of Circumstance* (1914) and *Moments of Vision* (1917). His verse is compellingly elegiac (nowhere more astonishingly powerful than in the guilty poems recalling his first wife after her death in 1912), Gothic, bereft of Christian faith, but constantly arguing with the 'President of the Immortals', and wonderfully unmisgiving about what W. H. Auden grudgingly acknowledged as the force of 'his rhythmical clumsiness, his outlandish vocabulary'. Hardy's prefaces and his critical comments on art, his own and other people's (not least in his autobiography, *The Life of Thomas Hardy*, published posthumously as if it were a biography by his second wife Florence Emily Hardy), show him making a principle of what he called 'disproportioning' and the 'idiosyncratic mode of regard'. 'Unadjusted impressions have their value', he writes in the Preface to *Poems of the Past and the Present*, 'and the road to a true philosophy of life seems to lie in humbly recording diverse readings of its phenomena as they are forced upon us by chance and change.' If his plain-speaking and his gruffly consonantal vocabulary make him the poetic father of Edward Thomas, Wilfred Owen and Philip Larkin (as well as, perhaps, of Auden in certain moods), his impressionism (and note the enthusiasm for the later paintings of Turner) marks him out as a significant modernist. Hardy was in his time a great clubman; he knew every literary person who mattered; but in old age, away in Dorchester, he became for the public the bufferish Sage of Wessex, as in Siegfried Sassoon's poem 'At Max Gate'. In 1909 he succeeded Meredith as President of the Society of Authors; he received the Order of Merit in 1910, was given honorary doctorates galore, became Honorary Fellow of Magdalene College, Cambridge, and The Queen's College, Oxford. He died at Max Gate, 11 January 1928. His ashes were interred in Westminster Abbey, but his heart was buried in the ancestral churchyard at Stinsford parish church.

Her Dilemma

(In —— Church)

The two were silent in a sunless church,
Whose mildewed walls, uneven paving-stones,
And wasted carvings passed antique research;
And nothing broke the clock's dull monotones.

Leaning against a wormy poppy-head,
So wan and worn that he could scarcely stand,
– For he was soon to die, – he softly said,
'Tell me you love me!' – holding long her hand.

She would have given a world to breathe 'yes' truly,
So much his life seemed hanging on her mind,
And hence she lied, her heart persuaded throughly
'Twas worth her soul to be a moment kind.

But the sad need thereof, his nearing death,
So mocked humanity that she shamed to prize
A world conditioned thus, or care for breath
Where Nature such dilemmas could devise.

10

Written 1866. Wessex Poems and Other Verses *(Harper & Brothers, September 1898).*

Neutral Tones

We stood by a pond that winter day,
And the sun was white, as though chidden of God,
And a few leaves lay on the starving sod,
    – They had fallen from an ash, and were gray.

Your eyes on me were as eyes that rove
Over tedious riddles of years ago;

And some words played between us to and fro –
    On which lost the more by our love.

The smile on your mouth was the deadest thing
    Alive enough to have strength to die;   10
And a grin of bitterness swept thereby
    Like an ominous bird a-wing....

Since then, keen lessons that love deceives,
    And wrings with wrong, have shaped to me
Your face, and the God-curst sun, and a tree,
    And a pond edged with grayish leaves.

Written 1867. Wessex Poems (1898).

FRIENDS BEYOND

William Dewy, Tranter Reuben, Farmer Ledlow late at plough,
    Robert's kin, and John's, and Ned's,
And the Squire, and Lady Susan, lie in Mellstock churchyard now!

'Gone,' I call them, gone for good, that group of local hearts and heads;
    Yet at mothy curfew-tide,
And at midnight when the noon-heat breathes it back from walls and leads,

They've a way of whispering to me – fellow-wight who yet abide –
    In the muted, measured note
Of a ripple under archways, or a lone cave's stillicide:

'We have triumphed: this achievement turns the bane to antidote,
    Unsuccesses to success,
Many thought-worn eves and morrows to a morrow free of thought.   10

'No more need we corn and clothing, feel of old terrestial stress;
    Chill detraction stirs no sigh;
Fear of death has even bygone us: death gave all that we possess.'

W. D. – 'Ye mid burn the old bass-viol that I set such vallie by.'
Squire. – 'You may hold the manse in fee,
    You may wed my spouse, my children's memory of me may decry.'

Lady. – 'You may have my rich brocades, my laces; take each household key;
    Ransack coffer, desk, bureau;
    Quiz the few poor treasures hid there, con the letters kept by me.'

Far. – 'Ye mid zell my favourite heifer, ye mid let the charlock grow,   20
    Foul the grinterns, give up thrift.'
Wife. – 'If ye break my best blue china, children, I shan't care or ho.'

All. – 'We've no wish to hear the tidings, how the people's fortunes shift;
    What your daily doings are;
    Who are wedded, born, divided; if your lives beat slow or swift.

'Curious not the least are we if our intents you make or mar,
    If you quire to our old tune,
If the City stage still passes, if the weirs still roar afar.'

– Thus, with very gods' composure, freed those crosses late and soon
    Which, in life, the Trine allow   30
(Why, none witteth), and ignoring all that haps beneath the moon,

William Dewy, Tranter Reuben, Farmer Ledlow late at plough,
   Robert's kin, and John's, and Ned's,
And the Squire, and Lady Susan, murmur mildly to me now.

Wessex Poems *(1898)*.

Nature's Questioning

When I look forth at dawning, pool,
   Field, flock, and lonely tree,
   All seem to gaze at me
Like chastened children sitting silent in a school;

Their faces dulled, constrained, and worn,
   As though the master's ways
   Through the long teaching days
Their first terrestrial zest had chilled and overborne.

Upon them stirs, in lippings mere
   (As if once clear in call,   10
   But now scarce breathed at all) –
'We wonder, ever wonder, why we find us here!

'Has some Vast Imbecility,
   Mighty to build and blend,
   But impotent to tend,
Framed us in jest, and left us now to hazardry?

'Or come we of an Automaton
   Unconscious of our pains? . . .
   Or are we live remains
Of Godhead dying downwards, brain and eye now gone?   20

'Or is it that some high Plan betides,
   As yet not understood,
   Of Evil stormed by Good,
We the Forlorn Hope over which Achievement strides?'

Thus things around.   No answerer I. . . .
   Meanwhile the winds, and rains,
   And Earth's old glooms and pains
Are still the same, and Life Death neighbours nigh.

Wessex Poems *(1898)*.

'I Look Into My Glass'

I look into my glass,
And view my wasting skin,
And say, 'Would God it came to pass
My heart had shrunk as thin!'

For then, I, undistrest
By hearts grown cold to me,
Could lonely wait my endless rest
With equanimity.

But Time, to make me grieve,
Part steals, lets part abide;
And shakes this fragile frame at eve   10
With throbbings of noontide.

Wessex Poems *(1898). (Last poem in the volume.)*

To Life

O life with the sad seared face,
    I weary of seeing thee,
And thy draggled cloak, and thy hobbling pace,
    And thy too-forced pleasantry!

I know what thou would'st tell
    Of Death, Time, Destiny –
I have known it long, and know, too, well
    What it all means for me.

But canst thou not array
    Thyself in rare disguise,   10
And feign like truth, for one mad day,
    That Earth is Paradise?

I'll tune me to the mood,
    And mumm with thee till eve;
And maybe what as interlude
    I feign, I shall believe!

Poems of the Past and Present *(Harper & Brothers, 1901).*

Long Plighted

Is it worth while, dear, now,
To call for bells, and sally forth arrayed
For marriage-rites – discussed, decried, delayed
    So many years?

Is it worth while, dear, now,
To stir desire for old fond purposings,
By feints that Time still serves for dallyings,
    Though quittance nears?

Is it worth while, dear, when
The day being so far spent, so low the sun,   10
The undone thing will soon be as the done,
    And smiles as tears?

Is it worth while, dear, when
Our cheeks are worn, our early brown is gray;
When, meet or part we, none says yea or nay,
    Or heeds, or cares?

Is it worth while, dear, since
We still can climb old Yell'ham's wooded mounds
Together, as each season steals its rounds
    And disappears?   20

Is it worth while, dear, since
As mates in Mellstock churchyard we can lie,
Till the last crash of all things low and high
Shall end the spheres?

Poems of the Past and Present *(1901)*.

THE SELF-UNSEEING

Here is the ancient floor,
Footworn and hollowed and thin,
Here was the former door
Where the dead feet walked in.

She sat here in her chair,
Smiling into the fire;
He who played stood there,
Bowing it higher and higher.

Childlike, I danced in a dream;
Blessings emblazoned that day;   10
Everything glowed with a gleam;
Yet we were looking away!

Poems of the Past and Present *(1901)*.

DE PROFUNDIS[1]

I

'Percussus sum sicut foenum, et aruit cor meum.'
Psalm ci[2]

Wintertime nighs;
But my bereavement-pain
It cannot bring again:
Twice no one dies.

Flower-petals flee;
But, since it once hath been,
No more that severing scene
Can harrow me.

Birds faint in dread:
I shall not lose old strength   10
In the lone frost's black length:
Strength long since fled!

Leaves freeze to dun;
But friends can not turn cold
This season as of old
For him with none.

DE PROFUNDIS I
1 Psalm 130.1: 'out of the depths have I cried unto thee, O Lord.'

2 actually Psalm 102.4: 'My heart is smitten and withered like grass.'

Tempests may scath;
But love can not make smart
Again this year his heart
Who no heart hath.   20

Black is night's cope;
But death will not appal
One who, past doubtings all,
Waits in unhope.

De Profundis II

'Considerabam ad dexteram, et videbam; et non erat qui cognosceret me.... Non est qui requirat animam meam.'

Psalm cxli[1]

When the clouds' swoln bosoms echo back the shouts of the many and strong
That things are all as they best may be, save a few to be right ere long,
And my eyes have not the vision in them to discern demonstration so clear,
The blot seems straightway in me alone; one better he were not here.

The stout upstanders say, All's well with us: ruers have nought to rue!
And what the potent say so oft, can it fail to be somewhat true?
Breezily go they, breezily come; their dust smokes around their career,
Till I think I am one born out of due time, who has no calling here.[2]

Their dawns bring lusty joys, it seems; their eves exultance sweet;
Our times are blessed times, they cry: Life shapes it as is most meet,   10
And nothing is much the matter; there are many smiles to a tear;
Then what is the matter is I, I say. Why should such an one be here?...

Let him to whose ears the low-voiced Best seems stilled by the clash of the First,
Who holds that if way to the Better there be, it exacts a full look at the Worst,
Who feels that delight is a delicate growth cramped by crookedness, custom, and fear,
Get him up and be gone as one shaped awry; he disturbs the order here.

1895–6

De Profundis III

'Heu mihi, quia incolatus meus prolongatus est! Habitavi cum habitantibus Cedar; multum incola fuit anima mea.'

Psalm cxix[1]

There have been times when I well might have passed and the ending have come –
Points in my path when the dark might have stolen on me, artless, unrueing –
Ere I had learnt that the world was a welter of futile doing:
Such had been times when I well might have passed, and the ending have come!

De Profundis II
1 Psalm 141.4: 'I looked on my right hand, and beheld; but there was no man that would know me...no man cared for my soul.'
2 as St Paul: 'one born out of due time', and 'not meet to be called an apostle', I Corinthians 15. 8–9.

De Profundis III
1 actually Psalm 120. 5–6: 'woe is me, that I sojourn in Mesech, that I dwell in the tents of Kedar! My soul hath long dwelt with him that hateth peace.'

Say, on the noon when the half-sunny hours told that April was nigh,
And I upgathered and cast forth the snow from the crocus-border,
Fashioned and furbished the soil into a summer-seeming order,
Glowing in gladsome faith that I quickened the year thereby.

Or on that loneliest of eves when afar and benighted we stood,
She who upheld me and I, in the midmost of Egdon[2] together,   10
Confident I in her watching and ward through the blackening heather,
Deeming her matchless in might and with measureless scope endued.

Or on that winter-wild night when, reclined by the chimney-nook quoin,
Slowly a drowse overgat me, the smallest and feeblest of folk there,
Weak from my baptism of pain; when at times and anon I awoke there –
Heard of a world wheeling on, with no listing or longing to join.

Even then! while unweeting that vision could vex or that knowledge could numb,
That sweets to the mouth in the belly are bitter, and tart, and untoward,
Then, on some dim-coloured scene should my briefly raised curtain have lowered,
Then might the Voice that is law have said 'Cease!' and the ending have come.   20

1896

Poems of the Past and Present *(1901). These poems retitled, later, as* In Tenebris *I, II, III.*

RETROSPECT

'I Have Lived with Shades'

I

I have lived with Shades so long,
And talked to them so oft,
Since forth from cot and croft
I went mankind among,
      That sometimes they
      In their dim style
      Will pause awhile
      To hear my say;

II

And take me by the hand,
And lead me through their rooms   10
In the To-be, where Dooms
Half-wove and shapeless stand:
      And show from there
      The dwindled dust
      And rot and rust
      Of things that were.

III

'Now turn,' they said to me
One day: 'Look whence we came,
And signify his name
Who gazes thence at thee.' –   20
      – 'Nor name nor race

---

2   Hardy's fictitious 'Wessex' heath.

Know I, or can,'
I said, 'Of man
So commonplace.

IV

'He moves me not at all;
I note no ray or jot
Of rareness in his lot,
Or star exceptional.
Into the dim
Dead throngs around
He'll sink, nor sound
Be left of him.'

V

'Yet,' said they, 'his frail speech
Hath accents pitched like thine –
Thy mould and his define
A likeness each to each –
But go! Deep pain
Alas, would be
His name to thee,
And told in vain!'

February 2, 1899

Poems of the Past and Present *(1901)*.

AN AUGUST MIDNIGHT

I

A shaded lamp and a waving blind,
And the beat of a clock from a distant floor:
On this scene enter – winged, horned, and spined –
A longlegs, a moth, and a dumbledore;[1]
While 'mid my page there idly stands
A sleepy fly, that rubs its hands...

II

Thus meet we five, in this still place,
At this point of time, at this point in space.
– My guests parade my new-penned ink,
Or bang at the lamp-glass, whirl, and sink.
'God's humblest, they!' I muse. Yet why?
They know Earth-secrets that know not I.

Max Gate, 1899

Poems of the Past and Present *(1901)*.

THE DARKLING THRUSH

I leant upon a coppice gate
When Frost was spectre-gray,

AN AUGUST MIDNIGHT
1   bumble-bee, or (dialect) cockchafer.

And Winter's dregs made desolate
    The weakening eye of day.
The tangled bine-stems scored the sky
    Like strings of broken lyres,
And all mankind that haunted nigh
    Had sought their household fires.

The land's sharp features seemed to be
    The Century's corpse outleant,   10
His crypt the cloudy canopy,
    The wind his death-lament.
The ancient pulse of germ and birth
    Was shrunken hard and dry,
And every spirit upon earth
    Seemed fervourless as I.

At once a voice arose among
    The bleak twigs overhead
In a full-hearted evensong
    Of joy illimited;   20
An aged thrush, frail, gaunt, and small,
    In blast-beruffled plume,
Had chosen thus to fling his soul
    Upon the growing gloom.

So little cause for carolings
    Of such ecstatic sound
Was written on terrestrial things
    Afar or nigh around,
That I could think there trembled through
    His happy good-night air   30
Some blessed Hope, whereof he knew
    And I was unaware.

            31st December 1900

            Poems of the Past and Present *(1901)*.

OBSERVATIONS, ON LIFE, ART AND POETRY

After looking at the landscape ascribed to Bonington[1] in our drawing-room I feel that Nature is played out as a Beauty, but not as a Mystery. I don't want to see landscapes, *i.e.*, scenic paintings of them, because I don't want to see the original realities – as optical effects, that is. I want to see the deeper reality underlying the scenic, the expression of what are sometimes called abstract imaginings.

The 'simply natural' is interesting no longer. The much decried, mad, late-Turner[2] rendering is now necessary to create my interest. The exact truth as to material fact ceases to be of importance in art – it is a student's style – the style of a period when the mind is serene and unawakened to the tragical mysteries of life; when it does not bring anything to the object that coalesces with and translates the qualities that are already there, – half hidden, it may be – and the two united are depicted as the All.

            (January 1887)

OBSERVATIONS...
1 Richard Parkes Bonington (1802–28).

2 Joseph Mallord William Turner (1775–1851). See Introduction.

Reading H. James's *Reverberator*[3]. After this kind of work one feels inclined to be purposely careless in detail. The great novels of the future will certainly not concern themselves with the minutiae of manners.... James's subjects are those one could be interested in at moments when there is nothing larger to think of.

(9 July 1888)

We dined at Walter Pater's. Met Miss——, an Amazon, more, an Atalanta, most, a Faustine.[4] Smokes: handsome girl: cruel small mouth: she's of the class of interesting women one would be afraid to marry.

(14 July 1888)

At the Old Masters, Royal Academy. Turner's water-colours: each is a landscape *plus* a man's soul.... What he paints chiefly is *light as modified by objects*. He first recognizes the impossibility of really reproducing on canvas all that is in a landscape; then gives for that which cannot be reproduced a something else which shall have upon the spectator an approximative effect to that of the real. He said, in his maddest and greatest days: 'What pictorial drug can I dose man with, which shall affect his eyes somewhat in the manner of this reality which I cannot carry to him?' – and set to make such strange mixtures as he was tending towards in 'Rain, Steam and Speed', 'The Burial of Wilkie', 'Agrippina landing with the ashes of Germanicus', 'Approach to Venice', 'Snowstorm and a Steamboat', etc. Hence, one may say, Art is the secret of how to produce by a false thing the effect of a true....

(9 January 1889)

Art consists in so depicting the common events of life as to bring out the features which illustrate the author's idiosyncratic mode of regard; making old incidents and things seem as new.

(March–April 1890)

Reflections on Art. Art is a changing of the actual proportions and order of things, so as to bring out more forcibly than might otherwise be done that feature in them which appeals most strongly to the idiosyncrasy of the artist. The changing, or distortion, may be of two kinds: (1) The kind which increases the sense of vraisemblance: (2) That which diminishes it. (1) is high art: (2) is low art.

High art may choose to depict evil as well as good, without losing its quality. Its choice of evil, however, must be limited by the sense of worthiness.

[...]

Art is a disproportioning – (*i.e.* distorting, throwing out of proportion) – of realities, to show more clearly the features that matter in those realities, which, if merely copied or reported inventorially, might possibly be observed, but would more probably be overlooked. Hence 'realism' is not Art.

(5 August 1890)

'Florence Emily Hardy', The Early Life of Thomas Hardy 1840–1891 *(Macmillan & Co., 1928), 242–3, 277, 278, 283–4, 294, 299.*

---

3   *The Reverberator* (1888).
4   Amazon: one of race of mythic female warriors. Atalanta: mythic speedy huntress who would only marry the man who could outstrip her (and killed all the ones she beat); defeated finally by the suitor with the golden apples. Faustine: poisonous heroine of Swinburne's poem 'Faustine', in *Poems and Ballads* (1866).

W. S. (Wilfrid Scawen) Blunt (1840–1922)

Wilfrid Scawen Blunt, explorer, Arabist, critic of colonialism, and poet, was born at Petworth House, Sussex, 17 August 1840, second son of a Grenadier Guards officer, Francis Scawen Blunt, and Mary Chandler, an Anglican clergyman's daughter. He had a Roman Catholic education at Stonyhurst and Oscott and entered the diplomatic service when he was eighteen, serving in embassies across Europe and in Buenos Aires. In 1869 he married Byron's pious Roman Catholic granddaughter Lady Anne Isabella Noel and left the diplomatic corps. When his brother died three years later he inherited the family estates in Sussex and began, with his intrepid wife, a life of travel and exploration instead. He became an expert on conditions in North Africa, Persia, India, and a vocal opponent of the imperialist excesses he observed, in books like *Ideas About India* (1885) and *The Secret History of the English Occupation of Egypt* (1911). He was deeply critical of the Egyptian manoeuvrings of Sir Evelyn Baring (later Lord Cromer). He wintered regularly in Egypt, from 1881 on his small estate on the edge of Cairo – going native in Arab dress, speaking Bedouin dialect, acting the part of respected tribal chief. His interest in colonial people led to his taking up the cause of Ireland. He failed in 1885 and 1886 to get elected to Parliament as a Home Ruler, and was imprisoned for two months in 1887 for inciting Irish tenants to resist eviction. His radical views inform his poetry, not least in his long pro-Irish poem 'The Canon of Aughrim'. The sonnets of *In Vinculis* (1889) – a small volume with 'The Canon of Aughrim' in it, dedicated 'To the Priests and Peasantry of Ireland, Who for Three Hundred Years Have Preserved the Tradition of a Righteous War For Faith and Freedom' – were mainly written in Galway and Kilmainham gaols (on the fly-leaves of Blunt's prayerbook). His novel in verse *Griselda* (1893) was not a success. His kind of reflective absorption in the incidental minutiae of life is better caught in his shorter runs, especially his sonnets, as in *Sonnets and Songs of Proteus* (1875) and *Esther* (1892). William Morris's Kelmscott Press brought out a very artsy-craftsy hand-printed volume of *The Love Lyrics and Songs of Proteus* in 1892. W. E. Henley and George Wyndham edited a selected *Poetry* in 1898. Illness slowed Blunt down as the years went on, but his polemics continued unabated to the end, especially in *My Diaries* (1919 and 1920). His wife, herself the author of worthwhile travel books, *The Bedouin Tribes of the Euphrates* (2 vols, 1879) and *A Pilgrimage to Nedj* (2 vols, 1881), died in Egypt at the end of 1917. Blunt died in Sussex, 10 September 1922, and was buried in Newbuildings Wood, Southwater, without – as he requested – any religious ceremony.

A Day in Sussex

The dove did lend me wings.   I fled away
From the loud world which long had troubled me.
Oh lightly did I flee when hoyden May
Threw her wild mantle on the hawthorn tree.
I left the dusty high road, and my way
Was through deep meadows, shut with copses fair.
A choir of thrushes poured its roundelay
From every hedge and every thicket there.
Mild, moon-faced kine looked on, where in the grass
All heaped with flowers I lay, from noon till eve.   10
And hares unwitting close to me did pass,
And still the birds sang, and I could not grieve.
Oh what a blessed thing that evening was!
Peace, music, twilight, all that could deceive
A soul to joy or lull a heart to peace.
It glimmers yet across whole years like these.

The Love Sonnets of Proteus *(C. Kegan Paul & Co., 1881).*

TO HESTER ON THE STAIR

1

Hester, creature of my love,
  What is this?   You love not me?
On the stair you stand above,
  Looking down distrustfully
    With the corners of your eyes
    Watching me in mute surprise,
  Me, your father, only me.

2

Hester, why this foolish terror,
  You who know me and my ways?
Was my love so writ in error   10
  That it needed your disgrace?
    Is your doubt of locks grown thin
    Or the beard which hides his chin
  His, your father's chin and face?

3

Hester, we were fools of passion
  When our last goodbyes were smiled.
Now you stand in your strange fashion
  By my kisses unbeguiled,
    With your light foot turned to flee
    While I press you to my knee,   20
  You, my child, my only child.

4

Listen, Hester, I am able
  Still to flatter and be fond:
You the wise crow of the fable
  Perched above me and beyond.
    Foolish! Not one word you speak
    To my praises of your cheek,
  Not one sound, one only sound!

5

Be it so.   My love you mock it,
  And my sighs are empty wind.
See, I shut my heart and lock it   30
  From your laughing eyes unkind.
    Yet, remember this last word,
    Love is two-edged like a sword.
  Mind this only, only mind!

Esther, Love Lyrics, and Natalia's Resurrection (Kegan Paul, Trench, Trübner & Co., 1892).

THE IDLER'S CALENDAR

May: The London Season

I still love London in the month of May,
  By an old habit, spite of dust and din.

I love the fair adulterous world, whose way
   Is by the pleasant banks of Serpentine.
   I love the worshippers at fashion's shrine,
The flowers, the incense, and the pageantry
   Of generations which still ask a sign
Of that dear god, whose votary am I.
I love the 'greetings in the market-place,'
   The jargon of the clubs.   I love to view   10
The 'gilded youth' who at the window pass,
   For ever smiling smiles for ever new.
I love these men and women at their task
   Of hunting pleasure.   Hope, mysterious too,
Touches my arm and points, and seems to ask
'And you, have you no Juliet in the masque?'

The Poetry of Wilfrid Blunt, *ed. W. E. Henley and George Wyndham*
(William Heinemann, 1898).

Lost Threads

Here lie the lost threads of a tangled life,
Enigmas meaningless and without clue,
Loose ends and knots, frayed edges of time's strife,
Essays in vain love ignorant of you.
Not so had my life been had Heaven's high blue
Apparelled us betimes in its romance,
Clothed us with one fair passion chaste and true,
Armed my weak soul with your dear countenance.
– Rage of my heart! How idly I declaim,
Now knowing your delights and sweetnesses,   10
Empty sad verse engarlanding your name.
Great griefs are silent as the wide lone seas;
Irrevocable loss lives bare of fame.
Else were I eloquent of thee and these.

The Poetical Works: A Complete Edition, *2 vols (Macmillan & Co., 1914), I.*

Alfred Tennyson

Tears, idle tears! Ah, who shall bid us weep,
Now that thy lyre, O prophet, is unstrung?
What voice shall rouse the dull world from its sleep
And lead its requiem as when Grief was young,
And thou in thy rapt youth, Time's bards among,
Captured our ears, and we looked up and heard
Spring's sweetest music on thy mourning tongue
And knew thee for Pain's paradisal bird.
We are alone without thee in our tears,
Alone in our mute chauntings. Vows are vain   10
To tell thee how we loved thee in those years
Nor dream to look upon thy like again.
We know not how to weep without thy aid,
Since all that tears would tell thyself hast said.

Poetical Works *(1914), I.*

John Addington Symonds (1840–93)

John Addington Symonds, born 5 October 1840 in Bristol, was the only son of John Addington Symonds, eminent West Country medical practitioner, lecturer in forensic medicine and psychologist, and his wife Harriet Sykes. Three brothers died at birth or soon after, but three sisters survived, one of whom, Charlotte, married the philosopher T. H. Green. When Symonds was four, their mother died of scarlet fever, and their father became a strongly intrusive presence. Symonds went to Harrow School (1854) and then to Balliol College, Oxford, to read Classics (1858), and where initial dilatoriness turned to great success. He gained First Classes in Classical Moderations and Finals; won the Newdigate Poetry prize ('The Escorial'); won a Fellowship by Examination at Magdalen College (1862) and the Chancellor's English Essay Prize (1863: 'The Renaissance'). All the time he was troubled by his own homosexual proclivities, which were schooled by eye-opening readings in Greek texts such as Plato's *Phaidros*, and egged on by works such as William Johnson Cory's *Ionica*. (Symonds wrote a fan letter to Cory, and received a long epistolary apologia for pederasty in return.) He fell deeply in love with lower-class choir-boys; shopped the Revd Dr Vaughan, the Headmaster of Harrow, to his father for pederastic designs on a boy (and thus smashed up Vaughan's church career); was himself shopped to the Magdalen Fellows as lover of males by a nasty man from Corpus whom he'd rebuffed, called C. G. H. Shorting. Guilty about the 'wolf' of his desires and the shaming débâcle at Magdalen, and with his father prompting him about the dangerous tendencies of what Symonds at the time called 'arcadian' love, he married Janet Catherine North in 1864, and fathered three daughters. He sought to sublimate his zest for male contact in private confessional records, unpublished poems with titles like *Phallus Impudicus*, foreign travel, lengthy scholarly researches in the Greek poets and the Italian Renaissance, and translations of Italian poets such as Michelangelo. But of course the love whose name he couldn't speak aloud – so that he substituted disguising female pronouns for the male ones in his own love sonnets, and his extremely explicit *Memoirs* were to be locked away from prying eyes in the London Library (and not published until Phyllis Grosskurth's edition of 1984) – shone brightly through his lectures, histories and translations. Reading Walt Whitman's *Leaves of Grass* (1865) confirmed his taste for male comradeship among the lower classes. Mrs Symonds apparently condoned such extra-mural passions for peasants, coachmen, gondoliers. Symonds's lifelong need to live in healthy resorts outside England – his lungs were extremely bad – conveniently took him to continental places where the law was more liberal in such matters than at home. Happily, too, for him, he had a private income to finance such wanderings. His finally settling in Davos in Switzerland (1880) and his writing about it helped make Davos and such resorts very fashionable with the English. In Davos he struck up his great friendship with the convalescing Robert Louis Stevenson, to whom his *Wine, Women and Song* (1884) – translations of medieval goliardic verse – is dedicated. His biggest work is the multi-volumed *Renaissance in Italy* (1875–86). The attack in 1887 in the *Contemporary Review* on 'The Greek Spirit in Modern Literature', by the Revd R. Tyrwhitt, Rector of St Mary Magdalen, Oxford (targeting Arnold's atheism and Symonds's homosexuality) seems to have prompted Pater to take cover (withdrawing as candidate to succeed Arnold as Oxford Professor of Poetry). Symonds's work on Greek pederasty, *A Problem in Greek Ethics* (1883), became a bourgeois gay men's cult book. From 1888 he spent much time in Venice in the house of his gay friend and biographer, Horatio F. Brown, whose book of crypto-pederastic verses, *Drift*, came out in 1900. His last great love affair was with a gondolier. He collaborated with Havelock Ellis's sober study of homosexuality, *Sexual Inversion* (1891) – Case XVII is Symonds. His *Life of Michelangelo Buonarroti* appeared in 1892. He died in Rome, 19 April 1893, of pneumonia, on the very day his *Walt Whitman: A Study* was published. Symonds's published poems – *Many Moods* (1878), *New and Old* (1880), *Animi Figura* (1882), *Vagabunduli Libellus* (1884) – lack the impudic force of his unpublished ones: repression and masking-tape are no better for his verses than they are for anyone else's. He is buried in the Protestant Cemetery in Rome, near to Keats. Benjamin Jowett, Master of his old College, composed a pious Latin epitaph.

A DREAM

'Εν ὀμμάτων ἀχηνίαις.[1]

I yearn for you, my dearest; for you came
   In visions of the night and stood by me:
   I took your hand, and set you on my knee,
And stroked your hair, and drank the sunny flame
Of your large eyes: I kissed your cool moist lips,
   And laid your cheek to mine, and asked you why
   You stayed so long away; for lovers die
In one short week of waiting, tears eclipse
The moonlight of their eyes, where hope hath lit
   Radiance reflected from the brows they love: 10
   And then you laughed, and playful seemed to prove
Whether or no I loved you, frowned and knit
   Brows all unused to anger, smiled again,
   And nestled to my side and breathed away my pain.

And then I woke. The dazzling summer sun
   Shot fiery arrows through the hot white blind,
   Withering the dream for which my spirit pined,
Urging me up life's weary race to run.
And you were gone. Oh, why did cruel sleep
   Show me my darling to confuse the morrow   20
   With sweetest recollection steeped in sorrow?
Might I not plod along the road and keep
My recreant thoughts from banished Paradise?
   Might I not glue my face to books, or fast
   Till long oblivion sealed the erring past?
Oh, it is hard! Prayer, penance, sacrifice
   Must slowly wipe away short sleep's delight,
   And years repair the ruin of a night.

New and Old: A Volume of Verse *(Smith, Elder, & Co., 1880).*

AN INVITATION TO THE SLEDGE

Come forth, for dawn is breaking;
   The sun hath touched the snow:
Our blithe sledge-bells are calling,
   And Christian waits below.

All day o'er snow-drifts gliding
   'Twixt grey-green walls of ice,
We'll chase the winter sunlight
   Adown the precipice.

Above black swirling death-waves
   We will not shrink nor blanch,
Though the bridge that spans the torrent   10
   Be built by an avalanche.

We'll talk of love and friendship
   And hero-hearted men,

A DREAM

1 'in the blank gaze of the eyes'. Aeschylus, *Agamemnon*, 418.

Mid the stems of spangled larches
   In the fairy-frosted glen.

With flight as swift as swallows
   We'll sweep the curdled lake,
Where the groans of prisoned kelpies
   Make the firm ice-pavement quake.   20

We'll thread the sombre forest,
   Where giant pines are crowned
With snow-caps on their branches
   Bent to the snowy ground.

Strong wine of exultation.
   Free thoughts that laugh at death,
Shall warm our wingèd spirits
   Though the shrill air freeze our breath.

With many a waif of music
   And memory-wafted song,   30
With the melody of faces
   Loved when the world was young,

With clear Hellenic stories
   And names of old romance,
We'll wake our soul's deep echoes
   While the hills around us dance:

Dance to the arrowy motion
   Of our sledge so firm and free,
Skimming the beaten snow-track
   As a good ship skims the sea.   40

Like love, like all that's joyous,
   Like youth, like life's delight,
This day is dawning o'er us
   Between a night and a night.

O friend, 'tis ours to clasp it!
   Come forth! No better bliss
For hearts by hope uplifted
   Hath heaven or earth than this!

New and Old *(1880)*.

VINTAGE

I found him lying neath the vines that ran
   Grape-laden o'er grey frames of oak and beech;
A fair and jocund Faun, whose beard began,
   Like dewy down on quince or blushing peach,
   To soften chin and cheek. He bade me reach
My hand to his, and drew me through the screen
Of clusters intertwined with glistening green.

Sunrise athwart us fell – a living fire,
   That touching turned our tendrilled roof to red;
Network of shade from many a flickering spire   10
   And solid orb upon the youth was shed;

With purple grapes and white his comely head
Was crowned, and in his hand a bunch he pressed
Against the golden glory of his breast.

Gourds with the grapes, and hops, and serpentine
  Wreaths of blue bindweed tangling built a bower,
Where lying we could watch 'twixt vine and vine
    Young men and maidens move, and singing shower
    On wattled crates the fruit whose hoary flower
With dew still glistened; for the kiss of night   20
Lay yet on vale and mountain misty-bright.

Some trod the press; some climbed the elms that hung
  Vine-burdened; and beneath, a beardless boy
Tuning his melancholy lute-strings sung
    A wild shrill song, that spake of only joy,
    But was so sad that virgins cold and coy
Melted, and love mid sorrow-sweetness fell
On careless hearts that felt the powerful spell.

New and Old (1880).

PERSONALITY

I

I know not what I am. – Oh dreadful thought! –
  Nor know I what my fellow-creatures are:
  Between me and the world without, a bar
  Impalpable of adamant is wrought.
Each self, from its own self concealed, is caught
    Thus in a cage of sense, sequestered far
    From comradeship, calling as calleth star
    To star across blank intermediate nought.
His own self no man sees, and none hath seen
    His brother's self. Nay, lovers, though they sigh   10
    'There is no room for ought to come between
'Our blended souls in this felicity,'
    Starting from sleep, shall find a double screen
    Built 'twixt two sundered selves – and both must die.

II

Yea, both shall carry with them to the void
  Without, the void more terrible within,
  Tormented haply by the smart of sin,
  And cursing what their wilful sense enjoyed.
Yet were they free to take or to avoid?
    Who knows! – Amid the dull chaotic din   20
    Of wrangling schools which argument can win
    Conviction, when blind faith hath been destroyed?
Freedom or servitude? – So fooled is man
    By blind self-ignorance, he cannot say
    If will alone beneath heaven's azure span
Its self-determined impulses obey;
    Or if each impulse, wild as wind at play,
    Be but a cog-wheel in the cosmic plan.

New and Old (1880).

Mathilde Blind (also 'Claude Lake') (1841–96)

Mathilde Blind, German-Jewish intellectual, independent woman-of-letters on the European model, one of her era's most potent crusading new thinkers and New Women, was born at Mannheim, 21 March 1841. Her German father, a Cohen, was a banker, who died when she was very young. Her mother then married Karl Blind, a leading revolutionary who was involved in the failed Baden uprising of 1848–9 and who, like so many German revolutionaries, including of course Karl Marx, sought political asylum with his family in London. Mathilde adopted his surname. All her life and work register her family's European socialist leanings (her seventeen-year-old brother Karl Blind tried to assassinate Bismarck – and committed suicide when the attempt failed). She was expelled from an English school as an atheist, was on close friendly terms with the European revolutionaries of her stepfather's acquaintance like Garibaldi and Mazzini, and with their English admirers such as Swinburne (though Swinburne complained that she hung on to his first editions of Matthew Arnold, and he clearly preferred her and her family's politics to her person and the amatory designs on him that people thought she entertained: he 'comes to tea with me and does not notice and recites poetry and goes away', she bemoaned to Edmund Gosse). She was great friends with Eleanor Marx. Shadowing George Eliot's demythologizing work, she translated D. F. Strauss's *The Old Faith and the New* (1873–4). Her poetic rewrite of the legend of St Oran, which sceptically takes up the questions of religious history, *The Prophecy of St Oran* (1881), was withdrawn by its publishers for being too 'atheistic'. Her subsequent volume, *The Fire on the Heather* (1886), is a long poem against the Scottish Highland land clearances and evictions of peasant families for the economic advantage of rich landowners. Her most ambitious poem is an epic of Darwinianism, *The Ascent of Man* (1888: Darwin's rival, the eminent evolutionist Alfred Wallace, wrote an introduction for the 1899 reprint). Mathilde Blind edited selections from Byron and Shelley (the story goes that she once reverently kissed the bit of Shelley's skull in William Rossetti's possession). From the 1860s on she was closely involved in feminist struggles. Her first collection of poems appeared (1867) under the gender-ambivalent name of Claude Lake. One of her best friends and allies was Mona Caird, the New Woman novelist and preacher of 'free unions' instead of marriage. Blind translated from French the influential diary of an angry woman, *The Journal of Marie Bashkirtseff* (1890). She was the first biographer of George Eliot, in the Eminent Women series (1883). A close associate of the Pre-Raphaelites, she lived for a long time with the Ford Madox Browns. She was an able writer of lyrical poems in addition to her obviously polemical verses. She'd never be the Christina Rossetti she so admired, nor, for that matter, the George Eliot she celebrated (she produced an action-packed prose romance, *Tarantella*, 1885), but she's a very solid and influential poetic presence. She suffered badly from headaches. She died in London, 26 November 1896, leaving her estate to Newnham College for Women at Cambridge, in particular to endow a Scholarship for Language and Literature.

AUTUMN TINTS

Coral-coloured yew-berries
  Strew the garden ways,
Hollyhocks and sunflowers
  Make a dazzling blaze
  In these latter days.

Marigolds by cottage doors
  Flaunt their golden pride,
Crimson-punctured bramble leaves
  Dapple far and wide
  The green mountain-side.

Far away, on hilly slopes
  Where fleet rivulets run,
Miles and miles of tangled fern,
  Burnished by the sun,
  Glow a copper dun.

For the year that's on the wane,
   Gathering all its fire,
Flares up through the kindling world
   As, ere they expire,
   Flames leap high and higher.   20

            Songs and Sonnets *(Chatto & Windus, 1893).*

THE DEAD

The dead abide with us! Though stark and cold
Earth seems to grip them, they are with us still:
They have forged our chains of being for good or ill;
And their invisible hands these hands yet hold.
Our perishable bodies are the mould
In which their strong imperishable will –
Mortality's deep yearning to fulfil –
Hath grown incorporate through dim time untold.

Vibrations infinite of life in death,
As a star's travelling light survives its star!   10
So may we hold our lives, that when we are
The fate of those who then will draw this breath,
They shall not drag us to their judgment bar,
And curse the heritage which we bequeath.

            Songs and Sonnets *(1893).*

MANCHESTER BY NIGHT

O'er this huge town, rife with intestine wars,
Whence as from monstrous sacrificial shrines
Pillars of smoke climb heavenward, Night inclines
Black brows majestical with glimmering stars.
Her dewy silence soothes life's angry jars:
And like a mother's wan white face, who pines
Above her children's turbulent ways, so shines
The moon athwart the narrow cloudy bars.

Now toiling multitudes that hustling crush
Each other in the fateful strife for breath,   10
And, hounded on by divers hungers, rush
Across the prostrate ones that groan beneath,
Are swathed within the universal hush,
As life exchanges semblances with death.

            Songs and Sonnets *(1893).*

A WINTER LANDSCAPE

All night, all day, in dizzy, downward flight,
   Fell the wild-whirling, vague, chaotic snow,
   Till every landmark of the earth below,
Trees, moorlands, roads, and each familiar sight

Were blotted out by the bewildering white.
　　And winds, now shrieking loud, now whimpering low,
　　Seemed lamentations for the world-old woe
That death must swallow life, and darkness light.

But all at once the rack was blown away,
　　The snowstorm hushing ended in a sigh;
　　Then like a flame the crescent moon on high
Leaped forth among the planets; pure as they,
Earth vied in whiteness with the Milky Way:
　　Herself a star beneath the starry sky.

Songs and Sonnets *(1893)*.

Once We Played

Once we played at love together –
　　Played it smartly, if you please;
Lightly, as a wind-blown feather,
　　Did we stake a heart apiece.

Oh, it was delicious fooling!
　　In the hottest of the game,
Without thought of future cooling,
　　All too quickly burned Life's flame.

In this give-and-take of glances,
　　Kisses sweet as honey dews,　　　　　　　　　　　　　　10
When we played with equal chances,
　　Did you win, or did I lose?

Was your heart then hurt to bleeding,
　　In the ardour of the throw?
Was it then I lost, unheeding,
　　Lost my heart so long ago?

Who shall say? The game is over.
　　Of us two who loved in fun,
One lies low beneath the clover,
　　One lives lonely in the sun.　　　　　　　　　　　　　　20

Birds of Passage: Songs of the Orient and Occident
(Chatto & Windus, 1895).

Robert (Williams) Buchanan (also 'Thomas Maitland') (1841–1901)

Robert Buchanan, poet, playwright, novelist and controversialist, was born in Carswell, Staffordshire, 18 August 1841, the only surviving child of socialist parents. His father was an evangelist for Robert Owen's utopian schemes who owned and edited socialist papers in Glasgow. After a troubled passage through several Glasgow schools, Buchanan took courses at Glasgow University, but when his father's finances ran out, he left university in 1860 to try for a literary career in London. His university friend David Gray went south too. They struggled. Gray died in 1861. Buchanan's account of his friend (in *David Gray and Other Essays*) greatly moved people like George

Eliot. With help and encouragement from the likes of George Eliot, G. H. Lewes, W. H. Dixon, Browning and Peacock, Buchanan slowly got on. Dickens published him in *All the Year Round*. After his early pseudo-classic phase (*Undertones*, 1863) and his Scottish verse story-telling (*Idyls and Legends of Inverbury*, 1865), his poems gradually settled down into the urban London version of what he called 'mystic realism', represented by *London Poems* (1866) and characteristic of his *Poetical Works* (3 vols, 1874). The poor are given a voice – often sentimental, to be sure – in Buchanan's numerous dramatic monologues in the Browningesque style. The emphasis of Buchanan's explanations of 'mystic realism' is on a kind of untranscendent humanist transcendence which sounds rather like George Eliot's or Ruskin's post-Christian aesthetics. 'Streets are not beautiful', he declares in the essay 'On Mystic Realism', appended to vol.3 of the *Poetical Works*, 'and this is the age of streets; trade seems selfish and common, and this is the age of trade; railways, educational establishments, poor houses, debating societies, are not romantic, and this is the age of all these. But if we strip off the hard outer crust of these things, if we pass from the unpicturesqueness of externals to the currents which flow beneath, who then shall say that this life is barren of poetry.' It is no surprise Buchanan admired the Brownings, Clough and Walt Whitman (whom he met in 1885). He managed, too, to combine his intense mystic and mythological involvements (as in *The Book of Orm*, 1870, and his epic poem *The City of Dream*, 1888) with the scathing hostility to Jesus and Christianity which he imbibed with his socialist mother's milk. He wrote large numbers of novels and plays, managed theatres, travelled variously in Scotland, Ireland and the USA, spent his earnings unwisely, and ended up bankrupt in 1900. He was in his own lifetime thought a more central literary figure than at any time since, and he had hopes of succeeding Tennyson as Poet Laureate (Alfred Austin, more intimate with the Prime Minister, Lord Salisbury, got it instead). He remains best known for his improvident, though still considerable, attacks on Swinburne and Rossetti and associated writers, in the sixties and early seventies.

Swinburne had insulted David Gray's memory; Buchanan (anonymously in the *Athenaeum*) attacked Swinburne's *Poems and Ballads* (1866) as filthy ('unclean for the sake of uncleanness'); William Michael Rossetti charged in to defend Swinburne in the *Spectator* (15 September 1866); Buchanan kept his powder dry, then, as Thomas Maitland, scattered his fire in a *Contemporary Review* piece (October 1871), 'The Fleshly School of Poetry: Mr D. G. Rossetti' (the Pre-Raphaelites were now an immoral *school*). The article became a pamphlet; Swinburne weighed in, at first a bit limply in a letter to the *Athenaeum* (16 December 1871) deploring 'The Stealthy School of Criticism', then, with something more like his usual pepperiness against critics, in *Under the Microscope* (1872), and a piece entitled 'The Devil's Due' in the *Examiner* (28 December 1875) – after which tirade Buchanan won £5 damages for libel. Buchanan rather spoiled his argument – an arresting one not unakin, perhaps, to Walter Bagehot's notorious argument that Browning's poetry was 'grotesque' (in his 1864 essay, 'Wordsworth, Tennyson, and Browning; or Pure, Ornate, and Grotesque Art in English Poetry') – by recanting in a letter to the *Academy* (1 July 1882): 'Mr Rossetti, I freely admit now, never was a fleshly poet at all; never, at any rate, fed upon the poisonous honey of French art', and by making further amends in 'A Note on Dante Rossetti' in *A Look Around Literature* (1887): 'hasty expressions and uninstructed abuse'; 'how false a judgement it was, how conventional, and Pharisaic a criticism, which chose to dub as "fleshly" the works of this most etherial and dreamy – in many respects this least carnal and most religious – of modern poets'. (For all that, Ezra Pound still labelled him 'foetid Buchanan' in his poem 'Hugh Selwyn Mauberley'.) Buchanan's wife, Mary Jay, died after twenty-one years of marriage and a long illness, in November 1882 (the *Selected Poems* of that year are dedicated to her). Her sister Harriet, Buchanan's theatrical collaborator as writer, manager and actress, devoted herself to Buchanan's welfare in later years. He died privately in poverty at Streatham, 10 June 1901. Harriet, ever staunch, wrote a memoir, *Robert Buchanan: Some Account of his Life, his Life's Work and Literary Friendships* (1903).

THE CITIES

I took my staff and wandered o'er the mountains,
And came among the heaps of gold and silver,
The gorgeous desolation of the Cities.

My trouble grew tenfold when I beheld
The agony and burden of my fellows,
The pains of sick men and the groans of hungry.

I saw the good man tear his hair and weep;
I saw the bad man tread on human necks
Prospering and blaspheming: and I wondered.

The silken-natured woman was a bond-slave;   10
The gross man foul'd her likeness in high places;
The innocent were heart-wrung: and I wondered.

The gifts of earth are given to the base;
The monster of the Cities spurned the martyr;
The martyr died, denying: and I wondered.

Poetical Works, *3 vols (Henry S. King & Co., 1874), III.*

SONG OF THE SLAIN

This is the Song of the Weak
    Trod 'neath the heel of the Strong!
This is the Song of the hearts that break
    And bleed as we ride along, –
From sea to sea we singing sweep, but this
    is the slain man's Song!

Southward, a shriek of pain,
    As the martyr'd races fall!
The wild man's land and his herds we gain,
    With the gold that's best of all, –   10
Because the leaves of the tree are black 'tis
    meet that they should fall!

Eastward, another cry,
    Wrung from the black and red!
But merrily our hosts go by,
    Trampling the quick and dead, –
'Tis meet that the heathen tribes should
    Starve, and the Christian dogs be fed.

Westward, close at the door,
    A cry for bread and light!   20
But lo, we hug our golden store
    And feast from morn to night: –
Our brother Esau must perish too, altho'
    his skin be white!

In the name of the Jingo-Christ
    We raise our savage song,
In gold the martyr's blood is priced
    Wherever we march along,
How should we heed our brother's cry, –
    he is weak and we are strong!   30

We have sow'd, and lo! we reap,
    We are strong, and lo! we slay;
We are lords of Earth and Deep,
    And this is our triumph-day, –
The broken wave and the broken heart are
    spent, and vanish away!

Ever the Weak must fall
    Under the strength of the Strong!
And God (they say), who is Lord of all,
    Smiles as we sweep along;   40

Yet tho' we are strong and our song is loud,
    this is the slain man's Song!

Complete Poetical Works, *2 vols (Chatto & Windus, 1901), II.*

THE SHOWER

I

Suddenly, as the busy crowd
  Surges and roars along the street,
Over the housetops broods the cloud,
  And down the first loose raindrops beat!
While black umbrellas here and there
Flutter up in the troubled air,
With pitter-patter of many feet
Into shelter the throngs retreat;
In a moment the rush and roar
Are still'd, and the Shower begins to pour,   10
The eager Shower, with its twofold sound –
The splash close by, and the murmur all round!

II

Splash, splash! while the murmurous sound
Gathers and deepens all around!
And on the streets with leaden strokes
Strikes the Rain, till the pavement smokes
And where the great drops plash and pelt
Quicksilver-rings are made and melt!
While under the archways, at open doors,
The wet folk gather, down it pours, –
The eager Shower, with its twofold sound, –
The splash close by, and the murmur around!   20

III

And now...how quiet all things look!
Still as a picture in a book!
And lo! the crowding people seem
Spell-bound, like figures in a Dream!
Silently they shelter and stare
On the rain-lash'd street, thro' the misty air: –
Trembling the little sempstress stands,
Holding her bandbox in her hands,
Lifting her skirt and peeping down
At her thin wet shoes with a shrug and a frown;   30
The fop his silk umbrella grips,
Holding it from him while it drips;
The city man with impatient glance
Looks at the clouded sky askance,
Mutters, and quietly unfolds
The evening newspaper he holds;
The loafer leaneth against the wall,
Straw in his mouth, with a grin for all;
The urchin, reaching out his foot,
Into the puddle dips his boot,   40
Or cap in hand thrusts out his bare
Head, that the drops may pelt his hair!
'Buses and cabs crawl slowly by,

Glistering moistly under the sky;
A mist steams up from the slippery ground,
While louder and louder grows the sound –
The splash close by, and the murmur around!

IV

Then, all of a sudden, the air grows bright;
The moist black pools flash back the light,
The sun shines cheerily over all,   50
And lo, the Shower has ceased to fall!
The spell is broken, and now once more
The crowd flows onward with busy roar!

Complete Poetical Works *(1901), II.*

NIETZSCHE[1]

Jupiter's gutter-snipe! A shrill-tongued thing
    Running beside the blood-stain'd chariot wheels,
Crying 'Hosannah to the pitiless King,
    The ravening Strength that neither spares nor feels!'

A slave that glorified the yoke and goad,
    Cast mud into the well of human tears,
Gibed at the Weak who perish on the road,
    Slain by the Law which neither heeds nor hears!

'All hail to the Eternal Might and Right,
    By which all life is sifted, slain, and shed!   10
Lord, make me hard like thee that day and night
    I may approve thy ways, however dread!'

So cried he, while, indifferent to his cries,
    Nature's triumphal Car went grinding past, –
And lo, the dust was blown into his eyes,
    And crush'd 'mid blood and mud, he sank at last.

Poor gutter-snipe! Answer'd with his own prayer,
    Back to primeval darkness he has gone; –
Only one living soul can help him there,
    The gentle human god he spat upon!   20

Complete Poetical Works *(1901), II.*

DOCTOR B.[1]

(On Re-reading a Collection of Poems)

Confound your croakers and drug concoctors!
    I've sent them packing at last, you see!
I'm in the hands of the best of doctors,
    Dear cheery and chirpy Doctor B.!

NIETZSCHE
1 Friedrich Wilhelm Nietzsche (1844–1900), anti-Christian philo-
sopher, notorious for advocating the 'will to power', and Übermens-
chlichkeit.

DOCTOR B.
1 Robert Browning, evidently.

None of your moping, methodistic,
    Long-faced ravens who frighten a man!
No, ever with treatment optimistic
    To *rouse* the sick, is the Doctor's plan!

In he comes to you, smiling brightly,
    Feels your pulse for the mere form's sake,   10
Bustles about the sick room lightly.
    Gives you no beastly drugs to take,

But blithely clapping you on the shoulder
    'Better?' he cries. 'Why, you're nearly well!'
And then you hear, with a heart grown bolder,
    The last good story he has to tell!

And, mind you, his learning is prodigious,
    He has Latin and Greek at his finger ends,
And with all his knowledge he's still religious,
    And counts no sceptic among his friends.   20

God's in His Heaven, and willy nilly
    All things come right in the end, he shows –
The rouge on the ladies of Piccadilly
    Is God's, as much as the blush of the rose!

And as for the wail of the whole world's sorrow,
    Well, men may weep, but the thrushes sing!
If you're sick to-day, there'll be jinks tomorrow,
    And life, on the whole, is a pleasant thing!

When out of spirits you're sadly lying,
    All dismal talk he puts bravely by: 30
'God's in His Heaven,' you hear him crying, –
    'All's right with Creation from star to sty!'

Full of world's wisdom and life's variety,
    Always alive and alert is he,
His patients move in the best society,
    And Duchesses swear by Doctor B.!

A bit too chirpy to some folks' thinking?
    Well, there *are* moods that he hardly suits! –
Once, last summer, when I felt sinking,
    I fear'd his voice and the creak of his boots!   40

If he *has* a fault which there's no denying,
    'Tis proneness to argue and prove his case, –
When under the shadow a man is lying,
    Such boisterous comfort seems out of place;

'Tis little solace, when one is going
    Into the long eternal Night,
To hear a voice, like a bugle blowing,
    Cry, 'Glory to God, for the world's all right!'

I long'd, I own, for a voice less cheery,
    A style less strident, a tone less free, –   50
For one who'd bend by my bedside dreary
    And hush his wisdom and weep with me!

> But bless your heart, when my health grew better,
>   I gladden'd the old boy's face to see;
> And still I consider myself the debtor
>   Of dear old chirpy Doctor B.!

Complete Poetical Works (1901), II.

THE FLESHLY SCHOOL OF POETRY: MR. D. G. ROSSETTI

Poems, by Dante Gabriel Rossetti, Fifth Edition. London: F. S. Ellis.

By 'Thomas Maitland'

If, on the occasion of any public performance of Shakespere's great tragedy, the actors who perform the parts of Rosencranz and Guildenstern were, by a preconcerted arrangement and by means of what is technically known as 'gagging,' to make themselves fully as prominent as the leading character, and to indulge in soliloquies and business strictly belonging to Hamlet himself, the result would be, to say the least of it, astonishing; yet a very similar effect is produced on the unprejudiced mind when the 'walking gentlemen' of the fleshly school of poetry, who bear precisely the same relation to Mr. Tennyson as Rosencranz and Guildenstern do to the Prince of Denmark in the play, obtrude their lesser identities and parade their smaller idiosyncrasies in the front rank of leading performers. In their own place, the gentlemen are interesting and useful. Pursuing still the theatrical analogy, the present drama of poetry might be cast as follows: Mr. Tennyson supporting the part of Hamlet, Mr. Matthew Arnold that of Horatio, Mr. Bailey that of Voltimand, Mr. Buchanan that of Cornelius, Messrs. Swinburne and Morris the parts of Rosencranz and Guildenstern, Mr. Rossetti that of Osric, and Mr. Robert Lytton that of 'A Gentleman.' It will be seen that we have left no place for Mr. Browning, who may be said, however, to play the leading character in his own peculiar fashion on alternate nights.

This may seem a frivolous and inadequate way of opening our remarks on a school of verse-writers which some people regard as possessing great merits; but in good truth, it is scarcely possible to discuss with any seriousness the pretensions with which foolish friends and small critics have surrounded the fleshly school, which, in spite of its spasmodic ramifications in the erotic direction, is merely one of the many sub-Tennysonian schools expanded to supernatural dimensions, and endeavouring by affectations all its own to overshadow its connection with the great original. In the sweep of one single poem, the weird and doubtful 'Vivien,' Mr. Tennyson has concentrated all the epicene force which, wearisomely expanded, constitutes the characteristic of the writers at present under consideration; and if in 'Vivien' he has indicated for them the bounds of sensualism in art, he has in 'Maud,' in the dramatic person of the hero, afforded distinct precedent for the hysteric tone and overloaded style which is now so familiar to readers of Mr. Swinburne. The fleshliness of 'Vivien' may indeed be described as the distinct quality held in common by all the members of the last sub-Tennysonian school, and it is a quality which becomes unwholesome when there is no moral or intellectual quality to temper and control it. Fully conscious of this themselves, the fleshly gentlemen have bound themselves by solemn league and covenant to extol fleshliness as the distinct and supreme end of poetic and pictorial art; to aver that poetic expression is greater than poetic thought, and by inference that the body is greater than the soul, and sound superior to sense; and that the poet, properly to develop his poetic faculty, must be an intellectual hermaphrodite, to whom the very facts of day and night are lost in a whirl of æsthetic terminology. After Mr. Tennyson has probed the depths of modern speculation in a series of commanding moods, all right and interesting in him as the reigning personage, the walking gentlemen, knowing that something of the sort is expected from all leading performers, bare their roseate bosoms and aver that *they* are creedless; the only possible question here being, if any disinterested person cares twopence whether Rosencranz, Guildenstern, and Osric are creedless or not – their self-revelation on that score being so perfectly gratuitous? But having gone so far, it was and is too late to retreat. Rosencranz, Guildenstern, and Osric, finding it impossible to risk an individual bid for the leading business, have arranged all to play leading business together, and mutually to praise, extol, and imitate each other; and although by these measures they have fairly earned for themselves the title of the Mutual Admiration School, they have in a great measure succeeded in their object – to the general stupefaction of a British audience. It is time, therefore, to ascertain whether any of these gentlemen has actually in himself the making of a leading performer. When the *Athenæum* – once more cautious in such matters – advertised nearly every week some interesting particular about Mr. Swinburne's health, Mr. Morris's holiday-making, or Mr. Rossetti's genealogy, varied with such startling statements as 'We are informed that Mr. Swinburne dashed off his noble ode *at a sitting*,' or 'Mr. Swinburne's songs have already reached a second edition,' or 'Good poetry seems to be in demand; the first edition of Mr. O'Shaughnessy's poems is exhausted;' when the *Academy* informed us that 'During the past year or two Mr. Swinburne has written several novels' (!), and that some review or other is to be praised for giving Mr. Rossetti's poems 'the attentive study which they demand' – when we read these things we might or might not know pretty well how and where they originated; but to a provincial eye, perhaps, the whole thing really looked like leading business. It would be scarcely worth while, however, to inquire into the pretensions of the writers on merely literary grounds, because sooner or later all literature finds its own level, whatever criticism may say or do in the matter; but it unfortunately happens in the present case that the fleshly school of verse-writers are, so to speak, public offenders, because they are diligently spreading the seeds of disease broadcast wherever they are read and understood. Their complaint too is catching, and carries off many young persons. What the complaint is, and how it works, may be seen on a very slight examination of the works of Mr. Dante Gabriel Rossetti, to whom we shall confine our attention in the present article.

Mr. Rossetti has been known for many years as a painter of exceptional powers, who, for reasons best known to himself, has shrunk from publicly exhibiting his pictures, and from allowing anything like a popular estimate to be formed of their qualities. He belongs, or is said to belong, to the so-called Pre-Raphaelite school, a school which is generally considered to exhibit much genius for colour, and great indifference to perspective. It would be unfair to judge the painter by the glimpses we have had of his works, or by the photographs which are sold of the principal paintings. Judged by the photographs, he is an artist who conceives unpleasantly, and draws ill. Like Mr. Simeon Solomon, however, with whom he seems to have many points in common, he is distinctively a colourist, and of his capabilities in colour we cannot speak, though we should guess that they are great; for if there is any good quality by which his poems are specially marked, it is a great sensitiveness to hues and tints as conveyed in poetic epithet. These qualities, which impress the casual spectator of the photographs from his pictures, are to be found abundantly among his verses. There is the same thinness and transparence of design, the same combination of the simple and the grotesque, the same morbid deviation from healthy forms of life, the same sense of weary, wasting, yet exquisite sensuality; nothing virile, nothing tender, nothing completely sane; a superfluity of extreme sensibility, of delight in beautiful forms, hues, and tints, and a deep-seated indifference to all agitating forces and agencies, all tumultuous griefs and sorrows, all the thunderous stress of life, and all the straining storm of speculation. Mr. Morris is often pure, fresh, and wholesome as his own great model; Mr. Swinburne startles us more than once by some fine flash of insight; but the mind of Mr. Rossetti is like a glassy mere, broken only by the dive of some water-bird or the hum of winged insects, and brooded over by an atmosphere of insufferable closeness, with a light blue sky above it, sultry depths mirrored within it, and a surface so thickly sown with water-lilies that it retains its glassy smoothness even in the strongest wind. Judged relatively to his poetic associates, Mr. Rossetti must be pronounced inferior to either. He cannot tell a pleasant story like Mr. Morris, nor forge alliterative thunderbolts like Mr. Swinburne. It must be conceded, nevertheless, that he is neither so glibly imitative as the one, nor so transcendently superficial as the other.

Although he has been known for many years as a poet as well as a painter – as a painter and poet idolized by his own family and personal associates – and although he has once or twice appeared in print as a contributor to magazines, Mr. Rossetti did not formally appeal to the public until rather more than a year ago, when he published a copious volume of poems, with the announcement that the book, although it contained pieces composed at intervals during a period of many years, 'included nothing which the author believes to be immature.' This work was inscribed to his brother, Mr. William Rossetti, who, having written much both in poetry and criticism, will perhaps be known to bibliographers as the editor of the worst edition of Shelley which has yet seen the light. No sooner had the work appeared than the chorus of eulogy began. 'The book is satisfactory from end to end,' wrote Mr. Morris in the *Academy*; 'I think these lyrics, with all their other merits, the most complete of their time; nor do I know what lyrics of any time are to be called *great*, if we are to deny the title to these.' On the same subject Mr. Swinburne went into a hysteria of admiration: 'golden affluence,' 'jewel-coloured words,' 'chastity of form,' 'harmonious nakedness,' 'consummate fleshly sculpture,' and so on in Mr. Swinburne's well-known manner when reviewing his friends. Other critics, with a singular similarity of phrase, followed suit. Strange to say, moreover, no one accused Mr. Rossetti of naughtiness. What had been heinous in Mr. Swinburne was majestic exquisiteness in Mr. Rossetti. Yet we question if there is anything in the unfortunate 'Poems and Ballads' quite so questionable on the score of thorough nastiness as many pieces in Mr. Rossetti's collection. Mr. Swinburne was wilder, more outrageous, more blasphemous, and his subjects were more atrocious in themselves; yet the hysterical tone slew the animalism, the furiousness of epithet lowered the sensation; and the first feeling of disgust at such themes as 'Laus Veneris' and 'Anactoria,' faded away into comic amazement. It was only a little mad boy letting off squibs; not a great strong man, who might be really dangerous to society. 'I *will* be naughty!' screamed the little boy; but, after all, what did it matter? It is quite different, however, when a grown man, with the self-control and easy audacity of actual experience, comes forward to chronicle his amorous sensations, and, first proclaiming in a loud voice his literary maturity, and consequent responsibility, shamelessly prints and publishes such a piece of writing as this sonnet on 'Nuptial Sleep': –

> *At length their long kiss severed, with sweet smart:*
> *And as the last slow sudden drops are shed*
> *From sparkling caves when all the storm has fled,*
> *So singly flagged the pulses of each heart.*
> *Their bosoms sundered, with the opening start*
> *Of married flowers to either side outspread*
> *From the knit stem; yet still their mouths, burnt red,*
> *Fawned on each other where they lay apart.*
>
> Sleep sank them lower than the tide of dreams,
> And their dreams watched them sink, and slid away.
> Slowly their souls swam up again, through gleams
> Of watered light and dull drowned waifs of day;
> Till from some wonder of new woods and streams
> He woke, and wondered more: for there she lay.

This, then, is 'the golden affluence of words, the firm outline, the justice and chastity of form.' Here is a full-grown man, presumably intelligent and cultivated, putting on record for other full-grown men to read, the most secret mysteries of sexual connection, and that with so sickening a desire to reproduce the sensual mood, so careful a choice of epithet to convey mere animal sensations, that we merely shudder at the shameless nakedness. We are no purists in such matters. We hold the sensual part of our nature to be as holy as the spiritual or intellectual part, and we believe that such things must find their equivalent in all; but it is neither poetic, nor manly, nor even human, to obtrude such things as the themes of whole poems. It is simply nasty. Nasty as it is, we are very mistaken if many readers do not think it nice. English society of one kind purchases the *Day's Doings*. English society of another kind goes into ecstasy over Mr. Solomon's pictures – pretty pieces of morality, such as 'Love dying by the breath of Lust.' There is not much to choose between the two objects of admiration, except that painters like Mr. Solomon lend actual genius to worthless subjects, and thereby produce veritable monsters – like the lovely devils that danced round Saint Anthony. Mr. Rossetti owes his so-called success to the same causes. In poems like 'Nuptial Sleep,' the man who is too sensitive to exhibit his pictures, and so modest that it takes him years to make up his mind to publish his poems, parades his private sensations before a coarse public, and is gratified by their applause.

It must not be supposed that all Mr. Rossetti's poems are made up of trash like this. Some of them are as noteworthy for delicacy of touch as others are for shamelessness of exposition. They contain some exquisite pictures of nature, occasional passages of real meaning, much beautiful phraseology, lines of peculiar sweetness, and epithets chosen with true literary cunning. But the fleshly feeling is everywhere. Sometimes, as in 'The Stream's Secret,' it is deliciously modulated, and adds greatly to our emotion of pleasure at perusing a finely-wrought poem; at other times, as in the 'Last Confession,' it is fiercely held in check by the exigencies of a powerful situation and the strength of a dramatic speaker; but it is generally in the foreground, flushing the whole poem with unhealthy rose-colour, stifling the senses with overpowering sickliness, as of too much civet. Mr. Rossetti is never dramatic, never impersonal – always attitudinizing, posturing, and describing his own exquisite emotions. He is the 'Blessed Damozel,' leaning over the 'gold bar of heaven,' and seeing

'Time like a pulse shake fierce
Thro' all the worlds;'

he is 'heaven-born Helen, Sparta's queen,' whose 'each twin breast is an apple sweet;' he is Lilith the first wife of Adam; he is the rosy Virgin of the poem called 'Ave,' and the Queen in the 'Staff and Scrip;' he is 'Sister Helen' melting her waxen man; he is all these, just as surely as he is Mr. Rossetti soliloquizing over Jenny in her London lodging, or the very nuptial person writing erotic sonnets to his wife. In petticoats or pantaloons, in modern times or in the middle ages, he is just Mr. Rossetti, a fleshly person, with nothing particular to tell us or teach us, with extreme self-control, a strong sense of colour, and a careful choice of diction. Amid all his 'affluence of jewel-coloured words,' he has not given us one rounded and noteworthy piece of art, though his verses are all art; not one poem which is memorable for its own sake, and quite separable from the dis-pleasing identity of the composer. The nearest approach to a perfect whole is the 'Blessed Damo-zel,' a peculiar poem, placed first in the book, perhaps by accident, perhaps because it is a key to the poems which follow. This poem appeared in a rough shape many years ago in the *Germ*, an unwholesome periodical started by the Pre-Raphaelites, and suffered, after gasping through a few feeble numbers, to die the death of all such publications. In spite of its affected title, and of numberless affectations throughout the text, the 'Blessed Damozel' has great merits of its own, and a few lines of real genius. We have heard it described as the record of actual grief and love, or, in simple words, the apotheosis of one actually lost by the writer; but, without having any private knowledge of the circumstance of its composition, we feel that such an account of the poem is inadmissible. It does not contain one single note of sorrow. It is a 'composition,' and a clever one. Read the opening stanzas: –

'The blessed damozel leaned out
    From the gold bar of Heaven;
Her eyes were deeper than the depth
    Of water stilled at even;
She had three lilies in her hand,
    And the stars in her hair were seven.

'Her robe, ungirt from clasp to hem,
    No wrought flowers did adorn,
But a white rose of Mary's gift,
    For service meetly worn;
Her hair that lay along her back
    Was yellow like ripe corn.'

This is a careful sketch for a picture, which, worked into actual colour by a master, might have been worth seeing. The steadiness of hand lessens as the poem proceeds, and although there are several passages of considerable power, – such as that where, far down the void,

> 'this earth
> Spins like a fretful midge,'

or that other, describing how

> 'the curled moon
> Was like a little feather
> Fluttering far down the gulf,' –

the general effect is that of a queer old painting in a missal, very affected and very odd. What moved the British critic to ecstasy in this poem seems to us very sad nonsense indeed, or, if not sad nonsense, very meretricious affectation. Thus, we have seen the following verses quoted with enthusiasm, as italicised –

> 'And still she bowed herself and stooped
>   Out of the circling charm;
> *Until her bosom must have made*
>   *The bar she leaned on warm,*
> And the lilies lay as if asleep
>   Along her bended arm.

> 'From the fixed place of Heaven she saw
>   *Time like a pulse shake fierce*
> *Thro' all the worlds.* Her gaze still strove
>   Within the gulf to pierce
> Its path; and now she spoke as when
>   The stars sang in their spheres.'

It seems to us that all these lines are very bad, with the exception of the two admirable lines ending the first verse, and that the italicised portions are quite without merit, and almost without meaning. On the whole, one feels disheartened and amazed at the poet who, in the nineteenth century, talks about 'damozels,' 'citherns,' and 'citoles,' and addresses the mother of Christ as the 'Lady Mary,' –

> 'With her five handmaidens, whose names
>   Are five sweet symphonies,
> Cecily, Gertrude, Magdalen,
>   Margaret and Rosalys.'

A suspicion is awakened that the writer is laughing at us. We hover uncertainly between picturesqueness and namby-pamby, and the effect, as Artemus Ward would express it, is 'weakening to the intellect.' The thing would have been almost too much in the shape of a picture, though the workmanship might have made amends. The truth is that literature, and more particularly poetry, is in a very bad way when one art gets hold of another, and imposes upon it its conditions and limitations. In the first few verses of the 'Damozel' we have the subject, or part of the subject, of a picture, and the inventor should either have painted it or left it alone altogether; and, had he done the latter, the world would have lost nothing. Poetry is something more than painting; and an idea will not become a poem because it is too smudgy for a picture.

   In a short notice from a well-known pen, giving the best estimate we have seen of Mr. Rossetti's powers as a poet, the *North American Review* offers a certain explanation for affectation such as that of Mr. Rossetti. The writer suggests that 'it may probably be the expression of genuine moods of mind in natures too little comprehensive.' We would rather believe that Mr. Rossetti lacks comprehension than that he is deficient in sincerity; yet really, to paraphrase the words which Johnson applied to Thomas Sheridan, Mr. Rossetti is affected, naturally affected, but it must have taken him a great deal of trouble to become what we now see him – such an excess of affectation is not in nature.[1] There is very little writing in the volume spontaneous in the sense that some of Swinburne's verses are spontaneous; the poems all look as if they had taken a great deal of trouble. The grotesque mediævalism of 'Stratton Water' and 'Sister Helen,' the mediæval classicism of 'Troy Town,' the false and shallow mysticism of 'Eden Bower,' are one and all essentially imitative, and must have cost the writer much pains. It is time, indeed, to point out that Mr. Rossetti is a poet possessing great powers of assimilation and some faculty for concealing the nutriment on which he feeds. Setting aside the 'Vita Nuova' and the early Italian poems, which are familiar to many readers by his own excellent translations, Mr. Rossetti may be described as a writer who has yielded to an unusual extent to the complex influences of the literature surrounding him at the present moment. He has the painter's imitative power developed in proportion to his lack of the poet's conceiving imagination. He reproduces to a nicety the manner of an old ballad, a trick in which Mr. Swinburne is also an adept. Cultivated readers, moreover, will recognise in every one of these poems the tone of Mr. Tennyson broken up by the style of Mr. and Mrs. Browning, and disguised here and there by the eccentricities of the Pre-Raphaelites. The 'Burden of Nineveh' is a philosophical edition of 'Recollections of the Arabian Nights;' 'A Last Confession' and 'Dante at Verona' are, in the minutest trick and form of thought, suggestive of Mr. Browning; and that the sonnets have been largely moulded and inspired by Mrs. Browning can be ascertained by any critic who will compare them with the 'Sonnets from the Portuguese.' Much remains, nevertheless, that is Mr. Rossetti's own. We at once recognise as his own property such passages as this: –

> 'I looked up
> And saw where a brown-shouldered harlot leaned
> Half through a tavern window thick with vine.
> Some man had come behind her in the room
> And caught her by her arms, and she had turned
> With that coarse empty laugh on him, as now
> He *munched her neck with kisses, while the vine*
> *Crawled in her back.*'

Or this: –

> 'As I stooped, her own lips rising there
> *Bubbled with brimming kisses at my mouth.*'

Or this: –

> 'Have seen your lifted silken skirt
> Advertise dainties through the dirt!'

Or this: –

> 'What more prize than love to impel thee,
> *Grip* and *lip* my limbs as I tell thee!'

Passages like these are the common stock of the walking gentlemen of the fleshly school. We cannot forbear expressing our wonder, by the way, at the kind of women whom it seems the unhappy lot of these gentlemen to encounter. We have lived as long in the world as they have, but never yet came across persons of the other sex who conduct themselves in the manner described. Females who bite, scratch, scream, bubble, munch, sweat, writhe, twist, wriggle, foam, and in a general way slaver over their lovers, must surely possess some extraordinary qualities to counteract their otherwise most offensive mode of conducting themselves. It appears, however, on examination, that

---

THE FLESHLY SCHOOL OF POETRY

1 'Why, sir, Sherry is dull, *naturally* dull; but it must have taken him a *great deal of trouble* to become what we now see him – such an excess of stupidity is not in nature.' – *Boswell's Life*. [Author's note]

their poet-lovers conduct themselves in a similar manner. They, too, bite, scratch, scream, bubble, munch, sweat, writhe, twist, wriggle, foam, and slaver, in a style frightful to hear of. Let us hope that it is only their fun, and that they don't mean half they say. At times, in reading such books as this, one cannot help wishing that things had remained for ever in the asexual state described in Mr. Darwin's great chapter on Palingenesis. We get very weary of this protracted hankering after a person of the other sex; it seems meat, drink, thought, sinew, religion for the fleshly school. There is no limit to the fleshliness, and Mr. Rossetti finds in it its own religious justification much in the same way as Holy Willie: —

> 'Maybe thou let'st this fleshly thorn
> Perplex thy servant night and morn,
>   'Cause he's so gifted.
> If so, thy hand must e'en be borne,
>   Until thou lift it.'

Whether he is writing of the holy Damozel, or of the Virgin herself, or of Lilith, or Helen, or of Dante, or of Jenny the street-walker, he is fleshly all over, from the roots of his hair to the tip of his toes; never a true lover merging his identity into that of the beloved one; never spiritual, never tender; always self-conscious and æsthetic. 'Nothing,' says a modern writer, 'in human life is so utterly remorseless – not love, not hate, not ambition, not vanity – as the artistic or æsthetic instinct morbidly developed to the suppression of conscience and feeling;' and at no time do we feel more fully impressed with this truth than after the perusal of 'Jenny,' in some respects the finest poem in the volume, and in all respects the poem best indicative of the true quality of the writer's humanity. It is a production which bears signs of having been suggested by Mr. Buchanan's quasi-lyrical poems, which it copies in the style of title, and particularly by 'Artist and Model;' but certainly Mr. Rossetti cannot be accused, as the Scottish writer has been accused, of maudlin sentiment and affected tenderness. The two first lines are perfect: —

> 'Lazy laughing languid Jenny,
> Fond of a kiss and fond of a guinea;'

And the poem is a soliloquy of the poet – who has been spending the evening in dancing at a casino – over his partner, whom he has accompanied home to the usual style of lodgings occupied by such ladies, and who has fallen asleep with her head upon his knee, while he wonders, in a wretched pun –

> 'Whose person or whose purse may be
> The lodestar of your reverie?'

The soliloquy is long, and in some parts beautiful, despite a very constant suspicion that we are listening to an emasculated Mr. Browning, whose whole tone and gesture, so to speak, is occasionally introduced with startling fidelity; and there are here and there glimpses of actual thought and insight, over and above the picturesque touches which belong to the writer's true profession, such as that where, at daybreak –

> 'lights creep in
> Past the gauze curtains half drawn-to,
> And *the lamp's doubled shade grows blue.*'

What we object to in this poem is not the subject, which any writer may be fairly left to choose for himself; nor anything particularly vicious in the poetic treatment of it; nor any bad blood bursting through in special passages. But the whole tone, without being more than usually coarse, seems heartless. There is not a drop of piteousness in Mr. Rossetti. He is just to the outcast, even generous; severe to the seducer; sad even at the spectacle of lust in dimity and fine ribbons. Notwithstanding all this, and a certain delicacy and refinement of treatment unusual with this poet, the poem repels and revolts us, and we like Mr. Rossetti least after its perusal. We are angry with the fleshly person at last. The 'Blessed Damozel' puzzled us, the 'Song of the Bower' amused us, the love-sonnet depressed and sickened us, but 'Jenny,' though distinguished by less special vicious-ness of thought and style than any of these, fairly makes us lose patience. We detect its fleshliness at a glance; we perceive that the scene was fascinating less through its human tenderness than because it, like all the others, possessed an inherent quality of animalism. 'The whole work' ('Jenny,') writes Mr. Swinburne, 'is worthy to fill its place for ever as one of the most perfect poems of an age or generation. There is just the same life-blood and breadth of poetic interest in this episode of a London street and lodging as in the song of "Troy Town" and the song of "Eden Bower;" just as much, and no jot more,' – to which last statement we cordially assent; for there is bad blood in all, and breadth of poetic interest in none. 'Vengeance of Jenny's case,' indeed! – when such a poet as this comes fawning over her, with tender compassion in one eye and æsthetic enjoyment in the other!

It is time that we permitted Mr. Rossetti to speak for himself, which we will do by quoting a fairly representative poem entire: –

LOVE-LILY

'Between the hands, between the brows,
    Between the lips of Love-Lily,
A spirit is born whose birth endows
    My blood with fire to burn through me;
Who breathes upon my gazing eyes,
    Who laughs and murmurs in mine ear,
At whose least touch my colour flies,
    And whom my life grows faint to hear.

'Within the voice, within the heart,
    Within the mind of Love-Lily,
A spirit is born who lifts apart
    His tremulous wings and looks at me;
Who on my mouth his finger lays,
    And shows, while whispering lutes confer,
That Eden of Love's watered ways
    Whose winds and spirits worship her.

'Brows, hands, and lips, heart, mind, and voice,
    Kisses and words of Love-Lily, –
Oh! bid me with your joy rejoice
    Till *riotous longing rest in me!*
Ah! let not hope be still distraught,
    But find in her its gracious goal,
Whose speech Truth knows not from her thought,
    Nor Love her body from her soul.'

With the exception of the usual 'riotous longing,' which seems to make Mr. Rossetti a burthen to himself, there is nothing to find fault with in the extreme fleshliness of these verses, and to many people who live in the country they may even appear beautiful. Without pausing to criticise a thing so trifling – as well might we dissect a cobweb or anatomize a medusa – let us ask the reader's attention to a peculiarity to which all the students of the fleshly school must sooner or later give their attention – we mean the habit of accenting the last syllable in words which in ordinary speech are accented on the penultimate: –

'Between the hands, between the brows,
    Between the lips of Love-Lil*ee!*'

which may be said to give to the speaker's voice a sort of cooing tenderness just bordering on a loving whistle. Still better as an illustration are the lines: —

> 'Saturday night is market night
> Everywhere, be it dry or wet,
> And market night in the Haymar-*ket!*'

which the reader may advantageously compare with Mr. Morris's

> 'Then said the king
> Thanked be thou; *neither for nothing*
> Shalt thou this good deed do to me;'

or Mr. Swinburne's

> 'In either of the twain
> Red roses full of rain;
> She hath for bondwo*men*
> All kinds of flowers.'

It is unnecessary to multiply examples of an affectation which disfigures all these writers – Guilden-stern, Rosencranz, and Osric; who, in the same spirit which prompts the ambitious nobodies that rent London theatres in the 'empty' season to make up for their dullness by fearfully original 'new readings,' distinguish their attempt at leading business by affecting the construction of their grand-fathers and great-grandfathers, and the accentuation of the poets of the court of James I. It is in all respects a sign of remarkable genius, from this point of view, to rhyme 'was' with 'grass,' 'death' with 'lièth,' 'love' with 'of,' 'once' with 'suns,' and so on *ad nauseam*. We are far from disputing the value of bad rhymes used occasionally to break up the monotony of verse, but the case is hard when such blunders become the rule and not the exception, when writers deliberately lay them-selves out to be as archaic and affected as possible. Poetry is perfect human speech, and these archaisms are the mere fiddlededeeing of empty heads and hollow hearts. Bad as they are, they are the true indication of falser tricks and affectations which lie far deeper. They are trifles, light as air, showing how the wind blows. The soul's speech and the heart's speech are clear, simple, natural, and beautiful, and reject the meretricious tricks to which we have drawn attention.

It is on the score that these tricks and affectations have procured the professors a number of imitators, that the fleshly school deliver their formula that great poets are always to be known because their manner is immediately reproduced by small poets, and that a poet who finds few imitators is probably of inferior rank – by which they mean to infer that they themselves are very great poets indeed. It is quite true that they are imitated. On the stage, twenty provincial 'stars' copy Charles Kean, while not one copies his father; there are dozens of actors who repro-duce Mr. Charles Dillon, and not one who attempts to reproduce Macready. When we take up the poems of Mr. O'Shaughnessy,[2] we are face to face with a second-hand Mr. Swinburne; when we read Mr. Payne's queer allegories,[3] we remember Mr. Morris's early stage; and every poem of Mr. Marston's[4] reminds us of Mr. Rossetti. But what is really most droll and puzzling in the matter is, that these imitators seem to have no difficulty whatever in writing nearly, if not quite, as well as their masters. It is not bad imitations they offer us, but poems which read just like the originals; the fact being that it is easy to reproduce sound when it has no strict connection with sense, and simple enough to cull phraseology not hopelessly interwoven with thought and spirit. The fact that these gentlemen are so easily imitated is the most damning proof of their inferiority.

2 'An Epic of Women.' By Arthur W. E. O'Shaughnessy. (Hotten.) [Author's note]

3 'The Masque of Shadows.' By John Payne. (Pickering.) [Author's note]

4 'Songtide, and other Poems.' By Philip Bourke Marston. (Ellis.) [Author's note]

What merits they have lie with their faults on the surface, and can be caught by any young gentleman as easily as the measles, only they are rather more difficult to get rid of. All young gentlemen have animal faculties, though few have brains; and if animal faculties without brains will make poems, nothing is easier in the world. A great and good poet, however, is great and good irrespective of manner, and often in spite of manner; he is great because he brings great ideas and new light, because his thought is a revelation; and, although it is true that a great manner generally accompanies great matter, the manner of great matter is almost inimitable. The great poet is not Cowley, imitated and idolized and reproduced by every scribbler of his time; nor Pope, whose trick of style was so easily copied that to this day we cannot trace his own hand with any certainty in the *Iliad*; nor Donne, nor Sylvester, nor the Della Cruscans. Shakspere's blank verse is the most difficult and Jonson's most easy to imitate, of all the Elizabethan stock; and Shakspere's verse is the best verse, because it combines the great qualities of all contemporary verse, with no individual affectations; and so perfectly does this verse, with all its splendour, intersect with the style of contemporaries *at their best*, that we would undertake to select passage after passage which would puzzle a good judge to tell which of the Elizabethans was the author – Marlowe, Beaumont, Dekkar, Marston, Webster, or Shakspere himself. The great poet is Dante, full of the thunder of a great Idea; and Milton, unapproachable in the serene white light of thought and sumptuous wealth of style; and Shakspere, all poets by turns, and all men in succession; and Goethe, always innovating, and ever indifferent to innovation for its own sake; and Wordsworth, clear as crystal and deep as the sea; and Tennyson, with his vivid range, far-piercing sight, and perfect speech; and Browning, great, not by virtue of his eccentricities, but because of his close intellectual grasp. Tell 'Paradise Lost,' the 'Divine Comedy,' in naked prose; do the same by *Hamlet, Macbeth*, and *Lear*; read Mr. Hayward's translation of 'Faust;' take up the 'Excursion,' a great poem, though its speech is nearly prose already; turn the 'Guinevere' into a mere story; reproduce Pompilia's last dying speech without a line of rhythm. Reduced to bald English, all these poems, and all great poems, lose much; but how much do they not retain? They are poems to the very roots and depths of being, poems born and delivered from the soul, and treat them as cruelly as you may, poems they will remain. So it is with all good and thorough creations, however low in their rank; so it is with the 'Ballad in a Wedding' and 'Clever Tom Clinch,' just as much as with the 'Epistle of Karsheesh,' or Goethe's torso of 'Prometheus;' with Shelley's 'Skylark,' or Alfred de Musset's 'A la Lune,' as well as Racine's 'Athalie,' Victor Hugo's 'Parricide,' or Hood's 'Last Man.' A poem is a poem, first as to the soul, next as to the form. The fleshly persons who wish to create form for its own sake are merely pronouncing their own doom. But *such* form! If the Pre-Raphaelite fervour gains ground, we shall soon have popular songs like this: –

> 'When winds do roar, and rains do pour,
> Hard is the life of the sail*or*;
> He scarcely as he reels can tell
> The side-lights from the binna*cle*;
> He looketh on the wild wa*ter*,' &c.,

and so on, till the English speech seems the speech of raving madmen. Of a piece with other affectations is the device of a burthen, of which the fleshly persons are very fond for its own sake, quite apart from its relevancy. Thus Mr. Rossetti sings: –

> 'Why did you melt your waxen man,
> Sister Helen?
> To-day is the third since you began.
> The time was long, yet the time ran,
> Little brother.
> (*O mother, Mary mother,*
> *Three days to-day between Heaven and Hell.*)'

This burthen is repeated, with little or no alteration, through thirty-four verses, and might with as much music, and far more point, run as follows: –

'Why did you melt your waxen man,
Sister Helen?
To-day is the third since you began.
The time was long, yet the time ran,
Little brother.
(*O Mr. Dante Rossetti,
What stuff is this about Heaven and Hell?*)'

About as much to the point is a burthen of Mr. Swinburne's, something to the following effect: –

'We were three maidens in the green corn,
Hey chickaleerie, the red cock and gray,
Fairer maidens were never born,
One o'clock, two o'clock, off and away.'

We are not quite certain of the words, as we quote from memory, but we are sure our version fairly represents the original, and is quite as expressive. Productions of this sort are 'silly sooth' in good earnest, though they delight some newspaper critics of the day, and are copied by young gentlemen with animal faculties morbidly developed by too much tobacco and too little exercise. Such indulgence, however, would ruin the strongest poetical constitution; and it unfortunately happens that neither masters nor pupils were naturally very healthy. In such a poem as 'Eden Bower' there is not one scrap of imagination, properly so-called. It is a clever grotesque in the worst manner of Callot, unredeemed by a gleam of true poetry or humour. No good poet would have wrought into a poem the absurd tradition about Lilith; Goethe was content to glance at it merely, with a grim smile, in the great scene in the Brocken. We may remark here that poems of this unnatural and morbid kind are only tolerable when they embody a profound meaning, as do Coleridge's 'Ancient Mariner' and 'Cristabel.' Not that we would insult the memory of Coleridge by comparing his exquisitely conscientious work with this affected rubbish about 'Eden Bower' and 'Sister Helen,' though his influence in their composition is unmistakable. Still more unmistakable is the influence of that most unwholesome poet, Beddoes, who, with all his great powers, treated his subjects in a thoroughly insincere manner, and is now justly forgotten.

The great strong current of English poetry rolls on, ever mirroring in its bosom new prospects of fair and wholesome thought. Morbid deviations are endless and inevitable; there must be marsh and stagnant mere as well as mountain and wood. Glancing backward into the shady places of the obscure, we see the once prosperous nonsense-writers each now consigned to his own little limbo – Skelton and Gower still playing fantastic tricks with the mother-tongue; Gascoigne outlasting the applause of all, and living to see his own works buried before him; Silvester doomed to oblivion by his own fame as a translator; Carew the idol of courts, and Donne the beloved of schoolmen, both buried in the same oblivion; the fantastic Fletchers winning the wonder of collegians, and fading out through sheer poetic impotence; Cowley shaking all England with his pindarics, and perishing with them; Waller, the famous, saved from oblivion by the natural note of one single song – and so on, through league after league of a flat and desolate country which once was prosperous, till we come again to these fantastic figures of the fleshly school, with their droll mediæval garments, their funny archaic speech, and the fatal marks of literary consumption in every pale and delicate visage. Our judgment on Mr. Rossetti, to whom we in the meantime confine our judgment, is substantially that of the *North American Reviewer*, who believes that 'we have in him another poetical man, and a man markedly poetical, and of a kind apparently, though not radically, different from any of our secondary writers of poetry, but that we have not in him a new poet of any weight;' and that he is 'so affected, sentimental, and painfully self-conscious, that the best to be done in his case is to hope that this book of his, having unpacked his bosom of so much that is unhealthy, may have done him more good than it has given others pleasure.' Such, we say, is our opinion, which might very well be wrong, and have to undergo modification, if Mr. Rossetti was younger and less self-possessed. His 'maturity' is fatal.

George Augustus Simcox (1841–1905)

George Augustus Simcox, Classicist and poet, was born in London. He was elected a Scholar of Corpus Christi College, Oxford, 26 March 1858 (his home address was then Newgate Street, London). At Oxford he had a formidable reputation for Classical brilliance. He won the Ireland Scholarship (1861), the Craven Scholarship (1862), and the Latin Essay Prize (1864), and became a Fellow of The Queen's College in 1865. He had, though, failed to get elected a Fellow of Balliol – a College put off, it might be supposed, by already pronounced eccentricities and idiocy in the practicalities of life (they became worse: he grew notoriously scruffy and loony, once gave a tutorial in his night-shirt, was prone to laugh maniacally in church, failed to keep appointments). J. A. Symonds held it against his friends for using Simcox's brilliance as a reason for his not applying for the Balliol Fellowship – and going to the less tolerant Magdalen instead, where malicious allegations about his homosexuality broke up his academic career. Simcox wrote for periodicals such as the *North British Review* and *Nineteenth Century*, did the standard and not-so-standard editing tasks (Demosthenes, 1872; the *Book of Revelation*, 1893; Juvenal, 1867), subscribing to the standard attitudes (he omitted the more notorious 2nd, 6th and 9th Satires of Juvenal from his edition, agreeing with their absence from the Oxford syllabus – which proceeded 'on the creditable hypothesis, that all candidates for a pass or honours either possess or cultivate the temper to which such reading is as painful as it ought to be'). Simcox was a loyal Anglican in a time of great defection to Rome (*A Letter to George Augustus Simcox, Esq., MA, From A Friend Who Has Lately been Received into the Catholic Church* was published in 1866). Simcox's verse tragedy *Prometheus Unbound* appeared in 1867 ('it may be a legitimate ambition', says the Preface, 'to continue the poetry of a period which it is impossible to reproduce'), *Poems and Romances* in 1869, and his big *History of Latin Literature from Ennius to Boethius* in two volumes in 1883. Simcox disappeared whilst on holiday at Ballycastle in Northern Ireland. It was thought he fell off the cliffs into the sea – an ironic fate for such a keen traipser across Europe and author of the Ruskinian *Recollections of a Rambler* (1874).

LOVE'S VOTARY

Others have pleasantness and praise,
    And wealth; and hand and glove
They walk with worship all their days,
    But I have only Love.

And therefore if Love be a fire,
    Then he shall burn me up;
If Love be water out of mire,
    Then I will be the cup.

If Love come worn with wayfaring,
    My breast shall be his bed;   10
If he come faint and hungering,
    My heart shall be his bread.

If Love delight in vassalage,
    Then I will be his thrall,
Till, when I end my pilgrimage,
    Love give me all for all.

Poems and Romances (Strahan & Co., 1869).

FALLING LEAVES

On a bare hill a thin elm's spindle crest
    Was glorified by kisses of the sky,
    Where harvest sunshine made the shrill wind die
Till evening, and the waning year had rest.

Only about a blackened empty nest
  Some lonely rooks kept an unrestful cry;
  Below the babbling brook of reeds was dry
In the green valley trending to the west,
  Green still; on either side the lands were ploughed,
Whence carrying scanty sheaves of ill-saved grain   10
On creaking wheels went by a broken wain,
  Whereon three harvest men who whistled loud;
  But in the shadow of a rising cloud
Two scarlet leaves fell in a pool of rain.

Poems and Romances (1869).

William John Courthope (also 'Novus Homo') (1842–1917)

William John Courthope, civil servant, literary scholar and poet, was born, 17 July 1842, elder son of the rector of South Malling, near Lewes, Sussex. His mother was a sister of John Charles Ryle, the crusading Evangelical, who became first Bishop of Liverpool. The Courthope children were brought up by their uncle after their father died in 1849. William John went to Harrow School and then to Oxford, where he was a Commoner of Corpus Christi College (1861) before becoming an Exhibitioner of New College (1862). Through another Old Harrovian, John Addington Symonds, he became a close friend of John Conington, first Corpus Christi Professor of Latin (who died 23 October 1869). He was a successful undergraduate Classicist, gaining First Classes in Moderations and Greats (Finals), and winning the Newdigate Prize (1864) and the Chancellor's English Essay Prize (1868: 'The Genius of Spenser'). He became a lawyer and civil servant, first of all in the Education Office (1869). He ended up as Senior Civil Service Commissioner. In 1870 – after Conington's death – he married Mary Scott, daughter of the Inspector of Hospitals in Bombay, and they had four sons and two daughters. From 1895 to 1900 Courthope was the elected Professor of Poetry at Oxford – doubtless on the strength of his volumes of light and frequently sub-Classical verses, *Poems* by Novus Homo (1865), *Ludibria Lunae* (1869: satirical about women's rights), *Paradise of Birds* (1870 – Aristophanes for the young), 'The Country Town' (1886, in the *National Review*: bucolics about his native Lewes), but especially for his editing of the last five volumes of the one-time standard ten-volume edition of Alexander Pope (1881–99). There was also his 1884 *Life of Addison* in the English Men of Letters series. Courthope produced a massive six-volume history of English poetry (1895–1910), and published his Oxford lectures as *Life in Poetry, Law in Taste* (1901). 'The Hop Garden' (*Blackwood's*, 1905) is a Virgilian celebration of the hops industry. He did a volume of imitations and translations of Martial's *Epigrams* (1914). He retired from the Civil Service in 1905 to live in Whiligh, Sussex, where he died, 10 April 1917. *The Country Town and Other Poems* appeared posthumously in 1920, with a Memoir by A. O. Prickard.

TOBACCO

Horace, you were born too soon![1]
Half the things beneath the moon,
That make living light to men,
Known are now and known were then.
Dewy eyes and waving hair,
All the sweets of dark and fair,
Garden shades, Falernian wine,[2]

TOBACCO
1 i.e., if the Roman poet Horace had lived in the age of tobacco he'd have written an Ode in its praise, as he praised so many other amenities, such as wine...

2 wine of Falernia, Italy.

Talk and friendship, nights divine,
These and many more were thine.
But our Raleigh was not born,[3]   10
Who bade sorrow cease to mourn,
Softened joy, tempestuous rage,
Mellowed youth and brightened age:
Taught us talk was made for two,
Not to turn, as boys will do
And at times the elders too,
Flowing, cheerful dialogue
Into fearful monologue.
Moan, ye wits! ye smokers, moan!
Had Tobacco but been known,   20
When the centuries were young,
When our Horace lived and sung;
Straight his stile he would have took,
Added to his odes a book;
How Prometheus but began
Half the kindly task for man;
Raleigh gave us life indeed,
Heavenly fuel in the weed,
For the fire that filled the reed.
How Augustus thronèd high   30
Round the tables in the sky,
When the goddesses are gone,
And the couches closely drawn,
Not alone his nectar sips,
But between his purple lips
Hangs his hookah, pleased and proud
Jove-like to compel a cloud.

Poems, *by Novus Homo (Wheeler & Day, Oxford, 1865).*

Edward Dowden (1843–1913)

Edward Dowden, cautious poet but prolific Shakespearian scholar and literary critic, was born into an Irish Protestant Ascendancy family in Cork, 3 May 1843, fourth son of John Wheeler Dowden, merchant and landowner, and Alicia Bennett. His elder brother John became Bishop of Edinburgh in 1886. Edward was a great success at Trinity College, Dublin (graduating 1863). In 1867, aged only twenty-four, he became the first Professor of English Literature at Trinity, a post he held until his death. His books on English literature multiplied profusely – editions of Shakespeare plays, biographies, critical essays and studies on now canonical authors such as Wordsworth, George Eliot, Robert Browning, Walt Whitman. His biggest book was his *Life of Shelley* (1886). But it was his first book, *Shakespeare, His Mind and Art* (1875), which became his best-known and most influential. His strongly moraliz-

ing and deeply biographical criticism helped found the professional study of English literature as a serious business. His study of Browning's *Sordello* (reprinted in his volume *Transcripts and Studies*) won him the poet's friendship. His pioneering enthusiasm for Whitman led to a deep and lasting friendship. Dowden resisted Irish Home Rule energetically, was at the centre of a lively intellectual coterie in Dublin, and married twice. His first wife, Mary Clarke (1869), bore him one son and two daughters. She died in 1892. In 1895 he married Elizabeth Dickinson, a widow, daughter of a Dean of St Patrick's Cathedral, and an old friend. Dowden never produced very much of his sweet but oddly steely verse, and his main poetic work remains only the *Poems* (1876). The thin volume *A Woman's Reliquary*, for his second wife, came out in 1913, the year when, on April 4, he died in Dublin.

3   Sir Walter Raleigh (1552–1618) introduced tobacco into England.

IN THE GARDEN

VI: A Peach

If any sense in mortal dust remains
When mine has been refined from flower to flower
Won from the sun all colours, drunk the shower
And delicate winy dews, and gained the gains
Which elves who sleep in airy bells, a-swing
Through half a summer day, for love bestow,
Then in some warm old garden let me grow
To such a perfect, lush, ambrosian thing
As this. Upon a southward-facing wall
I bask, and feel my juices dimly fed   10
And mellowing, while my bloom comes golden-grey:
Keep the wasps from me! but before I fall
Pluck me, white fingers, and o'er two ripe-red
Girl lips, O let me richly swoon away!

Poems *(Henry King, 1876)*.

IN THE GARDEN

VIII: Later Autumn

This is the year's despair: some wind last night
Utter'd too soon the irrevocable word,
And the leaves heard it, and the low clouds heard;
So a wan morning dawned of sterile light;
Flowers drooped, or showed a startled face and white;
The cattle cowered, and one disconsolate bird
Chirped a weak note; last came this mist and blurred
The hills, and fed upon the fields like blight.
Ah, why so swift despair! There yet will be
Warm noons, the honey'd leavings of the year,   10
Hours of rich musing, ripest autumn's core,
And late-heaped fruit, and falling hedge-berry,
Blossoms in cottage crofts, and yet, once more,
A song, not less than June's, fervent and clear.

Poems *(1876)*.

BURDENS

Are sorrows hard to bear, – the ruin
    Of flowers, the rotting of red fruit,
A love's decease, a life's undoing,
    And summer slain, and song-birds mute,
And skies of snow and bitter air?
These things, you deem, are hard to bear.

But ah the burden, the delight
    Of dreadful joys! Noon opening wide,
Golden and great; the gulfs of night,
    Fair deaths, and rent veils cast aside,   10

Strong soul to strong soul rendered up,
And silence filling like a cup.

Poems (1876).

The Inner Life

III: Seeking God

I said 'I will find God,' and forth I went
To seek Him in the clearness of the sky,
But over me stood unendurably
Only a pitiless, sapphire firmament
Ringing the world, – blank splendour; yet intent
Still to find God, 'I will go seek,' said I,
'His way upon the waters,' and drew nigh
An ocean marge weed-strewn, and foam-besprent;
And the waves dashed on idle sand and stone,
And very vacant was the long, blue sea;   10
But in the evening as I sat alone,
My window open to the vanishing day,
Dear God! I could not choose but kneel and pray,
And it sufficed that I was found of Thee.

Poems (1876).

From April to October

VIII: In July

Why do I make no poems? Good my friend
Now is there silence through the summer woods,
In whose green depths and lawny solitudes
The light is dreaming; voicings clear ascend
Now from no hollow where glad rivulets wend,
But murmurings low of inarticulate moods,
Softer than stir of unfledged cushat broods
Breathe, till o'erdrowsed the heavy flower-heads bend.
Now sleep the crystal and heart-charmèd waves
Round white, sunstricken rocks the noontide long,   10
Or 'mid the coolness of dim-lighted caves
Sway in a trance of vague deliciousness;
And I, – I am too deep in joy's excess
For the imperfect impulse of a song.

Poems (1876).

David and Michal

(2 Samuel vi.16.)[1]

But then you don't mean really what you say –
To hear this from the sweetest little lips,

DAVID AND MICHAL
1   Michal, Saul's daughter, despises King David for dancing before
Ark of Covenant.

O'er which each pretty word daintily trips
Like small birds hopping down a garden way,
When I had given my soul full scope to play
For once before her in the Orphic² style
Caught from three several volumes of Carlyle,
And undivulged before this very day!
O young men of our earnest school confess
How it is deeply, darkly tragical   10
To find the feminine souls we would adore
So full of sense, so versed in worldly lore,
So deaf to the Eternal Silences,
So unbelieving, so conventional.

Poems *(1876)*.

Margaret Veley (1843–87)

An Essex poet and story-teller, Margaret Veley was born, the second of four children, 12 May 1843, in Braintree, where she spent most of her life. Her mother, Sophia Ludbey, was daughter of a vicar; her father, Augustus Charles Veley, a solicitor who specialized in ecclesiastical work. Margaret remained the characteristically dutiful daughter, staying at home, nursing her two infirm sisters and her father. After he died in 1879, she moved with her mother to London. She was chronically shy, but still dissented modestly from the family's High Church proclivities. She started having things published from her late twenties on. Her first published poem, 'Michaelmas Daisies', appeared in the *Spectator*, April 1870; her first published story, 'Milly's First Love', in *Blackwood's* in September of the same year. She contributed widely to the journals but was in particular taken up by Leslie Stephen, editor of the *Cornhill*, which regularly published her stories and poems. 'A Japanese Fan' appeared there in September 1876. Her novel *For Percival* (1878) started out as a *Cornhill* story. Leslie Stephen edited her posthumous collection of poems *A Marriage of Shadows* (1888) and provided a Biographical Notice for it. Her poems may be quietly acquiescent in their spiritual and erotic struggles, but they tend to shrewdness and are never vague or over-weary in their troubledness. Margaret Veley died, 7 December 1887, of some sort of infection brought on by a chill. She was forty-four years old.

A JAPANESE FAN

How time flies! Have we been talking
    For an hour?
Have we been so long imprisoned
    By the shower
In this old oak-panelled parlour?
    Is it noon?
Don't you think the rain is over
    Rather soon?

Since the heavy drops surprised us,
    And we fled   10
Here for shelter, while it darkened
    Overhead;
Since we leaned against the window,
    Saw the flash
Of the lightning, heard the rolling
    Thunder crash;

You have looked at all the treasures
    Gathered here,
Out of other days and countries
    Far and near;   20
At those glasses, thin as bubbles,
    Opal bright –
At the carved and slender chessmen
    Red and white –
At the long array of china
    Cups and plates –
(Do you really understand them?
    Names and dates?)
At the tapestry, where dingy
    Shepherds stand,   30
Holding grim and faded damsels
    By the hand,
All the while my thoughts were busy

2 oracular: after mysteries associated with Orpheus.

With the fan
Lying here – bamboo and paper
   From Japan.
It is nothing – very common –
   Be it so;
Do you wonder why I prize it?
   Care to know?   40
Shall I teach you all the meaning,
   The romance
Of the picture you are scorning
   With a glance?
From Japan! I let my fancy
   Swiftly fly;
Now if we set sail to-morrow,
   You and I,
If the waves were liquid silver,
   Fair the breeze,   50
If we reached that wondrous island
   O'er the seas,
Should we find that every woman
   Was so white,
And had slender upward eyebrows
   Black as night?
Should we then perhaps discover
   Why, out there,
People spread a mat to rest on
   In mid air?   60

Here's a lady, small of feature,
   Narrow-eyed,
With her hair of ebon straightness
   Queerly tied;
In her hand are trailing flowers
   Rosy sweet,
And her silken robe is muffled
   Round her feet.
She looks backward with a conscious
   Kind of grace,   70
As she steps from off the carpet
   Into space;
Though she plants her foot on nothing
   Does not fall,
And in fact appears to heed it
   Not at all.
See how calmly she confronts us
   Standing there –
Will you say she is not lovely?
   Do you dare?   80
I will not! I honour beauty
   Where I can,
Here's a woman one might die for!
   – In Japan.

Read the passion of her lover –
   All his soul
Hotly poured in this fantastic
   Little scroll.
See him swear his love, and vengeance

Read his fate –   90
You don't understand the language?
   I'll translate.

'Long ago,' he says, 'when summer
   Filled the earth
With its beauty, with the brightness
   Of its mirth;
When the leafy boughs were woven
   Far above;
In the noonday I beheld her,
   Her – my love!   100
Oftentimes I met her, often
   Saw her pass,
With her dusky raiment trailing
   On the grass.
I would follow, would approach her,
   Dare to speak,
Till at last the sudden colour
   Flushed her cheek.
Through the sultry heat we lingered
   In the shade;   110
And the fan of pictured paper
   That she swayed
Seemed to mark the summer's pulses,
   Soft and slow,
And to thrill me as it wavered
   To and fro.
For I loved her, loved her, loved her,
   And its beat
Set my passion to a music
   Strangely sweet.   120

Sunset came, and after sunset
   When the dusk
Filled the quiet house with shadows;
   And the musk
From the dim and dewy garden
   Where it grows,
Mixed its perfume with the jasmine
   And the rose;
When the western splendour faded,
   And the breeze   130
Went its way, with good-night whispers
   Through the trees,
Leaning out we watched the dying
   Of the light,
Till the bats came forth with sudden
   Ghostly flight.
They were shadows, wheeling, flitting
   Round my joy,
While she spoke and while her slender
   Hands would toy   140
With her fan, which as she swayed it
   Might have been
Fairy wand, or fitting sceptre
   For a queen.
When she smiled at me, half pausing

In her play,
All the gloom of gathering twilight
    Turned to day!

Though to talk too much of heaven
    Is not well –   150
Though agreeable people never
    Mention hell –
Yet the woman who betrayed me –
    Whom I kissed –
In that bygone summer taught me
    Both exist.
I was ardent, she was always
    Wisely cool,
So my lady played the traitor,
    I – the fool' –   160
Oh, your pardon! But remember,
    If you please,
I'm translating – this is only
    Japanese.

'Japanese?' you say, and eye me
    Half in doubt;
Let us have the lurking question
    Spoken out.
Is all this about the lady
    Really said   170
In that little square of writing
    Near her head?
I will answer, on my honour,
    As I can,
Every syllable is written
    On the fan.
Yes, and you could learn the language
    Very soon –
Shall I teach you on some August
    Afternoon?   180

You are wearied. There is little
    Left to say;
For the disappointed hero
    Goes his way,
And such pain and rapture never
    More will know.
But he smiles – all this was over
    Long ago.
I am not a blighted being –
    Scarcely grieve –   190
I can laugh, make love, do most things
    But believe!

Yet the old days come back strangely
    As I stand
With the fan she swayed so softly
    In my hand.
I can almost see her, touch her,
    Hear her voice,
Till, afraid of my own madness,
    I rejoice   200
That beyond my help or harming
    Is her fate –
Past the reach of passion – is it
    Love – or hate?

This is tragic! Are you laughing?
    So am I!
Let us go – the clouds have vanished
    From the sky.
Yes, and you'll forget this folly?
    Time is ceased,   210
For you do not understand me
    In the least.
You have smiled and sighed politely
    Quite at ease, –
And my story might as well be
    Japanese!

Cornhill, 34 (1876), 379–84. A Marriage of Shadows and Other Poems
(Smith, Elder & Co., 1888).

A Town Garden

A plot of ground – the merest scrap –
    Deep, like a dry, forgotten well,
A garden caught in a brick-built trap,
    Where men make money, buy and sell;
And struggling through the stagnant haze,
    Dim flowers, with sapless leaf and stem,
Look up with something of the gaze
    That homesick eyes have cast on them.

There is a rose against the wall,
    With scanty, smoke-incrusted leaves;   10
Fair showers on happier roses fall –
    On this, foul droppings from the eaves.

It pines, but you need hardly note;
    It dies by inches in the gloom;
Shoots in the spring-time, as if by rote;
    Long has forgotten to dream of bloom.

The poorest blossom, and it were classed
    With colour and name – but never a flower!
It blooms with the roses whose bloom is past,
    Of every hue, and place, and hour.   20
They live before me as I look –
    The damask buds that breathe and glow,
Pink wild roses, down by a brook,
    Lavish clusters of airy snow.

Could one transplant you – (far on high
   A murky sunset lights the tiles) –
And set you 'neath the arching sky,
   In the green country, many miles,
Would you strike deep and suck up strength,
   Washed with rain and hung with pearls,   30
Cling to the trellis, a leafy length,
   Sweet with blossom for June and girls?

Yet no! Who needs you in those bowers?
   Who prizes gifts that all can give?
Bestow your life instead of flowers,
   And slowly die that dreams may live.
Prisoned and perishing, your dole
   Of lingering leaves shall not be vain –
Worthy to wreathe the hemlock bowl,
   Or twine about the cross of pain!   40

Harper's *(August 1883)*. A Marriage of Shadows *(1888)*.

SONNET

'Have not all songs been sung – all loves been told?
What shall I say when nought is left unsaid?
The world is full of memories of the dead –
Echoes and relics. Here's no virgin gold,
But all assayed, none left for me to mould
Into new coin, and at your feet to shed;
Each piece is mint-marked with some poet's head,
Tested and rung in tributes manifold.

'Oh for a single word should be mine own,
And not the homage of long-studied art,   10
Common to all, for you who stand apart!
Oh weariness of measures tried and known!
Yet in their rhythm, you – if you alone –
Should hear the passionate pulses of my heart!'

A Marriage of Shadows *(1888)*.

Arthur W. E. (William Edgar) O'Shaughnessy (1844–81)

Arthur O'Shaughnessy, fringe Pre-Raphaelite poet, was a Londoner, born 14 March 1844. At the age of seventeen he went to work as junior assistant in the British Museum Library. To the astonishment of real zoologists he was in 1863 promoted to an assistantship in the zoological department of the Natural History Museum, but in time he turned himself into a renowned expert on herpetology – reptiles and amphibians. He got to know D. G. Rossetti and other Pre-Raphaelites, had high cultural ambitions and was especially interested in French writing, and in writing, for his own part, in French. *An Epic of Women and Other Poems* (1870), though, seems to have taken people by surprise with its gorgeous, weird sexiness. The obsessive reworking of the Salome story in this volume's long poem 'The Daughter of Herodias' might well have been the stimulus for the late Victorian cult of this dangerous female. *Lays of France*, extravagant reworkings of the Lays of Marie de France, followed in 1872, and the far less rav-

ishing *Music and Moonlight* in 1874. In 1873 O'Shaughnessy married Eleanor Marston, sister of the blind poet Philip Bourke Marston, and together they produced a volume of stories for children (all dolls, nursery worlds, miniature places), *Toyland* (1875). She died, January 1879. In January 1881, on the verge of a second marriage, and newly appointed as English correspondent of *Le Livre*, O'Shaughnessy died, after a chill he got coming away from the theatre on a very cold night. He had recently become very interested in sculpture, and his Aestheticist tendencies are clearly evinced in his 'Thoughts in Marble' in the posthumous collection *Songs of a Worker* (1881) – 'thoughts in marble, or poems of form', he called them, celebrations of 'an art in which I have as yet failed to perceive either morality or immorality', and suggesting the kind of bridge-passage which undoubtedly leads from the aestheticizing side of Pre-Raphaelitism to the later formalist exclusions of Art for Art's Sake.

ODE

We are the music makers,
   And we are the dreamers of dreams,
Wandering by lone sea-breakers,
   And sitting by desolate streams; –
World-losers and world-forsakers,
   On whom the pale moon gleams:

Yet we are the movers and shakers
   Of the world for ever, it seems.

With wonderful deathless ditties
We build up the world's great cities,   10
   And out of a fabulous story
   We fashion an empire's glory:
One man with a dream, at pleasure,
   Shall go forth and conquer a crown;
And three with a new song's measure
   Can trample a kingdom down.

We, in the ages lying
   In the buried past of the earth,
Built Nineveh with our sighing,
   And Babel itself in our mirth;   20
And o'erthrew them with prophesying
   To the old of the new world's worth;
For each age is a dream that is dying,
   Or one that is coming to birth.

A breath of our inspiration
Is the life of each generation;
   A wondrous thing of our dreaming
   Unearthly, impossible seeming –
The soldier, the king, and the peasant
   Are working together in one,   30
Till our dream shall become their present,
   And their work in the world be done.

They had no vision amazing
Of the goodly house they are raising;
   They had no divine foreshowing
   Of the land to which they are going:
But on one man's soul it hath broken,
   A light that doth not depart;
And his look, or a word he hath spoken,
   Wrought flame in another man's heart.   40

And therefore to-day is thrilling
With a past day's late fulfilling;
   And the multitudes are enlisted
   In the faith that their fathers resisted,
And, scorning the dream of to-morrow,
   Are bringing to pass, as they may,
In the world, for its joy or its sorrow,
   The dream that was scorned yesterday.

But we, with our dreaming and singing,
   Ceaseless and sorrowless we!   50
The glory about us clinging
   Of the glorious futures we see,
Our souls with high music ringing:
   O men! it must ever be
That we dwell, in our dreaming and singing,
   A little apart from ye.

For we are afar with the dawning
   And the suns that are not yet high,

And out of the infinite morning
   Intrepid you hear us cry –   60
How, spite of your human scorning,
   Once more God's future draws nigh,
And already goes forth the warning
   That ye of the past must die.

Great hail! we cry to the comers
   From the dazzling unknown shore;
Bring us hither your sun and your summers,
   And renew our world as of yore;
You shall teach us your song's new numbers,
   And things that we dreamed not before: 70
Yea, in spite of a dreamer who slumbers,
   And a singer who sings no more.

Music and Moonlight: Poems and Songs (Chatto & Windus, 1874).

LIVING MARBLE

When her large, fair, reluctant eyelids fell,
   And dreams o'erthrew her blond head mutinous,
That lollingly surrendered to the spell
   Of sleep's warm death, whose tomb is odorous
   And made of recent roses; then unchid
I gazed more rapturously than I may tell
On that vain-hearted queen with whom I dwell,
   The wayward Venus who for days hath hid
   Her peerless, priceless beauty, and forbid,
With impious shames and child-like airs perverse,   10
   My great, fond soul from worshipping the sight
   That gives religion to my day and night –
Her shape sublime that should be none of hers.

*   *   *   *   *

The wonder of her nakedness, unspoiled
   By fear or feigning, showed each passionate limb
In reckless grace that failed not nor recoiled;
   And all the sweet, rebellious body, slim,
   Exuberant, lay abandoned to the whim
And miracle of unabashed repose.
   I joyed to see her glorious side left bare,   20
   Each snow-born flow'ret of her breast displayed,
One white hand vaguely touching one red rose,
   One white arm gleaming through thick golden hair.
   I gazed; then broke the marble I had made,
And yearned, restraining heart and holding breath,
That sleep indeed were endless, even as death.

Songs of a Worker (Chatto & Windus, 1881).

BLACK MARBLE

Sick of pale European beauties spoiled
   By false religions, all the cant of priests
And mimic virtues, far away I toiled

In lawless lands, with savage men and beasts.
Across the bloom-hung forest, in the way
　　Widened by lions or where the winding snake
Had pierced, I counted not each night and day,
　　Till, gazing through a flower-encumbered brake,
I crouched down like a panther watching prey –
　　Black Venus stood beside a sultry lake.　　　　　　　　　10

The naked negress raised on high her arms,
　　Round as palm-saplings; cup-shaped either breast,
Unchecked by needless shames or cold alarms,
　　Swelled, like a burning mountain, with the zest
Of inward life, and tipped itself with fire:
　　Fashioned to crush a lover or a foe,
　　　　Her proud limbs owned their strength, her waist its span,
Her fearless form its faultless curves. And lo! –
　　The lion and the serpent and the man
　　　　Watched her the while with each his own desire.　　　20

Songs of a Worker *(1881)*.

Andrew Lang (1844–1912)

Andrew Lang, Scottish man of letters of extraordinary range and bulk, was born in Selkirk, 31 March 1844, eldest son of John Lang, the Sheriff-Clerk, and Jane Penderleath Sellar, sister of an Edinburgh Latin Professor. Grandfather Andrew Lang, also Selkirk Sheriff-Clerk, had been a friend of Walter Scott. Lang's imagination was formed early by the Scottish stories and ballads which would impel one of his many literary careers, that of folklorist. He attended Selkirk Grammar School and Edinburgh Academy before matriculating in 1861 at St Andrews University. A session at Glasgow University qualified him for a Snell Exhibition in Classics at Balliol College, Oxford (1865). Armed with First Classes in Classical Moderations and Literae Humaniores Finals, he became a Fellow of Merton in 1868. Recuperating from lung trouble in France in 1874, he became friends with Robert Louis Stevenson – a crucial relationship which helped him resist the difficult ur-modernist realisms of James and Hardy in favour of simpler, historical romances. In 1875 he married Leonora Blanche Alleyne, whose family made money in the plantations of Barbados, and gave up his Merton Fellowship for the life of a glitzy hack in London journalism. He was a combative and contentious anthropologist – an advocate of the comparative anthropological rather than the comparative philological approach to myth – and a cranky monotheist, using his spiritualist beliefs (he was a founder of the Psychical Research Society) to explain the miraculous phenomena dotting the mythical scene. Much of his work was devoted to Homeric studies – translation, debates on the unity of the Homeric texts and the person of Homer. He wrote many Lives, much Scottish literary history. He busily anthologized fairy stories for the young, in volumes demarcated by colour: Yellow, Blue, and so on. As a current rhyme had it: 'Books Yellow, Red, and Green, and Blue/ All true, or just as good as true.' He produced novels – historical romances, shockers (*Much Darker Days* (1884), a Christmas chiller, is by 'A Huge Longway'), collaborative efforts (including *The World's Desire* (1890), about Odysseus's last voyage, with Rider Haggard; and *Parson Kelly* (1900), a Jacobite thriller, with A. E. W. Mason, later the author of the popular imperialist novel, *The Four Feathers*). And he knocked off poems – as short and sweet, witty and slick as his prose journalism, the essays and causeries he made money by: *Rhymes à la Mode* (1885), *Grass of Parnassus* (1888), *Ban and Arrière Ban* (1894), and so on. His first books of verses, *Ballads and Lyrics of Old France* (1872), *xxii Ballades in Blue China* (1880), and *xxxii Ballades in Blue China* (1884), put him in the forefront of the fashionable taste for old French modes, ballades, triolets, rondeaux. *Helen of Troy* (1882), in six books, was an experiment in the long narrative poem which ill suited his talent for the light touch, the momentary reference, and the short run, and he never repeated the effort. He was a *sportif* gent, in love with golf and fishing and cricket (said to be able to hammer out perfect journalistic pieces at odd moments in the pavilion). He was thought very well of by contemporaries. Oxford gave him an honorary doctorate (1904); Merton made him an Honorary Fellow (1890); Matthew Arnold tried to get him to stand as Oxford Professor of Poetry. He had no children, and died of angina in Scotland, 20 July 1912. He is buried in the cathedral precincts at St Andrews. His *Poetical Works* appeared in four volumes in 1923.

BALLADE OF ÆSTHETIC ADJECTIVES

There be 'subtle' and 'sweet', that are bad ones to beat,
There are 'lives unlovely', and 'souls astray';
There is much to be done yet with 'moody' and 'meet',
And 'ghastly', and 'grimly', and 'gaunt', and 'gray';
We should ever be 'blithesome', but never be 'gay',
And 'splendid' is suited to 'summer' and 'sea';
'Consummate', they say, is enjoying its day –
'Intense' is the adjective dearest to me!

The snows and the rose they are 'windy' and 'fleet',
And 'frantic' and 'faint' are delight and dismay;   10
Yea, 'sanguine', it seems, as the juice of the beet,
Are 'the hands of the king' in a general way:
There be loves that 'quicken', and 'sicken', and 'slay';
'Supreme' is the song of the bard of the free;
But of adjectives all that I name in my lay
'Intense' is the adjective dearest to me!

The matron intense – let us sit at her feet,
And pelt her with lilies as long as we may;
The maiden intense – is not always discreet:
But the singer intense, in his 'singing array',   20
Will win all the world with his roundelay:
While 'blithe' birds carol from tree to tree,
And art unto nature doth simper, and say –
' "Intense" is the adjective dearest to me!'

Envoy
Prince, it is surely as good as a play
To mark how the poets and painters agree;
But of plumage aesthetic that feathers the jay,
'Intense' is the adjective dearest to me!

Text of Poetical Works, *4 vols, ed. Mrs Leonora B. Lang*
(Longmans, Green & Co., 1923), I.

ON THE DEATH OF LORD TENNYSON

Silence! 'The best' (he said) 'are silent now,
That younger bearer of the laurel bough,
Who with his Thyrsis, kindred souls divine,
Harps only for Sicilian Proserpine:
For Arnold died, and Browning died, and he
The oldest, wisest, greatest of the three –
Dies, and what voice shall dirge for him to-day?
For the Muse went with him the darkling way,
And left us mute!... Peace! who shall rhyme or rave?
The violet blooms not on the new-made grave,   10
And not in this first blankness of regret
Are eyes of men who mourn their Master wet.
New grief is dumb: himself through many a year
Withheld the meed of his melodious tear
While Hallam slept. But no! the moment flies!
And rapid rhymers, when the Poet dies,

Wail punctual, and prompt, and unafraid,
In copious instant ditties ready made.
Oh, peace! Ye do but make our loss more deep,
Who wail above his unawaking sleep.   20

Text of Poetical Works *(1923), III.*

BALLADE OF CRICKET

To T. W. Lang

The burden of hard hitting: slog away!
Here shalt thou make a 'five' and there a 'four,'
And then upon thy bat shalt lean, and say,
That thou art in for an uncommon score.
Yea, the loud ring applauding thee shall roar,
And thou to rival THORNTON[1] shalt aspire,
When lo, the Umpire gives thee 'leg before,' –
'This is the end of every man's desire!'

The burden of much bowling, when the stay
Of all thy team is 'collared,' swift or slower,   10
When 'bailers' break not in their wonted way,
And 'yorkers' come not off as here-to-fore,
When length balls shoot no more, ah never more,
When all deliveries lose their former fire,
When bats seem broader than the broad barn-door, –
'This is the end of every man's desire!'

The burden of long fielding, when the clay
Clings to thy shoon in sudden shower's downpour,[2]
And running still thou stumblest, or the ray
Of blazing suns doth bite and burn thee sore,   20
And blind thee till, forgetful of thy lore,
Thou dost most mournfully misjudge a 'skyer,'
And lose a match the Fates cannot restore, –
'This is the end of every man's desire!'

Envoy

Alas, yet liefer[3] on Youth's hither shore
Would I be some poor Player on scant hire,
Than King among the old, who play no more, –
'*This* is the end of every man's desire!'

Rhymes à la Mode *(Kegan Paul, Trench & Co., 1885).*

THE HAUNTED HOMES OF ENGLAND[1]

The Haunted Homes of England,
    How eerily they stand,
While through them flit their ghosts – to wit,
    The Monk with the Red Hand;

BALLADE OF CRICKET
1 Charles Inglis ('Buns') Thornton (1850–1929), formidable batsman (and bowler) for Eton, Cambridge, Kent, Middlesex and the Gentlemen of England.
2 lines recalled by A. E. Housman, 'The rain, it streams on stone and hillock', below, p. [989].

3 rather.
THE HAUNTED HOMES OF ENGLAND
1 a kind of satirical coda to Felicia Hemans, 'The Homes of England' (1827): with its 'stately', 'merry', 'blessed', 'cottage', and 'free, fair' homes of England.

The Eyeless Girl – an awful spook –
   To stop the boldest breath,
The boy that inked his copybook,
   And so got 'wopped' to death!

Call them not shams – from haunted Glamis
   To haunted Woodhouselea,   10
I mark in hosts the grisly ghosts
   I hear the fell Banshie![2]
I know the spectral dog that howls
   Before the death of squires;
In my 'Ghosts'-guide' addresses hide
   For Podmore and for Myers![3]

I see the Vampire climb the stairs
   From vaults below the church;
And hark! the Pirate's spectre swears!
   O Psychical Research,   20
Canst *thou* not hear what meets my ear,
   The viewless wheels that come?
The wild Banshie that wails to thee?
   The Drummer with his drum?

O Haunted Homes of England,
   Though tenantless ye stand,
With none content to pay the rent,
   Through all the shadowy land,
Now, Science true will find in you
   A sympathetic perch,   30
And take you all, both Grange and Hall,
   For Psychical Research!

Ban and Arrière Ban: A Rally of Fugitive Rhymes *(Longmans,*
Green & Co., 1894).

Gerard Manley Hopkins (1844–89)

Gerard Hopkins (as his friends knew him), priest and poet, virtually unpublished in his own lifetime but taken up after the First World War as the most modern (though not modernist) seeming of the Victorians, was born, 28 July 1844, in Stratford, East London, son of a marine insurance agent who was also a poet, encyclopedist and London's Consul-General for Hawaii. The family were High Anglicans. Early on young Gerard acquired an obsession with Gothic architecture to add to his alert interest in the rhyming of nursery rhymes. At Highgate School he was taught by R. W. Dixon (who would later become one of his main

epistolary mainstays). He entered Balliol College, Oxford, in 1863 as an Exhibitioner and quickly fell in with the Balliol Ritualists. Small and beautiful (known as 'Skin' at school and 'Poppy' at Balliol), he loved life and pastries and Old Etonian Digby Mackworth Dolben. He was given to a lively daftness and to practical jokes (pepper through keyholes, and all that). He became a close Ruskin-influenced observer of nature and filled his notebooks with philologically speculative lists of words designed to prove the natural relations of words to things. His worry about bodies began early – his own body (he

---

2 Irish or Scottish family ghost: wails when family member dies.
3 F. W. H. Myers (1843–1901), poet and essayist, one of the founders of the Society for Psychical Research; Frank Podmore (1855–1901),

socialist and spiritualist; they collaborated on *Phantasms of the Living* (1886), a guide book of 'proven' psychic phenomena.

went in for body-building dumb-bells, was fearful for the fragility of his eyes, anxious about masturbation, given to hair-shirts and other punishments of the flesh, self-flagellation, fasting, doing without pudding on Holy Days) and other people's bodies (he was guiltily attracted to certain kinds of male, young and old, especially lower-class ones and foreigners, navvies, labourers, soldiers, buglers, Norwegians). At Oxford he formed his great and crucial friendship with his contemporary Robert Bridges (reading Classics at Corpus Christi). He was for a time at Oxford coached by Walter Pater of Brasenose, but his particularist blend of Christian aestheticism would lead him not into Paterian decadence but to follow John Henry Newman from High Anglicanism to Rome. Hopkins converted to Roman Catholicism in 1866 and started training as a Jesuit in 1868. He studied in Roehampton and at other Jesuit centres – Stonyhurst in Lancashire, St Beuno's in Wales. He worked as a training priest at Farm Street in London's Mayfair, St Aloysius in Oxford, and in Liverpool (1879–82). After that he taught at Stonyhurst College, before going as Professor of Greek to the new Catholic University College, Dublin. Everywhere Hopkins's fastidious snobbery and priggishness found ordinary humanity hard to stomach – Newman's Oratory School masters were 'the dregs of Great Britain'; Rhyl was sordidly full of human slime, St Aloysius too demotic, the Liverpool crowd 'base and bespotted' of figure and feature, Dublin filthy. Nature, though, was a different matter, lovely as the preferred male bodies which occasionally caught his eye (he naturally took to Whitman when he came across his poems), to be captured in extraordinary eye-on-the-object metaphors ('cocoa-dust-coloured handkerchiefs of ploughfields'), and in verses built on his personal deftly constructed system of so-called Sprung Rhythm, in lines syntactically disjunctive, densely repetitive and heavily rhyming (rhymes of all sorts – initial, median and end-rhymes; highly consonantal after Anglo-Saxon and the Welsh cynghanned; much influenced by the line-repeating Hebrew method found in the Psalms). Poetry was all about repetition ('oftening, over-and-overing, aftering') – a repeating reconstruction of God's world in words conceived of as, themselves, originating as systematic repeaters of the divine order and creation. God's philology; God's poetic; the divine 'instress'. Bridges wrote in his 1918 edition that Hopkins had been 'flattered when I called him *perittotatos*' – a Greek word meaning very clever in expression, but also very excessive and odd. He 'saw the humour of it – and one would expect to find in his work the force of emphatic condensation and the magic of melodious expression, both in their extreme forms'. The Jesuits did not recognize what Hopkins was up to. Their journal the *Month* rejected both 'The Wreck of the Deutschland' and 'Eurydice'. Hopkins's priestly career began with a theatrical gesture of poetic repression – the burning of many early poems (it was theatrical because Bridges had copies) – and continued in a religio-aesthetic restraint and estrangement reflected in his so-called 'terrible sonnets'. The Dublin years – 'hard wearying wasting wasted' – symptomatized the plight of an Englishman in a religious order which judged him eccentric, in a culture which had little time for what Yeats dismissed as 'English Aesthetic Catholicism', and of a poet cut off from the poetry public he was due. 'I am gall, I am heartburn.' 'Thou art indeed just, Lord' carries the jeremiad right up to the throne of God – a daring utterance of complaint only allowable to the truly submissive priest because it begins in and is sanctioned by the biblical words of the prophet Jeremiah himself. Hopkins's extensive correspondence with Bridges, Dixon and the Catholic poet Coventry Patmore at least allowed him to keep whistling in the dark as critic and explainer of his own work. Hopkins died in Dublin, 8 June 1889, aged only forty-four. Bridges inherited his papers, got some of the poems posthumously into collections, and in 1918, carefully judging his moment, brought out the first, momentous and reputation-making Oxford edition of the *Poems of Gerard Manley Hopkins*. The volume 'will be', Bridges wrote to Housman, 'one of the queerest in the world but ... full of genius and poetic beauty'.

From the 'AUTHOR'S PREFACE' (1918)

The poems in this book[1] are written some in Running Rhythm, the common rhythm in English use, some in Sprung Rhythm, and some in a mixture of the two. And those in the common rhythm are some counterpointed, some not.

Common English rhythm, called Running Rhythm above, is measured by feet of either two or three syllables and (putting aside the imperfect feet at the beginning and end of lines and also some unusual measures in which feet seem to be paired together and double or composite feet to arise) never more nor less.

Every foot has one principal stress or accent, and this or the syllable it falls on may be called the Stress of the foot and the other part, the one or two unaccented syllables, the Slack. Feet (and the

AUTHOR'S PREFACE

1   Hopkins was referring to the manuscript of his poems written 1876 and after.

rhythms made out of them) in which the Stress comes first are called Falling Feet and Falling Rhythms, feet and rhythm in which the Slack comes first are called Rising Feet and Rhythms, and if the Stress is between two Slacks there will be Rocking Feet and Rhythms. These distinctions are real and true to nature; but for purposes of scanning it is a great convenience to follow the example of music and take the stress always first, as the accent or the chief accent always comes first in a musical bar. If this is done there will be in common English verse only two possible feet – the so-called accentual Trochee and Dactyl, and correspondingly only two possible uniform rhythms, the so-called Trochaic and Dactylic. But they may be mixed and then what the Greeks called a Logaoedic Rhythm arises. These are the facts and according to these the scanning of ordinary regularly-written English verse is very simple indeed and to bring in other principles is here unnecessary.

But because verse written strictly in these feet and by these principles will become same and tame the poets have brought in licences and departures from rule to give variety, and especially when the natural rhythm is rising, as in the common ten-syllable or five-foot verse, rhymed or blank. These irregularities are chiefly Reversed Feet and Reversed or Counterpoint Rhythm, which two things are two steps or degrees of licence in the same kind. By a reversed foot I mean the putting the stress where, to judge by the rest of the measure, the slack should be and the slack where the stress, and this is done freely at the beginning of a line and, in the course of a line, after a pause; only scarcely ever in the second foot or place and never in the last, unless when the poet designs some extraordinary effect; for these places are characteristic and sensitive and cannot well be touched. But the reversal of the first foot and of some middle foot after a strong pause is a thing so natural that our poets have generally done it, from Chaucer down, without remark and it commonly passes unnoticed and cannot be said to amount to a formal change of rhythm, but rather is that irregularity which all natural growth and motion shews. If however the reversal is repeated in two feet running, especially so as to include the sensitive second foot, it must be due either to great want of ear or else is a calculated effect, the superinducing or *mounting* of a new rhythm upon the old; and since the new or mounted rhythm is actually heard and at the same time the mind naturally supplies the natural or standard foregoing rhythm, for we do not forget what the rhythm is that by rights we should be hearing, two rhythms are in some manner running at once and we have something answerable to counterpoint in music, which is two or more strains of tune going on together, and this is Counterpoint Rhythm. Of this kind of verse Milton is the great master and the choruses of *Samson Agonistes* are written throughout in it – but with the disadvantage that he does not let the reader clearly know what the ground-rhythm is meant to be and so they have struck most readers as merely irregular. And in fact if you counterpoint throughout, since one only of the counter rhythms is actually heard, the other is really destroyed or cannot come to exist and what is written is one rhythm only and probably Sprung Rhythm, of which I now speak.

Sprung Rhythm, as used in this book, is measured by feet of from one to four syllables, regularly, and for particular effects any number of weak or slack syllables may be used. It has one stress, which falls on the only syllable, if there is only one, or, if there are more, then scanning as above, on the first, and so gives rise to four sorts of feet, a monosyllable and the so-called accentual Trochee, Dactyl, and the First Paeon. And there will be four corresponding natural rhythms; but nominally the feet are mixed and any one may follow any other. And hence Sprung Rhythm differs from Running Rhythm in having or being only one nominal rhythm, a mixed or 'logaoedic' one, instead of three, but on the other hand in having twice the flexibility of foot, so that any two stresses may either follow one another running or be divided by one, two, or three slack syllables. But strict Sprung Rhythm cannot be counterpointed. In Sprung Rhythm, as in logaoedic rhythm generally, the feet are assumed to be equally long or strong and their seeming inequality is made up by pause or stressing.

Remark also that it is natural in Sprung Rhythm for the lines to be *rove over*, that is for the scanning of each line immediately to take up that of the one before, so that if the first has one or more syllables at its end the other must have so many the less at its beginning; and in fact the scanning runs on without break from the beginning, say, of a stanza to the end and all the stanza is one long strain, though written in lines asunder.

Two licences are natural to Sprung Rhythm. The one is rests, as in music; but of this an example is scarcely to be found in this book, unless in the *Echos*, second line. The other is *hangers* or *outrides*, that is one, two, or three slack syllables added to a foot and not counting in the nominal scanning. They are so called because they seem to hang below the line or ride forward or backward from it in another dimension than the line itself, according to a principle needless to explain here. These out-riding half feet or hangers are marked by a loop underneath them, and plenty of them will be found.

The other marks are easily understood, namely accents, where the reader might be in doubt which syllable should have the stress; slurs, that is loops *over* syllables, to tie them together into the time of one; little loops at the end of a line to shew that the rhyme goes on to the first letter of the next line; what in music are called pauses ⁊, to shew that the syllable should be dwelt on; and twirls ∼, to mark reversed or counterpointed rhythm.

Note on the nature and history of Sprung Rhythm – Sprung Rhythm is the most natural of things. For (1) it is the rhythm of common speech and of written prose, when rhythm is perceived in them. (2) It is the rhythm of all but the most monotonously regular music, so that in the words of choruses and refrains and in songs written closely to music it arises. (3) It is found in nursery rhymes,[2] weather saws,[3] and so on; because, however these may have been once made in running rhythm, the terminations having dropped off by the change of language, the stresses come together and so the rhythm is sprung. (4) It arises in common verse when reversed or counterpointed, for the same reason.

But nevertheless in spite of all this and though Greek and Latin lyric verse, which is well known, and the old English verse seen in *Pierce Ploughman* are in sprung rhythm, it has in fact ceased to be used since the Elizabethan age, Greene being the last writer who can be said to have recognized it. For perhaps there was not, down to our days, a single, even short, poem in English in which sprung rhythm is employed – not for single effects or in fixed places – but as the governing prin-ciple of the scansion. I say this because the contrary has been asserted: if it is otherwise the poem should be cited.

Preface, Poems of Gerard Manley Hopkins, *ed. Robert Bridges (Oxford University Press, London, 1918).*

THE HABIT OF PERFECTION

Elected Silence, sing to me
And beat upon my whorlèd ear,
Pipe me to pastures still and be
The music that I care to hear.

Shape nothing, lips; be lovely-dumb:
It is the shut, the curfew sent
From there where all surrenders come
Which only makes you eloquent.

Be shellèd, eyes, with double dark
And find the uncreated light:
This ruck and reel which you remark
Coils, keeps, and teases simple sight.

Palate, the hutch of tasty lust,
Desire not to be rinsed with wine:
The can must be so sweet, the crust
So fresh that come in fasts divine!

10

2 Hopkins's example: '*Díng, dóng, béll,* Pússy's ín the wéll: *Whó pút* her ín? Líttle Jóhnny Thín...' (letter to R. W. Dixon, 5 October 1878).

3 e.g. Réd sky at níght, shépherd's delíght [Example given by W. H. Gardner, editor with N. H. Mackenzie, of the 4th Oxford edition of the *Poems* (1967).]

Nostrils, your careless breath that spend
Upon the stir and keep of pride,
What relish shall the censers send
Along the sanctuary side!   20

O feel-of-primrose hands, O feet
That want the yield of plushy sward,
But you shall walk the golden street
And you unhouse and house the Lord.

And, Poverty, be thou the bride
And now the marriage feast begun,
And lily-coloured clothes provide
Your spouse not laboured-at nor spun.

Written 1866. First published in The Poets and the Poetry of the Century:
Robert Bridges and Contemporary Poets, *ed. A. H. Miles (1893).*
Text: Poems of Gerard Manley Hopkins, *ed. Bridges (1918).*

THE WRECK OF THE DEUTSCHLAND

To the
happy memory of five Franciscan nuns
exiles by the Falck Laws
drowned between midnight and morning of
Dec. 7th, 1875

Part the First

1

Thou mastering me
God! giver of breath and bread;
World's strand, sway of the sea;
Lord of living and dead;
Thou hast bound bones and veins in me, fastened me flesh,
And after it almost unmade, what with dread,
Thy doing: and dost thou touch me afresh?
Over again I feel thy finger and find thee.

2

I did say yes
O at lightning and lashed rod;   10
Thou heardst me truer than tongue confess
Thy terror, O Christ, O God;
Thou knowest the walls, altar and hour and night:
The swoon of a heart that the sweep and the hurl of thee trod
Hard down with a horror of height:
And the midriff astrain with leaning of, laced with fire of stress.

3

The frown of his face
Before me, the hurtle of hell
Behind, where, where was a, where was a place?
I whirled out wings that spell   20
And fled with a fling of the heart to the heart of the Host.

My heart, but you were dovewinged, I can tell,
　　Carrier-witted, I am bold to boast,
To flash from the flame to the flame then, tower from the grace to the grace.

4

　　I am soft sift
　　In an hourglass — at the wall
Fast, but mined with a motion, a drift,
　　And it crowds and it combs to the fall;
I steady as a water in a well, to a poise, to a pane,
But roped with, always, all the way down from the tall
　　Fells or flanks of the voel,¹ a vein
Of the gospel proffer, a pressure, a principle, Christ's gift.   30

5

　　I kiss my hand
　　To the stars, lovely-asunder
Starlight, wafting him out of it; and
　　Glow, glory in thunder;
Kiss my hand to the dappled-with-damson west:
Since, tho' he is under the world's splendour and wonder,
　　His mystery must be instressed, stressed;
For I greet him the days I meet him, and bless when I understand.   40

6

　　Not out of his bliss
　　Springs the stress felt
Nor first from heaven (and few know this)
　　Swings the stroke dealt —
Stroke and a stress that stars and storms deliver,
That guilt is hushed by, hearts are flushed by and melt —
　　But it rides time like riding a river
(And here the faithful waver, the faithless fable and miss).

7

　　It dates from day
　　Of his going in Galilee;   50
Warm-laid grave of a womb-life grey;
　　Manger, maiden's knee;
The dense and the driven Passion, and frightful sweat:
Thence the discharge of it, there its swelling to be,
　　Though felt before, though in high flood yet —
What none would have known of it, only the heart, being hard at bay,

8

　　Is out with it! Oh,
　　We lash with the best or worst
Word last! How a lush-kept plush-capped sloe
　　Will, mouthed to flesh-burst,   60
Gush! — flush the man, the being with it, sour or sweet,
Brim, in a flash, full! — Hither then, last or first,
　　To hero of Calvary, Christ,'s feet —
Never ask if meaning it, wanting it, warned of it — men go.

THE WRECK OF THE DEUTSCHLAND
1   a Vegetation-free hill or mountain (Welsh).

9

Be adored among men,
God, three-numberèd form;
Wring thy rebel, dogged in den,
Man's malice, with wrecking and storm.
Beyond saying sweet, past telling of tongue,
Thou art lightning and love, I found it, a winter and warm;   70
Father and fondler of heart thou hast wrung:
Hast thy dark descending and most art merciful then.

10

With an anvil-ding
And with fire in him forge thy will
Or rather, rather then, stealing as Spring
Through him, melt him but master him still:
Whether at once, as once at a crash Paul,[2]
Or as Austin,[3] a lingering-out swéet skill,
Make mercy in all of us, out of us all
Mastery, but be adored, but be adored King.   80

Part the Second

11

'Some find me a sword; some
The flange and the rail; flame,
Fang, or flood' goes Death on drum,
And storms bugle his fame.
But wé dream we are rooted in earth – Dust!
Flesh falls within sight of us, we, though our flower the same,
Wave with the meadow, forget that there must
The sour scythe cringe, and the blear share come.

12

On Saturday sailed from Bremen,
American-outward-bound,   90
Take settler and seamen, tell men with women,
Two hundred souls in the round –
O Father, not under thy feathers nor ever as guessing
The goal was a shoal, of a fourth the doom to be drowned;
Yet did the dark side of the bay of thy blessing
Not vault them, the million of rounds of thy mercy not reeve even them in?

13

Into the snows she sweeps,
Hurling the haven behind,
The Deutschland, on Sunday; and so the sky keeps,
For the infinite air is unkind,   100
And the sea flint-flake, black-backed in the regular blow,
Sitting Eastnortheast, in cursed quarter, the wind;
Wiry and white-fiery and whirlwind-swivellèd snow
Spins to the widow-making unchilding unfathering deeps.

14

She drove in the dark to leeward,
She struck – not a reef or a rock
But the combs of a smother of sand: night drew her

---

2   St Paul.   3   St Augustine.

Dead to the Kentish Knock;
And she beat the bank down with her bows and the ride of her keel;
The breakers rolled on her beam with ruinous shock;   110
And canvas and compass, the whorl and the wheel
Idle for ever to waft her or wind her with, these she endured.

15

Hope had grown grey hairs,
Hope had mourning on,
Trenched with tears, carved with cares,
Hope was twelve hours gone;
And frightful a nightfall folded rueful a day
Nor rescue, only rocket and lightship, shone,
And lives at last were washing away:
To the shrouds they took, – they shook in the hurling and horrible airs.   120

16

One stirred from the rigging to save
The wild woman-kind below,
With a rope's end round the man, handy and brave –
He was pitched to his death at a blow,
For all his dreadnought breast and braids of thew:
They could tell him for hours, dandled the to and fro
Through the cobbled foam-fleece. What could he do
With the burl of the fountains of air, buck and the flood of the wave?

17

They fought with God's cold –
And they could not and fell to the deck   130
(Crushed them) or water (and drowned them) or rolled
With the sea-romp over the wreck.
Night roared, with the heart-break hearing a heart-broke rabble,
The woman's wailing, the crying of child without check –
Till a lioness arose breasting the babble,
A prophetess towered in the tumult, a virginal tongue told.

18

Ah, touched in your bower of bone,
Are you! turned for an exquisite smart,
Have you! make words break from me here all alone,
Do you! – mother of being in me, heart.   140
O unteachably after evil, but uttering truth,
Why, tears! is it? tears; such a melting, a madrigal start!
Never-eldering revel and river of youth,
What can it be, this glee? the good you have there of your own?

19

Sister, a sister calling
A master, her master and mine! –
And the inboard seas run swirling and hawling;
The rash smart sloggering brine
Blinds her; but she that weather sees one thing, one;
Has one fetch in her: she rears herself to divine   150
Ears, and the call of the tall nun
To the men in the tops and the tackle rode over the storm's brawling.

20

She was first of a five and came
Of a coifèd sisterhood.

(O Deutschland, double a desperate name!
 O world wide of its good!
But Gertrude, lily, and Luther, are two of a town,[4]
 Christ's lily and beast of the waste wood:
From life's dawn it is drawn down,
Abel is Cain's brother and breasts they have sucked the same.)[5]   160

21

 Loathed for a love men knew in them,
  Banned by the land of their birth,
 Rhine refused them, Thames would ruin them;
  Surf, snow, river and earth
Gnashed: but thou art above, thou Orion of light;
 Thy unchancelling poising palms were weighing the worth,
  Thou martyr-master: in thy sight
Storm flakes were scroll-leavèd flowers, lily showers – sweet heaven was astrew in them.

22

 Five! the finding and sake
  And cipher of suffering Christ.[6]   170
 Mark, the mark is of man's make
  And the word of it Sacrificed.
But he scores it in scarlet himself on his own bespoken,
 Before-time-taken, dearest prizèd and priced –
  Stigma, signal, cinquefoil token
For lettering of the lamb's fleece, ruddying of the rose-flake.

23

 Joy fall to thee, father Francis,[7]
  Drawn to the Life that died;
 With the gnarls of the nails in thee, niche of the lance, his
  Lovescape crucified   180
And seal of his seraph-arrival! and these thy daughters
 And five-livèd and leavèd favour and pride,
  Are sisterly sealed in wild waters,
To bathe in his fall-gold mercies, to breathe in his all-fire glances.

24

 Away in the loveable west,
  On a pastoral forehead of Wales,[8]
 I was under a roof here, I was at rest,
  And they the prey of the gales;
She to the black-about air, to the breaker, the thickly
 Falling flakes, to the throng that catches and quails   190
  Was calling 'O Christ, Christ, come quickly':
The cross to her she calls Christ to her, christens her wild-worst Best.

25

 The majesty! what did she mean?
  Breathe, arch and original Breath.
 Is it love in her of the being as her lover had been?
  Breathe, body of lovely Death.
They were else-minded then, altogether, the men

---

4 St Gertrude (1265–1301/2) died at Eisleben, German birth place of Reformer (and Hopkins's bête-noire) Martin Luther (1483).
5 Cain killed his brother Abel, Genesis 4.

6 the five wounds of the crucified Christ.
7 St Francis of Assissi (the nuns were Franciscans).
8 St Beuno's.

Woke thee with a *We are perishing* in the weather of Gennesareth.[9]
Or is it that she cried for the crown then,
The keener to come at the comfort for feeling the combating keen?   200

26

For how to the heart's cheering
The down-dugged ground-hugged grey
Hovers off, the jay-blue heavens appearing
Of pied and peeled May!
Blue-beating and hoary-glow height; or night, still higher,
With belled fire and the moth-soft Milky Way,
What by your measure is the heaven of desire,
The treasure never eyesight got, nor was ever guessed what for the hearing?

27

No, but it was not these.
The jading and jar of the cart,   210
Time's tasking, it is fathers that asking for ease
Of the sodden-with-its-sorrowing heart,
Not danger, electrical horror; then further it finds
The appealing of the Passion is tenderer in prayer apart:
Other, I gather, in measure her mind's
Burden, in wind's burly and beat of endragonèd seas.

28

But how shall I ... make me room there:
Reach me a ... Fancy, come faster –
Strike you the sight of it? look at it loom there,
Thing that she ... There then! the Master,   220
Ipse, the only one, Christ, King, Head:
He was to cure the extremity where he had cast her;
Do, deal, lord it with living and dead;
Let him ride, her pride, in his triumph, despatch and have done with his doom there.

29

Ah! there was a heart right!
There was single eye!
Read the unshapeable shock night
And knew the who and the why;
Wording it how but by him that present and past,
Heaven and earth are word of, worded by? –   230
The Simon Peter of a soul! to the blast
Tarpeïan-fast,[10] but a blown beacon of light.

30

Jesu, heart's light,
Jesu, maid's son,
What was the feast followed the night
Thou hadst glory of this nun?[11] –
Feast of the one woman without stain.
For so conceivèd, so to conceive thee is done;
But here was heart-throe, birth of a brain,
Word, that heard and kept thee and uttered thee outright.   240

9   Palestinian lake; scene of disciples in storm, Jesus walking on   save the Capitol.
water, St Peter sinking in attempt to do likewise, Matthew 14. 22–32.   11   8 December: feast of Immaculate Conception of Blessed Virgin
10   Roman criminals were thrown to their death from the Tarpeian   Mary.
Rock – named after Tarpeia, in one legend a heroine killed trying to

31

Well, she has thee for the pain, for the
    Patience; but pity of the rest of them!
  Heart, go and bleed at a bitterer vein for the
    Comfortless unconfessed of them –
No not uncomforted: lovely-felicitous Providence
Finger of a tender of, O of a feathery delicacy, the breast of the
  Maiden could obey so, be a bell to, ring of it, and
Startle the poor sheep back! is the shipwrack then a harvest, does tempest carry the grain for thee?

32

I admire thee, master of the tides,
    Of the Yore-flood, of the year's fall;   250
  The recurb and the recovery of the gulf's sides,
    The girth of it and the wharf of it and the wall;
Stanching, quenching ocean of a motionable mind;
Ground of being, and granite of it: past all
    Grasp God, throned behind
Death with a sovereignty that heeds but hides, bodes but abides;

33

With a mercy that outrides
    The all of water, an ark
  For the listener; for the lingerer with a love glides
    Lower than death and the dark;   260
A vein for the visiting of the past-prayer, pent in prison,
The-last-breath penitent spirits – the uttermost mark
    Our passion-plungèd giant risen,
The Christ of the Father compassionate, fetched in the storm of his strides.

34

Now burn, new born to the world,
    Double-naturèd name,
  The heaven-flung, heart-fleshed, maiden-furled
    Miracle-in-Mary-of-flame,
Mid-numberèd he in three of the thunder-throne!
Not a dooms-day dazzle in his coming nor dark as he came;   270
    Kind, but royally reclaiming his own;
A released shower, let flash to the shire, not a lightning of fire hard-hurled.

35

Dame, at our door
    Drowned, and among our shoals,
  Remember us in the roads, the heaven-haven of the reward:
    Our King back, Oh, upon English souls!
Let him easter in us, be a dayspring to the dimness of us, be a crimson-cresseted east,
  More brightening her, rare-dear Britain, as his reign rolls,
    Pride, rose, prince, hero of us, high-priest,
Our hearts' charity's hearth's fire, our thoughts' chivalry's throng's Lord.   280

Written 1876. Poems *(1918).*

GOD'S GRANDEUR

The world is charged with the grandeur of God.
  It will flame out, like shining from shook foil;
  It gathers to a greatness, like the ooze of oil
Crushed. Why do men then now not reck his rod?

Generations have trod, have trod, have trod;
   And all is seared with trade; bleared, smeared with toil;
   And wears man's smudge and shares man's smell: the soil
Is bare now, nor can foot feel, being shod.

And for all this, nature is never spent;
   There lives the dearest freshness deep down things;   10
And though the last lights off the black West went
   Oh, morning, at the brown brink eastward, springs –
Because the Holy Ghost over the bent
   World broods with warm breast and with ah! bright wings.

Written 23 February–March 1877. Poems *(1918).*

SPRING

Nothing is so beautiful as Spring –
   When weeds, in wheels, shoot long and lovely and lush;
   Thrush's eggs look little low heavens, and thrush
Through the echoing timber does so rinse and wring
The ear, it strikes like lightnings to hear him sing;
   The glassy peartree leaves and blooms, they brush
   The descending blue; that blue is all in a rush
With richness; the racing lambs too have fair their fling.

What is all this juice and all this joy?
   A strain of the earth's sweet being in the beginning   10
In Eden garden. – Have, get, before it cloy,

   Before it cloud, Christ, lord, and sour with sinning,
Innocent mind and Mayday in girl and boy,
   Most, O maid's child, thy choice and worthy the winning.

Written May 1877. The Poets and the Poetry of the Century *(1893). Text:* Poems *(1918).*

IN THE VALLEY OF THE ELWY[1]

I remember a house where all were good
   To me, God knows, deserving no such thing:
   Comforting smell breathed at very entering,
Fetched fresh, as I suppose, off some sweet wood.

That cordial air made those kind people a hood
   All over, as a bevy of eggs the mothering wing
   Will, or mild nights the new morsels of Spring:
Why, it seemed of course; seemed of right it should.

Lovely the woods, waters, meadows, combes, vales,
All the air things wear that build this world of Wales;   10
   Only the inmate does not correspond:

IN THE VALLEY OF THE ELWY
1   'The kind people of the sonnet were the Watsons of Shooter's Hill,
nothing to do with the Elwy' (the Welsh river).

God, lover of souls, swaying considerate scales,
Complete thy creature dear O where it fails,
    Being mighty a master, being a father and fond.

Written by 23 May 1877. Poems *(1918).*

THE WINDHOVER:

To Christ our Lord

I caught this morning morning's minion, king-
    dom of daylight's dauphin, dapple-dawn-drawn Falcon, in his riding
    Of the rolling level underneath him steady air, and striding
High there, how he rung upon the rein of a wimpling wing
In his ecstasy! then off, off forth on swing,
    As a skate's heel sweeps smooth on a bow-bend: the hurl and gliding
    Rebuffed the big wind. My heart in hiding
Stirred for a bird, – the achieve of, the mastery of the thing!

Brute beauty and valour and act, oh, air, pride, plume, here
    Buckle! AND the fire that breaks from thee then, a billion   10
Times told lovelier, more dangerous, O my chevalier!

    No wonder of it: shéer plód makes plough down sillion
Shine, and blue-bleak embers, ah my dear,
    Fall, gall themselves, and gash gold-vermilion.

Written by 30 May 1877. Poems *(1918).*

PIED BEAUTY

Glory be to God for dappled things –
    For skies of couple-colour as a brinded cow;
        For rose-moles all in stipple upon trout that swim;
Fresh-firecoal chestnut-falls; finches' wings;
    Landscape plotted and pieced – fold, fallow, and plough;
        And áll trádes, their gear and tackle and trim.

All things counter, original, spare, strange;
    Whatever is fickle, freckled (who knows how?)
        With swift, slow; sweet, sour; adazzle, dim;
He fathers-forth whose beauty is past change: 10
                            Praise him.

Written Summer 1877. Poems *(1918).*

BINSEY[1] POPLARS

Felled 1879

My aspens dear, whose airy cages quelled,
    Quelled or quenched in leaves the leaping sun,
All felled, felled, are all felled;
    Of a fresh and following folded rank

BINSEY POPLARS
1   Small settlement on the River Thames on edge of Oxford.

Not spared, not one
That dandled a sandalled
Shadow that swam or sank
On meadow and river and wind-wandering weed-winding bank.

O if we but knew what we do
When we delve or hew –   10
Hack and rack the growing green!
Since country is so tender
To touch, her being só slender,
That, like this sleek and seeing ball
But a prick will make no eye at all,

Where we, even where we mean
To mend her we end her,
When we hew or delve:
After-comers cannot guess the beauty been.
Ten or twelve, only ten or twelve   20
Strokes of havoc únselve
The sweet especial scene,
Rural scene, a rural scene,
Sweet especial rural scene.

Dated, Oxford, 13 March 1879. Poems (1918).

FELIX RANDAL

Felix Randal the farrier, O is he dead then?¹ my duty all ended,
Who have watched his mould of man, big-boned and hardy-handsome
Pining, pining, till time when reason rambled in it and some
Fatal four disorders, fleshed there, all contended?

Sickness broke him. Impatient, he cursed at first, but mended
Being anointed and all; though a heavenlier heart began some
Months earlier, since I had our sweet reprieve and ransom²
Tendered to him. Ah well, God rest him all road ever he offended!

This seeing the sick endears them to us, us too it endears.
My tongue had taught thee comfort, touch had quenched thy tears,   10
Thy tears that touched my heart, child, Felix, poor Felix Randal;

How far from then forethought of, all thy more boisterous years,
When thou at the random³ grim forge, powerful amidst peers,
Didst fettle for the great grey drayhorse his bright and battering sandal!

Dated, Liverpool, 28 April 1880. Poems (1918).

'AS KINGFISHERS CATCH FIRE'

As kingfishers catch fire, dragonflies draw flame;
As tumbled over rim in roundy wells
Stones ring; like each tucked¹ string tells, each hung bell's

FELIX RANDAL
1   A parishioner of Hopkins.
2   confession, absolution, Eucharist.

3   built of rough stones.
'AS KINGFISHERS CATCH FIRE'
1   plucked (obsolete word).

Bow swung finds tongue to fling out broad its name;
Each mortal thing does one thing and the same:
  Deals out that being indoors each one dwells;
  Selves – goes itself; *myself* it speaks and spells,
Crying *What I do is me: for that I came.*

Í say more: the just man justices;   10
  Keeps gráce: thát keeps all his goings graces;
Acts in God's eye what in God's eye he is –
  Chríst. For Christ plays in ten thousand places,
Lovely in limbs, and lovely in eyes not his
  To the Father through the features of men's faces.

Undated in manuscript. Poems *(1918).*

SPELT FROM SIBYL'S LEAVES[1]

Earnest, earthless, equal, attuneable, | vaulty, voluminous, … stupendous
Evening strains to be tíme's vást, | womb-of-all, home-of-all, hearse-of-all night.
Her fond yellow hornlight wound to the west, | her wild hollow hoarlight hung to the height
Waste; her earliest stars, earlstars, | stárs principal, overbend us,
Fíre-féaturing heaven. For earth | her being has unbound; her dapple is at end, as-
tray or aswarm, all throughther, in throngs; | self ín self steepèd and páshed – qúite
Disremembering, dísmémbering | áll now. Heart, you round me right
With: Óur évening is over us; óur night | whélms, whélms, ánd will end us.

Only the beakleaved boughs dragonish | damask the tool-smooth bleak light; black,
Ever so black on it. Óur tale, O óur oracle! | Lét life, wáned, ah lét life wind   10
Off hér once skéined stained véined varíety | upon, áll on twó spools; párt, pen, páck
Now her áll in twó flocks, twó folds – black, white; | right, wrong; reckon but, reck but, mind
But thése two; wáre of a wórld where bút these | twó tell, each off the óther; of a rack
Where, selfwrung, selfstrung, sheathe- and shelterless, | thóughts agaínst thoughts ín groans grínd.

Written 1884–5. Poems *(1918). Hopkins called it 'the longest sonnet ever made'.*

(CARRION COMFORT)

Not, I'll not, carrion comfort, Despair, not feast on thee;
Not untwist – slack they may be – these last strands of man
In me ór, most weary, cry *I can no more.* I can;
Can something, hope, wish day come, not choose not to be.

But ah, but O thou terrible, why wouldst thou rude on me
Thy wring-world right foot rock? lay a lionlimb against me? scan
With darksome devouring eyes my bruisèd bones? and fan,
O in turns of tempest, me heaped there; me frantic to avoid thee and flee?

Why? That my chaff might fly; my grain lie, sheer and clear.
Nay in all that toil, that coil, since (seems) I kissed the rod,   10
Hand rather, my heart lo! lapped strength, stole joy, would laugh, chéer.
Cheer whom though? The hero whose heaven-handling flung me, fóot tród

SPELT FROM SIBYL'S LEAVES
1 Sibyls: female prophets of ancient Mediterranean world. Best known is the Sibyl of Cumae, who helped Aeneas visit the underworld.

Inspiring wind scattered the leaves in her cave; driven by the god Apollo, she read from these leaves, which were her prophecies.

Me? or me that fought him? O which one? is it each one? That night, that year
Of now done darkness I wretch lay wrestling with (my God!) my God.

Written 1885. Poems (1918). Bridges thought it the sonnet described by Hopkins as 'written in blood'
in May 1885. Title by Bridges.

No worst, there is none. Pitched past pitch of grief,
More pangs will, schooled at forepangs, wilder wring.
Comforter, where, where is your comforting?
Mary, mother of us, where is your relief?
My cries heave, herds-long; huddle in a main, a chief-
woe, world-sorrow; on an age-old anvil wince and sing –
Then lull, then leave off. Fury had shrieked 'No ling-
ering! Let me be fell: force I must be brief'.
O the mind, mind has mountains; cliffs of fall
Frightful, sheer, no-man-fathomed. Hold them cheap   10
May who ne'er hung there. Nor does long our small
Durance deal with that steep or deep. Here! creep,
Wretch, under a comfort serves in a whirlwind: all
Life death does end and each day dies with sleep.

Written 1885. Poems (1918).

To seem the stranger lies my lot, my life
Among strangers. Father and mother dear,
Brothers and sisters are in Christ not near
And he my peace/my parting, sword and strife.

England, whose honour O all my heart woos, wife
To my creating thought, would neither hear
Me, were I pleading, plead nor do I: I wear-
y of idle a being but by where wars are rife.

I am in Ireland now; now I am at a third
Remove. Not but in all removes I can   10
Kind love both give and get. Only what word

Wisest my heart breeds dark heaven's baffling ban
Bars or hell's spell thwarts. This to hoard unheard,
Heard unheeded, leaves me a lonely began.

Written, probably, 1885. Poems (1918).

I wake and feel the fell of dark, not day.
What hours, O what black hours we have spent
This night! what sights you, heart, saw; ways you went!
And more must, in yet longer light's delay.

With witness I speak this. But where I say
Hours I mean years, mean life. And my lament
Is cries countless, cries like dead letters sent
To dearest him that lives alas! away.

I am gall, I am heartburn. God's most deep decree
Bitter would have me taste: my taste was me;   10
Bones built in me, flesh filled, blood brimmed the curse.

Selfyeast of spirit a dull dough sours. I see
The lost are like this, and their scourge to be
As I am mine, their sweating selves; but worse.

Written, probably, 1885. Poems *(1918).*

Patience, hard thing! the hard thing but to pray,
But bid for, Patience is! Patience who asks
Wants war, wants wounds; weary his times, his tasks;
To do without, take tosses, and obey.

Rare patience roots in these, and, these away,
Nowhere. Natural heart's ivy, Patience masks
Our ruins of wrecked past purpose. There she basks
Purple eyes and seas of liquid leaves all day.

We hear our hearts grate on themselves: it kills
To bruise them dearer. Yet the rebellious wills   10
Of us we do bid God bend to him even so.

And where is he who more and more distills
Delicious kindness? – He is patient. Patience fills
His crisp combs, and that comes those ways we know.

Written, probably, 1885. Poems *(1918).*

My own heart let me more have pity on; let
Me live to my sad self hereafter kind,
Charitable; not live this tormented mind
With this tormented mind tormenting yet.

I cast for comfort I can no more get
By groping round my comfortless, than blind
Eyes in their dark can day or thirst can find
Thirst's all-in-all in all a world of wet.

Soul, self; come, poor Jackself, I do advise
You, jaded, let be; call off thoughts awhile   10
Elsewhere; leave comfort root-room; let joy size

At God knows when to God knows what; whose smile
's not wrung, see you; unforeseen times rather – as skies
Betweenpie[1] mountains – lights a lovely mile.

Written, probably, 1885. Poems *(1918).*

TOM'S GARLAND:

Upon the Unemployed

Tom – garlanded with squat and surly steel[1]
Tom; then Tom's fallowbootfellow piles pick[2]

MY OWN HEART...
1 verb – G.M.H. coinage = (?) to produce a dappled lighting effect in
a valley between mountains, or on sides of mountains split by a valley.

TOM'S GARLAND
1 Hopkins explained the *garland* as the hobnails on the Irish navvy's
boots.
2 pick-axe.

By him and rips out rockfire homeforth – sturdy Dick;
Tom Heart-at-ease, Tom Navvy: he is all for his meal
Sure, 's bed now. Low be it: lustily he his low lot (feel
That ne'er need hunger, Tom; Tom seldom sick,
Seldomer heartsore; that treads through, prickproof, thick
Thousands of thorns, thoughts) swings though. Commonweal
Little Í reck ho! lacklevel in, if all had bread:
What! Country is honour enough in all us – lordly head,   10
With heaven's lights high hung round, or, mother-ground
That mammocks,³ mighty foot. But nó way sped,
Nor mind nor mainstrength; gold go garlanded
With, perilous, O nó; nor yet plod safe shod sound;
        Undenizened, beyond bound
Of earth's glory, earth's ease, all; no one, nowhere,
In wide the world's weal; rare gold, bold steel, bare
        In both; care, but share care –
This, by Despair, bred Hangdog dull; by Rage,
Manwolf, worse; and their packs infest the age.⁴   20

Dated, Dromore, September 1887. Poems *(1918).*

THAT NATURE IS A HERACLITEAN FIRE¹ AND OF THE COMFORT OF THE RESURRECTION

Cloud-puffball, torn tufts, tossed pillows | flaunt forth, then chevy on an air-
built thoroughfare: heaven-roysterers, in gay-gangs | they throng; they glitter in marches.
Down roughcast, down dazzling whitewash, | wherever an elm arches,
Shivelights and shadowtackle in long | lashes lace, lance, and pair.
Delightfully the bright wind boisterous | ropes, wrestles, beats earth bare
Of yestertempest's creases; | in pool and rutpeel parches
Squandering ooze to squeezed | dough, crust, dust; stanches, starches
Squadroned masks and manmarks | treadmire toil there
Footfretted in it. Million-fuelèd, | nature's bonfire burns on.
But quench her bonniest, dearest | to her, her clearest-selvèd spark   10
Man, how fast his firedint, | his mark on mind, is gone!
Both are in an unfathomable, all is in an enormous dark
Drowned. O pity and indig | nation! Manshape, that shone
Sheer off, disseveral, a star, | death blots black out; nor mark
      Is any of him at all so stark
But vastness blurs and time | beats level. Enough! the Resurrection,
A heart's-clarion! Away grief's gasping, | joyless days, dejection.
      Across my foundering deck shone
A beacon, an eternal beam. | Flesh fade, and mortal trash
Fall to the residuary worm; | world's wildfire, leave but ash: 20
      In a flash, at a trumpet crash,
I am all at once what Christ is, | since he was what I am, and
This Jack, joke, poor potsherd, | patch, matchwood, immortal diamond,
      Is immortal diamond.

Dated, 26 July 1888, Dublin. Poems *(1918).*

---

3 Navvies 'in gangs and millions, mainly trench, tunnel, blast, and in
other ways disfigure, "mammock" the earth and . . . singly, and superfi-
cially stamp it with their footprints' (G. M. H.).
4 'And this state of things, I say, is the origin of Loafers, Tramps,
Cornerboys, Roughs, Socialists and other pests of society' (G. M. H.).

THAT NATURE IS A HERACLITEAN FIRE
1 early Greek philosopher Heraclitus thought everything is in a state
of fiery flux.

'Thou art indeed just, Lord'

*Justus quidem tu es, Domine, si disputem tecum; verumtamen
justa loquar ad te: Quare via impiorum prosperatur? &c.*[1]

Thou art indeed just, Lord, if I contend
With thee; but, sir, so what I plead is just.
Why do sinners' ways prosper? and why must
Disappointment all I endeavour end?

Wert thou my enemy, O thou my friend,
How wouldst thou worse, I wonder, than thou dost
Defeat, thwart me? Oh, the sots and thralls of lust
Do in spare hours more thrive than I that spend,

Sir, life upon thy cause. See, banks and brakes
Now, leavèd how thick! lacèd they are again   10
With fretty chervil, look, and fresh wind shakes

Them; birds build – but not I build; no, but strain,
Time's eunuch, and not breed one work that wakes.
Mine, O thou lord of life, send my roots rain.

Dated, 17 March 1889. Poems *(1918).*

Edward Carpenter (1844–1929)

Edward Carpenter, English Whitmanite, twentieth-century gay icon, rival of William Morris for post as *the* poetic prophet of the British Labour Movement, was born in Brighton, 29 August 1844, the second son of Charles Carpenter, a retired naval officer with Christian Socialist leanings, and his wife, née Wilson. Carpenter attended Brighton College (1854–63), with a year at the Lycée Imperial in Versailles, 1857. He spent time in Heidelberg before going up to Trinity Hall, Cambridge, to study Theology and Mathematics (1864). He was Tenth Wrangler (i.e. he came out tenth overall in the Maths Finals) in 1868, was ordained an Anglican deacon in 1869 and became Fellow of his College. When F. D. Maurice, leading Christian Socialist, became vicar of St Edward's in Cambridge (1870) he made Carpenter his curate. But a combination of socialist politics and awareness of his own homosexuality – a new self-consciousness assisted by his reading of Whitman – was provoking a crisis of conscience about practising as an Anglican clergyman. His Italian journey of 1873 inducted Carpenter into a neo-pagan fascination with sculpture. He published his poem *Narcissus* in November 1873, and at the end of the 1873–4 academic year he abandoned his Holy Orders and his

Fellowship, heading north for Leeds and the industrial, proletarian regions of England to teach workers in the brand-new University Extension movement. There were never enough workers in his classes for his taste. He wrote a five-act play, *Moses* (1875), made his first pilgrimage to meet Whitman in America (1877), settled in Sheffield (1878), moved in with his proletarian Sheffield friend Albert Fearnenough (1880), studied the Bhagavad Gita, and began work on the great unrhymed sequence of poems he called *Towards Democracy* – a book celebrating northern industrial life and panting with visionary socialist and homoerotic fervour that would, eventually, be on the shelf of every literate Socialist and Trade Unionist in the land. The first version of *Towards Democracy* appeared anonymously in Manchester in mid-1883. By this time Carpenter had fixed on the pattern of existence and desire he would sustain for the rest of his life – writing, manual labour, the romantic sexual-socialist cult of the proletarian male beloved. In the utopian simple-lifer small-holding at Millthorpe, near Chesterfield, that Carpenter purchased with an inheritance in 1883, Whitmanized male sex met Thoreau-ite Waldenism and William Morrisite socialism, with its attendant late Victorian package of vegetarianism, anti-vivisection, fruit-juice drinking and sandals-wearing. Carpenter made his second Whitman pilgrimage in 1884, founded the Sheffield Socialist Society (1885), set his collection of *Chants of Labour* (1888) to music. A visit to Ceylon in 1890 caused Carpenter to stir oriental peace of mind into the simple-lifer brew. *Towards Democracy* grew and grew, as did Carpenter's pamphlets and other writings idealistically combining socialism and homoerotics, with titles like *Homogenic Love and Its Place in a Free Society, Love's Coming of Age* (1896), *Iolaus, an Anthology of Friendship* (1902), *The Intermediate Sex* (1908). George Merrill, Carpenter's second grand proletarian passion, moved to Millthorpe in 1898. Millthorpe became a mecca for male homosexuals in the wake of the Wilde affair, in years legally dangerous for gay men in Britain. E. M. Forster had a visionary sexual awakening on his visit there. In 1922, now an immense cult figure within the politics of the Left and of gender, Carpenter retired, with Merrill, to Guildford. On his eightieth birthday in 1924 the British Trades Union Congress presented him with an Address. Merrill died in 1928. Carpenter, profoundly deaf as well as old, died 28 June 1929. He is buried in Guildford.

From: TOWARDS DEMOCRACY (1883–1905)

Heroes, lovers, judges; despised, outcast, ridiculed; princes and kings and destitute; drudges and slaves; mothers, free women and feminine neuters; actors, parsons, squires, capitalists, rich dinners, fine houses (it is all the same: I go back upon my own words), the parks and the opera; unobtrusive, unguessed, day by day, and year by year; talking loud, talking soft, in the fashion, and out; dreaming of duty, love, release, nature, organisation, hatred, death; ascetic, lusty, genial, maimed, incoherent, proud; by tradition military, money-broking, official, commercial, idle, literary, church, chapel and club; in all forms and in all places; weary yet unwearied; before dawn rising and through the window peering at the untroubled sky; weak yet indomitable; suffering yet filled with exceeding joy –

Age after age, under the Earth, hidden, the womb of the dead generations arising to life again, myriads of seeds, chrysalids, pupæ, cysts, rootlets, transparent white bulbs of souls in Hades, by faith working many miracles; thrills of magnetism through the whole vast frame, summer heat and winter cold and the kiss of the living air; death and decay and weakness and prostration and poisonous inbreaths, and nearer nearer nearer nearer life and joy everlasting.

Through the city crowd pushing wrestling shouldering, against the tide, face after face, breath of liquor, money-grubbing eye, infidel skin, shouts, threats, greetings, smiles, eyes and breasts of love, breathless, clutches of lust, limbs, bodies, torrents, bursts, savage onslaughts, tears, entreaties, tremblings, stranglings, suicidal, the sky, the houses, surges and crests of waves, white faces from afar bearing down nearer nearer, almost touching, and glances unforgotten and meant to be unforgotten.

First published, Towards Democracy *(John Heywood, Manchester and London, 1883), section XXVII. (In subsequent editions, section XIX; finally,* Towards Democracy, *Complete Edition (Swan, Sonnenschein, & Co., Bloomsbury, London; S. Clarke, Manchester, 1905), Part I, XIX.)*

England spreads like a map below me. I see the mud-flats of the Wash striped with water at low tide, the embankments grown with mugwort and sea-asters, and Boston Stump and King's Lynn, and the squaresail brigs in the offing.

Beachy Head stands up beautiful, with white walls and pinnacles, from its slopes of yellow poppy and bugloss; the sea below creeps with a grey fog, the vessels pass and are folded out of sight within it. I hear their foghorns sounding.

Flamborough Head stands up, dividing the waves. Up its steep gullies the fishermen haul their boats; in its caves the waters make perpetual music.

I see the rockbound coast of Anglesey with projecting ribs of wrecks; the hills of Wicklow are faintly outlined across the water. I ascend the mountains of Wales; the tarns and streams lie silver below me, the valleys are dark. Moel Siabod stands up beautiful, and Trifan and Cader Idris in the morning air.

I descend the Wye, and pass through the ancient streets of Monmouth and of Bristol. I thread the feathery birch-haunted coombs of Somerset.

I ascend the high points of the Cotswolds, and look out over the rich vale of Gloucester to the Malvern hills, and see the old city clustering round its Church, and the broad waters of the Severn, and the distant towers of Berkeley Castle.

The river-streams run on below me. The broad deep-bosomed Trent through rich meadows full of cattle, under tall shady trees runs on. I trace it to its birthplace in the hills. I see the Derbyshire Derwent darting in trout-haunted shallows over its stones. I taste and bathe in the clear brown moor-fed water.

I see the sweet-breathed cottage homes and homesteads dotted for miles and miles and miles. It comes near to them. I enter the wheelwright's cottage by the angle of the river. The door stands open against the water, and catches its changing syllables all day long; roses twine, and the smell of the woodyard comes in wafts.

The Castle rock of Nottingham stands up bold over the Trent valley, the tall flagstaff waves its flag, the old market-place is full of town and country folk. The river goes on broadening seaward. I see where it runs beneath the great iron swing-bridges of railroads, there are canals connecting with it, and the sails of the canal-boats gliding on a level with the meadows.

The great sad colorless flood of the Humber stretches before me, the low-lying banks, the fog, the solitary vessels, the brackish marshes and the water-birds; Hull stretches with its docks, vessels are unlading – bags of shell-fish, cargoes of oranges, timber, fish; I see the flat lands beyond Hull, and the enormous flights of pewits.

The Thames runs down – with the sound of many voices. I hear the sound of the saw-mills and flour-mills of the Cotswolds, I can see racing boats and hear the shouts of partisans, villages bask in the sun below me; Sonning and Maidenhead; anglers and artists are hid in nooks among tall willow-herbs; I glide with tub and outrigger past flower-gardens, meadows, parks; parties of laughing girls handle the oars and tiller ropes; Teddington, Twickenham, Richmond, Brentford glide past; I hear the songs, I hear Elizabethan echoes; I come within sound of the roar of London.

I see the woodland and rocky banks of the Tavy and the Tamar, and of the arrowy Dart. The Yorkshire Ouse winds sluggish below me; afar off I catch the Sussex Ouse and the Arun, breaking seaward through their gaps in the Downs; I look down from the Cheshire moors upon the Dee.

In their pride the beautiful cities of England stand up before me; from the midst of her antique elms and lilac and laburnum haunted gardens the grey gateways and towers of Cambridge stand up; ivy-grown Warwick peeps out of thick foliage; I see Canterbury and Winchester and Chester, and Worcester proud by her river-side, and the ancient castles – York and Lancaster looking out seaward, and Carlisle; I see the glistening of carriage wheels and the sumptuous shine of miles of sea frontage at Brighton and Hastings and Scarborough; Clifton climbs to her heights over the Avon; the ruins of Whitby Abbey are crusted with spray.

I hear the ring of hammers in the ship-yards of Chatham and Portsmouth and Keyham, and look down upon wildernesses of masts and dock-basins. I see the observatory at Greenwich and catch the pulses of star-taken time spreading in waves over the land. I see the delicate spider-web of the telegraphs, and the rush of the traffic of the great main lines, North, West, and South. I see the solid flow of business men northward across London Bridge in the morning, and the ebb at evening. I see the eternal systole and diastole of exports and imports through the United Kingdom, and the armies of those who assist in the processes of secretion and assimilation – and the great markets.

I explore the palaces of dukes – the parks and picture galleries – Chatsworth, Hardwicke, Arundel; and the numberless old Abbeys. I walk through the tall-windowed hospitals and asylums of the great cities and hear chants caught up and wandering from ward to ward.

I see all over the land the beautiful centuries-grown villages and farmhouses nestling down among their trees; the dear old lanes and footpaths and the great clean highways connecting; the fields, every one to the people known by its own name, and hedgerows and little straggling copses, and village greens; I see the great sweeps of country, the rich wealds of Sussex and Kent, the orchards and deep lanes of Devon, the willow-haunted flats of Huntingdon, Cambridge and South Lincolnshire; Sherwood Forest and the New Forest, and the light pastures of the North and South Downs; the South and Midland and Eastern agricultural districts, the wild moorlands of the North and West, and the intermediate districts of coal and iron.

The oval-shaped manufacturing heart of England lies below me; at night the clouds flicker in the lurid glare; I hear the sob and gasp of pumps and the solid beat of steam and tilt-hammers; I see streams of pale lilac and saffron-tinted fire. I see the swarthy Vulcan-reeking towns, the belching chimneys, the slums, the liquor-shops, chapels, dancing saloons, running grounds, and blameless remote villa residences.

I see the huge warehouses of Manchester, the many-storied mills, the machinery, the great bale-laden drays, the magnificent horses; I walk through the Liverpool Exchange; the brokers stand in knots; the greetings, the frock-coats, the rosebuds; the handling and comparing of cotton samples.

Leeds lies below me; I hear the great bell; I see the rush along Boar Lane and Briggate. I enter the hot machine shops, smelling of oil and wooldust. I see Sheffield among her hills, and the white dashing of her many water-wheels, and the sulphurous black cloud going up to heaven in her midst.

Newcastle I recognise, and her lofty bridge; and I look out over the river gates of the Mersey.

First published, Towards Democracy (1883), Section XLVI. (In subsequent editions, Section XXXVIII;
finally (1905), Part I, XXXVIII.)

In silence I wait and accept all – the glare of misapprehension I accept – I sit at the fashionable dinner-table and accept what is brought to me.

I am a painter on the house-side, the sight of the distant landscape pleases me, and the scraps of conversation caught from the street below. My back aches singling turnips through the long hot day; my fingers freeze getting potatoes.

I help the farmer drive his scared cattle home at midnight by the fitful flicker of lightning. I go mowing at early morning while the twilight creeps in the North East – I sleep in the hot hours – and mow again on into the night.

I am a seeing unseen atom traveling with others through space or remaining centuries in one place; again I resume a body and disclose myself.

I am one of the people who spend their lives sitting on their haunches in drawing-rooms and studies; I grow gradually feebler and fretfuler. I am a boy once more in tall hat and gloves walking wearily among crowds of well-dressed (hopelessly well-dressed) people, up and down a certain pro-menade.

I enter the young prostitute's chamber, where he is arranging the photographs of fashionable beauties and favorite companions, and stay with him; we are at ease and understand each other.

I dance at the village feast in the upper room of a public; my partner shows me the steps and figures. The elderly harper, so noble and dignified, accompanies his son's fiddle – or goes round to collect the pence – but all the while his thoughts are with his only daughter in Australia.

The wheel turns, but whatever it brings uppermost is well.

First published, Towards Democracy (1883), Section LIII. (In subsequent editions, section XLV;
finally (1905), Part I, XLV.)

Beautiful is the figure of the lusty full-grown groom on his superb horse: the skin of the animal is saturated with love.

Radiant health!

O kisses of sun and wind, tall fir-trees and moss-covered rocks! O boundless joy of Nature on the mountain tops – coming back at last to you!

Wild songs in sight of the sea, wild dances along the sands, glances of the risen moon, echoes of old old refrains coming down from unimagined times!

O rolling through the air superb prophetic spirit of Man, pulse of divine health equalising the universe, vast over all the world expanding spirit!

O joy of the liberated soul (finished purpose and acquittal of civilisation), daring all things – light step, life held in the palm of the hand! O swift and eager delight of battle, fierce passion of love destroying and destroying the body!

Eternal and glorious War! Liberation! the soul like an eagle – from gaping wounds and death – rushing forth screaming into its vast and eternal heaven.

See! the divine mother goes forth with her babe (all creation circles round) – God dwells once more in a woman's womb; friend goes with friend, flesh cleaves to flesh, the path that rounds the universe.

O every day sweet and delicious food! Kisses to the lips of sweet-smelling fruit and bread, milk and green herbs. Strong well-knit muscles, quick-healing glossy skin, body for kisses all over!

Radiant health! to breathe, O joy! to sleep, ah! never enough to be expressed!

For the taste of fruit ripening warm in the sun, for the distant sight of the deep liquid sea!

For the sight of the naked bodies of the bathers, bathing by the hot sea-banks, the pleasant consciousness of those who are unashamed, the glance of their eyes, the beautiful proud step of the human animal on the sand;

For the touch of the air on my face or creeping over my unclothed body, for the rustling sound of it in the trees, and the appearance of their tall stems springing so lightly from the earth!

Joy, joy and thanks for ever.

First published, Towards Democracy *(1883), Section LXXII. (In subsequent editions, Section LXIV; finally (1905), Part I, LXIV.)*

In a Manufacturing Town

As I walked restless and despondent through the gloomy city,

And saw the eager unresting to and fro – as of ghosts in some sulphurous Hades;

And saw the crowds of tall chimneys going up, and the pall of smoke covering the sun, covering the earth, lying heavy against the very ground;

And saw the huge refuse-heaps writhing with children picking them over,

And the ghastly half-roofless smoke-blackened houses, and the black river flowing below;

As I saw these, and as I saw again far away the Capitalist quarter,

With its villa residences and its high-walled gardens and its well-appointed carriages, and its face turned away from the wriggling poverty which made it rich;

As I saw and remembered its drawing-room airs and affectations, and its wheezy pursy Church-going and its gas-reeking heavy-furnished rooms and its scent-bottles and its other abominations –

I shuddered:

For I felt stifled, like one who lies half-conscious – knowing not clearly the shape of the evil – in the grasp of some heavy nightmare.

Then out of the crowd descending towards me came a little ragged boy:

Came – from the background of dirt disengaging itself – an innocent wistful child-face, begrimed like the rest but strangely pale, and pensive before its time.

And in an instant (it was as if a trumpet had been blown in that place) I saw it all clearly, the lie I saw and the truth, the false dream and the awakening.

For the smoke-blackened walls and the tall chimneys, and the dreary habitations of the poor, and the drearier habitations of the rich, crumbled and conveyed themselves away as if by magic;

And instead, in the backward vista of that face, I saw the joy of free open life under the sun:

The green sun-delighting earth and rolling sea I saw,

The free sufficing life – sweet comradeship, few needs and common pleasures – the needless endless burdens all cast aside,

Not as a sentimental vision, but as a fact and a necessity existing, I saw

In the backward vista of that face.

Stronger than all combinations of Capital, wiser than all the Committees representative of Labor, the simple need and hunger of the human heart.

Nothing more is needed.

All the books of political economy ever written, all the proved impossibilities, are of no account.

The smoke-blackened walls and tall chimneys duly crumble and convey themselves away;

The falsehood of a gorged and satiated society curls and shrivels together like a withered leaf,
Before the forces which lie dormant in the pale and wistful face of a little child.

First published, Towards Democracy, *2nd edn (John Heywood, Manchester and London, 1885). (In Second Section,*
'Of Joy in Thee' ('O Freedom, beautiful beyond compare': in 3rd edn, 1892); 'Part II: Children of Freedom', 1905.)

The Elder Soldier in the Brotherhood to the Younger

Dear comrade, at whose feet thus now I kneel,
Of you perhaps so soon to be seen no more –
Here I give you my charge, that afterwards remembering and desiring me,
You may find me again in these others.
Slowly out of their faces I will emerge to you – lo! I swear it,
By the falling rain and dimpled thunderclouds in the East I swear it –
[To become your life whom I have loved so long]
With love absorbing, joy and blessedness enclosing,
I will emerge to you.
That you now to other comrades, and these again to others,
Over the whole world may bear the glad covenant, perfected, finished –
To form an indissoluble union and compact, a brotherhood unalterable,
Far-pervading, fresh and invisible as the wind, united in Freedom –
A golden circle of stamens, hidden beneath the petals of humanity,
And guarding the sacred ark.
Through heroisms and deaths and sacrifices,
   Always for the poor and despised, always for the outcast and oppressed,
   Through kinship with Nature, and the free handling of all forms and customs,
   Through the treasured teaching of inspired ones – never lost and never wholly given to the
world, but always emerging –
   Through love, faithful love and comradeship, at last emancipating the soul into that other realm
(of freedom and joy) into which it is permitted to no mortal to enter –
   Thus to realise the indissoluble compact, to reveal the form of humanity.
   To you, dear comrade, I transmit this charge – bequeathed also to me –
   In love remaining faithful to you, as now, never to change,
   Through all times and vicissitudes faithful faithful to you.
   Here now at your feet, leaning on your knees, in your eyes deep-looking,
   All that I have said I confirm.

First published, Towards Democracy, *3rd edn. (T. Fisher Unwin, 1892), in 4th Section,*
'Little heart within thy cage' (1905: 'Part III: After Civilisation').

Parted Lips

Parted lips, between which love dwells –
   Only a little space of breath and shadow,
   Yet here the gate of all the world to me

First published, Towards Democracy, *3rd edn. (1892), in 4th Section, 'Little heart*
within thy cage' (1905: 'Part III: After Civilisation').

Robert (Seymour) Bridges (1844–1930)

Robert Bridges, Poet Laureate, prosodist, language refor-mer, hymn-writer, confidant and editor of Gerard Manley Hopkins, was born, 23 October 1844, at Walmer, Kent, into a prosperous land-owning family. He was the fourth son and eighth child of John Thomas Bridges and Harriet Affleck, daughter of a vicar (and baronet). Sale of the family lands upon John Bridges's premature death in 1853 (aged forty-seven) meant Robert would never be compelled to work for his living. In 1854 his mother mar-ried the Revd John Molesworth, vicar of Rochdale, so that the Lancashire vicarage became the family home. Mean-time, aged ten, Bridges entered Eton, where he became the complete House Captain. He played in the famous Wall Game, and was drawn both to Puseyism and to his poetic and Anglo-Catholic cousin Digby Mackworth Dol-ben. The beauty of holiness was to be subsumed for Bridges into the holiness of beauty, but he did nonetheless remain great friends with Gerard Hopkins, the future Jesuit poet, who entered Balliol in the same Oxford gen-eration as Bridges, who went up to Corpus Christi College to read Classics in October 1863. At Corpus, Bridges was a great oarsman, drifted away from Puseyism, was deeply upset by the death of his younger brother Edward in 1866 and his friend Dolben in 1867. (Bridges's poetry would be filled with fine elegiac strains.) He gained a Sec-ond Class in his Literae Humaniores Finals in 1867; went travelling in the Middle East; studied German in Germany (with his Corpus friend William Sanday, the great biblical scholar-to-be). He began serious medical studies at St Bartholomew's Hospital in London in 1871; produced his first volume of *Poems* privately in 1873 (later sup-pressed); graduated Bachelor of Medicine in 1874; trav-elled Italy for six months with another great friend, Harry Ellis Wooldridge, dedicatee of the 1873 *Poems*, later Slade Professor of Fine Art at Oxford (they shared a house until 1877). Bridges practised medicine in London hos-pitals, living with his mother in Georgian splendour in Bedford Square (where he entertained Hopkins not long after his first sermon at the Jesuits' Farm Street Church, August 1878). Pulmonary illness put a stop to Dr Bridges's London existence in June 1881. In 1882 he settled with his mother in the Manor House at Yattenden, Berkshire. Two years later he married Monica Waterhouse, daughter of the architect Alfred Waterhouse, and they had three children. Bridges conducted the Yattenden church choir, and even-tually produced, with Wooldridge, the influential *Yattenden Hymnal* (1895–9). A hundred hymns with music, beauti-fully printed by Horace Hart of the Oxford University Press, this traditionally Anglican collection, Reformation-minded, resistant to the enthusiasms of both Evangelical-ism and Romanism, containing several of Bridges's own hymns, especially his Latin translations (the music was mainly sixteenth and seventeenth century), reflected the instincts and interests of this rather retired writer's poems and critical writings. The aesthetic was Anglican and dignified (his essay 'A Practical Discourse on Some Principles of Hymn-Singing', 1899–1900, stresses the need for dignified hymn-tunes), and the prosodic polish was high. Questions of prosody preoccupied Bridges greatly – as his many published discussions of Milton's verse, his important correspondence with Hopkins and his most significant edition of Hopkins's *Poems* (1918) all show. The poems 'London Snow' and 'On a Dead Child' are examples of his work in stressed or accentual verse, whose principles he explicated, for example, in the 1921 edition of his book *Milton's Prosody*. Bridges's steady stream of verses from 1873, and verse-dramas from 1885 – sober in tone, prosodically experimental in form, displaying a reserved classicist's interest in romantic subjects like land-scape and weather – had little impact until the Oxford Uni-versity Press produced his *Poetical Works* in 1912. The world was nonetheless surprised at his being chosen as Poet Laureate in 1913 (the journals expected Rudyard Kipling). The founding of the Society for Pure English in the same year (with the lexicographer Henry Bradley, Sir Walter Raleigh and Logan Pearsall Smith) seemed more Bridges's thing. And after the Great War Bridges did indeed devote much of his time to writing SPE tracts. But being Laureate did wonders for his reputation as a poet. *The Spirit of Man* (1916), an anthology of verse and prose, 'designed to bring fortitude and peace of mind to his countrymen in wartime', was thought to be proper Laureate work, and proved a great seller. In 1924, turned eighty, Bridges spent some successful months at the Uni-versity of Michigan at Ann Arbor. His *New Poems* (1925) went down well, and his long poem in free Alexandrines ruminating on aesthetic and spiritual questions, *The Testa-ment of Beauty* (1929), was a runaway smash hit (fourteen impressions in its first year). That same year Bridges deliv-ered one of the first ever wireless broadcast lectures – on *Poetry* – and received the Order of Merit. He died, 21 April 1930, at Chilswell House, his home since 1907 on Boar's Hill, overlooking Oxford (a district known to local wags as Parnassus, because so many poetic persons lived there).

LONDON SNOW

When men were all asleep the snow came flying,
In large white flakes falling on the city brown,
Stealthily and perpetually settling and loosely lying,
   Hushing the latest traffic of the drowsy town;
Deadening, muffling, stifling its murmurs failing;
Lazily and incessantly floating down and down:
   Silently sifting and veiling road, roof and railing;
Hiding difference, making unevenness even,
Into angles and crevices softly drifting and sailing.
   All night it fell, and when full inches seven   10
It lay in the depth of its uncompacted lightness,
The clouds blew off from a high and frosty heaven;
   And all woke earlier for the unaccustomed brightness
Of the winter dawning, the strange unheavenly glare:
The eye marvelled – marvelled at the dazzling whiteness;
   The ear hearkened to the stillness of the solemn air;
No sound of wheel rumbling nor of foot falling,
And the busy morning cries came thin and spare.
   Then boys I heard, as they went to school, calling,
They gathered up the crystal manna to freeze   20
Their tongues with tasting,[1] their hands with snowballing;
   Or rioted in a drift, plunging up to the knees;
Or peering up from under the white-mossed wonder,
'O look at the trees!' they cried, 'O look at the trees!'
   With lessened load a few carts creak and blunder,
Following along the white deserted way,
A country company long dispersed asunder:
   When now already the sun, in pale display
Standing by Paul's high dome,[2] spread forth below
His sparkling beams, and awoke the stir of the day.   30
   For now doors open and war is waged with the snow;
And trains of sombre men, past tale of number,
Tread long brown paths as towards their toil they go:
   But even for them a while no cares encumber
Their minds diverted; the daily word is unspoken,
The daily thoughts of labour and sorrow slumber
At the sight of the beauty that greets them, for the charm they have broken.

Poems: Third Series (E. W. D. Bumpus, 1880).

ON A DEAD CHILD

Perfect little body, without fault or stain on thee,
   With promise of strength and manhood full and fair!
      Though cold and stark and bare,
The bloom and the charm of life doth awhile remain on thee.

Thy mother's treasure wert thou; – alas! no longer
   To visit her heart with wondrous joy; to be
      Thy father's pride; – ah, he
Must gather his faith together, and his strength make stronger.

LONDON SNOW   2   St Paul's Cathedral.
1   manna, the food God provided for the wandering Israelites, was
white, like 'hoar frost', Exodus 16.14.

To me, as I move thee now in the last duty,
  Dost thou with a turn or gesture anon respond;   10
        Startling my fancy fond
With a chance attitude of the head, a freak of beauty.

Thy hand clasps, as 'twas wont, my finger, and holds it:
  But the grasp is the clasp of Death, heart breaking and stiff;
        Yet feels to my hand as if
'Twas still thy will, thy pleasure and trust that enfolds it.

So I lay thee there, thy sunken eyelids closing, –
  Go lie thou there in thy coffin, thy last little bed! –
        Propping thy wise, sad head,
Thy firm, pale hands across thy chest disposing.   20

So quiet! doth the change content thee? – Death, whither hath he taken thee?
  To a world, do I think, that rights the disaster of this?
        The vision of which I miss,
Who weep for the body, and wish but to warm thee and awaken thee?

Ah! little at best can all our hopes avail us
  To lift this sorrow, or cheer us, when in the dark,
        Unwilling, alone we embark,
And the things we have seen and have known and have heard of, fail us.

Poems: Third Series *(1880)*.

I never shall love the snow again
      Since Maurice died:
With corniced drift it blocked the lane,
And sheeted in a desolate plain
      The country side.

The trees with silvery rime bedight
      Their branches bare.
By day no sun appeared; by night
The hidden moon shed thievish light
      In the misty air.   10

We fed the birds that flew around
      In flocks to be fed:
No shelter in holly or brake they found.
The speckled thrush on the frozen ground
      Lay frozen and dead.

We skated on stream and pond; we cut
      The crinching snow
To Doric temple or Arctic hut;
We laughed and sang at nightfall, shut
      By the fireside glow.   20

Yet grudged we our keen delights before
      Maurice should come.
We said, In-door or out-of-door
We shall love life for a month or more,
      When he is home.

They brought him home; 'twas two days late
      For Christmas day:

Wrapped in white, in solemn state,
A flower in his hand, all still and straight
  Our Maurice lay.   30

And two days ere the year outgave
  We laid him low.
The best of us truly were not brave,
When we laid Maurice down in his grave
  Under the snow.

   The Shorter Poems of Robert Bridges, *Book V (George Bell & Sons, 1894).*

The north wind came up yesternight
  With the new year's full moon,
And rising as she gained her height,
  Grew to a tempest soon.
Yet found he not on heaven's face
  A task of cloud to clear;
There was no speck that he might chase
  Off the blue hemisphere,
Nor vapour from the land to drive:
  The frost-bound country held   10
Nought motionable or alive,
  That 'gainst his wrath rebelled.
There scarce was hanging in the wood
  A shrivelled leaf to reave;
No bud had burst its swathing hood
  That he could rend or grieve:
Only the tall tree-skeletons,
  Where they were shadowed all,
Wavered a little on the stones,
  And on the white church-wall.   20

– Like as an artist in his mood,
  Who reckons all as nought,
So he may quickly paint his nude,
  Unutterable thought:
So Nature in a frenzied hour
  By day or night will show
Dim indications of the power
  That doometh man to woe.
Ah, many have my visions been,
  And some I know full well: 30
I would that all that I have seen
  Were fit for speech to tell. –

And by the churchyard as I came,
  It seemed my spirit passed
Into a land that hath no name,
  Grey, melancholy and vast;
Where nothing comes: but Memory,
  The widowed queen of Death
Reigns, and with fixed, sepulchral eye
  All slumber banisheth.   40
Each grain of writhen dust, that drapes
  That sickly, staring shore,
Its old chaotic change of shapes
  Remembers evermore.

And ghosts of cities long decayed
   And ruined shrines of Fate
Gather the paths, that Time hath made
   Foolish and desolate.
Nor winter there hath hope of spring,
   Nor the pale night of day,   50
Since the old king with scorpion sting
   Hath done himself away.

        *   *   *

The morn was calm; the wind's last breath
   Had fal'n: in solemn hush
The golden moon went down beneath
   The dawning's crimson flush.

The Shorter Poems, *Book V (1894)*.

L. S. (Louisa Sarah) Bevington (Mrs Ignatz Guggenheimer) (also 'Arbor Leigh') (1845–95)

Louisa Sarah Bevington, the anarchist poet, was born in 1845, eldest of the eight children (seven were girls) of Alexander Bevington and his wife Louisa, who were Quakers. She grew up in London. Her first pamphlet of poems, *Keynotes*, verses anguishing mildly about religion and society, appeared in 1876, under the pseudonym Arbor Leigh (she'd obviously been reading her Elizabeth Barrett Browning). She was a highly moralized rationalist, rather on the George Eliot plan. Like George Eliot she was greatly influenced by Herbert Spencer's social-evolutionary ethicity. In her mild-mannered way a finely radical critic of the orthodox, Christian, conservative, imperialist centre in British life, she was an important presence in radical London politics, alongside now better-remembered polemicists such as William Morris and G. B. Shaw. *Poems, Lyrics, and Sonnets* was published in 1882 under her own name. In 1883 she married a German artist, Ignatz Guggenheimer, though the marriage probably did not last. By the end of the eighties she had taken up with the London anarchists – a movement focused by the presence in the capital of the exiled Russian Prince Peter Kropotkin – and she wrote a great deal for anarchist papers such as *Freedom* and *Liberty*. Her *Why I Am An Expropriationist* appeared in 1894 together with Morris's *Why I Am A Communist* in a pamphlet from James Tochatti's 'Liberty' Press (the *Why I Am* series). A letter of Bevington's was used in order to prove that an anarchist attempt to blow up the Greenwich Observatory in 1894 – the germ of Conrad's novel *The Secret Agent* – was a police set-up. Bevington's *Liberty Lyrics* – for peace, freedom, the future, against money and religion, but always gently so – were published in 1895 by Tochatti. She died at the end of 1895. In her pamphlet *Anarchism and Violence*, published posthumously by Tochatti, she once again, and in characteristically measured strains, attacked the Church, property, credit, law, subjection. 'Bomb-throwing is not Anarchism'; but it is occasionally necessary in the fight against 'poverty, parasitism, degeneration, despair, and the wholesale tormenting of man by man'.

TWILIGHT

Grey the sky, and growing dimmer,
   And the twilight lulls the sea.
Half in vagueness, half in glimmer,
   Nature shrouds her mystery.

What have all the hours been spent for?
   Why the on and on of things?
Why, eternity's procession
   Of the days and evenings?

Hours of sunshine, hours of gloaming,
    Wing their unexplaining flight,   10
With a measured punctuation
    Of unconsciousness, at night.

Just at sunset was translucence,
    When the west was all aflame;
So I asked the sea a question,
    And a kind of answer came.

Is there nothing but Occurrence?
    Tho' each detail seem an Act,
Is that whole we deem so pregnant
    But unemphasizëd Fact?   20

Or, when dusk is in the hollows
    Of the hillside and the wave,
Are things just so much in earnest
    That they cannot but be grave?

Nay, the lesson of the twilight
    Is as simple as 'tis deep;
Acquiescence: acquiescence:
    And the coming on of sleep.

Keynotes, *by Arbor Leigh (Thomas Scott, Upper Norwood, London, 1876).*

'EGOISME À DEUX'[1]

When the great universe hung nebulous
    Betwixt the unprevented and the need,
Was it foreseen that you and I should be? –
        Was it decreed?

While time leaned onward through eternities,
    Unrippled by a breath and undistraught,
Lay there at leisure Will that we should breathe? –
        Waited a Thought?

When the warm swirl of chaos-elements
    Fashioned the chance that woke to sentient strife,   10
Did there a Longing seek, and hasten on
        Our mutual life?

That flux of many accidents but now
    That brought you near and linked your hand in mine, –
That fused our souls in love's most final faith, –
        Was it divine?

Poems, Lyrics, and Sonnets *(Elliot Stock, 1882).*

'EGOISME À DEUX'
1   Egoism for two.

STANZA

The sweetest song that a poet sings,
Though to your dull ear it be speech with wings,
He, singing, hears with a pent distress,
'Tis a cypher that stands for his speechlessness.

Poems, Lyrics, and Sonnets *(1882)*.

LOVE AND LANGUAGE

Love that is alone with love
    Makes solitudes of throngs;
Then why not songs of silences, –
    Sweet silences of songs?

Parts need words: the perfect whole
    Is silent as the dead;
When I offered you my soul
    Heard you what I *said?*

Poems, Lyrics, and Sonnets *(1882)*.

AM I TO LOSE YOU?

'Am I to lose you now?' The words were light;
    You spoke them, hardly seeking a reply,
    That day I bid you quietly 'Good-bye,'
And sought to hide my soul away from sight.
The question echoed, dear, through many a night, –
    My question, not your own – most wistfully;
    'Am I to lose him?' – asked my heart of me;
'Am I to lose him now, and lose him quite?'

And only you can tell me. Do you care
    That sometimes we in quietness should stand   10
    As fellow-solitudes, hand firm in hand,
And thought with thought and hope with hope compare?
What is your answer? Mine must ever be,
    'I greatly need your friendship: leave it me.'

Poems, Lyrics, and Sonnets *(1882)*.

Eugene (Jacob) Lee-Hamilton (1845–1907)

Eugene Lee-Hamilton was born in London, 6 January 1845, but brought up in France by his mother Matilda (Abadam) Lee-Hamilton, his father James having died when the boy was very young. His mother's second husband was Henry Ferguson Paget (they married in Paris), a Polish engineer in exile, father of Violet Paget, who became known as a novelist and critic under the name Vernon Lee. In 1864 Eugene returned to England as a student of French and German at Oriel College, Oxford. He never took a degree, but worked in the diplomatic corps in various embassies in France, Switzerland and Portugal, until in 1875 he had some sort of nervous collapse and

became bedridden for the next twenty years. He lived in Florence with his mother and half-sister Violet, estivating at Siena or Bagni di Lucca, talking a great deal, entertaining the cosmopolitan glitterati from his supine couch (Henry James was just one who would call by), writing numerous verses, especially sonnets, which were published in a steady stream, in volumes such as *Imaginary Sonnets* (1888) and *Sonnets of the Wingless Hours* (1894) – highly dyspeptic, morose verse, alert to the cosmic miseries to be found in the grim drama *The Fountain of Youth* (1891) as much as to personal pains and miseries. By 1896, though, he was ready to arise from his bed of sickness, visited North America, and returned, surprisingly renovated, to marry, in Hampshire in July 1898, Annie E. Holdsworth, the Jamaican-born feminist novelist. They lived in Italy, jointly produced poetry (the surprisingly cosy *Forest Notes*, 1899, has both names on its title page and is dedicated tweely 'To each Other and To *The little velvet-coated Creatures of the Woods*'), and they had a daughter; but, Lee-Hamilton's luck and poetic felicity being destined, clearly, to be very short-lived, she died very young in 1904. Her death is duly the subject of the elegiac sonnets of the posthumous *Mimma Bella* (1909). He translated Dante's *Inferno* (1898) and pro-duced a couple of novels, *The Lord of the Dark Red Star*, being the Story of the Supernatural Influences in the Life of an Italian Des-pot of the Thirteenth Century (1903) and *The Romances of the Fountain* (1905). In 1903 a large selection of his work came out as *Dramatic Sonnets, Poems, and Ballads*, introduced by William Sharp. But in his last years his grief over his dead daughter was unabated and, greatly depressed, he suffered a paralysing stroke, and died in Bagni di Lucca, 7 September 1907. He is buried in the new Protestant cem-etery in Florence. Annie Holdsworth carried on writing until at least 1913 (*The Book of Anna*). She died outside Eng-land, and her death-date remains unknown.

FAIRY GODMOTHERS

I think the Fairies to my christening came;
　But they were wicked sprites, and envious elves,
　Who brought me gall, as bitter as themselves,
In tiny tankards wrought with fairy flame.

They wished me love of books – each little dame –
　With power to read no book upon my shelves;
　Fair limbs – for palsy; – Dead Sea fruits by twelves
And every bitter blessing you can name.

But one good Elf there was; and she let fall
　A single drop of Poesy's wine of gold   10
In every little tankard full of gall:

So year by year, as woes and pains grow old,
　The little golden drop is in them all;
But bitterer is the cup than can be told.

Sonnets of the Wingless Hours *(Elliot Stock, 1894)*.

KING CHRISTMAS

Now Old King Christmas, bearded hoary-white,
　Comes with his holly and carousing noise,
　Barons of beef, mince pies, and wassail joys,
And flame surrounds the pudding blue and bright;

And now the fir-trees, as he comes in sight,
　Acclaimed by eager blue-eyed girls and boys,
　Burst into tinsel fruit and glittering toys,
And turn into a pyramid of light.

I love, in fancy, still to see them all,
　Those happy children round the dazzling tree   10
That fills the room with scents of fir and wax;

For still I love that life's sweet things should fall
　Into the lap of others; though, for me,
The gift of Christmas is but pain that racks.

Sonnets of the Wingless Hours *(1894)*.

WHAT THE SONNET IS

Fourteen small broidered berries on the hem
  Of Circe's mantle, each of magic gold;
  Fourteen of lone Calypso's tears that roll'd
Into the sea, for pearls to come of them;

Fourteen clear signs of omen in the gem
  With which Medea human fate foretold;
  Fourteen small drops, which Faustus, growing old,
Craved of the Fiend, to water Life's dry stem.

It is the pure white diamond Dante brought
  To Beatrice; the sapphire Laura wore   10
When Petrarch cut it sparkling out of thought;

The ruby Shakespeare hewed from his heart's core;
  The dark deep emerald that Rossetti wrought
For his own soul, to wear for evermore.

Sonnets of the Wingless Hours *(1894)*.

SUNKEN GOLD

In dim green depths rot ingot-laden ships,
  While gold doubloons that from the drowned hand fell
  Lie nestled in the ocean-flower's bell
With Love's gemmed rings once kissed by now dead lips.
And round some wrought-gold cup the sea-grass whips
  And hides lost pearls, near pearls still in their shell,
  Where sea-weed forests fill each ocean dell,
And seek dim sunlight with their countless tips.

So lie the wasted gifts, the long-lost hopes,
  Beneath the now hushed surface of myself,   10
In lonelier depths than where the diver gropes.
They lie deep, deep; but I at times behold
  In doubtful glimpses, on some reefy shelf,
The gleam of irrecoverable gold.

Apollo and Marsyas and Other Poems *(Elliot Stock, 1884)*.

SONG OF THE ARROW-POISONERS

    When nature was fashioned
      The vapours of Hell
    Crept through to the surface,
      Insidious and fell.

    Of plants that are deadly
      They fattened the root;
    The sap of destruction
      Filled berry and fruit;

    While trickles of horror,
      In numberless snakes,   10

Ran live through the grasses
   That summer awakes.

And tetanus followed
   The rattlesnake's grasp,
And palsy the ripple
   Of cobra and asp.

The juice of creation
   Is venom and blood,
And torture is master
   Of earth and of flood.   20

All nature is teeming
   With claw and with fang:
Above is the beauty,
   Beneath is the pang.

In shadow and flowers
   The leopardess lies;
Two living green embers
   Glow wild in her eyes.

The sea is all sunshine;
   The shark is beneath;   30
A wave of red water
   Wells up from his teeth.

But Man is the monarch
   Of torture and death;
The breath of his nostrils
   Is murder's own breath.

The hunter of hunters
   Who hunts his own race,
Relentless and savage,
   From off the earth's face.   40

So dip we the arrows
   In juices of night,
That madness and horror
   May follow their flight;

And waves as of lava
   May run in each vein,
Till lethargy deadens
   Unthinkable pain.

The Fountain of Youth: A Fantastic Tragedy in Five Acts *(Elliot Stock, 1891),*
   Act III, sc.i. The singers are female, a chorus of 'Venom-girls', handmaidens of the
   Indian Sorceress, worshippers of 'the great and all-pervading god of Cosmic Cruelty'.
   The drama is dedicated 'To Vernon Lee, With Her Brother's Love'.

Noon's Dream-Song

The day is long; the worn Noon dreams.
He shifts in vain, to ease his pain,
And through what seems, he hears a song:

A forest song, whose high note seems
To tell of pain, endured in vain,
And fills his dreams with things lost long.

A dead love seems to thrill that song;
Hope nursed in vain, years passed in pain,
Leaves fallen long, a tide that dreams.

Then, as he dreams, the shades grow long;   10
And, in his pain, he moans in vain
While fades the song of what but seems.

Forest Notes, *by Eugene and Annie Lee-Hamilton (Grant Richards, 1899).*

AMONG THE FIRS

And what a charm is in the rich hot scent
  Of old fir forests heated by the sun,
  Where drops of resin down the rough bark run
And needle litter breathes its wonderment.

The old fir forests heated by the sun,
  Their thought shall linger like the lingering scent,
  Their beauty haunt us, and a wonderment
Of moss, of fern, of cones, of rills that run.

The needle litter breathes a wonderment;
  The crimson crans¹ are sparkling in the sun;   10
  From tree to tree the scampering squirrels run;
The hum of insects blends with heat and scent.

The drops of resin down the rough bark run:
  And riper, ever riper, grows the scent:
  But eve has come, to end the wonderment
And slowly up the tree trunk climbs the sun.

Forest Notes *(1899).*

William Canton (1845–1926)

William Canton was born in China, 27 October 1845, the eldest son of Thomas and Mary Canton. His father, a colonial civil servant, died in Jamaica when William was nine. Canton went to school in France, studied for the Roman Catholic priesthood at Douai, but converted to Protestantism. From 1867 he hacked about in London, teaching, doing bits of journalism, getting excited by the great wave of contemporary interest in geology and other new sciences. His long poem 'Through the Ages: The Legend of a Stone Axe' (*New Quarterly*, 1873) attracted the scientists' interest by its effort to talk science in verse. From 1876 Canton worked as a journalist in Glasgow, but

came to London in 1891 where he would work for the rest of his life in variously Christian publishing and writing work – as general manager for Isbister the publisher, subeditor of the *Contemporary Review*, a big contributor of prose and verse to *Good Words*, official historian of the British and Foreign Bible Society, and author of popular little Bible Society story books. He was married twice – in 1874 to Emma Moore, who died in 1880, and in 1882 to Annie Taylor. The only child of the first marriage, a girl, died in 1877; the daughter of the second marriage, Winifred Vida (she had one brother), died at the age of eleven in 1901. The 'W.V.' books – for his daughter and

AMONG THE FIRS
1   cranberries (?).

about her and her dead sister, culminating in *In Memory of W.V.* (1901), a highly elegiac collection – earned Canton a wide audience. *A Lost Epic and Other Poems* appeared in 1887, *The Comrades, Poems Old and New* in 1902. The Victorian readers of Canton's poetry valued him most for his verses about and for children, and for attention to the long vistas of evolutionary time. His most interesting verses often defy the drifts of melancholy, sentiment and tweeness which are his stock-in-trade. 'All my life I've *trudged*', he declared, 'sometimes with satisfaction to myself, more often not.' He was granted a Civil List Pension in 1912. He died at his home in Hendon, in the northern reaches of London, 2 May 1926.

DAY-DREAMS

Broad August burns in milky skies,
   The world is blanched with hazy heat;
The vast green pasture, even, lies
   Too hot and bright for eyes and feet.

Amid the grassy levels rears
   The sycamore against the sun
The dark boughs of a hundred years,
   The emerald foliage of one.

Lulled in a dream of shade and sheen,
   Within the clement twilight thrown
By that great cloud of floating green,
   A horse is standing, still as stone.

He stirs nor head nor hoof, although
   The grass is fresh beneath the branch;
His tail alone swings to and fro
   In graceful curves from haunch to haunch.

He stands quite lost, indifferent
   To rack or pasture, trace or rein;
He feels the vaguely sweet content
   Of perfect sloth in limb and brain.

        A Lost Epic and Other Poems *(Blackwood, Edinburgh and London, 1887).*

A NEW POET

I write. He sits beside my chair
   And scribbles too in hushed delight;
He dips his pen in charmèd air;
   What is it he pretends to write?

He toils and toils; the paper gives
   No clue to ought he thinks. What then?
His little heart is glad; he lives
   The poems that he cannot pen.

Strange fancies throng that baby brain.
   What grave sweet looks! What earnest eyes!
He stops – reflects – and now again
   His unrecording pen he plies.

It seems a satire on myself –
   These dreamy nothings scrawled in air,
This thought, this work! Oh, tricksy elf,
   Wouldst drive thy father to despair?

Despair! Ah, no; the heart, the mind
   Persists in hoping, – schemes and strives
That there may linger with our kind
   Some memory of our little lives.   20

Beneath his rock i' the early world
   Smiling the naked hunter lay,
And sketched on horn the spear he hurled,
   The urus[1] which he made his prey.

Like him I strive in hope my rhymes
   May keep my name a little while. –
O child, who knows how many times
   We two have made the angels smile!

A Lost Epic *(1887)*.

Michael Field (Katherine Harris Bradley (1846–1914) and Edith Emma Cooper (1862–1913))

'Michael Field' was the collaborative writing name of a wealthy lesbian couple, Katherine Harris Bradley and her niece Edith Emma Cooper. Katherine Bradley's father was a Birmingham tobacco merchant who died when she was tiny. She was educated at home, at Newnham College, Cambridge, and the College de France in Paris. She more or less adopted her sister's elder daughter Edith when her mother became an invalid with the birth of her second daughter. In 1878 the pair attended classes together in Classics and philosophy at college in Bristol, where the family had moved from Kenilworth. In Bristol they argued for votes for women in the college debating society, supported the local anti-vivisection league, and became lovers. Bradley's first volume of verses, *The New Minnesinger* (1875), came out under the Elizabeth Barrett Browning-influenced name of Arran Leigh. In 1881 the pair's first joint volume appeared – *Bellerophon*, by Arran and Isla Leigh. Michael Field came into being with *Calirrhoe and Fair Rosamund* (1884) and from then on remained their public name. After their signal gesture of moving together to Reigate in 1888 – 'Against the world, to be/Poets, and lovers evermore', as their poem beginning 'It was deep April' has it – came *Long Ago* (1889), openly sapphic and lesbian, inspired by Henry Wharton's translations of Sappho (1885), which had for the first time in English put in the female pronouns for the beloved. Of all the many Sappho poems by women, the Michael Field versions and elaborations were the only ones to be openly lesbian. Bradley and Cooper moved freely around Europe (visiting the Paris morgue that so fascinated Dickens's *Uncommercial Traveller*; meeting the ageing Browning: my 'two dear Greek women' was his phrase for them) until Whym Chow their dog kept them quarantined at home (dogs – witness Elizabeth Barrett Browning and Flush – had this way of affecting Victorian women poets' lives; not to mention the lives of the men poets: Whym Chow killed Kipling's pet rabbit). They were familiar figures on London's aestheticist and symbolist fringe – they dined with Havelock (nutty-cutlet and sexology) Ellis, heard Pater lecture and Verlaine read (1893), met Wilde often. Many of their nineties volumes were issued by the arty *fin de siècle* publishers Elkin Mathews and John Lane. Godless (Bradley had to quit Ruskin's Guild of St George when she was discovered to be an atheist), they nonetheless found nineties decadence and naturalism not to their taste, and withdrew one of their poems from John Lane's *Yellow Book* in 1894. In an abrupt reversal of ideology in 1907, in a shift somehow connected with the loss of Whym Chow, they became Roman Catholic Christians. Father John ('Dorian') Gray, one-time Wilde associate and aestheticist poet, was instrumental in persuading them to go down his own path – switching from one kind of erotics to another, from bodily sensuality in verse to a kind of rococo religiosity. But then, pagan sensuousness was not all that far from the lush Roman practice such converts seemed to crave. In 1899 the pair moved to Richmond in Surrey. Michael Field continued to write until cancer killed Edith at the end of 1913 (she refused opium, in order to keep consciousness and writing going right to the end). Katherine carried on writing for her few remaining months, until cancer took her too, September 1914.

1 ur-ox; any extinct kind of oxen.

Ταῖς κάλαις ὕμμιν [τὸ] νόημα τὠμον
　　οὐ διάμειπτον[1]

Maids, not to you my mind doth change;
Men I defy, allure, estrange,
Prostrate, make bond or free:
Soft as the stream beneath the plane
To you I sing my love's refrain;
Between us is no thought of pain,
　　　Peril, satiety.

Soon doth a lover's patience tire,
But ye to manifold desire
Can yield response, ye know　　　　　　　　　　　　10
When for long, museful days I pine,
The presage at my heart divine;
To you I never breathe a sign
Of inward want or woe.

When injuries my spirit bruise,
Allaying virtue ye infuse
With unobtrusive skill:
And if care frets ye come to me
As fresh as nymph from stream or tree,
And with your soft vitality　　　　　　　　　　　　20
　　　My weary bosom fill.

　　　　　　　　　　　　　Long Ago (George Bell & Sons, 1889).

Ἄλλα, μὴ μεγαλύνεο δακτυλίω πέρι[1]

Come, Gorgo, put the rug in place,
　　And passionate recline;
I love to see thee in thy grace,
　　Dark, virulent, divine.
But wherefore thus thy proud eyes fix
　　Upon a jewelled band?
Art thou so glad the sardonyx
　　Becomes thy shapely hand?

Bethink thee! 'Tis for such as thou
　　Zeus leaves his lofty seat;　　　　　　　　　　　10
'Tis at thy beauty's bidding how
　　Man's mortal life shall fleet;
Those fairest hands – dost thou forget
　　Their power to thrill and cling?
O foolish woman, dost thou set
　　Thy pride upon a ring?

　　　　　　　　　　　　　　　　Long Ago (1889).

'Maids, not to you my mind doth change'
1 'My mind is unchangeable towards you, fair maidens' (Sappho).

'Come, Gorgo, put the rug in place'
1 'Foolish woman, don't pride yourself in a ring' (Sappho).

LA GIOCONDA[1]

Leonardo Da Vinci

The Louvre

Historic, side-long, implicating eyes;
A smile of velvet's lustre on the cheek;
Calm lips the smile leads upward; hand that lies
Glowing and soft, the patience in its rest
Of cruelty that waits and doth not seek
For prey; a dusky forehead and a breast
Where twilight touches ripeness amorously:
Behind her, crystal rocks, a sea and skies
Of evanescent blue on cloud and creek;
Landscape that shines suppressive of its zest
For those vicissitudes by which men die.

Sight and Song *(Elkin Mathews and John Lane at the Sign of the Bodley Head, 1892).*

SPRING

Sandro Botticelli[1]

The Accademia of Florence

Venus is sad among the wanton powers,
That make delicious tempest in the hours
Of April or are reckless with their flowers:
   Through umbrageous orange-trees
   Sweeps, mid azure swirl, the Breeze,
   That with clipping arms would seize
   Eôs,[2] wind-inspired and mad,
   In wind-tightened muslin clad,
   With one tress for stormy wreath
   And a bine between her teeth.   10
   Flora[3] foots it near in frilled,
   Vagrant skirt, with roses filled;
   Pinks and gentians spot her robe
   And the curled acanthus-lobe
   Edges intricate her sleeve;
   Rosy briars a girdle weave,
   Blooms are brooches in her hair:
   Though a vision debonair,
   Thriftless, venturesome, a grace
   Disingenuous lights her face;   20
   Curst she is, uncertain-lipped,
   Riggishly her dress is whipped
By little gusts fantastic. Will she deign
To toss her double-roses, or refrain?

LA GIOCONDA
1 the *Mona Lisa* of da Vinci (1452–1519).
SPRING
1 (1444–1510). His *Primavera* now in Uffizi Gallery, Florence.

2 Greek goddess of dawn.
3 Flora, Italian goddess of flowers and spring (in Ovid, Chloris, pursued by Zeus, turns into Flora and breathes out flowers: Botticelli's theme).

These riot by the left side of the queen;
Before her face another group is seen:
In ordered and harmonic nobleness.
Three maidens circle o'er the turf – each dress
Blown round the tiptoe shape in lovely folds
Of air-invaded white; one comrade holds   30
Her fellow's hand on high, the foremost links
Their other hands in chain that lifts and sinks.
Their auburn tresses ripple, coil or sweep;
Gems, amulets and fine ball-fringes keep
Their raiment from austereness. With reserve
The dancers in a garland slowly curve.
They are the Graces in their virgin youth;
And does it touch their Deity with ruth
That they must fade when Eros speeds his dart?
Is this the grief and forethought of her heart?   40

For she is sad, although fresh myrtles near
Her figure chequer with their leaves the drear,
Grey chinks that through the orange-trees appear:
    Clothed in spring-time's white and red,
    She is tender with some dread,
    As she turns a musing head
    Sideways mid her veil demure;
    Her wide eyes have no allure,
    Dark and heavy with their pain.
    She would bless, and yet in vain   50
    Is her troubled blessing: Love,
    Blind and tyrannous above,
    Shoots his childish flame to mar
    Those without defect, who are
    Yet unspent and cold with peace;
    While, her sorrow to increase,
    Hermes, leader of her troop –
    His short cutlass on the loop
    Of a crimson cloak, his eye
    Clear in its fatality –   60
    Rather seems the guide of ghosts
    To the dead, Plutonian coasts,
Than herald of Spring's immature, gay band:
He plucks a ripened orange with his hand.

The tumult and the mystery of earth,
When woods are bleak and flowers have sudden birth,
When love is cruel, follow to their end
The God that teaches Shadows to descend,
But pauses now awhile, with solemn lip
And left hand laid victorious on his hip.   70
The triumph of the year without avail
Is blown to Hades by blue Zephyr's gale.
Across the seedling herbage coltsfoot grows
Between the tulip, heartsease, strawberry-rose,
Fringed pinks and dull grape-hyacinth. Alas,
At play together, through the speckled grass
Trip Youth and April: Venus, looking on,
Beholds the mead with all the dancers gone.

Sight and Song *(1892)*.

A PEN-DRAWING OF LEDA[1]

Sodoma[2]

The Grand Duke's Palace at Weimar

'Tis Leda lovely, wild and free,
    Drawing her gracious Swan down through the grass to see
Certain round eggs without a speck:
One hand plunged in the reeds and one dinting the downy neck,
    Although his hectoring bill
    Gapes toward her tresses,
She draws the fondled creature to her will.

    She joys to bend in the live light
Her glistening body toward her love, how much more bright!
    Though on her breast the sunshine lies   10
And spreads its affluence on the wide curves of her waist and thighs,
    To her meek, smitten gaze
    Where her hand presses
The Swan's white neck sink Heaven's concentred rays.

                                        Sight and Song *(1892)*.

Sometimes I do despatch my heart
    Among the graves to dwell apart:
On some the tablets are erased,
Some earthquake-tumbled, some defaced,
And some that have forgotten lain
A fall of tears makes green again;
And my brave heart can overtread
Her brood of hopes, her infant dead,
And pass with quickened footsteps by
The headstone of hoar memory,   10
    Till she hath found
    One swelling mound
With just her name writ and *beloved*;
From that she cannot be removed.

            Underneath the Bough: A Book of Verses *(George Bell & Sons, 1893)*.

LOVE'S SOUR LEISURE

As a poem in my mind
Thy sweet lineaments are shrined:
From the memory, alas!
Sweetest, sweetest verse will pass;
And the fragments I must piece
Lest the fair tradition cease.
There is balmy air I trow
On the uplands of thy brow,
But the temple's veinèd mound
Is the Muses' sacred ground;   10

A PEN-DRAWING OF LEDA   2 Giovanni Antonio Bazzi (1477–1549).
1 impregnated by Zeus in form of a swan.

While the tresses pale are groves
That the laurelled godhead loves.
There is something in the cheek
Like a dimple still to seek,
As my poet timidly
Love's incarnate kiss would flee.
But the mouth! That land to own
Long did Aphroditè moan,
Ere the virgin goddess grave
From the temptress of the wave   20
That most noble clime did win;
Who, retreating to the chin,
Took her boy's bow for a line,
The sweet boundary to define,
And about the beauteous bays
Still in orbèd queenship plays.
I have all the charact'ry
Of thy features, yet lack thee;
And by couplets to confess
What I wholly would possess   30
Doth but whet the appetite
Of my too long-famished sight:
Vainly if my eyes entreat,
Tears will be their daily meat.

                                        Underneath the Bough *(1893)*.

Our myrtle is in flower;
    Behold Love's power!
The glorious stamens' crowded force unfurled,
    Cirque beyond cirque
At breathing, bee-like, and harmonious work;
The rose-patched petals backward curled,
    Falling away
To let fecundity have perfect play.

    O flower, dear to the eyes
        Of Aphrodite, rise   10
As she at once to bare, audacious bliss;
        And bid us near
Your prodigal, delicious hemisphere,
Where thousand kisses breed the kiss
        That fills the room
With languor of an acid, dark perfume!

                                        Underneath the Bough *(1893)*.

CYCLAMENS

    They are terribly white:
        There is snow on the ground,
    And a moon on the snow at night;
    The sky is cut by the winter light;
Yet I, who have all these things in ken,
Am struck to the heart by the chiselled white
    Of this handful of cyclamen.

                                        Underneath the Bough *(1893)*.

George R. (Robert) Sims (1847–1922)

Not much is known about George R. Sims – journalist, novelist, playwright, children's author, balladeer of London. He was born in the capital in 1847, and educated at Hanwell College and in Germany at the University of Bonn. From 1877 he wrote regularly for the *Referee* as 'Dagonet'. The name came from Tennyson's 'The Last Tournament' in *The Idylls of the King* series (*Contemporary Review*, December 1871): 'Dagonet, the fool, whom Gawain in his mood/Had made mock-knight of Arthur's Table Round'. Sims's first volume of poems, *The Dagonet Ballads* (1879), consisted mainly of poems taken from that paper. His interest in telling poetic stories of London life, especially about how the poor live – a concern continued in his *Ballads of Babylon* (1880) and *The Lifeboat and Other Poems* (1883) – is consistent with the themes of his journalism (which included an investigation of poverty for the *Daily News* in the manner pioneered by Henry Mayhew's *London Labour and the London Poor*) and those of his fiction, much of which does naturalistic accounts of London life rather in the grim and pessimistic mode of Sims's contemporary, Arthur Morrison. Sims married late-ish in life, in 1901. In *Who's Who* he said that his recreations were 'bull-dogs, badminton, motoring'. (And, as evidence of a certain kind of popularity at least: whereas many Victorian poetry books in Oxford's Bodleian Library have clearly not been read much, and some never – as uncut pages witness – Sims's trio of volumes has been read to the point of destruction.)

A GARDEN SONG

I scorn the doubts and cares that hurt
    The world and all its mockeries,
My only care is now to squirt
    The ferns among my rockeries.

In early youth and later life
    I've seen an up and seen a down,
And now I have a loving wife
    To help me peg verbena down.

Of joys that come to womankind
    The loom of fate doth weave her few,   10
But here are summer joys entwined
    And bound with golden feverfew,

I've learnt the lessons one and all
    With which the world its sermon stocks,
Now, heedless of a rise or fall,
    I've Brompton and I've German stocks.

In peace and quiet pass our days,
    With nought to vex our craniums,
Our middle beds are all ablaze
    With red and white geraniums.   20

And like a boy I laugh when she,
    In Varden hat and Varden hose,[1]
Comes slyly up the lawn at me
    To squirt me with the garden hose.

A GARDEN SONG
1 Dolly Varden, sex-kitten in Dickens' *Barnaby Rudge* (1841), wears 'the wickedest and most provoking head-dress that ever malicious milliner devised' (ch. 19), and has 'a heart-rending pair of shoes' (ch. 18).

Let him who'd have the peace he needs
    Give all his worldly mumming up,
Then dig a garden, plant the seeds,
    And watch the product coming up.

The Dagonet Ballads (Chiefly from 'The Referee') (E. J. Francis & Co., 1879).
                                    Ballads and Poems (John P. Fuller, 1883).

UNDERTONES

By a Lunatic Laureate

There's a feeling that comes with the daze of joy
    And goes with the knights of grief –
That stands on the top of a baby buoy,
    And floats with an anchor chief.
It rides on the back of a noted Bill,
    And fights where your collars fray;
It whispers in accents loud and shrill –
    To-morrow succeeds to-day.

We con the lessons of life betimes
    In the leaves of an open glade;   10
The frost on the window writes its rimes,
    We live and we learn be trayed.
The coals we heat and the apes we were
    Are gone where the Russians sleigh.
The moral is blown on the well-known air –
    To-morrow succeeds to-day.

In the bustle and jam of the daily strife,
    What matters if men preserve
The bosom of hope from the butcher's knife,
    And its train from the pointsman curve?   20
Remember the fate of the ready maid
    Who went where the preachers prey;
Take matter for thought from a new decayed –
    To-morrow succeeds to-day.

Ballads of Babylon (John P. Fuller, 1880). Ballads and Poems (1883).

CHRISTMASSING À LA MODE DE SLUMOPOLIS

I saw a lady up a court that leads to Drury-lane,
She held her head between her hands, and seemed to be in pain.
She'd two black eyes, a broken nose, and bruises half a score,
She sat and moaned upon a step beside an open door.
'What's up?' I said; 'you seem in grief.' She answered with a sigh,
'We've been a-keepin' Christmas, sir, and Bill has blacked my eye.'

'Your nose is damaged very much – you've lost a dozen teeth,
I see your head is sadly cut, your battered hat beneath;
Your face is very wan and white, excepting where it's black,
And, by the way you twist about, it's clear you've pains that rack.'   10
'It's nothin', sir,' she answered me, with quite an angry frown;
'We've been a-keepin' Christmas up, and Bill has knocked me down.'

'Why don't you seek your little home, and bandage up your head,
And bathe your face, and wash yourself, and lie upon the bed?
You must be cold upon the step, in such a shocking state –
Come, come, poor soul, go home at once, and seek your lawful mate.'
'I can't go home,' the woman growled, 'the landlord's turned us out –
We've been a-keepin' Christmas, sir – our things is up the spout.'[1]

'Well, where's your husband?' then I said; 'his place is by his wife;
He shouldn't leave you in the streets to risk your precious life.   20
He's blacked your eye and cut your head, but still he is your spouse,
And ought at least to remedy the fruits of his carouse.'
'My husband, sir,' the woman sobbed, 'in quod[2] he's got to stop,
He's been a-keepin' Christmas, sir, and jumpin' on a slop.'[3]

'Your children, surely, where are they – you are not quite alone?
A little boy, or little girl – come, don't sit there and moan.
Where are your children, what of them, they can't be drunk at least,
Or overcome, like you and Bill, with this the Church's feast?'
'I had a child,' the woman cried, 'poor little thing – it's dead –
I'd been a-keepin' Christmas, sir, and laid on it in bed.'   30

I left the woman with a coin – it went, no doubt, in gin –
And thought of how this time of joy is made a time of sin;
How homes are ruined, limbs are maimed, and helpless children killed,
While prison cells and workhouse wards with maddened fools are filled.
I thought of Christ's sweet carnival to heathen rites 'demeaned,'
And Christmas made the harvest-time of Drink – hell's fiercest fiend.

The Lifeboat and Other Poems *(J. P. Fuller, 1883)*.
Ballads and Poems *(1883)*.

THE LOST CORD[1]

(With a Thousand Apologies)

Seated one day in a carriage,
    I was frightened and ill at ease,
For a fellow, behaving wildly,
    Was up to his drunken sprees.

I knew not if he was playing,
    Or what I was doing then,
But I pulled the cord like winking
    While the lunatic shrieked 'Amen.'

It rattled against the ceiling
    As I clasped it in my palm,   10
Then it broke and fell on the cushion,
    Where it lay in a holy calm.

It startled the next compartment,
    On the lunatic's nerves it jarred;
It reached the length of the carriage,
    But it never reached the guard.

CHRISTMASSING À LA MODE DE SLUMOPOLIS
1 they've been pawned (slang).
2 in prison (slang).

3 criticizing a policeman (?) (slang).
THE LOST CORD
1 cf. Adelaide Anne Procter, ' A Lost Chord'.

It may be a grand invention
At the distant guard to get;
But I've tried it in twenty cases
And I've never succeeded yet.   20

The Lifeboat and Other Poems *(1883)*. Ballads and Poems *(1883)*.

(Mrs) Alice (Christiana Gertrude) Meynell (A. C. Thompson) (1847–1922)

Alice Meynell was an extremely prolific Roman Catholic journalist who also wrote poems – and was twice nominated for Poet Laureate (1895 and 1913). She was born at Barnes in London, 22 September 1847, daughter of Thomas Thompson, gent. Her mother, Christiana Weller, was a one-time concert pianist; her elder sister Elizabeth became, as Lady Butler, the famous painter of military scenes (her wonderfully pathetic *Roll Call*, depicting battered remnants of soldiery at the end of a day's fighting, was exhibited at the Royal Academy, 1874). The wealthy father, a Creolized Englishman, graduate of Trinity College, Cambridge, and a friend of Dickens, was forbidden by the terms of his inheritance (Jamaican sugar money) from paid employment; he devoted himself to his daughters' educational upbringing, much of it in Italy. A formidably silent man, he probably influenced Alice's strong poetic investment in silence. Around the end of the sixties, Mrs Thompson converted to Roman Catholicism, followed by Alice and, not long after, by all the others in the family. Alice's first volume, *Preludes*, appeared in 1875 under her maiden name A. C. Thompson (illustrated by her sister Elizabeth). Two years later, aged thirty, she married Wilfred Meynell, a Catholic journalist. From then she was known as A. M., or Alice Meynell. Her *Poems* (1893) and *Poems* (1913) are both dedicated to 'W. M.'. She bore eight children (one died), at the same time as doing her full share of editing and writing the couple's magazines, *The Pen: A Journal of Literature* (short-lived, 1880), the *Weekly Register* (1881–8), the monthly *Merry England* (1883–95). She was always rather vague about her children's names. She moved in grand and influential Roman Catholic circles, and built up a close Catholic literary acquaintance. She was great friends (to begin with at least) of the aged Catholic poet Coventry Patmore; helped stop the tormented Catholic genius Francis Thompson auto-destruct on opium (his 'Love in Dian's Lap' poems are for her); became very close indeed to yet another Catholic poet, Katharine Tynan. Her literary tastes and associates and admirers were not all Roman Catholics, of course. George Meredith was a close ally (attracted initially by A. M.'s *Pall Mall Gazette* pieces). Ruskin and Tennyson greatly liked her poems. But still, for every book she would produce on, say, Ruskin (as *John Ruskin*, 1900), there would be one on the Blessed Virgin Mary (as *Mary, the Mother of Jesus*, 1912). She was a *Catholic* writer. In the twentieth century she and her husband travelled widely. She lectured in the USA (1901–2); marched as a non-militant suffragette; was a pacifist in the Great War of 1914–18. Her poetic output was remarkably slight in bulk beside her torrential spates of journalism – though it is big on self-thinnings, reticence, little ones, renunciation (the sonnet 'Renouncement' is addressed to Father Dignam, the priest who received her into his church, but who eventually broke off all contact because of the sexual temptation proximity offered them both). She died at the age of seventy-five, in London, 27 November 1922.

To One Poem in a Silent Time

'De quel nom te nommer?'
Victor Hugo[1]

Who looked for thee, thou little song of mine?
This winter of a silent poet's heart
Is suddenly sweet with thee, but what thou art,
Mid-winter flower, I would I could divine.

To One Poem in a Silent Time
1 'What name shall I give you?'

Art thou a last one, orphan of thy line?
  Did the dead summer's last warmth foster thee?
  Or is Spring folded up unguessed in me,
And stirring out of sight, – and thou the sign?

Where shall I look – backwards or to the morrow
  For others of thy fragrance, secret child?   10
  Who knows if last things or if first things claim thee?

– Whether thou be the last smile of my sorrow,
  Or else a joy too sweet, a joy too wild?
    How, my December violet, shall I name thee?

Preludes, by A. C. Thompson, illustrated by Elizabeth Thompson
(Henry S. King & Co., 1875).

RENOUNCEMENT

I must not think of thee; and, tired yet strong,
  I shun the thought that lurks in all delight –
  The thought of thee – and in the blue Heaven's height,
And in the sweet passage of a song.
Oh, just beyond the fairest thoughts that throng
  This breast, the thought of thee waits, hidden yet bright;
  But it must never, never come in sight;
I must stop short of thee the whole day long.

But when sleep comes to close each difficult day,
  When night gives pause to the long watch I keep,   10
    And all my bonds I needs must loose apart,
Must doff my will as raiment laid away, –
  With the first dream that comes with the first sleep
    I run, I run, I am gathered to thy heart.

Written, 1875. Poems *(Elkin Mathews and John Lane, 1893).*

AFTER A PARTING

Farewell has long been said; I have forgone thee;
  I never name thee even.
But how shall I learn virtues and yet shun thee?
  For thou art so near Heaven
That Heavenward meditations pause upon thee.

Thou dost beset the path to every shrine;
  My trembling thoughts discern
Thy goodness in the good for which I pine;
  And, if I turn from but one sin, I turn
Unto a smile of thine.   10

How shall I thrust thee apart
  Since all my growth tends to thee night and day –
To thee faith, hope, and art?
  Swift are the currents setting all one way;
They draw my life, my life, out of my heart.

Written, 1877. First published, Scots Observer *(31 May 1890).* Poems *(1893). 1893 text.*

THE LADY POVERTY

The Lady Poverty was fair:
But she has lost her looks of late,
With change of times and change of air.
Ah slattern, she neglects her hair,
Her gown, her shoes; she keeps no state
As once when her pure feet were bare.

Or – almost worse, if worse can be –
She scolds in parlours, dusts and trims,
Watches and counts. Oh, is this she
Whom Francis met, whose step was free,   10
Who with Obedience carolled hymns,
In Umbria walked with Chastity?[1]

Where is her ladyhood? Not here,
Not among modern kinds of men;
But in the stony fields, where clear
Through the thin trees the skies appear,
In delicate spare soil and fen,
And slender landscape and austere.

Other Poems, *by Alice Meynell (privately printed at the New Year, 1896).*
Later Poems (John Lane, The Bodley Head, 1902). 1896 text.

CRADLE-SONG AT TWILIGHT

The child not yet is lulled to rest.
    Too young a nurse, the slender Night
So laxly holds him to her breast
    That throbs with flight.

He plays with her, and will not sleep.
    For other playfellows she sighs;
An unmaternal fondness keep
    Her alien eyes.

Saturday Review (6 July 1895). Other Poems (1896). Later Poems (1902). Text, 1896, 1902.

THE ROARING FROST

A flock of winds came winging from the North,
Strong birds with fighting pinions driving forth
    With a resounding call!

Where will they close their wings and cease their cries –
Between what warming seas and conquering skies –
    And fold, and fall?

Other Poems (1896). Later Poems (1902). Text, 1896, 1902.

THE LADY POVERTY
1   St Francis of Assisi.

Digby (Augustus Stewart) Mackworth Dolben (1848–67)

Digby Mackworth Dolben (the Mackworth being his mother's family name) was born in Guernsey, 8 February 1848, though the family home was Finedon Hall in Northamptonshire. He was the youngest child of four. After preparatory school at Cheam, he entered Eton College, aged thirteen, in January 1862. Robert Bridges, a cousin on both sides of his family, made him his fag. Bridges (who left the school in July 1863) became a sort of mentor to the younger boy – Dolben even dubbing him 'father'. Dolben's real father was deeply hostile to his son's being caught up in the massive wave of mid-century Anglo-Catholic enthusiasm. So were the Eton authorities. At one point Dolben was going to be withdrawn from the school over his Romanizing behaviour – crossing himself at meals, visiting Roman chapels in the neighbourhood, consorting with nearby Jesuits. His Aunt Annie, a strong Puseyite, was more encouraging, as was his ascetic cousin the Revd Euseby Cleaver. Bridges, at this time a Puseyite himself, shared Dolben's not at all whimsical desire for a High Anglican Brotherhood, a more distinctly religious version of the Pre-Raphaelite Brotherhood, which would involve 'our Monastery'. On promise of being on his best religious behaviour, Dolben was readmitted to 'our B. Lady of Eton', and kept up his camp Anglo-Catholic tone of which that phrase from a letter to Bridges is typical. His Romanizing drift proceeded: at the end of his last term, July 1864, he even sneaked off to a nunnery in preference to attending the Eton–Harrow cricket match. His 'sacramental ecstasies' elided easily into more earthly passions, especially desire for his school-fellow 'Marchie' Gosselin, to whom many poems were directed. Some of these Dolben destroyed, Bridges suggests in his Memoir in the *Poems* (1911), in a moment of guilty religious fervour, but the passion for Gosselin never died, and was, apparently, fuelled by the reading Dolben did in Greek literature for entrance to Oxford. All the religious men Dolben met were taken by his physical beauty and his religiosity. After Dolben's death Bridges's friend Gerard Manley Hopkins, who had met Dolben only once, wrote that 'there can very seldom have happened the loss of so much beauty (in body and mind and life)...seldom, I mean, in the whole world'. Dolben expressed his passions extremely. While at school he joined the Anglican Order of St Bene-

dict, led by the notorious Father Ignatius. He liked prowling about at night in his monkish habit. He even put it on for cycling excursions. He made a robed and barefoot pilgrimage to John Henry Newman's Oratory in Birmingham, probably in hopes of being received into the Roman Catholic Church at Newman's hands. Newman was not there. On the way, Dolben was 'mobbed' in Birmingham. Hearing of this, Gerard Hopkins didn't know whether to find it 'more funny or affecting to think of'. Dolben left Eton to be coached up to Balliol standards by private tutors (most them were too Protestant for his taste, because his father liked them that way). He was not physically strong; he was taken ill and fainted whilst sitting the Balliol matriculation exam, 2 May 1867, and thus failed to get in. He lowered his sights to Christ Church, but while residing yet again with a coaching clergyman, he drowned, 18 June 1867, in a swimming hole on the River Welland. He was supporting the non-swimmer son of his tutor on his back when he sank suddenly to his death. Reapers in nearby meadows came to his aid too late. There was considerable anxiety about the male eroticism of his verses: his family destroyed letters and poems; Bridges left some poems out of his 1911 edition and rewrote at least one of them. Gosselin's widow embargoed access to her husband's diaries. There was talk of attempts to make certain poems look as if addressed to girls. Marchie Gosselin is referred to throughout Bridges's Memoir as Archie Manning (for whom some Old Etonians searched in vain in the school lists). Bridges is anxious to fend off 'lamentable gossip', whilst recognizing that Dolben's sexuality is 'open to misrepresentation'. These sad attempts at clean-up and cover-up failed in their disguising purpose. Dolben was buried 'under the altar' at Finedon, 6 July 1867. Hopkins wrote to Bridges asking directions to the burial place, hoped to go and see where Dolben was drowned, and requested a sight of the letters in Bridges's possession. William (Johnson) Cory, the Eton master sacked for homosexual dealings with boys, copied out certain of Dolben's poems from manuscript and hailed one at least of them as 'better than Newman'. Bridges thought his cousin a genius; but then his Memoir also extols Dolben's mother as 'a fine example of...the indigenous grace of our country-houses'.

AFTER READING AESCHYLUS[1]

I will not sing my little puny songs.
It is more blessed for the rippling pool
To be absorbed in the great ocean-wave
Than even to kiss the sea-weeds on its breast.
Therefore in passiveness I will lie still,
And let the multitudinous music of the Greek
Pass into me, till I am musical.

Poems, ed. with Memoir, Robert Bridges (Oxford University Press, 1911).

SONNETS

(1)

One night I dreamt that in a gleaming hall
You played, and overhead the air was sweet
With waving kerchiefs; then a sudden fall
Of flowers; and jewels clashed about your feet.
Around you glittering forms, a starry ring,
In echo sang of youth and golden ease:
You leant to me a moment, crying – 'Sing,
'If, as you say, you love me, sing with these.' –
    In vain my lips were opened, for my throat
Was choked somewhere, my tongue was sore and dry,   10
And in my soul alone the answering note;
Till, in a piercing discord, one shrill cry,
As of a hunted creature, from me broke.
You laughed, and in great bitterness I woke.

(2)

I thank thee, Love, that thou hast overthrown
The tyranny of Self; I would not now
Even in desire, possess thee mine alone
In land-locked anchorage: nay rather go,
Ride the high seas, the fruitless human seas,
Where white-winged ships are set for barren shores,
Though freighted all, those lovely argosies,
And laden with a wealth of rarest stores.
    Go, draw them after thee, and lead them on
With thine own music, to the ideal west,   10
Where, in the youth of ages, vaguely shone
The term of all, the Islands of the Blest.
    I too dare steer, for once-loved haven's sake,
My tiny skiff along thy glorious wake.

(3)

A boyish friendship! No, respond the chimes,
The years of chimes fulfillèd since we parted,
Since 'au revoir' you said among the limes,
And passed away in silence tender-hearted.
I hold it cleared by time that not of heat,
Or sudden passion my great Love was born:

AFTER READING AESCHYLUS
1   main Greek composer of tragedies.

I hold that years the calumny defeat
That it would fade as freshness off the morn.
   That it was fathered not by mean desire
Of eye and ear, doth cruel distance prove. –   10
My life is cleft to steps that lift it higher,
And with my growing manhood grows my Love.
   Then come and tread the fruits of disconnection
To the sweet vintage of your own perfection.

(4)

O come, my king, and fill the palaces
Where sceptred Loss too long hath held her state,
With courts of Joyaunce, and a laughing breeze
Of voices. – If thou willest, come; – I wait
Unquestioning, no servant, but thy slave.
I plead no merit, and no claim for wages,
Nor that sweet favour which my sovereign gave
In other days, of his own grace: but pages
Are privileged to linger at the door
With longing eyes, while nobles kiss the hand   10
Of him the noblest, though elect no more
To touch the train, or at the throne to stand.
   But come, content me with the lowest place,
So be it that I see thy royal face.

Poems (1911).

O, a moon face
In a shadowy place.

Lean over me – ah so, – let fall
   About my face and neck the shroud
   That thrills me as a thunder-cloud
Full of strange lights, electrical.

Sweet moon, with pain and passion wan,
   Rain from thy loneliness of light
   The primal kisses of the night
Upon a new Endymion;[1]

The boy who, wrapped from moil and moan,
   With cheeks for ever round and fair,   10
   Is dreaming of the nights that were
When lips immortal touched his own.

I marked an old man yesterday,
   His body many-fingered grief
   Distorted as a frozen leaf:
He fell, and cursed the rosy way.

O better than a century
   Of heavy years that trail the feet,
   More full of being, more complete
A stroke of time with youth and thee.   20

Poems (1911).

'LEAN OVER ME . . .'
1 beautiful Greek boy kissed by moon goddess Selene whilst asleep – it was so pleasant, he asked for perpetual sleep. Subject of very influential Keats poem, 'Endymion'.

W. H. (William Hurrell) Mallock (1849–1923)

W. H. Mallock, satirical polemicist, novelist and poet, was born at Cheriton Bishop, Devon, into a heavily clerical Devonian clan, 7 February 1849. His father was the Revd William Mallock, his mother Margaret a Froude – daughter of an Archdeacon, sister of the well-known Froude brothers, Richard Hurrell and James Anthony Froude. William Hurrell was tutored privately before going to Balliol College, Oxford, in 1869 to read Classics. Benjamin Jowett, the Master of Balliol, rightly marked Mallock down as a dilettante. He did minimal work, netting only a Third Class in Honour Moderations (1871) and a Second in Literae Humaniores Finals (1874), but won the Newdigate Prize for poetry (topic: the Isthmus of Suez) as well as producing in 1872 the satirical guide to writing poems after the best models of the day, *Every Man His Own Poet: or, the Inspired Singer's Recipe Book*, by 'A Newdigate Prizeman' (published in Oxford by Thomas Shrimpton & Son of Broad Street). Mallock's most notorious work appeared in 1877 – *The New Republic*, a mock symposium on culture, faith and philosophy involving recognizable sages of the time, Carlyle, Ruskin, Jowett, Arnold, Pater, and so on. *The New Paul and Virginia, or Positivism on an Island* quickly followed (1878), satirically fingering T. H. Huxley, Frederic Harrison and the Comtean School. Mallock became the latest *enfant terrible*, the gentleman bad boy every country-house hostess wanted as guest. He moved in deeply shallow fashionable circles in London and on the Riviera. Novels, political and theological books, pamphlets, lectures gushed forth, increasingly conservative in tone. He said his writing's aim was 'to expose the fallacies of Radicalism and Socialism'. For its part the *Athenaeum* said that no novelists succeeded better than him in 'leaving a nasty taste on the palate and a nasty smell in the nose of his readers'. Mallock stood as an anti-common-ownership candidate for a Scottish parliamentary seat, but withdrew – dilettantishly – before election day. *Poems* (1880) consists of juvenile stuff done between the ages of seventeen and twenty and is predictably light and spry. *Verses* (1893) mocks and gibes and wisecracks along in a hardly less know-all boyish fashion. Mallock also produced *Lucretius on Life and Death in the Metre of Omar Khayyám* (1900) – he'd done a little guide to Lucretius for Blackwood in 1878. His American lectures of 1907 became *A Critical Examination of Socialism* (1908). Towards the end of his life he wrote an autobiography, *Memoirs of Life and Literature* (1920). He died – a bachelor – at Wincanton, Somerset, 2 April 1923. He was received into the Roman Catholic Church as he lay dying.

LINES ON THE DEATH OF A PET DOG

Belonging to Lady Dorothy Nevill

'Animula, vagula, blandula'[1]

I

Where are you now, little wandering
   Life, that so faithfully dwelt with us,
Played with us, fed with us, felt with us,
Years we grew fonder and fonder in?

II

You, who but yesterday sprang to us,
   Are we for ever bereft of you?
   And is this all that is left of you –
One little grave and a pang to us?

Dated June 1878. Poems *(Chatto & Windus, 1880).*

LINES ON THE DEATH OF A PET DOG

1 'wandering, charming, little soul': supposed last words of Emperor Hadrian.

TOO LATE!

I

What, dead – quite dead? And can you hear no prayer
　　Already? Have you in so short a space
　　Gone so far from your old abiding-place?
And is this all you have left me, this – to bear
　　The still accusings of that dear marred face?

II

How they make bitterer all my grief than gall!
　　Oh, loving eyes, for ever closed on me;
　　Worn face that look'st so unreproachfully!
Too late, too late, I would I could recall
　　Every unloving word I have said to thee!　　　　　　　　10

III

Have I been blind, never to recognise
　　The wounds I made till now? Ah, now I know
　　My cruel work in all that dumb great woe!
I see how piteous look thy poor closed eyes,
　　And know that it is I have made them so.

IV

Oh why, why did you love me all these years?
　　Why not grow cruel to me as I to you?
　　Had both been false, neither had had to rue
One thing, nor shed, as I do, hard vain tears.
　　Why have you taunted me by being so true?　　　　　　　20

V

Why have you let the whole remorse be mine?
　　Thy most sad mouth, why did it never say
　　One counter-word of anger? Lovingly,
Why did you let each patient, painful line,
　　Deepen in moanless silence day by day?

VI

Why will tears never come, till they must fail
　　Of ease and comfort, and can only sear?
　　Why am I moaning now to a deaf ear –
Moaning, as if my words could ever avail
　　To make one deep-grooved pain-line shallower?　　　　　30

An. æt. 20[1]

Poems *(1880).*

HUMAN LIFE

Like smoke I vanish, though I burn like flame;
　　I flicker in the gusts of wrong and right,
　　A shining frailty in the guise of might,
Before, a nothing – and behind, a name.

Verses *(Hutchinson & Co., 1893).*

TOO LATE!
1　in his 20th year.

CHRISTMAS THOUGHTS, BY A MODERN THINKER

(After Mr. Matthew Arnold)[1]

The windows of the church are bright;
   'Tis Christmas Eve; a low wind breathes;
And girls with happy eyes to-night
   Are hanging up the Christmas wreaths;

And village voices by-and-by
   Will reach my windows through the trees,
With wild, sweet music: 'Praise on high
   To God: on earth, good-will and peace.'

Oh, happy girls, that hang the wreaths!
   Oh, village fiddlers, happy ye!   10
Christmas to you still truly breathes
   Good-will and peace; but not to me.

Yes, gladness is your simple rôle,
   Ye foolish girls, ye labouring poor;
But joy would ill beseem my soul –
   To sigh, my part is, and endure.

For once as Rousseau stood, I stand
   Apart, made picturesque by grief –
One of a small world-weary band,
   The orphans of a dead belief.   20

Through graveyards lone we love to stray,
   And sadly the sad tombs explore,
And contradict the texts which say
   That we shall rise once more.

Our faith is dead, of course; and grief
   Fills its room up; and Christmas pie
And turkey cannot bring relief
   To such as Obermann and I.

Ah, Obermann, and might I pass
   This English Christmas-tide with thee,   30
Far by those inland waves whose glass
   Brightens and breaks by Meillerie;[2]

Or else amongst the sternest dells
   Alp shags with pine, we'd mix our sighs,
Mourn at the sound of Christmas bells,
   Sniff at the smell of Christmas pies.

CHRISTMAS THOUGHTS, BY A MODERN THINKER
1 The poem particularly draws on Arnold's two Obermann poems (1849, 1867) – worrying tributes to Etienne de Sénancour, doubting French author of volume of Swiss Letters (very Rousseau-esque and Goethean) *Obermann* (1804).
2 on French side of Lake Geneva.

But thou art dead; and long, dank grass
    And wet mould cool thy tired, hot brain;
Thou art lain down, and now, alas!
    Of course you won't get up again.   40

Yet, Obermann, 'tis better so;
    For if, sad slumberer, after all
You were to re-arise, you know
    'Twould make us feel so very small.

Best bear our grief this manlier way,
    And make our grief be balm to grief;
For if in faith sweet comfort lay,
    There lurks sweet pride in unbelief.

Wherefore, remembering this, once more
    Unto my childhood's church I'll go,   50
And bow my head at that low door
    I passed through standing, long ago.

I'll sit in the accustomed place,
    And make, while all the unlearnèd stare,
A mournful, atheistic face
    At their vain noise of unheard prayer.

Then, while they hymn the heavenly birth
    And angel voices from the skies,
My thoughts shall go where Weimar's earth
    For ever darkens Goethe's eyes;   60

Till sweet girls' glances from their books
    Shall steal towards me, and they sigh:
'How intellectual he looks,
    And yet how wistful! And his eye

Has that vain look of baffled prayer!'
    And then when church is o'er I'll run,
Comb misery into all my hair,
    And go and get my portrait done.

Verses (1893).

From: EVERY MAN HIS OWN POET: OR, THE INSPIRED SINGER'S RECIPE BOOK

Of the Nature of Poetry

Poetry as practised by the latest masters, is the art of expressing what is too foolish, too profane, or too indecent to be expressed in any other way. And thus, just as a consummate cook will prepare a most delicate repast out of the most poor materials, so will the modern poet concoct us a most popular poem from the weakest emotions, and the most tiresome platitudes. The only difference is, that the cook would prefer good materials if he could get them, whilst the modern poet will take the bad from choice. As far, however, as the nature of materials goes, those which the two artists work with are the same – *viz.*, animals, vegetables, and spirits. It was the practice of Shakespeare and other earlier masters to make use of all these together, mixing them in various proportions. But the moderns have found that it is better and far easier to employ each separately. Thus

Mr. Swinburne uses very little else but animal matter in the composition of his dishes, which it must be confessed are somewhat unwholesome in consequence: whilst the late Mr. Wordsworth, on the contrary, confined himself almost exclusively to the confection of primrose pudding, and flint soup, flavoured with the lesser-celandine; and only now and then a beggar-boy boiled down in it to give it a colour. The robins and drowned lambs which he was wont to use, when an additional piquancy was needed, were employed so sparingly that they did not destroy in the least the general vegetable tone of his productions; and these form in consequence an unimpeachable lenten diet. It is difficult to know what to say of Mr. Tennyson, as the milk and water of which his books are composed chiefly, make it almost impossible to discover what was the original nature of the materials he has boiled down in it. Mr. Shelley, too, is perhaps somewhat embarrassing to classify; as, though spirits are what he affected most, he made use of a large amount of vegetable matter also. We shall be probably not far wrong in describing his material as a kind of methyllated spirits; or pure psychic alcohol, strongly tinctured with the barks of trees, and rendered below proof by a quantity of sea-water. In this division of the poets, however, into animalists, spiritualists, and vegetarians, we must not be discouraged by any such difficulties as these; but must bear in mind that in whatever manner we may neatly classify anything, the exceptions and special cases will always far outnumber those to which our rule applies.

But in fact, at present, mere theory may be set entirely aside: for although in the case of action, the making and adhering to a theory may be the surest guide to inconsistency and absurdity, in poetry these results can be obtained without such aid.

The following recipes, compiled from a careful analysis of the best authors, will be found, we trust, efficient guides for the composition of genuine poems. But the tyro must bear always in mind that there is no royal road to anything, and that not even the most explicit directions will make a poet all at once of even the most fatuous, the most sentimental, or the most profane.

Recipes

The following are arranged somewhat in the order in which the student is recommended to begin his efforts. About the more elaborate ones, which come later, he may use his own discretion as to which he will try first; but he must previously have had some training in the simpler compositions, with which we deal before all others. These form as it were a kind of palæstra[1] of folly, a very short training in which will suffice to break down that stiffness and self-respect in the soul, which is so incompatible with modern poetry. Taking, therefore, the silliest and commonest of all kinds of verse, and the one whose sentiments come most readily to hand in vulgar minds, we begin with directions,

How To Make an Ordinary Love Poem

Take two large and tender human hearts, which match one another perfectly. Arrange these close together, but preserve them from actual contact by placing between them some cruel barrier. Wound them both in several places, and insert through the openings thus made a fine stuffing of wild yearnings, hopeless tenderness, and a general admiration for stars. Then completely cover up one heart with a sufficient quantity of chill church-yard mould, which may be garnished according to taste with dank waving weeds or tender violets: and promptly break over it the other heart.

How To Make a Pathetic Marine Poem

This kind of poem has the advantage of being easily produced, yet being at the same time pleasing, and not unwholesome. As, too, it admits of no variety, the chance of going wrong in it is very small. Take one midnight storm, and one fisherman's family, which, if the poem is to be a real

1 place of physical education, such as a gymnasium or wrestling school.

success, should be as large and as hungry as possible, and must contain at least one innocent infant. Place this last in a cradle, with the mother singing over it, being careful that the babe be dreaming of angels, or else smiling sweetly. Stir the father well up in the storm until he disappears. Then get ready immediately a quantity of cruel crawling foam, in which serve up the father directly on his re-appearance, which is sure to take place in an hour or two, in the dull red morning. This done, a charming saline effervescence will take place amongst the remainder of the family. Pile up the agony to suit the palate, and the poem will be ready for perusal.

How To Write an Epic Poem Like Mr. Tennyson
(The following, apart from its intrinsic utility, forms in itself a great literary curiosity, being the original directions from which the Poet Laureate composed the Arthurian Idylls.)

To compose an epic, some writers instruct us first to catch our hero. As, however, Mr. Carlyle is the only person on record who has ever performed this feat, it will be best for the rest of mankind to be content with the nearest approach to a hero available, namely a prig. These animals are very plentiful, and easy to catch, as they delight in being run after. There are however many different kinds, not all equally fit for the present purpose, and amongst which it is very necessary to select the right one. Thus, for instance, there is the scientific and atheistical prig, who may be frequently observed eluding notice between the covers of the 'Westminster Review;' the Anglican prig, who is often caught exposing himself in the 'Guardian;' the Ultramontane prig, who abounds in the 'Dublin Review;' the scholarly prig, who twitters among the leaves of the 'Academy;' and the Evangelical prig, who converts the heathen, and drinks port wine. None of these, and least of all the last, will serve for the central figure, in the present class of poem. The only one entirely suitable is the blameless variety. Take, then, one blameless prig. Set him upright in the middle of a round table, and place beside him a beautiful wife, who cannot abide prigs. Add to these, one marred goodly man; and tie the three together in a bundle with a link or two of Destiny. Proceed, next, to sur-round this group with a large number of men and women of the nineteenth century, in fancy-ball costume, flavoured with a great many very possible vices, and a few impossible virtues. Stir these briskly about for two volumes, to the great annoyance of the blameless prig, who is, however, to be kept carefully below swearing-point, for the whole time. If he once boils over into any natural action or exclamation, he is forthwith worthless, and you must get another. Next break the wife's reputation into small pieces; and dust them well over the blameless prig. Then take a few vials of tribulation and wrath, and empty these generally over the whole ingredients of your poem: and, taking the sword of the heathen, cut into small pieces the greater part of your minor characters. Then wound slightly the head of the blameless prig; remove him suddenly from the table, and keep in a cool barge for future use.

How To Write a Poem Like Mr. Matthew Arnold
Take one soulfull of involuntary unbelief, which has been previously well flavoured with self-satisfied despair. Add to this one beautiful text of Scripture. Mix these well together; and as soon as ebullition commences grate in finely a few regretful allusions to the New Testament and the lake of Tiberias, one constellation of stars, half-a-dozen allusions to the nineteenth century, one to Goethe, one to Mont Blane, or the Lake of Geneva; and one also, if possible, to some personal bereavement. Flavour the whole with a mouthful of 'faiths' and 'infinites,' and a mixed mouthful of 'passions,' 'finites,' and 'yearnings.' This class of poem is concluded usually with some question, about which we have to observe only that it shall be impossible to answer.

How To Write a Poem Like Mr. Browning
Take rather a coarse view of things in general. In the midst of this, place a man and a woman, her and her ankles, tastefully arranged on a slice of Italy, or the country about Pornic. Cut an opening across the breast of each, until the soul becomes visible, but be very careful that none of the body be lost during the operation. Pour into each breast as much as it will hold of the new strong wine of love: and, for fear they should take cold by exposure, cover them quickly up with a quantity of

obscure classical quotations, a few familiar allusions to an unknown period of history, and a half-destroyed fresco by an early master, varied every now and then with a reference to the fugues or toccatas of a quite-forgotten composer.

If the poem be still intelligible, take a pen and remove carefully all the necessary particles.

How To Write a Modern Pre-Raphaelite Poem

Take a packet of fine selected early English, containing no words but such as are obsolete and unintelligible. Pour this into about double the quantity of entirely new English, which must have never been used before, and which you must compose yourself, fresh as it is wanted. Mix these together thoroughly till they assume a colour quite different from any tongue that was ever spoken, and the material will be ready for use.

Determine the number of stanzas of which your poem shall consist, and select a corresponding number of the most archaic or most peculiar words in your vocabulary, allotting one of these to each stanza; and pour in the other words round them, until the entire poem is filled in.

This kind of composition is usually cast in shapes. These, though not numerous – amounting in all to something under a dozen – it would take too long to describe minutely here: and a short visit to Mr.——'s shop in King street, where they are kept in stock, would explain the whole of them. A favourite one, however, is the following, which is of very easy construction. Take three damozels, dressed in straight night-gowns. Pull their hair-pins out, and let their hair tumble all about their shoulders. A few stars may be sprinkled into this with advantage. Place an aureole about the head of each, and give each a lily in her hand, about half the size of herself. Bend their necks all different ways, and set them in a row before a stone wall, with an apple-tree between each and some large flowers at their feet. Trees and flowers of the right sort are very plentiful in church windows. When you have arranged all these objects rightly, take a cast of them in the softest part of your brain, and pour in your word-composition as above described.

This kind of poem is much improved by what is called a burden. This consists of a few jingling words, generally of an archaic character, about which we have only to be careful that they have no reference to the subject of the poem they are to ornament. They are inserted without variation between the stanzas.

In conclusion we would remark to beginners that this sort of composition must be attempted only in a perfectly vacant atmosphere; so that no grains of common-sense may injure the work whilst in progress.

How To Write a Narrative Poem Like Mr. Morris

Take about sixty pages-full of the same word-mixture as that described in the preceding; and dilute it with a double quantity of mild modern Anglo-Saxon. Pour this composition into two vessels of equal size, and into one of these empty a small mythological story. If this does not put your readers to sleep soon enough, add to it the rest of the language, in the remaining vessel.

How To Write a Satanic Poem, Like the Late Lord Byron

(This recipe is inserted for the benefit of those poets who desire to attain what is called originality. This is only to be got by following some model of a past generation, which has ceased to be made use of by the public at large. We do not however recommend this course, feeling sure that all writers in the end will derive far more real satisfaction from producing fashionable, than original verses; which two things it is impossible to do at one and the same time.)

Take a couple of fine deadly sins; and let them hang before your eyes until they become racy. Then take them down, dissect them, and stew them for some time in a solution of weak remorse; after which they are to be devilled with mock-despair.

How To Write a Patriotic Poem Like Mr. Swinburne

Take one blaspheming patriot, who has been hung or buried for some time, together with the oppressed country belonging to him. Soak these in a quantity of rotten sentiment, till they are completely sodden; and in the mean while get ready an indefinite number of Christian kings and priests.

Kick these till they are nearly dead; add copiously broken fragments of the Catholic church, and mix all together thoroughly. Place them in a heap upon the oppressed country; season plentifully with very coarse expressions; and on the top carefully arrange your patriot, garnished with laurel or with parsley: surround with artificial hopes for the future, which are never meant to be tasted. This kind of poem is cooked in verbiage, flavoured with Liberty, the taste of which is much heightened by the introduction of a few high gods, and the game of Fortune. The amount of verbiage which Liberty is capable of flavouring, is practically infinite.

Conclusion

We regret to have to offer this work to the public in its present incomplete state, the whole of that part treating of the most recent section of modern poetry, *viz.*, the blasphemous and the obscene, being entirely wanting. It was found necessary to issue this from an eminent publishing firm in Holywell street, Strand, where by an unforeseen casualty, the whole of the first edition was seized by the police, and is at present in the hands of the Society for the Suppression of Vice. We incline however to trust that this loss will have but little effect; as indecency and profanity are things in which, even to the dullest, external instruction is a luxury, rather than a necessity. Those of our readers, who, either from sense, self-respect, or other circumstances, are in need of a special training in these subjects, will find excellent professors of them in any public-house, during the late hours of the evening; where the whole sum and substance of the fieriest school of modern poetry is delivered nightly; needing only a little dressing and flavouring with artificial English to turn it into very excellent verse.

From: *A Newdigate Prizeman,* Every Man His Own Poet: or, The Inspired Singer's Recipe Book
(Thomas Shrimpton & Son, Oxford, 1872).

W. E. (William Ernest) Henley (1849–1903)

W. E. Henley, distinguished later-Victorian man of letters, was born in Gloucester, 23 August 1849, eldest of the five sons of a bookseller, William Henley. His mother, Emma Morgan, was a descendant of Joseph Warton, the eighteenth-century critic and translator. Henley attended Gloucester's Crypt Grammar School under the headmastership of the poet T. E. Brown. Crippled early on by some sort of tubercular disease – which meant a foot had to be amputated – he became a devotedly bookish youth. In 1873 he was sent to Edinburgh Infirmary in hopes that treatment under Joseph Lister would save his other leg from amputation. The hope proved well founded. He sent verses which he wrote during his twenty-months hospitalization – basis of his *In Hospital* sequence – to the *Cornhill Magazine* under Leslie Stephen. Some were published (July 1875), though not all, Stephen not caring, it seems, for the unrhymed ones. Stephen visited Henley in hospital taking along Robert Louis Stevenson (who is apparently the subject of the poem 'Apparition'), thus helping found one of Henley's closest associations. After leaving hospital Henley worked for a while on the *Encyclopedia Britannica*, but soon returned south to edit (1877–8) the weekly *London*, founded by Stevenson's friend George Glasgow Brown and himself. In January 1878, in Edinburgh, he married Anna Boyle. When *London* folded (it published much of

Henley's early verse as well as work by Stevenson), Henley hacked about for the *Athenaeum*, the *St James's Gazette*, the *Saturday Review* and *Vanity Fair*. He was so 'utterly unmarketable' as a poet, he said, 'that I had to own myself beaten in art, and to addict myself to journalism for the next ten years'. He edited the *Magazine of Art* (1882–6), promoting Rodin and Whistler; returned (1889) to Edinburgh to edit the weekly *Scots Observer*, which came south to London as the *National Observer* in 1891. The *Observer* had a most distinguished literary section, publishing J. M. Barrie, Hardy, Kipling, Arthur Morrison, Stevenson, H. G. Wells, Yeats, T. E. Brown, Alice Meynell. Henley was a great bringer-on of young talent. From 1894 he edited the *New Review*, a literary monthly which collapsed in 1898. After that he was an occasional contributor to the *Pall Mall Gazette*. Besides being a prolific literary and art critic – enthusiastic but bad-tempered (he even slagged off Stevenson) – Henley wrote plays (collaborating with Stevenson on four dramas); edited a dictionary of slang with J. S. Farmer (1894–1904); edited volumes of Burns, Byron, Shakespeare; contributed prefaces to large numbers of literary collections; edited *Lyra Heroica* (1891), a once very famous collection of English heroic verse, and several other collections of English prose and poetry. The original *In Hospital* sequence was published in 1888 in aid of a London East End Hospital, attracted the publisher David Nutt, and he brought it out, supplemented, in *A Book of Verses* (1888). Oscar Wilde praised the Hospital poems with faint damns: 'the beautiful poetry of a prose-writer'. (Much wittier was Wilde's reaction, in a letter of 7 March 1898, to Henley's hostile review of *The Ballad of Reading Gaol* – 'He is so proud of having written *vers libres* on his scrofula that he is quite jealous if a poet writes a lyric on his prison'.) *The Song of the Sword* followed (1892), expanded as *London Voluntaries* (1893). These volumes were revised up into *Poems* (1898), with a photograph of Rodin's sculpted head of the author. By 1909 this collection had gone into eleven impressions. The patriotic Boer War volume *For England's Sake: Verses and Songs in Time of War* (1900) included the anthology favourite 'Pro Rege Nostro' ('What have I done for you, England, my England?'), which was set to music in at least two versions (Stanford set the same volume's 'Last Post'). Henley's last published poetic effort was 'A Song of Speed', an early piece of motor-car enthusing. In 1899 he moved to Worthing for health reasons, and then (1901) to Woking. He died there, 11 June 1903, after an accident while leaving a moving train. His only child Margaret died in 1894, aged five. She was the 'Reddy' of J. M. Barrie's 'Sentimental Tommy', and, some people think, the Wendy of his *Peter Pan*. A *Collected Works* appeared in six volumes in 1908. A memorial – a bronze copy of the Rodin bust, set in marble – was unveiled in the crypt of St Paul's Cathedral in 1907.

In Hospital

On ne saurait dire à quel point un homme, seul dans son lit et malade, devient personnel.
Balzac[1]

I
Enter Patient

The morning mists still haunt the stony street;
The northern summer air is shrill and cold;
And lo, the Hospital, gray, quiet, old,
Where life and death like friendly chafferers meet.
Thro' the loud spaciousness and draughty gloom
A small, strange child – so agèd yet so young! –
Her little arm besplinted and beslung,
Precedes me gravely to the waiting room.
I limp behind, my confidence all gone.
The gray-haired soldier-porter waves me on,
And on I crawl, and still my spirits fail:
A tragic meanness seems so to environ
These corridors and stairs of stone and iron,
Cold, naked, clean – half-workhouse and half-jail.

II
Waiting

A square, squat room (a cellar on promotion),
Drab to the soul, drab to the very daylight;
Plasters astray in unnatural-looking tinware;
Scissors and lint and apothecary's jars.

Here, on a bench a skeleton would writhe from,
Angry and sore, I wait to be admitted:
Wait till my heart is lead upon my stomach,
While at their ease two dressers do their chores.

IN HOSPITAL
1 'One couldn't say at what point a man, alone on his sick-bed, becomes an individual.'

One has a probe – it feels to me a crowbar.
  A small boy sniffs and shudders after bluestone.
  A poor old tramp explains his poor old ulcers.
  Life is (I think) a blunder and a shame.

10

III
Interior

  The gaunt brown walls
Look infinite in their decent meanness.
There is nothing of home in the noisy kettle,
  The fulsome fire.

  The atmosphere
Suggests the trail of a ghostly druggist.
Dressings and lint on the long, lean table –
  Whom are they for?

  The patients yawn,
Or lie as in training for shroud and coffin.
A nurse in the corridor scolds and wrangles.
  It's grim and strange.

10

  Far footfalls clank.
 The bad burn waits with his head unbandaged.
 My neighbour chokes in the clutch of chloral . . .
  O a gruesome world!

IV
Before

Behold me waiting – waiting for the knife.
A little while, and at a leap I storm
The thick, sweet mystery of chloroform,
The drunken dark, the little death-in-life.
The gods are good to me: I have no wife,
No innocent child, to think of as I near
The fateful minute; nothing all-too dear
Unmans me for my bout of passive strife.
Yet am I tremulous and a trifle sick,
And, face to face with chance, I shrink a little:
My hopes are strong, my will is something weak.
Here comes the basket? Thank you. I am ready.
But, gentlemen my porters, life is brittle:
You carry Cæsar and his fortunes – steady!

10

V
Operation

You are carried in a basket,
  Like a carcase from the shambles,[1]
  To the theatre, a cockpit
  Where they stretch you on a table.

OPERATION
1 meat market/slaughter-house.

Then they bid you close your eyelids,
  And they mask you with a napkin,
  And the anæsthetic reaches
  Hot and subtle through your being.

And you gasp and reel and shudder
  In a rushing, swaying rapture,   10
  While the voices at your elbow
  Fade – receding – fainter – farther.

Lights about you shower and tumble,
  And your blood seems crystallising –
  Edged and vibrant, yet within you
  Racked and hurried back and forward.

Then the lights grow fast and furious,
  And you hear a noise of waters,
  And you wrestle, blind and dizzy,
  In an agony of effort,   20

Till a sudden lull accepts you,
  And you sound an utter darkness...
  And awaken...with a struggle...
  On a hushed, attentive audience.

VI
After

Likeas a flamelet blanketed in smoke,
So through the anæsthetic shows my life;
So flashes and so fades my thought, at strife
With the strong stupor that I heave and choke
And sicken at, it is so foully sweet.
Faces look strange from space – and disappear.
Far voices, sudden loud, offend my ear –
And hush as sudden. Then my senses fleet:
All were a blank, save for this dull, new pain
That grinds my leg and foot; and brokenly   10
Time and the place glimpse on to me again;
And, unsurprised, out of uncertainty,
I awake – relapsing – somewhat faint and fain,
To an immense, complacent dreamery.

VII
Vigil

Lived on one's back,
In the long hours of repose,
Life is a practical nightmare –
Hideous, asleep or awake.

Shoulders and loins
Ache- - -!
Ache, and the mattress,
Run into boulders and hummocks,
Glows like a kiln, while the bedclothes –
Tumbling, importunate, daft –   10
Ramble and roll, and the gas,

Screwed to its lowermost,
An inevitable atom of light,
Haunts, and a stertorous sleeper
Snores me to hate and despair.

All the old time
Surges malignant before me;
Old voices, old kisses, old songs
Blossom derisive about me;
While the new days   20
Pass me in endless procession:
A pageant of shadows
Silently, leeringly wending
On ... and still on ... still on.

Far in the stillness a cat
Languishes loudly. A cinder
Falls, and the shadows
Lurch to the leap of the flame. The next man to me
Turns with a moan; and the snorer,
The drug like a rope at his throat,   30
Gasps, gurgles, snorts himself free, as the night-nurse,
Noiseless and strange,
Her bull's eye half-lanterned in apron
(Whispering me, 'Are ye no' sleepin' yet?'),
Passes, list-slippered and peering,
Round ... and is gone.

Sleep comes at last –
Sleep full of dreams and misgivings –
Broken with brutal and sordid
Voices and sounds   40
That impose on me, ere I can wake to it,
The unnatural, intolerable day.

VIII

Staff-Nurse: Old Style

The greater masters of the commonplace,
REMBRANDT and good SIR WALTER[1] – only these
Could paint her all to you: experienced ease,
And antique liveliness, and ponderous grace;
The sweet old roses of her sunken face;
The depth and malice of her sly gray eyes;
The broad Scots tongue that flatters, scolds, defies;
The thick Scots wit that fells you like a mace.
These thirty years has she been nursing here,
Some of them under SYME,[2] her hero still.   10
Much is she worth, and even more is made of her.
Patients and students hold her very dear.
The doctors love her, tease her, use her skill.
They say 'The Chief' himself is half-afraid of her.

STAFF-NURSE: OLD STYLE   2   James Syme (1799–1870), famous Edinburgh surgeon.
1   Scott.

IX
Lady-Probationer

Some three, or five, or seven, and thirty years;
A Roman nose; a dimpling double-chin;
Dark eyes and shy that, ignorant of sin,
Are yet acquainted, it would seem, with tears;
A comely shape; a slim, high-coloured hand,
Graced, rather oddly, with a signet ring;
A bashful air, becoming everything;
A well-bred silence always at command.
Her plain print gown, prim cap, and bright steel chain
Look out of place on her, and I remain   10
Absorbed in her, as in a pleasant mystery.
Quick, skilful, quiet, soft in speech and touch . . .
'Do you like nursing?' 'Yes, Sir, very much.'
Somehow, I rather think she has a history.

X
Staff-Nurse: New Style

Blue-eyed and bright of face but waning fast
Into the sere of virginal decay,
I view her as she enters, day by day,
As a sweet sunset almost overpast.
Kindly and calm, patrician to the last,
Superbly falls her gown of sober gray,
And on her chignon's elegant array
The plainest cap is somehow touched with caste.
She talks BEETHOVEN; frowns disapprobation
At BALZAC's name, sighs it at 'poor GEORGE SAND's';   10
Knows that she has exceeding pretty hands;
Speaks Latin with a right accentuation;
And gives at need (as one who understands)
Draught, counsel, diagnosis, exhortation.

XI
Clinical

Hist? . . .
Through the corridor's echoes
Louder and nearer
Comes a great shuffling of feet.
Quick, every one of you,
Straight your quilts, and be decent!
Here's the Professor.

In he comes first
With the bright look we know,
From the broad, white brows the kind eyes   10
Soothing yet nerving you. Here at his elbow,
White-capped, white-aproned, the Nurse,
Towel on arm and her inkstand
Fretful with quills.
Here in the ruck, anyhow,
Surging along,
Louts, duffers, exquisites, students, and prigs –
Whiskers and foreheads, scarf-pins and spectacles! –
Hustles the Class! And they ring themselves

Round the first bed, where the Chief   20
(His dressers and clerks at attention!)
Bends in inspection already.

So shows the ring
Seen, from behind, round a conjuror
Doing his pitch in the street.
High shoulders, low shoulders, broad shoulders, narrow ones,
Round, square, and angular, serry and shove;
While from within a voice,
Gravely and weightily fluent,
Sounds; and then ceases; and suddenly   30
(Look at the stress of the shoulders!)
Out of a quiver of silence,
Over the hiss of the spray,
Comes a low cry, and the sound
Of breath quick intaken through teeth
Clenched in resolve. And the Master
Breaks from the crowd, and goes,
Wiping his hands,
To the next bed, with his pupils
Flocking and whispering behind him.   40

Now one can see.
Case Number One
Sits (rather pale) with his bed-clothes
Stripped up, and showing his foot
(Alas for God's Image!)
Swaddled in wet, white lint
Brilliantly hideous with red.

XII
Etching

Two and thirty is the ploughman.
He's a man of gallant inches,
And his hair is close and curly,
    And his beard;
But his face is wan and sunken,
And his eyes are large and brilliant,
And his shoulder-blades are sharp,
    And his knees.

He is weak of wits, religious,
Full of sentiment and yearning,   10
Gentle, faded – with a cough
    And a snore.
When his wife (who was a widow,
And is many years his elder)
Fails to write, and that is always,
    He desponds.

Let his melancholy wander,
And he 'll tell you pretty stories
Of the women that have wooed him
    Long ago;   20
Or he'll sing of bonnie lasses
Keeping sheep among the heather

With a crackling, hackling click
  In his voice.

XIII
Casualty

As with varnish red and glistening
  Dripped his hair; his feet looked rigid;
  Raised, he settled stiffly sideways:
  You could see his hurts were spinal.

He had fallen from an engine,
  And been dragged along the metals.
  It was hopeless, and they knew it;
  So they covered him, and left him.

As he lay, by fits half sentient,
  Inarticulately moaning,   10
  With his stockinged soles protruded
  Stark and awkward from the blankets,

To his bed there came a woman,
  Stood and looked and sighed a little,
  And departed without speaking,
  As himself a few hours after.

I was told it was his sweetheart.
  They were on the eve of marriage.
  She was quiet as a statue,
  But her lip was gray and writhen.   20

XIV
Ave, Caesar![1]

From the winter's gray despair,
From the summer's golden languor,
Death, the lover of Life,
Frees us for ever.

Inevitable, silent, unseen,
Everywhere always,
Shadow by night and as light in the day,
Signs she at last to her chosen;
And, as she waves them forth,
Sorrow and Joy   10
Lay by their looks and their voices,
Set down their hopes, and are made
One in the dim Forever.

Into the winter's gray delight,
Into the summer's golden dream,
Holy and high and impartial,
Death, the mother of Life,
Mingles all men for ever.

Ave, Caesar!
1 Hail Caesar!

XV
'The Chief'

His brow spreads large and placid, and his eye
Is deep and bright, with steady looks that still.
Soft lines of tranquil thought his face fulfill –
His face at once benign and proud and shy.
If envy scout, if ignorance deny,
His faultless patience, his unyielding will,
Beautiful gentleness, and splendid skill,
Innumerable gratitudes reply.
His wise, rare smile is sweet with certainties,
And seems in all his patients to compel   10
Such love and faith as failure cannot quell.
We hold him for another Herakles,[1]
Battling with custom, prejudice, disease,
As once the son of Zeus with Death and Hell.

XVI
House-Surgeon

Exceeding tall, but built so well his height
Half-disappears in flow of chest and limb;
Moustache and whisker trooper-like in trim;
Frank-faced, frank-eyed, frank-hearted; always bright
And always punctual – morning, noon, and night;
Bland as a Jesuit, sober as a hymn;
Humorous, and yet without a touch of whim;
Gentle and amiable, yet full of fight;
His piety, though fresh and true in strain,
Has not yet whitewashed up his common mood   10
To the dead blank of his particular Schism.
Sweet, unaggressive, tolerant, most humane,
Wild artists like his kindly elderhood,
And cultivate his mild Philistinism.

XVII
Interlude

O the fun, the fun and frolic
    That *The Wind that Shakes the Barley*
    Scatters through a penny whistle
    Tickled with artistic fingers!

Kate the scrubber (forty summers,
    Stout but sportive) treads a measure,
    Grinning, in herself a ballet,
    Fixed as fate upon her audience.

Stumps are shaking, crutch-supported;
    Splinted fingers tap the rhythm;   10
    And a head all helmed with plasters
    Wags a measured approbation.

Of their mattress-life oblivious,
    All the patients, brisk and cheerful,

'THE CHIEF'
1 Hercules.

Are encouraging the dancer,
And applauding the musician.

Dim the gases in the output
Of so many ardent smokers,
Full of shadow lurch the corners,
And the doctor peeps and passes.   20

There are, maybe, some suspicions
Of an alcoholic presence...
'Tak' a sup of this, my wumman!'...
New Year comes but once a twelve-month.

XVIII
Children: Private Ward

Here in this dim, dull, double-bedded room,
I play a father to a brace of boys,
Ailing, but apt for every sort of noise,
Bedfast, but brilliant yet with health and bloom.
Roden, the Irishman, is 'sieven past,'
Blue-eyed, snub-nosed, chubby, and fair of face.
Willie's but six, and seems to like the place,
A cheerful little collier to the last.
They eat, and laugh, and sing, and fight, all day;
All night they sleep like dormice. See them play   10
At Operations: – Roden, the Professor,
Saws, lectures, takes the artery up, and ties;
Willie, self-chloroformed, with half-shut eyes,
Holding the limb and moaning – Case and Dresser.

XIX
Scrubber

She's tall and gaunt, and in her hard, sad face
With flashes of the old fun's animation
There lowers the fixed and peevish resignation
Bred of a past where troubles came apace.
She tells me that her husband, ere he died,
Saw seven of their children pass away,
And never knew the little lass at play
Out on the green, in whom he's deified.
Her kin dispersed, her friends forgot and gone,
All simple faith her honest Irish mind,   10
Scolding her spoiled young saint, she labours on:
Telling her dreams, taking her patients' part,
Trailing her coat sometimes: and you shall find
No rougher, quainter speech, nor kinder heart.

XX
Visitor

Her little face is like a walnut shell
With wrinkling lines; her soft, white hair adorns
Her either brow in quaint, straight curls, like horns;
And all about her clings an old, sweet smell.
Prim is her gown and quakerlike her shawl.
Well might her bonnets have been born on her.
Can you conceive a Fairy Godmother

The subject of a real religious call?
    In snow or shine, from bed to bed she runs,
Her mittened hands, that ever give or pray,   10
Bearing a sheaf of tracts, a bag of buns,
All twinkling smiles and texts and pious tales:
A wee old maid that sweeps the Bridegroom's way,[1]
Strong in a cheerful trust that never fails.

XXI
Romance

'Talk of pluck!' pursued the Sailor,
    Set at euchre[1] on his elbow,
    'I was on the wharf at Charleston,
    Just ashore from off the runner.

'It was gray and dirty weather,
    And I heard a drum go rolling,
    Rub-a-dubbing in the distance,
    Awful dour-like and defiant.

'In and out among the cotton,
    Mud, and chains, and stores, and anchors,   10
    Tramped a squad of battered scarecrows –
    Poor old Dixie's bottom dollar!

'Some had shoes, but all had rifles,
    Them that wasn't bald, was beardless,
    And the drum was rolling *Dixie*,
    And they stepped to it like men, sir!

'Rags and tatters, belts and bayonets,
    On they swung, the drum a-rolling,
    Mum and sour. It looked like fighting,
    And they meant it too, by thunder!'   20

XXII
Pastoral

'Tis the Spring.
Earth has conceived, and her bosom,
Teeming with summer, is glad.

Thro' the green land,
Vistas of change and adventure,
The gray roads go beckoning and winding,
Peopled with wains, and melodious
With harness-bells jangling:
Jangling and twangling rough rhythms
To the slow march of the stately, great horses   10
Whistled and shouted along.

White fleets of cloud,
Argosies heavy with fruitfulness,
Sail the blue peacefully. Green flame the hedgerows.

VISITOR
1 Jesus Christ, bridegroom of the church at second Advent.

ROMANCE
1 a card game.

Blackbirds are bugling, and white in wet winds
Sway the tall poplars.
Pageants of colour and fragrance,
Pass the sweet meadows, and viewless
Walks the mild spirit of May,
Visibly blessing the world.   20

O the brilliance of blossoming orchards!
O the savour and thrill of the woods,
When their leafage is stirred
By the flight of the angel of rain!
Loud lows the steer; in the fallows
Rooks are alert; and the brooks
Gurgle and tinkle and trill. Thro' the gloaming,
Under the rare, shy stars,
Boy and girl wander,
Dreaming in darkness and dew.   30

It's the Spring.
A sprightliness feeble and squalid
Wakes in the ward, and I sicken,
Impotent, winter at heart.

XXIII
Music

Down the quiet eve,
Thro' my window, with the sunset
Pipes to me a distant organ
Foolish ditties;

And, as when you change
Pictures in a magic lantern,
Books, beds, bottles, floor, and ceiling
Fade and vanish,

And I'm well once more. . . .
August flares adust and torrid,   10
But my heart is full of April
Sap and sweetness.

In the quiet eve
I am loitering, longing, dreaming . . .
Dreaming, and a distant organ
Pipes me ditties.

I can see the shop,
I can smell the sprinkled pavement,
Where she serves – her chestnut chignon
Thrills my senses!   20

O, the sight and scent,
Wistful eve and perfumed pavement!
In the distance pipes an organ . . .
The sensation

Comes to me anew,
And my spirit, for a moment

Thro' the music breathes the blessèd
Airs of London.

XXIV
Suicide

Staring corpselike at the ceiling,
  See his harsh, unrazored features,
  Ghastly brown against his pillow,
  And his throat – so strangely bandaged!

Lack of work and lack of victuals,
  A debauch of smuggled whisky,
  And his children in the workhouse,
  Made the world so black a riddle

That he plunged for a solution;
  And, although his knife was edgeless,   10
  He was sinking fast towards one,
  When they came, and found, and saved him.

Stupid now with shame and sorrow,
  In the night I hear him sobbing.
  But sometimes he talks a little.
  He has told me all his troubles.

In his broad face, tanned and bloodless,
  White and wide his eyeballs glitter;
  And his smile, occult and tragic,
  Makes you shudder when you see it.   20

XXV
Apparition

Thin-legged, thin-chested, slight unspeakably,
Neat-footed and weak-fingered: in his face –
Lean, large-boned, curved of beak, and touched with race,
Bold-lipped, rich-tinted, mutable as the sea,
The brown eyes radiant with vivacity –
There shines a brilliant and romantic grace,
A spirit intense and rare, with trace on trace
Of passion, impudence, and energy.
Valiant in velvet, light in ragged luck,
Most vain, most generous, sternly critical,   10
Buffoon and poet, lover and sensualist:
A deal of Ariel, just a streak of Puck,
Much Antony, of Hamlet most of all,
And something of the Shorter-Catechist.[1]

XXVI
Anterotics

  Laughs the happy April morn
    Thro' my grimy, little window,
    And a shaft of sunshine pushes
  Thro' the shadows in the square.

APPARITION
1 Calvinist catechism book/reader or instructor.

Dogs are romping thro' the grass,
  Crows are cawing round the chimneys,
  And among the bleaching linen
  Goes the west at hide-and-seek.

Loud and cheerful clangs the bell.
  Here the nurses troop to breakfast.   10
  Handsome, ugly, all are women...
  O, the Spring – the Spring – the Spring!

XXVII
Nocturn

At the barren heart of midnight,
  When the shadow shuts and opens
  As the loud flames pulse and flutter,
  I can hear a cistern leaking.

Dripping, dropping, in a rhythm,
  Rough, unequal, half-melodious,
  Like the measures aped from nature
  In the infancy of music;

Like the buzzing of an insect,
  Still, irrational, persistent...   10
  I must listen, listen, listen
  In a passion of attention;

Till it taps upon my heartstrings,
  And my very life goes dripping,
  Dropping, dripping, drip-drip-dropping,
  In the drip-drop of the cistern.

XXVIII
Discharged

Carry me out
Into the wind and the sunshine,
Into the beautiful world.

O the wonder, the spell of the streets!
The stature and strength of the horses,
The rustle and echo of footfalls,
The flat roar and rattle of wheels!
A swift tram floats huge on us...
It's a dream?
The smell of the mud in my nostrils   10
Blows brave – like a breath of the sea!

As of old,
Ambulant, undulant drapery
Vaguely and strangely provocative,
Flutters and beckons. O yonder –
Scarlet? – the glint of a stocking!
Sudden a spire
Wedged in the mist! O the houses,
The long lines of lofty, gray houses,
Cross-hatched with shadow and light!   20

These are the streets....
Each is an avenue leading
Whither I will!

Free...!
Dizzy, hysterical, faint,
I sit, and the carriage rolls on with me
Into the wonderful world.

Dated, The Old Infirmary, Edinburgh, 1873–5. First, shorter, version, Cornhill (July 1875). Greatly revised in A Book of Verses *(David Nutt, 1888). 1888 text (*pavement! *in XXIII supplied from a later text, for 1888* pavemen).

The past was goodly once, and yet, when all is said,
The best of it we know is that it's done and dead.

Dwindled and faded quite, perished beyond recall,
Nothing is left at last of what one time was all.

Coming back like a ghost, staring and lingering on,
Never a word it speaks but proves it dead and gone.

Duty and work and joy – these things it cannot give;
And the present is life, and life is good to live.

Let it lie where it fell, far from the living sun,
The past that, goodly once, is gone and dead and done.   10

A Book of Verses *(1888)*.

RAIN

The sky saggs low with convoluted cloud,
Heavy and imminent, rolled from rim to rim.
A bank of fog blots out of sight the brim
Of the leaden sea, all spiritless and cowed.
The rain is falling sheer and strong and loud,
The strand is desolate, the distance grim
With threats of storm, the wet stones glimmer dim,
And to the wall the dank umbrellas crowd.
At home... the dank shrubs whisper dismal mooded,
Black chimney-shadows streak the shiny slates,   10
The eaves are strung with drops, and steeped the grasses,
A draggled fishwife screeches at the gates,
The baker hurries dripping on, and hooded
In her wet prints a pretty housemaid passes.

A Book of Verses *(1888)*.

A desolate shore,
The sinister seduction of the Moon,
The menace of the irreclaimable Sea.

Flaunting, tawdry and grim,
From cloud to cloud along her beat,
Leering her battered and inveterate leer,
She signals where he prowls in the dark alone,
Her horrible old man,

Mumbling old oaths and warming
His villainous old bones with villainous talk –   10
The secrets of their grisly housekeeping
Since they went out upon the pad
In the first twilight of self-conscious Time:
Growling, obscene and hoarse,
Tales of unnumbered Ships,
Goodly and strong, Companions of the Advance
In some vile alley of the night
Waylaid and bludgeoned –
Dead.

Deep cellared in primeval ooze,   20
Ruined, dishonoured, spoiled,
They lie where the lean water-worm
Crawls free of their secrets, and their broken sides
Bulge with the slime of life. Thus they abide,
Thus fouled and desecrate,
The summons of the Trumpet, and the while
These Twain, their murderers,
Unravined, imperturbable, unsubdued,
Hang at the heels of their children – She aloft
As in the shining streets,   30
He as in ambush at some fetid stair.

The stalwart Ships,
The beautiful and bold adventurers!
Stationed out yonder in the isle,
The tall Policeman,
Flashing his bull's-eye, as he peers
About him in the ancient vacancy,
Tells them this way is safety – this way home.

The Song of the Sword and Other Verses (David Nutt, 1892).

To W.R.

Madam Life's a piece in bloom
   Death goes dogging everywhere:
She's the tenant of the room,
   He's the ruffian on the stair.

You shall see her as a friend,
   You shall bilk him once and twice;
But he'll trap you in the end,
   And he'll stick you for her price.

With his kneebones at your chest,
   And his knuckles in your throat,   10
You would reason – plead – protest!
   Clutching at her petticoat;

But she's heard it all before,
   Well she knows you've had your fun,
Gingerly she gains the door,
   And your little job is done.

Written 1877. Poems (David Nutt, 1898).

Henry Bellyse Baildon (1849–1907)

Henry Bellyse Baildon, poet and university teacher, was born at Granton in 1849, the son of an Edinburgh chemist. He had a sister Frances with whom he remained close (did he marry?). They were distantly related to Elizabeth Large, second wife of the great Scottish explorer and missionary to the South Seas with the London Missionary Society, James Chalmers (killed and eaten, it was said, in Papua New Guinea, 1901), who was greatly admired by Robert Louis Stevenson as well as by Baildon ('that valiant Gospeller, the Great-heart of New Guinea'). In 1864–5 Baildon was a pupil, with Stevenson, at Mr Robert Thomson's school for backward or delicate boys in Frederick Street, Edinburgh, where the two boys collaborated on a school magazine, *The Trial* (or *Jack o' Lantern*). Baildon became honorary secretary of the Edinburgh Philosophical Society, lectured on literature and modern poetry for the Edinburgh University Extension Scheme, and became a lecturer in English at the University of Vienna, then at the University of Dundee. He published several volumes of verse – *First Fruits and Shed Leaves* (1873), which was brought out anonymously, and heavily panned by the *Scotsman* and the Edinburgh *Courant*; as well as *Rosamund: A Tragic Drama* (1875), *Morning Clouds: Being Divers Poems* (1877), *The Spirit of Nature* (1880), *The Rescue and Other Poems* (1893). *The Rescue*, his last volume, has a dedicatory letter to Stevenson, deprecating Baildon's abandonment by the Muses: 'So I can only send you from my stripped vineyard raisins for grapes; and when you "pree" them, as we say in Scotland, you must bethink you of Frederick Street and the Gardens and the short-lived *Jack o' Lantern*, and let the glow of old fellowship renew the bloom and plump the skin of these wizened berries!' Stevenson thought some of the work 'good stout poems, fiery and sound', but didn't at all like Baildon's affectation of dropping definite and indefinite articles ('The reader goes on with a sense of impoverishment: he has been robbed by foot-pads and goes scouting for his lost article!': letter of 15 January 1894). Stevenson used Baildon's house, Duncliffe, at Murrayfield, as the scene of the murder in his story 'Misadventures of John Nicholson'. Baildon published *Robert Louis Stevenson: A Life Study in Criticism* (1901).

ALONE IN LONDON

By her fault or by ill-fate,
Left in great London, desolate
Of helpers and of comforters,
Without one heart to beat with hers, –
Without one hand in tenderness
And sympathy her hand to press, –
A lone soul, left dispassionate,
Without one link of love or hate.

From her lodging poor and bare,
And high up in the smoke-dim air,   10
With cheerless heart, with aimless feet,
She descendeth to the street,
Where the people, coming, going,
Ceaseless as a river's flowing,
Seemed as imperturbable,
As though no heart-warm tear could well
Into those dry eyes, – no sob
Ever could those set lips rob
Of their sternness, – with blind stare
They passed a woman in despair.   20

With hopeless heart, with weary feet,
She wanders on from street to street,
Restless as a withered leaf

Fallen from its parent tree;
  Goaded by a sleepless grief,
Dogged by dull perplexity,
Passing along, in dumb despair,
Deserted street and silent square.

Into the shadow black and deep
  Of a doorway she doth shrink,
Crouching there, she cannot weep,
  Waiting there, she cannot think.
As a tide on river wall
  Lappeth ever wearily,
Round her soul despair doth call
  Constantly and drearily;
As round ancient gable peaks
A ghostly night-wind wails and shrieks,
So again and yet again
Rise the bitter gusts of pain.

Steps are heard upon the stone:
One cometh down the street alone,
And upon the footsteps follow,
'Mid the dark roofs, echoes hollow,
On he comes, all unaware
Of the dark misery lurking there;
He pauseth not, but passes on, –
She speaketh not, and he is gone.
She thinks, 'He would but reckon me
The vile thing that I would not be.'

Silence again. A wild intent
The pang woke in her as it went;
She goes, nought with her, down the street,
But haunting echoes of her feet.
  .   .   .   .   .   .

She stands where, far below, is heard
The river's one unchanging word;
She stands and listens, and doth know,
Beneath the waters seaward go.
Like an incantation drear
She hears them wash by wharf and pier.

Will none come to save her yet?
Her foot is on the parapet;
Upward to a starless heaven
One last, hopeless look is given:
On each hand stretches black and far
The line of roofs irregular,
And beneath, a vast night-wall,
Based in gloom funereal.

The blackness floweth up to meet
The wanderer's world-weary feet,
And afar, below it all,
Still the river seems to call,
'Mortal, since thou wouldst not live,
Come, for I have rest to give;
Over thee and thy dark woes

30

40

50

60

70

Silently my waves shall close,
Spreading changeless over all,
Like a mighty funeral pall.'

A moment, agonized and mute,
Rigid, yet irresolute   80
She stands; then, with a bitter cry,
Rent from her soul's last agony,
Sheer down the black abyss she falls; –

The river washes by its walls.

Morning Clouds: Being Divers Poems *(David Douglas, Edinburgh, 1877)*.

To a Cabbage Leaf

O leaf, vulgar and homely,
How art thou become so comely?
Proudest lady may not wear
Brighter jewels in her hair.
For, gathering into trembling spheres
The Morning's gift of happy tears,
Thou art decked all price beyond,
With liquid pearl and diamond.

Nature, who is but a sign
Of a Wisdom more divine,   10
Sends to me this lesson great,
Whereon I may meditate
(Lacking human speech, she tells
Only silent parables),
'On the lowly heart and true
Falls the spiritual dew.'

Morning Clouds *(1877)*.

A Moth

A clumsy clot of shadow in the fold
    Of the white blind, – a moth asleep or dead,
And hooked therein with still, tenacious hold,
    And dusky vans outspread.

Laid on my hand a wonder of dull dyes,
    A sombre miracle of mingled grain,
Grey etched on grey, faint as faint memories,
    Dim stain invading stain.

Each wing-edge scalloped clear as any shell's,
    With rippled repetitions ebbing in   10
Rhyme within rhyme, as when cathedral bells
    Remit their joyous din.

Complete is it of broken laceries,
    A pencilled maze of blending greys,

Mosaic of symmetric traceries,
   Assorted in sweet ways.

Black velvet grainings upon pearly ash,
   An elf-wrought broidery of hues they stole
From the black moss-blot, and the lichen-splash,
   From birch or beechen bole.   20

Strange-headed thing, in ruminative rest
   Stirring its flexile antlers dreamily,
With great ghoul-eyes and sable-feathered breast,
   In sleep's security.

'There rest thee, and sleep off thy drowsy fit,
   Till night shall triumph in the dusky glades,
And mass her conquering glooms, then rise and flit
   A shadow through the shades!'

Morning Clouds (1877).

A BLUEBOTTLE

In the sunlight, in the shadow,
   Buzzes, bustles,
   Fumes and fustles,
That bluebottle fly.
   Oh, good gracious!
   Time is precious!
Don't you stay. Good-bye!

What's the stir, sir?
Lost your purse, sir?
   Or mislaid your specs?   10
Got an old hat
For a new one?
Shares been sold at 'certain ruin'?
   What sharp troubles vex?

Has your son been rusticated?
Has your daughter wrongly mated,
   Lacking your consent?
Are your talents underrated?
Patent been anticipated?
What, dear sir, has aggravated   20
   You to this extent?
Is your wife's rich uncle shabby?
Have you overpaid the cabby?

Still abusing, random cruising,
Still unflagging, zig-a-zagging,
   Circling, swooping,
   Spiring, looping,
Unabating, oscillating;
   Stop a moment, pray!
Unavailing! He goes sailing   30
   (Heaven be thanked!) away.

Morning Clouds (1877).

Philip Bourke Marston (1850–87)

Philip Bourke Marston, the blind poet, was born in London, 13 August 1850, the son of John Westland Marston the playwright. He grew up, formidably precocious, in a very intense cultural ambience. His godparents were Philip James Bailey, the author of *Festus* (1839), one of the flagship poems of the 'Spasmodics', and Dinah Maria Mulock. Her very popular poem, 'Philip, my King', is addressed to Marston. He began to lose his sight at the age of three through excessive application of belladonna against scarlet fever, and perhaps also some blow to the head; but difficulties with ordinary schooling mattered less than early induction into London literary life. When he met Swinburne at the age of fourteen he could recite all the First Series of *Poems and Ballads* by heart. His devotion to D. G. Rossetti ('What a supreme man is Rossetti') inspired his own great commitment to the sonnet form. The admirees reciprocated the affection: there's a Rossetti sonnet 'To Philip Bourke Marston: Inciting Me to Poetic Work'. Marston's first volume, *Song-Tide, and Other Poems* (1871), sets the prevailing gloomy tone kept up by its successors *All in All* (1875) and *Wind-Voices* (1883). Sensitive to a fault, the poems' melancholy closely mirrors their author's rather Gothic life of saddening deprivations and morbid losses –

the gradual descent into total blindness; the shocking death of his fiancée Mary Nesbit from galloping consumption (November 1871); the sudden death from food-poisoning at the age of nineteen, late in 1872, of his close friend Oliver Madox Brown (the precocious painter and writer, son of Ford Madox Brown, and William Michael Rossetti's brother-in-law); the death of his two remaining sisters, Cicely in 1878, Eleanor (wife of Arthur O'Shaughnessy) early in 1879; Dante Gabriel Rossetti's death, April 1882, and James Thomson's in June of the same year (of a stomach haemorrhage which happened gruesomely in Marston's lodgings). Marston lived partly by selling short stories (sales in America helped on by his future biographer Louise Chandler Moulton). He suffered severe sunstroke on a summer holiday, had some kind of stroke early in 1887, and died 13 February 1887 (14 February according to Richard Le Gallienne's obituary sonnet in *My Ladies' Sonnets*, 1887), aged thirty-six. Swinburne's elegy appeared in the *Fortnightly Review*, January 1891. Mrs Moulton brought out the posthumous collection of verses, *Garden Secrets* (1887), and *A Last Harvest* (1891), and edited the *Collected Poems of Philip Bourke Marston*, with a Biographical Sketch (1892).

SPEECHLESS

Upon the Marriage of Two Deaf and Dumb Persons

Their lips upon each other's lips are laid;
    Strong moans of joy, wild laughter, and short cries
    Seem uttered in the passion of their eyes.
He sees her body fair and fallen head,
And she the face whereon her soul is fed;
    And by the way her white breasts sink and rise,
    He knows she must be shaken by sweet sighs;
Though all delight of sound for them is dead.
They dance a strange, weird measure, who know not
    The tune to which their dancing feet are led;   10
Their breath in kissing is made doubly hot
    With flame of pent-up speech; strange light is shed
    About their spirits, as they mix and meet
    In passion-lighted silence, 'tranced and sweet.

Song-Tide, and Other Poems *(Ellis & Green, 1871)*.

SORE LONGING

My body is athirst for thee, my love;
    My lips, that may not meet thy lips again,

Are flowers that fail in drought for want of rain;
My heart, without thy voice, is like a grove
Wherein no bird makes music, while, above
  The twilight deepens as the low winds wane;
  My eyes, that ache for sight of thee in vain,
Are hidden streams no stars make mirrors of.
I see thee but in memory, alas!
  So some worn seaman, restless in his sleep,   10
  In time of danger, o'er the raging deep,
Sees visionary lights, and cries, 'We pass
  The prayed-for land; reverse the helm, put back!'
  Yet still the ship bears on her starless track.

All in All: Poems and Sonnets *(Chatto & Windus, 1875).*

AFTER

I

A little time for laughter,
  A little time to sing,
  A little time to kiss and cling,
And no more kissing after.

II

A little while for scheming
  Love's unperfected schemes;
  A little time for golden dreams,
Then no more any dreaming.

III

A little while 'twas given
  To me to have thy love;   10
  Now, like a ghost, alone I move
About a ruined heaven.

IV

A little time for speaking,
  Things sweet to say and hear;
  A time to seek, and find thee near,
Then no more any seeking.

V

A little time for saying
  Words the heart breaks to say;
  A short, sharp time wherein to pray,
Then no more need for praying;   20

VI

But long, long years to weep in,
  And comprehend the whole
  Great grief that desolates the soul;
And eternity to sleep in.

All in All: Poems and Sonnets *(1875).*

THE OLD CHURCHYARD OF BONCHURCH[1]

(This old churchyard has been for many years slipping toward the sea, which it is expected will ultimately engulf it.)

The churchyard leans to the sea with its dead, –
It leans to the sea with its dead so long.
Do they hear, I wonder, the first bird's song,
When the winter's anger is all but fled;
The high, sweet voice of the west wind,
The fall of the warm, soft rain,
When the second month of the year
Puts heart in the earth again?

Do they hear, through the glad April weather,
The green grasses waving above them?   10
Do they think there are none left to love them,
They have lain for so long there, together?
Do they hear the note of the cuckoo,
The cry of gulls on the wing,
The laughter of winds and waters,
The feet of the dancing Spring?

Do they feel the old land slipping seaward,
The old land, with its hills and its graves,
As they gradually slide to the waves,
With the wind blowing on them from leeward?   20
Do they know of the change that awaits them,
The sepulchre vast and strange?
Do they long for the days to go over,
And bring that miraculous change?

Or they love, perhaps, their night with no moonlight,
With no starlight, no dawn to its gloom,
And they sigh – "Neath the snow, or the bloom
Of the wild things that wave from our night,
We are warm, through winter and summer;
We hear the winds blow, and say –   30
"The storm-wind blows over our heads,
But we, here, are out of its way." '

Do they mumble low, one to another,
With a sense that the waters that thunder
Shall ingather them all, draw them under,
'Ah! how long to our moving, my brother?
How long shall we quietly rest here,
In graves of darkness and ease?
The waves, even now, may be on us,
To draw us down under the seas!'   40

Do they think 't will be cold when the waters
That they love not, that neither can love them,
Shall eternally thunder above them?

THE OLD CHURCHYARD OF BONCHURCH
1   Isle of Wight.

Have they dread of the sea's shining daughters,
That people the bright sea-regions
And play with the young sea-kings?
Have they dread of their cold embraces,
And dread of all strange sea-things?

But their dread or their joy – it is bootless:
They shall pass from the breast of their mother;   50
They shall lie low, dead brother by brother,
In a place that is radiant and fruitless,
And the folk that sail over their heads
In violent weather
Shall come down to them, haply, and all
They shall lie there, together.

Wind-Voices (Elliot Stock, 1883).

TO JAMES THOMSON, AUTHOR OF 'THE CITY OF DREADFUL NIGHT'

I

Brother, and fellow-citizen with me
  Of this great city whose tremendous gloom
  Weighted on thee with the heaviness of doom,
I walk its ways to-day, and seem to see
Thy saddest eyes; again with thee to be
  As on that day when, in this very room,
  Thine eyes and ours who watched thee saw Death loom,
A mighty monarch, strong to set thee free.

Still, still the same, this 'City of Dreadful Night' –
  Still does it hear a sound of lamentation,   10
  As of a conquered, broken-hearted nation;
Still glowers the Sphinx, and breaks us with her might
Of unresponsive front. There is no light –
  There is no hope – God, there is *no* salvation.

II

No tears of mine shall fall upon thy face;
  Whatever City thou hast gained, at last,
  Better it is than that where thy feet passed
So many times, such weary nights and days.
Those journeying feet knew all its inmost ways;
  Where shapes and shadows of dread things were cast –   20
  There moved thy soul, profoundly dark and vast,
There did thy voice its hymn of anguish raise.

Thou wouldst have left that City of great Night,
  Yet travelled its dark mazes, all in vain;
But one way leads from it, which found aright,
  Who goes by it may not return again.
  There didst thou grope thy way, through thy long pain;
Hast thou, outside, found any world of light?

Wind-Voices (1883).

NOT ONLY ROOMS WHEREIN THY LOVE HAS BEEN

Not only rooms wherein thy Love has been
   Hold still for thee the memory of her grace,
   The benediction of her blessing face,
But other rooms that never saw thy Queen
Are full of her: Has not thy spirit seen
   A vision of her in this firelit place
   That never knew the witchery of her ways,
The perfect voice, the eyes intense, serene?

Ah, stood she not before the mirror there,
   Her loveliness all clothed in soft attire,
   Then turned to thee, low-kneeling by this fire,   10
And laid a gracious hand upon thy hair,
   While thy heart leaped to her, thy heart's desire,
And thy kiss praised her, and thy look was prayer?

A Last Harvest: Lyrics and Sonnets from the Book of Love
(Elkin Mathews, 1891).

Robert Louis (Lewis Balfour) Stevenson (1850–94)

Robert Lewis Balfour Stevenson – the Louis substitution came later – was born in Edinburgh, 13 November 1850, into a family of great Scottish engineers, men with a particular bent for designing lighthouses. His father, Thomas Stevenson, was engineer to the Board of Northern Lighthouses. His mother Margaret was a Balfour, her father the minister to a Midlothian parish, her grandfather an Edinburgh professor of philosophy and law. From the start Stevenson was a sick child, dogged by the pulmonary weaknesses which haunted and shaped his life as he went from doctor to doctor, infirmary to infirmary, rest-cure to rest-cure, always on the move for his lungs' sake. Much of his childhood was spent in his maternal grandfather's manse, at health resorts, as well as up lighthouses with his father. Schooling, much of it with private tutors, was intermittent because of his illness. At Mr Robert Thomson's school for delicate and backward boys in Frederick Street, Edinburgh, in the early sixties, Stevenson made friends with the future poet Henry Bellyse Baildon. He took up engineering studies at Edinburgh University (1867) but switched to law (1871). He was called to the Bar (1875), but never practised – by then already set on combining the search for the best place in Britain and Europe for his health with the nearest approach to bohemianism his frailties would allow: visiting artistic colonies in France, giving up formal social ways, living in practical defiance of Scottish Calvinism, writing hard, always clubbable. His great friendship with W. E. Henley, with whom he would collaborate on many dramas, began in an Edinburgh Infirmary in the winter of 1874–5 (Henley was there to save his one remaining leg from amputation). In London Stevenson haunted the artistic Savile Club,

becoming friends with the likes of Leslie Stephen, Cosmo Monkhouse, Andrew Lang, Edmund Gosse. His essays and stories were starting to appear all over the scene, in the *Academy, Vanity Fair, London, Temple Bar*, the *Cornhill*. In 1878 he became friends with the admired George Meredith and made the journey which became *Travels With a Donkey in the Cévennes* (1879). The same year he chased off to California after Mrs Fanny Osbourne, whom he'd met in Parisian artistic circles. They married the following year, when her divorce came through. She would come between her husband and Henley. In the eighties Stevenson was often at death's door, unable to get his breath, coughing blood. Wintering at Davos, in Switzerland, at the end of 1880, as ever for his health, he met John Addington Symonds and their firm friendship began. Poor health did not stop him writing. The *Virginibus Puerisque* essays, many of them from the *Cornhill*, were gathered in 1881. *Familiar Stories of Men and Books* and the stories *New Arabian Nights* appeared in 1882. Stevenson hit the popularity jackpot in 1883 with the Boys' Book for all ages, *Treasure Island. A Child's Garden of Verses*, full of that attention to the miniature world of the child and the child's-eye vision which stimulated and formed so much of the Victorian *imaginaire*, was published in 1885. (It was finished at Hyères with his right arm strapped to his chest, the writing done in awkward capitals with his left hand.) In 1886 came two of the most central Stevenson fictions – the hugely popular *Dr Jekyll and Mr Hyde*, one of the most important contributions to the whole western Doppelgänger canon, and *Kidnapped*, possibly Stevenson's finest Scottish novel. More poems, frequently occasional, never uncharming, some in 'Scots', tender by-products of a mainly prose career, many of them done in fatigued corners of a frequently wearied life, were collected as *Underwoods* (1887), *Ballads* (1890) and *Songs of Travel* (1896). In the summer of 1887 the Stevensons moved to America, settling in the Adirondacks for a year or so, before setting off by yacht for the South Seas (financed by advances from an American publisher for a book of travel letters). After many months cruising about down under, the Stevenson ménage finally settled in Samoa, at the property named Vailima, where Stevenson turned into a sort of feudal overlord-cum-storyteller, a kind of Lord Jim of letters (known locally as Tusitala, the Teller of Tales). Nothing was allowed to distract him from writing – neither his immersion in local politics, quarrels with German administrators, his wife's nervous breakdown, writer's cramp (he had to dictate to his amanuensis stepdaughter), nor even loss of voice (he had to resort to deaf-and-dumb sign language). He and his little tribe desperately needed the money from publication, especially in America. He died, suddenly, of a brain haemorrhage, 3 December 1894, leaving much of his work incomplete and unpublished. Sixty natives hacked a way to his chosen burial place up Mount Vaea. The *Vailima Letters*, whose advance took him to Samoa, came out in 1895, the novel *The Weir of Hermiston* in 1896. *A Family of Engineers* was among many Stevenson texts to appear for the first time in the massive 27-volume Edinburgh Edition (1894–8).

THE LAND OF COUNTERPANE

When I was sick and lay a-bed,
I had two pillows at my head,
And all my toys beside me lay
To keep me happy all the day.

And sometimes for an hour or so
I watched my leaden soldiers go,
With different uniforms and drills,
Among the bed-clothes, through the hills;

And sometimes sent my ships in fleets
All up and down among the sheets;   10
Or brought my trees and houses out,
And planted cities all about.

I was the giant great and still
That sits upon the pillow-hill,
And sees before him, dale and plain,
The pleasant land of counterpane.

A Child's Garden of Verses *(Longmans, Green, & Co., 1885)*.

MY SHADOW

I have a little shadow that goes in and out with me,
And what can be the use of him is more than I can see.
He is very, very like me from the heels up to the head;
And I see him jump before me, when I jump into my bed.

The funniest thing about him is the way he likes to grow –
Not at all like proper children, which is always very slow;
For he sometimes shoots up taller like an india-rubber ball,
And he sometimes gets so little that there's none of him at all.

He hasn't got a notion of how children ought to play,
And can only make a fool of me in every sort of way.   10
He stays so close beside me, he's a coward you can see;
I'd think shame to stick to nursie as that shadow sticks to me!

One morning, very early, before the sun was up,
I rose and found the shining dew on every buttercup;
But my lazy little shadow, like an arrant sleepy-head,
Had stayed at home behind me and was fast asleep in bed.

A Child's Garden of Verses *(1885)*.

BLOCK CITY

What are you able to build with your blocks?
Castles and palaces, temples and docks.
Rain may keep raining, and others go roam,
But I can be happy and building at home.

Let the sofa be mountains, the carpet be sea,
There I'll establish a city for me:
A kirk and a mill and a palace beside,
And a harbour as well where my vessels may ride.

Great is the palace with pillar and wall,
A sort of a tower on the top of it all,   10
And steps coming down in an orderly way
To where my toy vessels lie safe in the bay.

This one is sailing and that one is moored:
Hark to the song of the sailors on board!
And see on the steps of my palace, the kings
Coming and going with presents and things!

Now I have done with it, down let it go!
All in a moment the town is laid low.
Block upon block lying scattered and free,
What is there left of my town by the sea?   20

Yet as I saw it, I see it again,
The kirk and the palace, the ships and the men,
And as long as I live, and where'er I may be,
I'll always remember my town by the sea.

A Child's Garden of Verses *(1885)*.

TO ANY READER

Whether upon the garden seat
You lounge with your uplifted feet
Under the May's whole Heaven of blue;
Or whether on the sofa, you,
No grown up person being by,
Do some soft corner occupy:
Take you this volume in your hands
And enter into other lands,
For lo! (as children feign) suppose
You, hunting in the garden rows,   10
Or in the lumbered attic, or
The cellar – a nail-studded door
And dark, descending stairway found
That led to kingdoms underground:

There standing, you should hear with ease
Strange birds a-singing, or the trees
Swing in big robber woods, or bells
On many fairy citadels:
There passing through (a step or so
Neither mamma nor nurse need know!)   20
From your nice nurseries you would pass
Like Alice through the Looking-Glass
Or Gerda following Little Ray,
To wondrous countries far away.[1]
Well, and just this volume can
Transport each little maid or man,
Presto, from where they live away
Where other children used to play.

As from the house your mother sees
You playing round the garden trees,   30
So you may see, if you but look
Through the windows of this book,
Another child, far, far away
And in another garden, play.
But do not think you can at all,
By knocking on the window, call
That child to hear you. He intent
Is still on his play-business bent.
He does not hear, he will not look,
Nor yet be lured out of this book.   40
For long ago, the truth to say,
He has grown up and gone away;
And it is but a child of air
That lingers in the garden there.

A Child's Garden of Verses (1885): only lines 29–44. Longer version,
Poems by Robert Louis Stevenson, ed. George S. Hellman, 2 vols
(Boston, 1916), I, which then became standard. Text of Lines 1–28, from
Collected Poems, ed. Janet Adam Smith (Rupert Hart-Davis, 1950).

CHRISTMAS AT SEA

The sheets were frozen hard, and they cut the naked hand;
The decks were like a slide, where a seaman scarce could stand;
The wind was a nor'wester, blowing squally off the sea;
And cliffs and spouting breakers were the only things a-lee.

They heard the surf a-roaring before the break of day;
But 'twas only with the peep of light we saw how ill we lay.
We tumbled every hand on deck instanter, with a shout,
And we gave her the maintops'l, and stood by to go about.

All day we tacked and tacked between the South Head and the North;
All day we hauled the frozen sheets, and got no further forth;   10
All day as cold as charity, in bitter pain and dread,
For very life and nature we tacked from head to head.

TO ANY READER
1   Lewis Carroll's *Alice*; Hans Christian Andersen's 'The Snow Queen'
(1846).

We gave the South a wider berth, for there the tide-race roared;
But every tack we made we brought the North Head close aboard:
So's we saw the cliffs and houses, and the breakers running high,
And the coastguard in his garden, with his glass against his eye.

The frost was on the village roofs as white as ocean foam;
The good red fires were burning bright in every 'longshore home;
The windows sparkled clear, and the chimneys volleyed out;
And I vow we sniffed the victuals as the vessel went about.   20

The bells upon the church were rung with a mighty jovial cheer;
For it's just that I should tell you how (of all days in the year)
This day of our adversity was blessèd Christmas morn,
And the house above the coastguard's was the house where I was born.

O well I saw the pleasant room, the pleasant faces there,
My mother's silver spectacles, my father's silver hair;
And well I saw the firelight, like a flight of homely elves,
Go dancing round the china-plates that stand upon the shelves.

And well I knew the talk they had, the talk that was of me,
Of the shadow on the household and the son that went to sea;   30
And O the wicked fool I seemed, in every kind of way,
To be here and hauling frozen ropes on blessèd Christmas Day.

They lit the high sea-light, and the dark began to fall.
'All hands to loose topgallant sails,' I heard the captain call.
'By the Lord, she'll never stand it,' our first mate Jackson, cried.
… 'It's the one way or the other, Mr. Jackson,' he replied.

She staggered to her bearings, but the sails were new and good,
And the ship smelt up to windward just as though she understood.
As the winter's day was ending, in the entry of the night,
We cleared the weary headland, and passed below the light.   40

And they heaved a mighty breath, every soul on board but me,
As they saw her nose again pointing handsome out to sea;
But all that I could think of, in the darkness and the cold,
Was just that I was leaving home and my folks were growing old.

Scots Observer *(22 December 1888)*. Ballads *(Chatto & Windus, December 1890)*.

Say not of me that weakly I declined
The labours of my sires, and fled the sea,
The towers we founded and the lamps we lit,
To play at home with paper like a child.
But rather say: *In the afternoon of time*
A strenuous family dusted from its hands
The sand of granite, and beholding far
Along the sounding coast its pyramids
And tall memorials catch the dying sun,
Smiled well content, and to this childish task   10
Around the fire addressed its evening hours.

Underwoods *(Chatto & Windus, 1887)*.

I will make you brooches and toys for your delight
Of bird-song at morning and star-shine at night.
I will make a palace fit for you and me
Of green days in forests and blue days at sea.

I will make my kitchen, and you shall keep your room,
Where white flows the river and bright blows the broom,
And you shall wash your linen and keep your body white
In rainfall at morning and dewfall at night.

And this shall be for music when no one else is near,
The fine song for singing, the rare song to hear!   10
That only I remember, that only you admire,
Of the broad road that stretches and the roadside fire.

Songs of Travel, *in* The Works of Robert Louis Stevenson, *Edinburgh Edition, XIV,*
ed. Sidney Colvin (December 1895). Songs of Travel and Other Verses
(Chatto & Windus, 1896). Poem No. XI. (Included in Ralph Vaughan William's song-cycle,
Songs of Travel.)

I have trod the upward and the downward slope;
I have endured and done in days before;
I have longed for all, and bid farewell to hope;
And I have lived and loved, and closed the door.

Songs of Travel *(1895, 1896). No.XXII.*

If This Were Faith

God, if this were enough,
That I see things bare to the buff
And up to the buttocks in mire;
That I ask nor hope nor hire,
Nut in the husk,
Nor dawn beyond the dusk,
Nor life beyond death:
God, if this were faith?

Having felt thy wind in my face
Spit sorrow and disgrace,   10
Having seen thine evil doom
In Golgotha and Khartoum,
And the brutes, the work of thine hands,
Fill with injustice lands
And stain with blood the sea:
If still in my veins the glee
Of the black night and the sun
And the lost battle, run:
If, an adept,
The iniquitous lists I still accept   20
With joy, and joy to endure and be withstood,
And still to battle and perish for a dream of good:
God, if that were enough?

If to feel, in the ink of the slough,
And the sink of the mire,
Veins of glory and fire
Run through and transpierce and transpire,

And a secret purpose of glory in every part,
And the answering glory of battle fill my heart;
To thrill with the joy of girded men   30
To go on for ever and fail and go on again,
And be mauled to the earth and arise,
And contend for the shade of a word and a thing not seen with the eyes:
With the half of a broken hope for a pillow at night
That somehow the right is the right
And the smooth shall bloom from the rough:
Lord, if that were enough?

Songs of Travel (1895, 1896). No.XXVI.

My wife and I, in our romantic cot,
The world forgetting, by the world forgot,
High as the gods upon Olympus dwell,
Pleased with the things we have, and pleased as well
To wait in hope for those which we have not.
She burns in ardour for a horse to trot;
I pledge my votive powers upon a yacht;
Which shall be first remembered, who can tell,
　My wife or I?

Harvests of flowers o'er all our garden-plot,   10
She dreams; and I to enrich a darker spot
My unprovided cellar; both to swell
Our narrow cottage huge as a hotel,
That portly friends may come and share our lot –
　Of wife and I.

First published 1921 (in Poems by Robert Louis Stevenson: Hitherto Unpublished,
ed. George S. Hellman, III (Boston, 1921), and Sidney Colvin, Memories and Notes *(1921).*
Text, Collected Poems, *ed. Janet Adam Smith (1950). Probably written, Hyères,*
the Stevensons' home March 1883–July 1884.

Theo (Théophile Jules Henri/Theophilus Julius Henry) Marzials (1850–?after 1897)

Theo Marzials, composer, librarian and poet, was born Théophile Jules Henri Marzials in Brussels, 21 December 1850. His mother came from Yorkshire; his father was a French Protestant cleric from Toulouse, who became pastor of the Reformed French Chapel of Canterbury Cathedral. His boyhood was passed in Brussels and Switzerland. He also went to school in England. He studied music in Paris and Milan, had a reputable baritone voice, wrote popular songs ('Twickenham Ferry', 'Three Sailor Boys', 'That Sweet Story of Old') and set other people's words to music (e.g. 'The Garden' by Philip Bourke Marston), adapted operas into English, and created operas of his own. He wrote art criticism for the *Examiner*. At some point he started to be known as the more English-sounding Theophilus Julius Henry Marzials. In 1870 he became superintendent of the British Museum Music Room.

Around that time he came into contact with the Pre-Raphaelites, is alleged to have torn up his old poems, and produced the Pre-Raphaelite-influenced volume *The Gallery of Pigeons and Other Poems* (1873), only straightaway to turn against his mentors. 'Mr Marzials had no sooner published the volume than he saw the mistake which he had made, and resolved not to publish again until he had emancipated himself from alien bondage, and could write entirely from his own thought, and feeling, and observation. This time may now' – this is A. T. C. Pratt in *People of the Period* (1897) – 'be said to have gone by and in a year or two we may expect to have a new volume from his pen, including some of his earlier as well as the product of his later work.' This volume does not seem to have materialized. A *Selected Poems* was published by the American University of Beirut, ed. John M. Munro, in 1974.

A Tragedy

Death!
Plop.
The barges down in the river flop.
Flop, plop,
Above, beneath.
From the slimy branches the grey drips drop,
As they scraggle black on the thin grey sky,
Where the black cloud rack-hackles drizzle and fly
To the oozy waters, that lounge and flop
On the black scrag piles, where the loose cords plop,   10
As the raw wind whines in the thin tree-top.
Plop, plop.
And scudding by
The boatmen call out hoy! and hey!
And all is running in water and sky,
And my head shrieks – 'Stop,'
And my heart shrieks – 'Die.'

      *   *   *   *   *

My thought is running out of my head;
My love is running out of my heart;
My soul runs after, and leaves me as dead,   20
For my life runs after to catch them – and fled
They are all every one! – and I stand, and start,
At the water that oozes up, plop and plop,
On the barges that flop
And dizzy me dead.
I might reel and drop.
Plop
Dead.

And the shrill wind whines in the thin tree-top.
Flop, plop.   30

      *   *   *   *   *

A curse on him.
Ugh! yet I knew – I knew –
If a woman is false can a friend be true?
It was only a lie from beginning to end –
My Devil – my 'Friend'
I had trusted the whole of my living to!
Ugh! and I knew!
Ugh!
So what do I care,
And my head is as empty as air –   40
I can do,
I can dare,
(Plop, plop,
The barges flop
Drip, drop.)
I can dare, I can dare!
And let myself all run away with my head,
And stop.
Drop
Dead.   50
Plop, flop.

Plop.

The Gallery of Pigeons and Other Poems (S. King & Co., 1873).

LOVE'S MASQUERADES

Love, the Poet

In broad brocades, three laughing ladies sat,
    Hand in white hand, and marygold-girt head
    To warm white throat; their cheeks encrimsonèd;
And from their lips intent, the waifs of chat
Went twittering o'er the daisied terrace-plat
    Of Love's delights what time they might be wed;
    Then Love came by the marygold's bright bed
A gay court poet, peacock-plume in hat.

With soft hand feeling down his slender thigh,
    Where dangling hung his deadly chorded lute,   10
He 'gan recite of Tristram and Yseut:
    For whose sad loves the silenced dames thereby,
In tears forgot their lords long due from chase; –
And Poesy had stolen all love's space.

Love, the Rebuker

Out o'er the windings of a dark side-street,
    High in a closely curtain'd balcony,
A lady's lover coil'd about her feet,
    Drawing her mouth to his; and swooning by
She forced, to still her quick heart's throb and beat,
    His face against her burning throat; and high
The gold stars glimmer'd in the midnight heat
    Thro' close set citron jars and rosemary.

Then sudden, from the angle of the square,
Clear to the moonlight, through the death-still air   10
    Love like a wanton cried aloud for hire;
And struck with bitter loathing of their sin
The lovers wrench'd apart! – I' the room within,
    They heard a stealthy step creep nigher, nigher.

Love, the Traitor

And there was one came reeling from carouse,
    Hose at his heel, sword trailing through the mire,
    Brawling a drunken song, and all on fire
At ducats filch'd in some low gambling-house;
And hearing Love from habit drone for hire,
    Listless with rose-wreath toppling from her brows,
    Clear from the moonlight, nodding in a drowse
In the deep shade of the Cathedral spire,

He ran and woke her with a scurvy jest,
    And closed her to him; and Love laughed out clear   10
Her cruel harlot's laugh; and, hugging, press'd
    Her dagger in – and cried: 'Thou fool, rot here,
    Who takest love for lust,' and soar'd up sheer,
Leaving his life-blood blackening from his breast.

Love, the Ideal

At noon when every dame had sought her bed,
  High in an oriel, peacock-plume in hand,
  And mapped beneath her all the varied land,
Dreaming from out her dainty book she read,
Till of a sudden, with a flame-girt head,
  The one she dream'd of, on light pinions fann'd
  Over the sill, did gently swoop and stand
Beside her, quivering for her full mouth's red.

And in his warm god's arms her cheeks so glow'd
  She hardly mark'd how, writ in rose and gold,   10
Her own life's page was past, and hardly show'd.
  Then with a cry he vanish'd – shivering cold
The night wind swept the corridors; the bell
Boom'd for one dead, down from the spired chapelle.

The Gallery of Pigeons (1873).

I'd like to be the lavender
  That makes her linen sweet,
And swoon and sweeten in her breast,
  And faint around her feet.

She'd hardly think of me at all,
  And shake out lawn and sheet;
And yet I'd be the lavender,
  And make her linen sweet.

The Gallery of Pigeons (1873).

The lords of state, and the thieving sparrows,
  Have settled noisily back to town;
The girls with flowers and shrill calabrians[1]
  Drone in the distance, up and down.

I cannot write, or read, or practise;
  I sit and grumble and curse the May;
The lime's one legion of smelling blossom,
  And hides her windows over the way.

The Gallery of Pigeons (1873).

William Renton (1852–?after 1905)

William Renton is rather a mystery man. Born in Edinburgh in 1852 and educated in Germany, this fine poetic miniaturist of setting and mood was the author of *The Logic of Style* (1874), a revisionist Life of Jesus (*Jesus, Kes-* wick, 1876), and a prose romance, *Bishopspool* (1883). He lived until at least 1905, when he superintended the revised version of his 1876 poems *Oils and Watercolours*.

'THE LORDS OF STATE, AND THE THIEVING SPARROWS'
1 Southern Italians, from Calabria.

CLOUD GROUPINGS

I

Those clouds at even are swollen and pieced
With a hundred milky paps at least;
And wait the sun's last thirsty tremors shooting high
To tint them ruddier and to lip them dry.

II

Two clouds sail through the noonday space,
One fair, the other dusky in the face.
In such sweet equipoise they move,
The cloud beneath sleeps like the shadow of the cloud above.

III

Sweet are the pencillings of April skies,
Soft lashes upon closing April eyes: 10
Drabbled and flustered films, depending sheer
From streaky cloud, or washed on wrinkled slice
Of sandlike murk upreared to precipice.
Not such, these pointing streaks; yet not less dear;
Calm, unimpeached, while cloudlets pass and flee,
Pure silver skiffs on immemorial sea.

Oils and Watercolours *(Edmonton & Douglas, Edinburgh, 1876).*

THE FOAL

The mouse-brown foal that fain had fed
From off the green his mother crops
So quietly in her own place,
Craning in vain and bending, stops,
Intent upon his match with space,
And rises beaten by half a head.
And last he sets himself to slide
His spidery-slender limbs aside,
If so be now to reach the mead. –
He must stride   10
Ere he can feed.

Oils and Watercolours *(1876).*

CRESCENT MOON

The moon had risen an hour or more.
It was the younger moon, but shorn
Of those first pointing cusps she wore,
And bluff with blunted horn;
But poised upright
And golden bright,
Save where there hung a middle haze,
Soft as the golden air that lies
Upon the sunset's closing eyes
And plays   10

Between his glory-golden lids –
And none forbids.
And none forbade, as it did seem,
That this lorn haze should doat and dream
On such an eve of June
And cling about the middle moon,
That scarce was dimmer for such offending.
But none might stay its soft ascending,
Till each in turn the veilèd old
Was clear as dew,   20
And all the new
Was dusky gold;
And last, a wraith,
Exhaling like the breath
We breathed upon a golden jar,
Showed on the tip and went afar –
Upon the disc a moving spot
That would be, was, and now was not.

Oils and Watercolours *(1876)*.

After Nightfall

Ample the air above the western peaks;
Within the peaks a silence uncompelled.
It is the hour of abnegation's self,
In clear obeisance of the mountain thrones,
And cloudless self-surrender of the skies:
The very retrospect of skiey calm,
And selfless self-approval of the hills.

Oils and Watercolours *(1876)*.

The Shadow of Himself

At evening the horse comes down unled
   With pace that is but his second best,
And with harness only about his head:
   He is half undrest,
And on his way to bed.
But he takes his share of the space and the light,
   His brown skin glisters warm and good,
And his shadow stretches as full a height
   As a horse's should;

For on the wall   10
   As he slouches down
Stalks a phantom, tall as he is tall
   And black as he is brown;
With the very gait and the very speed
   Of his Highness shown,
And I fear me a greed
   That matches his own;
For if his head should stoop to treat
With the wayside grasses – in a heat

There stoops his friend's,
And their muzzles meet
On the very tuft for which he contends.

20

Oils and Watercolours (1876).

Dull December

Wearily cawing crows are heavily winging
From where within the hollow of the hill,
Beside the brook, the heifers graze and saunter.
And up the nodding team comes, stoutly breasting
The ridge – the ploughman halting hard behind –
Part hid as yet, but their breaths float and waver
Down by the ploughed land toward the blue sheeprack
Stranded afar upon the level meadow.
More downcastly they come, with griding share
And dangling wood-gear; now they near the turn;
The ploughman tilts his wain, the horses swerve
And jostle, and so bear up for the next furrow.

10

Oils and Watercolours (1876).

The Fork of the Road

An utter moorland, high, and wide, and flat;
A beaten roadway, branching out in grave distaste;
And weather-beaten and defaced,
Pricking its ears along the solitary waste –
A signpost; pointing this way, pointing that.

Oils and Watercolours (1876).

Oscar (Fingall O'Flahertie Wills) Wilde (1854–1900)

Oscar Wilde was born in Dublin, 16 October 1854, middle child of distinguished Protestant parents – Dr (later Sir) William Wilde, an ear–eye surgeon, and Jane Francesca Elgee, archdeacon's granddaughter, translator, flamboyantly breathy poet of the nationalist Young Ireland movement of the forties (writing as 'Speranza') and centre of a shiny salon at the Wilde house in Merrion Square. Like Samuel Beckett later, Wilde was sent to the Protestant Portora Royal School in Enniskillen in the Protestant north of Ireland, and then to Trinity College, Dublin. He graduated in Classics in 1874, winner of the Berkeley Gold Medal. He then went on a scholarship to study Classics at Magdalen College, Oxford, 1874–5 – a reputedly lazy, but successful, student (First Classes in Moderations and Finals: 'the Bad Boy doing so well in the End'). At Oxford he burnished a reputation for aesthetical decadence of life and epigrammatic wittiness of speech, toyed like so many others with the aesthetic and sensuous attractions of Roman Catholicism, and fell in love with Greece (he was rusticated for stretching a Greek visit with his Dublin Classics tutor Mahaffy into a term-time). His first published poem, 'Chorus of Cloud-Maidens' in the *Dublin University Magazine* (1875), was followed by a shower of verse, especially in Irish periodicals. He collected many of these in *Poems* (1881) at his own expense (copies to Matthew Arnold, Robert Browning, Gladstone) – a volume some readers decided was obscene, others merely an anthology of pastiche. At Oxford he evangelized the merits of Elizabeth Barrett Browning's 'Aurora Leigh'. He thought Arnold's 'Thyrsis' and 'Scholar-Gipsy' exquisite. Influences stuck to him like flies – Shelley, Pater, Swinburne, Baudelaire, Tennyson. His early, less decided poetic voice is Protestant Irish and Cromwellian, his later one more Impressionist and Decadent, rather French and Gautieresque. He travelled widely after graduation – lecturing in North America (1882), where his languorous English aestheticism annoyed as well as fascinated (and he decided England and the USA had much in common except language), residing in Paris for several months in 1883 (as well as later in 1891). He tinkered with his *Poems* (last edition, 1892), married Constance Lloyd (1884), settled in Chelsea, fathered two sons (Cyril, 1885, Vyvyan, 1886), edited the *Woman's World* (1887–9), and became extremely notorious as a key figure in the aestheticist movement (all long hair, peacocks' feathers, blue china and velvet trousers), much lampooned by *Punch* (and was widely thought to be a model for the satirized aesthete Bunthorne in Gilbert and Sullivan's *Patience*, 1881). The days of his great literary flowering – essays, stories, plays – began with the publication of *The Happy Prince* stories (1888). *Blackwood's* published 'The Portrait of Mr W. H.' in 1889. *The Picture of Dorian Gray* first appeared in *Lippincott's Monthly Magazine* (1890). In 1891 came the expanded *Dorian, Lord Arthur Savile's Crime and Other Stories*, the fairy-story volume *A House of Pomegranates*, and 'The Soul of Man Under Socialism'. *Lady Windermere's Fan* was produced in 1892, *A Woman of No Importance* in 1893, *An Ideal Husband* and *The Importance of Being Earnest* in 1895. In 1895, hugely successful, the wondrous epigrammatic undoer of conventional codes, a subversive Anglo-Irish wit in the great tradition of Swift and Sterne ('I throw probability out of the window for the sake of a phrase, and the chance of an epigram makes me desert truth', he admitted to Conan Doyle), he hubristically took to court the rough and dirty-fighting Marquess of Queensberry (he who composed the modern rules for boxing) for publicly accusing Wilde of sodomy with his son Lord Alfred Douglas – the beautiful boy Bosie. Wilde's fetchingly young, wildly gay, hugely extravagant lover, who was credited by Wilde with the translation of Wilde's French play *Salomé* into English, had been introduced to Wilde by the poet Lionel Johnson. The pair were the flamboyant apogee of nineties gay literary London and Paris (the homosexually anxious young French Protestant writer André Gide was apparently driven to breakdown by Wilde's restless irreverence – as well as encouraged in gay libertinism by Bosie and Wilde in Algiers, January 1895). Wilde lost his case – done down in court not least by Queensberry's fiercely Protestant barrister and Wilde's Trinity contemporary, Edward Carson. Wilde was subsequently tried (twice) for illegal homosexual activities (London rough-traders, the 'panthers' with whom Wilde had too liberally 'feasted', queuing up to bear witness against him), and he was sentenced to the legal maximum of two years hard labour. Most of it was passed in great physical and mental torment in Reading Gaol. Wilde's trials and imprisonment in 1895 made an awesomely dramatic full-stop for nineties poetry's pronounced excursion in decadence and homosexuality. Erstwhile Uranians and Wildeans eagerly denied Wilde thrice, running for cover, packing the overnight ferries to France (the atmosphere of treachery and panic was like a combination of the McCarthy era in 1950s America and the 1980s AIDS horror). Wilde's critically solipsistic life of Art for Art's Sake, his old ideal of art as ideologically useless, an imitation of art not of life, was also stopped in its tracks. *De Profundis*, the long prose letter composed in Reading Gaol, is an anguished meditation not least on how life has intruded calamitously into the Platonized pastoral of Paterian assumptions about art's beautiful isolativeness. *The Ballad of Reading Gaol* (1898) is a strong piece of poetic propaganda against capital punishment, astonishingly different from Wilde's earlier Pre-Raphaelite impressionism and lipstick-tracings ('I will never again out-Kipling Henley', Wilde said of the poem). Yeats, still critically of the nineties, cut savagely into the poem's discursively protesting stanzas for his *Oxford Book of Modern Verse* (1936), leaving only a balladic core of 39 stanzas out of 109. Wilde's mother died in Chelsea while he was in prison (he was refused parole to visit her death-bed). Released, he escaped to Europe, eventually settling in Paris, 1898, after finding that Bosie's affections lasted only as long as Wilde's money. Wilde's wife died in 1898, still, naturally, angry and estranged. In 1900 Wilde visited Rome, centre of all his old religio-aesthetic desires. He died in Paris, 30 November that year, unhappy, Bosie-less, paranoid about money. 'I am going under: the morgue yawns for me.' He received the last rites of the Roman Church. (If only his father had not forbidden his becoming a Roman while he was at Oxford, he said, 'the artistic side of the church and the fragrance of its teaching would have curbed my degeneracies'.) His divided and divisive reputation continues the contradictions of his life and writing – an Irish writer Irish critics have dismissed as a phoney Englishman; troubled gay icon; Catholic-leaning Protestant; revisionist aestheticizer. In post-prison exile he called himself Sebastian Melmoth – after St Sebastian, another iconic gay male, done to death by phallic arrows (they brought to mind the arrows on Wilde's prison uniform), and the wanderer in the Gothic novel *Melmoth the Wanderer* (1820). The novel's author was the Irishman Charles Maturin – a grand-uncle on Wilde's mother's side.

ON THE SALE BY AUCTION OF KEATS' LOVE LETTERS

These are the letters which Endymion wrote
To one he loved in secret, and apart.
And now the brawlers of the auction mart
Bargain and bid for each poor blotted note,

Ay! for each separate pulse of passion quote
   The merchant's price. I think they love not art
   Who break the crystal of a poet's heart
That small and sickly eyes may glare and gloat.

Is it not said that many years ago,
   In a far Eastern town, some soldiers ran
   With torches through the midnight, and began
To wrangle for mean raiment, and to throw
   Dice for the garments of a wretched man,
Not knowing the God's wonder, or His woe?   10

The Dramatic Review (23 January 1886). The Poems of Oscar Wilde,
First Collected Edition [vol. ix] (Methuen & Co., 1908).

FANTAISIES DÉCORATIVES: II. LES BALLONS

Against these turbid turquoise skies
   The light and luminous balloons
   Dip and drift like satin moons,
Drift like silken butterflies;

Reel with every windy gust,
   Rise and reel like dancing girls,
   Float like strange transparent pearls,
Fall and float like silver dust.

Now to the low leaves they cling,
   Each with coy fantastic pose,
   Each a petal of a rose   10
Straining at a gossamer string.

Then to the tall trees they climb,
   Like thin globes of amethyst,
   Wandering opals keeping tryst
With the rubies of the lime.

The Lady's Pictorial, Christmas Number (1887). The Poems of
Oscar Wilde (1908).

SYMPHONY IN YELLOW

An omnibus across the bridge
   Crawls like a yellow butterfly,
   And, here and there, a passer-by
Shows like a little restless midge.

Big barges full of yellow hay
   Are moored against the shadowy wharf,
   And, like a yellow silken scarf,
The thick fog hangs along the quay.

The yellow leaves begin to fade
   And flutter from the Temple elms,   10

And at my feet the pale green Thames
Lies like a rod of rippled jade.

*The Centennial Magazine, Sydney (5 February 1889); The Golden Grain Guide
(May 1889). The Poems of Oscar Wilde (1908).*

THE ARTIST

One evening there came into his soul the desire to fashion an image of *The Pleasure that abideth for a Moment.* And he went forth into the world to look for bronze. For he could only think in bronze.

But all the bronze of the whole world had disappeared, nor anywhere in the whole world was there any bronze to be found, save only the bronze of the image of *The Sorrow that endureth for Ever.*

Now this image he had himself, and with his own hands, fashioned, and had set it on the tomb of the one thing he had loved in life. On the tomb of the dead thing he had most loved had he set this image of his own fashioning, that it might serve as a sign of the love of man that dieth not, and a symbol of the sorrow of man that endureth for ever. And in the whole world there was no other bronze save the bronze of this image.

And he took the image he had fashioned, and set it in a great furnace, and gave it to the fire.

And out of the bronze of the image of *The Sorrow that endureth for Ever* he fashioned an image of *The Pleasure that abideth for a Moment.*

*First of six 'Poems in Prose', Fortnightly Review (ed. Frank Harris), n.s. LVI
(July 1894), 22–9. Lord Arthur Savile's Crime and Other Prose Pieces,
First Collected Edition [vol. VII] (Methuen & Co., 1908).*

THE BALLAD OF READING GAOL BY C.3.3[1]

*In Memoriam
C. T. W.[2]
Sometime Trooper of the Royal Horse Guards,
Obiit H.M. Prison, Reading, Berkshire,
July 7th, 1896.*

I

He did not wear his scarlet coat,[3]
　For blood and wine are red,
And blood and wine were on his hands
　When they found him with the dead,
The poor dead woman whom he loved,
　And murdered in her bed.

He walked amongst the Trial Men
　In a suit of shabby grey;
A cricket cap was on his head,
　And his step seemed light and gay;   10
But I never saw a man who looked
　So wistfully at the day.

I never saw a man who looked
　With such a wistful eye
Upon that little tent of blue
　Which prisoners call the sky,
And at every drifting cloud that went
　With sails of silver by.

I walked, with other souls in pain,
　Within another ring,   20
And was wondering if the man had done
　A great or little thing,
When a voice behind me whispered low,
　'That fellow's got to swing.'

THE BALLAD OF READING GAOL
1 Wilde's cell number at Reading Gaol.
2 Charles Thomas Wooldridge, wife murderer.

3 Royal Horse Guards uniform was dark blue trimmed with red. 'I could hardly have written "He did not wear his azure coat, for blood and wine are blue"' (O.W.).

Dear Christ! the very prison walls
  Suddenly seemed to reel,
And the sky above my head became
  Like a casque[4] of scorching steel;
And, though I was a soul in pain,
  My pain I could not feel.   30

I only knew what hunted thought
  Quickened his step, and why
He looked upon the garish day
  With such a wistful eye;
The man had killed the thing he loved,
  And so he had to die.

        *

Yet each man kills the thing he loves,
  By each let this be heard,
Some do it with a bitter look,
  Some with a flattering word.   40
The coward does it with a kiss,
  The brave man with a sword!

Some kill their love when they are young,
  And some when they are old;
Some strangle with the hands of Lust,
  Some with the hands of Gold:
The kindest use a knife, because
  The dead so soon grow cold.

Some love too little, some too long,
  Some sell, and others buy;   50
Some do the deed with many tears,
  And some without a sigh:
For each man kills the thing he loves,
  Yet each man does not die.

        *

He does not die a death of shame
  On a day of dark disgrace,
Nor have a noose about his neck,
  Nor a cloth upon his face,
Nor drop feet foremost through the floor
  Into an empty space.   60

He does not sit with silent men
  Who watch him night and day;
Who watch him when he tries to weep,
  And when he tries to pray;
Who watch him lest himself should rob
  The prison of its prey.

He does not wake at dawn to see
  Dread figures throng his room,
The shivering Chaplain robed in white,

The Sheriff stern with gloom,   70
  And the Governor all in shiny black,
    With the yellow face of Doom.

He does not rise in piteous haste
  To put on convict-clothes,
While some coarse-mouthed Doctor gloats, and notes
  Each new and nerve-twitched pose,
Fingering a watch whose little ticks
  Are like horrible hammer-blows.

He does not feel that sickening thirst
  That sands one's throat, before   80
The hangman with his gardener's gloves
  Comes through the padded door,
And binds one with three leathern thongs,[5]
  That the throat may thirst no more.

He does not bend his head to hear
  The Burial Office read,
Nor, while the anguish of his soul
  Tells him he is not dead,
Cross his own coffin, as he moves
  Into the hideous shed.   90

He does not stare upon the air
  Through a little roof of glass:
He does not pray with lips of clay
  For his agony to pass;[6]
Nor feel upon his shuddering cheek
  The kiss of Caiaphas.[7]

        II

Six weeks the guardsman walked the yard,
  In the suit of shabby grey:
His cricket cap was on his head,
  And his step was light and gay,   100
But I never saw a man who looked
  So wistfully at the day.

I never saw a man who looked
  With such a wistful eye
Upon that little tent of blue
  Which prisoners call the sky,
And at every wandering cloud that trailed
  Its ravelled fleeces by.

He did not wring his hands, as do
  Those witless men who dare   110
To try to rear the changeling Hope
  In the cave of black Despair:
He only looked upon the sun,
  And drank the morning air.

---

4 helmet.
5 at wrists, elbows, knees.
6 unlike Jesus, who did...

7 Jewish High Priest who advised that Jesus should die, John 18.14;
'any priest who assists at the cruel and unjust punishments of men'
(O.W.).

He did not wring his hands nor weep,
    Nor did he peek or pine,
But he drank the air as though it held
    Some healthful anodyne;
With open mouth he drank the sun
    As though it had been wine!   120

And I and all the souls in pain,
    Who tramped the other ring,
Forgot if we ourselves had done
    A great or little thing,
And watched with gaze of dull amaze
    The man who had to swing.

For strange it was to see him pass
    With a step so light and gay,
And strange it was to see him look
    So wistfully at the day,   130
And strange it was to think that he
    Had such a debt to pay.

The oak and elm have pleasant leaves
    That in the spring-time shoot:
But grim to see is the gallows-tree,
    With its adder-bitten root,
And, green or dry, a man must die
    Before it bears its fruit!

The loftiest place is the seat of grace
    For which all worldlings try: 140
But who would stand in hempen band
    Upon a scaffold high,
And through a murderer's collar take
    His last look at the sky?

It is sweet to dance to violins
    When Love and Life are fair:
To dance to flutes, to dance to lutes
    Is delicate and rare:
But it is not sweet with nimble feet
    To dance upon the air!   150

So with curious eyes and sick surmise
    We watched him day by day,
And wondered if each one of us
    Would end the self-same way,
For none can tell to what red Hell
    His sightless soul may stray.

                    *

At last the dead man walked no more
    Amongst the Trial Men,
And I knew that he was standing up
    In the black dock's dreadful pen,   160
And that never would I see his face
    For weal or woe again.

Like two doomed ships that pass in storm
    We had crossed each other's way:

But we made no sign, we said no word,
    We had no word to say;
For we did not meet in the holy night,
    But in the shameful day.

A prison wall was round us both,
    Two outcast men we were: 170
The world had thrust us from its heart,
    And God from out His care:
And the iron gin that waits for Sin
    Had caught us in its snare.

                    III

In Debtor's Yard the stones are hard,
    And the dripping wall is high,
So it was there he took the air
    Beneath the leaden sky,
And by each side a Warder walked,
    For fear the man might die.   180

Or else he sat with those who watched
    His anguish night and day;
Who watched him when he rose to weep,
    And when he crouched to pray;
Who watched him lest himself should rob
    Their scaffold of its prey.

The Governor was strong upon
    The Regulations Act:
The Doctor said that Death was but
    A scientific fact: 190
And twice a day the Chaplain called,
    And left a little tract.

And twice a day he smoked his pipe,
    And drank his quart of beer:
His soul was resolute, and held
    No hiding-place for fear;
He often said that he was glad
    The hangman's day was near.

But why he said so strange a thing
    No warder dared to ask: 200
For he to whom a watcher's doom
    Is given as his task,
Must set a lock upon his lips,
    And make his face a mask.

Or else he might be moved, and try
    To comfort or console:
And what should Human Pity do
    Pent up in Murderers' Hole?
What word of grace in such a place
    Could help a brother's soul?   210

                    *

With slouch and swing around the ring
    We trod the Fools' Parade!
We did not care: we knew we were

The Devil's Own Brigade:
And shaven head and feet of lead
  Make a merry masquerade.

We tore the tarry rope to shreds
  With blunt and bleeding nails;[8]
We rubbed the doors, and scrubbed the floors,
  And cleaned the shining rails: 220
And, rank by rank, we soaped the plank,
  And clattered with the pails.

We sewed the sacks,[9] we broke the stones,
  We turned the dusty drill:[10]
We banged the tins, and bawled the hymns,
  And sweated on the mill:[11]
But in the heart of every man
  Terror was lying still.

So still it lay that every day
  Crawled like a weed-clogged wave: 230
And we forgot the bitter lot
  That waits for fool and knave,
Till once, as we tramped in from work,
  We passed an open grave.

With yawning mouth the horrid hole
  Gaped for a living thing;
The very mud cried out for blood
  To the thirsty asphalte ring:
And we knew that ere one dawn grew fair
  The fellow had to swing.   240

Right in we went, with soul intent
  On Death and Dread and Doom:
The hangman, with his little bag,
  Went shuffling through the gloom:
And I trembled as I groped my way
  Into my numbered tomb.

        *

That night the empty corridors
  Were full of forms of Fear,
And up and down the iron town
  Stole feet we could not hear,   250
And through the bars that hide the stars
  White faces seemed to peer.

He lay as one who lies and dreams
  In a pleasant meadow-land,
The watchers watched him as he slept,
  And could not understand

How one could sleep so sweet a sleep
  With a hangman close at hand.

But there is no sleep when men must weep
  Who never yet have wept: 260
So we – the fool, the fraud, the knave –
  That endless vigil kept,
And through each brain on hands of pain
  Another's terror crept.

        *

Alas! it is a fearful thing
  To feel another's guilt!
For, right within, the Sword of Sin
  Pierced to its poisoned hilt,
And as molten lead were the tears we shed
  For the blood we had not spilt.   270

The warders with their shoes of felt
  Crept by each padlocked door,
And peeped and saw, with eyes of awe,
  Grey figures on the floor,
And wondered why men knelt to pray
  Who never prayed before.

All through the night we knelt and prayed,
  Mad mourners of a corse!
The troubled plumes of midnight shook
  Like the plumes upon a hearse: 280
And bitter wine upon a sponge
  Was the savour of Remorse.[12]

        *

The grey cock crew, the red cock crew,
  But never came the day:
And crooked shapes of Terror crouched,
  In the corners where we lay:
And each evil sprite that walks by night
  Before us seemed to play.

They glided past, they glided fast,
  Like travellers through a mist: 290
They mocked the moon in a rigadoon[13]
  Of delicate turn and twist,
And with formal pace and loathsome grace
  The phantoms kept their tryst.

With mop and mow,[14] we saw them go,
  Slim shadows hand in hand:
About, about, in ghostly rout
  They trod a saraband:[15]
And the damned grotesques made arabesques,
  Like the wind upon the sand!   300

---

8 oakum picking – breaking up old (navy) rope. Traditional prison work.

9 mail-bags (for the Post Office). Another prison tradition.

10 the crank – a pointless task (in prisoner's cell), involving turning a handle to operate a sand scooping (and dropping) device.

11 treadmill – a huge mill-wheel turned by prisoners' feet (usually grinding nothing).

12 Jesus, on cross, was offered vinegary wine on a sponge.

13 lively French dance.

14 face-pulling.

15 stately dance.

With the pirouettes of marionettes,
    They tripped on pointed tread:
But with flutes of Fear they filled the ear,
    As their grisly masque they led,
And loud they sang, and long they sang,
    For they sang to wake the dead.

'Oho!' they cried, 'The world is wide
    But fettered limbs go lame!
And once, or twice, to throw the dice
    Is a gentlemanly game,   310
But he does not win who plays with Sin
    In the secret House of Shame.'

                        *

No things of air these antics were,
    That frolicked with such glee:
To men whose lives were held in gyves,[16]
    And whose feet might not go free,
Ah! wounds of Christ! they were living things
    Most terrible to see.

Around, around, they waltzed and wound;
    Some wheeled in smirking pairs;   320
With the mincing step of a demirep[17]
    Some sidled up the stairs:
And with subtle sneer, and fawning leer,
    Each helped us at our prayers.

                        *

The morning wind began to moan,
    But still the night went on:
Through its giant loom the web of gloom
    Crept till each thread was spun:
And, as we prayed, we grew afraid
    Of the Justice of the Sun.   330

The moaning wind went wandering round
    The weeping prison-wall:
Till like a wheel of turning steel
    We felt the minutes crawl:
O moaning wind! what had we done
    To have such a seneschal?[18]

At last I saw the shadowed bars,
    Like a lattice wrought in lead,
Move right across the whitewashed wall
    That faced my three-plank bed,   340
And I knew that somewhere in the world
    God's dreadful dawn was red.

                        *

At six o'clock we cleaned our cells,
    At seven all was still,
But the sough and swing of a mighty wing

The prison seemed to fill,
For the Lord of Death with icy breath
    Had entered in to kill.

He did not pass in purple pomp,
    Nor ride a moon-white steed.   350
Three yards of cord and a sliding board
    Are all the gallows' need:
So with rope of shame the Herald came
    To do the secret deed.

                        *

We were as men who through a fen
    Of filthy darkness grope:
We did not dare to breathe a prayer,
    Or to give our anguish scope:
Something was dead in each of us,
    And what was dead was Hope.   360

For Man's grim Justice goes its way,
    And will not swerve aside:
It slays the weak, it slays the strong,
    It has a deadly stride:
With iron heel it slays the strong,
    The monstrous parricide!

                        *

We waited for the stroke of eight:
    Each tongue was thick with thirst:
For the stroke of eight is the stroke of Fate
    That makes a man accursed,   370
And Fate will use a running noose
    For the best man and the worst.

We had no other thing to do,
    Save to wait for the sign to come:[19]
So, like things of stone in a valley lone,
    Quiet we sat and dumb:
But each man's heart beat thick and quick,
    Like a madman on a drum!

                        *

With sudden shock the prison-clock
    Smote on the shivering air,   380
And from all the gaol rose up a wail
    Of impotent despair,
Like the sound that frightened marshes hear
    From some leper in his lair.

And as one sees most fearful things
    In the crystal of a dream,
We saw the greasy hempen rope
    Hooked to the blackened beam,
And heard the prayer the hangman's snare
    Strangled into a scream.   390

---

16   shackles.
17   prostitute.
18   official administrator of the law.

19   The prison clock apparently; though perhaps (also?) the bell of St
Lawrence's church, Reading, which on execution days began tolling at
7.45 a.m., and continued until after 8 a.m., the time of executions.

And all the woe that moved him so
   That he gave that bitter cry,
And the wild regrets, and the bloody sweats,
   None knew so well as I:
For he who lives more lives than one
   More deaths than one must die.

IV

There is no chapel on the day
   On which they hang a man:
The Chaplain's heart is far too sick,
   Or his face is far too wan,   400
Or there is that written in his eyes
   Which none should look upon.

So they kept us close till nigh on noon,
   And then they rang the bell,
And the warders with their jingling keys
   Opened each listening cell,
And down the iron stair we tramped,
   Each from his separate Hell.

Out into God's sweet air we went,
   But not in wonted way,   410
For this man's face was white with fear,
   And that man's face was gray,
And I never saw sad men who looked
   So wistfully at the day.

I never saw sad men who looked
   With such a wistful eye
Upon that little tent of blue
   We prisoners called the sky,
And at every happy cloud that passed
   In such strange freedom by.   420

But there were those amongst us all
   Who walked with downcast head,
And knew that, had each got his due,
   They should have died instead:
He had but killed a thing that lived,
   Whilst they had killed the dead.

For he who sins a second time
   Wakes a dead soul to pain,
And draws it from its spotted shroud,
   And makes it bleed again,   430
And makes it bleed great gouts of blood,
   And makes it bleed in vain!

        *

Like ape or clown, in monstrous garb
   With crooked arrows starred,
Silently we went round and round

   The slippery asphalte yard;
Silently we went round and round,
   And no man spoke a word.

Silently we went round and round,
   And through each hollow mind   440
The Memory of dreadful things
   Rushed like a dreadful wind,
And Horror stalked before each man,
   And Terror crept behind.

        *

The warders strutted up and down,
   And watched their herd of brutes,
Their uniforms were spick and span,
   And they wore their Sunday suits,
But we knew the work they had been at,
   By the quicklime on their boots.[20]   450

For where a grave had opened wide,
   There was no grave at all:
Only a stretch of mud and sand
   By the hideous prison-wall,
And a little heap of burning lime,
   That the man should have his pall.

For he has a pall, this wretched man,
   Such as few men can claim:
Deep down below a prison-yard,
   Naked for greater shame,   460
He lies, with fetters on each foot,
   Wrapt in a sheet of flame!

And all the while the burning lime
   Eats flesh and bone away,
It eats the brittle bone by night,
   And the soft flesh by day,
It eats the flesh and bone by turns,
   But it eats the heart alway.

        *

For three long years they will not sow
   Or root or seedling there: 470
For three long years the unblessed spot
   Will sterile be and bare,
And look upon the wondering sky
   With unreproachful stare.

They think a murderer's heart would taint
   Each simple seed they sow.
It is not true! God's kindly earth
   Is kindlier than men know,
And the red rose would but blow more red,
   The white rose whiter blow.   480

---

20 corpses of the executed were covered in quicklime in grave, to
speed decomposition.

Out of his mouth a red, red rose!
    Out of his heart a white!
For who can say by what strange way,
    Christ brings His will to light,
Since the barren staff the pilgrim bore
    Bloomed in the great Pope's sight?[21]

                        *

But neither milk-white rose nor red
    May bloom in prison-air;
The shard, the pebble, and the flint,
    Are what they give us there: 490
For flowers have been known to heal
    A common man's despair.

So never will wine-red rose or white,
    Petal by petal, fall
On that stretch of mud and sand that lies
    By the hideous prison-wall,
To tell the men who tramp the yard
    That God's Son died for all.

                        *

Yet though the hideous prison-wall
    Still hems him round and round,   500
And a spirit may not walk by night
    That is with fetters bound,
And a spirit may but weep that lies
    In such unholy ground,

He is at peace – this wretched man –
    At peace, or will be soon:
There is no thing to make him mad,
    Nor does Terror walk at noon,
For the lampless Earth in which he lies
    Has neither Sun nor Moon.   510

                        *

They hanged him as a beast is hanged!
    They did not even toll
A requiem that might have brought
    Rest to his startled soul,
But hurriedly they took him out,
    And hid him in a hole.

The warders stripped him of his clothes,
    And gave him to the flies:
They mocked the swollen purple throat,
    And the stark and staring eyes: 520
And with laughter loud they heaped the shroud
    In which the convict lies.

The Chaplain would not kneel to pray
    By his dishonoured grave:
Nor mark it with that blessed Cross

That Christ for sinners gave,
Because the man was one of those
    Whom Christ came down to save.

Yet all is well; he has but passed
    To Life's appointed bourne: 530
And alien tears will fill for him
    Pity's long-broken urn,
For his mourners will be outcast men,
    And outcasts always mourn.[22]

                        V

I know not whether Laws be right,
    Or whether Laws be wrong;
All that we know who lie in gaol
    Is that the wall is strong;
And that each day is like a year,
    A year whose days are long.   540

But this I know, that every Law
    That men hath made for Man,
Since first Man took his brother's life,
    And the sad world began,
But straws the wheat and saves the chaff
    With a most evil fan.

This too I know – and wise it were
    If each could know the same –
That every prison that men build
    Is built with bricks of shame,   550
And bound with bars lest Christ should see
    How men their brothers maim.

With bars they blur the gracious moon,
    And blind the goodly sun;
And they do well to hide their Hell,
    For in it things are done
That Son of God nor son of Man
    Ever should look upon!

                        *

The vilest deeds like poison weeds,
    Bloom well in prison-air;
It is only what is good in Man   560
    That wastes and withers there:
Pale Anguish keeps the heavy gate,
    And the Warder is Despair.

For they starve the little frightened child
    Till it weeps both night and day:
And they scourge the weak, and flog the fool,
    And gibe the old and grey,
And some grow mad, and all grow bad,
    And none a word may say.   570

21   incident in Wagner's opera *Tannhäuser* – the Pope's staff blossoms,
proving Tannhäuser is forgiven for love of Venus.
22   last 4 lines of this stanza are on Jacob Epstein's monument over

O. W.'s grave, Père Lachaise Cemetery, Paris. O. W. agreed with friend
Robert Ross the poem might end here, 'but the propaganda, which I
desire to make, begins there'.

Each narrow cell in which we dwell
    Is a foul and dark latrine,
And the fetid breath of living Death
    Chokes up each grated screen,
And all, but Lust, is turned to dust
    In Humanity's machine.

The brackish water that we drink
    Creeps with a loathsome slime,
And the bitter bread they weigh in scales
    Is full of chalk and lime,   580
And Sleep will not lie down, but walks
    Wild-eyed, and cries to Time.

                    *

But though lean Hunger and green Thirst
    Like asp with adder fight,
We have little care of prison fare,
    For what chills and kills outright
Is that every stone one lifts by day
    Becomes one's heart by night.

With midnight always in one's heart,
    And twilight in one's cell,   590
We turn the crank, or tear the rope,
    Each in his separate Hell,
And the silence is more awful far
    Than the sound of a brazen bell.

And never a human voice comes near
    To speak a gentle word:
And the eye that watches through the door
    Is pitiless and hard:
And by all forgot, we rot and rot,
    With soul and body marred.   600

And thus we rust Life's iron chain
    Degraded and alone:
And some men curse, and some men weep,
    And some men make no moan:
But God's eternal Laws are kind
    And break the heart of stone.

                    *

And every human heart that breaks,
    In prison-cell or yard,
Is as that broken box that gave
    Its treasure to the Lord,   610
And filled the unclean leper's house
    With the scent of costliest nard.[23]

Ah! happy they whose hearts can break
    And peace of pardon win!
How else may man make straight his plan
    And cleanse his soul from Sin?
How else but through a broken heart
    May Lord Christ enter in?

                    *

And he of the swollen purple throat,
    And the stark and staring eyes,   620
Waits for the holy hands that took
    The Thief to Paradise;[24]
And a broken and a contrite heart
    The Lord will not despise.[25]

The man in red who reads the Law
    Gave him three weeks of life,
Three little weeks in which to heal
    His soul of his soul's strife,
And cleanse from every blot of blood
    The hand that held the knife.   630

And with tears of blood he cleansed the hand,
    The hand that held the steel:
For only blood can wipe out blood,
    And only tears can heal:
And the crimson stain that was of Cain[26]
    Became Christ's snow-white seal.[27]

                    VI

In Reading gaol by Reading town
    There is a pit of shame,
And in it lies a wretched man
    Eaten by teeth of flame,   640
In a burning winding-sheet he lies,
    And his grave has got no name.

And there, till Christ call forth the dead,
    In silence let him lie:
No need to waste the foolish tear,
    Or heave the windy sigh:
The man had killed the thing he loved,
    And so he had to die.

And all men kill the thing they love,
    By all let this be heard,   650
Some do it with a bitter look,
    Some with a flattering word,
The coward does it with a kiss,
    The brave man with a sword!

                                            C. 3.3

*Written 1897 in Berneval, after Wilde's release from Reading Gaol, 18 May 1897.
Published 13 February 1898, by Leonard Smithers ('the most learned erotomaniac
in Europe': Wilde), in name of 'C.3.3': Wilde's prison-cell number.*

23   Mark 14; woman – traditionally Mary Magdalene – anoints Jesus's
head with spikenard (nard) from 'alabaster box', and has sins forgiven.
24   thief, crucified with Jesus, forgiven sins; 'today thou shalt be with
me in paradise', Luke 23.43.

25   Psalm 51.17.
26   murderer of brother Abel, Genesis 4.
27   'though your sins be as scarlet, they shall be as snow; though they
be red like crimson, they shall be as wool', Isaiah 1.18.

(Mrs) Margaret L. (Louisa) (Bradley) Woods
(1856–1945)

Margaret Louisa Woods, the novelist and minor poet, was born in Rugby in 1856, daughter of a master at Rugby School, the Revd George Granville Bradley, and his wife Maria Philpot. George Bradley would go on to be Dean of Westminster Abbey. Margaret was educated at home and at a school in Leamington run by a Miss Gawthorp. She married Henry George Woods, who was President of Trinity College, Oxford, from 1887. There is frequently an Oxford connexion to her verses. She contributed regularly to the journals, such as the *Fortnightly Review*. Her novels include *Esther Vanhomrigh* (1891) and *The Vagabond* (1894). Her Victorian poetry is mainly in *Lyrics and Ballads* (1889), *Aëromancy and Other Poems* (1896) and *Wild Justice: A Dramatic Poem* (1896) – which is about a violent father and a mother protecting her children from him. Womanly questions and issues, mildly addressed, are her staple. In 1907 her *Poems Old and New* appeared, and in 1914 a *Collected Poems* was issued by John Lane, the Bodley Head press.

SONG

Weep no more, for why should sorrow
  Spend a time too short for kisses?
Wilt thou weep because to-morrow
  Brings no hour so sweet as this is?
    O fond heart!
Soon 'tis fled and then we part.

Comes no hour so sweet as this is –
  Haste to harvest then such flow'rs
    All thine hours
Keep the fragrance of its kisses.   10

Time but treads the slow sun's measure,
  Lightning souls outstrip his fleetness,
Packing half a life-time's pleasure
  In a moment of completeness.
    Haste, O haste,
Ere such moments run to waste!

Soon shall come an hour for weeping,
  Days enough and long to spare
    For thy care,
And thy tears shall haunt thee sleeping.   20

Tears are longer than sweet laughter,
  Yet they pass, and being ended,
Like a radiance following after
  Stormy eves from suns descended,
    So their rain
Fades into this light again.

Aëromancy and Other Poems *(Elkin Mathews, 1896).*

UNDER THE LAMP

I

Under the lamp
In the midnight lonely
Desolation
Of the flaring street –
Illumination
To exhibit only
The obscene pavement's horrible slime,
Spittle of smokers, foulness of feet
That have stayed their tramp,
Their everlasting journey for a time.   10

The usual pair,
A shop-soiled, meagre,
Night-wandering woman;
Facing her, young and straight and slim
Under the long, loose overcoat,
A man grasps at her waist with eager
Hand, and the woman hangs off from him
With feigned reluctance, making a note
Here is no fellow-expert and common,
No counter-jumper to cheapen her ware,   20
Under the lamp.

A gentleman.
Ay, more's the pity!
O evil blending
Of alien creatures
By diverse ways to this one way come!
The smile of his mother is yet on his features
And the fair stamp of a delicate home.
Under the lamp
As plain is it written where he began,   30
As where this woman will have her ending,
Like a crushed worm in the mire of the city.

The harlot goes
With her customer,
From him importunate
Still does backward bear
With wavering eyelids, in half denial,
To raise her wretched price, the unfortunate.
Lamp after lamp
In garish, yellow, remorseless espial   40
Lights them towards her mean and sordid lair,
And each one in a mocking marriage throws
Distorted shadows of him and her
Mingled, upon the ugly pavement damp.

II

Now in his ears
Midnight is tolling
From the dark dome
With solemn resonance.
The fundamental, unregarded Powers
Whereby we are, it calls to our remembrance,   50

Infinity hovering above the hours.
    That sound he hears
In the foul street, is heard too in his home.

    Hearing, they close
    Their books, the father
    And mother of this man.
Here where they sit beside the musing fire,
    About them gather
Dead faces on the walls, in a half-gloom,
Each one a high tradition to inherit.   60
With a brave sweetness, born amid the snows,
A bunch of early violets in the room
Breathes odour, like its own delightful spirit.
    Here he began,
Here is his home, this raker in the mire.

    For him those two,
    Father and Mother,
    Toil have endured
    And hard renunciation.
How should they dream their blood would not breed true?   70
A beast, a flower, a type being once secured,
Will hold to it. O subtle generation
Of man, more secret, hazardous, unstable!
Alchemy, making gold of things far other,
Of pure gold a dross most lamentable.

    Darkly upwell
    To the Mother visions
    From the page put by –
The vile hidden commerce of the city,
The hunting, the pulling down of young prey   80
    By hounds of Hell,
Anguish unspeakable, impotent outcry
Of murdered innocence, devilish derisions
Of souls emptied of pity –
And the common men who make these ventures pay.

    Every man
    Who this ware of woman
    Goes forth to hire;
Who brutishly this marvellous human
Being, whose thread the ages span,   90
Wherein immortal secrets hide,
As fruit crushes between the teeth of his desire,
    And as the rind
Of fruit, his thirst being satisfied,
Flings carelessly into the road behind.

    She on her men
    With thanksgiving
    Looks – on the dead,
High and aloof, beside the fire the living.
Soldier or priest, they have marched under one banner,   100
Fought seas apart, yet the bugle-call was one,
    Answered to in like manner.
The boy is of their breed. Why doubt him then?

It were a shame to doubt. Yet for her son
She prays, her heart burning with tears unshed.

III

The strong Prayer
On lightning pinion
Flashes about his soul;
But what can it do there?
The Life, that up in endless evolution   110
Led Man and leads, is absent from his soul.
Fierce primal Powers have him in their dominion,
They that rough-hewed the world in chaos and strife,
A mad dance of birth and dissolution,
And nightmare shapes, shrieking for life, life!

They cling to their prey,
Their heart rejoices,
A prey have they wrung
From their enemy, the Everlasting Mind.
They drag him down, they fill him with utter   120
Madness and whisper him with flattering voices,
Bidding him scorn the men from whom he sprung
And think himself a better man than they.
The Prayer can to his soul no entrance find,
For it is closed as with an iron shutter.

It does not die,
That Prayer rejected.
Like a hovering dove
It is drawn up towards the invisible flight
Of benedictions, breathings of pure Love,   130
The Angels of the Earth, continually
Streaming above us, potent, unsuspected.
Yet, as the Mother's prayer not unfulfilled
Could float upon the night,
It enters where she neither knew nor willed.

On a mean bed
A boy lies reading,
His candle-end
Flickers on the gloom.
Darkness is round, has always been around him,   140
Drunkenness, lies, dishonesty;
But the persistent Life within him said,
'Come forth out of this tomb!'
And he all blind followed where it was leading.
In his lone night the Mother's Prayer has found him,
And he immediately
Knows there is light somewhere, somewhere a friend.

Life does not tire,
Begetting, conceiving,
Always the same.   150
Life does not tire in transformation,
Never the same.
The blind believing
Of the insect in her unknown progeny,

Her skilful, unerring preparation –
　　This is the first mystery.
And the last is the Spirit of Man that will aspire
To God, out of the dust from whence it came.

Collected Poems *(John Lane, The Bodley Head, 1914)*.

A WOMAN'S APOLOGY

'So altered are thy face and mind
'Twere perjury to love thee now.'
　　　　　Byron[1]

If always I had slept within your arms
　　More calmly had I slept.
The dark-winged Hours with hush of whispering flight
　　Had gently passed above
　　That sleep, till one all bright
Had stopped from Heaven's gate and shone on me like Love.

If always I had wept within your arms
　　More often had I wept,
Consoled as Earth is comforted with rain.
　　Hearts may have need of tears,   10
　　And tears quench in the brain
The irreparable dark fire that consumes and sears.

If always I had smiled within your arms
　　More softly had I smiled.
For we who crowd at Life's perpetual Show
　　Thus eager for the jest,
　　Are cowards, afraid to know
How Fate and our own souls stand in the obscure contest.

But since I never might within your arms
　　Live healed and reconciled,
Pardon I ask for this too little change,   20
　　Familiar looks, lest these
　　With superscription strange
Deface a sanctuary, tombs, relics, images.

Collected Poems *(1914)*.

John Davidson (1857–1909)

London-Scottish poet of nineties decadence, who reacted into Nietzscheanism and journalistic realism, John Davidson was born at Barrhead, Renfrewshire, 1 April 1857, fourth child and eldest son of Alexander Davidson (one of the seceders from the Calvinist Congregationalist churches of Scotland who in 1843 formed the anti-Calvinist Evangelical Union), and his wife Helen Crocket. He grew up in some poverty in the port of Greenock on the

A WOMAN'S APOLOGY
1   not Byron.

Clyde, near Glasgow; had intermittent schooling; worked in Greenock in the chemical lab at Walker's sugar factory (1870), as a town chemical analyst (1871), and four years at his old school, the Highlanders' Academy. He spent one session at Edinburgh University (1876–7); taught in Glasgow; tried and failed to live as a poet (inspired by meeting Swinburne at the house of Glasgow University Professor of English Literature, John Nichol); returned, on and off, to teaching; wrote poems; and published his book *The North Wall*, a novel, dedicated to Margaret McArthur, daughter of a Perth bobbin-manufacturer (Glasgow, 1885). He married Miss McArthur on 23 October 1885 (they had two sons). *Bruce*, Davidson's Scottish chronicle-play, was published in 1886. He would go on trying – and mostly failing – to make money with novels and dramas. The Spasmodic *Smith; a Tragedy* came out in 1888 – Davidson had been affected in the Nichol circle by the Spasmodics, especially the Glaswegian poet Alexander Smith (and *Smith* is dedicated to John Nichol). In 1890 the Davidsons moved down to London, where Davidson soon established himself as the rough Carlylean northern Celt amongst the softer Celtic Fringe of London poets. He joined in, but with fingers crossed, with the Yeats–Symons gang, the Rhymers' Club. He contributed to the first number of the decadents' flagship publication *The Yellow Book* (1894). 'Thirty Bob a Week' appeared in the second number. But he always wanted the Rhymers to have 'more blood and guts'. This desire was worked through in his own verses: *Fleet Street Eclogues* (1893), *Ballads and Songs* (1894), *A Second Series of Fleet Street Eclogues* (1896), *New Ballads* (1897), *The Last Ballad, and Other Poems* (1899), and so on. It culminated theoretically in his terse programmatic cry in the *Speaker*, 28 January 1899, for a return to 'Pre-Shakespearianism' in poetry (a label modelled, of course, on 'Pre-Raphaelitism') – i.e. prosiness, journalistic truth, 'the offal of the world'. 'It is difficult to believe', he wrote in his review of Yeats's *Wind Among the Reeds* (*Speaker*, 29 April 1899), 'that Mr Yeats has not been dead for many years.' Davidson's twentieth-century poems, more and more based on his prose writings, became increasingly blunt, disturbed, Nietzschean – corrosive *bricolages* of coarse and degraded modern life. No serious literary labour brought Davidson adequate money – even pursued assiduously, reviewing scarcely made enough 'to buy tobacco' – and he relied heavily on grants (£250 from the Royal Literary Fund in 1898; money from G. B. Shaw in 1906; a Civil List Pension in that year of £100 per annum). He was perturbed by madness in the family: his brother was put in an Edinburgh mental asylum in 1893, and Davidson had a severe mental breakdown in 1896. Recuperating at Shoreham was hard (it increased his 'misery and hypochondria'). In 1907 the Davidsons moved to Penzance ('A low-lying land of unworked tin mines ...grey, ghastly, scabby ruins, inhabited by a lazy, lying, Wesleyan shoal of pilchards'). He missed the stimulus of London ('only primeval everlasting things are interesting, and these frequent the flanks of mountains and the streets of cities'). He disappeared, 23 March 1909. By the time his body was recovered by fishermen in the sea off Mousehole, a bullet-hole in the head, it had been in the water for six months or so. Suicide seemed probable. The body was buried at sea. Along with poems by Symons and Dowson, it was 'Thirty Bob a Week', said T. S. Eliot, which prepared him for initiation into the French Symbolists such as Laforgue. 'From these men I got the idea that one could write poetry in an English such as one would speak oneself. A colloquial idiom.'

IN ROMNEY MARSH[1]

As I went down to Dymchurch Wall,
    I heard the South sing o'er the land;
I saw the yellow sunlight fall
    On knolls where Norman churches stand.

And ringing shrilly, taut and lithe,
    Within the wind a core of sound,
The wire from Romney town to Hythe
    Alone its airy journey wound.

A veil of purple vapour flowed
    And trailed its fringe along the Straits;
The upper air like sapphire glowed;
    And roses filled Heaven's central gates.

10

IN ROMNEY MARSH
1 Romney and Hythe, two of the original 'Cinque Ports' of South East England (the others were Hastings, Dover, Sandwich). In *Ballads and Songs*, this poem was preceded by 'Song of a Cinque Port'.

Masts in the offing wagged their tops;
    The swinging waves pealed on the shore;
The saffron beach, all diamond drops
    And beads of surge, prolonged the roar.

As I came up from Dymchurch Wall,
    I saw above the Downs' low crest
The crimson brands of sunset fall,
    Flicker and fade from out the west.   20

Night sank: like flakes of silver fire
    The stars in one great shower came down;
Shrill blew the wind; and shrill the wire
    Rang out from Hythe to Romney town.

The darkly shining salt sea drops
    Streamed as the waves clashed on the shore;
The beach, with all its organ stops
    Pealing again, prolonged the roar.

Speaker, *IX (17 March 1894), 308*. Ballads and Songs *(John Lane, 1894).*
Based on Davidson's article 'Romney Marsh' in Glasgow Herald *(3 March 1894), 4.*

THIRTY BOB A WEEK

I couldn't touch a stop and turn a screw,
    And set the blooming world a-work for me,
Like such as cut their teeth – I hope, like you –
    On the handle of a skeleton gold key;
I cut mine on a leek, which I eat it every week:
    I'm a clerk at thirty bob as you can see.

But I don't allow it's luck and all a toss;
    There's no such thing as being starred and crossed;
It's just the power of some to be a boss,
    And the bally power of others to be bossed: 10
I face the music, sir; you bet I ain't a cur;
    Strike me lucky if I don't believe I'm lost!

For like a mole I journey in the dark,
    A-travelling along the underground
From my Pillar'd Halls and broad Suburbean Park,
    To come the daily dull official round;
And home again at night with my pipe all alight,
    A-scheming how to count ten bob a pound.

And it's often very cold and very wet,
    And my missis stitches towels for a hunks;[1]
And the Pillar'd Halls is half of it to let –   20
    Three rooms about the size of travelling trunks.
And we cough, my wife and I, to dislocate a sigh,
    When the noisy little kids are in their bunks.

THIRTY BOB A WEEK
1   miser.

But you never hear her do a growl or whine,
    For she's made of flint and roses, very odd;
And I've got to cut my meaning rather fine,
    Or I'd blubber, for I'm made of greens and sod:
So p'r'aps we are in Hell for all that I can tell,
    And lost and damn'd and served up hot to God.   30

I ain't blaspheming, Mr. Silver-tongue;
    I'm saying things a bit beyond your art:
Of all the rummy starts you ever sprung,
    Thirty bob a week's the rummiest start!
With your science and your books and your the'ries about spooks,
    Did you ever hear of looking in your heart?

I didn't mean your pocket, Mr., no:
    I mean that having children and a wife,
With thirty bob on which to come and go,
    Isn't dancing to the tabor and the fife: 40
When it doesn't make you drink, by Heaven! it makes you think,
    And notice curious items about life.

I step into my heart and there I meet
    A god-almighty devil singing small,
Who would like to shout and whistle in the street,
    And squelch the passers flat against the wall;
If the whole world was a cake he had the power to take,
    He would take it, ask for more, and eat them all.

And I meet a sort of simpleton beside,   50
    The kind that life is always giving beans;
With thirty bob a week to keep a bride
    He fell in love and married in his teens:
At thirty bob he stuck; but he knows it isn't luck:
    He knows the seas are deeper than tureens.

And the god-almighty devil and the fool
    That meet me in the High Street on the strike,
When I walk about my heart a-gathering wool,
    Are my good and evil angels if you like.
And both of them together in every kind of weather
    Ride me like a double-seated bike.   60

That's rough a bit and needs its meaning curled.
    But I have a high old hot un in my mind –
A most engrugious[2] notion of the world,
    That leaves your lightning 'rithmetic behind:
I give it at a glance when I say 'There ain't no chance,
    Nor nothing of the lucky-lottery kind.'

And it's this way that I make it out to be:
    No fathers, mothers, countries, climates – none;
No Adam was responsible for me,
    Nor society, nor systems, nary one: 70
A little sleeping seed, I woke – I did, indeed –
    A million years before the blooming sun.

---

2 Davidson's coinage: presumably = *egregious*.

I woke because I thought the time had come;
  Beyond my will there was no other cause;
And everywhere I found myself at home,
  Because I chose to be the thing I was;
And in whatever shape of mollusc or of ape
  I always went according to the laws.

I was the love that chose my mother out;
  I joined two lives and from the union burst;   80
My weakness and my strength without a doubt
  Are mine alone for ever from the first:
It's just the very same with a difference in the name
  As 'Thy will be done.'[3] You say it if you durst!

They say it daily up and down the land
  As easy as you take a drink, it's true;
But the difficultest go to understand,
  And the difficultest job a man can do,
Is to come it brave and meek with thirty bob a week,
  And feel that that's the proper thing for you.   90

It's a naked child against a hungry wolf;
  It's playing bowls upon a splitting wreck;
It's walking on a string across a gulf
  With millstones fore-and-aft about your neck;
But the thing is daily done by many and many a one;
  And we fall, face forward, fighting, on the deck.

Yellow Book, *vol. 2 (July 1894).* Ballads and Songs *(1894).*

A LOAFER

I hang about the streets all day,
  All night I hang about;
I sleep a little when I may,
  But rise betimes the morning's scout;
For through the year I always hear
  Afar, aloft, a ghostly shout.

My clothes are worn to threads and loops;
  My skin shows here and there;
About my face like seaweed droops
  My tangled beard, my tangled hair;   10
From cavernous and shaggy brows
  My stony eyes untroubled stare.

I move from eastern wretchedness
  Through Fleet Street and the Strand;
And as the pleasant people press
  I touch them softly with my hand,
Perhaps to know that still I go
  Alive about a living land.

3 a sentence from the 'Lord's Prayer' (the Paternoster, 'Our Father
which art in heaven').

For, far in front the clouds are riven;
    I hear the ghostly cry,   20
As if a still voice fell from heaven
    To where sea-whelmed the drowned folks lie
In sepulchres no tempest stirs
    And only eyeless things pass by.

In Piccadilly spirits pass:
    Oh, eyes and cheeks that glow!
Oh, strength and comeliness! Alas,
    The lustrous health is earth I know
From shrinking eyes that recognise
    No brother in my rags and woe.   30

I know no handicraft, no art,
    But I have conquered fate;
For I have chosen the better part,
    And neither hope, nor fear, nor hate.
With placid breath on pain and death,
    My certain alms, alone I wait.

And daily, nightly comes the call,
    The pale, unechoing note,
The faint 'Aha!' sent from the wall
    Of heaven, but from no ruddy throat   40
Of human breed or seraph's seed,
    A phantom voice that cries by rote.

Ballads and Songs (1894).

A NORTHERN SUBURB

Nature selects the longest way,
    And winds about in tortuous grooves;
A thousand years the oaks decay;
    The wrinkled glacier hardly moves.

But here the whetted fangs of change
    Daily devour the old demesne –
The busy farm, the quiet grange,
    The wayside inn, the village green.

In gaudy yellow brick and red,
    With rooting pipes, like creepers rank,   10
The shoddy terraces o'erspread
    Meadow, and garth, and daisied bank.

With shelves for rooms the houses crowd,
    Like draughty cupboards in a row –
Ice-chests when wintry winds are loud,
    Ovens when summer breezes blow.

Roused by the fee'd policeman's knock,
    And sad that day should come again,
Under the stars the workmen flock
    In haste to reach the workmen's train.   20

For here dwell those who must fulfil
　　Dull tasks in uncongenial spheres,
Who toil through dread of coming ill,
　　And not with hope of happier years –

The lowly folk who scarcely dare
　　Conceive themselves perhaps misplaced,
Whose prize for unremitting care
　　Is only not to be disgraced.

Speaker, *XIII (9 May 1896), 509–10*. New Ballads *(John Lane, 1897)*.
Based on article 'A Suburban Philosopher', in Glasgow Herald *(22 April 1893), 9*.

IN THE ISLE OF DOGS[1]

While the water-wagon's ringing showers
Sweetened the dust with a woodland smell,
'Past noon, past noon, two sultry hours,'
Drowsily fell
From the schoolhouse clock
In the Isle of Dogs by Millwall Dock.

Mirrored in shadowy windows draped
With ragged net or half-drawn blind
Bowsprits, masts, exactly shaped
To woo or fight the wind,　　　　　　　　　　　　　　10
Like monitors of guilt
By strength and beauty sent,
Disgraced the shameful houses built
To furnish rent.

From the pavements and the roofs
In shimmering volumes wound
The wrinkled heat;
Distant hammers, wheels and hoofs,
A turbulent pulse of sound,
Southward obscurely beat,　　　　　　　　　　　　　20
The only utterance of the afternoon,
Till on a sudden in the silent street
An organ-man drew up and ground
The Old Hundredth tune.[2]

Forthwith the pillar of cloud that hides the past
Burst into flame,
Whose alchemy transmuted house and mast,
Street, dockyard, pier and pile:
By magic sound the Isle of Dogs became
A northern isle[3] –　　　　　　　　　　　　　　　30
A green isle like a beryl set
In a wine-coloured sea,
Shadowed by mountains where a river met
The ocean's arm extended royally.

IN THE ISLE OF DOGS
1　in East London dockland.
2　tune of hymn 'All people that on earth do dwell' – in early metrical
version of Psalm 100 (Geneva, 1551).

3　Bute – where Davidson spent boyhood holidays.

There also in the evening on the shore
An old man ground the Old Hundredth tune,
An old enchanter steeped in human lore,
Sad-eyed, with whitening beard, and visage lank:
Not since and not before,
Under the sunset or the mellowing moon,   40
Has any hand of man's conveyed
Such meaning in the turning of a crank.

Sometimes he played
As if his box had been
An organ in an abbey richly lit;
For when the dark invaded day's demesne,
And the sun set in crimson and in gold;
When idlers swarmed upon the esplanade,
And a late steamer wheeling towards the quay
Struck founts of silver from the darkling sea,   50
The solemn tune arose and shook and rolled
Above the throng,
Above the hum and tramp and bravely knit
All hearts in common memories of song.

Sometimes he played at speed;
Then the Old Hundredth like a devil's mass
Instinct with evil thought and evil deed,
Rang out in anguish and remorse. Alas!
That men must know both Heaven and Hell!
Sometimes the melody   60
Sang with the murmuring surge;
And with the winds would tell
Of peaceful graves and of the passing bell.
Sometimes it pealed across the bay
A high triumphal dirge,
A dirge
For the departing undefeated day.

A noble tune, a high becoming mate
Of the capped mountains and the deep broad firth;
A simple tune and great,
The fittest utterance of the voice of earth.   70

Speaker, *XVIII (13 August 1898), 204.* The Last Ballad, and Other Poems
(John Lane, 1899). Based on article, 'The Isle of Dogs to Sydenham', in
Glasgow Herald *(22 July 1893), 4.*

PRE-SHAKESPEARIANISM

Now is 'a voice of wailing heard and loud lament';[1] our young men see visions and dream dreams.[2]
All the woe of the world is to be uttered at last. Poetry has been democratised. Nothing could pre-
vent that. The songs are of the highways and the by-ways.[3] The city slums and the deserted villages
are haunted by sorrowful figures, men of power and endurance, feeding their melancholy not with
heroic fable, the beauty of the moon, and the studious cloisters, but with the actual sight of the

PRE-SHAKESPEARIANISM
1 as over Herod's 'slaughter of the innocents', Matthew 2.18.

2 as prophesied in Joel, more or less, Joel 3.28.
3 locations of feast-giver's search for humble guests, Matthew 22.9.

misery in which so many millions live. To this mood the vaunted sweetness and light of the in-effective apostle of culture[4] are like a faded rose in a charnel-house, a flash of moonshine on the Dead Sea. It is not now to the light that 'the passionate heart of the poet' will turn. In vain the old man cried: –

> Authors – essayist, atheist, novelist, realist, rhymester, play your part,
> Paint the mortal shame of nature with the living hues of art.
> Rip your brothers' vices open, strip your own foul passions bare;
> Down with Reticence, down with Reverence – forward – naked – let them stare.[5]

This ironical Balaam-curse has become a message.[6] It must all out. The poet is in the street, the hospital. He intends the world to know that it is out of joint. He will not let it alone. With whatever trumpet or jew's-harp he can command he will clang and buzz at its ear, disturbing its sleep, its pleasures; discoursing of darkness and of the terror that walks by night. 'Down with Reticence' – that kills the patient; 'down with Reverence' – for whatever has become abominable. Do they delight in this? No; it is only that it is inevitable. Democracy is here; and we have to go through with it.

The newspaper is one of the most potent factors in moulding the character of contemporary poetry. Perhaps it was first of all the newspaper that couched the eyes of poetry. Burns's eyes were open. Blake's also for a time; and Wordsworth had profound insight into the true character of man and of the world; but all the rest saw men as trees walking; Tennyson and Browning are Shakespearian. The prismatic cloud that Shakespeare hung out between poets and the world! It was the newspapers, I think, that brought us round to what may be called an order of Pre-Shakespear-ianism. It was out of the newspapers that Thomas Hood got 'The Song of the Shirt' – in its place the most important English poem of the nineteenth century; the 'woman in unwomanly rags plying her needle and thread' is the type of the world's misery. 'The Song of the Shirt' is the most terrible poem in the English language. Only a high heart and strong brain broken on the wheel of life, but master of its own pain and anguish, able to jest in the jaws of death, could have sung this song, of which every single stanza wrings the heart. Poetry passed by on the other side.[7] It could not endure the woman in unwomanly rags. It hid its head like the fabled ostrich in some sand-bed of Arthurian legend, or took shelter in the paradoxical optimism of 'The Ring and the Book.' It is true William Morris stood by her when the priest and the Levite passed by. He stood by her side, he helped her; but he hardly saw her, nor could he show her as she is. 'Mother and Son,' his greatest poem, and a very great poem, is a vision of a deserted Titaness in London streets; there was a veil also between him and the world, although in another sense, with his elemental Sigurds, he is the truest of all Pre-Shakespearians. But the woman in unwomanly rags, and all the insanity and iniquity of which she is the type, will now be sung. Poetry will concern itself with her and hers for some time to come. The offal of the world is being said in statistics, in prose fiction: it is besides going to be sung. James Thomson sang it; and others are doing so. Will it be of any avail? We cannot tell. Nothing that has been done avails. Poor-laws, charity organisations, dexterously hold the wound open, or tenderly and hopelessly skin over the cancer. But there it is in the streets, the hospitals, the poor-houses, the prisons; it is a flood that surges about our feet, it rises breast-high. And it will be sung in all keys and voices. Poetry has other functions, other aims; but this also has become its province.

Speaker, XIX (28 January 1899), 258–9. The Man Forbid and Other Essays, ed. E. J. O'Brien (Boston, 1910).

4   Matthew Arnold.
5   Tennyson, 'Locksley Hall Sixty Years After' (1886), 139–42.
6   Balaam's curse: Numbers 22–3.
7   as the priest and the Levite did with the wounded man in story of the Good Samaritan, Luke 10. 33–7.

A. (Agnes) Mary F. Robinson (Mme James Darmesteter; Mme Emile Duclaux) (1857–1949)

Agnes Mary Robinson was a Low-Midlander, born in Leamington Spa in Warwickshire, elder daughter of the architect to the Anglican diocese of Coventry. She was not a strong child, spent much of her time as a young girl reading, but was sent abroad to school in Brussels at the age of thirteen. She also studied in Italy, and then at University College, London. Her parents were cultured people who lionized Robert Browning and Oscar Wilde. The story is that she was offered the choice between a lavish ball and the publication of her poems as a coming-of-age present – and she chose the book: *A Handful of Honeysuckle* (1878). This launched her in literary London, where she became something of a renowned young literary beauty. She went on to publish many more poems – *The New Arcadia, and Other Poems* (1884); *An Italian Garden: A Book of Songs* (1886); *Songs, Ballads, and A Garden Play* (1888), *Retrospect and Other Poems* (1893), as well as the *Life of Emily Brontë* in the Eminent Women series (1883), and a novel, *Arden*, also in 1883. Her volume of *Collected Poems, Lyrical and Narrative* appeared in 1902. In 1888 she married a French scholar, James Darmesteter, Professor of Persian in Paris, and their home in that city became quite a *salon*. He died in 1894, and in 1901 she married Emile Duclaux, a French scientist, and moved to the Cantal region. After only three years he died, but she lived on until 1949, writing a bit (her last volume of poems is *Images and Meditations*, 1923). She is a coolly meditative, cosmically sceptical lyricist with a touch for confessional wryness, stories, and versions of Italian peasant songs. Her Introduction to her *Collected Poems* argues that the ballad and the love song are particularly the zone of women poets ('We women have a privilege in these matters') and high culture should not despise such forms. Her defence – 'some old wife or other, crooning over her fire of sticks, in Scotland or the Val d'Aosta, in Romania or Gascony, is probably at the beginning of most romantic ballads' – rather echoes the praise of the realism of ordinary life, the subject matter of Dutch paintings (and of *Adam Bede*, of course), by that other Low-Midlander from the area around Coventry, George Eliot, in Chapter 17 of *Adam Bede* (1859): 'I find a source of delicious sympathy in those faithful pictures of a monotonous homely existence…an old woman bending over her flower-pot, or eating her solitary dinner…[with] her stone jug, and all those cheap common things which are the precious necessities of life to her.'

MEN AND MONKEYS

The hawthorn lane was full of flower;
   Across the hedge, the apple-trees
   Sent down with every gust of breeze
A light, loose-petalled blossom-shower.

The wide green edges of the lane
   Were filmed with faint valerian; white
   Archangels tall, the bees' delight,
Sprang lustier for the morning's rain.

The scent of May was heavy-sweet;
   The noon poured down upon the land.   10
   The nightingales on either hand
Called, and were silent in the heat.

For even in the distant deep
   Green-lighted forest glades, the noon
   Grown heavy with excess of boon,
Weighed all the sultry earth to sleep.

The herds, the flowers, the nightingales
   All drowsed; and I upon the edge
   Of grass beneath the flowering hedge
Lay dreaming of its shoots and trails.   20

When, starting at the sound of feet,
   I saw the Italian vagrants pass;
   The monkey, man, and peasant-lass,
Who figure on our village street –

At race-time in the spring; nor song,
   Caper, nor hurdy-gurdy tune
   Seemed left in them this blazing noon
As wearily they trudged along.

Their sallow faces drawn, their eyes
   Fixed on the miles of dust that went   30
   Before them, their round shoulders bent
Beneath a load of vanities.

The man tramped first, upon his back
   The hurdy-gurdy, with an ape,
   Who strained his lean and eager shape
Towards the woman's gayer pack

Of rags and ribbons. What a sight
   Among the blossoms and the green!
   I think there never can have been
A stranger shadow in the light.   40

They did not pause to look upon
   The apple-blossom and the may;
   They only saw the dust that they
Raised in their dismal trudging on.

They did not even stop to hear
   The rare sweet call of the nightingale;
   The hurdy-gurdy's squeak and yell
Was too accustomed in their ear.

I watched them plod their stolid way
   Straight on; till suddenly I heard   50
   The monkey mimic the singing-bird,
And snatch a trail of the flowering may.

And down the road I saw him still
   Catching and clutching the blossom white,
   Waving his long, black arms in delight,
Until they passed over the brow of the hill.

The New Arcadia, and Other Poems *(Ellis & White, 1884).*

POSIES: I

To F.M.R.

I made a posy for my Love
   As fair as she is soft and fine:
The lilac thrift I made it of,
   And lemon-yellow columbine.

But woe is me for my despair,
   For my pale flowers, woe is me
A bolder man has given her
   A branch of crimson peony!

An Italian Garden: A Book of Songs *(T. Fisher Unwin, 1886).*

DEATH IN THE WORLD

The great white lilies in the grass
   Are pallid as the smile of death;
For they remember still – alas!
   The graves they sprang from underneath.

The Angels up in heaven are pale –
   For all have died, when all is said;
Nor shall the lutes of Eden avail
   To let them dream they are not dead.

An Italian Garden *(1886). Retitled, 'Pallor', in* Collected Poems,
by A. Mary F. Robinson (Madame Duclaux) (T. Fisher Unwin, 1902).

ALTERNATIVES

Dearest, should I love you more
   If you understood me?
If, when I am sick and sore,
Straightway you divined wherefore,
Then with herbs and healing store
   Of your love imbued me?

Nay, I have instead, you know,
   In your heart an arbour
Where the great winds never go

That about my spirit blow;   10
Where the sweet wild roses grow,
   Sweeter thrushes harbour.

What a joy at last to rest
   Safe therein from sorrow!
What a spur when sore distressed,
To at last attain your breast!
When the night is loneliest
   What a hope of morrow!

An Italian Garden *(1886).*

IN AFFLICTION

I watch the happier people of the house
   Come in and out, and talk, and go their ways;
I sit and gaze at them; I cannot rouse
   My heavy mind to share their busy days.

I watch them glide like skaters on a stream
   Across the brilliant surface of the world;
But I am underneath; they do not dream
   How deep below the eddying flood is whirl'd.

They cannot come to me, nor I to them;
  But, if a mightier arm could reach and save,   10
Should I forget the tide I had to stem?

Should I, like these, ignore the abysmal wave?
Yes! in the radiant air how could I know
How black it is, how fast it is, below?

Songs, Ballads, and A Garden Play (T. Fisher Unwin, 1888).
Retitled, 'Neurasthenia,' in Collected Poems *(1902).*

AN ORCHARD AT AVIGNON

The hills are white, but not with snow:
  They are as pale in summer time,
For herb or grass may never grow
  Upon their slopes of lime.

Within the circle of the hills
  A ring, all flowering in a round,
An orchard-ring of almond fills
  The plot of stony ground.

More fair than happier trees, I think,
  Grown in well-watered pasture land   10
These parched and stunted branches, pink
  Above the stones and sand.

O white, austere, ideal place,
  Where very few will care to come,
Where spring hath lost the waving grace
  She wears for us at home!

Fain would I sit and watch for hours
  The holy whiteness of thy hills,
Their wreath of pale auroral flowers,
  Their peace the silence fills.   20

A place of secret peace thou art,
  Such peace as in an hour of pain
One moment fills the amazed heart,
  And never comes again.

Songs, Ballads, and A Garden Play (1888).

Constance (Caroline Woodhill) Naden (1858–89)

Constance Naden was born, 24 January 1858, in Edgbaston in the prosperous suburbs of Birmingham, the only child of Thomas Naden, an architect, and his wife Caroline Anne. Her mother died a few days after giving birth, and the child was brought up by her rather well-off Baptist grandparents. The grandfather was reputedly a man of some literary taste. Constance attended a Misses Martin's day-school until she was sixteen or so (they were Unitarians). She at first wanted to be a water-colourist but didn't get far with the Birmingham Society of Artists. She learnt Latin privately and attended classes at the Midland Institute for Botany and German. In autumn 1881 she enrolled as a student at the Mason Science College in Birmingham. A keen joiner and disciple, she was greatly influenced in her free-thinking by James Hinton, the Baptist turned physician who developed a strong post-Christian combination of science and metaphysics. She became a devotee of Herbert Spencer the pioneer sociologist, and in the later eighties a disciple too of a Dr R. Lewins and his doctrine of 'Hylo-Idealism' or 'monistic positivism' (difficult to follow, these: but supposed to reconcile philosophy, poetry and science). Lewins wrote the foreword to Naden's *Complete Poetical Works* (1894). In 1887 she inherited her grandmother's property, sold up, travelled widely on the proceeds in the Near and Far East (she was severely ill in India), then bought a house off Grosvenor Square in London. In the metropolis she was, as she had been in Bir-

mingham, widely active in charity works, raising money for the Garrett Anderson Hospital for Women (Elizabeth Garrett Anderson was a friend). She was a member of numerous debating and intellectual societies. She lectured and wrote a lot, especially on Spencerian and Hylo-Idealistic topics. She was a free-thinking radical Irish Home-ruler, devoted to the cause of women's suffrage. Her first published poem was 'The Lady Doctor' (in the magazine *London Society*, 1877). Her first book of verses was *Songs and Sonnets of Springtime* (1881), her second '*A Modern Apostle*', '*The Elixir of Life*', '*The Story of Clarice*', *and Other Poems* (1887). She published articles and pamphlets of a philosophical, pseudo-philosophical and free-thinking sort (e.g. *What is Religion? A Vindication of Free Thought*, 1893), and her essays were gathered in several posthumous volumes. Her poems often deal satirically with scientific topics and with the New Woman. As a cosmic Darwinian, she breezily occupies a nice niche in the generally male ranks of Victorian comic poets, but her tone can be so relentlessly jokey and her mood so ironic that it is commonly hard to detect which side these verses are coming down on in the personal and social debates about women's role. Towards the end of 1889 she became seriously unwell with a mortal illness, perhaps connected with her old Indian sickness. This involved some sort of serious surgery, after which she died, 23 December 1889. She was only thirty-one.

CHANGED

They told me she was still the same,
  In form, and mind, and heart;
With freshly-dawning joy I came,
  And now in grief depart.

Still round the forehead, smooth and white,
  The golden tresses twine,
The face is fair, the step is light,
  As when I called her mine.

And yet the mouth that once I kissed
  Is not the same as then;   10
The smile of love I never missed
  Comes not for me again.

More measured is the silver voice,
  The words more fitly said;
But while she speaks, I half rejoice
  To feel my love is dead.

The eyes are deeper than before,
  And far more subtly sweet;
And yet I pray that mine no more
  Their altered glance may meet.   20

My dream is past. I loved a child,
  The woman I resign;
The world and she are reconciled,
  And now she is not mine.

Songs and Sonnets of Springtime (C. Kegan Paul & Co., 1881).

THE LADY DOCTOR

Saw ye that spinster gaunt and grey,
Whose aspect stern might well dismay
  A bombardier stout-hearted?
The golden hair, the blooming face,
And all a maiden's tender grace
  Long, long from her have parted.

A Doctor she – her sole delight
To order draughts as black as night,
  Powders, and pills, and lotions;
Her very glance might cast a spell   10
Transmuting Sherry and Moselle
  To chill and acrid potions.

Yet if some rash presumptuous man
Her early life should dare to scan,
  Strange things he might discover;
For in the bloom of sweet seventeen
She wandered through the meadows green
  To meet a boyish lover.

She did not give him Jesuit's bark,
To brighten up his vital spark,   20
  Nor ipecacuanha,
Nor chlorodyne, nor camomile,
But blushing looks, and many a smile,
  And kisses sweet as manna.

But ah! the maiden's heart grew cold,
Perhaps she thought the youth too bold,
  Perhaps his views had shocked her;
In anger, scorn, caprice, or pride,
She left her old companion's side
  To be a Lady Doctor.   30

She threw away the faded flowers,
Gathered amid the woodland bowers,
  Her lover's parting token:
If suffering bodies we relieve,
What need for wounded souls to grieve?
  Why mourn, though hearts be broken?

She cared not, though with frequent moan
He wandered through the woods alone
  Dreaming of past affection:
She valued at the lowest price   40
Men neither patients for advice
  Nor subjects for dissection.

She studied hard for her degree;
At length the coveted M.D.
  Was to her name appended;
Joy to that Doctor, young and fair,
With rosy cheeks and golden hair,
  Learning with beauty blended.

Diseases man can scarce endure
A lady's glance may quickly cure,   50
  E'en though the pains be chronic;
Where'er that maiden bright was seen
Her eye surpassed the best quinine,
  Her smile became a tonic.

But soon, too soon, the hand of care
Sprinkled with snow her golden hair,
  Her face grew worn and jaded;
Forgotten was each maiden wile,
She scarce remembered how to smile,
  Her roses all were faded.   60

And now, she looks so grim and stern,
We wonder any heart could burn
   For one so uninviting;
No gentle sympathy she shows,
She seems a man in woman's clothes,
   All female graces slighting.

Yet blame her not, for she has known
The woe of living all alone,
   In friendless, dreary sadness;
She longs for what she once disdained,   70

And sighs to think she might have gained
   A home of love and gladness.

       Moral
Fair maid, if thine unfettered heart
Yearn for some busy, toilsome part,
   Let that engross thee only;
But oh! if bound by love's light chain,
Leave not thy fond and faithful swain
   Disconsolate and lonely.

       Songs and Sonnets of Springtime *(1881).*

TO AMY, ON RECEIVING HER PHOTOGRAPH

When of some lovely landscape unforgot
   A shadowy sketch I see, my thought divines
   Clear sunshine gleaming through the pencilled lines,
And cool green shade, where seems a shapeless blot:
I know how morning pierced that sheltered grot,
   How noonday glowed between the tufted pines,
   And even so, your cold grey portrait shines
With tints unseen by those who know you not.

They cannot see the apple-blossom cheek,
   The eyes of midnight blue, the sun-lit hair;   10
Grave are the lips, and will not smile or speak:
   And yet to me the pictured face is fair:
I conned that May-tide bloom when last we met,
And all the eye saw then, the heart sees yet.

       Songs and Sonnets of Springtime *(1881).*

(Mrs) Dollie (Caroline Maitland) Radford (1858–1920)

Dollie Radford, socialist, Fabian, poet, essayist, playwright, and children's writer, was born Caroline Maitland, in Worcester, went to school in Malvern and then studied at the Queen's College for young women in Baker Street, London (founded in 1848 by the Christian Socialist F. D. Maurice: Charles Kingsley was the first English Literature lecturer). She married the Fabian poet and critic Ernest Radford (1857–1919) in 1883. (He was one of the Yeatsian Rhymers' Club members.) They had three children, Maitland, Margaret (who herself became a published poet) and Hester. They lived at 32 Well Walk, Hampstead, and also owned a cottage at Hermitage, near Newbury, Berkshire. There's a lovely account in Fiona MacCarthy's *William Morris* (1994), taken from Radford's MS diary, of her going through wind and rain to Hammersmith, 30 November 1884, to hear Morris lecture on 'How We Live, and How We Might Live', staying on to supper, and going home very late and wet, more than ever convinced of the 'seriousness and beauty of the Socialist movement'. Dollie Radford helped William Allingham's widow Helen edit his

Diary in 1907. During the First World War she met and became a great friend and ally of the impecunious D. H. Lawrence, giving him and his wife Frieda a roof over their heads in Hampstead and Hermitage, storing their furniture, lending books, giving general succour. Dr Maitland Radford gave Lawrence a great deal of free medical advice and help. After a few years' acquaintance Lawrence turned his usual ungratefully tetchy self with the Radfords (Ernest, who had to go into a mental home, becomes 'the madman' in Lawrence's letters). But at the height of a very warm friendship Lawrence was very keen on and perceptive about Dollie Radford's poems. 'They made me sad. They make me think of the small birds in the twilight, whistling brief little tunes, but so clear, they seem like little lights in the twilight, such clear, vivid sounds. I do think you make fine, exquisite verse' (this in a letter, 27 January 1916, probably about her *Poems*, 1910). Her several volumes before that are *A Light Load* (1891), *Good Night* (1895), *Songs and Other Verses* (1895), *One Way of Love: An Idyll* (1898), *A Ballad of Victory* (1907).

SONG

In the first light of the morning,
    When the thrush sang loud and clear,
And the black-bird hailed day's dawning,
    How I wished my love could hear.

When the sun shone on the sand there,
    And the roses bloomed above,

And the blue waves kissed the land there,
    How I longed to see my love.

Now the birds good-night are calling,
    And the moonbeams come and go,   10
And my tears are falling, falling,
    Because I want him so.

                A Light Load *(Elkin Mathews, 1891).*

SONG

When first I saw your face, love,
    I knew my search was done,
You passed my lonely place, love,
    The light I sought was won,
When your steadfast eyes looked down on me,
And I arose to follow thee.

And something in your smile, love,
    I knew to be a part
Of joy that for a while, love,
    Had slumbered in my heart: 10
To what sweet music it awoke,
When first you turned to me and spoke!

                A Light Load *(1891).*

SONG

I am wanting to send you a song, love,
    From over the sea,
But the way, Oh the way is so long, love,
    Between you and me,
All the music would die,
In the waves and the sky,
    Before it reached thee.

I am wanting to tell you my love, love,
    But you will forget
How you lifted your sweet eyes above, love,   10
    How their lashes were wet
When you wished me good-bye,
While the stars filled the sky,
    And my sad sails were set.

                A Light Load *(1891).*

SOLILOQUY OF A MAIDEN AUNT

The ladies bow, and partners set,
And turn around and pirouette
        And trip the Lancers.

But no one seeks my ample chair,
Or asks me with persuasive air
        To join the dancers.

They greet me, as I sit alone
Upon my solitary throne,
        And pass politely.

Yet mine could keep the measured beat,   10
As surely as the youngest feet,
        And tread as lightly.

No other maiden had my skill
In our old homestead on the hill –
        That merry May-time

When Allan closed the flagging ball,
And danced with me before them all,
        Until the day-time.

Again I laugh, and step alone,
And curtsey low as on my own   20
        His strong hand closes.

But Allan now seeks staid delight,
His son there, brought my niece to-night
        These early roses.

Time orders well, we have our Spring,
Our songs, and may-flower gathering,
      Our love and laughter.

And children chatter all the while,
And leap the brook and climb the stile
      And follow after.   30

And yet – the step of Allan's son,
Is not as light as was the one
      That went before it.

And that old lace, I think, falls down
Less softly on Priscilla's gown
      Than when I wore it.

A Light Load *(1891)*.

E. (Edith) Nesbit (Mrs Hubert Bland) (1858–1924)

Edith Nesbit, the children's writer, was the youngest of the six children of Sarah and John Nesbit, an agricultural chemist who ran an agricultural college in Kennington, just south of the River Thames in London. He died when Edith was four or so, which soon caused financial problems. His widow then took her children around Europe. Edith was educated at a number of continental convent schools, before coming back to Brighton. Her sister Mary was briefly the fiancée of the blind poet Philip Bourke Marston. Edith began publishing poems in the later seventies, not long before, in 1880, seven months pregnant, she married Hubert Bland, a socialist brush-manufacturer, keen sexual philanderer, later a journalist. The paid companion of Bland's mother was also pregnant by him at the time – and he used to spend half the week at his mother's home to be with her. He also had two children by Edith's friend Alice Hoatson, who moved in with the Blands. Edith became legal parent to those two illegitimate ones, as well as bearing four children of her own. Her own philandering did not quite match her husband's, but neither partner's anarchic sexual activity seems to have been much diminished by their subsequent joint conversion to Roman Catholicism. They were founder members of the Fabian Society (1884) and moved in distinctly socialist, Fabian and anarchist circles. Sidney and Beatrice Webb, G. B. Shaw, Eleanor Marx, Annie Besant, Olive Schreiner, H. G. Wells, were all among her friends. She seems never to have seen the need, though, for women's suffrage. Bland died in 1914. In 1917 Edith married Thomas Terry Tucker, a ship's engineer. She died of cancer at her home near Dymchurch in Kent in 1924. *The Railway Children* (1906) is the children's story she is most remembered for, but commercial success as a children's author had set in a little earlier with *The Story of the Treasure Seekers* (1899). She produced, all told, more than forty children's books, but certainly at first it was as a poet that she saw herself – protesting, stirring up sympathy for various plights, domestic and sexual ones like her own, and the difficulties of the poor such as preoccupied the Fabians. But her skill at the long humane narrative poem, such as 'Two Christmas Eves' in her first volume, *Lays and Legends* (1886), indicates the direction her talent would most profitably run in. Other Victorian volumes were *Leaves of Life* (1888), *A Pomander of Verse* (1895) and *Songs of Love and Empire* (1898). Her Christian-Socialist leanings are even better demonstrated in the early twentieth-century volumes, *Ballads and Lyrics of Socialism, 1883–1908*, published by the Fabian Society (1908), and *Jesus in London* (also 1908).

The Wife of All Ages

I do not catch these subtle shades of feeling,
    Your fine distinctions are too fine for me;
This meeting, scheming, longing, trembling, dreaming,
    To me mean love, and only love, you see;
In me at least 'tis love, you will admit,
And you the only man who wakens it.

Suppose *I* yearned, and longed, and dreamed, and fluttered,
    What would you say or think, or further, do?
Why should one rule be fit for me to follow,
    While there exists a different law for you?   10
If all these fires and fancies came my way,
Would you believe love was so far away?

On all these other women – never doubt it –
　　'Tis love you lavish, love you promised me!
What do I care to be the first, or fiftieth?
　　It is the *only one* I care to be.
Dear, I would be your sun, as mine you are,
Not the most radiant wonder of a star.

And so, good-bye! Among such sheaves of roses
　　You will not miss the flower I take from you;　　　　　　20
Amid the music of so many voices
　　You will forget the little songs I knew –
The foolish tender words I used to say,
The little common sweets of every day.

The world, no doubt, has fairest fruits and blossoms
　　To give to you; but what, ah! what for me?
Nay, after all I am your slave and bondmaid,
　　And all my world is in my slavery.
So, as before, I welcome any part
Which you may choose to give me of your heart.　　　　　　30

　　　　　　　　Lays and Legends *(Longmans, Green & Co., 1886)*.

VIES MANQUÉES[1]

A year ago we walked the wood –
　　A year ago to-day;
A blackbird fluttered round her brood
　　Deep in the white-flowered may.

We trod the happy woodland ways,
　　Where sunset streamed between
The hazel stems in long dusk rays,
　　And turned to gold the green.

A thrush sang where the ferns uncurled,
　　And clouds of wind-flowers grew:　　　　　　10
I missed the meaning of the world
　　From lack of love for you.

You missed the beauty of the year,
　　And failed its self to see,
Through too much doubt and too much fear,
　　And too much love of me.

This year we hear the bird's glad strain,
　　Again the sunset glows,
We walk the wild wet woods again,
　　Again the wind-flower blows.　　　　　　20

In cloudy white the falling may
　　Drifts down the scented wind,

VIES MANQUÉES
1　missed lives.

And so the secret drifts away
   Which we shall never find.

Our drifted spirits are not free
   Spring's secret springs to touch,
For now you do not care for me,
   And I love you too much.

Lays and Legends (1886).

Love's Guerdons[1]

Dearest, if I almost cease to weep for you,
   Do not doubt I love you just the same;
'Tis because my life has grown to keep for you
   All the hours that sorrow does not claim.

All the hours when I may steal away to you,
   Where you lie alone through the long day,
Lean my face against your turf and say to you
   All that there is no one else to say.

Do they let you listen – do you lean to me?
   Know now what in life you never knew,   10
When I whisper all that you have been to me,
   All that I might never be to you?

Dear, lie still. No tears but mine are shed for you,
   No one else leaves kisses day by day,
No one's heart but mine has beat and bled for you,
   No one else's flowers push mine away.

A Pomander of Verse (John Lane at the Bodley Head, London; A. C. McClurg & Co.,
Chicago, 1895).

J. K. (James Kenneth) Stephen (1859–92)

J. K. Stephen the parodist was born in London, 25 February 1859, second son of a lawyer who became a judge. He went to various schools in preparation for Eton, where he was a Colleger 1871–8, and a pupil of the notorious Oscar Browning. He was good at history and essay-writing, no good at Classics and maths. He excelled at the Eton Wall Game, became College 'Keeper of the Wall', or Captain, and for most of his life would go back to school with teams of Old Boys to play again this peculiar game. In 1878 he went up to King's College, Cambridge, to read History. He was President of the Debating Union, learned to play the newly popular game of tennis, won the Members' English Essay Prize and the Winchester Reading

Prize, and came out first equal in the First Class of the History Tripos of 1881. In summer 1883 he coached Edward, Prince of Wales at Sandringham, in preparation for the prince's entry to Trinity College, Cambridge. He was elected a Fellow of King's College in 1885, was called to the Bar, and eventually started to practise in Stone Buildings in London. But writing was a great distraction. He turned into a prolific contributor to the journals – *St James's Gazette, Saturday Review, Pall Mall Gazette* – making his name as a witty versifier and parodist. At Felixstowe in the winter of 1886–7 he banged his head severely and from then on started to go downhill. In 1888 he founded a literary-political weekly, the *Reflector*, to which the likes of George

Meredith, Edmund Gosse, Frederick Locker-Lampson and Augustine Birrell contributed, but which quite exhausted his funds after only eighteen numbers. He was appointed by his father as Clerk of Assize in the South Wales Circuit, but mounting ill-health was against him, and in 1891 he returned to Cambridge, where he did bits of teaching and lecturing for two terms. His collection of his rhymes in *Lapsus Calami* (April 1891) was rather a hit, certainly in Stephen's own world of Old Etonians and university men, and in various forms this gathering had run to five editions by March 1892. A second volume, *Quo Musa Tendis?*, came out in November 1891, the month when, seriously ill, Stephen was compelled to leave Cambridge. He died 3 February 1892. His older brother gathered most of his material – school and Cambridge verses, travel pieces and other memorabilia, as well as the satires and parodies which are his real forte – in *Lapsus Calami and Other Verses*, together with a biographical introduction. The book was published in Cambridge by Macmillan and Bowes, June 1896, followed by a second edition, January 1898.

A PARODIST'S APOLOGY

If I've dared to laugh at you, Robert Browning,
    'Tis with eyes that with you have often wept:
You have oftener left me smiling or frowning,
    Than any beside, one bard except.

But once you spoke to me, storm-tongued poet,
    A trivial word in an idle hour;
But thrice I looked on your face and the glow it
    Bore from the flame of the inward power.

But you'd many a friend you never knew of,
    Your words lie hid in a hundred hearts,   10
And thousands of hands that you've grasped but few of
    Would be raised to shield you from slander's darts.

For you lived in the sight of the land that owned you,
    You faced the trial, and stood the test:
They have piled you a cairn that would fain have stoned you:
    You have spoken your message and earned your rest.

Pall Mall Gazette *(June 1891)*. Lapsus Calami and Other Verses
(Macmillan and Bowes, Cambridge, 1896).

A SONNET

Two voices are there: one is of the deep;
It learns the storm-cloud's thunderous melody,
Now roars, now murmurs with the changing sea,
Now bird-like pipes, now closes soft in sleep:
And one is of an old half-witted sheep
Which bleats articulate monotony,
And indicates that two and one are three,
That grass is green, lakes damp, and mountains steep:
And, Wordsworth, both are thine: at certain times
Forth from the heart of thy melodious rhymes,   10
The form and pressure of high thoughts will burst:
At other times – good Lord! I'd rather be
Quite unacquainted with the A. B. C.
Than write such hopeless rubbish as thy worst.

Granta *(June 1891)*. Lapsus Calami and Other Verses *(1896)*.

A. E. (Alfred Edward) Housman (1859–1936)

A. E. Housman, elegantly divided literary man – both sparely elegiac poet and also what W. H. Auden in his sonnet 'A. E. Housman' called 'The Latin Scholar of his generation' – was born, 26 March 1859, in Fockbury, Worcestershire, eldest child of a Bromsgrove solicitor, Edward Housman, and his first wife Sarah Jane Williams. The family moved to Perry Hall, Bromsgrove, in 1860. Housman had four brothers and two sisters. His mother died on his twelfth birthday; two years later his father married a cousin, Lucy Housman. From Bromsgrove School Housman went in October 1877 on a Classical Scholarship to St John's College, Oxford, and quickly formed the most important friendship of his life, with Moses Jackson. In the Classical Moderations exams of 1879 he gained a First Class. He failed to win the Newdigate Prize for Poetry, but he was a notoriously promising scholar, already devoted as an undergraduate to editing Latin texts (*Propertius*). For some reason he deliberately failed his Literae Humaniores Finals (refusing even to attempt answers to some questions). Reasons for this act of intellectual suicide remain matter for speculation, but a sexual brush-off by Moses Jackson is a likely candidate. Cast down from his high pinnacle, Housman retreated to Bromsgrove, prepared for the Civil Service exams, and took up a clerkship in the Patent Office. He shared lodgings in London's Bayswater district with Jackson and his younger brother Adalbert. Housman's relation with Jackson was up and down – Housman moved digs after a quarrel; Jackson went off to India in 1887 as headmaster of a Karachi school; he ended up in Canada. A. J. Jackson died of typhoid, 12 November 1892. The poem 'A. J. J.' celebrates him, echoing in brief Tennyson's massive elegy for his male friend, 'In Memoriam A. H. H.' Perhaps Housman was thinking of the coincidence of names – Alfred Tennyson and Alfred Housman – which linked him with the Laureate (the scholarly notes to Vladimir Nabokov's novel *Pale Fire* (1962) notice this as a connexion hintful of shared poetic quality). While still a civil servant Housman built up an extraordinary world-wide reputation as a textual scholar in both Greek and Latin. In 1892 eminent Classicists from Europe and America united to shoo him into the Chair of Latin at University College, London. In 1911 he transferred to Cambridge as Kennedy Professor of Latin. His editions of Juvenal and Manilius became standard works; his great spate of reviews – scathing, wry, bitchy, comically merciless about others' errors – confirmed him as the heavyweight champion of textual accuracy and poetic good

sense. In 1896 this seemingly dry-as-dust Classicist surprised everyone with the emotional intensities of *A Shropshire Lad*, published at Housman's own expense, after rejection by all the likely publishers. Many of its 63 poems were written in early 1895, in a state, Housman said, of 'continuous excitement'. Speculation (more speculation) connects this excitement with the Oscar Wilde trials then proceeding. 'Oh who is that young sinner...?' (held back from publication) rampages angrily about Wilde's being sentenced to hard labour 'for the colour of his hair'. The cryptic disclosure of Housman's intense feelings for men in his verse is aided by the deceptive – some say Latinate – spareness of his highly monosyllabic style. Linguistic sobriety rebukes by strong contrast the languors and lushness of the current decadence of the nineties ('all that twaddle', F. W. Bateson called it in the best essay on Housman, 'The Poetry of Emphasis', in *A. E. Housman: A Collection of Critical Essays*, ed. C. Ricks, 1968). Housman famously preached up the tingle at the back of the neck (another thing about Housman that Nabokov was arrested by, incidentally) as the marker of good poetry (this was in his 1933 lecture, 'The Name and Nature of Poetry'). But his own public verse never unbuttoned its lip. The day in May 1914 when Housman read aloud in a lecture his only published translation of Latin verse, the Horace poem 'Diffugere Nives', came as a great surprise to his students. 'He read the ode aloud with deep emotion, first in Latin and then in an English translation of his own. "That", he said hurriedly, almost like a man betraying a secret, "I regard as the most beautiful poem in ancient literature", and walked quickly out of the room.' Housman's poetic output was small – 'In barrenness, at any rate, I hold a high place among English poets, excelling even Gray'. The volume emphatically titled *Last Poems* came out in 1922 (with 41 poems). Housman lived quietly in Trinity College, Cambridge, hard at work, especially on his five-volume Manilius edition; though he did spend a month or so in France every summer. Illness overtook him in the early 1930s, and he died in a Cambridge nursing home, 30 April 1936, having abandoned a course of lectures in mid-stream. His brother Laurence culled 48 poems from the manuscript remains for the posthumous *New Poems* (1936), and appended a further 18 to his 1937 Memoir, *A. E. H.* (including 'Oh who is that young sinner...?'). The reluctant half of what John Berryman called Housman's 'double genius' (in Berryman's 'Dream Song 205') would out, even if only posthumously.

A.J.J.

When he's returned I'll tell him – oh,
  Dear fellow, I forgot:
Time was you would have cared to know,
  But now it matters not.

I mourn you, and you heed not how;
  Unsaid the word must stay;
Last month was time enough, but now
  The news must keep for aye.

Oh, many a month before I learn
  Will find me starting still   10

And listening, as the days return,
  For him that never will.

Strange, strange to think his blood is cold
  And mine flows easy on,
And that straight look, that heart of gold,
  That grace, that manhood gone.

The word unsaid will stay unsaid
  Though there was much to say;
Last month was time enough: he's dead,
  The news must keep for aye.   20

*(Written upon death of Adalbert J. Jackson, 12 November 1892). More Poems
(Alfred A. Knopf, New York, 1936). Collected Poems (Jonathan Cape, 1939).*

R.L.S.

Home is the sailor, home from sea:
  Her far-borne canvas furled
The ship pours shining on the quay
  The plunder of the world.

Home is the hunter from the hill:
  Fast in the boundless snare

All flesh lies taken at his will
  And every fowl of air.

'Tis evening on the moorland free,
  The starlit wave is still: 10
Home is the sailor from the sea,
  The hunter from the hill.

*Academy (22 December 1894), 533; above an obituary of Robert Louis Stevenson,
who died 3 December 1894. Text, Collected Poems (1939). Picks up lines from
Stevenson's 'Requiem', in Underwoods (1887): 'Home is the sailor,
home from the sea / And the hunter home from the hill'.*

From: A SHROPSHIRE LAD

I
1887[1]

From Clee to heaven the beacon burns,
  The shires have seen it plain,
From north and south the sign returns
  And beacons burn again.

Look left, look right, the hills are bright,
  The dales are light between,
Because 'tis fifty years to-night
  That God has saved the Queen.

Now, when the flame they watch not towers
  About the soil they trod,   10

Lads, we'll remember friends of ours
  Who shared the work with God.

To skies that knit their heartstrings right,
  To fields that bred them brave,
The saviours come not home to-night:
  Themselves they could not save.[2]

It dawns in Asia, tombstones show
  And Shropshire names are read;
And the Nile spills his overflow
  Beside the Severn's dead.   20

We pledge in peace by farm and town
  The Queen they served in war,

A SHROPSHIRE LAD
1 Written June 1887–September 1890. 1887 was the fiftieth anniversary of Queen Victoria's accession to the throne.

2 'He saved others, himself he cannot save', Mark 15.31 (priests' mocking words, of Jesus).

And fire the beacons up and down
  The land they perished for.

'God save the Queen' we living sing,
  From height to height 'tis heard;
And with the rest your voices ring,
  Lads of the Fifty-third.

Oh, God will save her, fear you not:
  Be you the men you've been,   30
Get you the sons your fathers got,
  And God will save the Queen.

II[3]

Loveliest of trees, the cherry now
Is hung with bloom along the bough,
And stands about the woodland ride
Wearing white for Eastertide.

Now, of my threescore years and ten,
Twenty will not come again,
And take from seventy springs a score,
It only leaves me fifty more.

And since to look at things in bloom
Fifty springs are little room,
About the woodlands I will go
To see the cherry hung with snow.

IV[4]
Reveille

Wake: the silver dusk returning
  Up the beach of darkness brims,
And the ship of sunrise burning
  Strands upon the eastern rims.

Wake: the vaulted shadow shatters,
  Trampled to the floor it spanned,
And the tent of night in tatters
  Straws the sky-pavilioned land.

Up, lad, up, 'tis late for lying:
  Hear the drums of morning play;   10
Hark, the empty highways crying
  'Who'll beyond the hills away?'

Towns and countries woo together,
  Forelands beacon, belfries call;
Never lad that trod on leather
  Lived to feast his heart with all.

Up, lad: thews that lie and cumber
  Sunlit pallets never thrive;

Morns abed and daylight slumber
  Were not meant for man alive.   20

Clay lies still, but blood's a rover;
  Breath's a ware that will not keep.
Up, lad: when the journey's over
  There'll be time enough to sleep.

XII[5]

When I watch the living meet,
  And the moving pageant file
Warm and breathing through the street
  Where I lodge a little while,

If the heats of hate and lust
  In the house of flesh are strong,
Let me mind the house of dust
  Where my sojourn shall be long.

In the nation that is not
  Nothing stands that stood before;   10
There revenges are forgot,
  And the hater hates no more;

Lovers lying two and two
  Ask not whom they sleep beside,
And the bridegroom all night through
  Never turns him to the bride.

XVI[6]

It nods and curtseys and recovers
  When the wind blows above,
The nettle on the graves of lovers
  That hanged themselves for love.

The nettle nods, the wind blows over,
  The man, he does not move,
The lover of the grave, the lover
  That hanged himself for love.

XIX[7]
To an Athlete Dying Young

The time you won your town the race
We chaired you through the market-place;
Man and boy stood cheering by,
And home we brought you shoulder-high.

To-day, the road all runners come,
Shoulder-high we bring you home,
And set you at your threshold down,
Townsman of a stiller town.

Smart lad, to slip betimes away
From fields where glory does not stay   10

---

3 Written May or June 1895.
4 First draft, January 1895.
5 Written February/March 1895.

6 Written July or August 1895.
7 First draft, March 1895.

And early though the laurel grows
It withers quicker than the rose.

Eyes the shady night has shut
Cannot see the record cut,
And silence sounds no worse than cheers
After earth has stopped the ears:

Now you will not swell the rout
Of lads that wore their honours out,
Runners whom renown outran
And the name died before the man.   20

So set, before its echoes fade,
The fleet foot on the sill of shade,
And hold to the low lintel up
The still-defended challenge-cup.

XXVII[8]

'Is my team ploughing,
    That I was used to drive
And hear the harness jingle
    When I was man alive?'

Ay, the horses trample,
    The harness jingles now;
No change though you lie under
    The land you used to plough.

'Is football playing
    Along the river shore,   10
With lads to chase the leather,
    Now I stand up no more?'

Ay, the ball is flying,
    The lads play heart and soul;
The goal stands up, the keeper
    Stands up to keep the goal.

'Is my girl happy,
    That I thought hard to leave,
And has she tired of weeping
    As she lies down at eve?'   20

Ay, she lies down lightly,
    She lies not down to weep:
Your girl is well contented.
    Be still, my lad, and sleep.

'Is my friend hearty,
    Now I am thin and pine,
And has he found to sleep in
    A better bed than mine?'

Yes, lad, I lie easy,
    I lie as lads would choose;   30
I cheer a dead man's sweetheart,
    Never ask me whose.

XXX[9]

Others, I am not the first,
Have willed more mischief than they durst:
If in the breathless night I too
Shiver now, 'tis nothing new.

More than I, if truth were told,
Have stood and sweated hot and cold,
And through their reins in ice and fire
Fear contended with desire.

Agued once like me were they,
But I like them shall win my way   10
Lastly to the bed of mould
Where there's neither heat nor cold.

But from my grave across my brow
Plays no wind of healing now,
And fire and ice within me fight
Beneath the suffocating night.

XXXI[10]

On Wenlock Edge the wood's in trouble;
    His forest fleece the Wrekin heaves;
The gale, it plies the saplings double,
    And thick on Severn snow the leaves.

'Twould blow like this through holt and hanger
    When Uricon[11] the city stood:
'Tis the old wind in the old anger,
    But then it threshed another wood.

Then, 'twas before my time, the Roman
    At yonder heaving hill would stare: 10
The blood that warms an English yeoman,
    The thoughts that hurt him, they were there.

There, like the wind through woods in riot,
    Through him the gale of life blew high;
The tree of man was never quiet:
    Then 'twas the Roman, now 'tis I.

The gale, it plies the saplings double,
    It blows so hard, 'twill soon be gone:
To-day the Roman and his trouble
    Are ashes under Uricon.   20

---

8   First draft, May or June 1895. Said to be 'Thomas Hardy's favourite'.
9   Written March or April 1895.
10   Written November 1895.
11   Uriconium: Roman name for Wroxeter, Shropshire.

XL[12]

Into my heart an air that kills
  From yon far country blows:
What are those blue remembered hills,
  What spires, what farms are those?

That is the land of lost content,
  I see it shining plain,
The happy highways where I went
  And cannot come again.

XLIV[13]

Shot? so quick, so clean an ending?
  Oh that was right, lad, that was brave:
Yours was not an ill for mending,
  'Twas best to take it to the grave.

Oh you had forethought, you could reason,
  And saw your road and where it led,
And early wise and brave in season
  Put the pistol to your head.

Oh soon, and better so than later
  After long disgrace and scorn,   10
You shot dead the household traitor,
  The soul that should not have been born.

Right you guessed the rising morrow
  And scorned to tread the mire you must:
Dust's your wages, son of sorrow,[14]
  But men may come to worse than dust.[15]

Souls undone, undoing others, –
  Long time since the tale began.
You would not live to wrong your brothers:
  Oh lad, you died as fits a man.   20

Now to your grave shall friend and stranger
  With ruth and some with envy come:
Undishonoured, clear of danger,
  Clean of guilt, pass hence and home.

Turn safe to rest, no dreams, no waking;
  And here, man, here's the wreath I've made:
'Tis not a gift that's worth the taking,
  But wear it and it will not fade.

XLVI[16]

  Bring, in this timeless grave to throw,
No cypress, sombre on the snow;
Snap not from the bitter yew

His leaves that live December through;
Break no rosemary, bright with rime
And sparkling to the cruel clime;
Nor plod the winter land to look
For willows in the icy brook
To cast them leafless round him: bring
No spray that ever buds in spring.   10

  But if the Christmas field has kept
Awns the last gleaner overstept,
Or shrivelled flax, whose flower is blue
A single season, never two;
Or if one haulm whose year is o'er
Shivers on the upland frore,
– Oh, bring from hill and stream and plain
Whatever will not flower again,
  To give him comfort: he and those
  Shall bide eternal bedfellows   20
  Where low upon the couch he lies
  Whence he never shall arise.

XLVIII[17]

Be still, my soul, be still; the arms you bear are brittle,
  Earth and high heaven are fixt of old and founded
    strong.
Think rather, – call to thought, if now you grieve a little,
  The days when we had rest, O soul, for they were long.

Men loved unkindness then, but lightless in the quarry
  I slept and saw not; tears fell down, I did not mourn;
Sweat ran and blood sprang out and I was never sorry:
  Then it was well with me, in days ere I was born.

Now, and I muse for why and never find the reason,
  I pace the earth, and drink the air, and feel the sun. 10
Be still, be still, my soul; it is but for a reason:
  Let us endure an hour and see injustice done.

Ay, look: high heaven and earth ail from the prime
    foundation;
  All thoughts to rive the heart are here, and all are vain:
Horror and scorn and hate and fear and indignation –
  Oh why did I awake? when shall I sleep again?

LX[18]

Now hollow fires burn out to black,
  And lights are guttering low:
Square your shoulders, lift your pack,
  And leave your friends and go.

Oh never fear, man, nought's to dread,
  Look not left nor right:

12 Written ?1886 ?–September 1890.
13 Written after suicide of a Woolwich Military Academy cadet, Henry Clarkson Maclean, aged 19, 6 August 1895. 'I have absolutely ruined my own life', said the suicide note – reported in newspaper cutting H. kept. Strong suggestions of homosexual guilt.
14 Jesus is, traditionally, the 'man of sorrows' of Isaiah 53.3.
15 'Golden lads and girls all must,/As chimney-sweepers, come to dust', *Cymbeline* IV.ii. 262–3.
16 First draft, before September 1890.
17 Written January 1892–spring 1893.
18 Written August–December 1894.

In all the endless road you tread
  There's nothing but the night.

LXII¹⁹

'Terence,²⁰ this is stupid stuff:
You eat your victuals fast enough;
There can't be much amiss, 'tis clear,
To see the rate you drink your beer.
But oh, good Lord, the verse you make,
It gives a chap the belly-ache.
The cow, the old cow, she is dead;
It sleeps well, the horned head:
We poor lads, 'tis our turn now
To hear such tunes as killed the cow.²¹   10
Pretty friendship 'tis to rhyme
Your friends to death before their time
Moping melancholy mad:
Come, pipe a tune to dance to, lad.'

Why, if 'tis dancing you would be,
There's brisker pipes than poetry.
Say, for what were hop-yards meant,
Or why was Burton built on Trent?²²
Oh many a peer of England brews
Livelier liquor than the Muse,   20
And malt does more than Milton can
To justify God's ways to man.²³
Ale, man, ale's the stuff to drink
For fellows whom it hurts to think:
Look into the pewter pot
To see the world as the world's not.
And faith, 'tis pleasant till 'tis past:
The mischief is that 'twill not last.
Oh I have been to Ludlow fair
And left my necktie God knows where,   30
And carried half way home, or near,
Pints and quarts of Ludlow beer:
Then the world seemed none so bad,
And I myself a sterling lad;
And down in lovely muck I've lain,
Happy till I woke again.
Then I saw the morning sky:

Heigho, the tale was all a lie;
The world, it was the old world yet,
I was I, my things were wet,   40
And nothing now remained to do
But begin the game anew.

Therefore, since the world has still
Much good, but much less good than ill,
And while the sun and moon endure
Luck's a chance, but trouble's sure,
I'd face it as a wise man would,
And train for ill and not for good.
'Tis true, the stuff I bring for sale
Is not so brisk a brew as ale: 50
Out of a stem that scored the hand
I wrung it in a weary land.
But take it: if the smack is sour,
The better for the embittered hour;
It should do good to heart and head
When your soul is in my soul's stead;
And I will friend you, if I may,
In the dark and cloudy day.

There was a king reigned in the East:²⁴
There, when kings will sit to feast,   60
They get their fill before they think
With poisoned meat and poisoned drink.
He gathered all that springs to birth
From the many-venomed earth;
First a little, thence to more,
He sampled all her killing store;
And easy, smiling, seasoned sound,
Sate the king when healths went round.
They put arsenic in his meat
And stared aghast to watch him eat;   70
They poured strychnine in his cup
And shook to see him drink it up:
They shook, they stared as white's their shirt:
Them it was their poison hurt.
– I tell the tale that I heard told.
Mithridates, he died old.²⁵

A Shropshire Lad (Kegan Paul, Trench, Trübner, & Co., 1896). The volume contained 63 poems.

Oh who is that young sinner with the handcuffs on his wrists?
And what has he been after that they groan and shake their fists?
And wherefore is he wearing such a conscience-stricken air?
Oh they're taking him to prison for the colour of his hair.

19 Written September–October 1895.
20 H.'s original title for the 'Shropshire Lad' sequence was *The Poems of Terence Hearsay.*
21 'The tune the old cow died of': colloquialism for boringly repeated story.
22 Burton-upon-Trent: a centre of beer-brewing trade.
23 Milton's *Paradise Lost* desired to do this, Bk I, line 26.
24 Mithridates VI, last of the kings of Pontus of that name; great enemy of Rome; immune to poison because of a 'diet of prophylactics'.
25 by the sword of a guard; aged 69.

'Tis a shame to human nature, such a head of hair as his;
In the good old time 'twas hanging for the colour that it is;
Though hanging isn't bad enough and flaying would be fair
For the nameless and abominable colour of his hair.

Oh a deal of pains he's taken and a pretty price he's paid
To hide his poll or dye it of a mentionable shade;   10
But they've pulled the beggar's hat off for the world to see and stare,
And they're haling him to justice for the colour of his hair.

Now 'tis oakum for his fingers and the treadmill for his feet
And the quarry-gang on Portland in the cold and in the heat,
And between his spells of labour in the time he has to spare
He can curse the God that made him for the colour of his hair.

Written after the Wilde trials, 10 August–30 September 1895. First published in Laurence Housman,
A. E. H.: Some Poems, Some Letters and a Personal Memoir by His Brother
(Jonathan Cape, 1937). (It 'says something which A. E. H. very much wished to say,
but perhaps preferred not to say in his own lifetime': L. Housman, A. E. H., p. 213.)

The chestnut casts his flambeaux, and the flowers
    Stream from the hawthorn on the wind away,
The doors clap to, the pane is blind with showers.
    Pass me the can, lad; there's an end of May.

There's one spoilt spring to scant our mortal lot,
    One season ruined of our little store.
May will be fine next year as like as not:
    Oh ay, but then we shall be twenty-four.

We for a certainty are not the first
    Have sat in taverns while the tempest hurled   10
Their hopeful plans to emptiness, and cursed
    Whatever brute and blackguard made the world.

It is in truth iniquity on high
    To cheat our sentenced souls of aught they crave,
And mar the merriment as you and I
    Fare on our long fool's-errand to the grave.

Iniquity it is; but pass the can.
    My lad, no pair of kings our mothers bore;
Our only portion is the estate of man:
    We want the moon, but we shall get no more.   20

If here to-day the cloud of thunder lours
    To-morrow it will hie on far behests;
The flesh will grieve on other bones than ours
    Soon, and the soul will mourn in other breasts.

The troubles of our proud and angry dust
    Are from eternity, and shall not fail.
Bear them we can, and if we can we must.
    Shoulder the sky, my lad, and drink your ale.

Begun November–December 1895; last stanza April 1922. Last Poems *(Grant Richards Ltd., 1922).*

DIFFUGERE NIVES

Horace: Odes IV. 7.[1]

The snows are fled away, leaves on the shaws[2]
   And grasses in the mead renew their birth,
The river to the river-bed withdraws,
   And altered is the fashion of the earth.

The Nymphs and Graces three put off their fear
   And unapparelled in the woodland play.
The swift hour and the brief prime of the year
   Say to the soul, *Thou wast not born for aye.*

Thaw follows frost; hard on the heel of spring
   Treads summer sure to die, for hard on hers   10
Comes autumn, with his apples scattering;
   Then back to wintertide, when nothing stirs.

But oh, whate'er the sky-led seasons mar,
   Moon upon moon rebuilds it with her beams:
Come *we* where Tullus and where Ancus[3] are,
   And good Aeneas,[4] we are dust and dreams.

Torquatus,[5] if the gods in heaven shall add
   The morrow to the day, what tongue has told?
Feast then thy heart, for what thy heart has had
   The fingers of no heir will ever hold.   20

When thou descendest once the shades among,
   The stern assize and equal judgment o'er,
Not thy long lineage nor thy golden tongue,
   No, nor thy righteousness, shall friend thee more.

Night holds Hippolytus[6] the pure of stain,
   Diana steads him nothing,[7] he must stay;
And Theseus leaves Pirithous in the chain
   The love of comrades cannot take away.[8]

                            Quarto, 3 (1897). More Poems (1936). 1936 text.

The laws of God, the laws of man,
He may keep that will and can;
Not I: let God and man decree
Laws for themselves and not for me;
And if my ways are not as theirs
Let them mind their own affairs.
Their deeds I judge and much condemn,
Yet when did I make laws for them?
Please yourselves, say I, and they
Need only look the other way.   10
But no, they will not; they must still
Wrest their neighbour to their will,
And make me dance as they desire
With jail and gallows and hell-fire.
And how am I to face the odds
Of man's bedevilment and God's?
I, a stranger and afraid
In a world I never made.
They will be master, right or wrong;
Though both are foolish, both are strong.   20
And since, my soul, we cannot fly
To Saturn nor to Mercury,
Keep we must, if keep we can,
These foreign laws of God and man.

                            Written c.1900. Last Poems (1922).

DIFFUGERE NIVES
1 The poem is a loose translation of the Horace.
2 groves, thickets.
3 third and fourth kings of Rome.
4 Virgil's hero in *Aeneid.*

5 a rich Roman.
6 chaste son of Theseus, killed on false charge of stepmother rape.
7 Goddess Diana revealed the innocence too late.
8 Theseus had to leave his close friend in underworld after failed Persephone-kidnap bid.

The rain, it streams on stone and hillock,
　　The boot clings to the clay.[1]
Since all is done that's due and right
Let's home; and now, my lad, good-night,
　　For I must turn away.

Good-night, my lad, for nought's eternal;
　　No league of ours, for sure.
To-morrow I shall miss you less,
And ache of heart and heaviness
　　Are things that time should cure.　　　　10

Over the hill the highway marches
　　And what's beyond is wide:
Oh soon enough will pine to nought

Remembrance and the faithful thought
　　That sits the grave beside.

The skies, they are not always raining
　　Nor grey the twelvemonth through;
And I shall meet good days and mirth,
And range the lovely lands of earth
　　With friends no worse than you.　　　　20

But oh, my man, the house is fallen
　　That none can build again;
My man, how full of joy and woe
Your mother bore you years ago
　　To-night to lie in the rain.

Begun before 1899; first and last stanzas c.1902; finished April 1922.
Last Poems (1922).

(Sir) A. (Arthur) Conan Doyle (1859–1930)

Arthur Conan Doyle, patriotic poet, medical doctor, military reformer, spiritualist and creator of the most famous fictional detective of all time, was born in Edinburgh, 22 May 1859, into an artistic Irish Roman Catholic family. He was the eldest son of Mary Foley and Charles Altimont Doyle, civil servant and artist. Grandfather John Doyle was a portrait-painter and caricaturist; uncle Richard Doyle was an artist for *Punch*. Arthur Conan went to Stonyhurst College, the Roman Catholic boys' school, and then studied medicine at Edinburgh University, qualifying MB in 1881, MD in 1885. He practised as a physician in Southsea, 1882–5, but soon turned to fiction. His first book, the novel *A Study in Scarlet* (1887), introduced Sherlock Holmes to the world, but it was in the *Strand Magazine* stories (first one, 'A Scandal in Bohemia', July 1891) that the detective's violin, deer-stalker hat, cocaine-syringe, narrating chum Dr Watson, and fabulously swift powers of deduction (based, apparently, on the diagnostic practices of one of Doyle's Edinburgh teachers, Dr Joseph Bell) became extraordinarily popular. Doyle would have preferred fame as a historical novelist, especially for the Napoleonic-era adventures of Brigadier Gerard, but Holmes was his money-spinning albatross, brought back even from death at the Reifenbach Falls at the hands of the terrible Dr Moriarty, by irresistible, though vexing, popular demand. An energetic sportsman, cricketer, follower of boxing, lover of mechanical toys, early motor-racing enthusiast, Doyle was also, in the words of his best biographer the crime-writer John Dickson Carr (1949), a great patriot, anxious to share his admiration

for the tradition of British military prowess. His novel *The White Company* (1891) was designed as 'the first book to depict the most important figure in English military history, her bowman soldier'. The balladic verses Doyle collected in *Songs of Action* (1898) are brisk heroics in a sort of Kiplingesque vein, celebrating, not least, that bowman. A deep admirer of Kipling's short stories, Doyle had more mixed feelings about the verse – not helped by his desperate struggles to play 'The Road to Mandalay' on the banjo. His great liking for Robert Louis Stevenson's work involved no such musical difficulties. His relish for Henley's poetry – 'to my mind one of our first living poets' – seems to have a lot to do with his believing the one-legged poet to have been the original of Long John Silver in Stevenson's *Treasure Island*. Doyle wangled himself a medical role in the Boer War of 1899–1902; was highly critical in *The Great Boer War* (1900) of old-fashioned military tactics, useless against the Boers' guerilla methods; defended English conduct (concentration camps and so forth) against liberal critics in *The War in South Africa: Its Cause and Conduct* (1902). He was knighted in 1902, and his literary fame opened up for him a life of public causes. He twice stood unsuccessfully for Parliament as a Liberal Unionist; successfully campaigned as a kind of Holmesian amateur detective on behalf of men he thought wrongfully convicted in the courts; was a thorn in the military establishment's side with his calls for army and navy reforms; preached the defensive virtues of a Channel Tunnel; wrote against other people's colonialist evils in Africa (*The Crime of the Congo*, 1910); tried vainly to save the

'THE RAIN, IT STREAMS ON STONE AND HILLOCK'
1　lines recalling Andrew Lang's 'Ballade of Cricket', above, p. 852.

pro-German Irish Republican Roger Casement from his death sentence; authored a six-volume *History of the British Campaign in France and Flanders* (1916–20). He spent his last years mainly writing and lecturing around the world on spiritualism – the great religious hope of the First World War's bereaved and widowed. His first marriage (1885–1906), to Louise Hawkins – one son, one daughter – petered out in unhappiness (he became a keen activist in the Divorce Reform Union); his second, to old friend Jean Leckie – two sons, one daughter – was happier (it was she who got him to try the banjo). He died at home at Crowborough, Sussex, 7 July 1930, full of years and books, reluctantly famous as Holmes's author, and a poet only as a by-product of his larger nationalist enthusiasms – *Songs of Action* indeed.

THE SONG OF THE BOW

What of the bow?
    The bow was made in England:
Of true wood, of yew-wood,
    The wood of English bows;
        So men who are free
        Love the old yew-tree
And the land where the yew-tree grows.

What of the cord?
    The cord was made in England:
A rough cord, a tough cord,   10
    A cord that bowmen love;
        And so we will sing
        Of the hempen string
And the land where the cord was wove.

What of the shaft?
    The shaft was cut in England:
A long shaft, a strong shaft,
    Barbed and trim and true;

        So we'll drink all together
        To the grey goose-feather   20
And the land where the grey goose flew.

What of the mark?
    Ah, seek it not in England,
A bold mark, our old mark
    Is waiting over-sea.
        When the strings harp in chorus,
        And the lion flag is o'er us,
It is there that our mark will be.

What of the men?
    The men were bred in England: 30
The bowmen – the yeomen,
    The lads of dale and fell.
        Here's to you – and to you!
        To the hearts that are true
And the land where the true hearts dwell.

Songs of Action *(Smith, Elder & Co., 1898)*.

THE FRONTIER LINE

What marks the frontier line?
    Thou man of India, say!
Is it the Himalayas sheer,
The rocks and valleys of Cashmere,
Or Indus as she seeks the south
From Attoch to the fivefold mouth?
        'Not that! Not that!'
    Then answer me, I pray!
What marks the frontier line?

What marks the frontier line?   10
    Thou man of Burmah, speak!
Is it traced from Mandalay,
And down the marches of Cathay,
From Bhamo south to Kiang-mai,
And where the buried rubies lie?
        'Not that! Not that!'
    Then tell me what I seek:
What marks the frontier line?

What marks the frontier line?
    Thou Africander, say!   20
Is it shown by Zulu kraal,
By Drakensberg or winding Vaal,
Or where the Shiré waters seek
Their outlet east at Mozambique?
        'Not that! Not that!
        There is a surer way
To mark the frontier line.'

What marks the frontier line?
    Thou man of Egypt, tell!
Is it traced on Luxor's sand,   30
Where Karnak's painted pillars stand,
Or where the river runs between
The Ethiop and Bishareen?
        'Not that! Not that!'
        By neither stream nor well
We mark the frontier line.

'But be it east or west,
    One common sign we bear,
The tongue may change, the soil, the sky,
But where your British brothers lie,   40
The lonely cairn, the nameless grave,

Still fringe the flowing Saxon wave.
    'Tis that! 'Tis where
    They lie – the men who placed it there,
That marks the frontier line.'

Songs of Action *(1898)*.

A Ballad of the Ranks

Who carries the gun?
    A lad from over the Tweed.
Then let him go, for well we know
    He comes of a soldier breed.
So drink together to rock and heather,
    Out where the red deer run,
And stand aside for Scotland's pride –
    The man that carries the gun!
        For the Colonel rides before,
            The Major's on the flank,   10
        The Captains and the Adjutant
            Are in the foremost rank.

        But when it's 'Action front!'
            And fighting's to be done,
        Come one, come all, you stand or fall
            By the man who holds the gun.

Who carries the gun?
    A lad from a Yorkshire dale.
Then let him go, for well we know
    The heart that never will fail.   20
Here's to the fire of Lancashire,
    And here's to her soldier son!
For the hard-bit north has sent him forth –
    The lad that carries the gun.

Who carries the gun?
    A lad from a Midland shire.
Then let him go, for well we know
    He comes of an English sire.
Here's a glass to a Midland lass,
    And each can choose the one,   30
But east and west we claim the best
    For the man that carries the gun.

Who carries the gun?
    A lad from the hills of Wales.
Then let him go, for well we know,
    That Taffy is hard as nails.
There are several ll's in the place where he dwells,
    And of w's more than one,
With a 'Llan' and a 'pen,' but it breeds good men,
    And it's they who carry the gun.   40

Who carries the gun?
    A lad from the windy west.
Then let him go, for well we know
    That he is one of the best.
There's Bristol rough, and Gloucester tough,
    And Devon yields to none.
Or you may get in Somerset
    Your lad to carry the gun.

Who carries the gun?
    A lad from London town.   50
Then let him go, for well we know
    The stuff that never backs down.
He has learned to joke at the powder smoke,
    For he is the fog-smoke's son,
And his heart is light and his pluck is right –
    The man who carries the gun.

Who carries the gun?
    A lad from the Emerald Isle.
Then let him go, for well we know,
    We've tried him many a while.   60
We've tried him east, we've tried him west,
    We've tried him sea and land,
But the man to beat old Erin's best
    Has never yet been planned.

Who carries the gun?
    It's you, and you, and you;
So let us go, and we won't say no
    If they give us a job to do.
Here we stand with a cross-linked hand,
    Comrades every one;   70
So one last cup, and drink it up
    To the man who carries the gun!
        For the Colonel rides before,
            The Major's on the flank,
        The Captains and the Adjutant
            Are in the foremost rank.

        And when it's 'Action front!'
            And there's fighting to be done,
        Come one, come all, you stand or fall
            By the man who holds the gun.   80

Songs of Action *(1898)*.

Francis Thompson (1859–1907)

Francis Thompson was born, 18 December 1859, second son of a Roman Catholic convert family in Preston, Lancashire (his elder brother died as a baby; Francis had three younger sisters). His father, Charles Thompson, was a homoeopathic doctor, his uncle Edward Thompson a devotional writer who taught English at University College, Dublin, and was a sub-editor on the *Dublin Review*. Francis was sent in 1870 to Ushaw College with a view to training as a priest, but, this not working out, he entered Owens College, Manchester, in 1877 as a medical student. Here he kept failing his exams and acquired his lifelong opium habit (inspired, it's been suggested, by De Quincey's *Confessions of an English Opium Eater* – a gift from his mother). His mother died in 1880, his father remarried, and in November 1885 Francis left Manchester for life in London as a literary down-and-out – sleeping rough and in doss-houses; selling matches and cleaning shoes to scrape up a living; writing poems. Canon John Carroll, a friend from childhood, got him to send poems to the Meynells' Catholic paper *Merry England*. Browning enthused. The support of Wilfred and Alice Meynell straightened out Thompson's health and addiction problems somewhat – though he may also have been helped, as if he were a De Quincey or Dostoevsky character, by friendship with a prostitute. The modish nineties publisher Mathews & Lane brought out *Poems* (1893), with 'The Hound of Heaven' in it, and fellow Catholic Coventry Patmore's praising review in the *Fortnightly* helped Thompson's reputation spread beyond the Meynells' Catholic circle. Through the Meynells and their friends, he went to live with the Capuchin Friars of Pantasaph in North Wales, where he worked on his *Sister Songs* (1895) and *New Poems* (1897). At the end of 1896 he returned to London and literary work, but also to his old street life and addiction to opium, reinforced heavily now by drink. His physical condition deteriorated and he died, 13 November 1907, emaciated, physically broken, in the Catholic hospice of Saint John and Saint Elizabeth in St John's Wood. The rhetoric of Thompson's verses – clotted, archaizing, curiously akin at times to the lines of Gerard Hopkins, which, of course, he had not seen – harks back, at their best and also their worst, to the extravagances of seventeenth-century Counter-Reformation poets such as Richard Crashaw. This endeared him to his Catholic readers, if to no one else. Wilfred Meynell loyally compiled the three-volume *Works: Poems*, published by the Catholic firm of Burns and Oates in 1913.

THE HOUND OF HEAVEN

I fled Him, down the nights and down the days;
I fled Him, down the arches of the years;
I fled Him, down the labyrinthine ways
Of my own mind; and in the mist of tears
I hid from Him, and under running laughter.
   Up vistaed hopes I sped;
   And shot, precipitated,
Adown Titanic glooms of chasmèd fears,
  From those strong Feet that followed, followed after.
    But with unhurrying chase,
    And unperturbèd pace,
  Deliberate speed, majestic instancy,
    They beat – and a Voice beat
    More instant than the Feet –
'All things betray thee, who betrayest Me.'   10

    I pleaded, outlaw-wise,
By many a hearted casement, curtained red,
  Trellised with intertwining charities;
(For, though I knew His love Who followèd,
    Yet was I sore adread   20
Lest, having Him, I must have naught beside)

But, if one little casement parted wide,
   The gust of His approach would clash it to.
   Fear wist not to evade, as Love wist to pursue.
Across the margent of the world I fled,
   And troubled the gold gateways of the stars,
   Smiting for shelter on their changèd[1] bars;
      Fretted to dulcet jars
And silvern chatter the pale ports o' the moon.
I said to dawn: Be sudden – to eve: Be soon;   30
   With thy young skiey blossoms heap me over
      From this tremendous Lover!
Float thy vague veil about me, lest He see!
   I tempted all His servitors, but to find
My own betrayal in their constancy,
In faith to Him their fickleness to me,
   Their traitorous trueness, and their loyal deceit.
To all swift things for swiftness did I sue;
   Clung to the whistling mane of every wind.
      But whether they swept, smoothly fleet,   40
     The long savannahs of the blue;
      Or whether, Thunder-driven,
      They clanged his chariot 'thwart a heaven,
Plashy with flying lightnings round the spurn o' their feet: –
   Fear wist not to evade as Love wist to pursue.
      Still with unhurrying chase,
      And unperturbèd pace,
   Deliberate speed, majestic instancy,
      Came on the following Feet,
      And a Voice above their beat –   50
   'Naught shelters thee, who wilt not shelter Me.'

I sought no more that, after which I strayed,
      In face of man or maid;
But still within the little children's eyes
      Seems something, something that replies,
They at least are for me, surely for me!
I turned me to them very wistfully;
But just as their young eyes grew sudden fair
      With dawning answers there,
Their angel plucked them from me by the hair.   60
'Come then, ye other children, Nature's – share
With me' (said I) 'your delicate fellowship;
     Let me greet you lip to lip,
     Let me twine with you caresses,
       Wantoning
     With our Lady-Mother's vagrant tresses,
       Banqueting
     With her in her wind-walled palace,
     Underneath her azured daïs,
     Quaffing, as your taintless way is,   70
      From a chalice
Lucent-weeping out of the dayspring.'
      So it was done:
I in their delicate fellowship was one –

THE HOUND OF HEAVEN
1   *clangèd* in later text.

Drew the bolt of Nature's secrecies.
   I knew all the swift importings
   On the wilful face of skies;
   I knew how the clouds arise
   Spumèd of the wild sea-snortings;
    All that's born or dies   80
   Rose and drooped with – made them shapers
Of mine own moods, or wailful or divine –
   With them joyed and was bereaven.
   I was heavy with the even,
   When she lit her glimmering tapers
   Round the day's dead sanctities.
   I laughed in the morning's eyes.
I triumphed and I saddened with all weather,
   Heaven and I wept together,
And its sweet tears were salt with mortal mine;   90
Against the red throb of its sunset-heart
   I laid my own to beat,
   And share commingling heat;
But not by that, by that, was eased my human smart.
In vain my tears were wet on Heaven's grey cheek.
For ah! we know not what each other says,
   These things and I; in sound *I* speak –
Their sound is but their stir, they speak by silences.
Nature, poor stepdame, cannot slake my drouth;
   Let her, if she would owe me,   100
Drop yon blue bosom-veil of sky, and show me
   The breasts o' her tenderness:
Never did any milk of hers once bless
   My thirsting mouth.
   Nigh and nigh draws the chase,
   With unperturbèd pace,
   Deliberate speed majestic instancy
   And past those noisèd Feet
   A voice comes yet more fleet –
   'Lo! naught contents thee, who content'st not Me.'   110

Naked I wait Thy love's uplifted stroke!
My harness piece by piece Thou hast hewn from me,
   And smitten me to my knee;
   I am defenceless utterly.
   I slept, methinks, and woke,
And, slowly gazing, find me stripped in sleep.
In the rash lustihead of my young powers,
   I shook the pillaring hours
And pulled my life upon me; grimed with smears,
I stand amid the dust o' the moulded years –   120
My mangled youth lies dead beneath the heap.
My days have crackled and gone up in smoke,
Have puffed and burst as sun-starts on a stream.
   Yea, faileth now even dream
The dreamer, and the lute the lutanist;
Even the linked fantasies, in whose blossomy twist
I swung the earth a trinket at my wrist,
Are yielding; cords of all too weak account
For earth with heavy griefs so overplussed.
   Ah! is Thy love indeed   130
A weed, albeit an amaranthine weed,

Suffering no flowers except its own to mount?
      Ah! must –
      Designer infinite! –
Ah! must Thou char the wood ere Thou canst limn with it?
My freshness spent its wavering shower i' the dust;
And now my heart is as a broken fount,
Wherein tear-drippings stagnate, spilt down ever
      From the dank thoughts that shiver
Upon the sighful branches of my mind.   140
      Such is; what is to be?
The pulp so bitter, how shall taste the rind?
I dimly guess what Time in mists confounds;
Yet ever and anon a trumpet sounds
From the hid battlements of Eternity;
Those shaken mists a space unsettle, then
Round the half-glimpsèd turrets slowly wash again;
      But not ere him who summoneth
      I first have seen, enwound
With glooming robes purpureal, cypress-crowned;   150
His name I know, and what his trumpet saith.
Whether man's heart or life it be which yields
      Thee harvest, must Thy harvest fields
      Be dunged with rotten death?
        Now of that long pursuit
        Comes on at hand the bruit;
      That Voice is round me like a bursting sea:
        'And is thy earth so marred,
        Shattered in shard on shard?
      Lo, all things fly thee, for thou fliest Me!   160

      'Strange, piteous, futile thing!
Wherefore should any set thee love apart?
Seeing none but I makes much of naught' (He said),
'And human love needs human meriting:
      How hast thou merited –
Of all man's clotted clay the dingiest clot?
      Alack, thou knowest not
How little worthy of any love thou art!
Whom wilt thou find to love ignoble thee,
      Save Me, save only Me?   170
All which I took from thee I did but take,
      Not for thy harms,
But just that thou might'st seek it in My arms.
      All which thy child's mistake
Fancies as lost, I have stored for thee at home:
      Rise, clasp My hand, and come!'

  Halts by me that footfall:
  Is my gloom, after all,
Shade of His hand, outstretched caressingly?
  'Ah, fondest, blindest, weakest,   180
  I am He Whom thou seekest!
Thou dravest love from thee, who dravest Me.'

Poems *(Elkin Mathews & John Lane, 1893).*

THE WAY OF A MAID[1]

The lover whose soul shaken is
In some decuman[2] billow of bliss,
Who feels his gradual-wading feet
Sink in some sudden hollow of sweet,
And 'mid love's usèd converse comes
Sharp on a mood which all joy sums –
An instant's fine compendium of
The liberal-leavèd writ of love;
His abashed pulses beating thick
At the exigent joy and quick,   10
Is dumbed, by aiming utterance great
Up to the miracle of his fate.
The wise girl, such Icarian[3] fall
Saved by her confidence that she's small, –

As what no kindred word will fit
Is uttered best by opposite,
Love in the tongue of hate exprest,
And deepest anguish in a jest, –
Feeling the infinite must be
Best said by triviality,   20
Speaks, where expression bates its wings,
Just happy, alien, little things;
What of all words is in excess
Implies in a sweet nothingness;
With dailiest babble shows her sense
That full speech were full impotence;
And, while she feels the heavens lie bare,
She only talks about her hair.

New Poems *(Archibald Constable & Co., Westminster, 1897).*

THE END OF IT

She did not love to love; but hated him
For making her to love, and so her whim
From passion taught misprison to begin;
And all this sin

Was because love to cast out had no skill
Self, which was regent still.
Her own self-will made void her own self's will.

New Poems *(1897).*

TO A SNOW-FLAKE

What heart could have thought you? –
Past our devisal
(O filigree petal!)
Fashioned so purely,
Fragilely, surely,
From what Paradisal
Imagineless metal,
Too costly for cost?
Who hammered you, wrought you,
From argentine vapour? –   10
'God was my shaper.

Passing surmisal,
He hammered, He wrought me
From curled silver vapour,
To lust of His mind: –
Thou could'st not have thought me!
So purely, so palely,
Tinily, surely,
Mightily, frailly,
Insculped and embossed,   20
With His hammer of wind,
And His graver of frost.'

New Poems *(1897).*

UNTO THIS LAST[1]

A boy's young fancy taketh love
Most simply, with the rind thereof;
A boy's young fancy tasteth more

The rind, than the deific core.
Ah, Sweet! to cast away the slips
Of unessential rind, and lips

THE WAY OF A MAID
1 cf. the three 'too wonderful' things of Proverbs 30.18–19, which
include 'the way of a man with a maid'.
2 very large (originally tenth part or tenth cohort).

3 Like Icarus, who flew too near the sun and the wax holding his
wings of feathers together melted, so he fell to his death.
UNTO THIS LAST
1 title of John Ruskin's anti-capitalist book of 1860, and of Isa (Craig)
Knox's poem of 1874, based on Matthew 20.16.

Fix on the immortal core, is well;
But heard'st thou ever any tell
Of such a fool would take for food
Aspect and scent, however good,   10
Of sweetest core Love's orchards grow?
Should such a phantast please him so,
Love where Love's reverent self denies
Love to feed, but with his eyes,
All the savour, all the touch,
Another's – was there ever such?
Such were fool, if fool there be;
Such fool was I, and was for thee!
But if the touch and savour too
Of this fruit – say, Sweet, of you –   20
You unto another give
For sacrosanct prerogative,
Yet even scent and aspect were
Some elected Second's share;
And one, gone mad, should rest content
With memory of show and scent;
Would not thyself vow, if there sigh
Such a fool – say, Sweet, as I –
Treble frenzy it must be
Still to love, and to love thee?   30

Yet had I torn (man knoweth not,
Nor scarce the unweeping angels wot
Of such dread task the lightest part)
Her fingers from about my heart.
Heart, did we not think that she
Had surceased her tyranny?
Heart, we bounded, and were free!
O sacrilegious freedom! – Till
She came, and taught my apostate will
The winnowed sweet mirth cannot guess   40
And tear-fined peace of hopelessness;
Looked, spake, simply touched, and went.
Now old pain is fresh content,
Proved content is unproved pain.
Pangs fore-tempted, which in vain
I, faithless, have denied, now bud
To untempted fragrance and the mood
Of contrite heavenliness; all days
Joy affrights me in my ways;
Extremities of old delight   50
Afflict me with new exquisite
Virgin piercings of surprise, –
Stung by those wild brown bees, her eyes!

New Poems (1897).

Katharine Tynan (Mrs Hinkson) (1861–1931)

Katharine Tynan, immensely prolific romantic novelist (over a hundred titles to her name), poet (eighteen volumes), autobiographer (five volumes) and journalist, was an Irish Roman Catholic Parnellite and a central figure in the Irish literary Celtic Revival of the end of the nineteenth century. She was born near Dublin, 23 January 1861 – though there is some suggestion that this date knocked two years off her age – the daughter of Andrew Cullen Tynan, farmer and well-known Irish nationalist. She published poems from her mid-teens on. Her first volume of poems, *Louise de la Vallière* (1885), was published at her father's expense, but it launched a greatly reputed career. She was close to Wilfred and Alice Meynell. W. B. Yeats praised her – he admired her 'devout tenderness', and her innocently childlike use of images from 'the green world about her'. She lionized Christina Rossetti ('deferential enough to puff me up like a puff-paste', i.e. puff-pastry, was the older poet's reaction to a visit from the young hero-worshipper) and a flattering imitativeness is visible not least in her most famous poem, 'Sheep and Lambs' – almost a Catholic devotional classic ('All in the April evening'). In 1893 she married Henry Albert Hinkson, an Irish barrister who also wrote novels. She lived with him in England and in Ireland (after he was appointed a magistrate in County Mayo), and in Europe after his death in 1919. She had three children, her daughter Pamela Hinkson becoming a novelist in turn. A. E. (George Russell) wrote the Foreword to her *Collected Poems* (1930). She died in Wimbledon, 2 April 1931, aged seventy, or perhaps seventy-two.

THE VIOLET FARM

If I might choose my simple lot
Far from the town and quite forgot,
All in a sheltered nook and warm,
'Tis I would have a violet farm.

No daffodils should me entice,
Nor hyacinths with their breath of spice,

The tulip with her painted hood
For me should wither where she stood.

Instead of sheep upon the sward,
The modest violet I would herd.   10
Instead of golden heads arow,
Would see my violet harvest blow.

Under an arch of wild, wild cloud,
Below an opal mountain bowed,
All in a humid world and cool,
With winds and waters beautiful.

What airs across my farm should breathe!
'Tis sweet where pinks and roses wreath:
But pinks and roses are not sweet
Beside the hidden violet.   20

No shortest day of all the year
Should fade without a violet's cheer,
Invisible sweetness hid within
And folded up in swathes of green.

Though white and purple babes be born
When Daffodil his flaming horn
O'er quiet hills and vales shall sound
And stir the sleepers underground;

What country bliss can equal mine,
With violets for my flocks and kine,   30
With violets for my corn and store?
What could a mortal wish for more?

Under a mountain pansy-dark,
Loved of the eagle and the lark,
And set too low for fear or harm,
'Tis I would have a violet farm.

Poems *(Lawrence & Bullen, 1901).*

SHEEP AND LAMBS

All in the April evening,
    April airs were abroad;
The sheep with their little lambs
    Passed me by on the road.

The sheep with their little lambs
    Passed me by on the road;
All in the April evening
    I thought on the Lamb of God.

The lambs were weary, and crying
    With a weak, human cry.   10
I thought on the Lamb of God
    Going meekly to die.

Up in the blue, blue mountains
   Dewy pastures are sweet;
Rest for the little bodies,
   Rest for the little feet.

But for the Lamb of God,
   Up on the hill-top green,
Only a Cross of shame
   Two stark crosses between.   20

All in the April evening,
   April airs were abroad;
I saw the sheep with their lambs,
   And thought on the Lamb of God.

Poems *(1901)*.

The Foggy Dew

A splendid place is London, with golden store
For them that have the heart and hope and youth galore;
But mournful are its streets to me, I tell you true,
For I'm longing sore for Ireland in the foggy dew.

The sun he shines all day here, so fierce and fine,
With never a wisp of mist at all to dim his shine;
The sun he shines all day here from skies of blue,
He hides his face in Ireland in the foggy dew.

The maids go out to milking in the pastures gray,
The sky is green and golden at dawn of the day;   10
And in the deep-drenched meadows the hay lies new,
And the corn is turning yellow in the foggy dew.

Mavrone! if I might feel now the dew on my face,
And the wind from the mountains in that remembered place,
I'd give the wealth of London, if mine it were to do,
And I'd travel home to Ireland and the foggy dew.

Poems *(1901)*.

May (Emma Goldworth) Kendall (1861–1943)

May Kendall, the satirical poet, New Woman novelist, and philanthropic activist, was born in Bridlington on the sea-coast of Yorkshire in 1861 into a Wesleyan Methodist family, daughter of Eliza Goldworth Level and James Kendall, who was a Methodist minister. Her first published book was a volume of satirical essays and verses, *That Very Mab* (1885), done in collaboration with, or, at least, under the sponsorship of, the fairy-tale expert Andrew Lang. Her volumes of poems and stories and her three novels all appeared in the eighties and nineties, though she did have poems and stories later in the *Cornhill* *Magazine* and poems in Quaker journals. Her first volume proper of verse was *Dreams to Sell* (1887), gathering in her socially engaged, sharply critical poems from papers such as *Punch*; her second volume, *Songs from Dreamland*, generally similar in tone and social thrust, appeared in 1894. Her book of stories *Turkish Bonds* (1898) indicates her somewhat conventional period Liberalism (it's on the side of the Armenians who were massacred by the Turks: a central end-of-century Liberal cause). Thereafter her energies were greatly taken up by her work with the reformist Quaker Rowntree family of York, where she lived for most of her life. She was a researcher and speech-writer for B. Seebohm Rowntree, working quite voluntarily for him, refusing any salary. Among other tasks, she was employed to turn the dryness of statistics and mere social reportage into reader-friendly anecdotes for Rowntree's influential *How the Labourer Lives* (1913) and *The Human Needs of Labour* (1918). She got no public credit for this work. She seems never to have become a Quaker, but she did remain close to the Society of Friends and always took the *Friends' Quarterly Examiner*. In later life she became a notorious York eccentric, sharing her house at 10 Monkgate with an army of cats. The Rowntree Trust paid for her funeral. Her grave in York Cemetery is unmarked.

IN THE DRAWING-ROOM

Furniture with the languid mien,
　　On which life seems to pall –
With your insipid grey and green
　　And drab, your cheerless wall –
To think that she has really been
　　An hour among you all.

I wonder, since she went away,
　　Has no one ever guessed
Why constantly you look more grey,
　　More green, and more depressed.　　10
I know – you know, you had your day,
　　Now you need only rest.

Yon heavy, yellow easy-chair,
　　Right opposite the door,
Ah, how impassively you stare
　　Across the dreary floor;
Yet even you would be aware
　　If she should come once more.

I see the dingy curtains stir
　　With a faint memory;　　20
The grand piano dreams of her
　　In a drowsy minor key.
Rest tranquilly, old furniture,
　　To-night it may not be!

Songs from Dreamland *(Longmans, Green & Co., 1894).*

THE SANDBLAST GIRL AND THE ACID MAN

Of all the cities far and wide,
　　The city that I most prefer,
Though hardly through the fog descried,
　　Is Muggy Manchester.
Of all its buildings the most dear,
　　I find a stained glass factory –
Because the sandblast girl works here,
　　In the same room with me!

It made a most terrific din,
　　Of yore, that sandblasting machine,　　10
I cursed the room I laboured in,
　　And all the dull routine,
And the *old* sandblast girl, who broke,
　　Of coloured glass, so many a sheet,
In fruitless efforts to evoke
　　Tracery clear and neat.

That sandblast girl, at last she left –
　　They couldn't let her blunders pass.
But Maggie's hands are slim and deft,
　　They never break the glass!　　20
From ruby, orange, or from blue,
　　The letters stand out clear as pearl.
The fellows say they never knew
　　So smart a sandblast girl!

I raise my eyes: I see her stand,
　　A sheet of glass her arms embrace;
Out spurts the narrow stream of sand
　　On each uncovered space,
Till perfectly the work is done,
　　And clear again grows Maggie's brow –　　30
Till a fresh labour is begun,
　　She's merely human, now!

And sometimes when her hands are free,
　　While with my acid still I work,
She'll give a hasty glance at me,
　　Embossing like a Turk.
Her pretty hair so soft and brown
　　Is coiled about her shapely head,
And I look up and she looks down,
　　And both of us go red!　　40

She has a dress of navy blue,
　　A turn-down collar, white and clean
As though no smoke it travelled through,
　　And smuts had never seen.
I've noticed that white snowdrop bells
　　Have a peculiar look of her!
And nothing but her pallor tells
　　Of Muggy Manchester.

Just twenty shillings every week!
 And always somebody distressed   50
Wants helping; and you feel a sneak
 If you don't do your best.
Suppose that I began to hoard,
 And steeled my heart, my coffer hid,
I wonder if I could afford
 To —— Would she, if I did?

She has a mother to support,
 And I've a sister. Trade's not brisk,
And for a working man, in short,
 Life is a fearful risk.   60

The Clarion[1] I sometimes read,
 I muse upon in winter nights,
I wonder if they'll e'er succeed
 In putting things to rights!

I'm vastly better off than some!
 I think of how the many fare
Who perish slowly, crushed and dumb,
 For leisure, food and air.
'Tis hard, in Freedom's very van,
 To live and die a luckless churl.   70
'Tis hard to be an acid man,
 Without a sandblast girl!

       Songs from Dreamland *(1894).*

A BONUS ON SOAP

Alone he stood before the pane,
 He let the crowd sweep by;
But what in city stores could chain
 That gifted author's eye?

'Twas not the jam attracted it,
 The salmon, nor the spice.
Above a keg of soap was writ
 The following advice:

'*Come hither, nor in darkness grope.*
 Come hither – buy, peruse –   10
The age's most superior soap
 And most enlightened views.

'*New lustre on each countenance*
 Touched by this soap you'll find;
This philosophical romance
 Will kindle heart and mind.

'*Their hands were never half so clean,*
 All customers agree,
And their beliefs have never been
 So utterly at sea.   20

'*To spiritual heights you'll grow*
 From which you'll ne'er descend.
Such is the novel we bestow,
 The soap that we commend.'

'What higher longing could be mine?'
 That author sighed. 'Enough!
The higher life I intertwine
 With common household stuff.'

There dimmed his eye a happy tear:
 'I have not lived amiss,   30
That I should be so very near
 The nation's heart as this!'

He turned from that attractive sight,
 And noted, standing by,
A threadbare and dejected wight,
 Who checked a heavy sigh.

'Brother,' he said, 'a helping hand
 To soothe your grief permit:
Humanity's my watchword, and
 You are a part of it.   40

'A purer faith I might provide
 Upon this very spot.'
That other pensively replied,
 'Thank you; I'd rather not.

'A momentary weakness shook
 My spirit, but is gone.
My book wrapped up the soap *your* book
 Was made a bonus on!'

       Songs from Dreamland *(1894).*

THE SANDBLAST GIRL AND THE ACID MAN
1 socialist newspaper.

Mary E. (Elizabeth) Coleridge (also 'Anodos') (1861–1907)

Mary Coleridge was born in Hyde Park Square in London, 23 September 1861, into a family of strong literary antecedents and tastes. Her great-great-uncle was Samuel Taylor Coleridge, her great-aunt Sara Coleridge. Her father was a Clerk of Assize but with numerous artistic friends. Robert Browning, Millais, Ruskin, Alfred Tennyson, were in and out of the parental house. One of two sisters, she was a precocious child, avid for languages – Hebrew, German, French (later on, Greek). She never went to school. From the age of thirteen she was in the group of girls instructed by William Johnson Cory, the poet and classicist, recently sacked from Eton College for a too obviously homoerotic interest in the boys. She read intensively in the British Museum, especially concentrating on Elizabethan and Jacobean drama. From the age of twenty she began contributing poems and articles to periodicals – the *Monthly Packet* (edited by Charlotte M. Yonge), *Merry England* (edited by Alice and Wilfred Meynell), the *Cornhill*, *Contemporary Review*, the *Times Literary Supplement* (from 1902). She wrote five novels, her first one a romantic fantasy, *The Seven Sleepers of Ephesus* (1893), which Robert Louis Stevenson liked. Robert Bridges – incidentally, a former pupil of Cory at Eton – came across a manuscript group of Mary Coleridge's poems at the house of a friend and helped her get them published by Daniel Smith, the Oxford don (Worcester College), as *Fancy's following*

(1896). The following year, some of these poems were reissued by Elkin Mathews in his Shilling Garland series, bulked out (if that's the word) by a few new verses, as *Fancy's Guerdon*. Both volumes went in the name of 'Anodos' – the name of the main character in George MacDonald's *Phantastes* (1858). Mary Coleridge's close friend Henry Newbolt reported her reluctance ('as long as I live') to appear in print under her own name – for 'fear of tarnishing the name which an ancestor has made illustrious in English poetry'. Inspired by Tolstoy, Mary Coleridge spent much time from 1895 teaching literature to working women at the Working Women's College. She wrote a critical introduction to Bridges's edition of Canon W. H. Dixon's *Last Poems* (1905) – she sympathized immensely with Dixon's Anglo-Catholic form of Christian belief and practice – and a *Life* of Holman Hunt (published posthumously). She died, 25 August 1907, after an operation for appendicitis. Newbolt collected her *Poems* (many previously unpublished) in 1908. She was not at all a conventional feminist ('Woman with a big W bores me supremely'), and expressed a strongly Anglo-Catholic poetic affection for Mary the Mother of Jesus, which has not prevented her entry into the feminist canon (mightily assisted by the readings of her work in Sandra Gilbert and Susan Gubar, *The Madwoman in the Attic*, 1979).

SLOWLY

Heavy is my heart,
 Dark are thine eyes.
Thou and I must part
 Ere the sun rise.

Ere the sun rise.
 Thou and I must part.
Dark are thine eyes,
 Heavy my heart.

Fancy's following, *by Anodos (Daniel Smith, Oxford, 1896).*

GONE

About the little chambers of my heart
Friends have been coming – going – many a year.
 The doors stand open there.
Some, lightly stepping, enter; some depart.

Freely they come and freely go, at will.
The walls give back their laughter; all day long
   They fill the house with song.
One door alone is shut, one chamber still.

Fancy's following (1896).

THE OTHER SIDE OF A MIRROR

I sat before my glass one day,
   And conjured up a vision bare,
Unlike the aspects glad and gay,
   That erst were found reflected there –
The vision of a woman, wild
   With more than womanly despair.

Her hair stood back on either side
   A face bereft of loveliness.
It had no envy now to hide
   What once no man on earth could guess.   10
It formed the thorny aureole
   Of hard unsanctified distress.

Her lips were open – not a sound
   Came through the parted lines of red.
Whate'er it was, the hideous wound
   In silence and in secret bled.
No sigh relieved her speechless woe,
   She had no voice to speak her dread.

And in her lurid eyes there shone
   The dying flame of life's desire,   20
Made mad because its hope was gone,
   And kindled at the leaping fire
Of jealousy, and fierce revenge,
   And strength that could not change nor tire.

Shade of a shadow in the glass,
   O set the crystal surface free!
Pass – as the fairer visions pass –
   Nor ever more return, to be
The ghost of a distracted hour,
   That heard me whisper: – 'I am she!'   30

Fancy's following (1896).

I saw a stable, low and very bare,
   A little child in a manger.
The oxen knew Him, had Him in their care,
   To men He was a stranger.
The safety of the world was lying there,
   And the world's danger.

Poems, by Mary E. Coleridge, ed. Henry Newbolt (Elkin Mathews, 1908).

AN INSINCERE WISH ADDRESSED TO A BEGGAR

We are not near enough to love,
    I can but pity all your woe;
For wealth has lifted me above,
    And falsehood set you down below.

If you were true, we still might be
    Brothers in something more than name;
And were I poor, your love to me
    Would make our differing bonds the same.

But golden gates between us stretch,
    Truths opens her forbidding eyes;   10
You can't forget that I am rich,
    Nor I that you are telling lies.

Love never comes but at love's call,
    And pity asks for him in vain;
Because I cannot give you all,
    You give me nothing back again.

And you are right with all your wrong,
    For less than all is nothing too;
May Heaven beggar me ere long,
    And Truth reveal herself to you!   20

Poems *(1908)*.

THE CONTENTS OF AN INK-BOTTLE

Well of blackness, all defiling,
Full of flattery and reviling,
Ah, what mischief hast thou wrought
Out of what was airy thought,
What beginnings and what ends,
Making and dividing friends!

Colours of the rainbow lie
In thy tint of ebony;
Many a fancy have I found
Bright upon that sombre ground;   10
Cupid plays along the edge,
Skimming o'er it like a midge;
Niobe in turn appears,
Thinning it with crystal tears.[1]

False abuse and falser praise,
Falsest lays and roundelays!
One thing, one alone, I think,
Never yet was found in ink; –
Truth lies not, the truth to tell,
At the bottom of this well!   20

Poems *(1908)*.

THE CONTENTS OF AN INK-BOTTLE
1   essence of maternal grief – all her 12 children were killed – Niobe
was turned into a column of stone, which wept.

Two differing sorrows made these eyes grow dim:
   Woe, for which all must weep, while weep they can,
And that more poignant anguish known to him
   Whose grief's the jest of every other man.

Poems (1908).

WORDS

Words, dear companions! In my curtained cot
I cooed and twittered like a nesting bird;
And women spoke around me; but no word
Came to my baby lips – I knew you not.

Yet laughter did I know. I have not learned
To laugh more gaily since I first began.
The reasons of his mirth are born in man;
But man was born to laugh ere he discerned.

And tears I knew. Who taught me how to cry?
Was it my mother's heart that whispered me?   10
Tears have I wept since then that none could see,
Nor laughed, as then I laughed, ere they were dry.

Words, dear companions! As the spirit grew,
I loved you more and more with every hour.
I felt the sweep, the whirlwind of the power
HE gave to man, when man created you.

Words, dear companions! glittering, fair and brave!
Rapt in your rapture I was whirled along,
Strong in the faith of old, the might of song,
Struck through the silent portals of the grave.   20

Words, dear companions! Into you I drove
The dark dumb devil that besets the heart;
Nature in you rose to a heavenly art,
And wrought on earth an airy heaven of love.

Ah, when ye leave me, will there yet remain
The laughter and the weeping all untaught?
And will they, in the realm of perfect thought,
Teach me new words to sing of life again?

Poems (1908).

Amy Levy (1861–89)

Amy Levy was born in Clapham, 10 November 1861, the second daughter of Lewis and Isabelle Levy. She was the first Jewish student to be admitted to Newnham, the Cambridge women's college. At the early age of thirteen she'd had a poem in the *Pelican*, a feminist journal, and she continued publishing poems and stories at university. *Xantippe and Other Poems* appeared in Cambridge while she was still an undergraduate. The title poem is a Browningesque dramatic monologue by Socrates's unhappy wife. Also in her preferred monologue form is the title poem of her next volume, *A Minor Poet and Other Verse* (1884). Like several of her poems, 'A Minor Poet' is unhappily and proleptically suicidal. Levy left Cambridge after only two terms and returned home to write (and act as secretary to her father's Beaumont Trust, raising funds for education in London's East End). She is self-consciously a writer of London. She moved in London's radical, feminist, trade-union circles. The socialist, suffragist and equal-pay campaigner Clementina Black (sister of Constance Garnett, the great translator of Russian fiction) was a close friend. So was Eleanor Marx, who translated Levy's second novel, *Reuben Sachs* (1888), into German. Levy knew Oscar Wilde, and published in his *Woman's World* magazine. Features by her appeared in the *Jewish Chronicle*, the *Spectator*, *Victoria Magazine*, and the *Gentleman's Magazine*. She published three novels in all – *The Romance of a Shop* (1888), about four sisters setting up a photography business; *Reuben Sachs: A Sketch*, which satirizes the snobbishness and materialism of London Jews; and a rather flat romance about a governess in Italy, *Miss Meredith* (1889). Amy Levy was extremely depressive (one character in *Reu-*

ben Sachs curses God for having 'the cruelty to make me a woman'). Her increasing deafness can't have been a cheering factor. She took her own life (by inhaling charcoal fumes) in her parents' house at 7 Endsleigh Gardens in London, 10 September 1889, after correcting the proofs of her last volume, *A London Plane-Tree and Other Verse* (1889). She was twenty-seven. Always the subject of gossip and myth – people wrongly thought she had worked in a factory, lived in a garret, taught in London – Levy was rumoured to have killed herself after a suicide pact with her friend Olive Schreiner which only Levy stuck to. Elaine Feinstein, herself Jewish and a graduate of Newnham, has a lovely memorial poem, 'Amy Levy' (about Levy's being in between cultures – a Jewish stranger in Cambridge and a poetical stranger among her family in London) in *Daylight* (Carcanet, Manchester, 1997).

MAGDALEN[1]

All things I can endure, save one.
The bare, blank room where is no sun;
The parcelled hours; the pallet hard;
The dreary faces here within;
The outer women's cold regard;
The Pastor's iterated 'sin'; –
These things could I endure, and count
No overstrain'd, unjust amount;
No undue payment for such bliss –
Yea, all things bear, save only this: 10
That you, who knew what thing would be,
Have wrought this evil unto me.

It is so strange to think on still –
That you, that *you* should do me ill!
Not as one ignorant or blind,
But seeing clearly in your mind
How this must be which now has been,
Nothing aghast at what was seen.
Now that the tale is told and done,
It is so strange to think upon.   20

You were so tender with me, too!
One summer's night a cold blast blew,
Closer about my throat you drew
The half-slipt shawl of dusky blue.
And once my hand, on a summer's morn,
I stretched to pluck a rose; a thorn
Struck through the flesh and made it bleed
(A little drop of blood indeed!)
Pale grew your cheek; you stoopt and bound
Your handkerchief about the wound;   30

MAGDALEN
1   a fallen woman: generic name from Mary Magdalen in Gospels.

Your voice came with a broken sound;
With the deep breath your breast was riven;
I wonder, did God laugh in Heaven?

How strange, that *you* should work my woe!
How strange! I wonder, do you know
How gladly, gladly I had died
(And life was very sweet that tide)
To save you from the least, light ill?
How gladly I had borne your pain.
With one great pulse we seem'd to thrill, –   40
Nay, but we thrill'd with pulses twain.

Even if one had told me this,
'A poison lurks within your kiss,
Gall that shall turn to night his day:'
Thereon I straight had turned away –
Ay, tho' my heart had crack'd with pain –
And never kiss'd your lips again.

At night, or when the daylight nears,
I hear the other women weep;
My own heart's anguish lies too deep   50
For the soft rain and pain of tears.
I think my heart has turn'd to stone,
A dull, dead weight that hurts my breast;
Here, on my pallet-bed alone,
I keep apart from all the rest.
Wide-eyed I lie upon my bed,
I often cannot sleep all night;
The future and the past are dead,
There is no thought can bring delight.
All night I lie and think and think;   60
If my heart were not made of stone,
But flesh and blood, it needs must shrink
Before such thoughts. Was ever known
A woman with a heart of stone?

The doctor says that I shall die.
It may be so, yet what care I?
Endless reposing from the strife,
Death do I trust no more than life.
For one thing is like one arrayed,
And there is neither false nor true;   70
But in a hideous masquerade
All things dance on, the ages through.
And good is evil, evil good;
Nothing is known or understood
Save only Pain. I have no faith
In God or Devil, Life or Death.

The doctor says that I shall die.
You, that I knew in days gone by,
I fain would see your face once more,
Con well its features o'er and o'er;   80
And touch your hand and feel your kiss,
Look in your eyes and tell you this:

That all is done, that I am free;
That you, through all eternity,
Have neither part nor lot in me.

A Minor Poet and Other Verse *(T. Fisher Unwin, 1884).*

BALLADE OF AN OMNIBUS

To see my love suffices me.
Ballades in Blue China[1]

Some men to carriages aspire;
On some the costly hansoms wait;
Some seek a fly, on job or hire;
Some mount the trotting steed, elate.
I envy not the rich and great,
A wandering minstrel, poor and free,
I am contented with my fate –
An omnibus suffices me.

In winter days of rain and mire
I find within a corner strait;   10
The 'busmen know me and my lyre
From Brompton to the Bull-and-Gate.
When summer comes, I mount in state
The topmost summit, whence I see
Crœsus[2] look up, compassionate –
An omnibus suffices me.

I mark, untroubled by desire,
Lucullus'[3] phaeton and its freight.
The scene whereof I cannot tire,
The human tale of love and hate,   20
The city pageant, early and late
Unfolds itself, rolls by, to be
A pleasure deep and delicate.
An omnibus suffices me.

Princess, your splendour you require.
I, my simplicity; agree
Neither to rate lower nor higher.
An omnibus suffices me.

A London Plane-Tree and Other Verse *(T. Fisher Unwin, 1889).*

LONDON POETS

(In Memoriam)

They trod the streets and squares where now I tread,
With weary hearts, a little while ago;
When, thin and grey, the melancholy snow

BALLADE OF AN OMNIBUS
1   Andrew Lang, 'Ballade Amoureuse. After Froissart', *XXXII Ballades in Blue China* (1881).

2   archetypal rich man.
3   another archetypal rich man.

Clung to the leafless branches overhead;
Or when the smoke-veiled sky grew stormy-red
In autumn; with a re-arisen woe
Wrestled, what time the passionate spring winds blow;
And paced scorched stones in summer: – they are dead.

The sorrow of their souls to them did seem
As real as mine to me, as permanent.   10
To-day, it is the shadow of a dream,
The half-forgotten breath of breezes spent.
So shall another soothe his woe supreme –
'No more he comes, who this way came and went.'

                                    A London Plane-Tree *(1889).*

ON THE THRESHOLD

O God, my dream! I dreamed that you were dead;
Your mother hung above the couch and wept
Whereon you lay all white, and garlanded
With blooms of waxen whiteness. I had crept
Up to your chamber-door, which stood ajar,
And in the doorway watched you from afar,
Nor dared advance to kiss your lips and brow.
I had no part nor lot in you, as now;
Death had not broken between us the old bar;
Nor torn from out my heart the old, cold sense   10
Of your misprision and my impotence.

                                    A London Plane-Tree *(1889).*

LAST WORDS

Dead! all's done with!
        R. Browning[1]

These blossoms that I bring,
This song that here I sing,
These tears that now I shed,
I give unto the dead.

There is no more to be done,
Nothing beneath the sun,
All the long ages through,
Nothing – by me for you.

The tale is told to the end;
This, ev'n, I may not know –   10
If we were friend and friend,
If we were foe and foe.

LAST WORDS
1   'Too Late', *Dramatis Personae* (1864), l.37.

All's done with utterly,
All's done with. Death to me
Was ever Death indeed;
To me no kindly creed

Consolatory was given.
You were of earth, not Heaven....
This dreary day, things seem
Vain shadows in a dream,   20

Or some strange, pictured show;
And mine own tears that flow,
My hidden tears that fall,
The vainest of them all.

A London Plane-Tree *(1889)*.

IN THE MILE END ROAD[1]

How like her! But 'tis she herself,
  Comes up the crowded street,
How little did I think, the morn,
  My only love to meet!

Whose else that motion and that mien?
  Whose else that airy tread?
For one strange moment I forgot
  My only love was dead.

A London Plane-Tree *(1889)*.

CONTRADICTIONS

Now, even, I cannot think it true,
My friend, that there is no more you.
Almost as soon were no more I,
Which were, of course, absurdity!
Your place is bare, you are not seen,
Your grave, I'm told, is growing green;
And both for you and me, you know,
There's no Above and no Below.
That you are dead must be inferred,
And yet my thought rejects the word.   10

A London Plane-Tree *(1889)*.

IN THE MILE END ROAD
1   in East End of London.

(Sir) Henry (John) Newbolt (1862–1938)

Henry Newbolt, quintessential poet of Empire and of the muscular Christianity of the Victorian Public School, was born in Bilston, Staffordshire, 6 June 1862, oldest child of an Anglican clergyman, the Revd Francis Newbolt, and his wife Emily Stubbs. Newbolt's paternal grandfather was – of course – a naval officer. Newbolt was educated at Clifton School – whose myth he greatly cherished, and celebrated in his verse – and Corpus Christi College, Oxford, which he entered as a Classical Scholar in October 1881 (First Class in Classical Moderations; Second Class in Finals, 1885). He went into the Law – practising at the Bar for twelve years from 1887, contributing greatly to the *Law Digest*, but turning more and more to literature. He married Margaret Edina Duckworth, a vicar's daughter, in 1889. They had a son and a daughter. Newbolt became very close to Mary Coleridge. He admired Hardy to distraction – and the affective simplicity of his ballads is not a million miles away from Hardy's line in directness. His Napoleonic tale *Taken from the Enemy* appeared in 1892, and *Mordred: A Tragedy* in 1895. The next year Andrew Lang published six of Newbolt's poems in *Longman's Magazine*; and 'Drake's Drum' (in *St James' Gazette*, 1896) became an instant hit. *Admirals All* (1897) – twelve poems including 'Drake's Drum' – was a complete sell-out (four editions in two weeks, twenty-one in two years). Newbolt became a full-time man of letters. He edited the *Monthly Review* (1900–4), which first published Walter de la Mare. *Songs of the Sea* (1904), *Clifton Chapel and Other School Poems* (1908) and *Songs of the Fleet* (1910) sealed his fame for the British Empire as a kind of nautical Kipling. He held various government posts in the First World War, ending up as Comptroller of Wireless and Cables. After the War he chaired the Commission on English in National Education, and wrote the Introduction of the Report (1921), which chauvinistically established English and English Literature as the centre of British education (as opposed to Classics), challenged the Oxford idea of English Studies as necessarily involving 'philology' – the defeated Germans had stood for excellence in both Classics and philology – and also took Shakespeare back from the Germans ('unser Shakespeare'), to become the centre of the new English teaching. He was made a Companion of Honour in 1922, and in 1923 became official historian of wartime naval operations. He remained productive to the end, dying in London, 19 April 1938. 'Vitaï Lampada', dinned at school into every muddied oaf's games-playing soul, became a by-word for an outmoded Public School cult of male duty and unflinching imperial service, and for the badness of late Victorian verse which early modernism was setting its face against. Its emotional celebration of male bravery and individual staunchness to a national community – its patriarchalism – does not now seem the axiomatically bad thing it once did.

DRAKE'S DRUM[1]

Drake he's in his hammock an' a thousand mile away,
　(Capten, art tha sleepin' there below?),
Slung atween the round shot in Nombre Dios Bay,
　An' dreamin' arl the time o' Plymouth Hoe.
Yarnder lumes the Island, yarnder lie the ships,
　Wi' sailor lads a dancin' heel-an'-toe,
An' the shore-lights flashin', an' the night-tide dashin',
　He sees et arl so plainly as he saw et long ago.

Drake he was a Devon man, an' rüled the Devon seas,
　(Capten, art tha sleepin' there below?),　　　　　　　　　　10
Rovin' tho' his death fell, he went wi' heart at ease,
　An' dreamin' arl the time o' Plymouth Hoe.
'Take my drum to England, hang et by the shore,
　Strike et when your powder's runnin' low;

DRAKE'S DRUM
1　Sir Francis Drake, fabled naval adventurer, who defeated Spanish Armada attack on England, 1588. Newbolt tries to register Drake's Devonian accent.

If the Dons sight Devon, I'll quit the port o' Heaven,
    An' drum them up the Channel as we drummed them long ago.'

Drake he's in his hammock till the great Armadas come,
    (Capten, art tha sleepin' there below?),
Slung atween the round shot, listenin' for the drum,
    An' dreamin' arl the time o' Plymouth Hoe.   20
Call him on the deep sea, call him up the Sound,
    Call him when ye sail to meet the foe;
Where the old trade's plyin' an' the old flag flyin'
    They shall find him ware an' wakin', as they found him long ago!

St James' Gazette (1896). Admirals All (Elkin Mathews, 1897). (Shilling Garland series.)

VITAÏ LAMPADA[1]

There's a breathless hush in the Close to-night –
    Ten to make and the match to win –
A bumping pitch and a blinding light,
    An hour to play and the last man in.
And it's not for the sake of a ribboned coat,
    Or the selfish hope of a season's fame,
But his Captain's hand on his shoulder smote
    'Play up! play up! and play the game!'

The sand of the desert is sodden red, –
    Red with the wreck of a square that broke; –   10
The Gatling's[2] jammed and the Colonel dead,
    And the regiment blind with dust and smoke.
The river of death has brimmed his banks,
    And England's far, and Honour a name,
But the voice of a schoolboy rallies the ranks:
    'Play up! play up! and play the game!'

This is the word that year by year,
    While in her place the School is set,
Every one of her sons must hear,
    And none that hears it dare forget.   20
This they all with a joyful mind
    Bear through life like a torch in flame,
And falling fling to the host behind –
    'Play up! play up! and play the game!'

Admirals All (1897). Reprinted in Clifton Chapel and Other School Poems
(John Murray, 1908).

VITAÏ LAMPADA   2   Gatling gun.
1   Et quasi cursores vitae lampada tradunt (Lucretius, *De rerum naturae*,
II.79): 'And like runners they hand on the torch of life'.

Victor (Gustave) Plarr (1863–1929)

Victor Plarr, librarian and poet, was born at Le Kapferhammer, near Strasbourg, 21 June 1863, son of Dr Gustave Plarr, a distinguished Alsatian mathematician, and an English mother, Mary Jane Tompkins. The parental home was burned down in the Franco-Prussian War of 1870–1. Plarr remained throughout his life a staunchly French Republican sympathizer. The family settled in Scotland, and he was schooled first at Madras College, St Andrews, then at Tonbridge School in England. In 1882 he went to Oxford as a sort of private student before entering Worcester College, getting a Second Class in Modern History in 1886. After graduation he made a living by literary journalism, translating from French, and working editorially on *Seafaring*, a journal for merchant seamen. Poems of his appeared anonymously in that journal. His translation of *Scenes from the Alcestis of Euripides* came out in 1886. He lived in Blackheath in London and there are poems by him about Blackheath. In 1890 he became Librarian of King's College, London; and in 1897 he began his career as the wry but devoted Librarian of the Royal College of Surgeons ('among the pickled foetuses and bottled bones'). He was much given to sloping off into Lincoln's Inn Fields for a cigarette, as well as to borrowing money from colleagues (to pass on to indigent poets). He knocked about in literary London, was a member of the Rhymers' Club (his 'half-French, half-Celtic' character being the ground of his membership) and was great friends with Lionel Johnson and Ernest Dowson. He was not, though, decadent in his life (few librarians, perhaps, are) or Symbolist in his writing. His enthusiasm for Zola was high: he translated *Nana* (1894) and was on Zola's side in the Dreyfus affair. He had poems in the journals, notably the *Spectator*, and his first serious and mature volume of poems, *In the Dorian Mood*, was brought out by John Lane (1896). The *Dorian* in that title was far from being a marker of Wildeanism. Plarr's poems are nostalgic, anxious about the modern city ('A Nocturne at Greenwich'), and keen on beggars, gipsies and labouring men, but always urbane. He was the editor of *The Garland of New Poetry* (1891), published by Lane's old partner and now rival Elkin Mathews. The long mini-epic *The Tragedy of Asgard* (1905), a sort of cross between Wagner and J. R. R. Tolkien, continues Matthew Arnold's *Balder Dead*. Plarr mixed with Ezra Pound (he's 'Monsieur Verog' in Pound's 'Hugh Selwyn Mauberley'), became the memorialist of Ernest Dowson (1914), produced some tub-thumping verses prompted by the First World War and the reopening of old Alsatian wounds, had stories in the *Anglo-French Review*, and did lives of distinguished medics for medical journals (two volumes of these appeared posthumously in 1930). He had suffered for years with bronchitis, and died suddenly from it, 28 January 1929.

In a Norman Church

As over incense-laden air
   Stole winter twilight, soft and dim,
The folk arose from their last prayer –
   When hark, an ancient hymn!

Round yon great pillar, circlewise,
   The singers stand up, two and two –
Small lint-haired girls from whose young eyes
   The gray sea looks at you.

Now heavenward the pure music wins
   With cadence soft and silvery beat:
In flutes and subtile violins
   Are harmonies less sweet.

It is a chant with plaintive ring,
   And rhymes and refrains old and quaint:

'Oh Monseigneur Saint Jacques,'[1] they sing,
And 'Oh Assisi's Saint.'[2]

Through deepening dusk one just can see
The little white-capped heads that move
In time to lines turned rhythmically
And starred with names of love.   20

Bred in no gentle silken ease,
Trained to expect no splendid fate,
They are but pleasant children these,
Of very mean estate.

Nay, is that true? To-night perhaps
Unworldlier eyes had well discerned
Among those little gleaming caps
An aureole that burned.

For once 'twas thought the Gates of Pearl
Best opened to the poor that trod   30
The path of the meek peasant girl
Who bore the Son of God.

First published in The Book of the Rhymers' Club *(Elkin Mathews, 1892).*
In the Dorian Mood (John Lane, The Bodley Head, London;
George H. Richmond and Co., New York, 1896).

SHADOWS

A song of shadows: never glory was
But it had some soft shadow that would lie
On wall, on quiet water, on smooth grass,
Or in the vistas of the phantasy:

The shadow of the house upon the lawn,
Upon the house the shadow of the tree,
And through the moon-steeped hours unto the dawn
The shadow of thy beauty over me.

In the Dorian Mood (1896).

ON A READING OF MATTHEW ARNOLD

Arnold is dead, and everyone forgets
His gracious doctrine, his hellenic creed,
His faith in light and sweetness. 'Tis indeed
So easy to repudiate our debts
Of heart and brain! When what one most regrets
Is stint of love, and ease, and wealth, who need
Go wail for culture? 'Tis a colourless weed
Which no one in his table nosegay sets.

IN A NORMAN CHURCH   2   St Francis.
1   St James of Compostella.

Yet, great Oxonian, it were meet and fit
   Could we but halt upon our daily stage   10
Of petty duty, dull mechanic task,
   To meditate thy theme and hear thee ask,
'Is conduct all? Are grace, and light, and wit,
   Not chiefly good in this Bœotian[1] age?'

In the Dorian Mood (1896).

A NOCTURNE AT GREENWICH[1]

Far out, beyond my window, in the gloom
   Nightly I see thee loom,
Thou vast black city. Oh, but night is kind,
   Here where Thames' waters wind,
To the grim formless features of thy face.
   They do assume such grace
In the deep darkness, starred through leagues of night,
   With long streets, fringed with light,
Or with the lanthorns of the ships that aye
   Ascend the water-way,   10
Coasting from East and West, and North and South,
   To this, Earth's harbour-mouth.
Up from the darkness echoes sleepily
   The shipman's wandering cry,
Or, like a wild beast's call heard in a dream,
   The siren's undulant scream
Whistles the darkling midnight through and through,
   While with her labouring screw
Some dim leviathan of ships drops down
   Past storied Greenwich town,   20
Showing her swiftly-gliding starboard light,
   Green 'gainst the wide dark night.
Past the great hospital she drops, and past
   The marshes, still and vast,
Below the lines of Woolwich and the lines
   Of Bostal's shadowy pines,
On to that world of Saxon brine and fen,
   Old races, vanished men,
Where Thames, from heron-haunted shores set free,
   Merges in northern sea.   30
Here, in my chamber, 'mong my books, at peace,
   I watch thee without cease,
Thou ancient stream, mysterious as the sky
   Which starless glooms on high.
About me, on the volume-peopled wall,
   The famed old authors all
Sleep their just sleep, and in the hearth's clear beams
   Dante's medallion gleams,
And Brutus and great Tully o'er the shelves
   Commune among themselves.[2]   40

ON A READING OF MATTHEW ARNOLD
1 rude, unlettered (after rural types despised by Athenians).

A NOCTURNE AT GREENWICH
1 on the Thames. The painter James Whistler liked titling his London river scenes 'Nocturnes'.
2 busts of distinguished Romans above the bookshelves.

This silent music of what once hath been
　　Suits well with that night scene:
Nay, its essential sweetness sweeter grows,
　　Because that river flows
Through northern midnight, big with life and doom,
　　Out yonder in the gloom.

In the Dorian Mood *(1896)*.

Arthur (William) Symons (1865–1945)

Arthur Symons, ur-modernist, impressionist poet, theorist of Symbolism, chief spokesman for nineties decadence, was the second child (there was an older sister) of Cornish Wesleyan Methodist parents, the Revd Mark Symons and his wife Lydia Pascoe. Because of the Methodist practice of moving its ministers on every few years, Symons led a restless childhood and claimed that as the basis for his freedom from prejudice, which was in turn the basis of his cult of rootless cosmopolitan decadence. At an early age he fell precociously among literary men, was commissioned (in 1884) by R. J. Furnivall to edit some of the *Shakespeare Quarto Facsimiles*, and had by the age of twenty-one published his first article on French literature and his *Introduction to the Study of Browning*. Pater reviewed the Browning with enthusiasm and the two became friends and critical allies. Part of Symons's importance was his devoted Paterianism. His first volume of verse, *Days and Nights*, appeared in 1889, around which time he began visiting France regularly, becoming a friend as well as translator of Verlaine and Mallarmé. Symons was the main conduit for the encounter between the French Symbolists and the English-language poets who fed off them, Yeats, Pound and Eliot. The Rhymers' Club of the early nineties – a loose group including Yeats, John Davidson, Richard Le Gallienne, Victor Plarr, Lionel Johnson, Edward Garnett, Ernest Radford – was the chief sphere of Symons's Frenchifying influence. He brought Verlaine to England in 1893. In November of the same year his essay 'The Decadent Movement in Literature' established not only his critical knowledge but also his importance as a cultural missionary. In 1896 Symons edited the *Savoy*, one of the flagships of nineties decadence (Aubrey Beardsley was a main illustrator: W. H. Smith withdrew No. 3 from sale). He dedicated his pioneering manifesto *The Symbolist Movement in Literature* (1899) to Yeats as chief of the Rhymers

and chief representative of Symbolism in England. Symons also introduced Yeats to hashish and dance. The critical mission was incalculably important, but so also was Symons's own verse – *Days and Nights*, of course, and also its many successors: *Silhouettes* (1892 and 1896); *London Nights* (1895, 1897); *Amoris Victima* (1897); *Images of Good and Evil* (1899); *The Loom of Dreams* (1901); *The Fool of the World* (1906); *Love's Cruelty* (1923). (A *Poems* in two volumes appeared in 1902 and a *Collected Works* in nine volumes in 1924, with much heavy revising of the earlier versions.) Without Symons's poetry – impressionistically jotting, urban, a roué vision, doing for modern London the downbeat, corrupt job Baudelaire and Laforgue had done for Paris, and, what is more, inflecting the decay of the modern city through post-Browningesque rhythms of ordinary speech – the early Prufrockian–*Waste Land* Eliot would not have been at all like it is. Eliot said it was Symons's poetry which prepared him for the impact of Jules Laforgue. Pound praised Symons and his friends for 'knocking bombast, & rhetoric & Victorian syrup out of our verse'. Later on (in *For Lancelot Andrewes*, 1929), post-conversion Eliot deplored the nineties' 'liturgy of sin', in which Evil was only 'very good fun', but this was not only a chiming in with all the conservative publishers, booksellers and critics who had thought Symons scarily filthy, it was biting the hand that had fuelled his own verse so generously. Symons married Rhoda Bowser in 1901; made his base from 1906 a twelfth-century house in Wittersham in Kent; wrote, edited, translated, and globe-trotted intensely; had a severe nervous breakdown in 1908; spent two years or so in mental asylums; lived on for many years, but critically and practically always a late-Victorian-Edwardian; dying, eventually, at Wittersham, 22 January 1945.

THE STREET-SINGER

She sings a pious ballad wearily;
Her shivering body creeps on painful feet
Along the muddy runlets of the street;
The damp is in her throat: she coughs to free
The cracked and husky notes that tear her chest;

From side to side she looks with eyes that grope
Feverishly hungering in a hopeless hope,
For pence that will not come; and pence mean rest,
The rest that pain may steal at night from sleep,
The rest that hunger gives when satisfied;　　10

Her fingers twitch to handle them; she sings
Shriller; her eyes, too hot with tears to weep,

Fasten upon a window, where, inside,
A sweet voice mocks her with its carollings.

Days and Nights *(Macmillan & Co., 1889). Dedicated 'To Walter Pater In
All Gratitude and Admiration'.*

MAQUILLAGE

The charm of rouge on fragile cheeks,
Pearl-powder, and, about the eyes,
The dark and lustrous Eastern dyes;
The floating odour that bespeaks
A scented boudoir and the doubtful night
Of alcoves curtained close against the light.

Gracile and creamy white and rose,
Complexioned like the flower of dawn,
Her fleeting colours are as those
That, from an April sky withdrawn,   10
Fade in a fragrant mist of tears away
When weeping noon leads on the altered day.

Silhouettes *(Elkin Mathews & John Lane, 1892).*

THE ABSINTHE-DRINKER

Gently I wave the visible world away.
Far off, I hear a roar, afar yet near,
Far off and strange, a voice is in my ear,
Two voices, his and mine: the words we say
Fall strangely, like a dream, across the day.
And the dim sunshine is a dream. How clear,
New as the world to lovers' eyes, appear
The men and women passing on their way!

The world is very fair. The hours are all
Linked in a dance of mere forgetfulness.   10
I am at peace with God and man. O glide,
Sands of the hour-glass that I count not, fall
Serenely: scarce I feel your soft caress,
Rocked on this dreamy and indifferent tide.

Silhouettes *(1892).*

APRIL MIDNIGHT

Side by side through the streets at midnight,
Roaming together,
Through the incongruous night of London,
In the miraculous April weather.

Roaming together under the gaslight,
Day's work over,
How the Spring calls to us, here in the city,
Calls to the heart from the heart of a lover!

Cool the wind blows, fresh in our faces,
Cleansing, entrancing,   10

After the heat and the fumes and the footlights,
Where you dance and I watch your dancing.

Good it is to be here together,
Good to be roaming,
Even in London, even at midnight,
Lover-like in a lover's gloaming.

You the dancer and I the dreamer,
Children together,
Wandering lost in the night of London,
In the miraculous April weather.   20

Silhouettes *(1892).*

NORA ON THE PAVEMENT

As Nora on the pavement
Dances, and she entrances the grey hour
Into the laughing circle of her power,
The magic circle of her glances,
As Nora dances on the midnight pavement;

Petulant and bewildered,
Thronging desires and longing looks recur,
And memorably re-incarnate her,
As I remember that old longing,
A footlight fancy, petulant and bewildered;   10

There where the ballet circles,
See her, but ah! not free her from the race
Of glittering lines that link and interlace;
This colour now, now that, may be her,
In the bright web of those harmonious circles.

But what are these dance-measures,
Leaping and joyous, keeping time alone
With life's capricious rhythm, and all her own,
Life's rhythm and hers, long sleeping,
That wakes, and knows not why, in these
    dance-measures?   20

It is the very Nora;
Child, and most blithe, and wild as any elf,
And innocently spendthrift of herself,
And guileless and most unbeguiled,
Herself at last, leaps free the very Nora.

It is the soul of Nora,   30
Living at last, and giving forth to the night,
Bird-like, the burden of its own delight,
All its desire, and all the joy of living,
In that blithe madness of the soul of Nora.

London Nights *(Leonard C. Smithers, 1895). Volume dedicated to Paul Verlaine.*
Poem appeared earlier in The Second Book of the Rhymers' Club
(Elkin Mathews & John Lane, 1894).

HALLUCINATION: I

One petal of a blood-red tulip pressed
Between the pages of a Baudelaire:
No more; and I was suddenly aware
Of the white fragrant apple of a breast
On which my lips were pastured; and I knew
That dreaming I remembered an old dream.
Sweeter than any fruit that fruit did seem,
Which, as my hungry teeth devoured it, grew
Ever again, and tantalised my taste.
So, vainly hungering, I seemed to see   10

Eve and the serpent and the apple-tree,
And Adam in the garden, and God laying waste
Innocent Eden, because man's desire,
Godlike before, now for a woman's sake
Descended through the woman to the snake.
Then as my mouth grew parched, stung as with fire
By that white fragrant apple, once so fair,
That seemed to shrink and spire into a flame,
I cried, and wakened, crying on your name:
One blood-red petal stained the Baudelaire.   20

Poems, *2 vols (William Heinemann, 1902), I. (In 'London Nights' section.)*

NERVES

The modern malady of love is nerves.
Love, once a simple madness, now observes
The stages of his passionate disease,
And is twice sorrowful because he sees,
Inch by inch entering, the fatal knife.
O health of simple minds, give me your life,
And let me, for one midnight, cease to hear

The clock for ever ticking in my ear,
The clock that tells the minutes in my brain.
It is not love, nor love's despair, this pain   10
That shoots a witless, keener pang across
The simple agony of love and loss.
Nerves, nerves! O folly of a child who dreams
Of heaven, and, waking in the darkness, screams.

Poems *(1902), I. (In 'London Nights' section.)*

SONG

Her eyes say Yes, her lips say No.
Ah, tell me, Love, when she denies,
Shall I believe the lips or eyes?
Bid eyes no more dissemble,
Or lips too tremble
The way her heart would go!

Love may be vowed by lips, although
Cold truth, in unsurrendering eyes,
The armistice of lips denies.
But can fond eyes dissemble,   10
Or false lips tremble
To this soft Yes in No?

London Nights *(1895).*

BIANCA: VIII. MEMORY

As a perfume doth remain
In the folds where it hath lain,
So the thought of you, remaining
Deeply folded in my brain,
Will not leave me: all things leave me:
You remain.

Other thoughts may come and go,
Other moments I may know
That shall waft me, in their going,

As a breath blown to and fro,   10
Fragrant memories: fragrant memories
Come and go.

Only thoughts of you remain
In my heart where they have lain,
Perfumed thoughts of you, remaining,
A hid sweetness, in my brain.
Others leave me: all things leave me:
You remain.

London Nights *(1895).*

BIANCA: X. LIBER AMORIS

What's virtue, Bianca? Have we not
Agreed the word should be forgot,
That ours be every dear device
And all the subtleties of vice,
And, in diverse imaginings,
The savour of forbidden things,
So only that the obvious be
Too obvious for you and me,
And the one vulgar final act
Remain an unadmitted fact?   10

And, surely, we were wise to waive
A gift we do not lose, but save.
What moment's reeling blaze of sense
Were rationally recompense
For all the ecstasies and all
The ardours demi-virginal?
Bianca, I tell you, no delights
Of long, free, unforbidden nights,
Have richlier filled and satisfied
The eager moments as they died,   20
Than your voluptuous pretence
Of unacquainted innocence,
Your clinging hands and closing lips
And eyes slow sinking to eclipse
And cool throat flushing to my kiss;
That sterile and mysterious bliss,
Mysterious, and yet to me
Deeper for that dubiety.

Once, but that time was long ago,
I loved good women, and to know   30
That lips my lips dared never touch
Could speak, in one warm smile, so much.
And it seemed infinitely sweet
To worship at a woman's feet,
And live on heavenly thoughts of her,
Till earth itself grew heavenlier.
But that rapt mood, being fed on air,
Turned at the last to a despair,

And, for a body and soul like mine,
I found the angels' food too fine.   40
So the mood changed, and I began
To find that man is merely man,
Though women might be angels; so,
I let the aspirations go,
And for a space I held it wise
To follow after certainties.
My heart forgot the ways of love,
No longer now my fancy wove
Into admitted ornament
Its spider's web of sentiment.   50
What my hands seized, that my hands held,
I followed as the blood compelled,
And finding that my brain found rest
On some unanalytic breast,
I was contented to discover
How easy 'tis to be a lover.
No sophistries to ravel out,
No devious martyrdoms of doubt,
Only the good firm flesh to hold,
The love well worth its weight in gold,   60
Love, sinking from the infinite,
Now just enough to last one night.
So the simplicity of flesh
Held me a moment in its mesh,
Till that too palled, and I began
To find that man was mostly man
In that, his will being sated, he
Wills ever new variety.
And then I found you, Bianca! Then
I found in you, I found again   70
That chance or will or fate had brought
The curiosity I sought.
Ambiguous child, whose life retires
Into the pulse of those desires
Of whose endured possession speaks
The passionate pallor of your cheeks;
Child, in whom neither good nor ill
Can sway your sick and swaying will,

Only the aching sense of sex
Wholly controls, and does perplex,   80
With dubious drifts scarce understood,
The shaken currents of your blood;
It is your ambiguity
That speaks to me and conquers me,
Your swooning heats of sensual bliss,
Under my hands, under my kiss,
And your strange reticences, strange
Concessions, your elusive change,
The strangeness of your smile, the faint
Corruption of your gaze, a saint   90
Such as Luini[1] loved to paint.

What's virtue, Bianca? nay, indeed,
What's vice? for I at last am freed,

With you, of virtue and of vice:
I have discovered Paradise.
And Paradise is neither heaven,
Where the spirits of God are seven,
And the spirits of men burn pure,
Nor is it hell, where souls endure
An equal ecstacy of fire,   100
In like repletion of desire;
Nay, but a subtlier intense
Unsatisfied appeal of sense,
Ever desiring, ever near
The goal of all its hope and fear,
Ever a hair's-breadth from the goal.

So Bianca satisfies my soul.

London Nights *(1895)*.

THE LAST MEMORY

When I am old, and think of the old days,
And warm my hands before a little blaze,
Having forgotten love, hope, fear, desire,
I shall see, smiling out of the pale fire,
One face, mysterious and exquisite;
And I shall gaze, and ponder over it,
Wondering, was it Leonardo[1] wrought
That stealthy ardency, where passionate thought
Burns inward, a revealing flame, and glows
To the last ecstasy, which is repose?   10
Was it Bronzino, those Borghese eyes?[2]

And, musing thus among my memories,
O unforgotten! you will come to seem,
As pictures do, remembered, some old dream.
And I shall think of you as something strange,
And beautiful, and full of helpless change,
Which I beheld and carried in my heart;
But you, I loved, will have become a part
Of the eternal mystery, and love
Like a dim pain; and I shall bend above   20
My little fire, and shiver, being cold,
When you are no more young, and I am old.

Images of Good and Evil *(William Heinemann, 1899)*.

W. B. (William Butler) Yeats (1865–1939)

W. B. Yeats, Irish Protestant politician and mystic, a chief figure in the later nineteenth/early twentieth-century movements for Irish cultural identity and independence, is one of the small handful of modernist poets writing in Britain acknowledged by everyone to be truly great. He's also one of the few modern poets in English with long writing careers who didn't fall away or merely level off in quality with the years. He was born in Dublin, 13 June 1865, into a minor *rentier* family, eldest son of the painter John Butler Yeats (from a line of Church of Ireland clergymen) and Susan Pollexfen (whose people were ship-owners in Sligo). There were two more brothers (one dying in

infancy) and two sisters. The family moved to London and (when the Irish rents ceased because of new legislation to control them) back to Dublin. While his father was becoming a kind of Pre-Raphaelite portraitist, W. B. attended Godolphin School, Hammersmith. Holidays were spent in Sligo with the Pollexfens – in the first of the utopian Irish places Yeats spent a lifetime in acquiring. Back in Dublin Yeats attended the High School, then the School of Art. In 1885 his first poems and an article appeared in the *Dublin University Review*, and he became friends with the Irish poet Kathleen Tynan and the Fenian John O'Leary. The next year he attended his first seance

BIANCA: X. LIBER AMORIS
1   Bernadino Luini, Italian painter of religious frescoes, early 16th century.
THE LAST MEMORY
1   Leonardo da Vinci (1452–1519), painter of the *Mona Lisa*.

2   Il Bronzino (Agnolo di Cosimo di Mariano) (1502–72), Florentine painter. The Borghese family owned great collection of paintings, many still in the Borghese Palace, Rome.

and got hooked on the spiritualist practices and revelations that would massively fuel his poems. Once more in London with the family in 1887, he launched into a politico-aesthetic-religious career of intense energy: doing much hack reviewing (for little financial reward); gathering the materials that featured in his many collections of Irish fairy and folk tales; writing his own poems and *Dhoya* (a prose tale) and *John Sherman* (his only novel) – both of these anonymously published in 1891. Early on he visited William Morris at Kelmscott. He was encouraged by W. E. Henley (the one-legged spotter of talent, who published Yeats in his *National Observer*), fell in (and quickly out) with the London Theosophists, met Maud Gonne, the rich flame-haired nationalist writer and agitator to whom he unsuccessfully proposed marriage many times and who would be mythicized in his poems as both his Helen of Troy and his fallen muse (because of her demagogic street politics). Yeats's inspiration fed off such women, even when they rebuffed him sexually, as Maud Gonne repeatedly did (eventually he proposed marriage to her daughter Iseult, who preferred the Irish novelist, and broadcaster for Hitler's Third Reich, Francis Stuart). Yeats had numerous affairs, not least the on–off relationship with Olivia Shakespear. Through her he met Pound, who married her daughter Dorothy, and George Hyde-Lees, Dorothy's chum, who became (1917) the wife of Yeats's middle age. Yeats's women frequently shared his enthusiasm for seances and mediums. He was also drawn to Anglo-Irish women with Great Houses he could stay at, like the Gore-Booth sisters from Lissadell (as featured in the great twenties poem 'In Memory of Eva Gore-Booth and Con Markiewicz'), and, of course, Lady Augusta Gregory, whose Coole Park became perhaps Yeats's most important imaginative centre in Ireland – and with whom he was working hard at the end of the nineties to establish an Irish Celtic or Literary Theatre. Yeats was the most prominent London literary Celt of the nineties. With T. W. Rolleston he founded the London-Irish Literary Society. He also founded the Dublin Literary Society with John O'Leary as president. He was a member of the Irish Republican Brotherhood, and deeply embroiled in the baroque factionalism of nationalist and nationalist-cultural politics, not least the contentious centenary celebrations of the 1798 Nationalist Rising. He was the key figure in the Rhymers' Club, founded in 1890, the important alliance of young poetic turks and wannabee *poètes maudits* – Celtic, pseudo-Celtic, francophile, bohemian, radical and aspirant-Symbolist: Lionel Johnson (Yeats's most prominent friend of the early nineties), Ernest Dowson, John Davidson, Richard Le Gallienne, Ernest Radford, Victor Plarr, Arthur Symons (who displaced the drunken Johnson in Yeats's affections), Oscar Wilde (on the fringes of this fringe). Rather astonishingly, Yeats sought to hold together an aesthetic practice turbulently uniting Irish fairy traditionalism, his own spiritualist visionary trance-life, the esotericism of his kabbalistic friend MacGregor Mathers and the Hermetic Order of the Golden Dawn,

and also the anti-realism of French Symbolism. A man with bad eyesight, Yeats saw more intensely inwards. He was a constant self-reviser and his poetic moved rapidly on from the murmuring Celtic Twilight of *The Wanderings of Oisin and Other Poems* (1889), through *Poems* (1895, revised 1899), to the more astringent *The Wind Among the Reeds* (1899), via the stories of *The Secret Rose* (1897). These last two volumes mark an important milestone in Yeats's long process of self-making. They show him growing into the variegated personae or masks provided by a roster of idealized Irish alter-egos – poets, prophets, mythic Irish types, named variously Michael Robartes, Red Hanrahan, O'Sullivan Rua, Aedh, Mangan, and so on – personae who would become, in later versions of the same poems, simply He, the Lover, the Poet. Symons dedicated *The Symbolist Movement in Literature* (1899) to Yeats as 'the chief representative of that movement in our country'. In 1900, when Yeats turned thirty-five, he was thinking, mistakenly, that his future would lie mainly with the pioneering nationalist poetic drama of *The Countess Cathleen* sort (performed in Dublin, May 1899). At the end of 1898 he had felt extremely dismayed over Symbolism's future, when he attended with Symons the Paris premiere of Alfred Jarry's comic-satirical *Père Ubu*: 'After Stephane Mallarmé, after Paul Verlaine, after Gustave Moreau, after Puvis de Chavannes, after our own verse, after all our subtle colour and nervous rhythm, after the faint mixed tints of Conder [the painter on silk] what more is possible? After us the Savage God.' But after 1900 came nearly forty years of unflagging production: dramas, of course, but poems above all, maturing in *The Wild Swans at Coole* (1917), climaxing in *The Tower* (1928) and *The Winding Stair* (1929), all involving a continual refiguring of poetic and Irish history, of W. B. Yeats, his ageing, his women, the Great Houses he loved, his evolving Byzantine ideal, the hermeticism and neo-Platonism he fantasized. The doubts in his *Last Poems* (1940) about his residence in the world of images are particularly compelling. Yeats's vision is, like his practice of automatic writing (shared by George Hyde-Lees) and like his great mythopoeic textbook *A Vision* (1925), frequently dotty and cranky. In the thirties he was even drawn to a kind of fascism. But his 'icy ecstacy' (Symons's phrase for Jules Laforgue) never fails to stir one's imagination. He was made a Senator of the Irish Republic in 1922 (and helped design the new Irish coinage). He won the Nobel Prize for Literature in 1923. His *Collected Poems* and *Collected Plays* appeared in 1933 and 1934. He died, 28 January 1939, at Roquebrune, near Monaco – provoking one of the finest elegies in the English language, W. H. Auden's 'In Memoriam W. B. Yeats'. In 1948 his remains were removed to the churchyard of his great-grandfather's parish, Drumcliffe, near Sligo, 'Under Ben Bulben'. Yeats's volume of assorted memoir pieces, *Autobiographies*, was published in 1955 (earlier versions have been edited by Denis Donoghue as *Memoirs: Autobiography-First Draft; Journal*, 1972).

HE REMEMBERS FORGOTTEN BEAUTY

When my arms wrap you round I press
My heart upon the loveliness
That has long faded from the world;
The jewelled crowns that kings have hurled
In shadowy pools, when armies fled;
The love-tales wove with silken thread
By dreaming ladies upon cloth
That has made fat the murderous moth;
The roses that of old time were
Woven by ladies in their hair,   10
The dew-cold lilies ladies bore
Through many a sacred corridor
Where such grey clouds of incense rose
That only the gods' eyes did not close:
For that pale breast and lingering hand
Come from a more dream-heavy land,
A more dream-heavy hour than this;
And when you sigh from kiss to kiss
I hear white Beauty sighing, too,
For hours when all must fade like dew,   20
But flame on flame, deep under deep,
Throne over throne, where in half sleep,
Their swords upon their iron knees
Brood her high lonely mysteries.

The Savoy (July 1896) – as 'O'Sullivan Rua to Mary Lavell'. The Wind Among
the Reeds (Elkin Mathews, 1899) – as 'Michael Robartes Remembers
Forgotten Beauty'. 1899 text. Title, first in A Selection (Tauchnitz, Leipzig, 1913).

HE GIVES HIS BELOVED CERTAIN RHYMES

Fasten your hair with a golden pin,
And bind up every wandering tress;
I bade my heart build these poor rhymes:
It worked at them, day out, day in,
Building a sorrowful loveliness
Out of the battles of old times.

You need but lift a pearl-pale hand,
And bind up your long hair and sigh;
And all men's hearts must burn and beat;
And candle-like foam on the dim sand,   10
And stars climbing the dew-dropping sky,
Live but to light your passing feet.

Written 1895. First appeared in the story 'The Binding of the Hair', Savoy
(January 1896) – untitled; story (and poem) reprinted in The Secret Rose
(Lawrence & Bullen, 1897); The Wind Among the Reeds (1899) – as 'Aedh gives
His Beloved Certain Rhymes'. Text constant. Title, first in A Selection (1913).

THE LAKE ISLE OF INNISFREE

I will arise and go now, and go to Innisfree,
And a small cabin build there, of clay and wattles made:
Nine bean rows will I have there, a hive for the honey bee,
And live alone in the bee-loud glade.

And I shall have some peace there, for peace comes dropping slow,
Dropping from the veils of the morning to where the cricket sings;
There midnight's all a glimmer, and noon a purple glow,
And evening full of the linnet's wings.

I will arise and go now, for always night and day
I hear lake water lapping with low sounds by the shore;   10
While I stand on the roadway, or on the pavements grey,
I hear it in the deep heart's core.

Written 1890. National Observer *(13 December 1890).* The Countess Kathleen and
Various Legends and Lyrics *(T. Fisher Unwin, 1892). 1892 text.*

WHO GOES WITH FERGUS?

Who will go drive with Fergus now,
And pierce the deep wood's woven shade,
And dance upon the level shore?
Young man, lift up your russet brow,
And lift your tender eyelids, maid,
And brood on hopes and fears no more.

And no more turn aside and brood
Upon love's bitter mystery;
For Fergus rules the brazen cars,
And rules the shadows of the wood,   10
And the white breast of the dim sea
And all dishevelled wandering stars.

The Countess Kathleen and Various Legends and Lyrics *(1892).*
Oona's song in Sc.ii of the play The Countess Kathleen *(later titled*
The Countess Cathleen*). Acquired title in* Poems *(T. Fisher Unwin, 1912).*

THE MAN WHO DREAMED OF FAIRYLAND

I

He stood among a crowd at Drumahair,
His heart hung all upon a silken dress,
And he had known at last some tenderness
Before earth made of him her sleepy care;
But when a man poured fish into a pile,
It seemed they raised their little silver heads
And sang how day a Druid twilight sheds
Upon a dim, green, well-beloved isle
Where people love beside star-laden seas;
How Time may never mar their fairy vows   10
Under the woven roofs of quicken boughs; –
The singing shook him out of his new ease.

II

He wandered by the sands of Lisadill,[1]
His mind ran all on money cares and fears,
And he had known at last some prudent years
Before they heaped his grave under the hill;
But while he passed before a plashy place,
A lug-worm with its grey and muddy mouth
Sang how somewhere to north or east or south
There dwelt a gay, exulting, gentle race;   20
And how beneath those three times blessed skies;
A Danaan[2] fruitage makes a shower of moons
And as it falls awakens leafy tunes; –
And at that singing he was no more wise.

III

He mused beside the well of Scanavin,
He mused upon his mockers. Without fail
His sudden vengeance were a country tale
Now that deep earth had drunk his body in,
But one small knot-grass growing by the rim
Told where – ah, little, all-unneeded voice! –   30
Old Silence bids a lonely folk rejoice,
And chaplet their calm brows with leafage dim,
And how, when fades the sea-strewn rose of day,
A gentle feeling wraps them like a fleece,
And all their trouble dies into its peace; –
The tale drove his fine angry mood away.

IV

He slept under the hill of Lugnagall;
And might have known at last unhaunted sleep
Under that cold and vapour-turbaned steep,
Now that old earth had taken man and all: 40
Were not the worms that spired about his bones
A-telling with their low and reedy cry,
Of how God leans His hands out of the sky,
To bless that isle with honey in His tones,
That none may feel the power of squall and wave,
And no one any leaf-crowned dancer miss
Until He burn up Nature with a kiss
The man has found no comfort in the grave.

National Observer *(7 February 1891)*. The Countess Kathleen *(1892)*.

To Ireland in the Coming Times

Know, that I would accounted be
True brother of a company
Who sang to sweeten Ireland's wrong,
Ballad and story, rann[1] and song;
Nor be I any less of them,
Because the red rose bordered hem

The Man Who Dreamed of Fairyland
1   home of the Gore-Booths.
2   Danaë was seduced by Zeus in/as a shower of gold.

To Ireland in the Coming Times
1   verse.

Of her whose history began
Before God made the angelic clan,
Trails all about the written page,
For in the world's first blossoming age   10
The light fall of her flying feet
Made Ireland's heart begin to beat,
And still the starry candles flare
To help her light foot here and there;
And still the thoughts of Ireland brood,
Upon her holy quietude.

Nor may I less be counted one
With Davis, Mangan, Ferguson,[2]
Because to him who ponders well
My rhymes more than their rhyming tell   20
Of the dim wisdoms old and deep,
That God gives unto man in sleep.
For round about my table go
The magical powers to and fro,
In flood and fire and clay and wind,
They huddle from man's pondering mind,
Yet he who treads in austere ways
May surely meet their ancient gaze.
Man ever journeys on with them
After the red rose bordered hem.   30
Ah, fairies, dancing under the moon,
A druid land, a druid tune!

While still I may I write for you
The love I lived, the dream I knew.
From our birthday until we die,
Is but the winking of an eye.
And we, our singing and our love,
The mariners of night above,
And all the wizard things that go
About my table to and fro,   40
Are passing on to where may be,
In truth's consuming ecstasy,
No place for love and dream at all,
For God goes by with white foot-fall.
I cast my heart into my rhymes,
That you in the dim coming times
May know how my heart went with them
After the red rose bordered hem.

The Countess Kathleen and Various Legends and Lyrics *(1892) – as*
'Apologia addressed to Ireland in the coming days'. Title, Poems *(T. Fisher Unwin,*
1895). Text, 1892: with 1892's 'Irelana' *(line 3) corrected to* 'Ireland'.

2   Thomas Osborne Davis (1814–45), James Clarence Mangan, poets;
Sir Samuel Ferguson (1810–86), poet and Celtic scholar.

HE REPROVES THE CURLEW

O, curlew, cry no more in the air,
Or only to the water in the West;
Because your crying brings to my mind
Passion-dimmed eyes and long heavy hair
That was shaken out over my breast:
There is enough evil in the crying of wind.

The Savoy *(November 1896) – as 'Windlestraws I. O'Sullivan Rua to the Curlew'.*
The Wind Among the Reeds (1899) – as 'Hanrahan Reproves
the Curlew'. 1899 text. Title, first in A Selection *(1913).*

THE CAP AND BELLS

The jester walked in the garden:
The garden had fallen still;
He bade his soul rise upward
And stand on her window-sill.

It rose in a straight blue garment,
When owls began to call:
It had grown wise-tongued by thinking
Of a quiet and light footfall;

But the young queen would not listen;
She rose in her pale night gown;   10
She drew in the heavy casement
And pushed the latches down.

He bade his heart go to her,
When the owls called out no more;
In a red and quivering garment
It sang to her through the door.

It had grown sweet-tongued by dreaming
Of a flutter of flower-like hair;
But she took up her fan from the table
And waved it off on the air.   20

'I have cap and bells,' he pondered,
'I will send them to her and die';
And when the morning whitened
He left them where she went by.

She laid them upon her bosom,
Under a cloud of her hair,
And her red lips sang them a love song:
Till stars grew out of the air.

She opened her door and her window,
And the heart and the soul came through,   30
To her right hand came the red one,
To her left hand came the blue.

They set up a noise like crickets,
A chattering wise and sweet,
And her hair was a folded flower
And the quiet of love in her feet.

Written 1893. National Observer *(17 March 1894) – as 'Cap and Bell'.*
The Wind Among the Reeds (1899).

HE WISHES FOR THE CLOTHS OF HEAVEN

Had I the heavens' embroidered cloths,
Enwrought with golden and silver light,
The blue and the dim and the dark cloths
Of night and light and the half light,
I would spread the cloths under your feet:
But I, being poor, have only my dreams;
I have spread my dreams under your feet;
Tread softly because you tread on my dreams.

The Wind Among the Reeds (1899) – as 'Aedh Wishes
For The Cloths of Heaven'. Title, first in A Selection *(1913).*

THE SYMBOLISM OF POETRY

I

'Symbolism, as seen in the writers of our day, would have no value if it were not seen also, under one disguise or another, in every great imaginative writer,' writes Mr. Arthur Symons in *The Symbolist Movement in Literature*, a subtle book which I cannot praise as I would, because it has been dedicated to me; and he goes on to show how many profound writers have in the last few years sought for a philosophy of poetry in the doctrine of symbolism, and how even in countries where it is almost scandalous to seek for any philosophy of poetry, new writers are following them in their search. We do not know what the writers of ancient times talked of among themselves, and one bull is all that remains of Shakespeare's talk, who was on the edge of modern times; and the journalist is convinced, it seems, that they talked of wine and women and politics, but never about their art, or never quite seriously about their art. He is certain that no one who had a philosophy of his art or a theory of how he should write, has ever made a work of art, that people have no imagination who do not write without forethought and afterthought as he writes his own articles. He says this with enthusiasm, because he has heard it at so many comfortable dinner-tables, where some one had mentioned through carelessness, or foolish zeal, a book whose difficulty had offended indolence, or a man who had not forgotten that beauty is an accusation. Those formulas and generalisations, in which a hidden sergeant has drilled the ideas of journalists and through them the ideas of all but all the modern world, have created in their turn a forgetfulness like that of soldiers in battle, so that journalists and their readers have forgotten, among many like events, that Wagner spent seven years arranging and explaining his ideas before he began his most characteristic music; that opera, and with it modern music, arose from certain talks at the house of one Giovanni Bardi of Florence; and that the Pliade[1] laid the foundations of modern French literature with a pamphlet. Goethe has said, 'a poet needs all philosophy, but he must keep it out of his work,' though that is not always necessary; and certainly he cannot know too much, whether about his own work, or about the procreant waters of the soul where the breath first moved, or about the waters under the earth that are the life of passing things; and almost certainly no great art, outside England, where journalists are more powerful and ideas less plentiful than elsewhere, has arisen without a great criticism, for its herald or its interpreter and protector, and it is perhaps for this reason that great art, now that vulgarity has armed itself and multiplied itself, is perhaps dead in England.

All writers, all artists of any kind, in so far as they have had any philosophical or critical power, perhaps just in so far as they have been deliberate artists at all, have had some philosophy, some criticism of their art; and it has often been this philosophy, or this criticism, that has evoked their most startling inspiration, calling into outer life some portion of the divine life, or of the buried

THE SYMBOLISM OF POETRY
1 *Pléiade* later.

reality, which could alone extinguish in the emotions what their philosophy or their criticism would extinguish in the intellect. They have sought for no new thing, it may be, but only to understand and to copy the pure inspiration of early times, but because the divine life wars upon our outer life, and must needs change its weapons and its movements as we change ours, inspiration has come to them in beautiful startling shapes. The scientific movement brought with it a literature which was always tending to lose itself in externalities of all kinds, in opinion, in declamation, in picturesque writing, in word-painting, or in what Mr. Symons has called an attempt 'to build in brick and mortar inside the covers of a book'; and now writers have begun to dwell upon the element of evocation, of suggestion, upon what we call the symbolism in great writers.

II

In 'Symbolism in Painting,'[2] I tried to describe the element of symbolism that is in pictures and sculpture, and described a little the symbolism in poetry, but did not describe at all the continuous indefinable symbolism which is the substance of all style.

There are no lines with more melancholy beauty than these by Burns: –

> The white moon is setting behind the white wave,[3]
> And Time is setting with me, O!

and these lines are perfectly symbolical. Take from them the whiteness of the moon and of the wave, whose relation to the setting of Time is too subtle for the intellect, and you take from them their beauty. But, when all are together, moon and wave and whiteness and setting Time and the last melancholy cry, they evoke an emotion which cannot be evoked by any other arrangement of colours and sounds and forms. We may call this metaphorical writing, but it is better to call it symbolical writing, because metaphors are not profound enough to be moving, when they are not symbols, and when they are symbols they are the most perfect, because the most subtle, outside of pure sound, and through them one can best find out what symbols are. If one begins the reverie with any beautiful lines that one can remember, one finds they are like those by Burns. Begin with this line by Blake –

> The gay fishes on the wave when the moon sucks up the dew;[4]

or these lines by Nash:[5] –

> Brightness falls from the air,
> Queens have died young and fair,
> Dust hath closed Helen's eye;

or these lines by Shakespeare –

> Timon hath made his everlasting mansion
> Upon the beached verge of the salt flood;
> Who once a day with his embossed froth
> The turbulent surge shall cover;[6]

or take some line that is quite simple, that gets its beauty from its place in a story, and see how it flickers with the light of the many symbols that have given the story its beauty, as a sword-blade may flicker with the light of burning towers.

2 Y.'s essay of 1898: precedes this essay in *Ideas of Good and Evil*.
3 Burns actually wrote: –
   'The wan moon is setting ayont the white wave,'
but Yeats's version has been retained for the sake of his comments. [Footnote in 1937 version, in W. B. Yeats, *Essays and Introductions* (Macmillan, 1961).] Actually: 'The wan moon sets behind the white wave', in
'Open the Door to Me, O'.
4 'Like the gay fishes on the wave, when the cold moon drinks the dew', from 'Europe a Prophecy' (1794, Plate 14.
5 more usually, Nashe (Thomas), c.1567–1601.
6 *Timon of Athens*, V.i.214–17.

All sounds, all colours, all forms, either because of their pre-ordained energies or because of long association, evoke indefinable and yet precise emotions, or, as I prefer to think, call down among us certain disembodied powers, whose footsteps over our hearts we call emotions; and when sound, and colour, and form are in a musical relation, a beautiful relation to one another, they become, as it were one sound, one colour, one form, and evoke an emotion that is made out of their distinct evocations and yet is one emotion. The same relation exists between all portions of every work of art, whether it be an epic or a song, and the more perfect it is, and the more various and numerous the elements that have flowed into its perfection, the more powerful will be the emotion, the power, the god it calls among us. Because an emotion does not exist, or does not become perceptible and active among us, till it has found its expression, in colour or in sound or in form, or in all of these, and because no two modulations or arrangements of these evoke the same emotion, poets and painters and musicians, and in a less degree because their effects are momentary, day and night and cloud and shadow, are continually making and unmaking mankind. It is indeed only those things which seem useless or very feeble that have any power, and all those things that seem useful or strong, armies, moving wheels, modes of architecture, modes of government, speculations of the reason, would have been a little different if some mind long ago had not given itself to some emotion, as a woman gives herself to her lover, and shaped sounds or colours or forms, or all of these, into a musical relation, that their emotion might live in other minds. A little lyric evokes an emotion, and this emotion gathers others about it and melts into their being in the making of some great epic; and at last, needing an always less delicate body, or symbol, as it grows more powerful, it flows out, with all it has gathered, among the blind instincts of daily life, where it moves a power within powers, as one sees ring within ring in the stem of an old tree. This is maybe what Arthur O'Shaughnessy meant when he made his poets say they had built Nineveh with their sighing; and I am certainly never certain, when I hear of some war, or of some religious excitement, or of some new manufacture, or of anything else that fills the ear of the world, that it has not all happened because of something that a boy piped in Thessaly. I remember once asking a seer to ask one among the gods who, as she believed, were standing about her in their symbolic bodies, what would come of a charming but seeming trivial labour of a friend, and the form answering, 'the devastation of peoples and the overwhelming of cities.' I doubt indeed if the crude circumstance of the world, which seems to create all our emotions, does more than reflect, as in multiplying mirrors, the emotions that have come to solitary men in moments of poetical contemplation; or that love itself would be more than an animal hunger but for the poet and his shadow the priest, for unless we believe that outer things are the reality, we must believe that the gross is the shadow of the subtle, that things are wise before they become foolish, and secret before they cry out in the market-place. Solitary men in moments of contemplation receive, as I think, the creative impulse from the lowest of the Nine Hierarchies,[7] and so make and unmake mankind, and even the world itself, for does not 'the eye altering alter all'?

> Our towns are copied fragments from our breast;
> And all man's Babylons strive but to impart
> The grandeurs of his Babylonian heart.[8]

III

The purpose of rhythm, it has always seemed to me, is to prolong the moment of contemplation, the moment when we are both asleep and awake, which is the one moment of creation, by hushing us with an alluring monotony, while it holds us waking by variety, to keep us in that state of perhaps real trance, in which the mind liberated from the pressure of the will is unfolded in symbols. If certain sensitive persons listen persistently to the ticking of a watch, or gaze persistently on the monotonous flashing of a light, they fall into the hypnotic trance; and rhythm is but the ticking of a

---

7 the order of heavenly beings, according to the 5th-century pseudo-Dionysius's *De Hierarchia Celesti* (from seraphim down to angels).

8 Francis Thompson, 'The Heart: To my Critic who had objected to the phrase – "The heart's burning floors",' *Poems*, II (1913)

watch made softer, that one must needs listen, and various, that one may not be swept beyond memory or grow weary of listening; while the patterns of the artist are but the monotonous flash woven to take the eyes in a subtler enchantment. I have heard in meditation voices that were forgotten the moment they had spoken; and I have been swept, when in more profound meditation, beyond all memory but of those things that came from beyond the threshold of waking life. I was writing once at a very symbolical and abstract poem, when my pen fell on the ground; and as I stooped to pick it up, I remembered some phantastic adventure that yet did not seem phantastic, and then another like adventure, and when I asked myself when these things had happened, I found that I was remembering my dreams for many nights. I tried to remember what I had done the day before, and then what I had done that morning; but all my waking life had perished from me, and it was only after a struggle that I came to remember it again, and as I did so that more powerful and startling life perished in its turn. Had my pen not fallen on the ground and so made me turn from the images that I was weaving into verse, I would never have known that meditation had become trance, for I would have been like one who does not know that he is passing through a wood because his eyes are on the pathway. So I think that in the making and in the understanding of a work of art, and the more easily if it is full of patterns and symbols and music, we are lured to the threshold of sleep, and it may be far beyond it, without knowing that we have ever set our feet upon the steps of horn or of ivory.

IV

Besides emotional symbols, symbols that evoke emotions alone, – and in this sense all alluring or hateful things are symbols, although their relations with one another are too subtle to delight us fully, away from rhythm and pattern, – there are intellectual symbols, symbols that evoke ideas alone, or ideas mingled with emotions; and outside the very definite traditions of mysticism and the less definite criticism of certain modern poets, these alone are called symbols. Most things belong to one or another kind, according to the way we speak of them and the companions we give them, for symbols, associated with ideas that are more than fragments of the shadows thrown upon the intellect by the emotions they evoke, are the playthings of the allegorist or the pedant, and soon pass away. If I say 'white' or 'purple' in an ordinary line of poetry, they evoke emotions so exclusively that I cannot say why they move me; but if I say them in the same mood, in the same breath with such obvious intellectual symbols as a cross or a crown of thorns, I think of purity and sovereignty; while innumerable meanings, which are held to one another by the bondage of subtle suggestion, and alike in the emotions and in the intellect, move visibly through my mind, and move invisibly beyond the threshold of sleep, casting lights and shadows of an indefinable wisdom on what had seemed before, it may be, but sterility and noisy violence. It is the intellect that decides where the reader shall ponder over the procession of the symbols, and if the symbols are merely emotional, he gazes from amid the accidents and destinies of the world; but if the symbols are intellectual too, he becomes himself a part of pure intellect, and he is himself mingled with the procession. If I watch a rushy pool in the moonlight, my emotion at its beauty is mixed with memories of the man that I have seen ploughing by its margin, or of the lovers I saw there a night ago; but if I look at the moon herself and remember any of her ancient names and meanings, I move among divine people, and things that have shaken off our mortality, the tower of ivory, the queen of waters, the shining stag among enchanted woods, the white hare sitting upon the hilltop, the fool of faery with his shining cup full of dreams, and it may be 'make a friend of one of these images of wonder,' and 'meet the Lord in the air.'[9] So, too, if one is moved by Shakespeare, who is content with emotional symbols that he may come the nearer to our sympathy, one is mixed with the whole spectacle of the world; while if one is moved by Dante, or by the myth of Demeter,[10] one is mixed into the shadow of God or of a goddess. So too one is furthest from symbols when one is busy doing this or that, but the soul moves among symbols and unfolds in symbols when trance, or madness, or deep meditation has withdrawn it from every impulse but its

9   I Thessalonians 4.17.   10   goddess of fruit and crops.

own. 'I then saw,' wrote Gérard de Nerval[11] of his madness, 'vaguely drifting into form, plastic images of antiquity, which outlined themselves, became definite, and seemed to represent symbols of which I only seized the idea with difficulty.' In an earlier time he would have been of that multitude, whose souls austerity withdrew, even more perfectly than madness could withdraw his soul, from hope and memory, from desire and regret, that they might reveal those processions of symbols that men bow to before altars, and woo with incense and offerings. But being of our time, he has been like Maeterlinck, like Villiers de l'Isle-Adam[12] in *Axël*, like all who are preoccupied with intellectual symbols in our time, a foreshadower of the new sacred book, of which all the arts, as somebody has said, are begging[13] to dream, and because, as I think, they cannot overcome the slow dying of men's hearts that we call the progress of the world, and lay their hands upon men's heartstrings again, without becoming the garment of religion as in old times.

V

If people were to accept the theory that poetry moves us because of its symbolism, what change should one look for in the manner of our poetry? A return to the way of our fathers, a casting out of descriptions of nature for the sake of nature, of the moral law for the sake of the moral law, a casting out of all anecdotes and of that brooding over scientific opinion that so often extinguished the central flame in Tennyson, and of that vehemence that would make us do or not do certain things; or, in other words, we should come to understand that the beryl stone was enchanted by our fathers that it might unfold the pictures in its heart, and not to mirror our own excited faces, or the boughs waving outside the window. With this change of substance, this return to imagination, this understanding that the laws of art, which are the hidden laws of the world, can alone bind the imagination, would come a change of style, and we would cast out of serious poetry those energetic rhythms, as of a man running, which are the invention of the will with its eyes always on something to be done or undone; and we would seek out those wavering, meditative, organic rhythms, which are the embodiment of the imagination, that neither desires nor hates, because it has done with time, and only wishes to gaze upon some reality, some beauty; nor would it be any longer possible for anybody to deny the importance of form, in all its kinds, for although you can expound an opinion, or describe a thing, when your words are not quite well chosen, you cannot give a body to something that moves beyond the senses, unless your words are as subtle, as complex, as full of mysterious life, as the body of a flower or of a woman. The form of sincere poetry, unlike the form of the popular poetry, may indeed be sometimes obscure, or ungrammatical as in some of the best of the Songs of Innocence and Experience,[14] but it must have the perfections that escape analysis, the subtleties that have a new meaning every day, and it must have all this whether it be but a little song made out of a moment of dreamy indolence, or some great epic made out of the dreams of one poet and of a hundred generations whose hands were never weary of the sword.

The Dome *(April 1900)*. Ideas of Good and Evil *(The Macmillan Company, New York, 1903)*. *1903 text.*

Laurence Housman (1865–1959)

Laurence Housman is the archetypal younger brother, a decent progressive and a poet of humane feeling, who is inevitably overshadowed by his older brother A. E. Housman. He was born, 18 July 1865, at Perry Hall, Bromsgrove, the next-to-youngest child of the five sons and daughters of solicitor Edward Housman. He studied art at various London art schools, was very impoverished, and fell into writing quickly for a living. He became art critic of the *Manchester Guardian* in 1895; churned out plays (which tended to attract the censorious hand of the

11 French writer (decadent; suicidal), 1808–55.
12 Maurice Maeterlinck (1862–1949), Auguste Villiers de Lisle Adam (1838–89), like de Nerval: all in Arthur Symons, *The Symbolist Movement in Literature* (1899).
13 altered to *beginning* later.
14 by William Blake (1789, 1794).

Lord Chamberlain's Office); wrote novels; became rather well known as the dramatist of Queen Victoria's life (plays collected as *Victoria Regina*, 1934); was always looking for the subject that would turn a book into the necessary cash profit. On the left in politics, he was variously engaged in the women's suffrage movement before the Great War, and in pacifism in that War. For many years he attended Quaker meetings, and actually became a Quaker in 1952. He was his brother's literary executor and biographer. As invited by A. E. Housman's will, he culled the 48 poems of A.E.H.'s *More Poems* (1936) from the manuscript remains, and gathered 18 further poems for first publication in his pioneering 1937 Memoir, *A.E.H.* His autobiography *The Unexpected Years* (1937) enjoys the benefit of long years around the literary scene. His own poems seem, by contrast with his brother's, conventional and ordinary. The nineties poetry books, *Green Arras* (1896), *Spikenard* (1898), *The Little Land* (1899), read more like mere footnotes to decadence. There was a *Collected Poems* in 1937. Laurence Housman never married; lived for much of his life with a sister in Somerset; and died, 20 February 1959, in hospital in Glastonbury.

FAILURE

When you are dead, when all you could not do
    Leaves quiet the worn hands, the weary head,
Asking not any service more of you,
    Requiting you with peace when you are dead;

When, like a robe, you lay your body by,
    Unloosed at last, – how worn, and soiled, and frayed! –
Is it not pleasant just to let it lie
    Unused and be moth-eaten in the shade?

Folding earth's silence round you like a shroud,
    Will you just know that what you have is best: –   10
Thus to have slipt unfamous from the crowd;
    Thus having failed and failed, to be at rest?

Oh, having, not to know! Yet oh, my Dear,
    Since to be quit of self is to be blest,
To cheat the world, and leave no imprint here, –
    Is this not best?

Green Arras *(John Lane, 1896).*

AS THE FLOCKS FOR THE BROOKS

As the flocks for the brooks,
    As the river for the sea,
So mine eyes long for thy looks,
    I for thee.

As the sun drinks up the dew,
    As the fire burns up the coal,
So Love strikes through and through
    To my soul.

My spirit wastes like smoke,
    My body burns like fire;   10
Denial was but cloak
    To my desire.

Wherefore did strife seem good,
    Or strength a goal to gain?

When the fire came to the wood,
　　All was vain!

O Beloved, if thou get heat
　　By any pain in me,
Then is the pain most sweet:
　　Let it be!　　　　　　　　　　　　　　　　　　20

Only make this be true,
　　And plain that I may see:
As the sun draws up the dew
　　Draw thou me!

When far, feel thou me near!
　　When heavy of heart, oh, haste: –
Drain me to death, for fear
　　Lest I waste!

Lest, betwixt lip and lip
　　Of loves that thirst and cry,　　　　　　　　　30
The cup of offering slip,
　　And I die!

The Little Land: With Songs From its Four Rivers *(Grant Richards, 1899)*.

LOVE IMPORTUNATE

Dark was the night, and dark as night my heart,
When at my chamber door there knocked a hand.
Then, with glad start,
I rose, and oped:
Nay, not the one I hoped –
There Love Himself did stand.

Ah, me! those eyes I could not meet for shame, –
So, downward looking, saw the Feet that bled;
And knew He came,
Footsore and worn,　　　　　　　　　　　　　　10
A Lover to man's scorn:
Yet could not give Him bread!

Grieved, from His Feet I feared to lift mine eyes:
Patiently there He stood while I stayed dumb.
Till with sharp sighs
I cried, 'Oh, sweet,
Oh, fearful, bleeding Feet
Of Love, why are Ye come?'

'One welcome lacking ever must I roam,
And footsore needs must be,' my Lord confessed:　　20
'From many a home
A wanderer still,
Because your stubborn will
Denies my Heart its rest.'

Sadly I owned, nought had I here to give:
Nay, not a bed so made that He might lie.

Could one not live
From Love shut fast,
But to one's door at last
He needs must come to die?   30

'Why, then,' quoth Love, 'didst thou so watch and wait?
Whom Love hath made, loveless can find no rest.
In empty state
Can peace begin?
Is not thy heart an inn
Which lacks the looked-for guest?'

'Yet there be other inns,' I sighed: 'fair boards
Where open hearts for Thee the feast prepare
Which peace accords!'
'Let it be so;   40
That feast I will forego!'
Said Love. 'Thou art My care.'

Ah, what He further spake I may not tell!
But in the very place where once lay sin,
Love deigns to dwell;
Nor may I doubt
The door which once shut out
Can closelier shut Love in.

Text: The Collected Poems of Laurence Housman *(Sidgwick & Jackson, 1937).*
A reprise of George Herbert's poem 'Love, III'. In 'Spikenard' section of CP, but not in
Spikenard: A Book of Devotional Love Poems *(Grant Richards, 1898) – which has 2*
stanzas of Herbert's 'Love, III' as Epigraph.

(Joseph) Rudyard Kipling (1865–1936)

Rudyard Kipling – 'the most complete man of genius (as distinct from fine intelligence) that I have ever known', Henry James called him – was born in Bombay, 30 December 1865, the first child of John Lockwood Kipling, Professor of Architectural Sculpture at the Bombay Art School, and of Alice Macdonald. Both families were steeped in Midlands Wesleyanism. Grandfather Joseph Kipling was a Methodist minister in the Potteries. Grandfather George Macdonald was another, in Wolverhampton. *His* father James Macdonald, yet another Methodist pastor, was a friend of John Wesley. The Macdonald daughters, an astonishing group, became prominent in British aesthetic circles – Georgiana married Edward Burne-Jones; Agnes, Edward Poynter. Louisa was the mother of Stanley Baldwin, future Prime Minister. John Kipling was a pottery designer in Burslem when he met his wife. Rudyard was named after the Rudyard Lake they courted by. In 1871 Kipling and his younger sister Trix were sent back to England to be fostered for five unhappy years in Southsea. Kipling later called their grimly pious foster home the House of Desolation. Christmases at the Burne-Jones's in Fulham were better – William Morris perched on a rocking-horse telling the children of Burnt

Njal, and all that. In 1877 his mother returned to England and quickly took her offspring away from the dreaded Mrs Holloway. The new United Services College for officers' children at Westward Ho! in Devon, to which Kipling was sent in 1878, was not, perhaps, much better (its minor public school ethos is trashed in the novel *Stalky & Co.*, 1899). Kipling began writing in earnest at school (he edited the College magazine). Unbeknownst to him his parents brought out *Schoolboy Lyrics* (1881) in Lahore, where his father had become director of the School of Art and curator of the Museum. In 1882 his father got him a job on the Lahore *Civil and Military Gazette*, in whose pages his prolific career as poet and story-teller soon took off. In 1884 *Echoes*, a collection of brother–sister verse parodies, appeared, in 1885 *Quartette* – a Christmas annual by both the parents and children. Kipling's own first authorized collection of verse was *Departmental Ditties* (Lahore, 1886). The volumes of *Plain Tales from the Hills* and *Soldiers Three* both came out in 1888, in the Indian Railway Library series. The striking collection of curiously old–young stories *Wee Willie-Winkie* appeared in 1889. In that year Kipling returned to England and found his distinctive poetic voice in the tones of Cockney Music Hall, as described in the 'My Great and Only' piece in *Abaft the Funnel* (1909). *Barrack-Room Ballads and Other Verses* (1892) – containing poems such as 'Mandalay', 'Gunga Din' and 'Danny Deever', that became great imperial hits – made Kipling's name as the slangily blokeish spokesman for the ordinary soldierly servant of the British Empire. The thirteen original soldier poems first appeared in 1890 in the one-legged talent scout W. E. Henley's *Scots Observer*. It was part of Kipling's youthful good fortune to be made a member of the so-called 'Henley Regatta' of rising poetic stars. Early in 1892 Kipling married Caroline Balestier, an American, and moved to Brattleboro, Vermont, where he wrote the two hugely successful *Jungle Books* (1894–5). *The Jungle Book* and *The Yellow Book* were, Kipling's biographer Harry Ricketts has nicely observed, rivalrous contemporaries. Not dissimilarly, it has also been suggested, with force, that part of Kipling's appeal after the Wilde trial was his offer of an anti-effeminate heterosexual, though still aestheticized, vision of English manhood (Kipling's poem 'In Partibus' characteristically sneers at 'long-haired things/In velvet collar-rolls,/Who talk about the Aims of Art'; by contrast, 'It's Oh to meet an Army man/Set up, and trimmed and taut'). In 1896, year of *The Seven Seas* poems, the Kiplings and their two daughters moved back to England – base thereafter for a life of many travels. *Kim*, Kipling's greatest Indian fiction (arrestingly ur-modernist), was published in 1901, the *Just So Stories* in 1902, *Puck of Pook's Hill*, characteristically a mixture of prose and poems, in 1906. On the strength of an already prodigious output – including not least the novels *The Light that Failed* (1891) and *Captains Courageous* (1897) – Kipling was awarded the Nobel Prize for Literature (1907), first English writer so honoured. His imagination was greatly darkened by the death of his daughter Josephine in 1899, and even more by the death in action in 1915, in the Battle of Loos in France, of his third child and only son John, a very youthful officer in the Irish Guards, who had wangled his way into the army under-age with the connivance of his most patriotic father. Kipling's work for the Imperial War Graves' Commission (he devised the gravestone inscription for unknown soldiers: 'Known Only to God') and his history *The Irish Guards in the Great War* (1923) scarcely assuaged the hurt and the guilt. Kipling was a great friend of the African exploiter and colonizer Cecil Rhodes, edited a paper for British troops in the Boer War (1900), was indeed the celebrator of 'our far-flung battle-line' and 'the White Man's Burden' – but the deeply critical wrynesses and cool ironies about Victoria's and Edward's Christian Empire, which inevitably accompany his celebrations, make his popular representation as a mere imperialist undeserved and wronging. Henry James's awed ribaldry hit certain Kiplingesque nails on the head: 'he has come down steadily from the simple in subject to the more simple – from the Anglo-Indians to the natives, from the natives to the Tommies, from the Tommies to the quadrupeds, from the quadrupeds to the fish, and from the fish to the engines and screws.' T. S. Eliot's prefatory essay to his selection *A Choice of Kipling's Verse* (1941) rose importantly to the challenge which accessible, emotive, politically expressive, popular verse offered to an era which valued coolly modernist (and Eliotic) difficulty over such simplicities. Kipling died at the Middlesex Hospital, London, 18 January 1936, full of years and of many writings, in prose and poetry, a Grand Old Man of Letters, his autobiography *Something of Myself*, though, unfinished.

TOMMY

I went into a public-'ouse to get a pint o' beer,
The publican 'e up an' sez, 'We serve no red-coats here.'
The girls be'ind the bar they laughed an' giggled fit to die.
I outs into the street again an' to myself sez I:
　O it's Tommy this, an' Tommy that, an' 'Tommy, go away';
　But it's 'Thank you, Mister Atkins,' when the band begins to play –
　The band begins to play, my boys, the band begins to play,
　O it's 'Thank you, Mister Atkins,' when the band begins to play.[1]

I went into a theatre as sober as could be,
They gave a drunk civilian room, but 'adn't none for me;　　　　10
They sent me to the gallery or round the music-'alls,
But when it comes to fightin', Lord! they'll shove me in the stalls!
　For it's Tommy this, an' Tommy that, an' 'Tommy, wait outside';
　But it's 'Special train for Atkins' when the trooper's on the tide –
　The troopship's on the tide, my boys, the troopship's on the tide,
　O it's 'Special train for Atkins' when the trooper's on the tide.

TOMMY
1 Thomas (Tommy) Atkins, since Wellington's time, the traditional nickname for the English soldier.

Yes, makin' mock o' uniforms that guard you while you sleep
Is cheaper than them uniforms, an' they're starvation cheap;
An' hustlin' drunken soldiers when they're goin' large a bit
Is five times better business than paradin' in full kit.
    Then it's Tommy this, an' Tommy that, an' 'Tommy, 'ow's yer soul?'   20
    But it's 'Thin red line of 'eroes' when the drums begin to roll –
    The drums begin to roll, my boys, the drums begin to roll,
      O it's 'Thin red line of 'eroes' when the drums begin to roll.

We aren't no thin red 'eroes, nor we aren't no blackguards too,
But single men in barricks, most remarkable like you;
An' if sometimes our conduck isn't all your fancy paints,
Why, single men in barricks don't grow into plaster saints;
    While it's Tommy this, an' Tommy that, an' 'Tommy, fall be'ind,'
    But it's 'Please to walk in front, sir,' when there's trouble in the wind –   30
    There's trouble in the wind, my boys, there's trouble in the wind,
      O it's 'Please to walk in front, sir,' when there's trouble in the wind.

You talk o' better food for us, an' schools, an' fires, an' all:
We'll wait for extry rations if you treat us rational.
Don't mess about the cook-room slops, but prove it to our face
The Widow's Uniform is not the soldier-man's disgrace.
    For it's Tommy this, an' Tommy that, an' 'Chuck him out, the brute!'
    But it's 'Saviour of 'is country' when the guns begin to shoot;
    An' it's Tommy this, an' Tommy that, an' anything you please;
    An' Tommy ain't a bloomin' fool – you bet that Tommy sees!   40

      Scots Observer *(1 March 1870) – as 'The Queen's Uniform'.* Barrack-Room Ballads and
        Other Verses *(Methuen & Co., 1892).*

MANDALAY

By the old Moulmein Pagoda, lookin' eastward to the sea,
There's a Burma girl a-settin', and I know she thinks o' me;
For the wind is in the palm-trees, and the temple-bells they say:
'Come you back, you British soldier; come you back to Mandalay!'
    Come you back to Mandalay,
    Where the old Flotilla lay:
    Can't you 'ear their paddles chunkin' from
        Rangoon to Mandalay?
    On the road to Mandalay,
    Where the flyin'-fishes play,
    An' the dawn comes up like thunder outer   10
        China 'crost the Bay!

'Er petticoat was yaller an' 'er little cap was green,
An' 'er name was Supi-yaw-lat – jes' the same as Theebaw's Queen,[1]
An' I seed her first a-smokin' of a whackin' white cheroot,
An' a-wastin' Christian kisses on an 'eathen idol's foot:
    Bloomin' idol made o' mud –
    Wot they called the Great Gawd Budd –
    Plucky lot she cared for idols when I kissed 'er where she stud!
    On the road to Mandalay...

MANDALAY
1   The British invaded Northern Burma after the death of King Thee-
haw (whose wife was indeed Supi-yaw-lat), 1885.

When the mist was on the rice-fields an' the sun was droppin' slow,
She'd git 'er little banjo an' she'd sing *'Kulla-lo-lo!'*   20
With 'er arm upon my shoulder an' 'er cheek agin my cheek
We useter watch the steamers an' the *hathis*[2] pilin' teak.
    Elephints a-pilin' teak
    In the sludgy, squdgy creek,
    Where the silence 'ung that 'eavy you was 'arf afraid to speak!
    On the road to Mandalay...

But that's all shove be'ind me – long ago an' fur away,
An' there ain't no 'busses runnin' from the Bank to Mandalay;
An' I'm learnin' 'ere in London what the ten-year soldier tells:
'If you've 'eard the East a-callin', you won't never 'eed naught else.'   30
    No! you won't 'eed nothin' else
    But them spicy garlic smells,
    An' the sunshine an' the palm-trees an' the tinkly temple-bells;
    On the road to Mandalay...

I am sick o' wastin' leather on these gritty pavin'-stones,
An' the blasted Henglish drizzle wakes the fever in my bones;
Tho' I walks with fifty 'ousemaids outer Chelsea to the Strand,
An' they talks a lot o' lovin', but wot do they understand?
    Beefy face an' grubby 'and –
    Law! wot do they understand?   40
    I've a neater, sweeter maiden in a cleaner, greener land!
    On the road to Mandalay...

Ship me somewheres east of Suez, where the best is like the worst,
Where there aren't no Ten Commandments an' a man can raise a thirst;
For the temple-bells are callin', an' it's there that I would be –
By the Old Moulmein Pagoda, looking lazy at the sea;
    On the road to Mandalay,
    Where the old Flotilla lay,
    With our sick beneath the awnings when we went to Mandalay!
    O the road to Mandalay,   50
    Where the flyin'-fishes play,
    An' the dawn comes up like thunder outer
        China 'crost the Bay!

Scots Observer (21 June 1890). Barrack-Room Ballads (1892). Alternatively,
'On the Road to Mandalay'.

GENTLEMEN-RANKERS

To the legion of the lost ones, to the cohort of the damned,
    To my brethren in their sorrow overseas,
Sings a gentleman of England cleanly bred, machinely crammed,
    And a trooper of the Empress, if you please.
Yes,[1] a trooper of the forces who has run his own six horses,
    And faith he went the pace and went it blind,
And the world was more than kin while he held the ready tin,
    But to-day the Sergeant's something less than kind.
        We're poor little lambs who've lost our way,
            Baa! Baa! Baa!   10

2   elephants.

GENTLEMEN-RANKERS
1   originally, *Yea.*

We're little black sheep who've gone astray,
    Baa – aa – aa!
Gentlemen-rankers out on the spree,
Damned from here to Eternity,
God ha' mercy on such as we,
    Baa! Yah! Bah!

Oh, it's sweet to sweat through stables, sweet to empty kitchen slops,
    And it's sweet to hear the tales the troopers tell,
To dance with blowzy housemaids at the regimental hops
    And thrash the cad who says you waltz too well. 20
Yes, it makes you cock-a-hoop to be 'Rider' to your troop,
    And branded with a blasted worsted spur,
When you envy, O how keenly, one poor Tommy being cleanly
    Who blacks your boots and sometimes calls you 'Sir.'

If the home we never write to, and the oaths we never keep,
    And all we know most distant and most dear,
Across the snoring barrack-room return to break our sleep,
    Can you blame us if we soak ourselves in beer?
When the drunken comrade mutters and the great guard-lantern gutters
    And the horror of our fall is written plain, 30
Every secret, self-revealing on the aching white-washed ceiling,
    Do you wonder that we drug ourselves from pain?

We have done with Hope and Honour, we are lost to Love and Truth,
    We are dropping down the ladder rung by rung,
And the measure of our torment is the measure of our youth.
    God help us, for we knew the worst too young!
Our shame is clean repentance for the crime that brought the sentence,
    Our pride it is to know no spur of pride,
And the Curse of Reuben[2] holds us till an alien turf enfolds us
    And we die, and none can tell Them where we died. 40
    We're poor little lambs who've lost our way,
        Baa! Baa! Baa!
    We're little black sheep who've gone astray,
        Baa – aa – aa!
    Gentlemen-rankers out on the spree,
    Damned from here to Eternity.
    God ha' mercy on such as we,
        Baa! Yah! Bah!

National Observer *(29 November 1892)*. Macmillan's *(December 1892)*. Barrack-Room Ballads
(1892). Alternatively, 'Gentleman-Songsters' (also, 'The Whiffenpoof Song').

RECESSIONAL[1]

1897

God of our fathers, known of old,
    Lord of our far-flung battle-line,
Beneath whose awful Hand we hold
    Dominion over palm and pine –

2 Deuteronomy 27.13–26.
RECESSIONAL
1 Traditionally, a hymn sung as the clergy retire to the vestry at the

end of a church service. The poem is packed with biblical allusions to the relations between the 'Children of Israel' and their Lord God of Hosts, Jahweh.

Lord God of Hosts, be with us yet,
Lest we forget – lest we forget!

The tumult and the shouting dies;
   The Captains and the Kings depart:
Still stands Thine ancient sacrifice,
   An humble and a contrite heart.   10
Lord God of Hosts, be with us yet,
Lest we forget – lest we forget!

Far-called, our navies melt away;
   On dune and headland sinks the fire:
Lo, all our pomp of yesterday
   Is one with Nineveh and Tyre!
Judge of the Nations, spare us yet,
Lest we forget – lest we forget!

If, drunk with sight of power, we loose
   Wild tongues that have not Thee in awe,   20
Such boastings as the Gentiles use,
   Or lesser breeds without the Law –
Lord God of Hosts, be with us yet,
Lest we forget – lest we forget!

For heathen heart that puts her trust
   In reeking tube and iron shard,
All valiant dust that builds on dust,
   And guarding, calls not Thee to guard.
For frantic boast and foolish word –
Thy mercy on Thy People, Lord!   30

Written 17 July 1897. The Five Nations *(Methuen, 1903). Alternatively, 'After',*
and 'Retrocessional'.

My Great and Only

Out of my many visits to the hall – I chose one hall, you understand, and frequented it till I could tell the mood it was in before I had passed the ticket-poll – was born the Great Idea. I served it as a slave for seven days. Thought was not sufficient; experience was necessary. I patrolled Westminster, Blackfriars, Lambeth, the Old Kent Road, and many, many more miles of pitiless pavement to make sure of my subject. At even I drank my lager among the billycocks, and lost my heart to a bonnet. Goethe and Shakespeare were my precedents. I sympathised with them acutely, but I got my Message. A chance-caught refrain of a song which I understand is protected – to its maker I convey my most grateful acknowledgements – gave me what I sought. The rest was made up of four elementary truths, some humour, and, though I say it who should leave it to the press, pathos deep and genuine. I spent a penny on a paper which introduced me to a Great and Only who 'wanted new songs.' The people desired them really. He was their ambassador, and taught me a great deal about the property-right in songs, concluding with a practical illustration, for he said my verses were just the thing and annexed them. It was long before he could hit on the step-dance which exactly elucidated the spirit of the text, and longer before he could jingle a pair of huge brass spurs as a dancing-girl jingles her anklets. That was my notion, and a good one.

    The Great and Only possessed a voice like a bull, and nightly roared to the people at the heels of one who was winning triple encores with a priceless ballad beginning deep down in the bass: 'We was shopmates – boozin' shopmates.' I feared that song as Rachel feared Ristori.[1] A greater than

My Great and Only
1 Elisa Rachel (1821–58), renowned French tragic actress, and   Adelaide Ristori (1821–1906), Italian actress, who eclipsed her, Paris, 1855.

I had written it. It was a grim tragedy, lighted with lucid humour, wedded to music that maddened. But my 'Great and Only' had faith in me, and I – I clung to the Great Heart of the People – my people – four hundred 'when it's all full, sir.' I had not studied them for nothing. I must reserve the description of my triumph for another 'Turnover.'

There was no portent in the sky on the night of my triumph. A barrowful of onions, indeed, upset itself at the door, but that was a coincidence. The hall was crammed with billycocks[2] waiting for 'We was shopmates.' The great heart beat healthily. I went to my beer the equal of Shakespeare and Molière at the wings in a first night. What would my public say? Could anything live after the abandon of 'We was shopmates'? What if the redcoats did not muster in their usual strength. O my friends, never in your songs and dramas forget the redcoat. He has sympathy and enormous boots.

I believed in the redcoat; in the great heart of the people: above all in myself. The conductor, who advertised that he 'doctored bad songs,' had devised a pleasant little lilting air for my needs, but it struck me as weak and thin after the thunderous surge of the 'Shopmates.' I glanced at the gallery – the redcoats were there. The fiddle-bows creaked, and, with a jingle of brazen spurs, a forage-cap over his left eye, my Great and Only began to 'chuck it off his chest.' Thus:

> 'At the back o' the Knightsbridge Barricks,
>   When the fog was a-gatherin' dim,
> The Lifeguard talked to the Undercook,
>   An' the girl she talked to 'im.'

'*Twiddle-iddle-iddle-lum-tum-tum!*' said the violins.

'*Ling-a-ling-a-ling-a-ling-ting-ling!*' said the spurs of the Great and Only, and through the roar in my ears I fancied I could catch a responsive hoof-beat in the gallery. The next four lines held the house to attention. Then came the chorus and the borrowed refrain. It took – it went home with a crisp click. My Great and Only saw his chance. Superbly waving his hand to embrace the whole audience, he invited them to join him in:

> 'You may make a mistake when you're mashing a tart,[3]
>   But you'll learn to be wise when you're older,
> And don't try for things that are out of your reach,
>   And that's what the girl told the soldier, soldier, soldier,
> And that's what the girl told the soldier.'

I thought the gallery would never let go of the long-drawn howl on 'soldier.' They clung to it as ringers to the kicking bell-rope. Then I envied no one – not even Shakespeare. I had my house hooked – gaffed under the gills, netted, speared, shot behind the shoulder – anything you please. That was pure joy! With each verse the chorus grew louder, and when my Great and Only had bellowed his way to the fall of the Lifeguard and the happy lot of the Undercook, the gallery rocked again, the reserved stalls shouted, and the pewters twinkled like the legs of the demented ballet-girls. The conductor waved the now frenzied orchestra to softer Lydian strains. My Great and Only warbled piano:

> 'At the back o' Knightsbridge Barricks,
>   When the fog's a-gatherin' dim,
> The Lifeguard waits for the Undercook,
>   But she won't wait for 'im.'

'*Ta-ra-rara-rara-ra-ra-rah!*' rang a horn clear and fresh as a sword-cut. 'Twas the apotheosis of virtue.

> 'She's married a man in the poultry line
>   That lives at 'Ighgate 'Ill,

2   men wearing billycock hats (a kind of bowler).

3   (slang) to mash = to make a 'conquest'; a tart in Victorian times was a girl a male fancied.

An' the Lifeguard walks with the 'ousemaid now,
An' (*awful pause*) she can't foot the bill!'

Who shall tell the springs that move masses? I had builded better than I knew. Followed yells, shrieks and wildest applause. Then, as a wave gathers to the curl-over, singer and sung to fill their chests and heave the chorus through the quivering roof – alto, horns, basses drowned, and lost in the flood – to the beach-like boom of beating feet:

'Oh, think o' my song when you're gowin' it strong
An' your boots is too little to 'old yer;
An' don't try for things that is out of your reach,
An' that's what the girl told the soldier, soldier, so-holdier!'

Ow! Hi! Yi! Wha-hup! Phew! Whew! Pwhit! Bang! Wang! Crr-rash! There was ample time for variations as the horns uplifted themselves and ere the held voices came down in the foam of sound –

'That's what the girl told the soldier.'

Providence has sent me several joys, and I have helped myself to others, but that night, as I looked across the sea of tossing billycocks and rocking bonnets, my work, as I heard them give tongue, not once, but four times – their eyes sparkling, their mouths twisted with the taste of pleasure – I felt that I had secured Perfect Felicity. I am become greater than Shakespeare. I may even write plays for the Lyceum, but I never can recapture that first fine rapture that followed the Upheaval of the Anglo-Saxon four hundred of him and her. They do not call for authors on these occasions, but I desired no need of public recognition. I was placidly happy. The chorus bubbled up again and again throughout the evening, and a redcoat in the gallery insisted on singing solos about 'a swine in the poultry line,' whereas I had written 'man,' and the pewters began to fly, and afterwards the long streets were vocal with various versions of what the girl had really told the soldier, and I went to bed murmuring: 'I have found my destiny.'

But it needs a more mighty intellect to write the Songs of the People. Some day a man will rise up from Bermondsey, Battersea or Bow, and he will be coarse, but clearsighted, hard but infinitely and tenderly humorous, speaking the people's tongue, steeped in their lives and telling them in swinging, urging, dinging verse what it is that their inarticulate lips would express. He will make them songs. Such songs! And all the little poets who pretend to sing to the people will scuttle away like rabbits, for the girl (which, as you have seen, of course, is wisdom) will tell that soldier (which is Hercules bowed under his labours) all that she knows of Life and Death and Love.

And the same, they say, is a Vulgarity!

Written November 1889. Civil and Military Gazette *(Lahore, India, 11/13 January 1890).* Abaft the Funnel *(R. W. Dodge, New York, 1909), 297–304. Partly in Andrew Rutherford ed.,* Early Verse by Rudyard Kipling 1879–1889: Unpublished, Uncollected, and Rarely Collected Poems *(Clarendon Press, Oxford, 1986), 473–5.* Abaft the Funnel *text.*

Richard (Thomas) Le Gallienne (1866–1947)

Richard Le Gallienne, poet, critic, novelist, was born in Liverpool, 20 January 1866, the eldest son of John Gallienne and Jane Smith. The father ended up managing the Birkenhead Brewery. The son went to school locally, is said to have caught his love of poetry from his mother, hung around bookshops, disliked his job as a trainee chartered accountant, and began to write (encouraged by Oliver Wendell Holmes). His first little volume of verses, *My Ladies' Sonnets And Other 'Vain and Amatorious' Verses,*

With Some of Graver Mood, privately printed in Liverpool in 1887 with the help of friends from the office, appeared as from R. Le Gallienne, his family's old Channel Islands name – though indicative too of an astute sense of the francophile way literature was going. In 1888 he headed for London and the aesthetic life – working as secretary to the actor-manager Wilson Barrett, hanging about literary people like Meredith, Swinburne and Wilde. In 1889 his second small volume of verses, *Volumes in Folio,* was published in the retro hand-made-paper mode that would characterize the preciously nineties productions of Elkin Mathews and John Lane. John Lane published his *English Poems* in 1892. Le Gallienne's timid and tepid flavour – as asthmatic, so to say, as him – was clearly of the moment. He was a founder member of the Rhymers' Club clustering around Yeats in the early nineties – Lionel Johnson, Plarr, Davidson, Dowson, Wilde too. By 1891 he had a regular books column in the *Spectator*, as the revealingly named Log-roller. He was reader for the Bodley Head, and got the poems of such friends as Johnson and Davidson published, as well as people like Francis Thompson and Laurence Binyon. In 1893 he edited the poems of Arthur Henry Hallam (Elkin Mathews and John Lane, 1893). He helped produce *The Yellow Book*. The book of verses *Robert Louis Stevenson, An Elegy, and Other Poems Mainly Personal* appeared in 1895, his successfully selling novel *The Quest of the Golden Girl* in 1896, and *Rubaiyat of Omar Khayam: A Paraphrase* in 1897. In 1891 Le Gallienne married Mildred Lee, a Liverpool waitress, who died in 1894 leaving Le Gallienne to look after their daughter. This grief is the subject of many of his verses – and Mildred became 'Angel' in his autobiographical novel *Young Love* (1899). In 1897 he married Juliet Norregard, a Danish journalist and railway magnate's daughter. This was not a success and he escaped from both her and the collapsing nineties literary scene (which he helped define in *The Romantic Nineties*, 1925) by departing in 1901 for the USA. In 1911 he married Irma Perry, an American sculptor's ex-wife (their daughter Gwen became a portrait painter). He settled in Paris in the late twenties, living by writing about French life for American papers. He continued publishing poems; but these were, as ever, a minor string to his bow. He and his wife took refuge in Monte Carlo during the German occupation of France, and he died, 14 September 1947, at Menton, where they'd had various homes since the early thirties. He is buried in the Menton cemetery near Aubrey Beardsley, his old nineties ally on *The Yellow Book*.

HAPPY LETTER

Fly, little note,
And know no rest
Till warm you lie
Within that nest
Which is her breast;
Though why to thee
Such joy should be

Who carest not,
While I must wait
Here desolate,   10
I cannot wot.
O what I'd do
To come with you!

English Poems *(John Lane, 1892). Text of 4th edn (1900).*

THE WORLD IS WIDE

The world is wide – around yon court,
    Where dirty little children play,
Another world of street on street
    Grows wide and wider every day.

And round the town for endless miles
    A great strange land of green is spread –
O wide the world, O weary-wide,
    But it is wider overhead.

For could you mount yon glittering stairs
    And on their topmost turret stand, –   10
Still endless shining courts and squares,
    And lanes of lamps on every hand.

And, might you tread those starry streets
    To where those long perspectives bend,
O you would cast you down and die –
    Street upon street, world without end.

English Poems *([1892], 1900).*

A BALLAD OF LONDON

(To H. W. Massingham)[1]

Ah, London! London! our delight,
Great flower that opens but at night,

Great City of the Midnight Sun,
Whose day begins when day is done.

A BALLAD OF LONDON
1 Liberal newspaper editor (1860–1924).

Lamp after lamp against the sky
Opens a sudden beaming eye,
Leaping alight on either hand,
The iron lilies of the Strand.

Like dragonflies, the hansoms hover,
With jewelled eyes, to catch the lover;   10
The streets are full of lights and loves,
Soft gowns, and flutter of soiled doves.

The human moths about the light
Dash and cling close in dazed delight,
And burn and laugh, the world and wife,
For this is London, this is life!

Upon thy petals butterflies,
But at thy root, some say, there lies
A world of weeping trodden things,
Poor worms that have not eyes or wings.   20

From out corruption of their woe
Springs this bright flower that charms us so,

Men die and rot deep out of sight
To keep this jungle-flower bright.

Paris and London, World-Flowers twain
Wherewith the World-Tree blooms again,
Since Time hath gathered Babylon,
And withered Rome still withers on.

Sidon and Tyre were such as ye,
How bright they shone upon the Tree!   30
But Time hath gathered, both are gone,
And no man sails to Babylon.

Ah, London! London! our delight,
For thee, too, the eternal night,
And Circe Paris hath no charm
To stay Time's unrelenting arm.

Time and his moths shall eat up all.
Your chiming towers proud and tall
He shall most utterly abase,
And set a desert in their place.   40

Robert Louis Stevenson, An Elegy, and Other Poems Mainly Personal
(John Lane, London; Copeland & Day, Boston, 1895).

JENNY DEAD

Like a flower in the frost
   Sweet Jenny lies,
With her frail hands calmly crossed,
   And close-shut eyes.

Bring a candle, for the room
   Is dark and cold,
Antechamber of the tomb –
   O grief untold!

Like a snowdrift is her bed,
   Dinted the snow,   10
Faint frozen lines from foot to head, –
   She lies below.

Turn from off her shrouded face
   The frigid sheet....
Death hath doubled all her grace –
   O Jenny, sweet!

Robert Louis Stevenson, An Elegy *(1895).*

AN INSCRIPTION

Precious the box that Mary brake
Of spikenard for her Master's sake,[1]
But ah! it held nought half so dear
As the sweet dust that whitens here.
The greater wonder who shall say:
To make so white a soul of clay,
From clay to win a face so fair,
Those strange great eyes, that sunlit hair

A-ripple o'er her witty brain, –
Or turn all back to dust again.   10

Who knows – but, in some happy hour,
The God whose strange alchemic power
Wrought her of dust, again may turn
To woman this immortal urn.

Robert Louis Stevenson, An Elegy *(1895).*

AN INSCRIPTION
1 Mark 14.3. Cf. Isa (Craig) Knox, 'The Box'.

SONG

She's somewhere in the sunlight strong,
   Her tears are in the falling rain,
She calls me in the wind's soft song,
   And with the flowers she comes again.

Yon bird is but her messenger,
   The moon is but her silver car;
Yea! sun and moon are sent by her,
   And every wistful waiting star.

Robert Louis Stevenson, An Elegy *(1895)*.

John (Henry) Gray (1866–1934)

John Gray, stereotypical poet of the nineties (alleged model for Wilde's Dorian Gray) was born, 9 March 1866, in the East End of London in Bethnal Green, first of the nine children of working-class parents (his father was a carpenter at Woolwich Royal Naval Dockyard, who became a stores inspector at Woolwich Arsenal). Gray left school at thirteen to become an apprentice metal-worker at the Arsenal, but, a clever lad, he attended evening classes with great energy, acquired French, German and Latin, studied art and music, fell in love with Keats. He passed the Civil Service examinations (1882), joined the Post Office as a clerk, passed the London University matriculation exams (1887), and went into the Foreign Office, becoming eventually one of its librarians. Aesthetic and sexual proclivities led him to trawl deep in bohemian waters. He was intimate with Charles Ricketts and Charles Shannon, francophile art students hanging out with other *Valistes* (Wilde's word) in Whistler's old home, the Vale, Chelsea. Gray contributed a piece on the Goncourt brothers to the first number of Ricketts and Shannon's magazine *The Dial*, August 1889. Through these connexions, Gray met Felix Fénéon, who was Laforgue's benefactor and publisher, Rimbaud's editor and a leading Symbolist critic. Gray became the translator of Verlaine, Mallarmé, Rimbaud; and such influences rubbed off on him enough to make him, temporarily at least, a kind of quintessential English Symbolist and decadent poet. He was baptized a Roman Catholic, 14 February 1890, but quickly lapsed into apostasy, dandyism and sexual prodigality, coached by Wilde, to whom he was very close in the period 1891–3. He read his poems to the Rhymers' Club, became well known in literary London as a beautiful Cockney Wunderkind and languid reciter, was lured away from the Wildean rough-trade ambience by Marc-André [Alexander Michaelson] Raffalovich, wealthy and epicene self-publishing Russian-Jewish arriviste and promoter of 'Uranian' love ('You cannot be Oscar's friend and mine'). Raffalovich pampered Gray and paid for the German convent education of Gray's sisters. The two wrote three plays together. Wilde's contract with Elkin Mathews and John Lane to finance Gray's first volume, *Silverpoints* (1893), fell through, which didn't hamper the volume's reputation for camp preciosity, not least in respect of its lovely arty binding. Fondly *pasticheurs*, highly Paterian,

Baudelarian, Laforguean – often forecasting the tones of early Eliot – Gray's verses also exhibit older English likings (Gray would go on to edit Campion, Drayton, Suckling, Sidney). They anglicize their Laforguean realisms with a kind of Cockney street-wisdom ('Geranium, houseleek', 'metal Burns'), what Richard Le Gallienne hinted at in his perceptive review (reprinted in his *Retrospective Reviews: A Literary Log*, I, *1891–1893* (1896)): 'in spite of his neo-Catholicism and his hot-house erotics, Mr Gray cannot accomplish that gloating abstraction from the larger life of humanity which marks the decadent'. The Wilde trials of 1895 seem to have precipitated Gray's turn away from the Uranian battlefield and his return in great self-hatred and moral panic to his Roman Catholicism. (Raffalovich converted from Judaism, early 1896.) *Spiritual Poems: Chiefly Done Out of Several Languages* (1896) marked this revolution. On 28 October 1898 Gray entered the Scots College in Rome to study for the priesthood (sustained by weekly hampers of luxury foodstuffs from Raffalovich). He was ordained in 1901, was posted at first to the Edinburgh slums, lived chastely in Edinburgh in close proximity to Raffalovich and his renowned salon, writing hymns, editing Aubrey Beardsley's *Last Letters* (1904) – Beardsley's deathbed conversion to Rome was under the influence of Gray and Raffalovich – translating saintly prayers, writing poems for the Virgin Mary (*Ad Matrem: Poems by John Gray*, 1904), contributing to *Blackfriars* magazine. There were two further volumes of mainly not-religious poetry, *The Long Road* (1926) and *Poems* (1931), and an odd religious-utopian novel, *Park: A Fantastic Story* (1932). From 1907 until his death, Gray was priest of St Peter's, the gorgeously decorated church specially built for him with large amounts of Raffalovich's money in the fashionable Morningside district of Edinburgh. He was a sort of father confessor to 'Michael Field' in Bradley and Cooper's late Catholic convert period. 'Father Silverpoints', as they knew him, devised the inscription for their tombstone at Richmond, designed by Ricketts: 'United in blood, united in Christ'. Stunned by the unexpected death of Raffalovich, 14 February 1934, Gray faded away, and died himself, 14 June 1934, aged sixty-eight, a well-loved parish priest, and canon of the Roman diocese of St Andrews and Edinburgh.

LES DEMOISELLES DE SAUVE[1]

To S. A. S. Alice, Princesse de Monaco[2]

Beautiful ladies through the orchard pass;
Bend under crutched-up branches, forked and low;
Trailing their samet[3] palls o'er dew-drenched grass.

Pale blossoms, looking on proud Jacqueline,
Blush to the colour of her finger tips,
And rosy knuckles, laced with yellow lace.

High-crested Berthe discerns, with slant, clinched eyes
Amid the leaves pink faces of the skies;
She locks her plaintive hands Sainte-Margot-wise.

Ysabeau follows last, with languorous pace;   10
Presses, voluptuous, to her bursting lips,
With backward stoop, a bunch of eglantine.

Courtly ladies through the orchard pass;
Bow low, as in lords' halls; and springtime grass
Tangles a snare to catch the tapering toe.

The Dial, *2 (1892), p.24.* Silverpoints *(Elkin Mathews & John Lane, 1893).*

THE BARBER

I

I dreamed I was a barber; and there went
Beneath my hand, oh! manes extravagant.
Beneath my trembling fingers, many a mask
Of many a pleasant girl. It was my task
To gild their hair, carefully, strand by strand;
To paint their eyebrows with a timid hand;
To draw a bodkin, from a vase of kohl,
Through the closed lashes; pencils from a bowl
Of sepia to paint them underneath;
To blow upon their eyes with a soft breath.   10
They lay them back and watched the leaping bands.

II

The dream grew vague. I moulded with my hands
The mobile breasts, the valley; and the waist
I touched; and pigments reverently placed
Upon their thighs in sapient spots and stains,
Beryls and crysolites and diaphanes,[1]
And gems whose hot harsh names are never said.
I was a masseur; and my fingers bled
With wonder as I touched their awful limbs.

LES DEMOISELLES DE SAUVE

1 an area of Provence.

2 second wife of Prince Albert of Monaco, later King Albert I of Monaco; a friend of Frank Harris.

3 samite.

THE BARBER

1 a word from Laforgue: 'O géraniums diaphanes' – in *La Vogue*, 6 Dec. 1886 – where *geraniums* are probably sexual organs. Quoted by T. S. Eliot, 'The Metaphysical Poets' (1921).

III

Suddenly, in the marble trough, there seems   20
O, last of my pale mistresses, Sweetness!
A twylipped scarlet pansie.[2] My caress
Tinges thy steelgray eyes to violet.
Adown thy body skips the pit-a-pat
Of treatment once heard in a hospital
For plagues that fascinate, but half appal.

IV

So, at the sound, the blood of me stood cold.
Thy chaste hair ripened into sullen gold.
The throat, the shoulders, swelled and were uncouth.
The breasts rose up and offered each a mouth.   30
And on the belly pallid blushes crept,
That maddened me, until I laughed and wept.

Silverpoints *(1893)*.

THE VINES

To André Chevrillon[1]

'Have you seen the listening snake?'
Bramble clutches for his bride,
Lately she was by his side,
Woodbine, with her gummy hands.

In the ground the mottled snake
Listens for the dawn of day;
Listens, listening death away,
Till the day burst winter's bands.

Painted ivy is asleep,
Stretched upon the bank, all torn,   10

Sinewy though she be; love-lorn
Convolvuluses cease to creep.

Bramble clutches for his bride,
Woodbine, with her gummy hands
All his horny claws expands;
She has withered in his grasp.

'Till the day dawn, till the tide
Of the winter's afternoon.'
'Who tells dawning?' – 'Listen, soon.'
Half-born tendrils, grasping, gasp.   20

Silverpoints *(1893)*.

Je pleure dans les coins; je n'ai plus goût à rien;
Oh! j'ai tant pleuré, Dimanche, en mon paroissien!
Jules Laforgue[1]

Did we not, Darling, you and I,
Walk on the earth like other men?
Did we not walk and wonder why
They spat upon us so. And then

We lay us down among fresh earth,
Sweet flowers breaking overhead,
Sore needed rest for our frail girth,
For our frail hearts; a well-sought bed.

So Spring came, and spread daffodils;   10
Summer, and fluffy bees sang on;
The fluffy bee knows us, and fills
His house with sweet to think upon.

Deep in the dear dust, Dear, we dream.
Our melancholy is a thing
At last our own; and none esteem
How our black lips are blackening.

2   female genitalia.
THE VINES
1   French man of letters (1864–1957); writer on English literature.
'DID WE NOT, DARLING, YOU AND I'
1   'I weep in corners; I've no desire for anything; Oh! I've wept so

much on Sundays for boredom.' 'Figurez-vous un peu' (pub. 1890).
Laforgue is a central figure in Arthur Symons's *The Symbolist Movement in Literature* (1899), so influential on e.g. T. S. Eliot.

And none note how our poor eyes fall,
Nor how our cheeks are sunk and sere...

Dear, when you waken, will you call?...
Alas! we are not very near.   20

Silverpoints *(1893)*.

POEM

To Arthur Edmonds[1]

Geranium, houseleek, laid in oblong beds
On the trim grass. The daisies' leprous stain
Is fresh. Each night the daisies burst again,
Though every day the gardener crops their heads.

A wistful child, in foul unwholesome shreds,
Recalls some legend of a daisy chain
That makes a pretty necklace. She would fain
Make one, and wear it, if she had some threads.

Sun, leprous flowers, foul child. The asphalt burns.
The garrulous sparrows perch on metal Burns.[2]   10
Sing! Sing! they say, and flutter with their wings.
He does not sing, he only wonders why
He is sitting there. The sparrows sing. And I
Yield to the strait allure of simple things.

Silverpoints *(1893)*.

SPLEEN

The roses every one were red,
And all the ivy leaves were black.

Sweet, do not even stir your head,
Or all of my despairs come back.

The sky is too blue, too delicate:
Too soft the air, too green the sea.

I fear – how long had I to wait! –
That you will tear yourself from me.

The shining box-leaves weary me,
The varnished holly's glistening,   10

The stretch of infinite country;
So, saving you, does everything.

Silverpoints *(1893)*. *A close translation of Verlaine's poem*
'Spleen' in Romances sans Paroles *(1874)*.

APRIL (1896)

Joyful table; and thereon
    Cakes and fruits of every sort;
    For the Infant holds a court,
With the help of cousin John.

Mulberries there be, and pears;
    Pompous grapes and pomegrenades
    Full of rubies laid in grades;
All the apple-woman's wares.

Cakes abundant be and buns;
    Cakes of mace and marzipan;   10
    Saffron cake and cakes of bran;
Gingerbreads and sallylunns.

Cousin John comes offering peaches
    Filled with velvet honey,
    Tasting, oh, of plots so sunny,
Which alone the wild bee reaches.

Jamie leading John his brother,
    Were the Fishers first to come;
    Whence the Child for joy was dumb;
For so much they loved each other.   20

Simon Peter came alone,
    Being bold and somewhat rude,
    (For as much as he withstood
Simon earned the name of Stone.)

POEM
1 Civil Service friend of Gray; died 1894.

2 statue of the writer Robert Burns.

Then came Andrew, Mark and Luke:
   Frisking Mark and Luke the stolid;
   Andrew grave, judicious, solid,
Bearing tablets, style and book.

All the guests were fair and slightly,
   Serious as grown-up men;   30
   Mild, like lambkins in a pen;
All but one behaved politely.

Only Judas smeared his lips,
   Made his mouth in dreadful shapes,
   Snatched the peaches, tore the grapes,
Fed the parrot with the pips.

Kind Saint Anne and sweet Saint Mary
   Sat a little way apart.
   While she talked Saint Mary's heart,
Ah, her watchful heart was wary!   40

The Blue Calendar *(1896). Text,* The Poems of John Gray, *ed. Ian Fletcher
(ELT Press, Dept. of English, Univ. of North Carolina, Greensboro, NC,
USA, 1988). The* Blue Calendars *are a series of 4 small calendars (1895–8),
typically around 30 pages each, in plain blue paper covers, with a poem by Gray for
every month. Privately printed (the three I've seen: by W. R. Folkard & Son,
Bloomsbury, London), for distribution to friends. Very rare (I've not been able to
see a copy for 1896).*

Dora Sigerson (Mrs Clement Shorter) (1866–1918)

Dora Sigerson, fervently Irish poet, painter and sculptor, was the elder of two daughters who grew up in a cultured and republican Dublin family. Her mother, Hester Varian, was a poet and novelist; her father, Dr George Sigerson, translated Irish verse. Dora and her sister Katharine stayed loyal to Parnell when his publicized adultery split the Republican cause. Dora's first published verses were in the *Catholic Irish Monthly,* and her first volume, *Verses,* came out in 1893. In 1896 she married Clement Shorter, the critic, and editor of the *London Illustrated News.* She settled in London, where she knew many of the English writers of her day – Hardy, Swinburne, Meredith (who introduced her *Collected Poems,* 1907) – but her best friends were Irish: Katharine Tynan, Yeats, Alice Furlong. In time-honoured Irish émigré fashion her heart was always in Ireland. Her verse – twenty volumes of it – reflects this homesickness, especially the ballads and recycled legends which became her trademark. She died in 1918, heartbroken, it was said, after the failure of the 1916 Easter Rising of republicans in Dublin, worn out in working for prisoners and the cause. Her best-known sculpture is her memorial to the patriots of 1916, now in the Dublin graveyard where she is buried. Katharine Tynan's homage and recollections are in Sigerson's posthumous volume *The Sad Years and Other Poems* (1918). In 1923 her friends Katharine Tynan, Eva Gore-Booth and Alice Furlong brought out a memorial volume.

IN WINTRY WEATHER

Dear, in wintry weather,
How close we crept together!
The storms, with all their thunder,
Could not our fond hands sunder.
No sorrow followed after
Cold words or scornful laughter.
How close we crept together,
Through all the wintry weather!

Dear, when each rose uncurled
To its sweet narrow world,
You went to cull their glory;   10
You would not hear my story,
Too sweet the birds were singing,
Too fair the buds were swinging.
If I should come or go
You did not care to know.

When each sweet rose uncurled
To its unknown world,
How could you e'er remember
That in a bleak December,   20
Through all the bitter weather,
We crept so close together?

Verses, by Dora Sigerson (Elliot Stock, 1893).

A Summer's Day

Well, love, so be it as you say,
Just the hours of a summer's day,
And no sighing for what comes after,
Whether it is tears or laughter.

Take my hand, and we go together
Into love's land of golden weather.
You to be king and I for queen;
Right royally to reign, I ween.

Cool amber wine in cups of gold
Bring maids, in rosy fingers' hold,   10
Lip-pledged, but, you'll say ere your drinking,
My kiss were sweeter to your thinking.

And youths shall rob the spring for me
Of all the perfumed flowers that be;
I'll seek your eyes, and they refusing,
I'll answer only at your choosing.

So, love, your hand, and we away,
Just the hours of a summer's day,
And no weeping for what comes after –
If it be tears, we've had our laughter.   20

Verses (1893).

The Lover

I go through wet spring woods alone,
Through sweet green woods with heart of stone,
My weary foot upon the grass
Falls heavy as I pass.
The cuckoo from the distance cries,
The lark a pilgrim in the skies;
But all the pleasant spring is drear.
I want you, dear!

I pass the summer meadows by,
The autumn poppies bloom and die;   10
I speak alone so bitterly
For no voice answers me.
'O lovers parting by the gate,
O robin singing to your mate,
Plead you well, for she will hear,
"I love you, dear!"'

I crouch alone, unsatisfied,
Mourning by winter's fireside.
O Fate, what evil wind you blow.
Must this be so?   20
No southern breezes come to bless,
So conscious of their emptiness
My lonely arms I spread in woe,
I want you so.

The Fairy Changeling and Other Poems, *by Dora Sigerson (Mrs Clement Shorter)*
(John Lane: The Bodley Head, 1898). Titled 'The Deserted Lover' in Dora Sigerson Shorter,
Collected Poems, *Intro. George Meredith (Hodder & Stoughton, 1907).*

A VAGRANT HEART

O to be a woman! to be left to pique and pine,
When the winds are out and calling to this vagrant heart of mine.
Whisht! it whistles at the windows, and how can I be still?
There! the last leaves of the beech-tree go dancing down the hill.
All the boats at anchor they are plunging to be free –
O to be a sailor, and away across the sea!
When the sky is black with thunder, and the sea is white with foam,
The grey-gulls whirl up shrieking and seek their rocky home,
Low his boat is lying leeward, how she runs upon the gale,
As she rises with the billows, nor shakes her dripping sail.   10
There is danger on the waters – there is joy where dangers be –
Alas! to be a woman and the nomad's heart in me.

Ochone! to be a woman, only sighing on the shore –
With a soul that finds a passion for each long breaker's roar,
With a heart that beats as restless as all the winds that blow –
Thrust a cloth between her fingers, and tell her she must sew;
Must join in empty chatter, and calculate with straws –
For the weighing of our neighbour – for the sake of social laws.
O chatter, chatter, chatter, when to speak is misery,
When silence lies around your heart – and night is on the sea.   20
So tired of little fashions that are root of all our strife,
Of all the petty passions that upset the calm of life.
The law of God upon the land shines steady for all time;
The laws confused that man has made, have reason not nor rhyme.

O bird that fights the heavens, and is blown beyond the shore,
Would you leave your flight and danger for a cage to fight no more?
No more the cold of winter, or the hunger of the snow,
Nor the winds that blow you backward from the path you wish to go?
Would you leave your world of passion for a home that knows no riot?
Would I change my vagrant longings for a heart more full of quiet?   30
No! – for all its dangers, there is joy in danger too:
On, bird, and fight your tempests, and this nomad heart with you!

The seas that shake and thunder will close our mouths one day,
The storms that shriek and whistle will blow our breaths away.
The dust that flies and whitens will mark not where we trod.
What matters then our judging? we are face to face with God.

The Fairy Changeling and Other Poems *(1898).*

THE WIND ON THE HILLS

Go not to the hills of Erin[1]
When the night winds are about,
Put up your bar and shutter,
And so keep the danger out.

For the good-folk whirl within it,
And they pull you by the hand,
And they push you on the shoulder,
Till you move to their command.

And lo! you have forgotten
What you have known of tears,   10
And you will not remember
That the world goes full of years;

A year there is a lifetime,
And a second but a day,
And an older world will meet you
Each morn you come away.

Your wife grows old with weeping,
And your children one by one
Grow grey with nights of watching,
Before your dance is done.   20

And it will chance some morning
You will come home no more;
Your wife sees but a withered leaf
In the wind about the door.

And your children will inherit
The unrest of the wind,
They shall seek some face elusive,
And some land they never find.

When the wind is loud, they sighing
Go with hearts unsatisfied,   30
For some joy beyond remembrance,
For some memory denied.

And all your children's children,
They cannot sleep or rest,
When the wind is out in Erin
And the sun is in the West.

Ballads & Poems, *by Dora Sigerson (Mrs Clement Shorter)*
(James Bowden, 1899).

THE RAIN

This is the rhyme of the rain on the roof,
Tears, all tears, slow falling tears —
If this is the warp, then what is the woof?
Flesh that sorrows and flesh that fears.

THE WIND ON THE HILLS
1 Ireland.

Ah! poor humanity, weeping sore,
Guilt and sorrow, anger and shame,
Oh! who could peace on this earth restore?
Who shall punish and who shall blame?

Here where a God, loved much, was slain.
Since He hath failed, then who can win?   10
On the thirsting ground let them fall again,
Tears of sorrow and tears of sin.

As The Sparks Fly Upward: Poems and Ballads, *by Dora Sigerson Shorter*
(Alexander Moring, The De la Mare Press, [1904]).

Ernest (Christopher) Dowson (1867–1900)

Quintessential nineties bohemian poet Ernest Dowson was born in Lee, in London, the son of a Limehouse dry-dock owner. His education was private, parental and sporadic, but his early continental experience did help on his great love of French literature and culture (he spent much time with his invalid parents on the Riviera and in Italy). He entered The Queen's College, Oxford, in 1886, fell under the influence of Pater, became great friends with Lionel Johnson, and went down in March 1887, flunking his Honour Moderations (Classics) exam papers, in order to lead as far as would be possible a bohemian and aesthetic existence. For a time he worked in his father's declining business, but his heart was in writerly London. He fell in eagerly with the Rhymers' Club and was greatly friendly with Aubrey Beardsley. He contributed to each *Book of the Rhymers' Club* (1892 and 1894), to *The Yellow Book* (1894) and the *Savoy* (1896). 'Non sum qualis eram,' one of the twelve poems of Dowson's in the Rhymers' Club Books, the 'archetypal decadent poem of the 1890s', according to John Sloan, biographer of Rhymers' Club satirist John Davidson (typically, Davidson thought it over-rated), was said to have been written at a bar-room table in 1891 after several glasses of absinthe. It used to be speculated that the poem reflected Dowson's curious infatuation with Adelaide Foltinowicz, daughter of a Polish-German bar-owner in Soho with whom he fell in love in 1891 when she was only twelve. But did the alleged absinthe intake occur in London or in Paris? Dowson certainly travelled easily between the two capitals, and he did many translations from the French – Voltaire, Zola, Balzac, Edmond de Goncourt. His great idol was Verlaine after that poet's public lecture of 1893. Dowson's single volume of poems, *Verses*, appeared in 1896. He produced two novels (with Arthur Moore), *A Comedy of Masks* (1893) and *Adrian Rome* (1899). His play *Pierrot of the Minute* was published in 1897 with Beardsley illustrations – the year that his Lolita the bar-owner's daughter broke with him. The suicide of his parents did not make for cheerfulness and his alcoholism got worse in the later nineties. After 1895 he tended to spend most of his time bumming about in France. He sought out Wilde in his post-imprisonment exile in France – Wilde liked Dowson's verse and his company ('You were wonderful and charming all last night'), and it was Dowson who persuaded Wilde to try sex with women again (the Dieppe prostitute, said Wilde, 'was like chewing cold mutton'). Dowson was at the Paris performance of Wilde's *Salomé* (11 February 1896) with Beardsley. Down-at-heel, destitute, sick, alcoholic, Dowson died in London, 23 February 1900. 'Poor wounded fellow that he was: a tragic reproduction of all tragic poetry, like a symbol, or a scene. I hope bay leaves will be laid on his tomb, and rue, and myrtle, too, for he knew what love is', wrote Wilde.

VITAE SUMMA BREVIS SPEM NOS VETAT INCOHARE LONGAM[1]

They are not long, the weeping and the laughter,
    Love and desire and hate:
I think they have no portion in us after
    We pass the gate.

VITAE SUMMA BREVIS
1   Horace, *Carmina*, I.iv.15: 'The brevity of life forbids us to go in for any far-reaching hope.'

They are not long, the days of wine and roses:
   Out of a misty dream
Our path emerges for a while, then closes
   Within a dream.

Verses *(Henry King, 1896).*

NON SUM QUALIS ERAM BONAE SUB REGNO CYNARAE[1]

Last night, ah, yesternight, betwixt her lips and mine
There fell thy shadow, Cynara! thy breath was shed
Upon my soul between the kisses and the wine;
And I was desolate and sick of an old passion,
   Yea, I was desolate and bowed my head:
I have been faithful to thee, Cynara! in my fashion.

All night upon mine heart I felt her warm heart beat,
Night-long within mine arms in love and sleep she lay;
Surely the kisses of her bought red mouth were sweet;
But I was desolate and sick of an old passion,   10
   When I awoke and found the dawn was gray:
I have been faithful to thee, Cynara! in my fashion.

I have forgot much, Cynara! gone with the wind,
Flung roses, roses riotously with the throng,
Dancing, to put thy pale, lost lilies out of mind;
But I was desolate and sick of an old passion,
   Yea, all the time, because the dance was long:
I have been faithful to thee, Cynara! in my fashion.

I cried for madder music and for stronger wine,
But when the feast is finished and the lamps expire,   20
Then falls thy shadow, Cynara! the night is thine;
And I am desolate and sick of an old passion,
   Yea hungry for the lips of my desire:
I have been faithful to thee, Cynara! in my fashion.

Verses *(1896). Appeared earlier in* The Second Book of the Rhymers' Club
(Elkin Mathews & John Lane, 1894), with breast *for* heart *(l.7).*

SPLEEN

For Arthur Symons

I was not sorrowful, I could not weep,
And all my memories were put to sleep.

I watched the river grow more white and strange,
All day till evening I watched it change.

All day till evening I watched the rain
Beat wearily upon the window pane.

NON SUM QUALIS ERAM
1 Horace, *Carmina*, IV.i.3–4: 'I am no longer the man I was when
ruled over by the good Cynara.'

I was not sorrowful, but only tired
Of everything that ever I desired.

Her lips, her eyes, all day became to me
The shadow of a shadow utterly.   10

All day mine hunger for her heart became
Oblivion, until the evening came,

And left me sorrowful, inclined to weep,
With all my memories that could not sleep.

Verses *(1896)*.

Ah, dans ces mornes séjours
Les jamais sont les toujours.[1]
Paul Verlaine

You would have understood me, had you waited;
    I could have loved you, dear! as well as he:
Had we not been impatient, dear! and fated
        Always to disagree.

What is the use of speech? Silence were fitter:
    Lest we should still be wishing things unsaid.
Though all the words we ever spake were bitter,
        Shall I reproach you dead?

Nay, let this earth, your portion, likewise cover
    All the old anger, setting us apart: 10
Always, in all, in truth was I your lover;
        Always, I held your heart.

I have met other women who were tender,
    As you were cold, dear! with a grace as rare.
Think you, I turned to them, or made surrender,
        I who had found you fair?

Had we been patient, dear! ah, had you waited,
    I had fought death for you, better than he:
But from the very first, dear! we were fated
        Always to disagree.   20

Late, late, I come to you, now death discloses
    Love that in life was not to be our part:
On your low lying mound between the roses,
        Sadly I cast my heart.

I would not waken you: nay! this is fitter;
    Death and the darkness give you unto me;
Here we who loved so, were so cold and bitter,
        Hardly can disagree.

Verses *(1896)*. *Appeared earlier in* The Second Book of the
Rhymers' Club *(1894)*.

'YOU WOULD HAVE UNDERSTOOD ME, HAD YOU WAITED'
1 'Ah, on these grim visits, nevers turn out to be alwayses.'

TERRE PROMISE[1]

For Herbert P. Horne[2]

Even now the fragrant darkness of her hair
Had brushed my cheek; and once, in passing by,
Her hand upon my hand lay tranquilly:
What things unspoken trembled in the air!

Always I know, how little severs me
From mine heart's country, that is yet so far;
And must I lean and long across a bar,
That half a word would shatter utterly?

Ah might it be, that just by touch of hand,
Or speaking silence, shall the barrier fall;   10
And she shall pass, with no vain words at all,
But droop into mine arms, and understand!

Verses *(1896)*.

Lionel (Pigot) Johnson (1867–1902)

Lionel Johnson, critic, poet, friend of Yeats, and drunk, was born at Broadstairs, Kent, 15 March 1867, into an old military family with Anglo-Indian and aristocratic connexions. He was the third son of an infantry captain, William Victor Johnson (who was second son of a baronet and grandson of a general and baronet), and his wife Catherine Delicia Walters. One of Johnson's cousins was the novelist Olivia (Tucker) Shakespear, lover of Yeats and mother of Dorothy Shakespear, who became Ezra Pound's wife. He went on a scholarship to Winchester, 1880–6 (where he won all the English essay and poetry prizes and edited *The Wykehamist*), before going up to New College, Oxford (October 1886) on a Winchester Scholarship to read Classics. He gained a Second Class in Classical Moderations in 1888 and a First in Literae Humaniores in 1890. At Oxford he fell strongly under the influence of Pater and drifted steadily towards Roman Catholicism. After Oxford he headed straight for literary London, living in a kind of aesthetic colony at 20 Fitzroy Street with Herbert Horne, architect and critic, and Selwyn Image, the artist and poet, who ran the Century Guild, an arts and crafts promotion society, from that address. He paid off his university debts by hacking for the journals, kept polishing his poems, matured as a critic (his essay celebrating Pater was in the *Fortnightly Review*, September 1894), prepared his book on Hardy (which also appeared in 1894: 'very wonderful', Yeats thought). He soon fell in with Yeats and the London Celts, discovered his Irish roots, became from its start in 1890 a keen member of the Rhymers' Club, along with Dowson, Le Gallienne, Davidson, Symons, Plarr, Ernest Radford and other London bohemians, decadents and would-be Symbolists. His poems appeared in the first and the second *Book of the Rhymers' Club* (1892 and 1894). He was received into the Church of Rome, 22 June 1891; worked on a kind of guide book to Chelsea with Richard Le Gallienne (*Bits of Old Chelsea*, 1894); supported the causes of Irish nationalism, and visited Ireland in 1893, 1894 and 1898. He was Yeats's 'most intimate friend', at least for the first half of the nineties. Yeats relished not least Johnson's vast learning and copious reading. In the later part of the decade Johnson lodged variously in London's Inns of Court ('Oxford in London', he thought), sinking lower and lower into the alcoholism (two bottles of whisky a day: source of loud assertiveness about literature and religion and also of terrible glooms) which alienated his friends, including Yeats. Tiny (5′2″ – his growth allegedly restricted after childhood glandular fever), epicene ('like a minnow, or an anatomical preparation', thought Davidson), a creature of solipsistic night-time study (he slept all day), Johnson lost touch, Yeats reckoned, with the 'accident, the unexpected, the confusion of nature', imagining friendships and conversations, all oddly reminiscent of Pater's solipsistic 'Sebastian Van Storck'. 'In him more than all others one can study the tragedy of that generation. When the soul turns from practical ends and becomes

TERRE PROMISE
1 Promised Land.

2 architect, poet, critic (friend of Lionel Johnson too); founder of *The Century Guild Hobby Horse*; died, Italy, April 1916.

contemplative, when it ceases to be a wheel spun by the whole machine, it is responsible for itself, an unendurable burden. Not yet ready for the impression of the divine will, it floats in the unnatural emptiness between the natural and the supernatural orders. Johnson had refused rather than failed to live...' (thus Yeats in the *Memoirs*, ed. Denis Donoghue, 1972, pp. 96–7). Even the agonistic mournfulness of his verses seems paled and dilute. Had the times permitted, his published volumes, *Poems* (1895) and *Ireland: With Other Poems* (1897), would undoubtedly have been more openly homoerotic, more explicit about his 'Dark Angel'. His Latin poem to Wilde in gratitude for *Dorian Gray* and its 'poma sodorum' and 'peccata dulcia' (apples of Sodom, and sweet sins) only appeared posthumously in 1928. Johnson died of a ruptured blood vessel after falling drunkenly off a chair in the Green Dragon pub in Fleet Street: 'much falling he/Brooded upon sanctity', as Yeats's poem 'In Memory of Major Robert Gregory'

puts it, a bit cruelly. Yeats selected the *Twenty-One Poems*, published in 1905 by Elkin Mathews, Johnson's old publisher. *Poetical Works* appeared in 1915. In his Introduction to his *Selected Poems of Ezra Pound* (1928) T. S. Eliot dwells on the lingering 'shades' of Dowson and Johnson in Pound's early work, and reminds us that Pound edited and introduced a volume of Johnson ('hastily withdrawn' by the publisher). In Pound's 'Hugh Selwyn Mauberley', Monsieur Verog (i.e. Victor Plarr)

> Told me how Johnson (Lionel) died
> By falling from a high stool in a pub...
>
> But showed no trace of alcohol
> At the autopsy, privately performed –
> Tissue preserved – the pure mind
> Arose toward Newman as the whisky warmed.

VICTORY

To George Moore[1]

Down the white steps, into the night, she came;
Wearing white roses, lit by the full moon:
And white upon the shadowy lawn she stood,
Waiting and watching for the dawn's first flame,
Over the dark and visionary wood.
Down the white steps, into the night, she came;
Wearing white roses, lit by the full moon.

Night died away: and over the deep wood
Widened a rosy cloud, a chilly flame:
The shadowy lawn grew cold, and clear, and white.   10
Then down she drew against her eyes her hood,
To hide away the inexorable light.
Night died away: and over the deep wood
Widened a rosy cloud, a chilly flame.

Then back she turned, and up the white steps came,
And looked into a room of burning lights.
Still slept her loveless husband his brute sleep,
Beside the comfortless and ashen flame:
Her lover waited, where the wood was deep.
She turned not back: but from the white steps came,   20
And went into the room of burning lights.

Dated 1888. Ireland: With Other Poems *(Elkin Mathews, 1897).*

VICTORY
1 Irish writer (1852–1933).

THE CHURCH OF A DREAM

To Bernhard Berenson[1]

Sadly the dead leaves rustle in the whistling wind,
Around the weather-worn, gray church, low down the vale:
The Saints in golden vesture shake before the gale;
The glorious windows shake, where still they dwell enshrined;
Old Saints, by long dead, shrivelled hands, long since designed:
There still, although the world autumnal be, and pale,
Still in their golden vesture the old saints prevail;
Alone with Christ, desolate else, left by mankind.

Only one ancient Priest offers the Sacrifice,
Murmuring holy Latin immemorial: 10
Swaying with tremulous hands the old censer full of spice,
In gray, sweet incense clouds; blue, sweet clouds mystical:
To him, in place of men, for he is old, suffice
Melancholy remembrances and vesperal.

Dated 1890. Poems *(Elkin Mathews, 1895).*

THE AGE OF A DREAM

To Christopher Whall[1]

Imageries of dreams reveal a gracious age:
Black armour, falling lace, and altar lights at morn.
The courtesy of Saints, their gentleness and scorn,
Lights on an earth more fair, than shone from Plato's page:
The courtesy of knights, fair calm and sacred rage:
The courtesy of love, sorrow for love's sake borne.
Vanished, those high conceits! Desolate and forlorn,
We hunger against hope for that lost heritage.

Gone now, the carven work! Ruined, the golden shrine!
No more the glorious organs pour their voice divine;   10
No more rich frankincense drifts through the Holy Place:
Now from the broken tower, what solemn bell still tolls,
Mourning what piteous death? Answer, O saddened souls!
Who mourn the death of beauty and the death of grace.

Dated 1890. Poems *(1895).*

THE ROMAN STAGE

To Hugh Orange

A man of marble holds the throne,
With looks composed and resolute:
Till death, a prince whom princes own,
Draws near to touch the marble mute.

THE CHURCH OF A DREAM
1   Bernard Berenson (Bernhard Valvrojenski), connoisseur, collector,
art historian (1865–1959).

THE AGE OF A DREAM
1   artist in stained glass.

The play is over: good my friends!
Murmur the pale lips: *your applause!*
With what a grace the actor ends:
How loyal to dramatic laws!

A brooding beauty on his brow;
Irony brooding over sin: 10
The next imperial actor now
Bids the satiric piece begin.

Dated 1891. Poems (1895).

THE DARK ANGEL

Dark Angel, with thine aching lust
To rid the world of penitence:
Malicious Angel, who still dost
My soul such subtile violence!

Because of thee, no thought, no thing,
Abides for me undesecrate:
Dark Angel, ever on the wing,
Who never reachest me too late!

When music sounds, then changest thou
Its silvery to a sultry fire: 10
Nor will thine envious heart allow
Delight untortured by desire.

Through thee, the gracious Muses turn
To Furies, O mine Enemy!¹
And all the things of beauty burn
With flames of evil ecstasy.

Because of thee, the land of dreams
Becomes a gathering place of fears:
Until tormented slumber seems
One vehemence of useless tears.   20

When sunlight glows upon the flowers,
Or ripples down the dancing sea:
Thou, with thy troop of passionate powers,
Beleaguerest, bewilderest, me.

Within the breath of autumn woods,
Within the winter silences:
Thy venomous spirit stirs and broods,
O Master of impieties!

The ardour of red flame is thine,
And thine the steely soul of ice: 30
Thou poisonest the fair design
Of nature, with unfair device.

THE DARK ANGEL
1 'hast thou found me, O mine enemy?' I Kings 21.20.

Apples of ashes, golden bright;
Waters of bitterness, how sweet!
O banquet of a foul delight,
Prepared by thee, dark Paraclete![2]

Thou art the whisper in the gloom,
The hinting tone, the haunting laugh:
Thou art the adorner of my tomb,
The minstrel of mine epitaph.   40

I fight thee, in the Holy Name!
Yet, what thou dost, is what God saith:
Tempter! should I escape thy flame,
Thou wilt have helped my soul from Death:

The second Death,[3] that never dies,
That cannot die, when time is dead:
Live Death, wherein the lost soul cries,
Eternally uncomforted.

Dark Angel, with thine aching lust!
Of two defeats, of two despairs: 50
Less dread, a change to drifting dust,
Than thine eternity of cares.

Do what thou wilt, thou shalt not so,
Dark Angel! triumph over me:
Lonely, unto the Lone I go;
Divine, to the Divinity.

Dated 1893. Poems (1895). Appeared earlier in The Second Book of the
Rhymers' Club *(Elkin Mathews & John Lane, 1894).*

(Joseph) Hilaire (Pierre René) Belloc (1870–1953)

Hilaire Belloc, poet, novelist, radical-rightist and Roman Catholic polemicist, had a gloriously mixed cultural inheritance. He was born, a French citizen, at St Cloud, near Paris, 17 July 1870. His grandfather, Hilaire Belloc, was a French painter with pictures in the Louvre, who married French-Irish Louise Swanton. His mother, the writer Bessie Rayner Parkes, was a Roman Catholic convert from a great dissident clan of Birmingham Unitarians (her great-grandfather was Joseph Priestley, the Birmingham radical; her father, Joseph Parkes, helped found the Reform Club). Hilaire Belloc's sister achieved renown as the writer Marie Belloc-Lowndes. His father, Louis Belloc, died in 1872. Mrs Belloc brought her young family to London, lost heavily on the Stock Exchange, and retreated to Sussex. Here the young Hilaire acquired that love of the South Downs and tramping about in the open air which infected all his life and writing, and helped define the Georgian atmosphere of hob-nailed gents and poems washed down with pints of rural ale. At the age of ten Belloc was packed off to Cardinal Newman's Oratory School in Edgbaston, Birmingham. He left at sixteen, studied in Paris, worked as a young radical for the London Dock Strike of 1889, travelled about France on a new-fangled bicycle for the *Pall Mall Gazette*, walked infatuated across the United States to California in pursuit of Elodie Hogan, the Irish-American Catholic girl who later became his wife, and did his military service in the French artillery. He went up to Balliol College, Oxford, as a relatively mature student of twenty-two, funded by his sister and her fiancé Frederick Lowndes. A resounding success (Brackenbury History Scholar, a First in History Finals, President of the Debating Union), his views were already setting into his arresting mix of French Revolutionism, Roman Catholicism and anti-Semitism (he was an

2   the Apples of Sodom were full of ashes; bitter waters of Marah, Genesis 15.23; Paraclete: the Holy Ghost.

3   Revelation 20.6.

anti-Dreyfusard). *The Bad Child's Book of Beasts* (1896) was a great success, and it was volumes like that and *Cautionary Tales for Children* (1907), with such blackly comic little Rake's Progresses in verse for kiddies as 'Henry King Who Chewed Bits of String, and Was Early Cut Off in Dreadful Agonies', and 'Rebecca Who Slammed Doors for Fun and Perished Miserably', which made Belloc's name, rather than the heartfelt adult, and ideological, things he was clearly capable of (as in his first volume of poems, *Verses and Sonnets* (1896), and his *Verses* (1910)). Failing to get a permanent academic post in Oxford he drifted into journalism and into writing merely for money (there were some 150 books all told, often French and Catholic in theme – essays, travel books, novels, history, politics, religion: after all, he had three sons and two daughters to educate). He edited journals, campaigned against the Boer War, was Liberal MP for Salford for several years from 1906, turned against the party system in British politics, was embroiled in the exposure of the Liberal Government's Marconi shares scandal of 1912. His stance as defender of white-man Catholicism allied him closely with his friend G. K. Chesterton and also with G. K.'s more distasteful brother Cecil in his ur-fascistic obsession with the power of Jewish financiers. Belloc wrote himself almost into the ground, not least in his popular First World War *Land and Water* weekly, with its close analysis of military events. His oldest son was killed in the First World War, his youngest in the Second. He remained in mourning for his wife (black clothes, black-edged notepaper) from her death in 1914 to his, 17 July 1953 (his last years impaired by a brain-enfeebling stroke).

THE NIGHT

Most holy Night, that still dost keep
The keys of all the doors of sleep,
To me when my tired eyelids close
    Give thou repose.

And let the far lament of them
That chaunt the dead day's requiem
Make in my ears, who wakeful lie,
    Soft lullaby.

Bid them that guard the sacred moon
By my bedside their memories croon;
So shall I have strange dreams and blest
    In my brief rest.   10

Fold thy great wings about my face,
Hide day-dawn from my resting-place,
And cheat me with thy false delight,
    Most holy Night.

Verses and Sonnets *(Ward & Downey Limited, 1896).*

THE POOR OF LONDON

Almighty God, whose Justice, like a sun
Shall coruscate along the floors of heaven:
Raising what's low, perfecting what's undone,
Breaking the proud, and making odd things even.
The Poor of Jesus Christ along the street
In your rain sodden, in your snows unshod,
They have nor hearth, nor roof, nor daily meat,
Nor even the bread of men; Almighty God.

The Poor of Jesus Christ whom no man hears
Have called upon your vengeance much too long.   10
Wipe out not tears but blood: our eyes bleed tears:

Come, smite our damnèd sophistries so strong,
That thy rude hammer battering this rude wrong
Ring down the abyss of twice ten thousand years.

Verses and Sonnets (1896).

THE JUSTICE OF THE PEACE

Distinguish carefully between these two,
   This thing is yours, that other thing is mine.
You have a shirt, a brimless hat, a shoe
   And half a coat. I am the Lord benign
Of fifty hundred acres of fat land
To which I have a right. You understand?

I have a right because I have, because,
   Because I have – because I have a right.
Now be quite calm and good, obey the laws,
   Remember your low station, do not fight   10
Against the goad, because, you know, it pricks
Whenever the uncleanly demos kicks.[1]

I do not envy you your hat, your shoe.
   Why should you envy me my small estate?
It's fearfully illogical in you
   To fight with economic force and fate.
Moreover, I have got the upper hand,
And mean to keep it. Do you understand?

Verses and Sonnets (1896).

THE SOUTH COUNTRY

When I am living in the Midlands
   That are sodden and unkind,
I light my lamp in the evening:
   My work is left behind;
And the great hills of the South Country
   Come back into my mind.

The great hills of the South Country
   They stand along the sea;
And it's there walking in the high woods
   That I could wish to be,   10
And the men that were boys when I was a boy
   Walking along with me.

The men that live in North England
   I saw them for a day:
Their hearts are set upon the waste fells,
   Their skies are fast and grey;

THE JUSTICE OF THE PEACE
1   cf. the Lord to Saul (St Paul) on road to Damascus: 'it is hard for
thee to kick against the pricks': Acts 9.5, 26.14 ('pricks' = goads).

From their castle-walls a man may see
  The mountains far away.

The men that live in West England
  They see the Severn strong,
A rolling on rough water brown   20
  Light aspen leaves along.
They have the secret of the Rocks,
  And the oldest kind of song.

But the men that live in the South Country
  Are the kindest and most wise,
They get their laughter from the loud surf,
  And the faith in their happy eyes
Comes surely from our Sister the Spring
  When over the sea she flies;   30
The violets suddenly bloom at her feet,
  She blesses us with surprise.

I never get between the pines
  But I smell the Sussex air;
Nor I never come on a belt of sand
  But my home is there.
And along the sky the line of the Downs
  So noble and so bare.

A lost thing could I never find,
  Nor a broken thing mend:
And I fear I shall be all alone   40
  When I get towards the end.
Who will there be to comfort me
  Or who will be my friend?

I will gather and carefully make my friends
  Of the men of the Sussex Weald,
They watch the stars from silent folds,
  They stiffly plough the field.
By them and the God of the South Country
  My poor soul shall be healed.   50

If I ever become a rich man,
  Or if ever I grow to be old,
I will build a house with deep thatch
  To shelter me from the cold,
And there shall the Sussex songs be sung
  And the story of Sussex told.

I will hold my house in the high wood
  Within a walk of the sea,
And the men that were boys when I was a boy
  Shall sit and drink with me.   60

Verses (Duckworth & Co., 1910).

ON THE GIFT OF A BOOK TO A CHILD

Child! do not throw this book about!
   Refrain from the unholy pleasure
Of cutting all the pictures out!
   Preserve it as your chiefest treasure.

Child, have you never heard it said
   That you are heir to all the ages?
Why, then, your hands were never made
   To tear these beautiful thick pages!

Your little hands were made to take
   The better things and leave the worse ones: 10
They also may be used to shake
   The Massive Paws of Elder Persons.

And when your prayers complete the day,
   Darling, your little tiny hands
Were also made, I think, to pray
   For men that lose their fairylands.

Verses *(1910)*.

Further Reading

Place of publication: where not stated, assume London; usually, where an individual publisher has two centres, only the first location is cited.

Abbreviations: U = University; P = Press; UP = University Press; ed(s) = editor(s); *BJRL* = *Bulletin of the John Rylands Library*; *CI* = *Critical Inquiry*; *CJ* = *Cambridge Journal*; *EinC* = *Essays in Criticism*; *ELH* = *English Literary History*; *ELT* = *English Literature in Transition*; *MLQ* = *Modern Languages Quarterly*; *PMLA* = *Publications of the Modern Languages Association of North America*; *TP* = *Textual Practice*; *VP* = *Victorian Poetry*; *VS* = *Victorian Studies*.

Anthologies

Adams, W. Davenport, ed., *The Comic Poets of the Nineteenth Century: Poems of Wit and Humour by Living Writers* (George Routledge & Sons, 1876).

Amis, Kingsley, ed., *The New Oxford Book of Light Verse* (Oxford UP, Oxford, 1978).

Armstrong, Isobel; Bristow, Joseph; Sharrock, Cath, eds, *Nineteenth-Century Women Poets* (Clarendon P, Oxford, 1996).

Auden, W. H., ed., *Nineteenth Century Minor Poets* (Faber & Faber, 1967).

Breen, Jennifer, ed., *Victorian Women Poets 1830–1900: An Anthology* (Everyman, J. M. Dent, 1994).

Bristow, Joseph, ed., *The Victorian Poet: Poetics and Persona* (Croom Helm, 1987).

Dixon, W. Macneile, ed., *The Edinburgh Book of Scottish Verse 1300–1900* (Meiklejohn & Holden, 1910).

Geraths, Armin; Herget, Kurt; Collier, Gordon; Wächter, Bernd, eds, *Viktorianische Lyrik: Englisch/Deutsch* (Philipp Reclam Jun, Stuttgart, 1985).

Henley, W. E., ed., *Lyra Heroica: A Book of Verse for Boys* (David Nutt, 1891).

Houghton, W. E. and Stange, G. Robert, eds, *Victorian Poetry and Poetics* (Houghton Mifflin, Boston, 1968).

Karlin, Daniel, ed., *The Penguin Book of Victorian Verse* (Allen Lane, The Penguin Press, 1997).

Leighton, Angela and Reynolds, Margaret, eds, *Victorian Women Poets: An Anthology* (Blackwell, Oxford, 1995).

Maidment, Brian, ed., *The Poorhouse Fugitives: Self-Taught Poets and Poetry in Victorian Britain* (Carcanet, Manchester, 1987).

Miles, Alfred H., ed., *The Poets and the Poetry of the Century*, 10 vols (Hutchinson, 1892–7); 12 vols (G. Routledge & Sons; E. P. Dutton, New York, 1905–7).

Palgrave, Francis Turner, ed., *The Golden Treasury of the Best Songs and Lyrical Poems in the English Language* (first version, 1861), ed. Christopher Ricks (Penguin, Harmondsworth, 1991).

Palmer, Roy, ed., *A Touch on the Times: Songs of Social Change 1770 to 1914* (Penguin Education, Harmondsworth, 1974).

Quiller-Couch, Arthur, ed., *The Oxford Book of Victorian Verse* (Clarendon P, Oxford, 1925).

Ricks, Christopher, ed., *The New Oxford Book of Victorian Verse* (Oxford UP, Oxford, 1987).

Stanford, Derek, ed., *Pre-Raphaelite Writing: An Anthology* (Dent, 1973).

Thornton, R. K. R., ed., *Poetry of the 1890s* (Penguin, Harmondsworth, 1970; 2nd edn, with Marion Thain, 1997).

General

Adams, James Eli, *Dandies and Desert Saints: Styles of Victorian Manhood* (Cornell UP, Ithaca, NY, 1995).

Anderson, Amanda S., *Tainted Souls and Painted Faces: The Rhetoric of Fallenness in Victorian Culture* (Cornell UP, Ithaca, NY, 1993).

Arata, Stephen, *Fictions of Loss in the Victorian Fin de Siècle* (Cambridge UP, 1996).

Armstrong, Isobel, ed., *The Major Victorian Poets: Reconsiderations* (RKP, 1969).

Armstrong, Isobel, *Victorian Scrutinies: Reviews of Poetry, 1830–1870* (Athlone P, 1972).

Armstrong, Isobel, *Victorian Poetry: Poetry, Poetics and Politics* (RKP, 1993).

Ashton, Rosemary, *The German Idea: Four English Writers and the Reception of German Thought 1800–1860* (Cambridge UP, Cambridge, 1980).

Auerbach, Nina, *Women and the Demon: The Life of a Victorian Myth* (Harvard UP, Cambridge, MA, 1982).

Barreca, Regina, ed., *Sex and Death in Victorian Literature* (Macmillan, 1990).

Beddoe, Stella, 'Fairy Writing and Writers', in *Victorian Fairy Painting*, ed. Jane Martineau (Royal Academy of Arts, London; The U of Iowa Museum of Art, Iowa; The Art Gallery of Ontario, Toronto; in association with Merrell Holberton Publishers, London).

Bergonzi, Bernard, *The Turn of a Century: Essays on Victorian and Modern English Literature* (Macmillan, 1973).

Bivona, Daniel, *Desire and Contradiction: Imperial Visions and Domestic Debates in Victorian Literature* (Manchester UP, Manchester, 1990).

Blake, Kathleen, *Love and the Woman Question in Victorian Literature: The Art of Self-Postponement* (Harvester, Hemel Hempstead, 1983).

Bradley, Ian, *Abide With Me: The World of Victorian Hymns* (SCM Press, 1997).

Bristow, Joseph, *Effeminate England: Homoerotic Writing after 1885* (Oxford UP, Oxford, 1995).

Bristow, Joseph, ed., *Victorian Women Poets: Emily Brontë, Elizabeth Barrett Browning, Christina Rossetti: Contemporary Critical Essays* (New Casebooks, Macmillan, Basingstoke, 1995).

Buckley, Jerome H., *The Victorian Temper: A Study in Literary Culture* (Frank Cass, 1960).

Buckley, Jerome H., *The Triumph of Time: A Study of the Victorian Concepts of Time, History, Progress and Decadence* (Harvard UP, Cambridge, MA, 1967).

Burgin, Victor; Donald, James; Kaplan, Cora, eds, *Formations of Fantasy* (Methuen, 1986).

Butler, Lance St John, *Victorian Doubt: Literature and Cultural Discourses* (Harvester/Wheatsheaf, Hemel Hempstead, 1990).

Campos, Christophe, *The View of France: from Arnold to Bloomsbury* (Oxford UP, London, 1965).

Charlesworth, Barbara, *Dark Passages: The Decadent Consciousness in Victorian Literature* (U of Wisconsin P, Madison and Milwaukee, 1965).

Chesterton, G. K., *The Victorian Age in Literature* (Oxford UP, London, 1913).

Christ, Carol T., *The Finer Optic: The Aesthetic Peculiarity in Victorian Poetry* (Yale UP, New Haven, 1975).

Christ, Carol T., 'The Feminine Subject in Victorian Poetry', *ELH* 54 (1987), 385–401.

Clarke, G. W., ed., *Rediscovering Hellenism: The Hellenic Inheritance and the Victorian Imagination* (Cambridge UP, Cambridge, 1989).

Cohen, William A., *Sex Scandal: The Private Parts of Victorian Fiction* (Duke UP, Durham, NC, 1996).

Cosslett, Tess, ed., *Victorian Women Poets* (Longman Critical Reader, Longman, 1996).

Cox, Don Richard, *Sexuality and Victorian Literature* (U of Tennessee P, Knoxville, 1984).

Croft-Brooke, Rupert, *Feasting With Panthers: A New Consideration of Some Late Victorian Writers* (Holt, Rinehart & Winston, New York, 1967).

Davis, Lloyd, ed., *Virginal Sexuality and Textuality in Victorian Literature* (State U of New York P, NY, 1993).

De Jean, Joan, *Fictions of Sappho, 1546–1937* (Chicago UP, Chicago, 1987).

De Laura, David J., *Hebrew and Hellene in Victorian England: Newman, Arnold, and Pater* (U of Texas P, Austin, 1969).

De Shazer, Mary K., *Inspiring Women: Imagining the Muse* (Pergamon P, Elmsford, NY, 1986).

Deane, Seamus, *Strange Country: Modernity and Nationhood in Irish Writing Since 1790* (Clarendon P, Oxford, 1997).

Dickerson, Vanessa D., *Keeping the Victorian House* (Garland Publishing, New York, 1995).

Diehl, Joanne Feit, ' "Come Slowly – Eden": An Exploration of Women Poets and Their Muse', *Signs* 3 (1978), 572–87.

Dollimore, Jonathan, *Sexual Dissidence: Augustine to Wilde, Freud to Foucault* (Clarendon P, Oxford, 1991).

Dowling, Linda, *Language and Decadence in the Victorian Fin de Siècle* (Princeton UP, Princeton, 1986).

Dowling, Linda, *Hellenism and Homosexuality in Victorian Oxford* (Cornell UP, Ithaca, NY, 1994).

Edmond, Rod, *Affairs of the Hearth: Victorian Poetry and Domestic Narrative* (RKP, 1988).

Faas, Ekbert, *Retreat into the Mind: Victorian Poetry and the Rise of Psychiatry* (Princeton UP, Princeton, 1988).

Filmer, K., ed., *The Victorian Fantasists* (Macmillan, 1991).

Fletcher, Ian, and Bradbury, Malcolm, eds, *Decadence in the 1890's* (Stratford-upon-Avon Studies, Edward Arnold, 1979).

Flint, Kate, *The Woman Reader 1837–1914* (Clarendon P, Oxford, 1993).

Fraser, Hilary, *Beauty and Belief: Aesthetics and Religion in Victorian Literature* (Cambridge UP, Cambridge, 1986).

Gates, Barbara T., *Victorian Suicide: Mad Crimes and Sad Histories* (Princeton UP, Princeton, 1988).

Gilbert, Sandra M., and Gubar, Susan, *The Madwoman in the Attic* (Yale UP, New Haven, 1979).

Gilmour, Robin, *The Victorian Period: The Intellectual and Cultural Context of English Literature, 1830–1890* (Longman, 1993).

Griffiths, Eric, *The Printed Voice of Victorian Poetry* (Clarendon P, Oxford, 1989).

Harvey, John, *Men in Black* (U of Chicago P, 1995).

Hickock, Kathleen, *Representations of Women: Nineteenth-Century British Women's Poetry* (Greenwood P, Westport, CT, 1984).

Hickock, Kathleen, ' "Intimate Egoism": Reading and Evaluating Noncanonical Poetry by Women', *VP* 33 (1995), 13–30.

Homans, Margaret, *Women Writers and Poetic Identity: Dorothy Wordsworth, Emily Brontë, and Emily Dickinson* (Princeton UP, Princeton, 1980).

Hönnighausen, Lothar, *The Symbolist Tradition in English Literature: A Study of Pre-Raphaelitism and Fin de Siècle* (Cambridge UP, Cambridge, 1988).

Hough, Graham, *The Last Romantics* (Duckworth, 1949).

Hughes, Linda K., ed., *VP* (Spring 1995). Women Poets issue.

Hurley, Kelly, *The Gothic Body: Sexuality, Materialism, and Degeneration at the Fin de Siècle* (Cambridge UP, Cambridge, 1996).

Johnson, E. D. H., *The Alien Vision of Victorian Poetry: Sources of the Poetic Imagination in Tennyson, Arnold, Browning* (Princeton UP, Princeton, 1952).

Julian, J., *A Dictionary of Hymnology . . .* (Murray, 1892).

Kaplan, Fred, *Sacred Tears: Sentimentality in Victorian Literature* (Princeton UP, Princeton, 1987).

Kiberd, Declan, *Inventing Ireland: The Literature of the Modern Nation* (Jonathan Cape, 1995).

Knoepflmacher, U. C., *Ventures into Childhood: Victorians, Fairy Tales, and Femininity* (U of Chicago P, Chicago, 1998).

La Quesne, A. L; Landow, George P; Collini, Arnold; Stansky, Peter, *Victorian Thinkers: Carlyle, Ruskin, Arnold, Morris* (Oxford UP, Oxford, 1993).

Langbaum, Robert, *The Poetry of Experience: The Dramatic Monologue in Modern Literary Tradition* (Chatto & Windus, 1957).

Le Gallienne, Richard, *The Romantic Nineties* (Putnam, 1925).

Lecercle, Jean-Jacques, *Philosophy of Nonsense: The Intuitions of Victorian Nonsense Literature* (RKP, 1994).

Leighton, Angela, ' "Because men made the laws": The Fallen Woman and the Woman Poet', *VP* 27 (1989), 109–27.

Leighton, Angela, *Victorian Women Poets: Writing Against the Heart* (Harvester, Hemel Hempstead, 1992).

Leighton, Angela, ed., *Victorian Women Poets: A Critical Reader* (Blackwell, Oxford, 1996).

McGann, Jerome J., ed., *Victorian Connections* (U of Virginia P, Charlottesville, 1989).

Mermin, Dorothy, 'The Damsel, the Knight, and the Victorian Woman Poet', *CI* 13 (1986), 64–80.

Mermin, Dorothy, *Godiva's Ride: Women of Letters in England, 1830–1880* (Indiana UP, Bloomington and Indianapolis, 1993).

Mermin, Dorothy, ' "The fruitful feud of hers and his": Sameness, Difference and Genre in Victorian Poetry', *VP* 33 (Spring 1995), 149–68.

Michie, Elsie B., *Outside the Pale: Cultural Exclusion, Gender Difference, and the Victorian Woman Writer* (Cornell UP, Ithaca, NY, 1993).

Miller, J. Hillis, *The Disappearance of God* (Harvard UP, Cambridge, MA, 1963).

Millgate, Michael, *Testamentary Acts: Browning, Tennyson, James, Hardy* (Clarendon P, Oxford, 1992).

Moers, Ellen, *Literary Women* (Doubleday, Garden City, NY, 1976).

Morris, Kevin L., *The Image of the Middle Ages in Romantic and Victorian Literature* (Croom Helm, 1984).

Munich, Adrienne Auslander, *Andromeda's Chains: Gender and Interpretation in Victorian Literature and Art* (Columbia UP, New York, 1989).

Nelson, Walter W., *The Creative 1890s: Essays on W. E. Henley, Arthur Symons, Oscar Wilde, and William Butler Yeats* (W. W. Nelson, Lund, 1998).

Ostriker, Alicia, 'The Thieves of Language: Women Poets and Revisionist Mythmaking', *Signs* 8 (1982), 68–90.

Parker, Christopher, ed., *Gender Roles and Sexuality in Victorian Literature* (Scolar, Aldershot, 1995).

Pearce, Lynne, *Woman/Image/Text: Readings in Pre-Raphaelite Art and Literature* (Harvester, Hemel Hempstead, 1991).

Pierrot, Jean, *The Decadent Imagination 1880–1900*, trans. Derek Coltman (U of Chicago P, Chicago, 1981).

Pittock, Murray G. H., *Spectrum of Decadence: The Literature of the 1890s* (RKP, 1993).

Reed, John R., *Victorian Will* (Ohio UP, Athens, OH, 1989).

Richards, Bernard, *English Poetry of the Victorian Period 1830–1890* (Longman, 1988).

Roppen, Georg, *Evolution and Poetic Belief: A Study of Some Victorian and Modern Writers* (Oslo UP, Oslo, 1956).

Ryals, Clyde de L., *A World of Possibilities: Romantic Irony in Victorian Literature* (Ohio State UP, Columbus, 1990).

Sadoff, Dianne F., *Monsters of Affection: Dickens, Eliot and Brontë on Fatherhood* (Johns Hopkins UP, Baltimore, 1982).

Sambrook, James, ed., *Pre-Raphaelitism: A Collection of Critical Essays* (U of Chicago P, Chicago, 1974).

Schur, Owen, *Victorian Pastoral: Tennyson, Hardy, and the Subversion of Forms* (Ohio State UP, Columbus, 1989).

Showalter, Elaine, *The Female Malady: Women, Madness and English Culture, 1830–1980* (Virago, 1987).

Showalter, Elaine, *Sexual Anarchy: Gender and Culture at the Fin de Siècle* (Bloomsbury, 1991).

Smith, Timothy d'Arch, *Love in Earnest: Some Notes on the Lives and Writings of English 'Uranian' Poets from 1889 to 1930* (RKP, 1970).

Stanford, Derek, *Critics of the Nineties* (John Baker, 1970).

Stanford, Derek, *Introduction to the Nineties* (Institüt für Anglistik und Amerikanistik, Salzburg, 1987).

Stein, Richard L., *Victoria's Year: English Literature and Culture 1837–8* (Oxford UP, New York, 1987).

Stevenson, Lionel, *Darwin Among the Poets* ([1932] Russell & Russell, New York, 1963).

Stevenson, Lionel, *The Pre-Raphaelite Poets* (U of North Carolina P, Chapel Hill, 1972).

Stokes, John, *In the Nineties* (Harvester/Wheatsheaf, Hemel Hempstead, 1989).

Stokes, John, ed., *Fin de Siècle/Fin du Globe: Fears and Fantasies of the Late Nineteenth Century* (Macmillan, 1992).

Stott, Rebecca, *The Fabrication of the Late-Victorian Femme Fatale: The Kiss of Death* (Macmillan, 1992).

Sussmann, Herbert L., *Victorians and the Machine: The Literary Response to Technology* (Harvard UP, Cambridge, MA, 1968).

Sussmann, Herbert L., *Fact into Figure: Typology in Carlyle, Ruskin and the Pre-Raphaelite Brotherhood* (Ohio State UP, Columbus, 1979).

Sussmann, Herbert L., *Victorian Masculinities: Manhood and Masculine Poetics in Early Victorian Literature and Art* (Cambridge UP, Cambridge, 1995).

Swindells, Julia, *Victorian Writing and Working Women: The Other Side of Silence* (Polity P, Cambridge, 1985).

Symons, Arthur, *The Symbolist Movement in Literature* (1899; revised 1900 and 1919; intro. R. Ellmann; E. P. Dutton, New York, 1958).

Thornton, R. K. R., *The Decadent Dilemma* (Edward Arnold, 1983).

Tucker, Herbert F., ed., *A Companion to Victorian Literature and Culture* (Blackwell, Oxford, 1999).

Vance, Norman, *The Sinews of the Spirit: The Ideal of Christian Manliness in Victorian Literature and Religious Thought* (Cambridge UP, Cambridge, 1985).

Vance, Norman, *The Victorians and Ancient Rome* (Blackwell, Oxford, 1997).

Vicinus, Martha, *The Industrial Muse: A Study of Nineteenth-Century British Working-Class Literature* (Croom Helm, 1974).

Watson, J. R., *The English Hymn: A Critical and Historical Study* (Clarendon P, Oxford, 1997).

Wheeler, Michael, *Death and the Future Life in Victorian Literature and Theology* (Cambridge UP, Cambridge, 1990).

Woods, Gregory, *A History of Gay Literature: The Male Tradition* (Yale UP, New Haven, 1998).

Selected Reading on the Poets
(in alphabetical order of poet names)

C. F. Alexander

Wallace, Valerie, *Mrs Alexander: A Life of the Hymn-Writer Cecil Frances Alexander, 1818–1895* (Lilliput P, Dublin, 1995).

William Allingham

The Poems of William Allingham, ed. John Harold Hewitt (Dolmen P, Dublin; Oxford UP, London, 1967).

Letters of Dante Gabriel Rossetti to William Allingham, 1854–1870, ed. G. B. N. Hill (T. Fisher Unwin, 1897).

William Allingham: A Diary, ed. Helen Allingham and Dollie Radford (Macmillan, 1907).

Warner, Alan, *William Allingham: An Introduction* (Dolmen P, Dublin, 1971).

Matthew Arnold

Arnold: The Complete Poems, ed. K. Allott (Longman's Annotated English Poets, Longman, 1965; 2nd edn, ed. Miriam Allott, 1979).

The Complete Prose Works, ed. R. H. Super, 11 vols (U of Michigan P, Ann Arbor, 1960–77).

Collini, Stefan, *Arnold: A Critical Portrait* (Clarendon P, Oxford, 1988).

Dawson, Carl, ed., *Matthew Arnold: The Critical Heritage – The Poetry* (RKP, 1973).

Fulweiler, H. W., *Letters from the Darkling Plain: Language and the Grounds of Knowledge in the Poetry of Arnold and Hopkins* (U of Missouri P, Columbia, 1972).

Hamilton, Ian, *A Gift Imprisoned: The Poetic Life of Matthew Arnold* (Bloomsbury, 1988).

Honan, Park, *Matthew Arnold: A Life* (Weidenfeld & Nicolson, 1981).

James, D. G., *Matthew Arnold and the Decline of English Romanticism* (Clarendon P, Oxford, 1961).

Stange, G. Robert, *Arnold: The Poet as Humanist* (Princeton UP, Princeton, 1967).

Trilling, Lionel, *Matthew Arnold* (Allen & Unwin, 1939); with additional essay 'Matthew Arnold, Poet' (Harcourt, Brace, Jovanovich, New York, 1979).

William Edmonstoune Aytoun

Weinstein, M. A., *W.E. Aytoun and the Spasmodic Controversy* (Yale UP, New Haven, 1968).

William Barnes

The Poems of William Barnes, ed. Bernard Jones, 2 vols (Centaur P, 1962).

Select Poems of William Barnes, ed. and intro. Thomas Hardy (Henry Frowde, Oxford UP, London, 1908).

William Barnes: Selected Poems, ed. Andrew Motion (Penguin, Harmondsworth, 1994).

Forster, E. M., 'William Barnes', *Two Cheers for Democracy* (Edward Arnold, 1951), 209–12.

Hardy, Thomas, 'Poems of Rural Life in the Dorset Dialect', *New Quarterly Magazine* (October 1879), in *Thomas Hardy's Personal Writings*, ed. Harold Orel (Macmillan, 1967).

Hardy, Thomas, 'The Reverend William Barnes BD', *Athenaeum* (16 October 1886), in *Thomas Hardy's Personal Writings*, ed. Harold Orel (Macmillan, 1967).

Larkin, Philip, 'The Poetry of William Barnes', *Required Writing* (Faber & Faber, 1983).

Levy, William Turner, *Barnes, The Man and His Poems* (Longmans, Dorchester, 1960).

Thomas Lovell Beddoes

The Works of Thomas Lovell Beddoes, ed. Henry Wolfgang Donner (Oxford UP, London, 1935).

Donner, H. W., *Thomas Lovell Beddoes: The Making of a Poet* (Basil Blackwell, Oxford, 1935).

Ricks, Christopher, 'Thomas Lovell Beddoes: "A Dying Start"', *The Force of Poetry* (Oxford UP, Oxford, 1984), 135–62.

Hilaire Belloc

Complete Verse, ed. W. N. Roughead (Duckworth, 1970).

Speaight, Robert, *The Life of Hilaire Belloc* (Hollis & Carter, 1957).

L. S. Bevington

Oliver, Hermia, *The International Anarchist Movement in Late Victorian London* (Croom Helm, 1983).

Mathilde Blind

The Poetical Works, ed. Arthur Symons, with memoir by Richard Garnett (T. Fisher Unwin, 1900).

W. S. Blunt

The Poetical Works of Wilfred Scawen Blunt: A Complete Edition (Macmillan, 1914).

Longford, Elizabeth, *A Pilgrimage of Passion: The Life of Wilfred Scawen Blunt* (Weidenfeld & Nicolson, 1979).

Robert Bridges

Poetical Works, 6 vols (Smith, Elder, 1898–1905).

The Correspondence of Robert Bridges and W.B. Yeats, ed. Richard J. Finneran (Macmillan, 1977).

The Selected Letters of Robert Bridges, ed. Donald E. Stanford (U of Delaware P, Newark, NJ, 1984).

Guerard, Albert J., *Robert Bridges: A Study of Traditionalism in Poetry* (Harvard UP, Cambridge, MA, 1942; Russell & Russell, New York, 1965).

Ritz, Jean-Georges, *Robert Bridges and Gerard Hopkins, 1863–1889: A Literary Friendship* (Oxford UP, London, 1960).

Stanford, Donald E., *In the Classic Mode: The Achievement of Robert Bridges* (U of Delaware P, Newark, NJ, 1979).

Stanford, Donald E., 'Robert Bridges and the Free Verse Rebellion', *Journal of Modern Literature* 2 (1971), 19–32.

The Brontës

Alexander, Christine and Sellars, Jane, *The Art of the Brontës* (Cambridge UP, Cambridge, 1995).

Ratchford, Fanny E., *The Brontës' Web of Childhood* (Columbia UP, New York, 1941).

Taylor, Irene, *Holy Ghosts: The Male Muses of Emily and Charlotte Brontë* (Columbia UP, New York, 1990).

Winnifrith, Tom, *The Brontës and Their Background: Romance and Reality* (Macmillan, 1973).

Wise, T. J. and Symington, J. A., *The Brontës: Their Lives, Friendships and Correspondence*, 4 vols (Shakespeare Head, Oxford, 1933).

Anne Brontë

The Poems of Anne Brontë: A New Text and Commentary, ed. Edward Chitham (Macmillan, 1979).

Gérin, Winifred, *Anne Brontë* (Allen Lane, 1959; new edn, 1976).

Gilligan, Carol, *In a Different Voice* (Harvard UP, Cambridge, MA, 1982).

Scott, P. J. M., *Anne Brontë: A New Critical Assessment* (Barnes & Nobel, New York, 1983).

Branwell Brontë

Gérin, Winifred, *Branwell Brontë* (Thomas Nelson & Sons, Toronto, 1961).

Charlotte Brontë

Poems: A New and Enlarged Edition of the Shakespeare Head Brontë, ed. Tom Winnifrith (Shakespeare Head Press and Basil Blackwell, Oxford, 1984).

The Poems of Charlotte Brontë: A New Text and Commentary, ed. Victor A. Neufeldt (Garland, New York, 1985).

Alexander, Christine, *The Early Writings of Charlotte Brontë* (Blackwell, Oxford, 1983).

Gaskell, Elizabeth Cleghorn, *The Life of Charlotte Brontë*, 2 vols (Smith, Elder, 1857).

Gérin, Winifred, *Charlotte Brontë: The Evolution of Genius* (Clarendon P, Oxford, 1967).

Gordon, Lyndall, *Charlotte Brontë: A Passionate Life* (Chatto & Windus, 1994).

Emily Brontë

The Complete Poems, ed. Janet Gezari (Penguin, Harmondsworth, 1992).

The Poems of Emily Brontë, ed. Barbara Lloyd-Evans (Batsford, 1992).

Burlinson, Kathryn, ' "What Language Can Utter the Feeling": Identity in the Poetry of Emily Brontë', in *Subjectivity and Literature from the Romantics to the Present Day*, ed. Philip Shaw and Peter Stockwell (Pinter, 1991).

Chitham, Edward, *A Life of Emily Brontë* (Blackwell, Oxford, 1987).

Dingle, H., *The Mind of Emily Brontë* (M. Brian & O'Keeffe, 1974).

Gérin, Winifred, *Emily Brontë: A Biography* (Clarendon P, Oxford, 1971).

T. E. Brown

The Collected Poems of T.E. Brown, ed. H. F. Brown, H. G. Dakyns, W. E. Henley (Macmillan, 1900; reissued,

Manx Museum and The National Trust, Douglas, Isle of Man, 1976).

Norris, Samuel, *Two Men of Manxland: Hall Caine, Novelist, T.E. Brown, Poet* (Norris Modern Press, Douglas, Isle of Man, 1947).

Elizabeth Barrett Browning

Complete Works, 6 vols, ed. Charlotte Porter and Helen A. Clarke (Crowell, New York, 1900).

Letters, 2 vols, ed. Frederic G. Kenyon (Smith, Elder, 1897).

The Brownings' Correspondence, vols 1–, ed. Philip Kelley, Ronald Hudson, Scott Lewis (Wedgestone P, Winfield, Kansas; Athlone P, London, 1984–).

Aurora Leigh and Other Poems, ed. and intro. Cora Kaplan (Women's P, 1978).

Aurora Leigh, ed. Margaret Reynolds (Ohio UP, Athens, OH, 1992; W. W. Norton & Co, New York, 1996).

Case, Alison, 'Gender and Narration in *Aurora Leigh*', *VP* 29 (1991), 17–32.

Gelpi, Barbara Charlesworth, '*Aurora Leigh*: The Vocation of the Woman Poet', *VP* 19 (1981), 35–48.

Gilbert, Sandra M., 'From *Patria* to *Matria*: Elizabeth Barrett Browning's Risorgimento', *PMLA* 99 (1984), 194–211.

Karlin, Danny, *The Courtship of Robert Browning and Elizabeth Barrett Browning* (Oxford UP, Oxford, 1985).

Leighton, Angela, *Elizabeth Barrett Browning* (Harvester, Brighton, 1986).

Mermin, Dorothy, *Elizabeth Barrett Browning: The Origins of a New Poetry* (U of Chicago P, Chicago, 1989).

Morgan, Edwin, 'Women and Poetry', *CJ* 3 (1950), 643–73.

Woolf, Virginia, '*Aurora Leigh*', *The Common Reader*, Second Series (Hogarth, 1932), 202–13; *Collected Essays*, vol. 1 (Hogarth, 1966), 209–18.

Robert Browning

Poems, ed. Donald Smalley (Houghton Mifflin, Boston, 1956).

Robert Browning: The Poems, ed. John Pettigrew and Thomas J. Collins, 2 vols (Penguin, Harmondsworth, 1981).

The Poetical Works of Robert Browning, ed. Ian Jack, Margaret Smith, Rowena Fowler, Robert Inglesfield, Stefan Hawlin, Tim Burnett, vols 1– (Clarendon P, Oxford, 1983–).

The Poems of Robert Browning, 2 vols, ed. John Woolford and Daniel Karlin (Longman's Annotated English Poets, Longman, 1991).

Letters of Robert Browning and Elizabeth Barrett, 1845–1846, 2 vols, ed. Elvan Kintner (Harvard UP, Cambridge, MA, 1969).

Armstrong, Isobel, ed., *Robert Browning* (Writers and Their Background, G. Bell & Sons, 1974).

Bloom, Harold and Munich, Adrienne, eds, *Robert Browning: A Collection of Critical Essays* (Twentieth Century Views, Prentice-Hall, Englewood Cliffs, NJ, 1979).

Christ, Carol T., 'Browning's Corpses', *VP* 33 (Autumn–Winter 1995), 391–401.

Culler, A. Dwight, 'Monodrama and the Dramatic Monologue', *PMLA* 90 (1975), 366–85.

De Vane, William Clyde, *A Browning Handbook* ([1935]; 2nd edn, Appleton-Century-Crofts, New York, 1955).

Jack, Ian, *Browning's Major Poetry* (Clarendon P, Oxford, 1973).

Karlin, Danny, *The Courtship of Robert Browning and Elizabeth Barrett* (Oxford UP, Oxford, 1985).

Karlin, Danny, *Browning's Hatreds* (Clarendon P, Oxford, 1993).

Litzinger, Boyd and Knickerbocker, K. L., eds, *The Browning Critics* (U of Kentucky P, Lexington, 1965).

Litzinger, Boyd and Smalley, Donald, eds, *Browning: The Critical Heritage* (RKP, 1970).

Ryals, Clyde de L., *Browning's Later Poetry, 1871–1889* (Cornell UP, Ithaca, NY, 1975).

Ryals, Clyde de L., *The Life of Robert Browning: A Critical Biography* (Blackwell, Oxford, 1993).

Robert Buchanan

Cassidy, John A., 'Robert Buchanan and the Fleshly Controversy', *PMLA* 67 (1952), 65–93.

Forsyth, R. A., 'Nature and the Victorian City: The Ambivalent Attitude of Robert Buchanan', *ELH* 36 (1969), 382–415.

C. S. Calverley

The Complete Works of C.S. Calverley, With a Biographical Notice by Sir Walter J. Sendall (George Bell, 1901).

Ince, Richard Basil, *Calverley and Some Cambridge Wits of the Nineteenth Century* (G. Richards and H. Toulmin at the Cayme P, 1929).

Thomas Carlyle

Works: Centenary Edition, ed. H. D. Traill, 30 vols (Chapman & Hall, 1897–1904).

The Collected Letters of Thomas and Jane Welsh Carlyle, ed. C. R. Sanders and K. J. Fielding, vols 1– (Duke UP, Durham, NC, 1970–).

Sartor Resartus, ed. K. Mcsweeney and P. Sabor (Oxford World's Classics, Oxford, 1987).

Tennyson, G. B., *Sartor Called Resartus: The Genesis, Structure, and Style of Thomas Carlyle's First Major Work* (Princeton UP, Princeton, 1965).

Edward Carpenter

Brown, Tony, *Edward Carpenter and Late Victorian Radicalism* (Cass, 1990).

Delavenay, Emile, *D.H. Lawrence and Edward Carpenter: A Study in Edwardian Transition* (Heinemann, 1971).

Forster, E. M., 'Edward Carpenter', *Two Cheers for Democracy* (Edward Arnold, 1951), 217–19.

Smith, Timothy d'Arch, *Love in Earnest: Some Notes on the Lives and Writings of English 'Uranian' Poets from 1889 to 1930* (RKP, 1970).

Tsuzucki, Chushichi, *Edward Carpenter (1844–1929): Prophet of Human Fellowship* (Cambridge UP, Cambridge, 1980).

Lewis Carroll

Amor, Anne Clark, *Lewis Carroll: A Biography* (Dent, 1979).

Blake, Kathleen, *Play, Games, and Sport: The Literary Works of Lewis Carroll* (Cornell UP, Ithaca, NY, 1974).

Empson, William, 'Alice in Wonderland: The Child as Swain', *Some Versions of Pastoral: A Study of the Pastoral Form in Literature* (Chatto & Windus, 1935).

Lecercle, Jean-Jacques, *Philosophy of Nonsense: The Intuitions of Victorian Nonsense Literature* (RKP, 1994).

Sewell, Elizabeth, *The Field of Nonsense* (Chatto & Windus, 1952).

John Clare

The Early Poems of John Clare, ed. Eric Robinson, David Powell, Margaret Grainger, 2 vols (Clarendon P, Oxford, 1989).

The Later Poems of John Clare, ed. Eric Robinson, David Powell, Margaret Grainger (Clarendon P, Oxford, 1984).

John Clare's Autobiographical Writings, ed. Eric Robinson and John Lawrence (Oxford UP, Oxford, 1983).

The Letters of John Clare, ed. Mark Storey (Clarendon P, Oxford, 1985).

Barrell, John, *The Idea of Landscape and the Sense of Place 1730–1840: An Approach to the Poetry of John Clare* (Cambridge UP, Cambridge, 1972).

Brownlow, T, *John Clare and the Picturesque Landscape* (Oxford UP, Oxford, 1983).

Chilcott, T. J., *'A Real World and Doubting Mind': A Study of the Poetry of John Clare* (Hull UP, Hull, 1985).

Heaney, Seamus, 'John Clare's Prog', *The Redress of Poetry: Oxford Lectures* (Faber & Faber, 1995), 63–82.

Storey, Edward, *A Right to Song: The Life of John Clare* (Methuen, 1982).

Storey, Mark, *The Poetry of John Clare: A Critical Introduction* (Macmillan, 1974).

Storey, Mark, ed., *Clare: The Critical Heritage* (RKP, 1973).

Todd, Janet M., *In Adam's Garden: A Study of John Clare's Pre-Asylum Poetry* (U of Florida P, Gainesville, Florida, 1973).

Arthur Hugh Clough

The Poems of Arthur Hugh Clough, 2nd edn, ed. F. L. Mulhauser (Clarendon P, Oxford, 1974).

The Correspondence of Arthur Hugh Clough, ed. F. L. Mulhauser, 2 vols (Clarendon P, Oxford, 1957).

Biswas, Robindra Kumar, *Arthur Hugh Clough: Towards a Reconsideration* (Clarendon P, Oxford, 1972).

Greenberger, Evelyn Barish, *Arthur Hugh Clough: The Growth of a Poet's Mind* (Harvard UP, Cambridge, MA, 1970).

Scott, Patrick, 'The Victorianism of Clough', *VP* 16 (1978), 32–42.

Thorpe, Michael, ed., *Clough: The Critical Heritage* (RKP, 1972).

Williams, David, *Too Quick Despairer: A Life of A.H. Clough* (Rupert Hart-Davis, 1969).

Mary E. Coleridge
The Collected Poems, ed. Theresa Whistler (Rupert Hart-Davis, 1954).

Eliza Cook
The Poetical Works of Eliza Cook (Chandos Classics, Frederick Warne, 1870).

Thomas Cooper
Collins, P. A. W., *Thomas Cooper, the Chartist: Byron and the 'Poets of the Poor'* (Byron Foundation Lecture, 1969) (U of Nottingham, 1970).

William (Johnson) Cory
Johnson, Lionel, *Poetry and Fiction: Reflections of Three Nineteenth Century Authors: Herbert P. Horne, Hubert Crackanthorpe, William Johnson Cory* (Tragara P, Edinburgh, 1982).

John Davidson
The Poems of John Davidson, ed. Andrew Turnbull, 2 vols (Scottish Academic P, Edinburgh, 1973).
John Davidson: A Selection of His Poems, ed. and intro. Maurice Lindsay (Hutchinson, 1961).
Selected Poems and Prose of John Davidson, ed. John Sloan (Clarendon P, Oxford, 1995).
MacDiarmid, Hugh, 'John Davidson: Influences and Influence', in *John Davidson: A Selection of His Poems*, ed. Maurice Lindsay (Hutchinson, 1961), 47–54.
Sloan, John, *John Davidson, First of the Moderns: A Literary Biography* (Clarendon P, Oxford, 1995).
Townsend, James Benjamin, *John Davidson: Poet of Armageddon* (Yale UP, New Haven, 1961).

Charles Dickens
Ackroyd, Peter, *Dickens* (Sinclair-Stevenson, 1990).

R. W. Dixon
Bridges, Robert, *Three Friends: Memoirs of Digby Mackworth Dolben, Richard Watson Dixon, Henry Bradley* (Oxford UP, London, 1932).
Sambrook, A. J., *A Poet Hidden: The Life of Richard Watson Dixon* (Athlone P, 1962).

Sydney Dobell
Jolly, Emily, *The Life and Letters of Sydney Dobell* (Smith, Elder, 1878).

Austin Dobson
The Complete Poetical Works of Austin Dobson (Humphrey Milford, Oxford UP, London, 1923).
Dobson, Alban T. A., *Austin Dobson: Some Notes; With Chapters by Sir Edmund Gosse and George Saintsbury* (Humphrey Milford, Oxford UP, London, 1928).

Digby Mackworth Dolben
The Poems of Digby Mackworth Dolben, ed. Robert Bridges (Henry Frowde, Oxford UP, London, 1911; Humphrey Milford, Oxford UP, Oxford, 1915).

Uncollected Poems of Digby Mackworth Dolben (Whiteknights P, Reading, 1973).
The Poems and Letters of Digby Mackworth Dolben, 1848–1867, ed. Martin Cohen (Avebury P, Amersham, 1981).
Bridges, Robert, *Three Friends: Memoirs of Digby Mackworth Dolben, Richard Watson Dixon, Henry Bradley* (Oxford UP, London, 1932).

Alfred Domett
Kenyon, Frederic G. and Arnould, Joseph, eds, *Robert Browning and Alfred Domett* (Smith, Elder, 1906).

Ernest Dowson
Fowler, Rowena, 'Ernest Dowson and the Classics', *Yearbook of English Studies* 3 (1973), 243–52.
Longaker, John Mark, *Ernest Dowson* (U of Pennsylvania P, Philadelphia, and Oxford UP, London, 1944; 3rd edn, U of Pennsylvania P, Philadelphia, 1967).
Snodgrass, Chris, 'Ernest Dowson's Aesthetics of Contamination', *ELT* 26 (1983), 162–74.

A. Conan Doyle
The Poems of Arthur Conan Doyle: Collected Edition (John Murray, 1922).
Edwards, Owen Dudley, *The Quest for Sherlock Holmes: A Biographical Study of Arthur Conan Doyle* (Mainstream, Edinburgh, 1983).

George Eliot
The George Eliot Letters, ed. Gordon S. Haight, 9 vols (Oxford UP, London; Yale UP, New Haven, 1954–78).
Selected Letters, Poems and Other Writings, ed. A. S. Byatt and Nicholas Warren (Penguin, Harmondsworth, 1990).
Ashton, Rosemary, *George Eliot: A Life* (Hamish Hamilton, 1996).
Beer, Gillian, *George Eliot* (Harvester, Brighton, 1986).
Carroll, David, ed., *George Eliot: The Critical Heritage* (RKP, 1971).

Ebenezer Elliott
Briggs, Asa, 'Ebenezer Elliott, the Corn Law Rhymer', *CJ* 3 (1950), 686–95.
James, Louis, 'Working-Class Poets and Poetry', Appendix I, *Fiction for the Working Man 1830–1850* (Oxford UP, London, 1963), 171–9.

Michael Field
A Selection from the Poems of Michael Field (Poetry Bookshop, London, 1923).
The Wattlefold: Unpublished Poems by Michael Field, Collected by Emily S. Fortey (Basil Blackwell, Oxford, 1930).
Works and Days: From the Journal of Michael Field, ed. T. and D. C. Sturge Moore (John Murray, 1933).
Faderman, Lillian, *Surpassing the Love of Men* (Women's Press, 1981).
Prins, Yopie, 'A Metaphorical Field: Katherine Bradley and Edith Cooper', *VP* (Spring, 1995), 129–48.

White, Christine, ' "Poets and lovers evermore": Interpreting Female Love in the Poetry and Journals of Michael Field', *TP* 4 (1990), 197–212.

Edward FitzGerald

The Letters of Edward FitzGerald, ed. Alred McKinley and Annabelle Burdick Terhune, 4 vols (Princeton UP, Princeton, 1980).

Edward FitzGerald, Rubáiyát of Omar Khayyám: A Critical Edition, ed. Christopher Decker (U of Virginia P, Charlottesville, 1997).

Martin, Robert Bernard, *With Friends Possessed: A Life of Edward FitzGerald* (Faber & Faber, 1985).

W. S. Gilbert

Stedman, Jane W., *W.S. Gilbert: A Classic Victorian and His Theatre* (Oxford UP, Oxford, 1996).

John Gray

McCormack, Jerusha Hull, *John Gray: Poet, Dandy and Priest* (Brandeis UP/UP of New England, Hanover, NH, 1991).

Dora Greenwell

Poems, selected, with a biographical intro., by William Dorling (The Canterbury Poets, Walter Scott, 1889).

Bett, Henry, *Dora Greenwell* (Epworth P, 1950).

Arthur Henry Hallam

Remains in Verse and Prose of Arthur Henry Hallam, ed. Henry Hallam (1834).

The Writings of Arthur Hallam, ed. T. H. Vail Motter (Oxford UP, New York, 1943).

The Letters of Arthur Henry Hallam, ed. Jack Kolb (Ohio State UP, Columbus, 1981).

Griffiths, Eric, 'The Worth of Change: The Arthur Hallam Letters', *Tennyson Research Bulletin* 42 (November 1983), 71–80.

Janet Hamilton

Selected Poems and Prose (Akros, Edinburgh, 1995).

Thomas Hardy

The Complete Poetical Works of Thomas Hardy, ed. Samuel Hynes, 4 vols (Clarendon P, Oxford, 1982–95).

The Collected Letters of Thomas Hardy, ed. R. L. Purdy and M. Millgate, 5 vols (Clarendon P, Oxford, 1978–88).

The Personal Notebooks of Thomas Hardy, ed. Richard H. Taylor (Macmillan, 1979).

Bayley, John, *An Essay on Hardy* (Cambridge UP, Cambridge, 1978).

Cox, R. G., ed., *Thomas Hardy: The Critical Heritage* (RKP, 1970).

Davie, Donald, *Thomas Hardy and British Poetry* (RKP, 1973).

'Hardy, Florence Emily', *The Early Life of Thomas Hardy, 1840–1891* (Macmillan, 1928).

'Hardy, Florence Emily', *The Later Years of Thomas Hardy, 1892–1928* (Macmillan, 1930).

Hynes, Samuel, *The Pattern of Hardy's Poetry* (U of North Carolina P, Chapel Hill, 1956).

Miller, J. Hillis, *Thomas Hardy: Distance and Desire* (Harvard UP, Cambridge, MA, 1970).

Millgate, Michael, *Thomas Hardy: A Biography* (Oxford UP, Oxford, 1982).

Paulin, Tom, *Thomas Hardy: The Poetry of Perception* (Macmillan, 1975).

Taylor, Dennis, *Hardy's Poetry, 1860–1928* (Columbia UP, New York, 1981).

Frances Ridley Havergal

Poetical Works, ed. M. V. G. Havergal, 2 vols (James Nisbet & Co, 1884).

Swiss Letters and Alpine Poems, ed. Her Sister, J. Miriam Crane (James Nisbet & Co, 1881).

Letters, ed. M. V. G. Havergal (James Nisbet & Co, 1887).

Grierson, Janet, *Frances Ridley Havergal: Worcestershire Hymnwriter* (The Havergal Society, Bromsgrove, 1979).

Robert Stephen Hawker

Selected Poems, ed. Cecil Woolf (C. Woolf, 1975).

Brendon, Piers, *Hawker of Morwenstow: Portrait of a Victorian Eccentric* (Jonathan Cape, 1975).

Peters, Robert, *Hawker* (Unicorn P, Greensboro, 1984).

W. E. Henley

Buckley, Jerome Hamilton, *William Ernest Henley: A Study in the "Counter-Decadence" of the 'Nineties* (Princeton UP, Princeton, 1945).

Gates, Norman T., 'Henley and Free Verse in Modern Poetry', *Four Decades of Poetry 1890–1930* 2 (1979), 145–52.

James Henry

Lyons, J. B., *Scholar and Sceptic: The Career of James Henry, MD, 1798–1876* (Glendale P, Dublin, 1985).

Richmond, John, *James Henry of Dublin: Physician, Versifier, Pamphleteer, Wanderer, and Classical Scholar* (John Richmond, Blackrock, 1976).

Thomas Hood

Thomas Hood: Poems, ed. Clifford Dyment (Grey Walls P, 1948).

Thomas Hood, Poems Comic and Serious, ed. Peter Thorogood (Bramber P, Bramber, 1995).

Blunden, Edmund, 'The Poet Hood', *Review of English Literature* 1 (1960), 26–34.

Clubbe, John, *Victorian Forerunner: The Later Career of Thomas Hood* (Duke UP, Durham, NC, 1968).

Gerard Manley Hopkins

The Poems of Gerard Manley Hopkins, ed. W. H. Gardner and N. H Mackenzie, 4th edn (Oxford UP, Oxford, 1970).

The Poetical Works of Gerard Manley Hopkins, ed. Norman H. Mackenzie (Clarendon P, Oxford, 1990).

Gerard Manley Hopkins: Selected Poetry, ed. Catherine Philips (World's Classics, Oxford UP, Oxford, 1996).

The Journals and Papers of Gerard Manley Hopkins, ed. Humphrey House (Oxford UP, London, 1959).

The Correspondence of Gerard Manley Hopkins and Richard Watson Dixon, ed. C. C. Abbott, 2nd, revised impression (Oxford UP, London, 1955).

The Letters of Gerard Manley Hopkins to Robert Bridges, ed. C. C. Abbott, 2nd, revised edn (Oxford UP, London, 1955).

Bergonzi, Bernard, *Gerard Manley Hopkins* (Macmillan, 1977).

Bloom, Harold, ed., *Gerard Manley Hopkins, Modern Critical Views* (Chelsea House, New York, 1986).

Hartman, Geoffrey, ed., *Hopkins: A Collection of Critical Essays* (Twentieth Century Views, Prentice-Hall, Englewood Cliffs, NJ, 1966).

Heaney, Seamus, 'The Fire i' the Flint: Reflections on the Poetry of Gerard Manley Hopkins', *Preoccupations: Selected Prose 1968–1978* (Faber & Faber, 1980), 79–97.

Johnson, Margaret, *Gerard Manley Hopkins and Tractarian Poetry* (Ashgate, Aldershot, 1997).

Lock, Charles, 'Hopkins as a Decadent Poet', *EinC* 34 (1984), 129–54.

Milroy, James, *The Language of Gerard Manley Hopkins* (Deutsch, 1977).

Ong, Walter J., *Hopkins, the Self and God* (U of Toronto P, 1986).

Plotkin, Cary H., *The Tenth Muse: Victorian Philology and the Genesis of the Poetic Language of Gerard Manley Hopkins* (Southern Illinois UP, Carbondale, 1989).

Roberts, Gerald, ed., *Gerard Manley Hopkins: The Critical Heritage* (RKP, 1987).

Robinson, John, *In Extremity: A Study of Gerard Manley Hopkins* (Cambridge UP, Cambridge, 1978).

White, Norman, *Hopkins: A Literary Biography* (Clarendon P, Oxford, 1992).

A. E. Housman

The Collected Poems of A.E. Housman (Jonathan Cape, 1939; new edn, 1960).

The Poems of A.E. Housman, ed. Archie Burnett (Clarendon P, Oxford, 1997).

Collected Poems and Selected Prose, ed. Christopher Ricks (Allen Lane, The Penguin P, 1988).

A.E. Housman, Selected Prose, ed. John Carter (Cambridge UP, Cambridge, 1961).

Bayley, John, *Housman's Poems* (Clarendon P, Oxford, 1992).

Burnett, Archie, 'Poetical Emendations and Improvisations by A.E. Housman', *VP* 36 (Fall 1998), 289–97.

Gardner, Philip, ed., *A.E. Housman: The Critical Heritage* (RKP, 1992).

Graves, Richard Perceval, *A.E. Housman: The Scholar Poet* (RKP, 1979).

Leggett, Bobby Joe, *The Poetic Art of A.E. Housman: Theory and Practice* (U of Nebraska P, Lincoln, 1978).

Page, Norman, *A.E. Housman: A Critical Biography* (Macmillan, 1983).

Ricks, Christopher, ed., *A.E. Housman: A Collection of Critical Essays* (Twentieth-Century Views, Prentice-Hall, Englewood Cliffs, NJ, 1968).

Laurence Housman

The Collected Poems of Laurence Housman (Sidgwick & Jackson, 1937).

Mary Howitt

Mary Howitt: An Autobiography, ed. Margaret Howitt (W. Isbister, 1889).

Leigh Hunt

Thompson, James R., *Leigh Hunt* (Twayne's English Authors, Twayne, Boston, 1977).

Jean Ingelow

Poems (Humphrey Milford, Oxford UP, London, 1913).

Peters, Maureen, *Jean Ingelow: Victorian Poetess* (The Boydell P, Ipswich, 1972).

Lionel Johnson

The Complete Poems of Lionel Johnson, ed. Ian Fletcher (Unicorn P, 1953).

Lionel Johnson, Reviews and Critical Papers, ed. Robert Shafer (Elkin Mathews, 1921).

Fletcher, Ian, 'Johnson's "The Dark Angel"', in John Wain, ed., *Interpretations: Essays on Twelve English Poems* (RKP, 1955), 155–78.

Ellen Johnston

Boos, Florence, 'Cauld Engle-Cheek: Working-Class Women Poets in Victorian Scotland', *VP*, 33 (1995).

Klaus, H. Gustav, *Factory Girl: Ellen Johnston and Working-Class Poetry in Victorian Scotland* (Scottish Studies International, vol. 23) (Peter Lang, Frankfurt am Main, 1998).

Ernest Jones

Ernest Jones, Chartist: Selections from the Writings and Speeches of Ernest Jones, ed. John Saville (Lawrence & Wishart, 1952).

John Keble

Battiscombe, Georgina, *John Keble: A Study in Limitations* (Constable, 1963).

Martin, Brian W., *John Keble: Priest, Professor and Poet* (Croom Helm, 1976).

Tennyson, G. B., *Victorian Devotional Poetry: The Tractarian Mode* (Harvard UP, Cambridge, MA, 1980).

Fanny Kemble

Armstrong, Margaret, *Fanny Kemble: A Passionate Victorian* (Macmillan, New York, 1938).

Marshall, Dorothy, *Fanny Kemble* (Weidenfeld & Nicolson, 1977).

May Kendall

Briggs, Asa, *Social Thought and Social Action: A Study of the Work of B. Seebohm Rowntree* (Longmans, 1961).

Charles Kingsley

Charles Kingsley: His Letters and Memories of His Life, ed. by His Wife, Frances Eliza Grenfell Kingsley, 2 vols (Henry S. King & Co, 1877).

Chitty, Susan, *The Beast and the Monk: A Life of Charles Kingsley* (Hodder & Stoughton, 1974).

Cunningham, Valentine, 'Soiled Fairy: *The Water-Babies* in its Time', *EinC* 35 (April 1985), 121–48.

Rudyard Kipling

A Choice of Kipling's Verse, ed. and intro. T. S. Eliot (Faber & Faber, 1941).

Early Verse by Rudyard Kipling, 1879–1889, Unpublished, Uncollected, and Rarely Collected Poems, ed. Andrew Rutherford (Clarendon P, Oxford, 1986).

Dobrée, Bonamy, *Rudyard Kipling: Realist and Fabulist* (Oxford UP, London, 1967).

Eliot, T. S., 'Rudyard Kipling', *On Poetry and Poets* (Faber & Faber, 1957) (= the Introduction to *A Choice of Kipling's Verse* (1941)).

Green, Roger Lancelyn, ed., *Kipling: The Critical Heritage* (RKP, 1971).

Ricketts, Harry, *The Unforgiving Minute: A Life of Rudyard Kipling* (Chatto & Windus, 1999).

Rutherford, Andrew, *Some Aspects of Kipling's Verse* (British Academy, 1967).

Wilson, Angus, *The Strange Ride of Rudyard Kipling: His Life and Works* (Secker & Warburg, 1978).

Yeats, A. W., 'The Genesis of "Recessional"', *University of Texas Studies in English* 31 (1952), 97–100.

L.E.L.: Letitia Elizabeth Landon

Letitia Elizabeth Landon: Selected Writings, ed. Jerome J. McGann and Daniel Riess (Broadview P, Peterborough, Ontario, 1997).

Life and Literary Remains, 2 vols (Laman Blanchard, 1841).

Blain, Virginia, 'Letitia Elizabeth Landon, Eliza Mary Hamilton, and the Genealogy of the Victorian Poetess', *VP* 33 (Spring 1995), 31–51.

Stephenson, Glennis, *Letitia Landon: The Woman Behind LEL* (Manchester UP, Manchester, 1995).

Stevenson, Lionel, 'Miss Landon: "The Milk-and-Watery Moon of our Darkness", 1824–30', *MLQ* 8 (1947), 355–63.

Walter Savage Landor

The Complete Works of Walter Savage Landor, ed. T. Earle Welby, 16 vols (Chapman & Hall, 1927–36).

Davie, Donald, 'The Shorter Poems of Walter Savage Landor', *EinC* 1 (1951), 345–55.

Pinsky, Robert, *Landor's Poetry* (U of Chicago P, Chicago, 1968).

Super, Robert H., *Walter Savage Landor: A Biography* (New York UP, New York, 1954).

Andrew Lang

Dear Stevenson: Letters from Andrew Lang to Robert Louis Stevenson…, ed. Maryson Demoor (Peeters, Leuven, 1990).

Green, Roger Lancelyn, *Andrew Lang: A Critical Biography with a Short-Title Bibliography of the Works of Andrew Lang* (E. Ward, Leicester, 1946).

Edward Lear

Byrom, Thomas, *Nonsense and Wonder: The Poems and Cartoons of Edward Lear* (Dutton, New York, 1977).

Noakes, Vivien, *Edward Lear: The Life of a Wanderer* (Collins, 1968).

Orwell, George, 'Nonsense Poetry', *Tribune* (21 December 1945); *The Collected Essays, Journalism and Letters,* ed. Sonia Orwell and Ian Angus, vol. 4, *In Front of Your Nose 1945–1950* ([1968]; Penguin, Harmondsworth, 1970), 64–8.

Richard Le Gallienne

Whittington-Egan, Richard and Smerdon, Geoffrey, *The Quest of the Golden Boy: The Life and Letters of Richard Le Gallienne* (Unicorn P, 1960).

Amy Levy

The Complete Novels and Selected Writings of Amy Levy, 1861–1889, ed. Melvyn New (U of Florida P, Gainesville, 1993).

Scheinberg, Cynthia, 'Recasting "sympathy and judgement": Amy Levy and the Victorian Dramatic Monologue', *VP* 35 (Summer 1997), 173–91.

George Henry Lewes

Ashton, Rosemary, *G.H. Lewes: A Life* (Clarendon P, Oxford, 1991).

Ashton, Rosemary, ed., *Versatile Victorian: Selected Critical Writings of George Henry Lewes* (Bristol Classical P, 1992).

Frederick Locker(-Lampson)

Birrell, Augustine, *Frederick Locker-Lampson, a Character Sketch, with a Small Selection of Letters Addressed to Him…* (Constable, 1920).

Henry Francis Lyte

Garland, Henry James, *Henry Francis Lyte and the Story of 'Abide With Me'* (Torch Publishing, Manchester, 1957).

Skinner, B. G., *Henry Francis Lyte: Brixham's Poet and Priest* (U of Exeter P, Exeter, 1974).

T. B. Macaulay

The Life and Works of Lord Macaulay, Edinburgh Edition, 10 vols (Longmans, Green & Co, 1897).

Millgate, Jane, *Macaulay* (RKP, 1973).

George MacDonald

The Poetical Works of George MacDonald (Chatto & Windus, 1915).

Robb, David S., *George MacDonald* (Scottish Academic P, Edinburgh, 1987).

William McGonagall

Poetic Gems; More Poetic Gems; Last Poetic Gems, ed. D. W. Smith and J. L. Smith (David Winter & Son, Dundee, Duckworth & Co., London, 1968–9).

W. H. Mallock

Memoirs of Life and Literature, 2nd edn (Chapman & Hall, 1920).

James Clarence Mangan

The Collected Works of James Clarence Mangan, ed. Jacques Chuto et al., vols 1– (Irish Academic P, Blackrock, Dublin, 1996–).

Shannon-Mangan, Ellen, *James Clarence Mangan: A Biography* (Irish Academic P, Blackrock, Dublin, 1996).

Philip Bourke Marston

The Collected Poems of Philip Bourke Marston, ed. with biographical sketch, Louise Chandler Moulton (Ward, Lock & Bowden, 1892).

Osborne, Charles Churchill, *Philip Bourke Marston* (Times Book Club, Privately Printed, 1926).

Theo Marzials

Selected Poems, ed. John M. Munro (American U of Beirut, Beirut, 1974).

Gerald Massey

Shaw, David, *Gerald Massey: Chartist, Poet, Radical and Freethinker* (Buckland, 1955).

George Meredith

Selected Poems of George Meredith, ed. and intro. Graham Hough (Oxford UP, London, 1962).

Modern Love, ed. Stephen Regan (Daisy, Peterborough, 1988).

Modern Love, ed. Gillian Beer (Syrens, 1995).

The Letters of George Meredith, ed. C. L. Cline, 3 vols (Clarendon P, Oxford, 1970).

The Poems of George Meredith, ed. Phyllis B. Bartlett, 2 vols (Yale UP, New Haven, 1978).

Bernstein, Carol L., *Precarious Enchantment: A Reading of Meredith's Poetry* (Catholic U of America P, Washington, DC, 1979).

Fletcher, Ian, ed., *Meredith Now: Some Critical Essays* (RKP, 1971).

Fletcher, Pauline, ' "Trifles Light as Air" in Meredith's *Modern Love*', VP 34 (Spring 1996), 87–99.

Mermin, Dorothy M., 'Poetry as Fiction: Meredith's *Modern Love*', *ELH* 43 (1976), 100–19.

Simpson, A. L., 'Meredith's Pessimistic Humanism: A New Reading of *Modern Love*', *Modern Philology* 67 (1970), 341–56.

Williams, Ioan, ed., *Meredith: The Critical Heritage* (RKP, 1971).

Woolf, Virginia, 'On Re-Reading Meredith', *Collected Essays*, I (Hogarth, 1966), 233–7.

Alice Meynell

The Poems of Alice Meynell: Complete Edition, ed. Frederick Page (Oxford UP, London, 1940).

The Poems of Alice Meynell: Centenary Edition (Hollis & Carter, 1947).

Prose and Poetry, ed. Frederick Page, intro. V. Sackville-West (Jonathan Cape, 1947).

Badeni, June, *The Slender Tree: A Life of Alice Meynell* (Tabb House, Padstow, Cornwall, 1981).

Hamilton, George Rostrevor, 'Alice Meynell', *Poetry Review* 38 (1947), 325–30.

Schlack, Beverley Ann, 'The "Poetess of Poets": Alice Meynell Rediscovered', *Women's Studies* 7 (1980), 111–26.

William Morris

Collected Works, ed. May Morris, 24 vols (Longmans, Green, 1910–1915).

Boos, Florence S., ed., *VP*, 34, no. 3 (Autumn 1996). William Morris Centenary Number.

Faulkner, Peter, ed., *William Morris: The Critical Heritage* (RKP, 1973).

Fredeman, William, ed., *VP* 12, nos 3–4 (1975). William Morris Special Number.

MacCarthy, Fiona, *William Morris: A Life For Our Time* (Faber & Faber, 1994).

Perrine, Laurence, 'Morris' Guenevere: An Interpretation', *Philological Quarterly* 39 (1960), 234–41.

Talbot, Norman, 'Women and Goddesses in the Romances of William Morris', *Southern Review* (Adelaide) 3 (1969), 339–57.

Talbot, Norman, 'The "Pomona" Lyric and Female Power', *VP* (Spring 1997), 71–81.

Arthur J. Munby

Hudson, Derek, *Munby, Man of Two Worlds: The Life and Diaries of Arthur J. Munby 1828–1910* (John Murray, 1972).

Constance Naden

The Complete Poetical Works of Constance Naden, foreword Robert Lewins (Bickers & Sons, 1894).

Selections from the Philosophical and Poetical Works of Constance W. Naden, compiled by Emily and Edith Hughes (Bickers & Sons, 1893).

Hughes, William Richard, *Constance Naden: A Memoir* (Bickers & Sons, 1890).

Smith, Philip E., and Smith, Susan, 'Constance Naden: Late Victorian Feminist, Poet and Philosopher', *VP* 15 (1977), 367–70.

John Mason Neale

Chandler, Michael, *The Life and Work of John Mason Neale, 1818–1866* (Gracewing, Leominster, 1995).

Litvack, Leon B., *John Mason Neale and the Quest for Sobornost* (Clarendon P, Oxford, 1994).

E. Nesbit

Briggs, Julia, *A Woman of Passion: The Life of E. Nesbit* (Hutchinson, 1987; Penguin, Harmondsworth, 1989).

Henry Newbolt

Chitty, Susan, *Playing the Game: A Biography of Sir Henry Newbolt* (Quartet, 1997).

Jackson, Vanessa Furze, *The Poetry of Henry Newbolt: Patriotism is Not Enough* (ELT P, Greensboro, NC, 1994).

John Henry Newman

The Letters and Diaries of John Henry Newman, ed. C. S. Dessain, T. Gornall, I. T. Ker, 31 vols (Clarendon P, Oxford, 1961–78).

Hark, Ina Rae, 'Newman's Dream of Gerontius: Beyond Time and Sense', *Renascence* 28 (1975), 15–26.

Jay, Elizabeth, 'Newman's Mid-Victorian Dream', in *John Henry Newman: Reason, Rhetoric and Romanticism*, ed. David Nicholls and Fergus Kerr (The Bristol Press, Bristol, 1991).

Ker, I. T., *John Henry Newman: A Biography* (Clarendon P, Oxford, 1988).

Ryan, John K., 'Newman as Poet', *Thought (Fordham U Quarterly)* 20 (1945), 645–56.

Caroline Norton

Selected Writings, ed. J. Hoge and J. Marcus (Scolar Facsimiles and Reprints, Delaware, New York, 1978).

Acland, Alice S., *Caroline Norton* (Constable, 1948).

Arthur W. E. O'Shaughnessy

Poems of Arthur O'Shaughnessy, ed. William Alexander Percy (Yale UP, New Haven, 1923).

Paden, William D., 'Arthur O'Shaughnessy: The Ancestry of a Victorian Poet', *BJRL* 46 (1964), 429–47.

Bessie Rayner Parkes

Lowndes, Marie Adelaide Belloc, *'I, too, have lived in Arcadia': A Record of Love and of Childhood* (Macmillan, 1941).

Walter Pater

The Renaissance: Studies in Art and Poetry: The 1893 Text, ed. Donald L. Hill (U of California P, Berkeley, 1980).

Donoghue, Denis, *Walter Pater, Lover of Strange Souls* (Alfred A. Knopf, New York, 1995).

Eliot, T. S., 'The Place of Pater', in *The Eighteen-Eighties: Essays by Fellows of the Royal Society of Literature*, ed. Walter de la Mare (Cambridge UP, Cambridge, 1930).

Seiler, R. M., ed., *Walter Pater: The Critical Heritage* (RKP, 1980).

Shaffer, Elinor, *Walter Pater and the Culture of the Fin-de-Siècle* (Cambridge UP, Cambridge, 1995).

Coventry Patmore

Cohen, J. M., 'Prophet Without Responsibility: A Study in Coventry Patmore', *EinC* 1 (1951), 283–97.

Fisher, Benjamin F., ed., *VP* 34, no. 4 (Winter 1996). Patmore centenary number, *Coventry Patmore 1823–1896 In Memoriam*.

McElrath, Joseph R., 'Coventry Patmore's *The Angel in the House*: The Experience of Divine Love', *Cithara* 10 (1970), 45–53.

Patmore, Derek, *The Life and Times of Coventry Patmore* (Constable, 1949).

Praz, Mario, 'The Epic of the Everyday', *The Hero in Eclipse in Victorian Fiction*, trans. Angus Davidson (Oxford UP, London, 1956), 413–43.

Reid, John Cowie, *The Mind and Art of Coventry Patmore* (RKP, 1957).

Victor Plarr

The Collected Poems of Victor Plarr, ed. and intro. Ian Fletcher (Eric and Joan Stevens, 1974).

Winthrop Mackworth Praed

Hudson, Derek, *A Poet in Parliament: The Life of Winthrop Mackworth Praed* (John Murray, 1939).

Adelaide Anne Procter

Gregory, Gill, *The Life and Work of Adelaide Procter: Poetry, Feminism and Fathers* (Ashgate, Aldershot, 1998).

A. Mary F. Robinson

The Collected Poems, Lyrical and Narrative, of Mary Robinson (Madame Duclaux) (T. Fisher Unwin, 1902).

The Rossettis

Troxell, Janet Camp, ed., *Three Rossettis: Unpublished Letters to and from Dante Gabriel, Christina, William* (Harvard UP, Cambridge, MA, 1937).

Christina G. Rossetti

Complete Poems: A Variorum Edition, ed. R. W. Crump, 3 vols (Louisiana State UP, Baton Rouge, 1979–90).

Poems and Prose, ed. Jan Marsh (Everyman, J. M. Dent; Charles E. Tuttle, Vermont, 1994).

Family Letters, ed. W. M. Rossetti (Brown, Langham, 1908).

Battiscombe, Georgina, *Christina Rossetti: A Divided Life* (Constable, 1965).

Campbell, Elizabeth, 'Of Mothers and Merchants: Female Economics in Christina Rossetti's "Goblin Market"', *VS* 33 (1990), 393–410.

Carpenter, Mary Wilson, ' "Eat me, drink me, love me": The Consumable Female Body in Christina Rossetti's *Goblin Market*', *VP* 29 (1991), 415–34.

Garlick, Barbara, 'Christina Rossetti and the Gender Politics of Fantasy', in *The Victorian Fantasists*, ed. Kath Filmer (Macmillan, Basingstoke, 1991), 133–52.

Griffiths, Eric, 'The Disappointment of Christina G. Rossetti', *EinC* 47 (1997), 107–42.

Helsinger, Elizabeth K., 'Consumer Power and the Utopia of Desire: Christina Rossetti's "Goblin Market"', *ELH* 58 (1991), 903–33.

Holt, Terence, ' "Men sell not such in any town": Exchange in *Goblin Market*', *VP* 28 (1990), 51–67.

Jones, Kathleen, *Learning Not To Be First: The Life of Christina Rossetti* (Windrush P, Gloucestershire, 1991; Oxford UP, Oxford, 1992).

McGann, Jerome J., 'Christina Rossetti's Poems: A New Edition and a Revaluation', *VP* 23 (1980), 237–54.

McGann, Jerome J., 'The Religious Poetry of Christina Rossetti', *CI* 10 (1983), 127–44.

Marsh, Jan, *Christina Rossetti: A Literary Biography* (Jonathan Cape, 1994).

Marshall, Linda E., ' "Transfigured to His Likeness": Sensible Transcendentalism in Christina Rossetti's "Goblin Market"', *University of Toronto Quarterly* 63 (1994), 429–50.

Michie, Helena, 'There is No Friend Like a Sister: Sister-hood as Sexual Difference', *ELH* 56 (1989), 401–22.

Rosenblum, Dolores, *Christina Rossetti: The Poetry of Endurance* (Southern Illinois UP, Carbondale, 1983).

Thomas, Frances, *Christina Rossetti: A Biography* (Virago, 1994).

Woolf, Virginia, ' "I am Christina Rossetti" ', *The Common Reader: Second Series* (Hogarth 1932), 237–44; *Collected Essays*, vol. IV (Hogarth, 1967), 54–60.

Dante Gabriel Rossetti

The Complete Poetical Works of Dante Gabriel Rossetti, ed. with preface and notes William Michael Rossetti (Roberts Bros, Boston, 1887).

Letters, ed. O. Doughty and J. R. Wahl, 4 vols (Clarendon P, Oxford, 1965–7).

Dante Gabriel Rossetti and Jane Morris: Their Correspondence, ed. John Bryson with Janet Camp (Clarendon P, Oxford, 1976).

Barclay, John, 'Consuming Artifacts: Dante Gabriel Rossetti's Aesthetic Economy', *VP* 35 (Spring 1997), 1–21.

Bock, Carol A., 'D.G. Rossetti's "Found" and "The Blessed Damozel" as Explorations in Victorian Psycho-sexuality', *Journal of Pre-Raphaelite Studies* 1/2 (1981), 83–90.

Cooper, Robert M., *Lost on Both Sides: Dante Gabriel Rossetti; Critic and Poet* (Ohio UP, Athens, OH, 1970).

Fredeman, William E., ed., *VP* 20, nos 3–4 (1982). Dante Gabriel Rossetti issue.

Lottes, Wolfgang, ' "Take out the picture and frame the sonnet": Rossetti's Sonnets and Verses for His Own Works of Art', *Anglia* 96 (1978), 105–35.

Rees, Joan, *The Poems of Dante Gabriel Rossetti: Modes of Self-Expression* (Cambridge UP, Cambridge, 1981).

Ryals, Clyde de L., 'The Narrative Unity of The House of Life', *Journal of English and Germanic Philology* 69 (1970), 241–57.

Weatherby, Harold L., 'Problems of Form and Content in the Poetry of Dante Gabriel Rossetti', *VP* 2 (1964), 11–19.

John Ruskin

The Works of John Ruskin, Library Edition, ed. E. T. Cook and Alexander Wedderburn, 39 vols (George Allen, London; Longmans, Green, & Co, New York, 1903–12).

The Diaries of John Ruskin, ed. Joan Evans and John Howard Whitehouse, 3 vols (Clarendon P, Oxford, 1956–9).

Birch, Dinah, *Ruskin's Myths* (Clarendon P, Oxford, 1988).

Bradley, John Lewis, ed., *John Ruskin: The Critical Heritage* (RKP, 1984).

Casteras, Susan P., *John Ruskin and the Victorian Eye* (Harry N. Abrams/Phoenix Art Museum, New York, 1993).

Hunt, John Dixon, *The Wider Sea: A Life of John Ruskin* (Dent, 1982).

Johnson, Wendell Stacy, 'Memory, Landscape, Love: John Ruskin's Poetry and Poetic Criticism', *VP* 19 (1981), 19–34.

Landow, George P., *The Aesthetic and Critical Theories of John Ruskin* (Princeton UP, Princeton, 1971).

William Bell Scott

Fredeman, William E., *The Letters of Pictor Ignotus: William Bell Scott's Correspondence with Alice Boyd, 1859–1884* (John Rylands U Library of Manchester, Manchester, 1976).

Dora Sigerson Shorter

The Sad Years, And Other Poems, with tribute and memories by Katharine Tynan (Constable, 1918).

Lizzie Siddal

Poems and Drawings, ed. Roger C. Lewis and Mark S. Lasner (The Wombat P, Wolfville, Nova Scotia, 1978).

Bronfen, Elizabeth, *Over Her Dead Body: Death, Femininity and the Aesthetic* (Manchester UP, Manchester, 1992), 168–78.

Hassett, Constance W., 'Elizabeth Siddal's Poetry: A Problem and Some Suggestions', *VP* 35 (Winter 1997), 443–70.

Joseph Skipsey

Selected Poems of Joseph Skipsey, ed. Basil Bunting (Ceolfrith P, Sunderland, 1876).

Alexander Smith

Weinstein, M. A., *W. E. Aytoun and the Spasmodic Controversy* (Yale UP, New Haven, 1968).

Robert Louis Stevenson

Collected Poems, ed. Janet Adam Smith (Rupert Hart-Davis, 1950; 2nd edn, 1971).

The Letters of Robert Louis Stevenson, ed. Bradford A. Booth and Ernest Mehew, 8 vols (Yale UP, New Haven, 1994–5).

McLynn, Frank, *Robert Louis Stevenson: A Biography* (Hutchinson, 1993).

Maixner, Paul, ed., *Robert Louis Stevenson: The Critical Heritage* (RKP, 1981).

Sandison, Alan, *Robert Louis Stevenson and the Appearance of Modernism: A Future Feeling* (Macmillan, 1996).

Algernon Charles Swinburne

The Swinburne Letters, ed. Cecil Y. Lang, 6 vols (Yale UP, New Haven, 1959–62).

Fuller, Jean Overton, *Swinburne: A Critical Biography* (Chatto & Windus, 1968).

Harrison, Antony H., 'Swinburne's Losses: The Poetics of Passion', *ELH* 49 (1982), 689–706.

Hyder, Clyde K., ed., *Swinburne: The Critical Heritage* (RKP, 1970).

Hyder, Clyde K., *Swinburne as Critic* (RKP, 1972).

Lang, Cecil Y., ed., *VP* 9, nos 1–2 (1971). Swinburne Special Number.

McGann, Jerome J., *Swinburne: An Experiment in Criticism* (U of Chicago P, Chicago, 1972).

Ober, William B., 'Swinburne's Masochism: Neuropathology and Psychopathology', *Boswell's Clap and Other Essays: Medical Analyses of Literary Men's Afflictions* (Southern Illinois UP, Carbondale, 1979).

Peters, Robert L., *The Crowns of Apollo: Swinburne's Principles of Literature and Art: A Study in Victorian Criticism and Aesthetics* (Wayne State UP, Detroit, 1965).

Praz, Mario, *The Romantic Agony*, trans. Angus Davidson (Oxford UP, London, 1933), 240–70.

Rooksby, Rikky, *A.C. Swinburne: A Poet's Life* (Scolar Press, Aldershot, 1997).

Thomas, Donald, *Swinburne: The Poet in His World* (Weidenfeld & Nicolson, 1979).

John Addington Symonds

The Letters of John Addington Symonds, ed. Herbert M. Schueller and Robert L. Peters, 3 vols (Wayne State UP, Detroit, 1967–9).

Grosskurth, Phyllis, *John Addington Symonds: A Biography* (Longmans, 1964).

Grosskurth, Phyllis, ed., *The Memoirs of John Addington Symonds* (Hutchinson, 1984).

Arthur Symons

Beckson, Karl, *Arthur Symons: A Life* (Clarendon P, Oxford, 1987).

Alfred (Lord) Tennyson

The Poems of Tennyson, ed. Christopher Ricks (Longman's Annotated English Poets, 1969; 2nd edn, 3 vols, 1987).

In Memoriam: An Authoritative Text, Backgrounds and Sources, Criticism, ed. Robert H. Ross (W. W. Norton, New York, 1973).

In Memoriam, ed. Susan Shatto and Marion Shaw (Clarendon P, Oxford, 1982).

Tennyson's Maud: A Definitive Edition, ed. Susan Shatto (Athlone P, 1986).

The Letters of Alfred Lord Tennyson, ed. Cecil Y. Lang and Edgar F. Shannon Jr, 3 vols (Clarendon P, Oxford, 1982–90).

Albright, Daniel, *Tennyson: The Muses' Tug-of-War* (UP of Virginia, Charlottesville, 1986).

Bradley, A. C., *A Commentary on Tennyson's 'In Memoriam'* (3rd edn revised, Macmillan, 1910).

Buckley, Jerome Hamilton, *Tennyson: The Growth of a Poet* (Harvard UP, Cambridge, MA, 1967).

Colley, Ann C., *Tennyson and Madness* (U of Georgia P, Athens, GA, 1983).

Dunn, Richard J., 'Vision and Revision: In Memoriam XCV', *VP* 18 (1980), 135–46.

Eliot, T. S., 'In Memoriam', Introduction, *Poems of Tennyson* (Nelson Classics, 1936); reprinted *Selected Prose of T. S. Eliot*, ed. Frank Kermode (Faber & Faber, 1975).

Francis, Elizabeth A., ed., *Tennyson: A Collection of Critical Essays* (Twentieth Century Views, Prentice-Hall, Englewood Cliffs, NJ, 1980).

Hair, Donald S., *Tennyson's Language* (U of Toronto P, 1991).

Joseph, Gerhard, *Tennyson and the Text: The Weaver's Shuttle* (Cambridge UP, Cambridge, 1992).

Jump, John D., ed., *Tennyson: The Critical Heritage* (RKP, 1967).

Kincaid, James R., *Tennyson's Major Poems: The Comic and Ironic Patterns* (Yale UP, New Haven, 1975).

Martin, Robert Bernard, *Tennyson, The Unquiet Heart* (Clarendon P, Oxford, and Faber & Faber, 1980).

Paden, William D., *Tennyson in Egypt: A Study of the Imagery in His Earlier Work* (U of Kansas P, Lawrence, 1942).

Palmer, D. J., ed., *Tennyson* (Writers and Their Background, G. Bell & Sons, 1973).

Peltason, T., *Reading 'In Memoriam'* (Princeton UP, Princeton, 1985).

Pettigrew, John, *Tennyson: The Early Poems* (Edward Arnold, 1970).

Priestley, F. E. L., *Language and Structure in Tennyson's Poetry* (Andre Deutsch, 1973).

Rader, R. W., *Tennyson's 'Maud': The Biographical Genesis* (U of California P, Berkeley, 1963).

Ricks, Christopher, 'Tennyson's Methods of Composition', *Proceedings of the British Academy* 57 (1966–7), 209–30.

Ricks, Christopher, *Tennyson* (Macmillan, 1972).

Ricks, Christopher, 'Tennyson's Tennyson', *Essays in Appreciation* (Clarendon P, Oxford, 1996), 172–205.

Sacks, Peter M., *The English Elegy: Studies in the Genre From Spenser to Yeats* (Johns Hopkins UP, Baltimore, 1985).

Shannon, Edgar F., Jr, 'Poetry as Vision: Sight and Insight in "The Lady of Shalott"', *VP* 19 (1981), 207–33.

Tennyson, Hallam, *Alfred Lord Tennyson: A Memoir, By His Son*, 2 vols (Macmillan, 1897).

Thwaite, Ann, *Emily Tennyson: The Poet's Wife* (Faber & Faber, 1996).

Tucker, Herbert F., 'From Monomania to Monologue: "St Simeon Stylites" and the Rise of the Victorian Dramatic Monologue', *VP* 22 (1984), 121–37.

Tucker, Herbert F., *Tennyson and the Doom of Romanticism* (Harvard UP, Cambridge, MA, 1988).

Victorian Poetry, 18, no. 2 (Summer 1980), *In Memoriam* number.

Frederick Tennyson

Nicolson, Harold, *Tennyson's Two Brothers* (Cambridge UP, Cambridge, 1947).

Schonfield, Hugh J., ed., *Letters to Frederick Tennyson* (Leonard and Virginia Woolf, 1930).

Tennyson, Sir Charles, *The Somersby Tennysons*, Supplement, *VS* 7 (1963).

William Makepeace Thackeray

Ballads and Contributions to 'Punch': 1842–1850, ed. George Saintsbury (Henry Frowde, Oxford UP, London, [1910?]).

Bloom, Harold, ed., *William Makepeace Thackeray: Modern Critical Views* (Chelsea House, New York, 1987).

Peters, Catherine, *Thackeray's Universe: Shifting Worlds of Imagination and Reality* (Faber & Faber, 1987).

Tillotson, Geoffrey and Hawes, Donald, eds, *William Thackeray: The Critical Heritage* (RKP, 1995).

Francis Thompson

Poetical Works, ed. Wilfrid Meynell (Oxford UP, London, 1937).

The Letters of Francis Thompson, ed. John Evangelist Walsh (Hawthorn Books, New York, 1969).

Buchen, Irving H., 'Francis Thompson and the Aesthetics of the Incarnation', *VP* 3 (1965), 235–44.

Megroz, Rodolphe L., *Francis Thompson: The Poet of Earth in Heaven* (Faber & Gwyer, 1927).

Nichols, Louis L., 'Francis Thompson: Flight and Fall', *Thought (Fordham U Quarterly)* 36 (1961), 101–23.

Walsh, J. E., *Strange Harp, Strange Symphony: The Life of Francis Thompson* (W. H. Allen, 1968).

James Thomson (B.V.)

Poems and Some Letters of James Thomson, ed. Anne Ridler (Centaur P, 1963).

The Speedy Extinction of Evil and Misery: Selected Prose of James Thomson (B.V.), ed. William David Schaeffer (U of California P, Berkeley, 1967).

Byron, Kenneth Hugh, *The Pessimism of James Thomson (B.V.) in Relation to His Times* (Mouton, the Hague, 1965).

Campbell, Ian, ' "And I burn too": Thomson's *City of Dreadful Night*', *VP* 16 (1978), 123–33.

Crawford, Robert, 'James Thomson and T. S. Eliot', *VP* 23 (Spring 1985), 23–41.

Dobell, Bertram, *The Laureate of Pessimism: A Sketch of the Life and Character of James Thomson ('B.V.')* (Kennikat P, Port Washington, New York, 1970).

Leonard, Tom, *Places of the Mind: The Life and Work of James Thomson ('B.V.')* (Jonathan Cape, 1993).

Schaefer, W. D., *James Thomson (B.V.): Beyond 'The City'* (U of California P, Berkeley, 1965).

Sharpe, William, 'Learning to Read *The City*', *VP* 22 (1984), 65–84.

Martin F. Tupper

Buchmann, Ralf, *Martin F. Tupper and the Victorian Middle Class Mind* (Verlag A. Francke Ag, Bern, 1941).

Hudson, Derek, *Martin Tupper: His Rise and Fall* (Constable, 1949).

Charles (Tennyson) Turner

Collected Sonnets, ed. F. B. Pinion and M. Pinion (Macmillan, 1988).

Nicolson, Harold, *Tennyson's Two Brothers* (Cambridge UP, Cambridge, 1947).

Tennyson, Sir Charles, *The Somersby Tennysons*, Supplement, *VS* 7 (1963).

Katharine Tynan

Memories (E. Nash & Grayson, 1924).

The Poems of Katharine Tynan, ed. Monk Gibbon (Figgis, Dublin, 1963).

Yeats, W. B., *Letters to Katharine Tynan*, ed. Roger McHugh (Clonmore & Reynolds, Dublin, 1953).

John Leicester Warren, Lord de Tabley

Pitts, G., 'Lord de Tabley: Poet of Frustration', *West Virginia U Philological Papers* 14 (1963), 57–73.

Taplin, Gardner B., *The Life, Works and Literary Reputation of Lord de Tabley* (Harvard UP, Cambridge, MA, 1946).

Walker, Hugh, *John B. Leicester Warren, Lord de Tabley: A Biographical Sketch* (Chapman & Hall, 1903).

Augusta Webster

Brown, Susan, 'Economical Representations: Dante Gabriel Rossetti's "Jenny", Augusta Webster's "Castaway", and the Campaign Against the Contagious Diseases Act', *Victorian Review* 17 (1991), 78–95.

Brown, Susan, 'Determined Heroines: George Eliot, Augusta Webster, and Closet Drama by Victorian Women', *VP* 33 (Spring 1995), 89–109.

Oscar Wilde

The Collected Works of Oscar Wilde, 15 vols, ed. Robert Ross; intro. J. Bristow [= 14–vol. edn (1908) supplemented] (Routledge/Thoemmes, 1993).

Selected Letters of Oscar Wilde, ed. Rupert Hart-Davis (Oxford UP, Oxford, 1989).

Beckson, Karl, ed., *Oscar Wilde: The Critical Heritage* (RKP, 1970).

Bloom, Harold, ed. *Oscar Wilde: Modern Critical Views* (Chelsea House, New York, 1985).

Danson, Lawrence, *Wilde's Intentions: The Artist in His Criticism* (Clarendon P, Oxford, 1998).

Ellmann, Richard, ed., *Oscar Wilde: A Collection of Critical Essays* (Twentieth Century Views) (Prentice-Hall, Englewood Cliffs, NJ, 1969).

Ellmann, Richard, *Oscar Wilde* (Hamish Hamilton, 1987).

Fryer, Jonathan, *André and Oscar: Gide, Wilde and the Gay Art of Living* (Constable, 1997).

Gillespie, Michael Patrick, *Oscar Wilde and the Poetics of Ambiguity* (UP of Florida, Gainesville, 1996).

Heaney, Seamus, 'Speranza in Reading: On "The Ballad of Reading Gaol" ', *The Redress of Poetry: Oxford Lectures* (Faber & Faber, 1995).

Shewan, Rodney, *Oscar Wilde: Art and Egotism* (Macmillan, 1977).

James R. Withers

Aspland, Janet E., 'A Memoir', in J. R. Withers, *Fairy Revels and Other Poems* (B. Diver, Cambridge; George Simpson, Newmarket, 1901).

William Wordsworth

The Poetical Works of William Wordsworth, ed. Ernest de Selincourt and Helen Darbishire, 5 vols (Clarendon P, Oxford, 1940–9; vols I–III revised, 1952–4).

The Cornell Wordsworth, eds Stephen Gill et al., vols 1– (Cornell UP, Ithaca, NY, 1975–).

Further Reading

Place of publication: where not stated, assume London; usually, where an individual publisher has two centres, only the first location is cited.

Abbreviations: U = University; P = Press; UP = University Press; ed(s) = editor(s); *BJRL* = *Bulletin of the John Rylands Library*; *CI* = *Critical Inquiry*; *CJ* = *Cambridge Journal*; *EinC* = *Essays in Criticism*; *ELH* = *English Literary History*; *ELT* = *English Literature in Transition*; *MLQ* = *Modern Languages Quarterly*; *PMLA* = *Publications of the Modern Language Association of North America*; *TP* = *Textual Practice*; *VP* = *Victorian Poetry*; *VS* = *Victorian Studies*.

Anthologies

Adams, W. Davenport, ed., *The Comic Poets of the Nineteenth Century: Poems of Wit and Humour by Living Writers* (George Routledge & Sons, 1876).

Amis, Kingsley, ed., *The New Oxford Book of Light Verse* (Oxford UP, Oxford, 1978).

Armstrong, Isobel; Bristow, Joseph; Sharrock, Cath, eds, *Nineteenth-Century Women Poets* (Clarendon P, Oxford, 1996).

Auden, W. H., ed., *Nineteenth Century Minor Poets* (Faber & Faber, 1967).

Breen, Jennifer, ed., *Victorian Women Poets 1830–1900: An Anthology* (Everyman, J. M. Dent, 1994).

Bristow, Joseph, ed., *The Victorian Poet: Poetics and Persona* (Croom Helm, 1987).

Dixon, W. Macneile, ed., *The Edinburgh Book of Scottish Verse 1300–1900* (Meiklejohn & Holden, 1910).

Geraths, Armin; Herget, Kurt; Collier, Gordon; Wächter, Bernd, eds, *Viktorianische Lyrik: Englisch/Deutsch* (Philipp Reclam jun, Stuttgart, 1985).

Henley, W. E., ed., *Lyra Heroica: A Book of Verse for Boys* (David Nutt, 1891).

Houghton, W. E. and Stange, G. Robert, eds, *Victorian Poetry and Poetics* (Houghton Mifflin, Boston, 1968).

Karlin, Daniel, ed., *The Penguin Book of Victorian Verse* (Allen Lane, The Penguin Press, 1997).

Leighton, Angela and Reynolds, Margaret, eds, *Victorian Women Poets: An Anthology* (Blackwell, Oxford, 1995).

Maidment, Brian, ed., *The Poorhouse Fugitives: Self-Taught Poets and Poetry in Victorian Britain* (Carcanet, Manchester, 1987).

Miles, Alfred H., ed., *The Poets and the Poetry of the Century*, 10 vols (Hutchinson, 1892–7); 12 vols (G. Routledge & Sons; E. P. Dutton, New York, 1905–7).

Palgrave, Francis Turner, ed., *The Golden Treasury of the Best Songs and Lyrical Poems in the English Language* (first version, 1861), ed. Christopher Ricks (Penguin, Harmondsworth, 1991).

Palmer, Roy, ed., *A Touch on the Times: Songs of Social Change 1770 to 1914* (Penguin Education, Harmondsworth, 1974).

Quiller-Couch, Arthur, ed., *The Oxford Book of Victorian Verse* (Clarendon P, Oxford, 1925).

Ricks, Christopher, ed., *The New Oxford Book of Victorian Verse* (Oxford UP, Oxford, 1987).

Stanford, Derek, ed., *Pre-Raphaelite Writing: An Anthology* (Dent, 1973).

Thornton, R. K. R., ed., *Poetry of the 1890s* (Penguin, Harmondsworth, 1970; 2nd edn, with Marion Thain, 1997).

General

Adams, James Eli, *Dandies and Desert Saints: Styles of Victorian Manhood* (Cornell UP, Ithaca, NY, 1995).

Anderson, Amanda S., *Tainted Souls and Painted Faces: The Rhetoric of Fallenness in Victorian Culture* (Cornell UP, Ithaca, NY, 1993).

Arata, Stephen, *Fictions of Loss in the Victorian Fin de Siècle* (Cambridge UP, 1996).

Armstrong, Isobel, ed., *The Major Victorian Poets: Reconsiderations* (RKP, 1969).

Armstrong, Isobel, *Victorian Scrutinies: Reviews of Poetry, 1830–1870* (Athlone P, 1972).

Armstrong, Isobel, *Victorian Poetry: Poetry, Poetics and Politics* (RKP, 1993).

Ashton, Rosemary, *The German Idea: Four English Writers and the Reception of German Thought 1800–1860* (Cambridge UP, Cambridge, 1980).

Auerbach, Nina, *Women and the Demon: The Life of a Victorian Myth* (Harvard UP, Cambridge, MA, 1982).

Barreca, Regina, ed., *Sex and Death in Victorian Literature* (Macmillan, 1990).

Beddoe, Stella, 'Fairy Writing and Writers', in *Victorian Fairy Painting*, ed. Jane Martineau (Royal Academy of Arts, London; The U of Iowa Museum of Art, Iowa; The Art Gallery of Ontario, Toronto; in association with Merrell Holberton Publishers, London).

Bergonzi, Bernard, *The Turn of a Century: Essays on Victorian and Modern English Literature* (Macmillan, 1973).

Bivona, Daniel, *Desire and Contradiction: Imperial Visions and Domestic Debates in Victorian Literature* (Manchester UP, Manchester, 1990).

Blake, Kathleen, *Love and the Woman Question in Victorian Literature: The Art of Self-Postponement* (Harvester, Hemel Hempstead, 1983).

Index of Titles and First Lines

Index to the Notes

Main entries on poets are signified by page numbers in **bold** print.

Thompson, Francis **992**, 1042; and Meynell 898; and
    Patmore 557; 'Love in Dian's Lap' 898; 'To a Snow-
    flake' *xxxix*; 'Unto this Last' *xli*
Thomson, James *xxxvi*, 726–7, 931; *City of Dreadful
    Night, The xxxvi*, 726; imitated by Ebenezer Elliott 19;
    'In the Room' *xliv*; ' "Melencolia" of Albrecht Dürer,
    The' 746n; *Seasons* 29
Thornbury, George W. 333
Thornton, Henry 71
Thornton, Henry Sykes 71
Thornton, R.K.R.: *Poetry of the 1890s xlv*
Times: M. Collins writes letters to 604
Times Literary Supplement: M. Coleridge contributes to
    1002
Tinsley's Magazine: M. Collins contributes to 604; Gilbert
    contributes to 759
Tochatti, James 881
Tolstoy, Leo 481
Toynbee, Arnold 481
*Tracts for the Time*s 25, 90
Train: L. Carroll contributes to 684
translations, Victorian *xlii*
Traveller: Hunt contributes to 21
Trial, The: Baildon and Stevenson write for 927
Trollope, Anthony: on Dickens 329; and Dobson 796; and
    Locker 516
Trophonius 561n
True Sun: Dickens contributes to 329
Tupper, Martin F. *xxxvii*, **301–2**
Turgenev, Ivan 569
Turner, Charles (Tennyson) *xliii*, 14, **178–9**, 235n;
    'Higher Criticism, The' *xl*; *Leben Jesu xl*; *Poems by Two
    Brothers* (with Alfred Tennyson) 174, 178, 194; *Vie de
    Jésus xl*
Turner, J.M.W.: *Fighting Temeraire, The xliv–xlv*; Hardy
    admires 803; Monkhouse writes on 799; Ruskin
    admires 481
Turner, Sharon: *History of the Anglo-Saxons* 638
Tynan, Kathleen **997**; and Meynell 898; and Shorter
    1048; and Yeats 1020; 'Sheep and Lambs' *xxxix*, 997
Tyrwhitt, R.: 'Greek Spirit in Modern Literature, The'
    816

Ulverston Advertiser: Bigg edits 638
United Irishman: Mangan contributes to 125
Useful and Instructive Poetry 684

Vanity Fair: Henley contributes to 911; Stevenson
    contributes to 935
Vanolis, Bysshe *see* Thomson, James
Vasari, Giorgio: *Lives of the More Excellent Painters, Sculptors
    and Architects* 345n, 360n
Vaughan, Charles 816
Vaughan, Henry: *Sacred Poems* 39
Veley, Margaret *xxxix*, **844**; 'Sonnet' *xli*
Venables, George Stovin 318
Verlaine, Paul: Dowson admires 1052; and Symons 1016;
    Gray as translator of 1044

Victoria, Queen: corresponds with McGonagall 585;
    drawing lessons from Lear 378; and Tennyson 194;
    pension for MacDonald 578
Victoria Magazine: Levy contributes to 1006
Victoria Press 588, 645
Victoria Regia: Procter edits 588
Virgil: *Aeneid* 50n, 55, 58n, 524n, 529n, 537n, 710,
    988n; and Henry 55
Vizetelly, Henry *xxxviii*
Volsunga-saga: Morris and Magnusson translate 710
Voltaire 1052

Wagner, Richard: *Tannhäuser* 956n
Walker, Patricius *see* Allingham
Wallace, Alfred 820
Wallis, Henry 609
Walpole, Horace 796
Ward, Mrs Humphrey 794
Waring, Anna Laetitia **554–5**
Warren, John Leicester, Lord de Tabley (M.A., G.F.
    Preston, W.P. Lancaster) 507, **752**
Watts, G.F. 481
Watts, Isaac 605n; *Divine and Moral Songs for Children*
    384; hymn book 426; influence on Withers 384
Watts-Dunton, Theodore 609; admires Skipsey 703; and
    Rossetti 619; on Ebenezer Jones 507; tutor to
    Swinburne 775
Webb, Philip 710
Webb, Sidney and Beatrice 977
Webster, Augusta *xxxix*, 662, **768**
Weekly Register: Meynell edits 898
Wellington, Arthur Wellesley, 1st duke of 252n, 253n,
    257n
Wells, H.G. 911, 977
Wesley, John 308n
Wesleyans 141
Westminster Review: S.F. Adams contributes to 140;
    G. Eliot assistant on 414; Havelock Ellis promotes Ashe
    757; Lewes contributes to 414; Pater contributes to 794
Wharton, Henry 889
Wheeler, Rosina Doyle 130
Whistler, James 1015n; and Swinburne 774; and Rossetti
    618; promoted by Henley 911; Ruskin attacks 481
Whitman, Walt: Buchanan admires 822; Hopkins
    admires 854; influence on Carpenter 871, 872; *Leaves of
    Grass* 816; selected by W.M. Rossetti 650; study by
    Dowden 841
Whyte-Melville, G.J. 139n
Wilde, Oscar *xliii*, **947–8**, 1042; and Bradley and Cooper
    889; and Levy 1006; 'Ballad of Reading Gaol, The'
    xxxvi, *xliv*, 912, 948; on Browning 333; and Dowson
    1052; and Gray 1044; and Pater 794; on Henley 912;
    on Meredith 609; 'On the Recent Massacres of
    Christians in Bulgaria' 710; *Picture of Dorian Gray, The*
    794, 948, 1044; *Salomé* 948, 1052; on Siddal's suicide
    647; on Skipsey 703
Wills, William Henry (Harry) 9–10, 329, 588
Withers, James R. **384**